The Adolescent

Development, Relationships, and Culture

F. PHILIP RICE

Late, University of Maine

KIM GALE DOLGIN

Ohio Wesleyan University

Boston ■ New York ■ San Francisco
Mexico City ■ Montreal ■ Toronto ■ London ■ Madrid ■ Munich ■ Paris
Hong Kong ■ Singapore ■ Tokyo ■ Cape Town ■ Sydney

Senior Series Editor: *Stephen Frail*
Executive Marketing Manager: *Pam Laskey*
Production Editor: *Pat Torelli*
Editorial Production Service: *Pine Tree Composition*
Composition Buyer: *Linda Cox*
Manufacturing Buyer: *JoAnne Sweeney*
Electronic Composition: *Pine Tree Composition*
Interior Design: *Ellen Pettengell*
Art: *Jim Atherton*
Anatomical Art: *Jay Alexander, I-Hua Graphics*
Photo Researcher: *Katharine S. Cebik*
Cover Administrator: *Linda Knowles*
Cover Designer: *Susan Paradise*

For related titles and support materials, visit our online catalog at www.ablongman.com.

Library of Congress Cataloging-in-Publication Data

Rice, F. Philip.
The adolescent : development, relationships, and culture / F. Philip Rice, Kim Gale Dolgin. — 12th ed.
p. cm.
Includes bibliographical references and index.
ISBN 13: 978-0-205-53074-8
ISBN 10: 0-205-53074-5
1. Teenagers—United States—Social conditions. 2. Adolescent psychology—United States. 3. Adolescence. I. Dolgin, Kim Gale. II. Title.
HQ796.R543 2008
305.235—dc22

2007012609

Printed in the United States of America

10 9 8 7 6 5 4 3 2 1 Q-WC-V 11 10 09 08 07

Credits appear on pages 509–510, which constitute an extension of the copyright page.

For my mother, Florence

CONTENTS

CHAPTER 3 ADOLESCENT DIVERSITY: SOCIOECONOMIC STATUS AND ETHNICITY 48

PART TWO PHYSICAL

CHAPTER 4 BODY ISSUES: SEXUAL MATURATION AND PHYSICAL GROWTH 74

CHAPTER 5 BODY ISSUES: HEALTH-RELATED BEHAVIORS AND ATTITUDES 94

PART THREE INTELLECTUAL

CHAPTER 6 TRADITIONAL APPROACHES TO COGNITIVE DEVELOPMENT: PIAGET AND ELKIND 116

CHAPTER 7 NEW APPROACHES TO COGNITIVE DEVELOPMENT: INFORMATION PROCESSING, DECISION MAKING, AND ASSESSMENT ISSUES 136

PART FOUR PSYCHOSEXUAL

CHAPTER 8 SELF-CONCEPT, IDENTITY, ETHNICITY, AND GENDER 158

CHAPTER 9 SEXUAL VALUES AND BEHAVIOR 186

PART FIVE FAMILIAL

CHAPTER 10 ADOLESCENTS AND THEIR FAMILIES 222

CHAPTER 11 DIVORCED, PARENT-ABSENT, AND BLENDED FAMILIES 244

PART SIX SOCIAL

CHAPTER 12 SOCIAL DEVELOPMENT: THE CHANGING NATURE OF FRIENDSHIP AND ROMANCE 266

CHAPTER 13 ADOLESCENT SOCIETY, CULTURE, AND SUBCULTURE 296

CHAPTER 14 THE DEVELOPMENT OF MORAL VALUES 320

PART SEVEN EDUCATIONAL AND VOCATIONAL

CHAPTER 15 EDUCATION AND SCHOOL 344

CHAPTER 16 WORK AND VOCATION 366

PART EIGHT PSYCHOSOCIAL PROBLEMS

CHAPTER 17 ADOLESCENT ALIENATION 392

CHAPTER 18 SUBSTANCE ABUSE, ADDICTION, AND DEPENDENCY 418

FEATURES

PERSONAL ISSUES

CROSS-CULTURAL CONCERNS

RESEARCH HIGHLIGHTS

IN THEIR OWN WORDS

PREFACE

I began using *The Adolescent: Development, Relationships, and Culture* when I got my first college teaching position at the University of Minnesota in 1981. With only occasional one-year forays to "try something new," I have always returned to it. In my opinion, it has been the most comprehensive, best-written adolescence text available for 30 years. I was quite honored, therefore, when I was asked to come on as co-author of the text for the tenth edition.

As with the previous two editions, I have remained faithful to the feel of the book yet have taken somewhat different approaches to certain issues. For instance, long-time readers will recognize a continuing shift in the discussion of adolescent girls. Another major change is in the coverage of cognitive development: The chapter on Piaget has been reframed to indicate his historical significance, and the chapter on information processing/current perspectives has been reworked to focus more squarely on the cognitive changes that occur during adolescence, rather than on basic information processing theory.

Several changes in format begun in the last edition will continue in this one. First, each chapter now begins with a series of interesting **Wouldn't you like to know . . .** questions that highlight some of the most intriguing information in the chapter. Answers to these questions are provided at relevant points throughout the chapter. Second, the text now includes **In Their Own Words** boxes—first-person narratives written by adolescents about their experiences that illustrate and personalize the information. Third, a brief **Epilogue** has been added that describes the differences between young adulthood and adolescence and discusses the new stage of life known as emerging adulthood. I hope it brings a nice closure to the text. Fourth, where possible, a section called **Useful Websites** has been added at the end of the chapter, providing useful online references.

One new modification has been made in the pedagogical aids. For many years the chapters have closed with a list of thought provoking questions which were designed to help students reflect on what they had read and to make the material more personally meaningful to themselves. In this edition, those questions have been sub-divided into three sections. The first contains **Personal Reflection** questions, which are most similar to the questions that have been present in previous versions of the text. The next section is composed of **Group Discussion** questions, which can be used to facilitate small-group interaction in or out of class. The questions could also be posted in a chat room or electronic bulletin board. The final section contains **Debate Questions;** these are controversial statements that are intended to be springboards for discussion and dispute.

I hope that you will find the new amalgamated twelfth edition of *The Adolescent* even better than it was before. I have added approximately 700 new references in this edition and 600 in the last and have, of course, updated the data and terminology to be as current as possible. In addition, the following new topics have been included or expanded in this edition:

- Emerging adulthood
- Adolescent cohorts of the 20th century
- The Children's Internet Protection Act
- An international perspective on adolescent concerns
- Violent computer games
- Teens who murder family members
- The use of scaffolding in course-related bulletin boards
- Criteria used by adolescents to assess entry into adulthood
- Schooling in areas of concentrated poverty
- Homeless youth
- Health concerns of Native American adolescents
- Filipino American adolescents
- Southeast Asian adolescents
- Resiliency
- Racial differences in the timing of puberty
- The female athlete triad
- Body dissatisfaction in adolescent boys
- Bullying and off-time maturation
- The climbing adolescent obesity rate
- Voluntary ban on sodas in school cafeterias
- Government action to improve adolescent health
- Is the personal fable a bad thing?
- Why does egocentrism develop?
- The role of executive control in cognitive development
- Adolescents' over-use of heuristics
- Stability of IQ scores across adolescence
- Culture fair and culture free IQ tests
- The dynamic testing movement
- The new SAT

Role strain and low self-esteem
Multiracial teens
Ethnic identity in Caucasian teens
Parent–child relations and sexual behavior
The effects of parent–child communication on sexual behavior
Friends with benefits
Coercive and unwanted sexual activity
Trichomoniasis
A new perspective on teenage mothers
Biological bases of sexual orientation
Hooking up on college campuses
Induction
The "tough love" parenting style used by some parents
Overly indulgent parenting
Styles of grandparent adolescent interaction
Effects of physical abuse on adolescents
The degree to which adolescents mislead their parents
Long-term effects of divorce
Loss of contact with significant others post divorce
Adolescents raised largely or solely by grandparents
Adolescents raised by widows or widowers
Adolescents who experienced open vs. closed adoptions
Parental effects on peer relationships
Different meanings of "popularity"
Characteristics of popular adolescents
Relational and reputational aggression
Bullies and their victims
Successful anti-bullying programs
Cyberbullying
The development of dating
Academic success and social standing
Effects of participation in structured extracurricular activities
Effects of participation in athletics
Notable youth subcultures: flappers, hippies, skateboarders, and hip hoppers
Adolescents as consumers
Adolescent cell phone use, including text messaging
Adolescent Internet use
College student credit card debt
Internet addiction
Moral reasoning and epistemological development
Changes in prosocial behavior during adolescence
Religiosity and moral development
Effects of violent television on adolescents
Effects of advertising on adolescent behavior
Why do teens like scary media?
Cheating in college
The No Child Left Behind Act and secondary education
Alternative school choices: home schooling, private schools, charter schools
Reasons for truancy
Tracking
Uses and utility of computers in schools
New school violence statistics
Summer school vs. summer employment
New data on the effects of after-school employment
Adolescent's own perceptions of the benefits of employment
The link between SSRIs and suicide
Family relationships in suicidal youth
Outcomes of juvenile arrests
Juveniles in adult prisons
Adolescent self-mutilation
LAAM
Club drugs
Characteristics of the best drug prevention programs
Tobacco advertising
Adolescent use of smokeless tobacco
Binge drinking

PLAN FOR THE TEXT

The organization of the text is the same as that of the previous edition.

Part One: Adolescence

Three major chapters are included in Part One: Adolescents in Social Context, Adolescents in Theoretical Context, and Adolescent Diversity. Chapter 1 places adolescent development, relationships, and culture in a social context and discusses the revolutionary changes in society and how they affect the lives of adolescents. Seven changes are discussed: the prolongation of adolescence, the computer revolution, changes in the world of work, changes in education the changing nature of the family, the sexual revolution, and the violence revolution. Chapter 2 places adolescence in a theoretical context and discusses the multidisciplinary views of adolescence. Chapter 3 places adolescence in both an ethnic and a socioeconomic context. It considers adolescents of low socioeconomic status along with adolescents who belong to these minority groups: African Americans, Hispanic Americans, Native Americans, and Asian Americans. There is also a section on immigrants and refugees.

Part Two: Physical

This part has two chapters of great interest to students: Sexual Maturation and Physical Growth, which discusses the biochemical and biological aspects of puberty, and Health Behaviors and

Attitudes, which addresses topics such as physical attractiveness, weight, nutrition, and exercise.

Part Three: Intellectual
The two chapters in Part Three are Traditional Approaches to Cognitive Development: Piaget and Elkind and New Approaches to Cognitive Development: Information Processing, Decision Making, and Assessment Issues.

Part Four: Psychosexual
The all-important topics of Self-Concept, Identity, Ethnicity, and Gender are discussed in Chapter 8, and Sexual Values and Behavior are covered in Chapter 9.

Part Five: Familial
The subject of Adolescents and Their Families is found in Chapter 10, and Chapter 11 looks at Divorced, Parent-Absent, and Blended Families.

Part Six: Social
Coverage of social development includes three chapters: The Changing Nature of Friendship and Romance; Adolescent Society, Culture, and Subculture; and The Development of Moral Values.

Part Seven: Educational and Vocational
Chapter 15, Education and School, covers developments in secondary education. Work and Vocation, the second chapter in this part, discusses the many issues involved in vocational choice.

Part Eight: Psychosocial Problems
Adolescent Alienation, as expressed through running away, depression, suicide, and juvenile delinquency, is discussed in this section along with Substance Abuse, Addiction, and Dependency.

Again, the text concludes with a brief Epilogue describing the life tasks of young adulthood and emerging adulthood.

FEATURES

Other important features, highly praised by adopters of the book, have been retained from previous editions, including five different types of boxes that present many new topics and examples (see pages xi–xii). **Personal Issues** discuss topics of individual interest to students. **Cross-Cultural Concerns** show comparisons between different racial and ethnic groups on a wide variety of subjects. **Research Highlights** continues the discussion of current research issues of special interest. **In Their Own Words** presents excerpts of journal entries written by college students that illustrate concepts in the text, and **Wouldn't you like to know . . .** boxes ask and answer questions intended to stimulate students' interest in the course material. Together, these boxed features add variety and interest to the text.

Other valuable features include the following:

Broad Research Base
The discussions are substantiated with over 3,000 citations, most of which are original research studies; however, the emphasis in the text is on discussing the subjects, not summarizing one research study after another.

Pedagogical Aids
This book has been written with the teaching-learning process in mind. Each chapter begins with a detailed outline. **Key Terms** appear in text in bold type and are defined in the margin on or near the same page where first mentioned; they appear again in the **Glossary** at the end of the book and at the end of each chapter that first introduces them. Each chapter discussion is followed by a detailed, numbered **Summary. Thought Questions** at the end of each chapter may be used in class discussions, in essay assignments, or to foster debate. The **Suggested Reading** list that concludes each chapter enables students and instructors to do extra reading on topics, as desired. Similarly, the addition of **Useful Websites** to many chapters provides readers with more source materials.

Eclectic Orientation
This text presents not one theory of adolescence but many, discussing the contributions, strengths, and weaknesses of each.

Comprehensive Coverage
The book is as comprehensive as possible within the confines of one text. The adolescent is discussed within the context of contemporary society. Material includes both theory and life experiences of adolescents and discusses physical, intellectual, emotional, psychosexual, social, familial, educational, and vocational aspects of adolescent development and behavior. It also reviews psychosocial problems of adolescents.

Adolescents in Contemporary Society
How modern society and social forces shape the lives of adolescents today is an important topic. Adolescents are discussed in social, theoretical, and ethnic contexts, not as though they were isolated from the social forces around them.

Cultural Diversity
Adolescents are not all alike, any more so than are adults. A wide variety of ethnic, racial, and cultural groups are discussed.

Adolescent Society and Culture

This book includes not only adolescent development and relationships but also group life and culture. Subjects include cultural versus subcultural societies, dress, social activities, and group life in and out of school. The importance of the automobile, telephone, and music in adolescents' lives is also emphasized.

Gender Issues and Concerns

Gender issues are raised in relation to a wide range of topics: physical attributes and body image, cognitive abilities and intelligence, eating disorders, social development and dating, sexual values and behavior, education, work and vocation, and others.

Personal Applications

The Thought Questions at the end of each chapter are designed to bring out students' attitudes, feelings, and responses to the subjects discussed. Students are encouraged to reflect on their own adolescent years, to talk about adolescents they know (either their own friends or their children), and to react in a critical way to the issues discussed. The *In Their Own Words* boxes also bring a personal focus to the topics discussed.

TEXTBOOK ANCILLARIES

Instructor's Manual/Test Bank

Written by Kathleen Clarke of Cape Cod Community College and Jane P. Sheldon of University of Michigan–Dearborn, this Instructor's Manual/Test Bank includes a wealth of resources. The Instructor's Manual contains detailed outlines, objectives, discussion questions, and media resources for each chapter of the text. The Test Bank contains over 50 test items per chapter in multiple-choice and essay formats. A page reference to the text discussion, a skill level, and a difficulty rating scale are included for each item.

Computerized Test Bank (Available for Windows and Macintosh)

The Test Bank also is available in electronic format. TestGen 5.0 is an integrated suite of testing and assessment tools for Windows and Macintosh. Instructors can use TestGen to create professional-looking exams in just minutes by building them from the existing database of questions, by editing questions, or by adding their own. TestGen also allows instructors to prepare printed, network, and online tests. This supplement is available for download from Supplements Central; contact your Allyn & Bacon representative for more details.

PowerPoint Presentation Package

Written by co-author Kim Dolgin, this PowerPoint package is an excellent tool for enhancing lectures. This supplement also is available for download from Supplements Central. Contact your Allyn & Bacon representative for more details.

Companion Website (www.ablongman.com/riceadolescent12e)

Authored by Robin Frye of Monroe Community College, this companion website for *The Adolescent* contains learning objectives and practice tests with multiple-choice, true/false, and essay questions.

Research Navigator Guide for Psychology

This easy-to-read guide points students in the right direction as they explore the tremendous array of information about psychology available on the Internet, and provides a wide range of annotated web links for further exploration. This guide also contains an access code to Research Navigator, Allyn & Bacon's online collection of academic and popular journals. Research Navigator offers students three exclusive databases (EBSCO's ContentSelect, the *New York Times* on the Web, and Link Library) of credible and reliable source content to help students first initiate, and then focus, their research efforts.

ACKNOWLEDGMENTS

I gratefully acknowledge the special help of the following people at Allyn and Bacon, who provided valuable guidance in writing and producing this book: Stephen Frail and Allison Rowland.

I would also like to thank the following individuals, who reviewed the previous edition or this edition at various stages and offered useful suggestions: Becky M. Atkinson, Samford University; Peter J. Byrne, Maria College; John T. Coggins, Purdue University North Central; Nancy A. Dash, Mott Community College; Mark Durm, Athens State University; Laurie S. Hunter, Francis Marion University; Fred Johnson; Margaret Johnson, Salem State College; Joline Jones, Worcester State College; Shelley Dean Kilpatrick, UCLA/RAND Center for Adolescent Health Promotion; David A. Lawson, Liberty University; William M. McGuigan, Penn State University; Elizabeth Pemberton, University of Delaware; Peggy Perkins, University of Nevada, Las Vegas; M. Cecil Smith, Northern Illinois University; and Rob Weisskirch, California State University, Fullerton.

Finally, I would like to thank my family for putting up with a wife and mom who was more frantic than usual during the time I was revising the text. Thanks for pitching in, guys, and for keeping your good humor even when there were no clean pants to wear and I had to ask you to take on extra chores. I'd also like to especially thank my mom who had to forego my visiting her this past summer so that I could get the text finished. I love you all.

CHAPTER 1 ADOLESCENTS IN SOCIAL CONTEXT

WOULDN'T YOU LIKE TO KNOW . . .

- ▶ When does adolescence begin and end?
- ▶ How is the American adolescent population changing?
- ▶ Is your state losing or gaining in adolescent population?
- ▶ Who invented the Internet and why?
- ▶ Can you expect to put in more or fewer hours on the job than your parents do?
- ▶ Are you more or less likely to get married than people of your parents' generation?
- ▶ What are three negative effects of the sexual revolution?
- ▶ Are you more or less likely to be a victim of a violent crime than you were 10 or 20 years ago?

The word adolescence comes from the Latin verb *adolescere,* which means "to grow" or "to grow to maturity." **Adolescence** is the period of growth between childhood and adulthood. The transition from one stage to the other is gradual and uncertain, and while the time span is not the same for every person, most adolescents eventually become mature adults. In this sense, adolescence is likened to a bridge between childhood and adulthood over which individuals must pass before they take their places as full-grown, responsible adults.

> **ANSWERS WOULDN'T YOU LIKE TO KNOW ...**
>
> **When does adolescence begin and end?**
>
> Adolescence begins at about 12 years of age, when the body starts maturing toward puberty. The end of adolescence is much less clearly delineated: Some individuals leave home at 17 and support themselves (adults?), whereas others live at home and are supported by their parents well into their twenties (adolescents?).

Most people place the beginning of adolescence at the time at which children *begin* to physically mature into individuals capable of reproduction—that is, when they begin to sexually mature. People call this "hitting puberty." Actually, this is a misnomer, since **puberty** correctly means to be physically capable of procreating, and the physical changes that are associated with "hitting puberty" begin quite a few years before children become fertile. In any case, most children reach puberty when they are between 11 and 13 years of age, and this is considered the lower boundary of adolescence. (By the way, in Latin, the word *puberty* means "to grow hair," which is a great descriptor of this maturation process!)

The upper boundary of adolescence is less clear. Different criteria can be used, and none are universally agreed upon. Some people believe that adolescence ends once physical maturity is reached. Others believe that it ends once an individual attains full legal status and can thereby vote, drink alcohol if desired, be drafted, get married, and so on. (A problem with this designation is that these legal markers do not occur at the same age: You can be drafted at 18 but be prohibited from drinking until 21.) Another more vague criterion puts the end of adolescence when most others treat the individual as an adult, according him or her respect and independence in decision making.

Adolescents themselves tend to focus on achieving emotional independence from their parents and taking responsibility for their own actions (Arnett, 1997). Most adults tend to think of adolescence as ending with a combination of attaining financial independence, attaining emotional independence, and attaining a change in perspective in which one focuses on issues that are less adolescent and more adult. Therefore, in this text we will consider full-time college students adolescents and discuss them periodically.

Adolescence, then, is not monolithic and uniform. There is a tremendous difference between an insecure, gangly, 12-year-old middle school student and a fully grown, confident 20-year-old college sophomore. Because of this, we distinguish *early adolescence* from *middle adolescence* and *late adolescence. Early adolescence* refers to individuals who are about 11 to 14 years old, and *middle adolescence* refers to those who are 15 to 17. We will use the term *late adolescence* to mean those adolescents who are 18 or older, with full cognizance that some 18-, 19-, and 20-year-olds are adults. Adults are (theoretically) mature in all ways—physically, emotionally, socially, intellectually, and spiritually—whereas adolescents still have significant growth to achieve in some areas.

When do adolescents believe they fully become adults? Some feel they have to wait too many years to "get into the club." Whereas many middle-aged and elderly adults say they feel younger than they really are and young adults typically "feel their age," adolescents most commonly feel older and more mature than their chronological age (Galambose, Kolaric, Sears, and Maggs, 1999; Montepare and Lachman, 1989). Since their parents and teachers usually do not share this assessment, however, many adolescents chafe under what they perceive to be excessive control by the adults around them.

Two other words that we will use frequently in this text are *teenager* and its shortened form, *teen.* Both of these terms, strictly speaking, mean only someone in the teen years: 13 to 19 years of age. The word **teenager** is of fairly recent origin. It first appeared in the *Readers' Guide to Periodical Literature* in the 1943–1945 issue. However, because children (especially girls) sometimes mature physically before 13 years of age, there are some discrepancies. An 11-year-old girl may look and act like a teenager, but a 15-year-old boy, if not yet sexually mature, may still act and look like a child. In this text, the words *teenager, teen,* and *adolescent* will be used interchangeably.

The word **juvenile** is generally used in a legal sense to signify one who is not yet considered an adult in the eyes of the law—in most states, anyone up to 18 years of age. The legal rights of 18-year-olds are confusing, however, for they vary from state to state. The Twenty-Sixth Amendment gave 18-year-olds the right to vote, and in some areas, they are called for jury duty. They may obtain credit in their own names at some stores and banks, but at others, they have to obtain cosigners. Many landlords still require the parents of 18-year-olds to cosign leases. The net result is confusion.

APPROACHES TO STUDYING ADOLESCENTS

There are various approaches to the study of adolescents. The first is the *biological* approach, which discusses the process of sexual maturation and physical growth that take place during puberty. It involves the maturation and functions of the male and female organs, the development of secondary sexual characteristics, and the growth trends in height and weight that take place during adolescence. As their bodies change, adolescents develop new concerns about their nutrition, weight, and physical attractiveness. In short, they are not always pleased with what is happening to their bodies. We will focus on the biological approach in Part Two of this book (Chapters 4 and 5).

The second approach to the study of adolescents is the *cognitive* approach, which deals with two aspects: (1) the qualitative changes that take place in the way adolescents think and (2) the quantitative changes that take place in intelligence and information processing. Of concern also is the effect that cognitive changes have on the adolescent's personality and behavior. Researchers interested in cognition study such topics as intelligence, Scholastic Assessment Test (SAT) scores, memory ability, thinking, problem solving, and decision making. We will take up the cognitive approach in Part Three (Chapters 6 and 7).

The third approach to the study of adolescents is the *psychosexual* approach, which deals with the development of emotions and of the self, including the development of self-concept, self-esteem, gender, and identity. It is concerned also with mental health and the effects of stress on the adolescent. During adolescence, individuals must integrate newfound sexual feelings into their self-concept and learn to manage their sexuality. We will examine the psychosexual approach in Part Four (Chapters 8 and 9).

The fourth way to view adolescents is to examine them in the context of their *social relationships*. We will do this in Parts Five and Six of this book. Part Five (Chapters 10 and 11) is concerned with the way that families influence teenagers. We will look at parent-adolescent conflicts, sibling relationships, and parenting styles. The effects of different family constellations—single-parent families, blended families, and adoptive families—are also considered. Part Six (Chapters 12, 13, and 14) deals with peer, friendship, and romantic relationships. Topics such as conformity, fads, and cliques and crowds are discussed. The section closes with a look at the development of moral values. Although this topic could just as readily have been placed in the cognitive development section, it has been located here to emphasize that morality is an intrinsically social phenomenon, since we develop our moral beliefs through interactions with others and since our moral beliefs dictate how we treat other people.

Some of the most important connections that adolescents have with the broader social world are discussed in Part Seven (Chapters 15 and 16). Adolescents spend many of their waking hours in school, interacting with teachers and administrators as well as peers. The school is the institution that provides adolescents with many of the skills they will need to function as independent adults, including social and job-related skills. The special needs of school dropouts are also considered in Chapter 15. Often while in school, and certainly after they graduate, most adolescents are employed. Pathways to career decisions, career education, the costs and benefits of youth employment, and youth unemployment are discussed in Chapter 16.

Part Eight, the text's penultimate section, deals with many of the serious problems faced by today's adolescents: suicide, delinquency, running away from home, and substance abuse. (Another serious concern, teenage pregnancy, is discussed with sexuality in Chapter 9.) Although certainly not all adolescents encounter these problems, surprisingly high percentages do. And even if they do not experience these problems themselves, they almost certainly know someone who does. Thus, a text on adolescent psychology would not be complete without an examination of the causes, symptoms, and treatments of these problems.

Finally, in order to provide a sense of closure, the text ends with a brief Epilogue about the differences between adolescence and young adulthood. The epilogue also contains a description of "emerging adults," those individuals who are in some ways between adolescence and adulthood. Emerging adulthood has become an increasingly more common bridge stage in modern times and is now normative enough that it deserves discussion since it, not young adulthood proper, will be the next phase of life for many adolescents.

The approach taken in this book is an *eclectic approach* to the study of adolescents. That is, the approach is interdisciplinary, emphasizing not one aspect of adolescent development but all of them, recognizing that no single approach contains all the facts. As such, the contributions of biologists, psychologists, educators, sociologists, anthropologists, and medical personnel are all

adolescence the period of growth from childhood to maturity.

puberty the developmental stage at which one becomes capable of reproduction.

teenager in a strict sense, includes only the teen years: ages 13 to 19.

juvenile one who is not yet considered an adult in the eyes of the law.

important. If we are to get a complete view of adolescents, we must stand in different places and look at adolescents from different perspectives.

THE CHANGING FACE OF AMERICAN ADOLESCENCE

Because of fluctuations in immigration rates and birthrates, the absolute size of the juvenile population in the United States is continuously changing. Between the late 1960s and the mid 1980s, the number of juveniles declined to a low of about 63 million individuals. Since that time, it has been slowly but steadily increasing. If the forecasts are accurate, this trend will continue at least through 2050, such that there will be about 80 million U.S. juveniles by 2025 (Snyder and Sickmund, 2006). This represents a 36 percent increase between 2000 and 2050 (see Figure 1.1). Growth in the teenage population closely mirrors that of the more inclusive juvenile population.

Although this change seems large, it is actually small in comparison to the increases in some other age groups. The change in the number of elderly individuals, in particular, has been much greater. Therefore, over the next 25 or 30 years, adolescents will make up a slightly smaller fraction of the U.S. population, despite their increase in absolute number.

Again, due to different immigration rates and birthrates, the racial and ethnic makeup of American adolescents is also changing. During the next 25 years, the relative increases in the numbers of Asian American, African American, Hispanic American, and Native American juveniles will greatly outstrip the number of non-Hispanic Caucasian juveniles. The American adolescent population is becoming increasingly multiracial and multiethnic. (Adolescent diversity is discussed in Chapter 3.)

Juveniles and their families are also on the move. While many states have experienced significant increases in their juvenile populations, numerous others have shown declines (see Figure 1.2). These changes reflect the overall movement of the U.S. population away from the north central and northeast states to the western and southern states.

ANSWERS WOULDN'T YOU LIKE TO KNOW . . .

How is the American adolescent population changing?

Although there are increasingly more adolescents in the United States, they now make up a smaller proportion of the total population because people are living longer and the birthrate is dropping. The racial/ethnic makeup of American adolescents is also changing. More and more are of African, Hispanic, or Asian descent.

OUR SOCIETY IN REVOLUTION

The society in which adolescents grow up has an important influence on their development, relationships, adjustments, and problems. The expectations of the society mold their personalities, influence their roles, and guide their futures. The structure and functions of the society either help them fulfill their needs or create new problems by stimulating further tension and frustration. Because adolescents are social beings who are part of a larger society, we need to understand this social order and some of the ways it influences them.

Certainly, much of the adolescent experience is reasonably constant. After all, for eons, individuals have had to cope with reaching puberty and all that goes with it. But not everything about being an adolescent is so predictable. The world is constantly changing—sometimes quite rapidly and sometimes more gradually.

FIGURE 1.1 U.S. JUVENILE POPULATION PROJECTION

Source: Data from U.S. Bureau of the Census (2000).

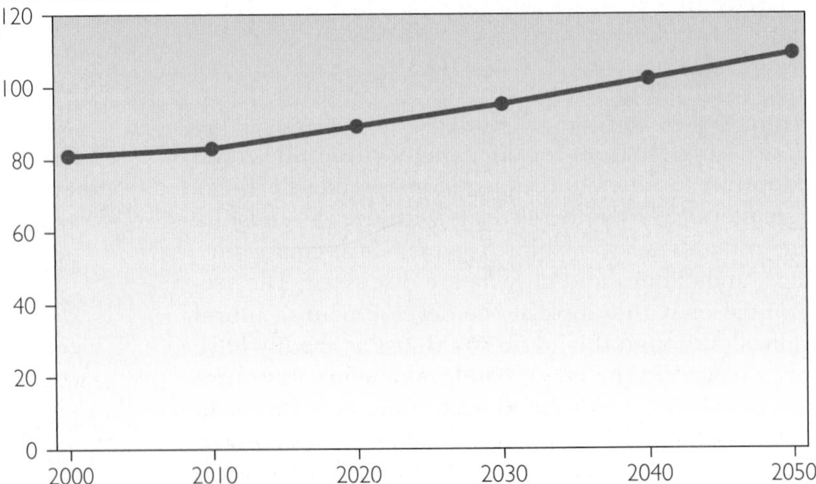

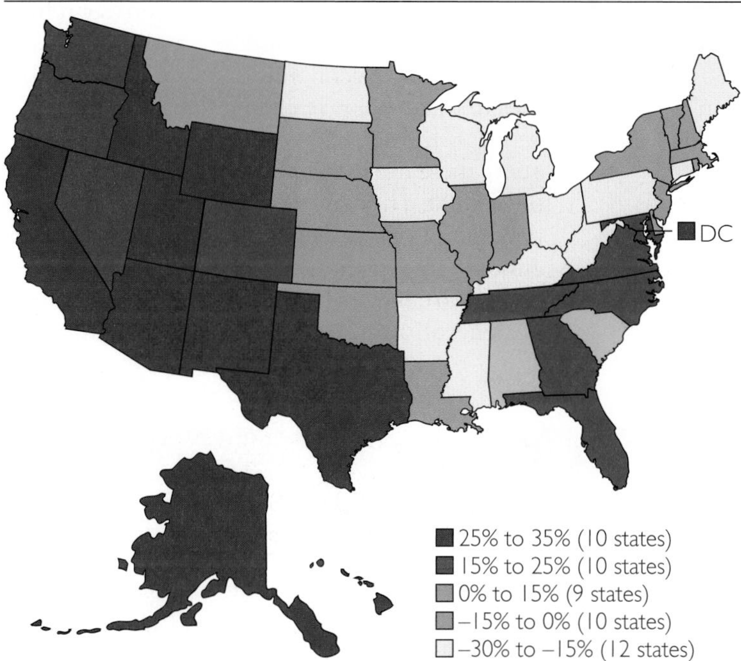

FIGURE 1.2 PROJECTED CHANGE IN U.S. JUVENILE POPULATION: 1995 TO 2015 (IN PERCENT)

Source: Snyder and Sickmund (2006).

ANSWERS WOULDN'T YOU LIKE TO KNOW . . .

Is your state losing or gaining in adolescent population?

Check Figure 1.2 to see if your home state is gaining or losing in adolescent population. If you live in the West, it is likely gaining, and if you live in the Midwest or the Northeast, it is likely losing.

Today's adolescents are facing a number of new conditions that are different from those faced by past generations. Some of these conditions are the result of gradual evolution and thus outgrowths of what has come before; others would have been unanticipated even 50 years ago. These societal changes are interrelated, each change playing off of and influencing the others.

Because of these sometimes rapid changes and singular events, different **cohorts** of adolescents have had different characteristics. It is easier to speak definitively about those cohorts from the past than more current ones, as there is not enough historical distance to know absolutely what events and issues will have been most important in shaping present- and near-present-day adolescents. The following are the descriptors most frequently given to the major adolescent cohorts since the early 1900s.

The Lost Generation: These were individuals who were adolescents or young adults during or just after World War I and hence were born between the mid-1880s and 1900. They were traumatized by the large number of casualties of World War I and disdainful of Victorian ideas about morality and propriety.

The G.I. Generation: This is the generation of Americans who were children during the Depression and youth during World War II. An enormous percentage of young men either enlisted or were drafted into the armed services, and many young women enlisted as well. Those who remained in the United States took on many formerly male occupations. (A popular song of the day was "Rosie the Riveter.")

The Silent Generation: Born too late to serve in World War II and too early to be unconventional and antiauthoritarian (about 1925–1940), this group is characterized as being conservative and traditionalist. However, it should be recognized that many of the heros and icons of the more freewheeling groups that came after—such as the Reverend Martin Luther King, Jr., John Lennon, and Jerry Garcia—were actually members of this cohort.

The Baby Boomers: This group was born during the years after World War II, after the GIs came home and began their adult civilian lives. They are a very large generation, as the birthrate was very high and they grew up in a largely prosperous economic time. Boomers were born from the

cohort A group of individuals who are born at approximately the same time and who share traits because they experienced the same historical events.

mid-1940s until the early to mid-1960s. They comprised the first rock and roll generation in the 1950s and the hippie nation in the late 1960s.

Generation X: The name reflects this generation's feelings of cynicism and alienation. It is a small generation that was born from the mid-1960s until about 1980. Members of generation X were therefore adolescents in the 1980s and 1990s. They are generally the children of baby boomers, and as a group they were not enamored of the world their parents left to them. They often felt neglected by their parents, who were searching for personal self-fulfillment, and pessimistic about their own economic opportunities and abilities to make positive changes in the world.

Generation Y: Also known as the Millennial Generation, these are individuals born from about 1980 until 2000. They (most of you) are too young to personally remember the Cold War and young enough that computers, the Internet, and cell phones are integral parts of life. Many members of generation Y were also raised by attentive

CROSS-CULTURAL CONCERNS THE MAJOR CRISES FACING THE WORLD'S ADOLESCENTS

According to the United Nations Population Fund, the largest adolescent generation in all of history—1.2 billion individuals—is coming of age. Their most pressing global needs include the promotion of gender equality and universal access to education, health services, and reproductive and sexual health information. Meeting these goals will not only improve the lives of the youth themselves but will help stem the AIDS pandemic and reduce worldwide poverty. While some of the issues faced by adolescents in other nations are different from those faced by American youth, some are eerily similar. For example, it is a global, not an American, concern that adolescents are leaning too much upon peers and the media for advice on how to survive in the "new" world they are facing rather than relying upon tradition.

Gender inequality is one pervasive theme; female adolescents face discrimination in much of the world. In many societies, families do not invest as much in their daughters' health or education as they do sons'. In many geographic areas, females are not allowed to own property. Because of poverty and a lack of employment opportunities, girls and women are vulnerable to sexually exploitive practices such as child marriage, sexual coercion, and sexual trafficking. Child brides almost never continue their education and, because of the large age difference between themselves and their husbands, have subordinate positions in the household and are usually not allowed to socialize outside the family. They have little opportunity to leave abusive husbands. In societies in which women have few rights and little social standing, sexual coercion is commonplace and females are held responsible for its occurrence. Annually, between 700,000 and 4,000,000 adolescent girls are forced into the sex trade and have bleak existences filled with degradation and illness.

Because premarital sexual activity has become more commonplace around the globe, HIV/AIDS and other STDs have become diseases of the young. Half of all new cases of AIDS are among people between the ages of 15 and 24; this translates to 6000 young people each day becoming infected, most of them female. The highest rates are in sub-Saharan Africa. Another way that the AIDS epidemic has affected adolescents is that many have lost family members to the virus. If a family member is ill, it is likely that a child (usually a daughter) will have to drop out of school to care for the family member. If a child or adolescent is left an orphan, he or she often must turn to theft or prostitution to survive.

It is important to provide reproductive health information to adolescents to help prevent the spread of STDs. Schools cannot be relied on to provide this information since many youth in developing nations do not attend classes. Different countries have tried different approaches, often using the mass media to get the message out. The most common themes involve abstinence, faithfulness to a single partner, and condom use.

These practices would also, of course, help reduce the number of adolescent pregnancies. Early pregnancy is a serious health risk for young adolescent girls. It is the leading cause of death for young women aged 15 to 19 worldwide. Most of these deaths are due to complications from labor and delivery, but a significant minority are due to botched abortions. Some young adolescents who survive childbirth are permanently disabled from the experience.

The good news is that issues of adolescent well-being are being taken very seriously. The biggest problems have been identified, steps are being taken, and globally progress is being made to improve adolescent outcomes. Real strides have been made in the last decade.

Source: Data from the United Nations Population Fund, 2003.

"helicopter parents," who were very child centered.

Generation ?: Members of the most recent living generation, consisting of those born after 2000, are of course not adolescents yet. They will be the first generation raised solely in the post–9/11 era, a time that feels very different from the more optimistic era that came just before it. Only time will tell what impact that event and others will have on this generation.

Let's briefly consider seven environmental changes that are affecting or will affect the contemporary adolescent experience: the prolongation of adolescence, the presence of the Internet, the changing job market, the need for a prolonged education, the changing family constellation, the sexual revolution, and the rise of violence. Each of these issues will be considered in more depth later in the textbook. The purpose of presenting them here, right up front, is to get you thinking about the social forces that are working to shape the current (and recent) cohorts of adolescents.

THE PROLONGATION OF ADOLESCENCE

Since the 1970s, individuals' full entrance into adulthood has been more and more delayed, as they have taken longer to complete their education, settle on a career, move out of their parents' home, marry, and have children (Arnett, 2000). In other words, adolescence has expanded and become increasingly prolonged. It is not unusual to be at least partly financially dependent upon one's parents well into one's twenties or to marry when close to thirty. With this delay has also come not only a pushing back of significant life events but also a disruption of the lockstep sequence in which these events have traditionally occurred (Fussell, 2002). For example, it is less likely that a female will have a child prior to marriage if she marries at 19 instead of at 27. As another example, someone who completes his or her education at age 20 is less likely to work at a full-time job before then than someone who keeps working toward a degree until he or she is 28.

Many reasons can explain this prolongation: More skills are needed to get a good job; there is increased societal permissiveness toward premarital sexual activity; inexpensive, effective birth control is available; and so on. The fact that the period of adolescence is more protracted is bound to lead to changes in the experiences that adolescents have.

THE REVOLUTION IN INFORMATION TECHNOLOGY

Adolescents today live in a society undergoing rapid technological changes. Probably no other society has so revered technological innovation while placing so little restraint on it than that of the United States. During the last 100 years, Americans have witnessed unprecedented advances: the introduction of electricity, radio, television, automobiles, airplanes, nuclear energy, robots, and satellite communication.

Of all these changes, none has had as profound an effect as the introduction of the computer. The first computers were less powerful than today's personal computers (PCs) yet occupied whole rooms and cost millions of dollars. It's easy to forget that the first personal computer was introduced in 1980. Since that time, the use of computers has skyrocketed. More than half of all U.S. workers today use computers on the job (Bureau of Labor Statistics, 2003). In 2003, 78 percent of American adolescents were using computers at home, and over 93 percent used computers at school (U.S. Bureau of the Census, 2003). Even 52 percent of prekindergarten and kindergarten students were using computers at school.

The Internet

One of the most important reasons for using the computer is the *Internet*. The researchers who created the Internet needed a safe way to store and communicate sensitive government information in the event of a nuclear war. The solution was a network that lacked a central computer to store its billions of bytes of information or to direct the actions of remote computers. Each computer site on the network stands alone but is also interconnected to the others. Thus, the destruction of one site (in the event of war) would not prevent the free interchange of information or destroy the data stored at other sites.

Today, the result is a decentralized network of data stored on thousands of computers that make up the network and that speak a common language. If a particular computer breaks, the rest of the computers connected to the network can use any number of other connections to maintain their link.

Estimates put more than 100 billion users on the Internet (Internet World Stats, 2006). The Internet is open 24 hours a day, 365 days a year. It's a way to meet people; find adventure; share ideas and experiences; look for a job, a date, or a mate; ask questions; or give advice. The information resources of thousands of universities, government agencies, and researchers are at your fingertips. It's like a shopping mall that never closes where you can shop for everything from automobiles to food. It's cyberspace: the final frontier. Cyberspace has no borders or defined boundaries; it is a system where you can

ANSWERS WOULDN'T YOU LIKE TO KNOW ...

Who invented the Internet and why?

The Internet was invented by the U.S. military as a way of protecting its computer network from sabotage. Since the Web is diffuse and decentralized, it is hard to destroy.

go to meet people, communicate, learn, explore, and get information. Cyberspace is the place for those who connect to each other electronically to share their thoughts and feelings. Once online, you can have private and group conversations, join in lively discussions with nationally known experts, play online games, browse through the articles of hundreds of periodicals and online magazines, go on a shopping spree, make flight or hotel reservations, or track investments with the latest stock market quotes and investment advice.

More than 85 percent of American adolescents are current Web users; more than 90 percent have used the Web at some point (Lenhart, Madden, and Hitlin, 2005). The most common reasons adolescents get on the Web is to communicate with others (via e-mails, text messaging, and chat rooms), to visit entertainment sites, and to play games.

As is obvious from the Internet's explosive growth, there is much good to be gained from spending time online. The sheer quantity of available information is staggering: you can learn about almost anything you want. It is like having a fantastic library at your fingertips, one in which you can checkout any books, pictures, or sound clips you'd like. You can take virtual tours of the world's great museums and watch and listen to video clips of policy makers announcing important decisions. (Of course, the information on the Web is of uneven quality, and users must learn how to judge the accuracy of sites and weigh the value of the information they find.) This informational benefit is especially important to more isolated individuals who otherwise might not have access to educational materials. The Internet also lets you inexpensively keep in touch with others, even those far away. For example, posting pictures to your Web page is a way to let your friends see what you did on your vacation or what your new girlfriend looks like. The Web allows you to purchase esoteric items that might not be available in your community, or listen to a live-stream radio program from a city on another continent.

There are, however, a number of potential downsides to Internet use.

Potential Hazards of Internet Use

Inappropriate Materials

One unfortunate downside to the Internet is that it makes a wide variety of inappropriate materials readily available to children and adolescents. For instance, one can find sexually explicit materials such as photographs and videos of singles, couples, and groups involved in various sex acts. Some photographic and artistic materials contain examples of bestiality and pedophilia. Fictional and nonfictional accounts of sexual encounters may include incest, group sex, or bondage. Users can find personal ads of individuals seeking same-sex and opposite-sex partners for one-night stands. Catalogs for sexual devices and clothing as well as advertisements for pay-for-service organizations ranging from phone sex to escort services are also offered.

There's nothing on the Internet that isn't available in other places, but the Internet is not as controllable and thus online materials are more accessible to adolescents and children than some other sources. Furthermore, sometimes even searches intended to visit only innocuous sites result in matches that contain graphic and explicit materials. Finkelhor and his colleagues (Finkelhor, Mitchell, and Wolak, 2000) found that 25 percent of the adolescents they sampled had been exposed to Web-based pornography, *even when they were not looking to do so,* and 20 percent had received a sexual solicitation online.

Violent and destructive materials are also included on the Internet. Recipes for bombs and other destructive devices can be found. There has been at least one example of an adolescent who found an Internet recipe for a bomb similar to that used in Oklahoma City in 1995 and purchased materials at the local hardware store with the intent of seeing if it worked. The Internet may also contain posts encouraging drug use, self-mutilation, or eating-disordered behavior. Radical activist groups also provide materials on the Internet. Such materials may come from neo-Nazi groups or state militia organizations or include information on gang-related activity.

Parents and lawmakers have sought to pass legislation that will help protect children from these kinds of exposures. The Communications Decency Act was passed into law in February 1996. Within days, several civil rights organizations challenged the law on the grounds that it violated the First Amendment. The court overturned the law, and on June 26, 1997, the U.S. Supreme Court, in a 7–2 decision, concurred that it violated the right of free speech and upheld the lower court's finding. A second version of the law, the Child Online Protection Act, was passed in 1998 but was also struck down by the Supreme Court in 2004. A much narrower statute, the Children's Internet Protection Act (CIPA), was passed by Congress in 2000. It was directed not at Internet site producers, but at libraries and public schools. It directed these institutions to ensure that children would not be exposed to "harmful" material if the institutions wished to continue receiving federal funds; what is "harmful" would be determined by local community standards. The act was jointly challenged by the

One drawback of Internet use is the opportunity for adolescents to view pornography and other objectionable material.

American Civil Liberties Union (ACLU) and the American Library Association, although in 2003 the U.S. Supreme Court upheld the law. Libraries and schools have complied with the law by installing blocking software, which they are permitted to remove for adult users who request that they do so (American Library Association, 2006).

Effects on Children and Adolescents

Using the Internet also gives adolescents opportunities to explore their identities that were unavailable in the past. Several authors have speculated that Internet users will develop multiple "virtual selves" (Anderson, 2002). Certainly, you can present yourself any way you wish on the Web. You can develop multiple screen personalities with different races and genders and describe your appearance any way you like. The impact of doing so on the development of a teen's true identity is unclear at this time.

Also on the downside, differential access to the Internet will increase the divide between rich and poor (U.S. Department of Commerce, 1999). Lack of familiarity with computers, networking, and information accessing will only put lower-income adolescents further behind their middle-class peers and make it even more difficult for them to get high-paying jobs.

Another interesting result of the computer revolution is that a technology gap has been created between children and their parents. Many parents don't understand computers and are afraid of them. As a result of these parents' slow assimilation of computer knowledge, the technology gap has widened. Parents must often go to their children for help with the computer problems they are facing.

THE REVOLUTION IN THE WORKPLACE

The United States is a materialistic society. Most individuals believe that it is important to own a nice home and to have many possessions in order to lead a good life. Given this value and the corresponding drive to accommodate ever-increasing material needs, the employment situation in this country continues to evolve.

Multiple Jobholders and Overtime Work

Even though real wages have gone up, Americans are putting in more and more hours at work. Some of these workers are in hard financial straits. Others desire a higher standard of living than they can afford working one 40-hour-a-week job. The recent past has seen increases in the number of workers who hold two jobs—usually one full-time job and a secondary part-time job—as well as increases in the amount of overtime put in by workers with single jobs. Americans spend more time working than most of their European counterparts; in fact, most Europeans spend less time working now than they did in 1970, whereas Americans spend about 20 percent more time working (Office of Economic Cooperation and Development, 2004). We work longer hours each week than most Europeans and we take less vacation time.

Obviously, working this number of hours cuts down on the amount of time workers can spend with their families and children. As one wife said, "When my husband is giving 80 hours a week to his job, what is there left for me?" (Rice, counseling notes).

ANSWERS WOULDN'T YOU LIKE TO KNOW . . .

Can you expect to put in more or fewer hours on the job than your parents do?

If current trends continue, you will likely spend more hours on the job than your parents do or your grandparents did. (So much for technology ensuring increased leisure!)

Working Women

Another indicator of Americans' attempting to keep up with the high cost of living is the increase in the number of women, even women with young children, who are working outside the home. In 2001, 73.9 percent of women worked outside the home. Some 80 percent of married women with children 6 to 17 years of age worked outside the home as did 63 percent of all married women with children under the age of 6. Mothers who were divorced were even more likely to be employed: 87 percent of those with children 6 or older worked and 76 percent of those with children younger than 6 did so (U.S. Bureau of the Census, 2002).

Increasing employment among mothers has intensified the demand for child care. In some cases, the adolescents or older children in the family are expected to take over childrearing duties while their parents are at work.

Adolescent Employment

One reason that Americans work longer hours than Europeans is that more American adolescents are employed. The proportion of high school students who work has been rising steadily. Generally speaking, working students have had the support of parents, teachers, and social scientists. The conventional wisdom seems to argue that working is actually good for students. With the blessing of society, then, American youths have gone to work. Nearly 3 million 15- to 17-year-olds work during the school year, and 4 million work during the summer months. These adolescents work an average of 17 hours a week while school is in session and 29 hours a week during the summer (Herman, 2000; Stringer, 2003).

Many experts, however, are beginning to feel that *many adolescents are devoting too much time to jobs and not enough to school* (Marsh and Kleitman, 2005). It is not unusual for a 16-year-old to earn $250 a week in the summer and spend the entire sum on car expenses, tickets to concerts, clothing, DVDs, and CDs. These spending patterns do not help prepare adolescents for adult self-sufficiency.

The effects of adolescent employment are fully reviewed in Chapter 16, but for now, suffice it to say that credible data suggest that working after school is associated with lowered school achievement and with increased delinquency and substance abuse rates. Employed teenagers are also less likely to get adequate sleep

The number of adolescents who hold part-time jobs has been rising steadily. An after-school job often conflicts with schoolwork and responsibilities at home, especially if the job takes more than 20 hours per week.

and sufficient exercise than their nonworking peers. Any adolescent who works may be somewhat at risk for negative outcomes, but this is particularly true of those adolescents who work long hours.

Advertising and Consumption

The mass media are partly responsible for creating a generation of consuming adolescents. Today's children have been surrounded, as no other generation before, by messages in newspapers and magazines, on radio and television, and in pop-ups on their computers, urging the purchase of the newest antiperspirant, breakfast food, or shampoo. More than 99 percent of U.S. households own televisions, and more than two-thirds of adolescents have television sets in their bedrooms (Rideout, Roberts, and Foehr, 2005).

Today's youths constitute a huge consumers' market. The increasing wealth of this age group has caused more and more businesses to cater directly to youths. Clothes, cosmetics, automobiles, CDs and DVDs, sunglasses skis, snowmobiles, motorcycles, magazines, grooming aids, sports equipment, cigarettes, and thousands of other items are given the hard sell to attract the dollars of increasing numbers of adolescents.

Adolescent buying power has been growing at an enormous rate. Adolescents are not only earning more money themselves, but parents are giving them more cash and they are more influential in regard to family purchases. American teens directed the spending of $190 billion dollars in 2006, a 25 percent increase since 2001 (MarketResearch.com, 2005). Most of their money (about one-third) goes to clothing and accessories and food (Coinstar, 2003). Adolescent girls spend more time shopping than adults: The average teenage girl goes to a mall 54 times a year and spends 90 minutes per visit, 40 percent more time than other shoppers (Munk, 1997; Voight, 1999).

Even so, many adolescents save at least some of their money. About 25 percent say that they save most of the money they receive, and 56 percent say that they save about half of their earnings (Dolliver, 1999). When teens save, it is most often for the major expenditures of college and a car.

Families that have not been able to keep up with the struggle for money, status, and prestige seem poorer than ever. As a result, adolescents in those families often feel abandoned and rejected. Youths who come from extremely poor families are more likely to be nonjoiners in school activities, are seldom elected to positions of prestige, and often seek status through antisocial behavior (U.S. Bureau of the Census, 2005). These youths struggle for identity and sometimes become problems because they find an identity that middle-class society rejects.

THE EDUCATION REVOLUTION

Expanding technology and social complexity have increased the need for higher education and thus lengthened the period of adolescent dependency. It is vital that adolescents graduate from high school and college if they are to get well-paying jobs. If U.S. adolescents wish to be competitive with their peers in other technological nations, they must spend more days and years in school, put in more hours doing homework, and tackle more complex information. It is imperative that they devote more time to learning new technological skills.

This essential increase in education means that the period of dependency on parents has lengthened. In 2000, more than half (56 percent) of men between the ages of 18 and 24 lived at home with one or both of their parents; more than 40 percent of unmarried 18- to 24-year-old women did as well (Fields and Casper, 2001). The result has been the delayed independence of these young people.

Educational Attainment

Considerable progress has been made in educating students through high school age. In 2000, 84 percent of the population age 25 and older had completed four years or more of high school. This figure represents 85 percent of Whites, 79 percent of African Americans, and 57 percent of Latinos. The percentage of students who have completed high school has doubled in the past 40 years. The number of students earning college degrees has not kept pace, however. In 2000, 26 percent of people age 25 and older had completed four or more years of college. This number represents 26 percent of Whites but only 17 percent of African Americans and about 11 percent of Latinos. Still, the percentage of students of all races who have completed four years or more of college has tripled since 1960 (U.S. Bureau of the Census, 2002; see Figure 1.3). There is still a long way to go, however.

Part of the problem of raising higher educational levels is the rapid increase in costs. Although the amount of financial aid available in the forms of grants and loans has increased, as well, it has not kept pace. The cost of a college education is rising faster than the standard of living. Many students are burdened with repaying huge loans years after they graduate from college.

Embracing the New Technology

One of the most exciting changes in education is happening as teachers become more experienced with computers and introduce new uses for them. Educators across the nation continue to embrace the new electronic technologies that are available. Many are

FIGURE 1.3 EDUCATIONAL ATTAINMENT BY AGE 25: 1960–2000

Source: Data from U.S. Bureau of the Census (2002).

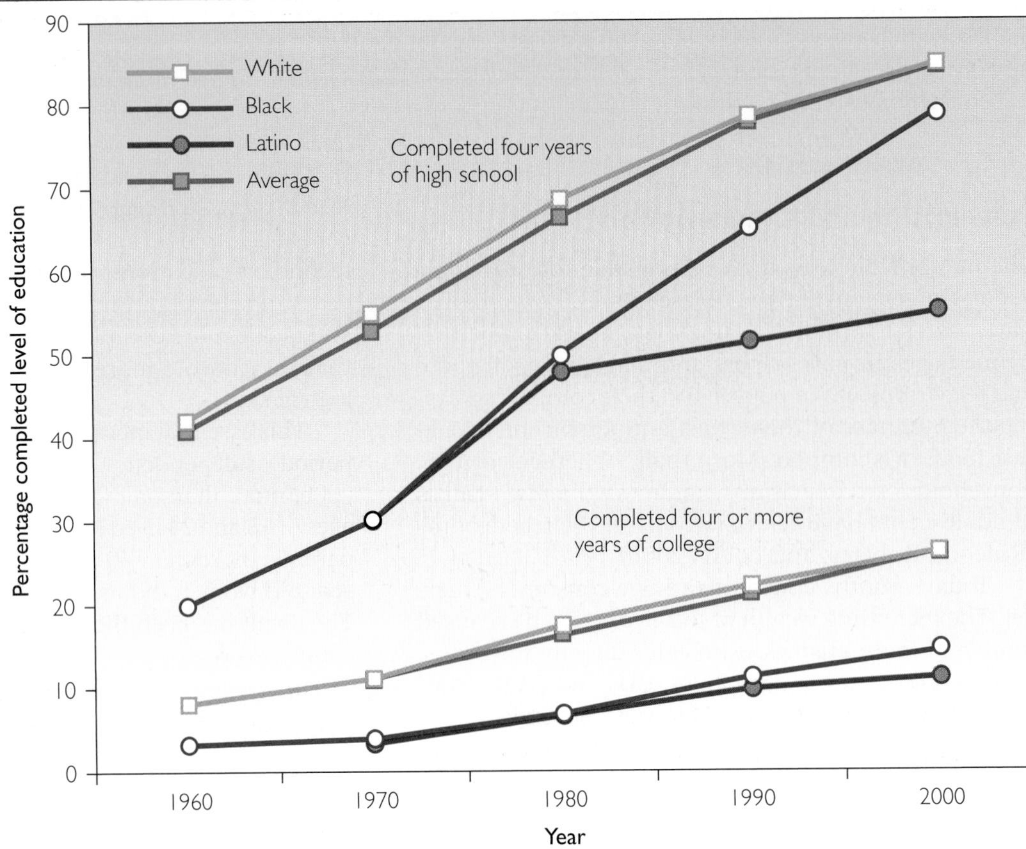

developing dynamic lesson plans that include significant uses of online resources outside the classroom for research in the development of background materials. In addition to using computers for research, many teachers employ computers in science classrooms as test equipment, in foreign-language labs for interactive work with students in other countries, in virtual field trips to the countries students are studying, in math labs to model complex mathematical equations, and in the administrative offices for more traditional office applications. Students can send e-mail messages worldwide in minutes to correspond with those in other lands. In Internet relay chats, individuals can participate in live, interactive discussions via the keyboard. The changes that have been made in education over the past 30 years have been significant and inspiring, but none will likely have more effect on educational processes than classroom computers.

Innovations in Career Education

Another educational trend that will affect adolescents is an increasing awareness of the need for career preparation while in high school. Not all students graduate from high school, and of those who do, many do not go on to college. As good-paying jobs require ever more specialized skills, schools are positioning themselves to provide those skills to students.

At the present time, American schools still do far less to facilitate graduates' entrance into the working world than do the schools in many European nations (Kerckhoff, 2002). However, increased opportunities for apprenticeships, as well as other innovations, may someday close that gap. (These new approaches are discussed more fully in Chapter 15.)

THE FAMILY REVOLUTION

Changes in Marriage and Parenthood

Trends in marriage and parenthood have changed over the last few decades. The marriage rate has declined, the age at which people marry has gone up, and the number of children per family has decreased.

Marriage Rates

As shown in Figure 1.4, more and more adults are electing to remain single than was true in the past. Today's adolescents are more likely to remain single

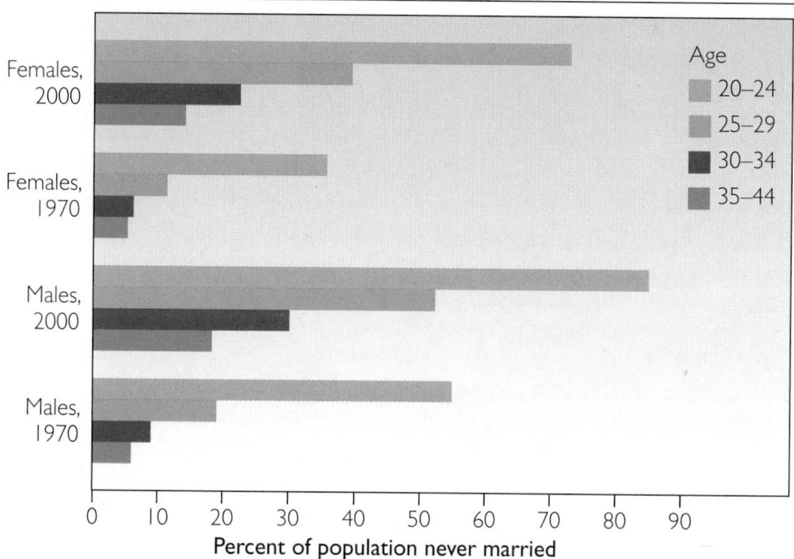

FIGURE 1.4 PERSONS NEVER MARRIED BY AGE AND SEX: 1970 AND 2000

Source: Fields and Casper (2001).

ANSWERS WOULDN'T YOU LIKE TO KNOW . . .

Are you more or less likely to get married than people of your parents' generation?

Fewer individuals are marrying than in the past, and they are waiting longer before they do so.

for more years than either their parents or their grandparents.

Age at Marriage

Even when individuals choose to marry, they are waiting longer before doing so. The median age of marriage for men in 1970 was 23.2; in 2004, it was 27. The median age of marriage for women in 1970 was 20.8; in 2004, it was 26 (Fields and Casper, 2001; Popenoe and Whitehead, 2005). Furthermore, the gap in median age of marriage for men and women has narrowed substantially.

The reasons for the trend to delay marriage include an increase in premarital sex, more opportunities for higher education, decreased negative attitudes toward singlehood, and an increase in nonmarital cohabitation. This trend is significant because those who wait until their mid to late twenties to marry have a greater chance of marital success than those who wed earlier. The delay of marriage has also resulted in a marked increase in unmarried young adults in the population. More than one-third of the men and one-fourth of the women in the United States have not married by 30 years of age.

In any case, even those adolescents who do eventually marry (which is the majority of them) will spend more years as single adults than those in previous generations.

Family Size

Declining birthrates since 1965 have resulted in smaller families. The average number of people per family was 3.67 in 1960, 3.19 in 1985, and 2.62 in 2000. More than half of families in 2000 had no children of their own under 18 years of age at home. An additional 20 percent of families had only one child of their own at home who was under 18 years of age.

These figures seem almost incredible: More than 70 percent of U.S. families had one or no children under age 18 living at home. The fact is, women in the United States are having fewer children. At the beginning of the twentieth century, the average married woman had five children. Today, the average number of total births to an ever-married woman between the age of 15 to 55 has declined to 1.8 (Dye, 2005; U.S. Bureau of the Census, 2002).

Adolescents who come from smaller families enjoy several advantages. Parents are more likely to give ample attention and care to each child. Adolescents who come from small families also have a greater opportunity to continue higher education, since parents' resources are more available to them. An important consideration is whether the children who are born into the family are wanted and are there by choice rather than chance. The psychological impact on the parents is lessened considerably if parenthood is chosen and welcomed. Not surprisingly, unwanted children are more likely to be neglected and abused. Marital delay and smaller family size go hand in hand since couples tend to have fewer children if they wait until they are older to wed.

The characters in HBO's popular TV series *Entourage* illustrate the trend to delay marriage. More than one-third of American men and one-fourth of American women have not married by age 30.

Changes in Family Dynamics

Not only has the likelihood of marriage and the structure of the family changed, but the expectations that individuals bring to marriage have changed as well.

Romantic Love

Adolescents today have grown up in a time where the fulfillment of romantic love and companionship—not economic necessity—are considered to be the primary functions of getting married.

This emphasis on personal relationships has placed more burden on the family unit. When people establish a family for love, companionship, and emotional security but do not find fulfillment, they become disappointed and experience feelings of failure and frustration. This is one reason for the high rate of divorce in the United States. Rather than stay together for the sake of the family, couples often separate if their personal needs and expectations are not met.

The Democratic Family

The family has also gradually become more democratic. Throughout most of our nation's history, the American family was patriarchal, with the father considered as head of the household, having authority over and responsibility for other members of the family. As head of the household and owner of the property, his wife and children were expected to reside with him or near his family, according to his choice. One characteristic of the traditional patriarchal family was a clear-cut distinction between the husband's and the wife's role in the family. The husband was the breadwinner and was usually responsible for clearly defined chores that were considered "man's work." The wife was responsible for "woman's work," such as housecleaning, cooking, sewing, childrearing, and other responsibilities. Children were expected to be submissive and obedient to their parents and to follow their directions, including assuming a considerable responsibility in the performance of family chores.

Gradually, a more democratic form of the family evolved. This change came about for several reasons. First, the rise of the feminist movement brought some economic power and freedom to women. Women gained the power to own property and to borrow money. Also, increasing educational opportunities for women and the gradual increase in the percentage of married women working outside the home encouraged the adoption of more egalitarian sex roles in the family. As more wives earned incomes, more husbands were asked to take on greater responsibilities for homemaking and child care. The general trend was toward a more equal voice in decision making and a more equitable distribution of family responsibility. Third, the demand for equality of sexual expression resulted from the recognition of the sexual capabilities of women. With such recognition, marriages could be based on the mutual exchange of love and affection. The development of efficient contraceptives also freed women from unwanted pregnancies and enabled them to have personal lives of their own as well as social lives with their husbands.

The Child-Centered Family

The child-study movement after World War II catalyzed the development of the child-centered family. No longer was the focus on what a child could do to serve his or her family but rather a matter of what the family could contribute to the total development of the child. The rights and needs of children as important members of the family were emphasized. As children matured, they demanded a greater voice in family decision making, which sometimes led to rebelliousness against their parents.

Nonmarital Cohabitation

Another significant change in marriage trends in the United States is the increase in the number of couples who cohabit before marriage. According to the government, there were 4.6 million unmarried cohabiting couples in the United States in 2003, which represents a 160 percent increase since 1980 (Fields, 2004). By the late 1990s, more than 40 percent of all adult women had been in at least one nonmarital, cohabiting relationship (Fields and Casper, 2001). About 40 percent of these couples had some children under 15 years of age living in the households. Approximately 20 percent of all the cohabitating couples were under age 25 (Fields, 2004). (A complete discussion of nonmarital cohabitation is found in Chapter 12 of this book.)

Adolescents will be affected by this rise in cohabitation for two main reasons: (1) They will be more likely to be raised by nonwed, cohabitating couples than in the past, and (2) they will be more likely to cohabitate someday themselves.

Out-of-Wedlock Births

Another trend worth noting is the dramatic rise in the number of births to unwed and never-wed mothers. This means that teens are more likely to become parents themselves prior to marriage and that they are also more likely to be raised by single, never-wed mothers. (This issue is discussed more fully in Chapters 9 and 11.) Suffice it for now to say that unwed mothers are more likely to be unhappy and to have a low standard of living. Moreover, their children are less likely to receive adequate prenatal care and to attend high-quality schools, and they are more likely to develop a variety of problems than children raised by married mothers.

Divorce

The divorce rate in the United States has been declining slightly since 1980 (U.S. Bureau of the Census, 2004; see Figure 1.5). In spite of this downward trend, the United States has the highest divorce rate in the world. Almost one-third of American adults have been divorced at least once (Krieder and Fields, 2002), and more than two-thirds of American children have experienced their parents' divorce (Fields, 2003). The high divorce and separation rates, plus a rise in out-of-wedlock births, means that over one-half of all children who were born in the 1980s and 1990s will spend a considerable amount of time living with only one parent. Adolescents in these cohorts will most likely have less contact with their fathers than those in previous cohorts. Since most divorced adults remarry, these teenagers are more likely to live in a blended, stepfamily situation than those from previous generations.

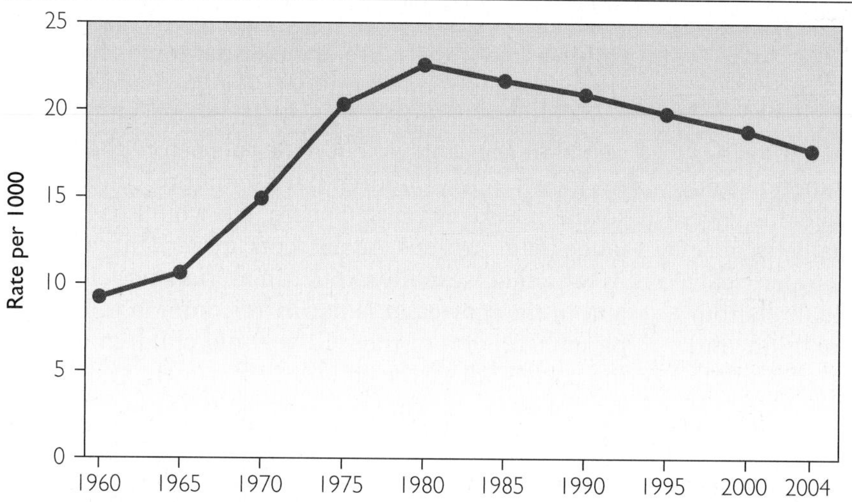

FIGURE 1.5 DIVORCE RATES: 1960–2004.

Source: Data from U.S. Bureau of the Census (2006).

THE SEXUAL REVOLUTION

The so-called sexual revolution began in earnest in the 1970s with the development of the birth control pill and the rise of the feminist movement. This revolution has had both positive and negative effects.

Positive Effects of the Sexual Revolution

Development of Scientific Knowledge of Sexual Functioning

For years, scientists had studied the human body and how it functions, and researchers had studied the various body systems. Somehow, though, a scientific study of the sexual response system was considered off limits. Much attention was devoted to human reproduction but little to sexual arousal, response, and expression.

This all changed when the research team of Masters and Johnson began to observe in the laboratory the physical details of human sexual arousal. For the first time, reports were given on the physiological changes in human sexual response that occur under sexual stimulation. Since the pioneering work of Masters and Johnson (1966), other clinicians have made significant contributions to the field.

This knowledge of the sexual response system enables individuals to understand better the stages of sexual response. In turn, this increased understanding may enhance the pleasure of sexual relationships and help solve many sexual problems. Knowing exactly what is to take place, medical personnel are now able to assist individuals in dealing with problems of sexual dysfunction. The study of the human sexual response system also exploded some sexual myths, one of which was that human females are not really sexual beings and are not able to respond sexually to the extent that males are. This fact tended to free females from the harmful philosophy that sex is a woman's duty and a man's pleasure. Today, women and men are now seen as equals in their sexual responsiveness.

Treatment of Sexual Dysfunction

Scientific knowledge has enabled medical authorities to understand the causes of sexual dysfunction and how to treat it. Countless millions of individuals have not been able to express themselves sexually because of some problem or another. Now, with proper treatment, most people can enjoy normal sexual relationships. Problems such as orgasm dysfunction and inhibited sexual desire in both men and women; premature ejaculation, erectile dysfunction, and ejaculatory inhibition in men; and painful intercourse (dyspareunia) in women are treatable sexual functions.

Development of Contraceptives

Numerous birth control measures have been made widely available, including pills, implants, spermicides, condoms, diaphragms, patches, and new sterilization techniques. The development of contraceptives freed women from the burden of bearing one child after the other and enabled couples to plan their families rather than having them by chance.

Willingness to Deal with Unwanted Sexual Behavior

In recent years, people have become more willing to openly discuss the issues of sexual harassment and rape. Individuals who used to suffer the pain and humiliation of rape in silence are now coming forth to confront their aggressors. The sexual abuse of children is also finally being faced and dealt with in a more helpful and healthful manner. Although American society still has a long way to go in reducing the incidence of sexual abuse of women and children, much progress has been made.

Flexibility of Gender Roles

Due in part to the sexual revolution, gender roles have undergone some drastic changes. Traditionally, society defined what was meant by *femininity* and *masculinity*. People were stereotyped and pressured to live up to certain roles according to their genders. These gender-role stereotypes placed limitations on the relationships that people were capable of forming and on career and personal achievements.

Today, gender roles in the family are becoming more flexible and men and women are interchanging roles. Similarly, housekeeping and child-care roles have expanded to include both sexes. Gender roles regarding choice of vocation have also changed, so that many women now occupy positions of leadership that were formerly reserved for men.

Negative Effects of the Sexual Revolution

Unfortunately, the more open sexual topics have become, the more opportunity there has been for this freedom to be abused. The media expose children to sexual images and violent materials before they learn to ride tricycles. Children have scant protection from sexual messages that 20 years ago would have been taboo for grown-ups. Adolescents are certainly affected by watching sexually explicit materials on television and in the movies. It is hardly uncommon to hear of parents' reports of their 12-year-old children attending parties where the children experiment sexually as part of the party games. A girl from Kansas said, "In fifth grade, my friends and I decided we would have sex with boys. Now we can't get our reputations back. Now we're sluts of the school." Another girl remarked,

"It's confusing, you're pressured to have sex but when you do, you're a whore" (Pipher, 1996).

An Earlier Beginning to Premarital Sexual Behavior

Researchers have noticed significant changes in premarital sexual attitudes and behavior over the last 40 years. Not only are youths more likely to have premarital intercourse but the age of their initial intercourse is years younger than in the past. Research indicates that more than half of American teens have lost their virginity by their senior year in high school (Centers for Disease Control, 2006). In addition, oral sex has become a common activity among even younger adolescents (Remez, 2000).

Unfortunately, many early and middle adolescents are not emotionally prepared to deal with intercourse. They are emotionally devastated when a relationship sours, they are unknowledgeable about birth control, they are not sufficiently concerned about sexually transmitted diseases, and they are uncertain as to how to set limits. Much early sexual behavior is therefore either unwanted or unsatisfactory.

Nonmarital Pregnancy

At present, more than 800,000 adolescent pregnancies, most of them unplanned, occur each year in the United States. Although this is down from peak rates in the early 1990s, the American adolescent pregnancy rate is still far higher than that found in most of the rest of the industrialized world (Singh and Darrock, 2000). Almost half a million babies are born to these adolescent girls annually, most of them to unwed, single mothers. More than 95 percent of these mothers keep their children and raise them themselves rather than giving them up for adoption (Henshaw, 2003).

Almost no one considers this an ideal situation. Adolescent mothers are more likely to face continuing economic hardship, to fail to continue their education, and to fail to establish their own independent households than other adolescent females. In addition, their children are similarly likely to be impoverished, to be deprived of prenatal care, and to have poor developmental outcomes. We must continue working to find ways to further reduce adolescent pregnancy rates.

Sexually Transmitted Diseases and AIDS

One of the most important consequences of the sexual revolution has been the rapid spread of sexually transmitted diseases (STDs). In today's world, gonorrhea is more common than chicken pox, measles, mumps, whooping cough, tetanus, rubella, tuberculosis, and trichinosis combined. The Centers for Disease Control estimates that 19 million new sexually transmitted infections develop each year in the United States, half of them to persons less than 25 years of age (Centers for Disease Control, 2004b). Adolescents are at high risk for STDs because they have multiple sex partners, do not consistently use safer sexual practices, and are frequently ignorant of STDs' symptoms. Many are unaware that several of the disorders are often asymptomatic (meaning that you might have an STD even though you exhibit no symptoms) and so unknowingly pass them on to their partners.

ANSWERS WOULDN'T YOU LIKE TO KNOW ...

What are three negative effects of the sexual revolution?

Unfortunately, the sexual revolution has brought with it a number of negative effects: high rates of STDs and adolescent pregnancies, a too-early onset of sexual activity (for which most teens are unprepared), and a proliferation of sexual messages on television and in movies. As a result, adolescents are confused about sexuality.

Unfortunately, while many STDs are merely unpleasant and uncomfortable, some can have serious consequences—ranging from serious illness through infertility to death. A number of them are becoming harder to treat since the organisms that cause them are becoming resistant to the available treatments. As with adolescent pregnancy, the adolescent STD situation is a national crisis that cannot be trivialized or ignored.

Confusion about Sex

Adolescents are more and more confused about their sexuality. They are encouraged to learn about and discuss it and some are stimulated to sexual arousal, but they are not quite certain how and if they should express their sexuality when they are confronted with the dangers of losing their reputations, having their hearts broken, or contracting a dangerous STD.

Sex has been demystified, which may be a good thing, but it is also being marketed, which is not a good thing. Adolescents have moved from viewing sex as forbidden and terrifying to seeing sex as accessible and interesting but still terrifying. Sex education and counseling are needed more than ever.

THE VIOLENCE REVOLUTION

Another social change taking place in the United States is the increased fear of violence experienced by many individuals—adolescents as well as children and adults. Even before the tragedy of 9/11, there was a growing perception among many Americans that their neighborhoods and schools were not as safe as they would like. New fears of terrorism and global unrest have only augmented this anxiety.

Violent Crime

The violent crime rate in the United States fell precipitously during the mid to late 1990s and, in fact, is now lower than at any time in the past 30 years (U.S. Bureau of Justice Statistics, 2000). Even so, there is an overall perception that the United States is becoming an ever more dangerous place to live. Well-publicized shootings in a number of high schools have made many adolescents fearful for their own safety; there is a sense that violence can erupt anytime, anywhere and that there is nowhere to hide from it.

In fact, adolescents have reason to be afraid: Even though crime rates have decreased, teenagers are more likely to be assaulted, raped, and robbed than persons in all other age groups (U.S. Bureau of Justice Statistics, 2000).

Violence in Society

Not only are significant percentages of adolescents involved in violent crime, but all of them have been exposed year after year to physical violence and disturbances in the world: the murders or attempted assassinations of national leaders, the bombings of embassies, terrorism at home and on a global scale, and war in over a dozen countries. Television and the press have provided constant exposure to violence. The mass media have created an age of instant news: Television viewers share in the experiences of starving Africans, terrorist bombings, wars, and massive earthquakes. Today's youths have not just heard about killings; they have seen them in the nightly news. They have been bombarded with sensory information that affects emotions and feelings as well as cognitive

RESEARCH HIGHLIGHT COMPUTER GAMES

Computer games first appeared in the 1970s, and since then, their use has skyrocketed as they have incorporated more complex themes and better graphics. Given the perception that many of these games have also become increasingly violent—for instance, requiring players to use weapons to kill large numbers of sometimes innocent opponents—many parents and educators are concerned about their effects on adolescents. Concern is ubiquitous enough that in 2000 the U.S. Senate held hearings on the topic, and a number of prominent researchers testified about the harm that violent games could cause (e.g., Funk, 2000).

No doubt, many of the most popular video and computer games are violent. One study examined the preferences of 9- to 12-year-olds and found that almost half of the games they played involved aggression (Buchman and Funk, 1996). Other studies using older subjects found an even greater percentage of playing time devoted to violent games, including some in which the violence was directed toward women (Dietz, 1998).

There is much less research about the harmful effects of violent video and computer games than there is about the effects of violent television. However, since the data clearly indicate that watching violent television promotes aggression in children and adolescents, there is legitimate cause for concern about the effects of violent computer games. Anderson and Dill (2000) suggest three reasons that playing violent games might be even worse than watching violent TV:

1. When playing a violent computer game, the player takes on the role of the hero, who succeeds by killing "the bad guys." Because the player and the hero are one and the player sees the world through the hero's eyes, he or she identifies with the hero. Previous research has shown that the more a television viewer identifies with an aggressive hero, the more deleterious the effects of televised violence.
2. Computer and video games require active participation, which is not part of regular television viewing. This increased participation promotes the development of aggressive scripts and develops the habit of selecting violent responses.
3. Computer and video games actively reward a player's aggressive actions. By killing, the player earns points and moves closer to succeeding at his or her goal.

Still, as Kirsh (2006) points out, the data are so scanty as to make any definitive claims impossible at this time. Unfortunately, much of the little research that there is was collected using old gaming systems whose graphics were much less realistic than today's and whose levels of violence were considerably less. Also, as of yet no one has systematically examined the effects of the different types of violent games on youth. For example, games with a first-person perspective may be more or less harmful than those that give a third-person perspective, and games in which the objective is to avoid being violent might have different effects than those in which the entire point is to kill as many creatures as possible. We simply do not know yet. However, most psychologists who work with adolescents believe that further research will provide conclusive and overwhelming evidence that playing violent computer and video games is harmful to teenagers.

perceptions. As a result of this constant exposure to violence, many adolescents become insensitive to the violence that goes on around them, and they begin to feel that violence is a necessary and accepted part of their lives.

Violence in the Home

Part of the violence that adolescents are exposed to may be traced back to violence in the home. Adolescents who are brought up in violent families where spouse abuse and child abuse are common tend to become abusive parents and mates themselves. Youths generally model the marital aggression that they witness in their homes. Children who observe their fathers hitting their mothers are more likely to be perpetrators as well as victims of severe marital aggression. The greater the frequency of violence, the greater the chance that the young victims will grow up to be violent parents or partners. Moreover, teenagers who are exposed to violence are more likely to use violence against their parents (Holden, Geffner, and Jouriles, 1998).

Violent Deaths

The most disturbing development in recent years relates to adolescent mortality factors. When young people die, most die violent deaths: Among adolescents age 15 to 24 who die, more than three-fourths die violently. Death from accidents, suicides, and homicides has exceeded disease as the leading cause of death for youths (Centers for Disease Control, 2006). Young people are the only age group in the United States that has not enjoyed improved health status over the past 30 plus years; the reason is the increase in violent deaths.

ANSWERS WOULDN'T YOU LIKE TO KNOW . . .

Are you more or less likely to be a victim of violent crime than you were 10 or 20 years ago?

The violent crime rate has dropped significantly, such that you are now less likely to be assaulted or murdered than you were in the 1980s and early 1990s. Even so, the publicity given to school and gang shootings, as well as terrorist incidents, has increased adolescents' level of fear.

A CAVEAT TO UNDERSTANDING ADOLESCENCE

Throughout this text and already in this chapter, we have made statements such as "Adolescents whose parents have divorced are more anxious than those whose parents have remained married" and "Adolescents who watch a lot of violent television are more aggressive than those who do not." Statements such as these describe **correlations,** or relationships between factors

correlation a description of a relationship between two factors that does not imply a causal relationship between them.

A greater percentage of adolescents have become involved in violent crime in recent years. This 15-year-old is accused of opening fire inside a California school, killing two classmates and wounding thirteen others.

or situations. A correlation can be **positive,** meaning that as one factor increases, so does the other. For example, the sentence "Income level and years of schooling are positively correlated" means that the higher someone's income, the more years he or she probably attended school. A correlation can also be **negative,** meaning that as one factor increases, the other decreases. For example, the statement "Weight and popularity are negatively correlated in Caucasian adolescent girls" means that the heavier a girl is, the less likely she is to be popular.

The most important thing to understand about correlations is that they do not imply *causation.* Many individuals will read a statement such as "Adolescents with high IQ scores do well in school" to mean that having a high IQ score *causes* someone to get good grades. This is a common mistake in interpretation.

Whenever a correlation exists, there are three possible explanations for its occurrence. One is that A might cause B. Having a high IQ score might indeed help you get good grades. Equally possible, however, is that B might cause A. That is, getting good grades and learning a lot in school might help you do well on an IQ test. There is a third possibility as well: that A and B are not directly related to each other. Instead, some other factor, C, might cause both A and B. For example, an adolescent whose parents spend a good deal of time talking with him or her about how to solve problems might do well in school and have a high IQ. Having these discussions might promote getting good grades and doing well on an IQ test. It is only coincidental that A and B occur together. The lesson is this: When you read this text (or another text or a newspaper or magazine article), do not make the mistake of assuming that the factor described in the first half of a correlation caused the second factor.

Why do we describe so many correlations if we cannot draw causal conclusions from them? The answer is that many of the issues we are most interested in—gender differences, age differences, ethnic differences, and socioeconomic differences—cannot be studied in such a way as to make reaching a causal conclusion possible. In order to be able to validly draw a causal conclusion, the researcher must have conducted a **true experiment.** In a true experiment, the researcher has control over the situation and its participants. He or she can ensure that the groups of participants are identical in all relevant ways before the study begins and that they have the same experiences while the study is ongoing (with the exception of the one issue being examined).

For example, if an educational psychologist wanted to determine whether viewing a particular "Don't drink and drive" film would decrease adolescents' inebriated driving behavior, she could set up an experiment. She could go to a high school and randomly divide all the students into two groups. (This is how researchers usually ensure that the participant groups are comparable before the intervention is performed.) She could then show one group of students the drunk-driving film and

RESEARCH HIGHLIGHT TEENS WHO KILL FAMILY MEMBERS

Another side of family violence is that which is perpetrated by the adolescent himself or herself. It includes *parricide,* the killing of a parent (which in turn includes both *patricide,* the murder of a father, and *matricide,* the killing of a mother) and *siblicide,* the murder of a sibling. Although literary examples abound of such behavior—for example, Oedipus Rex, Cain and Abel—in fact such behavior is sensational but uncommon. About 300 to 400 deaths per year are due to parricide (Sacks, 1994); roughly equal numbers of siblicides occur (Underwood and Patch, 1999).

Most parricides—90 percent—are committed by White males who are 14 to 17 years of age (Shon and Targonski, 2003). Matricides are less common than patricides and matricides by females are especially rare. The most common profile of a perpetrator is a 17- or 18-year-old male from a middle- or upper-middle-class family who has no history of violent behavior. He usually acts alone and not in immediate self-defense, although most typically he has been repeatedly abused by his parent(s) (Hart and Helms, 2003). Most of these adolescents do not have psychological disorders, nor are they mentally retarded (Hart and Helms, 2002).

Adolescents use different weapons when attacking their mothers and fathers, most likely because their fathers are usually bigger and stronger than themselves whereas their mothers are not. Guns are used more consistently in father homicides: Guns are more quickly lethal and can accomplish their task from a distance. Mothers are attacked with a broader range of weapons (Hart and Helms, 2003).

Siblicides are in some ways similar to and some ways different from parricides. Perpetrators and victims tend to be older, so that adolescents are not the individuals most commonly involved. Whatever the age, brothers are more likely to be involved as both the victim and the murderer; when sisters are involved, they are more likely to be victims than perpetrators. As with parricide, guns are the weapon of choice. Usually the murder closely follows an argument; alcohol or other drugs are unlikely to be in use (Underwood and Patch, 1999).

the other group a film about car maintenance. After waiting a period of time, perhaps three months, the researcher could survey all of the students, asking how often within the past month they had driven while intoxicated. If the students who watched the alcohol-related film were less likely to have driven while inebriated than the students who saw the neutral film, she could then validly conclude that watching the film *caused* a decrease in driving while drinking.

Much of the time, however, researchers do not have this degree of control. In particular, they cannot be sure that the different participant groups they have identified (rich versus poor, males versus females) are the same in all ways except for the issue being examined. Why? In a true experiment, the participants are randomly assigned to conditions, but in a **quasi-experiment,** pre-existing groups of individuals are studied. The researcher cannot say to a 14-year-old girl, "OK, for the purposes of my experiment, today you are a 14-year-old boy. Get in that group over there." If 14-year-old girls end up scoring differently than 14-year-old boys, because experimental control was not maintained, the researcher will not be able to infer that this difference is because of gender. For example, if we give 14-year-old girls and boys a math test, we might find that the boys do better than the girls. Does this have anything directly to do with gender? Maybe yes, maybe no. It might be that the boys, as a group, have taken more math classes, been more encouraged by their teachers, or not been teased by their peers for doing well in math. Without maintaining control, we cannot determine that gender *per se* caused the observed difference between the groups; other unspecified circumstances might have been more responsible. Again, it's essential not to jump to causal conclusions when you read quasi-experimental or correlational data.

positive correlation a description of a relationship in which when one factor increases, so does the other.

negative correlation a description of a relationship in which when one factor increases, the other decreases.

true experiment a study in which the researcher maintains control to ensure there are no significant differences among his or her groups of participants before the study begins and that the different groups of participants have identical experiences (except for the one issue of interest).

quasi-experiment a study in which the researcher compares pre-existing groups.

SUMMARY

1. *Adolescence* is the period of growth between childhood and adulthood. It is usually considered to begin with puberty, but its ending is less clearly defined. It is often divided into early adolescence (age 11 to 14), middle adolescence (15 to 17), and late adolescence (18 and over).
2. The various approaches to the study of adolescents are the biological approach, the cognitive approach, the psychosexual approach, and the social approach.
3. The number of juveniles in the United States has been steadily increasing and will continue to do so. For a number of years, the increase had been slower, however, than that for other age groups, which means adolescents had been making up an ever-smaller segment of the population. The relative size of the adolescent population has now stabilized; however, the American adolescent population is becoming increasingly diverse.
4. Because individuals born at about the same time experience the same historic events, different generations sometimes take on a predominant characteristic. There have been a number of identifiable cohorts since the beginning of the twentieth century, including the Lost Generation, the G.I. Generation, the Baby Boomers, and the members of Generation X.
5. Seven current societal changes are affecting the adolescent experience: the prolongation of adolescence, the presence of the Internet, the changing job market, the need for a prolonged education, the changing family constellation, the sexual revolution, and the increased fear of violence.
6. In recent decades, adolescence has become greatly prolonged. Individuals in their twenties are less likely to be financially independent, to live in their own homes, to be married, or to have children than were adolescents in the past.
7. The Internet has had a profound effect on U.S. society. Cyberspace has opened up the world to adolescents in a way that would have been unimagined in

the past. Almost any fact can be found, and people around the globe can be contacted.

8. Unfortunately, many materials that are inappropriate for children and adolescents have also become available on the Internet. Unintended exposure to pornography can be unsettling and even dangerous.
9. The world of work continues to evolve. The average employed full-time worker puts in more hours now than at any other time in the past 50 years. An increasingly greater number of women, even mothers, are employed outside the home. Adolescents are ever more likely to hold down jobs after school. These changes all have the potential of decreasing contact between family members.
10. Adolescents today have more money of their own to spend, and the consumer industry has responded by directing marketing and products their way.
11. Because high-paying jobs demand increasingly sophisticated skills, education is becoming more prolonged. More and more adolescents are graduating from high school, and to a lesser degree, more are graduating from college. Career-focused education is becoming more common.
12. Fewer individuals are marrying, and more are remaining single longer before they marry. Of those who do marry, they are having fewer children. Most families have become more democratic and child centered.
13. More adolescents are being raised for at least part of their life in a single-parent home. This is due to increases in both the nonmarital birthrate and the divorce rate.
14. Members of U.S. society are more open today about sexuality than they were in the past. This has had some positive effects—for example, the increased availability of information and contraception—but it has had some negative consequences, as well—such as rises in the prevalence of adolescent pregnancy and sexually transmitted diseases.
15. In part due to terrorism, Americans have an increased awareness of the violence around them. Even though the crime rate is not climbing, individuals are more fearful of their personal safety than in the past.
16. It is important to understand that a *correlation* between two factors does not imply that they are causally related. Much of the research done about adolescence is quasi-experimental, not true experimental research.

KEY TERMS

adolescence 2	positive correlation 20
cohort 5	puberty 2
correlation 19	quasi-experiment 21
juvenile 2	teenager 2
negative correlation 20	true experiment 20

THOUGHT QUESTIONS

Personal Reflection

1. Are you an adolescent? If not, when did adolescence end and why? If you are an adolescent, when do you anticipate adolescence ending? Why then?
2. How has the Internet affected your life? How much time do you spend online and what activities do you do? Do you always accurately portray yourself or do you perform identity experiments?
3. Did you ever consider *not* going to college? Why did you choose to continue your education?
4. Ideally, how many hours per week would you like to work? Would you be willing to work 45 hours per week on a regular basis if your job was otherwise good? 50 hours per week?
5. Have you ever cohabitated? Would you? Why or why not?

Group Discussion

6. What criteria should be used to determine when adolescence ends? Why are they important? Is there an upper age limit to adolescence?
7. How greatly will the so-called "graying of America" affect the adolescent experience?
8. Who is affected by adolescence becoming more prolonged? Who benefits? Who is harmed?
9. What can society do to encourage more students to go on to college?
10. The nuclear family was the standard in U.S. society for a long time. Why have so many alternative family structures become common in recent decades?
11. What have been the most important social changes during the years you've been growing up? How have these changes affected your life?

Debate Questions

12. Today's adolescents have too much independent spending money.
13. The sexual revolution has been more positive than negative.
14. Many young people are taking too long to become true adults.
15. Society is not any more violent than in the past.
16. The adolescent experience of the present generation is quite unique.

SUGGESTED READING

Arnett, J. J. (2004). *Emerging Adulthood: The Winding Road from the Late Teens through the Twenties.* New York: Oxford University Press.

Buckingham, D., and Willett, R. (Eds.). (2006). *Digital Generations: Children, Young People, and the New Media.* Mahwah, NJ: Erlbaum.

Chilman, C. S. (2001). *Adolescent Sexuality in a Changing American Society: Social and Psychological Perspectives.* Westport, CT: Greenwood Press.

Cornbleth, C. (2003). *Hearing America's Youth: Social Identities in Uncertain Times.* New York: Peter Lang.

Graff, H. J. (1995). *Conflicting Paths: Growing Up in America.* Cambridge, MA: Harvard University Press.

Hoffman, A. M., and Summers, R. W. (2000). *Teen Violence: A Global Perspective.* Westport, CT: Greenwood Press.

Mortimer, J. T., and Larson, R. W. (2002). *The Changing Adolescent Experience: Societal Trends and the Transition to Adulthood.* Cambridge, England: Cambridge University Press.

CHAPTER 2 ADOLESCENTS IN THEORETICAL CONTEXT

WOULDN'T YOU LIKE TO KNOW . . .

- How did the first psychologist who studied adolescents characterize them?
- What did Sigmund Freud think about adolescents?
- What do most psychologists believe is *the* most important task of adolescence?
- In what ways are adolescents more intelligent than children?
- To what extent does merely observing others' behavior influence adolescents?
- How does modern American society marginalize adolescents?
- How does modern American culture make the adolescent transition to adulthood more difficult than it otherwise might be?
- Is adolescence inevitably a difficult time of life?

Another way to answer the question *What is adolescence?* (from Chapter 1) is to look at adolescence from different points of view. In this book, we will draw on the studies of biologists, psychiatrists, psychologists, economists, sociologists, social psychologists, and anthropologists. This chapter will begin by surveying the views of a few representative and influential scholars from these disciplines. Later on, we will revisit some of these views as we take a closer look at various aspects of adolescence. By understanding different viewpoints, we gain a truer, more complete picture of adolescence.

The theories presented in this chapter are arranged in order from most to least biologically based. The more biological theorists—primarily biologists and psychologists—believe that adolescents are the way they are because of their genes, hormones, or evolutionary history. These theorists downplay environmental influences and tend to believe that the adolescent experience is similar regardless of where someone is raised. The less biologically based theorists—psychologists, anthropologists, and sociologists—believe that both immediate personal experience and culture shape adolescence. It follows that they believe that adolescents may be very different from each other, depending on the specific events that have occurred during their lives.

Hall theorized that adolescence is a turbulent time of life—one characterized by vacillations between emotional extremes.

BIOLOGICAL VIEWS OF ADOLESCENCE

A strictly *biological view* of adolescence defines this period as one of physical and sexual maturation, during which important growth changes take place in the child's body. In this section, we will outline these physical, sexual, and physiological changes; their reasons (when known); and their consequences.

The biological view also emphasizes biogenetic factors as the primary cause of any behavioral and psychological change in the adolescent. Growth and behavior are under the control of internal maturational forces, leaving little room for environmental influences. Development occurs in an almost inevitable, universal pattern, regardless of the sociocultural environment. According to some theoreticians, these patterns were formed as a result of evolutionary pressures and natural selection.

G. Stanley Hall: *Sturm und Drang*

If there is a "father of adolescent psychology," it is G. Stanley Hall (1844–1924), as he was the first person to take a scientific approach to the study of adolescence. His two-volume book—*Adolescence: Its Psychology and Its Relation to Physiology, Anthropology, Sociology, Sex, Crime, Religion, and Education*, published in 1904—is considered by many to be the first serious work in the field.

Hall was captivated by Charles Darwin's theory of evolution: namely, that humans evolved from more primitive life forms through a process of *natural selection* ("the survival of the fittest"). Like Darwin, Hall believed that "ontogeny recapitulates phylogeny," which means that an individual's growth and development (ontogeny) mirrors or parallels (recapitulates) the evolutionary history (phylogeny) of its species. Hall applied this idea to the study of human, particularly adolescent, behavior.

According to Hall, after moving through the animal, hunter, and savagery stages—infancy, childhood, and preadolescence, respectively—adolescents found themselves in a period of ***sturm und drang.*** This German phrase means "storm and stress," and it reflects Hall's view of the turbulent nature of adolescence. He believed that adolescents are on an emotional seesaw: giddy one moment and depressed the next, apathetic today and impassioned tomorrow. These vacillations between emotional extremes, Hall thought, lasted until a person was in his or her early twenties. Furthermore, little could be done to prevent them since they were genetically based.

Although psychologists no longer subscribe to Hall's views that adolescence is inevitably difficult, he was instrumental in inspiring others to study adolescence. Moreover, his negative views of the adolescent experience were picked up by others, such as Sigmund Freud (see pp. 27–28).

ANSWERS WOULDN'T YOU LIKE TO KNOW . . .

How did the first psychologist who studied adolescents characterize them?

G. Stanley Hall, the "father of adolescent psychology," thought that adolescents were by nature emotionally volatile and unstable.

Arnold Gesell: Spiral Growth Patterns

Arnold Gesell (1880–1961) is known for observations of human development from birth to adolescence that he and his staff made at the Yale Clinic of Child Development and later at the Gesell Institute of Child Development. His best-known book on adolescence is *Youth: The Years from Ten to Sixteen* (Gesell and Ames, 1956). Gesell was a student of G. Stanley Hall's and learned much from him.

Gesell was interested in the behavioral manifestations of development. He observed the actions and behavior of children and youths at different ages and constructed descriptive summaries of the stages of development. In his summaries, he described what he felt were the norms of behavior in their chronological sequences.

Gesell believed that genes determine the order of appearance of behavioral traits and developmental trends. Thus, abilities and skills appear without the influence of special training or practice (Thelen and Adolph, 1992). This concept implies a sort of biological determinism that prevents teachers and parents from doing anything to influence human development. Because maturation is regarded as a natural ripening process, it is assumed that time alone will solve most of the minor problems that arise in raising children. Difficulties and deviations will be outgrown, claimed Gesell, so parents were advised against overreacting to misbehavior (Gesell and Ames, 1956).

Gesell did try to allow for individual differences, accepting that each child is born unique, with his or her own "genetic factors or individual constitution and innate maturation sequences" (Gesell and Ames, 1956, p. 22). But he emphasized that "acculturation can never transcend maturation" because maturation is of primary importance. In spite of accepting individual differences and the influence of environment on individual development, Gesell nevertheless considered many trends and sequences to be universal among humans.

Although Gesell tried to emphasize that changes are gradual and overlap, his descriptions often indicate profound and sudden changes from one age to the next. He emphasized also that development is not only upward but also spiral, characterized by both upward and downward changes that cause some repetition at different ages. For example, both the 11- and 15-year-old are generally rebellious and quarrelsome, whereas the 12- and 16-year-old are fairly stable.

One of the chief criticisms of Gesell's work concerns his sample. He drew his conclusions from boys and girls of high socioeconomic status in New Haven, Connecticut. He contended that such a homogenous sample would not lead to false generalizations. (This is in keeping with his belief that environmental influences are unimportant.) However, even when only physical factors are considered, children differ so greatly in the level and timing of growth that it is difficult to establish precise norms for any age level. Nevertheless, Gesell's books were used by thousands of parents and exerted tremendous influence on childrearing practices during the 1940s and 1950s. The books were considered the "child-development bibles" for many students and teachers during those years.

PSYCHOANALYTICAL AND PSYCHOSOCIAL VIEWS OF ADOLESCENCE

Sigmund Freud was a Viennese physician who became interested in neurology, the study of the brain, and nervous disorders. He was the originator of psychoanalytical theory. His daughter, Anna Freud, applied his theory to adolescents. Freud's perspective, while intrinsically psychological in nature, has a strong biological flavor because he believed that "biology is destiny." That is, he believed that males and females, due to differences in the anatomy of their genitals, would necessarily have dissimilar experiences and hence turn out different from each other.

Sigmund Freud: Individuation

Sigmund Freud (1856–1939) was not greatly involved with theories on adolescence, for he considered the early years of a child's life to be the formative ones. He did, however, deal briefly with adolescence in his *Three Essays on the Theory of Sexuality* (Freud, 1953b). He described adolescence as a period of sexual excitement, anxiety, and sometimes personality disturbance. According to Freud, puberty is the culmination of a series of changes destined to give infantile sexual life its final, adult form. During the period of infancy, when pleasure is linked with oral activities (the **oral stage**), children derive pleasure from sexual objects outside their own

sturm und drang "storm and stress"; used to describe the volatile adolescent temperament.

oral stage the first psychosexual stage in Sigmund Freud's theory of development: from birth to one year, during which the child's chief source of pleasure and satisfaction comes from oral activity.

bodies: their mother's breasts. From these objects, they derive physical satisfaction, warmth, pleasure, and security. While the mother feeds her infants, she also cuddles, caresses, kisses, and rocks them (Freud, 1953b).

Gradually, children's pleasures become autoerotic; that is, children begin to derive pleasure and satisfaction from activities that they can carry on by themselves. As they give up sucking at their mother's breasts, they find they can still derive pleasure from other oral activities. They learn to feed themselves, for example. At around age 2 or 3, much concern and pleasure center on anal activities and elimination (the **anal stage**). This period is followed by a developing interest in their own bodies and in the examination of their sex organs during the **phallic stage** (ages 4 and 5) of development.

During the next period, which Freud termed the **latency stage** (roughly from 6 years of age to puberty), children's sexual interests do not appear to be as intense. Although Freud believed that children's sexual urges had temporarily dried up, more recent research suggests that they merely go underground (Thanasiu, 2004). Children's source of pleasure gradually shifts from self to other people. They become more interested in cultivating the friendship of others, especially those of the same sex.

At puberty (the **genital stage**), this process of "object finding" is brought to completion. Along with maturation of the external and internal sexual organs comes a strong desire to resolve the sexual tension that follows. This resolution demands a love object; therefore, Freud theorized, adolescents are drawn to other people—usually members of the opposite sex—who can resolve their tensions.

Freud believed that beginning with the phallic stage (4 to 6 years old), males and females have different personalities and engage in different behaviors due to differences in their anatomy. Their progression through the phallic stage is necessarily dissimilar. Boys undergo what Freud termed *the Oedipal complex*. (The name comes from the protagonist in the Greek tragedy *Oedipus Rex*. In that play, Oedipus is a king who kills his father and marries his mother.) Essentially, boys become jealous of their mothers' attention toward their fathers and believe, unconsciously, that their fathers must be equally jealous of their mothers' attention toward them. Boys fear that their fathers will try to hurt them and remove them as sexual rivals (which is called *castration anxiety*). In order to reduce this anxiety, they *identify* with their fathers. **Identification** involves absorbing their fathers' beliefs, behaviors, and values and serves two functions: (1) It reduces castration anxiety, since such imitation is flattering to the fathers and reduces conflict between father and son, and (2) it teaches the boy how to behave like a man, enabling him to find a wife of his own when he matures. Because castration anxiety is so stressful, boys work very hard at identification and develop well-rounded personalities.

Girls do not become jealous of their fathers, nor do they experience the Oedipal complex; instead, they must work their way through *the Electra complex*. (Electra was also a character in a Greek tragedy. She incited her brother to kill her mother to avenge her father's murder.) According to Freud, girls at this age are attracted to their fathers because they are seen as strong and powerful and because they are male. Once girls come to recognize the differences between male and female genitals, they become envious of boys because of their perception that penises are better than vulvas (which is called *penis envy*). Girls become hostile toward their mothers, whom they blame for their inferior genitals and because they resent the attention that their fathers give to their mothers. Girls only reluctantly identify with their mothers: They have attracted husbands, which is good, but they are only females, which is bad. Freud blamed the Electra complex and its resulting weak identification for the many negative personality traits—such as a low level of morality, excessive modesty, and lack of sex drive—that he thought were intrinsic to women.

Freud believed that by the end of childhood, children have identified with their same-sex parents and are very emotionally dependent on them. A central task of adolescence, then, is to break these close emotional ties so that adolescents can become independent adults. This process, termed **individuation,** involves a differentiation of an individual's behavior, feelings, judgments, and thoughts from those of parents. At the same time, the parent-child relationship moves toward growing cooperation, equality, and mutuality as the child becomes an autonomous person within the family context (Mazor and Enright, 1988).

Few psychologists endorse Freud's views today. He was a product of Victorian times, in which it was presupposed that women were weak, inferior beings. His theory, while groundbreaking in its willingness to acknowledge the import of human sexuality, swung too far in the other direction and overemphasized the role of sexual urges in controlling behavior. In addition, **psychoanalytic theory** is very negative, claiming that people are all ruled by selfish, hostile, demanding urges. This negativism most likely arose because Freud developed his theory by working with hospitalized mental patients, rather than more typical individuals. Also, most psychologists would say that Freud exaggerates the importance of early experiences and sees personality as more fixed than it really is.

Still, it is important to recognize Freud's enormous contribution to our understanding of behavior. If he had done nothing except invent the concept of the unconscious, he would be remembered for centuries.

ANSWERS WOULDN'T YOU LIKE TO KNOW . . .

What did Sigmund Freud think about adolescents?

Sigmund Freud believed that adolescents are anxious and moody because they are plagued by newly awakened sexual urges.

Anna Freud: Defense Mechanisms

Anna Freud (1895–1982), daughter of Sigmund Freud, was more concerned with the period of adolescence than her father was. She elaborated more on the process of adolescent development and the changes in the psychic structure of the child at puberty (Freud, 1946, 1958).

Adolescence was characterized by Anna Freud as a period of internal conflict, psychic disequilibrium, and erratic behavior. Adolescents are, on the one hand, egoistic, regarding themselves as the sole object of interest and the center of the universe but, on the other hand, also capable of self-sacrifice and devotion. They form passionate love relations, only to break them off suddenly. They sometimes desire complete social involvement and group participation and at other times solitude. They oscillate between blind submission to and rebellion against authority. They are selfish and material minded but also full of lofty idealism. They are ascetic yet indulgent, inconsiderate of others yet touchy themselves. They swing between optimism and pessimism, between indefatigable enthusiasm and sluggishness and apathy (Freud, 1946).

According to Anna Freud, the reasons for this conflicting behavior are the psychic disequilibrium and internal conflict that accompanies sexual maturation at puberty (Blos, 1979). At puberty, the most obvious change is an increase in the instinctual drives. This is due partly to sexual maturation, with its accompanying interest in genitalia and the increase of lustful impulses. But the flare-up in instinctual drives at puberty also has a physical base not confined solely to the sexual life. Aggressive impulses are intensified, hunger becomes voracious, and naughtiness sometimes erupts into criminal behavior. Oral and anal interests, long submerged, appear. Habits of cleanliness give way to grime and disorder. Modesty and sympathy are replaced by exhibitionism and brutality. Anna Freud compared this increase in instinctual forces at puberty to the similar condition of early infancy. Early infantile sexuality and rebellious aggression are "resuscitated" at puberty (Freud, 1946, p. 159).

The drives to satisfy one's desires, referred to as the **id,** increase during adolescence. These instinctual urges present a direct challenge to the individual's ego and superego. By **ego,** Anna Freud meant the sum of those mental processes that aim to safeguard the individual. The ego is the evaluative, reasoning power of the individual. By **superego,** Anna Freud meant the conscience that results from identification with the same-sex parent (see Figure 2.1.). Therefore, the renewed vigor of the instincts at adolescence directly challenges the reasoning abilities and the powers of conscience of the individual. The careful balance achieved between these psychic powers during latency is overthrown as open warfare breaks out between the id and superego. The ego, which previously has been able to enforce a truce, has as much trouble keeping the peace now as does a weak-willed parent when confronted by two strong-willed children who are quarreling. If the ego allies itself completely with the id, "no trace will be left of the previous character of the individual and the entrance into adult life will be marked by a riot of uninhibited gratification of instinct" (Freud, 1946, p. 163). If the ego

anal stage the second psychosexual stage in Sigmund Freud's theory of development: the second year of life, during which the child seeks pleasure and satisfaction through anal activity and the elimination of waste.

phallic stage the third psychosexual stage in Sigmund Freud's theory of development: from about the fourth to the sixth year, during which the genital area is the chief source of pleasure and satisfaction.

latency stage the fourth psychosexual stage in Sigmund Freud's theory of development: from about 6 to 12 years of age, during which sexual interests remain hidden while the child concentrates on school and other activities.

genital stage the last psychosexual stage in Sigmund Freud's theory of development, during which sexual urges result in seeking other persons as sexual objects to relieve sexual tension.

identification the taking on of parental values, beliefs, and behaviors.

individuation the formation of personal identity by the development of the self as a unique person separate from parents and others.

psychoanalytical theory Freud's theory that the structure of personality is composed of the id, ego, and superego and that mental health depends on keeping the balance among them.

id according to Sigmund Freud, those instinctual urges that a person seeks to satisfy according to the pleasure principle.

ego according to Sigmund Freud, the rational mind that seeks to satisfy the id in keeping with reality.

superego according to Sigmund Freud, that part of the mind that opposes the desires of the id by enforcing moral restrictions that have been learned to try to attain a goal of perfection.

FIGURE 2.1 ACCORDING TO ANNA FREUD, THE CONFLICT AMONG ID, EGO, AND SUPEREGO INCREASES DURING ADOLESCENCE

sides completely with the superego, the id's impulses will be confined within the narrow limits prescribed for the child, but a constant expenditure of psychic energy on anticathexes (emotionally charged activities) and defense mechanisms will be needed to hold these impulses in check.

Unless this id-ego-superego conflict is resolved at adolescence, the consequences can be emotionally devastating to the individual. Anna Freud discussed how the ego uses **defense mechanisms** to win the battle. The ego represses, displaces, denies, and reverses the instincts and turns them against the self; it produces phobias and hysterical symptoms and builds anxiety by means of obsessional thinking and behavior. According to Anna Freud, the rise of asceticism and intellectualism at adolescence is a symptom of mistrust of all instinctual wishes. Anna Freud did believe, however, that harmony among the id, ego, and superego is possible and does occur finally in most normal adolescents. This balance is achieved if the superego is sufficiently developed during the latent period—but does not inhibit the instincts too much, which would cause extreme guilt and anxiety—and if the ego is sufficiently strong and wise to mediate the conflict (Freud, 1946).

Erik Erikson: Ego Identity

Erik Erikson (1902–1994) modified Sigmund Freud's theory of psychosexual development as a result of findings of modern sociopsychology and anthropology. While Erikson retained many of Freud's concepts, including the id-ego-superego triangle of personality components, he placed considerably less emphasis on the id's basic biological urges than did Freud. Instead, Erikson believed that the ego was the driving force behind much of behavior.

Erikson described eight stages of human development (Erikson, 1950, 1968, 1982). In each stage, the individual has a psychosocial task to master. Confronting each task produces conflict, with two possible outcomes. If the conflict is resolved successfully, a positive quality is built into the personality and further development takes place. If the conflict persists or is resolved unsatisfactorily, the self is damaged because a negative quality is incorporated into it. According to Erikson, the overall task of the individual is to acquire a *positive ego identity* as he or she moves from one stage to the next (Erikson, 1950, 1959). Table 2.1 lists Erikson's eight stages, along with the age at which each stage occurs and a description of its possible positive and negative outcomes.

Although we are most concerned with *identity formation*—the event associated with stage 5, adolescence—it is useful to understand the four stages that come before it. Each stage builds on the previous ones, and the positive resolution of a stage is more assured if the previous stages have been successfully negotiated. Adolescents who feel optimistic and secure, who are independent and curious, and who feel pride in their accomplishments—all qualities learned earlier in life in previous stages—are more likely to be able to effectively form an identity.

The areas of interest shown in this girl's bedroom demonstrate that she has established a sense of personal identity, as defined by Erikson.

Identity formation neither begins nor ends with adolescence but is a lifelong process. Its roots go back in childhood to the experiences a child has with his or her parents. Children begin to form self-concepts through these interactions: If their parents love them and treat them as worthy, they feel worthy; if their parents neglect or reject them, they are likely to believe themselves flawed. As children mature, interactions with peers and other meaningful adults continue to shape their sense

defense mechanisms according to Anna Freud, unrealistic strategies used by the ego to protect itself and to discharge tension.

TABLE 2.1 ERIKSON'S STAGES OF PERSONALITY

AGE GROUP	STAGE	OUTCOMES
1. **Infants** (birth–2 years)	Basic trust vs. mistrust	Optimism and serenity vs. pessimism and anxiety
2. **Toddlers** (2–4 years)	Autonomy vs. shame and doubt	Self-trust and independence vs. dependency and fear
3. **Preschoolers** (4–6 years)	Initiative vs. guilt	Curiosity and energy vs. boredom and apathy
4. **Grade-schoolers** (6–11 years)	Industry vs. inferiority	Ability to feel pride in accomplishment and to work hard vs. shame at lack of accomplishment
5. **Adolescents** (11–early 20s)	Identity vs. diffusion	A sense of one's current and future self vs. lack of commitment and instability
6. **Young adults** (early 20s–40)	Intimacy vs. isolation	Close, meaningful relationships vs. loneliness
7. **Middle-aged adults** (40–65 years)	Generativity vs. stagnation	Growth and giving to others vs. stasis and meaninglessness
8. **Elderly adults** (65+ years)	Ego integrity vs. despair	Acceptance of mortality vs. fear of death

of who they are. The community both molds and gives recognition to newly emerging individuals.

Erikson emphasized that the identity search is a normative crisis, a normal phase of increased conflict. The experimenting individual becomes the victim of an identity consciousness that is the basis for the self-consciousness of youth. During this time, the individual must establish a sense of *personal identity* and avoid the dangers of *identity diffusion.* To establish identity requires individual effort in evaluating personal assets and liabilities and in learning how to use these to achieve a clearer concept of who one is and what one wants to become. Adolescents who are actively engaged in identity exploration are more likely to evidence a personality pattern characterized by self-doubt, confusion, impulsivity, and conflict with parents and other authority figures (Kidwell, Dunham, Bacho, Pastorino, and Portes, 1995).

One intriguing aspect of Erikson's theory is his concept of adolescence as a **psychosocial moratorium,** a societally sanctioned intermediary period between childhood and adulthood, during which the individual through free role experimentation may find a niche in society (Erikson, 1959). Adolescence becomes a period of analyzing and trying various roles without the responsibility for assuming any one. Erikson acknowledged that the duration and intensity of adolescence vary in different societies, but that eventually a failure to establish identity results in deep suffering. Interestingly, at present, the length of time it takes many individuals to create an identity has been increasing until well into the late twenties, so that a new stage of life—**emerging adulthood**—is being established. This newly recognized stage of life will be discussed at the end of this text.

The adolescent who fails in the search for an identity will experience self-doubt and role confusion; such an individual may indulge in a self-destructive, one-sided preoccupation or activity. He or she will likely be preoccupied with the opinions of others or may turn to the other extreme of no longer caring what others think. He or she may withdraw or turn to drugs or alcohol in order to relieve the anxiety that identity diffusion creates.

Erikson emphasized that although the identity crisis is most pronounced at adolescence, a redefinition of one's ego identity may also take place at other periods of life—when individuals leave home, marry, become parents, get divorced, or change occupations, for example. The extent to which people are able to cope with these changes in identity is determined partly by the success with which they have first mastered the adolescent identity crises (Erikson, 1959).

Erikson's work on identity will be extensively discussed in Chapter 8.

ANSWERS WOULDN'T YOU LIKE TO KNOW ...

What do most psychologists believe is *the* most important task of adolescence?

Most psychologists believe that forming a personal identity is the single most important task of adolescent development.

COGNITIVE VIEWS OF ADOLESCENCE

Cognition is the act or process of knowing. It is the mental activity or thinking involved in understanding. The cognitive theorists are discussed here (after the more biologically based theorists) because enhanced thinking skill depends in part on physical brain development. (No one believes that a 6-month-old could be taught to play chess.)

Jean Piaget, who began his career as a field biologist, retained a very biological flavor in his views. He is often described as an **organismic psychologist;** that is, he believed that both brain maturation and personal experience drive cognitive development. Robert Selman's work is less intrinsically biologically based, although his stage theory rests on the increasing cognitive sophistication that comes with maturation and experience. Lev Vygotsky, the last cognitive theorist discussed, is known for his emphasis on the environmental determinants of cognitive growth.

Jean Piaget: Adaptation and Equilibrium

Jean Paul Piaget (1896–1980) was a Swiss psychologist who became interested in human cognitive development. More than anyone before him, Piaget changed people's conceptions and understandings of the cognitive resources of children. Piaget showed that from birth onward, intellectual competencies undergo continual development that never ends (Beilin, 1992).

Piaget began his work in Alfred Binet's Paris laboratory, where modern intelligence tests originated. He disagreed with Binet's insistence that intelligence is fixed and innate and began to explore higher-level thought processes (Piaget and Inhelder, 1969). Piaget became more interested in how children reached conclusions than in whether their answers were correct. Instead of asking questions and scoring them right or wrong, Piaget questioned children to find the logic behind their answers. Through painstaking observation of his own, as well as other, children, he began to construct his theory of cognitive development (Piaget, 1951, 1967, 1971, 1972).

Piaget taught that cognitive development is the combined result of environmental influences and the maturation of the brain and nervous system. He used five terms to describe the dynamics of development. A **schema** represents the original patterns of thinking, or the mental structures that people use for dealing with what happens in the environment. For example, when children see something they want, they learn to reach out to grasp it. They form a schema that is needed in the situation. By forming new schema and linking them together, children learn to adapt to their environment.

Adaptation is including and adjusting to new information that increases a person's understanding of the world around him or her. Adaptation takes place through two means: assimilation and accommodation. **Assimilation** means acquiring new information by integrating it into already existing structures in response to new environmental stimuli. **Accommodation** involves adjusting to new information by creating new schema to replace the old. For example, a child's pet golden cocker spaniel might give birth to a litter of black puppies. The child will thereby learn that cocker spaniels can be black as well as golden (assimilation). And if the child tries to pet a new puppy and it nips at him or her (something the mother would never do), he or she will learn that some dogs bite and some do not (accommodation).

Equilibrium involves achieving a balance between assimilation and accommodation. It means feeling comfortable, because the reality that a person experiences is compatible with what he or she has been taught to believe. *Disequilibrium* arises when there is dissonance between reality and a person's comprehension of it, when further accommodation is necessary. Children resolve the conflict by acquiring new ways of thinking so that what they understand agrees with what they observe. The desire for equilibrium becomes the motivation that pushes children through the stages of cognitive development. Piaget outlined four stages of cognitive development, which will be discussed next.

Sensorimotor Stage (Birth to 2 Years)

During the sensorimotor stage, children learn to coordinate their physical actions and sensory experiences. Infants' senses of touch, hearing, vision, taste, and smell bring them into contact with various objects. As a result, they learn to reach for a ball, move their arms and hands to pick up an object, and move their head and eyes to follow a moving object.

Preoperational Stage (2 to 7 Years)

During the preoperational stage, children acquire language and learn to use symbols, such as maps, to represent the environment. Preoperational children can deal with the world symbolically but still cannot think logically. The stage is termed *preoperational* because young children have not yet developed the mental operations needed for logical thought.

Concrete Operational Stage (7 to 11 Years)

During the concrete operational stage, children show some capacity for logical reasoning, though it relates only to things actually experienced. They intuitively understand a number of **mental operations,** overarching logical principles. For example, they understand that two glasses might contain the same amount of water even if they are different shapes because the fact that one is taller than the other *compensates* for the fact that it is thinner than the other. They also have learned that objects can belong to more than one category—a woman can be both a mom and a teacher—and that some categories are nested inside one another. Children are not as easily fooled by appearances as they previously were.

Formal Operational Stage (11 Years and Older)

During the formal operational stage, adolescents move beyond concrete, actual experiences and begin to think in more logical, abstract terms. They are able to engage in introspection, thinking about their thoughts. They are able to use systematic, propositional logic in solving problems and drawing conclusions. They are also able to use inductive reasoning, bringing a

psychosocial moratorium a socially sanctioned period between childhood and adulthood during which an individual is free to experiment to find a socially acceptable identity and role.

emerging adulthood the stage of life, generally extending through one's twenties, in which one is between adolescence and full adulthood.

cognition the act or process of knowing.

organismic psychologist someone like Piaget, who believes that both brain maturation and environmental experience are needed for cognitive development.

schema the original patterns of thinking; the mental structures that people use for dealing with what happens in the environment.

adaptation including and adjusting to new information that increases understanding.

assimilation incorporating a feature of the environment into an existing mode or structure of thought.

accommodation involves adjusting to new information by creating new structures to replace old.

equilibrium according to Piaget, achieving a balance between schemas and accommodation.

mental operations abstract reasoning principles that allow children to think logically.

ANSWERS WOULDN'T YOU LIKE TO KNOW ...

In what ways are adolescents more intelligent than children?

Adolescents are more intelligent than children because they can think abstractly and hypothetically. They are also more logical and can imagine things and events they have not actually experienced.

number of facts together and constructing theories on the basis of these facts. Adolescents can also use deductive reasoning in scientifically testing and proving theories and can use algebraic symbols and metaphorical speech as symbols. Additionally, they can think beyond what is to what might be, projecting themselves into the future and planning for it.

We will discuss Piaget's stages of cognitive development in detail in Chapter 6.

Robert Selman: Social Cognition

Social cognition is the ability to understand social relationships. This ability elicits the understanding of others—their emotions, thoughts, intentions, social behavior, and general point of view. Social cognition is basic to all human relationships. Knowing what other people think and feel is necessary in getting along with them and in understanding them (Feldman and Ruble, 1988; Gnepp and Chilamkurti, 1988).

As the ability slowly develops, the question arises as to whether social knowledge and physical knowledge are gained in the same way. Certainly, much of both are acquired through observation, trial and error, exploration, direct firsthand experiences, and discovery. Gaining social knowledge, however, is more difficult. Physical knowledge is objective and factual; social knowledge is quite arbitrary, determined by a specific social situation, as well as by social, cultural, and even subcultural definitions and expectations. Because social rules are less uniform, less specific, and more situation dependent than physical phenomena, they are less predictable and more complicated to understand.

What is the relationship between general cognitive abilities and social problem-solving skills? The person who has superior intellectual problem-solving skills does not necessarily have superior social problem-solving skills. Social problem-solving skills may be learned or taught, separate from intellectual abilities. As Selman (1980) wrote, "The development of social conceptions, reasoning, thought—social cognition—is distinct from, though not unrelated to, the development of nonsocial cognition."

FIGURE 2.2 SELMAN'S FIVE STAGES OF SOCIAL ROLE TAKING

Source: R. E. Muuss, *Theories of Adolescence,* 6th ed. (New York: McGraw-Hill, 1995), pp. 249, 251, 254, 256, 258. Copyright © 1995 McGraw-Hill Publishing Company. Used by permission of The McGraw-Hill Companies.

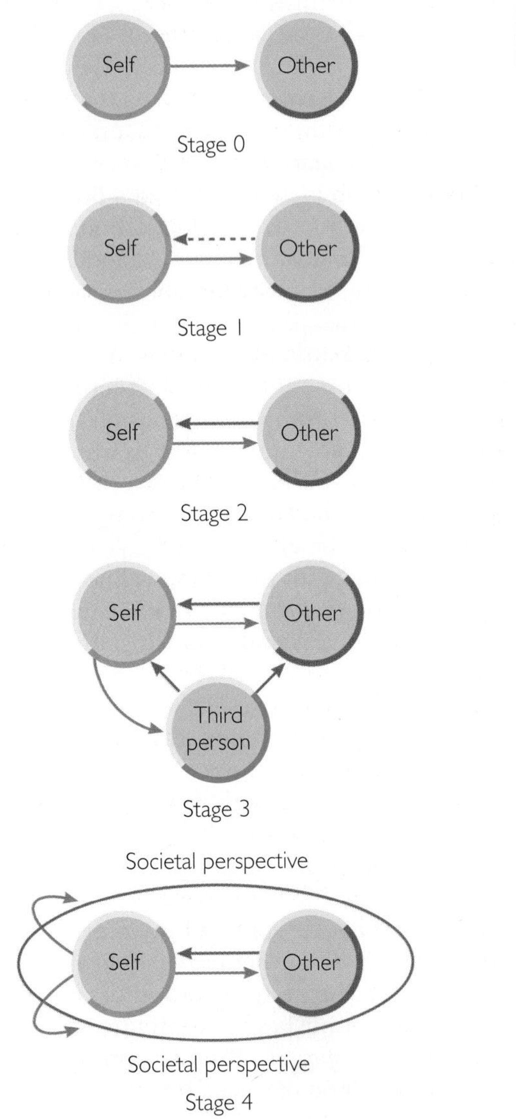

One of the most useful models of social cognition is that of Robert Selman (1942–), who has advanced a theory of **social role taking** (see Figure 2.2). To Selman (1977, 1980), social role taking is the ability to understand the self and others as subjects, to react to others as to the self, and to react to the self's behavior from others' points of view. He suggests children move through five stages of development.

Stage 0: Egocentric undifferentiated stage (ages 3 to 6). Until about age 6, children cannot make a clear distinction between their own interpretation of a social situation and the point of view of another, nor can they understand that their own perception may not be correct.

When asked how someone else feels in a particular situation, their responses reflect how *they* feel.

Stage 1: Differential or subjective perspective-taking stage, or social-informational stage (ages 6 to 8). Children at this stage develop an awareness that others may have a different social perspective, but they have little understanding of the reasons for others' viewpoints (LeMare and Rubin, 1987). Children believe that if others had the same information, they would feel as they do. However, they begin to distinguish between unintentional and intentional behavior and to consider the causes of actions (Miller and Aloise, 1989). They are capable of inferring other people's intentions, feelings, and thoughts, but they base their conclusions on physical observations that may not be correct, not realizing that people may hide their true feelings.

Stage 2: Self-reflective thinking or reciprocal perspective taking (ages 8 to 10). Preadolescents at stage 2 can take the perspective of another individual. Preadolescents thus become capable of making inferences about the perspectives of others; they can reflect about their own behavior and their own motivation as seen from the perspective of another person. This ability introduces an awareness that no single individual's social perspective is necessarily correct or valid in an absolute sense. In other words, another person's point of view may be as correct as one's own. Preadolescents think only within a two-person frame of reference—"I think; you think"—and cannot take a more general third-person perspective (Muuss, 1988b).

Stage 3: The third person or mutual perspective-taking stage (ages 10 to 12). Children can see their own perspectives, that of their partners, as well as that of a neutral third person. As third-person observers, they can see themselves as both object and actor (subject). They can understand a more generalized perspective that might be perceived by the majority of a group. Friendship now is viewed not as mutual back-scratching, but as a series of interactions over an extended period of time. Conflicts are seen as emerging from different personality characteristics (Muuss, 1982).

Stage 4: In-depth and societal perspective-taking stage (adolescence to adulthood). There are two distinguishing features of adolescents' conceptions of other people. First, they become aware that motives, actions, thoughts, and feelings are shaped by psychological factors. This notion of psychological determinants now includes the idea of the unconscious processes, although adolescents may not express this awareness in psychological terminology. Second, they begin to appreciate the fact that a personality is a system of traits, beliefs, values, and attitudes with its own developmental history.

During adolescence, the individual may move to a still higher and more abstract level of interpersonal perspective taking, which involves the coordination of all possible third-person perspectives—a societal perspective. The adolescent can conceptualize that each person can consider the shared point of view of the "generalized other"—that is, the social system—which, in turn, makes possible the accurate communication with an understanding of other people. Furthermore, the individual becomes aware of the idea that law and morality as a social system depends on the concept of consensual group perspective (Selman, 1980).

Before we move on to consider ecological, psychosocial, and anthropological views of human development, let's summarize and compare the various stages of development outlined by some of the theorists we have discussed so far. Figure 2.3 compares the stages of Freud, Erikson, Piaget, and Selman. Notice which stages correspond to adolescence.

Lev Vygotsky: Social Influences on Cognition

Lev Vygotsky (1896–1934), a Russian psychologist who was originally trained as a teacher, had a view of cognitive development very different from that of Piaget. Whereas Piaget thought that cognitive development is an individual achievement brought about by the child's private explorations of his or her environment, Vygotsky (1978) believed that cognitive skill is developed through social interaction. According to Vygotsky, children learn best when they are paired with a more skilled partner and they work together collaboratively to solve some problem. Learning is most rapid when the task is beyond the child's grasp but not so hard as to be overwhelming. This level of learning is called the **zone of proximal development.** Learning is also enhanced if the more expert helper provides **scaffolding** for the child—that is, if he or she provides assistance and then gradually

social cognition how people think and reason about their social world as they watch and interact with others; their understanding and ability to get along with other people.

social role taking according to Selman, the social roles that individuals take on that reflect their understanding of themselves, their actions to others, and their abilities to understand others' points of view.

zone of proximal development the level of learning at which a task that is too difficult for a child to complete by himself or herself is manageable with help.

scaffolding the assistance provided to help a child master a task; it is gradually withdrawn as the child gains competence.

FIGURE 2.3
COMPARISON OF PIAGET'S, FREUD'S, ERIKSON'S, AND SELMAN'S STAGES

The life cycle	Piaget's cognitive stages	Freud's psychosexual stages	Erikson's psychosocial stages	Selman's social role-taking stages
Late adulthood	↑	↑	Ego integrity vs. despair	↑
Middle adulthood			Generativity vs. stagnation	In-depth and societal perspective-taking
Early adulthood			Intimacy vs. isolation	↑
Adolescence	Formal operational	Genital	Identity vs. identity confusion	
↑	↑	↑	↑	Third person or mutual perspective-taking (age 10–12)
Middle and late childhood	Concrete operational	Latency	Industry vs. inferiority	Self-reflective thinking or reciprocal perspective-taking (age 8–10)
↑	↑	↑	↑	Differential or subjective perspective-taking, or social-information (age 6 to 8)
Early childhood	Preoperational	Phallic	Initiative vs. guilt	Egocentric undifferentiated (age 0–6)
Infancy	Sensorimotor	Anal Oral	Autonomy vs. shame, doubt Trust vs. mistrust	

withdraws that help as the child becomes able to complete the task alone. Vygotsky's theory has clear implications for teaching in that it strongly suggests that cooperative, group learning is a useful adjunct to or should even replace solitary, individual endeavors.

SOCIAL-COGNITIVE LEARNING VIEW OF ADOLESCENCE

Social learning theory is concerned with how the individuals around us shape our tendency to perform or not to perform various behaviors.

Albert Bandura: Social Learning Theory

Albert Bandura (1925–) has been concerned with the application of social learning theory to adolescents. His view emphasizes that children learn through observing the behavior of others and by imitating this pattern—a process referred to as **modeling.** As children grow, they imitate different models from their social environment. In many studies, parents are listed as the most significant adults in the lives of adolescents and hence the persons most likely to be modeled (Blyth, Hill, and Thiel, 1982; Galbo, 1983). Siblings are also mentioned as significant others, as are extended family members such as aunts and uncles.

Many aspects of behavior may be modeled from parents. Some of these are good, constructive behaviors; for example, adolescents are more likely to participate in community service activities if their parents do so (Keith, Nelson, Schlabach, and Thompson, 1990). In other instances, however, adolescents copy the destructive behaviors that they observe their parents do. For example, adolescents whose fathers gamble heavily are more likely to gamble heavily themselves (Vachon, Vitaro, Wanner, and Tremblay, 2004), and it is well known that parents who physically dis-

ANSWERS WOULDN'T YOU LIKE TO KNOW ...

To what extent does merely observing others' behavior influence adolescents?

Adolescents (along with adults and children) are greatly affected by observing others, especially respected others. They have an almost instinctive drive to copy, or model, what they see others do.

cipline their offspring are likely to raise children who hit others when they are angry (e.g., Bandura, 1973; Johnson and O'Leary, 1987).

The Role of Reinforcement

The most well-known learning theory, Skinner's (1938) *operant conditioning theory,* emphasizes the dual roles of **reinforcement** (reward) and punishment on influencing the behaviors we perform. It is common sense that if a teenager is praised by his or her friends for skipping class, he or she will be more likely to skip class in the future. On the other hand, if the teen is caught and gets two weeks' worth of detention, that punishment might be sufficient to prevent him or her from skipping class again.

Bandura expanded on this idea, speaking of **vicarious reinforcement** and **self-reinforcement.** Vicarious reinforcement consists of the positive or negative consequences that one observes others experiencing. Observing that others are rewarded for aggressive behavior

modeling learning by observing and imitating the behavior of another.

reinforcement positive reinforcements are influences that increase the probability that the preceding response will occur again. Negative reinforcements are influences that increase the probability that the preceding response will stop.

vicarious reinforcement learning from observing the positive or negative consequences of another person's behavior.

self-reinforcement the act of learners rewarding themselves for activities or responses that they consider of good quality.

RESEARCH HIGHLIGHT SCAFFOLDING IN COURSE-RELATED BULLETIN BOARDS

More and more college professors are using chat rooms and bulletin boards to facilitate discussions among the students in their classes (Berge, 2000). This is usually done in the hope that the students will learn from each other, and that the questions they pose will trigger a greater understanding of the course material. However, Vygotsky (1978) was quite clear in stating that individuals learn best from *experts* who *scaffold* their attempts at problem solving, not from other novices. Do online peer discussions foster learning? Can they?

The answers seem to be "Not always" and "Yes, they probably can, but only if the professor sets up the situation correctly." Students do not always know how to ask the kinds of questions that promote learning (van der Meij, 1998) and they may not have enough knowledge to be helpful (Land, 2000; van der Meij, 1990). Still, a number of studies had shown that it was possible for a teacher to provide external scaffolds that help students ask each other useful questions in a face-to-face classroom environment (King, Staffieri, and Adelgais, 1998), and so it seemed possible that online interactions could be similarly facilitated.

Choi, Land, and Turgeon (2005) attempted to do so for an online college course that contained several mandatory online discussion sessions. They developed scaffolds to help students ask three different types of questions of each other during these sessions (clarification/elaboration questions, counterarguments/disagreements, and probing, hypothetical questions); the intent was to prompt the students to ask the sorts of questions that would help their peers gain a deeper understanding of the course material. While the prompts succeeded in getting the students to ask *more* questions of each other, the questions were not of higher quality. The authors explained the lack of positive effects by the limited knowledge that the students had of the subject material (they were novices, not experts) and the fact that the initial answers that the students were responding to were already of high quality, with few obvious flaws. Perhaps most important, many of the students failed to utilize the prompts; previous research has shown that this is a common problem (e.g., Greene and Land, 2000). Azevedo and his colleagues (e.g., Azevedo, Cromley, Winters, Moos, and Greene, 2005) have shown that dynamic, rather than static, prompts can significantly aid self-directed computer-assisted learning, and so interactive, individualized prompts might be the key to improving the quality of student-student chat room or bulletin board interactions. In any case, as Vygotsky believed, without intervention and guidance, novices are not as helpful to each other as are trained experts.

increases the possibility that the observer will also show aggression. Bandura (1973) observed that self-reinforcement was as effective as external reinforcement in influencing behavior. Once the performance of a desired response pattern, such as shooting and making baskets with a basketball, acquired a positive value, adolescents could administer their own reinforcement by producing the baskets and then feeling good afterward. Adolescents who set reasonable goal levels of performance and reach that level feel proud and satisfied internally and become less dependent on parents, teachers, and bosses to give them rewards.

The work of social learning theorists is of great importance in explaining human behavior. It is especially important in emphasizing that *what adults do and the role models they represent are far more important in influencing adolescent behavior than what they say.* Teachers and parents can best encourage human decency, altruism, moral values, and a social conscience by exhibiting these virtues themselves.

Social-Cognitive Theory

In the 1980s, Bandura expanded his social learning theory to include the role of cognition (Bandura, 1986, 1989). Rather than describing individuals as determined strictly by environmental influences, Bandura emphasized that they, in large measure, *determine their own destinies* by choosing their future environments as well as other goals they wish to pursue. People reflect on and regulate their own thoughts, feelings, and actions to achieve their goals. In short, the way they interpret environmental influences determines how they act. For example, consider again the behavior of aggressive boys. Research has shown that aggressive boys are biased in favor of attributing hostile intent to others in various situations (Crick and Dodge, 1996). Aggressive boys are not careful in processing information that would help them to determine whether the intent of the action against them was hostile or benign. They pay less attention to information that would help them reach a more accurate inference about someone else's motives. Therefore, they are more likely to infer hostile intent when they come to conclusions quickly. In other words, it is not just what happens to these boys that determines the level of their aggression, but it is also the way they interpret others' intentions.

Social-cognitive theory emphasizes that individuals can actively control the events that affect their lives, rather than having to passively accept whatever the environment provides; they partially control the environment by the way they react to it. A placid, pleasant, easy-to-care-for adolescent may have a very positive influence on parents, encouraging them to act in a friendly, warm, and loving manner. However, an overactive, temperamental, hard-to-care-for adolescent who is easily upset may stimulate parents to be hostile, short-tempered, and rejecting. From this point of view, children—however involuntarily—are partly responsible for creating their own environments. Because of individual differences, different people, at different developmental stages, interpret and act on their environments in differing ways that create different experiences for each person (Bandura, 1986).

THE IMPACT OF CULTURE ON ADOLESCENTS

We will now consider a set of theorists who hold the perspective that adolescents' development is strongly influenced by the culture and society in which they are raised. (Vygotsky could easily have been placed in this section.) If you recall, Hall and Gesell underscored the importance of biology in influencing development; Freud and Piaget wrote of the interplay between biology and experience; and Bandura was concerned with the effects of those individuals who directly interact with the adolescent. This next set of researchers discuss the importance of cultural norms, traditions, and values in influencing behavior.

Robert Havighurst: Developmental Tasks

In *Developmental Tasks and Education* (1972), Robert Havighurst (1900–1991) outlined what he felt were the major developmental tasks of adolescence. His developmental task theory is an eclectic one, combining previously developed concepts.

Havighurst sought to develop a psychosocial theory of adolescence by combining consideration of individuals' needs with societal demands. What individuals need and society demands constitute the **developmental tasks.** They are the skills, knowledge, functions, and attitudes that individuals have to acquire at certain points in their lives through physical maturation, social expectations, and personal effort. Mastery of the tasks at each stage of development results in adjustment and preparation for the harder tasks ahead. Mastery of adolescent tasks results in maturity. Failure to master the adolescent tasks results in anxiety, social disapproval, and inability to function as a mature person.

According to Havighurst, there exists a teachable moment—a correct time for teaching any task. Some of the tasks arise out of biological changes, others from societal expectations at a given age or the individual's motivation at certain times to do particular things. Furthermore, developmental tasks differ from culture to culture. There are significant differences in developmental tasks in the upper, middle, and lower classes of the United States. Adolescents may face different tasks at different points in their lives (Klaczynski, 1990). Also, the demands and opportunities differ in various cultures, so that success is culturally defined, and the competencies required may differ (Brown, Larson and Saraswathi, 2002).

Havighurst (1972) outlined eight major tasks that American youths face during the adolescent period:

1. *Accepting one's physique and using the body effectively:* One characteristic of adolescents is their emerging, often extreme, self-consciousness about their physical selves as they reach sexual maturity. Adolescents need to accept their physiques and the pattern of growth of their own bodies, to learn to care for their bodies, and to use their bodies effectively in sports and athletics, recreation, work, and everyday tasks.

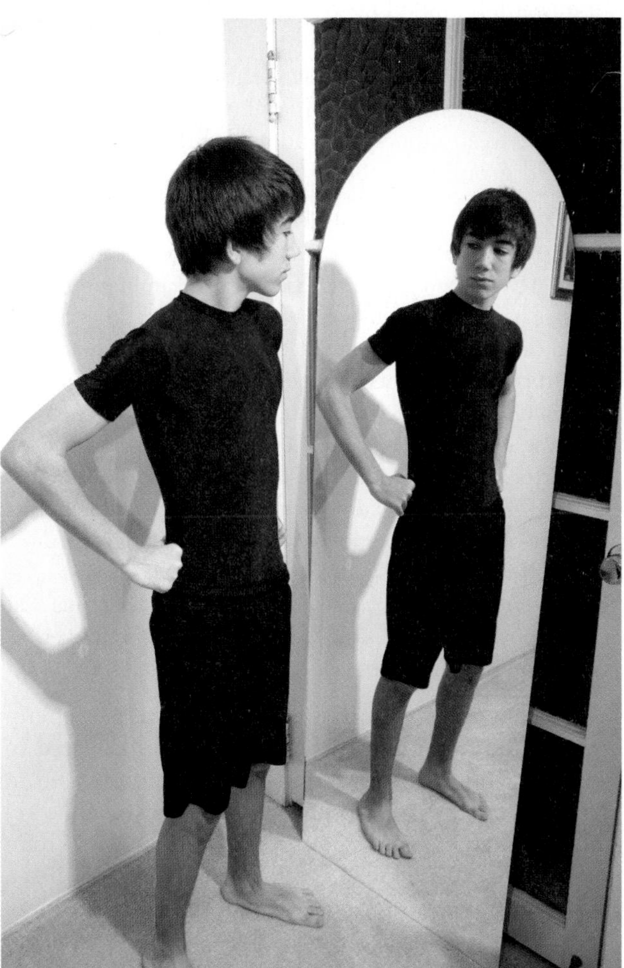

One of the major developmental tasks during the adolescent period, as defined by Havighurst, is accepting one's physique and using it effectively.

2. *Achieving new and more mature relations with age-mates of both sexes:* Adolescents must move from the same-sex interests and playmates of middle childhood to establish heterosexual friendships. Becoming an adult means also learning social skills and behaviors required in group life.
3. *Achieving a masculine or feminine social sex role:* What is a man? What is a woman? What are men and women supposed to look like? How should they behave? What are they supposed to be? Psychosexual social roles are established by each culture, but because masculine-feminine roles in Western culture have undergone rapid changes, part of the adolescent maturing process is to reexamine the changing sex roles of their culture and to decide what aspects they must adopt.
4. *Achieving emotional independence from parents and other adults:* Adolescents must develop understanding, affection, and respect without emotional dependence. Typically, the frequency and duration of contacts between parents and adolescents decrease (Larson, Richards, Moneta, Holmbeck, and Duckett, 1996), and closeness with parents declines (Holmbeck, 1996).
5. *Preparing for an economic career:* One of the primary goals of adolescents is to decide on a career, prepare for that career, and then become independent by earning their own living. Part of the task is to discover what they want out of life.
6. *Preparing for marriage and family life:* Patterns of marriage and family living are being readjusted to changing economic, social, and religious characteristics of society. The majority of youths desire a happy marriage and parenthood as one important goal in life and so they need to develop the positive attitudes, social skills, emotional maturity, and necessary understanding to make marriage work.
7. *Desiring and achieving socially responsible behavior:* This goal includes the development of a social ideology that takes into account societal values. The goal also includes participation in the adult life of the community and nation. Adolescents must find their place in society in a way that gives meaning to their lives (Havighurst, 1972).

developmental tasks the skills, knowledge, functions, and attitudes that individuals have to acquire at certain points in their lives in order to function effectively as mature persons.

8. *Acquiring a set of values and an ethical system as a guide to behavior—developing an ideology:* This goal includes the development of a sociopolitico-ethical ideology and the adoption and application of meaningful values, morals, and ideals in one's personal life.

Havighurst felt that many modern youths have not been able to achieve identity and therefore suffer from aimlessness and uncertainty.

Kurt Lewin: Field Theory

Kurt Lewin's (1890–1947) theory of adolescent development is outlined in his article "Field Theory and Experiment in Social Psychology: Concepts and Methods" (1939). This field theory attempts to explain why adolescents vacillate between mature and childish behavior and why they are so often unhappy.

Lewin's (1939) core concept is "that behavior (*B*) is a function (*f*) of the person (*P*) and of his environment (*E*)" (p. 34). To understand an adolescent's behavior, you must consider the individual's personality and the environment as interdependent factors. The sum total of all possible behaviors is called the life space (*LSp*). Unfortunately, not all areas of the life space are available to individuals.

Lewin compared the life space of a child with that of an adult. The child's life space is structured by what is forbidden and what is beyond his or her ability. As the child matures and becomes more capable, fewer restrictions are placed on freedom, so the life space expands into new regions and experiences. By the time the child reaches adolescence, more regions have become accessible, but it is unclear which ones the adolescent is supposed to enter. Thus, the life space remains undefined and unclear. The adult's space is considerably wider, but it is still bounded by activities beyond ability or forbidden by society.

According to Lewin, adolescence is a period of transition during which group membership changes from childhood to adulthood. The adolescent belongs partly to the child group and partly to the adult group. Muuss (1988b) wrote:

> Parents, teachers, and society reflect this lack of clearly defined group status; and their ambiguous feelings become obvious when they treat the adolescent at one time like a child and at another time like an adult. Difficulties arise because certain childish forms of behavior are no longer acceptable. At the same time some of the adult forms of behavior are not yet permitted either, or if they are permitted, they are new and strange to the adolescent. The adolescent is in a state of "social locomotion," moving into an unstructured social and psychological field. Goals are no longer clear, and the paths to them are ambiguous and full of uncertainties—the adolescent may no longer be certain that they even lead to the desired goals. (p. 147)*

This "lack of cognitive structures" helps explain uncertainty in adolescent behavior. Lewin referred to the adolescent as the "marginal man," represented in Figure 2.4 by the overlapping area (Ad) of the child region (C) and the adult region (A). Being a marginal man implies that the adolescent may at times act more like a child, often when he or she wants to avoid adult responsibilities; at other times, he or she acts more like an adult and requests adult privileges.

FIGURE 2.4 THE ADOLESCENT AS A MARGINAL MAN

(a) During childhood and adulthood, the "adults" (A) and "children" (C) are viewed as relatively separated groups. The individual child (c^1, c^2) and the individual adult (a^1, a^2) are sure of their belonging to their respective groups. *(b)* In adolescence, the adolescent is seen as belonging to a group (Ad) that can be viewed as an overlapping region of the children's (C) and the adults' (A) groups, belonging to both of them, or the adolescent is seen as standing between them, not belonging to either one.

Source: K. Lewin, "Field Theory and Experiment in Social Psychology: Concepts and Methods," *American Journal of Sociology, 44* (1939): 868–897. Copyright © the University of Chicago Press. Used by permission of the University of Chicago Press.

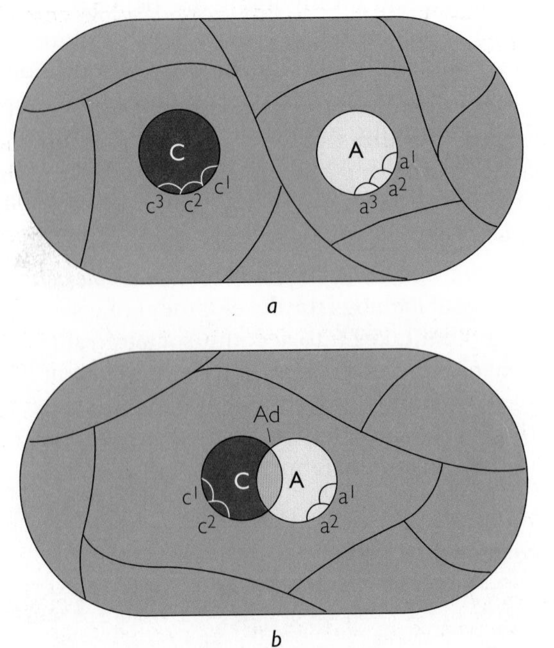

*R. E. Muuss, *Theories of Adolescence,* 5th ed. (New York: McGraw-Hill, 1988). Copyright © 1988 McGraw-Hill Publishing Company. Quotations in this chapter are used by permission of the McGraw-Hill Companies.

ANSWERS WOULDN'T YOU LIKE TO KNOW . . .

How does modern American society marginalize adolescents?

Lewin claimed that American society marginalizes adolescents by denying them the pleasures of childhood before offering to them the pleasures of adulthood.

One of the strengths of Lewin's field theory is that it assumes both personality and cultural differences, so it allows for wide individual variations in behavior. It also allows for varying lengths of the adolescent period from culture to culture and from social class to social class within a culture (Muuss, 1988b).

Urie Bronfenbrenner: An Ecological Model

Adolescents develop within the multiple contexts of their families, communities, and countries. They are influenced by peers, relatives, and other adults with whom they come in contact, and by the religious organizations, schools, and groups to which they belong. They are also influenced by the media, the cultures in which they are growing up, national and community leaders, and world events. They are partly a product of environmental and social influences.

Urie Bronfenbrenner (1917–2005) developed an ecological model for understanding social influences (1979, 1987). His perspective has firmly taken root over the past 30 years, and at present, it is one of the most widely accepted and utilized approaches. As you can see in Figure 2.5, social influences may be grouped into a series of systems extending beyond the adolescent. The adolescent is at the center of the systems.

The Microsystem

The most immediate influences on the adolescent are within the **microsystem** and include those with whom he or she has immediate contact. For most adolescents, the immediate family is the primary microsystem, followed by friends and school. Other components of the microsystem are health services, religious groups, neighborhood play areas, and various social groups to which the adolescent belongs.

Microsystems change as the adolescent moves in and out of different social settings. For example, the adolescent may change schools, stop going to church or synagogue, drop out of some activities, and join others. In general, the peer microsystem increases in influence during adolescence, providing powerful social rewards in terms of acceptance, popularity, friendship, and status. The peer group may also exert negative influences, encouraging irresponsible sex, drug use, theft, gang membership, or cheating. A healthy microsystem offers positive learning and development that prepares the adolescent for success in adult life.

The Mesosystem

The **mesosystem** involves reciprocal relationships among microsystem settings. For example, what happens at school influences what happens at home and vice versa. An adolescent's social development is understood best when the influences from many sources are considered in relation to each other. A mesosystem analysis would look at the frequency, quality, and influence of interactions, such as how family experiences are related to school adjustments, how family characteristics are related to peer pressures, or how church or synagogue attendance is related to intimacy with the opposite sex.

The Exosystem

The **exosystem** is composed of those settings in which the adolescent does not play an active role but that nevertheless influence him or her. For example, what happens to the parents at work influences the parents, and they, in turn, influence the adolescent's development. The parents' bosses determine the rate of pay, work and vacation schedules, and the community in which the work will take place. If the company decides to move an employee, it affects the whole family. All of these factors influence the parents' relationships with their adolescent.

Similarly, community organizations affect the adolescent in many ways. For instance, the school board establishes the curriculum and the school calendar and hires the teachers. The town government may open or close a youth center or a swimming pool. Those in the exosystem make decisions that affect the adolescent, whose parents are concerned that their adolescent's best interests are kept in mind.

The Macrosystem

The **macrosystem** includes the ideologies, attitudes, mores, customs, and laws of a particular culture. It includes a core of educational, economic, religious, political, and social values. The macrosystem

microsystem includes those persons with whom the adolescent has immediate contact and who influence him or her.

mesosystem the reciprocal relationships among microsystem settings.

exosystem that part of an ecological system that includes settings in which the adolescent does not have an active role as a participant but that influence him or her nevertheless.

macrosystem the ideologies, attitudes, mores, customs, and laws of a particular culture that influence the individual.

FIGURE 2.5
BRONFENBRENNER'S ECOLOGICAL MODEL FOR UNDERSTANDING SOCIAL INFLUENCES

Source: Data from Bronfenbrenner (1979).

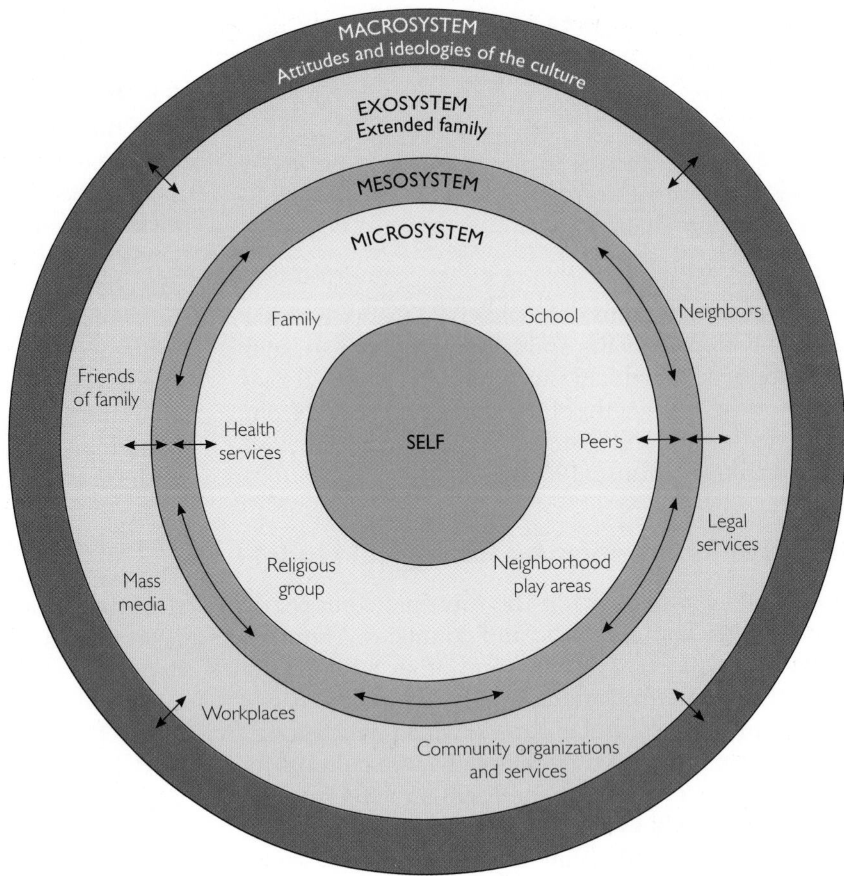

determines who is an adult and who is an adolescent. It sets standards of physical attractiveness and gender-role behavior, and influences health practices such as smoking. It also influences educational standards and relationships between races and ethnic groups.

Macrosystems differ in various countries and in racial, ethnic, or socioeconomic groups. There are also differences within each group. In Sweden, for example, it is against the law for parents to hit children, yet the practice is condoned by some groups in the United States. Middle-class parents in the United States often have different goals and philosophies of childrearing than do those in low-socioeconomic-status groups. Rural families may have different parenting values than urban families (Coleman, Ganong, Clark, and Madsen, 1989). These values and customs have differential effects on adolescents. In talking about social development, then, we have to discuss issues and concerns in the contexts in which adolescents are growing up.

Margaret Mead and Ruth Benedict: Anthropological Views

The theories of Margaret Mead (1901–1978), Ruth Benedict (1887–1948), and other cultural anthropologists have been called **cultural determinism** and **cultural relativism** because, like Bronfenbrenner, anthropologists emphasize the importance of the broader *social environment* in determining the personality development of the child. Since social institutions, economic patterns, habits, rituals, and religious beliefs vary from society to society, culture is relative.

Anthropologists emphasize that the sociocultural milieu determines the course of adolescence and strongly influences the degree to which adolescents feel welcomed by the adult community. In modern society, adolescence has become a prolonged stage of development; its completion is imprecise and its privileges and responsibilities are often illogical and confused. This is in contrast to nontechnological societies, where puberty rites mark a definite and early introduction into adulthood (Weisfeld, 1997).

Research on adolescents has revealed that their feelings of satisfaction depend partly on having some control over their lives, being able to have choices, and taking responsibility for their own behavior (Barker and Galambos, 2005). This is exactly what being an adult involves. This process is often delayed in modern industrial societies.

Cultural Continuity versus Discontinuity

Anthropologists challenge the basic truths of all age and stage theories of child and adolescent development (such as those of Freud and Erikson). Mead, for

PERSONAL ISSUES WHEN DO THEY BECOME ADULTS?

Adulthood is the stage of life recognized by cultures all over the world. In many nontechnological societies, the major criterion for attaining adulthood is that one has married (Schlegel and Barry, 1991). In addition, in Western societies, significant life changes, such as completing one's education, becoming a full-time worker, and establishing one's own home, have been assumed to be markers of social maturity (Goldscheider and Goldscheider, 1999). Are these the criteria used by adolescents and young adults?

The answer appears to be, largely, "no." A number of studies have shown that adolescents are more likely to believe that psychological, cognitive traits are more important than these social role markers. For example, Arnett (2001) found that almost 90 percent of the adolescents in his study believed that "accepting responsibility for one's actions" was necessary for adulthood, whereas fewer than 15 percent believed that "marriage" was needed. Similarly, the single most commonly cited marker for adulthood given by adolescents in Barker and Galambos's (2005) study was "the ability to act responsibly"; this beat out living independently, being financially independent, or being out of school.

When do adolescents think that they will begin to accept responsibility and hence become adults? That depends upon their age. Generally, the older the teen, the older that the person believes that adulthood will strike (Galambos and Vitunski, 2000). Most adolescents think that adulthood will descend upon them at an earlier age—perhaps 20 or 21—than they later will. Arnett (2001), however, discovered that somewhat fewer than half of the individuals in their twenties that he sampled felt as if they were "adults."

The findings of these studies are consistent with research suggesting that adulthood is an emerging process. This is a period of time (often in midadolescence) when youths begin to consider themselves adults—cognitively, emotionally, and behaviorally.

example, discovered that Samoan children follow a relatively continuous growth pattern, with no abrupt changes from one age to the other. They are not expected to behave one way as children, another way as adolescents, and yet another way as adults. Samoans never have to change abruptly their ways of thinking or acting; they do not have to unlearn as adults what they learned as children, so adolescence does not represent an abrupt change or transition from one pattern of behavior to another. This principle of *continuity of cultural conditioning* may be illustrated with three examples from Benedict (1938) and Mead (1950):

1. *Responsible versus nonresponsible roles:* The responsible roles of children in nontechnological societies can be contrasted with the nonresponsible roles of children in Western culture. Children in primitive societies learn responsibility quite early. Play and work often involve the same activity; for example, by "playing" with a bow and arrow, a boy learns to hunt. His adult hunting "work" is a continuation of his youthful hunting "play." In contrast, children in Western culture must assume drastically different roles as they grow up: They shift from nonresponsible play to responsible work and must do it rather suddenly.

2. *Submissive versus dominant roles:* The submissive role of children in Western culture is contrasted with the dominant role of children in many nontechnological societies. Children in Western culture must replace their childhood submission and adopt its opposite—dominance—as they become adults. Mead (1950) showed that Samoan children are not taught submission as children and then suddenly expected to become dominant when reaching adulthood. On the contrary, a 6- or 7-year-old Samoan girl dominates her younger siblings and in turn is dominated by the older ones. The older she gets, the more she dominates and disciplines others and the fewer there are to dominate her (the parents never try to dominate her). When she becomes an adult, she does not experience the dominance-submission conflict that the adolescent in Western society generally does.

3. *Similar versus dissimilar sex roles:* The similarity of sex roles of children and adults in many nontechnological cultures is contrasted with the dissimilar sex roles of children and adults in Western culture. Mead indicated that the Samoan girl experiences no real discontinuity of sex roles as she passes from childhood to adulthood. She has the opportunity to experiment and become familiar with sex with almost no taboos (except against

cultural determinism the influence of a particular culture in determining the personality and behavior of a developing individual.

cultural relativism variations in social institutions, economic patterns, habits, mores, rituals, religious beliefs, and ways of life from one culture to another.

ANSWERS WOULDN'T YOU LIKE TO KNOW ...

How does modern American culture make the adolescent transition to adulthood more difficult than it otherwise might be?

Modern American culture is discontinuous, which means that adolescents must change their behaviors as they mature. Change is more difficult to cope with than continuity.

incest). Therefore, by the time she reaches adulthood, the Samoan female is able to assume a sexual role in marriage very easily. By contrast, in Western culture, infant sexuality is denied and adolescent sexuality is repressed; sex is considered sinful and dangerous. When adolescents mature sexually, they must unlearn those earlier attitudes and taboos to become sexually responsive adults.

Storm and Stress Revisited

Although the research on which Mead based her conclusions has been criticized by some (e.g., Freeman, 1983), her 1950 book, *Coming of Age in Samoa,* rocked the academic world. Since Hall's time, it had been taken for granted that adolescence was inevitably troublesome. Evidence of the existence of even one society in which adolescence was tranquil severely undermined any and all biologically based interpretations of adolescent behavior.

In showing the continuity of development of children in some cultures, in contrast to the discontinuity of development of children in Western culture, anthropologists and some psychologists (Roll, 1980) cast doubt on the universality of ages and stages of growth of children in all cultures.

Anthropologists challenge the inevitability of the storm and stress of adolescence by minimizing the impact of physical changes and by focusing on the interpretation of those changes. Menstruation is a case in point. One tribe may teach that the menstruating girl is a danger to the tribe (she may scare the game or dry up the well); another tribe may consider her condition a blessing (she could increase the food supply or the priest could obtain a blessing by touching her). A girl taught that menstruation is good will react and act differently than a girl who is taught that it is a curse. Therefore, the stress and strains of pubescent physical changes may be the result of certain cultural interpretations of those changes and not due to any inherent biological tendencies.

As another example, anthropologists believe that it is specific conditions within Western society, not biology, that prompts parent-adolescent tension (Mead, 1974). In particular, the furious pace of social change, the diversity of available opinions, and the rapidity of technological development all converge, Mead and others would argue, to devalue parental views. Furthermore, early physiological puberty and the need for prolonged education allow many years for the development and assimilation of a peer-group culture in which adolescent values, customs, and mores may be in conflict with those in the adult world (Finkelstein and Gaier, 1983).

RESEARCH HIGHLIGHT HOW TROUBLED ARE ADOLESCENTS?

Early theoreticians, philosophers, and writers almost unanimously declared that adolescents were disrespectful, angry, immoderate, and disruptive. Even today, many American adults certainly believe that adolescents are more problematic than younger children (Buchanan, Eccles, Flanagan, Midgley, Feldlaufer, and Harold, 1990), and they believe teens to be lazy, rude, and selfish (Public Agenda, 1999). How accurate are these views?

After reviewing the available literature, Arnett (1999) concluded that those who believe in adolescent storm and stress are usually referring to one or more of three different types of behavior: (1) conflicts with others, especially parents and other authority figures, (2) mood swings, and (3) participation in risky behaviors. In each case, it appears that these problems are *more common* among adolescents than among persons of other ages. Certainly, this doesn't mean such behaviors are universal. Not all adolescents are depressed, but a disproportionate number are. Not all adolescents engage in unsafe sexual practices or drive without seatbelts, but too many do. Nonetheless, this finding does, in part, substantiate the notion of *sturm und drang.*

Perhaps the most correct conclusion is that adolescents are *more likely* to experience significant difficulties than either children or adults. The opposite is also likely true: If a person was moody or behaved recklessly during some part of his or her life, it was most likely during adolescence. Yet there is little reason to fear, as some adolescents do, that life will be one long downhill slide after reaching adulthood. At the same time, though, it is important to keep in mind that the majority of adolescents do not get into serious trouble and that even when problems occur, they are often sporadic or transitory (Offer and Schonert-Reichl, 1992).

Adolescents in many non-Western societies are given important responsibilities. This Cambodian girl is harvesting rice to help feed her family.

ANSWERS WOULDN'T YOU LIKE TO KNOW ...

Is adolescence inevitably a difficult time of life?

Those theorists with a biological bent tend to believe that adolescence is inevitably a difficult time of life; those who believe that the environment plays a greater role are less pessimistic. Research data indicate that adolescents are less happy than adults and children but are not uniformly or consistently miserable.

It might interest you to know that Mead believed adolescents should be given more freedom to make their own choices and live their own lives. By requiring less conformity and less dependency and by tolerating individual differences within the family, adolescent-parent conflict and tension could be minimized (Mead, 1950). Also, Mead wrote that youths can be accepted into adult society at younger ages. Gainful employment, even part time, would promote greater financial independence. Parenthood should be postponed, advocated Mead, but not necessarily sex or marriage. Adolescents should be given a greater voice in the social and political life of the community. These measures would eliminate some of the discontinuities of cultural conditioning of children growing up in Western society and would allow for a smoother, easier transition to adulthood.

The later writings of Mead (1970, 1974) and others were modified to show an appreciation of universal aspects of development (e.g., incest taboos) and more acknowledgment of the biological role in human development. Today, extreme positions are generally disregarded by both geneticists and anthropologists. They basically agree that a composite view that acknowledges both biogenetic factors and environmental forces comes closest to the truth.

SUMMARY

1. G. Stanley Hall was the "father of adolescent psychology." He believed that adolescent behavior was shaped by evolutionary forces and that adolescents were destined to be disrespectful and temperamental. He said that adolescence was a time of *sturm und drang,* or "storm and stress."
2. Arnold Gesell emphasized the importance of genetics and maturation in development.
3. Sigmund Freud made a significant contribution in his emphasis on early childhood experiences and unconscious motivations in influencing behavior. The desire to satisfy sexual instincts and psychic needs of affection is a strong motivating factor in influencing adolescent behavior. Similarly, Freud's explanations of the need to separate emotionally from parents, to establish heterosexual friendships with peers, and to find a love object for emotional fulfillment are helpful.
4. Anna Freud proposed that adolescents enter into a period of psychic disequilibrium when they enter puberty because the id becomes stronger and dominates behavior. Because of this unbalance, adolescents are forced to employ psychological defense mechanisms to reduce tension.
5. Erik Erikson outlined an eight-stage sequence of personality development over the lifespan. He coined the term *identity* to describe the adolescent's search for goals, self-understanding, and sense of unity. The identity search is now considered one of the major tasks that adolescents face.
6. Jean Piaget believed that individuals learn by developing new cognitive structures that help them adapt to their environment. He outlined four stages of cognitive development. Preadolescents are in the *concrete operational stage;* they can think logically about things they have actually experienced. Adolescents are in the *formal operational stage* and can think abstractly.
7. Robert Selman emphasized social cognition, the ability to understand social relationships, and the stages that people pass through in developing this ability. He described how, unlike younger children, adolescents can take a third-person perspective, even a generalized societal perspective, when judging others' behavior.

8. Lev Vygotsky believed that learning is a social, rather than an individual, process. He suggested that cognitive development proceeds most quickly if novices are teamed with experts to solve problems together.
9. Albert Bandura's social learning theory emphasized the importance of modeling and vicarious reinforcement in the learning process. His later emphasis on cognitive factors in shaping the environment was an important contribution.
10. Robert Havighurst outlined the major developmental tasks of adolescence. They include accepting one's changing body, developing more meaningful relationships with others, achieving emotional independence from parents, and achieving socially responsible behavior.
11. Kurt Lewin believed that adolescents are unhappy and confused because they are unclear as to what they are allowed to do and must give up many of the pleasures of childhood without yet gaining the benefits that come with adulthood.
12. Uri Bronfenbrenner described the adolescent's world as a series of nested environments. He urged researchers to look beyond the adolescent's immediate contacts and interactions and examine the effects of more distant aspects of the environment. He believed that overall cultural values greatly influence adolescent development.
13. Margaret Mead and Ruth Benedict and other anthropologists provide evidence that there are few universal patterns of development and that adolescent turmoil is not universal. Cultural comparisons emphasize the positive and negative elements in each culture that aid or prevent the adolescent from becoming an adult.

KEY TERMS

accommodation 33
adaptation 33
anal stage 28
assimilation 33
cognition 32
cultural determinism 42
cultural relativism 42
defense mechanisms 30
developmental tasks 38
ego 29
emerging adulthood 32
equilibrium 33
exosystem 41
genital stage 28
id 29
identification 28
individuation 28
latency stage 28
macrosystem 41
mental operations 33
mesosystem 41
microsystem 41
modeling 36
oral stage 27
organismic psychologist 32
phallic stage 28
psychoanalytical theory 28
psychosocial moratorium 32
reinforcement 37
scaffolding 35
schema 33
self-reinforcement 37
social cognition 34
social role taking 34
sturm und drang 26
superego 29
vicarious reinforcement 37
zone of proximal development 35

THOUGHT QUESTIONS

Personal Reflection

1. Would you describe your own adolescence as a period of storm and stress? Why or why not?
2. Think of the Eriksonian stages that you have already passed through in your lifespan. Did you have a favorable or an unfavorable outcome at each stage? What experiences seemed to contribute to these outcomes?
3. What aspects of your identity have you formed? Which are you still working on? Which have you put off for the time being?
4. Give specific examples of how you adapted cognitively through assimilation and accommodation.
5. Give several examples of the ways in which you have modeled yourself after your parents. Did you consciously try to do this or did it just happen?

Group Discussion

6. To what extent do basic biological urges, such as sexual desire and aggression, underlie behavior? Support your idea with examples.
7. Why is adolescence the time when most individuals begin to feel the need to break away from their parents? Why not earlier or later?
8. How might increased skill at perspective taking influence interpersonal relationships? Do you see any downside to having this skill? Explain.
9. Do you figure out problems best when working alone or when working with others? Do the characteristics of the people you are working with matter? Support your answers with examples.
10. Which of Havighurst's developmental tasks should be accomplished during early adolescence? Which should take longer? Why?
11. Drawing from as many theories as possible, explain why some adolescents act aggressively.
12. What cultural values do you believe can ease the transition from childhood to adolescence and from adolescence to adulthood?

Debate Questions

13. Is adolescent development more a matter of physical maturation or environmental experience?
14. Is adolescence a more difficult period of life than other developmental stages?
15. Does good or ill come from generating developmental norms as Gesell did?

16. Does emerging sexuality underlie most adolescent stress?
17. Are adolescents really "marginalized," as Lewin suggested?
18. Do the micro- and mesoenvironments or do the macro- and exoenvironments have a greater effect on adolescents' school achievement?

SUGGESTED READING

Bronfenbrenner, U. (2006). *Ecology of Human Development: Experiments by Nature and Design.* Cambridge, MA: Harvard University Press.

Coté, J. E. (1994). *Adolescent Storm and Stress: An Evaluation of the Mead-Freeman Controversy.* Hillsdale, NJ: Erlbaum.

Erikson, E. H. (1994). *Identity and the Life Cycle.* New York: W. W. Norton.

Muuss, R. E. H., and Porton, H. (1998). *Adolescent Behavior and Society: A Book of Readings.* New York: McGraw-Hill.

Rieber, R. W., and Robinson, D. K. (Eds.). (2004). *The Essential Vygotsky.* New York: Kluwer Academic Press.

Serulniko, A. (2000). *Piaget for Beginners.* London, England: Writers and Readers.

CHAPTER 3 ADOLESCENT DIVERSITY

Socioeconomic Status and Ethnicity

WOULDN'T YOU LIKE TO KNOW . . .

- How is the racial/ethnic composition of the United States changing?
- What is the *cycle of poverty?*
- How do the lives of low-socioeconomic-status (SES) adolescents differ from the lives of middle-class adolescents?
- In what ways have the lives of African Americans improved over the past 20 years?
- How do African American families differ from White families?
- What is arguably the greatest problem facing American Latinos?
- Are most Mexican Americans farmers or migrant workers?
- What values and beliefs distinguish Native American culture?
- How did U.S. immigration law disrupt the family lives of Chinese immigrants?
- From what area of the world have the most recent immigrants to the United States come? From what area have the most recent refugees to this country come?

One of the most common myths about adolescents is that they are all alike. Adolescents cannot be discussed as one homogenous group any more than any other age group. Not only do they come from a wide variety of ethnic and cultural backgrounds but also the environments in which they are raised are different and the circumstances of their lives are quite varied.

Many sections of this book refer to cultural differences among adolescents. Differences between low-socioeconomic-status and middle-class adolescents are highlighted, as are some differences between non-Caucasian and Caucasian adolescents. Unfortunately, much of the research with adolescents has been conducted with White, middle-class youths. Although these are the majority, they are not representative of all. So before we get into more detailed discussion of adolescence, let's look at the wide cultural diversity that exists among several representative minority groups.

We begin with low-socioeconomic-status adolescents of whatever race or national origin. The low-socioeconomic-status category cuts across racial and ethnic boundaries, affecting 12.4 percent of the population (U.S. Bureau of the Census, 2005a). In terms of sheer number, there are more poor White adolescents than Asian American, African American, Hispanic American, and Native American adolescents. A greater *proportion* of non-White adolescents are poor, however.

The discussion will continue with a consideration of the adolescents in four recognized racial/ethnic groups: African Americans, Hispanic Americans, Asian Americans, and Native Americans. Figure 3.1 shows the sizes of these groups. There are almost equal numbers of Latinos and non-Hispanic Black Americans, at 14 percent and 13 percent respectively. (Note that the term *Latino* does not denote people of a given skin color but those with a Spanish-speaking heritage; Latinos can be Black or White.) There are many fewer Asian Americans and Pacific Islanders (4 percent) and a very small proportion of Native Americans (about 1 percent). The remaining 66 percent of the U.S. population consists of White non-Latinos. Figure 3.1 also shows that due to differences in both immigration and birthrates among the groups, the percentage of non-Latino White Americans is expected to decrease. By the year 2050, Whites are expected to make up just over half of the U.S. population.

ANSWERS WOULDN'T YOU LIKE TO KNOW . . .

How is the racial/ethnic composition of the United States changing?

The United States is becoming more Asian and more Latino. While the percentages of Americans in these groups are increasing, the Black and Native American populations are expected to remain stable and the relative size of the Caucasian population is expected to decrease.

A word of caution is in order as we begin. Even though we will be making general statements about various minority groups, all individuals within a minority group are not alike. Tremendous diversity exists within minority groups, just as it exists among minority groups and within the White middle-class majority. In describing minority groups, the intent is to provide the background for better understanding, *not* to create or reinforce stereotypes. You likely know individuals from these minority groups to whom these descriptions apply only partially or perhaps not at all.

ADOLESCENTS OF LOW SOCIOECONOMIC STATUS

Various terms have been applied to youths who are of lower social classes and poor, among them *disadvantaged, poverty class, low socioeconomic status,* and *working class.* In this book, the term **low socioeconomic status (low SES)** is used because it refers to

FIGURE 3.1 RACIAL/ETHNIC MAKEUP OF THE UNITED STATES: 2000 AND 2050

Source: Data from U.S. Bureau of the Census (2005b).

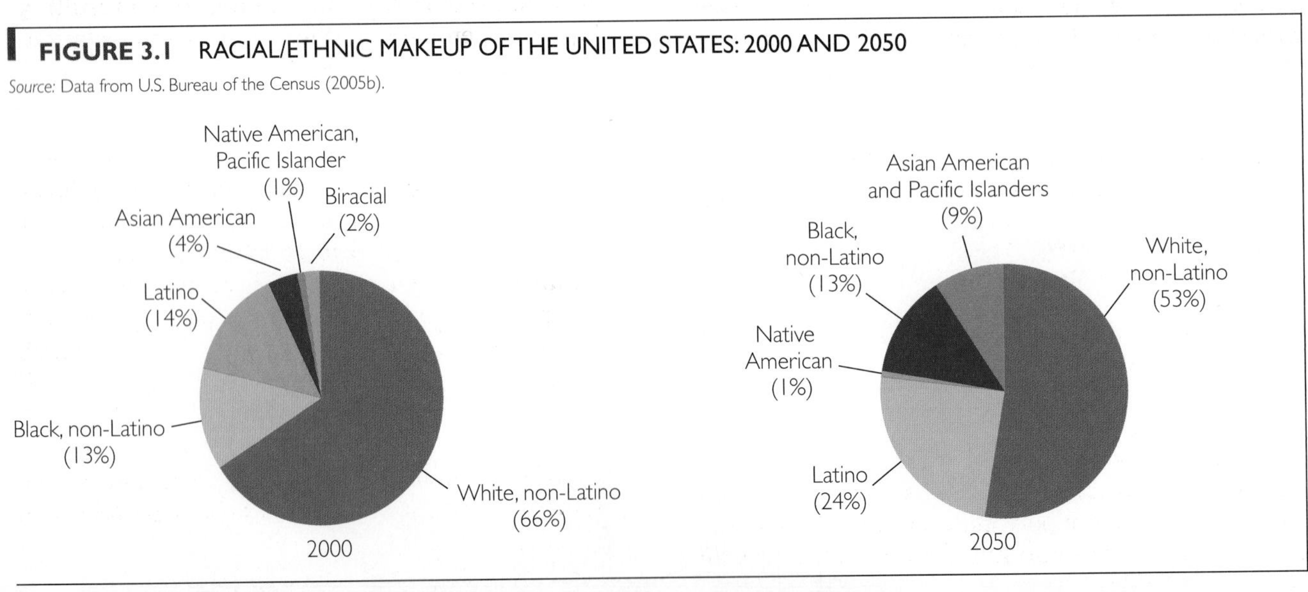

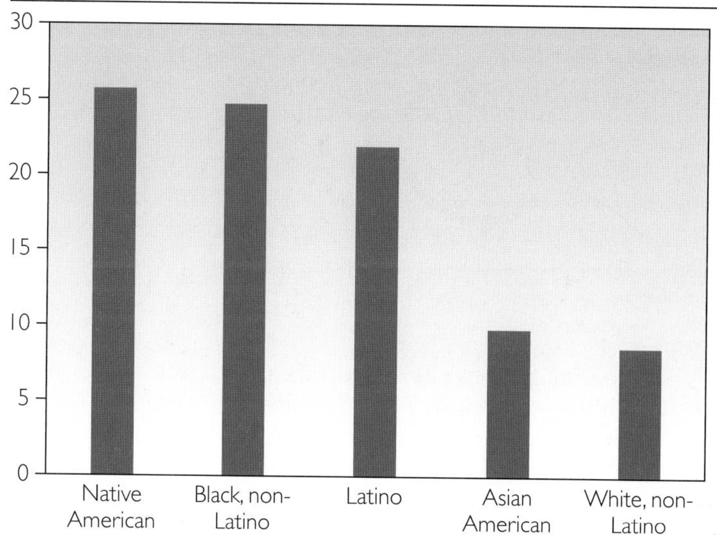

FIGURE 3.2 POVERTY RATES BY RACE AND ETHNICITY: 2004

Source: Data from U.S. Bureau of the Census (2005a).

two important aspects of the living condition: low social standing and low income.

These two factors do not always go together. Someone with a relatively low income may have a fairly high social standing (an artist or a poet, for example), and conversely, someone with a high income might be disfavored socially (a drug dealer, for instance). Generally, though, individuals who have very little money are marginalized by society in terms of status. Thus, they have only limited access to leisure facilities, educational advantages, work opportunities, health and medical care, and proper living conditions.

Compared with the general U.S. population, low-SES adolescents are disproportionally from non-White families (see Figure 3.2). In addition, these families are typically larger than average, have fewer wage earners, and have more female heads of household. They reside more often in the South, in farm areas, or in cities and less often in suburban areas.

Socioeconomic status (SES) plays an important role in the lives of adolescents. Awareness of different levels of SES influences adolescents' self-perceptions as well as their perceptions of the external world. Children, adolescents, and adults learn their worth, in part, by comparing themselves with others. Also, their self-attitudes are influenced greatly by the attitudes held by others toward them (Pearlman, 1995).

Limitations of Low Socioeconomic Status

Four important limitations are imposed on the lives of adolescents who have low socioeconomic status.

Limited Alternatives

Youths of low socioeconomic status are not exposed to a variety of social and cultural settings. Vocationally, they have fewer opportunities. Poverty limits their educational and career attainments. Socially, they are the nonjoiners, seldom going beyond the borders of kinship and neighborhood groups. Their limited experience and knowledge make it difficult to get out of or go beyond the narrow world in which they are growing up. Limited vision and experience restrict the possibilities and opportunities in their lives.

Helplessness, Powerlessness

In the working world, the skills of low-SES citizens are limited. They can exercise little autonomy or influence in improving their conditions, and they have little opportunity or knowledge to receive additional training. They are the most easily replaced workers. These individuals have little political or social influence in their communities and, sometimes, inadequate legal protection of their rights as citizens.

Deprivation

Adolescents of low socioeconomic status are aware of the affluence around them and the benefits received by others. The media make them constantly aware of their own abject status and "failure," often resulting in bitterness, embarrassed withdrawal and isolation, and social deviation and rebellion.

Insecurity

Low-SES individuals are at the mercy of life's unpredictable events: sickness, loss of work, injury, legal problems, school difficulties, family difficulties, and others. The lower their socioeconomic status, the more vulnerable they are to the stresses of life. They strive just to provide themselves with the basic necessities of life and they never feel secure about their lives, in general.

low socioeconomic status (low SES) those persons who are of low social class and status, including cultural deprivation and low income.

FIGURE 3.3 THE CYCLE OF POVERTY

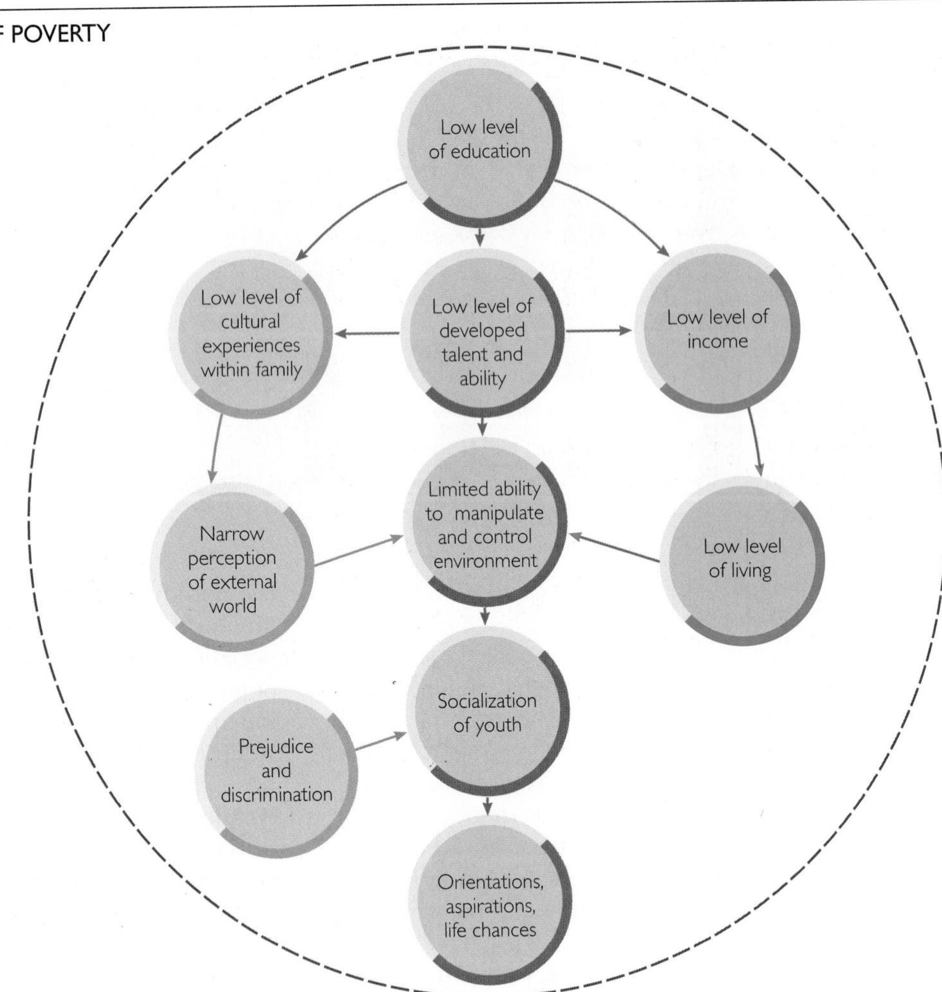

Cycle of Poverty and Deprivation

The net effect of the limitations imposed on the lives of low-socioeconomic-status youths is to perpetuate poverty (Knapp and Shields, 1990). Figure 3.3 illustrates this cycle of poverty. The cycle begins at the top, with a low level of education. Moving clockwise, having little education results in earning a low income, which results in having a low standard of living, which results in having a limited ability to manage or control the external environment. Therefore, adolescents are socialized to expect low education, a low level of living, and powerlessness. Their worldview perpetuates the lifestyle to which they have become accustomed.

Starting at the top of Figure 3.3 again and moving counterclockwise, having a low level of education results in having a low level of developed talent and ability and a low level of cultural experiences in the family. This, in turn, results in a narrow perception of the external world, which, along with the low level of living, contributes to limited ability to manage and control the environment. Because of discrimination and limitations imposed on them, parents, in one way or another, teach their children not to expect a very high income, level of living, or much education. Low-SES adolescents tend to be caught in a self-perpetuating cycle of poverty. This is especially true if adolescents' parents have themselves been poor for their entire lives. Individuals who start off being economically advantaged and then fall into poverty tend to be more optimistic about their children's future. Given that, they are more likely to socialize their children in ways that will help them succeed scholastically and economically.

Low Level of Education

The abilities to read and understand, to analyze situations and think critically about them, and to perform numerical calculations are important both to the individual and to society. Individuals with sound basic skills are more likely to attend and complete high school, perhaps go on to college, secure employment and higher wages, and live generally productive lives. Individuals who are frustrated by deficiencies in their abilities to read and write are less likely to complete school, less likely to succeed in the labor market, and more likely to engage in behaviors with negative social consequences, such as depending on public assistance and committing crime.

A recent meta-analysis that examined the findings from 74 studies looking at the relationship between ed-

PERSONAL ISSUES WHY ARE SOME PEOPLE POOR?

The impact of poverty on the lives of adolescents is huge. The reasons for that poverty must be considered. Why are some people poor?

The following questionnaire will enable you to express your ideas. You can then compare your answers with those of a group of 220 undergraduates at the University of Canterbury in New Zealand (Stacey, Singer, and Ritchie, 1989).

Instructions

Circle the number by each reason that best expresses your opinion. In the scale below, a rating of 1 means you feel the reason is extremely important. A rating of 7 means you feel the reason is not important at all. Thus, the low numbers indicate high importance and the high numbers represent low importance, with 4 indicating moderate importance.

Internal Factors

Lack of effort and laziness 1 2 3 4 5 6 7

Poor money management 1 2 3 4 5 6 7

Lack of intelligence 1 2 3 4 5 6 7

Lack of physical attractiveness 1 2 3 4 5 6 7

Societal Factors

Economic and taxation systems are at fault 1 2 3 4 5 6 7

Salaries and wages are too low 1 2 3 4 5 6 7

Economic system does not create enough jobs 1 2 3 4 5 6 7

Financial system is prejudiced against them 1 2 3 4 5 6 7

Family Factors

Little money in the family 1 2 3 4 5 6 7

Little emphasis in the family on success 1 2 3 4 5 6 7

Family is unable to provide opportunities 1 2 3 4 5 6 7

Strain in family life 1 2 3 4 5 6 7

Luck

Bad luck 1 2 3 4 5 6 7

Factors beyond their control 1 2 3 4 5 6 7

Some persons are doomed to be poor 1 2 3 4 5 6 7

Unlucky in gambling, speculation, and taking chances 1 2 3 4 5 6 7

After filling out the questionnaire, add the numbers in each of the four categories and divide by four. This will give you the average score for each category. If your "Internal Factors" score was as high or higher than your other scores, you believe that poor people are responsible for their own poverty.

A similar poll conducted in 2001 by a team of researchers from National Public Radio, the Kaiser Family Foundation, and Harvard University's Kennedy School of Government concluded that about half of Americans believe that poverty is primarily caused by personal factors such as laziness; the other half believe that social policy and circumstances beyond an individual's control are primarily responsible for poverty (National Public Radio, 2003).

Source: Adapted from B. G. Stacey, M. S. Singer, and G. Ritchie, "The Perception of Poverty and Wealth among Teenage University Students," *Adolescence, 24* (1989): 193–207. Used by permission.

ANSWERS WOULDN'T YOU LIKE TO KNOW . . .

What is the *cycle of poverty*?

The term *cycle of poverty* refers to the vicious circle that characterizes the experiences of impoverished people, who find it difficult to move into the middle class. For example, if you are poor, you will likely go to an inadequately funded high school. Even if you work hard, you will likely learn less than your middle-class peers. Because of this, you will be less likely to go to college or get a good job. And if you can't get a good job, you will have no legitimate way to earn money and raise your standard of living.

ucational achievement and poverty found a moderate influence of socioeconomic status and student achievement at the student level and a very large influence at the school level (Sirin, 2005). This confirms that families who live in areas of concentrated poverty are likely to have children who do not do well in school. Although the effect at the individual student level was smaller, it was still one of the best overall predictors of academic achievement. These SES effects were even stronger for Caucasian than for non-Caucasian students. Schools in higher-SES neighborhoods provide better materials, more experienced teachers, and lower teacher-student ratios than those in lower-SES neighborhoods: all of these help students learn more effectively. Coupled with the facts that lower-income parents often have lower expectations for their children and fewer personal resources to help them academically, at present this relationship is almost inevitable.

Family Instability and Female-Headed Households

Partly as a result of early marriages and economic struggles, low-SES families are much less stable than families of higher SES. The rates of divorce and separation increase as one goes down the socioeconomic scale (Bramlett and Mosher, 2002). Pregnancy rates, especially unintended pregnancy rates, also are higher among those of lower socioeconomic status. Poorer pregnant teenagers are less likely to obtain abortions than middle-class teens. These two factors together mean that more poor teenage girls become mothers than middle-class teenage girls. Entering into single parenthood at an early age binds these individuals to poverty (U.S. Department of Health and Human Services, 1995).

Due to high divorce and out-of-wedlock pregnancy rates, female-headed households are prevalent and persistent among the poor. Much research indicates that although a single-parent family may not be entirely disadvantaged (a father may be a financial burden or a source of friction), the overall effects of the absence or only occasional presence of a father are usually detrimental to the emotional and social development of adolescents. The fact that being raised in a one-parent family is a risk factor for a variety of problems (McLanahan and Sandefur, 1994) will be discussed quite fully in Chapter 11. For now, suffice it to say that being poor increases the chances that you will be raised in a one-parent home, and that being raised in a one-parent home increases the chances that you will end up economically disadvantaged as an adult.

Homelessness

A large number of people who are very poor are also homeless. Homelessness has increased in recent years for several reasons. First, there has been a decrease in the amount of available low-cost housing; older, less expensive units are torn down and replaced with far more expensive ones. Second, there has been a decline in the amount of government aid directed at housing assistance. Third, escalating health-care costs have pushed many families over the edge so that they cannot afford the housing that they used to (National Coalition for the Homeless, 2006).

Homelessness affects adolescents in many ways. Homeless adolescents are subject to both physical and emotional stress. Many turn to prostitution, drug dealing, and other crimes in order to survive. A number are in need of psychiatric treatment. School performance is low due to irregular attendance. Many homeless youths have multiple problems and they face a bleak future without some direct intervention.

Childrearing Goals and Philosophies

Families of low SES tend to be hierarchical, with rigid parent-adolescent relationships. The parents are seen as closed and inaccessible due to the stress that results from economic hardship. Most parents become more rigid and punitive when placed under stress (Abell, Clawson, Washington, Bost, and Vaughn, 1996). The home atmosphere is one of imperatives and absolutes, physical discipline, and psychological distance by the adults. Parent-child interaction patterns are oriented toward maintaining order, obedience, and discipline. The discipline—which is generally harsh and inconsistent—emphasizes physical punishment (even of adolescents) rather than verbal explanations and requests. As a group, adolescents from low-SES families report more problems with parents than do those from more privileged families.

Almost all parents want to bring up their children to live decent, obedient, honest lives. They want their children to rise above them economically, and a good report card from school seems to promise upward movement. There is a great deal of concern, therefore, over obedience, respect for adults, conformity to externally imposed standards, and staying out of trouble. Parents of low socioeconomic status are concerned with overt

Given the shortage of low-cost housing in some cities, many very poor families must turn to homeless shelters to house and feed their children.

behavior, with the immediate situation, and not with what behavior means in terms of future development.

Peer Orientation

Because adolescents from low-SES families tend to maintain weaker ties with parents than do youths from middle-class families, they form stronger, more lasting peer relationships. Those who report a low evaluation of parents and low self-esteem tend to be more peer oriented than those who have a high evaluation of parents (Vitaro, Brendgen, and Tremblay, 2000). This may be so for at least two reasons.

First, adolescents do not gain status through their familial identifications. The parents of these youths are not doctors, professors, or business executives. The adolescents, then, do not acquire status from the identity of their parents. In fact, they are keenly aware of their parents' lack of status in the community, and therefore their own lack of status. When a group in an achievement-oriented society cannot gain status in socially acceptable ways, then theft, narcotics, assault, vandalism, and other antisocial expressions may become the means of gaining status and recognition. The peer group replaces the family as the adolescent's primary reference group.

Second, low-SES adolescents may become more peer oriented than parent oriented because of their need for security. In the roughest neighborhoods, they need their gangs to protect lives.

Social Outcasts

Many low-SES adolescents are socialized differently from middle-class youths. They have their own manner of dress, speech, and behavior. Those who seem loud, ill mannered, or aggressive are scorned by middle-class society. On the other hand, those who withdraw, have low self-esteem, and are shy do not participate in many social functions and groups and are often ignored. In addition, inappropriate clothing and inadequate cleanliness invite criticism from middle-class peers.

Ordinarily, school is an important part of the social world of adolescents, but prejudicial treatment by middle-class adults and students can make low-SES adolescents social outcasts. They are likely to find themselves more and more socially isolated as they proceed through the grades, and, as a result, tend to seek friendships with out-of-school youths. Sometimes the association with other out-of-school youths influences adolescents to drop out of school.

Mental Health

The lack of emotional security and lack of stability in low-SES homes and particular patterns of childrearing lead to a high rate of psychological problems and mental illness among low-income adolescents. (Najman, Aird, Bor, O'Callaghan, Williams, and Shuttlewood, 2004). Furthermore, if they are hospitalized, low-SES adolescents are less likely to receive adequate treatment, are assigned less-skilled staff members, are treated for shorter periods with less intensive techniques, and are less likely to improve in psychotherapy (Tarnowski, Brown, and Simonian, 1999).

> **ANSWERS WOULDN'T YOU LIKE TO KNOW . . .**
>
> **How do the lives of low-socioeconomic-status (SES) adolescents differ from the lives of middle-class adolescents?**
>
> Low-SES adolescents are less likely to be raised by both their biological parents than middle-class youths. In addition, their parents are less likely to be home after school and more likely to be strict with them when they are home. Low-SES adolescents are more likely to experience both physical and psychological illnesses than middle-class teens, and they are also less likely to finish high school.

Physical Health

Poverty also leads to physical health problems. Poor health care, substandard nutrition, and exposure to environmental toxins are all more common in situations in which income is inadequate. These problems can lead to increased school absenteeism as well as fatigue, which creates an inability to pay attention even when in attendance. Among students with these problems, academic performance is likely to suffer, and students who do poorly in school frequently rebel, drop out, begin using drugs, or father or bear a child.

What should you take from the prior discussion? You should come away with an understanding that being raised in a family with meager economic resources is very stressful and that poor adolescents are more likely than middle-class youth to have grappled with a variety of problems while growing up. Later chapters will detail the basic fact that poverty-class adolescents are substantially more likely to exhibit problem behavior than middle-class adolescents. Understand that this is not due to bad genes or poor moral values but rather to the strain of living in a family that can barely make ends meet. Also remember, however, that many poor adolescents beat the odds. They avoid problem behavior, maintain high levels of physical and psychological well-being, graduate from high school, and move successfully into adult roles (Bowen and Chapman, 1996; Galbo and Demetrulias, 1996; Jarrett, 1995).

MINORITY ADOLESCENTS

The backgrounds of adolescents from minority groups are quite varied: Some are first-generation Americans who do not speak English in their homes, others have relatives who fled war or persecution in their homelands several generations ago, others have ancestors who were brought to the United States as slaves, and still others have parents who arrived here as wealthy, well-educated professionals. They may be rich or poor or middle class, and they may live on a farm or in a suburb or in the inner city.

Despite these differences, minority adolescents share one important quality: They are readily identifiable because they look different from Caucasian Americans. Given this, they may be targeted for prejudice and hostility. Even when they are not, minority youths are often acutely aware of the potential for prejudice to rear its ugly head at any moment. They feel different and sometimes marginalized. And this feeling of difference often affects them more than the specifics of their cultural backgrounds.

Much research suggests that it is the experience of being in the minority, rather than cultural differences per se, that most strongly influences Black, Asian, and Latino youths in the United States. If a White American adolescent were to move, say, to Japan or Nigeria, he or she would experience many of the same strains that an adolescent from a minority group does in the United States. It is difficult to have others view you as different from them—especially when their behavior suggests that *different* means "not quite as good as us." It is also difficult when others are oblivious to cultural differences and expect you to behave in ways that are foreign to what you have been taught at home.

Because minority youths are more likely to be poor than White youths, they are more likely to experience the stressors described earlier in this chapter. In addition to substandard living conditions, minority youths often face neighborhood and school violence, drug and alcohol abuse, academic underachievement, delinquency, and adolescent pregnancy (Vargas and Willis, 1994).

As a group, then, it is not surprising that minority adolescents experience disorders of psychological health more often than their majority counterparts. Depression, for example, is more common among African American and Hispanic American teens than among White teens. Native Americans are two to three times more likely to experience alcoholism and have higher suicide rates than Whites (Gonzales and Kim, 1997). The fact that Asian American youth, who are less likely to be economically disadvantaged than adolescents from other minority groups, do not show elevated rates of psychological disturbance underscores the importance of socioeconomic status, not ethnicity per se, in creating difficulties.

The following sections describe some of the issues of particular relevance to individuals in specific minority groups. Keep in mind that diversity is just as great within ethnic groups as between them and that poverty and discrimination are more responsible for ethnic-group differences than are differences in values and culturally prescribed behaviors.

African American Adolescents

Most Blacks have been in the United States for generations, having descended from enslaved Africans. More recently, Black immigrants have arrived from Latin America and the Caribbean. Each of these groups has its own culture. Here, we will concentrate on African Americans.

Legacy of Discrimination

For generations, African American families, especially those of lower SES, were forced to assume an inferior role in order to get along in White society. In the past, getting along meant sitting in the back of the bus and avoiding all "Whites-only" restaurants, restrooms, recreational facilities, theaters, and playgrounds. African American parents had to teach their children the so-called Black role. As one mother bluntly put it, "You have to let them know before they get out of their own backyard." African American children left their homes for school at their peril if they had not learned where they could sit and what they could or could not do if they got hungry or thirsty. At 5 years old, just as surely as at 15 or 25 years old, they had to know their place. One of the important lessons to learn was that no matter how unjustly they were treated, they had to control anger and conceal hostility. They had to be subservient and polite in the face of provocation, and walk with their eyes straight ahead, unmoved by taunts and jeers. Above all, they had to ignore insults and never argue or get in a fight with a White person. Black parents felt that they had to use severe measures to instill fear in their children as their best protection, or White society would punish them more severely.

Richard Wright (1937) wrote of his "first lesson in how to live as a Negro." Describing how he was badly cut as a result of a fight with White boys who threw bottles at him and his friends, he wrote:

> I sat brooding on my front steps, nursing my wound and waiting for my mother to come home from work. . . . I could just feel in my bones that she would understand. . . . I grabbed her hand and babbled out the whole story. She examined my wound, then slapped me.
>
> "How come yuh didn't hide?" she asked me. "How come yuh always fightin?"
>
> I was outraged and bawled. Between sobs I told her that I didn't have any trees or hedges to hide behind. . . .
>
> She grabbed a barrel stave, dragged me home, stripped me naked, and beat me till I had a fever of one hundred and two. She would smack my rump with the stave, and, while the skin was still smarting, impart to me gems of Jim Crow wisdom. I was never to throw cinders any more. . . . I was never, never under any conditions to fight white folks again. And they were absolutely right in clouting me with the broken milk bottle. (Wright, 1937)

Not all African American families used these means to protect their children from the wrath of Whites. Upper-class African American families told their children to avoid fights or brawls with Whites, not because it was dangerous but because it was beneath their social status. These families tried to isolate their children from racial discrimination as much as possible by outsegregating the White segregationists.

New Realities

The reality of the Black experience has changed greatly and continues to evolve. In the second half of the twentieth century, a series of sweeping judicial decisions that promised to desegregate Blacks and Whites contributed to the formation of a new conception of Black people in the minds of Blacks and Whites alike. Changes were seen in the emergence of a significant Black middle class, the rise of political leadership among Blacks, enfranchisement, the regulation of fair employment practices, and increased interest in African heritage and culture.

Today, 72 percent of Black adults have graduated from high school, and about 14 percent have gone on to earn college degrees. (McKinnon and Bennett, 2005). (This is slightly higher than the national average for high school graduation, but significantly lower for higher degrees.)

The trend toward higher education is continuing, as more and more African Americans are entering and graduating from college. Poverty rates among Blacks, are down compared to historic highs, but they are still about twice as high as for Whites. Still, nearly one-third of African American families have annual incomes in excess of $50,000 (U.S. Bureau of the Census, 2005b).

Many factors determine the level of self-esteem and self-image of African American adolescents, including graduating from high school, having positive relationships with their families, and enjoying family approval.

Contemporary Segregation

On May 17, 1954, the U.S. Supreme Court overruled the principle of "separate but equal" opportunity in education. In 1956, Dr. Martin Luther King, Jr., launched his passive resistance movement against the segregated bus system of Montgomery, Alabama. Although the court battles have been fought and won, there is still considerable disparity today between White and Black income, education, and other standards of living. Segregation continues to be a fact of life.

More African Americans live in the South than in the Northeast, Midwest, or West. This is part of the legacy of slavery. In many cases, families have lived in particular areas for generations. In terms of absolute numbers, more African Americans live in New York, California, Texas, Florida, and Georgia than in other states. However, as a percentage of the total population, Blacks are most heavily represented in Mississippi, Louisiana, South Carolina, Georgia, and Maryland. In addition, African Americans are more likely to live in metropolitan areas, especially in central cities, than non-Hispanic Caucasians (55 percent versus 22 percent) (McKinnon and Bennett, 2005). In many communities, neighborhoods are still segregated.

Unequal Education

In spite of the legal efforts to ensure equal education for all citizens, African American adolescents still do not enjoy that privilege. In terms of the total number of years of schooling, young African Americans have been catching up with Whites. (See Figure 3.4.) If quality of education is considered, however, African Americans still lag far behind Whites.

This difference is largely due to the socioeconomic differences between Blacks and Whites. If income levels are equated, there is much less racial difference in educational attainment. African American parents who are financially better off, close to their children, and involved in their schooling are much more likely to have adolescents who remain in school and do well (Brody, Stoneman, and Flor, 1995).

Occupational Aspirations

Although there has been an increase in the number of African Americans reaching higher socioeconomic levels in recent decades, several authors have pointed out that the actual *percentage* of Blacks who have moved into the middle-class has declined.

However, one study found that African American youths who were successful in high school and enrolled in college were optimistic about their future (Ganong, Coleman, Thompson, and Goodwin-Watkins, 1996). The African Americans in this study expected to be making about $10,000 a year more at the age 35 than did the European American students. They also expected to attain a higher level of education, and the

FIGURE 3.4 EDUCATIONAL ATTAINMENT AMONG AFRICAN AMERICANS AND WHITES, AGED 25 AND OLDER: 1960 TO 2004

Source: Data from U.S. Bureau of the Census (2005b).

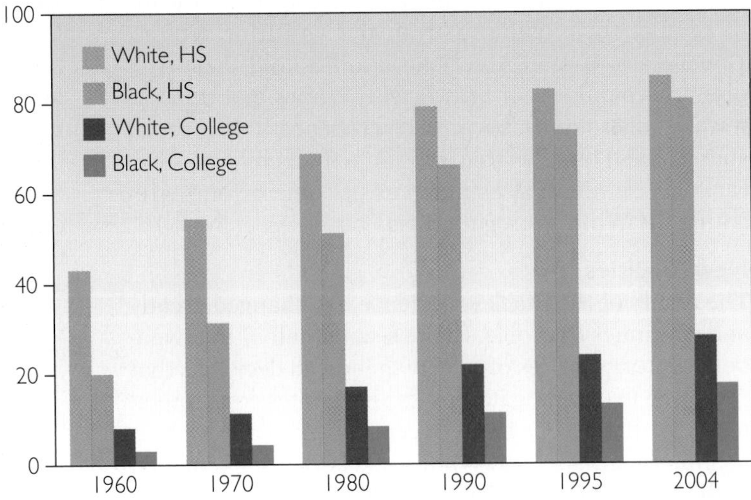

predicted probability of being successful was higher than that of Whites. The African Americans in this study clearly showed high aspirations, but it is unclear why they had greater optimism than their White peers. It may be partly due to the fact that intelligent, academically oriented Black youths are channeled by their families (and their own desire for economic advancement) toward careers that are prestigious and that pay well, such as law and medicine. Another possible explanation is that African American young adults view education as their main chance for successful careers—an access to the American Dream. African American students are aware of barriers they may face, and more perceive that education is a prerequisite to success. They may therefore be willing to work harder so that they can advance. Finally, the explanation may be that these African American young adults overestimate the economic value of the education they receive.

Desegregation Efforts

Traditionally, most African Americans lived in segregated neighborhoods and therefore had little opportunity for interracial contact. But changes in public attitudes and legislation paved the way for decreased segregation. Over the past 25 years, the segregation of African Americans declined by all five of the measures used by the U.S. Census Bureau to assess segregation (Iceland, Weinberg, and Steinmetz, 2002). Despite this decline, however, residential segregation was still higher for African Americans than for the other groups across all measures. Segregation remains strongest in large urban areas in the Midwest and Northeast.

Unemployment Rates

Unemployment rates are considerably higher for Black men and for Black teenagers than they are for the population at large. (Black women are actually slightly more likely to be employed than women at large; McKinnon and Bennett, 2005.) In fact, in the summer of 2006, while the overall teenage unemployment rate was at 15 percent, the almost 28 percent of African American teens who were seeking jobs could not find them (Employment Policies Institute, 2006). These higher rates are due to a complicated interaction of lower education, physical distance to available jobs, lack of transportation, discrimination, and lack of skills.

ANSWERS WOULDN'T YOU LIKE TO KNOW . . .

In what ways have the lives of African Americans improved over the past 20 years?

African Americans are less likely to live in segregated housing, less likely to be poor, and more likely to attend college than they were 20 years ago. On the other hand, the wage gap between Blacks and Whites has widened, and it is often the case that the public schools Blacks attend are less well funded than those attended primarily by Whites.

Income

In spite of the fact that the incomes of both Whites and African Americans have been increasing, the income gap between Whites and non-Whites has *widened,* not closed (see Figure 3.5). In every occupational category, African Americans are paid less than Whites for the same work. Unequal income is the result of unequal education, segregation, and discrimination and is still a reality. Legally, African American adolescents are entitled equal rights with White youths; in actuality, complete equality is still a goal to be attained.

Adolescent Pregnancy

Teenage pregnancy and motherhood (issues that will be discussed at length later in this text) are generally harmful to the adolescents involved. Adolescent mothers are less likely to graduate from high school and

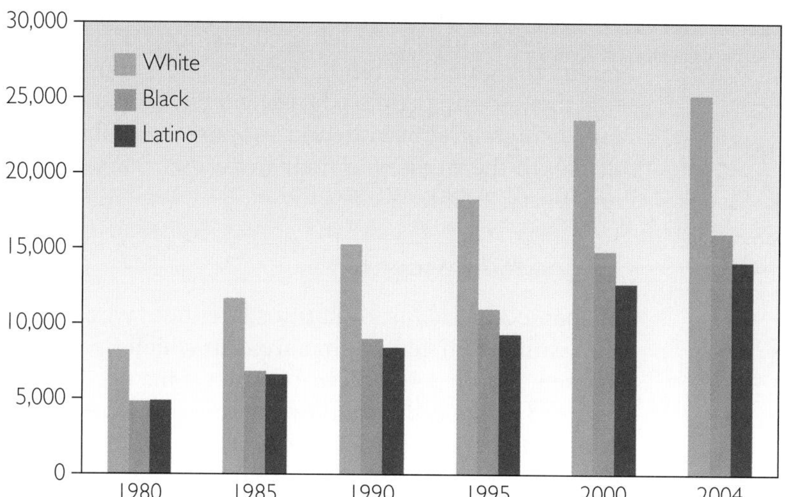

FIGURE 3.5 AVERAGE FULL-TIME WAGES BY RACE AND HISPANIC ORIGIN: 1980–2004.

Source: Data from U.S. Bureau of the Census (2000b).

more likely to become or remain impoverished than other adolescent girls (Hofferth, Reid, and Mott, 2001). Since African American adolescent girls are about three times as likely to get pregnant as Caucasian girls and about 1.5 times as likely to get pregnant as Latina

resiliency an individual's ability to succeed in spite of adversity and hardship

RESEARCH HIGHLIGHT THOSE WHO MAKE IT

There has been a tremendous amount of research on the factors that contribute to **resiliency,** the ability of a person to bounce back despite much hardship (Sandler, 2001). The traits and protective factors that have been identified as promoting resiliency cut across ethnic and socioeconomic groups. Some of the ones most commonly identified include the following:

Individual Characteristics:

1. "Resilient personalities": Resilient adolescents are often found to be assertive, verbally expressive, energetic, creative, and self-confident (Hart, Atkins, and Fegley, 2003). They are warm and outgoing, responsible, and reflective rather than impulsive and believe that they are masters of their own fates (Werner, 1998).
2. Genetic endowment: Research has shown a substantial genetic component to resiliency, often at or above the 50 percent mark (e.g., Kim-Cohen, Moffett, Caspi, and Taylor, 2004). Presumably, some nervous systems are designed to withstand stress more effectively than others.
3. High goal setters: They are achievement oriented, do well in school, and have set high career goals for themselves (Lewis, 2004).
4. Intelligent: Resilient youth tend to be bright (Asendorph and van Aken, 1999). Their intelligence allows them to think of solutions to the obstacles before them and to be flexible.
5. Possess deep interests: These interests give them joy and feelings of accomplishment and may provide them access to a mentor (Dolgin, 2006).
6. Are spiritual or are involved in a religious organization: Religious institutions provide mentorship, moral guidance, and support to vulnerable teens (Crawford, Wright, and Masten, 2004).

Family Characteristics

1. Parents provide emotional support: Resiliency is fostered when children know that their parents are there for them and express approval of them.
2. Parents foster self-sufficiency and independence.
3. Children are expected to assume responsibility (Werner, 1998).
4. Role models are present.

Community Resources

1. Involved, caring teachers
2. Stable friendships
3. Presence of mentors
4. Presence of safe havens

It is important to keep in mind that there are many adolescents who are raised under very difficult conditions who surpass their own backgrounds and who break out of the cycle of poverty.

ANSWERS WOULDN'T YOU LIKE TO KNOW . . .

How do African American families differ from White families?

When most African Americans think of the family in which they were raised, that group likely includes their aunts, uncles, cousins, grandparents, and even their parents' close friends. Their family likely had flexible gender roles, and it was more likely than average that they regularly attended church.

girls (Ventura, Mosher, Curtin, Abma, and Henshaw, 2001), adolescent pregnancy is a particularly crucial issue for the Black community. Approximately two-thirds of all births to Black women are to unwed mothers (National Center for Health Statistics, 2002).

Family Strengths

African American families are beset by many problems due to racial discrimination and the economic conditions under which many live. These families struggle to survive against the backdrop of high unemployment, disproportionate numbers of poor, and retrenchment of social programs important to them. However, African American families also show a number of positive characteristics that have enabled them to function and survive in a hostile social environment.

Strong Kinship Bonds Extended families are common in many minority populations. African Americans, in general, are exposed to more stress than Whites, but family members rely on one another for care, strength, and mutual support (Taylor, 2000).

Extended family members tend to live near one another, they share a strong sense of family obligation, there is a fluidity of household boundaries such that households absorb relatives and friends at need, there is much interactions, and a good deal of direct help and aid is given.

Favorable Attitude toward the Elderly At all socioeconomic levels, African Americans have a more favorable attitude toward the elderly than do Whites (Slaughter-Defoe, Kuehne, and Straker, 1992). One reason for the high degree of respect for the elderly family members is the strong kinship bond just discussed.

Adaptable Roles Husband-wife relationships in African American families are more egalitarian than in other races, with African American husbands sharing significantly in the performance of household tasks. Roles of all family members are flexible. For instance, an uncle or grandfather can assume the vacated position of a father or mother.

Strong Religious Orientation Religion has been a source of solace for downtrodden people, as well as a vehicle for rebellion and social advancement. The African American church—through preaching and teaching, symbols, belief systems, and rituals—remains the glue that binds families and communities together. Young people who attend church have a relatively high level of faith and support that helps them deal with the stresses in their lives (McCreary, Slavin, and Berry, 1996).

Latino Adolescents

Hispanic Americans, or Latinos, are those whose families came from geographic areas in which Spanish is spoken. About 14 percent of Americans are Latino. Figure 3.6 shows a breakdown of the world areas from which Hispanic American citizens originated. As you can see, about 60 percent of Latino citizens' families came from Mexico and about 10 percent came from Puerto Rico. Given this, these two ethnic groups will be discussed in the following sections.

Before we discuss these specific groups, however, it's essential to discuss an overarching problem in the Latino community: inequities in educational attainment.

Educational Concerns

Hispanic Americans are less likely to graduate from high school than other American citizens. Because educational attainment is essential to getting a good job, it is not surprising that the poverty rate is high among Latinos. The main reason that Latinos as a group struggle in school is because English is not the primary language spoken in most Hispanic students' homes. More than three-fourths of Hispanic families speak Spanish in their homes (Ramirez, 2004). Spanish-speaking children and adolescents must fight to understand teachers and textbooks not written in their native tongue; they must also try to put their thoughts on paper in a language with which they may not be comfortable.

Latino students are more likely than others to be held back in elementary school. And by middle school,

FIGURE 3.6 ANCESTRAL HOMELANDS OF HISPANIC AMERICANS: 2000

Source: Data from Guzman, 2001

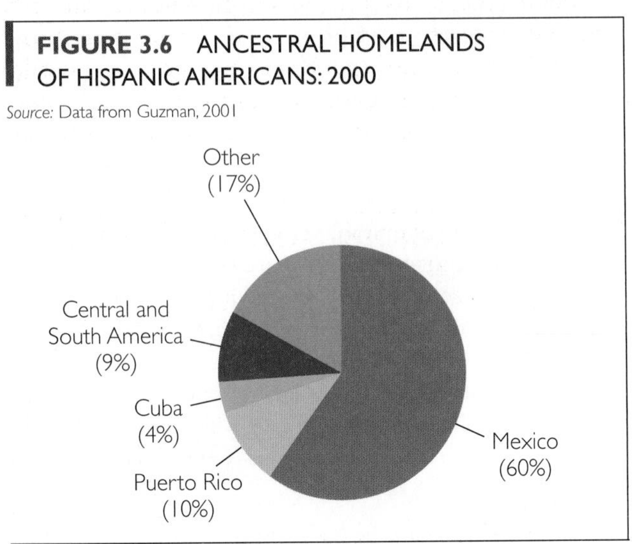

> **ANSWERS WOULDN'T YOU LIKE TO KNOW . . .**
>
> **What is arguably the greatest problem facing American Latinos?**
>
> The most pressing problem for the Latino community is the mismatch between Latino children and the schools they attend. As a result of language difficulties, inadequate funding, and cultural misunderstanding, needed skills are not being learned and diplomas are not being earned. This situation only perpetuates the levels of social isolation and high unemployment.

Latino students are likely to be several years behind in reading and math. Because of this, they are more likely to be tracked into general high school curricula, which do not prepare them for college. It is hardly surprising, then, that the dropout rate for Latino students in high school is double the rate for Blacks and three times that for non-Hispanic Whites. To further exacerbate the problem, Latino youths are more likely to drop out of school at an earlier age than youths from other ethnic groups.

Finally, Latino youths are less likely to go to college and graduate school than other adolescents (see Table 3.1). They receive only about 4 percent of the nation's B.A. degrees and 2 percent of the Ph.D.s (U.S. Bureau of the Census, 2003a).

In addition to the obvious language barrier, other issues that contribute to Latinos' lower level of academic achievement include inequities in school funding, school segregation, low numbers of Hispanic school personnel, lack of multicultural training for teachers, misplacement of students in special education classes, lack of availability of postsecondary financial assistance, and lack of school safety (President's Advisory Commission on Educational Excellence for Hispanic Americans, 1996).

Mexican American Adolescents

Mexican Americans are the second-largest minority group in the United States. They are also a young group: 35 percent of the Mexican American population is less than 18 years old (Guzman, 2001 1999a). Mexican Americans are concentrated in the Southwest in the states of California, Texas, New Mexico, and Arizona, but they are also moving in large numbers to cities in the Northeast and Midwest.

TABLE 3.1 ACADEMIC ACHIEVEMENT BY RACE AND ETHNICITY: 2000

RACE/ ETHNICITY	HIGH SCHOOL GRADUATES	ENROLLED IN COLLEGE
Whites	78.50%	44.40%
Blacks	71.30%	34.70%
Latinos	57.20%	25.30%

Source: Data from U.S. Bureau of the Census (2003a).

> **ANSWERS WOULDN'T YOU LIKE TO KNOW . . .**
>
> **Are most Mexican Americans farmers or migrant workers?**
>
> No. Most Mexican Americans live in urban areas. Only a minority are migrant workers. And not all migrant workers are Mexican American or even Latino; there are a significant number of Black migrant workers.

Segregation and Housing Mexican American youths are primarily urbanized: About 80 percent live in urban areas. Many live in cities and go to work as migrant workers on farms. The majority of Mexican Americans are segregated in residential ghettos called **colonias** or **barrios** (neighborhoods) (Hobbs and Stoops, 2002).

Families Mexican American marriages are more stable than those of either Whites or African Americans (U.S. Bureau of the Census, 2002). The greater stability holds true even when statistical allowances are made for differences in age, age at first marriage, education, and place of residence. Apparently, the traditional Mexican American family is highly cohesive. The mother is especially close to the children and plays an important role in their care (Martinez, 1988). Extended families are common. There is some evidence, however, that the traditional emphasis on the family is beginning to decline. Mexican American women, especially those who are more acculturated and who did better in school, are beginning to show interest in having prestigious, well-paying careers (Reyes, Kobus, and Gillock, 1999).

Culture The traditional Mexican culture, and hence the Mexican American culture, is different from that of the American mainstream in several ways:

1. Families are more patriarchal and traditional sex roles are emphasized (Valentine and Mosley, 1998).
2. There is a greater emphasis on **familialism:** devotion to one's family and respect for one's parents and grandparents (Niemann, Romero, Arredondo, and Rodriguez, 1999).
3. There is a strong commitment to Catholicism (Valentine and Mosley, 1999).

colonias or barrios colonies or districts of Spanish-speaking people.

familialism devotion to one's family and respect for one's parents and grandparents.

Mexican American culture places a strong emphasis on familialism, or devotion to one's family. The traditional Mexican American family is highly cohesive, and extended families are common.

Familialism is expressed by keeping children emotionally and physically close. Children in Mexican American families are given less freedom than those in non-Hispanic families, and Mexican American parents are granted the right to discipline their children as they see fit. Even as adults, children ask their parents for advice and listen respectfully to them. There are many positive aspects to familialism, but one downside is a lack of trust in people outside one's extended family. Maintaining this attitude can make it more difficult for Mexican Americans to succeed in the broader American society (Chandler, Tsai, and Wharton, 1999). Fortunately, this distrust of outsiders seems to have diminished in the past 20 years.

Niemann et al. (1999) asked Mexican Americans to compare their culture with the culture of their non-Hispanic neighbors. In addition to the differences already noted, they mentioned a love of celebration, a strong work ethic, and pride in their bilingualism. Unfortunately, the majority also mentioned being treated with discrimination and hostility by individuals such as store clerks and police.

Socialization of Adolescents Mexican American parents often emphasize some values that hinder the advancement of adolescents in the individualistic, highly competitive, materialistic U.S. society. An emphasis on family ties and dependency, submission to authority, living in the present, and politeness are not conducive to independence, achievement, deferred gratification, and success. For example, the older son's role in the Mexican American family is often an extension of that of the father: protector, orderer, and guardian of the younger children. Family dependency is antithetical to initiative and autonomy. Mexican American daughters are closely supervised and taught to take their place in the home (Villarruel, 1998). The emphasis on honor and respectful conduct leads to extraordinary courtesy and politeness. Young people are taught to show respect, obedience, and humility. (In traditional homes, the answer to the parent's call is "*Mande usted*"—"At your command.")

In school or work, Mexican American adolescents are not prodded to take risks but to be careful not to bring shame on themselves or their families. This is one reason comparisons between Mexican American and White American adolescents show that the latter are much more competitive. Mexican Americans are concerned with personal gain but more often avoid competitive behavior. Furthermore, Mexican American children are not expected to defer gratification but to live in the present. Such an orientation is not conducive to upward mobility.

Heterosexual Relationships When Mexican American males reach adolescence, they are expected to take an interest in females and to talk and act in the sexual sphere to demonstrate their virility. There are those girls who the males exploit for sexual purposes to prove their ***machismo*** (manhood) and those who they idealize and think to marry. Dating is frowned on, but the practice is difficult to suppress in the United States. However, a matchmaker (*portador*) is sometimes still called into service when mate selection reaches a serious stage.

The importance of modesty is highly emphasized, especially for girls, who are not supposed to learn about sexual relations by either conversation or experience. The result is a low level of knowledge about human sexuality (Meneses, Orrell-Valante, Grendelman, Oman, and

Irwin, 2006; Villarruel, 1998). Mothers do not discuss sex with their daughters, and many do not even discuss menstruation. The uninformed daughter is left on her own to learn about menstruation and sexual relations.

Mexican American adolescents are encouraged to preserve their virginity until marriage. This socialization partially explains the later age of first premarital sex of Mexican American adolescent women relative to their non-Hispanic White counterparts (Slonim-Nevo, 1992).

When unmarried Mexican American adolescent girls do get pregnant, they have more contact and receive more support from their extended families than do White adolescent mothers. They are also less likely to live alone and are more likely to live with a boyfriend or to marry and live with their spouse than are White adolescents. This is consistent with Mexican American familistic orientation, where the family is perceived as the center of emotional security (Codega, Pasley, and Kreutzer, 1990).

Puerto Rican Adolescents

Nearly 3 million Puerto Ricans live in the United States. About 70 percent of them live in the Northeast, with New York City having the largest population. One-fifth of the Puerto Ricans living in the United States are adolescents.

Although Puerto Rican Americans are more likely to have graduated from both high school and college than Mexican Americans, they are more likely to live in poverty (27 percent of families and 44 percent of children). Puerto Rican Americans also have the highest rates of both divorce and adolescent births of any ethnic or racial group (U.S. Bureau of the Census, 1999a).

As United States citizens, Puerto Ricans may enter the country and travel freely within it. This fact, combined with overpopulation and much poverty on their island, contributed to a rapid immigration of Puerto Ricans to the mainland in the decades following World War II. In recent years, immigration has declined, however.

The island of Puerto Rico, which is near Cuba, has a population of nearly 4 million people. It was a Spanish colony from the 1500s until 1898, when it was ceded to the United States at the end of the Spanish American War. Puerto Rico is a commonwealth; so while the residents enjoy many of the privileges of American citizens, they are not allowed to vote in presidential elections or to elect senators or congresspersons. The Puerto Rican culture is derived from the cultures of several historic populations: the native Taíno Indians, the African slaves who began settling there in the 1500s, and the Spanish explorers. The most important cultural values include **fatalism** (the belief that one cannot change one's destiny or fate), acceptance of hierarchies, masculine superiority, and a need for personal respect and dignity (Gibbons, Brusi-Figueroa, and Fisher, 1997).

Family Life Puerto Ricans have a profound sense of family. Most traditional women view motherhood as their central role. Their concept of motherhood is based on the female capacity to bear children and on the notion of ***marianismo,*** which presents the Virgin Mary as a role model. *Marianismo* implies that a woman finds her identity and derives her life's greatest satisfaction through motherhood.

Ideal family relations are described by two interrelating themes—family interdependence and family unity. Family interdependence fits within the Puerto Rican orientation to life, which stresses that the individual cannot do everything and still do it well. Older Puerto Rican women especially adhere strongly to the value of family interdependence. It influences patterns of mutual assistance with their children as well as expectations of support. The older women expect their adult children to take care of them during old age.

Family unity emphasizes the desirability of close and intimate kin ties—members get along well and keep in frequent contact during separations. Puerto Ricans believe that the greater the degree of unity in the family, the greater emphasis family members will place on interdependence and familial obligation.

Still, Puerto Rican Americans are less likely to be married than other Latinos, both because they are less likely to marry at all and because their marriages are more likely to end in divorce. Often when individuals are under stress, their idealized situation and the one they find themselves in are not the same.

Education, Employment, and Income The problems confronting Puerto Rican families are partly a result of the adverse economic and social conditions under which they live. In 2000, 25 percent of adult Puerto Ricans had less than 12 years of schooling. Only 13 percent had 4 years of college or more. Puerto Ricans had the highest rate of unemployment of all Hispanics (Ramirez, 2004). As a consequence, income was low.

Implications for Adolescents Considering the prevalence of single-parent households, Puerto Rican adolescents often lack parental role models with whom they can identify. Identity formation among minority adolescents includes discovering, on a personal basis, what it means to be a member of a specific group. But characteristics of the group are changing or are often confusing (McLoyd, 1990). Puerto Rican adolescents

machismo Spanish term for maleness or manhood.

fatalism the belief that one cannot change one's destiny or fate.

marianismo in Puerto Rican society, the implication that a woman finds her greatest satisfaction through motherhood.

experience an identity crisis compounded by strong intercultural and intergenerational conflicts. They experience conflict between the cultural values represented by their parents and the cultural values they experience on the city streets. They also face language and socioeconomic barriers to acculturation.

Many Puerto Rican youths are compelled to live in abject poverty, in the poorest slum areas of the city, where crime rates are astronomical, drug use is rampant, and good schools and quality education are scarce. These realities are often the reason why many disillusioned families return to Puerto Rico. The problems these youths face have been linked to higher prevalence of mental disorders, anxiety and depression, drug and alcohol abuse, delinquency, and lower self-esteem, compared with populations of African Americans and Whites (Hajat, Lucas, and Kington, 2000).

Native American Adolescents

In 2000, about 2.4 million Native Americans lived in the United States. Although their number is growing faster than the U.S. population as a whole, Native Americans still constitute just over 1 percent of the population. About half of all Native Americans live in rural areas, including their own reservations, with the remaining half split between urban and suburban areas. Most Native Americans live in the western half of the United States. California, Oklahoma, Arizona, New Mexico, Washington, and Alaska are home to more Native Americans than any other states (Ogunwole, 2006; Hobbs and Stoops, 2002).

Arizona and Oklahoma represent two extremes in tribal representation. Arizona has the second largest number of Native Americans, as well as the largest single tribe—the Navaho, who live on the largest reservation in the United States. Oklahoma, in contrast, has the largest number of tribes—about 60. This land was once Indian Territory, to which Native Americans from all over the country were moved when their tribal lands were coveted by Whites. Because these displaced Native Americans were newcomers living on land next to their White neighbors (who had also recently immigrated), most Oklahoma Native Americans lived among the general population, although there are some remote reservations in the state. In states such as New Mexico and the Dakotas, the majority of Native Americans are still living on their original reservations. In other states—such as North Carolina, California, and New York—the majority either resisted movement to reservations or now live on land where government control has terminated.

Since the beginning of World War II, there has been a rapid migration of Native Americans to urban areas. In 1940, only 7.2 percent of the total Native American population lived in cities; in 1999, the figure was 50 percent. This rapid migration was the result of youths leaving reservations during World War II to join the armed services and adults going to work in wartime factories. The government encouraged migration and offered assistance through a relocation program that sought to promote rapid integration into White American life (Fixico, 2000). This relocation created many problems, however. Urbanization increased Native Americans' level of employment, quality of housing, and perceived quality of life, but it has not been a panacea for poverty, discrimination, and alienation. One of the major problems of contemporary Native American youths is the inability to reconcile the cultural conflict between the way of life on the reservation and the way of life in urban America. We will examine this conflict in greater detail in a later section.

Health and Standard of Living

Native Americans have the lowest standard of living of any minority group in the United States, with unemployment high and income low. Approximately one-third live below the poverty level (U.S. Bureau of the Census, 1999a). Unemployment on some reservations runs as high as 80 to 90 percent. In most Native American communities, the pattern is one of bare subsistence, with the result that some of the worst slums in the United States are on reservations.

Although federally recognized tribes are entitled (due to treaty agreements) to health services from the national government, many Native Americans cannot or do not take advantage of these services. First, the Indian Health Service operates out of tribal lands and reservations, and many Native Americans do not live in these areas. In addition, factors such as poverty, inadequate sewage disposal, suspicion toward authorities, and cultural barriers increase the probability of illness and decrease the chances of adequate treatment (Office of Minority Health, 2006).

Native American individuals are more likely than others to die from a variety of causes, including all types of accidents, liver disease, diabetes, pneumonia and influenza, suicide, homicide, and tuberculosis (National Center for Health Statistics, 2001). Suicide is a leading cause of death among Native American youths 15 to 19 years old, with a rate two to three times the national average (CDC, 2003). The rate varies tremendously from tribe to tribe, however. Eating disorders, particularly bulimia, are common among Native American girls (Crago, Shisslak, and Estes, 1996).

Substance abuse, particularly alcoholism, is rampant in Native American culture, resulting in a very high rate of *fetal alcohol syndrome* (*FAS*) in babies of both adult and adolescent mothers (Backover, 1991). FAS is believed to be the leading cause of mental retardation in the United States (McShane, 1988). Even though the alcoholism rate among the Native American population as a whole is comparatively high, the fact remains that a relatively small minority of Native Americans are alcoholic. The very complex problem of alcoholism (or substance abuse) among Native Americans—as well as among others—goes well beyond simple comparisons of cold statistics (Mitchell, O'Nell, Beals, Dick, Keane, and Manson, 1996).

Despite these negative conditions, there is much room for optimism that economic strides can be made. Native American lands include many beautiful areas as well as very valuable ones. They contain much valuable timber and uranium.

Education

The record of Native American education is one of broken promises, inadequate resources, poor teachers, and, worst of all, the use of education as a tool to destroy a culture and a way of life. By the beginning of the twentieth century, the Bureau of Indian Affairs (BIA) was operating 147 reservation day schools, 81 reservation boarding schools, and 25 off-reservation boarding schools for Native Americans in various parts of the country as a part of the government's trust responsibility. However, the goal was complete assimilation. "Kill the Indian and Save the Man" was the motto. Regimentation, reading, writing, arithmetic, the manual trades, and home economics were drilled into the students.

Life at boarding schools was regimented, as well. Estranged from family, under the rule of an alien culture, and unable to talk to teachers (who did not know dialects), academic performance was poor. As many as 75 percent of Native American children in boarding schools were far from home and had school-related social or emotional problems. About one-third of the children in these schools were physically disabled (McShane, 1988).

In addition, the BIA operated a number of day schools located on or near the reservations. These schools also presented problems. Physical facilities were notoriously inadequate, texts and supplies were scarce and outdated, and little money was available to hire competent staff. The schools conducted all classes in English, yet some of the children spoke little or no English. The dropout rate was very high.

At the secondary level, the school curriculum did not acknowledge ethnic diversity. A report on education in Native American schools in Alaska stated that "education which gives the Indian, Eskimo, and Aleut knowledge of—and therefore pride in—their historic and cultural heritage is non-existent" (Henninger and Esposito, 1971).

The Indian Education Act of 1972 (known as Title IV) resulted in some improvements. This legislation established funding for special bilingual and bicultural programs, culturally relevant teaching materials, proper training and hiring of counselors, and establishment of an Office of Indian Education in the U.S. Department of Education. Most importantly, the act required participation of Native Americans in the planning of all relevant educational projects (O'Brien, 1989).

Native American education has improved remarkably in the past 30 years or so. During the 1998–1999 school year, the Office of Indian Education Programs directly served more than 53,000 students in 185 schools scattered over 23 states and more than 60 reservations. At present, more than 115 of these schools are controlled and operated by the tribes, not the office. More than 400,000 additional students were served indirectly, in good part through the provision of financial aid and scholarships. Twenty-six tribal colleges and universities were also funded. Navajo Community College, on the Navajo Reservation in Arizona, and Sinte Gleska (Spotted Tail) University, on the Rosebud Reservation in South Dakota, are two of the better-known of these institutions. In 1999, approximately 145,000 Native Americans were enrolled in colleges and universities located all over the United States (U.S. Bureau of the Census, 2002).

Family Life

Since there are more than 550 federally recognized Native American tribes, there is no such institution as a typical Native American family. Despite the attempt to impose Western family models on them, various family forms still exist among the different tribal groups. Some families are **matrilineal** (with descent through the mother's line) (Keshna, 1980). For many Native Americans, the extended family is the basic unit for carrying out family functions. This is often true despite the absence of extended kin in the same household. Children may be raised by relatives residing in different, noncontiguous households. The existence of multiple households sharing family functions is quite common.

Children

Most Native Americans view children as assets to the family. Children are taught that family and tribe are of the utmost importance. Grandmothers are very important; in fact, people who are aged, in general, are looked up to for wisdom and counsel. The aged occupy the important position of relating traditions, beliefs, and customs through the role of storyteller. Children are taught that listening, rather than speaking, is a sign of respect and the best way to learn. They are also taught to be independent (there are no rigid schedules for eating and sleeping), to be patient and unassuming, to maintain a rather severe reserve rather than to show emotions. The ability to endure pain,

matrilineal descent through the mother's line.

For many Native American tribes, the extended family is the basic family structure. Elderly family members, especially grandmothers, are often teachers of traditions and customs.

hardship, hunger, and frustration is emphasized, as are bravery and courage (Gilliland, 1995).

Cultural Conflict

For years, official government policy adopted the assimilation model—that is, the ultimate goal of full acceptance of Native Americans in the U.S. society by the dominant group. However, that acceptance was to come about as members of the minority group became more like members of the majority. Native Americans were considered heathens and savages, and so White Americans sought to civilize them so that they could find their acceptance into the dominant society (Williams, Himmel, Sjoberg, and Torrez, 1995).

Today, however, Native Americans are making a determined effort to retain and to teach their cultural values to their young people. Religion has always been important, but many practices were banned when the federal government conducted its 60-year (1870–1930) program of enforced enculturation ("The Denial of Indian Civil and Religious Rights," 1975).

ANSWERS WOULDN'T YOU LIKE TO KNOW . . .

What values and beliefs distinguish Native American culture?

Native Americans value cooperation and modesty more than individual achievement and bravado. They also show great respect for the elderly. Native Americans are not materialistic. They believe in focusing on the here and now, rather than in worrying about the future.

Puberty rites or equivalent rites of passage are still practiced by some tribes and form part of religious rituals today. When the federal government banned all Native American assemblies from 1870 to 1930, except between July 1 and July 4, the Apache changed the individual rite that marked a girl's first menstruation to a group rite in which all girls who had come of age during the year participated. The mandatory rite marks a transition in status from childhood to adulthood and makes the young woman eligible for marriage. Navaho boys and girls go through a religious ceremony at about the time of appearance of secondary sex characteristics. Through this ceremony, they are introduced to full participation in ceremonial life.

Native American values are often at variance with White American culture. The Native American is present oriented, not concerned about the future or with time. Whites are future oriented, concerned about time and planning ahead. Native Americans see human life as being in harmony with nature. Whites tend to seek conquest over nature. Native American life is group oriented, emphasizing cooperation, whereas Whites emphasize individualism and competition.

As a result of conflicting cultures, Native American youths today are faced with an identity crisis: whether to accommodate themselves to the White world and learn to compete in it or to retain traditional customs and values and live apart from the White world (Markstrom-Adams, 1990). Over 150 years of determined government effort has not succeeded in destroying Native American culture and society. Yet the longer Native American youths are isolated, the greater their chances are of remaining the most deprived minority in the United States. Certainly, one answer is to help all people appreciate and understand the values of Native American culture and the importance of preserving a rich heritage. The adolescent who is proud of being a Native American, as many are, and who is respected by White society, can contribute richly to a Western culture that prides itself on being culturally diverse.

Sadly, the original inhabitants of the United States have been shunted to the margins of the nation's life. As a consequence, most contemporary Native American youths suffer psychological strain under the impact of cultural change. Progress has been slow because these people are caught between two cultures and immobilized from going in either direction easily. The following poem, "Thoughts to Ponder," was written by Marie Ann Begay, a Navaho and a senior at Del Norte High School in Albuquerque, New Mexico:

Sitting here
A thought came into my mind
Living in two worlds—
That seems hard sometimes,
Especially if you are an Indian.
You feel like two persons
Trying to struggle for something
That you don't care about at times.

I ask myself what I am doing here,
But all odds add up to my own benefits
And a look at the new side.
Even though I should be
Riding or running in the open countryside
With the fresh clean air racing along with me,
Seeing the rain fall in the distance
And thunder that shakes the earth—

But here I am sitting trying to get
What I think is good for an Indian
Who's trying to make it
In the White Men's world and his own.

FIGURE 3.7 AREAS OF ORIGIN OF FOREIGN-BORN INDIVIDUALS RESIDING IN THE UNITED STATES: 1999

Source: Data from U.S. Bureau of the Census (2005b).

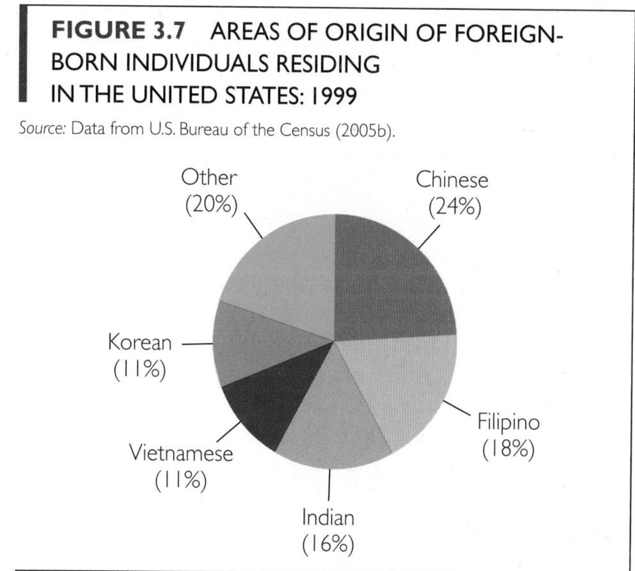

Asian American Adolescents

Asian Americans, in general, differ from Hispanic Americans and African Americans in that they have been more successful at achieving the so-called American Dream. Asian Americans have a higher average family income than all other groups, including non-Hispanic Caucasians (Reeves and Bennett, 2004). Asian and Pacific Americans are also more likely to have earned college degrees. Even though they comprise only about 4 percent of the U.S. population, they earn 10 percent of the nation's doctorate degrees and more than 20 percent of the doctorates in engineering and computer science. This is not to suggest that Asian Americans have not faced discrimination—they have. Nonetheless, they have managed to weave their way into mainstream society in spite of hardships. Some of this success may be due to the fact that their own cultural values are sufficiently compatible with those of mainstream American society to allow upward mobility.

Another explanation may be that marriages among Asian Americans tend to be stable. More than 80 percent of Asian American children live with both of their biological parents. More than half of all Asian Americans are foreign born; it is therefore not surprising that most live in the Western states near where they entered the United States. Many Asian American immigrants came from educated, middle-class backgrounds; many others, however, were peasants looking for a better way of life or fleeing political oppression.

The families of Asian Americans originally immigrated from all over the Asian continent. As shown in Figure 3.7, the largest numbers trace their ancestries to China, the Philippines, or India. About two-thirds of Asian Americans are foreign born; about half of those are naturalized citizens (Reeves and Bennett, 2004).

Chinese American Adolescents

There are about 2 million Chinese Americans in the United States. A minority of modern Chinese Americans are descendants of Chinese who immigrated to the United States during the period of open immigration from 1820 to 1882; many more are new or second-generation immigrants. After 1882, a series of exclusion acts were passed that restricted Asian immigration. It was not until 1965 that the national origin quota system that discriminated against Asians was abolished. Since that time, Chinese have immigrated in large numbers.

Until that time, Chinese men entered the United States without their wives and children. Custom required that a man marry before he left China and that his wife remain in the house of her husband's parents. The man's duty was to send money to his waiting family and to return home eventually. Frequently, years passed before he returned. Many hoped to earn enough to bring their families to the United States, but under the Immigration Act of 1882, no Chinese women, except a minority of exempt classes and wives of U.S. citizens, were permitted to enter. This restriction continued until 1943. As a result, Chinese men who remained in the United States were condemned to a life without intimate family relations.

ANSWERS WOULDN'T YOU LIKE TO KNOW ...

How did U.S. immigration law disrupt the family lives of Chinese immigrants?

For 50 years, U.S. immigration law forbade Chinese women to immigrate to the United States, with few exceptions. Therefore, Chinese men would come to this country to work, leaving their wives, children, and parents at home.

Family and Children Well-educated Chinese Americans have lower rates of divorce, mental illness, and public assistance—and higher family income—than the general U.S. population. In comparison to other minorities, Chinese Americans have more conservative sexual values, a lower fertility rate, fewer out-of-wedlock births, and more conservative attitudes toward the role of women.

Most Chinese Americans today have a strong sense of family ties. They feel a high sense of duty to family, responsibility for relatives, and self-blame when a young person fails to live up to expectations. A child who misbehaves brings shame to the family name.

Chinese American parents tend to be more controlling than Caucasian parents. However, due to their cultural heritage, their adolescent children are generally more accepting of this intrusion than Caucasian adolescents would be (Lam, 2003). Harmony and absence of conflict within the home are highly valued, more so than openness and communication (Shek, 2001).

Chinese children are taught that everyone has to work for the welfare of the family. They are given a great deal of responsibility and are assigned specific chores. Adolescents are responsible for supervising young children and for working around the house or in the family business. In spite of effects of acculturation, even second-generation Chinese youths still place a great deal of emphasis on the family as the most important unit (Feldman, Mont-Reynaud, and Rosenthal, 1992).

Youths Traditionally, rebellion among Chinese youths was almost unknown. Respect for elders was so deeply ingrained that youths never questioned their parents' authority or broke rules to bring dishonor on their families. If parents forbade something, it was wrong.

Contemporary Chinese American youths are more vocal than previous generations, more inclined to speak out and to rebel against authority. As these youths become more dissociated from their parents, antisocial behavior increases (Chiu, Feldman, and Rosenthal, 1992). Young and newly arrived immigrants from Hong Kong and Taiwan, and American-born Chinese school dropouts became estranged from both the Chinese American community and White America. Some became involved in delinquent activity, and some joined gangs (Tsunokai, 2005).

Education Chinese Americans have always stressed the importance of education and hard work as the means of getting ahead. A study was conducted of the school performance of first- and second-generation Chinese American students and their Westernized peers in Australia and the United States. Results indicated that Chinese American high schoolers of both generations reported that they put more effort into school and reported higher grades than did their White American and Australian peers. Family factors were associated with both high achievement and greater effort (Rosenthal and Feldman, 1991). The emphasis is on becoming able to earn a good deal of money and to gain prestige from entering such technical professions as engineering, pharmacy, and dentistry (Leong, 1991).

About 48 percent of today's Asian Americans who are 25 years or older have a bachelor's degree or higher—almost twice, the rate among all Americans (Reeves and Bennett, 2004). So great is the drive for educational accomplishment that Asian Americans outscore all other groups on standardized math exams and are well represented at the nation's top universities (National Center for Education Statistics, 2001).

Filipino American Adolescents

The Philippine Islands were under U.S. rule for 44 years and gained independence in 1946. There has therefore been a substantial American presence in the Philippines for more than 100 years, and there has been much interaction between the two peoples. However, the inequality of the relationship, the fact that the United States ruled the Philippines, led many Filipinos to feel shamed and led to feelings of less ethnic pride than is found among persons from other ethnic groups (Rotheram-Borus, Lightfoot, Moraes, Dopkins, and LuCoeur, 1998). Nonetheless, it is relatively common for Filipino American children to spend time living with relatives in the Philippines to experience that part of their heritage (Agbayani-Siewart, 2002). Unlike the majority of other Asians, most Filipinos are Catholic, a result of Spanish influence dating from the 1500s.

IMMIGRANTS AND REFUGEES

The United States is a country of **immigrants** and **refugees.** Ninety-nine percent of Americans can trace their ancestry to a foreign land. In 2000, more than 28 million foreign-born individuals resided in the United States, representing just over 10 percent of the total U.S. population (Schmidley, 2001). As shown in Figure

Many Chinese American families emphasize the importance of intergenerational family ties. Even adolescent children place a great deal of value on the family unit.

3.7, more than half were born in Asia. Foreign-born residents are more likely to live in urban areas than native-born Americans, and they tend to have larger families. Although some are highly educated, approximately one-third do not possess a high school diploma. Given this lack of education and because of language barriers, foreign-born Americans are more likely to be unemployed than native-born Americans, and when they do work, they earn less money (U.S. Bureau of the Census, 2000a).

Immigrants come to the United States primarily because they believe they can find better lives here. Refugees, however, are fleeing political persecution or dire poverty. Since 1975, the United States has admitted, if not always welcomed, more than 2 million refugees—more than all the other countries in the world combined (United Nations High Commissioner for Refugees, 2005). Figure 3.8 illustrates the areas from which the most recent refugees have arrived. As you can see, about one-third of all legally admitted refugees in 2004 were from Cuba, and about 25 percent were from Africa. This is a change from the trend seen for most of the past 30 years, during which the majority of refugees came from Southeast Asia.

Regardless of country of origin, immigrants and refugees—along with their adolescent children—face many difficulties. They have come to a country where most people speak a different language, behave in different ways, practice different traditions, and hold somewhat different values. Even individuals who were educated in their homelands may face difficulty, as their degrees might not be considered valuable in the United States. Refugees face the added difficulty of whatever trauma they endured before arriving in the United States—perhaps seeing their home destroyed or living through starvation or war. They may even feel guilty because they survived to make their journey whereas many of their friends and family members did not. Refugees may desperately miss those family members they lost or left behind.

Although immigrants and refugees come from all over the world, in the next section, we will focus on the experiences of those from Southeast Asia. More research has been conducted on the experiences of Southeast Asian immigrants than on other immigrant groups because as noted, a large percentage of refugees to the United States during the past 30 years have been from that region. Many of the issues they have faced are typical of the issues faced by all refugees, regardless of country of origin.

Southeast Asian Refugee Experience

The Southeast Asian refugee exodus from the countries of Vietnam, Cambodia (now Kampuchea), and Laos is one of the largest such movements in modern history. Today, more than 1.5 million former Southeast Asian refugees live in the United States.

There were two very different waves of Southeast Asian immigration to the United States. The first was prompted by the fall of the South Vietnamese city of Saigon in 1975. Refugees from Saigon were almost entirely Vietnamese. They were generally well-educated, young, urban dwellers, in good health, and in the company of family. The second wave of refugees included a much greater proportion of Hmong, Khmer, Lao, and Chinese-Vietnamese ethnic groups. They were generally less well educated, less literate, and of rural origin. Escape attempts from the countries of origin were typically long and traumatic (Kinze, Frederickson, Ben, Fleck, and Karls, 1984).

Acculturation Stress

Major research findings indicate that most newly arrived Amerasians experience acculturative stress, primarily in the areas of spoken English, employment, and limited formal education (Nwadiora and McAdoo, 1996). *Acculturation* is a multifaceted phenomenon involving numerous dimensions and factors. The

immigrants people who leave their native land to come to live in the United States for any reason.

refugees people who leave their native land to come to live in the United States because they are fleeing political oppression or death.

FIGURE 3.8 COUNTRIES OF ORIGIN OF REFUGEES RESETTLED IN THE UNITED STATES: 2004

Source: Data from U.S. Bureau of the Census, 2005b.

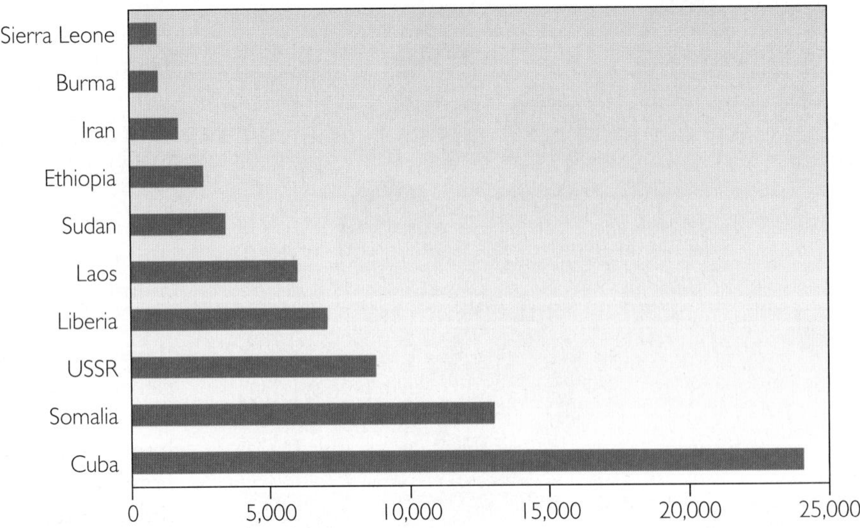

acculturation rate of Southeast Asian refugee adolescents is influenced by five different cultures that are in continuous interplay: (1) the Southeast Asian culture, (2) the U.S. culture, (3) the refugee culture, (4) the U.S. adolescent culture, and (5) the refugee adolescent culture.

Many Southeast Asian American adolescents are confronted with traditional values from the old country, contemporary values from the new country, and transitional values that represent a mixture of some traditional and contemporary traits.

There are major differences between the traditional Asian values and the contemporary urban industrial values. The degree of acculturation of each individual refugee adolescent depends on the following variables: (1) years in the United States, (2) cultural compatibility of the country of origin and

RESEARCH HIGHLIGHT COMPARISON OF TRADITIONAL ASIAN VALUES AND URBAN INDUSTRIAL VALUES

Traditional Asian Values	**Urban Industrial Values**
Group/community emphasis	Individual emphasis
Extended family	Nuclear family/blended family
Interdependence	Independence
Person-to-person orientation	Person-to-object orientation
Past → present → future	Future → present → past
Age	Youth
Conformity/cooperation	Competition
Harmony with nature	Conquest over nature
Fatalism	Master of one's own fate
Logic of the heart	Logic of the mind
Balance	Change
Patience/modesty	Aggression/assertion
Pragmatic outlook	Theoretical outlook
Suppression of emotion	Expression of emotion
Rigidity of role and status	Flexibility of role and state
Eastern	*Western*

Source: E. Lee, "Cultural Factors in Working with Southeast Asian Refugee Adolescents," *Journal of Adolescence, 11* (June 1988): 167–179. Reprinted by permission.

Immigrants and refugees face many difficulties, including learning a new language, behaving in different ways, practicing new traditions, and even holding different values.

ANSWERS WOULDN'T YOU LIKE TO KNOW ...

From what area of the world have the most recent immigrants to the United States come? From what area of the world have the most recent refugees to this country come?

Within the past decade, most immigrants to the United States have come from Latin America whereas most refugees have come from Eastern Europe. Both of these trends will likely change as the political and social situations in other nations fluctuate.

the "host community," (3) age at time of immigration, (4) language usage at home, (5) school environment, and (6) acculturation rate of parents and family members.

Acculturation stress is not solely induced by the process of acculturation but also by the difference perceived by Southeast Asian adolescents' friends and family members. A Vietnamese adolescent girl who arrived in the United States in 1989 as an infant may be perceived as "too Vietnamese" by her American friends, "too old-fashioned" by her Vietnamese peers, and "too American" by her parents. Her American friends may expect her to go out after school, to date American boys, to drive a car, and to be more independent. Her parents may expect her to speak only Vietnamese at home, to take care of her grandparents and younger siblings after school, to clean the house, and to marry someone chosen by the family. Many such adolescents deal with the conflict by rejecting both the new and the old cultures and establishing a "third culture" with a combination of the two with their refugee experiences.

Disparity between adolescents' and parents' values and expectations often erupt into major conflicts. Southeast Asian parents expect their children to be quiet, obedient, polite, humble, hardworking, and respectful to them and other extended family members. Good sons and daughters are expected to take care of younger siblings and aged parents and to bring honor to the family. Such value orientation is not only different but very opposite to American values, which have strong emphasis on independence, self-reliance, assertiveness, open communication, and competition. Three major intergenerational conflicts deserve special attention:

1. *Conflicts concerning dating and marriage:* Many parents insist on taking an active part in the choice and approval of dating and marital partners of their children. Many adolescents are pressured to date and marry within their own ethnic group.
2. *Conflicts concerning career choices:* Some career plans of the children are expected and are acceptable and some are not. Parents highly value professional careers such as medicine, law, engineering, and so forth. They often disapprove of nonprofessional jobs such as factory worker, sales, and careers in music or writing.
3. *Conflicts caused by role reversal:* Southeast Asian refugee adolescents usually are much more educated than their parents, who had little or no opportunity to attend school. In addition, many monolingual parents depend on their English-speaking adolescents as the "cultural brokers" to deal with the outside world. Such dependence can evoke anger and resentment on both parts and may lead to prolonged family stress.

Assessment of Strengths

Southeast Asian families arrive in the United States with many problems associated with their refugee experience. They also bring thousands of years of Asian culture and specific coping strategies in response to stress. Despite the hardships of the refugee experience, many refugees manage to endure and cope effectively without serious psychological problems. Family strengths—such as the support of extended family members and siblings, a powerful sense of obligation and self-sacrifice, the strong focus on educational achievement, the strong work ethic, and the loyalty of family members and friends—can be respected (Lee, 1982). Furthermore, religious beliefs in Buddhism provide strength to endure suffering caused by war and trauma.

The support system in the refugee community also plays an important role in determining the facility with which each family resolves transition. Many refugee youths are in frequent contact with community education and social service agencies. Being cut off from their families, villages, and countries, many Southeast Asian refugees feel the need to cluster together and to form community organizations as secondary sources of security (Bankston and Zhou, 1997).

SUMMARY

1. American adolescents are a diverse group. Experiential and subcultural differences can be identified between high-socioeconomic-status and low-socioeconomic-status groups. People of different ethnicities also have different histories and somewhat different values.
2. Low socioeconomic status cuts across ethnic boundaries, affecting more than 10 percent of U.S. families. Low-SES youths are both culturally disadvantaged and have low income. There are four limitations on their lives: limited experience and opportunities; little autonomy or influence, which results in a sense of helplessness and powerlessness; feeling a sense of failure because of their status amid those who are more affluent; and feeling insecure, at the mercy of life's unpredictable events. The net effect of these limitations is to perpetuate a cycle of poverty.
3. Adolescents from low-SES families often achieve only a low level of education; they therefore do not acquire the basic skills to acquire high-paying jobs.
4. Low-SES families are more unstable, resulting in large numbers of female-headed households. Parents tend to be harsh disciplinarians and more concerned with keeping children out of trouble than with personal growth.
5. Adolescents from minority groups have a wide variety of lifestyles and backgrounds. However, they share a legacy of prejudice and discrimination, are more likely to be impoverished, and are more likely to experience physical and psychological health problems than non-Hispanic White adolescents.
6. African American adolescents are gradually overcoming the legacy of prejudices and discrimination against them. Nevertheless, many African Americans still live in segregated neighborhoods and have not achieved equality of education, rates of employment, and income, although some achieve a high level of success in spite of the handicaps they face. Unwed adolescent pregnancy among African Americans continues to be a major problem.
7. African American family strengths include strong kinship bonds, favorable attitudes toward the elderly, adaptable roles, and a strong religious orientation.
8. Mexico is the ancestral home of most of American Latinos. The most outstanding issue facing Latino children and youths is the educational difficulty they face if they are not proficient in English.
9. Mexican American families are very stable. *Familialism*, or devotion to one's family, is a strong cultural ethic. Traditionally, the culture favors strong, well-defined gender roles. "Good" girls are expected to be modest and to remain sexually inexperienced until marriage.
10. The second-largest group of Latinos came to the United States mainland from Puerto Rico. Cultural values include fatalism, the need to maintain dignity, and a belief in strongly delineated gender roles. Puerto Rican Americans have a high poverty rate.
11. Native Americans comprise the smallest minority group in the United States, making up about 1 percent of the country's population. As a group, they are the least well-off Americans. They have the highest poverty rate of any culture group.
12. There are many individual Native American tribes, all with unique cultures. Common values, however, include matrilinealism, a strong sense of responsibility to one's extended family, respect for the elderly and for nature, and greater concern for the present than the future.
13. The ancestors of Asian Americans immigrated to the United States from countries as disparate as India, China, Korea, and Vietnam. Although they have experienced discrimination, as a group, Asian Americans are highly educated and financially well off.
14. Chinese American families are extremely cohesive; individuals are expected to act in a manner consistent with their family's best interest.
15. More than 37 million foreign-born individuals currently reside in the United States. Approximately 2 million of them are refugees who have been admitted during the past 25 years. New immigrants must cope with language barriers, cultural differences, and often economic hardship. Refugees face the additional difficulty of having experienced trauma and loss.
16. Many Southeast Asian immigrants were refugees. The stresses that they face include the difficulties of acculturation because there are major differences between traditional Asian values and contemporary urban industrial values. Conflicts arise over dating and marriage, career choices, and role reversal.

KEY TERMS

colonias or barrios 61	*machismo* 62
familialism 61	*marianismo* 63
fatalism 63	matrilineal 65
immigrants 68	refugees 68
low socioeconomic status (low SES) 50	resiliency 59

THOUGHT QUESTIONS

Personal Reflection

1. Were you ever financially poorly off as a child or adolescent? If so, do you remember how that made you feel? If not, did you notice that other children were not as well off financially? How did you feel about their situation?
2. Did you ever experience discrimination for any reason at any point in your life? Why? How did it make you feel? Could you successfully resolve the situation?
3. To what extent do you think that poverty is due to individuals' personal lack of ability or responsibility as opposed to lack of opportunity?
4. Think about having been raised in a home with uncaring, dysfunctional parents who didn't monitor your behavior or care about your education. Imagine that you lived in a neighborhood where many of the families were much the same. Do you think you would be as successful as you are today?
5. How important is your ethnicity, whatever it might be, to you? How different were your family's values from the cultural mainstream? Did you ever feel tugged in two directions?
6. How long ago did your family immigrate to the United States? Under what circumstances did they come? Do the stories your family tells emphasize the opportunities or the challenges they faced when they arrived in America?

Group Discussion

7. How is it possible for adolescents from poor families to break the cycle of poverty and deprivation?
8. Why are low-SES parents more likely than middle-class parents to harshly discipline their children?
9. Describe the discrimination faced by ethnic minorities in the community in which you were raised. Use examples to support your answer.
10. Do you believe that reparations are due to African Americans to because of past slavery and discrimination? How about to Native Americans, for broken treaties and confiscated lands?
11. What should the government do, if anything, to ease immigrants' transition to life in the United States?

Debate Questions

12. All immigrants should be required to take classes in English.
13. There is adequate opportunity so that no one has to remain impoverished.
14. Discrimination is not a major problem anymore.
15. Poor parenting and dysfunctional family life are the primary cause of adolescent maladjustment.
16. It is the government's responsibility to help raise people out of poverty.

SUGGESTED READING

Benokraitis, N. V. (Ed.). (2001). *Contemporary Ethnic Families in the United States: Characteristics, Variations, and Dynatics.* Englewood Cliffs, NJ: Prentice Hall.

Dinnerstein, L., and Reimers, D. M. (1999). *Ethnic Americans.* New York: Columbia University Press.

Iceland, J. (2003). *Poverty in America: A Handbook.* Berkeley: University of California Press.

Kelen, J. A., and Kelen, L. G. (2002). *Faces and Voices of Refugee Adolescents.* Logan: Utah State University Press.

Piper, M. (2003). *The Middle of Everywhere: Helping Refugees Enter the American Community.* New York: Harcourt Brace Jovanovich.

Plous, S. (2002). *Understanding Prejudice and Discrimination.* New York: McGraw-Hill.

Rumbaut, R. G., and Portes, A. (Eds.). (2001). *Ethnicity: Children of Immigrants in America.* Berkeley: University of California Press.

Steinberg, S. (2001). *The Ethnic Myth: Race, Ethnicity, and Class in America.* Boston: Beacon Press.

CHAPTER 4 BODY ISSUES

Sexual Maturation and Physical Growth

WOULDN'T YOU LIKE TO KNOW . . .

▶ Why does puberty start?

▶ Which hormones are adults referring to when they describe adolescence as a time of "raging hormones"?

▶ What is the major difference between males' and females' sex hormones?

▶ Besides the obvious, what are the differences between males' and females' reproductive organs?

▶ What is usually the first sign of puberty?

▶ Why are girls often taller than boys during early adolescence?

▶ Besides the obvious, what are the differences between males' and females' bodies?

Imagine that you are taking a walk in your local park and are observing people running, walking, biking, and skateboarding by you. Being a people-watcher by nature, you check each one out as he or she passes by. It takes you no time at all to figure out each person's general age: That one's a kid, that one's old, that one's a teen, that one's grown up but young. How do you do it so quickly?

Certainly, there are contextual clues, such as behavior and clothing style, but mostly you can tell by looking at people's bodies. Children just don't look like adolescents, and until late adolescence, adolescents don't look like adults. Why not? What kinds of changes happen to the body so that its shape and size change so much? Look again, and you'll notice that except for clothing and hair style, male and female children don't look very different from each other. That's certainly not true of adolescent boys and girls and adult men and women!

In this chapter, we will examine how and why female and male bodies grow, change, and become so different from each other. We will also talk about less obvious, internal changes that occur during puberty and set the stage for understanding the changes in behavior that occur during adolescence.

BIOCHEMICAL BASIS OF PUBERTY

Ultimately, the physical changes associated with adolescence occur because the brain starts directing various **endocrine glands** to increase their production of **hormones:** chemical messengers that flow through the bloodstream and affect what other cells do (see Figure 4.1). We still do not know exactly what triggers the brain to do this, but it is surely an interplay between heredity and environmental factors, such as food availability and stress. For whatever reason, the **hypothalamus**—a part of the brain intimately connected with puberty and sexuality—becomes more active and begins to direct the body to produce more sex hormones (Ellis, 2004).

The Hypothalamus

The hypothalamus is a small area of the forebrain about the size of a marble. It is the motivational and emotional control center of the brain, regulating such functions as eating, drinking, hormonal production, menstrual cycles, pregnancy, and sexual behavior. Electrical stimulation of the hypothalamus can produce sexual thoughts and feelings. Stimulation of the hypothalamus in male rats can produce extraordinary sexual interest and performance!

We are most concerned here with the role of the hypothalamus in hormonal production and regulation. It produces a chemical called **gonadotropin-releasing hormone (GnRH),** which controls the secretion of the hormones LH and FSH by the pituitary.

The Pituitary Gland

The **pituitary gland** is a small gland about the size of a pea that is located in the brain just beneath the hypothalamus. It consists of three lobes: anterior,

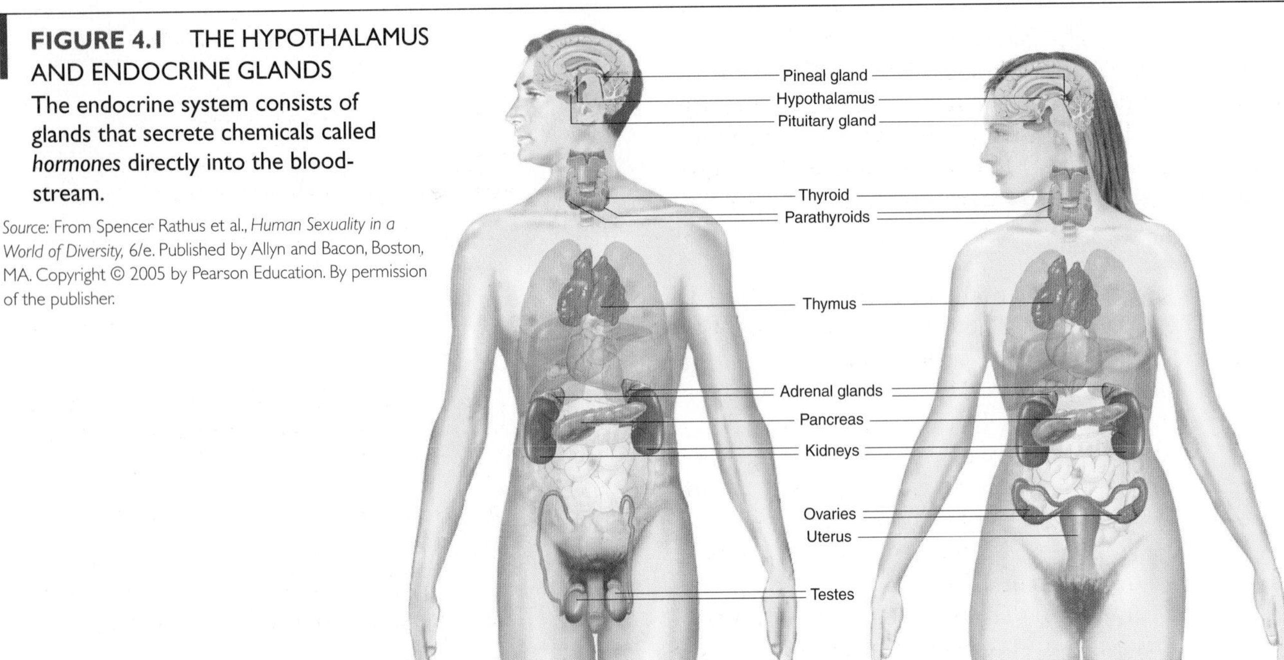

FIGURE 4.1 THE HYPOTHALAMUS AND ENDOCRINE GLANDS The endocrine system consists of glands that secrete chemicals called *hormones* directly into the bloodstream.

Source: From Spencer Rathus et al., *Human Sexuality in a World of Diversity,* 6/e. Published by Allyn and Bacon, Boston, MA. Copyright © 2005 by Pearson Education. By permission of the publisher.

ANSWERS WOULDN'T YOU LIKE TO KNOW ...

Why does puberty start?

No one knows why puberty begins precisely when it does, but it has to do with changes in the region of the brain called the *hypothalamus*.

intermediary, and posterior. The anterior pituitary lobe is known as the master gland of the body, for it produces several hormones that control the action of the other glands.

Gonadotropic hormones secreted by the anterior pituitary are so named because they influence the gonads, or sex glands. The two gonadotropic hormones are **follicle-stimulating hormone (FSH)** and **luteinizing hormone (LH).** FSH stimulates the growth of egg cells in the ovaries and sperm in the testes. FSH and LH in the female control the production and release of female sex hormones by the ovary. LH in the male controls the production and release of male sex hormones by the testes.

One important pituitary hormone is the **human growth hormone (HGH),** also called the *somatotropic hormone (SH)*. It affects the growth and shaping of the skeleton. An excess causes giantism; a deficiency causes dwarfism.

The Gonads

The **gonads,** or sex glands, secrete a number of sex hormones. The **ovaries** in the female secrete a whole group collectively known as **estrogens** (meaning "producing mad desire") that stimulate the development of female secondary sex characteristics such as breast development, the growth of pubic hair, and the distribution of fat on the body. These hormones also maintain the normal size and function of the uterus and the vagina. By interacting with the pituitary, they control the production of various pituitary hormones. Studies have also shown that estrogens influence olfactory sensitivity, which is greatest midway between menstrual periods when estrogen levels are the highest (Doty, 2001).

A second female hormone, **progesterone,** is produced in the ovaries by a new cell growth called the **corpus luteum** (meaning "yellow body") for about 13 days following ovulation. The corpus luteum forms under the stimulus of LH from the pituitary, following the rupture of the ovum, or egg cell, from the ovarian follicle. Progesterone is an extremely important hormone. It controls the length of the menstrual cycle from ovulation until the next menstruation. It is of primary importance in preparing the uterus for pregnancy and maintaining the pregnancy itself. A proper amount of progesterone is necessary to inhibit premature uterine contractions; it is often prescribed when there is a danger of spontaneous abortion.

The **testes** in the male, under the stimulation of LH from the pituitary, begin the production of the male sex hormones, or **androgens.** One male hormone, **testosterone,** is responsible for the development and preservation of masculine secondary sexual characteristics—including facial and body hair, voice change, and muscular and skeletal development—and

endocrine glands structures in the body that produce hormones.

hormones biochemical substances secreted into the bloodstream by the endocrine glands that act as an internal communication system that tells the different cells what to do.

hypothalamus a small area of the brain that controls motivation, emotion, pleasure, and pain in the body; that is, it controls eating, drinking, hormonal production, menstruation, pregnancy, lactation, and sexual response and behavior.

gonadotropin-releasing hormone (GnRH) a hormone secreted by the hypothalamus that controls the production and release of FSH and LH from the pituitary.

pituitary gland master gland of the body located at the base of the brain.

gonadotropic hormones hormones that are secreted by the pituitary and that influence the gonads, or sex glands.

follicle-stimulating hormone (FSH) a pituitary hormone that stimulates the maturation of the follicles and ova in the ovaries and of sperm in the testes.

luteinizing hormone (LH) a pituitary hormone that stimulates the development of the ovum and estrogen and progesterone in females and of sperm and testosterone in males.

human growth hormone (HGH) a pituitary hormone that regulates body growth.

gonads the sex glands: testes and ovaries.

ovaries female gonads, or sex glands, that secrete estrogen and progesterone and produce mature egg cells.

estrogens feminizing hormones produced by the ovaries and, to some extent, by the adrenal glands.

progesterone a female sex hormone produced by the corpus luteum of the ovary.

corpus luteum a yellow body that grows from the ruptured follicle of the ovary and becomes an endocrine gland that secretes progesterone.

testes the male gonads that produce sperm and male sex hormones.

androgens a class of masculinizing sex hormones produced by the testes and, to a lesser extent, by the adrenals.

testosterone a masculinizing sex hormone produced by the testes and, to a lesser extent, by the adrenals.

for the development of the male sex organs—the seminal vesicles, prostate gland, epididymis, penis, and scrotum.

Estrogens and androgens are found in both boys and girls but in negligible amounts prior to puberty. They are produced by the adrenals and the gonads in moderately increasing amounts during childhood. As the ovaries mature, the production of ovarian estrogens increases dramatically and begins to show the cyclic variation in level during various stages of the menstrual cycle. The level of androgens in the female's bloodstream also increases but not as much. As the testes mature in the male, the production of testosterone increases dramatically, whereas the level of the estrogens in the male's bloodstream increases only slightly. Figure 4.2 shows the increases in hormones at puberty.

It is the ratio of the levels of the male to female hormones that is largely responsible for development of male or female characteristics. An imbalance in the natural hormonal state in a growing child can produce deviations in primary and secondary sexual characteristics and affect the development of expected masculine or feminine physical traits. For example, a female with an excess of androgens may grow a mustache and body hair, develop masculine musculature and strength, develop an enlarged clitoris, or have other masculine characteristics. A male with an excess of estrogens or with an androgen deficiency may show decreased potency and sex drive and an enlargement of the breasts.

The Adrenal Glands

If the testes produce the male hormone androgen and the ovaries produce the female hormones estrogen and progesterone, how is it that adolescents of both genders have both androgens and estrogens in their bodies? The answer is because of their adrenal glands. The **adrenal glands,** located just above the kidneys (the term *adrenal* means "on the kidneys"), are capable of producing small amounts of both masculine and feminine sex hormones. Since both males and females have adrenal glands, both male and female bodies can produce androgens and estrogens.

FIGURE 4.2 HORMONE SECRETION WITH AGE

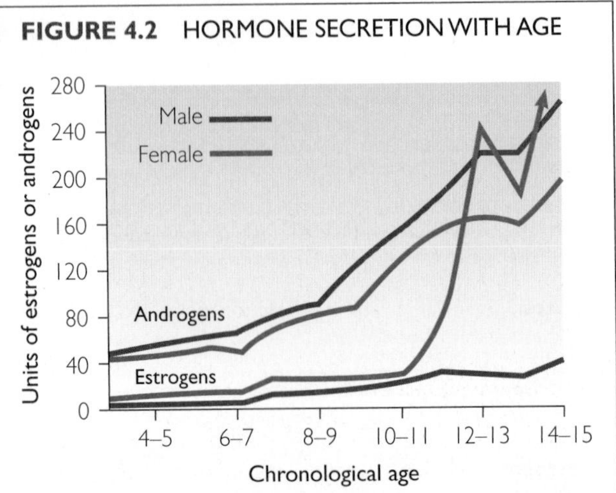

Sex Hormone Regulation in Males

The hypothalamus, pituitary gland, and testes function together in the male to control hormonal production. Under the influence of GnRH from the hypothalamus, the pituitary secretes FSH and LH. The follicle-stimulating hormone stimulates sperm growth in the testes (**spermatogenesis**), as does LH. Without the luteinizing hormone, sperm production begins but the cells fail to fully mature. However, the chief function of LH is to stimulate the testes to produce testosterone.

The level of testosterone is kept fairly constant by a phenomenon known as a *negative feedback loop* (see Figure 4.3.). The GnRH stimulates the production of LH, which, in turn, stimulates secretion of testosterone. As the level of testosterone builds, the hypothalamus, sensitive to the amount of testosterone present, reduces the production of GnRH, which, in turn, reduces the production of LH and testosterone. When the level of testosterone declines, the hypothalamus picks up this signal to increase secretion of GnRH, which stimulates greater production of LH and testosterone. The system acts much like a furnace with a thermostat to control the temperature of a room: An increase in temperature shuts the furnace down; a decrease turns it on.

An additional substance, **inhibin,** regulates FSH levels in another negative feedback loop (Plant, Winters, Attardi, and Majumdar, 1993). Inhibin is produced in the testes by cells called **Sertoli cells.** As the level of inhibin builds, FSH production is suppressed, which results in a decline of sperm production. With the discovery of inhibin, researchers have shown considerable interest in the possibility of using it as a male contraceptive because it inhibits sperm production. Whether the idea is practical remains to be seen.

Sex Hormone Regulation in Females

The hypothalamus, pituitary gland, and ovaries also work together in a negative feedback loop to control hormonal production in females. The gonadotropin-releasing hormone from the hypothalamus stimulates the pituitary to produce FSH and LH. These hormones act on the ovary to stimulate the growth of follicles and egg cells and to stimulate the secretion of ovarian estrogen and progesterone. As the level of estrogen builds, it inhibits the production of GnRH, which, in turn, reduces the production of FSH. Estrogen and progesterone levels of females vary with different stages of the menstrual cycle, as we will see later in this chapter.

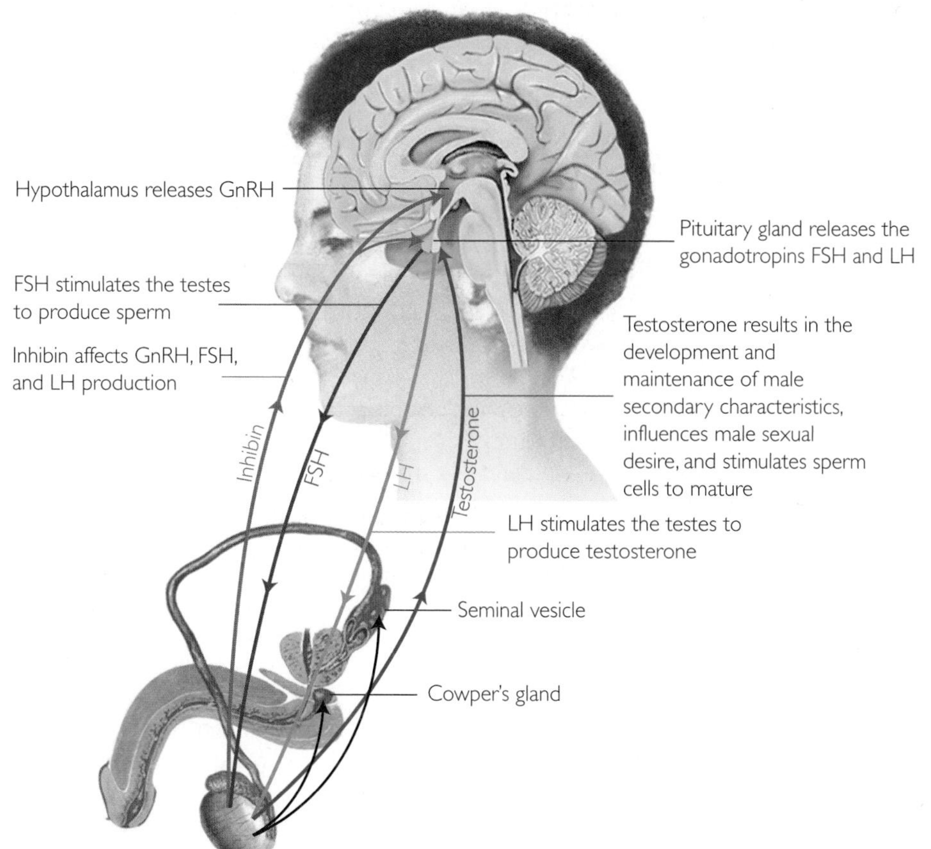

FIGURE 4.3 NEGATIVE FEEDBACK LOOPS

ANSWERS WOULDN'T YOU LIKE TO KNOW . . .

Which hormones are adults referring to when they describe adolescence as a time of "raging hormones"?

When frustrated adults say that adolescence is a time of "raging hormones," they are probably thinking of androgens, the male sex hormones, and estrogens and progesterones, the female sex hormones. The other hormones involved include gonadotropin-releasing hormone, leutinizing hormone, and follicle-stimulating hormone.

ANSWERS WOULDN'T YOU LIKE TO KNOW . . .

What is the major difference between males' and females' sex hormones?

The major difference between the hormonal systems of males and females is that the level of testosterone in males stays fairly constant, whereas the secretion of estrogen and progesterone in females is cyclic.

The increased presence of human growth hormone, the gonadotropic hormones, and the sex hormones in the bloodstream has a profound effect on the size and shape of the body. Since the purpose of puberty is, after all, to physically mature the body so that it will be capable of reproduction, it makes sense to begin with the changes that occur in the sex organs.

MATURATION AND FUNCTIONS OF MALE SEX ORGANS

Figure 4.4 depicts the primary male sex organs: the testes, scrotum, epididymis, seminal vesicles, prostate gland, Cowper's glands, penis, vas deferens, and

adrenal glands ductless glands, located just above the kidneys, that secrete androgens and estrogens in both men and women, in addition to the glands' secretion of adrenaline.

spermatogenesis the process by which sperm are developed.

inhibin a hormone produced in the testes to regulate FSH secretion and sperm production.

Sertoli cells cells in the testes that produce the hormone inhibin.

FIGURE 4.4 THE MALE REPRODUCTIVE SYSTEM
The external male sex organs include the penis and the scrotum.

Source: From Spencer Rathus et al., *Human Sexuality in a World of Diversity,* 6/e. Published by Allyn and Bacon, Boston, MA. Copyright © 2005 by Pearson Education. By permission of the publisher.

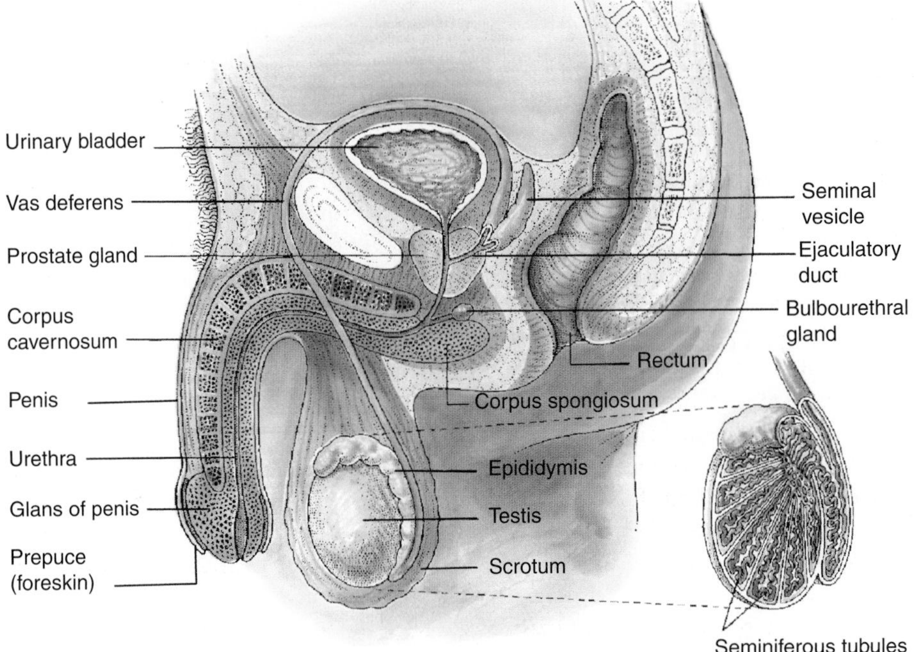

urethra. A number of important changes occur in these organs during adolescence. The growth of the testes and **scrotum** (the pouch of skin containing the testes) accelerates, beginning at about age 11½, becoming fairly rapid by age 13½, and slowing thereafter. These ages are averages. Rapid growth may start between 9½ and 13½ years, ending between ages 13 and 17. During this time, the testes increase 2½ times in length and about 8½ times in weight. The **epididymis** is a system of ducts, running from the testes to the vas deferens, in which sperm mature and are stored. Before puberty, the epididymis is relatively large in comparison with the testes; after maturity, the epididymis is only about one-ninth the size of the testes.

Spermatogenesis

The most important change within the testes themselves is the development of mature sperm cells. Again, this begins when FSH and LH from the pituitary stimulate production and growth. The total process of spermatogenesis, from the time the primitive spermatogonium is formed until it is ready to leave the seminephrous tubules, is about 10 days.

Following spermatogenesis, the sperm migrate by contraction of the seminiferous tubules to reach the epididymis, where they may remain for as long as six weeks. During ejaculation, muscle contractions and cilliary action conduct the sperm from the scrotum into the male's trunk through the **vas deferens.** They eventually reach the **seminal vesicles** and **prostate glands.** It is here that they are made more mobile by the addition of the *seminal fluid,* passing with it through the **urethra** and out of the penis. The seminal fluid—a nutrient-rich alkaline fluid with a milky appearance—keeps the sperm alive, healthy, and mobile and serves as a vehicle for carrying the sperm out of the penis. About 70 percent of the seminal fluid comes from the seminal vesicles; the remaining 30 percent comes from the prostate glands.

The Developing Penis

The **penis** doubles in length and girth during adolescence, with the most rapid growth taking place between ages 14 and 16. Genital growth usually takes 3 years to reach the adult stage, but some males complete this development in about 2 years and others take more than 4½ years. In the adult male, the flaccid (limp) penis averages from 3 to 4 inches in length and slightly over 1 inch in diameter. The tumescent (erect) penis, on the average, is 5½ to 6½ inches in length and 1½ inches in diameter; sizes vary tremendously from male to male.

Adolescent boys are often concerned with the dimensions of their penis, for they associate masculinity and sexual capability with penis size. These insecurities are often heightened because the scrotum starts to develop before the penis does. Mistakenly believing that their testes and penis should grow in sync, many young male teens fear that their penis will remain small forever.

In fact, the size of the flaccid penis has little to do with the size of the erect penis, for the small penis enlarges much more in proportion to its size than does the large penis. Moreover, the size of the erect penis has little to do with sexual capability, for the vagina has few nerve endings, and female sexual excitation comes primarily from stimulation of the external genitalia. The degree of pleasure experienced by both the man and the woman has nothing to do with the size of the male organ.

PERSONAL ISSUES USE OF STEROIDS BY ATHLETES

Athletes sometimes take synthetic male hormones called **anabolic steroids** to increase their strength and endurance. Ever since several competitors were disqualified from the 1988 Olympics because of the illegal use of anabolic steroids, attention has focused on the use of these drugs by athletes of all ages. It is feared that the use of androstenedione—a nonprescription, over-the-counter food supplement thought to help build muscle mass—by baseball greats Mark McGwire and Barry Bonds will further increase adolescent interest in these drugs. Steroids can be taken in pill form, rubbed on in cream form, or injected through a syringe.

There is no question that steroids increase muscle mass and reduce body fat. Unfortunately, they produce many serious physical side effects, as well. All abusers risk the development of liver tumors, jaundice, high blood pressure, weakening of tendons (resulting in tears and ruptures), heart attacks, strokes and blood clots, headaches, muscle cramps, severe acne, and baldness. And athletes who share needles are at increased risk for contracting hepatitis and HIV (human immunodeficiency virus), which causes AIDS (acquired immune deficiency syndrome). Males who abuse steroids are also likely to experience reduced sperm count, impotence, enlargement of the prostate gland, and increased breast size. Females who take steroids often find that their breasts shrink, that their clitorises enlarge, that they develop menstrual irregularities, that their voices deepen, and that their body and facial hair becomes more profuse. Adolescents who use steroids are at great risk for permanently shortened stature, since the presence of so much excess male hormone shuts down the production of human growth hormone.

Steroids also have emotional side effects. Abusers are subject to severe mood swings, paranoia, depression, and anxiety. They often develop hostile, irritable moods and are prone to fits of rage. Sometimes, these feelings result in fighting and other types of destructive behavior, such as property destruction.

The number of adolescents who use steroids is, fortunately, low. Although the number of twelfth-grades who used steroids had been steadily rising from 1.1 percent in 1991 to 2.5 percent in 2000, the most recent figures (2005) indicate a decline back to 1.5 percent. Most teenagers who use steroids are male. High school students perceive these drugs as risky, and most (about 90 percent) disapprove of their use. Teenagers believe that steroids are easy to obtain, although perhaps not quite as easy to obtain as they were a few years ago (Johnson, O'Malley, Bachman, and Schulenberg, 2006).

The head of the penis (*glans penis*) is covered by a loose fold of skin, the *prepuce* or *foreskin,* often removed surgically through *circumcision* for hygienic or religious reasons. Circumcision is not an obligatory health measure today, as long as the foreskin can be retracted and the penis is kept clean. If the prepuce is not retracted and the glans washed, a cheeselike substance known as *smegma* collects, acting as a breeding ground for irritants and disease.

Erection of the penis is possible from infancy; it may be caused by tight clothing, local irritation, the need to urinate, or manual stimulation. Sexual thoughts and stimulation are added to this list during puberty. Furthermore, erections become much more obvious and potentially embarrassing once the penis begins to grow. It is very common for adolescent males to experience undesired, uncontrollable erections, which they hope nobody else notices.

The Cowper's Glands

The **Cowper's glands,** which also mature during adolescence, secrete an alkaline fluid that lubricates and neutralizes the acidity of the urethra for easy and safe passage of the semen. A drop or two of this fluid may be observed at the opening of the glans during sexual excitement and before ejaculation. Because the fluid often contains sperm, conception is possible whenever intercourse occurs, even if the male withdraws prior to ejaculation.

scrotum the pouch of skin containing the testes.

epididymis a system of ducts, running from the testes to the vas deferens, in which sperm mature and are stored.

vas deferens the tubes running from the epididymis to the urethra that carry semen and sperm to the ejaculatory duct.

seminal vesicles twin glands that secrete fluid into the vas deferens to enhance sperm viability.

prostate glands two glands that secrete a portion of the seminal fluid.

urethra the tube carrying the urine from the bladder to the outside; in males, it also carries the semen to the outside.

penis the male organ for coitus and urination.

Cowper's glands small twin glands that secrete a fluid to neutralize the acid environment of the urethra.

anabolic steroids the masculinizing hormone testosterone taken by athletes to build muscle mass.

Nocturnal Emissions

Although male infants and children get erections, ejaculation isn't possible until puberty. Most adolescent boys experience **nocturnal emissions,** or "wet dreams," as do most adult men. In fact, Kinsey and colleagues (1948) reported that almost 100 percent of men have erotic dreams, and about 83 percent of them have dreams that culminate in orgasm. These dreams occur most frequently among males in their teens and twenties, but about half of all married men continue to have them.

Research has revealed that a boy's first ejaculation—termed **semenarche** or **spermarche**—is a memorable event (Downs and Fuller, 1991; Stein and Reiser, 1994). Many boys feel surprised at the occurrence because it often happens earlier than they imagine it will. (Most boys begin to ejaculate somewhat before their thirteenth birthday.) In addition to confusion, boys report feelings of pleasure and maturity. Still, most boys do not tell anyone that they have begun ejaculating. Those boys who are most informed about pubertal changes express the most positive feelings about semenarche (Paddack, 1987).

MATURATION AND FUNCTIONS OF FEMALE SEX ORGANS

The primary internal female sex organs are the ovaries, fallopian tubes, uterus, and vagina. The external female sex organs are known collectively as the **vulva.** They are the mons veneris (mons pubis), the labia majora (major or large outer lips), the labia minora (small inner lips), the clitoris, and the **vestibule** (the cleft region enclosed by the labia minora). The **hymen** is a fold of connective tissue that partly closes the vagina in the virginal female. The **Bartholin's glands,** situated on either side of the vaginal orifice, secrete a drop or so of fluid during sexual excitement. Figure 4.5 depicts the female sexual organs.

FIGURE 4.5 THE FEMALE REPRODUCTIVE SYSTEM
This cross-section locates many of the internal sexual organs that compose the female reproductive system. Note that the uterus is normally tipped forward.

Source: From Spencer Rathus et al., *Human Sexuality in a World of Diversity,* 6/e. Published by Allyn and Bacon, Boston, MA. Copyright © 2005 by Pearson Education. By permission of the publisher.

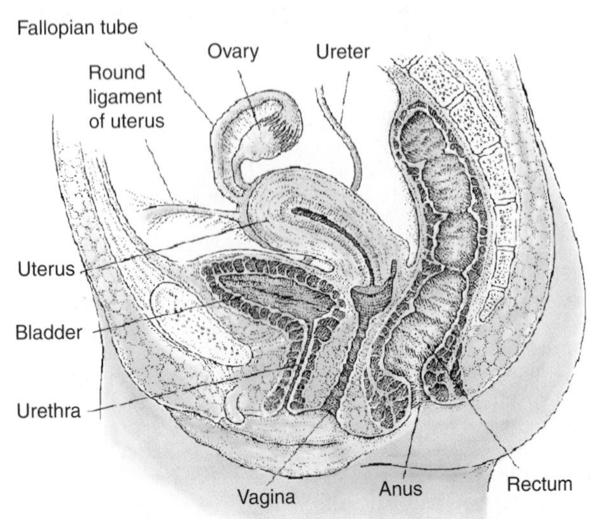

The Developing Vagina

The **vagina** matures at puberty in a number of ways. It increases in length and its mucous lining becomes thicker, becomes more elastic, and turns a deeper color. The Bartholin's glands begin to secrete their fluids, and the inner walls of the vagina change their secretion from basic to acidic.

Changes in the Vulva and Uterus

The **labia majora,** practically nonexistent in childhood, enlarge greatly, as do the **labia minora** and the **clitoris.** The **mons veneris** becomes more prominent through the development of a fatty pad.

A dramatic change also takes place in the **uterus,** which doubles in length, showing a straight-line increase during the period from 10 to 18 years of age. The uterus of the mature nonpregnant female is a hollow, thick-walled, muscular organ shaped like a pear, about 3 inches long, 2½ inches at the top and narrowing to a diameter of 1 inch at the cervix. Note from Figure 4.5 that the uterus sits at a right angle, tilted forward, to the vagina, not straight up and down.

Ovarian Changes

The ovaries increase greatly in size and weight. Every infant girl is born with about 400,000 follicles in each ovary. By puberty, this number has declined to about 80,000 in each ovary. Ordinarily, one follicle ripens into an ovum (egg) every 28 days for a period of about 40 years, which means that only about 500 ova ripen during the woman's reproductive years. The **fallopian tubes**—each only a little larger than a human hair in diameter—transport the ova from the ovaries to the uterus.

Menarche and the Menstrual Cycle

On average, the adolescent girl begins her menstrual cycle at 12 to 13 years of age, although she may mature considerably earlier or later (9 to 18 years is an extreme range). **Menarche** (the onset of menstruation) usually does not occur until after maximum growth rates in height and weight have been achieved. Because of superior nutrition and health care, girls start menstruating earlier today than in former generations. An increase in body fat may stimulate menarche; vigorous exercise tends to delay it (Ellis, 2004; Petridou, Syrigou,

ANSWERS WOULDN'T YOU LIKE TO KNOW . . .

Besides the obvious, what are the differences between males' and females' reproductive organs?

Males have a number of internal reproductive structures that females do not. Males have tubes in which their sperm mature (the epididymis) and a tube that carries the sperm from the testes into the body cavity (the vas deferens). Males also have three glands—the prostate, the seminal vesicles, and the Cowper's gland—that females do not. In addition to a vagina, uterus, and ovaries, female bodies possess fallopian tubes that transport eggs into the uterus. They also have a number of external structures—such as the labia minora and majora, clitoris, and Bartholin's glands—that collectively comprise the vulva.

Toupadakin, Zaritzanos, Willet, and Trichopoulos, 1996). Although the data are not entirely consistent, there is some evidence of racial and ethnic differences in the timing of menarche. Daniels et al. (1998), for example, found that African American girls hit puberty several months earlier than Caucasian girls.

The menstrual cycle may vary in length from 20 to 40 days, averaging about 28 days. There is considerable difference in the length of the cycle when different women are compared, and any one woman may show widespread variations. A truly regular cycle is quite rare.

The menstrual cycle has four phases: the menstrual phase, the follicular phase, the ovulatory phase, and the luteal phase. As Figure 4.6 shows, hormones control the cycle. During the *menstrual phase*—which begins with the first day of menstrual bleeding—estrogen, progesterone, FSH, and LH levels are all at minimums. This signals the hypothalamus to resume production of GnRH. GnRH, in turn, stimulates the pituitary gland to begin production of FSH. The *follicular phase* extends from just after menstruation until a follicle ripens and an egg matures. During this phase, the pituitary continues to secrete FSH. The follicle-stimulating hormone stimulates development of the follicles and one or more ova and induces the secretion of increasing levels of estrogen. When estrogen is at a peak, the hypothalamus acts on the pituitary to reduce the level of FSH and to secrete a surge of LH. The increased estrogen level results in a thickening of the inner lining of the uterus (the endometrium) to receive a possible fertilized egg.

Approximately 14 days before the onset of the next menstrual period, the spurt in LH production results in *ovulation,* during which a mature ovum erupts from its follicle and passes into the fallopian tube. The *ovulatory phase* is the shortest of the cycle.

The *luteal phase* follows ovulation and continues to the beginning of the next menstrual period. During the luteal phase, LH secretion from the pituitary stimulates growth of the follicle from which the ovum has erupted. This follicle develops into the *corpus luteum,* which secretes progesterone during the remainder of this phase (see Figure 4.7).

A high progesterone level causes the pituitary to cease production of LH, and the LH level drops. But with no LH, the corpus luteum degenerates and dies. Without a corpus luteum to produce progesterone, the level of this hormone drops, as well. At the conclusion of the luteal phase, a woman's body contains relatively little FSH, LH, estrogen, or progesterone. This triggers menstruation, and the cycle begins anew.

While many, but by no means all, adolescents know that ovulation occurs on about day 14 of a 28-day menstrual cycle, they have no idea when it occurs during a cycle that is longer or shorter. Many believe that ovulation always occurs in the middle of a girl's cycle—that is, on day 17 of a 34-day cycle or on day 12 of a 24-day cycle. This is a serious misconception! Ovulation almost always occurs 14 days before the beginning of the *next* menstrual period; that would be day 20 of a 34-day cycle or day 10 of a 24-day cycle. Ovulation is *not* closely tied to the beginning of the current menstrual cycle. This is an

nocturnal emissions male ejaculation during sleep.

semenarche a recently coined term for a boy's first ejaculation; derived from the term *menarche.*

vulva collective term referring to the external genitalia of the female.

vestibule the opening cleft region enclosed by the labia minora.

hymen the tissue partly covering the vaginal opening.

Bartholin's glands glands on either side of the vaginal opening that secrete fluid during sexual arousal.

vagina the canal from the cervix to the vulva that receives the penis during intercourse and acts as the birth canal through which the baby passes to the outside.

labia majora major or large lips of tissue on either side of the vaginal opening.

labia minora smaller lips or tissue on either side of the vagina.

clitoris a small shaft containing erectile tissue, located above the vaginal and urethral openings, that is highly responsive to sexual stimulation.

mons veneris mound of flesh (literally "mound of Venus") in the female located above the vagina, over which pubic hair grows.

uterus the womb in which the baby grows and develops.

fallopian tubes tubes that transport the ova from the ovaries to the uterus.

menarche first menstruation.

PERSONAL ISSUES STRESS AND PUBERTAL TIMING

Research has helped develop a new understanding of early menarche, especially regarding the role of environmental stress in the timing of puberty:

1. Girls whose parents are warm and supportive undergo puberty at later ages than girls whose parents are cold and rejecting (e.g., Romans, Martin, Gendall, and Herbison, 2003).
2. Compared with girls from intact families, those from divorced families have an earlier onset of menarche (e.g., Quinlan, 2003).
3. Higher maternal reports of interparental conflict are significantly related to earlier menarche (e.g., Jorm, Christensen, Rogers, Jacomb, and Easteal, 2004).
4. Depressive mood and poor family relations predict age of menarche (e.g., Ellis and Garber, 2000).
5. These findings are not limited to young women in the United States but have been replicated elsewhere. For example, Hulanicka (1999) described the same pattern occurring among girls in Poland.
6. Several researchers have suggested that the absence of a girl's father hastens the onset of menarche. In accord with the fact that the absence of a highly involved father promotes early puberty in girls, Kanazawa (2001) found that girls in polygynous cultures—cultures in which men are typically less involved with their children—reach menarche earlier than girls in more monogamous societies.

How do family stress and family conflict lead to early menarche? Researchers propose that family conflict predisposes girls to lower metabolism and weight gain, triggering the early onset of menarche (Belsky, Steinberg, and Draper, 1991; Moffitt, Caspi, Belsky, and Silva, 1992). In addition, stress during childhood has been shown to provoke changes in the hypothalamus, the part of the brain that triggers puberty (Dobson, Ghuman, Prabhakar, and Smith, 2003).

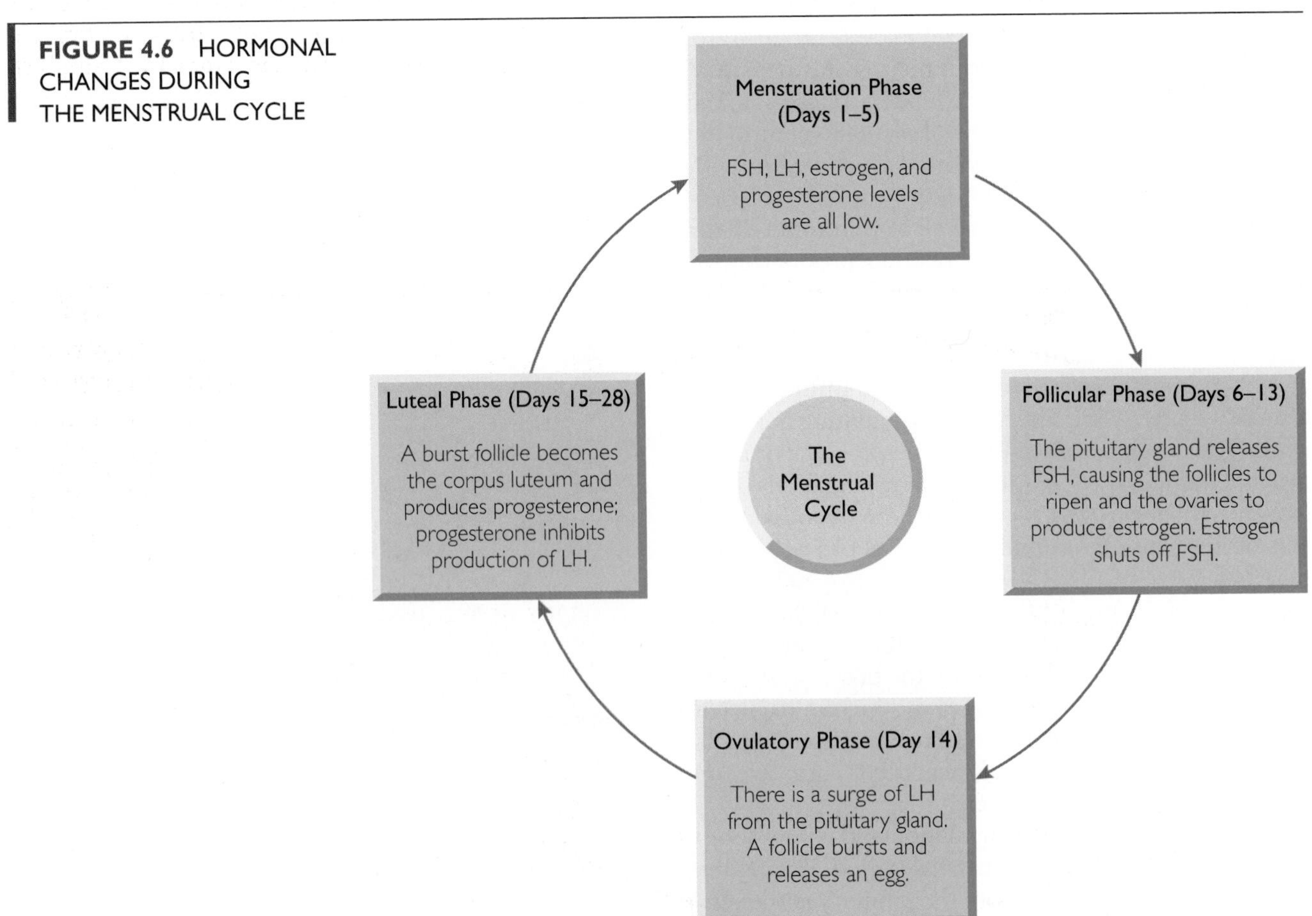

FIGURE 4.6 HORMONAL CHANGES DURING THE MENSTRUAL CYCLE

PERSONAL ISSUES PREPARING GIRLS FOR MENSTRUATION

Adolescent girls who are prepared for menstruation in a positive way are more likely to consider it a positive experience. What is the best preparation?

[One] study asked adolescent girls who had been menstruating for one to three years how they would prepare younger girls for the event, and how they would advise parents to prepare their daughters. To this end, 157 9th-grade girls rated their own experience of menarche. . . . The girls emphasized the need for emotional support and assurance that menstruation was normal and healthy—not bad, frightening, or embarrassing. They stressed the pragmatics of menstrual hygiene and the subjective experience of menstruation (how it would actually feel), while downplaying the biological aspects and the link between menstruation and self-definition as a woman. Most girls had talked about menstruation with their mothers, but few had discussed it with their fathers. They saw mothers as critically important but often unable to meet their needs. Many girls felt uncomfortable talking about menstruation with fathers, wanting them to be supportive but silent; others believed that fathers should be excluded completely. Responses suggested several ways early preparation could be revised, including a shift in focus from the biology of menstruation to the more personal, subjective, and immediate aspects of the experience. Responses also supported a conceptualization of menstrual education as a long-term, continuous process, beginning well before menarche and continuing long after.

Source: E. Koff and K. Rierdan, "Preparing Girls for Menstruation: Recommendations from Adolescent Girls," *Adolescence, 30* (1995): 795–811.

important piece of information because although pregnancy can occur at any point in the cycle, it is most likely to occur on the day of ovulation or one day later. If a girl's periods are at all irregular (which is true for most adolescent girls), then she cannot predict when she will ovulate. To do so, she would have to be able to count backward from a date that she does not yet know.

A girl may menstruate **anovulatory** (without ovulation) when her menstrual cycle begins, until the ovaries mature enough to discharge mature ova and until the endocrine glands secrete enough of their hormones to make ovulation possible. The first periods may be scanty and irregular, spaced at varying intervals until a rhythm is established. It is not uncommon for the flow to last only a day or so for the first few periods. Later, it may last from two to seven days, with the mean usually about five days. The total amount of blood lost averages 1.5 ounces (3 tablespoons). A normal range is from 1 to 5 ounces. Only part of the menstrual fluid is blood. The total discharge amounts to approximately 1 cup (6 to 8 ounces) and is composed partly of mucus and broken-down cell tissue (Warner, Critchley, Lumsden, Campbell-Brown, Douglas, and Murray, 2004).

anovulatory without ovulation.

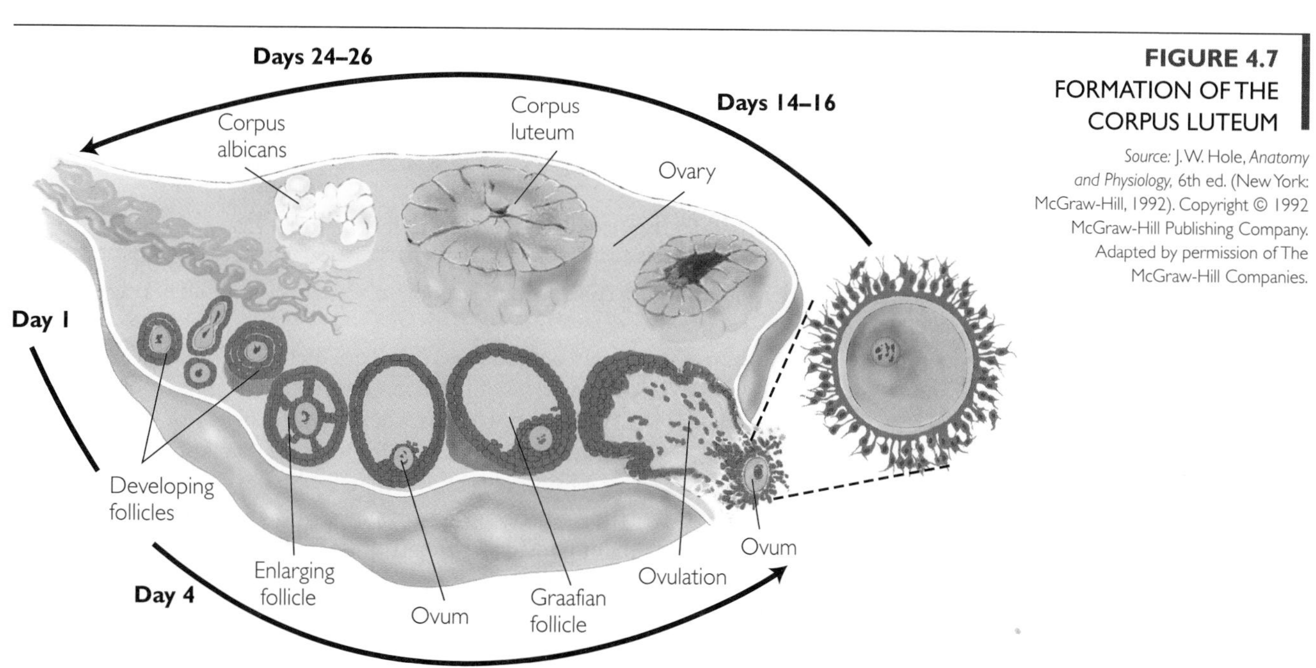

FIGURE 4.7 FORMATION OF THE CORPUS LUTEUM

Source: J. W. Hole, *Anatomy and Physiology*, 6th ed. (New York: McGraw-Hill, 1992). Copyright © 1992 McGraw-Hill Publishing Company. Adapted by permission of The McGraw-Hill Companies.

Menstrual Concerns

Menarche is a big event in a girl's life. It signals as nothing else can that she is growing up. Some girls—especially those who feel they have been waiting a long time for menstruation to start—view the event in a highly positive light. As one student explained:

> When it happened, I thought FINALLY! It seemed like all of my friends had had their periods for years. I felt very left out when they'd sit around and talk about it (even though they didn't make it sound very pleasant). I even practiced wearing pads so I'd be ready. When I woke up on a Saturday morning with a tell-tale stain, I called my three best friends right then and there—at 7:30 in the morning. I was so happy! I giggled on and off all day, because I felt I wasn't a kid anymore.

Contrary to this report, many girls have a negative view of menstruation. This is more common among early maturers, who are generally less informed about what to expect and how to manage than their peers who mature later (Chrisler and Zittel, 1998; Gallant and Derry, 1995). Negative views typically stem from three sources: off-putting messages received from others, fear of embarrassment, and anticipated discomfort.

Unfortunately, many girls are negatively conditioned even before menses (Frank and Williams, 1999; Merskin, 1999). Studies of advertisements of menstrual products showed that the ads depicted menstruation as a "hygienic crisis" that is managed by an "effective security system" that affords protection and "peace of mind." Failure to provide adequate protection places the woman at risk for soiling, staining, embarrassment, and odor. Such ads encourage guilt, insecurity, and diminished self-esteem (Havens and Swenson, 1988; Simes and Berg, 2001).

Regardless of whether they are privately pleased that they are physically maturing, many girls do not want to share this information with the world at large. Many college-age women laughingly recall how they timed bathroom trips so that no one would suspect they had their period or how they would only buy pads or tampons from a female cashier, even if they had to wait in a much longer line. Fortunately, this desperation to hide one's periods seems to wane by late adolescence.

Some adolescent girls do experience physical difficulties with their menstrual periods (McEvoy, Chang, and Coupey, 2004). These physical problems usually fall into one of four categories. *Dysmenorrhea* is painful or difficult menstruation: menstrual cramps or abdominal pain, with or without other symptoms such as backache, headache, vomiting, fatigue, irritability, sensitivity of the genitals or breasts, pain in the legs, swelling of the ankles, or skin irritations such as pimples. *Menhorrhagia* is excessive bleeding. Both of these conditions are believed to be caused by an excess of **prostaglandins:** hormones that cause smooth muscle contractions. Therefore, almost all girls who experience these conditions can be helped by taking **antiprostaglandins,** which are drugs that destroy or inhibit these chemicals. Ibuprofen is an antiprostaglandin that is available without prescription; aspirin, too, is a mild prostaglandin inhibitor (Mehlisch, Ardia, and Pallotta, 2003).

Amenorrhea is absence of flow. This may be due to a physical cause, such as vigorous exercise that changes the percentage of body fat and alters hormonal secretion. It may also be caused by an endocrine disorder or a change of climate, overwork, emotional excitement, and other factors. *Metrorrhagia*—bleeding from the uterus at times other than during a menstrual period—is not common. It demands a medical checkup to determine physical and/or emotional causes (Altchek, 1988).

Generally, girls who have been menstruating for some time have more positive attitudes about

RESEARCH HIGHLIGHT MENSTRUAL IRREGULARITY IN ATHLETES

Extensive research has established that *amenorrhea,* or irregular menstruation, is common in female athletes: ballet dancers, distance runners, swimmers, and others (Putukian, 1998). In fact, more than 10 percent of girls who vigorously exercise, and as many as half of girls who are runners, may develop amenorrhea (DeSouza and Metzger, 1991). It is generally believed that a lack of body fat causes these conditions (Warren and Perlroth, 2001). The current evidence suggests that exercise-induced amenorrhea rapidly reverses once training is discontinued (Stager, 1984). When physical training is reduced or stopped, either as a result of a vacation or an injury, amenorrheic athletes report a resumption of normal menstrual cycles.

However, in recent years there has been a growing concern over what has been termed the "female athlete triad": a combination of disordered eating behavior, amenorrhea, and **osteoporosis** (Reinking and Alexander, 2005). The bone mineral loss in athletes who have sustained amenorrhea can be quite dramatic and resemble that of postmenopausal women (Tietz, Hu, and Arendt, 1997).

It should be noted that *moderate* exercise has been found to reduce menstrual problems such as cramps and discomfort (Golub, 1992).

menstruation than do premenstrual young women (McGrory, 1990). This suggests that the reality of managing one's period is not as bad as it is reputed to be. Still, some adolescent girls experience new mood swings with the onset of their menstrual period. Although not nearly as ubiquitous as most people imagine (most women experience only mild symptoms), many adolescent girls will find themselves more irritable or depressed in the few days before they get their period. Some may also find that they retain fluid, gain weight, have an increased appetite, or feel their breasts swell and ache (Wittchen, Becker, Lieb, and Krause, 2002). There is a tendency, however, to mistakenly attribute a premenstrual sour mood with hormonal fluctuations. It is important to remember that all people, male and female, have emotional ups and downs. A girl who feels low the day before she gets her period might be experiencing the effects of low hormone levels or she might be reacting to breaking up with her boyfriend, just as she would midcycle. Many people attribute *all* bad moods during the premenstrual period to biology, when that is certainly not always the case (Baines and Slade, 1988).

DEVELOPMENT OF SECONDARY SEXUAL CHARACTERISTICS

We began this chapter by observing that it is easy to tell the differences between male and female bodies, even when they are clothed. The physical differences in the reproductive organs, however, are largely invisible in clothed individuals. The same sex hormones that cause changes in the reproductive structures during puberty also cause the **secondary sexual characteristics** to develop. These are the features that, although not absolutely necessary for reproduction, differentiate male and female bodies. They include the presence or absence of body hair, angular or more rounded body contours, an enlarged or smaller larynx (voice box), and increased muscle mass or body fat.

Table 4.1 gives the sequence of development for boys and girls. The development of some of the primary sexual characteristics is also included to give a picture of the total sequence of development (primary characteristics are marked with an asterisk). The ages provided in the table are averages. Actual ages may extend several years before and after, with individual differences having a hereditary base (Akinboye, 1984; Westney, Jenkins, Butts, and Williams, 1984). Although the average girl matures about two years before the average boy, the rate of development is not always consistent.

prostaglandins hormones that cause smooth muscle contractions and contribute to dysmenorrhea and menhorrhagia.

antiprostaglandins drugs that destroy prostaglandins and can reduce menstrual distress.

osteoporosis a condition in which the bones become brittle due to calcium loss.

secondary sexual characteristics features not directly related to reproduction that distinguish male from female bodies.

TABLE 4.1 SEQUENCE OF DEVELOPMENT OF PRIMARY AND SECONDARY SEXUAL CHARACTERISTICS

BOYS	AGE SPAN		GIRLS
Beginning growth of testes, scrotum, pubic hair Some pigmentation, nodulation of breasts (later disappears) Height spurt begins Beginning growth of penis*	11.5–13	10–11	Height spurt begins Slight growth of pubic hair Breasts, nipples, elevated to form "bud" stage
Development of straight, pigmented pubic hair Early voice changes Rapid growth of penis, testes, scrotum, prostate, seminal vesicles* First ejaculation of semen* Kinky pubic hair Age of maximum growth Beginning growth of axillary hair	13–16	11–14	Straight, pigmented pubic hair Some deepening of voice Rapid growth of vagina, ovaries, labia, uterus* Kinky pubic hair Age of maximum growth Further enlargement, pigmentation, elevation of nipple, areola to form "primary breast" Menarche*
Rapid growth of axillary hair Marked voice change Growth of beard Indentation of frontal hairline	16–18	14–16	Growth of axillary hair Filling out of breasts to form adult conformation, secondary breast stage

*Primary sexual characteristics are marked with asterisks.

Generally speaking, the average age of sexual maturity has been decreasing over the years, primarily due both to the better health care of today's generation of youth (Gilger, Geary, and Eisele, 1991) and to the fact that today's youths are heavier. While many studies have found an overall link between increased body mass and early puberty (e.g., Anderson, Dallal, and Must, 2003), that link appears stronger for girls than for boys (Biro, Khoury, and Morrison, 2006). In addition, African American girls hit puberty earlier on average than Caucasian girls; this may be due to a combination of the fact that African American girls are more likely to have higher levels of body fat (Kaplowitz, Slora, Wasserman, Pedlow, and Herman-Giddens, 2001) and that their bodies produce more **leptin,** a hormone associated with the onset on puberty (Wong et al., 1998).

Males

The development of secondary sexual characteristics in boys is a gradual process. The appearance of pubic hair starts with sparse, straight hair at the base of the penis, and then the hair gradually becomes more profuse and curled, forming an inverse triangle and spreading up to the umbilicus. Figure 4.8 shows the developmental process. Axillary (underarm) hair usually first appears about two years after the appearance of pubic hair, with the growth of the beard coming near the end of the total sequence, and the indentation of the hairline (this does not occur in girls) arriving as the final development. Muscular development, widening of the shoulders and chest, and other changes in body contours continue. Usually, a boy has reached 98 percent of his adult height during his seventeenth year.

Changes in the boy's voice are due to the rapid growth of the larynx (the Adam's apple) and the lengthening of the vocal cords across it. The vocal cords nearly double in length, lowering the pitch one octave. Volume also increases, and the tonal quality is more pleasant. Roughness of tone and unexpected pitch changes may last until 16 or 18 years of age.

Before and during the period when sexual maturation takes place, some boys (and girls) suffer what has been referred to as the *locker-room syndrome.* After physical education class, middle-schoolers are herded into the showers, where they have to undress and bathe in front of others. The range in normal developmental rates is great enough so that some boys are completely underdeveloped and others are ahead of their classmates. The adolescent boy with little pubic or axillary hair, no noticeable beard, an undeveloped penis, or a childlike body feels inferior to his more fully developed friends. Those who have started to develop may feel self-conscious at their new more sexual physique. Involuntary erection in front of others is especially embarrassing, as is noticeable body odor. Furthermore, as many as 70 percent of boys experience **gynecomastia:** a temporary enlargement of their breasts due to excessive amounts of estrogen in their systems (Lazala and Saenger, 2002). In fact, almost everything having to do with body development can become a source of embarrassment.

Females

Development of pubic hair in girls is similar to the process that occurs with boys. On average, girls are about 12 years of age when straight, pigmented pubic hair begins to grow, first along the labia, then, becoming more abundant and kinky, spreading over the mons in an inverse triangular pattern. By late adolescence, pubic hair spreads to the medial surface of the thighs. Figure 4.9 shows the developmental sequence (Katchadourian, 1977).

FIGURE 4.8 STAGES OF PUBIC HAIR DEVELOPMENT IN ADOLESCENT BOYS
Stages are (*1*) prepubertal (not shown) in which there is no true pubic hair; (2) sparse growth of downy hair mainly at base of penis; (3) pigmentation, coarsening, and curling with an increase in amount of hair; (4) adult hair, but limited in area; (5) adult hair with horizontal upper border and spread to thighs.

Source: Adapted from J. M. Tanner, *Growth at Adolescence,* 2nd ed. (Oxford: Blackwell Scientific Publications, 1962), as reprinted in H. Katchadourian, *The Biology of Adolescence* (San Francisco: W. H. Freeman, 1977), p. 67.

2

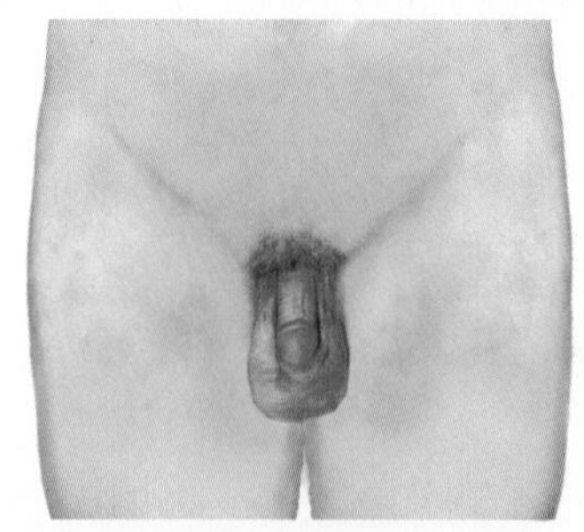

3

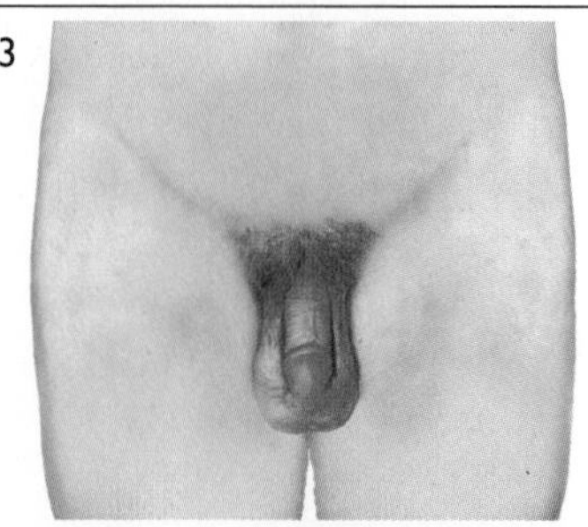

4

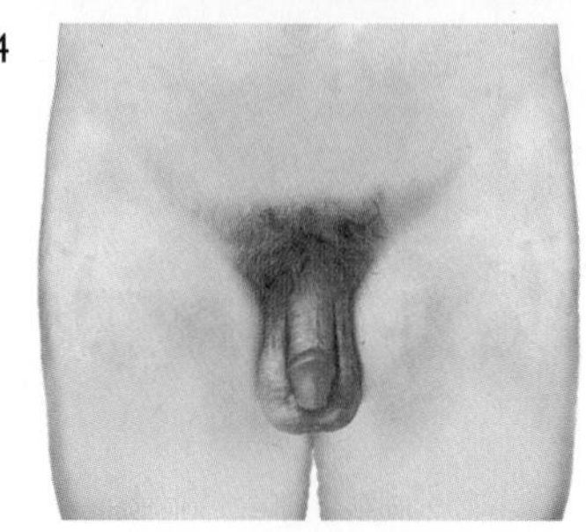

5

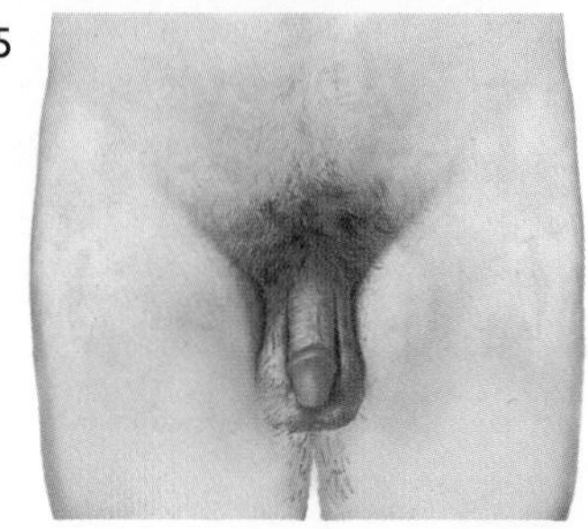

2

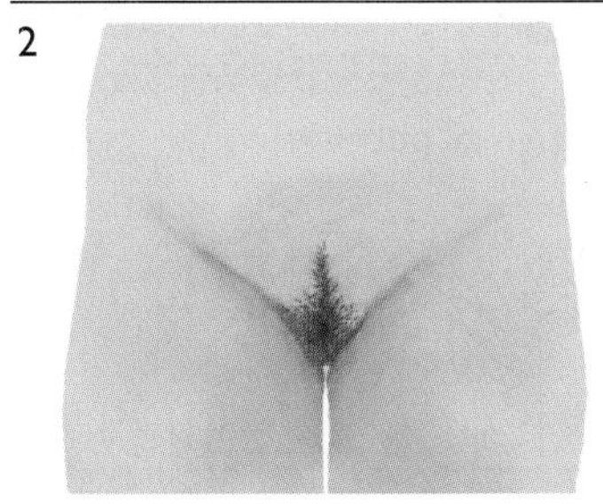

3

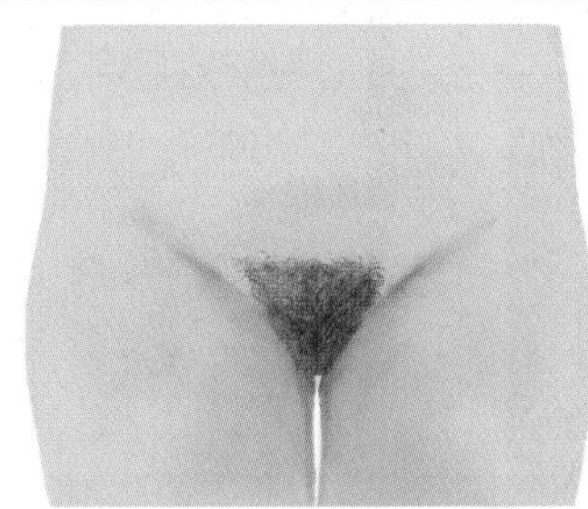

4

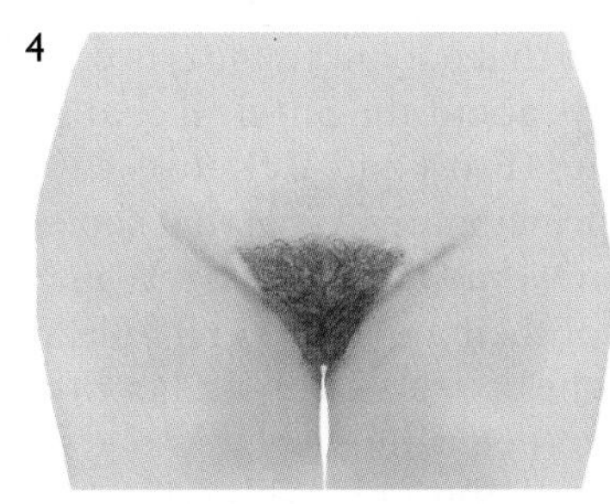

5

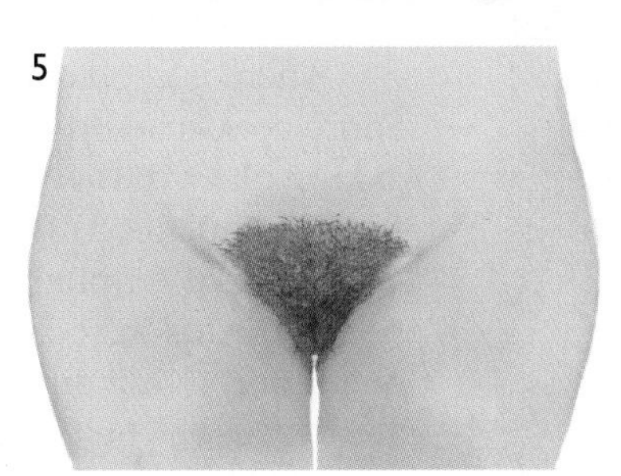

FIGURE 4.9 STAGES OF PUBIC HAIR DEVELOPMENT IN ADOLESCENT GIRLS

(*1*) Prepubertal (not shown) in which there is no true pubic hair; (*2*) sparse growth of downy hair mainly at sides of labia; (*3*) pigmentation, coarsening, and curling with an increase in the amount of hair; (*4*) adult hair, but limited in area; (*5*) adult hair with horizontal upper border.

Source: Adapted from J. M. Tanner, *Growth at Adolescence,* 2nd ed. (Oxford: Blackwell Scientific Publishers, 1962), as reprinted in H. Katchadourian, *The Biology of Adolescence* (San Francisco: W. H. Freeman, 1977), p. 57.

The facial hair of girls appears first as a slight down on the upper lip, then spreads to the upper part of the cheeks, and finally to the sides and lower border of the chin. The hair is less pigmented and of finer texture than that of men, but brunettes may have a darker, heavier down than blonds. Axillary hair grows about two years after pubic hair and is generally coarser and darker in brunettes than in blonds. Body hair, especially on the arms and legs, is the last to develop. Ordinarily, girls do not have noticeable hair on their chests, shoulders, or backs, except in cases of glandular disturbance.

One of the most noticeable changes in girls is the development of the breasts. It takes place in five stages:

1. *Prepubertal stage:* There is a flat appearance to the breasts.
2. *Bud stage:* Elevation, enlargement, and pigmentation of the nipple and surrounding areola begin, usually starting about two and one-half years before menarche.
3. *Primary stage:* An increase in the underlying fat surrounding the nipple and areola cause the areola to project in a mound above the level of the chest wall.
4. *Secondary or mature stage:* The mammary gland tissue develops, producing larger, rounder breasts. The areola recedes and is incorporated in the breast itself so that only the papilla (nipple) protrudes. This mature stage usually comes after menarche. Regardless of when development starts, it usually takes three years before the papilla projects out from the surrounding breast.
5. *Adult stage:* Development is complete.

IN THEIR OWN WORDS

"I think that most of my friends were envious of my chest, but they didn't have a clue. I hated the stares—I still do. I can't walk down the street in the summer without some jerk making a comment. It was worse when I was in middle school. I grew really big by seventh grade, and I was the only one in my class who was so developed. I especially hated when we had to do laps in gym because I bounced so much. It was pretty uncomfortable, and the guys would watch me and crack jokes. I even quit soccer because I didn't like to run with anyone watching me. I wore tight sports bras all the time, trying to make myself look smaller. I couldn't wear tube tops or spaghetti straps like the other girls, and I always resented that because they are so cute!"

"I was really scrawny and small back in middle and high school—definitely a late bloomer. I'd played lots of baseball as a kid but couldn't make the team even in seventh grade because I was just too small. There was this group of guys who rode the same bus I did, and they gave me a hard time. There were three of them, and they were all bigger than me. They were on me all the time for being a sexless wimp (and worse). One day, their horsing around got worse. As we started fighting, one grabbed my shirt and it tore and half fell off. One of the guys laughed and said, 'He's all right! Look at all that pit hair!' After that, they started called me 'Pit,' but they stopped hassling me. I guess you could say my armpit hair proved I was a real man."

leptin a hormone that helps trigger puberty.

gynecomastia a phenomenon experienced by some young male adolescents in which their breasts temporarily swell as they enter puberty.

Many adolescent girls are concerned about the size and shape of their breasts, due in large part to society's scrutiny of women's physiques.

Many adolescent girls are concerned about the size and shape of their breasts. Some girls who are flat chested feel self-conscious because they are influenced by society's emphasis on full breasts as a mark of beauty and sexuality. Girls who have unusually large breasts are also self-conscious when they suffer unkind remarks and stares.

Also of concern to girls are the changes that take place in body contours. The most noticeable change other than breast development is the widening and rounding of the hips. This is due to the broadening of the pelvis and the increased deposit of fat in the subcutaneous tissue of this area. These changes occur over about an 18-month period, usually starting at about the same time that the first breast buds appear. During the time when girls are acquiring subcutaneous fat on their hips, boys seem to lose body fat across the hips. Girls stop growing in height, on average, at age 16, plus or minus 13 months (Tanner, 1991).

ANSWERS WOULDN'T YOU LIKE TO KNOW . . .

What is usually the first sign of puberty?

In most boys, the first sign that puberty is beginning is that their testes and scrotum begin to grow. The first sign in girls is that they start sprouting and growing taller.

There is good evidence that adolescent girls become more concerned than boys about the physical changes taking place in their bodies (Frost and McKelvie, 2004; Tiggemann, 2005). The principal reason is that society places great emphasis on women's physiques. Women are rewarded in society for their appearance. It follows, therefore, that a girl will be concerned about her body fat because it helps her to determine whether she fits in socially and what her self-concept will be. The adolescent girl's concern is with meeting cultural standards of physical appearance and obtaining the approval of friends. As a consequence, glamour and popularity become important concerns. (This is discussed more fully in the next chapter.)

Results of Sexual Maturation

One of the most immediate results of sexual maturation is a developing preoccupation with sex. Attention becomes focused on sex, new sexual sensations, and on people of the opposite gender. Adolescent boys and girls spend a lot of time thinking about sex, looking at pictures of sexy individuals, and talking about the opposite sex.

These awakening sexual interests motivate adolescent boys to devote much time and attention to grooming and clothes, to body building and care, or to various attempts to attract the attention of girls. They may read pornography or go on the Web to find sexually explicit sites. Girls worry about their hair, experiment with makeup, flirt, and sigh over romantic movies or "chick flicks." They also spend endless hours discussing the hottest boys in class with their best friends.

Needless to say, it doesn't end there—with thoughts and fantasies. Most adolescents engage in some form of sexual behavior, such as kissing, petting, masturbation, and intercourse. (These topics are fully discussed later in the text.)

GROWTH IN HEIGHT AND WEIGHT

One of the earliest and most obvious physical changes of adolescence is the growth spurt that begins in early adolescence. This growth in height is accompanied by an increase in weight and changes in body proportion.

Growth Trends

As you can see in Figure 4.10, girls grow most in height and weight at approximately 12 years of age; boys grow most in height and weight at approximately age 14 (Abassi, 1998; Tanner, 1990). Girls are usually shorter and lighter than boys during childhood; however, because they start to mature earlier, they are, on average, taller than boys between ages 12 and 14 and heavier than boys between ages 10 and 14. Girls reach 98 percent of their adult height by the time they are almost 17, but boys do not do this until they are close to 18.

Determinants of Height

What determines the total mature height of an individual? A number of factors are believed to be important (Rowe, 2002), but one of the most important is heredity. Tall parents tend to have tall children; short parents tend to have short children. The most important environmental factor is nutrition. Children who are better nourished during the growth years become taller adults than those who are not nourished as well. Studies have shown that children from higher socioeconomic groups grow taller than those from poorer families. The reason is better nutrition—not income, job, or education.

The age when sexual maturation begins also affects the total height finally achieved. Boys and girls who are early maturers tend to be a little shorter as adults than those who are later maturers. Sexual maturation results in the secretion of sex hormones from the gonads; the hormones inhibit the pituitary from further production of human growth hormone. A later maturer has a longer time to grow before the sex hormones stop the pituitary from stimulating further growth. In addition, because limb bones tend to grow longer faster than they grow wider, late maturers are usually relatively narrower and less stocky than those who stop growing sooner.

Evidence indicates that the total process of growth is speeding up. Children and adolescents in industrialized nations today experience the growth spurt earlier, grow faster, attain a greater total adult height, and attain this height earlier than did children and adolescents 100 years ago. The normal, healthy girl is ½ to 1 inch taller and reaches menarche 10 months earlier than her mother. Girls at the turn of the 20th century reached their adult height at age 18 or 19; the average today has dropped to age 16. One researcher reported an increase in adult height of males of 2½ to 3½ inches during the last century. In 1880, males did not reach their final height until 23 to 25 years of age; today, their adult height is reached at age 18 (Tanner, 1968). The average height of U.S. sailors in the war of 1812 is estimated at 5 feet, 2 inches, which explains why the decks of the U.S.S. *Constitution* did not need to be more than 5 feet, 6 inches high.

FIGURE 4.10 INCREASE IN HEIGHT

Source: Adapted from J. M. Tanner, *Growth at Adolescence*, 2nd ed. (Oxford: Blackwell Scientific Publishers, 1962), as reprinted in H. Katchadourian, *The Biology of Adolescence* (San Francisco: W. H. Freeman, 1977), p. 55.

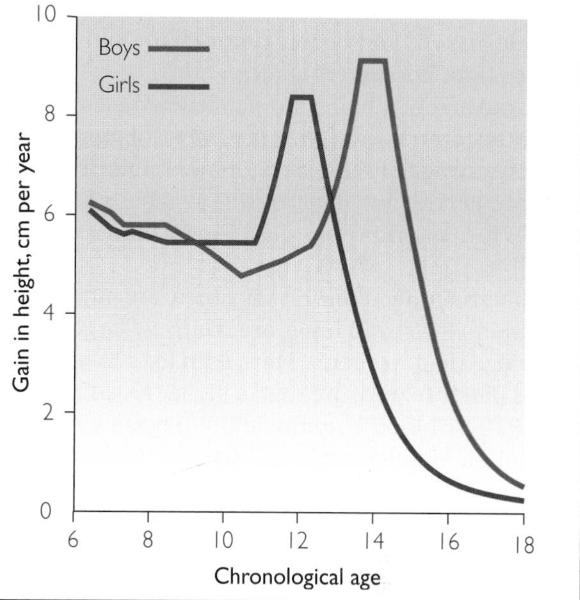

ANSWERS WOULDN'T YOU LIKE TO KNOW . . .

Why are girls often taller than boys during early adolescence?

Your sixth-grade class photo didn't lie: Girls are typically taller than boys throughout much of middle school because they hit their adolescent growth spurt about two years earlier.

This accelerated growth pattern, referred to as the **secular trend,** has tapered off, at least in the United States (Sun et al., 2005) and other developed countries (e.g., Simsek, UlUkol, and Gulnar, 2005). Apparently, there is a limit to the ultimate size of human beings.

Other Physical Changes

There are yet other ways in which mature male and female bodies are different. The high level of testosterone in males prompts their bodies to develop differently than those of females, who have a lower level of testosterone. Testosterone causes bones to grow thicker and to become more prominent. Men, therefore, have a relatively larger chin and more pronounced eyebrow ridges than women. Men's voice is deeper because their larynx enlarges more. Testosterone also encourages muscle growth, and so men generally have larger muscles than women. Lastly, testosterone fosters the growth of hair over a wide range of the body: Men typically have hairier arms,

secular trend the trend to mature sexually at earlier ages.

legs, chests, and backs than women. Paradoxically, testosterone causes the hairline on the forehead to recede, leaving men with a more exposed forehead than women. Since adolescent females do have testosterone in their systems, they experience increased bone and muscle growth and become more hairy but to a lesser degree than adolescent males.

Conversely, a high estrogen level causes girls' bodies to become more feminine. Most obviously, estrogen encourages breast development and prompts the body to lay down a layer of *subcutaneous* ("under the skin") fat. In addition, girls' hips widen to facilitate childbirth.

Internally and thus invisibly, there are other changes, too. Men's heart and lungs are relatively larger for their body size than women's. Thus, men tend to have higher blood pressure measures and a higher **basal metabolic rate.** Their blood contains more oxygen-carrying hemoglobin. Men have relatively more "fast-twitch" muscle fibers than women— the muscle cells that are strong but that do not sustain their contraction as long. Women have relatively more "slow-twitch" fibers—the muscle cells that contract with less initial force but that can sustain their pull.

ANSWERS WOULDN'T YOU LIKE TO KNOW . . .

Besides the obvious, what are the differences between males' and females' bodies?

By the end of middle adolescence, it's not just the genitals that are different anymore. Girls' bodies are smaller, less boney, less muscular, and less hair covered than male bodies. Girls also have developed breasts and wide hips, whereas boys have developed broad shoulders.

Together, these differences make it likely that late-adolescent boys and mature men will be stronger than women. (Of course, due to genetic variations and factors such as exercise, some women are stronger than some men.) Mature male bodies are designed for quick bursts of strength and energy; they can take in and carry more oxygen, utilize it more quickly, and fuel their large muscles. On the other hand, women's bodies are built for the "long haul." Female endocrinology lessens their risk of heart attack, arteriosclerosis, and stroke.

basal metabolic rate the speed at which the body burns calories when at rest.

SUMMARY

1. Adolescence is a period of sexual maturation and physical growth. The changes that occur prepare the body for reproduction and cause female and male children's bodies (which are quite similar except for the reproductive organs) to become distinctly different from each other.
2. Puberty is triggered by changes in the hypothalamus that cause it to signal particular endocrine glands to secrete hormones that stimulate and regulate the growth process.
3. The pituitary gland secretes HGH, the gonadotropic hormones FSH and LH, and LTH. FSH and LH stimulate the growth of egg cells in the ovaries, sperm in the testes, and the sex hormones. HGH affects the growth and shaping of the skeleton.
4. The ovaries secrete the hormones estrogen and progesterone. Estrogen stimulates the development of female sex characteristics and progesterone regulates the menstrual cycle and acts on the breasts.
5. The testes secrete the male hormone testosterone, which stimulates the development of male characteristics.
6. The adrenal glands secrete both androgens and estrogen.
7. The hypothalamus secretes GnRH, which controls the secretion of LH and FSH by the pituitary.
8. The level of testosterone and estrogen is regulated by negative feedback of these hormones, which tells the hypothalamus and gonads when enough of the hormones has been secreted.
9. Numerous changes occur in the male sex organs at puberty. The testes, scrotum, penis, prostate glands, and Cowper's glands enlarge. The testes increase the production of testosterone and begin the production of mature sperm (spermatogenesis).
10. Once boys become teenagers, it is quite normal for them to have nocturnal emissions, or spontaneous ejaculations while they sleep at night.
11. Numerous changes occur in the female sex organs. The vagina, labia, clitoris, uterus, and Bartholin's glands enlarge and mature. The ovaries increase the secretion of estrogen and progesterone and begin the production of mature ova.
12. Most girls begin to menstruate early in adolescence. The menstrual cycle is controlled by rising and ebbing hormonal levels. FSH and estrogen levels are higher in the first half of the monthly cycle; later, a surge of LH causes the progesterone level to rise as the FSH and estrogen levels drop off.
13. It is important for parents to provide good information about menstruation to their daughters before they get their period. Doing so will alleviate anxiety and helps girls develop a good attitude about their maturing body. Positive attitudes about menstruation are associated with having fewer menstrual problems, as well.
14. Sexual maturation at puberty also includes the development of secondary sexual characteristics: in men, the appearance of pubic hair, the height spurt, voice changes, muscular development, and the growth of axillary hair, including the beard; in women, the

appearance of pubic hair, breasts, and a more rounded female figure. Boys and girls can become self-conscious about their development, especially if they do not believe their growth is normal.

15. One of the most obvious physical changes of adolescence is the growth spurt that begins in early adolescence. The growth in height is accompanied by changes in body proportion. Both heredity and environmental factors determine the total mature height achieved. Generally, the earlier sexual maturation occurs, the sooner the growth spurt slows down and stops. Girls usually begin their growth spurt about two years earlier than boys.
16. Both boys and girls today are maturing at younger ages than did those of previous generations. This secular trend is due primarily to better nutrition and health care.
17. Testosterone causes many changes in physique in both boys and girls, encouraging bone, muscle, and hair growth. In girls, estrogen promotes breast development and development of a layer of subcutaneous fat.

KEY TERMS

adrenal glands 78
anabolic steroids 81
androgens 77
anovulatory 85
antiprostaglandins 86
Bartholin's glands 82
basal metabolic rate 92
clitoris 82
corpus luteum 77
Cowper's glands 81
endocrine glands 76
epididymis 80
estrogens 77
fallopian tubes 82
follicle-stimulating hormone (FSH) 77
gonadotropic hormones 77
gonadotropin-releasing hormone (GnRH) 76
gonads 77
gynecomastia 88
hormones 76
human growth hormone (HGH) 77
hymen 82
hypothalamus 76
inhibin 78
labia majora 82
labia minora 82
leptin 88
luteinizing hormone (LH) 77
menarche 82
mons veneris 82
nocturnal emissions 82
osteoporosis 86
ovaries 77
penis 80
pituitary gland 76
progesterone 77
prostaglandins 86
prostate glands 80
scrotum 80
secondary sexual characteristics 87
secular trend 91
semenarche or spermarche 82
seminal vesicles 80
Sertoli cells 78
spermatogenesis 78
testes 77
testosterone 77
urethra 80
uterus 82
vagina 82
vas deferens 80
vestibule 82
vulva 82

THOUGHT QUESTIONS

Personal Reflection

1. To men: When you had your first nocturnal emission, did you understand what was happening? Were you prepared for it? How did you feel? With whom did you discuss it?
2. To women: When you first started to menstruate, did you understand what was happening? Were you prepared for it? How did you feel? With whom did you discuss it?
3. When did you first become self-conscious about your body? Was it timed with the onset of puberty?
4. When you were an adolescent, were you shorter or taller than your classmates? How did you feel? Explain.

Group Discussion

5. Explain why withdrawal is not a safe method of birth control, taking into account the action of the Cowper's glands.
6. Explain why there is no completely safe period of the month when a woman cannot get pregnant.
7. Why don't some female athletes menstruate?
8. Comment on the attitudes in U.S. society toward female breasts. What effect do these attitudes have on adolescent girls? Boys?

Debate Questions

9. Should female and male athletes be allowed to take testosterone to improve their abilities? What might be some of the effects?
10. All newborn male babies should be circumcised for health reasons.
11. Would it be a good or a bad idea for families to more formally celebrate an adolescent's menarche or first ejaculation?
12. Should schools be required to educate students about the physical changes that will accompany puberty before these changes happen?

SUGGESTED READING

Bancroft, J., and Reinisch, J. M. (Eds.). (1990). *Adolescence and Puberty.* New York: Oxford University Press.

Heffner, L. J., and Schust, D. J. (2006). *The Reproductive System at a Glance.* Oxford, UK: Blackwell.

Kipke, M. D. (1999). *Adolescent Development and the Biology of Puberty: Summary of a Workshop on New Research.* Washington, DC: National Academy Press.

Martin, K. (1996). *Puberty, Sexuality and the Self: Girls and Boys at Adolescence.* New York: Routledge.

Plant, T. M., and Lee, P. A. (Eds.). (1995). *The Neurobiology of Puberty.* Malden, MA: Blackwell Science.

Seiffge-Krenke, I. (1998). *Adolescents' Health: A Developmental Perspective.* Mahwah, NJ: Erlbaum.

CHAPTER 5 BODY ISSUES

Health-Related Behaviors and Attitudes

WOULDN'T YOU LIKE TO KNOW . . .

- How healthy are adolescents?
- Why don't adolescents take better care of themselves?
- Are most adolescents happy with their bodies?
- Do most teens think they are fat?
- Is it hard to reach puberty earlier or later than everyone else?
- Why are more and more teens obese?
- What types of teens are at risk for developing anorexia?
- What kinds of foods should adolescents eat?
- Why can't you and your friends stay awake during 8 o'clock classes?

Adolescence is intrinsically a very healthy time of life. By the time we have reached the teenage years, we have passed through the fragile, vulnerable stages of infancy and early childhood but not yet developed the debilitating, chronic health concerns of older adulthood. Health not only comes from our physiology but also from the health-related behavioral choices that we make.

The choices we make during adolescence are crucially important. For one, it is choosing good behaviors that primarily determines our physical well-being during adolescence. In addition, many of the habits that we establish during adolescence linger into adulthood and help determine our health for the rest of our lives. Since many of these choices depend on and reflect adolescents' attitudes about their bodies, in this chapter we will not only describe the kinds of choices that adolescents make but also discuss teenagers' perceptions of their bodies and health needs.

HEALTH STATUS

Mortality

One of the most common ways to understand health concerns is to examine **mortality** or death rates. The *number* of deaths tells us how relatively healthy a certain group is, and the *causes* of death tell us where the most significant problems lie. Figure 5.1 shows the death rates of American children, adolescents, and adults. As you can see, the rate for younger adolescents (ages 10 to 14) is very low, but the rate for older adolescents (ages 15 to 19), while still less that those of the adults, is quite a bit higher (Centers for Disease Control, 2006).

The reason for this rise can be inferred from Figure 5.2, which depicts the leading causes of death of American adolescents. The single most common reason that adolescents die is because they are involved in car accidents. (Note, however, that adolescents who wear seatbelts and drive only when sober are much less likely to die or be seriously injured in motor vehicle accidents.) About three-fourths of adolescent deaths are due to nonmedical reasons: Accidents, taken together, account for just about half of the deaths, and violence (homicide and suicide) accounts for about one-fourth (Centers for Disease Control, 2005). This pattern is a change from the past, when most adolescent deaths were due to natural causes (Ozer, Park, Paul, Brindis, & Irwin, 2003). Older adolescents are more likely to die from both accidents and violence than younger adolescents; hence, their increased mortality rate. Males, who are more likely to be violent and to take risks, are more likely to die than females. Remember, too, that accidents and violence can result in injury and disability as well as death and so greatly contribute to the health concerns of living adolescents.

Health Decisions

Every day, each of us makes decisions that affect our health. We can make good decisions, such as following a healthy diet, exercising regularly, keeping medical appointments, and getting adequate sleep. Or we can make bad decisions and engage in risky behaviors, such as using drugs, practicing unsafe sex, and performing thrilling but risky stunts. The health decisions adolescents make result from a complex interplay of factors:

FIGURE 5.1 DEATH RATES OVER THE LIFESPAN

Source: Data from Centers for Disease Control (2006).

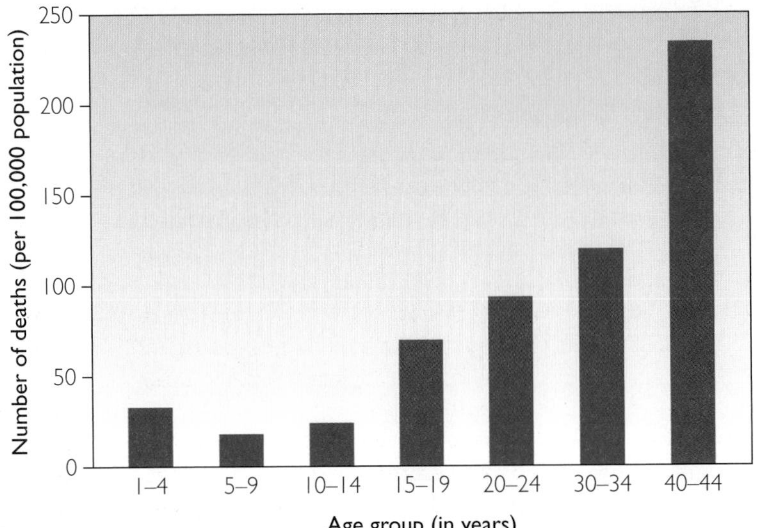

FIGURE 5.2 LEADING CAUSES OF DEATH OF AMERICAN ADOLESCENTS

Source: Data from Centers for Disease Control (2005).

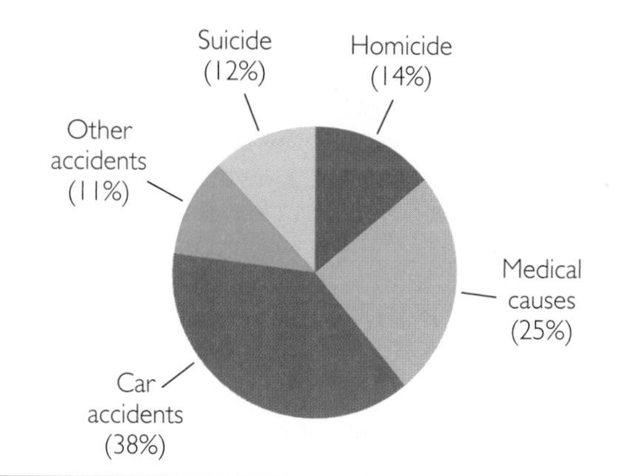

ANSWERS WOULDN'T YOU LIKE TO KNOW . . .

How healthy are adolescents?

Adolescents are not as healthy as they could be, since many of them put themselves in situations that increase their health risks. The majority of the serious health problems that teenagers face are preventable.

1. *Their own knowledge of the health consequences of particular behaviors.* This knowledge is, of course, based on what parents, peers, doctors, and teachers have taught teens, as well as the messages they have received from the media and society at large.

mortality rate the probability of dying.

RESEARCH HIGHLIGHT IMPROVING ADOLESCENT HEALTH

Can we improve the overall health level of American adolescents? The U.S. government is trying to do just that as part of its *Healthy People 2010* initiative. The Centers for Disease Control have identified 21 critical health objectives for adolescents and young adults (Centers for Disease Control, 2004). The specific targets include reducing adolescent deaths, especially those caused by car accidents, homicides, and suicides; reducing adolescent substance abuse; decreasing the numbers of adolescents who have sexually transmitted diseases or who are involved in pregnancies; and increasing adolescent fitness levels.

What is especially interesting about the government's approach is that the government has acknowledged that poor health is a multifaceted phenomenon, stemming from multiple sources. In particular, government scientists identified nine societal institutions that affect adolescent health and recommended using all of these institutions to enact positive change.

1. *Families:* Reducing poverty, reducing access to guns in the household, having parents model good health behaviors and monitor their adolescents more closely could all have positive impacts upon adolescents' health.
2. *Schools:* Enhancing physical education, maintaining clean and safe buildings, serving nutritious foods, and providing students with accurate health-related information could make a difference.
3. *Colleges and universities:* College students, too, do not always have the most healthful lifestyles. They frequently drink to excess, do not get enough sleep, and engage in unsafe sexual practices.
4. *Health-care providers:* Adolescent access to health care could be improved by making medical insurance more affordable, easing fears about confidentiality so that adolescents will come in for treatment, enhancing preventative interventions, and making services physically accessible to teenagers.
5. *Community organizations:* Service to adolescents would be enhanced if services were affordable, convenient, culturally sensitive, and compassionate.
6. *Faith-based organizations:* In particular, these groups can help individuals from outside the community link with and gain the trust of community members.
7. *The media:* It would be beneficial if television and other media promoted healthy lifestyles and did not glamorize dangerous, risky behaviors.
8. *Employers:* Since long work hours are associated with poor health outcomes in teenagers, employers can limit the amount of time that they will allow any individual adolescent to work each week.
9. *Government agencies:* These groups develop policies, provide funding, and implement programs that can help efforts to improve adolescent health.

As this model illustrates, many of the avenues to improving adolescent health are indirect. Namely, creating safer communities, decreasing poverty, believing in the chance for a good life, having increased knowledge and decision-making skills, feeling connected to others, and gaining access to adequate services all lead to improved health by enhancing the overall quality of adolescents' lives. These same kinds of interventions can also serve to reduce levels of delinquency, school dropout, and pregnancy among teens.

2. *Their own abilities to judge risks and make rational decisions.* Cognitive development is taken up in later chapters of this book, but it is important to state here that adolescents' abilities to think abstractly, to appreciate the long-term consequences of actions, to evaluate information, and to weigh personal risk are not fully developed.
3. *Their parents' behaviors.* Adolescents mimic their mothers' and fathers' actions and values. So if parents are unconcerned about their own health, then their adolescents are likely to be lackadaisical, as well. Another factor is that parents who closely monitor and supervise their children do not give them as much opportunity to engage in dangerous behaviors.
4. *The resources available to teens and their families.* Some families may have the desire to lead a healthy lifestyle but not the means. For instance, some families have no choice but to live in a dangerous, polluted, or violent neighborhood. Likewise, some cannot afford to get regular medical and dental checkups.
5. *Peer pressure.* Peers can convince each other to be sexually active, to drink alcohol or use drugs, or to do something dangerous, like swim where there is a strong current. Conversely, peers can encourage each other to use condoms, to avoid drugs, and to participate in sports or exercise.
6. *Societal values.* Adolescents receive messages that it's important, for instance, to be slender and that it's cool to smoke and drink. The images they see on television and in movies and the advertisements directed at them in magazines and other media often encourage less than ideal health behaviors.

ANSWERS WOULDN'T YOU LIKE TO KNOW . . .

Why don't adolescents take better care of themselves?

Adolescents are often oblivious to the risks of extreme dieting, driving without wearing a seatbelt, and using drugs. They feel personally invulnerable, finding it hard to believe that anything bad will happen to them. Moreover, some of the risks they face are simply too far in the future for them to worry about. Finally, parents and friends often encourage poor health habits, as do the mass media. The fact that popular singers and actors are often shown drinking alcohol and smoking doesn't help, either.

Adolescent Health in the Third World

The health issues facing adolescents living in the less developed parts of the world are quite different than those confronting American teenagers (Call, Aylin, Hein, McLoyd, Petersen, & Kipke, 2002). Some of the problems of Third World teens stem directly from poverty and political instability. For example, adolescents in much of Asia, Africa, and Latin America are more likely to be malnourished and to contract illnesses than American youths. In many parts of the world, where political instability is the reality, war and terrorism take their toll on lives and health and disrupt the government's ability to provide needed health services. In addition, numerous children and adolescents in sub–Saharan Africa are infected with the human immunodeficiency virus (HIV) that leads to AIDS (acquired immune deficiency syndrome). Countless more have been left orphans because their parents have succumbed to this disease.

Other negative health consequences can be attributed to Westernization and rapid cultural change. For example, Third World youths today are smoking in greater and greater numbers. This is due, in good part, to the fact that American tobacco companies, which are facing ever greater restrictions in the United States, are increasingly turning their marketing efforts overseas (Verma and Saraswathi, 2002). And as sexual values change, adolescents from Southeast Asia, China, the Indian subcontinent, Latin American, and Africa (not to mention North America and Europe) are engaging in more nonmarital sex and beginning at earlier ages (Brown, Larson, and Saraswathi, 2002). This has greatly increased the likelihood that these teens will develop sexually transmitted infections.

BODY IMAGE

The health-related choices that adolescents make are linked to the way they feel about themselves. Those who feel good about themselves are likely to avoid harmful behaviors, whereas those who do not, will not. Unfortunately, during adolescence, a large part of our self-esteem is tied up with how physically attractive we feel. Even more unfortunately, the standards we measure ourselves against are often unreasonably high. The following discussion focuses on adolescents' concept of physical attractiveness and their feelings about their own bodies.

Physical Attractiveness

Physical attractiveness and body image have an important relationship to the adolescent's positive self-evaluation, popularity, and peer acceptance

(Davison and McCabe, 2006). Physical attractiveness influences personality development, social relationships, and social behavior. Attractive adolescents are generally thought of in positive terms: warm, friendly, successful, and intelligent (Langlois, Kalakanis, Rubenstein, Larson, Hallam, and Smoot, 2000; Zebrowitz, Hall, Murphy, and Rhodes, 2002).

Partly as a result of differential treatment, attractive adolescents appear to have higher self-esteem and healthy personality attributes, are better adjusted socially, and possess a wider variety of interpersonal skills (Perkins and Lerner, 1995). Physical attractiveness is significantly related to the self-esteem of both males and females (Frost and McKelvie, 2004). Research has shown that adolescents who are ranked as physically attractive are also rated by teachers and by themselves as having better peer and parent relations than adolescents who are not considered as attractive (Lerner et al., 1991). Research has also shown that physical appearance affects girls' self-esteem more than boys' (Williams and Currie, 2000) and affects girls' social status more, as well.

Body Types and Ideals

Three body types have been identified: ectomorph, endomorph and mesomorph. Most people are a mixture rather than a pure type, but identifying the pure types helps considerably in any discussion of general body build.**Ectomorphs** are tall, long, thin, and narrow, with a slender, bony, lanky build.**Endomorphs** are at the other extreme, with soft, round, thick, heavy trunks and limbs and a wrestler-type build.**Mesomorphs** fall between these two types. They have square, strong, well-muscled bodies, with medium-length limbs and wide shoulders. They represent an athletic type of build and participate in strenuous physical activity more frequently than the other types.

The vast majority of Caucasian adolescent girls are dissatisfied with their bodies and would like to be ectomorphic (Button, Loan, Davies, and Sonuga-Barke, 1997; Gardner, Friedman, and Jackson, 1999). This feeling of dissatisfaction becomes more and more pronounced over the course of adolescence (Rosenblum and Lewis, 1999). Most researchers agree that the media is largely responsible for girls' desire to be slender (Levine and Harrison, 2004). The women portrayed as desirable in movies, television programs, television commercials, and magazines are uniformly tall, narrow, and small waisted. Incessant exposure to these images sends a clear message to girls and women: If you wish to be considered pretty, you must be thin. One study, for example, showed that after even a *brief* exposure to models with ideally slim physiques, subjects displayed increased body dissatisfaction (Thornton and Maurice, 1997). Thus, the cumulative effect of hundreds of hours of viewing can be pervasive and powerful.

ectomorph tall, slender body build.

endomorph short, heavy body build.

mesomorph medium, athletic body build.

Adolescents come in all shapes and sizes. The girl at the far left is a muscular mesomorph, while the boy at the far right is endomorphic. Standing next to him is a tall, slender, ectomorphic girl.

PERSONAL ISSUES PLASTIC SURGERY AMONG ADOLESCENTS

During the 1990s, it became more common for adolescents who were unhappy with their bodies to resort to the most extreme measure to correct their "flaws": plastic surgery. More than 223,000 adolescents aged 18 years or younger underwent cosmetic or reconstructive surgery in 2003. The most common procedure, accounting for about one-half of all operations, was *rhinoplasty,* or nose reshaping. Breast reduction was also popular; more than 16,000 teens—3,000 of them boys—had their breasts surgically reduced that year. Breast augmentation, surgery to correct protruding ears, and liposuction to reduce fat deposits accounted for most of the rest of the procedures. Adolescents now represent about 4 percent of all cosmetic surgery patients (American Society of Plastic Surgeons, 2004; Zuckerman, 2005).

The American Society of Plastic Surgeons recommends that such procedures be limited to adolescents who initiate the requests (that is, who are not being pushed into an operation by their parents), who have realistic goals and expectations, and who are sufficiently mature to handle the initial discomfort and disfigurement associated with surgery (Plastic Surgery Information Service, 2000b).

Adolescents who desire plastic surgery need to understand that changing one's appearance is not a quick fix for becoming popular, enjoying athletic success, or regaining a lost boyfriend or girlfriend. The physical changes are permanent, the procedures are costly, and there is a risk of complications or unsatisfactory results. A far better solution, in most cases, is to encourage self-confidence based on the sum of the individual's positive traits and to discourage the fixation on physical perfection.

Dissatisfaction with one's body spills over into dissatisfaction with one's self, especially for girls. In other words, girls who perceive themselves as being overweight have lower self-esteem than other girls (Guiney and Furlong, 1999) and are also more likely to feel depressed (Siegel, 2002). In fact, Siegel, Yancy, Aneshensel, and Schuler (1999) found that poor body image was the main reason adolescent girls in their study were more depressed than adolescent boys. This lowered sense of self-esteem may result, in part, from the fact that overweight individuals enjoy less satisfactory interactions with peers. Teenage girls certainly fear that they will be less attractive to boys, and less likely to date, if they are overweight. Interestingly, although teenage boys agree that a thin shape is more desirable in a girl than a plump one, thin girls are no more likely to date than heavier ones (Paxton, Norris, Wertheim, Durkin, and Anderson, 2005).

Furthermore, research suggests that appearance anxiety in women is related to negative social experiences in childhood and early adolescence. For example, studies have found that weight-related teasing by parents and peers increases a youth's body dissatisfaction (Barker and Galambos, 2003; Paxton, Schultz, Wertheim, and Muir, 1999). This dissatisfaction is, in turn, related to appearance anxiety in late adolescence and early adulthood (Keelan, Dion, and Dion, 1992).

Body dissatisfaction among adolescent girls varies along racial and ethnic lines. African American females are less likely than girls of other races and ethnicities to judge themselves as being overweight (White, Kohlmaier, Varnado-Sullivan, and Williamson, 2003). Caucasian girls are quite dissatisfied with their body shapes, but Asian American and Hispanic American girls are more so. In particular, even very lean Hispanic and Asian American females are apt to be unhappy with their weight and wish they were smaller (Robinson, Killen, Litt, and Hammer, 1996).

ANSWERS WOULDN'T YOU LIKE TO KNOW . . .

Are most adolescents happy with their bodies?

Most adolescents are not especially happy with their bodies. This is especially true of late-adolescent Caucasian, Latino, and Asian girls.

In contrast, boys are most likely to prefer having a mesomorphic body type (Ricciardelli and McCabe, 2004). In contrast to girls, generally only heavy adolescent boys feel that they are overweight (Field et al., 1999). Body dissatisfaction in more slender boys instead results from a lack of sufficient muscularity (Carlson Jones and Crawford, 2005). Tall men with good builds are considered more attractive than short men, and boys who are short or heavy are subjected to stigmatization and other psychosocial stressors (Barker and Galambos, 2003; Sandberg, 1999). Men with muscular, mesomorphic body builds are more socially accepted than those with different builds.

Adolescent males tend to feel better and better about their bodies as they move through adolescence (Allgood-Merten, Lewinsohn, and Hops, 1990), whereas adolescent females do not (Richards, Boxer, Petersen, and Albrecht, 1990). Therefore, not only are boys more satisfied with their bodies than girls during early adolescence (Rosenblum and Lewis, 1999), but these differences are even greater during late adolescence (Pritchard, King, and Czajka-Narins, 1997).

Media images of excessively slender women encourage adolescent girls to be overly critical of and dissatisfied with their own weight.

ANSWERS WOULDN'T YOU LIKE TO KNOW ...

Do most teens think they are fat?

Adolescent girls tend to think that they are fat because their ideal is to be extremely slender. Adolescent boys are more divided about feeling too fat or too thin; their preference is to be lean but athletic.

EARLY AND LATE MATURATION

As noted in the previous chapter, there is a great deal of variation in the age at which adolescents undergo puberty. Figure 5.3 further illustrates this point. The timing with which an adolescent experiences the physical changes of puberty can have a profound effect on how he or she feels about his or her body and self. For good or ill, it can also affect how others treat him or her and the expectations that they have of him or her. This is especially true for someone who is either earlier or later than average. Much research has been devoted to understanding the effects of the timing of puberty on adolescents' self-esteem and behavior, including health-related behavior.

Early-Maturing Boys

There has been a long-standing belief, based on older data, that early maturation is a positive experience for boys (Ge, Conger, and Elder, 2001). It seems logical that this would be the case. After all, early-maturing boys are large for their age, stronger, more muscular, and better coordinated than later-maturing boys, so they enjoy a considerable athletic advantage. Early-maturing boys are better able to excel in competitive sports and their athletic skills enhance their social prestige and position. They enjoy considerable social advantages in relation to their peers, participate more frequently in extracurricular activities in high school, and are often chosen for leadership roles. Early-maturing boys also tend to show more interest in girls and to be popular with them because of superior looks and more sophisticated social interests and skills. Early sexual maturation thrusts them into heterosexual relationships at an early age.

Data highlight the fact that some early-maturing boys cannot handle the freedom they are granted. Because they are less closely supervised by their parents and tend to associate more with older peers, early-maturing boys are more likely than others to engage in delinquent acts (Dubas, Garber, and Pedersen, 1991), to use drugs and alcohol (Wichstrøm, 2001), and to exhibit a broad range of psychopathological symptoms (Graber, Lewinsohn, Seeley, and Brooks-Gunn, 1997). These problems seem most likely to appear when the boys are experiencing detectable stressors in their lives. These problems by no means affect all early maturers, but they are common enough to raise the group average above that of later-developing males.

Late-Maturing Boys

Late-maturing boys often experience socially induced inferiority. A boy who has not reached puberty at age 15 may be 8 inches shorter and 30 pounds lighter than his early-maturing male friends. Accompanying this size difference are marked differences in body build, strength, and coordination. Because physical size and motor coordination play such an important role in social acceptance, late maturers develop negative self-perceptions and self-concepts (Alsaker, 1992; Richards and Larson, 1993). They are characterized as less attractive and popular; more restless, bossy, and rebellious against parents; and as having feelings of inadequacy, rejection, and dependency. They often become self-conscious and some withdraw because of their social rejection.

Late maturers sometimes overcompensate by becoming overly eager for status and attention. At other

FIGURE 5.3 VARIATIONS IN PUBESCENT DEVELOPMENT
All three girls are 12¾ years and all three boys are 14¾ years of age but in different stages of puberty.

Source: Adapted from J. M. Tanner, *Scientific American* (Sept. 1973): 38.

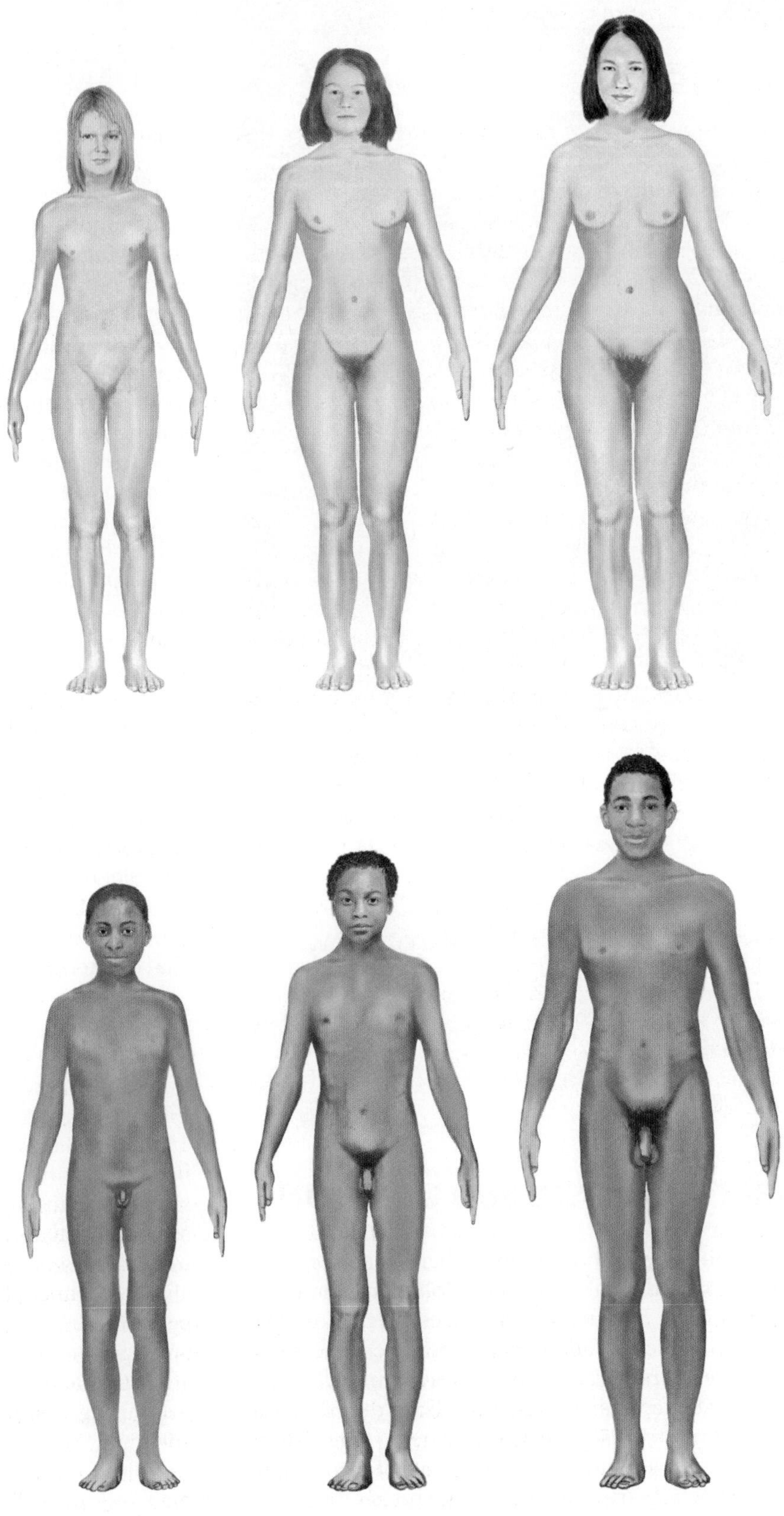

times, they try to make up for their inadequacies by belittling, attacking, or ridiculing others or by using attention-getting devices. An example would be the loud, daring show-off with a chip on his shoulder, ready to fight at the least provocation.

Early-Maturing Girls

Early maturation is not as positive an experience for female adolescents as for male adolescents (Graber, Petersen, and Brooks-Gunn, 1996). Since girls usually reach puberty about two years before boys, the earliest-maturing girls are considerably out of step with their peers. Because they are taller and more developed sexually, they tend to feel awkward and self-conscious. Early maturers are also *heavier* than their friends, which, as discussed in an earlier section, is perceived negatively by most female adolescents. Being so different from their peers adversely affects these girls' self-esteem (Alsaker, 1992).

Given these stresses and the fact that early-maturing girls are more likely to hang around with older boys, they are at increased risk for a variety of problems. Early-maturing females are more likely to experience internalizing disorders, such as anxiety and depression (Graber, Lewinsohn, Seeley, and Brooks-Gunn, 1997; Hayward, Killen, Wilson, and Hammer, 1997). They are also more likely to be disruptive in school (Simmons and Blyth, 1987) and to perform delinquent acts (Caspi, Lynam, Moffit, and Silva, 1993). Finally, they are more likely to engage in early sexual behavior (Flannery, Rowe, and Gulley, 1993) and to drink (Tschann, Adler, Irwin, Milstein, Turner, and Kegeles, 1994). As with early-maturing boys, early maturation makes girls susceptible to other stressors in their lives (Ge, Congev, and Elder, 1996).

These effects are not limited to girls in the United States. For example, in a Slovakian study, Prokopcakova (1998) found that early-maturing girls were more likely to drink alcohol, smoke cigarettes, smoke marijuana, and spend more time with boys than their on-time or late-maturing peers.

Late-Maturing Girls

Late-maturing girls are at a distinct social disadvantage in junior high school and high school. They look like little girls and resent being treated as such. They are largely bypassed and overlooked in invitations to boy-girl parties and social events. Girls who experience menarche at ages 14 to 18 are especially late daters. As a consequence, late-maturing girls may be envious of their friends who are better developed. They are generally on the same level with normal-maturing boys and so have much in common with them as friends. However, they avoid large, mixed groups of boys and girls, and their activities reflect the interests of those of younger age groups with whom they spend their time.

ANSWERS WOULDN'T YOU LIKE TO KNOW ...

Is it hard to reach puberty earlier or later than everyone else?

It's easiest to deal with puberty if you are in the middle of the pack. Early maturers may get teased and find themselves in trouble because they often hang out with misbehaving older peers. Late maturers may also get teased and may be excluded by peers because they appear immature and childlike.

One advantage is that late-maturing girls do not experience the sharp criticism of parents and other adults as do girls who develop early. The chief disadvantage seems to be the temporary loss of social status because of their relative physical immaturity.

Off-Time Maturation

Research on the timing of puberty suggests that being *off time* is problematic, whether one is early or late, male or female. This notion has been termed the *deviance hypothesis* (Brooks-Gunn, Petersen, and Eichorn, 1985). While the problems individual adolescents have will differ, depending on the interaction between maturity rate and gender, being out of step with one's peers leads to confusion and stress.

The undesirable behaviors that result from this upset may be superficially similar, but the same activity may be differently motivated for late and early maturers. Williams and Dunlop (1999), who found high delinquency rates in both early- and late-maturing boys, suggest that early maturers are motivated to misbehave when egged on by older peers, whereas late maturers misbehave in order to raise their self-esteem and gain social status. *All* adolescents want to be liked and admired by their peers, and they will engage in compensatory behaviors to ensure their acceptance.

In fact, it might be the presence or lack of acceptance that determines whether or not off-time maturers will have problems. In a recent study, Nadeem and Graham (2005) found that it was the early-maturing boys who were perceived as misfits or victims by peers who got into trouble. Apparently, the combination of being physically developed while at the same time not behaving in a sufficiently "masculine" fashion encouraged peer bullying, and the stress of this bullying provoked problematic behavior. Similarly, the small size of late-maturing boys can make them easy targets for bullies (Olweus, 1991). Off-time maturation may therefore interact with peer acceptance to affect adjustment.

WEIGHT

Obesity

Few adolescents desire to be obese, and even many children are concerned about their weight. For example, Ricciardelli, McCabe, Holt, and Finemore (2003) asked 500 Australian 8- to 11-year olds whether they worried about their weight and whether they had ever dieted to lose weight. The boys' and girls' answers were almost identical: about 45 percent sometimes, often, or always thought about their weight, and virtually the same number had attempted to lose weight by dieting. Almost as many young children report exercising to lose weight (Ricciardelli and McCabe, 2001).

Regardless, adolescent**obesity** is on the rise in the United States: The obesity rate rose significantly between the years of 1999 and 2004 (Ogden, Carroll, Curtin, McDowell, Tubak, and Flegal, 2006). Furthermore, the amount by which adolescents are overweight continues to rise; that is, overweight adolescents weigh more than they used to (Jolliffe, 2004).

As Figure 5.4 shows, teenage obesity rates began climbing rapidly in the mid-1970s. African American girls and Mexican American boys have the highest rates (both above 25 percent), and Caucasian girls and boys have the lowest rates (about 12 percent). Even these rates are too high, however, as they represent a tripling of obesity among teens since the mid-1960s (Ozer, Park, Paul, Brindis, and Irwin, 2003).

As most people know, obesity carries numerous serious health risks, even for children and adolescents. In particular, adolescent obesity is associated with a significantly increased risk for Type 2 diabetes, a disease previously almost unknown in children. Also, overweight adolescents are more likely than their slender peers to develop high blood pressure and have a high cholesterol level, both of which are precursors to heart disease (U.S. Department of Health and Human Services, 2001). In addition, of course, overweight adolescents face social rejection and have lowered self-esteem.

The causes of obesity and the reasons it is becoming more common are complex. In order to understand this health crisis, we need to look (1) within individual adolescents; (2) at their interactions with others; (3) at the environments in which they spend their time; and (4) at broader societal influences.

Personal Contributors to Being Overweight

A number of personal characteristics make individuals more likely to become overweight. These characteristics include their genetic makeup, their motivation to eat excessively, their eating patterns, their preference for high-calorie foods, and their lack of physical activity.

Genetic Contributors to Obesity

Several studies have provided clear evidence for a genetic link to body weight. For example, we know that biological siblings raised in different households are nearly as similar to each other in weight as pairs raised together (Grilo and Pogue-Geile, 1991) and that adopted children are more similar in weight to their biological parents than to their adoptive parents (Stunkard et al., 1986).

Motivation to Eat

Obese individuals often eat for different reasons than their more normal-weight peers. For instance, eating is a greater positive reinforcement for obese people

FIGURE 5.4 TEENAGE OBESITY RATES: 1966 TO 2000

Source: Data from Centers for Disease Control (2006).

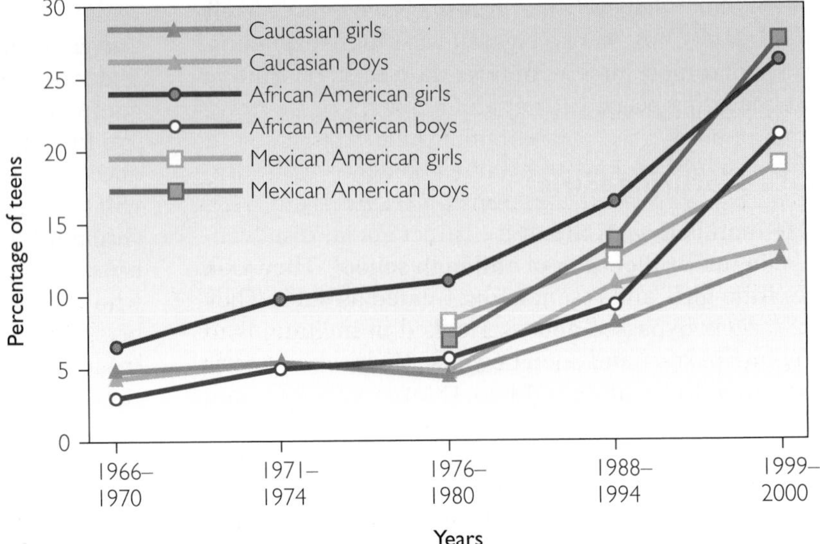

IN THEIR OWN WORDS

"As far as I can remember, my body weight has been tightly connected to my self-esteem. This started while I was in high school. Dieting was something every girl practiced at some time or another. Not eating was something to be proud of! I must say that I was a normal weight, and this was true for all the other girls in my class, but we all thought we were extremely fat. Going to the gym after classes was a must, even though we all hated it.

"There was this notion that as long as you are skinny, you are beautiful. Plus, the boys were constantly making jokes about the overweight girls in school. Well, I do not think that what the boys thought of us was what motivated us the most. What motivated us was the thought that being skinny means being beautiful and sexy. When I was not eating, I was feeling good about myself, and when I ate, I was miserable. There were days when I could not think of anything else but food. If I ate a sandwich, I used to feel guilty and be mad at myself. I had these nightmares about becoming fat and everyone laughing at me.

"I used to buy these magazines with skinny girls in them, and every time I looked at them, even though I was hungry, my appetite disappeared. I wanted to look like them so much! I cannot believe I was so stupid—thinking that being thin would solve all my problems and make me happy.

"Even nowadays, I still watch my weight very closely. I don't think I suffer from an eating disorder, but this feeling of guilt when I eat a piece of pizza is still there. But I've learned to live with it."

because they find it to be a more pleasurable activity than do people of normal weight. Jacobs and Wagner (1984) found that the reinforcement values of spending time with friends and family were higher for obese people than for people of normal weight. For other people, eating is a negative reinforcement of disturbed emotions—that is, it can eliminate anxiety, depression, and upset. Oral activity becomes a means of finding security and release from tension (Heatherton, Herman, and Polivy, 1992).

For still other people, eating becomes a means of punishment. They have poor self-esteem or hate themselves. Weight gain becomes a way of reinforcing their own negative self-conceptions and proving they are right in feeling that way.

Eating Patterns

Since most heavy teens are unhappy with their weight, they frequently try to control their eating. For instance, they may not allow themselves to eat breakfast and have only a small lunch (Keski-Rahkonen, Viken, Kapiro, Rissanen, and Rose, 2004), but then they get so hungry later in the day that they binge and eat late at night. Others frequently snack, even when they are not especially hungry. Some eat rapidly and so consume more food than normal in a set period of time (Marcus and Kalarchian, 2003).

Food Preferences

Most of us have a variety of foods to select from when we are hungry. Those of us who reach for ice cream and potato chips are more likely to gain weight than those who enjoy fruits and other less calorie-laden alternatives. Some of the increase in average adolescent weight can be attributed to increased consumption of fast food. American adolescents now eat in fast-food restaurants almost one day out of every three (Bowman, Gortmaker, Ebbeling, Pereira, and Ludwig, 2004). Research has shown that overweight teens eat more in fast-food restaurants than their more slender counterparts, and that their total calorie intake is greater on days in which they eat at fast-food establishments than on days they do not (Ebbeling, Sinclair, Pereira, Garcia-Lago, Feldman, and Ludwig, 2004).

Lack of Exercise

Adolescents' physical activity and sports participation will be discussed in a later section. Suffice it here to say that doing exercise both burns calories while you are doing it and increases the body's **metabolic rate** (the rate at which it burns calories) for a period of time even after you have finished.

Interpersonal Interactions and Being Overweight

Parents and peers can both influence adolescents' tendency to gain weight.

Family Contributors

Parents greatly influence what foods their children eat and how much they participate in physical activity. For example, parents can insist that the entire family eat dinner together and prepare healthy meals; alternatively, parents can leave their adolescents to fend for themselves, with the result that they live on peanut butter sandwiches, hot dogs, and fast food. Some parents use high-caloric foods as rewards and inadvertently train their children to expect cookies and candy when they have had success. Similarly, parents can

obesity overweight; excessively fat.

metabolic rate the rate at which the body utilizes food and oxygen.

model athletic participation by taking walks or playing tennis with their children, or they can spend their time watching television with them.

Peer Contributors

Peers influence one another's weight, as well. For example, they help set behavioral norms, such that teenagers whose friends participate in sports are more likely to do so, as well. Conversely, teens whose friends hang out at fast-food restaurants or who make snacking a large part of the social scene will be discouraged from maintaining a normal weight.

Environmental Influences

The places in which adolescents find themselves may or may not be conducive to weight gain.

Schools

As mentioned earlier, adolescents spend much of their lives in school. School policies can therefore determine what they eat during those hours. What foods are served at lunch? Are vending machines available? If so, what foods do they contain? Are students allowed to leave the building to eat lunch elsewhere? (If they are, they are likely headed to a fast-food restaurant.) Recently (in 2006), America's largest beverage distributors agreed to halt sales of sodas to elementary and middle schools, and they agreed to sell only diet sodas in high schools. These steps will help ensure that younger adolescents drink more water, juice, and low-fat milk and will likely reduce high schoolers' sugar consumption.

School policies can also promote students' physical activity levels. For example, they encourage students who live within a close radius to the school to walk by discontinuing bus service. Alternatively, they can ensure that students must regularly enroll in physical education classes that make them sweat.

Community

Communities can also encourage or discourage obesity. Do they provide parks and rec centers? Do they offer public basketball courts? Are these facilities open for extensive hours? Are there sidewalks, which encourage walking, and bike paths, which encourage riding?

Broader Social Influences

Obesity has increased, in part, because food (and especially calorie-dense food) is far more available than in the past. In addition, we can now buy foods that are already or almost entirely prepared and ready for consumption, and this convenience encourages impulsive eating. What's more, the portion sizes served in restaurants have increased enormously (Nielsen and Popkin, 2003).

Lack of activity is also an issue. Adolescents today spend more time in front of the TV and computer monitor than they did in the past, burning relatively fewer calories as they do. We have also become more and more dependent on automobiles to take us where we wish to go and as a result spend less time walking.

> **ANSWERS WOULDN'T YOU LIKE TO KNOW ...**
>
> Why are more and more teens obese?
>
> Ever greater numbers of teens are obese, in part, because not only is junk food more available (even in school and at home), but it also comes packaged in larger portions. In addition, adolescents get less exercise than they did in the past because they spend more time sitting in front of the television, playing video games, and visiting chat rooms.

EATING DISORDERS

Due to societal stereotypes of physical attractiveness, most adolescent girls desire to be slim. In fact, it has become the norm for adolescent girls to begin dieting in early adolescence (Tyrka, Graber, and Brooks-Gunn, 2000). Sometimes the desire to be thin is carried to such an extreme that an eating disorder develops. No longer a rarity, eating disorders are the third most common type of chronic illness among adolescent girls (Rosen, 2003). Two such disorders are discussed here: anorexia nervosa and bulimia.

Anorexia Nervosa

Anorexia nervosa is a life-threatening emotional disorder characterized by an obsession with food and weight. It is sometimes referred to as the *starvation sickness* or *dieter's disease.*

In order to be diagnosed as anorexic, an individual must be at least 15 percent under normal body weight for his or her height and build. In addition, an individual must show an excessive fear of gaining weight and becoming fat and have a distorted body image such that he or she does not perceive himself or herself as being underweight. Furthermore, a female must experience *amenorrhea,* or the absence of menstrual cycling (American Psychiatric Association, 2000). It is not uncommon for anorexics to be clinically depressed (Kennedy, Kaplan, Garfinkel, Rockert, Toner, and Abbey, 1994) and to exhibit obsessive-compulsive traits (Fisher, Fornari, Waldbaum, and Gold, 2002). Some anorexics also engage in binging and purging behaviors.

ANSWERS WOULDN'T YOU LIKE TO KNOW . . .

What types of teens are at risk for developing anorexia?

Early adolescent Caucasian girls who are perfectionists and who have controlling, overly protective parents are at the highest risk for developing anorexia.

Anorexia is also associated with numerous medical conditions: slow heartbeat, cardiac arrest (a frequent cause of death), low blood pressure, dehydration, hypothermia, electrolyte abnormalities, metabolic changes, constipation, and abdominal distress (Becker, Grinspoon, Klibanski, and Herzog, 1999). Once the illness has progressed, anorexics become thin and emaciated in appearance. They feel cold, even in warm weather. The body grows fine silky hair to conserve body heat. A potassium deficiency may cause malfunction of the kidneys. Researchers have also found brain abnormalities coupled with impaired mental performance and lessened reaction time and perception speed due to malnutrition.

Although some anorexics have only one bout with the disorder, between 30 and 40 percent relapse (Herzog et al., 1999). Ultimately, more than 10 percent of anorexics die because of medical problems associated with malnutrition (Nye and Johnson, 1999; Reijonen, Pratt, Patel, and Greydanus, 2003). Their obsession with dieting is combined with a compulsion to exercise, which leads to social isolation and withdrawal from family and friends (Davis, 1999). Hunger and fatigue are usually denied, and any attempt to interfere with the regime is angrily resisted. Anorexics are very difficult to treat (Woodside, 2005).

Anorexia is less common among African American than Caucasian girls, even though African American girls tend to be heavier (Henriques, Calhoun, and Cann, 1996; Walcott, Pratt, and Patel, 2003). Anorexia is also much less common in males. Those males who do develop the disorder are often athletes, dancers, or models who must control their weight (Rolls, Federoff, and Guthrie, 1991). Wrestlers, body builders, and long-distance runners are especially at risk (Garner, Rosen, and Barry, 1998). Some 95 percent of anorexics are female, usually between the ages of 12 to 18. The disorder has become more common and now affects about 1 percent of all adolescent females (Dolan, 1994). It occurs among individuals from all economic classes and a wide variety of age groups.

Much of the recent research into the cause of anorexia has focused on anorexics' relationships with their families. Families with anorexic daughters are often described as noncohesive and unsupportive (Tyrka, Graber, and Brooks-Gunn, 2000). They raise their daughters to be excessively full of feelings of guilt (Berghold and Lock, 2002), and mothers transfer their own concerns about weight and attractiveness to their daughters (Hirokane, Tokomura, Nanri, Kimura, and Saito, 2005). In other words, girls are more likely to diet if their mothers do as well, and they are more likely to engage in extreme weight-loss measures if their mothers are dissatisfied with their own bodies (Benedikt, Wertheim, and Love, 1998; Hill and Pallin, 1998). Eating disorders have also been linked to sexual abuse (Fornari and Dancyger, 2003).

Some of this research is longitudinal, and so it is possible to say that impaired family relationships are a strong predictor of disordered eating symptoms—stronger even than weight (Archibald, Graber, and Brooks-Gunn, 1999). This effect holds true in early adolescence but not in middle and late adolescence (Archibald, Linver, Graber, and Brooks-Gunn, 2002).

The fact that anorexia nervosa appears at puberty after the development of sexual characteristics suggests that sexual conflict is a central issue in the illness. Apparently, anxiety develops over feminine physiological changes. The girl's developing body symbolically demands coming to terms with her female sexual identification. She has the task of integrating her new body image with her concept of female sexual roles. If she cannot accept her female sexual identity, she seeks to repress her physical development to a stage of prepubertal development. She then actually distorts her body image through extreme weight loss and takes on a slim, masculine appearance. She may become severely emaciated in appearance, removing all outward signs of her secondary sex characteristics. In addition, she stops menstruating. These efforts represent the youth's desperate attempt to halt her sexual development. Instead of progressing forward through adolescence, she regresses to a prepubertal stage of development.

Anorexics have a pervasive sense of inadequacy and distorted body images that often lead to depression. They have low self-esteem and high anxiety (Button, 1990), reflecting negative attitudes about physical attractiveness (Canals, Carbajo, Fernandez, Marti-Henneberg, and Domenech, 1996). Anorexics are often described as compliant, self-doubting, dependent, perfectionistic, and anxious (McVey, Pepler, Davis, Flett, and Abdolell, 2002; Nye and Johnson, 1999). They are not very attuned to their body's internal signals of hunger (Wonderlich, Lilenfeld, Riso, Engel, and Mitchell, 2005). Adolescents with anorexia nervosa rarely look at themselves and, even when forced to, rarely perceive their body images

anorexia nervosa an eating disorder characterized by an obsession with food and with being thin.

accurately. They view their bodies with disgust, which is a projection of how they actually feel about themselves.

What are the various forms of treatment for anorexia nervosa? Medical treatment monitors the physical condition of the anorexic and tries to return her weight to the safe range. Behavior modification uses rewards and deprivation, contingent on eating behavior and weight gain. Family therapy seeks to solve underlying family interaction problems and to improve relationships with the anorexic (Dare, Eisler, Russell, and Szmukler, 1990). Individual counseling can be used to help the individual resolve her emotional conflicts. A recent review found that family therapy was most effective overall (Le Grange and Lock, 2005). The goals are to eliminate the anorexic symptoms and to enable the patient to feel and act as an independent person who likes herself, is confident about her capabilities, and is in control of her life. Accomplishing these goals may require long-term therapy (Lask, Waugh, and Gordo, 1997).

Bulimia

Bulimia is a binge-purge syndrome. The name comes from the Greek *bous limos,* which means "ox hunger" (Ieit, 1985). The first cases of bulimia that appeared in the literature were in connection with anorexia nervosa (Vandereycken, 1994). Some clinicians diagnosed bulimia as a subgroup of anorexia; however, since binge eating occurs in both obese and normal-weight individuals, bulimia is now designated a separate eating disorder (American Psychiatric Association, 2000).

In order to be diagnosed with bulimia, an individual must (1) participate in repeated episodes of binge eating over which he or she has no control; (2) engage in excessive compensatory behaviors to avoid gaining weight, such as fasting, vomiting, and abusing laxatives; and (3) unduly allow his or her weight to influence self-esteem. Moreover, the binging must occur at least twice per week over a period of at least three months (American Psychiatric Association, 2000).

Bulimia is characterized by a compulsive and rapid consumption of large quantities of high-calorie food in a short period of time (Holleran, Pascale, and Fraley, 1988). One study of the frequency and duration of binging episodes among bulimic clients in an outpatient setting revealed an average of 13.7 hours spent in binge eating each week (Mitchell, Pyle, and Eckert, 1981). Binging and purging may occur many times daily. Caloric consumption ranged from 1,200 to 11,500 calories per episode, with carbohydrates as the primary food. Many clients report losing the ability to perceive a sense of fullness. Episodes usually take place secretly, often in the afternoon or evening and sometimes at night. Induced vomiting is the usual aftermath of binge-eating episodes. Bulimics use laxatives, diuretics, enemas, amphetamines, compulsive exercising, or fasting to offset the huge food intake.

Bulimics are unhappy with the appearance of their bodies and yearn to attain the thin shape glamorized by society (Ruuska, Kaltiala-Heino, Rantanen, and Koivisto, 2005). However, they lack control over eating. The bulimic feels driven to consume food and, because of a concern about body size, to purge afterward. Binges usually follow periods of stress and are accompanied by anxiety, depressed mood, and self-deprecating thoughts during and after the episode (Davis and Jamieson, 2005; Wegner, Smyth, Crosby, Wittrock, Wonderlick, and Mitchell, 2002).

Who develops bulimia? It is more common, by far, in girls than boys; only about 10 percent of bulimics are male (Nye and Johnson, 1999). Bulimia tends to develop in mid to late adolescence and last into the twenties, which is a somewhat later age range than anorexia (Reijonen, Pratt, Patel, and Greydanus, 2003). Girls from lower-income families are relatively more likely to develop bulimia than girls from upper-income families (Gard and Freeman, 1996).

Bulimics wish to be perfect, yet they have a poor self-image, have a negative self-worth, are shy, and lack assertiveness (Bardone, Vohs, Abramson, Heatherton, and Joiner, 2000). Like anorexics, they are often perfectionistic and unsatisfied with the way they look. They believe themselves to be unattractive (Young, Clopton, and Bleckley, 2004). They feel pressured by others to be thin.

Because of unrealistic standards and the drive for perfection, pressure builds up, which is relieved through lapses of control during binge-purge episodes. This is followed by feelings of shame and guilt, which contribute to the sense of low self-esteem and depression. Bulimics are often difficult to treat because they resist seeking help or sabotage treatment.

The families of bulimics are somewhat different than those of anorexics. Whereas the families of anorexics tend to be overprotective, repressed, and enmeshed, the families of bulimics are better described as chaotic, stressful, and disengaged (Johnson and Flach, 1985; Tyrka, Graber, and Brooks-Gunn, 2000). The parents of bulimics typically place a great deal of emphasis on attractiveness, physical fitness, achievement, and success (Roberto, 1986).

Some of the most promising treatment programs involve cognitive-behavioral approaches that help clients identify unrealistic and self-defeating cognitions and assumptions (Phillips, Greydanus, Pratt, and Patel, 2003). Correcting these irrational beliefs is an essential step toward changing the bulimic's behavior. Family therapy has also been found useful (Vanderlinden and Vandereycken, 1991). Therapists have found that antidepressants can reduce binging and purging behaviors (Freeman, 1998).

TABLE 5.1 COMPARISON OF ANOREXIA NERVOSA AND BULIMIA

CHARACTERISTIC	ANOREXIA NERVOSA	BULIMIA
Weight	Emaciated	Near normal
Prevalence	1% of adolescent girls	2% to 3% of adolescent girls
Age of Onset	Teens	Late teens, early twenties
Race/Ethnicity	Primarily Caucasian	No racial/ethnic differences
Eating Behavior	Barely eats	Periodically consumes large quantities and then purges
Personality	Dependent, anxious, perfectionistic	Moody, impulsive, unable to tolerate frustration
Emotional State	Denial	Guilt and shame
Desire to Change	No desire to change	Great desire to change
Behavior Motivation	Desire for control and rejection of femininity	Desire to be perceived as attractive
Family Background	Enmeshed and repressed	Conflicted and stress filled
Treatment Success	Very difficult to treat	Somewhat easier to treat

Many individuals find it difficult to distinguish between anorexia nervosa and bulimia. To help clarify the differences, Table 5.1 provides a point-by-point comparison of these two disorders.

HEALTH-RELATED BEHAVIORS

Being healthy requires not only avoiding unhealthy behaviors but also practicing healthy behaviors. In order to stay healthy, adolescents must eat well, exercise sufficiently, and get enough sleep. But what does that mean?

Nutrition

Adults sometimes think that adolescents are constantly eating. The fact is, during the period of rapid growth, adolescents *need* greater quantities of food, as well as certain nutrients, to take care of bodily requirements.

The stomach increases in size and capacity in order to be able to digest the increased amounts of food needed by adolescents. Research shows that the caloric requirement for girls may increase, on average, by 25 percent from ages 10 to 15 and then decrease slightly and level off. The caloric requirement for boys may increase, on average, by 90 percent from ages 10 to 19. Active adolescent boys need between 2,500 and 3,000 calories a day; girls, with their smaller stature and lower basal metabolic rate, need about 2,200.

Adolescents also need the right nutrients. Most studies of nutrition during adolescence show that many adolescents have inadequate diets (Venkdeswaran, 2000). The deficiencies may be summarized as follows:

ANSWERS WOULDN'T YOU LIKE TO KNOW . . .

What kinds of foods should adolescents eat?

The healthiest diet for adolescents includes a lot of fruits and vegetables (the green, red, and yellow kinds), whole grains (brown rice, not white bread), lean meats and fish, and lowfat dairy products. It includes little processed sugar, saturated fats (butter and ice cream), and starches (potatoes).

1. Insufficient calcium, due primarily to the inadequate intake of milk and dairy products—adolescents need 1,200 to 1,500 milligrams of calcium daily, which is equivalent to about three servings of dairy products.
2. Insufficient iron, especially in girls—girls need more iron than males (15 milligrams versus 12 milligrams) due to the blood loss that occurs with menstruation. Iron can be found in red meat, eggs, beans, and dark green vegetables, such as spinach.
3. Inadequate protein, primarily in girls who are dieting.
4. Too little Vitamin A, which can be found in yellow and green fruits and vegetables.
5. Insufficient Vitamin B6, which can be found in seeds, whole grains, and legumes.

bulimia an eating disorder characterized by binge-eating episodes and purging.

In an attempt to be slim and attractive, many adolescent girls constantly diet. Unfortunately, carrot sticks and diet soda do not provide adequate nutrition.

Adolescent girls have nutritional deficiencies more often than boys. One reason for this deficit is that girls eat less and so are less likely to get the necessary nutrients (Newell, Hammig, Jurick, and Johnson, 1990). Another reason is that girls diet more often (Adams, Sargent, Thompson, Richter, Corwin, and Rogan, 2000), depriving themselves of necessary nutrients. The additional need for some nutrients because of menstruation or pregnancy sometimes also imposes special problems.

Why do so many adolescents, both boys and girls, have inadequate diets? Here are some of the reasons:

1. They *skip breakfast* because of lack of time in the morning, because they would rather sleep late, and for other reasons.
2. *Snacks,* which make up about one-fourth of the daily intake of food, *do not compensate for meals missed.* This is because snacks are primarily fats, carbohydrates, and sugars, and because the intake from snacks is not sufficient to make up for the food missed.
3. They eat only *small quantities of nutritious foods,* especially fruits, vegetables, milk, cheese, and meat. Girls usually need more eggs and whole-grain cereal than they eat. One-quarter of all vegetables eaten by teens are french fries (Washington State Department of Health, 2000)—hardly the most nourishing choice! Very few adolescents (20 percent) eat enough fruits and vegetables (Grunbaum, Kann, Kirchen, Williams, Ross, and Lowry, 2002). Since a diet low in fruits and veggies poses significant long-term health risk (Frazao, 1999), adolescents should be encouraged to eat more of these foods.
4. *Inadequate knowledge of nutrition* influences the development of poor nutrition practices. Many times, high school boys and girls know so little about nutrition that they cannot select a well-balanced meal in a cafeteria.
5. *Social pressures* may cause poor eating habits. Girls, in particular, may encourage each other to follow extreme, controversial diets in order to lose weight. Friends may also pressure one another to follow strict vegan and macrobiotic diets. While it is certainly possible to eat healthy under these regimens, adolescents need to consciously work to ensure an adequate protein intake.
6. *Troubled family relationships and personal adjustments* seem to accompany poor eating habits. Adolescents from broken or troubled homes may not have parents at home to cook for them or to see that they get an adequate diet. Those with emotional problems may have nervous stomachs, ulcers, or more complex reasons for not eating properly.
7. The *family is poor* and cannot afford to buy proper food. Altogether, about 12 percent of families in the United States are below the poverty level (U.S. Bureau of the Census, 2003b).

How can teens be encouraged to eat better? Parents and other adults can model good eating habits and prepare nourishing meals. Since most teens cannot be bothered to count milligrams of calcium and other nutrients, they need to be taught guidelines that will help them take in the good (vitamins, minerals, protein) and leave out the bad (saturated fats, sugars). One widely used model is the U.S. Department of Agriculture's My Pyramid (see Figure 5.5). Adolescents who follow this model will take in all the nutrition they need. Also, making sensible selections within each food group will allow getting the proper nutrients without consuming excess calories.

FIGURE 5.5 MY PYRAMID
The government's newest eating recommendations.
Source: http://www.mypyramid.gov.

Exercise

American adolescents as well as adults are in the midst of a nationwide fitness craze—or at least, we say we are. Working out and staying in shape have become immensely popular—to talk about. The trendiest clothes include active wear and expensive athletic shoes. Every sizable community has fitness centers, gyms, pools, tennis courts, and bike trails.

Unfortunately, all the talk and attention has not translated into increased activity. Only about one-half of American adolescents regularly participate in vigorous physical activity. About 25 percent report no vigorous activity at all, and about 14 percent get no exercise at all. Adolescent girls are less likely to be physically active than adolescent boys, and Black females are even less likely to exercise than White females. The overall amount of physical activity declines during the course of adolescence, which means older teens get even less exercise than younger ones (Aaron, Stortin, Robertson, Kriska, and LaPorte, 2002; U.S. Department of Health and Human Services, 2001).

Benefits of Exercise

People are finding that exercising is fun and beneficial in a variety of ways. One most obvious benefit is to *build physical fitness.* Exercise tones up the body system, builds muscles, strengthens the heart and lungs, and improves circulation. It also relieves nervous tension, depression, and anxiety. Similarly, a desire to *lose weight* motivates many adolescents to exercise. Nearly everyone knows that exercising consumes calories and that exercise can also depress the appetite (Vartanian and Herman, 2006; Watkins, 1992).

In addition, exercise *promotes psychological and mental health* (Carruth and Goldberg, 1990). Possessing a physically fit body that meets the cultural ideals of thinness and beauty can enhance body image and self-esteem (Ferron, Narring, Cauderay, and Michaud, 1999). Exercise may improve self-esteem by promoting feelings of competence and mastery (Maton, 1990). There is a positive correlation between physical activity and feelings of competence, including social competence. Also, physically active adolescents are less likely to feel depressed or anxious than less-active youth (Kirkcaldy,

Shephard, and Siefen, 2002; Sears, Sheppard, Scott, Lodge, and Scott, 2000). Boys and girls seem to benefit equally in this way from participation in sports and exercise (Gore, Farrell, and Gordon, 2001).

There is evidence that physical activity patterns developed in adolescence may continue into adulthood. A comparison of the physical activity levels of 453 young adult men, age 23 to 25, with their childhood fitness scores revealed that those who were physically active as adults had better childhood physical fitness test scores than those who were not physically active (Dennison, Straus, Mellits, and Charney, 1988).

How much exercise do adolescents need? According to the U.S. Surgeon General, they should average at least 30 minutes of moderately intense physical activity on all or most days of the week (U.S. Department of Health and Human Services, 2001). How can they best be encouraged to do this? The best way appears to be to enroll them in organized, after-school physical activities (Sallis, Prochaska, Taylor, Hill, and Geraci, 1999). This suggests that schools should place an emphasis on intramural as well as varsity sports. In addition, girls' participation could be increased by providing them environments in which they can be both awkward and sweaty without fear of embarrassment, since embarrassment is a barrier to athletic participation (Grieser et al., 2006).

Sleep

Not only do adolescents need exercise to remain healthy, but they need adequate sleep, as well. In fact, however, many teenagers do not get as much sleep as they should.

Mary Carskadon and her colleagues have intensely studied adolescent sleep patterns and their consequences. In one study, they compared the sleep habits of students doing poorly in school (earning mostly Cs or lower) with those of students doing well. They found that compared to the A and B students, the C and D students got about 40 minutes less sleep per night and stayed up later on weekends (Wolfson and Carskadon, 1998). And no wonder: The participants who reported getting less sleep were both more tired and depressed during the day than those who reported getting more sleep. Students who lack sleep are also more inattentive (Fallone, Acebo, Arendt, Seifer, and Carskadon, 2001), which surely cannot help school performance. The seriousness of adolescent sleep deprivation was underscored even more strongly in one of Carskadon's more recent studies. About two-thirds of the adolescents she sampled reported driving badly due to tiredness, and 20 percent claimed that they had actually fallen asleep while behind the wheel! Males were more likely to drive while excessively tired than females (Carskadon, 2002b).

Although most adolescents believe that they should stay up later than they did when they were children, teenagers actually need *more* sleep than preteens (9 hours), not less (Carskadon, Harvey, and Duke, 1980). Yet adolescents stay up later than children—and older adolescents stay up later than younger adolescents—because they are under increasing pressure to juggle the responsibilities of homework, sports, and jobs (Carskadon, 2002a). They are also more likely to socialize during late hours and to stay up late to play video games or watch TV (Owens, Stohl, Patton, Reddy, and Crouch, 2006). Another issue is that parents become less likely to enforce early bedtimes as their children age (Mercer, Merritt, and Cowell, 1998).

> **ANSWERS WOULDN'T YOU LIKE TO KNOW . . .**
>
> **Why can't you and your friends stay awake during 8 o'clock classes?**
>
> You're probably falling asleep in your early classes because you're staying up too late and not getting enough sleep. However, it's not entirely your fault, since the adolescent brain is primed to desire sleep at a later hour than the adult brain. Not leaving your term paper to the last minute couldn't hurt, though.

Why do so many adolescents, even those who are not especially busy, stay up late? Carskadon's research indicates that there is a real biological underpinning to this behavior. She found that an adolescent's peak secretion of **melatonin**—the hormone that your brain produces to make you sleepy—occurs two hours later during the night than that of a child or an adult (Carskadon, Wolfson, Acebo, Tzischinsky, and Seifer, 1998). This delay has been tied directly to pubertal status. When girls of the same age who had and had not entered puberty were compared, only the ones who had begun to develop had later melatonin surges (Carskadon, Vieira, and Acebo, 1993).

Ironically, as bedtimes get later, waking times get earlier. Middle schools generally start earlier in the morning than elementary schools, and high schools begin earlier yet, often before 8:00 A.M. (Most school districts have staggered starting times so that they can use the same school buses for students at all three levels.) Since adolescents' biological clocks are set so as to encourage them to sleep late, it is not surprising that middle school and high school students are not often alert during their first few class periods. These adolescent sleep experts, therefore, advocate starting adolescents' school days later and enforcing an earlier "lights out" (Carskadon, Wolfson, Acebo, Tzischinsky, and Seifer, 1998).

ACNE

Although **acne** is not a serious medical concern, it is often an upsetting aspect of adolescent development. Many teens spend countless dollars purchasing and then endless hours applying creams, astringents, and special soaps to try to control their acne. In addition, having acne can lead to self-consciousness and even social withdrawal, particularly when youths are teased or otherwise embarrassed by the condition of their skin. As such, having acne is an important adolescent phenomenon.

Skin Gland Development

Three kinds of skin glands can cause problems for the adolescent:

1. **Merocrine** sweat glands, distributed over most of the skin surfaces of the body
2. **Apocrine** sweat glands, located in the armpit, mammary, genital, and anal regions
3. **Sebaceous** glands, which are the oil-producing glands of the skin

During the adolescent years, the merocrine and apocrine sweat glands secrete a fatty substance with a pronounced odor that becomes more noticeable. The result is body odor. The sebaceous glands develop at a greater speed than the skin ducts through which they discharge their skin oils. As a result, the ducts may become plugged and acne can develop. Almost 85 percent of adolescents develop acne at some point (University of California at Los Angeles Medical Center, 2000).

Acne can take a variety of forms, depending on its severity. Whiteheads and blackheads result when oil glands becomes blocked. In the case of blackheads, the plugs oxidize and turn dark. (Blackheads are not dark because they contain embedded dirt.) If the plug becomes infected, then a**papule**—a tender, inflamed, pink bump—or a**pustule**—a pus-filled pimple—will form. Large pustules, called**cysts,** can leave permanent scars. Acne is most common on the face, upper back, and chest.

Causes

Acne is triggered by the increased amount of testosterone present during adolescence. Boys tend to develop acne more than girls because they have more testosterone in their systems. Acne has little to do with personal hygiene, since most people wash their faces once or twice per day. Masturbation does not cause acne, either. And contrary to popular belief, most people can eat chocolate or greasy foods without exacerbating their acne. On the other hand, oily cosmetics, the friction caused by rubbing the skin, and stress can make acne worse.

Treatment

Mild cases of acne often respond to over-the-counter medications. Creams containing benzoyl peroxide kill the bacteria that cause pustules and can reduce oil production. Salicylic acid helps keep pores from becoming clogged. More severe cases of acne require prescription medication. Topical vitamin A solutions (Retin-A) are one option; oral antibiotics, such as tetracycline and erythromycin, are another. Estrogen-containing birth control pills are usually effective, as well, because estrogen counters the effects of testosterone.

Individuals with acne tend to want to scrub with harsh, abrasive soaps and douse their faces with harsh astringents in an attempt to wash away blackheads and dry out the skin. Neither remedy is desirable, however, since both will irritate the skin and often make acne worse. Instead, individuals with acne should treat their skin gently by using mild soap and avoiding scouring (National institute of Arthritis and Musculoskeletal and Skin Diseases, 2006).

melatonin the hormone that the brain produces to induce sleep.

acne pimples on the skin caused by overactive sebaceous glands.

merocrine glands sweat glands distributed over the entire body.

apocrine glands sweat glands located primarily in the armpits and groin whose secretions cause body odor.

sebaceous glands oil-producing skin glands whose secretions can cause acne if the glands' pores become blocked.

papules tender, raised red bumps that are precursors to pimples.

pustules the medical term for *pimples*.

cysts large, deep pimples that can cause scarring.

SUMMARY

1. Adolescence is intrinsically a healthy time of life. Most of the health concerns that teens face are due to their own behaviors and are thus preventable. The three leading causes of death for American adolescents are car accidents, homicide, and suicide.
2. Adolescents often make poor health-related decisions because they lack knowledge and fail to perceive the hazards that risky behaviors entail. They may also bow to peer pressure and societal messages that glorify unhealthy and even dangerous activities.

3. Adolescents in developing countries face different health risks than American adolescents. Malnutrition, lack of medicine and health services, and war-related violence are of more concern in the Third World than in the United States.
4. Adolescents are concerned about body image: physical attractiveness, body-type concepts of the ideal, body weight, and timing of their own development in relation to what is considered normal. Adolescents who are physically attractive are treated in more positive ways, develop more positive self-perceptions and personalities, and are more popular and better adjusted socially.
5. The three body types are ectomorph, mesomorph, and endomorph. Boys prefer to be mesomorphic: solid and muscular. Girls hope to be ectomorphic: tall and slender. A soft, round, endomorphic build is least preferred by both genders.
6. Most adolescents are not happy with their bodies. This is more true of girls than boys, and their discontentment increases over the course of adolescence. Unfortunately, not liking one's body can have a negative effect on one's overall level of self-esteem.
7. The timing of physical maturation is important. Some adolescents mature earlier or later than average, with a differential effect. Early-maturing boys may enjoy athletic, social, and community advantages but they are also under more pressure to act older than their age and are at a heightened risk to engage in antisocial activities at a young age. Late-maturing boys suffer socially induced inferiority.
8. Girls who mature in elementary school tend to feel awkward and self-conscious because they look different. Early maturity results in precocious heterosexual interests. Late-maturing girls are at a social disadvantage. They look like little girls, resent being treated as such, and are envious of their friends who have matured. These social advantages are temporary and are overcome when maturation takes place.
9. Current research suggests that off-time maturation—whether relatively early or relatively late—puts adolescents at risk for poor psychological and behavioral adjustment.
10. An ever-increasing number of American adolescents are obese, which poses health risks and increases their likelihood of social rejection. Obesity is on the rise because adolescents are eating more and exercising less than they did in the past.
11. Anorexia nervosa is a life-threatening emotional disorder characterized by an obsession with food and weight. Symptoms include constant preoccupation with food and dieting, body image disturbances, excess weight loss, amenorrhea, hyperactivity, moodiness, isolation, and strong feelings of insecurity, helplessness, depression, and loneliness. Anorexia is also associated with numerous medical conditions.
12. Anorexia is found primarily in teenage girls and usually appears at puberty. Anorexics often have disturbed relationships with their parents.
13. Bulimia is a binge-purge syndrome characterized by compulsive and rapid consumption of large quantities of high-calorie food, followed by efforts to purge the food.
14. Bulimics are unhappy with the appearance of their bodies, yet they are impulsive, lack control over eating, and are anxious and depressed with low self-esteem. Bulimics usually come from families that are characterized by strife and conflict.
15. Nutrition is extremely important to individual health. Adolescents may suffer a variety of deficiencies: calcium, iron, protein, and vitamins A, C, and B6. There are a number of reasons for deficiencies: Adolescents skip breakfast; snacks of junk food do not make up for meals missed; small quantities of the right foods are eaten; inadequate knowledge of nutrition results in poor food selection; social pressures and troubled family relationships result in poor eating habits; or the family cannot afford to buy good food.
16. Exercise is not only fun but physically and psychologically beneficial. Many adolescents participate in sports of some kind, but too many American youths do not get sufficient exercise.
17. Most adolescents do not get enough sleep because they stay up late and get up early. This sleep deprivation has both psychological and academic ramifications.
18. Adolescents worry about body odor and acne caused by the increased secretion of skin glands during puberty. Prompt attention and treatment of acne may prevent its becoming severe.

KEY TERMS

acne 112
anorexia nervosa 106
apocrine glands 113
bulimia 108
cysts 113
ectomorph 99
endomorph 99
melatonin 112
merocrine glands 113
mesomorph 99
metabolic rate 105
mortality 96
obesity 104
papules 113
pustules 113
sebaceous glands 113

THOUGHT QUESTIONS

Personal Reflection

1. Do you ever think about your own health? Do you have any health problems? What steps do you take to ensure that you stay healthy? What changes could you make to stay healthy or become healthier?
2. Did you mature earlier or later than your classmates? How did you feel? How did it affect you? What happened? What did you do?
3. Have you ever been overweight? What helped you deal with this condition?
4. What changes should you make in your diet and why? What are you eating too much or too little of?
5. Do you eat breakfast? Lunch? Why or why not?

6. Do you follow a regular routine of exercise? Why or why not? What prevents you from doing so, if you do not?
7. Do you usually get enough sleep? If not, why not? What effects have you noticed when you fail to get enough sleep?

Group Discussion

8. Have you known anyone who died during adolescence? If so, what was the cause? Was it either accidental or violence related?
9. What are the similarities and differences between the health issues faced by American adolescents and those in the developing world?
10. Why is adolescents' self-esteem so tied to their feelings about their appearance? Why does that change as youths move into adulthood?
11. Have you ever known anyone who was anorexic? Describe the person and explain why you think the person became that way.
12. Have you ever known anyone who was bulimic? Describe the eating behavior of the person, something about the personality of the individual, and why you think the individual was bulimic.
13. What do nutritionists consider to be a balanced diet?
14. What helps most in the prevention and/or treatment of acne?

Debate Questions

15. In order to improve adolescent health, should schools require that all students participate in more extensive physical education activities?
16. Should adolescents who desire it be permitted to have plastic surgery procedures?
17. In order to decrease adolescent obesity, should school cafeterias serve only healthy, nutritious foods?
18. Can the media be held responsible for the widespread body dissatisfaction and high prevalence of eating disorders found in today's adolescents?
19. Cigarette companies are not allowed to advertise on television. Should fast-food commercials also be banned?

SUGGESTED READING

Burniat, W., Coke, T. J., Lissau, I., and Poskitt, E. M. E. (Eds.). (2002). *Child and Adolescent Obesity: Causes and Consequences, Prevention and Management.* New York: Cambridge University Press.

Carskadon, M. A. (Ed.). (2002). *Adolescent Sleep Patterns: Biological, Social, and Psychological Influences.* New York: Cambridge University Press.

Hayward, C., Hurrelmann, K., Curie, C., and Rasmussen, V. (2003). *Gender Differences at Puberty.* New York: Cambridge University Press.

Kalodner, C. R. (2003). *Too Fat or Too Thin? A Reference Guide to Eating Disorders.* Westport, CT: Greenwood.

Rew, L. (2003). *Adolescent Health: A Multidisciplinary Approach.* Thousand Oaks, CA: Sage.

Romer, D. (Ed.). (2003). *Reducing Adolescent Risk: Toward an Integrated Approach.* Thousand Oaks, CA: Sage.

Smoll, F. L., and Smith, R. E. (2002). *Children and Youth in Sports: A Biopsychological Perspective.* Dubuque, IA: Kendall/Hunt.

Thompson, J. K., and Smolak, L. (Eds.). (2001). *Body Image, Eating Disorders, and Obesity in Youth: Assessment, Prevention, and Treatment.* Washington, DC: American Psychological Association.

USEFUL WEB SITES

ACNE.org
www.acne.org

This site contains "Answers to Frequently Asked Questions" about acne, a list of common myths about acne, and many links to other related sites.

Anorexia Nervosa and Related Eating Disorders (ANRED)
www.anred.com

This site, which is especially clearly written, contains information on the three most well-known eating disorders (anorexia, bulimia, and obesity) as well as information on less common disorders.

Kansas State University Nutrition Links
www.oznet.k-state.edu/humannutrition/nutlink/n2.htm

This site provides numerous links to other sites concerned with all aspects of nutrition.

National Eating Disorder Association (NEDA)
www.edap.org/p.asp?webpage_10=294

Click on the button at the top of the page, labeled "Eating Disorder Information." This site is especially useful for those interested in information about eating disorders in males and body image.

National Institute of Arthritis and Musculoskeletal and Skin Diseases (NIAMS)
www.niams.nih.gov/hi/topics/acne/acne.htm

This site is an up-to-date, comprehensive information source about acne.

CHAPTER 6 TRADITIONAL APPROACHES TO COGNITIVE DEVELOPMENT

Piaget and Elkind

WOULDN'T YOU LIKE TO KNOW . . .

- Can babies think?
- Why do preschoolers seem so selfish?
- Why are children in grade school smarter than those in preschool?
- Why are adolescents sometimes described as "junior scientists"?
- Why do adolescents often have extreme political views?
- Why do adolescents often say one thing and then do another?
- Why are adolescents so self-conscious?
- Are adults actually smarter than adolescents, or do they just know more?
- What can be done to promote high levels of reasoning in adolescents?

The word cognition literally means "the act of knowing or perceiving." So, in discussing the cognitive development of adolescents, we seek to discuss the process by which they grow in knowledge. More specifically, we will look at their ability to understand, think, and perceive, and to utilize these abilities in solving the practical problems of everyday living.

There are basically three approaches to this study of cognition. The first is the *Piagetian approach,* which emphasizes the broad patterns and qualitative changes in the way adolescents think. The second is the *information-processing approach,* which examines the progressive steps, actions, and operations that take place when the adolescent receives, perceives, remembers, thinks about, and uses information. The third approach is the *psychometric approach,* which measures quantitative changes in adolescent intelligence. The Piagetian approach is discussed in this chapter along with the views of David Elkind, a researcher who discussed how adolescent cognitive development shapes individuals' personalities.

A discussion of the information-processing approach and the psychometric approach is covered in Chapter 7.

During Piaget's sensorimotor stage, children under 2 years old begin to move from a body-centered world to an object-centered world, where simple motor activities, such as picking up objects, become intriguing.

PIAGET'S STAGES OF COGNITIVE DEVELOPMENT

As we discovered in Chapter 2, Piaget divides cognitive development into four major stages (Overton and Byrnes, 1991; Piaget, 1971):

1. The *sensorimotor stage* is from birth to about age 2.
2. The *preoperational stage* is from about age 2 to age 7.
3. The *concrete operational stage* is from about age 7 to about age 11 or 12.
4. The *formal operational stage* is from age 11 or 12 on.

The differences among the four stages have primarily to do with (1) what one can think about, (2) how flexible one's thinking is, and (3) how much one can use correct logic. In the sensorimotor stage, the individual cannot think without performing movement: To think *is* to move. Thought, therefore, is quite inflexible and so the infant does not engage in logic. In the preoperational stage, the young child can think entirely in his or her mind; he or she doesn't have to take physical action in order to imagine or consider. Thinking is *pre*operational, however, as the child at this age lacks the **mental operations** needed for flexible thinking. His or her logic is inadequate, frequently leading to erroneous conclusions. Once the child enters the concrete operational stage, those mental operations are in place. As the name of the stage indicates, however, the individual can only use these mental operations when thinking about real, concrete objects or actual behavior. Such thought is flexible and logical. Finally, with the onset of the formal operational stage, the individual can think abstractly and hypothetically. He or she can reason and draw logical conclusions even when thinking about things that he or she has not actually experienced.

Let's look at each stage in more depth.

Sensorimotor Stage

During the **sensorimotor stage,** learning is related to the mastery of sensory-motor sequences. The infant moves from a self-centered, body-centered world to an object-centered world as the senses of vision, touch, taste, hearing, and smell bring him or her into contact with things having various properties and relationships to other objects. The child becomes intrigued with such simple motor activities as picking up objects,

ANSWERS WOULDN'T YOU LIKE TO KNOW . . .

Can babies think?

Babies can't think in the sense that you and I can. Their thinking is limited to the sensations they feel, the movements they make, and the relationship between the two. Babies are caught up in the need to learn the boundaries of their own bodies and how they can affect the world around them.

ANSWERS WOULDN'T YOU LIKE TO KNOW . . .

Why do preschoolers sometimes seem so selfish?

Preschoolers can seem selfish because they are egocentric. They simply cannot imagine what is going through another person's mind. Rather, they assume that what they want is what you want and that what they like is what you like. They are not deliberately ignoring others' feelings, however.

falling backward on a pillow, and blowing. Thinking, if any, occurs as a stimulus-response connection with the physical world, although the latter part of this period marks a transition to symbolic play, imitation, and the mental representation of objects. Elkind (1967) labeled the principal cognitive task during this period the *conquest of the object.*

Preoperational Stage

The **preoperational stage** is the period when language is acquired. Children begin dealing with their world by learning and manipulating symbols, as well as through motor activity and direct interactions with the environment. Symbolic play, or *internalized imitation,* emerges. Elkind (1967) labeled the principal preoperational task the *conquest of the symbol.*

During this period, there is evidence of transductive reasoning rather than more mature inductive or deductive reasoning. **Transductive reasoning** occurs when the child proceeds from particular to particular, without generalization, rather than from the particular to the general **(inductive reasoning)** or from the general to the particular **(deductive reasoning).** Transductive reasoners tend to infer cause and effect where none exists. If, for example, a 4-year-old girl meets a mean man who has a beard, she may assume that all men with beards are mean because beards make people mean. She would then worry if her father said he was planning on growing a beard because doing so would make him mean. Similarly, a young boy who once noticed he had a sore throat as he was combing his hair might thereafter believe that brushing his hair would make him sick.

These examples also illustrate the concept of **syncretism,** or trying to link ideas that are not always related. For example, Mommy had a baby the last time she went to the hospital, so the next time she goes to the hospital, you mistakenly expect Mommy will bring home another baby.

Preoperational thinking is also *egocentric;* that is, children have difficulty understanding why someone else cannot see something in the same way they do. For example, suppose you have already had three cookies and your sister has only had one. There is one more cookie on the plate. Whom do you believe should eat the last cookie if you are in the preoperational stage? You, of course, because you are still hungry. At this stage, you cannot put yourself in your sister's place and imagine how she feels. Syncretism coupled with egocentrism leads to a related phenomenon called **animism.** Young children assume that inanimate objects—especially those that share features such as eyes and faces with animals—have feelings and are, in essence, alive. Since children get lonely when they are left alone, they assume that their dolls and teddy bears get lonely, too.

Related to all the preceding characteristics is **centering,** which refers to children's tendencies to focus attention on one detail and their inability to shift attention to other aspects of a situation (Muuss, 1988b). For example, you may conclude there is more water in a shallow dish than in a glass because the dish is wider, even though you have already seen all the water poured from the glass into the dish (see Figure 6.1). You ignore the greater height of the glass and the demonstration of pouring.

mental operations logical processes that allow for flexible thought.

sensorimotor stage the first stage of cognitive development, according to Piaget, lasting from birth to about 2 years of age.

preoperational stage the second stage of cognitive development, according to Piaget, lasting from 2 to 7 years of age.

transductive reasoning proceeding from particular to particular in thought, without making generalizations.

inductive reasoning gathering individual items of information and putting them together to form hypotheses or conclusions.

deductive reasoning beginning with an hypothesis or premise and breaking it down to see if it is true.

syncretism the act of trying to link ideas.

animism the preoperational belief that inanimate objects have humanlike properties and emotions.

centering the tendency of children to focus attention on one detail and their inability to shift attention to other aspects of the situation.

FIGURE 6.1 UNDERSTANDING THE PRINCIPLE OF CONSERVATION OF VOLUME
(a) The child agrees that glasses A and B have the same amount of water. *(b)* The water from B is poured into the dish. The child is unable to understand that glass A and the dish still have the same amount of water, because the dish appears broader even though it is shallower. The child is unable to retain one aspect (the amount) when another aspect changes (the height of the water column and the width of the column).

As a result of their inability to maintain more than one relationship in their thinking at a time, children make errors of judgment, give inadequate or inconsistent explanations, and show a lack of logical sequence in their arguments and a lack of comprehension of constants. There is evidence of thinking but still an absence of operational thinking.

Concrete Operational Stage

Early adolescents are usually in the **concrete operational stage** of cognitive development. And as we will see, even older adolescents and adults sometimes think in ways characteristic of concrete, rather than formal, operations. It is therefore important to understand what individuals in this stage can and cannot do.

During the concrete operational stage, children show a greater capacity for logical reasoning, although at a very concrete level. One of the reasons they can think more logically is that they are able to arrange objects into **hierarchical classifications** and comprehend **class inclusion relationships** (the inclusion of objects in different levels of the hierarchy at the same time). This gives children the ability to understand the relations of the parts to the whole, the whole to the parts, and the parts to the parts.

For example, suppose you are given a randomly organized array of blue and red squares and black and white circles. If you understand inclusion relationships, you discover there are two major collections (squares and circles) and two subtypes of each (blue versus red squares and black versus white circles). There is a hierarchy whose higher level is defined by shape and whose lower level is defined by color. This enables you to say that all squares are either blue or red; that there are more squares than blue squares; that there are more squares than red squares; that if the red squares are taken away, the blue ones are left; and so on.

Children at this stage learn that different objects may be grouped by size, by alphabetical order, or by age, or that an object may simultaneously belong to more than one class. A child may be a girl, a fourth-grader, an athlete, and a redhead, all at the same time. Children learn that some relationships are *symmetrical*, or *reciprocal*—such as two brothers are brothers to each other. In dealing with numbers, children learn that different combinations of numbers make the same total and that *substitutions* may be made with the same result. In dealing with liquids and solids, they learn that a change in shape does not necessarily change volume or mass; the amount is conserved.

For the first time, children can make **transitive inferences.** Transitive inference problems can be very easy or very difficult, but they all have a similar form. A typical transitive inference problem is "Oranges cost more than grapefruit, and grapefruit cost more than apples. Do apples cost more than oranges?" In order to solve such a problem, you must be able to perform

seriation, or mentally arrange items in order from large to small or small to large. Preoperational children can seriate (although it is often difficult for them), but they cannot perform the mental manipulations necessary for transitive inferences.

Piaget calls this stage the *concrete operational stage* of cognitive development because it involves concrete elements (objects, relations, or dimensions) and operations (such as addition or subtraction) as well as rules, or *properties,* that describe the way the operations may be performed. Elkind (1967) called the major cognitive task of this period *mastering classes, relations, and quantities.*

Four mental operations are especially important:

1. *Reversibility:* All actions, even mental actions, have an opposite. For example, "canaries" and "turtles" can be lumped together into the category of "pets," and "pets" can be divided into the subcategories of "canaries" and "turtles." Understanding reversibility, in effect, lets you think backward, imagining an item's state before some action was performed on it. For example, when we see a wet washcloth, we know that it must have been dunked in water, since removing the water would make it dry again.
2. *Identity* or *nullifiability:* This operation involves understanding that if we do something to an object and then do its opposite, the net effect is that the object is unchanged. For example, imagine that you have six pennies. If your brother gives you two more but then your sister takes two of them away, you will be back to having six pennies. Another way of thinking about identity is that anything plus zero stays the same. So, if you take a glass a water and pour it into a differently shaped container, you will still have the same amount you started with (assuming you didn't add any water or spill any water).
3. *Associativity:* This operation involves understanding that the same outcome can result from different combinations or clusterings or actions. For instance, if we want to make fruit salad, we can mix blueberries and strawberries and then add some pineapple. If we instead mix the strawberries and pineapple and only later add the blueberries, the results will be identical.
4. *Combinativity:* Classes can always be combined to form larger, broader categories. For example, "boxes" and "jars" can be conceptually combined to form the category "containers" (Muuss, 1988b).

Piaget used **conservation problems** to determine whether children had entered the concrete operational stage of cognitive development. *Conservation* refers to the recognition that properties of things such as weight and volume are not altered by changing their container or shape. Conservation tasks involve some manipulation of the shape of matter that does not alter the mass or volume of the matter (Piaget and Inhelder, 1969). A typical conservation problem is represented by the balls of clay in Figure 6.2. In this example, the child is asked to confirm that A and B are the same size. Then, while the child watches, B is changed to B_1, then to B_2, then to B_3. The child is asked to compare A with B_1, then with B_2, and with B_3, each time stating whether A and B are still the same. Children in the preoperational stage are guided by the shapes they see. Using the operations described above, children in the concrete operational stage preserve a recognition of the equality between A and B that transforms their physical shape.

FIGURE 6.2 CONSERVATION OF MASS

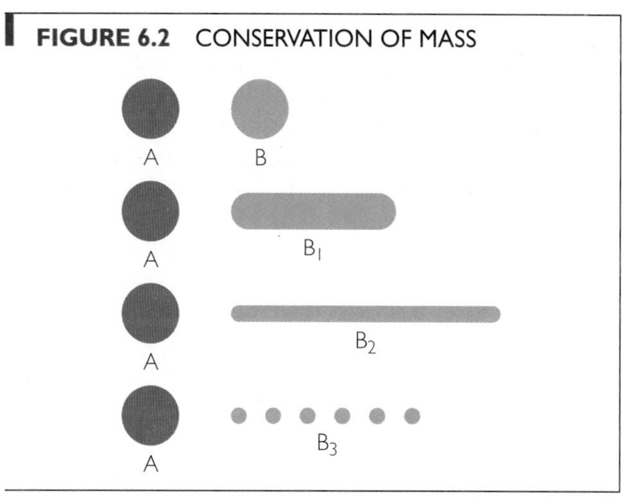

concrete operational stage the third stage of cognitive development, according to Piaget, lasting from 7 to 11 or 12 years of age.

hierarchical classification the ability to divide objects into nested series of categories.

class inclusion relationships understanding that objects can be fit into different levels of hierarchies.

transitive inferences the ability to solve problems such as "Tom is taller than Fred, and Fred is taller than Marty. Is Tom taller than Marty?"

seriation the ability to line things up in order from large to small or small to large.

conservation problems tests used by Piaget to determine whether children had mastered concrete operations, such as understanding that changing an object's appearance does not alter its fundamental properties.

ANSWERS WOULDN'T YOU LIKE TO KNOW . . .

Why are children in grade school smarter than those in preschool?

Grade-schoolers are smarter than preschoolers because they better understand hierarchies and part/whole relationships. They can arrange items in their minds from small to large. They can also think backward and infer the past from the present. Finally, they know that not all changes in appearance are meaningful. Taken together, these skills mark a big change in development.

It is important to remember that *the child's thinking is still linked to empirical reality* (Piaget, 1967). Children have made some progress toward extending their thoughts from the actual toward the potential (Elkind, 1970), but the starting point must still be real because concrete operational children can reason only about those things with which they have had direct, personal experience. When children have to start with any hypothetical or contrary-to-fact proposition, they have difficulty. Elkind (1967) also pointed out that one of the difficulties at this stage is that the child can deal with only two classes, relations, or quantitative dimensions at the same time. When more variables are present, the child flounders. This ability to consider more than two variables at once is achieved only during the formal operations stage that follows.

Formal Operational Stage

The last stage of cognitive development, the **formal operational stage,** begins during early adolescence. Piaget subdivided the stage of formal operations further into substages III-A, almost full formal function (11 or 12 to 14 or 15 years), and III-B, full formal function (14 or 15 years and up). The division of the adolescent period at the age of 14 or 15 implies another restructuring and a disequilibrium, which then leads to a higher level of equilibrium and intellectual structure during late adolescence.

Substage III-A appears to be a preparatory stage in which adolescents may make correct discoveries and handle certain formal operations. Their approach is still crude, however. They are not yet able to provide systematic and rigorous proof of their assertions. This substage has been titled *emergent formal operational thought*. At this time, adolescents are able to exhibit formal operations in some situations but not in others.

By the time adolescents reach substage III-B, they have become capable of formulating more elegant generalizations and advancing more inclusive laws. Most of all, they are now able to provide more systematic proof for their assertions (Muuss, 1988b). This second substage is the true or consolidated stage of formal operational thought wherein the adolescent or adult demonstrates such thought across a variety of situations. Many adolescents and adults never truly reach the second substage. Most seem to remain fixated somewhat in substage III-A, often thinking formally only in situations with which they are familiar (Flavell, Miller, and Miller, 1993).

The attainment of formal operations is not an all-or-nothing proposition. Between the ages of 11 or 12 and 14 or 15, considerable modification, systemization, and formalization of thought processes can be observed. The complexity of the problems that the individual can handle increases substantially during these years and reaches an equilibrium after substage III-B has been attained (Muuss, 1988b). Some adolescents and adults never reach this formal operational stage because of limited intelligence or a lack of needed experiences.

Elkind (1967) called this final stage the *conquest of thought*. During this stage, the thinking of the adolescent differs radically from that of the child (Piaget, 1972). The concrete operational child can perform mental operations and has some understanding of classes and relations. However, his or her ability to use induction and deduction is significantly limited. A child at this stage will get lost when asked to juggle multiple dimensions of a problem at the same time or to ignore his or her own past experiences in problem solving. An adolescent, however, is able to superimpose propositional logic on the logic of classes and relations. In other words, formal operations adolescents are able, through inductive reasoning, to systematize their ideas and deal critically with their own thinking to be able to construct theories about it. Furthermore, they can test these theories logically and scientifically, considering several variables, and are able to discover truth, scientifically, through deductive reasoning (Inhelder and Piaget, 1958). In this sense, adolescents are able to assume the role of scientists because they have the capacity to construct and test theories.

The difference between the way children approach problems and the logical, systematic approach of adolescents is given in the following example:

> E. A. Peel . . . asked children what they thought about the following event: "Only brave pilots are allowed to fly over high mountains. A fighter pilot flying over the Alps collided with an aerial cableway and cut a main cable, causing some cars to fall to the glacier below. Several people were killed." A child at the concrete-operational level answered: "I think the pilot was not

During Piaget's formal operational stage, which begins in early adolescence, the individual's thinking begins to differ radically from that of a child. He or she becomes able to construct theories and can test these theories using scientific methods.

> very good at flying." A formal-operational child responded: "He was either not informed of the mountain railway on his route or he was flying too low. Also his flying compass may have been affected by something before or after take-off, thus setting him off course causing collision with the cable."
>
> The concrete-operational child assumes that if there was a collision the pilot was a bad pilot; the formal-operational child considers all the possibilities that might have caused the collision. The concrete-operational child adopts the hypothesis that seems most probable or likely to him. The formal-operational child constructs all possibilities and checks them out one by one. (Kohlberg and Gilligan, 1971, pp. 1061, 1062)

One of the experiments Piaget conducted, which led to discovering the strategies adolescents use in solving problems, involved a pendulum. Adolescent participants were shown a pendulum suspended by a string (see Figure 6.3). The problem was to discover what factors would affect the oscillatory speed of the pendulum. The participants were asked to investigate four possible effects: changing the length of the pendulum, changing its weight, releasing the pendulum from various heights, and starting the pendulum with various degrees of force. The adolescents were allowed to solve the problem in any way they chose.

The adolescents showed three basic characteristics in their problem-solving behavior. First, they planned their investigations systematically. They began to test all possible causes for variation in the pendulum swings: long or short string, light or heavy weight, high or low heights, and various degrees of force of push. Their search was *exhaustive*. Second, they recorded the outcomes accurately and with little bias under the different experimental conditions. Third, they were able to draw logical conclusions. The adolescents intuitively knew to vary only one feature of the pendulum at a time—for instance, the length of the string, the force with which they pushed the pendulum, or the weight. They realized that if they changed more than one feature at a time, then they would be unable to ascertain which feature caused any observed change in speed. Psychologists call this approach **hypothetico-deductive reasoning,** but it is more often referred to as *the scientific method*.

Younger subjects given the same problem may come up with the right answer by trial and error but they will not use systematic and scientific procedures or be able to give a logical explanation of the solution. Children tend to form conclusions that seem warranted by the facts. But often these conclusions are premature and false because the children have not considered all of the important facts and are not able to reason logically about them. Even when presented

formal operational stage the fourth stage of cognitive development, according to Piaget, during which people develop abstract thought independent of concrete objects.

hypothetico-deductive reasoning a way to solve problems using the scientific method; only one factor at a time is varied while all else is held constant.

FIGURE 6.3 THE PENDULUM PROBLEM

This simple pendulum consists of a string, which can be shortened or lengthened, and a set of varying weights. The other variables that at first might be considered relevant are the height of the release point and the force of the push given by the subject.

Source: "The Pendulum Problem" from *The Growth of Logical Thinking: From Childhood to Adolescence* by Jean Piaget. Copyright © 1958 by Basic Books, Inc. Reprinted by permission of Basic Books, a member of Perseus Books, L.L.C.

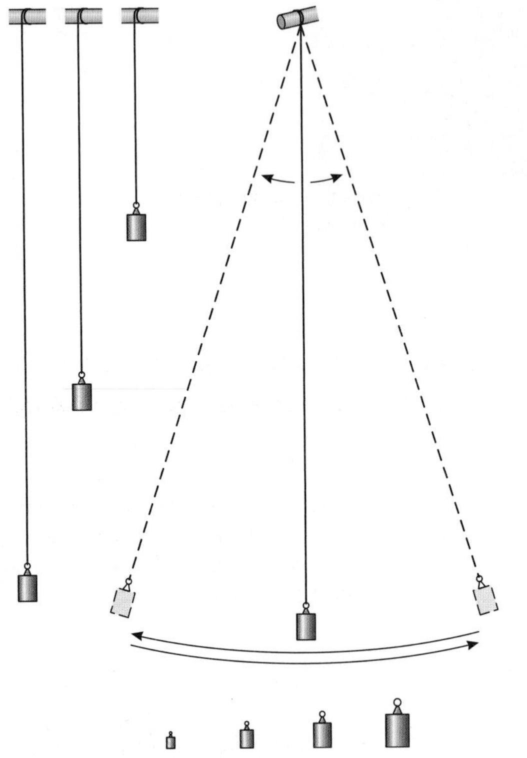

ANSWERS WOULDN'T YOU LIKE TO KNOW ...

Why are adolescents sometimes described as "junior scientists"?

Some cognitive psychologists consider adolescents to be "junior scientists" because they spontaneously and intuitively use the scientific method to solve problems. In other words, they know that in order to discover which element of a situation is causing some effect, they must change only one feature at a time while keeping everything else constant.

with contrary evidence, younger children tend to hold tenaciously to the initial hypothesis and try to make the circumstances fit these preconceived notions.

One striking characteristic of adolescents' thinking is the ability to be flexible. They can be quite versatile in their thoughts and in dealing with problems. They can also devise many interpretations of an observed outcome. Because they can anticipate many possibilities prior to an actual event, they are not surprised by unusual outcomes. They are not stuck with their preconceptions. In contrast, younger children are confused by atypical results inconsistent with their simple perceptions of events.

It has already been suggested that the preoperational child begins to utilize symbols. The formal operational adolescent, however, now begins to utilize a second symbol system: *a set of symbols for symbols.* For example, metaphorical speech or algebraic symbols are symbols for other words or numbers. The capacity to symbolize symbols makes the adolescent's thought much more flexible than the child's. Words can now carry double or triple meanings. Cartoons can represent a complete story that would otherwise have to be explained in words. It is no accident that algebra is not taught in elementary school or that children have difficulty understanding political cartoons or religious symbols until approximately junior high age (Elkind, 1970).

Another important difference between concrete operational children and formal operational adolescents is that the latter are able to orient themselves toward what is abstract and not immediately present. They are able to escape the concrete present and think about the abstract and the possible. This facility enables adolescents to project themselves into the future, to distinguish present reality from possibility, and to think about what might be. Not only do adolescents have the capacity to accept and understand what is given, but they also have the ability to conceive of what might be possible and reflect on the blatantly impossible. Because they can construct ideas, they have the ability to elaborate on what they received, generating new or different ideas and thoughts. They become inventive, imaginative, and original in their thinking. Possibility dominates reality. "The adolescent is the person who commits himself to possibilities . . . who begins to build 'systems' or 'theories' in the largest sense of the term" (Baker, 1982). This ability to project themselves into the future has many important consequences for their lives.

In summary, formal thinking, according to Piaget, involves five major aspects: (1) introspection (thinking about thought), (2) abstract thinking (going beyond the real to the possible), (3) combinatorial thinking (being able to consider all important facts and ideas), (4) logical reasoning (the ability to form correct conclusions using induction and deduction), and (5) hypothetical reasoning (formulating hypotheses and examining the evidence for them, considering numerous variables). See Figure 6.4 for an overview of the abilities that distinguish the concrete operational and formal operational stages.

FIGURE 6.4 CHARACTERISTICS OF CONCRETE OPERATIONAL AND FORMAL OPERATIONAL THOUGHT

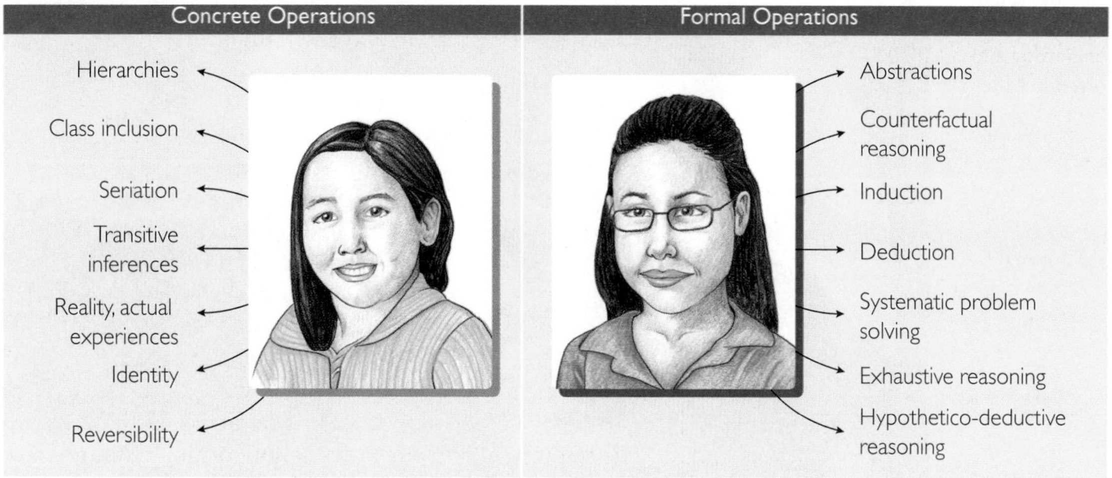

Concrete Operations	Formal Operations
Hierarchies	Abstractions
Class inclusion	Counterfactual reasoning
Seriation	Induction
Transitive inferences	Deduction
Reality, actual experiences	Systematic problem solving
Identity	Exhaustive reasoning
Reversibility	Hypothetico-deductive reasoning

EFFECTS OF ADOLESCENT THOUGHT ON PERSONALITY AND BEHAVIOR

Parents and siblings alike often bemoan the fact that their sweet, polite son/daughter/brother/sister turned into a brat once he or she became a teenager. This stereotype is the stuff of sitcoms and comic strips. But how accurate is this perception? Does the adolescent personality take a turn for the worse? In Chapter 2, we discussed the fact that teenagers are often more moody and even depressed than children and adults. In this chapter, we will describe common changes in adolescent personality and behavior that historically have been tied to cognitive development.

ANSWERS WOULDN'T YOU LIKE TO KNOW ...

Why do adolescents often have extreme political views?

Adolescents are often drawn to extreme views—political and otherwise—because they are idealistic. This idealism springs from their newfound ability to think hypothetically and imagine how the world could be. Hypothetical thinking also allows teens to come up with new solutions to old problems.

Idealism

As they become oriented to the adult world, adolescents' powers of reflective thinking enable them to better evaluate what they learn. They become much more capable of moral reasoning. They become impatient with those who don't agree with them and who appear inactive in the face of injustice. Furthermore, their ability to differentiate the possible from the real enables them to distinguish not only what the adult world is but also what it might be like, especially under ideal circumstances. This ability of adolescents to grasp what is and what might be makes them *idealistic*. They compare the possible with the actual, discover that the actual is less than ideal, and become critical observers of things as they are and ultracritical of adults.

For a while, some adolescents develop somewhat of a *messianic complex*. In all modesty, they attribute to themselves essential roles in the salvation of humanity. They may make a pact with God, promising to serve Him without return but planning to play a decisive role in the cause they espouse (Piaget, 1967). They see themselves as engaging in a major effort to reform the world, usually in verbal discussions and, for some, in group movements. Some adolescents get caught up in political idealism and become preoccupied with the utopian reconstruction of society.

At the same time that adolescents become political idealists, they also become champions of the underdog. It may be the adolescents' own inner turmoil that accounts for their empathic capacities for the suffering of others. Due to their own insecurities, they can easily identify with the weak, the poor, and the oppressed victims of selfish society. Thus, the social injustices that they perceive mirror their own internal, individual struggles. Elkind (1967) has stated that most young adolescents rebel primarily on a verbal level, doing little to work for the humanitarian causes they espouse. Only later in adolescence do many young people begin to tie their ideals to appropriate actions and to be more understanding, tolerant, and helpful.

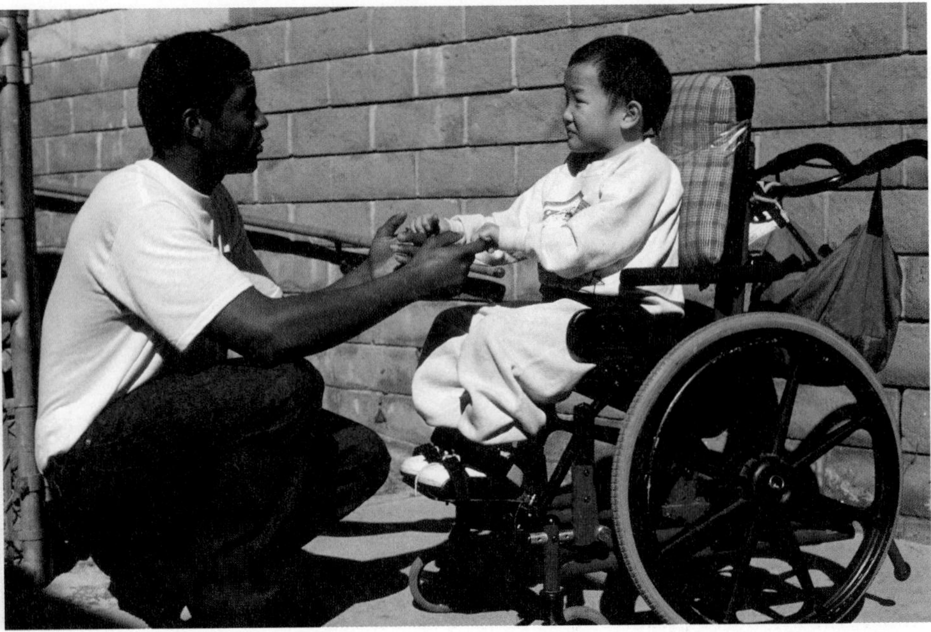

Idealism in adolescents results from their newfound ability to distinguish between what is and what might be. They become champions of the underdog and often become involved in helping people with problems.

Long-Term Values

A prominent characteristic of adolescence is that individuals begin to take on adult roles. Adolescents begin to see themselves as equals with adults, to develop a life program, to be concerned with the future, and to have ideas about changing society. At first, the adolescent personality is highly egocentric, but that egocentricism is gradually broken down. Along with formal reasoning comes the development of values with long-term implications rather than immediate gratification and goal satisfaction.

Hypocrisy

Because of the discrepancy between what they say and what they do, adolescents are sometimes accused of **hypocrisy.** Elkind (1978) gave two examples to illustrate this tendency.

First, a teenage boy complains at great length about his brother going into his room and taking his things. He berates his father for not punishing the culprit; yet the same adolescent feels no compunction about going into his father's study, using his father's computer and calculator, and playing music on his father's stereo without asking.

Second, a group of young people are involved in a "Walk for Water" drive, in which sponsors pay them for each mile walked. The money is for testing the water of Lake Ontario and for pollution control. Elkind described how pleased he was that these youths were not as valueless and materialistic as they were sometimes described to be. The next day, however, a drive along the route the youths had walked revealed a roadside littered with fast-food wrappers and soft drink and beer cans. City workers had to be hired to clean up the mess. The question was: Did the cost of cleaning up amount to more money than was collected? Here was an example of hypocrisy at its finest. On the one hand, the youths objected to pollution, yet they were among the chief offenders in defacing their environment (Elkind, 1978).

The behavior of these adolescents was hypocritical to the extent that it revealed a discrepancy between idealism and behavior. But this assumes that they had the capacity to relate general theory to specific practice, which young adolescents are not necessarily able to do. Early adolescents have the capacity to formulate general principles, such as "Thou shalt not pollute," but lack the experience to see the application of these general rules to specific practice. This is due to intellectual immaturity rather than to a character deficit. Youths tend to believe that if they can conceive and express high moral principles, then they have attained them, and nothing concrete need be done. This attitude confuses and upsets adults, who insist that ideals have to be worked for and cannot be attained instantly. This attitude is, in turn, considered cynical and hypocritical by youths (Elkind, 1978).

The ability of adolescents to think about themselves, their own thoughts, and society also leads to another manifestation of hypocrisy: pretending to be what they are not. Teenagers are expected to like school yet they rarely do. They are expected to conform to parental viewpoints and beliefs even when they do not agree with them. They are expected not to

ANSWERS WOULDN'T YOU LIKE TO KNOW ...

Why do adolescents often say one thing and then do another?

Adolescents often say one thing and do another because while their minds are focusing on lofty ideals, their bodies are performing mundane, everyday behaviors, and they don't always see the connection between the two. Adults unknowingly encourage hypocrisy by asking adolescents to pretend to have feelings that they do not have.

express hurt or anger when they really are. They are expected not to engage in behavior that will hurt or disappoint parents, so they do not dare talk to them. They are pressured not to be, not to feel, not to desire. They are expected to deny themselves and so they behave hypocritically. Their newly achieved capacity to envision what *should be* enables them to go beyond their real selves and to pretend to be what others expect them to be.

Pseudostupidity

Elkind (1978) pointed out that young adolescents also often demonstrate what he has called **pseudostupidity:** the tendency to approach problems at much too complex a level and fail, not because the tasks are difficult but because they are too simple. It's as if they approach most problems as if they are trick multiple-choice test questions. They overanalyze the situation, searching for nuances that are probably not to be found, and they can become paralyzed because tasks seem so difficult. For instance, a young adolescent might spend 20 minutes staring at a restaurant's menu, unable to decide what to have. Likewise, a high-schooler might find choosing which classes to take or what clothes to wear overwhelming.

In other words, the ability to perform formal operations gives young adolescents the capacity to consider alternatives, but this newfound capacity is not completely under control. Thus, adolescents appear stupid because they are, in fact, bright but not yet experienced.

Egocentrism

Another effect of adolescents' intellectual transformation is their development of a new form of **egocentrism** (deRosenroll, 1987; Vartanian and Powlishta, 1996). This egocentrism is manifested in two ways: through the development of what have been termed the imaginary audience and the personal fable (Lapsley, FitzGerald, Rice, and Jackson, 1989).

ANSWERS WOULDN'T YOU LIKE TO KNOW ...

Why are adolescents so self-conscious?

Adolescents are self-conscious because they believe that everyone else is looking at them all the time. And not only do they believe that others are paying attention to them, but they believe that they are playing to a tough, critical audience. Being subject to such scrutiny is enough to make almost anyone feel insecure.

As adolescents develop the capacity to think about their own thoughts, they become acutely aware of themselves, their person, and their ideas. As a result, they become egocentric, self-conscious, and introspective. They direct their thoughts toward themselves rather than toward others (Goossens, Seiffge-Krenke, and Marcoen, 1992). They become so concerned about themselves that they may conclude that others are equally obsessed with their appearance and behavior. "It is this belief that others are preoccupied with his appearance and behavior that constitutes the egocentrism of the adolescent" (Elkind, 1967, p. 1029). As a result, adolescents feel they are "on stage" much of the time. Thus, a great deal of their energy is spent "reacting to an **imaginary audience**" (Buis and Thompson, 1989).

The need to react to an imaginary audience helps account for the extreme self-consciousness of adolescents (Peterson and Roscoe, 1991). Whether in the lunchroom or on the bus going home, most youths feel that they are the center of attention. Sometimes, groups of adolescents react to this audience by loud and provocative behavior because they believe everyone is watching them and they want to look cool. Reacting to an imaginary audience also contributes to conformity. For example, peers can't laugh at your shoes if they are wearing the same shoes that you are. Finally, the concept of the imaginary audience drives

hypocrisy discrepancy between what people say and do.

pseudostupidity the tendency to approach problems at much too complex a level and to fail, not because the tasks are difficult, but because they're too simple. Adolescents appear stupid when they are, in fact, bright but not yet experienced.

egocentricism the inability to take the perspective of another or to imagine the other person's point of view.

imaginary audience adolescents' belief that others are constantly paying attention to them.

IN THEIR OWN WORDS

"The concept of the imaginary audience was certainly something I experienced as an adolescent. I think that this was in part due to the fact that I was a very late-maturing boy and thus pretty self-conscious about my looks. Excessive grooming was often a part of my routine. I can remember that before dances, I would spend so much time messing with my hair that my arms would actually begin to hurt!"

"I was never much of a diary or bad-poetry girl, but I was a big fan of writing horrible, horrible, *letters to celebrities and sometimes even sending them. I remember writing to some of the* Friends *cast members about how much I could relate to the show and how I totally understood the characters and thought I could be much better friends with them than I could with my classmates. I was thirteen!"*

"At my house, I had a basketball hoop on my garage. When I would go out to play alone, I would imagine how all of my classmates showed up and watched as I played against someone famous like Michael Jordan. Every time that I made a shot, I would act like the crowd was going wild. When I began to grow tired, I would do a countdown, as if the clock was running out and I was trailing by 2 points with 5 seconds left. Then I would try to make the shot that would either win the game for me or send me 'to the showers' in defeat. It was obvious that I had a serious case of an imaginary audience!"

many adolescents to exhibit an increased need for privacy; the only time they can relax and feel at ease is when they are literally unobservable and by themselves.

Elkind (1967) also discussed what he termed the **personal fable:** adolescents' beliefs in the uniqueness of their own experiences. Because of their imaginary audiences and their beliefs that they are important to so many people, adolescents come to regard themselves as special and unique. Some have a unique sense of their own immortality and invulnerability to harm (Dolcini et al., 1989). This may be why so many adolescents believe that unwanted pregnancies happen only to others, never to them (Arnett, 1990), or that they won't be in a car accident, even if they drive very aggressively.

Egocentrism may also be linked to adolescents' desires for social reform and to their efforts to assume adult roles (White, 1980). Not only do they try to adapt themselves to the social environment but they also try to adjust the environment to themselves. They begin to think how they might transform society. Inhelder and Piaget (1958) wrote:

> The adolescent goes through a phase in which he attributes an unlimited power to his own thoughts so that the dream of a glorious future or of transforming the world through ideas (even if this idealism takes a materialistic form) seems to be not only fantasy but also an effective action which in itself modifies the empirical world. This is obviously a form of cognitive egocentrism. (p. 345)

RESEARCH HIGHLIGHT IS A PERSONAL FABLE ENTIRELY A BAD THING?

When Elkind (1967) first described the personal fable, he emphasized its negative qualities. If you believe you are special and *unique,* you may feel lonely and misunderstood. If you suppose yourself *invulnerable,* then you don't think that bad things can happen to you and you engage in risky behaviors. If you think you are *omnipotent,* then of course you are right and others are wrong. But is the personal fable entirely a bad thing? Recent research suggests that it is not, or at least that not all of it is.

Aalsma, Lapsley, and Flannery (2006) recently concluded a study that examined the correlations among the strengths of the different aspects of the personal fable and various aspects of mental health in sixth through twelfth graders. On one hand, their findings indicate that feelings of *uniqueness* are negatively associated with mental health; in particular, those adolescents who felt most unique were most likely to be depressed and to have suicidal thoughts. On the other hand, adolescents who felt omnipotent had positive mental profiles: They felt worthy, strong, able to cope, and were well-adjusted. The relationship of invulnerability to mental health was more complex. Teenagers who believed they were invulnerable were more prone to engage in dangerous, risky behavior and to use drugs. However, they also tended to feel good about themselves.

The researchers were careful to note that these relationships may well hold true for adults as well as adolescents. Their study was not designed to compare adolescent and adult egocentrism. Future research will be needed to see if these patterns are exclusive to teenagers.

Introspection

As adolescents gain the ability to think abstractly and hypothetically, as they become more interested in society's ills, as they come to believe that everyone is staring at them, and as they develop a personal fable that says they are deeper and more sensitive than the people around them, they begin to spend more time in **introspection.** When we add up all of these other cognitive changes, it makes sense that adolescents become fascinated with their own thoughts and feelings. They *are* smarter than they used to be, and they *can* now think about complex issues that were formerly beyond them. Moreover, their thoughts are worth examining in detail because they are undoubtedly better than other people's thoughts. In their minds, adolescents replay interactions they have had with friends and nonfriends: Was there some subtle meaning to the way Carrie said hi this morning? Would it have been better if I had passed a note to Tony in geometry instead of asking Marcy to speak to him for me? The adolescent world is full of intricate problems that careful thought can help solve.

Self-Concept

The capacity of adolescents to think about themselves is also necessary to the process of developing self-concepts and identities. In doing this, adolescents have to formulate a number of postulates about themselves, such as "I am physically attractive," "I'm smart in school," or "I'm popular." These postulates are based on a number of specifics, such as "I'm attractive because I have pretty hair." Because of formal operational thinking, they are able to entertain a number of simultaneous ideas and to test each one—for example, by asking a friend: "What do you think of my hair?" or "Do you think I have ugly hair?" Gradually, they begin to sort out what they feel is truth from error about themselves and to formulate total concepts of self.

CRITIQUE OF PIAGET'S THEORY

Piaget did his research in the early part of the twentieth century, so it is not surprising that at the beginning of the twenty-first century, criticisms of his work have evolved and the field of cognitive development has moved on to new theories. Although no one doubts Piaget's assertion that adolescent thinking greatly surpasses that of younger children, the specifics of his claims about formal operational thought have been questioned on numerous fronts.

Criticisms of Piaget's First Two Stages

In general, modern researchers find that young children are more cognitively advanced than Piaget believed (Berk, 2006). More subtle measurements than he was capable of indicate that a number of abilities emerge at early ages than he envisioned (e.g., Wang, Baillargeon, and Paterson, 2005), both during the sensorimotor and preoperational periods. In addition, many psychologists who study cognitive development now believe that infants are endowed with considerable stores of built-in, prewired knowledge (e.g., Carey and Markman, 1999) and do not have to learn everything that they will come to know from scratch.

Age and Development

One question asked by investigators concerns the age at which formal operational thought replaces the concrete operational stage. Piaget (1972) himself advanced the possibility that in some circumstances, the appearance of formal operations may be delayed to 15–20 years of age and "that perhaps in extremely disadvantageous conditions, such a type of thought will never really take shape" (p. 7). Piaget (1971) acknowledged that social environment can accelerate or delay the onset of formal operations. In fact, fewer economically deprived adolescents achieve formal thought than do their more privileged counterparts, and there is a complete absence of formal operations among the mentally retarded. The percentage of adolescents demonstrating formal operational thinking is often below 50 percent (Kuhn, 1979). When a larger proportion (60 to 70 percent) have shown formal thinking, they have been drawn from gifted samples or from older, more academic, college students.

It is important for adults, especially parents and teachers, to realize that not all same-aged adolescents are at the same stage of development (Flavell, 1992). Many have not yet achieved formal operations. These youths cannot yet understand reasoning that is above their level of comprehension; to ask them to make decisions among numerous alternatives or variables that cannot be grasped simultaneously is to ask them to do the impossible. A very few youths may make the transition to formal operations by age 10 or 11, but only about 40 percent have progressed beyond concrete operations by high school graduation (Lapsley, 1990).

personal fable adolescents' belief that they are invulnerable and that their feelings are special and unique.

introspection thinking about one's thoughts and feelings.

Consistency

Even those individuals who can use formal operations don't consistently do so. In particular, people regress when they are angry, upset, or rushed (Neimark, 1975). Someone who looks under his or her bed 15 times for a lost set of keys is hardly gathering data and using it in a logical, systematic way. Likewise, the person who repeatedly pushes the button on a vending machine that has eaten his or her dollar bill has not accepted that that particular strategy is not working and is thus failing to operate at the formal operational level.

ANSWERS WOULDN'T YOU LIKE TO KNOW . . .

Are adults actually smarter than adolescents, or do they just know more?

While it's true that adults have had more time than teens to learn facts and gain experiences, they also seem to think in better ways. They better appreciate the complexity and murkiness of many issues, and they can better deal with conflicting information. Also, many adults (but certainly not all) tackle problems before they become crises. Thus, most experts agree that adults *are* smarter than adolescents.

Beyond Formal Operations

Piaget believed that the formal operational stage was the fourth and final level of cognitive development. Although people would continue to learn more and to make better decisions as they matured—presumably, because they had collected more experiences and had more data to draw on—all the "hardware" they would ever have would be in place by midadolescence. Many, if not most, researchers now disagree with this contention (Commons, Richards, and Kuhn, 1982).

There is currently no one, consistent, uniform conception of postformal cognitive development. Riegel (1973) and Basseches (1980) have proposed that some adults enter into a state of cognitive **dialectics.** A dialectical thinker is one who can integrate two or more conflicting pieces of data; a formal thinker, in contrast, tends to assume that one argument is right and the other is wrong. A dialectical thinker also understands that many aspects of the world are interconnected—that if you make a change in one place, it might have ramifications elsewhere. A formal thinker tends to wear mental "blinders" and hone in on the specific problem with which he or she is concerned, ignoring the ripple effects of solutions. This approach often leads to the extreme stances associated with idealism.

For example, imagine that both a formal reasoner and a dialectical reasoner are asked their opinions about a new law allowing unrestricted logging on state-owned land. The formal reasoner might say, "It's a terrible law; think of the wildlife that will be killed!" or he or she might say, "Great! We need that lumber for houses. It will help the economy." The dialectical thinker will more likely say, "Well, it's good in that it will help decrease unemployment among loggers, but on the other hand, that habitat is irreplaceable and beautiful. Maybe we can work something out that will allow more logging but still protect the forest." The world appears more simple and straightforward to formal operations thinkers than it does to dialectical thinkers. The positive side of this formal operations simplicity is that it allows individuals to make decisions and take action, rather than be paralyzed by complexities. The negative aspect of this simpler approach is that people risk being hideously wrong and shortsighted in the solutions they enact. (This last point provides another example of dialectical reasoning about an issue.)

In contrast to Piaget, Arlin (1975) suggests there is a fifth stage of cognitive development: the **problem-finding stage.** This new stage is characterized by cre-

Parents can create a stimulating and supportive home environment that facilitates their child's cognitive development.

ative thought, the envisioning of new questions, and the discovery of new problem-solving methods in thought. It represents an ability to discover problems not yet delineated, to formulate these problems, or to raise general questions for ill-defined problems. Persons in the problem-finding stage are proactive and discover problems before they become imminent.

Evidence indicates that not all subjects in formal operations have reached the problem-finding stage. In her research with college seniors, Arlin (1975) found that all subjects high in problem finding had reached formal operational thinking, but not all subjects who had reached formal thinking were high in problem finding. This fact demonstrates that sequencing was evident. In other words, formal operations had to be accomplished before individuals could move on to the next stage.

Culture and Environment

Cross-cultural studies have shown that formal thought is more dependent on social experience than is sensorimotor or concrete operational thought. The attainment of the first three Piagetian stages appears to be more or less universal, but full attainment of formal thinking, even in college students and adults, is far from guaranteed (Cole, 1990). Adolescents from various cultural backgrounds show considerable variability in abstract reasoning abilities. Some cultures offer more opportunities to adolescents to develop abstract thinking than others, by providing a rich verbal environment and experiences that facilitate growth by exposure to problem-solving situations. Cultures that provide stimulating environments facilitate the acquisition of cognitive skills necessary to deal with the abstract world.

Social institutions such as the family and school accelerate or retard the development of formal operations. Factors such as maternal intelligence, sociodemographic status, and the quality of the home environment have been found to relate to children's cognitive development (Ardila, Rosselli, Matute, and Guajardo, 2005).

Parents who encourage exchanges of thoughts, ideational explorations, academic excellence, and the attainment of ambitious educational and occupational goals are fostering cognitive growth. Schools that encourage students to acquire abstract reasoning and develop problem-solving skills enhance cognitive development.

dialectics an advanced form of reasoning that allows one to create new and better insights by integrating conflicting data.

problem-finding stage the fifth stage of cognitive development characterized by the ability to be creative, to discover, and to formulate problems.

RESEARCH HIGHLIGHT WHY DOES EGOCENTRISM DEVELOP?

Extensive research has confirmed the existence of the imaginary audience and the personal fable. The data, however, call into question the idea that this egocentrism is closely tied to formal operational thought. Although a number of studies have found an association between formal operational thought and adolescent egocentrism (Hudson and Gray, 1986), many studies have failed to show the predicted peak in either the imaginary audience or the personal fable in adolescents just entering the formal operational stage (see Vartanian, 2000, for a review). In addition, often gender differences in egocentrism are found—even though there are not gender differences in the emergence of formal operational thought (Pesce and Harding, 1986). Therefore, competing views as to why this egocentrism develops have been proposed.

Lapsley and Murphy (1985), for example, proposed a *social-cognitive* rationale for adolescent egocentrism. They suggested that changes in level of social perspective-taking, à la Selman (1980), were responsible for increased adolescent self-consciousness. In particular, they suggested that entry into Selman's third level, which is characterized by the ability to simultaneously consider one's own perspective and others' perspectives on a social situation, was crucial to the development of egocentrism. While evidence tying the imaginary audience to Selman's level 3 is lacking, there is some support linking it to the personal fable (Jahnke and Blanchard-Fields, 1993).

A second theoretical explanation has been deemed "the New Look" (Lapsley, 1993); it posits that egocentrism, especially the imaginary audience, arises from the adolescent identity search (O'Connor, 1995) and the need that adolescents have to separate themselves from their parents. Data suggest that adolescents who feel threatened by loss are more prone to egocentrism (Vartanian, 1997). This explanation is also appealing in that it can more readily account for the gender differences in egocentrism mentioned previously; since female adolescents tend to be more connected to their parents than male adolescents, they should, by this model, exhibit the personal fable and imaginary audience more strongly than males do (Vartanian, 2000).

FIGURE 6.5 PIAGET'S WATER-LEVEL AND ROD-AND-FRAME TASKS

The water-level task

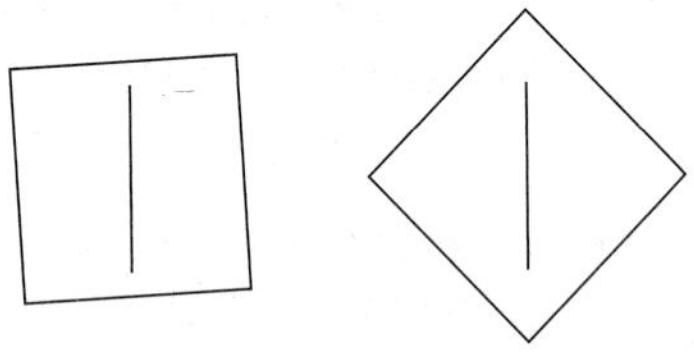

The rod-and-frame task

ANSWERS WOULDN'T YOU LIKE TO KNOW . . .

What can be done to promote high levels of reasoning in adolescents?

The highest levels of reasoning are attained when individuals are given the chance to discuss, argue, and debate with people whose views are different from their own. Giving adolescents the opportunity to formulate their own ideas and opinions and then gently challenging them is one way to promote such reasoning. (Socrates taught this way thousands of years ago.) Giving teens the opportunity to actively learn by doing, experimenting, and questioning is extremely helpful, as well.

Motivation and Response

Caution should be exercised in using the results of formal operations tests to predict the scholastic behavior of adolescents. Test models describe what adolescents are *capable* of doing intellectually—not necessarily what they *will* do in a specific situation. Fatigue, boredom, or other factors affecting motivation may prevent adolescents from displaying full cognitive performance in any given situation (Klaczynski, Byrnes, and Jacobs, 2001). Also, Piaget's models are qualitative, not quantitative, measurements. They are used to describe thought problems and do not necessarily duplicate or predict in depth the performance of adolescents.

A good example of this involves gender differences in people's ability to solve Piaget's water-level problem. It measures spatial perceptual ability, as does the related rod-and-frame task. In the water-level problem, the subject is shown a picture of a person drinking a glass of water and asked to draw the water line on the glass. In the rod-and-frame task, the subject is asked to adjust the position of a rod inside a tilted frame so that it is vertical. To do well, the subject must ignore the orientation of the surrounding frame. Figure 6.5 illustrates these problems.

Men and boys often outperform women and girls on both of these tasks as they are traditionally presented. However, a variety of manipulations eliminate the male advantage. For example, when a human figure is substituted for the rod in the rod-and-frame task, women outperform men. When instructions highlight the spatial aspects of the tasks, women's performances suffers; when those aspects are downplayed, females' performance improves. Training procedures can also decrease gender differences on these two tasks (Brannon, 1999). In sum, these findings underscore the importance of context, confidence, and motivation on performance.

WHAT CAN WE RETAIN FROM FORMAL OPERATIONS?

The substantive list of criticisms presented in this chapter may seem to suggest that Piaget was just plain wrong about cognitive development and that his work is now irrelevant. Although movement into the formal operational stage as originally conceived by Piaget cannot account for all of the changes that occur in adolescent reasoning (Moshman, 1997), his work cannot be completely discounted. Piaget was correct about these crucial aspects of adolescent cognition:

- Children become significantly and qualitatively more intelligent beginning at about 11 years of age. (These changes will be discussed more fully in the next chapter.) This change takes time and develops throughout much of adolescence.
- Deductive reasoning greatly improves during adolescence (Klaczynski, 1993) and leads to finding better answers in shorter periods of time (Foltz, Overton, and Ricco, 1995).
- Being able to think about hypothetical or even blatantly untrue situations improves substantially

during adolescence (Markovitz and Bouffard-Bouchard, 1992).

- Use of prepositional logic increases during adolescence (Ward and Overton, 1990).
- Exhaustive combinatorial reasoning improves during adolescence, as documented by evidence from studies of probabilistic reasoning (Dixon and Moore, 1996).
- Metacognition—the ability to think about one's own thoughts—improves during adolescence (Moshman, 1994).

And even though the field of cognitive development has moved on, much of the research currently being conducted about adolescent cognition was inspired by issues and questions first raised by Piaget. While many of his specific findings have been called into question, his work is the bedrock upon which more modern research rests.

SUMMARY

1. Piaget divided cognitive development into four major periods: the sensorimotor stage, the preoperational stage, the concrete operational stage, and the formal operational stage.
2. During the sensorimotor period, children learn about the effects that their actions have on their senses and perceptions.
3. The preoperational stage is the period during which language is acquired so that children can deal with the world by manipulating symbols.
4. During the concrete operational stage, children show a greater capacity for logical reasoning but only when they are thinking about reality and experiences they have actually had. They come to understand hierarchical relationships, to be able to make transitive inferences, and to understand mental operations such as reversibility and identity.
5. During the formal operational stage, children are able to use logic and abstract concepts independent of concrete objects. They become capable of introspection (thinking about thought), abstract thinking (going beyond the real to what is possible), logical thinking (being able to consider all important facts and ideas and to form correct conclusions), and hypothetical reasoning (formulating hypotheses and examining the evidence for them).
6. The ability to do formal thinking has several effects on adolescents' thoughts and behavior. The ability to grasp what is and to project what might be often makes them idealistic and rebellious.
7. Individuals with formal reasoning ability are more likely to develop long-term values than those who have not reached this stage.
8. Because of the discrepancy between what they say and what they do, adolescents are sometimes accused of hypocrisy.
9. Sometimes adolescents demonstrate pseudostupidity—the tendency to approach problems at too complex a level.
10. Adolescents become egocentric and develop an imaginary audience and personal fable. They are very self-conscious and feel that they are on stage much of the time. Personal fables refer to adolescents' beliefs in the uniqueness of their own experiences and their own invulnerability.
11. Adolescents spend a lot of time in introspection, thinking about their own thoughts and feelings.
12. Because they have reached formal operational thinking, adolescents begin to think about themselves and to develop an identity.
13. Not all adolescents reach formal operational thinking, and not all same-aged adolescents are at the same stage of development.
14. There is some evidence that a fifth stage of cognitive development exists. It is sometimes described as a dialectical stage and sometimes as a problem-finding stage. Dialectical thinkers can handle conflicting information, lack of clarity, and complexity. Problem finders can discover problems not yet delineated.
15. Adolescents from various cultures show considerable variability in abstract reasoning abilities. Social institutions such as the family and school accelerate or retard the development of formal operations. The amount of urbanization, literacy, and education all relate to formal thought development.
16. Motivation and familiarity with test content greatly affect whether individuals use formal operational modes of thinking when trying to solve problems.
17. The school can play a role in developing formal operational thinking.
18. Although adolescent cognitive development is not precisely as Piaget described it, his basic findings are fundamentally correct—namely, that adolescents show qualitative cognitive change, that they think more abstractly than younger children, that they reason in a more deductive fashion, that they more exhaustively generate solutions to problems and more logically evaluate those solutions, and that they are more aware of their own thought processes.

KEY TERMS

animism 119	imaginary audience 127
centering 119	inductive reasoning 119
class inclusion relationships 120	introspection 129
concrete operational stage 120	mental operations 118
conservation problems 121	personal fable 128
deductive reasoning 119	preoperational stage 119
dialectics 130	problem-finding stage 130
egocentrism 127	pseudostupidity 127
formal operational stage 122	sensorimotor stage 118
hierarchical classification 120	seriation 121
hypocrisy 126	syncretism 119
hypothetico-deductive reasoning 123	transductive reasoning 119
	transitive inferences 120

THOUGHT QUESTIONS

Personal Reflection

1. Think of personal examples in which you, a sibling, or a friend demonstrated three or more of the following: the imaginary audience, the personal fable, adolescent hypocrisy, idealism, and pseudostupidity.
2. Do you feel that the imaginary audience inhibited your own personal creativity when you were younger? Does it still do so?
3. What did your parents do to encourage you to develop formal operational thinking? What kinds of opportunities did they provide?
4. Are you satisfied with your level of cognitive sophistication? In what ways would you like to become smarter or wiser? Do these match either dialectics or problem seeking?

Group Discussion

5. If you give two children the same amount of ice cream but in different-sized bowls, what are they likely to do? Why?
6. Come up with several real-life, practical examples of how the cognitive limitations of the preoperational stage would affect a 5-year-old's behaviors and decisions.
7. Describe how a preschooler, a grade-schooler, and a middle-schooler would each go about playing Twenty Questions. How would their choices of questions differ from each other?
8. Imagine that you are taking one of Piaget's conservation tests—the one in which there are two identical glasses of water and then water from one of the glasses is poured into a tall, narrow test tube. Devise three separate arguments to convince someone that there is still the same amount of water in the two containers.
9. Another test that Piaget used to assess whether adolescents were capable of formal operational thinking that is not described in the text is the *chemistry experiment.* It involves showing a child five test tubes, each filled with a colorless liquid. Behind a screen, the tester pours some of the tubes' contents together. She then holds up a beaker filled with a yellow liquid. The child is asked to make a yellow liquid himself or herself. What would be the differences between how a concrete operational child and a formal operational child would approach this task?
10. Why is it necessary to reach the formal operational stage before individuals can move on to the problem-finding or dialectical stage?
11. What if any are the drawbacks of being in the dialectical-reasoning stage? How about being in the problem-seeking stage?

Debate Questions

12. Debate this statement: "Many adolescents are functioning at a cognitive level that renders them unable to practice most forms of birth control effectively."
13. Should middle schools encourage Piagetian-style individual exploration or Vygotskian-style collaboration?
14. Adolescents should be taught in advance about the personality changes they will likely experience as a result of cognitive development.
15. Idealism is, in balance, more good than bad.

SUGGESTED READING

Elkind, D. (1981). *Children and Adolescents: Interpretive Essays on Jean Piaget.* 3rd ed. New York: Oxford University Press.

Elkind, D. (1998). *All Grown Up and No Place to Go: Teenagers in Crisis.* New York: Perseus Books.

Jardine, D. W. (2005). *Piaget & Education: Primer.* New York: Peter Lang Publishing.

Montangero, J., Maurice-Naville, D., and Cornu-Wells, A. (1997). *Piaget or the Advance of Knowledge.* Mahwah, NJ: Erlbaum.

Pass, S. (2004). *Parallel Paths to Constructivism: Jean Piaget and Lev Vygotsky.* Greenwich, CT: Information Age Publishing.

Piaget, J. (2001). *Language and Thought of the Child.* London, England: Routledge.

Serulinkov, A. (2000). *Piaget for Beginners.* New York: Writers & Readers. York: Plume.

USEFUL WEB SITES

Jean Piaget Society
www.piaget.org

The Jean Piaget Society is a scholarly organization devoted to furthering the work begun by Piaget. It contains a short biography of Piaget, extensive reference lists for students and professionals, and links to many other valuable pages about cognitive development.

Psi Café: Jean Piaget
www.psy.pdx.edu/PsiCafe/KeyTheorists/Piaget.htm

Includes links to biographies of Piaget, descriptions of his work, critiques of his theory, reprints of some of his most important works, and other Piaget cites.

CHAPTER 7 NEW APPROACHES TO COGNITIVE DEVELOPMENT

Information Processing, Decision Making, and Assessment Issues

WOULDN'T YOU LIKE TO KNOW . . .

- ▶ Why do adolescents take greater risks than adults do?
- ▶ How are adolescents' memory skills better than children's?
- ▶ Why can adolescents think more quickly than children?
- ▶ How does reasoning improve during adolescence?
- ▶ How can parents and teachers help adolescents learn to make good decisions?
- ▶ Why do adolescents sometimes become skeptical of authority?
- ▶ What is the most mature way to view truth?
- ▶ Why are adolescents sometimes more emotional than adults?
- ▶ What does it mean to be *intelligent?*
- ▶ How well do IQ tests measure intelligence?

In the previous chapter, we discussed Piaget's traditional views of cognitive development. In this chapter, we will build on that discussion and consider contemporary views of cognitive development. Much of the current research concerning cognitive development is based on the **information-processing approach,** in which scientists study how individuals perceive, attend to, retrieve, and manipulate information (hence the name). Other researchers are trying to discover how adolescents reason and make difficult decisions. In addition, there has recently been a surge of interest in the effects of brain development on adolescent cognitive ability. The chapter concludes with a section on intelligence and assessment.

Overall, the current research differs from that done by Piaget in a number of consistent ways. First, whereas Piaget was most interested in developing an overview of cognitive development—a broad description of the intellectual gains that we make as we mature—researchers today are more focused on a microlevel analysis of the processes underlying those grand changes. They have taken this route because the mechanisms proposed by Piaget do not (to most psychologists' satisfaction) adequately account for the great intellectual differences observed between individuals at different stages in Piaget's scheme.

A second point about which current researchers disagree with Piaget is the stage concept itself. Piaget strongly believed in a stage approach to cognitive development, proposing that individuals grow in a steplike fashion. According to the stage theory, individuals mature rapidly for a period of time, and then their growth greatly slows and their achievement levels off. Most of today's researchers believe that change is more gradual and continuous. Also, what appear to be major strides are actually the gradual accumulation of smaller accomplishments (see Figure 7.1).

FIGURE 7.1 DISCONTINUOUS VERSUS CONTINUOUS GROWTH: STAGES OF DEVELOPMENT VERSUS GRADUAL CHANGE

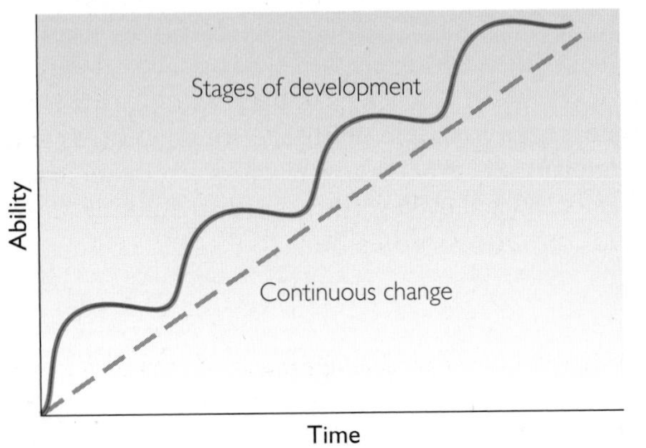

A third point of departure between most of current researchers and Piaget is a belief that knowledge and skills are *domain specific*. Piaget believed that once a person had acquired a cognitive skill, he or she could apply it broadly in a wide range of circumstances. The current thought, however, is that many skills can only be used in contexts similar to the ones in which they were acquired (Wellman and Gellman, 1998). Researchers today believe that cognitive structures are specialized, rather than general.

Finally, whereas Piaget believed that the central feature of adolescent cognitive development was the development of the ability to think abstractly, the most current conceptualizations instead emphasize increased executive control (Keating, 2004; Kuhn, 2006). In other words, older adolescents are better able to monitor and control their own learning and thinking behaviors than are children and younger adolescents. Because of this, they are more efficient and more likely to succeed at cognitive tasks.

INFORMATION PROCESSING

The information-processing approach to cognition emphasizes the progressive steps, actions, and operations that take place when the adolescent receives, perceives, remembers, thinks about, and utilizes information (Siegler, 1995). Adolescents differ in the speed of processing information (just as different computers process information at different speeds). The processing speed continues to improve in early adolescence (Hale, 1990). For example, 10-year-olds are slower than 15-year-olds in processing information, but 15-year-olds process information about as fast as young adults do.

One way we can understand information processing in humans is to compare it with the actions of a computer. Information is coded and fed, in an organized way, into a computer, where it is stored in memory. When any of that information is required, the computer is asked to produce it. The machine searches for the relevant information and displays or outputs the items requested.

Information processing by adolescents is similar in fashion but far more sophisticated. The adolescent receives information, organizes it, stores it, retrieves it, thinks about it, and combines it in such a way as to answer questions, solve problems, and make decisions. The most elaborate computer used in creating *artificial intelligence* cannot match the capacity of the human mind and nervous system in the input and output of information (Keating, 1990).

Steps in Information Processing

Figure 7.2 illustrates how information processing can be divided into a series of logical steps. The diagram shows information flowing in one direction only, from

FIGURE 7.2 STEPS IN INFORMATION PROCESSING

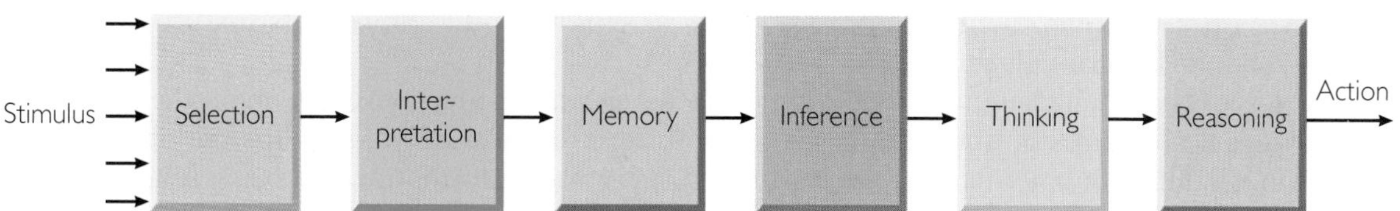

the time a stimulus is received until an action is begun. The general flow is in one direction, but there may be some flow backward as well as forward. For example, an adolescent may receive and select some information and take it in and out of memory to think about it over a long period of time before making a decision and instituting action. Nevertheless, the flowchart helps us to understand the total process. Next we'll look at the steps in more detail.

ANSWERS WOULDN'T YOU LIKE TO KNOW . . .

Why do adolescents take greater risks than adults do?

Some adolescents take risks because they feel invulnerable and charmed (the personal fable). Others are willing to take greater risks than adults because they are less upset at the thought of negative consequences. These adolescents are fatalistic and assume that bad things are likely to occur regardless of what they do. Why, then, bother to be careful?

Stimuli

Every person is constantly bombarded with stimuli—audible, visual, and tactile. As you walk down the street, for instance, you are exposed to sounds, sights, and even physical contact when someone bumps into you or touches you. Your senses are your *receptors,* your contacts with the world outside yourself. Through them, you receive all information. The sensory organs mature early in life and develop little during adolescence in terms of their raw abilities to take in information.

Selection

People do not really hear, see, or feel all of the stimuli they are exposed to, primarily because they cannot focus attention on everything at once, and they may not be interested in much of what is happening. For example, you may dimly hear a horn honking, but you may not notice the color and make of the car from which the sound is emitted or care about who is doing the honking. However, if you hear someone call your name, your attention is directed immediately to the source, and you see that the person calling your name is your good friend, driving her blue car, which you have seen many times before. Your friend pulls over, you walk over to talk, and your attention is directed to the conversation rather than to the hundreds of other sights and sounds around you. Thus, people are interested in some happenings but not others, so they are motivated to direct their attention to that which they select.

The ability to direct one's attention improves during adolescence (Hamilton, 1983; Harnishfeger, 1995). Eighteen-year-olds are better than younger children at sustaining attention and ignoring distraction. They are also better at ignoring irrelevant information and focusing on the important aspects of what they are attending to (Lehman, Morath, Franklin, and Elbaz, 1998).

Interpretation

People make judgments about everything they are exposed to, partly according to their past experiences. For instance, an adolescent girl brought up by an alcoholic father may perceive her boyfriend as drunk when he has one beer. Another girl may not consider him inebriated at all. These two girls will interpret information differently according to their perceptions of it. Adolescents, as well as adults, may sometimes make faulty judgments because of inaccurate perceptions or insufficient information. Therefore, there is often the need to make additional inquiry, to gain further information, or to check perception against fact to make sure the perception is accurate.

The interpretational biases of adolescents may make them prone to risky behavior. It is generally recognized that adolescents, especially young adolescents, are more likely to take risks than adults. This is true, in part, because adolescents are not as adept as adults at determining exactly how risky a certain behavior is, often because they lack the necessary experience (Millstein and Halpern-Felsher, 2002a). It is also true,

information-processing approach an approach to studying cognition that focuses on the perception, attention, retrieval, and manipulation of information.

however, because adolescents do not view the risks as being as significant as adults do and so are less concerned about them (Gerrard, Gibbons, Benthin, and Hessling, 1996; Millstein and Halpern-Felsher, 2002b). In addition, some adolescents may engage in risky behaviors because they are so pessimistic about their chance of leading a long, healthy, happy life (Chapin, 2001). Apparently, these adolescents' interpretation of the importance of the consequences, not a sense of low risk itself, is what allows them to smoke, to drink excessively, and to drive without wearing a seatbelt.

Memory

Information that is useful must be remembered long enough to undergo additional processing. The process of remembering involves a series of steps (Fitzgerald, 1991). The most widely accepted model is a three-stage one (Murdock, 1974): sensory storage, short-term storage, and long-term storage. Information is seen as passing from one compartment to another, with decreasing amounts passed on at any one time to the next stage. Figure 7.3 illustrates the three-stage model of memory.

Information is held only briefly (as little as a fraction of a second) in the mind before the image begins to decay and/or is blocked out by other incoming sensory information. Information that has not already faded from the sensory store is read out to **short-term storage.** Because of the limited capacity of the short-term store, information to be held longer must be further rehearsed and transferred to the relatively permanent **long-term storage.** For all practical purposes, long-term storage capacity is infinite. In the process of retrieval, stored information is obtained by searching, finding, and remembering, either through recall or recognition. Memory efficiency depends on all three of these processes and is usually at a maximum during adolescence and young adulthood.

Information received by the senses is held briefly in one of several specific types of **sensory storage.** Auditory information is held in an auditory sensory store, referred to as *echoic memory.* Visual information is held in a visual sensory store, called *iconic memory.* Other sensory stores include those for tactile information and for smell. Research evidence indicates that *the ability to retrieve information from the sensory store does not change much* as children and adolescents mature (Wickens, 1974).

FIGURE 7.3 THREE-STAGE MODEL OF MEMORY

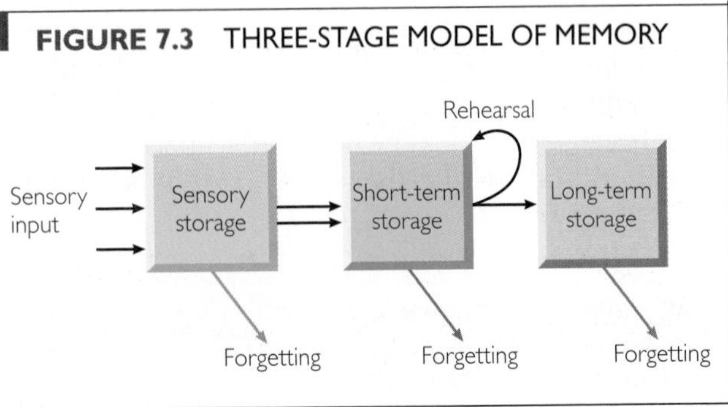

There is often some confusion about the difference between short-term and long-term memory. Short-term memory involves information still being rehearsed and focused on in the conscious mind. Long-term memory is characterized by how deeply the information has been processed, not by how long the information has been held. Deep processing, in which perceived information has been passed into layers of memory below the conscious level, constitutes secondary memory. For example, when you memorize a word list, the words under immediate consideration are at the primary or short-term memory stage. Words already looked at, memorized, and tucked away are at the secondary or long-term memory level, though they were learned only a short time before. Specific words recalled several days or months later are recalled from secondary memory. Secondary memory can last for 30 seconds or for years. These two layers of memory are used synonymously in this discussion with short-term and long-term memory, though some secondary memory stores may be recalled after relatively short time intervals.

When measuring primary or short-term memory, the subject is presented with a short string of digits, letters, or words and then tested for the total that can be recalled immediately. The most recent research indicates that short-term memory continues to improve during adolescence and into early adulthood (Fry and Hale, 1996). For example, Kail (2000) found that one's short-term memory span increases throughout adolescence. This seems to be true of both verbal and visiospatial memories (Swanson, 1999; Zald and Iacono, 1998).

The most significant changes in memory storage occur in long-term ability or in the capacity to shift information from short- to long-term storage. Adolescents take longer to retrieve information from memory than young adults do (Kail, 1991). Also, they are less likely than young adults to use effective memory strategies; for example, teenagers don't use retrieval cues to help them cluster their recall as efficiently as do older persons (Lehman, Morath, Franklin, and Elbaz, 1998). However, adolescents are more efficient at deep processing than older adults and show superior ability in long-term memory. Interestingly enough, subjects of all ages (20 to 79) can best remember sociohistoric events that occurred when they were 15 to 25 years old, indicating that these are the most impressionable years as far as memory is concerned.

Some of the changes that occur in memory during adolescence can be attributed to the fact that compared to children, older adolescents are less likely to clutter up their memories with irrelevant information.

ANSWERS WOULDN'T YOU LIKE TO KNOW . . .

How are adolescents' memory skills better than children's?

Adolescents can store more bits of information in their working memory than children. Also, adolescents are better at laying down new memories than children, in part because they can better focus their attention on the information that they want to remember.

ANSWERS WOULDN'T YOU LIKE TO KNOW . . .

Why can adolescents think more quickly than children?

Adolescents can think more quickly than children because more of their neurons are *myelinated,* or covered with an insulating fatty material. This coating speeds up neural transmission and results in quicker thinking.

For example, Bjorklund and Harnishfeger (1990) presented children and adolescents with sentences whose last words were missing; each sentence was constructed in such a way that there was only one sensible, obvious choice for the last word (e.g., *Bananas are the color* . . .). Each subject was asked to supply the missing last word. Sometimes, the correct answer was the obvious choice, but other times, the subject was told that his or her answer was wrong and that another, unexpected word was correct. Each subject was told to remember the correct last word for each sentence. At the end of the procedure, each subject was asked to list the correct-ending words and also the words that he or she had guessed, even if they were incorrect. The older subjects generally remembered only the correct words, as they had been instructed; the younger subjects remembered both the correct words and their incorrect guesses. Because the older subjects had concentrated on remembering the correct words only, they recalled more of the correct-ending words than did the children.

Processing Speed

Age changes in both attention span and memory are likely accounted for by the same mechanism: mental processing speed. **Processing speed** refers to how fast the brain perceives and utilizes information. It influences how fast you notice the details of a stimulus and how fast you think. Kail (1991) found that 12- and 13-year-old adolescents were substantially slower—a full standard deviation slower—than adults on a wide variety of processing speed tasks, including mental addition, mental rotation, memory search, and the performance of simple motor skills. This simple change in processing speed, which is probably linked to neural development and myelinization (Kail, 2000), causes improvements in short-term memory (Kail, 1997). Enhanced short-term memory, in turn, leads to increases in intelligence, reasoning, and problem solving (Demetriou, Christou; Spanoudis, and Platsidou, 2002). Fry and Hale (1996) labeled this series of enhancements a "developmental cascade."

Higher-Order Thought Processes

After information has been retrieved from memory stores, it must be manipulated in some way. In a lengthy review of the literature, Moshman (1997) differentiates among three higher-order thought processes: inference, thinking, and reasoning. Each improves during adolescence.

Inference—the most basic of the thought processes—is the ability to generate new thoughts from old information. Even very young children make unconscious inferences, but the ability to draw on what one already knows to infer new facts continues to improve with age. For example, Barnes, Dennis, and Haefele-Kalvaitis (1996) asked 147 six- to fifteen-year-olds to make inferences after having been read a story. The adolescents were better able to infer information not explicitly stated than the younger children were.

Thinking is more advanced in that it is the conscious, deliberate coordination of information (Moshman, 1997). You are thinking when you struggle with a problem, try to decide between two options, or plan the itinerary of your vacation. Adolescents think more clearly than children; for example, they are more planful

short-term storage (short-term memory) the process by which information is still in the conscious mind, being rehearsed and focused on (also called *primary memory*).

long-term storage (long-term memory) the process by which information is perceived and processed deeply so it passes into the layers of memory below the conscious level (also called *secondary memory*).

sensory storage (sensory memory) the process by which information is received and transduced by the senses, usually in a fraction of a second.

processing speed the pace at which the brain perceives and manipulates information.

inference to develop new thoughts from old information.

thinking the conscious, deliberate manipulation of information.

(Lachman and Burack, 1993). Several studies have demonstrated that older adolescents are more deliberative and systematic when using information than younger adolescents (e.g., Nakajima and Hotta, 1989), and that—as Piaget claimed—they are more likely to manipulate one variable at a time when solving problems (Kuhn and Dean, 2005).

One way that adolescents' thinking improves is that they are better able to use *negative information*—that is, information that refutes their hypotheses—than younger children. During early and middle childhood, individuals search for and base their decisions on the confirming evidence that they find; during adolescence, individuals search for and rely more on disconfirming evidence. For example, imagine that you have been asked to decide whether all pears are green. To help you, you have been given a large stack of pictures of pear trees. If you were 8 or 9 years old, you would point to a lot of pictures of green pears and gleefully say that they are *all* green. If you were 15, you would either show those same pictures and say "They seem to be but I'm not certain," or you would find the one picture at the bottom of the stack that showed a red pear. You would then conclude that not all pears are green because you would understand that one counterexample is enough to disprove a premise, even if there are hundreds of confirming pieces of evidence. Adolescents rely on **negation** rather than **affirmation** (Mueller, Sokol, and Overton, 1999), and they use an **elimination strategy** rather than the younger child's **confirmation strategy** (Foltz, Overton, and Ricco, 1995).

Adolescents may be more able than children to incorporate negative information into their judgments, but like adults, adolescents are not very good at doing this when they are personally or emotionally involved in the situation (Kuhn, 1989). Klaczynski and Gordon (1996), for example, found that adolescents were better able to find logical flaws in arguments that were inconsistent with their religious beliefs than those that were in accord with them. This **self-serving bias** probably serves the same function in adolescence that it does in adulthood: Seeing the data as more consistent with your opinion than it really is enhances self-esteem, allows one to feel self-righteous, and promotes optimism (Schaller, 1992).

The most sophisticated cognitions involve the third type of thought process: **reasoning.** Reasoning occurs when you constrain and limit your thinking along lines that you believe are rational and useful. You do this based on prior experiences with both successful and unsuccessful thinking strategies.

Finding parallels between similar problems is one form of reasoning known as reasoning by *analogy: Grass is to green as sky is to ....* As with many cognitive skills, young children have some ability to form analogies, but this skill improves during adolescence (Nippold, 1994).

ANSWERS WOULDN'T YOU LIKE TO KNOW ...

How does reasoning improve during adolescence?

Adolescents are better than children at seeing similarities between problems; this lets them use their past experiences more effectively to solve current dilemmas. Adolescents are also better than children at *deducing* answers, or beginning with general truths and logically deriving specific answers to problems. Adolescents are better able to do the opposite, too: drawing general conclusions from specific examples.

Another form of reasoning involves deliberately following the rules of logic, or making *deductions.* This is the type of reasoning that Piaget (1963) focused on in his discussions of formal operations. The fact that formal operational thinking begins in adolescence indicates a growth in logical, deductive reasoning ability. This increased use of deduction has been confirmed by more recent studies, such as those by Moshman and Franks (1986), which demonstrated that older adolescents can better follow a logical argument than younger adolescents, and Byrnes and Overton (1988), which showed that older adolescents better comprehend *if/then* statements than younger ones.

Although adolescents best use deduction when solving problems in which the content is familiar (Klarczynski and Narasimhan, 1998), they can create and test hypotheses when the content is unfamiliar or counterfactual (Ward and Overton, 1990). In fact, Moshman (1999) has concluded that most of the deductive improvement that occurs during adolescence comes from an increasing ability to suspend one's own beliefs. A third form of reasoning, induction (the ability to drawing general conclusions from a series of examples), also appears to improve during adolescence (e.g., Caspo, 1997; Galotti, Komatsu, and Voelz, 1997).

Finally, an advanced type of reasoning occurs when one uses **principles** to solve problems. Principles differ from rules in that rules are more precise. For example, the statement *Any number times 0 equals 0* is a rule because it is always true. If you apply the rule, you will always get the same answer. Principles are more abstract; thus, two individuals using the same principle might propose different solutions to a dilemma. Two people who believe in the principle "One should be kind to others" might easily treat their neighbors differently. While one might conclude that kindness involves doing extensive favors, the second might believe that exchanging pleasantries and doing small favors is sufficient. Adolescents are much more likely than children to engage in principle-based reasoning (Moshman, 1993). The development of principled moral reasoning has been extensively studied and will be discussed further in Chapter 14.

Problem Solving

One of the practical results of information processing is *problem solving.* This begins with *problem finding,* which means determining the problem so that the individual can determine what needs to be done. The second step is *evaluating the elements of the problem* so that the person knows the information and tasks with which he or she has to work. This step usually requires insightful reorganization and thinking about various facets of the problem. The third step is *generating a list of solutions and evaluating* them ahead of time by trying to foresee the effects or consequences each solution will produce. This will enable the individual to make a choice.

Some of the differences between adolescents and children in problem-solving ability can be attributed to the nature of adolescents' information processing. Adolescents are better able to remember more information, consider all possible relationships, think about them logically, and generate and evaluate different variables and solutions ahead of time before deciding on a solution and course of action. Children usually do not get sufficient information, remember enough of it, think about it logically enough, or consider all possible relations before arriving at solutions. Their information-processing ability is limited in relation to that of adolescents (Kuhn, 2006).

Furthermore, researchers have found that when adolescents get together in groups to solve problems, more satisfactory solutions are found. Sometimes, the process takes longer than when an individual is solving a problem, but the problem is usually solved with greater understanding and results are more satisfactory. Much research has documented the power of peer collaboration in problem solving (e.g., Tudge and Winterhoff, 1993).

The information-processing approach brings us closer to understanding why and how adolescents think in more advanced ways than when they were children. Such an approach sheds light on what abilities are developed when individual adolescents become more efficient problem solvers.

The Role of Knowledge

"Garbage in, garbage out" is an apt saying when it comes to problem solving. In order to accurately manipulate facts in your mind, you must *know* those facts. Part of the reason that adolescents are smarter than children is simply that they know more information and have had more experiences (Byrnes, 2003). They can thus draw on that information and those experiences to find analogies to new problems they are facing. For example, suppose you get a new pie recipe from a friend but forget to ask how long it needs to be baked. If you have made a lot of pies in your lifetime, you can guess that the baking time is about an hour. But if you have never baked one before, you will be clueless.

As noted earlier, adolescents do better at solving problems when the content is familiar. Obviously, as we get older, more and more content is familiar to us and so our problem-solving ability is enhanced.

DECISION MAKING

One of the characteristics of an intelligent, mature person is the ability to *make good decisions.* Some decisions made during adolescence may have lifelong consequences. Important decisions may pertain to education, career, choice of mate, leisure activities, drug use, medical care, and health habits. Adolescence is a period of challenge and change—a time when both deliberate and unintentional decisions are made that affect the course of the adolescents' lives. Furthermore, adolescents begin to question parental authority and want to make some decisions on their own regarding choice of friends, leisure activities, curfews, and study habits. The consequences of these decisions depend partly on the degree to which good judgment is exercised (Mann, Harmoni, and Power, 1989).

The Process

Decision making is a complicated process involving information search and processing to understand available options (Moore, Jensen, and Hauck, 1990). It involves problem solving to find novel or creative solutions. Ross (1981) proposed that decision makers must master five skills: (1) identifying alternate courses of action, (2) identifying appropriate criteria for considering alternatives, (3) assessing alternatives by criteria, (4) summarizing information about alternatives, and (5) evaluating the outcome of the decision-making process.

negation a strategy used to disprove.

affirmation a strategy used to confirm.

elimination strategy looking for evidence that disproves a hypothesis.

confirmation strategy looking for examples that match a hypothesis.

self-serving bias looking at the world in a way that favors one's own opinion.

reasoning logical, constrained, useful thinking.

principles abstract, theoretical guidelines.

One of the major decisions during adolescence is to choose a college or a vocation, an important decision that has lifelong consequences.

ANSWERS WOULDN'T YOU LIKE TO KNOW . . .

How can parents and teachers help adolescents learn to make good decisions?

Parents and teachers can help adolescents learn to make good decisions by letting them practice. Good decision making is a skill that needs to be honed. Adolescents need to be given opportunities to make decisions for themselves and to learn from their mistakes along the way.

One study of decision making during adolescence revealed that, in comparison with the early adolescent, the middle adolescent understands very well what is involved in the activity of decision making. The early adolescent has little recognition that decision-making activity involves clearly specifying goals, considering options, and checking before taking action to implement a decision. This conclusion is consistent with other research findings that young adolescents are less likely than older adolescents to generate options, to anticipate the consequences of decisions, and to evaluate the credibility of sources (Ormond, Luszez, Mann, and Beswick, 1991).

Many researchers have found a relationship between age and decision-making ability. Older adolescents formulate more options, pay more attention to future outcomes, consult more with experts, and are more aware of the implications of advice received from someone with vested interest. Other studies of adolescents have identified such cognitive changes as improvement in memory and improved ability to process information and apply knowledge (Friedman and Mann, 1993).

The breadth of experience plays an important role in the quality of decisions that are made. There is an old saying that "Experience is the world's best teacher." It has been demonstrated that adolescents who have had many opportunities to make decisions for themselves are better at doing so than adolescents who have not (Jacobs and Potenza, 1990; Quadrel, Fischoff, and Davis, 1993). Parents who involve their adolescents in family decision making are helping to prepare them for mature adult life. So important is this skill that many schools have developed programs to help teach adolescents critical-thinking skills (Ennis, 1991).

The Nine Cs of Decision Making

One of the most helpful decision-making models was developed by Mann and his colleagues (1989). They listed nine elements of competent decision making (the nine Cs of decision making): choice, comprehension, creativity, compromise, consequentiality, correctness, credibility, consistency, and commitment.

Choice

Willingness to choose is an important prerequisite to decision making. Having high self-esteem gives adolescents the courage and confidence to make choices (Brown and Mann, 1991). If their locus of control is internal rather than external, their decision-making authority resides within themselves. In general, older adolescents (15 to 17 years old) have higher internality than young adolescents (12 to 14 years old) (Mann, Harmoni, Power, and Beswick, 1986). Some adolescents relinquish personal control in their desire to conform to peer groups. Peer pressures generally reach a peak at about 12 to 13 years of age, so group conformity is greatest during those years. (Conformity is more fully addressed in Chapter 13.) Other adolescents may relinquish chances to choose because, due to newfound thinking abilities, making choices is simply too overwhelming. (See also the next section of this chapter.)

Comprehension

Comprehension refers to the understanding of decision making as a cognitive process. Often termed **metacognition,** this refers to one's ability to think about and understand one's own thinking and learning. If you know that you study better with soft music than with loud music or that it will take you longer to get through a chapter in your physics text than it will to read a chapter in a best-selling novel, you have some metacognitive skills.

Metacognition is now also referred to as *executive control.* As mentioned earlier, many researchers believe that advances in executive control (or metacognition) are largely responsible for the cognitive advances seen during adolescence (Keating, 2004). As Klaczynski (2005) puts it, adolescents become more analytical in their reasoning; they are deliberate and self-reflective when they think. Instead of responding reflexively, they actively, consciously manipulate their own thought processes.

Creativity

The best solutions are often not the most obvious ones, and the first answer you come up with when solving a complex problem is rarely the best one. According to Sternberg and Williams (1996), creativity is not one cognitive skill but a set of three clusters of abilities. The first cluster, **synthetic ability,** contains the skills of generating novel, interesting ideas and finding connections among problems to see analogies. Many people think that these abilities are the defining characteristics of creative persons, but Sternberg and Williams do not believe that these abilities are sufficient. The second cluster of skills they describe are termed **analytic ability.** These are the skills of critical thinking, which allow you to evaluate the ideas you have generated (because not all ideas are equally good). Finally, **practical ability** is needed in order to make ideas work. Practical ability allows you to take abstract ideas and turn them into real-world applications. After all, ideas must be implemented if they are to do any good. Something real must come out of them.

Are adolescents creative individuals? While there are factors that should push them toward creativity—for example, they often reject the traditional and are capable of new ways of thinking—there are also factors that prevent them from being as creative as they might be. In particular, adolescents are often driven to conform to their peers due to pressure from the imaginary audience. It is probably fair to say that adolescents are capable of being quite creative but that they do not always exercise this ability.

Compromise

Decision making often involves a willingness to accept compromises—to negotiate a mutually acceptable solution in a dispute with family or friends. This includes the willingness to consider the other person's point of view as important.

Consequentiality

Competent decision making involves the willingness to think about the potential consequences of choosing actions for oneself and others. Older adolescents are more likely than younger adolescents to anticipate the consequences of their actions (Halpern-Felsher and Cauffman, 2001) and to learn from their mistakes (Byrnes, Miller, and Reynolds, 1999).

Correctness

Making a correct choice is the prime test of decision making (Klayman, 1985). Unfortunately, even adults do not always make the best decisions. This is in part because we rely too much on *heuristics,* or rules of thumb, when making decisions. A good example of this involves the "sunk-cost fallacy," a situation that arises when people do more of a disliked activity if they paid for it than if it was free. In one study, 63 percent of adults watched a boring movie longer if they paid for it than if it were shown gratis; 73 percent of 16-year-olds and a whopping 84 percent of 12-year olds did the same (Klaczynski and Cottrell, 2004). Clearly, then, the tendency to avoid this mistake increases as we get older, but most individuals, even adults, still make a poor choice. Similarly, adolescents (just like adults) are mistakenly likely to conclude that a pretty, cheerful girl is more likely to be a cheerleader than to be in the band even though there are more female band members than cheerleaders (Jacobs and Potenza, 1991). These errors are most likely to be made in social than nonsocial contexts, showing that individuals have learned stereotypes (Jacobs and Klaczynski, 2002).

metacognition the ability to think about one's own thought processes.

synthetic ability the aspect of creativity that involves generating new ideas.

analytic ability the aspect of creativity that involves evaluating ideas.

practical ability the aspect of creativity that involves turning abstract ideas into practical applications.

Credibility

Credibility involves the ability to accept the authenticity of the information relating to choice alternatives. Young adolescents are less able to recognize the vested interests of those who offer advice and are less likely to question the expertise or credibility of the source. Older adolescents are more likely to check new information against previous knowledge.

Consistency

A competent decision maker is expected to show some consistency and stability in patterns of choices.

Commitment

Commitment involves a willingness to follow through on decisions. Older students (ages 16 to 20) are more likely to follow through than younger students (ages 14 to 15) (Mann, Harmoni, and Power, 1989).

In summary, many adolescents are aware of the steps involved in systematic decision making and have the capacity for creative problem solving. Research has shown that late adolescents with more experience have greater competence than early adolescents. By age 15, adolescents who have achieved a reasonable degree of autonomy are competent in decision making. However, there is sometimes a gap between competence and involvement in decision making. Low self-esteem, peer pressure, structured family situations (Brown and Mann, 1988), and legal restraints may interfere with adolescents' involvement in making personal decisions. In order to develop this skill, adolescents must be taught how to make decisions and then given the opportunity to do so (Baron, 1989).

EPISTEMOLOGICAL UNDERSTANDING

A major change in reasoning that occurs during adolescence involves how teenagers think about *facts* and *truth*. As adolescence progresses, individuals become much more sophisticated in how they perceive and reason about information and knowledge. They come to understand that truth is not objective but subjective. More specifically, they discover that one *constructs* his or her understanding of the truth rather than *uncovers* it. The great strides in thinking about knowledge—**epistemology**—that occur during adolescence rely on the abstract reasoning capacity and the metacognitive abilities that emerge during the formal operations stage.

Boyes and Chandler (1992; see also Chandler, Boyes, and Ball, 1990) have devised a four-level scheme of epistemic development that is appealing because it speaks to a diverse set of changes that occur during childhood and adolescence.

ANSWERS WOULDN'T YOU LIKE TO KNOW ...

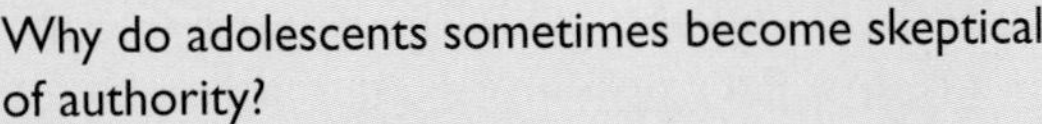
Why do adolescents sometimes become skeptical of authority?

Some adolescents lose respect for authority because they realize that what comprises truth sometimes changes and that experts can be wrong. In a sense, they view all opinions as equally valid because they understand that our knowledge of truth is imperfect.

Level 1

In early childhood, when children are in Piaget's preoperational stage of cognitive development, they are **naive realists.** They believe that there are absolute, universal truths in the world, and they have difficulty distinguishing fact from opinion. Naive realists believe that when people have diverging opinions, it is because they are working with different pieces of information. The 4-year-old who says "Just try my vanilla ice cream; you'll think it's better than chocolate" after you announce that chocolate is your favorite flavor is demonstrating naive realism. Note that this stage is reminiscent of stage 1 of Selman's (1980) theory of social role taking (see Chapter 2).

Level 2

During middle childhood, when individuals are in the concrete operational stage, they become **defensive realists.** They are still realists because they continue to cling to the belief that there are absolute, universal truths, but they now recognize that people can hold different opinions and draw different conclusions even when they are working with the same information. They defend their belief in realism by arguing that people are biased (and hence misrepresent and distort the truth) and by differentiating between fact and opinion. Defensive realists see facts as unambiguously, universally true and opinions as variable. Some individuals never progress beyond this epistemic stage.

Level 3

Once adolescents enter the formal operations stage, they become either **dogmatists** or **skeptics,** at least in the short run. Boyes and Chandler (1992) see these opposite types as being rooted in the same awareness: that truth is always constructed and that facts are open to multiple valid interpretations. This is an unsettling revelation at best, and adolescents feel beset by uncertainty. They wonder: "If you can't tell the true from the false, if you cannot be certain who is right and who is wrong, how can you make good choices?"

Skeptical adolescents react to this uncertainty by rejecting rationality. They take the attitude that if they cannot be certain about what to do or whom to believe,

ANSWERS WOULDN'T YOU LIKE TO KNOW . . .

What is the most mature way to view truth?

The most mature conceptualization of truth is that while you can never be certain of a fact or know that something is irrefutably right, you can recognize that some pieces of information are more likely to be right than others.

then all opinions and positions are equally valid and they don't have to listen to anyone (or to anyone in particular). They lose respect for authority and have little patience for those who parade around as experts. Because they have lost faith in logic, these adolescents behave *impulsively* (without reasoning through situations), *intuitively* (doing what their emotions, rather than their logic, tells them to do), and *indifferently* (without attempting to choose a good course of action, "going with the flow"). They are apt to *conform* to others, letting the majority make their decisions for them, and they become rebellious or disengaged.

In contrast to the skeptics, *dogmatists* flee from their uncertainty, rigidly clinging to one set of beliefs. They are intolerant of other views because they find them threatening, and they do not want to question their own beliefs. They conform to the views of those they have chosen as allies. They insist that their way of thinking is right and that any who disagree with them are wrong.

Whereas skeptics believe that anyone who believes too deeply in anything is foolish, dogmatists believe that anyone who espouses something different than they do is misguided. Clearly, neither of these positions is desirable. Boyes and Chandler (1992) view skepticism and dogmatism as short-term costs associated with entry into formal operations. Again, many people never outgrow this stage of reasoning.

Level 4

Finally, some individuals progress to the stage of **postskeptical rationalism.** Postskeptical rationalists understand that absolute certainty of the truth is not needed for rational behavior. Although one cannot be completely certain what is right, it is clear that some possibilities are more likely right than others. Postskeptical rationalists believe that you do the best you can with the information available. You recognize, however, that others may draw different conclusions from that data or reject as false some of the data that you use.

Researchers disagree as to how quickly individuals can move through these four levels of epistemic development. Boyes and Chandler (1992) found evidence of rationalism in some of the high school juniors they studied, but King, Kitchener, Davidson, Parker, and Wood (1983) found that it took several years of college experience before rationalism emerged.

IN THEIR OWN WORDS

"I definitely saw the world in dichotomies. I thought that the world had a few truths, such as Good/Evil and Just/Unjust. At the time, it was surprising to me that adults did not view things the same way. To me, it was obvious that problems existed in the world and that solutions were easy. Becoming dogmatic in my religion and my beliefs, I held firm to the fact that I was right and those who disagreed with me were wrong. I was very argumentative with my mom, family, and friends. I was not afraid to be controversial if it meant that I held onto my beliefs. I felt that my faith and my thoughts were truth in the world."

"Boy, was I a skeptic! In some ways, I still am. I used to argue with my dad and my teachers and say stuff like 'You don't really know that; you just think that.' I thought that my opinion was just as good as anyone else's. I got into a huge fight with my English teacher. She loved Shakespeare, and I thought his plays sucked. She told me that most scholars agreed that he was one of the greatest writers of all time. I told her that I thought his plays were stupid and boring and that I didn't care what anyone else thought. I didn't think that anyone had anything worthwhile to tell me. I needed to figure it all out for myself. I still think that a lot of so-called experts are just full of bullshit. I like to think things out for myself."

BRAIN DEVELOPMENT DURING ADOLESCENCE

Why do adolescents make these cognitive gains? It might be, in part, because they have had time to acquire a substantial amount of knowledge. It might be,

epistemology one's beliefs about knowledge.

naive realism the belief that there are absolute, universal truths; creates difficulty in distinguishing fact from opinion.

defensive realism the belief that there are absolute truths but people are biased; differentiates between opinion and fact.

dogmatism clinging rigidly to one belief.

skepticism the rejection of rationality; complete disbelief.

postskeptical rationalism the belief that truth is constructed but that some beliefs are more valid than others.

in part, that they have had time to practice their cognitive skills or that they have learned which cognitive strategies are most successful. Or it might be, in part, due to physical maturation of the brain (Byrnes, 2003).

For many years, scientists believed that brain development was largely completed during early childhood (Straugh, 2003). They now know that this is not the case and that a number of key brain structures do not mature until the individual is in his or her twenties (Casey, Giedd, and Thomas, 2000; Giedd et al., 1999a). Most of the identified changes occur in the **cerebrum.** As the largest structure in the human brain, the cerebrum is mostly what you see when you look at an intact brain. The cerebrum is divided into two hemispheres (or halves) that are connected by the **corpus callosum,** a band of nerve fibers that transmits information back and forth. Each hemisphere is divided into four lobes (or sections; see Figure 7.4).

Each type of lobe contributes to thinking in a different way, and three of the lobes—the **parietal lobe,** the **frontal lobe,** and the **temporal lobe**—continue to develop into adolescence. The cells in the parietal lobe become active when a person is working on problems involving *spatial reasoning* (Kandel, Schwartz, and Jessel, 1991), such as figuring out whether your car will fit into that small parking space or which way you need to turn in order to get to your friend's house. The frontal lobe is involved in higher-order thought processes, such as planning and impulse control. People whose frontal lobe has been damaged act before they think and are unconcerned with long-term consequences. In contrast, if you bite your tongue instead of telling off your boss when he or she is being unreasonable or if you begin studying for finals more than a week before they occur, you have a well-functioning frontal lobe. The most well-known function of the temporal lobe (or in most people, the left temporal lobe) is language. (The right hemisphere of the temporal lobe is more concerned with interpreting nonverbal communication.)

Not only do these lobes continue to mature throughout adolescence, but the connections among them continue to develop, as well. For example, the nerve fibers running from the frontal and temporal lobes become thicker and more myelinated (Paus et al., 1999). (*Myelin* is a fatty covering that helps nerve impulses travel more quickly.) The corpus callosum—that band of tissue connecting the left and right cerebral hemispheres—also thickens (Giedd et al., 1999b). This enables different areas of the brain to share information more efficiently with each other.

Deep inside the temporal lobe are two other structures that are now known to mature during adolescence: the **hippocampus** and the **amygdala.** The hippocampus is involved with learning, memory, and motivation. The amygdala interprets incoming sensory information and causes us to respond in primal, emotional ways to that information. It is also concerned with memory, especially emotional memory. An individual who has a strong amygdala and a weak frontal lobe may, for example, anger easily and lash out at others or perhaps cry at a small setback. Interestingly, the hippocampus matures more quickly in girls and the amygdala matures more quickly in boys (Giedd, Castellanos, Rajapakse, Vaituzis, and Rapaport, 1997).

Maturation of these brain structures is a two-step process. First, the cells rapidly grow and proliferate. This growth is so rapid that the resulting interconnections are termed *exuberant synapses.* Growth continues until the adolescent is about 16. At that point, the number of cells and interconnections are cut back. Some cells grow larger and stronger, and the surrounding, less used cells die off. (Imagine a fast-growing oak sapling creating so much shade that its slower-growing siblings die off; it now has more room to expand and get even larger.) The cell loss that occurs can be quite dramatic. The brain actually loses 7 to 10 percent of its cells, and in some specific areas, half of all cells disappear (Durston et al., 2001). To repeat the theme that inhibition is associated with maturity, the number of excitatory synapses that are eliminated is much greater than the number of inhibitory synapses. In fact, the ratio of excitatory to inhibitory synapses drops from 7:1 to 4:1 during adolescence. This, in turn, highlights the importance of the environment in adolescent brain development, since which interconnections are strengthened and which are lost is a function of the experiences that the adolescent is having.

A number of researchers have hypothesized that the kinds of brain changes just described could account for much of the cognitive advancement seen during adolescence (e.g., Case, 1992; Kail, 2000; Waltz et al., 1999). Increased processing speed, memory improvements, more sophisticated use of language, and enhanced self-awareness are the sorts of cognitive effects to be expected from these types of brain changes. At the same time, some of the less positive aspects of adolescent behavior—such as increased risk taking, moodiness, and impulsiveness—also correlate with the uneven growth of the brain.

ASSESSING COGNITION

In addition to the Piagetian and information-processing approaches already described, there is a third perspective from which we can study cognitive development: the **psychometric approach.** Psychometricians are interested in the measurement of knowledge and thinking ability. To this end, they have devised many tests, some of which are given to enormous numbers of children and adolescents. Tests that are designed to measure intelli-

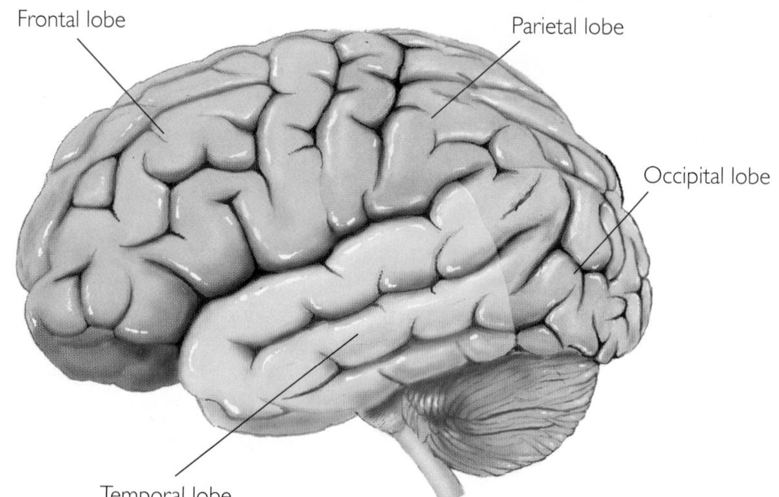

FIGURE 7.4 THE CEREBRAL LOBES

ANSWERS WOULDN'T YOU LIKE TO KNOW ...

Why are adolescents sometimes more emotional than adults?

Adolescents may be more emotional than adults because the amygdala (the emotional center) develops faster than the frontal lobes (the center of planning and impulse control). This is even more true of boys than girls.

gence, which are usually termed *IQ tests* (for **intelligence quotient**), are widely used by schools to determine students' eligibility for special academic programs. The other main type of test, **achievement tests,** are intended to measure mastery of particular subject matter, such as reading comprehension or geometry.

Questions about these types of tests and the utility of testing in general have recently become the subject of public debate, in large part because the Bush administration has made the frequent, mandatory achievement testing of all American schoolchildren part of its educational agenda. Although tests are usually labeled as being either *intelligence* or *achievement* tests, many are, in fact, blends of the two. In order to do well on such a test, you must be bright and capable of quick thought *and* you must possess relevant knowledge.

Theories of Intelligence

Intelligence has almost as many definitions as experts who try to measure it. It has been described as an innate capacity to learn, think, reason, understand, and solve problems. Piaget (1963) described it as the ability to adapt to one's environment. At the present time, two very different theories of intelligence are generally accepted. Let's describe each in turn.

Triarchic Theory of Intelligence

Sternberg (1997) and his colleagues at Yale University arranged abilities into the following three major groupings in his triarchic theory of intelligence:

1. *Componential intelligence:* Componential intelligence includes general learning and comprehension abilities, such as good vocabulary; high reading comprehension; the ability to do test items

cerebrum the largest part of the human brain.

corpus callosum a fibrous band of tissue that connects the two cerebral hemispheres of the brain.

parietal lobe the cerebral lobe that is the center for solving problems involving spatial relationships.

frontal lobe the cerebral lobe that is the center for higher-order thought processes, such as planning and impulse control.

temporal lobe the cerebral lobe that is the center for producing and understanding language.

hippocampus the part of the brain involved with learning, memory, and motivation.

amygdala the part of the brain that creates primitive emotional responses to the environment.

psychometric approach an approach to cognitive development that focuses on the measurement of knowledge and thinking ability.

intelligence quotient (IQ) calculated by dividing the mental age (MA) by the chronological age (CA) and multiplying by 100.

achievement tests tests designed to assess mastery of specific subject matter or skills.

such as analogies, syllogisms, and series; and the ability to think critically. This is the traditional concept of intelligence as measured on tests.

2. *Experiential intelligence:* Experiential intelligence includes the ability to select, encode, compare, and combine information in meaningful ways to create new insights, theories, and ideas.
3. *Contextual intelligence:* Contextual intelligence includes adaptive behavior in the real world, such as the ability to size up situations, achieve goals, and solve practical problems (Sternberg and Wagner, 1986).

Research has demonstrated that adolescents who are taught in a manner that taps into each of these three types of intelligence learn more than those who are taught in a more traditional, memory-based fashion (Sternberg, Torff, and Grigorenko, 1998).

Eight (or Ten?) Frames of Mind

Harvard professor Howard Gardner objects to assessing intelligence in only two dimensions: *linguistic* and *logical-mathematical abilities* (Gardner, 1993). In his classic book *Frames of Mind* (1993), he outlines seven types of intelligence:

1. *Linguistic intelligence*
2. *Logical-mathematical intelligence*
3. *Spatial intelligence:* Spatial intelligence is the ability to form spatial images and to find one's way around in an environment. The sailors in the Caroline Islands of Micronesia navigate among hundreds of islands using only the stars and their bodily feelings. Intelligence testers in Micronesia would have to come up with an entirely different list of intelligences and testing methods.
4. *Musical intelligence:* Musical intelligence is the ability to perceive and create pitch and rhythmic patterns. There are individuals who are otherwise classified as mentally retarded who can play a song on a piano after hearing it once, or who have an extraordinary talent as a trombonist yet not be able to read a newspaper.
5. *Body-kinesthetic intelligence:* Body-kinesthetic intelligence is the gift of fine motor movement, as seen in a surgeon or dancer.
6. *Interpersonal intelligence:* Interpersonal intelligence is the understanding of others, how they feel, what motivates them, and how they interact. Certain people interact well with others because of their empathetic understanding; others, such as politicians, are highly skilled at understanding others and manipulating them.

According to Gardner, one of the dimensions for assessing intelligence involves music and the ability to perceive and create pitch and rhythmic patterns.

7. *Intrapersonal intelligence:* Intrapersonal intelligence centers on the individual's ability to know himself or herself and to develop a sense of identity.

And in his most recent work, Gardner (1999) considers the possibility of three additional types of intelligence: existential, spiritual, and naturalistic. He most clearly endorses **naturalistic intelligence,** which is the ability to identify plants and animals.

Gardner insists that people have to develop a completely different concept of who is bright and how to measure brightness. His concept is unique because he claims independent existence for different intelligences in the human neural system. He would like to stop measuring people according to some unitary dimension called "intelligence." Instead, he would like to think in terms of different intellectual strengths.

Do these various types intelligence improve between childhood and adulthood? Verbal, spatial, and

ANSWERS WOULDN'T YOU LIKE TO KNOW . . .

What does it mean to be *intelligent?*

There is no one agreed upon definition of *intelligence*, and the two most prominent theories of intelligence are quite different from each other. When most people use the word *intelligent*, they are referring to someone who can easily learn new information, who can solve problems well and make good choices, and who can be flexible and adapt to new situations.

mathematical abilities surely do. Interpersonal intelligence improves, too; the effects this change has on friendship and other relationships will be discussed in Chapter 12. Dramatic changes also occur in self-awareness, which will be discussed in Chapter 8. Musical intelligence appears to increase sharply during adolescence (Hassler, 1992), and kinesthetic ability also increases until early adulthood (Visser and Geuze, 2000).

Intelligence Tests

The most well-known intelligence tests are the Stanford-Binet and the Wechsler Scales. As you will see from the discussion that follows, neither is based on Sternberg's or Gardner's theory of intelligence. (Both tests predate these theories.) And while aspects of each theory are captured by the questions on the tests, the tests measure a much narrower swath of abilities than either theory proposes. In Sternberg's terms, the tests measure largely *componential intelligence;* in Gardner's terms, they measure *linguistic intelligence* and *logical-mathematical intelligence.*

Stanford-Binet

The first intelligence test was devised by Alfred Binet, a professor at the University of Sorbonne, in France. The members of the Paris Ministry of Education had been faced with a difficult problem. Their goal was to provide extensive education for all intelligent children and more practical, less academic kinds of schooling for less intelligent children. They wanted to be fair about choosing the children who would be given advanced academic training, so they asked Binet to devise a test to sort out children who were more intelligent from those who were less intelligent. Binet and his collaborators were able to construct a set of questions that could be answered by most children at a given age.

Revisions of Binet's test were made by Lewis Terman, of Stanford University, and the name was changed to Stanford-Binet test. It is used with individuals from age 2 through late adulthood. The fifth edition of the Stanford-Binet was published in 2003. This test provides separate verbal intelligence and performance (nonverbal) intelligence subscores as well as an overall, composite IQ score.

The Wechsler Scales

The most widely used measure of intelligence is the Wechsler Adult Intelligence Scale (WAIS-III), which may be used with people 16 years and older (Kaplan and Saccuzzo, 2005). Younger adolescents are usually given the Wechsler Intelligence Scale for Children (WISC-III). The WAIS-III divides intelligence into two components: verbal skills and performance/manipulation skills. Seven subtests constitute the verbal component: Information, Comprehension, Arithmetic, Similarities, Digit Span, Vocabulary, and Letter-Number Sequencing (see Table 7.1). Seven tests—Digit Symbol, Picture Completion, Block Design, Matrix Reasoning, Symbol Search, Picture Arrangement, and Object Assembly—compose the performance scores (again, see Table 7.1).

Changes with Age

Although IQ can change greatly from earlier on in childhood into adolescence (Schneider, Perner, Bullock, Stefanick, and Zeiglev, 1999), by the time individuals have reached the teenage years their IQ scores have usually stabilized (Kaufman and Lichtenbeger, 2002). The differences in childhood IQ and adolescent IQ can be explained by the environmental experiences that the individual has had. For example, if he or she has experienced significant stress (such as would be caused by living in poverty, experiencing a parent's protracted illness or death, or having parents who are chronically fighting), his or her IQ is very likely to decrease over time (e.g., Gutman, Sameroff, and Cole, 2003). This underscores that IQ score is not a product only of biology, but also of the environment. Both past experiences and immediate circumstances can effect how well one does on an IQ test.

Factors Influencing Test Results

One reason for variations in IQ and other measures of intelligence is that it is sometimes difficult to get valid test results. Results vary not only because intelligence may vary but also because of factors influencing test scores (Richardson, 2002). One of the most important influences is the presence of *anxiety* in the subjects tested. Anxious youths do not do as well on tests as those with greater emotional security (Zeidner, 1995).

Motivation also has a marked influence on test results (Wentzel, 1996). An otherwise bright student, poorly motivated to do well on a test, will not measure up to his or her capacity and will do much worse than he or she might (Goff and Ackerman, 1997). Furthermore, the tests are not free of cultural bias. Tests to

naturalistic intelligence the ability to identify plants and animals.

TABLE 7.1 SUBTESTS OF THE WECHSLER ADULT INTELLIGENCE SCALE (WAIS-III)

VERBAL SUBTESTS	PERFORMANCE SUBTESTS
Arithmetic—Perform mathematical calculations	Block Design—Arrange colored blocks to mimic specific patterns
Comprehension—Give solutions to social and practical problems	Digit Symbol—Use a key to translate symbols into numbers
Digit Span—Repeat a set of digits either forward or backward	Object Assembly—Assemble a puzzle
Information—Answer questions about general information and common knowledge	Picture Arrangement—Arrange a set of pictures into a coherent story
Similarities—Use inductive reasoning skills (How is A similar to B?)	Picture Completion—Find the missing part in a picture (e.g., a dog without a tail)
Vocabulary—Define words	
Letter-Number Sequencing—Remember the order of presented numbers and letters	Matrix Reasoning—Fill in a missing element in a symbolic sequence

Source: Adapted from L. R. Aiken, *Psychological Testing and Assessment* (7th ed., pp. 163–164) (Boston: Allyn & Bacon, 1991).

measure IQ were originally designed to measure innate general intelligence apart from environmental influences. But research over a long period has shown that sociocultural factors play a significant role in the outcome of the tests (Richardson, 2002). The tests' language, illustrations, examples, and abstractions are designed to measure intelligence according to middle-class standards. For example, some of the questions on IQ tests ask about "basic" knowledge, information more readily available to middle-class children who have been read to and to those whose parents have a large working vocabulary (Martinez, 2000). Many adolescents from low-socioeconomic-status families grow up in a world where words used are so different that understanding middle-class expressions on an intelligence test is difficult. Thus, some adolescents do poorly not because they are less intelligent but because they do not comprehend language foreign to their backgrounds and experiences (Berry and Bennett, 1992; Berry, Poortinga, Segal, and Dasen, 1992).

The amount of anxiety and motivation are factors that influence test results. There is also the effect of cultural bias, in which cultural standards and language favor the students from middle-class, nonminority backgrounds.

Efforts to develop culturally unbiased tests have been very frustrating. The general approach has been to use language familiar to the particular minorities for which the test is designed or to make the test completely nonverbal. The most well-known example of such a test is called the Raven Progressive Matrix Test, or the RPM. Items in this test are composed of several rows of symbols; the rightmost symbol of the bottom row is missing, and the test-taker's job is to select which symbol would complete that row so that its pattern matches that of the rows above. Although its nonverbal nature was thought to ensure that it was culturally fair, many researchers now disagree with that assertion. Carpenter, Just, and Shell (1990), for example, concluded that, although the symbols themselves are culture free, the manipulations required to derive the correct answer are not. Persons familiar with the concept of reading from left to right (as opposed to from top to bottom or right to left) and with subtraction and addition and other mathematical concepts will find the problems much easier than those who are not. In general, these tests have not been very successful.

A relatively new approach that is being endorsed by some is termed *dynamic testing* (Lidz, 2001). It is based on Vygotsky's approach to intelligence in that it taps ability to improve performance based upon social interaction. Children are first tested on their ability to perform some task; they are then coached in as helpful a manner as possible and, finally, asked to try the task again on their own. Dynamic testing differs from traditional intelligence testing in that each child is treated as an individual rather than in a fixed, consistent manner and in that the children are given feedback as to how they initially did. Researchers who have used dynamic testing assessments have found that the results are good predictors as to how well children can learn in school (Sternberg and Grigorenko, 2002).

ANSWERS WOULDN'T YOU LIKE TO KNOW . . .

How well do IQ tests measure intelligence?

IQ tests often do a good job of measuring the subset of intellectual abilities that they are designed to measure: memory, vocabulary, spatial perception, and so on. If someone does well on a given test, we can assume that he or she has the related skills. The reverse, however, is less true: If someone does poorly on an IQ test, he or she might lack these skills or other factors might be involved.

Uses and Misuses of IQ Tests

Great caution must be used when interpreting intelligence test scores. First, as stated earlier, a test score reflects, at best, a snapshot of a person's ability at a particular point in time. If you have ever had to take an exam when you were tired, grumpy, or didn't feel well, then you know that people do not always perform their best when test taking. Second, even if a person's score is an accurate reflection of how well he or she can perform on a particular test, it may not reflect his or her intelligence *per se* but instead his or her aptitude or background. How do you think your score would change if you were given an IQ test in a language in which you were not completely fluent or that contained questions about a culture with which you were not familiar? Clearly, you would do worse on such a test than on one more reflective of your own background.

RESEARCH HIGHLIGHT INTELLECTUALLY DIFFERENT ADOLESCENTS

About 95 percent of the population have IQ scores that fall between 70 and 130. The remaining 5 percent are evenly divided between top and bottom, such that 2.5 percent have IQs above 130 and 2.5 percent have IQs below 70. Those with IQs above 130 are referred to as *gifted,* whereas those with the lowest scores are *mentally retarded.* Adolescence can be an especially challenging time for an individual in either group.

Individuals with cognitive limitations are subjected to increased pressures during adolescence. They find school more challenging than ever, since they have fallen further behind their peers than in the past. These students will remain locked into preoperations or concrete operations while their classmates move into formal operations. Students with cognitive disabilities also have low self-esteem and feel less in control of their own lives than intellectually normal adolescents (Wehmeyer and Palmer, 1997). Adolescents who are mentally retarded and have been integrated into schools with typical adolescents (that is, *mainstreamed*) are more content with their social lives than mentally retarded adolescents in segregated schools (Heiman, 2000), but they are still less socially accepted than the average teenager (Freeman and Alkin, 2000). Individuals who are mentally retarded are sometimes shunned by former friends who, because of the insecurities of adolescence, have become concerned about how being friends with a mentally retarded individual will affect their own social standing.

Sexuality is another issue that confronts adolescents with cognitive disabilities to an even greater degree than average adolescents. Many adults view mentally disabled individuals as perpetually childlike and asexual. Because of this erroneous assumption, parents and teachers are unlikely to discuss puberty and sexuality with retarded adolescents. Unschooled as to the appropriate channels for their sexual feelings and having been taught to do what others tell them to do, mentally retarded adolescents are particularly vulnerable to sexual exploitation.

Although the issues confronting gifted teenagers are less severe than the issues confronting those with mental challenges, they stem from the same roots: stereotyping by others and the desire to conform and fit in. There is the widespread presumption that gifted adolescents are perfectionistic, nerdy, teachers' pets. In fact, gifted adolescents are as well or better adjusted on the whole than intellectually average teens (Garland and Zigler, 1999; Nail and Evans, 1997) and no more perfectionistic (LoCicero and Ashby, 2000). Students who are gifted also find that other students try to take advantage of them by wanting to copy their schoolwork and that teachers ignore them in class (Moulton, Moulton, Housewright, and Bailey, 1998). The desire to fit in makes some gifted teens—especially females—try to hide their talents and to drop out of activities in which they excel (Patrick, Ryan, Alfeld-Liro, Fredricks, Hruda, and Eccles, 1999).

All adolescents have a tremendous need to be liked and understood by their peers and the adults who are important to them. Being intellectually different can make this more difficult to accomplish. When conformity is king, being different in *any* way can be problematic.

At the same time, IQ tests can be put to good use. In fact, an adolescent who does poorly on an IQ test probably has *some* issue that is keeping him or her from doing well. Whatever that issue is—be it worry over personal problems, lack of motivation, a background that has failed to provide expected learning opportunities, or low intelligence—it is important to identify it so that appropriate services can be provided to the student. Thus, IQ tests can serve as screening devices and call attention to adolescents in need.

In addition, IQ tests do predict—even if the means are indirect and not causally related to intelligence—various important aspects of a person's situation. For instance, IQ scores do, to a certain degree, predict an adolescent's popularity with peers (Scarr, 1997). And, as one might expect, IQ does predict school achievement (Brody, 1997). In good part because of this, IQ also predicts level of entry into the job market and occupational status (Neisser et al., 1996). It does not, however, predict success on the job (Wagner, 1997) since other factors such as work ethic and motivation so strongly play into job performance.

ACHIEVEMENT TESTS

An achievement test is designed to measure how well someone has mastered a set of facts or skills. Most of the tests that you took in elementary, middle, and high school were achievement tests, as will be most of the tests that you will take in college. For instance, midterms and final exams are usually designed to assess whether you have learned the course material (although if they require you to draw inferences beyond what was actually taught, they may be tapping into intelligence, as well). The mandatory competency tests that are now given to American schoolchildren as a result of recent federal education legislation (the No Child Left Behind Act) are also examples of achievement tests; so are the SAT area tests in biology, literature, and the like. The ACT (see the following Highlight box) was originally intended to be an achievement test, but like the SAT, it has both aptitude and achievement components.

The Scholastic Assessment Test (SAT)

One of the most widely used tests in the United States is the *SAT.* (It used to be called the *Scholastic Assessment Test* and, prior to that, the *Scholastic Aptitude Test.* It is now named the *Scholastic Reasoning Test,* and the abbreviation *SAT* is still used even though it no longer fits.) The SAT is used by a majority of colleges as one basis for admission. Approximately 1.3 million high school seniors took the test in 2002.

Beginning in March 2000, the SAT was substantially modified. Previously, the exam consisted of a Math and a Verbal section. The entire test took 2½ hours to take, and the maximum scores was 1600 (800 on each of the two sections). The most significant change involved the inclusion of a writing section (with both multiple-choice questions and an essay) that was based largely upon the former SAT II Writing Subject Test. In addition, analogy questions were removed from the Verbal (now called Critical Reading) section, and the Mathematics section now includes several items requiring knowledge from high school Algebra II, and questions requiring students to make quantitative comparisons (decide which of two formulas yielded the larger value or indicate whether the question was impossible to answer) were omitted. The maximum possible score is now 2400 (800 on each of three sections), and the test takes substantially longer to complete.

The combined verbal and math scores often determine eligibility not only for college admission but also for scholarships and financial aid. The Educational Testing Service (ETS), which produces the SAT, claims that in combination with high school records, the SATs have proved to be better predictors of students' first-year performances in college than any other measurement. Nevertheless, the protests against the use or misuse of this test are significant (e.g., Lemann, 2000).

There are two primary objections to the SAT. First, the test is not neutral in terms of race/ethnicity, socioeconomic status, and gender (e.g., Freedle, 2003). Asian Americans consistently outscore Caucasians, and both of these groups outscore African and Hispanic Americans. In addition, males outscore females on both the verbal and quantitative sections of the test (e.g., Jackson and Rushton, 2006). As shown in Figure 7.5, SAT test scores are higher for individuals who come from higher-level socioeconomic backgrounds (College Board, 2003).

The second primary objection has to do with the claim that the test measures basic abilities acquired over a student's lifetime and is thus immune to last-minute cramming and is "coach-proof." A study by the Federal Trade Commission's Bureau of Consumer Protection showed that special coaching can improve SAT scores by an average of 25 points. More than 80 coaching schools in one nationwide chain tutored 30,000 students in a single year, in 10-week courses, and improved scores by an average of 25 points. The schools claim that in individual cases they can improve scores up to 100 points. In contrast, a study sponsored by the College Board, the parent organization of the SAT, found that students who were coached are only slightly more likely to show large score gains than uncoached students (Powers and Rock, 1999). Still, it seems clear that reviewing mathematical formulas that one has forgotten or becoming familiar with the instructions on a timed test—whether one is

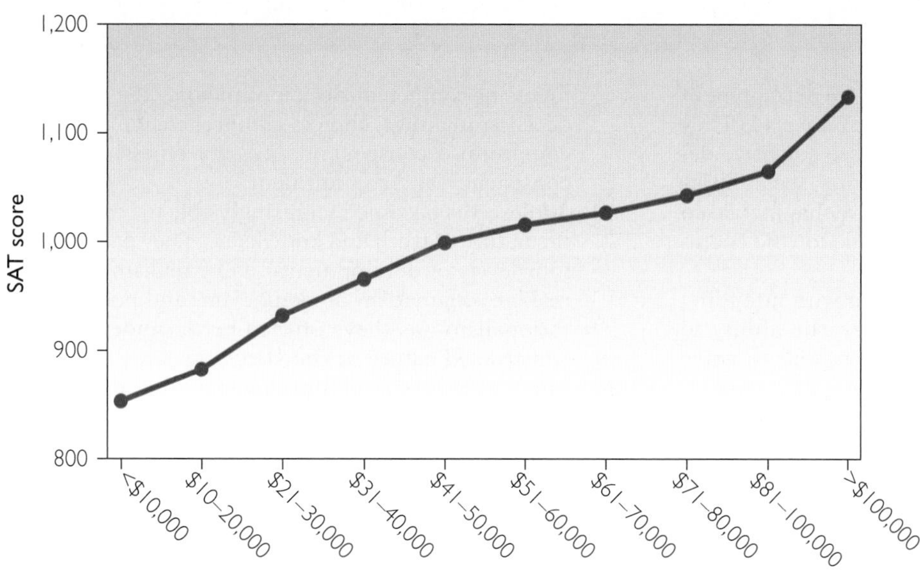

FIGURE 7.5
RELATIONSHIP BETWEEN ANNUAL FAMILY INCOME AND SAT SCORE

Source: Data from College Board (2003).

formally coached or one spends time on one's own—should be able to influence one's score.

The SAT measures both aptitude and achievement. The fact is, any timed test measures mental quickness (aptitude), and a student must have learned specific mathematical principles in order to do well on the quantitative section and specific vocabulary words to do well on the verbal section (achievement). While aptitude itself may not be coachable, learning certain test-taking skills may help one do better on aptitude tests. Achievement is, of course, enhanced by coaching.

If coaching can raise a student's score, should the SAT be relied on as a basic measure of scholastic aptitude? Should admission to college depend partly on a skill gained by those who can afford a coaching course? In all fairness, the College Entrance Examination Board has long issued warnings against making admissions decisions on the basis of the SAT score alone. The ETS itself has stated that an individual's score can vary plus or minus 30 to 35 points, a spread of 60 to 70 points. For these reasons, most schools rely equally or more on student essays, interviews, and other admission procedures (Laird, 2005). In addition, more and more colleges and universities are making taking the SAT optional rather than required, and in, 2001, Richard Atkinson, president of the University of California, urged that the SAT be widely dropped as a college admissions requirement (Atkinson, 2001).

RESEARCH HIGHLIGHT THE AMERICAN COLLEGE TESTING (ACT) ASSESSMENT PROGRAM

The American College Testing (ACT) Assessment Program is the second most widely used college admissions test, administered to more than 2 million students each year. It consists of three parts: (1) the Academic Tests, (2) the Student Profile Section (SPS), and (3) the ACT Interest Inventory. The Academic Tests are English Usage Tests, Mathematics Usage Tests, Reading Tests, and the Science Reasoning Test.

The Student Profile Section is a 192-item inventory of demographics, high school activities and accomplishments, and academic and extracurricular plans for college. The UNIACT is a survey of students' vocational preferences.

The ACT Academic Tests yield standard scores of 1 to 36, which are averaged to create the ACT Composite. The mean composite score in 2005 was 20.9 (ACT, 2006). The SPS has been shown to be valid, with follow-up studies showing a 69 to 70 percent match between students' choices of major on the SPS and actual choices at the end of the freshman year (Laing, Valiga, and Eberly, 1986).

SUMMARY

1. Current views on adolescents' cognitive development differ from Piaget's views in four main ways: (1) They are more process oriented; (2) they see cognitive development as more continuous; (3) they see abilities as domain specific; and (4) they believe that increased executive control is largely responsible for the cognitive advances of adolescence.
2. Information processing is concerned with attending to and interpreting stimuli, memory, the ability to make inferences, to think, to reason, and to solve problems.
3. Both the ability to sustain attention and the ability to ignore distractions improve during adolescence.
4. Adolescents perceive risk differently than adults. Although (contrary to Elkind) they do not perceive themselves as being at less risk than adults do, they do not fully appreciate the magnitude of the consequences of that risk as much as adults do. Hence, adolescents are more likely than adults to engage in risky behavior.
5. Information received by the senses is put into the sensory store, where it begins to decay in a fraction of a second. That which has not faded is passed on to the short-term store. Information that is held for a period of time is then transferred to the long-term store.
6. Sensory storage improves only slightly during adolescence. Short-term memory does improve. The long-term memory of adolescents is better than that of children, in part because adolescents have learned to ignore irrelevant information. Young adults' memory is better than that of adolescents, but adolescents' memory is superior to that of elderly adults.
7. Improvements in mental processing speed likely account for adolescents' improved attention span and memory ability.
8. After information has been retrieved from memory, it is used to make inferences, to think, and to reason. Each of these thought processes improves during adolescence.
9. Adolescents are better able than children to use negative information and an elimination strategy when solving problems. However, they do so inconsistently, exhibiting self-serving biases in their reasoning.
10. Reasoning involves making explicit inferences, deliberately following rules of logic, and using principles to solve problems.
11. In order to solve a problem, an individual must determine what the problem is, evaluate the elements of the problem, generate a list of potential solutions, and then evaluate those solutions. Adolescents are better at problem solving than children, in part because they know more.
12. Decision makers must master five skills: Identify alternate courses of action, identify appropriate criteria for considering alternatives, assess alternatives, summarize information about the alternatives, and self-evaluate the outcome of the decision-making process.
13. A helpful decision-making model was developed by Mann and his colleagues. Their model listed nine elements of competent decision making (the nine Cs of decision making): choice, comprehension, creativity, compromise, consequentiality, correctness, credibility, consistency, and commitment.
14. Adolescents become increasingly able to reason about the nature of truth and knowledge. They pass through four levels of development—naive realism, defended realism, dogmatism or skepticism, and postskeptical rationalism—as they come to better understand the constructed nature of knowledge.
15. Three of the four cerebral lobes mature during adolescence: the parietal, the temporal, and the frontal lobes. The corpus callosum, which connects the cerebrum's two hemispheres, also grows at this stage. These changes in the brain may account for the development of spatial reasoning, language abilities, and impulse control in adolescence and adulthood.
16. During adolescence, more neurons in the brain become myelinated. This results in faster and more selective neural transmission.
17. The hippocampus—the part of the brain involved in setting down new memories—continues to develop throughout adolescence.
18. The amygdala—a part of the brain that reacts emotionally to stimuli—grows earlier in adolescence than the frontal lobe, which moderates emotional response.
19. There is no agreed upon definition of *intelligence*.
20. Sternberg groups intelligence into three categories: componential intelligence, experiential intelligence, and contextual intelligence.
21. Gardner identifies eight types of intelligence: linguistic intelligence, logical-mathematical intelligence, spatial intelligence, musical intelligence, body-kinesthetic intelligence, interpersonal intelligence, intrapersonal intelligence, and naturalistic intelligence.
22. IQ tests measure subsets of the intellectual abilities that comprise intelligence. The two most commonly used individual IQ tests are the Stanford-Binet and the Wechsler Scales.
23. Although often stabilized by adolescence, intelligence scores may vary considerably during one's lifetime. Scores should be considered only as a result on a test taken at a particular time.
24. Anxiety, the degree of motivation, and sociocultural factors, among others, may influence test results.
25. Culture-fair tests and dynamic testing have both been used to reduce bias against minorities and the poor.
26. Adolescence can be difficult for people who are mentally retarded (with IQs below 70) and people who are gifted (with IQs above 130). Mentally retarded teenagers fall increasingly further behind their intellectually-average peers and face decreasing social acceptance. Gifted teens, especially girls, may feel pressured to fit in and to hide their abilities.
27. Achievement tests differ from aptitude tests in that they measure actual mastery of specific skills and knowledge rather than learning potential.

28. The SAT is the most widely used college admission test; it provides a common yardstick for evaluating students from across the United States. However, questions about fairness and the fact that students' scores can be improved by taking test preparation courses have led to criticism as to the SAT's fairness.
29. The ACT is the second most widely used college admission test. It consists of three parts: (a) the academic tests, (b) the student profile section, and (c) the ACT interest inventory.

KEY TERMS

achievement tests 149	naive realism 146
affirmation 142	naturalistic intelligence 150
amygdala 148	negation 142
analytic ability 145	parietal lobe 148
cerebrum 148	postskeptical rationalism 147
cognitive monitoring 142	practical ability 145
corpus callosum 148	principles 142
defensive realism 146	processing speed 141
dogmatism 146	psychometric approach 148
elimination strategy 142	reasoning 142
epistemology 146	self-serving bias 142
frontal lobe 148	sensory storage 140
hippocampus 148	short-term storage 140
inference 141	skepticism 146
information-processing approach 138	synthetic ability 145
intelligence quotient (IQ) 149	temporal lobe 148
long-term storage 140	thinking 141
metacognition 145	

THOUGHT QUESTIONS

Personal Reflection

1. Selective attention means each person notices something different, depending on interest and motivation. What sorts of things do you notice and remember most easily?
2. Are you a risk taker? Why or why not?
3. Do you use the confirmation strategy or the elimination strategy when solving a problem? If you go back and forth, when do you use each?
4. When was the last time you can remember using deduction to solve a problem? Induction? Provide examples.
5. When you are faced with problems, what techniques do you find most helpful in making decisions or arriving at solutions?
6. Are you an epistemological realist or rationalist? Explain how so.

Group Discussion

7. In what ways is the human mind similar and dissimilar to a computer?
8. Were you and your friends more impulsive when you were younger? If so, why do you think your rash tendencies have diminished?
9. How would you describe an intelligent person? What factors distinguish a person who is intelligent from one who is not?
10. Have you ever taken IQ tests at different times, only to discover that your scores changed? Why did they change? Explain.
11. Imagine going through a school day as an adolescent who is cognitively impaired. How would other students treat you? How would teachers treat you? What would you find particularly difficult? What part of your day would you enjoy most?

Debate Questions

12. Componential intelligence is more important than experiential or contextual intelligence.
13. Some of Gardner's types of intelligence are more important than others.
14. All students should be given intelligence tests and then they and their parents should be told their test scores.
15. The SAT or ACT should be required for admission to all colleges.

SUGGESTED READING

Gardner, H. (1999). *Intelligence Reframed: Multiple Intelligences for the Twenty-First Century.* New York: Basic Books.

Jacobs, J. E., and Klaczynski, P. A. (Eds.). (2005) *The Development of Judgment and Decision Making in Children and Adolescents.* Mahweh, NJ: Erlbaum.

Moshman, D. (1999). *Adolescent Psychological Development: Rationality, Morality, and Identity.* Mahwah, NJ: Erlbaum.

Pressley, M., and Memory de Schneider, W. (1997). *Introduction to Memory Development during Childhood and Adolescence.* Mahwah, NJ: Erlbaum.

Sternberg, R. J. (2003). *Wisdom, Intelligence, and Creativity Synthesized.* New York: Cambridge University Press.

CHAPTER 8 SELF-CONCEPT, IDENTITY, ETHNICITY, AND GENDER

WOULDN'T YOU LIKE TO KNOW . . .

- Why is having a good self-concept important?
- How much does getting good grades affect self-esteem?
- Do adolescents become delinquent because they have low self-esteem?
- What kinds of parents raise children with high levels of self-esteem?
- Do adolescent girls and boys have different levels of self-esteem?
- What identity status is most common among college students?
- How does the development of an ethnic identity affect someone's self-esteem?
- What is the difference between *sex* and *gender?*
- Why is it good to have a blend of masculine and feminine traits?

Since Erik Erikson first proposed that finding an identity was *the* major life task of adolescence, researchers have been examining the ways in which teenagers go about this process of self-discovery. Even before they have developed identities, however, adolescents bring from childhood certain views of themselves. How someone would describe himself or herself is a good indication of this self-view.

The **self** is that part of an individual's personality of which he or she is aware. **Self-concept** is a conscious, cognitive perception and evaluation by an individual of himself or herself; it is one's thoughts and opinions about oneself. Self-concept has been called the individual's "self-hypothesized identity" (Wayment and Zetlin, 1989). Erikson (1968) referred to it as the individual's "ego identity," or the individual's self-perceived, consistent individuality.

Self-concept is more limited in scope than *identity,* which is more complete, more coherent, and more forward projecting, as it includes long-term goals. Self-concept, and later identity, form the basis for **self-esteem,** a related term that refers to how one feels about oneself. People with high self-esteem like themselves; people with low self-esteem do not.

Thus, self-esteem is necessary for the "survival of the soul"; it is the ingredient that gives dignity to human existence. It grows out of human interaction in which the self is considered important to someone. The ego grows through small accomplishments, praise, and success (Lazarus, 1991).

This chapter begins by reviewing the research on changes in self-concept and self-esteem that occur during adolescence. A detailed discussion of the identity search then follows. Since in modern American society, gender and ethnicity play such a significant role in an individual's self-concept, this chapter concludes with sections examining ethnic and gender differences in self-perception and identity.

FIGURE 8.1 SIX DIFFERENT SELVES

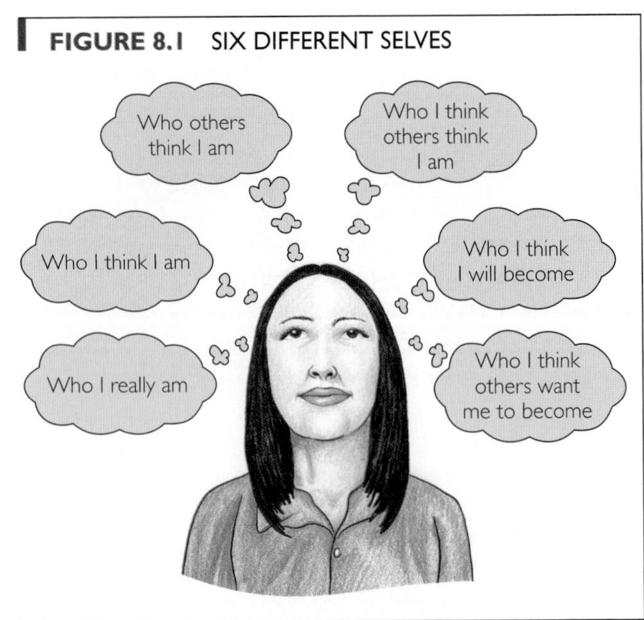

SELF-CONCEPT AND SELF-ESTEEM

The first step in the development of a self-concept is when a person recognizes that he or she is a distinct, separate individual. This awareness begins in early childhood. Self-concept also implies a developing awareness on a person's part of who and what he or she is. It describes what individuals see when they look at themselves, in terms of their self-perceived physical characteristics, personality skills, traits, roles, and social statuses. It might be described as the system of attitudes they have about themselves. It is the sum total of their self-definitions or self-images (Harter, 1990).

Self-concept is often described as a *global entity:* how someone feels about himself or herself in general (DuBois, Felner, Brand, Phillips, and Lease, 1996). But it has also been described as made up of *multiple self-conceptions,* with concepts developed in relation to different roles (Griffin, Chassin, and Young, 1981). Thus, a person may rate himself or herself as a son or daughter, student, athlete, friend, and so forth. Self-concept is equally comprised of beliefs about different aspects of the self, such as social skills, athletic prowess, and morality. These conceptions of different aspects of the self may differ, which helps to explain how behavior varies in different circumstances.

Adolescents gather evidence that helps them evaluate themselves: Am I competent? Am I attractive to the opposite sex? Am I intelligent? From this evidence, they form hypotheses about themselves and check out their feelings and opinions through further experiences and relationships. They compare themselves with their own ideals and those of others.

Whether individuals have an accurate self-concept is significant. As Figure 8.1 illustrates, all people have six different selves: the people they are, the people they think they are, the people others think they are, the people they think others think they are, the people they think they will become, and the people they think others want them to become. Self-concepts may or may not be close approximations of reality, and self-concepts are always in the process of change, particularly during childhood and adolescence. Allport (1950) emphasized that personality is less a finished product than a transitive process. It has some stable features, but at the same time, it is undergoing change. Allport coined the word **proprium,** which he defined as "all aspects of per-

PERSONAL ISSUES LOVING OURSELVES AND OTHERS

Some theorists emphasize that by promoting or enhancing self-esteem alone, people focus attention on themselves, and this promotes a certain type of self-consciousness, self-preoccupation, and selfishness. When people focus their attention on others in order to enhance their own self-esteem, this is fundamentally a selfish type of attention, with the concern for others serving a secondary part of what is occurring. These theorists emphasize that the maxim "We cannot love others until we love ourselves" is actually 180 degrees wrong. Ironically and paradoxically, this idea would be more true, more relevant, and less harmful if we were to reverse it—"We cannot love ourselves until we love others." Theorists suggest that we should focus our attention on the welfare of others and establish intimate, emotional, and compassionate connections with others (Burr and Christensen, 1992).

sonality that make for inward unity." This is the self that is at the core of personal identity.

Fifty years ago, Strang (1957) outlined four basic dimensions of the self. First, there is the *overall, basic self-concept,* which is the adolescent's view of his or her personality and "perceptions of his abilities and his status and roles in the outer world" (p. 68).

Next are the individual's *temporary or transitory self-concepts.* These ideas of self are influenced by the mood of the moment or by a recent or continuing experience. A recent low grade on an examination may leave a person with a temporary feeling of being stupid; a critical remark from parents may produce a temporary feeling of deflated self-worth.

Third, there are the adolescent's *social selves*—the selves he or she thinks others see, which, in turn, influences how the individual sees himself or herself. If youths have the impression that others think they are stupid or socially unacceptable, they tend to think of themselves in these negative ways. Their perceptions of others' feelings color their views of themselves (Harter, Stocker, and Robinson, 1996). Self-concept comes partly from an involvement of the self with thers, in intimacy, group participation, cooperation, and competition. It evolves through social interactions, encompassing both continuity of self and identification with something beyond the self.

Part of self-concept is the sense of social status, the positions in which individuals place themselves in the social system in the present or the future. For example, adolescents from low socioeconomic-status backgrounds who see themselves as not belonging there but as members of a higher socioeconomic class are molding new identities because of their higher aspirations.

The fourth dimension is the **ideal self,** which is the kind of person an adolescent would like to be. His or her aspirations may be realistic, too low, or too high. An ideal self that is too low impedes accomplishment; one that is too high may lead to frustration and self-depreciation. Having a realistic self-concept leads to self-acceptance, mental health, and accomplishment of realistic goals.

Importance of Having a Good Self-Concept

Why is having a good self-concept important? Self-concept is important because it motivates and directs one's behavior. If you believe that you are athletic and coordinated, you are more likely to try to learn to ski than if you view yourself as clumsy and graceless. Likewise, if you view yourself as intelligent and hard working, you are more likely to sign up for hard courses than if you think you are limited in these areas.

In their discussion of the link between motivation and self-concept, Oyserman and Markus (1990a, 1990b) focus on an adolescent's **possible selves.** These are the people he or she might be someday; they refer to the future, not to the present. Each of us has **hoped-for selves,** or the people we wish to become; **expected selves,** the people we think we will likely become; and

self a person's personality or nature of which that person is aware.

self-concept a person's conscious, cognitive perception and evaluation of himself or herself; one's thoughts and opinions about oneself.

self-esteem a person's impression or opinion of himself or herself.

proprium the self-identity that is developing in time.

ideal self the kind of person an individual would like to be.

possible selves the different selves we envision ourselves becoming.

hoped-for selves the people we hope to be in the future.

expected selves the people we think we will likely be in the future.

PERSONAL ISSUES PERFECTIONISM

Generally, the wish to excel is an admirable attribute. Normal perfectionists derive real pleasure from their accomplishments, but they feel free to be less precise if a situation permits. *Maladaptive perfectionists* pursue excellence to an unhealthy extreme. They hold the irrational belief that they must be perfect to be accepted. Their standards are beyond reason—they strain toward impossible goals that are never reached. Plagued by self-criticism, their self-worth is further lowered. Because in their own eyes they never measure up, they become defensive and angry when faced with possible criticism, a behavior that frustrates and alienates others and causes the very disapproval that they fear. Over time, they are filled with fear and emotional turmoil, and experience more pain than rewards. Even academic success, which many attain, does nothing to promote self-confidence (Halgin and Leahy, 1989). Perfectionism is closely associated with the development of eating disorders (Pearson and Gleaves, 2006). Developing a healthy identity, then, involves wanting to be a good person while at the same time not demanding flawlessness from oneself.

ANSWERS WOULDN'T YOU LIKE TO KNOW ...

Why is having a good self-concept important?

Having a positive self-concept not only makes it easier for a person to be friendly and outgoing, but it also gives him or her the confidence to try new activities and to take on challenges. Having a positive self-concept leads to having high self-esteem, as well.

feared selves, the people we dread becoming. For example, you may hope to become a world-famous violinist, expect to become a high school music teacher, and fear becoming an unemployed street musician.

Oyserman and Markus (1990a, 1990b) assert that adolescents who lack positive expected selves drift into unproductive, antisocial behavior. It seems that if one has no hope for happy outcomes, then one will engage in self-destructive activities. If the most optimistic future you envision for yourself is none too good, why bother trying? Conversely, if you believe that you can attain your dreams, then you will be willing to work hard at improving your chances. In addition, having a balancing set of feared selves can also prompt responsible behavior. Being aware that very bad outcomes can occur is energizing, and acknowledging negative consequences can help one avoid antisocial actions. For instance, you may wish to get rich (a hoped-for self) but robbing a bank may land you in jail and make you a convict (feared self). Researchers have shown that an adolescent's possible selves influence his or her delinquency, tobacco use, and alcohol consumption (Aloise-Young, Hennigan, and Leong, 2001; Oyserman and Saltz, 1993).

Self-Esteem

Having built concepts of themselves, adolescents then must deal with the esteem with which they view themselves. When they examine themselves, what value do they place on the selves they perceive? Does this appraisal lead to self-acceptance and approval, to a feeling of self-worth? If so, then they have enough self-esteem to accept and live with themselves. If people are to have high self-esteem, there must be a correspondence between their self-concepts and their *self-ideals.*

With the onset of puberty, most young people begin to make a thorough assessment of themselves, comparing not only their body parts but also their motor skills, intellectual abilities, and social skills with those of their peers and their ideals or heroes. This critical self-appraisal is accompanied by self-conscious behavior that makes adolescents vulnerable to embarrassment. It can lead to an imaginary audience. As a consequence, teenagers are preoccupied with attempting to reconcile their selves as they perceive them with their ideal selves. By late adolescence, most have managed to sort themselves out—to determine what they can most effectively be and to integrate their goals into their ideal selves.

Carl Rogers (1961) was one of the most important theorists in the development of a theoretical and practical structure of self-ideals. He pictured the end point of personality development as a basic congruence between objective reality and one's self-perception. This result allows freedom from internal conflict and anxiety; when individuals discover who they are and what they perceive themselves to be and want to be begin to merge, they are then able to accept themselves, without conflict. Their self-perceptions and relationships with others elicit self-acceptance and self-esteem. Psychological maladjustment occurs when there is a divergence between the selves they are being in relationship to others and the selves they perceive they are or want to be.

Mental Health

A positive self-perception, or high self-esteem, is a desired outcome of the human developmental process. It has been linked to long-term mental health and emotional well-being (Klein, 1995). Individuals whose self-esteem has never sufficiently developed manifest a number of symptoms of emotional ill health (Koenig, 1988). There is a well-established link between low self-esteem and depression in adolescence (Dori and Overholser, 1999) and a separate, equally strong link between low self-esteem and suicidal behavior (Grøholt, Ekeberg, Wichstrøm, and Haldorson 2000).

Individuals with low self-esteem may evidence psychosomatic symptoms and anxiety (Byrne, 2000). Low self-esteem has also been found to be a factor in drug abuse and in unwed pregnancy (Kalil and Kunz, 1999; Parker and Benson, 2005). In fact, unwed pregnancy is often an effort on the part of young women to enhance their self-esteem (Streetman, 1987). Low self-esteem is also associated with the eating disorders anorexia nervosa and bulimia (Sassaroli and Ruggiero, 2005).

Sometimes, the adolescent with low self-esteem tries to develop a false front, or facade, with which to face the world. This is a compensating mechanism used to overcome feelings of worthlessness by convincing others that one is worthy. The youth tries to put on an act to impress people. Putting on an act, however, is a strain. To act confident, friendly, and cheerful when one feels the opposite is a constant struggle. The anxiety that the person might make a false step and let the guard slip creates considerable tension.

Another reason for anxiety is that people with low self-esteem show a shifting and unstable identity. Adolescents with low self-esteem are self-conscious and overly vulnerable to criticism or rejection, which testifies to their sense of inadequacy (Rosenthal and Simeonsson, 1989). They may be deeply disturbed when laughed at, when blamed, or when others have a poor opinion of them. The more vulnerable they feel themselves to be, the higher are their anxiety levels. Such adolescents report, "Criticism hurts me terribly" or "I can't stand to have anyone laugh at me or blame me when something goes wrong." As a result, they feel awkward and uneasy in social situations and avoid embarrassment whenever they can.

Interpersonal Competence and Popularity

Those with poor self-concepts are often rejected by other people. Acceptance by others, especially by best friends, is positively related to self-concept scores. Acceptance of self is positively and significantly correlated with acceptance of, and by, others (Harter, Stoker, and Robinson, 1996). Thus, there is a close relationship between self-acceptance and popularity.

Poor social adjustment, which is related to low self-concept and self-esteem, manifests itself in a number of ways. Adolescents with low self-esteem are often socially invisible (see Chapter 17). They are not noticed or selected as leaders, and they do not participate often in class, clubs, or social activities. They do not stand up for their own rights or express their opinions on matters that concern them. These adolescents more often develop feelings of isolation and loneliness. A vicious cycle can develop when these feelings reinforce negative self-concepts and low self-esteem.

The other problem faced by low-self-esteem adolescents is that they experience a good deal of role strain (de Bruyn and van den Boom, 2005; Fenzel, 2000). Most young adolescents experience stress when they make the transition to middle school, with its new expectations, enlarged peer group, and larger, more impersonal size. But whereas more popular teens can lean on friends for social support, less popular adolescents find themselves being picked on, teased, and bullied by their peers. Thus, less popular teenagers experience the double whammy of transition stress and peer neglect or hostility.

Progress in School

Increasing evidence supports the theory that there is a correlation between self-concept and achievement in school. Successful students feel a greater sense of personal worth and somewhat better about themselves (Garzarelli, Everhart, and Lester, 1993). However, the relationship is reciprocal. Those who have high self-esteem tend to have higher academic achievement, and those who are academic achievers have higher self-esteem (Liu, Kaplan, and Risser, 1992). Grades appear to affect self-esteem somewhat more than self-esteem affects grades (Hoge, Smit, and Crist, 1995). One reason is that students who have confidence in themselves have the courage to try and are motivated to live up to what they believe about themselves. Students who have negative attitudes about themselves impose limitations on their own achievement. They feel they "can't do it anyhow" or are "not smart enough" (Fenzel, 1994).

Recently, attention has been focused on the strategies children use in school to portray themselves as unable to do schoolwork. By procrastinating, deliberately not trying, allowing others to keep them from studying, and using other self-defeating strategies, students can

feared selves the people we are afraid of becoming in the future.

ANSWERS WOULDN'T YOU LIKE TO KNOW . . .

How much does getting good grades affect self-esteem?

Getting good grades enhances self-esteem, but having high self-esteem and confidence in your own abilities helps you earn good grades.

convey that circumstances, rather than lack of ability, are the reasons for poor performance. Survey data from 256 eighth-grade students indicated that boys used those strategies more so than girls, and low achievers more so than high achievers (Midgley and Urdan, 1995).

Other studies emphasize that participation in extracurricular activities is also related to increased self-esteem. Whether the participation is *because* of higher self-esteem or whether it *contributes* to higher self-esteem is sometimes questionable, but the two are nevertheless correlated. Also, participation in extracurricular activities is related to a higher grade-point average and lower absenteeism from school (Fertman and Chubb, 1992). This is in keeping with other research findings that participation in high school activities, especially athletic activities, is associated with higher self-esteem in both boys and girls (Steitz and Owen, 1992).

African American males are less likely to develop positive self-concepts from high achievement because of the attitudes of the group toward good grades (Osborne, 1995). Thus, to understand how academic achievement influences social self-image, we must consider the individual within the context of his or her peer group; that is, we must consider how peer attitudes toward achievement will affect an individual's social self-image. Peer influences may either encourage or discourage academic success, depending on the dominant value within the peer group. Peers who place a high value on academics influence each other to do well in school (Roberts and Petersen, 1992).

The positive attitudes and support of significant others—mothers, fathers, grandparents, older siblings, special friends, teachers, or school counselors—can have an important influence on students' academic self-concepts. Students who feel that others have confidence in their academic abilities have confidence in themselves.

Vocational Aspirations

For some people, the selection of an occupation is an attempt to fulfill the sense of self. The desire and expectation to get ahead vocationally also depend on self-esteem. Adolescents who have determined some career goals for themselves have higher self-esteem than do those without any career goals (Chiu, 1990; Munson, 1992). Both those with low and high self-esteem consider it important to get ahead, but those with low self-esteem are less likely to expect they will succeed. They are more likely to say, "I would like to get ahead in life, but I don't think I'll ever get ahead as far as I want." They do not believe that they possess those qualities essential for success.

Is there a difference in the types of positions desired by low- and high-self-esteem adolescents? In general, those with low self-esteem want to avoid positions in which they will be forced to exercise leadership and avoid jobs in which others dominate them; they want to be neither power wielders nor power subjects. Avoiding leadership or supervision by others is a way of avoiding criticism or judgment.

Educational and vocational aspirations depend partly on self-image, which in turn may be derived from family background. This will be discussed more fully in a later chapter, but for now let it suffice to say that adolescents from lower-SES backgrounds are likely to have lower vocational aspirations than those from higher-SES backgrounds (Trusty, Robinson, Plata, and Ng, 2000). There are multiple reasons for this fact, but it stems in part from lower-SES youths having difficulty seeing themselves as successful workers (Sarigiani, Wilson, Petersen, and Vicary, 1990).

Delinquency

For many years, psychologists and sociologists believed there was a close relationship between low self-esteem and delinquency. Namely, it was thought that being delinquent was an attempt to compensate for having poor feelings about oneself. This idea was first proposed by Kaplan (1980) as the **self-enhancement thesis.** He argued that individuals who were unsuccessful at following the so-called straight-and-narrow path would not receive positive reinforcement for their behavior and would therefore have lowered self-esteem. Thus, teens who got bad grades, didn't get along with more normal peers, and couldn't seem to do anything right would feel badly about themselves and suffer from low self-esteem. In order to feel better about themselves, they would associate with deviant teens, who would reinforce and praise them for these same delinquent behaviors. Association with deviant peers would encourage their behavior to become even more deviant and, with further reinforcement, their self-esteem would rebound. In sum, Kaplan suggested that adolescents with low self-esteem would become delinquents and that after they had done so, their self-esteem would rise.

Research conducted in the 1990s, however, failed to find this link (Heaven, 1996). In fact, findings have varied dramatically. Delinquents' self-esteem has been found to increase, to decrease, and not to change; it has

ANSWERS WOULDN'T YOU LIKE TO KNOW ...

Do adolescents become delinquent because they have low self-esteem?

Delinquents do not necessarily have low self-esteem. In fact, in some studies, they have been found to have an inflated sense of their own talents and abilities.

been found to be low and high and unremarkable. Jang and Thornberry (1998), who conducted a longitudinal study of urban adolescents, found that low self-esteem did not predict association with delinquent peers; however, the self-esteem of those youths who chose delinquents as friends rose even though their own delinquency did not. When an association has been found between delinquency and low self-esteem, it often shows up in girls but not boys (Esbensen, Deschenes, and Winfree, 1999; Rigby and Cox, 1996).

However, results from a very recent study may finally provide an explanation for the contradictory findings. Donnellan and his colleagues (2005) conducted research in which they separated out the effects of self-esteem and **narcissism** (a personality trait that denotes that a person is overly vain and self-absorbed). They found a strong relationship between *low* self-esteem and delinquent behavior and aggression. High self-esteem did not predict delinquency: narcissism did. Since previous research did not distinguish between normal, healthy high self-esteem and pathological narcissism, it appeared that high self-esteem was related to aggression when in fact it was not.

Development of a Positive Self-Concept

How can a positive self-concept be developed? Let's look at several factors that contribute to its achievement.

Significant Others

The idea that self-concept is determined in part by others' views of us, or the way we think others view us, is generally accepted (Juhasz, 1989). However, not all people exert an equally strong influence. *Significant others* are those individuals who occupy a high level of importance. They are influential and their opinions are meaningful (Lackovic-Grgin and Dekovic, 1990). Their influence also depends on their degree of involvement and intimacy, the social support they provide (Blain, Thompson, and Whiffen, 1993), and the power and authority given to them by others.

Parents

A variety of researchers have found that the affective quality of family relations during adolescence is associated with high levels of self-esteem (Robinson, 1995). This has been found true not only in the United States, but in many other nations as well (Farruggia, Chen, Greenberger, Dhitrievan, and Macek, 2004).

self-enhancement thesis an explanation for delinquency based on the need for troubled youths to enhance their self-esteem.

narcissism the trait of being excessively vain and self absorbed.

A positive relationship with his father will help the adolescent boy develop high self-esteem and a stable self-image. This is also true of the adolescent girl's relationship with her father.

Adolescents with higher self-esteem report greater intimacy with their mothers and fathers; in other words, they feel close to and get along with their parents (Field, Lang, Yando, and Vendell, 1995). Adolescent self-esteem has been associated with parental willingness to grant autonomy (Linver and Silverberg, 1995), parental acceptance, flexibility (Klein, 1992), communication (Caughlin and Malis, 2004) and shared satisfaction, as well as parental support, participation, and control (Barber, Chadwick, and Oerter, 1992; Robinson, 1995).

In short, regardless of either race or ethnicity, authoritative parents raise children with high self-esteem (Dekovic and Meeus, 1997). We will discuss a number of these factors in more detail.

Maternal Relationship and Identification The quality of mother-adolescent relationships is clearly an important factor in adolescent self-esteem (Hahn-Smith and Smith, 2001; Turnage, 2004). Older adolescent girls who feel close to their mothers see themselves as confident, wise, reasonable, and self-controlled. Those who feel distant from their mothers perceive themselves in negative terms: rebellious, impulsive, touchy, and tactless. These findings indicate that the degree of maternal identification influences self-concept.

Paternal Relationship and Identification Fathers are important, too, in an adolescent's development. Although in the past it had been assumed that children's relationships with their mothers was more important to their psychological adjustment than their relationships to their fathers, most recent research finds that this is not the case (Rohner and Veneziano, 2001). Studies generally show that both relationships serve the same functions or that father-child relationships serve different but equally vital roles in adolescent development. Fathers' effects on their sons' and their daughters' self-esteem appears to stem from different behaviors: Fathers enhance their daughters' self-esteem most by expressing physical affection to them, but they increase their sons' self-esteem by sustaining contact with them (Barber and Thomas, 1986).

Parental Interest, Concern, and Discipline A key factor in determining whether parents have a positive effect in helping their adolescents build a healthy self-concept is the warmth, concern, and interest they show them. Parents who care and show interest are more likely to have adolescents who have high self-esteem. The parents of high-self-esteem adolescents are strict but consistent and they demand high standards, yet they are also flexible enough to allow deviations from rules under special circumstances. There seems to be a combination of warmth and firm discipline (Buri, 1989).

ANSWERS WOULDN'T YOU LIKE TO KNOW . . .

What kinds of parents raise children with high levels of self-esteem?

Parents who are warm, supportive, caring, and authoritative are most likely to raise children with high levels of self-esteem.

Divorced and Blended Families When children perceive conflict between parents or between themselves and their parents, lower self-esteem can be expected. Amato (1986) found lower self-esteem among adolescents from conflicted families and from those where the parent-adolescent relationship was poor. However, one of the significant findings was that loss of self-esteem when parents divorce is usually temporary. Amato (1988) also found no significant association between adult self-esteem and having experienced parental divorce or death as a child.

The well-being of children can best be assessed by the adequacy of *nurturing, love, and training* they receive, rather than in terms of particular family structures (Hutchinson, Valutis, Brown, and White, 1989). One study found that adolescents who had experienced parental divorce were significantly more likely to have encountered parental hostility and/or lack of care, inadequate supervision when not in school, lack of concern by teachers, and greater financial hardship. In turn, lower self-concepts and/or social skills were found to be associated with these kinds of life experiences (Parish, 1993; Parish and Parish, 1991).

Socioeconomic Status

The effects of socioeconomic status (SES) on self-esteem are variable. Generally, low-SES students have lower self-esteem than high-SES students, and the effects of SES appear to be stronger with increasing age.

The effects of socioeconomic status appear to be more indirect than direct (Dusek and McIntyre, 2003). It is not so much that teenagers view themselves harshly *because* they are poor but rather that they are doing poorly in school because of their economic situation. Also, economic hardship reduces affective parental support and may thus convey a negative appraisal of the adolescent, thereby lowering his or her self-esteem (Ho, Lempers, and Clark-Lempers, 1995). Finally, teenagers from low-income families are less likely to be able to afford the latest fashions, nor are they as able as more wealthy peers to join the kinds of clubs and organizations that can lead to increased popularity. They have a legitimate reason to worry about how they are being judged by their classmates, and this, of course, can decrease self-esteem.

Race/Ethnicity

In the 1950s, eminent psychologist Kenneth Clark (1953) reported the results of groundbreaking research that indicated that African American children had lower levels of self-esteem than Caucasian children. He presented young Black children with both Black and White dolls and asked them to indicate which of the dolls were nice, which were pretty, which they would like to play with, and so on. The Black children preferred the White dolls, indicating that they felt bad about themselves and about Black individuals in general. Clark's research was instrumental in convincing the members of the U.S. Supreme Court to declare segregation unconstitutional in their seminal 1954 decision *Brown v. Board of Education.*

Does race still factor into self-esteem today? Research findings suggest that with the increase of racial pride brought about by the civil rights movement, self-esteem among African Americans has risen. In fact, most research now shows that African American adolescents have higher self-esteem than adolescents from any other group, including Caucasians (Twenge and Crocker, 2002). (This is generally not found to be true for adolescents from other racial minorities.)

Overall, there is some evidence that African American youths have higher self-esteem when not exposed to White prejudices (Martinez and Dukes, 1991). When surrounded primarily by those with similar physical appearance, social-class standing, family background, and school performance, African Americans rate themselves much higher in self-esteem than when surrounded by Whites (Comer, 1993; Dreyer, Jennings, Johnson, and Evans, 1994). African American students in segregated schools have higher self-esteem than African American students in integrated schools. The desegregated school has many advantages, but enhancing self-esteem is not one of them.

The self-esteem of minority adolescents is enhanced if they have a positive ethnic identity. (This will be discussed more fully later in this chapter.) Adolescents who have not yet become comfortable with their own ethnicity have lower self-esteem (Phinney, 1992).

Adolescents from different ethnic backgrounds may base their overall self-esteem on different factors. One study, for example (Erkut, Marx, Fields, and Sing, 1999), found that African American girls based their self-worth predominately on their scholastic abilities, that Chinese American girls based their self-worth primarily on their close friendships, and that Caucasian and Puerto Rican American girls derived their self-worth mainly from their appearance.

Gender

Most research on the effects of gender on self-esteem find that in adolescence, girls' self-esteem is somewhat lower than boys'. This was confirmed in a recent meta-analysis of hundreds of studies on this topic by Kling, Hyde, Showers, and Buswell (1999). They found that males had modestly higher self-esteem than females overall and that this difference was greatest in late adolescence. These findings are consistent with the belief that girls' self-esteem drops more than boys' during the teenage years (AAUW, 1992; Marsh, 1989). This pattern of lower self-esteem in girls is not limited to the United States but has been replicated in other countries, as well. For example, Bolognini, Plancherel, Bellschart, and Halfon (1996) found that Swiss adolescent girls had lower self-esteem than Swiss adolescent boys.

ANSWERS WOULDN'T YOU LIKE TO KNOW ...

Do adolescent girls and boys have different levels of self-esteem?

Although there are few gender differences in self-esteem during childhood, in adolescence, boys often have higher self-esteem than girls. This is probably because adolescent girls are more preoccupied and less satisfied with their appearance than boys are at this age.

Girls' self-esteem is also based on different factors than boys'. Girls' self-esteem is tied much more strongly to their perceived physical attractiveness (Wade and Cooper, 1999) and to their feelings of interconnectedness with others—their social networks (Josephs, Markus, and Tafarodi, 1992). Boys' self-esteem is most strongly related to their feelings of achievement and athletics (Wigfield, Eccles, MacIver, Reuman, and Midgley, 1991).

Why do adolescent girls have lower self-esteem than adolescent boys? Some researchers point to the fact that traits viewed as masculine are seen by American society as more desirable than those seen as feminine (Markus and Kitayama, 1994). Other researchers point to the negative effects of the media on girls' body image (Kilbourne, 1995), and still others suggest that it is harder to maintain high self-esteem when it is largely based on others' impressions of you. In any case, these differences are important even if they are rather small, since self-esteem helps determine one's moods, goals, and life plans.

Physical Disabilities

As might be expected, adolescents with physical disabilities and negative body images have more difficulty developing positive self-concepts and self-esteem than do those who are more average (Koff, Rierdan, and Stubbs, 1990). (The importance of physical attractiveness and body image was discussed in Chapter 5.) It is certain that the degree of physical attractiveness and acceptance of one's physical self are influential factors in the development of a total self-concept.

IN THEIR OWN WORDS

"I remember not having much self-esteem in early adolescence. . . . I was shy and very quiet, and I was a major tomboy. So, when the other girls started to wear make-up and dresses, I was all of the sudden different from them. I didn't want to change the way I was! I enjoyed being a tomboy and having fun. As I entered middle school, my self-esteem first took a large drop because I didn't know anyone there and felt very isolated. After a little while, however, I found a group of people that I liked who liked me back, and slowly my self-esteem started to rise. It took a while, but now I feel that I have a good amount of self-esteem."

Stress

One study of 2,154 North Dakota high school students between ages 14 and 19 revealed that as the number of negative life events increased, the level of self-esteem decreased (Youngs, Rathge, Mullis, and Mullis, 1990). Negative life events included the death of a close family member, failing an exam, change in school or residence, illness, work problems, problems in relationships, and family changes such as gaining a new family member or divorce. These findings are significant because if stress has a negative impact on self-esteem, this, in turn, affects many aspects of the adolescent's life, as we have seen. Not surprisingly, disruptions in self-esteem are negatively associated with adjustment in early adolescence (Tevendale, DuBois, Lopez, and Prindiville, 1997).

Changes in Self-Concept during Adolescence

To what extent does self-concept change during adolescence? Overall, self-concept gradually stabilizes (Cole et al., 2001). Adolescents are extremely sensitive, however, to important events and changes in their lives. One study found a lowered self-concept of high school juniors after they and their families had moved a long distance to another town. The more recent and frequent the move, the greater the negative effect on self-concept (Hendershott, 1989).

Research indicates that self-esteem is lowest in early adolescence, and this appears to be true across lines of race/ethnicity, gender, and socioeconomic status. There are numerous reasons for this drop. With cognitive development comes the ability to see oneself more realistically, rather than in the inflated way that is typical of younger children (Marsh, 1989); therefore, in adolescence, one may all of a sudden feel that one doesn't look so good. In addition, once puberty has occurred, adolescents become very interested in finding girlfriends or boyfriends, and so they become concerned about and dissatisfied with their own appearance. This is more true of girls than of boys, contributing to the greater decline in girls' self-esteem at this time (Allgood-Merten, Lewinsohn, and Hope, 1990; Pliner, Chaiken, and Flett, 1990).

Most important, perhaps, is the fact that students leave elementary school for middle school at this time. The move from a protected elementary school, where a child had few teachers and one set of classmates, to a much larger, more impersonal junior high, where teachers, classmates, and even classrooms are constantly shifting, can be disturbing to youths' self-image. Research has shown that school level is a more critical factor than age. In one study, sixth-graders in elementary schools felt better about themselves than sixth-graders who attended middle schools (Wigfield and Eccles, 1994). Many studies have reinforced the finding that the transition from elementary to junior high or middle school can be a stressful event in the lives of early adolescents (Fenzel, 1989; Mullis, Mullis, and Normandin, 1992).

Self-image and self-esteem can be improved by helpful events (Markstrom-Adams and Spencer, 1994). For instance, summer-camp experiences have been found to be helpful in improving the self-concepts of young adolescents. Studies have reported good results with *assertiveness training* of high school and college-level students who are timid, withdrawn, and incapable of dealing with other students, teachers, and relatives (e.g., Waksman 1984).

In summary, the concept of the self is not completely solidified by adolescence, although recognizable trends and traits persist. With increasing age, these recognizable traits become more stable. However, self-concept is subject to change under the influence of powerful forces (see Figure 8.2). Assisting the adolescent who has a negative identity to find a mature and positive image of self is a major undertaking, but it can be done in some cases. It is certain that the change is easier during adolescence than in adulthood.

IDENTITY

No doubt, one of the most important tasks an adolescent faces is to form an identity. As you may recall from Chapter 2, the concept of identity was first proposed by Erik Erikson (see pp. 30–32). Identity is, in a sense, one's life story (McAdams, 2001). Society expects young people to decide on a college and/or a job,

FIGURE 8.2 FACTORS THAT AFFECT ADOLESCENTS' SELF-ESTEEM

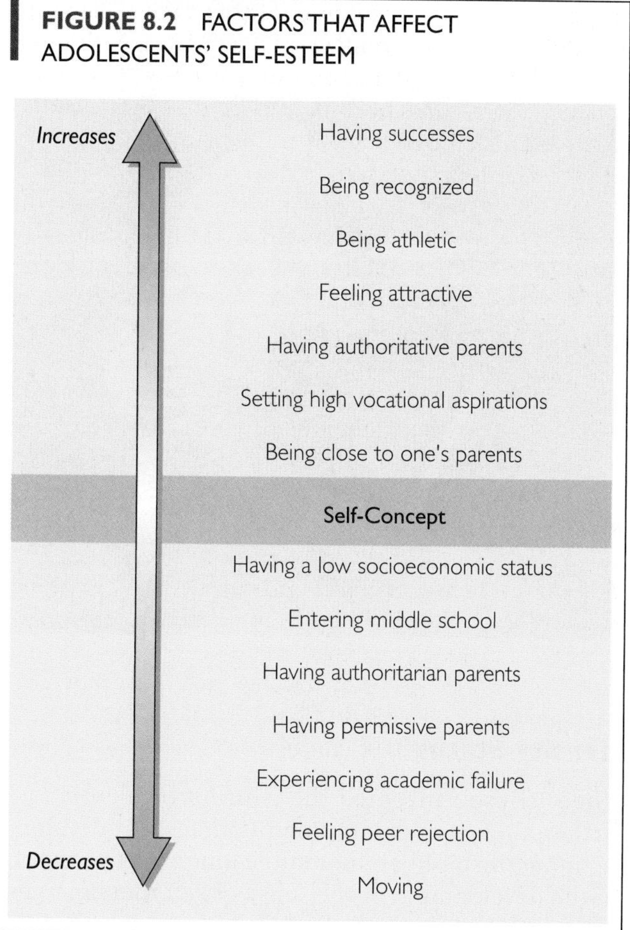

to become romantically involved, and to make choices regarding political philosophies and religious practices (Rotheram-Borus, 1989). Erikson described the task of identity formation as one of making choices by exploring alternatives and committing to roles (Adams, Gulotta, and Montemayor, 1992). Then, as one moves through adolescence, if these values, beliefs, goals, and practices are no longer appropriate, one can engage in a task of identity redefinition and refinement. Self-identity is clearly not stable, but is instead an ongoing process of self-reflection and change as one moves through life (Baumeister, 1991).

Seven Conflicts

You must make scores of decisions before you will have developed a fully formed identity: Where should you live? Do you want to have children? How important is religion in your life? Even so, Erikson felt that seven issues were of primary importance, some of which may seem more obvious than others:

1. *Temporal perspective versus time confusion:* Gaining a sense of time and of the continuity of life is critical for the adolescent, who must coordinate the past and the future and form some concept of how long it takes people to achieve their life plans. It means learning to estimate and allocate his or her time. A true sense of time does not develop until relatively late in adolescence—at around age 15 or 16.
2. *Self-certainty versus self-consciousness:* This conflict involves developing self-confidence based on past experiences so that a person believes in himself or herself and feels that there is a reasonable chance of accomplishing future aims. To do this, adolescents go through a period of increasing self-awareness and self-consciousness, especially in relation to their physical self-images and social relationships. When development follows a relatively normal course, children acquire confidence in themselves and their abilities. They develop confidence in their ability to cope in the present and in anticipation of future success.
3. *Role experimentation versus role fixation:* Adolescents have opportunities to try out the different roles they are to play in society. They can experiment with many different identities, personality characteristics, ways of talking and acting, ideas, goals, or types of relationships. Identity comes through opportunities for such experimentation. Those who have developed too much inner restraint and guilt, who have lost initiative, or who have prematurely experienced role fixation never really find out who they are (Erikson, 1968).
4. *Apprenticeship versus work paralysis:* Similarly, the adolescent has an opportunity to explore and try out different occupations before deciding on a vocation. The choice of job plays a large part in determining a person's identity (Erikson, 1968). Furthermore, a negative self-image in the form of inferiority feelings can prevent a person from mustering the necessary energy to succeed at school or on the job.
5. *Sexual polarization versus bisexual confusion:* Adolescents continue to attempt to define what it means to be male and female. Erikson believed it is important that adolescents develop a clear identification with one sex or the other as a basis for future heterosexual intimacy and as a basis for a firm identity. Furthermore, he emphasized that for communities to function properly, men and women must be willing to assume their so-called proper roles; sexual polarization, then, is necessary (Erikson, 1968). Much of present-day analysis (and much criticism!) of Erikson relates to his emphasis on the need for sexual polarization.

According to Erikson, a coherent self-identity is formed as the adolescent chooses values, beliefs, and goals. These choices are made by exploring alternatives and committing to roles.

6. *Leadership and followership versus authority confusion:* As adolescents expand their social horizons through schoolwork, social groups, and new friends, they begin to learn to take leadership responsibilities as well as how to follow others. At the same time, they discover there are competing claims on their allegiances. The state, employer, parents, and friends all make demands, with the result that adolescents experience confusion in relation to authority. To whom should they listen? Whom should they follow? To whom should they give their primary allegiance? Sorting out the answers requires an examination of personal values and priorities.
7. *Ideological commitment versus confusion of values:* Construction of an ideology guides other aspects of behavior. Erikson (1968) referred to this struggle as the "search for fidelity." He emphasized that individuals need something to believe in or to follow.

If the individual is able to resolve these seven conflicts, then a firm identity will emerge. The crisis is past when he or she no longer has to question at every moment his or her own identity—when he or she has subordinated childhood identity and found a new self-identification (Erikson, 1950). Erikson acknowledged that finding an acceptable identity is much more difficult during a period of rapid social change because the older generation is no longer able to provide adequate role models for the younger generation.

Identity Status

When Erikson invented the concept of identity, he furthered our understanding of adolescent development and inspired an incredible amount of research on the development of the sense of self that emerges during adolescence. Of all of that research, the most influential was conducted by James Marcia (1966, 1976, 1991, 1994). According to Marcia, the criteria used to establish the attainment of a mature identity are two variables: crisis and commitment, in relation to occupational choice, religion, and political ideology. "*Crisis* refers to the adolescent's period of engagement in choosing among meaningful alternatives, *commitment* refers to the degree of personal investment the individual exhibits" (Marcia, 1966; emphasis added). A *mature identity* is achieved when the individual has experienced a crisis and has become committed to an occupation and ideology.

Marcia (1966) revealed four basic identity statuses: identity diffused, foreclosure, moratorium, and identity achieved. Table 8.1 shows the four identity statuses, which we will examine in more detail in the following sections.

Identity Diffused

Subjects who are **identity diffused** have not experienced a crisis period, nor have they made any commitment to an occupation, a religion, a political philosophy, sex roles, or personal standards of behavior (Archer and Waterman, 1990). They have not experi-

TABLE 8.1 THE FOUR IDENTITY STATUSES AS DERIVED FROM THE EGO IDENTITY DIMENSIONS

	COMMITMENT DIMENSION	
EXPLORATION DIMENSION	**PRESENCE OF COMMITMENTS**	**ABSENCE OF COMMITMENTS**
Explored alternatives in the past	Identity achievement	Identity diffusion
Currently exploring alternatives	—	Moratorium
Never explored alternatives	Foreclosure	Identity diffusion

Source: S. L. Archer, "The Status of Identity: Reflections on the Need for Intervention," *Journal of Adolescence, 12* (1989): 345–359. Reprinted by permission.

enced an identity crisis in relation to any of these issues, nor have they gone through the process of reevaluating, searching, and considering alternatives.

Diffusion is developmentally the most unsophisticated identity status and is usually a normal characteristic of early adolescents. Given time and increasing pressure from parents, peers, and schools, most young people eventually begin to grapple with these issues. Adolescents who continue to express no interest in commitment may be masking an underlying insecurity about identity issues (Berzonsky, Nurmi, Kinney, and Tammi, 1999). Lacking self-confidence, they mask their feelings with expressions of apathy. Diffused individuals usually have low self-esteem, are unduly influenced by peer pressure, and lack meaningful friendships. They drift from interest to interest, relationship to relationship. They are selfish and hedonistic.

If an adolescent has tried to make identity commitments and has failed, the response may be anger directed against parents or religious or political leaders. Older adolescents who become social dropouts, who are rebelling against all established values, and who have adopted a nihilistic attitude fall into this category. Identity-diffused adolescents who avoid anxiety, crisis, and commitment by using alcohol and drugs try to deny that any problem exists.

Foreclosure

Subjects in **foreclosure** have not experienced a crisis, but they have made commitments to occupations and ideologies that are not the result of their own searching but are ready-made and handed down to them, frequently by parents. They often have identified closely with same-sex parents (Cella, DeWolfe, and Fitzgibbon, 1987). They become what others want them to become, without really deciding for themselves. An example of this type of identity status is the youth who wants to be a doctor because his or her parent is a doctor. Foreclosed adolescents are not able to distinguish between their own goals and the ones their parents plan for them. In one study, foreclosed adolescents reported a strong emotional foundation within the family, but it was such a close relationship that it reflected enmeshment. Foreclosed adolescents exhibited significantly lower levels of healthy separation than others (Papini, Mucks, and Barnett, 1989).

Foreclosed individuals are often authoritarian and intolerant. They are conformists and conventional thinkers (Berzonsky, 1989; Kroger, 2003). They seek security and support from significant others or familiar settings (Kroger, 1990). When put under stress, however, they perform poorly. Their security lies in avoiding change or stress. As one researcher observed, the "total lack of conflict during adolescence is an ominous sign that the individual's psychological maturity may not be progressing" (Keniston, 1971, p. 364). It has been suggested also that foreclosure is a means of reducing anxiety. Persons who are too uncomfortable with uncertainty make choices without a lengthy process of consideration. They may marry while still in school, as well as make early decisions about vocations without lengthy consideration.

Some researchers suggest that identity statuses may not be comprised of homogeneous groups of people, raising the possibility of the need for subcategories (Kroger, 1995). For example, some research has raised the possibility of distinguishing individuals who are firm versus developmental foreclosures, based on their willingness to respond to changing environmental circumstances. *Firm foreclosures* are not likely to change statuses. *Developmental foreclosures* could be expected to enter a moratorium phase at some future time, rather than remaining under the

identity diffused according to Marcia, those adolescents who have not experienced a crisis and explored meaningful alternatives or made any commitments in finding an acceptable identity.

foreclosure according to Marcia, establishing an identity without search or exploration, usually according to what has been handed down by parents.

IN THEIR OWN WORDS

"I am fully immersed in the moratorium stage—a not-altogether fun place to be! Coming into college, I remember people around me telling me how much time I had to figure out what I wanted to do in life. Well . . . time is rapidly running out and I still don't know what I want to do with myself. I was encouraged when I learned that nobody usually gets stuck in this stage, because right now, it feels like I may never know what to do with myself. I am consumed with thoughts of my future and where I will be in 10 years. So, basically to sum up the last 10 years, I have gone from worrying about looks and popularity to worrying about a job and money. The fact that there is no one clear answer to this is what makes it so hard, I think. I have a good amount of self-esteem."

guidance of parents. Current longitudinal and cross-sectional investigations of identity development in later adolescence and young adulthood indicate that fewer than one-half of foreclosed individuals would shift from those statuses over one- to six-year intervals (Kroger, 2003). Those who have the potential to outgrow their foreclosure status are more secure and have less need for approval than those who do not (Kroger, 1995).

Do individuals in cultures that neither encourage nor support identity crises have identities? Of course, but the identity is a foreclosed one. An identity does not have to be achieved in these cultures to be functional. Going through the decision-making process necessary to achieve an identity is unnecessary if one has no choices to make. If there is only one possible occupation (say, farmer), if everyone has the same beliefs, and if everyone marries, for instance, then there will be no real crises to face. It is certainly easier to remain foreclosed in a foreclosure society.

Moratorium

The word **moratorium** means a period of delay granted to someone who is not yet ready to make a decision or assume an obligation. During adolescence, it is a period of exploration of alternatives before commitments are made. Some subjects with a moratorium identity status are involved in continual crises. As a consequence, they seem confused, unstable, and discontented. They are often rebellious and uncooperative. Some moratorium-status individuals avoid dealing with problems, and they may have a tendency to procrastinate until situations dictate a course of action (Berzonsky, 1989). Because these individuals experience crises, they tend to be anxious (Meeus, Iedama, Helsen, and Vollebergh, 1999). One study even showed that death anxiety is higher in moratorium-status adolescents than in those in the other three statuses (Sterling and Van Horn, 1989). Adolescents in this status category are often uncertain they have selected the right major in college and may be unhappy with their college experience and education. Granted, it is not uncommon or even especially undesirable for adolescents to "try on" a variety of identities (even radically different identities) before finding the one that best fits them (Muuss, 1988b). Thus, they may dabble in exotic religions, wear unusual and attention-calling clothing, and choose impractical careers. However, most individuals become reasonably conventional by the end of this identity search.

Why do adolescents move from being foreclosed or diffused into a state of moratorium? Going to college encourages exploration. Students in college are actively and thoughtfully confronted with the crisis of making an occupational commitment and stimulated to rethink their ideologies. In addition, college is an environment in which individuals meet people who are different from themselves. Being confronted with persons who have dissimilar values and desires often triggers a rethinking of your own views and may make you less certain of your beliefs. Being met with conflicting opinions—especially those of people whom you respect—stimulates identity growth (Bosma and Kunnen, 2001).

Identity Achieved

Subjects whose status is **identity achieved** have experienced a psychological moratorium, have resolved their identity crises by carefully evaluating various alternatives and choices, and have come to conclusions and decisions on their own. They have been highly motivated to achieve and have been able to do so because they have attained high levels of intrapsychic integration and social adaptation. Once an identity has been achieved, there is self-acceptance, a stable self-definition, and a commitment to a vocation, religion, and political ideology. There is harmony within oneself and an acceptance of capacities, opportunities, and limitations. There is a more realistic concept of goals.

Research with high school students indicates that few have achieved an identity by the time of graduation. Living at home and possessing limited life and work experiences are not conducive to identity achievement. Most but not all 18-year-olds know that they have yet to find an identity. As one student wrote in her journal:

ANSWERS WOULDN'T YOU LIKE TO KNOW . . .

What identity status is most common among college students?

Most college students have a moratorium status and so are actively trying to figure out what they want from their lives.

When I was a senior in high school, I just knew that I was going to be a doctor. I had planned on a career in medicine as long as I could remember. I would have bet a million dollars that that's what I was going to do. What a joke! I hated all the science courses I had to take in college, and I struggled to even pass. Now that I'm a junior, I'm still not sure what I want to do with my life—but it's not to be a doctor! I want to do something where I work with people, but that's all I'm sure of.

Adolescents who have a foreclosure status are often certain of their career plans and feel that they have achieved their identities. If they move on to a moratorium status, however, they usually rethink and reject their initial plans. Even at the college level, 80 percent of students change their majors during their four years (Waterman, 1992). In general, however, the percentage of adolescents who are identity achievers increases with age (Waterman, 1999).

Components of Identity

Identity has many components—*physical, sexual, social, vocational, moral, ideological,* and *psychological* characteristics—that make up the total self (Grotevant, 1987). Thus, individuals may identify themselves by their physical appearance, their gender, their social relationships and membership in groups, their vocations and work, and their religious and political affiliations and ideologies. *Identity* may be described in terms of the *total concept of self.* It is personal because it is a sense of "I-ness," but it is also social, for it includes "we-ness," or one's collective identity. Identity is intrinsically both an individual and a social process (Adams and Marshall, 1996). Adolescents who have a positive identity have developed a sense of accepting themselves; furthermore, identity development is associated with the development of intimacy and an acceptance of others. Adolescents are attracted to those with identity statuses similar to their own (Goldman, Rosenzweig, and Lutter, 1980). Identity achievement also helps in developing committed relationships: Intimacy alters identity—it helps people grow (Kacerguis and Adams, 1980).

Other adolescents adopt a **negative identity** that is at odds with the cultural values of the community. In a sense, a negative identity is a variant of the foreclosure status. Whereas a foreclosure may be thought of as slavishly following authority figures' desires, someone with a negative identity will sit when told to stand. He or she will derive satisfaction from rebelling against and defying more obedient, mainstream individuals. The individual with a negative identity can be viewed as a "reverse foreclosure" in that he or she bases his or her behavior on what parents, teachers, and members of society at large want—but does the opposite. Slackers, truants, juvenile delinquents, and those with oppositional defiant disorder are the types of individuals who might have a negative identity. Protinsky (1988) found that adolescents who exhibit behavioral problems score much lower on measures of general identity than those who do not have such problems.

Other adolescents will behave in ways to reduce the anxiety of uncertain or incomplete identities. Some will try to *escape* through such intense immediate experiences as drug abuse or wild parties. These emotional experiences temporarily blot out the search for identity. An adolescent may substitute a *temporary identity* by becoming a joiner, a goof-off, a clown, or a bully. Some will seek to strengthen their identity temporarily through vandalism, competitive sports, or popularity contests. Those who are cognitively dogmatic may become bigots or superpatriots and seek to build a temporary *fortress identity.* Ensuring a *meaningless identity* by engaging in fads is another possibility. For some youths, having a meaningless identity is better than no identity at all.

Some aspects of identity are more easily formed than others. Physical and sexual identities seem to be established earliest. Young adolescents become concerned with their body image before they become interested in choosing a vocation or examining their moral values and ideologies. Similarly, they must deal with their own sexual identity both before and after puberty.

Vocational, ideological, and moral identities are established more slowly. These identities depend on

moratorium according to Marcia, a period of time in the life of adolescents who are involved in a continual crisis, who continue to search for an identity, and who have not made any commitments.

identity achieved according to Marcia, those adolescents who have undergone a crisis in their search for an identity and who have made a commitment.

negative identity an identity based on rejecting parenting and societal values.

adolescents reaching more advanced levels of cognitive growth and development that enable them to explore alternative ideas and courses of action. In addition, reformulation of these identities requires independence of thought. The exploration of occupational alternatives is the most immediate and concrete task as adolescents finish high school or enter college. Religious and political ideologies are usually examined during late adolescence, especially the college years, but identities in these areas may be in a state of flux for years (Cote and Levine, 1992).

Critique

Since Marcia's four-status scheme was first developed in the 1960s, criticisms have been raised. Some have come from the fact that his four identity statuses do not capture the entirety of the identity concept, as envisioned by Erikson. Namely, critics say that Marcia focuses too much on the crisis/commitment aspect of identity and too little on its other crucial components. For example, van Hoof (1999) states that Marcia's scheme is inadequate because it fails to address the sense of personal continuity so central to identity. Similarly, Glodis and Blasi (1993) feel that the four statuses do not adequately capture the integration of different parts of the self, or the sense of unity that comes with having an identity.

In addition, it is now recognized that identity statuses do not always develop in exact sequence. It was originally believed that a developmental progression would be the norm. Most adolescents would enter the identity crisis from the foreclosure status, moving through a moratorium phase, out of which achievement status would be attained. The diffusion status during adolescence was seen as an aberration in this natural progression, hopefully a transient one.

Note that there are three important variations from this developmental sequence. First, a significant number of individuals enter adolescence in the diffusion status; some of them remain there. Second, some individuals seem never to make the transition to the moratorium and achievement statuses, remaining firmly entrenched within the foreclosure status. Third, certain individuals who attain an achievement status appear to regress to a lower status years later (Marcia, 1991). This suggests that individuals may go through the developmental sequence of identity more than once during a lifetime. A person may have found identity achievement at a certain period of life, then later in life go through another moratorium stage or stage of identity diffusion before identity achievement is accomplished (Stephen, Fraser, and Marcia, 1992).

Identity as a Process

Erikson's and Marcia's approaches to identity are status, or *outcome,* approaches. Their research did not concentrate on the *process* by which adolescents find their identities. Much of the current research about adolescent identity formation—and hence, much of the current criticism of Erikson's and Marcia's work—focuses on this process.

Grotevant (1992) was one of the first researchers (and one of the most influential) to discuss identity from this process perspective. He emphasizes that exploration is the key to finding an identity; one needs to gather information about oneself and about the environment in order to make life choices. (This certainly does not contradict Erikson's view.)

Burke (1991) envisions an **identity control system** that consists of two interpersonal and three intrapersonal components. The interpersonal components include one's *social behavior* and the *interpersonal feedback* one gets from others. The intrapersonal factors are *self-concept,* one's **identity standards,** and a **comparator** that assesses the similarity between the two. As individuals behave and get feedback on their behavior, their self-concept is affected. The comparator matches one's self-perceptions against the standards one has for who one wants to be. If there is a discrepancy between the two, then one's behavior, standards, or self-concept must be modified to increase consistency.

Adolescents in the different identity states handle discrepancies in different ways. Diffused individuals have yet to develop identity standards. Foreclosured youths overemphasize the feedback from their parents and significant others and form standards early on; they discount discordant feedback if it does not match their already established identity standards. Moratoriums are actively seeking feedback and are willing to adjust their identity standards. Like those in foreclosure, individuals who are identity achieved have solidified their identity standards, but they developed these standards more slowly and based them more on broad-based feedback (Kerpelman, Pittman, and Lamke, 1997).

Berzonsky (1997; Berzonsky and Kuk, 2000) has identified three styles of identity searching. Youths with an *informational style* seek out diagnostic information and accommodate their plans and behaviors, if necessary. This style characterizes moratorium and identity-achieved individuals. Others have a *normative style;* they are resistant to change and block out discrepant information. This style is characteristic of foreclosured adolescents. Diffused individuals are most likely to exhibit an *avoidant style* of identity searching. They put off making decisions and evade feedback; when they do make changes, these changes are superficial and short lived. These styles appear consistent across both genders and among youths in at least three different countries: the United States, Finland, and the Czech Republic (Berzonsky, Macek, and Nurmi, 2003).

Ethnic Identity

Ethnic identity is the sum total of group members' feelings about those symbols, values, and common histories that identify them as a distinct group. It is an individual's sense of self as a member of an ethnic group and the attitudes and behaviors associated with that sense (Helms, 1990). Ethnic development is the process of development from an unexamined ethnic identity through a period of exploration to arrive at an achieved ethnic identity (Yeh and Huang, 1996). The development of an ethnic identity is an essential human need. It provides a sense of historical continuity and a sense of belonging (Smith, E. J., 1991). It positively influences academic achievement (Arellano and Pedilla, 1996), helps individuals stand up to the strains of discrimination (Phinney and Chavira, 1995), and bolsters psychological well-being (Umaña-Taylor, Diversi, and Fine, 2002).

Acculturation Options

Acculturation is the adjustment of minority groups to the culture of the dominant group (Sodowsky, Lai, and Plake, 1991). A problem experienced by adolescents from ethnic-minority families and from immigrant families is that the culture into which they were born is not always valued or appreciated by the culture in which they are raised (Feldman, Mont-Reynaud, and Rosenthal, 1992). In the early stages of forging an identity, ethnic minorities and immigrants often find conflict between their ethnic cultures and the values of the larger society in which they live. The central question is the way in which minority ethnic groups relate to the dominant culture and to one another (Hiraga, Cauce, Mason, and Ordonez, 1993).

There are four possible ways in which ethnic group members can participate in a culturally diverse society. *Separation* involves exclusive focus on the cultural values and practices of the ethnic group and little or no interaction with the dominant society. *Assimilation* is the outcome when ethnic group members choose to identify solely with the culture of the dominant society and to relinquish all ties to their ethnic cultures. *Integration* is characterized by strong identification and involvement with both the dominant society's culture and the traditional ethnic culture. *Marginality* is defined by the absence or loss of one's culture of origin and the lack of involvement with the dominant society.

Which type of participation contributes most to the positive development of identity and self-esteem in adolescents? One study of high school and college students from a diverse, inner-city school sought an answer to this question. The students were from mixed backgrounds: Asians, African Americans, Hispanics, and Whites (Phinney, Chavira, and Williamson, 1992). Results indicated that among the four acculturation options, integration is the most adaptive, resulting in better psychological adjustment and higher self-esteem. A healthy relationship between endorsement of integration and self-esteem indicates that a more positive self-concept is associated with identification with a person's mainstream culture as well as his or her own culture. In contrast, endorsement of assimilation was found to be related to a lower self-esteem among the Asian and foreign-born participants. Thus, giving up your ethnic culture can have a negative impact on your self-concept. The idea of separation (an ethnic group should keep to itself and not mix with mainstream society) was given little support by the students, with no difference among ethnic groups or by socioeconomic status. Of all four alternatives, marginality—in which a person identifies neither with his or her own ethnic group nor the dominant culture—is the least satisfactory alternative (Phinney, 1992).

More recently, Phinney and Devich-Navarro (1997) revised the concept of integration by dividing it into two new types: **blended biculturalism** and **alternating biculturalism.** In addition, they posited a third new acculturation option, **fusion.** A blended bicultural person finds commonalities between his or her ethnic culture and the mainstream society; this individual usually acts in ways congruent with both cultures. An alternating bicultural is someone who moves back and forth between the two cultures, sometimes acting in the way the ethnic culture proscribes and sometimes in the way the mainstream culture proscribes. Fusion occurs when someone truly blends both cultures into a new, coherent whole. Figure 8.3 illustrates these different acculturation patterns.

identity control system a construct that describes the process of developing an identity.

identity standards one's beliefs about how one should behave.

comparator the component of the identity control system that compares one's self-concept with one's identity standards.

blended biculturalism the state in which one finds the commonalities between one's ethnic and mainstream identities.

alternating biculturalism the state in which one vacillates between following one's ethnic beliefs and those of the societal mainstream.

fusion the state in which one has merged one's ethnic traditions and those of the cultural mainstream into a new whole.

FIGURE 8.3 ETHNIC ACCULTURATION PATTERNS

Source: J. Phinney and M. Devich-Navarro, "Variations in Bicultural Identification among African American and Mexican American Adolescents," *Journal of Research on Adolescence,* 7 (1997): 3–32. Used with permission of Blackwell Publishing. All rights reserved.

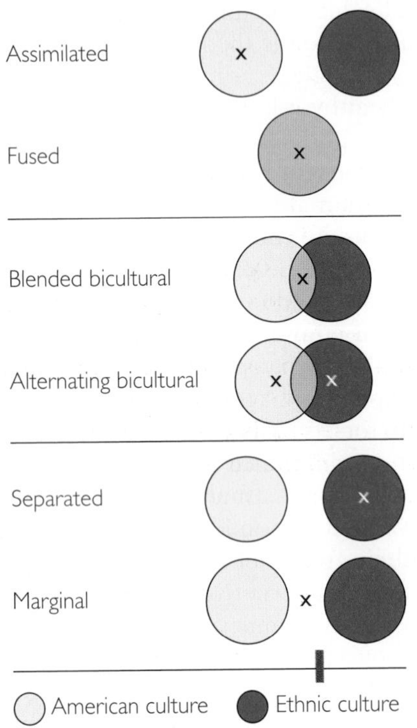

Ninety percent of the African American and Mexican adolescents in Phinney and Devich-Navarro's study (1997) were bicultural. The blended bicultural teenagers felt both American and ethnic. They believed the United States to be a diverse country and felt generally positive toward people in other ethnic groups. Ethnicity was not especially salient for them, and they did not perceive their biculturality to be problematic. The teenagers who had chosen an alternating bicultural pattern felt more ethnic than American. They took pleasure in their ethnicity but experienced more conflict in negotiating between their ethnic culture and mainstream American society. Separated adolescents felt distant from the mainstream culture, which they perceived as White. They felt they were actively excluded from full membership in society at large and were negative about people from other ethnic groups. The authors found no assimilated, fused, or marginal individuals in their sample of 98 tenth- and eleventh-graders.

Developing an Ethnic Identity

Children are not born understanding the concept of ethnicity; it must be learned. Tse (1999) has proposed a four-stage model of ethnic identity development. Very young children are *ethnically unaware.* They don't know that people have different ethnicities and assume everyone is just like them. This period is typically short lasting and ends by the time a child enters school. Children in the second stage are *ethnically ambivalent.* They downplay the importance of their ethnic background and don't strongly identify with

Adolescents who are experiencing an ethnic identity search typically segregate themselves by ethnicity, at least temporarily.

their ethnic group. During adolescence, *ethnic emergence* develops. In this stage, individuals realize that they can't fully join the mainstream. This can lead to feelings of anger and resentment and motivates many to immerse themselves in their ancestral culture. For instance, they may take courses or read books about their cultural history, spend most of their time socializing with others who share their ethnicity, and visit their ancestral homeland. Finally, when individuals realize that they are a product of two cultures—their ethnic culture and the mainstream American culture in which they were raised—they *incorporate* their ethnic identities, feeling both American and ethnic.

Quintana, Casañeda-English, and Ybarra (1999) base their conception of developing ethnic awareness on Selman's (1977) model of social cognition. (See Chapter 2 for a review of Selman's theory.) Initially, very young children believe that race/ethnicity is based solely on physical characteristics, such as skin color and eye shape. When they enter school, children come to know that other traits—such as native language, preferred foods, and countries of origin—distinguish groups, as well. At some point during elementary school, children become sensitive to more subtle, less essential differences between groups. They note socioeconomic differences and become aware of discrimination. During early adolescence, they learn the attitudes and perspectives of their particular groups; they see the world through these ethnic lenses. Eventually, many individuals develop a multicultural perspective and a bicultural identity. They come to understand the views of other groups.

ANSWERS WOULDN'T YOU LIKE TO KNOW . . .

How does the development of an ethnic identity affect someone's self-esteem?

Adolescents who are integrated—either blended biculturals or fused biculturals—have higher self-esteem than adolescents who have assimilated.

CROSS-CULTURAL CONCERNS PARENTAL ETHNIC SOCIALIZATION

As the numbers of ethnic minority children continue to increase, the socialization of these children in adolescence has become a topic of growing interest and concern. On the basis of research, it appears that minority parents face three distinct challenges. Their children need to be socialized both to their own culture and the mainstream culture, and they need to understand prejudice and discrimination. The first challenge, the learning of one's own culture, would seem to be the least problematic, in that it is presumably learned naturally in the home. Yet we know from several studies of African American families that some explicit cultural teaching is needed. A second socialization theme involves teaching children to get along in the mainstream culture or helping them to succeed in society at large. African American parents generally teach their children to be bicultural. Part of getting along in society involves developing the skills necessary to be successful; to accomplish this, children are encouraged to work hard and do well. The final theme common to all research on African American socialization is explicit teaching to prepare children to be aware of prejudice and discrimination. Racial barriers and blocked opportunities need to be emphasized.

In one study on ethnic socialization, parents were interviewed and given a series of questions:

1. Do you try to teach your son or daughter about the cultural practices of your ethnic group?
2. Have you tried to teach your son or daughter how to get along in mainstream American culture?
3. Have you talked to him or her about how to deal with experiences like name calling or discrimination?
4. Have you personally tried to prepare your daughter or son to live in a culturally diverse society? (Phinney and Chavira, 1995)

In-depth interviews with 60 American-born Japanese American, African American, and Mexican American high school students, ages 16 to 18, and one parent of each adolescent revealed significant ethnic group differences. African American parents more frequently reported discussing prejudice with their child. Japanese American and African American parents emphasized adaptation to society more than Mexican American parents. Interestingly enough, youths who were socialized to be aware of racial barriers and cautioned about appropriate interracial behavior attained higher grades and a greater sense of personal efficacy (Phinney and Chavira, 1995).

Ethnic Identity and Multiracial Teens

Early theoretical research on multiracial adolescents painted a bleak picture of their situation: They were thought to be betwixt and between, marginalized by members of both of their parent ethnicities and as a result having low self-esteem and a poor sense of self (Bracey, Bámaca, and Umaña-Taylor, 2004). More recent empirical research has provided a different view: Some studies have found that multiracial adolescents have high self-esteem (e.g., Brown, 2001), while others have found no consistent differences in the self-concepts of monoracial and multiracial youth (e.g., Phinney and Alipuria, 1996). Those multiracial adolescents who have a well-developed sense of ethnic identity are those who are most likely to have high self-esteem (Bracey, Bámaca, and Umaña-Taylor, 2004).

Ethnic Identity and Caucasian Adolescents

Do Caucasian students have an ethnic identity? Many, if not most, do not (Phinney and Alipuira, 1990; St. Louis and Liem, 2005). This is because their own ethnicity is often not salient or important to them. (Self-esteem is generally tied to White adolescents' ethnic identity only when they are in a situation in which they find themselves in the minority [Roberts et al., 1999]—a situation analogous to that of most minority adolescents, who find themselves surrounded by majority culture.) Of course, some Caucasian adolescents do strongly identify themselves as being part of an ethnic or religious group (the junior author fondly remembers her years in Minnesota, where many individuals are fervently and proudly *Norwegian American*), and their ethnic identities can be important sources of pride for them.

In sum, the research on ethnic identity strongly demonstrates that having a positive ethnic identity is strongly related to healthy self-esteem in non–Caucasian American adolescents (Smith, Walker, Fields, Brookins, and Seay, 1999). Integration—that is, feeling good about and comfortable with both the ethnic and mainstream aspects of heritage—is most closely associated with having a positive self-concept.

GENDER

The word **sex,** when used by psychologists and sociologists, refers to a person's anatomical physical attributes. If you have a penis and a scrotum, you are male; if you have a vagina and labia, you are female. Sex is determined by chromosomes and prenatal hormones; it is a biological phenomenon. Thus, each person is born having a biological sex.

From his or her first day of life, each person is assigned a **gender.** Gender is a much more inclusive concept than sex. It entails all of the cultural associations and expectations that go along with one's biological sex. It is a psychological and social phenomenon. Some of these cultural expectations are directly based on biology: for instance, that only women can get pregnant and give birth and that male athletes are apt to have more muscle mass than female athletes. Some cultural expectations are more indirectly tied to biology: for example, that women should be nurturing in order to care for children and that males should compete with each other to attract mates. Still other cultural expectations have little or nothing to do with biology or evolutionary history: that only women should enjoy wearing skirts (but not in Scotland) and that only men should participate in contact sports.

How one feels about his or her sex and gender is an important part of identity. Understanding society's characterization of your gender and developing your own personal code as to how someone of your gender should behave is therefore a central component of the identity search.

> **ANSWERS WOULDN'T YOU LIKE TO KNOW ...**
>
> What is the difference between *sex* and *gender?*
>
> Sex is a purely biological concept: male or female. *Gender* is a social construction that includes expectations about what males and females should be like.

Biological Sex

Biological sex is genetically and hormonally determined. The fetus becomes a male or female depending on whether it has XY or XX chromosomes and on the prenatal balance between the male and female hormones in the bloodstream. Hormones can have a definite influence on physical characteristics even after birth. Male hormones can be administered to a woman, encouraging the growth of a beard, body hair, the clitoris, and the development of masculine muscles, build, and strength. Similarly, female hormones can be administered to a man, encouraging breast development, increasing voice pitch, and leading to other female traits. Femaleness or maleness, then, is somewhat tenuous and may be partially altered.

Hormones alter physical characteristics, but do they influence sex-typed behavior? If human females are exposed to excessive androgenic (masculinizing sex hormones) influences prior to birth, they become more tomboyish, more physically vigorous, and more assertive than other females. They will prefer boys rather than girls as playmates and will choose strenuous activities over the relatively docile play of most prepubertal girls. Similarly, adolescent boys born to mothers who receive estrogen and progesterone during pregnancies tend to exhibit less assertiveness and physical activity, and may be rated lower on general masculine-type behavior (Rabin and Chrousos, 1991). This suggests that changes in prenatal hormonal levels in humans may have marked effects on gender-role behavior; after birth, however, hormonal changes have much less effect on masculine/feminine characteristics already evident.

Cognitive-Developmental Theories

Cognitive-developmental theories suggest that gender identification has its beginning in the gender that is assigned to the child at birth and subsequently accepted by him or her while growing up. At the time of birth, gender assignment is made largely on the basis of genital examination. From that point on, the child is considered a boy or a girl. If genital abnormalities are present, gender assignment may prove to be erroneous if it is not in agreement with sex chromosomes and gonads that are present. However, even if erroneous, gender identification usually follows the sex in which the child is reared.

The assignment of gender influences how the child feels about herself or himself and how others feel about the child. The cognitive theories, of course, focus on the child's self-perceptions. They hold that the child's self-categorization as a boy or girl is the basic organizer of the gender identification attitudes that are developed. For example, the child who recognizes that he is a male begins to act consistently with male gender expectations. He begins to structure his own experiences according to his accepted gender and to act out appropriate sex roles. Sex differentiation takes place gradually as children learn to be masculine or feminine according to culturally established gender identification expectations and their interpretations of them (Trepanier-Street, Romatowski, and McNair, 1990).

The most widely accepted variant of the cognitive-developmental perspective on gender is called **gender schema theory.** It proposes a multistep developmental process. First, children learn that they are boys or girls (even if they are unclear as to exactly what those labels mean). Next, children recognize that not only people but things and behaviors are also labeled as boy things or girl things. Children are naturally more curious about items and behaviors that match their labels than they are about items and behaviors that do not. They therefore pay more attention to and learn more about gender-appropriate objects and behaviors than gender-inappropriate ones. It is a well-established aspect of human nature that we come to like things that we are familiar with; they make us feel comfortable. It follows, then, that children will begin to prefer gender-appropriate actions and will perform them more frequently than gender-inappropriate actions (Martin, Ruble, and Szkrybalo, 2002).

A child's sex-role identity begins with the cognitive assignment of gender made at birth. However, society also plays an important role, ascribing certain qualities of femininity or masculinity to the child.

Societal Influences

Children do not develop their attitudes about gender in a vacuum; they are surrounded by parents, teachers, other adults, friends, and less-than-friendly peers who make their views of appropriate masculine and feminine behaviors known. Even people that children don't know and with whom they don't directly interact—such as the producers of TV shows and movies and musicians whose songs are heard on the radio and

sex one's biological endowment as a male or a female.

gender the psychological/sociological construct of what it means to be a man or a woman.

gender schema theory a revised cognitive-developmental approach to gender that emphasizes the stages of labeling, attention, and interest.

whose videos are seen on TV—bombard them with images of men and women. Through these observances and interactions, children learn the **gender roles** prescribed by their society: that is, the behaviors that men and women are expected to engage in with different frequencies. For example, being aggressive is part of the American male gender role, whereas being emotional is part of women's. Eating is not part of anyone's gender role because males and females eat with more or less equal frequency. (Eating or avoiding eating certain foods, however, may be part of one's gender role. In some social circles, it is perceived as more masculine to eat bratwurst than to eat crustless cucumber sandwiches.) Individuals are described as **masculine** or **feminine** based on how consistently they fulfill gender-role expectations.

Masculinity

Traditionally, masculine men were supposed to be aggressive, strong, forceful, self-confident, virile, courageous, logical, and unemotional (Brannon, 1999). Pleck (1976) captured the traditional American male gender role in four directives. A man is supposed to be "The Big Wheel"; that is, he must be successful and have a high status. He is also expected to be "The Sturdy Oak"; like John Wayne, Clint Eastwood, and Arnold Schwartzenegger, he is required to constantly evidence toughness, self-confidence, and self-reliance. A man is allowed and expected to "Give 'Em Hell," as well—to be daring and to be ready to solve his problems with violence if needed. Finally, a man is told "No Sissy Stuff"; in other words, any interest or behavior that is in any way feminine should be shunned at all costs. It is especially important for a man to avoid any expression of caring or gentleness toward other men (Rabinowitz, 1991; Salt, 1991).

Although many members of American society have moved away from this rigid conceptualization of masculinity, some subgroups have not. For example, male youths who join delinquent street gangs tend to be very concerned about appearing masculine. Many of the practices that form their initiation rites—such as having to fight and needing to demonstrate their courage by engaging in dangerous acts (such as running along subway tracks)—are reminiscent of old-fashioned masculine ideals (Hunt and Laidler, 2001).

Femininity

What are the traditional concepts of femininity as taught by middle and upper-middle classes of U.S. society? In the past, women were supposed to be submissive, sensitive, tender, affectionate, sentimental, dependent, and emotional. A feminine female was never aggressive, loud, or vulgar in speech or behavior. She was expected to be soft-hearted, to cry easily, to get upset at times over small things, and to like frivolous things. She was expected to be dependent and submissive and to be interested primarily in her home. Today, few social groups hold these stereotypes of femininity, indicating that significant changes have taken place in people's concepts.

Social Learning Theory

Social learning theory suggests that a child learns sex-typed behavior the same way he or she learns any other type of behavior: through a combination of reward, punishment, direct instruction, and modeling. From the beginning, boys and girls are socialized differently. Boys are expected to be more active, hostile, and aggressive. They are expected to fight when teased and to stand up to bullies. When they act according to expectations, they are praised; when they refuse to fight, they are criticized for being a "sissy." Similarly, girls are condemned or punished for being too boisterous and aggressive and are rewarded when they are polite and submissive. As a consequence, boys and girls grow up manifesting different behaviors (see Table 8.2).

Traditional gender roles and concepts are taught in many ways as a child grows up. For instance, television plays a significant role in the socialization process (for both young and old). Television commercials and programming contain considerable gender bias and sexism (Calvert, 1999). Another way of reinforcing gender roles is giving children gender-specific toys that may influence vocational choices. For example, boys might be persuaded to be scientists, astronauts, and football players, and girls might be inclined to be nurses, teachers, and flight attendants (Blakemore and Centers, 2005).

Without realizing it, many teachers still develop traditional masculine/feminine stereotypical behavior in school. Studies of teachers' relationships with boys and girls reveal that teachers, in general, encourage boys to be more assertive in the classroom (Sadker and Sadker, 1995). When the teacher asks questions, the boys call out comments without raising their hands, literally grabbing the teacher's attention. Most girls sit patiently with their hands raised, but when a girl calls out, the teacher reprimands her: "In this class, we don't shout out answers; we raise our hands." The message is subtle but powerful: Boys should be assertive academically; girls should be quiet.

Children also find appropriate gender roles through the processes of identification and modeling, especially with parents. Parental **identification** is the process by which a child adopts and internalizes parental values, attitudes, behavioral traits, and personality characteristics. Identification begins shortly after birth because of the child's early dependence on parents. This dependency, in turn, usually leads to close emotional attachment. Gender-role learning takes place almost

TABLE 8.2 HOW CHILDREN LEARN SEX-TYPED BEHAVIORS

MECHANISM	MALE EXAMPLE	FEMALE EXAMPLE
Reward	A boy is cheered by his team for making the winning tackle in a football game. The next day, he practices running fast so that he can make more tackles in the future.	A girl is praised by her teacher for working so quietly at her desk. The girl continues to work without getting up and speaking to others.
Punishment	A father ridicules his son for crying when his pet dies. The boy subsequently avoids crying in front of others.	Other girls refuse to play with a preschooler who plays too rough. The preschooler plays more gently the next day.
Instruction	A grandfather teaches his grandson how to fish. The boy spends his afternoons fishing in the stream behind his house.	A mother teaches her daughter how to knit. The girl makes a scarf for her aunt on her birthday.
Modeling	A boy watches an interview of a sports star who uses foul language. The boy begins cursing when speaking to his friends.	A girl overhears her older sister putting down some girls who dress unfashionably. She later criticizes unfashionable girls to her own friends.

unconsciously and indirectly in this close parent-child relationship. Children listen and observe how each parent behaves, speaks, dresses, and acts differently in relation to the other parent, to other children, or to people outside the family. Thus, children learn what a mother, a wife, a father, a husband, a woman, and a man *is* through example and through daily contacts and association.

One particular example of how parents influence their children's view of gender roles involves maternal employment. Adolescent girls whose mothers are employed outside the home are more likely to have an untraditional view of gender roles than girls whose mothers are full-time homemakers (Nelson and Keith, 1990) and are more likely to pursue nontraditional careers (Phillips and Imhoff, 1997). This is especially true if the father is supportive and approves of female employment. Boys are similarly affected (Christian, 1994). If their own mothers are employed and their fathers are supportive of this, boys are more likely not only to endorse women's employment but also to select nontraditional careers themselves.

Peers may play a particularly important role in the development of children's gender identities. Maccoby (1990) observed that boys and girls behave quite similarly when viewed alone, but in same-sex play groups, they behave very differently. Same-sex play groups are a frequent occurrence because from a very young age, when left to their own devices, most children prefer to play with others of the same sex. Girls gravitate toward other girls because boys play too roughly for them and don't listen to their suggestions; boys prefer to play with other boys because girls don't like to play fun games. These male and female same-sex groups develop very distinct cultures. Boys play competitively and physically; they like to win and to show who is the best. Girls like to talk, take turns, and cooperate. The messages that boys and girls get from their peers are very different, and Maccoby (1990) believes that many gender differences in behavior can be traced to these early social groupings.

Gender Stereotypes

Gender stereotypes are harmful to the people being stereotyped as well as the people doing the stereotyping. Individuals may feel pressured to live up to stereotypes that do not suit their personalities or abilities. Adolescents may feel this pressure especially intensely, since they value conformity and peer opinions more than children and adults. Trying to be someone you are not is stressful and unsatisfying, and trying to do things that do not suit you usually leads to failure. Belief in rigid gender roles is also limiting in that it prevents one from exploring supposedly inappropriate behaviors that one might, in fact, enjoy.

gender roles the behaviors that are supposedly characteristic of men and women.

masculinity personality and behavioral characteristics of a male according to culturally defined standards of maleness.

femininity personality and behavior characteristics of a female according to culturally defined standards of femaleness.

identification the process by which an individual ascribes to himself or herself the characteristics of another person.

Trying to be a macho man is sometimes harmful and has been associated with suicide, health and emotional problems, stress, and substance abuse. Do these adolescents fit the macho stereotype?

Fortunately, during the past quarter century, gender stereotypes have broken down somewhat and individuals have gained more freedom to pursue their interests, regardless of whether those interests are typical of their gender. Due to peer pressure, this remains less true during early and mid adolescence than at other points in the lifespan. Even so, teenagers grant each other somewhat more gender-role flexibility today than they did in the past.

Androgyny

A gradual mixing of male and female traits and roles seems to be emerging as the ideal, thereby producing **androgyny,** or male and female in one (Bem, 1974). Androgynous people are not sex-typed with respect to roles (although they are distinctly male or female in gender). They match their behavior to the situation rather than being limited by what is culturally defined as male or female. An androgynous male feels comfortable cuddling and caring for a young boy; an androgynous female feels comfortable pumping gas and changing the oil in her car. Androgyny expands the range of human behavior, allowing individuals to cope effectively in a variety of situations.

Being androgynous has more benefits for females than for males because many masculine traits are valued more highly than feminine traits. For instance, women who take on masculine characteristics such as assertiveness and independence are generally rewarded for these traits; however, men who are emotionally expressive or passive or who embrace untraditional occupations are generally devalued. Men therefore have less reason to become androgynous than women (Skoe, 1995).

Although the concept of androgyny was an improvement over exclusive notions of femininity and masculinity, it has turned out to be less of a panacea than many of its early proponents envisioned (Doyle and Paludi, 1995). Some theorists believe androgyny should be replaced with gender-role transcendence—the belief that when an individual's competence is at issue, it should not be conceptualized on the basis of masculinity, femininity, or androgyny but rather on a person basis. Thus, rather than merging gender roles or stereotyping people as masculine or feminine, we should begin to think about people as people.

Gender in Adolescence

What happens to an individual's sense of gender when he or she hits adolescence? Usually he or she becomes *more* gendered; that is, he or she begins to act in a more gender-stereotypical way and to hold more stereotypical beliefs. This is termed the **gender intensification hypothesis** (Basow and Rubin, 1999). This effect is stronger in girls than in boys, probably because girls' sex-role behavior is less stereotypical in middle childhood than boys' and so they have more ground to make up (Huston and Alvarez, 1990). Also, once they hit puberty, girls tend to be very concerned that boys will find them attractive, and "femininity" is seen as part of attractiveness.

How do these findings relate back to identity? If girls are shaped by biology, societal messages, and reinforcement to have stereotypically feminine traits—or to believe that they *should* have stereotypically feminine traits—then they will limit their identity choices to conform to those qualities. They will therefore shy away from choosing careers that require assertiveness and competition and feel that they must necessarily become wives and mothers. If boys believe they will only be valued if they are stereotypically masculine, they will throw themselves into their work and undervalue the relationships in their lives. Clearly, the choices we make are done so against a backdrop of gender.

There appear to be few gender differences in the *processes* individuals use to form an identity. In fact, a review of the literature concluded that gender differences in identity formation were small and mainly confined to two issues: family-career priorities and sexual values (Kroger, 1997). This may be due to the fact that more and more individuals are androgynous or gender transcendent. Indeed, gender-role orientation may be more influential than gender per se in influencing identity formation (Bartle-Haring and Strimple, 1996).

ANSWERS WOULDN'T YOU LIKE TO KNOW ...

Why is it good to have a blend of masculine and feminine traits?

People who possess both traditionally masculine and traditionally feminine traits have the flexibility to act appropriately in more circumstances than those who do not. It is thus a good thing to be androgynous, especially if you are female.

androgyny a blending of male and female characteristics and roles.

gender intensification hypothesis the proposal that adolescents feel more pressure than children to behave in gender-stereotypical ways.

SUMMARY

1. Self-concept is one's perception of oneself; it is who a person thinks he or she is. Having a good self-concept allows you to like yourself, to feel comfortable around others, and to participate willingly in a variety of activities.
2. Self-esteem refers to how much you like yourself; it is based on your self-concept.
3. Self-esteem influences mental health, interpersonal competence, social adjustment, progress in school, and vocational aspirations.
4. Warm, authoritative, involved parents raise children with the highest level of self-esteem.
5. In general, adolescents from lower-SES families have lower self-esteem than those from higher-SES families.
6. Adolescent girls' self-esteem is lower than that of boys. Girls' self-esteem relies more on their perceived physical attractiveness and social relationships than boys'.
7. Self-concept decreases in early adolescence and then later rises. This decrease is associated most strongly with the move to middle or junior high school.
8. The central developmental task of adolescence is the formation of a coherent identity.
9. Erikson outlined seven major conflicts that are central to the self-identity search.
10. Marcia described four basic identity statuses: identity diffused, foreclosed, moratorium, and identity achieved.
11. Adolescents who are identity diffused have not experienced a crisis, explored alternatives, or made a commitment in a given area.
12. Foreclosure status is typical of adolescents who have made a commitment without exploring alternatives. They are not able to distinguish between their own values and goals and those of their parents.
13. Adolescents in a moratorium status are exploring alternatives with the expectation of making a decision. Using adolescence as a period of moratorium can be a very positive experience.
14. Adolescents who are identity achieved have experienced a crisis and moratorium, have evaluated various alternatives, and have come to conclusions and decisions on their own.
15. The newest research on identity focuses on the process of identity development. Burke has suggested that an individual compares his or her self-concept with his or her identity standards based on feedback from others. Berzonsky has compared individuals with informational, normative, and avoidant styles of information gathering.
16. Part of one's identity is one's ethnic identity. Acculturation options for ethnic minorities include separation, assimilation, integration, and marginality. Integration can take the form of blended biculturalism or alternating biculturalism. Integration is related to higher self-esteem more than are the other options.
17. Ethnic identity develops by progressing through several stages. Individuals begin by being ethnically unaware; next, they are ambivalent. Their ethnicity then emerges, and they finally incorporate their ethnicity into their self-concept. Changes in thinking about ethnicity may parallel changes in social cognition.

18. Sex is a biological endowment: male or female. Gender is the sum of biology and cultural beliefs; it is a way of categorizing people and is more psychological and behavioral in nature.
19. The biological basis of gender includes both heredity and hormonal influences. Both affect physical characteristics. Hormones can accentuate or minimize certain masculine/feminine traits already in evidence.
20. Gender schema theory emphasizes the role of self-labeling on attention, interest, and competence.
21. Cultural influences are a major determinant of gender identity and roles. Concepts of masculinity and femininity vary from culture to culture and have undergone changes in the United States.
22. Social learning theory says that children learn sex-typed behavior through a combination of rewards, punishment, instruction, and modeling. Boys and girls learn sex-typed behavior as defined by their culture and as taught and exemplified by significant others.
23. Parental identification says that children learn appropriate gender roles by identifying with parents and internalizing parental values, attitudes, traits, and personality characteristics.
24. Traditional concepts are changing. Men are becoming more expressive and women more independent and assertive. What is emerging is a gradual mixing of male and female traits and roles to produce androgyny, which has advantages for both sexes.
25. There are few differences in the process used by persons of each gender to form an identity, although women and men often come to different decisions regarding sexual values and the relative importance of family and career.

KEY TERMS

alternating biculturalism 175
androgyny 182
blended biculturalism 175
comparator 174
expected selves 161
feared selves 162
femininity 180
foreclosure 171
fusion 175
gender 178
gender intensification hypothesis 182
gender roles 180
gender schema theory 179
hoped-for selves 161
ideal self 161
identification 180
identity achieved 172
identity control system 174
identity diffused 170
identity standards 174
masculinity 180
moratorium 172
narcissism 165
negative identity 173
possible selves 161
proprium 160
self 160
self-concept 160
self-enhancement thesis 164
self-esteem 160
sex 178

THOUGHT QUESTIONS

Personal Reflection

1. In what ways does your concept of yourself differ from what you want to be like?
2. Have your feelings about yourself changed much as you have become older? Why or why not?
3. How do your parents feel about you? How do their views affect your feelings about yourself?
4. What events in your life have most influenced how you feel about yourself?
5. Everyone has an ethnic heritage. Is yours important to your identity and self-concept? Why or why not?

Group Discussion

6. In which of Marcia's identity statuses are most of your friends? Can you come up with specific issues for which they are in each of the four identity statuses?
7. Of the four possible ways in which ethnic group members can participate in a culturally diverse society (separation, assimilation, integration, and marginality), which one appeals most to you? Why do you feel that that is the best way of participating in a culturally diverse society?
8. How do people learn sex-typed behavior according to (a) cognitive-developmental theory, (b) social learning theory, and (c) parental identification theory?
9. What changes should be made in traditional sex roles?
10. Will equality result in people having identical personalities and gender roles? Explain.
11. Do you think it is harder for women to find identity achievement than it is for men? Why or why not?

Debate Questions

12. All children should be encouraged to be androgynous.
13. There is no such thing as too much self-esteem.
14. Being an identity foreclosure is better than being identity diffused.
15. Society would benefit if Caucasian adolescents were encouraged to develop ethnic identities.

SUGGESTED READING

Beal, C. R. (1994). *Boys and Girls: The Development of Gender Roles.* New York: McGraw-Hill.

Dublin, T. (Ed.). (1996). *Becoming American, Becoming Ethnic: College Students Explore Their Roots.* Philadelphia: Temple University Press.

Harter, S. (1999). *The Construction of the Self: A Developmental Perspective.* New York: Guilford Press.

Kimmel, M. (2000). *The Gendered Society.* Oxford, England: Oxford University Press.

Kimmel, M., and Aronson, A. (2003). *Men and Masculinities: A Social, Cultural, and Historical Encyclopedia.* Santa Barbara, CA: ABC-CLIO.

Kroger, J. (2000). *Identity Development: Adolescence through Adulthood.* Newbury Park, CA: Sage.

Lerner, R. M., and Hess, L. E. (Eds.). (1999). *The Development of Personality, Self, and Ego in Adolescence.* New York: Garland Press.

Simon, B. (2004). *Identity in Modern Society: A Social Psychological Perspective.* Oxford, England: Blackwell.

Winters, L. I., and De Bose, H. L. (2002). *New Faces in a Changing America: Multiracial Identity in the 21st Century.* Thousand Oaks, CA: Sage.

USEFUL WEB SITES

National Association for Self-Esteem
www.self-esteem-nase.org

This Web site provides research summaries, a booklist, an online newsletter, and a discussion forum. It also contains pages directed toward parents who wish to ensure their children develop high self-esteem.

The Psi Café: Erik Erikson Page
www.psy.pdx.edu/PsiCafe/KeyTheorists/Erikson.htm

This Web page provides a good deal of information on Erik Erikson and his theory of identity formation. It provides multiple links to other pages.

CHAPTER 9 SEXUAL VALUES AND BEHAVIOR

WOULDN'T YOU LIKE TO KNOW . . .

- At what age do most American teens lose their virginity?
- What is the sexual ethic of most American teens?
- Do adolescent girls and boys have different attitudes about sex?
- How often are adolescent girls pressured into having sex?
- What types of birth control are most often used by American teens?
- When teens have ready access to contraceptives, are they more likely to have sex?
- How often do sexually active teens develop sexually transmitted diseases (STDs)?
- How likely is it that a sexually active teen will develop AIDS?
- How many American girls get pregnant every year, and what do most of them do?
- What makes someone straight or gay?
- How effective is abstinence-only sex education in reducing sexual behavior, unwanted pregnancies, and STDs?

The onset of puberty is accompanied by an increasing interest in sex. At first, this interest is self-centered, focusing on the adolescent's bodily changes and observable happenings. Most adolescents spend a lot of time looking in the mirror or examining body parts in detail. This early concern is centered on developing an acceptable body image rather than on erotic sensations or expression.

Gradually, young adolescents become interested not only in their own development but also in that of others. More and more questions arise concerning the development, changes, and sexual characteristics of the opposite sex. Adolescents also become fascinated with basic facts about human reproduction. Both boys and girls slowly become aware of their own developing sexual feelings and drives and how these are aroused and expressed. Most adolescents begin some experimentation: touching themselves, playing with their genitals, exploring new developments. Often by accident, they experience orgasm through self-manipulation. Interest in sex as erotic feeling and expression increases. Adolescents begin to compare their ideas with those of others and spend a lot of time talking about sex, telling crude jokes, viewing sexually explicit Web sites, and exchanging sex-oriented literature. Adults are sometimes shocked at the language and jokes. Many parents have been horrified at finding "dirty" books hidden under their children's mattresses. These activities, however, are motivated by a desire to understand human sexuality; they are adolescents' means of understanding, expressing, and gaining control over their sexual feelings.

Gradually, adolescents become more interested in sexual experimentation with others. Part of this interest is motivated by curiosity; part by a desire for sexual stimulation and release; and part by a need for love, affection, intimacy, and acceptance from another person. In some adolescents, the need for emotional fulfillment and reassurance is a stronger motive for sexual participation than is physical fulfillment.

Sexual ethics in the United States have changed greatly since the late 1960s/early 1970s, the time of the so-called sexual revolution. Some of these changes have been positive. For instance, most adolescents today are far more open and honest about sex and have little hesitancy in talking about it. This attitude should contribute to their having more satisfying sex lives. Along with this new morality have come some changes in sexual attitudes and behavior. Research documents the increasing sexual permissiveness of youths, especially of girls, and the fact that society now is pluralistic as far as sexual morality is concerned. People now tolerate and accept not one standard of sexual behavior but many. In general, adolescents now accept an individual ethic—the fact that all people must decide on their own standards for themselves.

These changes have brought some problems, as well. Along with increased sexual activity have come increases in sexually transmitted diseases, abortions, and unwed pregnancies. The reason for these increases is that adolescents are more sexually active and most do not consistently use effective methods of birth control and disease prevention.

Today's adolescents, like those of past generations, are confronted with the task of making sexual decisions. Youths have the same sexual drives and urges today that other generations have had, but the difference is that these urges are being constantly stimulated and the guidelines for their control or expression are less clearly defined. Despite the abundance of sex seen on television and in movies and the number of discussions of sex in magazines, many adolescents are still uninformed or misinformed about their sexuality. Consequently, there is a need for positive programs of sex education to counteract the half-truths and distortions and to help adolescents wade through a jungle of moral confusion.

CHANGING ATTITUDES AND BEHAVIOR

How sexually active are American teens? Do most lose their virginity while in high school? Middle school? Apart from intercourse, what else are they doing? This section explores the actual sexual behavior of American teens.

Premarital Sexual Behavior

According to the Centers for Disease Control (CDC) (2006), only about 4 to 9 percent of teenagers have experienced sexual intercourse by age 13, but about 40 percent of girls and 45 percent of boys have had sex by tenth grade. Sexual activity increases during the mid-teenage years, however, so that by senior year, more than half of adolescents are sexually active (about 60 percent). Only about 15 to 20 percent of American 20-year-olds are virgins (Mosher, Chandra, and Jones, 2005).

Most sexually active adolescents have partners near their own ages. Typically, boys have partners one to two years younger than themselves. Girls are more likely to have partners older than themselves: Two-thirds of girls have partners one to three years their senior and about one-fourth have partners 3 to 5 years their senior (Alan Guttmacher Institute, 1999). In other words, most teens have sex with other teens or with very young adults.

When asked why they had intercourse the first time, 43 percent of high school males attributed it to opportunity; 23 percent answered that they were in love. Among the females, 54 percent said they were in love and only 11 percent said that they had the opportunity and were ready. A very small percentage of both boys and girls said they had sex because of a desire for physical pleasure, and only a small number indicated peer pressure as a consideration. Girls, on average, lose their virginity at age 17; boys at age 16 (Kaiser Family Foundation, 1998).

Other data suggest a distressingly high incidence of unwanted first intercourse, at least on the part of female teenagers. About 7 percent of young women reported having been forced into it, and almost 25 percent said that their first experience was unwanted and done solely to please a partner. The younger the girl at age of first intercourse, the more likely this was to be true: 70 percent of the girls who had had intercourse before 13 described the incident as either forced or unwanted (Alan Guttmacher Institute, 1999). It is not surprising, then, that males generally report that their first experience with intercourse was more satisfying than females do (Sprecher, Barbee, and Schwartz, 1995). Males recall it as being more physically satisfying and less guilt provoking than females. Both males and females remember the experience as being more emotionally intense if their sexual partner was someone for whom they felt affection.

Overall, today's adolescents are having sex earlier than their grandparents but not their parents. Most of the increase in teenage sexual activity that has occurred since the 1960s is because of the increased sexual activity rates of Caucasian females; rates for other groups did not change nearly as much. Intercourse rates, which had risen steadily through the 1980s, actually declined during the 1990s (see Figure 9.1). This change was mostly due to *male* behavior. Most researchers believe that these declines are mostly due to increased awareness of and fear of sexually transmitted diseases (STDs).

ANSWERS WOULDN'T YOU LIKE TO KNOW...

At what age do most American teens lose their virginity?

Most American teens are no longer virgins by their seventeenth birthday.

Since the average age of marriage is now in the mid-20s, few Americans are waiting until they marry to have sex, but most sexually active high school students show no signs of having large numbers of partners. The preferred pattern is *serial monogamy,* in which one dates and has intercourse with only one partner at a time. Most adolescents say that their sexual behavior occurs in the context of a relationship that is important to them. Even so, about 15 percent of high school students are involved in concurrent relationships (Kelley, Borawski, Flocke, and Keen, 2003), and the

CROSS-CULTURAL CONCERNS ADOLESCENT SEXUAL BEHAVIOR IN PREINDUSTRIAL SOCIETIES

American adolescents are about as sexually active as those in most Westernized, industrial countries, but how does their behavior compare to that of adolescents in preindustrial, nontechnological societies? Although there are profound differences in the values among these various societies, it is fair to conclude that American adults are *less* tolerant of adolescent sexual behavior than adults in the majority of nontechnological cultures.

When Schlegel and Barry (1991) reviewed accounts of 186 diverse, non-Western societies, they found that 60 to 65 percent of preliterate societies tolerated heterosexual intercourse for both male and female adolescents, at least with a limited number of other adolescents. Eventual spouses were usually included among individuals' early sex partners. Allowance of complete promiscuity was rare. Some groups, such as the Kikuyu of East Africa, allowed mutual masturbation and petting but forbade intercourse.

Schlegel and Barry also found that cultures that were tolerant of adolescent heterosexual activity were characterized as being the least technologically advanced, as having egalitarian relationships between the sexes, as being matrilineal, as being places where women contributed significantly to the family's wealth, and as allowing individuals to choose their own spouses. Restrictive societies, in contrast, had the opposite traits as well as the custom of exchanging wealth at the time of marriage.

In a minority of the cultures, homosexual behaviors were either tolerated or encouraged. The Kimam of Melanesia, for instance, believe that young boys need semen to mature into mature men; boys in this and other similar societies fellate older males in order to ingest their semen.

In sum, the cultures studied exhibited wide variation in tolerance of adolescent sexual activity. Some were completely restrictive and disallowed any contact between adolescent boys and girls. The most common pattern, however, was to view adolescent sexual behavior as merely another aspect of teenage life. Amusement was a more common reaction than anger.

FIGURE 9.1 RATES OF SEXUAL INTERCOURSE BY RACE AND SEX, 1993–2005

Source: Data from Centers for Disease Control (2006).

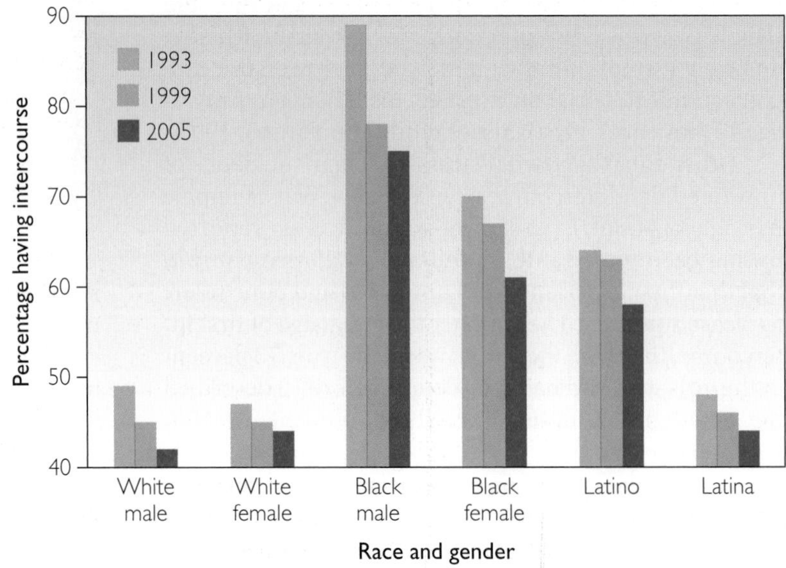

percentage is higher in college. (See Personal Issues box, "Hooking Up on College Campuses.") Teenage boys are still more likely than teenage girls to separate sex from love (Feldman, Turner, and Araujo, 1999).

Correlates

Not all teens are equally likely to be sexually active. Let's look at what factors are associated with adolescent sexual activity.

Age

The older they are, the more likely adolescents are to have had premarital **coitus,** or sexual intercourse (Centers for Disease Control, 2006).

Race/Ethnicity

Other things being equal, African Americans report a higher incidence of premarital coitus than Whites. African Americans begin at an earlier age, are more sexually active, and are less likely to link emotional commitment and sex (Miller, Norton, Curtis, Hill, Schvaneveldt, and Young, 1997). Asian American adolescents are less likely to be sexually active than teens from other racial and ethnic groups and often postpone even kissing and petting until their 20s (Okazaki, 2002). Hispanic American adolescents are less restrictive than Asian Americans but more so than either African Americans or Whites (Feldman, Turner, and Araujo, 1999). When differences in socioeconomic status are taken into account, differences in race and ethnicity become less significant (Bingham, Miller, and Adams, 1990).

Religion

Religiosity and a lower level of sexual permissiveness go together, at least for girls. (The evidence for males is more mixed.) However, it is less clear that religiosity itself is *causally* related to lessened sexual activity; the relationship might be merely correlational (Rostosky, Wilcox, Wright, and Randall, 2004). Still, a large number of adolescents who indicate that they are abstinent claim to be so due for religious reasons (Kaiser Family Foundation, 1998).

Boyfriend or Girlfriend

Adolescents who report having a boyfriend or girlfriend are more likely to have premarital sexual intercourse than those who do not (Scott-Jones and White, 1990).

Early Dating and Steady Dating

Adolescents who begin dating early and who develop steady relationships early are more likely to have more permissive attitudes concerning premarital sex, to be more sexually active, and to have sexual relations with more partners than are those who date and go steady at later ages (Dorius, Heaton, and Steffen, 1993).

Young Age at First Intercourse

Those who are youngest at first intercourse tend to be more permissive subsequently than are those who report older ages at first intercourse.

Liberality

A high level of social liberalism is correlated with a high level of sexual permissiveness (Costa, Jessor, Donovan, and Fortenberry, 1995).

Age at Puberty

The earlier a girl reaches menarche, the younger she will likely be when she first has intercourse (Billy, Brewster, and Grady, 1994). Similarly, boys who reach puberty at an early age are more likely to become sexually active sooner than boys who do not (Halpern, Udry, Campbell, Suchrindran, and Mason, 1994). Given the fact that hormones are partially responsible for both self-concept as an adult and for sexual desire, this correlation is reasonable.

Parental Standards and Relationships

A number of characteristics of the relationships that adolescents have with their parents influence adolescents' sexual behaviors. (See Miller, Benson, and Galbraith, 2001, for a review.) Parents who have warm, close relationships with their adolescent children have offspring who remain abstinent, delay intercourse, and have fewer sex partners. This is partially a direct effect—the teen's attitude matches that of his or her parents—and partially an indirect effect in that the teen has better overall impulse control, doesn't associate with deviant peers, avoids drug use, and is involved in prosocial activities, all of which themselves help reduce teenage sexual activity rates. Similarly, parents who regulate and monitor their children's behavior, such as by setting rules and enforcing curfews, are less likely to have sexually active teens. (Parents who were perceived as being *excessively* strict have children who were *more* sexually active, though.) Also, contrary to some folk wisdom, talking to adolescents about sex does not implicitly give them permission to be sexually active (a point to which we will return later): Parents who clearly speak to their children about their sexual values have children who delay intercourse and have fewer sexual partners. For example, in a study of urban, African American teens, Jaccard, Dittus, and Gordon (1996) found that sexual activity rates were only one-twelfth as high if adolescents had warm parents who clearly communicated their conservative sexual values to them.

Many variables correlate with adolescent premarital sexual behavior. Being able to discuss sexual matters with one's parents has the highest influence in early adolescence, whereas the influence of friends has a greater effect in later adolescence.

Peer Standards

Adolescents tend to form sexual standards close to those of their peers, and they are more likely to engage in sex when peers discuss their experiences (Billy and Udry, 1985). Also, adolescents who are members of deviant peer groups are more likely to engage in early sexual activity (Underwood, Kupersmidt, and Coie, 1996). Miller et al. (1997) simultaneously compared many predictors of adolescent sexual activity and found that believing that one's friends were sexually active was among the strongest predictors of adolescent sexual activity. Effect of friends on sexual behavior peaks in the early college years (Treboux and Busch-Rossnagel, 1995).

Siblings

Adolescents, particularly girls, are influenced by the attitudes and behavior of their same-sex and older siblings (East, Felice, and Morgan, 1993). Younger siblings are systematically more sexually active at a given age than older siblings (Rodgers, Rowe, and Harris, 1992).

Gender

Girls tend to be less permissive than boys, although this double standard is being eliminated slowly. For example, the average age of first intercourse for girls has been declining. Girls do, however, place more emphasis on the quality of a relationship before intercourse takes place (Wilson and Medora, 1990). Among those who have experienced sexual intercourse, males and females are equally likely to be sexually active, as measured by having recent and frequent sexual intercourse (DeGaston, Weed, and Jensen, 1996).

coitus sexual intercourse.

Problem Behaviors

Problem behaviors—such as delinquency, drug use, and promiscuity—are typically clustered, so that a teenager who engages in one problem behavior is more likely to engage in others, as well. Given this pattern, it is not surprising that those youths who take drugs are more likely to have premarital sexual intercourse than those who do not take drugs (Weinbender and Rossignol, 1996). One of the strongest predictors of high-risk sexual activity is alcohol use (Harvey and Spigner, 1995). Interestingly, this association between deviancy and sexual behavior does not appear to hold for low-income African American adolescents (Black, Ricardo, and Stanton, 1997), probably because adolescent sexual intercourse is more normative and accepted in that subgroup.

Father Absence

Girls, in particular those who grow up in a father-absent home, are more likely to seek sexual relationships as a means of finding affection and social approval than are girls in father-present homes (Miller, Norton, Curtis, Hill, and Schaneveldt, 1997).

Divorced and Reconstituted Families

Adolescents from divorced and reconstituted families report more sexual experience than those from intact families (Upchurch, Aneshensel, Sucoff, and Levy-Storms, 1999; Young, Jensen, Olsen, and Cundick, 1991).

Parents' Education

Adolescents of parents with a high school education or less are more likely to have experienced intercourse and more permissive attitudes than those with more education (Sieving, McNeely, and Blum, 2000).

Educational Expectations

The higher adolescents' educational expectations, the less likely they are to have premarital sexual intercourse (Ohannessian and Crockett, 1993). Adolescents who spend a lot of time studying, especially girls, are less likely to be sexually active (Whitbeck, Yoder, Hoyt, and Conger, 1999). Adolescent factory workers have a higher frequency of premarital intercourse than do adolescent students (Huerta-Franco, deLeon, and Malacara, 1996). The higher the parents' educational aspirations for their children, the less sexually active those children tend to be (Miller and Sneesby, 1988).

Socioeconomic Status

There is a higher instance of early coital behavior among youths of low socioeconomic status who have less-educated parents (Murry, 1996; Upchurch, Aneshensel, Sucoff, and Levy-Storms, 1999).

Other Mutual Sexual Behaviors

In many people's minds, the term *virgin* conjures up someone with little or no sexual experience. This is not the case with many virginal adolescents, however.

RESEARCH HIGHLIGHT JUST HOW COMMON IS ORAL SEX?

During the past several years, a number of well-respected newspapers and magazines have reported that a large percentage of middle school students are engaging in oral sex (e.g., Jarrell, 2000; Stepp, 1999). Is this, in fact, true?

The available data suggest that it is. A Canadian study conducted in 2002 found that approximately 30 percent of the nineth-graders and just over 50 percent of the eleventh-graders said that they had participated in oral sex; the numbers were similar for male and female students (McKay, 2004). U.S. data suggest that between 36 and 49 percent of American teens between the ages of 15 and 19 have engaged in oral sex (Bersamin, Walker, Fisher, and Grube, 2006; Gates and Sonenstein, 2000). This makes oral sex a more common activity than vaginal intercourse, and for many teens, this activity precedes sexual intercourse.

There are also some data suggesting that, like President Bill Clinton, adolescents do not consider oral sex "sex." (If you recall, Clinton claimed that he had not had sex with Monica Lewinsky, even though they had engaged in oral sex.) A survey conducted by a popular teen magazine found that only 60 percent of male and female 15- to 19-year-olds considered oral sex to be sex (Remez, 2000). To the remaining 40 percent of sampled teens, *virginity* was equivalent to "never having had vaginal sexual intercourse."

Having oral sex does pose fewer risks than having intercourse; namely, pregnancy is unlikely and the chances of contracting some, but not all, STDs are reduced. However, because many teens erroneously believe that oral sex is risk free—which it is not—they may be putting themselves at risk for gonnorhea, Chlamydia, genital herpes, and genital warts. Furthermore, because they do not perceive themselves as vulnerable, youths might be slow to seek treatment for these conditions.

In one study of 2,000 high school students, approximately 30 percent of the virgins reported that they had either masturbated a partner or been masturbated by a partner and approximately 10 percent had engaged in oral sex (Schuster, Bell, and Kanouse, 1996). Although neither of these behaviors carries much risk of pregnancy, many STDs can be transmitted orally. More recently, a flurry of press reports have suggested that oral sex has become a much more common recreational activity for adolescents (see the Highlight box).

Masturbation

Masturbation refers to any type of self-stimulation that produces erotic arousal, regardless of whether that arousal proceeds to orgasm. It is commonly practiced among both males and females, married and unmarried. The reported incidences of masturbation vary somewhat among studies.

In a study of female and male college students, twice as many males as females said they had masturbated, and of the males who masturbated, they did so more frequently than the females (Leitenberg, Detzer, and Srebnik, 1993). This and other studies indicate that a greater percentage of males than females masturbate. Among those who masturbate, males do so more often than females and more frequently fantasize erotic experiences (Smith, Rosenthal, and Reichler, 1996). According to one survey, teenage boys masturbate about five times a week (LoPresto, Sherman, and Sherman, 1985). By the end of adolescence, virtually all males and about three-fourths of females have masturbated to orgasm.

Practically all competent health, medical, and psychiatric authorities now say that masturbation is a normal part of growing up. It does not have any harmful physical and mental effects nor does it interfere with normal sexual adjustment. In fact, women who have never masturbated to orgasm before marriage have more difficulty reaching orgasm during coitus in the first year of marriage than do those who have masturbated to orgasm. Masturbation serves as a useful function in helping the individual learn about his or her body, learn how to respond sexually, develop sexual identity, and achieve sexual release. The only ill effect from masturbation comes not from the act itself but from guilt, fear, or anxiety when the adolescent believes the practice will do harm or create problems. These negative emotions can do a great deal of psychological damage. Youths who continue to believe that masturbation is unhealthy or harmful, yet continue to practice it, will eventually feel anxiety.

SEX AND ITS MEANING

With an increasing number of adolescents having sexual intercourse at younger ages, the question arises regarding the meaning attached to these relationships.

ANSWERS WOULDN'T YOU LIKE TO KNOW . . .

What is the sexual ethic of most American teens?

Most American teens believe that "sex with affection" is permissible. Certainly, some teens engage in intercourse with individuals they do not care about, but this is not considered ideal.

Has the increase in premarital sexual intercourse been accompanied by enhanced emotional intimacy, development of loving feelings, and increasing commitment?

For years, research had shown that the preferred standard for youths is permissiveness with affection (Christopher and Cate, 1988). However, there are a significant number of adolescents today who engage in coitus without affection or commitment (Manning, Longmore, and Giordano, 2004).

What Are Adolescents Seeking?

When adolescents say they want sex, what are their primary motives? It is easy to say that they want a quick fix to relieve biological drives. But often, adolescent sexuality is driven by emotional needs that have nothing to do with sex (Hajcak and Garwood, 1988). These emotional needs include the desire to receive affection, ease loneliness, gain acceptance, confirm masculinity or femininity, bolster self-esteem, express anger, or escape from boredom. Sex becomes a means of expressing and satisfying nonsexual emotional needs. (See Figure 9.3.)

When adolescents use sex as an effort to cope, other problems are created. When efforts do not result in emotional fulfillment, the result may be increased depression, lower self-esteem, decreased intimacy, hypersensitivity, and diminished sexual satisfaction. The danger is that adolescents develop immature, unsatisfactory relationships and sexual habits that carry into adulthood (Hajcak and Garwood, 1988).

Sexual Pluralism

When questioning the meaning attached to present-day sexual practices, it is important to recognize that there are individual and social differences in sexual attitudes and behavior. We Americans live in a **pluralistic society:** Our society accepts not one but a number of standards of sexual behavior.

There have been many efforts to categorize these standards, but the work of Reis is particularly

pluralistic society a society in which there are many different competing standards of behavior.

noteworthy (Reis, 1971). He outlined four standards of sexual permissiveness in our culture: abstinence, double standard, permissiveness with affection, and permissiveness without affection. A current analysis of the sexual behavior of today's adolescents would seem to require an expansion of Reis's categories to include the following:

- Abstinence
- Double standard
- Sex with affection, commitment, and responsibility
- Sex with affection and commitment but without responsibility
- Sex with affection but without commitment
- Sex without affection
- Sex with ulterior motives

The exact meaning of *abstinence* may vary depending on the point at which sexual activity ceases and abstaining begins. Some adolescents allow kissing only with affection; others kiss without affection. Kissing can be perfunctory, whether light kissing, heavy kissing, or French kissing. Some adolescents feel that necking is allowed (all forms of kissing and embracing) but disallow petting (body caresses below the neck). Others allow caressing of the breasts but not of the genitals. Others engage in genital stimulation, even mutual masturbation to orgasm, but stop short of actual coitus. Some adolescents are technical virgins—meaning they never allow the penis to enter the vagina but engage in oral-genital, interfemoral stimulation (penis between the thighs), or other activity except vaginal intercourse itself.

The *double standard* refers to one standard of behavior for males, another for females. As will be seen in a later discussion, differences in standards between males and females, though present, are slowly being eliminated.

Some adolescents will engage in sex only with affection, commitment, and responsibility. They are in love; they are committed to each other and accept the responsibility and consequences of their actions. Responsibility in this case includes the use of dependable means of contraception to prevent unwanted pregnancies. In case of accidental pregnancy, they are willing to take responsibility for whatever course of action they decide to pursue. But what does *commitment* mean? Interpretations vary. Some adolescents will have intercourse only if engaged, others only if they have an understanding to marry, others only if they are living together, and others if they are committed to exclusive dating and going steady. The distinguishing feature of this standard is that sex includes love and responsibility as well as a defined degree of commitment.

Some adolescents want sex with affection and commitment but without responsibility. They are in love, have committed themselves to one another, usually on a temporary basis only, but assume no real responsibility for their actions. These adolescents are less likely to use birth control and to have thought through what they would do in the case of an unwanted pregnancy.

Sex with affection but without commitment has become the standard of many adolescents. They would not think of making love unless they really loved (liked) and felt affection for each other. They may or may not show responsibility in the practice of birth control but have made no promises or plans for the future. They are affectionate, are having intercourse, and that's it, at least for the time being.

Of course, there are degrees of affection: One can *like* or one can *love*. A recently coined term is *friends with benefits*. Friends with benefits are friends with whom one has sex (oral sex or intercourse); there is no implied commitment and no intent to move the relationship into a romantic partnering (Hughes, Morrison, and Asada, 2005). These relationships are quite common on college campuses: Research puts the incidence at between 50 and 60 percent of undergraduates (Mongeau, Ramirez, and Vorrell, 2003, cited in Hughes, Morrison, and Asada, 2005).

Sex without affection characterizes people having sexual intercourse without emotional involvement, without the need for affection. They engage in sex for sex's sake because they like it, enjoy it, and do so without any strings attached. Some may be having sex for motives they do not recognize or understand. Some who practice this standard have already had sex with a large number of partners. Some of these people see nothing wrong with this and enjoy it. Others are promiscuous but feel conflict and guilt that they have difficulty controlling. Some people who have sex without affection are responsible in the use of contraceptives; others are irresponsible.

Sex with ulterior motives may include a number of different motives:

- *To punish:* "She made me mad, so just for spite, I did it." In this case, sex becomes an expression of hostility, anger, or revenge. Some adolescents have sex and strive for pregnancy to get even with parents or to punish a former lover.
- *To win or return favors:* "I spent fifteen dollars on you tonight; now what do I get?" "I can't thank you enough for the coat." This is really the prostitution of sex: giving sex as payment.
- *To control behavior:* "If I sleep with you, will you marry me?" "Let's have a baby; then our parents will have to give us permission to marry."

- *To build up the ego:* "Wait until the others find out whom I slept with last night." "I bet you five dollars I can score." "I'll show you who's irresistible."
- *To exploit selflessly:* The other person is used for physical satisfaction without regard for that person's well-being or for the consequences. "I don't care if you're not feeling well. You belong to me and I want sex now!"

All of these standards of behavior are being practiced in American culture. Most adolescents feel that what the other person does sexually is his or her own business; no one else has a right to interfere or judge. The only qualification they make is "as long as no one is hurt." Because intercourse involves two people, however, no ethic can be completely individualistic. At the very least, it must take into account one's sex partner. Of course, a person's actions may also affect many others: a child conceived out of wedlock, families and relatives, and others in the community if one needs to turn to them for help or assistance. There is no such thing as behavior that does not affect someone else.

Not everyone who goes to bed with someone else does so out of love. Sex can mean "I love you," "I need you," "I don't care about you," or "I hate you and want to hurt you." Sex can therefore be either loving or hateful, helpful or harmful, satisfying or frustrating. The outcome will depend partially on motives, meanings, and relationships. Sex is more than what a person does; it expresses what that person is and feels. Morality is defined by how one human being deals with another human being—responsibly or irresponsibly.

ANSWERS WOULDN'T YOU LIKE TO KNOW...

Do adolescent girls and boys have different attitudes about sex?

Most adolescent girls have a more conservative attitude about sexuality than adolescent boys. Girls are more likely to want to care deeply about a person with whom they are sexually involved. Girls are also more likely to be concerned about their reputation (and to get a bad reputation) if they have multiple partners.

Gender Differences in Sexual Ethics

Although gender differences in motivation for sexual behavior are diminishing, they are still present: Males generally accept sex without love more readily than females (Feldman, Turner, and Araujo, 1999). When discussing why they are sexually active, women emphasize a desire for emotional closeness whereas men emphasize pleasure and relief from sexual tension (Leigh, 1989). Exacerbating this situation is the fact that male adolescents are more likely than females to describe their relationships as "casual"; what he terms "casual," she views as "steady" or "regular" (Rosenthal, Moore, and Brumer, 1990). Unfortunately, these differences create a formula for feelings of hurt and betrayal.

RESEARCH HIGHLIGHT HOOKING UP ON COLLEGE CAMPUSES

Hooking up is a fact of life for many college students. Hooking up occurs when two people who either have just met or who are casual acquaintances meet at a bar or a party and leave to engage in some form of sexual behavior with no expectation of a prolonged, future relationship. Hookups usually occur when both parties have been drinking alcohol. Paul, McManus, and Hayes (2000) found that nearly 80 percent of the students on the college campus they studied had hooked up at least once, and that nearly half of the men and one-third of the women had engaged in sexual intercourse during a hookup. But are students really glad they are doing so?

The answer is likely "not as much as you'd think." Lambert, Kahn, and Apple (2003) conducted a study in which they asked college students how comfortable they were with their college's norm of hooking up, and both women and men reported being uncomfortable with the commonness of the practice (although men were more comfortable than women). In other words, they believed that they were out of step with their peers, who they took to be more liberal than themselves in their attitudes toward hooking up. This discrepancy was greater for men than for women. In short, many students felt that they were engaging in hooking-up behavior primarily due to the need to conform. Furthermore, men were less comfortable with engaging in hooking-up behaviors than women believed them to be, and women were less comfortable with engaging in hooking-up behaviors than men believed them to be. This is very troubling, because it means that much unwanted sexual activity is occurring.

Many adolescents continue to believe that sexual activity is more acceptable for males than for females (Crawford and Popp, 2003). Girls are more likely than boys to be concerned about their reputation if it becomes commonly known that they are sexually active (Hillier, Harrison, and Warr, 1997). Their fears are justified, since girls who have multiple sex partners are belittled by their peers (Graber, Brooks-Gunn, and Galen, 1998). This double standard is by no means confined to the United States. Girls in other Western countries, such as Great Britain and Russia, report the same concern (Ivchenkova, Efimova, and Akkuzina, 2001; Jackson and Cram, 2003).

ANSWERS WOULDN'T YOU LIKE TO KNOW . . .

How often are adolescent girls pressured into having sex?

Large numbers of adolescent girls—and quite a few adolescent boys—are pressured into unwanted sexual activity. Although sexual assault while on dates is all too common, most of the time the coercion is not physical.

Sexual Aggression

It is distressing to read the research about adolescents' experiences with sexual aggression because almost all studies indicate that it is quite common. According to the Centers for Disease Control, about 9 percent of high school students reported having been hit or physically hurt by their boyfriend or girlfriend during the previous year (dating violence). The rates were highest for Black and twelfth-grade students. Almost the same number—7.5 percent—said that they had been physically forced to have sexual intercourse in the same time period. Forcible rape was more commonly experienced

RESEARCH HIGHLIGHT THE NATURE OF RAPE

There are three varieties of rape. **Stranger rape,** the kind of rape most often envisioned, occurs when a person is assaulted by someone he or she does not know. **Acquaintance rape** is rape perpetrated by a person the victim does know: perhaps a co-worker, someone who lives in the same apartment building or on the same block, or a cashier at a grocery store. **Date rape** is a form of sexual assault that occurs on a voluntary, prearranged date or after a woman meets a man on a social occasion and voluntarily goes somewhere with him (Koss, Gidyca, and Wisniewski, 1987). Date rape has become an increasing problem in high schools and on college campuses (Klingman and Vicary, 1992). One student wrote:

> Charlie and I went parking after the movie. He asked me to get in the back seat with him, which I did, because I trusted him and felt safe with him. We necked and petted a while and then he became violent. He ripped off my panties, pinned me down on the seat, and forced himself on me. I couldn't do anything about it. He had the nerve to ask me afterward if I enjoyed it. (from a student paper)

Men who rape women are likely to have a history of repeated episodes of sexual aggression, where they use physical force to gain sexual ends. They are generally more aggressive than other men, and some are hostile to all women. Some exhibit symptoms of sexual sadism in which they experience arousal from a woman's emotional distress (Heilbrun and Loftus, 1986). Greendlinger and Byrne (1987) found that the likelihood of college men committing rape was correlated with their coercive fantasies, aggressive tendencies, and acceptance of the rape myth (i.e., that women like to be forced).

This is in keeping with other studies that show that belief in the rape myth is associated with assigning more blame to the victims (Blumberg and Lester, 1991). Denial of the validity of women's feelings about sexuality results in pro-rape attitudes by men (Feltey, Ainslie, and Geib, 1991; Kershner, 1996).

In one study, high school students viewed a photograph of a rape victim in provocative clothing and a photograph of a rape victim dressed conservatively. The students were more likely to indicate that the provocatively dressed victim was responsible for her assailant's behavior, that the assailant's behavior was justified, and that the act of unwanted sexual intercourse was not rape (Cassidy and Hurrell, 1995).

Rape is a traumatic experience for the victims as well as their families. A rape victim often becomes acutely disorganized and experiences much distress, which she shows through words and tears. As she tries to put her life back to normal, she may experience depression, fear, and anxiety for months or even years. About one-fifth of rape victims have made a suicide attempt—a rate eight times higher than that of women who have not been raped. A female's recovery is enhanced if she gains crucial support from parents, partners, and others. Professional counseling helps and is sometimes obtained through rape crisis centers (Koss, 1993).

Source: Based on F. P. Rice, *Human Sexuality* (Dubuque, IA: Wm C. Brown, 1989).

by females than males (11 percent vs. 4 percent), more common for Blacks than Whites, and higher among the older students (Centers for Disease Control, 2006). Rates are much higher when *coercive,* as well as forcible, rape is counted because in many cases physical violence is not used. Instead, for example, threats of violence or severe inebriation prevent a person from legally consenting to sexual activity. In one study, for example, 30 percent of sexually active, female middle and high school students in New England reported having been either forced or coerced into engaging in sexual intercourse (Shrier, Pierce, Emans, and DuRant, 1998).

Rates are much higher yet when *unwanted* sexual activity is considered. This occurs when a person consents to sex even though he or she would rather not. Sometimes the individual feels obligated to his or her partner or is afraid his or her partner might end the relationship. Sometimes teens are afraid of being labeled as "gay" if they don't take advantage of a heterosexual opportunity when it presents itself (Rhynard, Krebs, and Glover, 1997). Sometimes they are disinhibited due to drugs or alcohol.

Adolescent boys also participate in unwanted sexual activity, although the frequency is lower. In a Canadian study, 22 percent of the males sampled claimed to have participated in unwanted sexual activity of some sort (Rhynard Krebs, and Glover, 1997), and in the New England study just described 10 percent of male students reported having had unwanted intercourse (Shrier, Pierce, Emans, and DuRant, 1998).

Women use a variety of rejection strategies to avoid unwanted sexual activity (Perper and Weis, 1987). These include avoiding enticing behavior, avoiding intimate situations, ignoring sexual signals the man gives, using diversion and distraction, making excuses ("I have a big exam tomorrow"), saying no, and physical rejection. Women also use delaying themes ("I'm not ready yet" "I need an emotional relationship!") and threats ("I won't see you again if you don't stop" "I'll leave!").

Some adolescents are able to say no to unwanted sex easier than others. A study of almost 2,500 tenth-grade White, Hispanic, and African American adolescents found no racial or ethnic differences in the ability to say no. Females said they were more likely than males to believe they could say no to unwanted sex. Having a less permissive attitude toward sex, giving low importance ratings to peer influence, and, for females, having a generalized sense of self-efficacy are all predictors of the ability to say no (Zimmerman, Sprecher, Langer, and Holloway, 1995).

CONTRACEPTIVES AND SEXUALLY TRANSMITTED DISEASES

With almost one-third of 16-year-old girls and over two-thirds of 17-year-old girls having premarital coitus, the rate of use of contraceptives is extremely important. Estimates are that 90 percent of adolescent girls who are sexually active and who do not use contraception will become pregnant within one year (Alan Guttmacher Institute, 1999). Countless more will develop STDs that might have been prevented.

Use of Contraceptives among Adolescents

What percentage of sexually active young people are using some form of protection against pregnancy and sexually transmitted diseases? More and more are doing so than in the past.

In 1988, the National Survey of Family Growth revealed that only 35 percent of 15- to 19-year-old females or their partners used any method of contraception (including withdrawal) at first intercourse (Forrest and Singh, 1990). In that same year, only 32 percent of 15- to 19-year-old females or their partners reported currently using contraceptives (Mosher, 1990). More recent figures indicate that 74 percent of teenage couples use some form of birth control, mostly condoms, when they first have intercourse and that 96 percent of adolescent girls use contraception at least sporadically (Martinez, Mosher, and Dawson, 2004). Still, adolescent girls are significantly less likely to consistently use birth control than older women (Glei, 1999), and sporadically is not good enough. When asked if they used contraceptives when they most recently had sexual intercourse, only 70 percent of females and 81 percent of males reported that they had (Abma and Sonenstein, 2001).

These figures indicate that a large number of youths are not protected against unwanted pregnancy and STDs. As a result, 1 of every 5 sexually active women aged 15 to 19 becomes pregnant each year in the United States (Martinez, Mosher, and Dawson, 2004); 4 out of

stranger rape forced, unwanted sexual intercourse with someone the victim doesn't know.

acquaintance rape forced, unwanted sexual intercourse with someone the victim knows.

date rape forced, unwanted sexual intercourse with a date.

FIGURE 9.2 PERCENT OF SEXUALLY ACTIVE HIGH SCHOOL STUDENTS WHO HAVE USED DIFFERENT TYPES OF BIRTH CONTROL

Source: Martinez, A. J. C., Mosher, W. D., & Dawson, B. S. (2004). Teenagers in the United States: Sexual activity, contraceptive use, and child bearing, 2002. National Center for Health Statistics. *Vital Health Statistic, 23.*

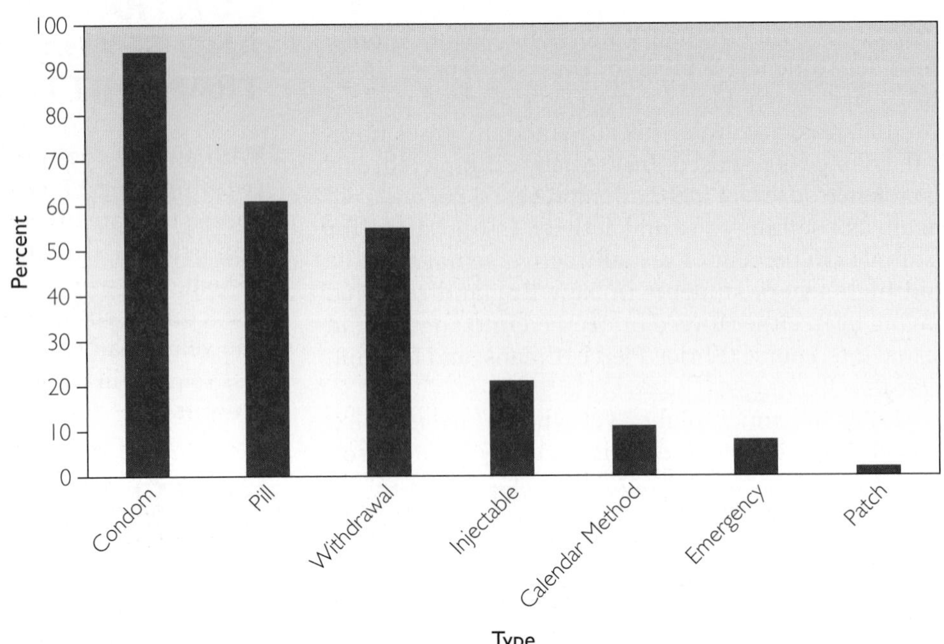

5 of these young women are unmarried (Darroch and Singh, 1999).

The most common contraceptive method used by American adolescents is the condom (94 percent); next most common is the birth control pill (61 percent). Withdrawal, an unreliable method, is the next most popular method (55 percent). All other means—the rhythm method, injectables, IUDs, and the like—are used by only a small number of teens (Martinez, Mosher, and Dawson, 2004). See Figure 9.2.

Sexually active adolescents who value personal achievement and have conventional lifestyles are more likely to use contraceptives regularly than their less conventional peers (Hollander, 1996). Teenage girls who feel they can communicate with their partner about sex and who are accepting of their own sexuality are also relatively likely to use contraception (Tschann and Adler, 1997).

Many health officials believe that condoms should be the contraceptive of choice for adolescents because they not only greatly reduce the risk of pregnancy but also substantially decrease the probability of contracting an STD. In contrast, the pill and other hormonal methods do not reduce the chances of disease transmission. Condoms are being used increasingly by sexually active teenagers, probably due to the fear of contracting the human immunodeficiency virus (HIV), which causes acquired immune deficiency syndrome (AIDS). This use is sporadic, however: Only about one-fourth of female teens use condoms each time they have sex.

ANSWERS WOULDN'T YOU LIKE TO KNOW . . .

What types of birth control are most often used by American teens?

Condoms are the most widely used birth control method used by American teens; birth control pills run a close second. (For many years, the order was reversed.) Although long-lasting hormonal methods, such as patches and injections, are becoming more widely used, their use is still negligible compared to that of condoms and the pill.

An individual's preferred birth control method is a function of race/ethnicity, age, and sexual orientation. Black teens, for example, are relatively more likely to favor condoms than birth control pills; the reverse is true for White teens (Grunbaum, Kann, Kinchen, Williams, Ross, and Lowry, 2002). Older teens are more likely to use oral contraceptives than younger teens (Santelli et al., 1997), and gay teens are less likely to use condoms than their heterosexual peers (Blake, Ledsky, Lehman, Goodenow, Sawyer, and Hack, 2001).

Why aren't condoms used more often? Reasons include negative experiences with condoms (breakage, decreased sensation, etc.) (Furby, Ochs, and Thomas,

PERSONAL ISSUES SEXUAL HARASSMENT IN HIGH SCHOOL

In 1993, the American Association of University Women (AAUW) conducted a survey of 1,600 middle and high school students and found that 87 percent of the girls and 71 percent of the boys had been sexually harassed by peers at school. This harassment took many forms, including exposing oneself, making sexual jokes and gestures, displaying sexually graphic pictures, writing lewd comments on bathroom walls, spreading sexual rumors (including that the target was gay), spying on the victim while he or she was showering, touching in a sexual way, brushing up against someone, or pulling at his or her clothing. The researchers repeated their survey in 2001 (AAUW, 2001); the major change they found is that boys were more likely to report having been harassed in 2001 than in 1993.

The AAUW researchers found that this harassment was not merely unpleasant; it often resulted in real, negative consequences for the victims. When harassment is sufficiently severe, students skip or drop classes, their grades suffer, they become truant, they lose friends, and they suffer from fear, loneliness, and anger.

Teachers, as well as peers, have the opportunity to harass. How commonly does this happen? In one study, 105 college students were asked to complete a survey estimating the seriousness and frequency of harassment by teachers when they were in high school. According to this study, *sexual harassment* was defined as "any unwanted sexual leers, suggestions, comments, or physical contact that a person might find objectionable in the context of a teacher-student relationship." The results of this study indicated that most respondents did not think that sexual harassment by teachers was frequent or serious in their high schools, although half cited examples of such incidents happening to those they knew. Most of the examples involved unwanted comments or sexual looks, with touching and affairs the least frequent type of incidents. Although most of the incidents involved male teachers and female students, there were examples of female teachers behaving in a sexually inappropriate manner with male students. In addition, there were a few cases of male-to-male harassment.

Over one-third of the respondents said they had known of a sexual relationship between a teacher and a high school student. The majority of the students felt that both the student and the teacher were equally interested in the affair. Apparently, most students thought it was possible for high school students and their teachers to engage in mutually consenting sexual relationships despite differences in age and status. This finding, in conjunction with other comments, provides evidence that respondents often disclaim instances of sexual harassment in high school (Corbett, Gentry, and Pearson, 1993).

Sexual harassment can be especially damaging when the perpetrators are teachers and other adults who have considerable authority over adolescents (Lee, Cloninger, Linn, and Chen, 1995). So, what should you do if you are a victim of harassment? There are several useful strategies:

1. Find out about your school's sexual harassment policy. Most student handbooks tell you whom to go to for assistance if you are harassed and the steps you should take in filing a report, if you should choose to do so.
2. Keep a written record or log of the incidents. Make sure your entries are specific as to the time, place, and nature of the harassment. If possible, note any witnesses to the incident. A log of this sort will be extremely useful if you choose to take formal action at some later point.
3. Write the harasser a letter (keeping a copy for yourself) in which you tell him or her that you are uncomfortable with his or her actions. It is entirely possible that the harasser will be appalled at your accusations and stop these behaviors immediately, especially if he or she has committed only minor actions (e.g., lingering looks, putting a hand on your shoulder). Even if he or she has committed more egregious actions, he or she may likely stop because you have signaled that you will not passively accept this behavior. Let others know that you have sent such a letter.
4. Speak to the department chairperson or the harasser's superior. And if the situation doesn't improve or if you feel that the actions were so inappropriate as to deserve punishment, make a formal complaint through the appropriate channels. You have the legal right to attend school without enduring sexual harassment. No one has the right to make you feel victimized.

1997), a generalized disregard for risk, a lack of self-efficacy and an unwillingness to take responsibility for oneself, and the perception that condoms are ineffective (Christ, Raszka, and Dillon, 1998). Condoms are used more frequently in casual sexual relationships than in long-term relationships (Landry and Camelo, 1994).

Interestingly, one study found that if an adolescent suggested using a condom during sex, the odds were better than 50:50 that his or her partner would assume that this meant the teen knew he or she had an STD. Moreover, about half of the teens said they would believe that their partner was specifically suspicious of them and about 20 percent said they would feel insulted (Kaiser Family Foundation, 2000).

ANSWERS WOULDN'T YOU LIKE TO KNOW ...

When teens have ready access to contraceptives, are they more likely to have sex?

No! Access to contraception does *not* increase sexual activity rates among teens. It does, however, reduce pregnancy rates.

Why Contraceptives Are Not Used

Getting sexually active teenagers to consistently use effective contraceptives is a challenge. Even sexually active teenagers who say they do not want pregnancy often do not use contraceptives consistently. Users have to be knowledgeable of the method, be willing to admit that they are sexually active, and be willing and able to obtain contraceptives as needed. Some students are misinformed about what are supposedly safe times to have sex and the likelihood of pregnancy. Many do not believe pregnancy will happen to them. There is a small percentage of unmarried adolescents who really want to get pregnant because they believe they are in love and that pregnancy will ensure marriage. Because some have moral objections to intercourse, they deny the consequences of pregnancy or romanticize about the thrills of maternity, or they hesitate to obtain help for fear of parental disapproval (Milan and Kilmann, 1987).

Should Adolescents Have Contraceptives?

On June 9, 1977, the U.S. Supreme Court affirmed that no state could legally restrict the distribution of contraceptives to minors, that nonprescription devices could be dispensed by those other than registered pharmacists, and that such devices could be openly displayed and advertised (Beiswinger, 1979; *Carey*, 1977). The courts also ruled that clinics do not have to notify parents before prescribing contraceptives for adolescents, regardless of age.

Several types of contraceptives, including condoms, are openly sold in drug and grocery stores. Despite their availability, many sexually active adolescents fail to use contraceptives, increasing the rates of both adolescent pregnancy and STDs.

Family-planning clinics are a good source of information about contraceptives for adolescents engaging in sexual intercourse. However, adolescents often do not go to clinics until after they are sexually active or even pregnant.

ANSWERS WOULDN'T YOU LIKE TO KNOW . . .

How often do sexually active teens develop sexually transmitted diseases (STDs)?

Estimates are that as many as one in four sexually active teens will develop an STD *each year.*

Whether adolescents should have access to contraceptives has been a controversial subject. Some adults are worried that the availability of contraceptives will increase teen promiscuity. Nevertheless, most adults agree that contraceptives should be made available to everyone, including teenagers (Princeton Survey Research Associates, 1997).

The availability of contraceptives, then, has almost no influence on whether youths have sex, but it may be a major determinant as to whether a particular girl gets pregnant (Furstenberg, Mariarz Geitz, Teitler, and Weiss, 1997; Schuster, Bell, Berry, and Kanouse, 1998). One of the major goals of sex education should be to provide information about contraception. Some who oppose sex education argue that they are afraid if teenagers "know too much," they will use their knowledge to "get into trouble." Evidence indicates, however, that contraceptive knowledge has no influence on sexual behavior. What really influences behavior are the values and morals accepted by individuals and the groups to which youths belong. The fact remains that contraceptives are readily available to teenagers, but youths frequently fail to use them.

Sexually Transmitted Diseases

People of all ages (children, youths, and adults) may be exposed to sexually transmitted diseases through sexual contact (Nevid and Gotfried, 1995). But STDs are very much an adolescent problem. Essentially, all sexually active teens are at risk of contracting a sexually transmitted disease due to biological vulnerability and a variety of risk-taking behaviors (Rosenthal, Biro, Cohen, Succop, and Stanberry, 1995). Many STDs, such as Chlamydia and gonorrhea, are more widespread among adolescents than adults (Centers for Disease Control, 2000a). A full 50 percent of the new cases of STDs contracted by persons in this country each year are contracted by individuals 15 to 24 years of age (Weinstock, Berman, and Cates, 2004).

There are more than 25 different infectious organisms that can be transmitted sexually. Chlamydia, gonorrhea, AIDS, syphilis, and hepatitis B are all among the 10 most frequently reported infections in the United States (Donovan, 1997). Unfortunately, few adolescents are aware how very susceptible they are to STD infection.

As shown in Figure 9.3, HPV (human papiloma virus) is the most commonly contracted STD with more than 4.5 million new cases each year. Fortunately, most infections are asymptomatic, do not require treatment, and clear up on their own. Sometimes HPV causes genital warts, which are contagious and

FIGURE 9.3 YEARLY INCIDENCE OF THE FIVE MOST COMMON STDS IN THE AMERICAN 15- TO 24-YEAR-OLD POPULATION

Source: Data from Weinstock, Berman, and Cates, (2004).

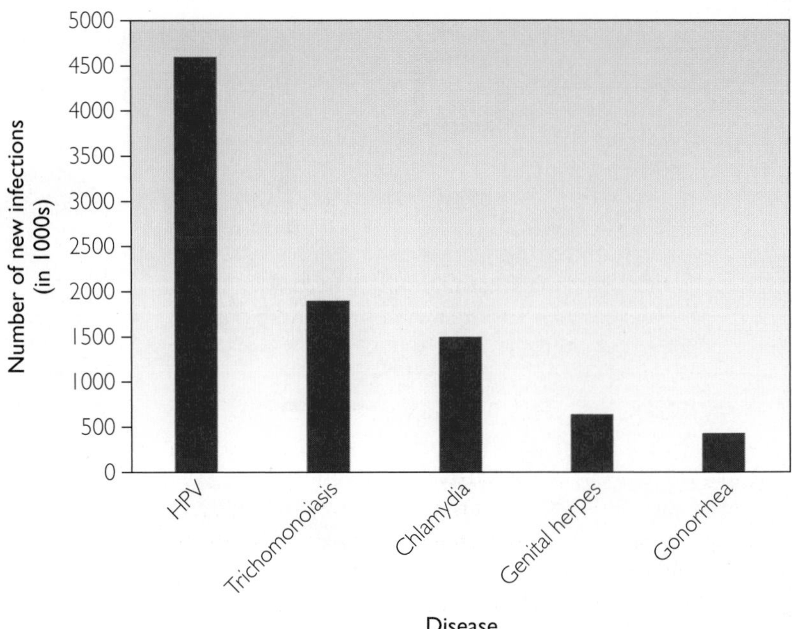

unsightly but painless. More seriously, HPV is associated with cervical cancer in women, and so for that if for no other reason it is best to minimize one's chance of infection.

The second most likely STD for an adolescent to contract is trichomoniasis, which is caused by a single-celled protozoan. The vagina is the most common site of infection in women, and the urethra (urine canal) is the most common site of infection in men. Most men with trichomoniasis do not have noticeable symptoms; women are likely to have a vaginal discharge with a strong odor.

Adolescent girls are more at risk for STDs than boys, since a boy is less likely to develop an STD after having sex with an infected girl than vice versa (Rosenthal, Biro, Succop, Bernstein, and Stanberry, 1997). In addition, females are more likely to develop serious complications due to STDs than males. This is because females are more often asymptomatic and the symptoms they do have are often not obvious; hence, they are less likely to seek treatment until serious harm has been done to their bodies.

African American females are more likely to develop an STD than White females, and White females are at more risk than Latino females (Centers for Disease Control, 2004b). The two best predictors of STD risk are the number of sexual partners one has and regularity of condom use (Rosenthal, Biro, Succop, Bernstein, and Stanberry, 1997).

Many STDs do not always cause symptoms, which means individuals frequently have STDs but don't know it. These individuals may unwillingly infect others. Because of the rapid increase in and high fatality rate of AIDS, much of the public focus during the past decade has been on this disease. Other untreated STDs can also lead to infertility and death and should be taken very seriously. Table 9.1 illustrates some of the main symptoms of and outcomes of untreated STDs.

AIDS

AIDS is the sixth-leading cause of death among Americans 15 to 24 years old. Although the actual AIDS rate amongst adolescents is relatively low, most young adults who have AIDS most likely acquired the virus during their teenage years (MacKay, Fingerhut, and Duran, 2000). Also, the actual adolescent HIV infection rate is most likely significantly higher than can be inferred from the young adult AIDS prevalence, since many HIV-infected young adults will not have developed symptoms (National Institute of Allergy and Infectious Diseases, 2002). African American youths are more likely to become infected with HIV (66 percent of adolescent cases) than either Caucasian or Latino youths (24 percent and 8 percent, respectively).

Causation and Diagnosis of AIDS

AIDS is caused by the human immunodeficiency virus. When HIV gets into the bloodstream, it attacks particular white blood cells, called *T-lymphocytes*. T-lymphocytes stimulate the body's immune system and ability to fight disease. As HIV multiplies, more and more T-lymphocytes are destroyed. The immune system progressively weakens, leaving the body vulnerable to a variety of other so-called opportunistic

PERSONAL ISSUES HOW MUCH DO YOU KNOW ABOUT AIDS?

Take the following quiz and find out how much you know about AIDS. Answer *yes* or *no* to each statement.

1. You can get AIDS from sharing needles.
2. You can infect another person with HIV during sex.
3. You can get AIDS from sex without a condom.
4. You can get AIDS from holding hands.
5. You can reduce your chance of HIV infection by using condoms.
6. Only gay men can get AIDS.
7. You can get AIDS from casual contact with students in class.
8. There is a cure for AIDS/HIV infection.
9. A pregnant women can infect her unborn baby.
10. You can reduce your chance of infection by abstinence.
11. You can reduce your chance of infection by not having sex with intravenous drug users.
12. You can reduce your chance of infection by taking birth control pills.
13. You can tell if a person is infected by their appearance.
14. You can get AIDS from public toilets.
15. You can get AIDS from donating blood.
16. You can get AIDS from insect bites.
17. You can transmit HIV to another person without knowing you are a carrier.
18. You can get AIDS from oral sex.
19. You can get AIDS from receiving a blood transfusion.
20. You can get AIDS from hugging an infected person.

Answers: 1. Yes, 2. Yes, 3. Yes, 4. No, 5. Yes, 6. No, 7. No, 8. No, 9. Yes, 10. Yes, 11. Yes, 12. No, 13. No, 14. No, 15. No, 16. No, 17. Yes, 18. Yes, 19. Yes, 20. No

diseases. Not everyone who is exposed to the virus gets AIDS, however. About three months after exposure, the presence of HIV in the body can be detected by a blood test that determines whether HIV antibodies are present in one's blood (the ELISA or EIA test).

A person is considered to have AIDS when symptoms develop. The incubation period for AIDS may be from a few years to up to 10 years. The average latency time from viral infection to time of illness is about 5 to 7 years (Ahlstrom, Richmond, Townsend, and D'Angelo, 1992). An adolescent can be exposed to the human immunodeficiency virus, carry it for years without knowing it, and not come down with AIDS until after adolescence has passed. For this reason, only a small

TABLE 9.1 FACTS ABOUT COMMON STDS

DISEASE	CAUSE	SYMPTOMS	TREATMENT	OUTCOMES
Chlamydia	Bacterium	Thin, clear discharge in males; females are generally asymptomatic	Antibiotics	Urethral damage in males; infertility and pelvic inflammatory disease in females if untreated
Gonorrhea	Bacterium	Thick, puslike discharge in males; often asymptomatic in females	Antibiotics	Pelvic inflammatory disease and infertility in females
Syphilis	Bacterium	Chancre sore followed by a rash	Antibiotics	About half of untreated individuals die of heart disease
Genital warts	Papilloma virus	Warts around and inside the genitals	Topical treatments, lasers	Linked to cervical cancer in women
Genital herpes	Herpes virus	Small, painful blisters on the genitals	No cure; acyclovir moderates symptoms	Narrowing of urethra; meningitis in rare cases; increases susceptibility to HIV virus

percentage of cases are reported during adolescence itself. However, increasing numbers of young adults who engaged in high-risk behavior during their adolescent years are reported to have AIDS (Anderson, Kann, Holtzman, Arday, Truman, and Kolbe, 1990).

Diagnosing AIDS can be difficult. Some people apparently remain well after being infected with the virus; they have no physical symptoms. Even at this stage, however, they can spread the virus to others without knowing that they are infected. It is important to note that abnormalities of the immune system may develop weeks or months before any symptoms develop. As the virus gradually destroys the body's immune system, other infections invade the body. It is these secondary diseases that eventually cause death. The AIDS patient not only experiences rapid swelling and soreness of the lymph glands in the neck, groin, and armpit but also sudden loss of appetite, weight loss, persistent and unexplained diarrhea or bloody stools, night sweats, and/or fever, chronic fatigue, shortness of breath, severe headaches, persistent dry cough, reddish-purplish bumps on the skin, and chronic white coating on the tongue and throat. Physical manifestations may be divided into the following five major categories (Ognibene, 1984):

1. *Infectious:* Various infectious agents cause pneumonia, esophagitis, oral and anal ulcerations, mass lesions of the central nervous system, meningitis, encephalitis, peritonitis, and infections of the eyes, liver, spleen, lungs, and lymph nodes.
2. *Hematologic:* AIDS reduces both white and red blood cells, lowering the body's resistance to infections and causing anemia.
3. *Neurological:* AIDS patients may experience various infections of the central nervous system, which produce progressive dementia, seizures, aphasia, and other signs of neural deterioration.
4. *Nutritional and gastrointestinal:* Patients develop severe diarrhea, resulting in weight loss.
5. *Neoplastic:* Kaposi's sarcoma is a rare cancer that produces a proliferation in the cells lining the heart, blood vessels, and lymph glands. Violet lesions or lumps occur on the skin and mucous membranes.

Treatment and Transmission of HIV/AIDS

To date, there is no cure for AIDS. However, increasingly better drug therapies are being developed that slow the onset of immunodeficiency and its related symptoms. The most successful treatment is called HAART, which stands for *highly active anti-retroviral therapy.* It is composed of two different types of drugs: nucleoside reverse transcriptase (RT) inhibitors and protease inhibitors. These drugs greatly reduce the virus's ability to replicate itself. HAART is not a cure or an ideal solution; it is extremely costly and can cause devastating side effects (Deeks, Smith, Holodniy, and Kahn, 1997; Katzenstein, 1997).

ANSWERS WOULDN'T YOU LIKE TO KNOW . . .

How likely is it that a sexually active teen will develop AIDS?

Adolescents rarely develop AIDS because the disease often takes many years to develop after someone has been infected with HIV. However, a large percentage of the people who develop AIDS while in their twenties (which is a large percentage of AIDS cases) became infected with HIV while in their teens.

HIV may be found in the semen, blood, vaginal secretions, urine, saliva, tears, and breast milk of an infected individual. The disease may be transmitted from an infected mother to her unborn child, to her child at the time of birth, and after birth through breastfeeding. HIV can also be acquired by contact with infected blood or blood products, usually through needle sharing by intravenous (IV) drug users. Finally, the virus can be passed between individuals engaging in either hetero- or homosexual activity in which body fluids are exchanged, especially blood and semen. The skin itself is a barrier against the virus. However, small, unseen tears in the lining of the vagina or rectum may occur, thus providing an opening for the virus to enter directly into the bloodstream.

It is important to know that infected students can remain in school as long as they feel well enough to attend and are not infectious with other diseases such as chicken pox. If an open cut or sore on one child is exposed to the blood or body fluids of a child infected with AIDS, there is a possible occurrence of infection. People who have AIDS can remain in virtually any occupation without special restriction as long as they do not have associated symptoms such as open sores. They can share telephones, computers, office equipment, desks, tools, papers, vehicles, toilets, showers, uniforms, eating facilities, coffee pots, and water fountains. Remember: *AIDS cannot be contracted by casual contact.*

Other than total abstinence, condoms have been widely promoted as the best method of preventing the spread of AIDS. Only latex condoms, not natural skin condoms, provide protection against HIV. Before use, a condom should be inspected for holes and imperfections; if any irregularities are detected, the condom should not be used. In addition, care must be taken when putting on a condom to be sure that it is not snagged on a fingernail or torn. The user should also hold on to the top of the condom when withdrawing the penis from the vagina or anus to prevent leakage and slippage. When used with a spermicidal foam, jelly, or cream, the contraceptive efficiency of condoms is increased. Spermicides are also damaging to any HIV that may be present. When correctly used, condoms greatly reduce the chance of spreading HIV and other STDs. However, they do not reduce this risk to zero.

With no medical procedure available to cure or prevent the spread of AIDS, it is imperative that people learn to recognize and change behaviors that place them at risk of contracting the disease. Individuals who recognize that their behavior places them at risk will be more likely to change than individuals who do not. Thus, if programs are to be effective in promoting change in individuals who engage in risky sexual behavior, sexual practices that decrease the likelihood of contracting AIDS need to be specified clearly, and participants must be encouraged to apply this information to themselves (Brown, Baranowski, Kulig, Stephenson, and Perry, 1996; Jurich, Adams, and Schulenberg, 1992).

UNWED PREGNANCY AND ABORTION

A high rate of premarital sexual intercourse accompanied by a lack of efficient use of contraceptives has caused an explosion of out-of-wedlock pregnancies.

ANSWERS WOULDN'T YOU LIKE TO KNOW . . .

How many American girls get pregnant every year, and what do most of them do?

About 1 in 5 sexually active girls ages 15 to 19 gets pregnant each year. In 1999, 860,000 American girls became pregnant. The vast majority of adolescent pregnancies are unplanned and unwanted. Even so, in most cases, the girl will have the baby and then raise it herself.

Incidence of Teen Pregnancy

With the exception of the Russian Federation, the United States has the highest rate of teen pregnancy among industrialized societies (Singh and Darrock, 2000). Adolescent pregnancy is widely recognized in U.S. society as one of the most complex and serious health problems.

The good news is that the teenage pregnancy rate fell throughout the 1990s and early 2000s. By the end of the decade, the rate was lower than it had been at any time since records were first collected in 1972 (see Figure 9.4). Throughout the 1970s and 1980s, more than 1 million American teenagers became pregnant each year; in 1999, only 856,000 did (Henshaw, 2003). And while 856,000 pregnancies is still a lot, it represents a 15 percent decrease from previous years. Of this number, 122,000 were miscarriages or stillbirths, 250,000 were induced abortions, and the remaining 485,000 were babies born alive (see Figure 9.5). Although the U.S. teenage pregnancy rate declined

The United States has the second highest rate of teen pregnancy in the industrialized world. Most girls decide to keep their children and either drop out of school or juggle motherhood and school responsibilities.

FIGURE 9.4 NUMBER OF PREGNANCIES AMONG AMERICAN TEENAGERS: 1974 TO 1999

Source: Data from Henshaw (2003).

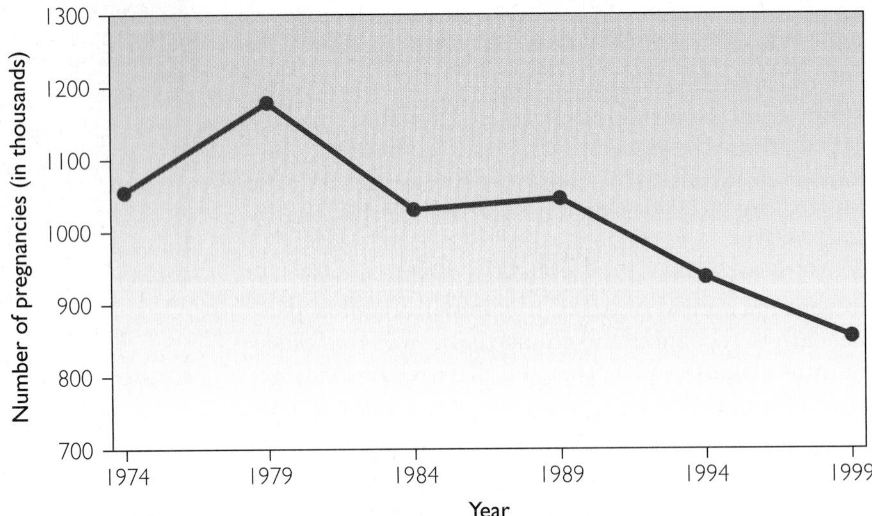

during the 1990s and into the early 2000s, about 1 in 5 of all sexually active 15- to 19-year-old girls gets pregnant each year.

The decline in adolescent pregnancies that occurred in the 1990s differed among girls by race/ethnicity. Pregnancy rates declined most markedly for Caucasian and African American teenagers (by 26 percent and 23 percent, respectively) and less so for Hispanic teenagers (5 percent). Still, African American girls are about three times as likely to get pregnant as Caucasian girls and about 1.5 times as likely to get pregnant as Latinas (Ventura, Mosher, Curtin, Abma, and Henshaw, 2001).

As Figure 9.6 illustrates, the U.S. adolescent birthrate is much higher than that of many other countries. Almost 80 percent of births among American teens are unplanned (Henshaw, 1999). A decline in the teenage birthrate has resulted from a reduction in second births to teenage mothers to 20% (Blakc et al., 2006). The birthrate is highest for Hispanic American teens (Ryan, Franzetta, and Manlove, 2005).

FIGURE 9.5 OUTCOMES OF PREGNANCIES BY AMERICAN TEENAGERS: 1999

Source: Data from Ventura, Mosher, Curtin, Abma, and Henshaw (2001).

Abortions (29%)
Live births (57%)
Miscarriages (14%)

Causation Theories

Why are American adolescents so much more likely to get pregnant than their counterparts in other Western countries? Darroch and her colleagues (2001) compared the situation in the United States with the situations in four other developed nations and drew the following conclusions:

1. American teens are no more likely to be sexually active than European teens. Thus, differences in pregnancy rates are *not* due to higher rates of intercourse.
2. American adolescents are less likely to use contraceptives than adolescents in other countries. And when they do use contraceptives, they are less likely to rely on the methods that most reliably prevent pregnancy: the birth control pill and long-lasting hormonal methods (injectables and implants). European teens are more likely to "double up" and use both condoms and hormonal methods simultaneously, thus minimizing their risks of both pregnancy and STDs.
3. The poverty rate is higher in the United States than in many developed countries. This is significant because in all of the studied nations, poverty was associated with a higher pregnancy rate.
4. The U.S. government provides fewer health-care services to middle-class citizens than do other

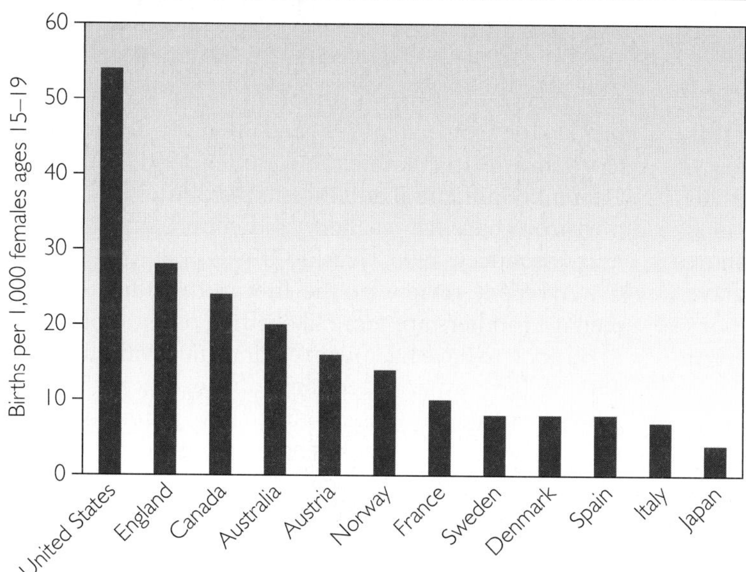

FIGURE 9.6 BIRTHRATES AMONG ADOLESCENTS IN SELECTED COUNTRIES

Source: Data from Singh and Darrock (2000).

Western countries. Thus, because American teens do not uniformly have access to free or low-cost prescription contraceptives, they are less likely to use them and more likely to become pregnant.

5. Primary-care physicians in the United States are less likely to concern themselves with birth control than primary-care physicians in other nations. American adolescent girls must often go to a gynecologist or separate clinic to receive prescription birth control.
6. Youths in other countries are more likely to receive assistance from outside sources as they make the transition from adolescence to adulthood. For example, they are more likely to receive vocational training and get help finding jobs. Such assistance reduces the rate of poverty, which in turn reduces the rate of teenage pregnancy.
7. Parental leave policies in the other nations provide incentives to postpone childbearing. In particular, the wages one receives while on leave are proportional to one's regular salary. Since it is much easier to subsist on 60 percent of a higher salary than on a lower one, many couples decide to put off having children. There is therefore a real economic incentive to delay childbearing.
8. Attitudes toward adolescent sexual behavior are more accepting in many European nations. Because there is less shame associated with being sexually active, adolescents feel more free to admit to themselves that they intend to have sex and hence to prepare for it by obtaining birth control.
9. American society is more tolerant of adolescent childbearing than other nations.
10. In contrast to the abstinence-only approach to sex education adopted by many American school districts, comprehensive sex education is favored in other nations. (Sex education is discussed in more detail later in this chapter.)

It is clear from this review that many things could be done to reduce the rate of teenage pregnancy in the United States.

Pregnancy-Resolution Decisions

There are four possible outcomes to an adolescent pregnancy: (1) The adolescent can choose to have and keep her baby; (2) the adolescent can elect to have an abortion; (3) the adolescent might miscarry; and (4) the adolescent can have the baby and then give it up for adoption. These options are arranged in order from most to least common.

Abortion

Teenagers obtain approximately 20 percent of the abortions performed in the United States (Jones, Darroch, and Henshaw, 2002). As would be expected, the adolescent abortion rate dropped during the 1990s as the adolescent pregnancy rate fell. The abortion rate, however, fell more sharply than the pregnancy rate. Some of this drop was due to the fact that fewer pregnant adolescents opted to abort their fetuses, but a much greater contributor to the decline was the greater availability of emergency contraception—the so-called morning-after pill (Jones, Darroch, and Henshaw, 2002).

Which teens choose abortion? The strongest correlate of abortion is income level; namely, the higher the adolescent's socioeconomic status, the more likely it is that she will choose abortion over childbirth (Murry, 1995). Most minors who have an abortion do so with at least one parent's knowledge. A large majority of parents support their daughter's abortion decision (Henshaw and Kost, 1992). In fact, a majority of the states have passed laws requiring parental involvement in a minor's abortion decision. Table 9.2 details these different restrictions.

Parenthood

About 95 percent of adolescent mothers decide to keep their babies (Hanson, 1992; Namerow, Kalmuss, and Cushman, 1993). Those who decide to place their babies for adoption generally feel quite comfortable with this decision. Certainly, they fare somewhat better than parents who keep their babies based on a set of social-democratic outcomes assessed some months after birth.

One study compared the coping responses and psychosocial adjustments of pregnant adolescents who intended to relinquish their infants with parenting adolescents who wanted to keep their infants (Stern and Alvarez, 1992). Pregnant adolescents who intended to relinquish their infants showed better overall levels of self-image than pregnant adolescents intending to parent. Other research has found that adolescents who choose to raise their babies are more likely to be clinically depressed prior to their pregnancy than those who give their babies up for adoption or have an abortion (Miller-Johnson et al., 1999) and are more likely to have low self-esteem (Plotnick and Butler, 1991). Coping is even more difficult if adolescents encounter lack of support from parents, teachers, and counselors (Caldwell and Antonucci, 1996; Gruskin, 1994).

A recent review of the literature indicated that teenage mothers are more likely than other adolescents to be poor, to have had poor relationships with their parents, to have experienced child abuse, to have parents who are substance abusers, and to have parents who fail to monitor their behavior. These young women tend to be followers with poor social skills. They falsely believe that having a baby will improve their relationship with their baby's father. In addition, they desire the love that a baby will give them, not realizing how difficult and demanding a job parenting can be. These youths are uncomfortable with their own sexuality and hence dislike discussing birth control with their partners (Garrett and Tidwell, 1999).

Adolescent Mothers

What motivates adolescent girls to choose motherhood? One reason is to have someone to love. One young mother said: "I planned on having this baby. She was no accident. I always wanted a baby so that I

TABLE 9.2 STATE LAWS REGULATING PARENTAL INVOLVEMENT IN MINORS' ABORTIONS

CONSENT REQUIREMENTS	NOTIFICATION REQUIREMENTS
States That Require Consent of Both Parents	**States That Require Notification of Both Parents**
Mississippi, North Dakota	Minnesota
States That Require Consent of One Parent	**States That Require Notification of One Parent**
Alabama, Arizona, Arkansas, Idaho, Indiana, Kentucky, Louisiana, Massachusetts, Michigan, Missouri, Ohio, Pennsylvania, Rhode Island, Tennessee, Texas, Virginia, Wisconsin, Wyoming (Laws in Alaska, California, and New Mexico are currently enjoined.*)	Colorado, Florida, Georgia, Kansas, Maryland, Nebraska, Ohio, Oklahoma, South Dakota, West Virginia (Laws in Illinois, Montana, Nevada, New Hampshire, and New Jersey are currently enjoined.*)
States That Allow Relatives Other Than Parents to Give Consent	**States That Allow Notification of Relatives Other Than Parents**
North Carolina, South Carolina	Delaware, Iowa
States That Do Not Require Parental Consent or Notification	
Connecticut, District of Columbia, Hawaii, Maine, New York, Oregon, Vermont, Washington	

*If a state's laws are currently enjoined, it means that the state legislature passed a law requiring parental consent or notification but the law has been rejected by the state's court system and is not in effect.

Source: Data from the Alan Guttmacher Institute (2006).

could have someone to care for. Now I can give her all the love that I never had myself." Another motive is for the young mother to fulfill herself through her child, and yet another is to cement her relationship with the father of her child. Regardless, the reality of motherhood is rarely what these young women expect: Babies are demanding, not giving, and adolescent co-parents rarely live happily every after.

Most Americans consider young teenage motherhood a tragedy (Zachry, 2005). The single mother who decides to keep her baby may become entrapped in a downward spiral consisting of failure to continue her education, repeated pregnancies (Kuziel-Perri and Snarey, 1991), failure to establish a stable family life, and dependence on others for support (Hanson, 1992). If she marries, the chances of her remaining married are only about one in five. And while most adolescent mothers now complete high school, they are unlikely to go on to college. The National Longitudinal Survey of Youth found that early childbearing lowers the educational attainment of young women. Having a child before age 20 significantly reduces schooling—by almost 3.0 years (Klepinger, Lundberg, and Plotnick, 1995). Finally, teen mothers are unlikely to get good jobs to support themselves and their families and are likely to require public assistance for years (Ahn, 1994; Blau and Gulotta, 1993; Klaw and Saunders, 1994).

The costs of adolescent childbearing are enormous, and members of three generations generally share in these costs. First, there are direct costs to the young mother in terms of loss or delayed education, abrupt changes in her developmental trajectory, and lost economic opportunities. Many young fathers are also negatively affected by early pregnancies and by family formation. Second, the parents of these young parents are also affected: They usually feel immediate disappointment and shock, face disruption of their own life plans, often share a large portion of the child-care responsibilities for a child not their own, and have the burden of additional costs (Cross and Aday, 2006). Third, for the children born to adolescent mothers, the cost often includes increased likelihood of life in poverty in a single-parent family, a poor educational prognosis, poor developmental prognosis, and increased probability of becoming adolescent parents themselves (Pogarsky, Thornberry and Lizotte, 2006). Most adolescents simply do not know how to be good parents, which harms their children's development.

More recently, a new perspective is gaining ground: that although it is indisputably true that teenage mothers fare poorly compared to other teenage girls, motherhood is not the causal reason for their poor outcomes. Instead, the theory is that these girls were more distressed than average to begin with—that motherhood is a symptom of their distress, rather than a cause of their problems (e.g., Oxford, Gilchrist, Gillmore, and Lohr, 2006). They are more likely to have used drugs, been abused, been delinquent, and so on. The theory is that these young women would have problems whether or not they were trying to raise children. As an example, one author recently argued that the unwed teenage mothers she studied became more interested in their education, not less interested, after they had children to care for (Zachry, 2005). Still, even given that these adolescents are largely coping with numerous problems before they become mothers, motherhood is for most an additional stress.

Adolescent Fathers

Since most adolescent mothers became pregnant by having sexual intercourse with male teenagers only two to three years older than themselves (Coley and Chase-Lansdale, 1998), there are a substantial number of teenage fathers as well as teenage mothers. Who are these adolescents? What kind of relationships do they have with their children and the mothers of their children?

In many ways, adolescent boys who become fathers are demographically similar to adolescent girls who become mothers. They are more often poor, live in low-income neighborhoods, and have done poorly in school. They are often dropouts and have engaged in seriously delinquent behavior (Fagot, Pears, Capaldi, Crosby, and Leve, 1998; Stouthamer-Loeber and Wei, 1998).

Many teenage fathers say they want to maintain contact with and to support their children and the mothers of their children. But in reality, contact steadily decreases after the child's birth. For example, one study (Larson, Hussey, Gilmore, and Gilchrist, 1996) found that fewer than 40 percent of teenage fathers were living with their child and the child's mother when that child was one year of age; only about one-fourth had been living constantly together as a family unit since the child had been born.

Why such low levels of involvement? Teenage mothers and fathers have somewhat different views on this issue. Adolescent fathers cite maternal resistance as the major barrier to their participation; adolescent mothers, on the other hand, are more likely to cite paternal disinterest. It is possible that *both* viewpoints are correct: The fathers may perceive the mothers' frustration and anger at lack of financial support as a more generalized lack of desire for their presence, and the mothers may interpret the fathers' embarrassment at being unable to contribute more money and their discomfort of handling children as an unwillingness to be involved (Rhein et al., 1997). Both parents also frequently give the father's involvement with drugs as a reason for his lack of involvement.

Adolescent boys who father children find their lives profoundly changed. Some help the mothers with child-care responsibilities, and others drop out of school to help support their children.

Teenage fathers are usually poor, which makes it impossible for many of them to contribute substantial amounts of money to their children. Typically, teenage fathers leave school earlier, have lower earnings, and work fewer weeks per year than other teenage males in their neighborhoods (Nock, 1998). Also, the adolescents who father children frequently have problems that began before the pregnancy. Compared with nonfathers, teenage fathers are twice as likely to be delinquents (Stouthamer-Loeber and Wei, 1998) and more than three times as likely to be drug users (Guagliardo, Huang, and D'Angelo, 1999). Unfortunately, antisocial behavior prior to fatherhood is a strong predictor of poor parenting (Florsheim, Moore, Zollinger, MacDonald, and Sumida, 1999). Teenage fathers are often the sons of absent fathers themselves; they may or may not have a male parental model and, in fact, may have numerous models of pregnancy outside of marriage (Leadbetter, 1994; Leadbetter, Way, and Raben, 1994). Many adolescent fathers compound the problem by dropping out of school (Resnick, Wattenberg, and Brewer, 1992).

In light of these considerations, professionals need to increase their attempts to assist teenage fathers. Society can no longer demand that teenage fathers become responsible parents without providing them with the understanding and guidance needed to assist them in successfully managing the crisis of premature parenthood. There is documented evidence that teenage fathers respond favorably to appropriate outreach initiatives, and that such efforts enable teenage fathers to enhance their own lives and to contribute positively to society and to the well-being of their children (Kiselica and Sturmer, 1993).

HOMOSEXUALITY

Homosexuality refers to a sexual orientation in which one has a sexual interest in those of the same biological sex. Alfred Kinsey was one of the first social scientists to emphasize that there are degrees of **heterosexuality** (sexual orientation to those of the opposite sex) and homosexuality. Figure 9.7 shows Kinsey's seven-level continuum of sexual behavior. Kinsey found that many persons have a mixture of homosexuality and heterosexuality, and so are to some degree *bisexual*. Some of these persons, for example, live a typical heterosexual life with a spouse and children and yet enjoy homosexual sex on the side.

Homosexuality does not describe physical appearance, sex roles, or personality any more than does heterosexuality. Many homosexual men are masculine in appearance and actions; some are outstanding athletes. Many lesbians are feminine in appearance and behavior. A person cannot tell by physical or behavioral characteristics if someone is homosexual. Some may display stereotyped heterosexual sex roles in society and in their families; others may exhibit some of the physical and personality characteristics of the opposite sex and assume opposite-sex roles.

How many individuals are exclusively homosexual? Different researchers give somewhat different figures (in part, because they use different definitions of homosexuality), but most estimates fall into the range of 2 to 5 percent of adult males and 1 to 2 percent of adult females (e.g., Laumann, Gagnon, Michael, and Michaels, 1994). How many adolescents are homo-

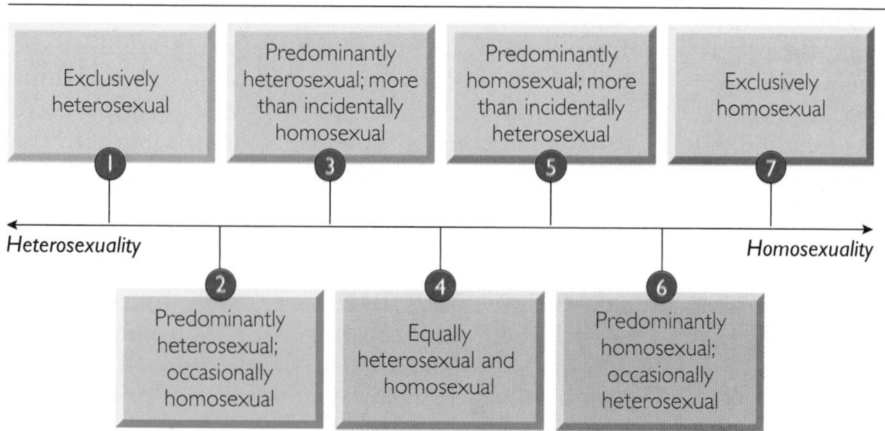

FIGURE 9.7 KINSEY'S CONTINUUM OF HETEROSEXUALITY-HOMOSEXUALITY

Source: Kinsey (1948).

sexual? About the same percentage of adolescent and adult males are gay, as the majority of gay men recognized their homosexual orientation early in life (Bailey and Zucker, 1995). It is less typical for lesbians to be aware of their homosexuality during adolescence, and so fewer adolescent females know that they are gay (Diamond and Savin-Williams, 2000).

Although homosexuality is considered deviant by some in U.S. culture, it is not so regarded by people in some other cultures. The American Psychiatric Association (APA) does not consider homosexuality a mental disorder. "For a mental condition to be considered a psychiatric disorder," a decision of the APA read, "it should regularly cause emotional distress or regularly be associated with generalized impairment of social functioning; homosexuality doesn't meet these criteria" (McCary and McCary, 1982, p. 457).

Causation Theories

Although the question of causation is usually posed as "What causes homosexuality?" it could just as well be asked, "What causes heterosexuality?" The answer is an interplay of biological, personal, and social factors. There is no single determinant of sexual orientation. Also, sexual orientation in females is likely determined by a different constellation of causes than sexual orientation in males (Baumeister, 2000).

Biological Theories

One's biology can influence one's sexual orientation in any of three ways: (1) due to genetic differences; (2) due to exposure to atypical concentrations of prenatal sex hormones; and (3) due to differences in brain structure. These three avenues are not unrelated or mutually exclusive. The presence of a certain pattern of genes, for instance, could influence brain growth or influence response to prenatal hormonal levels; similarly, prenatal hormones could affect brain development. What do the data suggest?

Most researchers agree that sexual orientation is, in part, a genetic phenomenon, at least in some individuals. (For a review, see Rahman, Glenn, and Wilson, 2003). For example, in one study, the sexual orientations of individuals who had homosexual twins were examined. The researchers found that if an individual had an identical twin who was gay, there was approximately a two-thirds probability that the individual was also gay. However, if an individual had a fraternal twin who was gay, the likelihood of him or her also being gay was less than one-third. Identical twins, who developed from the same egg, are genetically more similar than fraternal twins, who are no more closely related than different-aged siblings. The fact that identical twin pairs are more likely to share the same sexual orientation than fraternal twin pairs suggests a genetic component to this phenomenon. However, since not all of the identical twins in the research had a homosexual orientation, environmental factors must be partially involved, as well (Whitman, Diamond, and Martin, 1993).

Another possibility is that prenatal hormone levels affect sexual orientation (Meyer-Bahlburg et al., 1995). Research has demonstrated that elevated and lowered testosterone levels can affect brain development in human fetuses (Reiner, 1997). In particular, an elevated prenatal testosterone level causes the developing hypothalamus (the part of the brain most involved with sex drive) to develop specialized receptor cells that are sensitive to androgens (Fernandez-Guasti, Kruijver, Fodor, and Swaab, 2000).

This leads to a discussion of whether differences in brain anatomy can lead to differences in sexual orientation. The most well-known research in this area was

homosexuality sexual orientation to those of the same sex.

heterosexuality sexual orientation to those of the opposite sex.

conducted by Simon LeVay (1991), who found a bundle of nerve fibers in the hypothalamus that were three times as large in heterosexual males as in homosexual males and females. His research was imperfect, however; he had only a small sample of hypothalamuses to study and many of them had been collected from the brains of individuals who had died of AIDS. LeVay's findings, therefore, are not considered conclusive. Other researchers have continued to pursue similar lines of investigation. For example, studies have shown that several parts of the hypothalamus are indeed larger in homosexual than heterosexual men. Swaab and Hofman (1995) found that the suprachiasmic nucleus, a region involved in sexual behavior, is larger and more elongated in homosexual men; this shape is more characteristic of women. Allen and Goski (1992) found that a portion of the anterior commisure that is larger in women than in men is also larger in gay men than in straight men. Finally, Scamvougeas et al. (1994) found that a part of the corpus callosum, the band of nerve fibers that connects the left and right hemispheres of the cerebrum, is larger in homosexual men than in heterosexual men; it is also larger in women than in men.

Psychoanalytic Theories/Parenting Theories

Traditionally, homosexuality was thought to be caused by problems in parent-child relationships in the family. The troubled relationships were thought to cause problems in identifying with the parent of the same sex. However, a study of 322 gay men and women from different sections of the country revealed that two-thirds perceived their relationships with their fathers as extremely satisfactory or satisfactory; three-fourths perceived their relationships with their mothers as extremely satisfactory or satisfactory (Robinson, Skeen, Flake-Hobson, and Herman, 1982). Only 4 percent never or hardly ever felt loved by their mothers, and 11 percent did not feel loved by their fathers.

In fact, there is little evidence that parents have much effect in any way upon their children's sexual orientation. More than 90 percent of the sons of gay fathers are heterosexual, as are more than 90 percent of women raised by lesbians (Bailey, Bobrow, Wolfe, and Mikach, 1995; Golombok and Tasker, 1996).

CROSS-CULTURAL CONCERNS GAY ADOLESCENTS FROM RACIAL/ETHNIC MINORITY GROUPS

As difficult as it may be for gay Caucasian adolescents to find acceptance, it is often even more difficult for adolescents from racial/ethnic minority groups, whether they be African American, Hispanic American, or Asian American (Savin-Williams, 1996). The reasons for this additional difficulty vary by group.

The African American community is relatively negative toward homosexuality, and this attitude is likely rooted in two sources: the strong influence of conservative Christian doctrine (Gallagher, 1997) and the reluctance to in any way reinforce the negative stereotype of Blacks being hypersexual. Given that many African Americans (like Americans from other culture groups), believe the stereotype that gays are promiscuous, they disparage homosexual behavior out of fear that it will encourage the perception of Blacks as sexually immoral (Collins, 1990).

Cultures that endorse strictly defined gender roles are also generally less tolerant of homosexual behavior because of the common misunderstanding that masculinity and femininity are closely tied to sexual orientation. Hispanic culture proscribes different gender roles for males and females (*machismo* versus *etiqueta*), and so is relatively intolerant of homosexuality (Carrier, 1989).

Within the Asian American community, there is the commonly held belief that individuals should subsume their desires to the well-being of their families. Homosexuality is seen as a violation of that belief, since exclusive homosexuality precludes marriage. Refusing to marry has implications for the family as a whole, since it prevents the conception of heirs and negates the possibility of solidifying families ties within the community (Chan, 1992).

In contrast, many Native American tribes have traditionally accepted homosexual behavior. In fact, research going back to the 1960s found that more than 50 percent of all Native American tribes condoned male homosexuality and that more than 15 percent condoned lesbianism (Pomeroy, 1965). This level of acceptance was explained by the belief that each individual is considered to have been given a unique life quest by the gods; therefore, individual differences have generally been well tolerated. This acceptance has continued today, and Native American gay youths are less likely to experience family strain than youths from other ethnic/racial groups.

> **ANSWERS WOULDN'T YOU LIKE TO KNOW . . .**
>
> What makes someone straight or gay?
>
> Sexual orientation is a complex phenomenon, and many factors work together to determine whether someone is gay or straight. Moreover, the factor that seems to determine sexual orientation in one individual may not be important for another. Most experts agree that a combination of biology, personal experiences, and societal values contribute to the determination of sexual orientation.

Social Learning Theories

Behaviorists would emphasize that homosexuality is simply the result of learning. According to behavioral theories, psychological conditioning through reinforcement or punishment of early sexual thoughts, feelings, and behavior is what influences sexual preference. Thus, a person may lean toward homosexuality if he or she has unpleasant heterosexual experiences and rewarding same-sex experiences. According to this view, a girl who is raped or whose first attempts at heterosexual intercourse are quite painful might turn to homosexuality.

In one study, 686 homosexual men, 293 homosexual women, 337 heterosexual men, and 140 heterosexual women were interviewed intensively for three to five hours (Bell, Weinberg, and Hammersmith, 1981). The researchers tried to gain data that would uncover the causes of homosexuality. They then analyzed the data statistically using a technique called *path analysis* to establish cause and effect. They could not find any common threads running through the backgrounds of their homosexual participants. Some had had negative heterosexual experiences; many had not. Some got along well with their parents; others did not. Some had had a positive homosexual experience that triggered their recognition of their own homosexuality; others knew they were gay long before they had had any same-sex contact. The lack of any consistent environmental factors led these researchers to conclude that homosexuality must have a biological basis, a view most researchers hold today (Rahman, Glenn, and Wilson, 2003).

The fact is, no one knows for certain the causes of homosexuality. There are a number of plausible causative factors, but no single factor emerges as a consistent reason. Perhaps one explanation may be that there are many different types of homosexuals. They are not a homogeneous group, so what contributes to one person's homosexuality may not contribute to another's (Diamond and Savin-Williams, 2003). The tendency in some people seems to be there from childhood. They recognize that they are gay by early adolescence. In most cases, the children of homosexuals do not grow up to be homosexuals, indicating that modeling and imitation alone cannot account for individuals becoming homosexuals or heterosexuals. Most homosexuals do not choose their sexual preference. In fact, many deny it and fight against it for years because they are afraid of public and personal recrimination. In all probability, there is no single cause of homosexuality.

Identity Adjustment

In one study of gay male adolescents, declaring their homosexuality, or coming out, was conceptualized in three stages: (1) sensitization; (2) awareness of guilt, denial, confusion, and shame; and (3) acceptance

> **IN THEIR OWN WORDS**
>
> *I realized that I was attracted to girls at quite a young age: in fact, I was 11. Now, this is not very typical for lesbians. What can I say: I always liked to do things differently. The bad thing is the shock I felt when I realized that not everyone saw homosexuality was normal; I was unprepared. I remember that kids used words like* fag *and* dyke *very loosely and they directed them toward feminine guys and masculine girls. It became clear that gays were considered abnormal and strange people. I was floored by this realization.*
>
> *Research says parents are usually the last people that gay teens come out to; I think they are right. I was feeling very isolated as is typical of many gay teens, and so I turned to the Internet. I found communities of gay teens who were just looking for someone to relate to. I saw a posting of a girl who was bisexual, so I e-mailed her. I was not aware at the time that my mother was reading my e-mails. She called me into her room and asked me to sit down and unfolded a piece of paper that happened to be the e-mail I sent to the girl. My mother went on to tell me that I was too young to make that decision, that I would never really be happy, and that my friends would probably not hang out with me. She suggested therapy.*
>
> *Unsurprisingly, I started high school deep in the closet. Then, when I was 16, my friends and I were just discussing life one night and I cautiously brought up my bisexuality. The conversation grew and by the end of it my friends were assuring me that they were my friends no matter what and that nothing would change that. That started a change in me. I stopped feeling so hopeless and lost. My friends enabled me to feel comfortable with who and what I am.*

Some adolescent homosexuals readily accept their sexual orientation. Others do so after a period of denial. Still others are never able to accept their sexual preference. Becoming involved in the gay/lesbian community may help encourage these individuals in the expression of their identity.

(Newman and Muzzonigro, 1993). Some homosexuals accept their orientation fairly readily. Others go through a period of denial after which they accept their preferences, establish close friendships with their own sex, and are much happier and psychologically better adjusted because of it. The unhappiest are those who are never able to accept their condition, but lead separated, secretive lifestyles, seeking fleeting, anonymous sexual encounters. They are often isolated, lonely, unhappy people—terribly afraid of rejection—even by other homosexuals.

Some adolescents are unable to move beyond labeling themselves as gay or lesbian and to become involved in the gay/lesbian community. Gay and lesbian adolescents negotiate the extent and nature of the costs and rewards associated with expressing a lesbian/gay identity. In other words, when the perceived benefits outweigh the perceived costs, identity expression is fostered. Alternatively, when the perceived costs of identity expression outweigh the perceived benefits, gay and lesbian youths will remain fixated, subject to identity confusion and otherwise psychologically disadvantaged (Waldner-Haugrud and Magruder, 1996).

Unfortunately, many gay and lesbian adolescents find it extremely difficult to come out to their parents. They fear abandonment or even abuse (Cohen and Savin-Williams, 1996), especially from their fathers (Savin-Williams and Dubé, 1998). Unfortunately, these fears do not appear to be unrealistic. Some 60 to 80 percent of gay and lesbian teens eventually disclose to their mothers but only 50 to 65 percent disclose to their fathers. Rarely, though, is a parent the first to be told; more commonly, a same-sex friend is selected (Savin-Williams, 1998).

Gay and lesbian adolescents experience additional stressors, as well. They are at heightened risk for harassment and victimization in school (Williams, Connolly, Peplar, and Craig, 2005), and males are at increased risk for AIDS. When these stressors are coupled with rejection by family and friends and the pain of acknowledging an atypical identity, it is not surprising that homosexual teens are much more likely than straight teens to be depressed and to attempt suicide (Hershberger, Pilkington, and D'Augelli, 1997).

SEX KNOWLEDGE AND SEX EDUCATION

With the large number of adolescent pregnancies and the increased incidence of HIV and other STDs, it has become even more important for adolescents to receive adequate sex education. Where do adolescents receive their information about sex?

Sources of Sex Information

Researchers surveyed 700 male and female respondents ranging in age from 9 to 73 years of age to determine, among other things, the source of their sexuality information. About a fourth of the respondents said their primary source of information was siblings; about 20 percent said their primary source was teachers; about 12 percent said their primary source was parents; about 5 percent said their primary source was relatives; and about a third of the respondents said they received their sexual information from other sources (e.g., friends, mass media, literature, and miscellaneous sources) (Ansuini, Fiddler-Woite, and Woite, 1996). Similarly, another study, in which 13- to 15-year-olds were asked from whom they learned a lot about sex, found that the two most common responses were "media" such as television and magazines (61 percent) and "friends" (60 percent). Teachers were more important sources than parents (45 percent versus 40 percent, respectively). Religious institutions were of minor importance (13 percent) (Shibley-Hyde and DeLamater, 2000). Physicians were not mentioned by many adolescents as a source of information about sexuality.

The Role of Parents

Some people believe that the proper place for sex education is in the adolescent's own home. Unfortunately, many parents do not speak with their children about sexual matters (Raffaelli, Bogenschneider, and Flood, 1998). And when they do, the conversation is all too often limited to the physical changes associated with puberty, such as menstruation, and impersonal topics such as pregnancy and STDs (Baumeister, Flores, and Marin, 1995). The topics that most teenagers want to hear about—masturbation, nocturnal emission, how to use contraceptives, and orgasm—are rarely mentioned (Rosenthal and Feldman, 1999).

Mothers are much more likely than fathers to discuss sex with their children (DeIorio, Kelley, and Hockenberry-Eaton, 1999), and mothers spend more time talking with their daughters about sex than with their sons (Noller and Callin, 1990). Adolescents feel better about discussing sex with their mothers, most likely because mothers are more open, they are more likely to try to make teens comfortable, they encourage questions, and they treat sexual matters as they would any other health issue (Feldman and Rosenthal, 2000). These are the characteristics common to all individuals who have meaningful conversations about sex with teens.

Most research reveals that parents are an important source of transmission of values and attitudes and do have an influence on adolescent attitudes and behavior, especially by way of example. As far as providing formal sex education is concerned, however, many parents are deficient, for a number of reasons:

1. *Some parents are too embarrassed to discuss the subject, or they deal with it in negative ways.* Many parents have been brought up to feel that all sex is wrong and dirty, and they become intensely uncomfortable any time the subject is mentioned. If they do discuss sex, the messages they give their children are negative ones, which interfere with sexual satisfaction. Some adolescents also feel embarrassed talking to their parents, so do not discuss the subject with them.

RESEARCH HIGHLIGHT ADOLESCENT SEXUAL FOLKLORE

Over the years, students in the Adolescent Psychology and Human Sexuality classes at Ohio Wesleyan University were asked to relate the sexual myths that they had heard in the corridors of their middle and high schools. Here is a sampling of the misinformation shared among American youths:

1. You can't get a girl pregnant if you have sex standing up.
2. You can't get pregnant if you douche with cola after having sex.
3. Plastic food wrap makes a workable condom.
4. You can't get a girl pregnant if you have sex in a hot tub.
5. A girl can't get pregnant the first time she has intercourse.
6. A girl can't get pregnant if her period is irregular.
7. Wearing "tighty whities" can make a guy sterile.
8. If a male masturbates frequently, then he won't have enough sperm stored to cause a pregnancy.
9. The withdrawal method works.

Needless to say, even modern adolescents don't have all the facts they need about sex and reproduction. Sadly, erroneous beliefs such as these explain, in part, the high levels of adolescent pregnancies and STDs.

2. *Some parents have difficulty overcoming the incest barrier between themselves and their adolescents.* The taboo on parent-child sexual behavior may be so strong that any verbalization about sex in this relationship becomes almost symbolic incest. It has been found that even in families where there has been some communication about sex with young children, this communication drops as the children approach adolescence.
3. *Some parents are uninformed and do not know how to explain sexuality to their children.* In one study, 90 adolescents and 73 mothers were asked to define in their own words seven terms related to sexual development: *ejaculation, hormones, menstruation, copulation, puberty, semen,* and *wet dreams.* Results suggested that the mothers were not able to adequately define the sexual development terms and thus were poorly prepared to teach their children about sex or to reenforce information the adolescents learned in school (Hockenberry-Eaton, Richman, Dilorio, Rivero, and Maibach, 1996). One mother remarked, "I don't understand menstruation myself, so how can I explain it to my daughter?"
4. *Some parents are afraid that knowledge will lead to sexual experimentation; they do not tell their children because they want to keep them innocent.* The old argument "Keep them ignorant and they won't get into trouble" couldn't be more wrong. Youths who are uninformed are more likely to get into trouble. There is no evidence to show that sexual knowledge per se leads to sexual experimentation. There is a lot of evidence, however, to show that ignorance leads to trouble.
5. *Some parents tell too little too late.* Most parents are shocked to learn that the time to explain the basic physical facts about reproduction is *before* puberty. Most children ought to know about fertilization and how it takes place in humans by ages 7 to 9. For some children, this is too late; they ask questions during the preschool period that demand a simple, honest explanation. The parent who says "Wait until you are older" is running the risk of telling too little too late. The time to explain about menstruation is before the girl starts her menses, not after. As one boy said, "All the way through my childhood, whenever I asked questions about sex, my parents would say: 'Wait until you're older.' Now that I'm 18 and I ask them something, they remark, 'For Pete's sake, you're 18 years old, you ought to know that!'"
6. *Some parents set a negative example at home.* It is not just the words parents use that are important; it is also the lives they lead and the examples they set. One adolescent remarked, "My parents never came out and actually told me the facts of life. . . . But indirectly they told me plenty. They made me feel that sex was dirty and something to be ashamed of or embarrassed about."

Of course, some parents talk more to their teens about sex than others. Politically conservative, religious parents report more discussion with their teens about the negative consequences of sex than their liberal and nonreligious counterparts. In general, nonreligious parents report more discussion about where to obtain birth control than religious parents do. Parents who have daughters, older teens, and teens in romantic relationships are more likely to speak with their children about sex than those whose children are males, are younger teens, and whose teens are not in romantic relationships. (Swain, Ackerman, and Ackerman, 2006).

Parents can do a better job by becoming better informed and more comfortable when talking about sexuality. Reading or attending classes in human sexuality can help parents tremendously. The schools can play an important role by teaching parents so they can do a better job of teaching their children. Parents can also help support family life and sex education programs in the schools to supplement their own efforts.

The Role of Schools

Nationwide surveys have revealed that the vast majority of American adults favor teaching sex education in the schools (Sexuality Information and Education Council of the United States, 1999). Specifically, more than 90 percent favor teaching sex education in high school, and more than 80 percent favor teaching it in middle school. According to these respondents, sex education courses should contain information about puberty, abstinence, HIV and other STDs, relationships, contraception, sexual orientation, and abortion. Similar results have been found in studies of Canadian adults (McKay, Pietrusiak, and Holowaty, 1998). Because so many parents do an inadequate job and adolescents need more reliable sources of information than peers, the public schools have a responsibility, for several reasons:

1. *Family life and sex education are natural parts of numerous courses already offered to adolescents.* Biology courses should cover the reproductive system when other bodily systems are discussed; not to do so is hypocritical. It is difficult to study sociology or social problems without including a study of the family as the basic social unit or of social problems such as illegitimacy, early mar-

riage, or divorce. Health education usually includes such topics as menstrual hygiene, masturbation, acne, sexually transmitted disease, and body odor. Literature courses may stimulate discussion about youths in today's world, moral values, interpersonal relationships, or other topics properly belonging to family life and sex education. Discussions of sex or sex behavior are hard to avoid in a course in the modern novel or in poetry. Even the study of the Bible as literature contains a sexual aspect. Thus, if existing courses are taught honestly, family life and sex education will have a place in many of them.

2. *Preparing youths for happy marriage and responsible parenthood is an important educational goal.* It is certain that having a happy marriage and being a good parent are among the most important personal goals of the average person. If the school does not prepare youths for this goal, as well as for a vocation, is it preparing them for living as well as for making a living?

3. *The school is the only social institution that reaches all youths and therefore has a unique opportunity to reach youths who need family life and sex education the most.* Some parents do an excellent job, but the majority of parents do not. Are their children to be deprived of proper information, attitudes, examples, and guidance? One would hope not. Other community youth-service organizations, such as churches and scouts, have a responsibility also, for family life and sex education of youths is a community responsibility. None of these groups, however, reaches as many youths as schools.

4. *The school, as the professional educational institution, is or can be equipped to do a fine job.* This does not mean that all teachers are qualified to teach or that the individual school already has the expertise and resources to develop a program, but it does mean that the school is able to train teachers, develop curricula, and provide the necessary resources once priorities and needs are established.

Support for Sex Education

Some individuals are opposed to sex education in the schools because they believe that talking about sex tacitly gives adolescents permission to engage in sexual behaviors. Are they correct? The answer is a resounding no! In a review of 47 studies about the effects of teaching sex education, Grunseit and colleagues (Grunseit, Kippax, Aggleton, Baldo, and Slutkin, 1997) found that only 3 reported an increase in student sexual activity after having taken such a course. Seventeen of the studies reported modest *decreases* in early intercourse, number of sex partners, and rates of pregnancy and STDs. Most of the courses seemed to have little effect on teenage sexual activity. Furthermore, Singh (1986) found a negative correlation between the number of students receiving sex education in a state and the adolescent pregnancy rates in that state.

Numerous public opinion polls have shown that sex education in the schools has strong support. Most studies place support for sex education in the public

RESEARCH HIGHLIGHT CONDOM AVAILABILITY IN HIGH SCHOOLS

The American Journal of Public Health released a study examining the impact of condom availability on students' sexual activity in a large sample of Massachusetts high schools (Blake, Ledsky, Goodenow, Sawyer, Lohrmann, and Windsor, 2003). Fifteen percent of the 60 schools studied made condoms available to their students, and 85 percent did not. (The first finding of this study, therefore, was that few public high schools in Massachusetts offered condoms to their students.) Most of the schools that provided condoms did so through the school nurse or other personnel, such as a physical education teacher.

Of great interest was the question, Does having easy access to condoms increase adolescents' sexual activity? The answer to this question was no. Forty-two percent of the students from schools that did provide condoms reported being nonvirgins, compared to 49 percent of the students at the schools that did not provide condoms. Furthermore, fewer students from the schools that provided condoms reported having recently had sexual intercourse than those in the control schools.

The researchers were also interested in learning whether providing condoms increased their usage, and it did seem to have this effect. More than 70 percent of the students in schools that provided condoms had used one when they had last had intercourse, while only 56 percent of students in the other schools reported having used a condom the last time they had had sex. The students who attended the schools that provided condoms were also more likely to use other forms of birth control than the other students.

In sum, providing condoms did not make having sexual intercourse more likely, just more safe.

FIGURE 9.8 PARENTS' PREFERENCES FOR TOPICS IN HIGH SCHOOL SEX EDUCATION

Source: Data from Kaiser Family Foundation (2000).

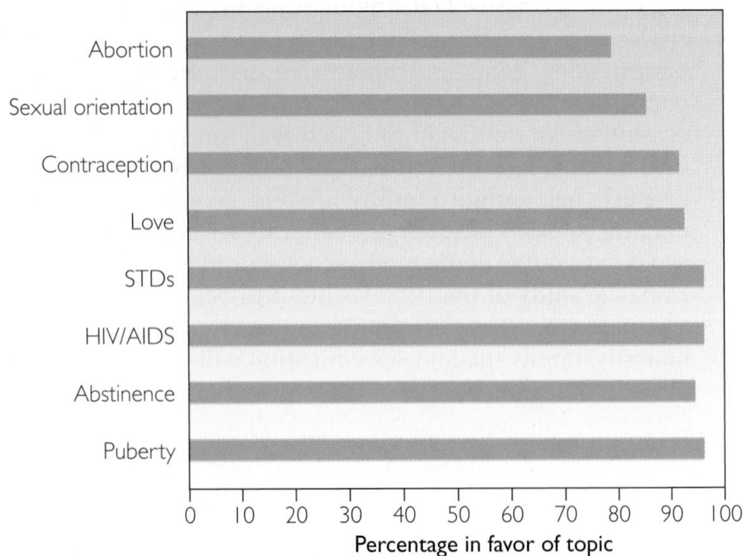

> **ANSWERS WOULDN'T YOU LIKE TO KNOW ...**
>
> **How effective is abstinence-only sex education in reducing sexual behavior, unwanted pregnancies, and STDs?**
>
> Although abstinence-only sex education is becoming more and more common, it is *not* as effective as more comprehensive approaches at reducing sexual behavior, unwanted pregnancies, and STDs.

middle and high schools at more than 90 percent (SEICUS, 2005). The majority of parents favor comprehensive sex education; that is, they would like to see the schools provide information on a wide variety of topics, such as the facts of puberty, the benefits of abstinence, HIV and other STDs, and birth control and abortion (see Figure 9.8).

Approaches to Sex Education

To what extent are the schools providing sex education programs? The number of states that mandate sex education has increased since the late 1970s, largely due to concern over HIV/AIDS. There are, however, wide differences in how sex education is approached and what information is presented.

In 1998, Landry and colleagues surveyed a nationally representative sample of 825 school districts and found that approximately 70 percent had a districtwide sex education policy (Landry, Kaeser, and Richards, 1999). The most common policy (51 percent) was to teach sex education using an *abstinence-preferred model.* Schools in these districts attempted to teach students that practicing celibacy during their teenage years is the most desirable behavior; some information about STDs and birth control was provided, as well. Another 35 percent of the districts had an *abstinence-only policy* and provided little or no information about birth control. In these schools, discussions about sex were generally negative and focused on the harmful consequences that can result. The remaining 14 percent of the districts had *comprehensive* sex education policies, in which abstinence was presented as one option but other broader, more inclusive curricula were also typically included.

In sum, the schools are not doing what the majority of parents want them to do. More than one-third of the school districts with sex education policies favor abstinence-only programs, and this number is growing. The federal government alone earmarked $250 million to fund abstinence-only programs between 1998 and 2002. It is therefore legitimate to ask how successful this type of curriculum is compared to the other models. In actuality, little research supports the abstinence-only approach. Most studies show that it is less effective than abstinence-preferred or comprehensive sex education programs (Rabasca, 1999).

The failure of many sex education programs to reduce the rates of teenage pregnancy and STDs almost certainly lies in the fact that these programs are inadequate. There is an urgent need to develop programs that promote safe, healthy behavior. A review of the literature has identified seven characteristics common to successful sex education programs:

1. They focus on promoting risk-reducing behaviors.
2. Based on established principles of learning theory, they work by establishing incentives for healthy behaviors and then teaching students how to perform these behaviors.

3. They employ active learning techniques, such as role-playing and group discussion.
4. They address the media and peer influences that promote high-risk behaviors.
5. They are tailored to the specific population of students enrolled in the course.
6. They promote healthy values and encourage abstinence.
7. They teach communication skills (Kirby et al., 1994).

A nationwide study of sex education in public schools in grades seven through twelve revealed a gap between what teachers thought should be taught at different grade levels and what was actually being taught (Darroch, Landry, and Singh, 2000). Virtually all teachers thought that sex education should cover sexual decision making, abstinence, birth control methods, prevention of pregnancy, and AIDS and other STDs. Many of the schools covered these topics but not until the ninth or tenth grade. Teachers thought the topics should be covered by grades seven or eight at the latest. The major problem teachers faced in providing sex education was negative pressure from the state government (Landry, Kaeser, and Richards, 1999).

SUMMARY

1. According to the best available data, 40 to 45 percent of American adolescents have engaged in sexual intercourse by tenth grade, and by 17, more than half have done so. By age 20, 80 to 85 percent of Americans are no longer virgins.
2. When asked why they had intercourse the first time, about half of the males attributed it to curiosity and readiness for sex and 25 percent answered affection for their partner. Among the females, it was the reverse: About half cited affection for their partner, and many fewer attributed it to curiosity and readiness for sex.
3. Most sexually active young people show no signs of having large numbers of partners.
4. Premarital sexual behavior is correlated with age, race/ethnicity, religiosity, having a boyfriend or girlfriend, early dating and steady dating, age at first intercourse, liberality, age at menarche, parental relationships, peer standards, sibling influence, gender, drug usage, father absence, and parents' education, education expectations, and socioeconomic status.
5. Adults in preindustrial societies are generally tolerant of adolescent heterosexual activity. This is most true in groups where women have high status.
6. Many adolescents who have never experienced sexual intercourse do engage in other intense forms of sexual activity. Thirty percent report that they have either masturbated a partner or been masturbated by a partner. More than that report that they have either given or received oral sex from a partner.
7. Almost all adolescent boys and many girls masturbate regularly. The practice is not harmful and should be considered normal.
8. Although the preferred standard of sexual activity among youths is permissiveness with affection, many adolescents engage in coitus without affection or commitment. Generally speaking, women are less likely to have sex without affection than are men.
9. Not all adolescents have the same sexual standards. American society is pluralistic; it accepts not one but a number of different standards of sexual behavior.
10. Although the sexual double standard is slowly becoming obsolete, American adolescents still endorse it. That is, sexual activity is still more acceptable for males than females.
11. Both male and female adolescents report participating in unwanted sexual activity. Although little of this activity is due to the threat of physical force or harm, the incidence of sexual aggression is disturbingly high.
12. The majority of high school students, male and female, report being sexually harassed by their peers. Most of the harassers are male.
13. Sexually active adolescents are more likely to use contraceptives now than in the past. Still, most use them only sporadically. Most contraceptive-using adolescents rely on condoms.
14. Getting sexually active teenagers to use effective contraceptives is a huge challenge. There are various reasons why contraceptives are not used: anxiety, ignorance, lack of responsibility, ambivalent feelings about sex, a desire to get pregnant, and rape. The availability of contraceptives does not increase promiscuity, but it does decrease unwanted pregnancy and STD rates.
15. The incidence of STDs among adolescents has reached epidemic proportions. These diseases can have lifelong health consequences if not treated; unfortunately, they may be asymptomatic, especially in females.
16. AIDS is the most serious sexually transmitted disease. Adolescents can and do contract HIV, the virus that causes AIDS, but they will not likely exhibit the symptoms of AIDS until they are adults.
17. About three quarters of a million teenage girls got pregnant in each of the last 5 years; this is down from a high of more than one million adolescent pregnancies/year

in the 1980s. About 30% of pregnant teenage girls get an abortion.

18. American teens are far more likely to get pregnant or to cause a pregnancy than European teens, even though they are no more sexually active. This is due to the fact that European teens are more likely to use birth control consistently.
19. The future outlook for teenagers who have and keep their children is more bleak than that of teens who do not. Teenage parents are more likely to be poor for much of their lives, and their children will not fare well, either. Children born to and raised by adolescent mothers are unlikely to do well in school and are less apt to be healthy than other children.
20. Adolescent fathers are generally either unwilling or unable to contribute much care to their children. These fathers are often poor, and many have histories of drug use or delinquency.
21. There are three major categories of theories of the causes of homosexuality: biological theories, psychoanalytical theories, and social learning theories. In all probability, there is no single cause of homosexuality. Support is strongest for biological theories.
22. Gay and lesbian adolescents face many hardships, including being frequently harassed. These youths' families often fail to offer them emotional support, especially when the families first learn of the youths' sexual orientation.
23. Peers and the media contribute more to adolescents' sexual knowledge than either parents or teachers.
24. Parents are not doing a good job of sex education for various reasons: They are too embarrassed, they have difficulty overcoming the incest barrier, they are uninformed, they are afraid knowledge will lead to sexual experimentation, they tell too little too late, or they set a negative example at home.
25. Some 85 percent of parents support offering sex education in the schools. An increasing number of schools offer sex education, but an abstinence-only approach has become more common. This is unfortunate, since abstinence-preferred and comprehensive programs are more successful at reducing teenage pregnancy.
26. Teaching sex education does not increase sexual activity or pregnancy rates among adolescents. The best programs decrease those the rates.

KEY TERMS

acquaintance rape 196	homosexuality 210
coitus 190	pluralistic society 193
date rape 196	stranger rape 196
heterosexuality 210	

THOUGHT QUESTIONS

Personal Reflection

1. How have your sexual values and behaviors changed as you've matured? Why?
2. How closely do your own sexual behaviors match your sexual ethics? If there is a mismatch, why?
3. Did the availability of birth control or abortion affect your own sexual decisions as a high school or middle school student? How?
4. Have you ever felt pressured to have sex when you didn't want to? Have you ever pressured anyone else?
5. Did your parents tell you about sex when you were growing up? What did they tell you? How did they tell you?
6. Did you have sex education in school? Comment on the program.

Group Discussion

7. Do parents have much influence over the sexual behavior of their adolescents?
8. What are some myths about masturbation that you heard while you were growing up?
9. Has the increase in premarital sexual intercourse been accompanied by lessening of emotional intimacy, loving feelings, and decreasing commitment in relationships? Support your answer.
10. Was sexual harassment by peers a problem in the high school that you attended? Explain.
11. Why don't more sexually active adolescents consistently use effective contraceptives? What can be done to improve this situation?
12. Has the AIDS epidemic made any differences in the sexual behavior of your friends? Why or why not?
13. What can be done to reduce the number of unwed pregnancies?
14. What are the alternatives to abortion for teenage pregnancy? What do you think of them?
15. Do you know any gay men or lesbian women? What are the most serious problems they face?
16. Comment on this statement: "Adolescents' primary source of sex information is their friends." How do you feel about this?

Debate Questions

17. High school health clinics should distribute contraceptive information and condoms.
18. Middle and high schools should be required to attend a comprehensive sex education class.
19. Oral sex is sex and should be strongly discouraged for high school students.
20. Parental consent should be required before adolescents can obtain abortions.
21. Pediatricians should routinely question their adolescent patients about their sex lives and screen them for STDs if they are sexually active.

SUGGESTED READING

Emery, B., and Lloyd, S. (1999). *The Dark Side of Courtship.* Thousand Oaks, CA: Corwin Press.

Evans, R. (2006). *Teenage Pregnancy and Parenthood.* New York: Routledge.

Gottfried, T. (2001). *Teen Fathers Today.* Evergreen, CO: Century Books.

Harris, M. B. (Ed.). (1997). *School Experiences of Gay and Lesbian Youth: The Invisible Minority.* New York: Harrington Park Press.

Huegel, K. (2003). *GLBTQ: The Survival Guide for Queer and Questioning Teens.* Minneapolis, MN: Free Spirit Publishing.

Irvine, J. (2004). *Talk About Sex: The Battles over Sex Education in the United States.* Berkeley: University of California Press.

Levy, B. (1998). *Dating Violence: Young Women in Danger.* Seattle, WA: Seal Press.

Luker, K. (1996). *Dubious Conceptions: The Politics of Teenage Pregnancy.* Cambridge, MA: Harvard University Press.

USEFUL WEB SITES

Alan Guttmacher Institute
www.agi-usa.org

A nonprofit organization dedicated to tracking and improving sexual and reproductive health; it publishes three journals, all available online. The site provides information about topics such as sexual education, adolescent pregnancy, law and public policy, contraception, and sexual behavior. One section of the site is devoted solely to adolescent sexuality.

Henry J. Kaiser Family Foundation
www.kff.org

This well-known philanthropic organization is concerned with major health-care issues, including sexual health. Its site contains reports of survey research conducted by the foundation, as well as fact sheets and research reviews about topics such as sex education, sexually transmitted diseases, adolescent health, and abortion.

Sexuality Information and Education Council of the United States (SEICUS)
www.seicus.org

SEICUS is a nonprofit organization that promotes comprehensive sex education. On the site is information about sexually transmitted diseases and current legislative initiatives concerning sex education. The organization also produces an e-newsletter.

CHAPTER 10 ADOLESCENTS AND THEIR FAMILIES

WOULDN'T YOU LIKE TO KNOW . . .

- What traits characterize the best parents?
- Do most teens find it easier to talk with their mothers or their fathers?
- Do adolescents want their parents to be affectionate and demonstrative?
- How can teens get their parents to trust them?
- Is it possible to be *too close* to one's family?
- What is the best way to discipline adolescents?
- How much say should adolescents have in making family plans?
- Are adolescent-parent conflicts mostly due to adolescents' desire for greater freedom?
- What are most parent-adolescents arguments about?

Virtually all adolescents find themselves part of a family. The specific makeup of that family may be unique. For instance, a teen might be raised by both of his biological parents, by only his father or only his mother, or by a biological parent and a stepparent. He may or may not have interactions with siblings, aunts, uncles, grandparents, cousins, and the like. Yet regardless of makeup, the function and importance of every family is the same. The family is probably the single most important influence in an adolescent's life.

Relationships with kin tend to be more long lasting and intense than those with nonkin. The older members of your family have probably known you since your birth. When children are young, their parents or their parents' surrogates have almost complete control over their behavior; these elders set the rules and provided the opportunities. Because many family members typically share the same physical space, they come into frequent contact with each other (whether they want to or not). And since families share financial resources as well as space, the behavior of one family member often affects one or more of the others. If you share a bathroom with your sister, for instance, when she leaves it a mess, it will inconvenience you. But if she damages the family car, it will likely cause real hardship for your whole family. Therefore, interactions with family members are frequently impassioned.

This chapter begins by describing what youths need and expect from their parents. After that, the focus will turn to parent-adolescent conflict. The next section will focus on adolescent-sibling relationships and the relationships of youths with other relatives in the family. Finally, discussion on maltreatment of adolescents will include the topics of child abuse, sexual abuse, incest, and neglect.

PARENTING ADOLESCENTS

Almost all research indicates that parents have an enormous influence on adolescents' behavior (Steinberg, 2001). Parents vary in their behavior, however, and some patterns of behavior are more beneficial than others.

What Kind of Parents Do Adolescents Want?

What kind of parents do adolescents want and need? A compilation of research findings indicates that youths want and need parents who display the following qualities (Newman, 1989):

"Are interested in us and available to help us when needed."
"Listen to us and try to understand us."
"Let us know they love us."

ANSWERS WOULDN'T YOU LIKE TO KNOW . . .

What traits characterize the best parents?

The best parents show love and concern for their children, grant them privacy and a certain degree of freedom, and set rules and standards of behavior.

"Show approval of us."
"Accept us as we are, faults and all."
"Trust us and expect the best of us."
"Treat us like grown-ups."
"Guide us."
"Are happy people with good dispositions and a sense of humor, who create a happy home, and who set a good example for us."

These comments map well onto the three key components of parenting identified by researchers. The first is **connection** or the presence of a warm, stable, loving, attentive bond between parents and child. Connection provides a sense of security that allows an adolescent to explore the world outside the family. The second component is **psychological autonomy,** the freedom to form one's own opinions, have privacy, and make decisions for oneself. If autonomy is lacking, adolescents are vulnerable to problem behavior and have trouble becoming independent adults. Finally, children must have **regulation.** Successful parents monitor and supervise their children's behavior and set rules that limit that behavior. Regulation teaches children self-control and helps them avoid antisocial behavior (Barber, 1997).

Let's examine these qualities in more detail.

Connection

Parental Interest and Help

Some of the ways adolescents know that their parents care about them is by the interest their parents show in them, by the amount of quality time spent with them, and by their willingness to stand beside them and help them as needed (Amato, 1990; Gecas and Seff, 1990). Positive parental support is associated with close relationships with parents and siblings, high self-esteem, academic success, and advanced moral development (e.g., Barber, Maughan, Olsen, and Thomas, 2002). Lack of parental support may have exactly the opposite effect: low self-esteem, poor schoolwork, impulsive behavior, poor social adjustment, and deviant and antisocial behavior or delinquency (Herman, Dornbusch, Herron, and Herting, 1997). For instance, consider this reaction expressed by a high school basketball player:

> I'm the star player on the school basketball team, but never once has either parent come to see me play.

They're either too busy or too tired or can't get a baby sitter for my younger sister. The crowds cheer for me, the girls hang around my locker, some kids even ask me for my autograph. But it doesn't mean much if the two most important people in my life don't care. (Rice, counseling notes)

Adolescents want attention and companionship from their parents (Henry, Wilson, and Peterson, 1989).

Some parents overdo the companionship. Adolescents want to spend time with their own friends and do not want their parents to be pals. They need adult interest and help, not adults trying to act like adolescents. Adolescents need time to be alone, and to be alone with their peers.

In general, parents spend less time with their adolescents as their adolescents get older. Although they continue to provide emotional support and warmth, they are less involved in their children's activities. For example, in one study, measures of maternal and parental demandingness, responsiveness, values toward achievement, involvement in schoolwork, and involvement in school functions were obtained from both adolescents and their parents. Results showed that both adolescents and their parents perceived mothers to be more involved in parenting than were fathers in both ninth and twelfth grades. Additionally, both mothers and fathers perceived themselves to be higher in all aspects of parenting than their adolescents perceived them to be. In the longitudinal study, both adolescents and parents perceived levels of parenting to drop between ninth and twelfth grades—except values toward achievement, which did not change (Paulson and Sputa, 1996).

The attention adolescents get from their parents depends partially on the birth order and spacing of the children. Middle-born adolescents sometimes feel cheated of parental attention and support and express a sense of being "pushed around" in terms of family rules and regulations (Arnstein, 1978). Middle-born adolescents are less likely than first- or last-borns to say that they would turn to their parents for help (they are more likely to nominate a sibling), and they are less likely than their older and younger siblings to identify themselves as being a member of their family when asked an open-ended question (Salmon and Daly, 1998).

Listening and Empathetic Understanding

Empathy refers to the ability to identify with the thoughts, attitudes, and feelings of another person. It is *emotional sensitivity* to others, the vicarious sharing of experiences of another person and the emotions associated with them (Decety and Jackson, 2004).

Some parents are completely insensitive to their adolescents' feelings and moods. They are unaware of what their adolescents are thinking and feeling and so act without taking those thoughts and feelings into account. When their adolescents are upset, they have no idea why. One possible consequence of this insensitivity is that children grow up as insensitive as the parents. The children's own feelings have never been considered, so they don't learn to consider other people's feelings. Older adolescents perceive their parents as more empathic than younger adolescents, perhaps because the worst conflicts are behind them (Drevets, Benton, and Bradley, 1996).

Communication with parents deteriorates to some extent during adolescence. Adolescents have reported that they spend less time interacting with their parents compared to when they were younger. They disclose less information to their parents and communication with parents is often difficult (Beaumont, 1996). Perhaps one reason for this lack of communication is that many parents do not listen to their teens' ideas, accept their opinions as relevant, or try to understand their feelings and points of view. Adolescents want parents who will talk *with* them, not *at* them, in a sympathetic way:

"We want parents we can take our troubles to and be sure they'll understand. Some parents won't listen or let their children explain. They should try to see things a little more from our point of view."

"We wish our parents would lose an argument with us once in a while and listen to our side of problems." (Rice, counseling notes)

Basically, adolescents are saying that they want sympathetic understanding, an attentive ear, and parents who feel that their children have something worthwhile to say (Noble, Adams, and Openshaw, 1989). Research indicates that the respect parents show for adolescent opinions contributes greatly to the climate and happiness of the home.

A number of studies have found that adolescents spend more time talking with their mothers than with their fathers and that they are more likely to go to their mothers for advice on a wide variety of topics (e.g., Ackard, Neumark-Sztainer, Story, and Perry, 2006; Greene, 1990). This is especially true of daughters. Mothers are more likely to be available to talk and are

connection the presence of a warm, stable, loving, attentive bond between parents and child.

psychological autonomy the freedom to form one's own opinions, have privacy, and make decisions for oneself.

regulation parental monitoring, supervision, and rule setting.

empathy the ability to identify with the thoughts, attitudes, and feelings of another person.

ANSWERS WOULDN'T YOU LIKE TO KNOW ...

Do most teens find it easier to talk with their mothers or their fathers?

Most teens find their mothers easier to talk to than their fathers because they believe that their mothers will be more understanding.

perceived as listening with more sympathy and less judging than fathers. Communication is one key to harmonious parent-youth relationships (Masselam, Marcus, and Stunkard, 1990).

Some parents feel threatened when their adolescent disagrees, does not accept their ideas, or tries to argue. Parents who refuse to talk and close the argument by saying, "I don't want to discuss it; what I say goes," are closing the door to effective communication, just as are adolescents who get angry, stamp out of the room, refuse to discuss a matter reasonably, and go into their rooms to pout.

Given the limited communication between parents and adolescents—along with the fact that parents and adolescents frequently have different perceptions of the same event—even empathic, caring parents are often unaware of the stresses that their adolescent children are experiencing. Several studies (Hartos and Power, 1997; O'Brien and Iannotti, 1993) have shown that mothers consistently underestimate the magnitude of the stressors felt by their adolescent children. Since parents cannot help their children deal with problems that they don't know exist, it's not surprising that the greater the awareness gap, the more the problems exhibited by the adolescent.

Love and Positive Affect

Affect, which refers to the emotions or feelings that exist among family members, may be positive or negative. **Positive affect** between family members refers to relationships characterized by emotional warmth, affection, love, and sensitivity. Family members show that they matter to one another and are responsive to one another's feelings and needs. **Negative affect** is characterized by emotional coldness, rejection, and hostility. Family members don't seem to love one another—or even like one another. In fact, they may hate one another, be indifferent to one another's feelings and needs, and act as though they really don't care about the other members of the family. There is little affection, positive emotional support, empathy, or understanding.

Most adolescents need a great deal of love and demonstration of affection from parents (Barber and Thomas, 1986). Sometimes, however, parents themselves were brought up in unexpressive families where affection was seldom bestowed. As a consequence, the parents seldom hug their children, hold them, or kiss them. They don't express positive, warm feelings at all. As one girl expressed it: "I don't remember my parents ever telling me that they loved me. They just assumed I knew, but I wish they could have told me, and showed it once in a while."

Two possibilities may result: Either the adolescents are so starved for love and affection that their needs become very great when they become adults, or they remain cold and aloof themselves, finding it difficult to express affection to their own spouses or children. Adolescents emphasize that they need both intrinsic support (encouragement, appreciation, being pleased

CROSS-CULTURAL CONCERNS EXTENDED FAMILIES

When Americans of European descent hear the word *family,* they will most likely envision what anthropologists and sociologists call the *nuclear family.* A nuclear family is composed of a married couple and any children they might have together. Of course, in modern American society—with its proliferation of out-of-wedlock births, divorces, and remarriages—many white Americans think of *single-parent families, split families,* and *blended families,* as well. Individuals with other ancestral backgrounds, however, may find that the *extended family* more quickly comes to mind.

The extended family structure is common throughout much of the world. Families in many parts of Asia, Africa, and Latin America follow an extended family model. Many Native American people have also traditionally followed and continue to embrace this pattern. Some extended families are three generational: Grandparents, parents, and children share the same household. Others are composed of adult siblings and their spouses and children. In some parts of the world, extended families consist of a husband, his several wives, and their children.

The extended family has the advantage of involving more adults in the sharing of economic burdens, household labor, and child care. Because of this, extended families are more common among low-socioeconomic-status Americans than among middle-class Americans. This trend is most apparent among African Americans, who have enjoyed the benefits of the extended family for generations.

Most adolescents need a great deal of love and affection from their parents. Perceptions of parental support, both intrinsic and extrinsic, correlate positively with life satisfaction for adolescents.

with the child, trust, and love) and extrinsic support (external expressions of support, such as hugging and kissing, taking the child to dinner or a movie, and buying the child something special). Adolescents' perceptions of parental support, particularly intrinsic support and closeness, are positively correlated with life satisfaction for the adolescents (Young, Miller, Norton, and Hill, 1995).

Adolescents use a variety of tactics to elicit demonstrations of the love they crave (Flint, 1992). They demonstrate mutual trust (by being honest, by discussing times they did the wrong things), they are polite (they listen and don't talk back), they show concern and caring (they compliment their parents and help them out), and they demonstrate affection. Older adolescents rely on mutual trust-enhancing behaviors more than younger adolescents, and they demonstrate more concern and caring. Adolescents are typically more polite to their fathers and more demonstrative to their mothers.

ANSWERS WOULDN'T YOU LIKE TO KNOW ...

Do adolescents want their parents to be affectionate and demonstrative?

Although most teens don't want to get a hug and a kiss from their mom on the front steps of their middle school, they do want and need demonstrations of caring from their parents. If teens don't get enough love, they will likely grow up to be insecure in all their future relationships.

Acceptance and Approval

An important component of love is unconditional acceptance. One way to show love is to know and accept adolescents exactly as they are, faults and all. Adolescents need to know they are valued, accepted, and liked by their parents. They also want parents to have tolerance for individuality, intimacy, and interpersonal differences in the family (Bomar and Sabatelli, 1996).

There must be a determined effort by parents both to show approval and to achieve enough objectivity to see the child as a human being, entitled to human attributes. Adolescents do not want to feel that their parents expect them to be perfect before they will love them, nor can they thrive in an atmosphere of constant criticism and displeasure.

Negative feelings between parents and adolescents may exist for a variety of reasons. Some children are resented, rejected, and unloved by parents from the time they are born, because they were unplanned and unwanted in the first place. One girl explained:

> My mother always tells me how upset she was when she found out she was pregnant with me. She had to give up a successful career when I was born. Carrying me destroyed her figure. Giving birth was painful. I was a fussy baby who cried a lot and kept her awake nights. Growing up, I was a pain in the butt most of the time, according to her. She's resented me all these years and she lets me know it. (Rice, counseling notes)

Other parents may be upset at the way their children have turned out. One father complained:

> I hate to admit it but I'm very disappointed in my son. He's not at all like me. When I was in school, I played

affect feelings that exist among family members.

positive affect a relationship characterized by emotional warmth, affection, love, empathy, care, sensitivity, and emotional support.

negative affect a relationship characterized by negative feelings of emotional coldness, rejection, hostility, anger, and insensitivity among family members.

football and other sports. My son prefers music and books. He has long hair, an earring in his left ear, and looks like a sissy. I wish I could be proud of him but I'm not. He really embarrasses me. (Rice, counseling notes)

Trust

"Why are our parents always so afraid we are going to do the wrong thing? Why can't they trust us more?"

"Our parents could trust us more than they often do. They should tell us what we need to know about dating without being old-fashioned. Then they should put us on our own and expect the best of us so we have something to live up to." (Rice, counseling notes)

Some of the most annoying evidences of distrust are parents' opening the children's e-mail, reading their diaries, and listening in on their telephone conversations. One girl complained:

My mother is forever going through my room under the pretense of "cleaning." I don't like to have my desk straightened up (it's where I keep my diary) or my bureau rummaged through. . . . Don't you think a 16-year-old girl needs privacy? (Rice, counseling notes)

Some parents seem to have more difficulty trusting their adolescents than others do. Such parents tend to project their own fears, anxiety, and guilt onto the adolescent. The most fearful parents are usually those who are the most insecure or who had difficulties themselves while growing up. Mothers who themselves have conceived or borne children out of wedlock are those most concerned about their own daughters' dating and sexual behavior. Most adolescents feel that parents should trust them completely unless they have given the adults reason for distrust.

Recent research suggests that parents' trust is based primarily on the amount and kind of knowledge they have about their adolescent. Knowledge of their child's daily activities accounts for more trust than knowledge of their child's past misbehaviors. Adolescents who spontaneously tell their parents about their daily lives elicit the most trust of all (Kerr, Stattin, and Trost, 1999).

Attachment Style

The characteristics mentioned in the previous sections are not randomly distributed. Parents who demonstrate a lot of affection are more likely to listen than those who do not, and parents who approve of their children are more likely to trust them. It is common, therefore, to cluster these characteristics and, borrowing a term originally used to refer only to the bond between infants and their caregivers, to speak of an adolescent's **attachment style.**

ANSWERS WOULDN'T YOU LIKE TO KNOW . . .

How can teens get their parents to trust them?

The best thing a teenager can do to elicit trust from his or her parents is to talk to them about the things going on in his or her life.

There are three main attachment patterns: secure, anxious, and avoidant (Ainsworth, Blehar, Waters, and Wall, 1978). Individuals with **secure attachments** have parents who are consistently warm and nurturing; securely attached persons are trusting and open to others. Individuals with **anxious attachments** are, as the label indicates, nervous and insecure in their relationships; they need frequent indications that they are loved and are fearful of desertion. Anxiously attached individuals usually come from backgrounds in which their parents were there for them only inconsistently. Individuals with **avoidant attachments** are aloof and distant; they are afraid of being hurt and so they emotionally seal themselves off. Parents of avoidantly attached individuals are often cold and rejecting.

Adolescents who are securely attached to their parents feel competent (Papini and Roggman, 1992) and get along with others (Kenny, 1994). They do well in school, have high self-esteem, are less likely to engage in problematic behaviors (Noom, Dekovic, and Meeus, 1999), and are unlikely to be depressed (Kenny, Lomax, Brabeck, and Fife, 1998). The differences between securely attached adolescents and anxiously or avoidantly attached adolescents are most pronounced during periods of stress (Rice and Whaley, 1994).

Autonomy

One goal of every adolescent is to be accepted as an autonomous adult. This is accomplished through a process called **separation-individuation,** during which the parent-adolescent bond is transformed but maintained (Fleming and Anderson, 1986; Josselson, 1988). The adolescent establishes individuality and connectedness with parents at the same time (Grotevant and Cooper, 1985). Thus, adolescents seek a differentiated relationship with parents, while communication, affection, and trust continue (Quintana and Lapsley, 1990). For example, they develop new interests, values, and goals and may develop points of view that are different from parents in order to experience distinctiveness. Nevertheless, the adolescents are still part of a family. Adolescents and their parents continue to expect emotional commitment from each other (Newman, 1989).

Individuation is a fundamental organizing principle of human growth (Gavazzi and Sabatelli, 1990). It involves the ongoing efforts of an individual to build self-understanding and identity in relation to other people. In making the transition from childhood to adulthood, the adolescent needs to establish a degree of **autonomy** and identity in order to assume adult roles and responsibilities. Adolescents who remain too dependent on their parents are not as able to develop satisfactory relationships with peers (Schneider and Younger, 1996).

There are two aspects of autonomy. **Behavioral autonomy** involves becoming independent and free enough to act on your own without excessive dependence on others for guidance. **Emotional autonomy** means becoming free of childish emotional dependence on parents. Research indicates that behavioral autonomy, the ability to make decisions for oneself, increases sharply during adolescence (Feldman and Wood, 1994). Adolescents desire behavioral autonomy in some areas, such as clothing selection or choice of friends, but follow their parents' leads in other areas, such as formulating educational plans. Adolescents want and need parents who will grant them behavioral autonomy in slowly increasing amounts as they learn to use it, rather than all at once. Too much freedom granted too quickly may be interpreted as rejection. Youths want to be given the right to make choices, to exert their own independence, to argue with adults, and to assume responsibility, but they do not want complete freedom. Those who have it worry about it because they realize they do not know how to use it.

The shift to emotional autonomy during adolescence is not as dramatic as the shift to behavioral autonomy. Much depends on parental behavior. Some parents continue to encourage overdependency. Parents who have an unhappy marriage sometimes turn to their children for emotional satisfaction and become overly dependent on them. Parents who encourage dependency needs that become demanding and excessive, even into adulthood, are interfering with their child's ability to function as an effective adult. Some adolescents who have been dominated by their parents begin to accept and to prefer being dependent. The result is prolonged adolescence. Some adolescents, for example, may prefer to live with their parents after marriage or may never achieve mature social relationships, establish a vocational identity of their own choosing, or develop a positive self-image as separate, independent people.

The opposite extreme from overdependence is detachment by parents, so that the adolescent cannot depend on them at all for guidance and advice. As in so many other areas of life, a middle ground should be established.

Connectedness and autonomy may at first seem to be mutually exclusive. How can one feel close to one's parents yet be independent from them? Most researchers, however, see the two traits as complementary (Montemayor and Flannery, 1991) and believe that the healthiest families balance independence and emotional support (Grotevant and Cooper, 1985). Families whose members lean too heavily toward connectedness—they spend most of their time together, expect to know details about every aspect of each others' lives, and so on—are described as **enmeshed.** Conversely, families whose members are isolated from each other—no one knows what the others do during the day, who their friends are, what they think about important events—are termed **disengaged** (Olson, 1988).

Regarding adolescents and family **cohesion,** then, more is not necessarily better. Much depends on the adolescent's age and the stage of the family life cycle. Ordinarily, family cohesion is tightest in the early stages of marriage while the children are very young. Children like to feel that they are part of a closely knit family unit. As the children become adolescents, most families become less cohesive (Ohannesian and Lerner, 1995). When children leave home during the launching stage,

attachment style the kind of emotional bond an adolescent has with his or her parents; described as secure, anxious, or avoidant.

secure attachments youths are trusting and open to others; fostered by parents who were consistently warm and nurturing.

anxious attachments youths are nervous and insecure in relationships; fostered by inconsistent parenting.

avoidant attachments youths are aloof and distant, afraid of being hurt; fostered by cold, rejecting parents.

separation-individuation the process by which the adolescent becomes separated from parents and becomes a unique individual.

autonomy independence or freedom.

behavioral autonomy becoming independent and free enough to act on one's own without excessive dependence on others.

emotional autonomy becoming free of childish emotional dependence on parents.

enmeshed families those whose members are too heavily connected with each other.

disengaged families those whose members are isolated from each other.

cohesion the degree to which family members are connected to one another.

ANSWERS WOULDN'T YOU LIKE TO KNOW . . .

Is it possible to be too close to one's family?

Yes, it is. Although there can never be too much love, there can be too much togetherness. Everyone in the family needs some privacy and time to be alone or with his or her own friends.

family cohesion (at least as far as it involves youths) is usually at its lowest ebb (Larson and Lowe, 1990).

The lower level of family cohesion in adolescence is due to the adolescent striving to become autonomous, to carve out a life for himself or herself in the process of separation-individuation. At the same time, parents are separating from the adolescent in their increasing need for privacy as they create a new life for themselves (Demick, 2002). The result of these simultaneous separating processes is a lower level of cohesion at the adolescent stage of the family life cycle.

Furthermore, research indicates that the spatial distance in parental-adolescent dyads is greater for older adolescent families compared with younger adolescent families (Bulcroft, Carmody, and Bulcroft, 1996). This lends support to the idea that older adolescents strive for more autonomy and separateness, and for more personal space, compared with younger adolescents (Larson and Lowe, 1990). Thus, there is a clear and important relationship between the developmental stage of the family and the spatial distance in the family. This conclusion is even more evident in the research of Larson and Lowe (1990), who found that older adolescents and their parents maintained, on average, a 70 percent greater distance between themselves than did younger adolescents and their parents.

What degree of family cohesiveness is necessary for a functional family and what degree is necessary for a dysfunctional family? The most functional family situation seems to be that which is characterized by a high degree of family cohesiveness as children grow, with a gradual shift to a more balanced degree of closeness as children become adolescents, thus allowing formation of budding identities in adolescents who strive to become persons in their own right.

Regulation

Guidance and Control

More than 35 years ago, Diana Baumrind (1971) described four basic patterns by which parents exercise control over their children. These four patterns arise from two different, independent dimensions of parenting: control and warmth. The first dimension, **control,** has to do with the degree to which parents manage their children's behavior. At one extreme, for example, are parents who exercise a lot of control: They dictate many aspects of their children's behavior, and they expect their children to unquestioningly obey their commands. At the other end of the controlling continuum are parents who set few rules and impose few consequences if those rules are violated. The second dimension, **warmth,** reflects the degree to which parents are affectionate and supportive as opposed to rejecting and unresponsive.

When these two dimensions are combined in different ways, four separate parenting styles are determined (see Figure 10.1):

1. **Authoritative parents** listen to their children and take their wants and desires into account when making rules and decisions. These parents are not really democratic, however: If consensus cannot be reached, they have the ultimate say. If you were raised in a family that had frequent family conferences, in which issues were hashed out and everyone's opinion was solicited, then you were most likely raised in an authoritative home.
2. **Authoritarian parents** are strict disciplinarians. They make decisions based on what *they* want and what *they* believe is right; there is little discussion about rules and family practices. Children find themselves in big trouble if they do not live up to their parents' expectations. If your parents frequently said "You'll do it because I said so," without offering any other explanation for their demands, you were likely raised in an authoritarian home.
3. **Permissive parents** are overindulgent. They believe that the best way to express their love is to give in to their children's wishes. They permit their children to decide almost everything for themselves and tend to not monitor their children closely. They don't like to say no or to disappoint their children. It follows that not much happens to the children if they do something that goes against their parents' preferences. If your parents let you stay up as late as you wanted (even when

FIGURE 10.1 THE FOUR PRIMARY PARENTING STYLES

Source: Based on Baumrind (1971).

	Controlling	Undemanding
Warm	Authoritative parents	Permissive parents
Cold	Authoritarian parents	Uninvolved parents

you were only 7 or 8) and didn't give you any chores to do (or did them for you), you were probably raised in a permissive home.

4. **Uninvolved parents** do not seem to care about their children, as they let their children do whatever they (the children) wish. However, these parents do so out of indifference rather than (misguided) love. They seem to want to be bothered as little as possible. Often, parents are uninvolved because they are overwhelmed by the stresses in their own lives or because their children were unwanted.

What effect does each method of control have on the adolescent? What methods are most functional?

Few ideas are agreed upon more readily by developmental psychologists than the idea that authoritative parenting is best (Steinberg, 2001). In fact, it is better to have one parent who is authoritative and one who is not (even though this means there will be parental disagreement) than it is to have two parents who use another parenting style (Fletcher, Steinberg, and Sellers, 1999). Authoritative parents exercise authority but

control the degree to which parents manage their child's behavior.

warmth the love, approval, and emotional support that parents give their children.

authoritative parents parents who respect their children's wishes but who maintain control in the home.

authoritarian parents parents who set many rules and harshly enforce them.

permissive parents parents who exercise little control over their children's behavior.

uninvolved parents parents who seem disinterested in their children and thus do not supervise them or give them much affection.

RESEARCH HIGHLIGHT IS IT OK TO MISLEAD ONE'S PARENTS?

Adolescence is a time when individuals actively seek autonomy and independence, when they strive to "grow up" and experience new things. Parents frequently disagree with their teenage children as to the pace at which this maturation should take place and the specific activities appropriate for them. Given this, and given the perceived need for conformity to peers and for being cool, it is almost inevitable that adolescents will find themselves in the situation of wanting to do something of which their parents may disapprove. One "solution" to this dilemma is to mislead them, either by outright lying or by neglecting to tell them about the upcoming activity. Recently, as an outgrowth of interest in parental monitoring, there has been a burst of research activity concerning the issue of adolescent deception.

Perhaps the most basic question asks whether it is common for adolescents to lie to their parents. The answer appears to be yes. Jensen, Arnett, Feldman, and Cauffman (2004) asked high school and college students whether they had lied to their parents about six issues (e.g., parties, alcohol) during the previous year. Between one-third and two-thirds of the high school students and 28 to 50 percent of the college students reported about lying about each issue; approximately 80 percent of the students had lied at least once during the previous year. Sons lied somewhat more than daughters.

Do adolescents think that it is morally acceptable to lie to their parents? Sometimes. It depends both on the issue and the motivation for lying. Adolescents feel most obligated to tell their parents about those issues that they believe to be legitimately their parents' concern and least obligated to tell them about issues that are purely personal, and hence not their parents' business (Smetana, Metzger, Gettman, and Campione-Barr, 2006). Of course, parents and adolescents do not always agree about into which realm issues fall, but these disagreements become smaller as adolescents age. Lying is more acceptable when the motives are altruistic or prosocial rather than spiteful (Jensen, Arnett, Feldman, and Cauffman, 2004).

Still, what may be acceptable and normative in small doses is not necessarily good in larger ones. Consistent with most previous research, Frijns, Frinkenauer, Vermilst, and Engels, (2005) found that adolescents who made a habit of keeping secrets from their parents were more likely to have low self-esteem, exhibit depressed moods, be stressed, be aggressive, and have low levels of self-control than their more honest peers. They suggested three possible reasons for these negative associations. First, keeping secrets is stressful, hard work. Second, parents can't help their adolescents as well as they should if they are uninformed about what is really going on in their lives. Third, keeping secrets undermines feelings of belongingness and cohesiveness with the family.

In any event, honesty is generally the best policy!

PERSONAL ISSUES CORPORAL PUNISHMENT

Corporal punishment or *physical punishment* refers to the use of physical force with the intention of causing a child pain, but not injury, for purposes of correction or control of the child's behavior. Corporal punishment of children by parents is a normative form of discipline in U.S. society. In fact, not only are spanking and slapping children considered acceptable but they are generally believed to be quite necessary and highly effective. One study found that 84 percent of the national sample of adults agreed that a good, hard spanking is sometimes necessary. Parents who refuse to use corporal punishment on children are viewed as too lenient and ineffective—in essence, poor parents. Although the prevalence of corporal punishment declines with the age of the child, it still remains high even during adolescence. Almost half of the children in early adolescence experience corporal punishment by a parent (Turner and Finkelhor, 1996). Widely accepted or not, it is important to note that a recent meta-analysis of 70 studies of the effects of corporal punishment (studies conducted between 1961 and 2000) indicated that physical discipline had both negative behavioral and negative emotional consequences (Paolucci and Violata, 2004). Other forms of discipline are more effective and do not yield these negative effects.

ANSWERS WOULDN'T YOU LIKE TO KNOW . . .

What is the best way to discipline adolescents?

The best way to discipline adolescents is to talk to them about the reasons that their actions are unacceptable. Making threats and handing out punishments tend to make children and adolescents aggressive, and withdrawing love and affection makes them insecure.

express concern through guidance. **Induction** (Hoffman, 2000) is the technique most frequently used by authoritative parents. Induction involves talking with the child, explaining why the action in question was inappropriate and how it affected others in a negative way. The purpose of the discussion is to induce feelings of guilt over the behavior so that it will not be repeated. Not only is induction the most effective disciplinary technique, but it is one that adolescents are receptive to: They may not enjoy these discussions, but they believe them appropriate responses on their parents' part and the discussions do not make them angry (Padilla-Walker and Carlo, 2004).

Authoritative parents also encourage individual responsibility, decision making, and autonomy. Adolescents are involved in making their own decisions while listening to and discussing the reasoned explanations of their parents. Adolescents are also encouraged to detach themselves gradually from their families. As a result, the authoritative home atmosphere is likely to be one of respect, appreciation, warmth, acceptance, and consistent parenting (Necessary and Parish, 1995). This type of home is associated with conforming, trouble-free nondelinquent behavior for both boys and girls.

This finding about the effectiveness of authoritative parenting is so robust that it not only holds true for American adolescents, including those from a wide range of racial and ethnic groups, but it also holds true cross-culturally, as well (Khalique and Rohner, 2002; Rohner and Britner, 2002). For example, in their comparative study of American, Swiss, Hungarian, and Dutch adolescents, Vazsonyi, Hibbert, and Snider (2003) found that parents who were relatively authoritative had adolescent children who were better adjusted than those who were relatively authoritarian or permissive. This pattern also holds true for families from non-Western cultures (e.g., Feldman and Rosenthal, 1994), and for ethnic minorities within the United States as well (Steinberg, 2001).

The usual effect of *authoritarian parenting* is to produce a combination of rebellion and dependency. Adolescents are taught to follow their parents' demands and decisions without question and not to try to make decisions themselves. Adolescents in such environments usually are more hostile to their parents, often deeply resent their control and domination, and less often identify with them. When they succeed in challenging parent authority, youths may become rebellious, sometimes overtly aggressive and hostile, especially if the parents' discipline has been harsh, unfair, or administered without much love and affection. Thus, the effects on children growing up in autocratic homes differ. The meeker ones are cowed and remain codependent; the stronger ones are rebellious. Both usually show some emotional disturbances and have problems. Those who rebel often leave home as soon as they can; some become delinquent (Fischer and Crawford, 1992).

Authoritarian parents are often inflexible. Inflexible parents believe there is only one right way, and that is their way. Such parents are unyielding and refuse to change their ideas and behavioral responses. They won't discuss different points of view or allow disagreements, so they and their adolescents can never

ANSWERS WOULDN'T YOU LIKE TO KNOW . . .

How much say should adolescents have in making family plans?

Parents should definitely allow adolescents to have a say in making family plans. Doing so demonstrates respect for their opinions and gives them practice in decision making. However, adolescents should not have as much or more say in these decisions than their parents.

understand one another. They expect all of their children to fit narrow molds, to act, think, and be alike. They are intolerant of children who are different.

Inflexible parents are often perfectionists, and thus are regularly critical and displeased with their adolescents' performances on most things. The results are the destruction of the adolescents' self-esteem and the creation of intolerable tension and stress. Many such adolescents grow up with a great deal of anxiety and fear they will be doing something wrong or not be able to measure up.

Authoritarian parents rely heavily on punishment, and the effect of using punitive measures to exercise control is usually negative. Adolescents can get (metaphorically) beaten down by their parents' harshness, and adolescents with authoritarian parents are more likely to become clinically depressed than other adolescents (Aquilino and Supple, 2001). Furthermore, adolescents who grow up in homes where parents use harsh and physical punishment will usually model their parents' aggressive behavior. Family violence seems to beget more violence in and outside the home (Walker-Barnes and Mason, 2004).

There is also a relationship between harsh discipline in the home and adolescents' relationships with their peers. Adolescents who exercise little restraint in their social behavior, partly because they model the aggressive behavior of their parents, are not as well liked by peers as adolescents who have learned restraint from positive models at home (Feldman and Wentzel, 1990; Kaufmann, Gesten, and Santa Lucia, 2000).

Although, as noted before, the evidence strongly suggests that authoritative parenting works best across a broad array of cultural and ethnic groups, it is also true that the negative effects of authoritarian parenting are not as consistent in some groups as in others (e.g., Asian Americans and African Americans). This may be in part because the broad term *authoritarian* does not capture the subtle differences in how parents in different ethnic groups exercise strict control. Brooks-Gunn and Markman (2005), for example, found evidence that older African American mothers sometimes use a strategy they termed "tough love," a variant of authoritarianism different from that used by younger African American mothers that could be quite successful. It is also likely due to the fact that the different cultural backgrounds of individuals from these groups means that adolescents and parents have different expectations about normative behavior, and hence attribute different meanings to the parents' disciplinary behaviors than Caucasian adolescents would; this could serve to mitigate the negative effects of authoritarianism (Mason, Walker-Barnes, Tu, Simons, and Martinez-Arrue, 2004). For example, Asian American adolescents whose parents were authoritarian tend to do well in school, although in one recent study they did not do as well as those who had more authoritative parents (Lee, Daniels, and Kissinger, 2006).

At the other extreme is the *permissive* home, in which adolescents receive little guidance and direction, are given few restrictions from parents, and are expected to make decisions for themselves. There are actually three forms of overindulgence: (1) material overindulgence, in which children are given nearly every possession they desire, regardless of the cost or their need for it; (2) relational overindulgence, which occurs when parents excessively attend to their child's every whim so that the child never learns to do anything independently for himself or herself; and (3) structural overindulgence, which results when parents set no rules or limits on a child's behavior (Clarke, Dawson, and Bredehoft, 2004). Often these types of permissiveness go together.

The specific effects of the different sorts of permissiveness vary, of course, but the overall outcome is the same: Pampered adolescents will be ill prepared to accept frustrations or responsibility or show proper regard for others. They often become domineering, self-centered, and selfish, and get into trouble with those who will not indulge them the way their parents have. Without limits on their behavior, they feel insecure, disoriented, and uncertain. If adolescents interpret the parents' lack of control as disinterest or rejection, they blame the parents for not warning or guiding them. Lax discipline, rejection, and lack of parental affection also have been associated with delinquency. In fact, in one recent study, juvenile delinquents from permissive homes were less empathic, had lower grades, and were more likely to use drugs than those from authoritarian homes (Steinberg, Blatt-Eisengart, and Cauffman, 2006). Adolescents raised by uninvolved parents are similar to those raised by permissive parents, but the effects are more extreme.

In addition to setting rules and meting out punishments, parents regulate their children's behavior by *monitoring* them. Successful parents know what their children do, where they go, and with whom they spend their time (Jacobson and Crockett, 2000). Moreover, adolescents are less likely to get into trouble if they believe

induction parental control through offering alternative choices.

that their parents will find out about it. Monitored adolescents are less likely to participate in delinquent behavior (Snyder, Dishion, and Patterson, 1986), engage in sexual behavior (Ensminger, 1990), and use drugs (Brown, Mounts, Lamborn, and Steinberg, 1993). Permissive parents, of course, expend less effort in monitoring their children than either autocratic or authoritative parents.

PARENT-ADOLESCENT TENSION

The amount of tension between parents and adolescents is greater than that between parents and younger children (Kim, Conger, and Lorenz, 2001). Even so, most families that enjoy good relationships when their children are small will continue to do so when their children become teens (Noack and Buhl, 2004). Given that adolescents are striving to increase their autonomy, a certain amount of conflict is normal and inevitable. One might even argue that conflict contributes to healthy development. Working out disagreements forces adolescents to clarify their identities, to take others' perspectives, to grapple with moral issues, to learn how to compromise, and to handle frustration and anger (Walker and Taylor, 1991). In the following sections, we will discuss some of the major causes of parent-adolescent tension.

Differences in Outlook

Parent-adolescent misunderstandings arise from the two different types of outlooks that adults and youths typically have. Table 10.1 shows a comparison of these outlooks. And while not all adults or youths fit the types described, enough are similar to the two descriptions to make these differences a major source of conflict.

Table 10.1 reveals some significant differences between middle-aged parents and adolescent children. From a vantage point reached after many years of experience, parents feel that youths are irresponsible, reckless, and naive, too inexperienced even to recognize that they are foolish to take chances. Parents worry that their youths will have accidents, get hurt, or get in trouble with the law. Youths feel their parents are overly cautious and worry too much.

Middle-aged parents tend to compare today's youths and life-styles with their own past. Parents often suffer from a perennial *cultural lag*—a situation that renders them relatively poorly informed. Children and teenagers show a tendency to generalize the inefficiency of parents as instructors and have started to question their reliability as educators in general. In fact, adolescents sometimes feel they have to socialize parents to bring them up to date on modern views.

Parents also become a little cynical about human character and somewhat disillusioned about trying to change the world and everybody in it; they realistically learn to accept some things as they are. Adolescents are still extremely idealistic and impatient with adults who are part of the establishment and accept and like things as they are. Adolescents want to reform the world overnight and become annoyed when their parents do not agree with their crusade.

Recall from Chapter 6 (Traditional Approaches to Cognitive Development) that adolescents are enthralled with their new cognitive abilities. They can now think abstractly, hypothetically, and counterfactually. They can imagine alternatives that do not, in fact, exist. Parental behaviors that were once taken for granted are now questioned. Adolescents often believe that they have intuited solutions to problems that are better than those proposed by their elders. While sometimes they have, more often, their solutions are not realistic because they lack experience and do not yet comprehend the complexities of the world. Adolescents may feel misunderstood, however, when their suggestions are not embraced.

Adolescents also grow to be wary of adults, primarily because they feel most adults are too critical and will

TABLE 10.1 MIDDLE-AGED ADULT VERSUS ADOLESCENT OUTLOOKS

MIDDLE-AGED ADULT GENERATION	ADOLESCENT GENERATION
Is careful/experienced	Is daring and adventurous; sometimes takes foolish chances
Holds to past; has tendency to compare present with yesterday	Considers past irrelevant; lives in present
Is realistic; sometimes skeptical about life and people	Is idealistic, optimistic
Is conservative in manners, morals, and mores	Is liberal; challenges traditional ideas; experiments with new customs
Is generally contented and satisfied; accepts status quo	Is critical with things as they are; desires to reform, change
Wants to stay youthful; fears age	Wants to be grown-up, but dislikes idea of ever being old
Tends to be restrictive on views of what is age-appropriate behavior	Tends to be more accepting than adults of actions that violate social expectations of age-appropriate behavior

ANSWERS WOULDN'T YOU LIKE TO KNOW ...

Are adolescent-parent conflicts really mostly due to adolescents' desire for greater freedom?

Although adolescent-parent arguments are due, in part, to adolescents' wanting greater freedom, they are also due to the fact that middle-aged parents are fighting their own psychological battles and have different perspectives on life than their teenage children.

not understand them. Youths feel they have good ideas, too, and know more about some things than their parents do, and, because they want to be grown-ups, they may scoff at parental suggestions or ideas. Adults react to criticism and rejection with anger and hurt.

Finally, some aging adults become oversensitive about growing old or being considered aged. Because they hate to think of getting old, they focus more and more attention on staying young. If parents carry this insecurity to extremes in their dress and behaviors, they succeed mostly in attracting the embarrassed shame of their own teenagers and the amused ridicule of other youths.

Focus of Conflict

In spite of personality differences, research indicates that parent-adolescent relationships are usually harmonious (Noack and Buhl, 2004; Steinberg, 1990). When conflict occurs, arguments usually involve one or more of five broad topics (Holmbeck, Paikoff, and Brooks-Gunn, 1995; Laursen, 1995).

Social Life and Customs

Adolescents' social lives and the social customs they observe probably create more conflict with parents than any other area (Smetana and Asquith, 1994). These are the most common sources of friction:

- Choice of friends or dating partners
- How often they are allowed to go out, going out on school nights, and frequency of dating
- Where they are allowed to go and the type of activity they can attend
- Curfew hours
- The age they are allowed to date, ride in cars, and participate in certain events
- Going steady
- Choice of clothes and hairstyles

One of the most common complaints of parents is that adolescents are never home and do not spend any time with the family.

Responsibility

Parents become the most critical of adolescents who do not evidence enough responsibility. Parents expect adolescents to show responsibility in the following:

- Performing family chores
- Earning and spending money
- Caring for personal belongings, clothes, and room
- Using the family automobile
- Using the telephone
- Doing work for others outside the home
- Using family property or belongings (furniture, tools, supplies, equipment, etc.)

Adolescents and their parents can come into conflict over many different issues: choice of friends, curfews, chores, grades, and use of bad language, among others.

School

Adolescents' school performance, behavior at school, and attitudes toward school receive much attention from parents. Specifically, parents are concerned about these issues:

- Grades and level of performance (whether the youths are performing according to their potential)
- Study habits and homework
- Regularity of attendance
- General attitude toward school studies and teachers
- Behavior in school

Family Relationships

Conflict arises over the following:

- Immature behavior
- General attitude and level of respect shown to parents
- Quarreling with siblings
- Relationships with relatives, especially aged grandparents in the home
- Degree of orientation toward family or amount of autonomy from family (Barber and Delfabbro, 2000)

Social Conventions

Parents are concerned especially with these behaviors:

- Drinking, smoking, and using drugs
- Language and speech
- Sexual behavior
- Staying out of trouble
- Going to church or Sunday school

As will be discussed in Chapter 14 on moral development, parents and their teenage children rarely disagree about basic moral values, such as whether it is wrong to cheat or hurt others (Reisch et al., 2000). Instead, they disagree about behaviors that are socially acceptable to one group (adolescents) but not to the other (adults). For example, adolescents usually find it more acceptable to curse and use coarse language than adults.

Conflicts usually occur when people's expectations are violated. These violations are especially likely during adolescence because the adolescent is changing rapidly (hence, parental expectations may be out of date) and because the adolescent may have an inflated sense of his or her own maturity and abilities (Collins, Laursen, Mortensen, Luebker, and Ferreira, 1997). Adolescents expect to be granted autonomy at an earlier age than their parents believe is appropriate (Feldman and Quatman, 1988). This is perhaps because they feel older than they really are (Montepare and Lachman, 1989).

ANSWERS WOULDN'T YOU LIKE TO KNOW ...

What are most parent-adolescent arguments about?

Most parent-adolescent arguments are about having consideration for other family members, doing schoolwork and chores, and performing social conventions. Parents and adolescents often have different senses of what is typical or proper, and so their expectations differ.

Variables Affecting Conflict

The focus of conflict in any one family will depend on a number of factors. The three most obvious factors are the *adolescent's gender,* the *parent's gender,* and the *adolescent's age.*

The first of these, adolescent gender, does not by itself seem to contribute greatly to the overall amount of conflict in a family (Bosma et al., 1996), although it does interact with the other two factors to produce different patterns. For example, girls argue with their fathers most often while in early adolescence, whereas sons argue most with their fathers while in late adolescence (Comstock, 1994). Also, adolescent girls and boys may argue with their parents about somewhat different issues; in one recent study, for example, sons argued more with their parents about behavioral problems than did daughters, who argued more (with fathers, at least) about peer and friend issues (Renk, Liljequist, Simpson, and Phares, 2005).

Adolescents have different types of conflicts with their mothers than with their fathers because they tend to have different kinds of relationships with them. Adolescents typically perceive their fathers to hold more authority than their mothers (Youniss and Smollar, 1985). This, coupled with the fact that they usually spend more time with their mothers, means that they tend to argue more with their mothers (Laursen and Collins, 1994; Montemayor, 1986). But again, conflict does not necessarily imply dislike or lack of closeness. Most adolescents feel closer to and communicate more openly with their mothers than with their fathers (Ackard, Neumark-Sztainer, Story, and Perry, 2006), and mothers exert more influence over adolescents (Greene, 1990).

As adolescents age, they are apt to agree more and argue less with their parents. By the time a child is 18 or 19, his or her parents are usually willing to grant the autonomy and freedom he or she desires. It is earlier, during middle and especially early adolescence, that conflict is more likely. At those ages, adolescents likely desire freedoms that their parents feel are inappropriate and want to shrug off responsibilities that their parents feel they are ready to assume. A recent metanalytic review of the literature confirmed this trend: The conflict rate does decrease over the course of adolescence. However, the conflicts become more intense and emotional as the adolescents mature (Laursen, Coy, and Collins, 1998).

The total *atmosphere within the home* influences conflict. Conflict of all types is more frequent in authoritarian homes than in authoritative homes. In authoritarian homes, there is more conflict over spending money, social life, activities outside the home, and home chores. Conflict between parents also affects the home atmosphere and has a detrimental effect on adolescents. The level of parent-adolescent conflict is determined partially by family context. A family atmosphere of warmth and supportiveness promotes successful negotiation of disagreements between parents and adolescent children and thereby helps keep conflict at a low to moderate level. Under hostile, coercive conditions, however, parents and adolescents will be unlikely to resolve disagreements and conflict will escalate to dysfunctional levels (Rueter and Conger, 1995).

The *socioeconomic status* of the family is another variable affecting conflict. Low-socioeconomic-status families are more often concerned about obedience, politeness, and respect, whereas middle-income families are more concerned with developing independence and initiative. Low-socioeconomic-status families may also worry more about keeping children out of trouble at school; middle-class parents are more concerned about grades and achievement (Hoff, Laursen, and Tardif, 2002). Poverty-class parents are more likely to be authoritarian and to use harsh and inconsistent discipline practices (Leyendecker, Harwood, Comparini, and Yalcinkaya, 2005).

As previously mentioned, *ethnicity* is also correlated with family interaction patterns. For example, since Asian American adolescents are likely to believe that their parents have more of a right to supervise their studying habits and academic progress than other teens, they are less likely to fight over these issues (Lee, Daniels, and Kissinger, 2006).

The *community environment* in which the child grows up will determine what parents worry about. An adolescent growing up in an area where there is high delinquency or considerable drug abuse will find parents more concerned with these problems.

Another factor influencing conflict is *parental workload.* Adolescent conflict is highest when both parents are stressed. This is particularly true in dual-career families, in which both the mother and father may be stressed because of their jobs (Galambos, Sears, Almeida, and Kolaric, 1995). When both parents work outside the home to support the family, there is a reduction of parental attention and monitoring provided to the adolescent. This lack of proper supervision of the adolescent is the major cause of difficulty in some families. Some parents do a good job in parenting their adolescents even though both work; other parents virtually neglect this responsibility almost entirely, and their adolescents are left on their own to fend for themselves.

The variables influencing parent-adolescent conflict are almost countless, but the ones mentioned here indicate how many factors may be involved. Not all parents and adolescents quarrel about the same things or to the same extent.

Conflicts with Parents versus Conflicts with Peers

Adolescents spend more time arguing and fighting with their parents than they do with their peers (Fuhrman and Buhrmester, 1992), and their arguments with their parents are more emotional and heated (Laursen, 1993). Arguments with parents tend to involve clear winners and losers, whereas with friends the resolution is more likely to include a compromise (Adams and Laursen, 2001). These differences likely stem from two sources. First, parents and adolescents have more things to argue about—more divergent expectations—than friends and adolescents. Second, friendships are voluntary alliances that can be terminated whereas family ties are intrinsically more permanent (Collins, Laursen, Mortensen, Luebker, and Ferreira, 1997). In short, you can yell at your mother without worrying that she will abandon you for some other child, but you can't yell at your friend because he or she may likely end the relationship.

Results of Conflict

Again, it is important to emphasize that constant, intense adolescent-parent conflict is abnormal (Smetana, 1996). Research with families of adolescents not under clinical treatment has consistently shown that despite arguments with parents, adolescents characterize their family relationships by closeness, positive feelings, and flexibility. Studies on the frequency and intensity of family conflict, however, including both marital conflict and parent-adolescent conflict, emphasize that high levels of conflict affect family cohesion and have an adverse effect on adolescent development. Adolescents in families with high levels of conflict are more likely to evidence antisocial behavior, immaturity, and low self-esteem than those in families with low levels of conflict (Barber and Delfabbro, 2000).

Parents actually seem to experience more stress from having arguments with their adolescents than the adolescents do. In one study, 40 percent of parents reported experiencing two or more negative effects—decreased self-esteem, increased anxiety, and so on—as a result of conflict with their teenage children (Steinberg and Steinberg, 1994). It is the parents, not the children, who cannot easily stop thinking about these disputes.

RELATIONSHIPS WITH OTHER FAMILY MEMBERS

Parents, of course, are usually not an adolescent's only relatives. Most adolescents have siblings, grandparents, aunts, uncles, and cousins. They may also have stepparents and half- and stepsiblings. (These relationships are discussed in the next chapter.) The influence of siblings and grandparents, in particular, can be quite significant.

Adolescent-Sibling Relationships

Research efforts have concentrated on exploring parent-adolescent relationships in the family, and less information is available, on adolescent-sibling relationships. Yet the relationships between brothers and sisters are vitally important because they may have a lasting influence on development and on the individual's ultimate adult personality and roles. Let's examine the number of ways in which sibling relationships are important.

First, older siblings are likely to serve as role models for younger brothers and sisters. They have a strong influence on the development of younger brothers and sisters. This influence can be good or bad. For example, economically disadvantaged inner-city youths who had close relationships with supportive, well-adjusted, older siblings were less likely to be delinquent and did better in school than similar youths who did not have comparable older siblings (Widmer and Weiss, 2000). Conversely, adolescent girls whose older sisters were teenage mothers were more likely to be sexually active themselves than girls whose older sisters were not mothers as teens (East and Khoo, 2005). Having deviant older siblings may be an even stronger influence on an adolescent's proclivity toward deviancy behavior than having antisocial parents (Ardelt and Day, 2002).

Next, older siblings often serve as surrogate parents and caregivers (Dunn, Slomkowski, and Beardsall, 1994). If older children feel useful, accepted, and admired because of the care they give younger children, this added appreciation and sense of usefulness contributes positively to their own sense of self-worth. Older siblings act as teachers and foster their younger siblings' cognitive development (Azmitia and Hesser, 1993). They also nurture and give advice (Buhrmester and Fuhrman, 1990; Tucker, Barber, and Eccles, 1997). Older brothers and sisters are also often expected to protect younger siblings from the aggression of older children (Tisak and Tisak, 1996). Many adolescents learn adult roles and responsibilities by having to care for younger brothers and sisters while growing up.

Third, older siblings often provide companionship, friendship, and meet one another's needs for affection and meaningful relationships. For example, Seginer (1998) found that adolescents who were not popular with

Adolescents frequently serve as role models and teachers to their younger siblings.

their peers but who had warm, affectionate relationships with siblings were as satisfied with their overall levels of social support as adolescents who were popular. Older brothers and sisters can act as confidants, help one another, and share many experiences. This is particularly true for girls, who are closer to their siblings and report getting more emotional support from them (Moser, Paternite, and Dixon, 1996).

If siblings are six or more years apart in age, they tend to grow up like single children. If there is less than six years' difference, however, they are often a threat to each other's power and command over their parents, rivalry is more pronounced, and conflicts tend to be more severe. One study of 274 high school junior and senior boys and girls explored the sources of conflict among siblings and the conflict resolution strategies that were used (Goodwin and Roscoe, 1990). The 10 most common sources of conflict were something the sibling said, teasing, possessions, duties and chores, name-calling, wearing other's clothing, invasion of privacy, special treatment by parents, embarrassment in front of friends, and conflict over privileges. The primary methods of resolving conflict between siblings involved yelling, arguing, ignoring, compromising, and talking about the conflict. More boys than girls used physical force or the threat of physical force as a means of conflict resolution.

Do relationships with siblings tend to be more frictional during early adolescence than later? Almost all sibling relationships experience some tension and conflict (Lempers and Clark-Lempers, 1992), but this typically lessens as siblings age. As adolescents mature, they accept their siblings in a calmer, more rational manner, with the result that conflicting relationships generally subside and are replaced by friendlier, more cooperative ones (Fuhrman and Buhrmester, 1992).

Relationships with Other Relatives

Relationships with grandparents can also have positive effects on adolescents. Baranowski (1982) discussed three of these:

1. Grandparents may be significant agents in providing a sense of continuity in an adolescent's life, in linking the past to the present, and in transmitting knowledge of culture and family roots, and thus having a positive impact on the adolescent's search for identity (Kopera-Frye and Wiscott, 2000).
2. Grandparents may have a positive impact on parent-adolescent relations by conveying information about the parents to the adolescent. Adolescents also turn to grandparents as confidants and arbiters when they are in conflict with their parents (Lussier, Deater-Deckard, Dunn, and Davies, 2002).
3. Grandparents help adolescents understand aging and accept the aged. Adolescents who see their grandparents frequently and have a good relationship with them are more likely to have positive attitudes toward the elderly (Harwood, Hewstone, Paolini, and Voci, 2005).

Mueller, Wilhelm, and Elder (2002) have identified five different grandparenting styles. The closest grandparents they labeled *influential;* as the term implies, these grandparents are highly involved in their grandchildrens' lives, the majority of them seeing their grandchildren almost daily. They serve as confidants, friends, and mentors, and they tend to provide financial resources to their grandchildren. The next-closest relationship is held by *supportive* grandparents. The largest difference between supportive grandparents and influential grandparents is that supportive grandparents do not play a role in disciplining their grandchildren and do not see themselves as authority figures to them. *Passive* grandparents see their grandchildren less frequently (generally at least once/month) and enjoy them, but they do not materially help them nor do they assume quasi-parental responsibilities for them. *Authority-oriented* grandparents are more distant fonts of family wisdom who have less direct involvement with their grandchildren. Lastly, *detached* grandparents do not know their grandchildren well, and although they may have fond feelings for them, they are largely uninvolved in their lives.

In addition, with increases in both the divorce rate and births to never-married women, it is becoming more common for grandparents to actively help parent or even solely raise their grandchildren. This phenomenon will be discussed more fully in the next chapter.

What determines the nature of the grandparent-grandchild relationship? Physical proximity certainly makes it easier to maintain contact (Uhlenberg and

Grandparents often have positive effects in relationships with their adolescent grandchildren. A grandparent may help in the adolescent's search for identity by linking the past to the present and may serve as an arbiter in conflicts with the adolescent's parents.

Hammill, 1998). The relationship of parent and grandparent is also of key importance, as parents are generally the gatekeepers of grandchild-grandparent contact. Since daughters usually remain closer to their parents than sons, grandchildren often spend more time with their mothers' parents than with their fathers' (Chan and Elder, 2000). Also, relationships with grandparents tend to improve during the course of adolescence (Crosnoe and Elder, 2002), most likely as autonomy issues are resolved and family relations as a whole improve.

Children of all ages, including adolescents, are sometimes the victims of physical abuse, sexual abuse, emotional abuse, and neglect.

MALTREATMENT

Maltreatment of children may include either child abuse or child neglect. **Child abuse** means nonaccidental physical injury and assault, sexual abuse, and/or mental and emotional injury of the child. The child may be physically attacked, burned, hit, beaten, banged against a wall or the floor, or battered, leading to fractures, lacerations, or bruises. **Sexual abuse** includes very suggestive language, use of pornography, fondling, petting, masturbation, exhibitionism, voyeurism, oral sex, or full vaginal or anal intercourse. **Emotional abuse** includes constant screaming at the child, calling him or her foul names, criticizing, making fun, comparing the child with siblings, or ignoring the child. **Child neglect** means failure to provide even minimal care of the child, including adequate food, clothing, shelter, and medical care, as well as failure to provide for a child's emotional, social, intellectual, and moral needs. Thus, maltreatment is a multidimensional concept that includes both attack and neglect.

Physical Abuse

Parents who physically attack and hurt their children have a devastating effect on them both emotionally and physically. Some children die of the abuse; others are permanently maimed. The children are hurt and terrified and are deeply scarred emotionally by the rage and hatred directed against them. Pathological fear, shyness, passive dispositions, deep-seated hostility, sullenness, and a cold, indifferent inability to love others are often the results. Adolescents who are physically abused are more likely to use violence themselves, even as adults. Fagan (2005) found that adolescents who had been physically abused while teenagers were 50 percent more likely to engage in general crime and to use drugs than nonvictims. Even more startlingly, she found a doubling or tripling in the amount of violent crime that physically abused individuals committed against the general public or against intimate partners. Adolescent girls who have been physically abused often continue to find themselves on the receiving end of violence: They choose abusive dating partners and are traumatized in their romantic relationships (Reuterman and Burcky, 1989). They also are more likely than other adolescent girls to engage in risky sexual behavior (Elliott, Avery, Fishman, and Hoshiko, 2002). Finally, adolescents who have been physically abused are more likely to develop clinical depression and to have suicidal thoughts than adolescents without a history of abuse (Danielson et al., 2005).

Sexual Abuse

The effects of sexual abuse on children and adolescents have been well documented. Researchers in the area of child sexual abuse have noted that the constellation of symptoms observed among abuse survivors matches the diagnostic criteria for postraumatic stress disorder (PTSD) (Banyard and Williams, 1996).

Both clinical and community studies have found high levels of depression, anxiety, sexual problems, and suicidal threats and behavior in sexual abuse victims (Paolucci, Genius, and Violato, 2001). In addition, sexual abuse victims appear highly susceptible to substance abuse (Martin et al., 2005), eating disorders (Johnson, Cohen, Kotler, Kasen, and Brook, 2002), and self-abusive behavior (Cyr, McDuff, Wright, Theriault, and Cinq-Mars, 2005).

Sexual abuse also seems to be an important background factor in some patterns of adolescent antisocial behavior. People who are sexually abused—primarily females—have been found to score higher than controls on measures of hostility and aggression and are more likely to become delinquent (Kendall-Tackett, Williams, and Finklehor, 1993). They have also been reported to manifest elevated levels of school problems, including truancy and dropping out before completing high school. In addition, they are more likely than controls to run away from home during adolescence. There is evidence that many prostitutes have been sexual abuse victims, particularly those abused at relatively young ages and with greater violence. Females are more often sexually abused than males, but much sexual abuse of both males and females remains undetected and underreported. Most experts agree that at least 20 percent of all women and between 5 and 10 percent of all men were sexually abused before the age of 18 (Finkelhor, 1994).

Incest

Much of child and adolescent sexual abuse is incestuous; that is, it takes place between persons who are closely related. Although most people assume that father-daughter incest is the most common form, in fact, sister-brother, cousin-cousin, and stepfather-stepdaughter incest are all more common (Canavan, Meyer, and Higgs, 1992). The most prolonged, severe effects occur when the abuser is a father or stepfather, when the abuse involved penetration, and when the abuse was prolonged (Wyatt and Newcomb, 1990). Father-daughter incest usually occurs in families characterized by other problems; often, for example, the father is physically abusive to his spouse or to his children (Alter-Reid, Gibbs, Lachenmeger, Sigal, and Massoth, 1986). The father is usually the dominant member of the household, and he frequently has experienced some setback, such as the loss of his job, prior to the onset of the abuse (Waterman, 1986).

The long-term consequences of incest are similar to those of other forms of sexual abuse. However, due to the intense sense of betrayal that they experience, victims of incest are generally more strongly affected by the experience than victims of nonincestuous sexual abuse (Banyard and Williams, 1996; Rind and Tromovitch, 1997). Common reactions include an inability to trust others; low self-esteem; increased risks for developing depression, eating disorders, and substance abuse; and diffuse physical symptoms such as stomach pain (Holifield, Nelson, and Hart, 2002; Luster and Small, 1997). It is not unusual for incest survivors to find it difficult to trust others, and so they often have trouble forming intimate relationships. It appears that men who were incest victims as boys are even more strongly affected than women who were incest victims as girls (Garnefski and Diekstra, 1997).

Neglect

Neglect is the most common form of maltreatment of children and adolescents. It may take many forms (Doueck, Ishisaka, and Greenaway, 1988). *Physical neglect* may involve failure to provide enough food or a proper diet, adequate clothing, health care, adequate shelter, or sanitary conditions in the home, or to require personal hygiene. *Emotional neglect* may include showing inadequate attention, care, love, and affection, or failing to provide for the child's need for approval, acceptance, and companionship. *Intellectual neglect* may include allowing the child to stay out of school frequently for no reason, failing to see that the child goes to school or does homework, or failing to provide intellectually stimulating experiences and materials. *Social neglect* may include inadequate supervision of social activities, lack of concern about the child's companions and playmates, unwillingness to get the child involved in social groups and activities, or failure to socialize the child to get along with others. *Moral neglect* may include the failure to provide a positive moral example for the child, or any type of moral education and guidance.

The stories of parental neglect are legion. One couple went on vacation for several weeks at a time and left their 12-year-old daughter alone in the house unsupervised. Another mother spent days with her boyfriend, leaving her 15-year-old son to care for himself. One

child abuse may include not only physical assault of a child but also malnourishment, abandonment, neglect, emotional abuse, and sexual abuse.

sexual abuse may include very suggestive language, use of pornography, fondling, petting, masturbation, exhibitionism, voyeurism, oral sex, or full vaginal or anal intercourse.

emotional abuse may include constant screaming at the child, calling him or her foul names, giving constant criticism and put-downs, making fun, constantly comparing the child with siblings, ignoring the child, and refusing to talk or listen to him or her.

child neglect failure to provide even minimal care of a child, including adequate food, clothing, shelter, and medical care, as well as for the child's emotional, social, intellectual, and moral needs.

mother let her daughter's teeth decay until they fell out without making any attempt to get dental care (Rice, counseling notes).

Some cases of neglect are more subtle: The parents reject their children emotionally and fail to show that they love or care for them. Such situations can be just as devastating as actual abuse (Wolock and Horowitz, 1984).

Emotional abuse has been linked to substance abuse (Moran, Vuchinich, and Hall, 2004). Children who have been emotionally abused tend to have low self-esteem, to be depressed, to have difficulties in school, and to have poor peer relations (Sneddon, 2003).

SUMMARY

1. Good parents are emotionally connected to their children, give them opportunities for psychological autonomy, and monitor their behavior.
2. Parents express the love they have for their children by being interested in them, helping them, listening to them, being sensitive to their needs, trusting them, and accepting them for who they are.
3. Adolescents who have a secure attachment to their parents are more successful than adolescents with either an anxious or avoidant attachment.
4. Adolescents want parents who will accept them as autonomous adults and let them establish individuality and independence through the process of separation-individuation. Autonomy consists of two aspects: behavioral autonomy and emotional autonomy. The desire for behavioral autonomy arises during adolescence before the shift to emotional autonomy.
5. *Cohesion* refers to the degree to which family members are connected or separated. Families that are extreme—either completely disengaged or completely enmeshed—function less adequately than do families that are nearer the center of the scale. Family cohesion is greatest when children are young, and declines as adolescents grow up and seek to become autonomous adults.
6. There are four basic patterns of family control: authoritative, authoritarian, permissive, and uninvolved.
7. The authoritative pattern of control has the most positive effect on adolescents.
8. Authoritarian control tends to produce a combination of rebellion and dependency. The effect of punitive measures is usually negative.
9. Adolescents raised by permissive parents are often selfish and irresponsible.
10. Uninvolved parents typically produce adolescent children who feel rejected and insecure.
11. The most functional families are those in which the parents are flexible, adaptable, and tolerant in their ideas and behavior.
12. Parents and adolescents often find themselves in conflict because they are in the midst of very different stages of life. They have different perspectives on the issues they are confronting, which makes misunderstandings inevitable.
13. Overall, parent-adolescent relationships are usually harmonious, but when conflict occurs, it may be in any one of the following five areas: social life and customs, responsibility, school, family relationships, and social conventions.
14. A number of variables affect conflict: age and sex of the adolescent, the atmosphere within the home, the socioeconomic status of the family, ethnicity, the community environment in which the child grows up, and family size, and parental workload.
15. While moderate levels of conflict are normal, high levels are not.
16. Older siblings affect the development of children: They serve as role models and surrogate parents, provide companionship, and meet one another's needs for affection and meaningful relationships.
17. Siblings also are sometimes jealous, compete for parental affection, and have conflict with one another.
18. Relationships with grandparents can have a positive effect on adolescents. Grandparents can be influential, supportive, passive, authority oriented, or detached.
19. *Child abuse* includes nonaccidental physical injury and assault, sexual abuse, and/or mental and emotional injury of the child. *Sexual abuse* may include suggestive language, pornography, fondling, petting, masturbation, exhibitionism, voyeurism, oral sex, or vaginal or anal intercourse. *Emotional abuse* may include screaming at the child, calling names, criticism and put-downs, making fun, unfavorable comparisons of the child, and refusal to talk or to listen. *Child neglect* means failure to provide even minimal care of the child; failure to provide adequate food, clothing, shelter, and medical care; and failure to provide for the child's emotional, social, intellectual, and moral needs.
20. Adolescents who have been abused are more likely to be depressed, anxious, and violent than other teenagers. They are more likely to use drugs and to develop eating disorders. Without treatment, many of these problems carry on into adulthood.

KEY TERMS

affect 226
anxious attachments 228
attachment style 228
authoritarian parents 230
authoritative parents 230
autonomy 229
avoidant attachments 228
behavioral autonomy 229
child abuse 240
child neglect 240
cohesion 229
connection 224

control 230	positive affect 226
disengaged families 229	psychological autonomy 224
emotional abuse 240	regulation 224
emotional autonomy 229	secure attachments 228
empathy 225	separation-individuation 228
enmeshed families 229	sexual abuse 240
induction 232	uninvolved parents 231
negative affect 226	warmth 230
permissive parents 230	

THOUGHT QUESTIONS

Personal Reflection

1. Were your parents authoritative, authoritarian, permissive, or uninvolved? Why do you characterize them that way? Provide examples to support your answer.
2. Do you want to be the same kind of parent that your mother was? That your father was? What do you think you will do differently than they did? Why?
3. How did your parents express their warmth and concern for you? Which means of expression meant the most to you? Why?
4. When you were an adolescent, what sort of discipline did your parents use on you? Was it effective? Why or why not?
5. Did you find it easier to talk to your mother or your father? Were there some topics you discussed more with one than with the other?

Group Discussion

6. What issues did you and your parents most frequently argue about? Did the same issues come up over and over again, or were they constantly changing?
7. What keeps parents from listening to adolescents and understanding them?
8. What sorts of home responsibilities or family chores should be expected of adolescents? Should they be paid for doing these chores? Why or why not?
9. If you have an adolescent brother or sister living at home, what are the major sources of conflict between him or her and your parents?
10. Do you know any adult who was abused as a child? What have been some of the effects?
11. What do you think is the ideal role for grandparents to play within the family?

Debate Questions

12. Parents should unquestioningly act as if they trust their adolescent children unless they have been given clear reason to do otherwise.
13. Teenagers should always obey their parents.
14. Parents should give their adolescent children advice, whether or not their children want to hear it.
15. Siblings should be required to "be friends" and spend a lot of time together.

SUGGESTED READING

Barber, B. K. (Ed.). (2002). *Intrusive Parenting: How Psychological Control Affects Children and Adolescents.* Washington, DC: American Psychological Association.

Crosson-Tower, C. (2001). *Understanding Child Abuse and Neglect* (5th ed.). Boston, MA: Allyn & Bacon.

Ferrara, F. F. (2001). *Childhood Sexual Abuse: Developmental Effects across the Lifespan.* Pacific Grove, CA: Brooks-Cole.

Fontenelle, D. H. (2000). *Keys to Parenting Your Teenager.* Hauppauge, NY: Barrons.

Glasser, W. (2003). *For Parents and Teenagers: Dissolving the Barrier between You and Your Teen.* Chatsworth, CA: Quill.

Lipinski, B. (2001). *Heed the Call: Psychological Perspectives on Child Abuse.* Seattle: Pacific Meridian.

USEFUL WEB SITES

Child Abuse Prevention Network
http://child-abuse.com/

This site is primarily designed to help professionals in the field of child abuse. However, it contains a listing of useful e-lists and support groups for laypersons with an interest in this topic.

Child Welfare Information Gateway
www.childwelfare.gov

This site, created and maintained by the U.S. Department of Health and Human Services, was designed to be useful to parents as well as educators and other professionals. It is full of current information about child abuse; namely, it provides information about individual state statutes, the steps to take if you suspect child abuse or neglect, information about how to seek help, national statistics of abuse, a database, and links to other sites. It also provides information about adoption.

Ohio State University Family and Consumer Sciences Extension Service
www.hec.ohio-state.edu/famlife/adolescence/parads.htm

The Department of Family and Consumer Sciences at The Ohio State University provides this site, which contains a series of articles written to help parents learn to better interact with their teenage children. Topics include Communicating with Your Teen, Monitoring: Staying Involved in Your Teen's Life, and Understanding Teens.

CHAPTER 11 DIVORCED, PARENT-ABSENT, AND BLENDED FAMILIES

WOULDN'T YOU LIKE TO KNOW . . .

- How many adolescents have divorced parents?
- What are the short-term effects of divorce on adolescents and how long do these effects last?
- Are children from divorced families more likely to have long-term behavioral problems than children from intact families?
- Are children whose parents got divorced more likely to get divorced themselves someday?
- In terms of the children's well-being, should unhappy parents stay together or get divorced?
- What is better for adolescents: If their parents have joint custody or if one parent has sole custody?
- How well do children fare when they are raised by never-married mothers?
- Do adolescents benefit when their mothers get remarried?
- How well do adolescents in blended families get along with their stepsiblings?

Fewer and fewer American adolescents have the experience of living in the same home as both of their biological parents for the duration of their childhood. In fact, it is no longer the norm to be raised in a single house by both one's biological mother and biological father, and it is even more atypical to be raised in what has historically been known as a traditional family, in which one's biological father goes off to work while one's biological mother stays home and minds the kids. Because so many adolescents have undergone their parents' divorce, are being raised by single parents, or are part of a blended, reconstituted family, it is worthwhile to consider the impact of these events on adolescent development. In this chapter, we will examine each of these family constellations.

WITH WHOM DO AMERICAN ADOLESCENTS LIVE?

As Figure 11.1 illustrates, almost all American adolescents (96 percent) below the age of 19 reside with at least one of their biological parents, and about two-thirds (68 percent) live with both of their biological parents (U.S. Census Bureau, 2005a). Some 23 percent live with only their biological mothers, and just 4.5

FIGURE 11.1 ADOLESCENT RESIDENTIAL PATTERNS BY RACE AND ETHNICITY

Source: Data from U.S. Bureau of the Census (2005a).

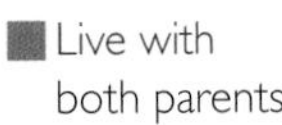

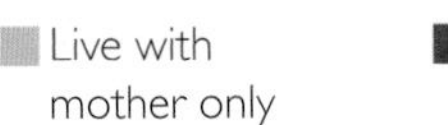

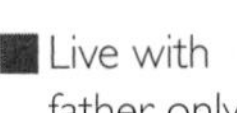

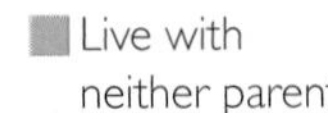

All Adolescents

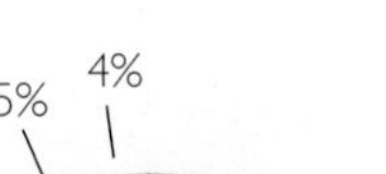

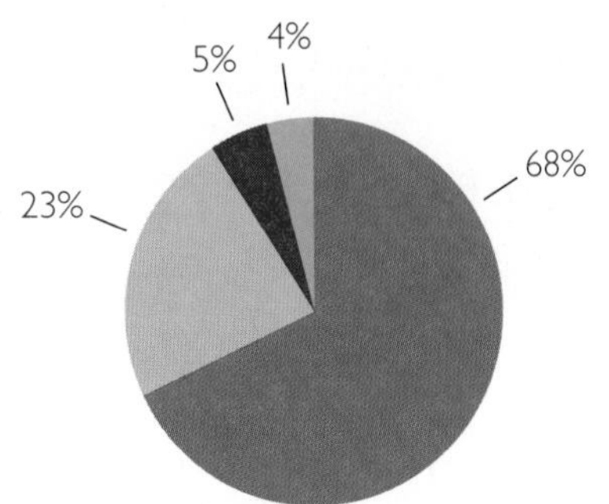

African American Adolescents

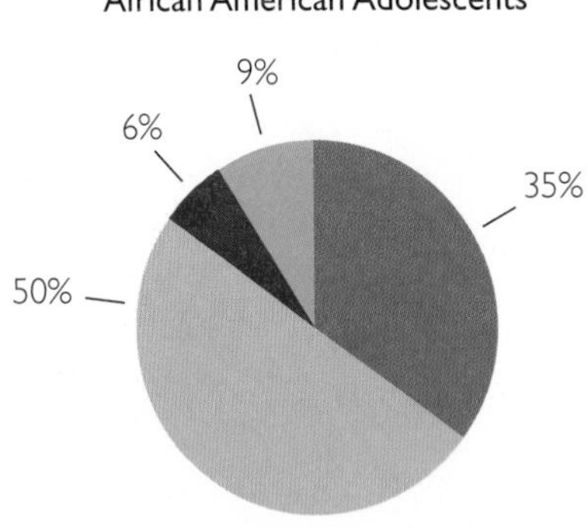

Asian American Adolescents

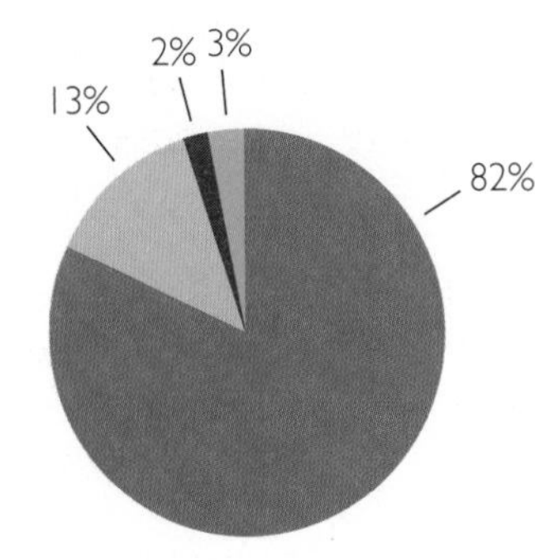

Hispanic American Adolescents

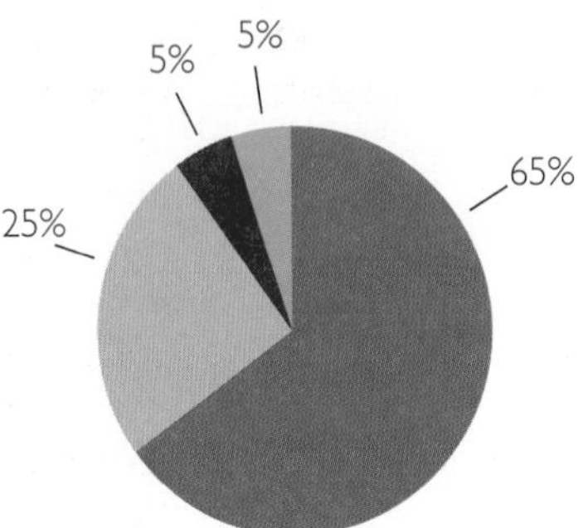

White, Non-Hispanic American Adolescents

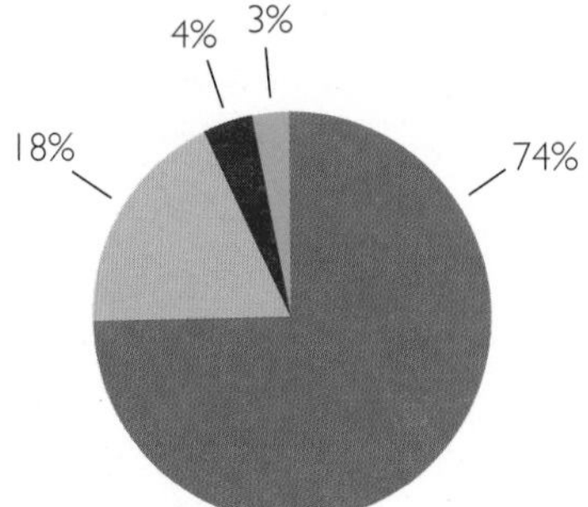

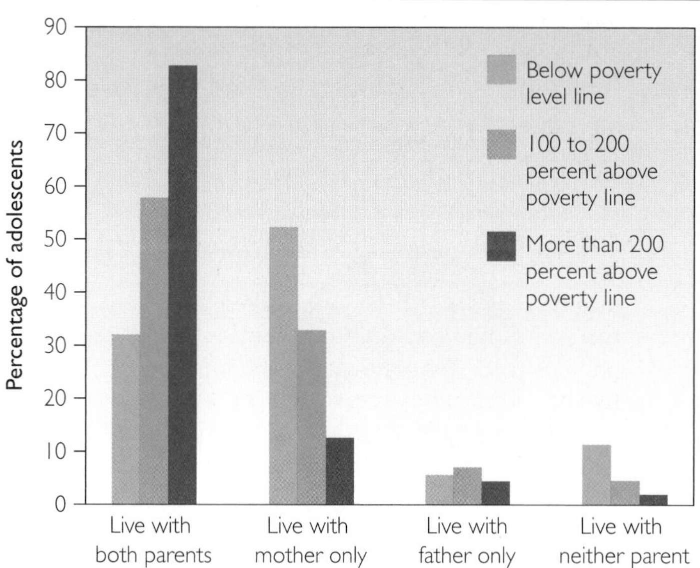

FIGURE 11.2 ADOLESCENT RESIDENCE AS A FUNCTION OF FAMILY INCOME LEVEL

Source: Data from U.S. Bureau of the Census (2002).

percent live with only their biological fathers. Residential patterns vary considerably by race and ethnicity. Asian American and non-Hispanic Caucasian teens, for example, are more likely than average to live with both parents, whereas half of all African American adolescents live apart from their biological fathers.

These racial/ethnic differences are, in part, a result of the economic disparity between cultural subgroups. As shown in Figure 11.2, middle-class adolescents are far more likely to live with both biological parents than those from lower socioeconomic levels. Conversely, lower-income youths are far more likely to live with only their mothers or with neither parent than middle-income youths (U.S. Census Bureau, 2002).

There are four possible reasons that an adolescent might live with only one of his or her biological parents. First, the parents might be married but living apart due to certain circumstances, such as one parent working in another city or state. Second, a parent may have died. Third, the parents might be divorced or legally separated. Finally, the child might have been born to a single mother who has never been wed to the child's father. As Figure 11.3 depicts, the latter two reasons are by far more common than the first two (U.S. Census Bureau, 2002). Again, there is significant racial/ethnic variation in the reasons for living with one parent. Divorce is the most common reason in Asian American and non-Hispanic Caucasian homes, whereas out-of-wedlock birth is the most common reason in Hispanic and African American homes. And as noted earlier, family income level correlates with the reason for parental absence: The higher the income level, the more likely the parents were divorced as opposed to never wed (see Figure 11.4).

DIVORCE AND ADOLESCENTS

As divorce becomes more common, the question arises as to how it affects adolescents. A range of factors are involved.

Attitudes toward Divorce

Data indicate that nearly half of all American marriages end in divorce (National Marriage Project, 2005). The great majority of these marriages involve children, some of whom are already adolescents and some of whom have yet to grow into adolescents.

A large number of mental health practitioners view divorce as a major, negative event that stimulates insecurity, confusion, and painful emotions.While the majority of these practitioners feel that most children are not permanently harmed by divorce, others insist that the upset interferes with long-term emotional and social growth (Wallerstein and Lewis, 2004).

Short-Term Emotional Reactions

Immediate emotional reactions to parents divorcing have been well documented (Kelly, 2003). One is shock and disbelief if adolescents have not realized the extent of the marital problem. One female college student remarked, "My mother called me the other day to tell me she and daddy are getting divorced. I can't believe it. I didn't even know they were having problems" (Rice, counseling notes). Another reaction is fear, anxiety, and insecurity about the future: "Will my father move away? Will I get to see him?" "Will I have to

FIGURE 11.3 REASONS ADOLESCENTS LIVE WITH ONE BIOLOGICAL PARENT BY RACE AND ETHNICITY

Source: Data from U.S. Bureau of the Census (2002).

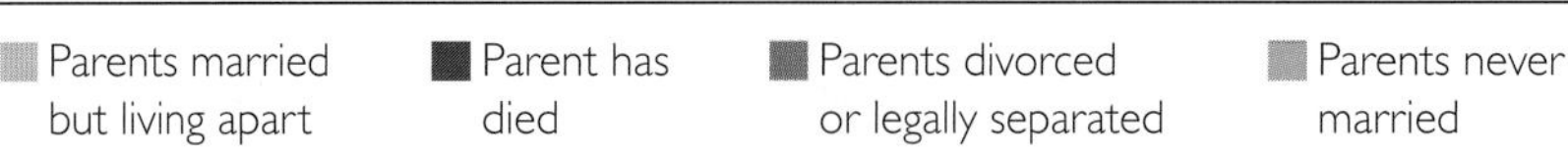

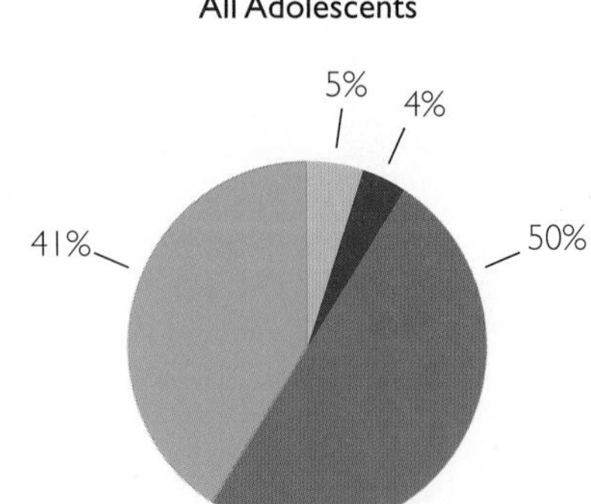

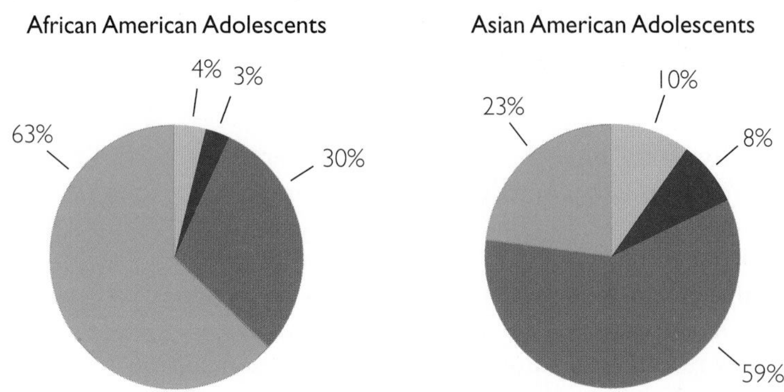

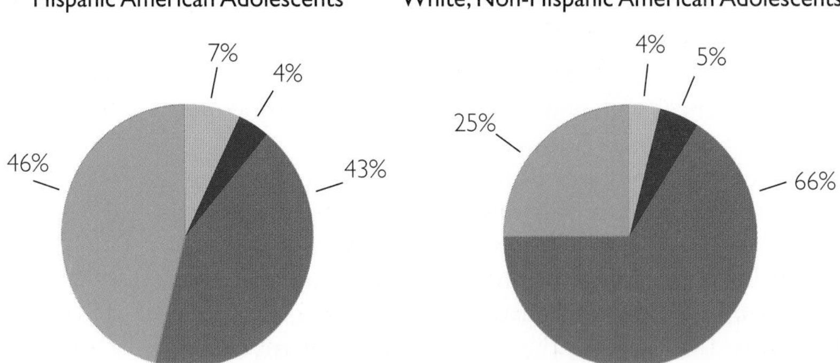

go to another school?" "Who am I going to live with?" "How am I going to be able to go to college?"

Anger and hostility are also common emotional reactions among adolescents, especially toward the parent they blame for the divorce. One girl asked her mother, "Why did you make daddy leave?" Another, age 12, asked, "Why did you leave my father all alone?" A son told his father, "I hate you for leaving mom for that other woman" (Rice, counseling notes). Sometimes the anger is directed toward both parents: "You've ruined my whole life. I have to leave all my friends and my school." Some youths are so caught up in their own pain that they forget (at least temporarily) the distress that their parents are feeling.

Another common feeling among adolescents is one of self-blame and guilt. If parental conflict has been about the children, they may feel partly responsible for their parents breaking up or that the parent is leaving because he or she wants to get away from the children. They may also feel self-conscious and bewildered that their parents are getting divorced, and they try to hide that fact from their friends.

After separation occurs, adolescents have to adjust to the absence of one parent, often one on whom they

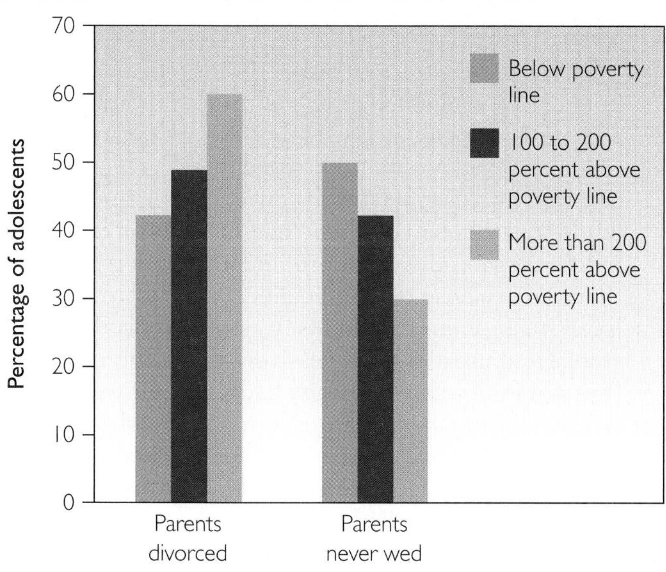

FIGURE 11.4 REASONS ADOLESCENTS LIVE WITH ONE BIOLOGICAL PARENT BY FAMILY INCOME LEVEL

Source: Data from U.S. Bureau of the Census (2002).

ANSWERS WOULDN'T YOU LIKE TO KNOW ...

What are the short-term effects of divorce on adolescents, and how long do these effects last?

Most adolescents whose parents divorce experience a range of emotions—among them fear, anger, depression, guilt, and resentment—and are, at times, entirely overwhelmed by the experience. (A minority of youths, however, feel relieved and happy.) It is not uncommon for youths to lose interest in school and other activities during this time of upheaval. It usually takes one to two years for adolescents to adjust to their parents' divorce.

ANSWERS WOULDN'T YOU LIKE TO KNOW ...

How many adolescents have divorced parents?

Roughly one out of six adolescents has experienced his or her parents' divorce. Interestingly, almost as many have mothers who have never been married.

have depended deeply for affection and help. One adolescent girl remarked, "The hardest thing for me was to get used to being without my father. I never realized how much I needed him until he left" (Rice, counseling notes). Divorce is often followed by a period of mourning and grief, not unlike the feeling arising when one loses a parent by death. Feelings of sadness, dejection, and depression are common.

If parents begin to date again and get emotionally involved with another person, adolescents may become jealous and resentful because they have to share their parent with another adult. If parents remarry, as the majority do, the adolescents are confronted with a new adjustment to a stepparent.

Burns and Dunlop (1999) found that these negative emotions, which were almost universal near the time of divorce, do not last. Three years after their parents divorced, most of the adolescents studied reported that their sadness and shock had greatly diminished; these feelings were replaced with those of relief and gladness that the conflict was over. Ten years after the divorce, gladness and relief dominated the teens' emotions, although many still retained anger toward one of their parents (usually their father).

Long-Term Effects

Many people believe that children whose parents divorce can be scarred for life by the experience. This common conviction was reinforced by Judith Wallerstein's best-seller *Second Chances: Men, Women, and Children a Decade after Divorce* (Wallerstein and Blakeslee, 1989), based on a 15-year follow-up to a landmark clinical investigation. Wallerstein found that almost half of the children in her California study were, on reaching young adulthood, "worried, underachieving, self-deprecating, and sometimes angry young men and women. Many were involved in maladaptive pathways, including multiple relationships and impulsive marriages that ended in divorce" (Wallerstein, 1991, p. 354). There were among these young adults some who had seemed calm and untroubled at earlier ages. This led Wallerstein to remark that the long-term effects of divorce on children cannot be predicted from how the children react earlier in life.

ANSWERS WOULDN'T YOU LIKE TO KNOW ...

Are children from divorced families more likely to have long-term behavioral problems than children from intact families?

In short, yes: Children from divorced families are more likely to exhibit long-term behavioral difficulties than children from intact families. Nonetheless, 75 to 80 percent do not experience significant problems.

These rather pessimistic conclusions were challenged because other studies produced different results. Critics noted the limitations of the California study, such as its small size, the lack of a nondivorced control group, and the fact that the sample was not selected on a probability basis and was overrepresented by families that sought clinical help (Cherlin and Furstenberg, 1989).

Given the continued high rate of marital disruption and continuing controversy over what impact it has on children (Gill, 1992), scholars called for better evidence to test Wallerstein's and others' hypotheses about the long-term effects of parental divorce. In the intervening 15 to 20 years, much more research on this topic has been conducted—most of it confirming and extending Wallerstein's and Blakeslee's findings: Children and adolescents whose parents divorce are at heightened risk for a variety of problem behaviors, when they are minors and when they are adults.

Although the differences are not always large, as a whole, children of divorced parents do worse in school, are more likely to engage in delinquency, get along less well with their peers, engage in more precocious sexual activity, and are more likely to use drugs (Hines, 1997; McLanahan and Sandefur, 1994). A recent meta-analysis of divorce-outcome studies published in the 1990s found that, compared to children with continuously married parents, children with divorced parents scored significantly lower on measures of academic achievement, acceptable conduct, psychological adjustment, self-concept, and social relations (Amato, 2001). These negative outcomes are likely regardless of the child's age at the time of the divorce (Wallerstein and Lewis, 1998). Many studies have concluded that boys' behavior is more affected than girls'.

Furthermore, the influence of having experienced one's parents' divorce extends into adulthood. Compared to adults raised in intact families, adults whose parents divorced when they were children are less likely to attend college and more likely to cohabitate without marriage, to have children at an early age, and to suffer from poor mental health. These differences are not all merely continuations of the problems that emerge during adolescence. In fact, the gap between individuals raised in intact families and those raised by divorced parents increases during adulthood (Cherlin, Chase-Lansdale, and McRae, 1998).

This pattern is not confined to the United States, but has been validated cross-culturally. For example, in a large European study, Huurre, Junkkari, and Aro (2006) tracked nearly 1,500 individuals as they moved through adolescence into their early thirties. Adults whose parents had divorced had been less likely to attend college and were more likely to be unemployed than those whose parents had not. They were also less likely to be married themselves and more likely to smoke and use alcohol excessively. In addition, women (but not men) whose parents had divorced were more likely to suffer from depression and psychosomatic symptoms than women from intact families. These effects held even when socioeconomic status and other factors were controlled.

One specific aspect of Wallerstein and Blakeslee's (1989) findings that has been confirmed by other researchers is the long-term effect of parental divorce on children's future marital relationships. In 2001, Amato and DeBoer reported the results of a large, longitudinal study of adults that found that those who were the children of divorced parents were at twice the risk of getting divorced themselves, compared to those who were raised in intact families. The adults raised by parents who had low levels of marital satisfaction but did not divorce were not at such risk. Interestingly, the risk of divorce was most elevated if one's parents showed only a low level of discord prior to their divorce.

Relationships with siblings, too, seem to suffer. Another study (Riggio, 2001) found that there were long-term disruptions in sibling relationships among individuals whose parents had divorced when they were adolescents.

Researchers have been trying to sort out causes for this phenomenon (Glenn and Kramer, 1987). One explanation is offered by social learning theory. Children tend to model their behavior after that of their parents. Thus, children may imitate parental behavior that is detrimental to successful marriage and prone to divorce.

Two other explanations have been offered, as well. One is that when children of divorce marry, they are highly apprehensive about it and have a lower commitment to their marriages, so are more likely to fail than offspring from intact families. They tend to be hesitant and cautious about marriage, often saying they will not marry. However, they are just as likely to marry as are other people. They are strongly impelled toward marriage, but often hedge their bets against failure by withholding full commitment to marriage.

Another explanation is that they marry at an earlier age than children from intact families. This may be because of emotional need or the desire to escape an unpleasant home situation. Marriage at early ages has been

> **ANSWERS WOULDN'T YOU LIKE TO KNOW . . .**
>
> **Are children whose parents get divorced more likely to get divorced themselves someday?**
>
> Again, yes: Children whose parents get divorced are more likely to divorce themselves someday.

found to be significantly related to marital failure (Booth and Edwards, 1985).

It is important to underscore that most adolescents whose parents divorce have no long-term adjustment problems. Divorce is a risk factor; it increases the odds that problems will develop but does not guarantee that they will (Amato, 2000). In general, children whose parents have divorced are two to three times as likely to develop problems as children from intact families (Kelly, 2003), so that whereas approximately 10 percent of children from never-divorced families have serious adjustment problems, approximately 20 to 25 percent of children whose parents have divorced do (Hetherington and Kelly, 2002).

Moreover, the alternative to divorce—that is, for the parents to remain in a conflict-ridden, unhappy marriage—is no better for children's development. Several studies (e.g., Morrison and Coiro, 1999) have shown that children whose parents have divorced are better off than those raised in intact but discordant households. Furthermore, children brought up in intact homes fraught with conflict are no more likely to experience stable marriages themselves than those whose parents chose to divorce (Amato and Booth, 2001).

Factors Influencing the Effects of Divorce

Many factors contribute to the lower well-being of adolescents who have experienced parental divorce. First, there is the trauma and conflict leading up to the divorce. Since adults who are happily married and content with their lives do not divorce, children whose parents divorce have witnessed parental battles and experienced significant tension within the home. Next is the trauma of the divorce itself. Even in the most harmonious of circumstances, divorce brings pain and uncertainty. Children ask themselves questions such as: Where will we live? Will Dad still love me? and Who will I stay with? Finally, there are the long-term lifestyle changes that result from divorce. Children will likely spend far less time with one of their parents, or they will move back and forth between two households. Moreover, the family's financial situation usually deteriorates following divorce, and the family may move to a new home in a new neighborhood. The parents' behavior toward their children likely changes, as well. (Each of these issues will be discussed in more detail later in this section.)

> **ANSWERS WOULDN'T YOU LIKE TO KNOW . . .**
>
> **In terms of the children's well-being, should unhappy parents stay together or get divorced?**
>
> The most important factor in determining the children's well-being is the amount of discord that they experience at home. If the parents' getting divorced will diminish the conflict in the home, then that is preferable to subjecting the children to an ongoing hostile family situation. But if getting divorced does not relieve or increases the parents' acrimony, then it is not the better solution.

Many but not all of these issues revolve around *conflict.* Multiple forms of family conflict—including frequent disagreements with parents, marital conflict, parental aggression, and conflict between nonresidential fathers and mothers—consistently and adversely affected adolescent outcome. For many adolescents in divorced families and stepfamilies, conflict had been a routine part of their lives. Many adolescents suffered lingering effects from sustained predivorce marital discord and accompanying family process, including inconsistent parenting, interspousal aggression, parent-child aggression, and deteriorating parent-child relationships. These problems are compounded by persistent postdivorce tensions and hostilities between parents as adolescents are drawn into conflicts, feel caught between parents, and are either pressured to take sides or to try to remain close to both parents and subsequently experiencing loyalty conflicts. In other words, the data corroborate mounting evidence that family conflicts—manifested in diverse ways, and persisting over stages of the life course—impair adolescent well-being (Demo and Acock, 1996).

Heredity and Temperamental Differences

There are variations in how adaptable individuals are to change—namely, in the quality of their coping skills, their level of self-esteem, and their willingness to go to others for help. These personality attributes may well affect how a given child will adjust to his or her parents' divorce (Hetherington and Stanley-Hagan, 1999). Some children are simply more resilient than others. There is substantial evidence that personality traits such as these are, in part, genetic and that they do contribute to psychological well-being and adjustment. Kendler, Walters, Neale, Kesslar, Heath, and Eaves (1995), for example, report that genetic differences influence one's tendency to respond to stress with depression.

Predivorce Economic Circumstances

As a whole, families that are headed for divorce are qualitatively different from families that are destined to remain intact. In particular, individuals who have a low level of education, earn less money, and marry at a young age (characteristics that frequently occur together) are more likely to divorce than those who do not fit this profile (Pryor and Rogers, 2001). Furthermore, declining economic circumstances (or becoming more poor regardless of one's starting point) also increase the probability of divorce (O'Connor, Pickering, Dunn, and Golding, 1999). This means that children whose parents have divorced are more likely to have experienced poverty or a decline in their standard of living than children whose families are stable. Moreover, the stressful circumstances that were experienced prior to the divorce will likely contribute to any negative outcomes seen after the divorce.

Predivorce Parental Behavior

In addition to parental conflict, as mentioned earlier, additional aspects of parents' predivorce behavior are detrimental to the children living in the household. For example, even prior to a divorce, mothers whose marriages will end behave more negatively toward their children than mothers whose marriages will succeed, and neither mothers nor fathers in marriages destined to dissolve exercise as much control over their children as those whose marriages will continue (Hetherington, 1999a). In addition, adults are generally physically and psychologically distressed for a period of time leading up to a divorce, and being under stress clearly decreases the quality of parenting. Alcohol or substance abuse on the part of one spouse may also be involved, as it is frequently cited as a reason for divorce (Ostermann, Sloan, and Taylor, 2005). It follows that children whose parents have divorced are more likely to have been raised by a substance-abusing parent than children whose parents have remained married. Again, the fact that these stressors were present in a household prior to a divorce can explain the origin of any problems displayed by a child after the fact.

Postdivorce Economic Resources

In most cases, children's economic status worsens after their parents' divorce. Most children live full or part time with their mothers after their parents have separated, and women's standard of living declines by an average of 27 percent postdivorce (Peterson, 1996). This drop in income frequently means that children lose not only the security of their family as they have known it but also the lifestyle to which they have

RESEARCH HIGHLIGHT ADOLESCENT CHILDREN RAISED BY GAY AND LESBIAN PARENTS

Many people assume that adolescent children raised by gay and lesbian parents will more likely have problems than children raised by heterosexuals, including (1) an abnormal sexual identity, (2) adjustment and personality problems, (3) impaired relationships, and (4) increased likelihood of being sexually abused (American Psychological Association, 1995). Are these concerns legitimate? Let's examine each in turn:

1. *Abnormal sexual identity: Sexual identity* is a broad term that encompasses gender identity (positive feelings about being male or female), sex-typed behavior (doing and enjoying so-called masculine activities if male and feminine activities if female), and sexual orientation (one's sexual preference in a partner). Contrary to popular belief, there is *no* evidence that children raised by homosexuals are more likely to develop an abnormal sexual identity—in any sense of the term—than children raised by heterosexuals. Most children raised by gay parents are themselves heterosexual (Bailey, Bobrow, Wolfe, and Mikach, 1995; Patterson, 1994).
2. *Adjustment problems:* Researchers have compared the personalities, autonomy, behavioral problems, depression rates, moral development, and intelligence of children raised by gay versus straight parents. *No* meaningful differences have been found (American Psychological Association, 1995; Fitzgerald, 1999).
3. *Social relationships:* Although many children of gay parents are undoubtedly teased and harassed about their parents' sexual orientation, overall, the peer relationships of these youths are fine (Green, Mandel, Hotvedt, Gray, and Smith, 1986). Just as having heterosexual parents doesn't shield children from teasing, having homosexual parents doesn't guarantee it.
4. *Sexual abuse:* There is no reason to believe that children of gay parents are more likely to be sexually abused than other children. The notion that gay men are more likely to be child molesters than straight men is an erroneous assumption. It is simply untrue (Jenny, Roesler, and Poyer, 1994).

In sum, children raised by gays and lesbians do not behave any differently than children raised by heterosexuals. And while there has been very little long-term research in this area, it appears that these children remain as normal and well adjusted as other children into adulthood (Tasker and Golombok, 1995).

become accustomed. It is not unusual, for instance, for children to move to a smaller home after a divorce, often in a different neighborhood or school district. They may also have to give up music lessons or need to take a job to help with expenses.

Postdivorce Parental Behavior

The effect of divorce on adolescents depends partly on how their parents are affected. The psychological adjustment of parents, especially of the custodial parents, greatly influences the adjustment of their adolescents (Hetherington, 1999a). The more upset the parents are, the more likely adolescents will be disturbed. Some parents are very relieved by the divorce and this has a positive effect on adolescents.

Divorce is a very difficult experience for couples, even under the best circumstances. Under the worst circumstances, it results in emotional trauma and a high degree of shock and disorientation. The newly divorced face loneliness and social readjustment as they seek new friendships and companionship (Pinquart, 2003). The divorced woman with children is faced with role strain and an overload of work, now that she must perform all family functions herself (Bird and Harris, 1990). Contacts with an ex-spouse may continue to be troublesome. Positive support from one's own parents is helpful, and grandparents can have an important effect on the adolescent's adjustments, as well. Because the adjustment of parents after divorce affects the adjustment of adolescents, parents need to get help if they can't make a happy transition themselves (Guidubaldi and Perry, 1985).

It is generally agreed that after a divorce, the quality of parenting goes down. For example, right after the divorce, parents may become less affectionate and more autocratic with their children; they may be inconsistent in their demands and enforcement of rules (Hetherington, 1991). In the long run, divorced custodial mothers tend to engage in less monitoring of their children's behavior and use less effective discipline strategies (Simons, Lin, Gordon, Conger, and Lorenz, 1999).

Some parents feel guilty about the divorce and want to make it up to their children (Raphael, Cubis, Dunne, Lewin, and Kelly, 1990). If this desire leads to a parent's spoiling his or her child, the intent may be good but the outcome will not. Adolescents may enjoy being spoiled at the time, but being plied with expensive gifts, being allowed to stay out until 3:00 A.M., and being excused from chores do not help teenagers become mature, responsible adults. Often, it is the noncustodial parent who tries to make the most of the limited time he or she has with the child and, in effect, buy the child's affection.

Any understanding of the effects of divorce on adolescents must take into account the parents' changed position following a divorce. If a parent is quite upset, if her income is severely reduced, if she must often leave her adolescents alone while she goes to work outside the home, the children are going to be affected, not because of the divorce, as such, but because of the subsequent effect on that parent and her changed relationship with her children.

Amicability of the Divorce

As stated earlier, children benefit from their parents' divorce if it removes them from a conflict-ridden situation (Hetherington, 1999a; Morrison and Coiro, 1999). Unfortunately, the conflict between parents does not always cease once their divorce has been finalized. The stress often continues and the children may feel caught in the middle. Adolescents are particularly upset over the fighting if their parents are trying to get them to take sides or exploit them as spies, go-betweens, and informers in winning over the other parent. In most cases, adolescents love both of their parents and do not want to have to choose sides.

Although custody arrangements will be discussed in the next section, it is worth mentioning here that, *post* divorce, most adolescents do not see one of their parents—usually their fathers—nearly as often as they formerly did. In addition, they are less likely to spend as much time with members of the noncustodial parent's extended family: If you only see your father six days a month, then you most likely see your paternal grandparents and your cousins from his side of the family less as well. In addition, many children and adolescents lose contact with their friends due to the fact that their custodial parent physically relocates them (moves). In one recent study (Braver, Ellman, and Fabricius, 2003), approximately 30 percent of the respondents said they moved more than an hour's drive away from their former home with their custodial parent, and there were numerous negative outcomes associated with those moves. Relatedly, Hetherington and Kelly (2002) reported that the custodial mothers in their study moved an average of four times in the six years following their divorce. Even if some of those moves are within the same relatively small geographic area, the likelihood of a child's having to change schools, thereby losing contact with friends and teachers, is great.

Custody and Living Arrangements

Some of the most difficult decisions made during a divorce are those concerning child custody. Custody is comprised of two separate issues: **Legal custody** refers to the right of a parent to make decisions affecting a child, and **residential custody** refers to where and

legal custody the parent has the right to make important decisions about the child's life, such as which school he or she will attend.

residential custody where and with which parent the child will live.

Until recently, the mother automatically was granted custody of the children, unless there were concerns about her competency. Today, the father's chances of custody are enhanced. Rallies such as the one shown have helped change this pattern.

with which parent the child will live. Emotional attachments, fairness, and economic consequences for children and parents are among the issues involved in arriving at a custody disposition.

Until the 1980s, in the majority of the cases, it was assumed that the mother would receive both legal and residential custody, unless there were circumstances that would keep her from being a competent parent. Today, the odds of father custody are enhanced when children are older, especially when the oldest child is male, when the father is the plaintiff, and when a court investigation has occurred during divorce proceedings. Odds of the father getting custody are reduced by higher educational levels of mothers, higher incomes for mothers, and support delinquency prior to final divorce judgments. It is not surprising that substantial policy debates concerning legal and custody arrangements at divorce are common (Fox and Kelly, 1995).

The greatest fear of adolescents who have good relationships with both parents is that divorce will result in their losing contact with a parent. This is not an unreasonable fear: Between 18 and 25 percent of children lose all contact with their fathers within two to three years after the divorce occurs (Kelly, 2003). This is clearly not beneficial. The data are quite compelling that adolescents who remain in close contact with their noncustodial fathers, especially when those fathers are authoritative, involved in their schoolwork, and support them financially, do better scholastically and have fewer behavioral problems than adolescents whose fathers do not (Amato and Gilbreth, 1999; Menning, 2002). For this reason, parents need to make it clear that they are not divorcing their children and that they will continue to be active, concerned, and caring parents. Of course, if a parent is poorly adjusted, extremely immature, or abusive in any way, tight restrictions on child visitation may be necessary (Warshak, 1986). Under the best circumstances, disturbance is minimized if the adolescent can see a parent any time he or she needs or wants to.

Divorce often results in reduced attachment to the noncustodial parent. In general, adolescents from intact families view themselves as more positively emotional attached to their fathers than do those from divorced and remarried families. Thus, divorce may have an impact on the emotional bonds adolescents have with their fathers, and remarriage does not seem to mediate this impact (McCurdy and Scherman, 1996).

In many instances, **joint custody** is awarded to the parents. *Joint legal custody* means both parents are responsible for caring for the adolescent and making decisions concerning his or her welfare. This is now the most common outcome of divorce proceedings (Hardcastle, 1998). *Joint residential custody* means that a child alternates between living with each parent. Research has shown that in cases of joint custody, fathers are more likely to be active in parenting than are noncustodial fathers and that children are often, as a result, better adjusted (Bauserman, 2002).

ANSWERS WOULDN'T YOU LIKE TO KNOW ...

What is better for adolescents: If their parents have joint custody or if one parent has sole custody?

The main benefit of joint residential custody is that the children get to remain in close contact with both parents. This benefit is negated, however, if the children find themselves caught between parents who do not get along. Neither joint custody nor single-parent custody is uniformly better for adolescents.

Such arrangements require a high degree of maturity and flexibility on the part of the parent, or discussions will result in squabbles and a continuation of the marital stress. If desired by both parents, and if they are able to get along together, there is general agreement that joint custody is a helpful solution to a difficult problem (Kolata, 1988).

Which type of arrangement is best? There is no clear-cut answer to this question. For most of twentieth century, it was assumed that mothers made better parents than fathers, and so almost all custody decisions were made in the mother's favor. Then, in the last 30 years, a number of studies showed that same-sex pairings worked best—that is, that daughters were better off if raised by mothers and sons were better off if raised by fathers (Camara and Resnick, 1988). Many other studies, however, did not find this effect (Guttman and Lazar, 1998). The research comparing adolescents in joint custody with those in single-parent custody have had mixed results: Some have shown little overall difference in outcomes as a function of type of custody (Hines, 1997) while others have shown benefits (Bauserman, 2002). What matters more is the quality of the relationship of the child with each parent and the quality of the relationship of the parents with each other after the divorce. The benefits of joint custody are largely negated if the situation is strained and the parents argue and fight (Lee, 2002).

Maccoby and colleagues (1993) studied the post-divorce roles of mothers and fathers in the lives of their children to determine the effect of those roles on children's adjustments. These researchers found that the factors most powerfully associated with good adolescent adjustment were (1) having a close relationship with a residential parent who monitored well and remained involved in decisions regarding the young person's life and (2) not feeling caught in the middle of parental conflict. The effect on adolescents depended on how conflict was managed and the extent to which the child felt caught between parents as a result of the conflict. In this study, mothers carried the primary responsibility for residential care and economic support after the divorce, but fathers remained substantially involved in their children's lives.

What appears to be most important is not the amount of time spent with both parents but the degree to which both parents remain actively engaged in the adolescent's life and continue to function *as parents* (Simons, Lin, Gordon, Conger, and Lorenz, 1999). Functioning as a parent involves more than having fun, going on outings, and providing economic support. It also means providing discipline, giving advice, and fostering maturity. Engaged parents share in the negative as well as the positive aspects of the parental role.

SINGLE-PARENT/GRANDPARENT-HEADED FAMILIES

As we have seen, divorce may have different effects on different adolescents, depending on a number of factors. What do we know about adolescents raised in other types of single-parent homes? Far less than we should, especially since nearly one in three births in the United States in the 1990s was to an unmarried woman (Bumpass and Raley, 1995). Given this fact, it is surprising that so little of the research literature has specifically examined the differences between adolescents raised by single mothers who were never wed and those raised by mothers who were married but got divorced (Amato, 2000).

Furthermore, the literature that does look at this issue is confounded by parental age: Much of the research concerning the children of unwed mothers focuses on the children of unwed *adolescents,* whereas the divorce research usually examines children of *older parents.* Since adolescent mothers are generally less successful than older mothers, whatever their marital status, it is very hard to separate the effects of being raised by an unwed mother from those of being raised by a teenage mother.

Racial and economic factors are involved, as well. Most single Black mothers have never been married, whereas most single White mothers have been married and then divorced; never-wed mothers, as a whole, are worse off economically than divorced mothers (Amato, 2000). These two factors may be related to each other.

In any event, in 2000, more than 4.5 million American children and adolescents lived in households headed not by parents, but by grandparents. About 5 percent of White, non-Hispanic children and adolescents, 9 percent of Hispanic children, and 15 percent

joint custody when two parents share decision-making privileges (joint legal custody) and/or living with a child (joint residential custody).

IN THEIR OWN WORDS

"I came from a wonderful family—living proof that single parenthood does not automatically lead to endless despair and troubles. My mom is my role model. She provided a wonderful home for my brother and I to grow up. She sacrificed her own needs and wants for ours. We are indebted to her for life.

"After the divorce, my mother was committed to family each hour of the day. While we were sleeping, she was studying to pass her certification for public accounting. During the days, she was an at-home mom who was there when we got home from school and willing to drive us to a friend's house or sports game. She would help us with homework and talk to us in the evenings. My mom did such a great job that things were never out of step—I never actually realized how bad our family's situation was until just a few years ago.

"Yet extended family support was also key for our successful development. I knew from an early age that I belonged to my family. My maternal grandparents have always been there for us. My grandfather pulled his double-duty, while my grandmother was always willing to take some burden off of my mom. Aunts and uncles would take us on vacation. They gave us a childhood full of experiences that my mother could not provide alone."

of Black children had these living arrangements. Most of the time the mother is present as well as the grandparent(s), but 25 percent of the time she is not (U.S. Census Bureau, 2000e). Therefore, while it is common for women in all ethnic groups to turn to their own mothers for support when they find themselves single mothers (Szinovacz, 1998), this phenomenon is most strongly practiced in African American families. African Americans are more likely to emphasize extended family ties than Caucasian Americans (Hill, 1998) as such ties are a part of African cultural heritage (Hunter, 1997). In addition, first-time African American mothers are apt to be younger than first-time Caucasian mothers (Hamilton, Ventura, Martin, and Sutton, 2005) and so have less experience with childrearing and resources of their own.

Apfel and Seitz (1991) studied the helping arrangements of 120 inner-city Black adolescent mothers and their own mothers and found that they each fell into one of four types. The most common arrangement was a *parental supplement* pattern; it occurred in about half of the families. In these homes, mothers and grandmothers essentially coparented, although the grandmothers did not necessarily share a residence with their daughter and grandchild. The grandchildren benefited from the situation in that they had the care of two parents, one of them quite experienced; the adolescent mothers benefited because they could continue their education and because they had a helpmate to assume a good deal of the child-care burdens. On the downside, Apfel and Seitz found that the coequal nature of the relationship could cause tension between mother and daughter when there were disagreements and could lead to the child/grandchild's confusion about whom to obey.

Twenty percent of families followed a *supportive primary parenting model.* In this arrangement, the mothers were responsible for the full-time care of their children. Grandmothers helped with expenses, occasionally babysat, and sometimes lent a hand with the mothers' household responsibilities. Family members might all share a residence, or they might live near each other. Some of the families settled into this arrangement because it was the mother's wish to do so: Some of the young mothers wanted to live with their boyfriends or assume an adult, independent role. In other cases, it was more the choice of the grandmothers, who were uninterested in assuming the task of childrearing or who did not want to make things too easy for their daughters and hence encourage additional pregnancies. The benefits of this model are that the mother is provided some support, and the child is provided some additional care; the risk of this model is that the young mother will be overwhelmed when trying to manage so much on her own. The child may be poorly cared for or neglected, and the mother may find that she cannot finish her education or find time for job training.

The third arrangement was for the grandmother to be a *parental replacement* for her daughter; this occurred in about 10 percent of the families. As the name suggests, in these families the grandmothers assumed total parental responsibilities and the mother herself played a rather insignificant role. Sometimes this model is chosen by mutual agreement; for example, both mother and grandmother wanted the mother to go off to college. Sometimes the grandmother took over, gradually or abruptly, because her daughter was negligent. Some families drifted into this pattern, whereas others consciously chose to adopt it. Both mother and child may benefit from this model, the child by having a more competent, nurturing parent than he or she might otherwise have and the mother by being able to concentrate on her own development. However, families run the risk of conflict (if the grandmother does not wish to become the full-time parent or if the mother does not wish to relinquish her role), and the child may have to make a wrenching adjustment in the future if the mother returns to resume her parental role.

Apfel and Seitz (1991) termed the final pattern the *parental apprentice* model; it, too occurred in about 10 percent of the families. In this situation, the grandmother acted as mentor to her daughter. These grandmothers believed that, although their daughters had the potential to be good parents, they did not yet have the skills and knowledge needed to do a good job. The grandmothers acted as teachers and gradually turned responsibility over to the mothers. This model appeared to have numerous benefits: The adolescent mother was given the training she needed, the child became strongly attached to his or her mother, the mothers and grandmothers were not in conflict about who was the primary parent, and the child received high-quality care. Furthermore, grandmothers and mothers following the *apprentice* model tended to have warm, close relations. (Of course, they could have entered into this relationship *because* they had warm relations rather than developing these relations as a result of it.) The risk of this approach is that the emphasis in these homes was so strongly on parenting that the young mother's education and economic future may have been jeopardized. It is also possible that resentments develop between grandmother and mother.

It is clear, then, that not all children raised by never-wed mothers are raised solely (or even primarily) by these mothers. The presence of grandparents in these children's lives—and, in fact, in any child's life—can make a profound difference in their development and in the well-being of their adolescent mothers (Taylor and Roberts, 1995).

Although there are definite benefits to the grandchild to having a highly involved grandparent, there are often costs to that grandparent. Many studies have shown that raising grandchildren often takes a strong toll on the grandmother's well-being (Ross and Aday, 2006). Custodial and near-custodial grandparents (corresponding to the *parental supplement* and *primary supportive parenting* models) exhibit higher rates of depression and worse physical health and report being under more stress than noncustodial grandparents (e.g., Burnett, 1999; Minkler and Fuller-Thomson, 1999). This is especially true if their grandchild has emotional or behavioral difficulties, as is often the case if the child had been previously raised by an inattentive mother (Emick and Hayslip, 1999). Still, many custodial grandparents report immense satisfaction from their role, stating that their grandchildren give them a renewed reason for living and that they feel content knowing that their grandchild is being well cared for (Pruchno, 1999).

Single-Parent Families Resulting from Parental Death

Another type of family that has not been well studied is the single-parent family that results from parental death. More than 2 million American children and adolescents under age 18 have experienced a parent's death (Christ, Siegel, and Christ, 2002). While experiencing a parent's death is in some ways similar to experiencing one's parents' divorce—there are feelings of separation and loss, the child's life is disrupted, economic circumstances likely change—with parental death, the loss is complete and permanent and there is no hope for continued contact (at least in this lifetime). On the other hand, unless the parent committed suicide, there is less of a sense of betrayal, as the separation is not voluntary. How similar, then, are the effects of divorce and parental death on children?

Surprisingly little is known about the effects of parental death on adolescent adjustment, and most of what is known relates to short-term changes rather than long-term outcomes. Adolescents are likely to experience sadness (*dysthymia*) for up to a year after the death of a parent, but only a minority will become clinically depressed (Dowdney, 2000). They often develop fears about the safety of their remaining parent, and many develop symptoms of posttraumatic stress syndrome, especially if the death was a violent,

IN THEIR OWN WORDS

"My dad died when I was eleven. Things were worse than awful—Dad was gone and we moved out of state so that my mom could be close to her family. So much went wrong all at the same time! I lost all my friends, my school, my neighborhood, and my dad in one week. For months, I was obsessed with guilt for not being a better daughter while I had the chance; to this day I still kick myself for turning down his invitation to go see a ball game with him a few days before he died. I was miserable and lonely. I had had lots of friends in my old school but was a social loser in my new one because I was unfriendly and cried a lot.

"Over time, though, I began to realize that if I had to lose my dad, I'd rather lose him the way I did—because he died, not because of divorce. There's no anger or sense of betrayal when someone dies, or at least only irrational anger. We were sad and worried, but I didn't feel abandoned. My situation wasn't anyone's fault. I didn't have to watch my dad remarry and love other kids and be with them. I didn't have to watch him choose to move away from us for a better-paying job. I mean, it would have been better to have had my parents get a happy divorce—the kind where they live next door to each other and you see both of your folks all the time and they stay friends. But I don't know any people who ended up in that situation for more than a little bit of time."

unexpected one (Cerel, Fristad, Weller, and Weller, 2000). Not surprisingly, interest in school work and other activities drops. Adolescent boys are more likely to react aggressively and by acting out than girls (Dowdney, Wilson, Maughan, Allerton, Schofield, and Skuse, 1999). One of the most important determinants of the adolescents' reactions is the success that their surviving parent has with their own coping: Having a strong, calm parent to rely on makes the grieving interval more bearable (Stoppelbein and Greening, 2000). Another important variable is the degree to which the child's life remains similar to the way it was prior to the parent's death (Hope and Hodge, 2006).

We can only speculate about the long-term effects of parental absence due to death versus other causes, as virtually no research has been done on this issue. Little seems to have been added since Hetherington produced her classic (1972) study, which found that daughters of widows have more positive views of men than daughters of divorcees. Although there are some studies on the effects of maternal absence, they do not specifically examine mother absence due to death. It seems likely that the long-term effects of parental absence due to a parent's death would be influenced by the same mediating and moderating factors that influence adolescents' reactions to parental absence due to other reasons: frequency and distance of relocating, strength of a social support network, behavior of the remaining parent, child's innate resiliency, and degree of change to economic circumstances. At this point in time, though, we do not know.

EFFECTS OF BEING RAISED IN A ONE-PARENT FAMILY

Being raised in a one-parent family, of any sort, is a risk factor for a variety of problems (McLanahan and Sandefur, 1994). Adolescents raised in single-parent families are more likely to exhibit emotional and personality problems, to engage in delinquent acts, to be involved in early pregnancies, to use drugs, to do poorly in school, and to be aggressive than those raised in two-parent homes. This research has been replicated outside of the United States, notably in Australia and Great Britain (Pryor and Rogers, 2001) and in several Scandanavian countries (e.g., Nævdal and Thuen, 2004).

Two issues, the development of masculinity/femininity and school achievement, rate special attention.

Development of Masculinity/Femininity

The common assumption has been that boys who lack an effective father figure and who are raised by their mothers are more likely to score lower on measures of masculinity, to have unmasculine self-concepts and sex-role orientations, and to be more dependent, less aggressive, and less competent in peer relationships than those whose fathers are present (Beaty, 1995; Mandara, Murray, and Joyner, 2005). The younger a boy is when he is separated from his father and the longer the separation, the more the boy will be affected in his early years. As a boy gets older, however, the early effects of father absence decrease. By late

RESEARCH HIGHLIGHT SINGLE FATHERS

About one in seven American children who live with only one parent live with their fathers. Fathers are far less likely to be single parents than mothers because they nearly never raise children born out of wedlock and because 85 to 90 percent of sole-custody decisions grant custody to mothers. Usually, a father will retain custody because the mother has died, is deemed an unfit parent, or doesn't get along well with her children. Adolescents are more likely than younger children to live with their fathers, and sons are more likely than daughters to live with their fathers (Cancian and Meyer, 1998).

Single fathers have one clear advantage over single mothers: They are more likely to have an adequate income (Richards and Schmeige, 1993). They are therefore more likely to avoid the numerous stresses that come with poverty. Instead, single fathers' stress more often comes from learning to take on responsibilities that were formerly assumed by their wives (Grief, 1985; Maccoby and Mnookin, 1992).

Although there are exceptions, most research suggests that children raised by their fathers turn out similarly to those raised by their mothers (Amato and Keith, 1991); for example, they do equally well in school (McLanahan and Sandefur, 1994). This similarity exists despite the fact that there are differences in how single mothers and fathers rear their children. Mothers, for instance, more closely supervise and monitor their children than fathers, but fathers are more effective disciplinarians (Buchanan, Maccoby, and Dornbusch, 1992). Since it is becoming increasingly common for fathers to raise children as single parents, it is reassuring to know that they are every bit as capable as mothers of doing a good job.

In single-parent families, many children are faced with being on their own at home because their parents work. Although this is associated with many negative effects on the adolescent, the development of independence and autonomy may be one positive result.

childhood, father-absent boys may score as high as their father-present counterparts on measure of sex-role adoption and preference.

The effect of father absence depends largely on whether boys have male surrogate models (Klyman, 1985). Father-absent boys with a father substitute such as an older male sibling are less affected than those without a father substitute. Male peers, especially older ones, may become important substitute models for paternally deprived boys. Young father-absent male children seek the attention of older males and are strongly motivated to imitate and please potential father figures.

The effects of father absence on daughters seem to be just the opposite. Daughters are affected less when young but more during adolescence. A lack of meaningful male/female relationships in childhood can make it more difficult for them to relate to the opposite sex later on.

One of the most well-known studies in the field of adolescent psychology was conducted by Mavis Hetherington in 1972. She was the first researcher to explicitly compare the cross-sex relationships of adolescent girls raised by married women, divorced women, and widows. She found that daughters of divorcees were more flirtatious than girls raised by the other two types of women and that they were more likely to begin dating at an early age. These girls had likely interpreted their mothers' unhappiness at being divorced as being unhappy because they lacked a romantic attachment. The daughters of widows, in contrast, were stiff and cautious in their dealings with males. They set high standards that had to be met before they were willing to get involved, perhaps because their mothers had glorified their dead husbands.

ANSWERS WOULDN'T YOU LIKE TO KNOW . . .

How well do children fare when they are raised by never-married mothers?

Never-wed mothers are often young when they have children and thus face ongoing financial struggles. But when income levels are equated between never-married mothers and divorced mothers, few differences are observed in their children.

Influences on School Performance, Achievement, and Vocation

Adolescents raised by single parents are less likely to do well in school than adolescents raised in two-parent homes (Amato, 2001). This is especially true for girls, and especially true for mathematics (Murray and Sandqvist, 1990). Partly because of this, and partly due to twin economic issues—single-mother households typically are lower income, and absent fathers are frequently unwilling or unable to contribute financially to their children's education (Popenoe, 1996)—adolescents from one-parent homes are less likely to attend college than other teenagers. This is even more true for adolescent girls than boys (Krohn and Bogan, 2001). Other factors, such as lowered self-esteem and decreased belief in one's ability to succeed academically, doubtless also contribute to this phenomenon.

Furthermore, since doing well in school is vital to obtaining interesting, well-paying jobs, it follows that children, especially girls, raised in one-parent families are less likely to obtain satisfactory employment after they have finished their education (Keith and Finlay, 1988).

BLENDED FAMILIES

More than 50 percent of divorced women who have children remarry within 5 years of their divorce, and more than three-fourths do so within 10 years of the divorce (Bramlett and Mosher, 2002). The high rate of divorce and remarriage means that nearly half of marriages are now second marriages for one or both of the partners. The median age of spouses in these remarriages is in the early or middle 30s, with children being of elementary or preadolescent age at the time their parents remarry (U.S. Bureau of the Census, 2000e). It has been estimated that almost one-fourth of all American children under the age of 18 will spend some time living in a stepfamily; if unmarried, cohabitating families are counted, the estimate rises to almost one-third (Bumpass, Raley, and Sweet, 1995).

Unfortunately, more than half of remarriages end in divorce, as the divorce rate for second marriages is higher than that for first marriages. As a result, many children end up undergoing more than one parental divorce. It is no longer unusual for children to have several sets of stepparents and perhaps stepsiblings and half-siblings, as well (Tzeng and Mare, 1995).

There are many different combinations of blended families. Family relationships in remarriage can become quite complicated. Children may have natural parents and siblings, stepparents and stepsiblings, grandparents and stepgrandparents, plus other relatives. Adult spouses relate to one another, to their own natural parents and grandparents, and to their new in-laws, and they may continue to relate to their former in-laws and other family members. It is understandable why family integration is difficult.

Adolescents in remarried family households who perceive their families to be more flexible report greater satisfaction with both the overall remarried family household and the parent-stepparent subsystem. Flexibility allows households to adopt to the changing needs of households and individual family members (Henry and Lovelace, 1995).

ANSWERS WOULDN'T YOU LIKE TO KNOW . . .

Do adolescents benefit when their mothers get remarried?

Boys tend to benefit, as they once again have a male role model in the home. Girls do not adjust as well; they often feel that their stepfather intrudes on their relationship with their mother.

Children are usually not pleased when their biological parents remarry, and so they do not gladly welcome their new stepparents. Their behavior often puts a strain on the newlyweds (Lagoni and Cook, 1985). In fact, the presence of children from prior marriages increases the possibility of divorce among remarried couples (Fine, 1986). When remarrieds divorce, it is often because they want to leave the stepchildren, not the new spouse (Meer, 1986).

In a majority of cases, at least one spouse has children when the remarriage begins. The mother most often

RESEARCH HIGHLIGHT OPEN AND CLOSED ADOPTIONS

From the 1930s until the 1980s, most adoptions were *closed* adoptions; that is, birth records were sealed, all parties were advised to minimize the fact of the adoption, and children were usually placed with parents who looked similar to themselves so as to maintain the illusion that the child was biologically related to the adoptive family (Bussiere, 1998). Although practices still vary widely by state, the trend has clearly been to move toward *open* adoption (which was the common practice prior to the 1930s). *Open adoption* has numerous meanings, ranging from providing the adoptive parents biographical and medical information about the biological mother through third-party letter exchange all the way to visitations between adoptive parents and biological mother or biological mother and child. Openness has become more the norm as the number of infants available for adoption has decreased due to abortion and an increase in the number of women who are willing to raise a child as a single parent; because of these changes, biological mothers now have a greater ability to negotiate prior to adoption the terms that they, rather than the adoptive parents, would like (Hartman and Laird, 1990). In many states, adopted children are legally permitted to view their adoption records when they reach the age of majority.

Are adolescents interested in obtaining information about their birth parents? A study by Wrobel, Grotevant, and McRoy (2004) suggests that they are. Approximately two-thirds of the adopted adolescents Wrobel and colleagues studied indicated that they had at least some interest in searching for their birth parents. There was some indication that girls were more interested in searching than boys, and older adolescents were more likely to have actively begun to take steps than younger ones. There was no evidence that the adolescents who were interested in finding their birth parents were more poorly adjusted or less happy with their adopted families than those who did not wish to search. The more information that the adolescents already had about their birth parents, the more eager they were to search; in other words, information piqued rather than slaked their curiosity. Most of the adoptive parents in their study were supportive of their children's desires to search. Wrobel, Grotevant, and McRoy concluded that a desire to search for one's birth parents is a normative state for adoptive teenagers and is not indicative of unhappiness or maladjustment.

gets residential custody, so her children are living with her and her husband, who becomes a stepfather (Bramlett and Mosher, 2002). The husband's children are usually living with his ex-wife, creating family ties with her household and the possibility of hostility and conflict. The wife's ex-spouse as noncustodial father usually comes to visit his children, so he has contact with his ex-wife and her new husband, which may result in problems and tension. Being a stepparent is far more difficult than being a natural parent, because children have trouble accepting a substitute parent.

Stepmothers, more often than stepfathers, experience greater difficulties in rearing their stepchildren than in rearing their biological children. This is true regardless of whether their biological children are from a previous marriage or from the current marriage. Several reasons explain stepmothers' difficulties. First, biological fathers often expect stepmothers (i.e., their new wives) to do more of the childrearing than vice versa; stepfathers are thus able to remain uninvolved when there is disciplining to be done. A second reason is that noncustodial biological mothers tend to stay more involved with their children than noncustodial biological fathers; this creates the potential for greater conflict between stepmothers and biological mothers than is typical between stepfathers and biological fathers (Hetherington, 1999a). Finally, fairytales and folklore have developed the stereotype of the cruel stepmother—a myth that may be hard to overcome (Claxton-Oldfield and Butler, 1998).

Despite these issues, stepmothers must try to develop friendly relationships with their stepchildren during infrequent visits—a difficult task at best (Ambert, 1986). All of the adults are coparenting, with three or four parent figures as opposed to two. The children are continually adjusting to those in two households—three or four adult figures and two or more models of relationship patterns with the opposite sex. Both children and adults must contend with the attitudes and influences of other family members.

A great deal of research has confirmed that daughters tend to have a harder time adjusting to their parents' remarriage than sons. Girls tend to be more resistant to both stepmothers and stepfathers, and their adjustment difficulties are both more severe and more sustained (Hetherington and Jodl, 1994). Rather than acting out, they often withdraw and behave in a sullen, uncommunicative fashion (Hetherington, 1993). A preadolescent girl who is close to her mother is especially likely to resist the addition of a new stepfather (Hetherington, 1993).

Adolescent stepchildren particularly have difficulty accepting their new stepfather or stepmother. They may be jealous of the attention their own parent gives his or her mate (who is the stepparent). They may view the stepparent as an intruder or as just one more adult who will try to curtail their freedom (Hetherington, 1999a). They may also feel their primary loyalty is toward their own parents and that the stepparent is an intruder (Moore and Cartwright, 2005). This was dramatically illustrated in the case of a new wife who was greeting her husband's older daughter for the first time. The woman was anxious to make a good impression. "I'm your new mother," she cooed. "The hell you are," replied the daughter and stamped out of the room (Rice, counseling notes).

Because of the high rate of divorce and remarriage, there are many second marriages. In most blended families, it takes time and effort to work out problems and build good stepparent/stepchildren relationships.

This case is not unusual. One of the typical reactions of a stepchild to a stepparent is rejection: "You're not my father" or "You're not my mother." This apparent rejection is hard for the stepparent to take and sometimes leads to a battle of wills. In many cases, the stepparent who initially tried to be kind and concerned will pull back in the face of continued hostility. He or she may display less warmth and support and give up trying to control or monitor the adolescent's behavior (Anderson, Greene, Hetherington, and Clingempeel, 1999).

Given these strains and the fact that the relationships between the children and both their biological parents and stepparents will cool down for some time after a remarriage (Hetherington, 1993), it is no wonder that stepchildren look much more like children raised in single-parent homes rather than those raised in intact homes (Amato, 2001). Like the children whose parents divorced but did not remarry, stepchildren are more likely to do poorly in school, to be involved in a teenage

PERSONAL ISSUES STEPPARENTS VERSUS NATURAL PARENTS

Many stepparents are disappointed, surprised, and bewildered when they find few similarities between being stepparents and natural parents. Let's review important differences between the two:

- *Stepparents may have unrealistic expectations of themselves and of their stepchildren.* After all, they have been parents before, so they anticipate that they will fit into the stepparent role very nicely. They are bewildered if their stepchildren don't accept them immediately and show them due respect. This creates anger, anxiety, guilt, and low self-esteem. They feel there is something wrong with the stepchildren or they blame themselves. They need to realize it may take several years before they and their stepchildren accept one another and develop satisfactory relationships.
- *Parents and stepparents may enter into their new families with a great deal of regret and guilt over their failed marriages.* They feel sorry that they have put their children through the trauma of divorce. As a result, parents tend to be overindulgent and not as strict as they would be otherwise, so they have more trouble controlling and guiding the children's behavior (Amato, 1987). Often, they try to buy the children's cooperation and affection.
- *Stepparents are faced with the necessity of dealing with children who have been socialized by another set of parents.* They don't have a chance to bring them up from infancy as they see fit (unless a stepchild is quite young). The children resent the stepparent coming in and trying to change things.
- *Stepparent roles are not clearly defined.* Stepparents are neither parents nor friends. In the beginning, efforts to take over the parental role may be rejected by older children. Stepparents can't be just friends, because they are confronted with parental responsibilities and hope to make a contribution to the lives of these children. They are required to assume many of the responsibilities of parents: support, physical care, recreational opportunities, and going to sports events and school functions. They may have the responsibilities of parents but few of the privileges and satisfactions.
- *Stepparents expect thanks and gratitude for all of the things they do but may get criticism and rejection instead.* They usually offer the same care as they give their own biological children, yet most biological children and stepchildren seem to take such help for granted. One stepfather complained, "I would like to have a little appreciation and thanks once in a while" (Rice, counseling notes).
- *Stepparents are faced with unresolved emotional issues from their prior marriages and divorces.* Stepparents are still influenced by what happened in their previous families. They may still have a lot of anger, resentment, and hurt, which can come out in destructive ways in their new families. They may need therapy to resolve some of the negative feelings that were created by the separation and divorce.
- *Family cohesion tends to be lower in stepfamilies than in intact families.* Life in reconstituted families tends to be stressful and chaotic during the years following remarriage. Fortunately, things usually settle down in time.

pregnancy, to drop out of school, to use drugs, and to eventually divorce themselves than children from intact families (Hanson, McLanahan and Thomson, 1996; McLanahan and Sandefur, 1994). As before, *more likely* does not mean *usually:* even so, the rates at which children whose parents have divorced (and remarried or not) experience these problems are roughly double the rates for adolescents from intact families, or 20 to 25 percent (Amato, 2001).

Does a parent's remarriage change sibling relationships? How well do half-siblings and stepsiblings get along? Let's begin with the effects on the relationship between the siblings who lived together before the remarriage—the full biological siblings from the original marriage. A number of studies have shown than full biological siblings who are raised in stepfamilies tend to be less close than those raised in intact homes (e.g., Hetherington and Clingempeel, 1992). Boys are especially likely to become more distanced from their siblings, male and female. This distance carries over into adulthood, such that full siblings raised in blended families are more estranged than full siblings raised in intact homes even after they move out of their childhood households (Hetherington, 1999a).

Two-thirds of children whose parents remarry either immediately or eventually gain either a half-sibling or a stepsibling (Bumpass, 1984), which clearly has the potential to be unsettling. For example, the adolescent who is used to being the oldest child in the household may lose that status and the privileges that go with it. Still,

ANSWERS WOULDN'T YOU LIKE TO KNOW ...

How well do adolescents in blended families get along with their stepsiblings?

The relationships between stepsiblings are usually cordial and friendly but rather superficial. Stepsiblings generally co-exist without a lot of tension, but they do not become very close to one another.

most stepsiblings get along reasonably well (Beer, 1992). Their relationships tend to be more casual and less intense than those of full or half-siblings (Hetherington, 1999b), however, and involve fewer positive and fewer extremely negative interactions. Half-siblings are most often treated the same as full siblings, and they have the same kinds of relationships (Anderson, 1999).

ADOPTED ADOLESCENTS

Another kind of family, not discussed elsewhere, involves adopted adolescents and their parents. More than 1.5 million families in the United States include adopted children (Kreider, 2003).

How well do these adolescents fare? It depends on who you compare them with. Adopted adolescents, as a whole, have fewer problems and better educational attainment than adolescents raised in single-parent families (Fergusson, Lynskey, and Horwood, 1995), for several reasons. They tend to be better off economically and hence go to better schools, receive higher-quality health care, and so on than adolescents raised by only single parents. Moreover, adopted families tend to be more stable than single-parent families, and interactions between adopted parents and their children tend to be warm and nurturing. Adopted adolescents are not as successful as children raised by their biological parents in intact families. Adopted youths do not do as well in school, are more prone to conduct disorders, and are not as popular with their peers (Kirschner, 1996; Wierzbicki, 1993). These differences are most pronounced during middle childhood and midadolescence and decline later in life (Brodzinsky, 1987). Of course, single-parents can also adopt children, or adopted children may end up in single-parent homes if their parents divorce. In those instances, adopted children look similar to other children raised in single-parent families.

What explains the different patterns? Grotevant, Ross, Marchel, and McCoy (1999) have pointed both to preadoption and postadoption contributing factors. Many adopted adolescents likely received inadequate prenatal care while their birth mothers were pregnant, as there is an increased likelihood that these mothers were young, impoverished, or substance abusers. Adopted children may also have been neglected or abused after birth and prior to having been adopted.

Once they have been adopted, adopted adolescents may face more complex attachment issues and experience more conflict over regulation issues than other teenagers, as indicated by statements such as "You can't tell me what to do—you're not really my mother!" Adopted individuals may also find it more difficult to cope with increasing autonomy if they feel they have been abandoned before. They may also face added social stigma due to their adopted status. Most importantly, having been adopted often makes the identity search more difficult. It is harder to form an identity—to figure out who you are—when pieces of information are missing (Grotevant, 1997). This is especially true of adolescents who underwent closed adoptions and know little or nothing about their birth parents. Adolescents who underwent open adoptions and who have had contact with their birth parents will not have this problem but may instead experience conflicted loyalties to relatives with different values and lifestyles.

One group that might seem particularly at risk is that of transracially adopted adolescents. After all, their identity searches will be that much more disrupted than those of intraracially adopted adolescents, and their adopted parents may be ill equipped to help them become comfortable with their ethnic identities. Contrary to this argument, transracial adoptees are just as successful as intraracial adoptees. They feel just as good about themselves and have resolved their ethnic identifications (Levy-Schiff, Zoran, And Shulman, 1997; Vroegh, 1997).

SUMMARY

1. About 30 percent of American adolescents live with only one of their biological parents, more often their mother. About 50 percent of these teenagers have parents who are divorced, and about 40 percent have mothers who were never married to their biological fathers.
2. Most experts agree that divorce has both short-term and long-term effects on adolescent development.
3. Short-term emotional reactions include shock and disbelief, fear, anxiety, insecurity about the future, anger and hostility, self-blame and guilt, mourning and grief, and jealousy and resentfulness.

4. Although the large majority of children whose parents divorce grow up well adjusted, experiencing one's parents' divorce often impairs family relationships and increases the probability of a wide variety of adjustment problems during adolescence and young adulthood.
5. A number of factors influence the effects of divorce: the individual adolescent's temperament, the behavior and economic circumstances of the family before the divorce, the quality of parenting after the divorce, the economic resources available to the child after the divorce, and the amicability of the parents after the divorce.
6. Joint custody is not uniformly better or worse than single-parent custody. Joint custody can work well if the parents get along; it does not work well if the adolescent is caught between fighting parents.
7. There is little research directly comparing children raised by never-wed mothers and divorced mothers, and the research that does exist often compares children from different socioeconomic statuses and races/ethnicities. Still, it appears that the effects of being raised by a single parent—whether as the result of a divorce or out-of-wedlock birth—are similar.
8. Single fathers are, on average, as successful as parents as single mothers.
9. Many adolescents raised by single mothers, especially African American children, are cared for exclusively or in good part by their grandmothers.
10. Most divorced adults eventually remarry, which means large numbers of adolescents will grow up in blended families.
11. The biggest complication in remarriage is children. Being a stepparent is far more difficult than being a natural parent because children have trouble accepting a substitute parent.
12. Relations are typically more strained between stepmothers and stepchildren than between stepfathers and stepchildren, primarily because stepmothers are more involved in their stepchildren's lives.
13. While a son is more likely to have trouble adjusting to his parents' divorce, a daughter is more likely to have trouble adjusting to her parents' remarriage.
14. Adolescents raised in blended families are more similar to those raised by single parents than to adolescents raised in intact, two-parent homes.
15. Full-sibling relationships often become less supportive if siblings' parents remarry. Relations with stepsiblings are usually cordial but not close.
16. Adopted adolescents fare better than adolescents raised in single-parent homes, but they do have more adjustment problems than adolescents raised by both of their biological parents.

KEY TERMS

legal custody 253
residential custody 253
joint custody 254

THOUGHT QUESTIONS

Personal Reflection

Think about questions 1–5 if your parents are divorced; if they are not, ask these questions of a friend whose parents are. Think about questions 6–7 if your mother and father were never married; if your parents were married, ask these questions of a friend raised by an unwed mother.

1. How did your parents' divorce affect you as it was happening? What emotions did you experience? Give some examples to illustrate your explanation.
2. What upset you the most when your parents were first divorced? Compile a list of do's and don'ts for parents who are divorcing.
3. What custody arrangements did you have? Were they, in your opinion, ideal? Why or why not?
4. Looking back, did you benefit from your parents' divorce in any ways? Explain.
5. Are you a different person because of your parents' divorce? Why or why not?
6. Were you content with your family situation (having an unwed mother) as you were growing up? Did you feel different or ostracized in any way? Use examples to explain.
7. Did you have close relationships with any adult men as you were growing up (uncles, grandfathers, etc.)? Was the fact that these relationships were with men as opposed to women important to you? Why or why not?

Group Discussion

8. Did your peers have negative stereotypes about an adolescent raised in a one-parent home? Did you? If so, what were they?
9. What are the appropriate roles for residential stepmothers and stepfathers? Nonresidential stepmothers and stepfathers? What should characterize the relationship each has with his or her stepchildren?
10. Draw up a list of the advantages and disadvantages of having stepsiblings.
11. If you were adopted, when did you begin to have an interest in your birth family? How strongly interested were you? How did your adoptive parents react? Was any of the information you received helpful?
12. If you were not adopted, do you think you would want to develop a relationship with your birth parents? What would be the possible costs and benefits?

Debate Questions

13. Society should make it more difficult for married couples to divorce.
14. Parents who divorce should not be permitted to relocate far from their children's other biological parent.
15. The main reason for the decreased outcomes for adolescents raised in single-parent families is poverty and economic hardship.
16. Stepparents should leave disciplining to a child's biological parents.

SUGGESTED READING

Emery, R. L. (1999). *Marriage, Divorce and Children's Adjustment.* 2nd ed. Thousand Oaks, CA: Corwin.

Ganong, L. H., & Coleman, M. (2003). *Stepfamily Relationships: Development, Dynamics, and Interventions.* New York: Springer.

Hetherington, E. M. (1999). *Coping with Divorce, Single-Parenting, and Remarriage: A Risk and Resiliency Perspective.* Mahwah, NJ: Lawrence Erlbaum.

Howard, J. A., and Smith, S. L. (2003). *After Adoption: The Needs of Adopted Youth.* Washington, DC: Child Welfare League of America.

Mason, M. A., Skolnick, A., and Sugarman, S. D. (2002). *All Our Family: New Policies for a New Century. A Report of the Berkeley Family Forum.* 2nd ed. Oxford, England: Oxford University Press.

Papernow, P. L. (2002). *Becoming a Stepfamily: Patterns of Development in Remarried Families.* Hillsdale, NJ: Analytic Press.

Steinberg, G., & Hall, B. (2000). *Inside Transracial Adoption.* Indianapolis, IN: Perspectives Press.

Tasker, F. L., and Golombok, S. (1998). *Growing Up in a Lesbian Family: Effects on Child Development.* New York: Guilford.

Teyber, E. (2001). *Helping Children Cope with Divorce.* 2nd ed. Lexington, MA: Lexington Books.

USEFUL WEB SITES

Family Pride Coalition
www.familypride.org

The Family Pride Coalition is a nonprofit organization whose purpose is to "advance the well-being of lesbian, gay, bisexual and transgender parents and family members." The site contains news articles, advocacy information, a newsletter, a bookstore, contact information for local parents' support groups, and links to other sites of interest to gay and bisexual parents.

Stepfamily Association of America
www.saafamilies.org

The Web site of this nonprofit organization is geared to both laypersons and professionals interested in stepfamilies. It contains a large list of recommended books and articles and is home to a number of forums in which individuals can share ideas about different aspects of stepparenting.

CHAPTER 12 SOCIAL DEVELOPMENT

The Changing Nature of Friendship and Romance

WOULDN'T YOU LIKE TO KNOW . . .

- How often do adolescents feel lonely?
- What are early adolescent friendships usually like?
- Do adolescents pressure each other to conform?
- What makes some adolescents so popular?
- Is it good for adolescents to have cross-sex friendships?
- Do teenage boys fall in love as easily as teenage girls?
- How common is dating violence among adolescents?
- Is going together good or bad for teenagers?
- Is living together a good test of marital compatibility?
- How many adolescents get married?

Adolescence is a time of profound changes in relationships with peers. As teenagers break away from their families, they spend increasingly more time with their friends. And because their social cognitive skills are more sophisticated than when they were younger (see the section on Robert Selman's work in Chapter 2), they have a better understanding of others and their peers have a better understanding of them. This opens the door to having more intimate, meaningful interactions. What's more, when adolescents change schools—going from grade school to middle school and then from middle school to high school—they are usually exposed to a new and larger, more diverse group of peers. Finally, with physical maturation and emerging sexual interests come the desire for romantic as well as platonic attachments.

This chapter is concerned with the nature of close peer relationships during adolescence. It begins by examining changes in friendship and then moves to romantic pairings. Because nonmarital cohabitation has become quite common among late adolescents, that phenomenon is also discussed, and since some adolescents marry, the experience of early marriage will be considered, as well.

COMPANIONSHIP

The need for close friends becomes crucial during adolescence. Until adolescence, children's dependence on peers is rather loosely structured. Children seek out playmates of their own ages with whom they share common interests or activities. They engage them in friendly competition and win or lose some measure of their respect and loyalty, but emotional involvement with them is not intense. Children do not depend primarily on one another for emotional satisfaction. They look to their parents for fulfillment of their emotional needs and seek their praise, love, and tenderness. Only if they have been unloved, rejected, and adversely criticized by parents will they turn to friends or parent substitutes for emotional fulfillment.

During adolescence, this picture changes. Sexual maturation brings new feelings and needs for emotional fulfillment and for emotional independence and emancipation from parents. Adolescents now turn to their peers to find the support formerly provided by their families (Helsen, Vollebergh and Meevs, 2000).

The Need for Friends

The positive aspects of peer relationships among adolescents are well documented. Many studies have found that the quality and stability of adolescents' friendships are related to self-esteem (e.g., Keefe and Berndt, 1996). Involvement of peers has been found to be related positively to many indicators of psychological and social adjustment (Bishop and Inderbitzen, 1995). Numerous studies have indicated that social support is directly related to well-being and serves to buffer the effects of unusual stress.

There is also reason to believe that adolescence is a time of life when the potential for stress arising from peer relationships is particularly high. Adolescents are oriented toward their peers and rely on them for a sense of self-worth. Peer conformity increases during the early adolescent years. Being neglected or rejected by peers during adolescence is linked to serious problems such as delinquency, drug abuse, and depression (Merten, 1996). Early adolescence may be an especially vulnerable time for experiences in social stress for peers (Moran and Eckenrode, 1991).

The first needs of adolescents are for relationships with others with whom they can share common interests (Hortacsu, 1989). As they grow older, they desire closer, caring relationships that involve sharing mature affection, problems, and their most personal thoughts (Pombeni, Kirchler, and Palmonari, 1990). They need close friends who stand beside them and for them in an understanding, caring way. Friends share more than secrets or plans; they share feelings and help each other resolve personal problems and interpersonal conflicts (Berndt, 2004). As one boy said, "He is my best friend. We can tell each other things we can't tell anyone else; we understand each other's feelings. We can help each other when we are needed" (Rice counseling notes).

During adolescence, success in forming and maintaining peer relationships is positively implicated in social and psychological adjustment and achievement. An important element in success in peer relationships is the willingness of friends to be prosocial—that is, to help and provide emotional support, advice, and information (Estrada, 1995). Girls, however, expect more from their friends than boys do (Claes, 1992), and their level of attachment and intimacy with friends is greater, at least during early and middle adolescence (Azmitia, Kamprath, and Linnet, 1998).

Research has indicated that young adolescents prefer to disclose their emotional feelings to parents. Much depends on the openness of family communication. However, as they get older, adolescent self-disclosure to friends increases and becomes greatest among older adolescents. Females of all ages exhibit greater emotional disclosure to both parents and peers than do males. This finding is consistent with traditional masculine stereotypes that emphasize that males are not to express emotional concerns and feelings (Papini, Farmer, Clark, Micka, and Barnett, 1990).

One of the reasons friendships are crucial is that adolescents are insecure and anxious about themselves (Hartup and Stevens, 1999). They lack personality definition and secure identities. Consequently, they gather

PERSONAL ISSUES BEING ALONE VERSUS BEING LONELY

There is a tremendous difference between *being alone* and *being lonely,* although sometimes people—especially adolescents—confuse the two. *Being alone* literally means to be physically apart from others. *Being lonely* reflects the subjective feeling that one is not receiving enough support or companionship; one can feel lonely when standing in a crowd.

Loneliness in adolescence is most strongly tied to feelings of distance from peers, rather than from parents. Not having a best friend and feeling distant from the larger peer network can both contribute to a youth's feelings of loneliness (Hoza, Bukowski, and Beery, 2000).

Although adolescents generally do not prefer to be alone (Buchholz and Catton, 1999) and are less happy when they are alone (Larson, Csikszentmihalyi, and Graef, 1982), numerous benefits can be derived from solitude. For example, one can use time alone for private reflection (crucial to the adolescent identity search), for concentrating on a difficult task, or for rest and renewal.

Many teenagers seem to feel that they should spend all of their free time socializing with friends and that there is something wrong with a teen who chooses to be alone. This idea should be more actively discouraged. It is possible for an individual to enjoy the company of others yet enjoy private time, as well (Burger, 1995).

friends around them from whom they gain strength. From them, they learn the necessary personal and social skills and societal definitions that help them become part of the larger adult world. They become emotionally bound to others who share their vulnerabilities and their deepest selves. They become comrades in a hostile world.

Loneliness

One of the greatest problems of adolescents is the problem of loneliness. One adolescent girl commented, "I'm really lonely. My mom and dad both work, so are not home a lot. My brother is six years older than I am, so we don't have too much in common. If it weren't for some friends, I wouldn't have anyone to talk to." Adolescents describe their loneliness as emptiness, isolation, and boredom. They are more likely to describe themselves as lonely when feeling rejected, alienated, isolated, and not in control of a situation (Woodward and Kalyan-Masih, 1990). Boys seem to have a greater problem with loneliness than do adolescent girls (Koenig and Abrams, 1999), probably because it is more difficult for boys to express their feelings.

Adolescents are lonely for a variety of reasons. Some have trouble knowing how to relate to others; they have high levels of social anxiety (Goossens and Marcoen, 1999). Some have a poor self-image and feel very vulnerable to criticism. They anticipate rejection and avoid actions that might cause them embarrassment (Cacciopo et al., 2000). Given this, a vicious cycle can develop: An adolescent may become depressed because he or she is lonely, and being depressed makes it even more difficult to establish new relationships, essentially ensuring further loneliness (Brage, Meredith, and Woodward, 1993). Some adolescents have had a history of victimization and so have been conditioned to mistrust peers and are therefore cynical about relating to them (Boivin, Hymel, and Bukowski, 1995). They avoid social contact and intimacy so others can't take advantage of them. Still other adolescents feel a lack of support from parents, which makes it harder to make friends. Whenever adolescents perceive the social risks of forming friendships to be greater than the potential benefits, they have difficulty establishing meaningful relationships (East, 1989).

For the most part, also, youths are lonelier than older people (Medora and Woodward, 1986). Part of loneliness is situational; it is socially conditioned because the youth culture emphasizes that if you are alone on Friday night, you will be miserable, so adolescents end up feeling that way (Meer, 1985). It becomes a self-fulfilling prophesy.

Different adolescents cope with their loneliness in different ways. Those who are more independent engage in individual pursuits, keep busy, and readjust their thinking so they are more content. Those who are more dependent attempt to extend their social contacts, try to be with others more, rely on external sources of support, seek adult help, or resort to religion, physical activities, or professional help (Woodward and Kalyan-Masih, 1990). Still others withdraw.

It is important to realize that *almost all* adolescents, including college students, feel lonely some of the time and that many feel lonely a good part of the time. Also, objectively, lonely adolescents are, as a whole, no less attractive or socially desirable than more socially embedded adolescents (Cacciopo et al., 2000). They are as bright, as good looking, and as athletic. Loneliness comes from inside oneself, from a tendency to withdraw and disengage rather than reach out to others.

ANSWERS WOULDN'T YOU LIKE TO KNOW ...

How often do adolescents feel lonely?

Adolescents commonly experience feelings of loneliness. In fact, feeling lonely is more common in adolescence than in childhood or adulthood.

It is therefore important for all adolescents to develop strategies to help them deal with bouts of loneliness in positive, productive ways. Some good choices include keeping yourself busy with activities that you find enjoyable (for example, favorite hobbies or exercising), interacting with friends and loved ones, and helping others who are in need.

Family and Peer Relationships

The ability to form close friendships is partly learned in the family. There is a significant correlation between relationships with parents and adolescents' social adjustments (Markiewicz, Doyle, and Bregden, 2001).

Many studies have tied the quality of parent-child **attachments** to the quality of peer relationships (e.g., Zimmerman, 2004). Attachments are the earliest form of love that children experience, usually between themselves and their parents. Adolescents who had healthy, secure attachments have intrinsic trust in others, and so relate warmly to them (Waters and Cummings, 2000). On the other hand, adolescents who never developed healthy attachments to their parents are rigid and hostile in their dealings with peers (Zimmerman, 1999).

The effect of parent-child closeness can also be explained by the fact that teens who are close to their parents tend to have high self-esteem (Sim, 2000). Having high self-esteem, in turn, allows one to be outgoing and to think of oneself as likeable, thus allowing one to approach and be open to peers.

Parents can also influence friendship by actively encouraging or discouraging it. For example, Way and her colleagues (Way and Chen, 2000; Way and Greene, 2005) have found that Asian American parents are less likely to encourage their adolescent children to have close nonfamilial relationships than are Latino or African American parents. Hence, Asian American youth are less likely to spend as much time with friends or to be as close to them as are teens from these other groups.

Early Adolescent Friendships

The need for companionship causes young adolescents to choose a best friend or two, almost always of the same sex. The adolescent will spend long hours conversing with this friend on his or her cell phone; will attend school, club, and athletic events with him or her; and will strive to dress like, look like, and act like this person. Usually, this best friend is from a similar socioeconomic, racial, and home background; from the same neighborhood, school, and school grade; of the same age; and with numerous interests, values, and friends in common. Best friends usually get along well because they are similar and thus compatible. Successful friendships are based on each person's meeting the needs of the other (Zarbatany, Ghesquiere, and Mohr, 1992). If best friends meet each other's needs, the bonds of friendship may be drawn tightly.

Why are adolescent friends so similar? One reason is that adolescents consciously select people who are like them (Urberg, Degirmencioglu, and Tolson, 1998). Those who are like us affirm who we are and what choices we make; they bolster our self-esteem. The other reason that adolescent friends are so similar is that once they become friends, they influence and encourage each other to engage in mutually satisfying activities so that they can be together. However, contrary to many adults' imaginings, friends rarely coerce each other into doing things (Berndt, 1992). Rather, they provide information, give

RESEARCH HIGHLIGHT FACTORS CONTRIBUTING TO ADOLESCENT LONELINESS

A number of factors contribute to adolescent loneliness:

- A sense of separation and alienation from parents
- Parental divorce
- New cognitive abilities leading to an awareness of self
- An increasing sense of freedom, which is frightening
- The search for self-identity
- The struggle for meaningful goals
- Marginal status of adolescents in society
- Fierce competitive individualism leading to feelings of failure and rejection
- Excessive expectation of popularity
- Low self-esteem, resulting in pessimism about being liked and accepted by others
- Apathy and aimlessness, low educational and occupational aspirations, a cycle of failure and withdrawal
- Severe individual shyness and self-consciousness

ANSWERS WOULDN'T YOU LIKE TO KNOW . . .

What are early adolescent friendships usually like?

Early adolescent friendships are usually same sex, volatile, and based on individual similarities.

or withhold approval, and are respected models for each other. Friendships usually end if one friend puts too much unwanted pressure on the other.

Early adolescent friendships are intense, emotional, and sometimes stormy. Adolescents expect that their close friends will be there for them, and they react with anger and frustration when they are not. Because early adolescents are often somewhat egocentric, they may have unrealistic expectations about the level of support their friends should give them. They may fight with their friends or even break off friendships if they are unsatisfied with how their friends come through for them. The friendships of young adolescents are, therefore, often tempestuous and unstable.

Although the rigid single-sexed structure of friendship breaks down during adolescence (Dunphy, 1963), adolescents continue to have predominantly same-sex friends (Hartup, 1983). Intimacy truly begins to distinguish friendships between males and females at this age (Berndt and Perry, 1990). Adolescent girls report that their friendships are more intimate than boys' (Blyth and Foster-Clark, 1987) and that they disclose more than boys do (Dolgin and Kim, 1994). Boys believe that they will be teased if they disclose much to their friends (Berndt, 1990; Youniss and Smollar, 1985); so when boys do talk, it largely takes the form of bragging about their achievements (Stapley and Haviland, 1989). Adolescent girls are more likely to turn to friends for emotional support than boys are (Lederman, 1993). When males seek support, they expect concrete, material help from their friends; they also expect their friends to stand by them when they are in trouble with authority figures (Douvan and Adelson, 1966). During adolescence, girls begin to experience stress in their friendships. Girls are more concerned than boys about their friends' faithfulness (Schneider and Couts, 1985).

Adolescents need close friends who will share secrets, plans, and feelings and who will help with personal problems. These best friends are usually quite similar, coming from the same type of socioeconomic and racial/ethnic background, living in the same neighborhood, going to the same school, and sharing interests and values.

IN THEIR OWN WORDS

"My best friend is a male [writes a female student]. We have been through so much together that I feel he has always been a part of my life. When we were not together, we spoke on the phone for hours. There was only one awkward moment in our relationship: when we thought we wanted something more than to just be friends. We had just broken up with our girlfriend/boyfriend, and I guess we both needed to be loved. So we decided to love each other. We kissed and I felt like I was kissing my brother and he told me he felt like he was kissing his sister. So, we ended the whole thing before it began and went back to normal.

"I lived with him through every love affair he ever had. He was seeking my advice and I was happy to give it to him. One girl left him once and he called me, crying. I tried to convince him that it wasn't his fault.

"He, on the other hand, was my conscience releaser. At home, I was a good girl, but outside, I was quite wild. He was always covering my back and supporting me in my initiatives. When I smoked my first cigarette, he was the first to know and he just accepted it as something I did."

"I was known as a dork ever since the time that I got glasses and braces in the same year. I hung out with the cool kids but was never really accepted into their group. Once, one guy I hung out with called me and asked for my X-box controller—but then didn't invite me over to play video games at his house. At the lunch table, I usually sat at the end closest to the garbage cans so that everyone could pass down their trash to me to throw it away for them. On the few occasions that I didn't sit by the garbage cans, trash was still passed to me and I had to get up and walk it to the trash cans. Now that I'm in college, I'm at least somewhat popular, and at least if I put anyone's trash in the garbage, it's because I want to be a nice guy."

attachment the early emotional bond formed between child and parent.

PERSONAL ISSUES ADOLESCENT RELATIONSHIPS AND ADJUSTMENTS

From a developmental perspective, the relative influence of peers depends on the child's age. Children are more dependent on parents during middle through late childhood and more dependent on peers during early to middle adolescence. During later adolescence, individuals exhibit greater resistance to peer pressure and greater capacity for autonomous behavior. For many adolescents, the shift toward a peer social orientation does not necessarily involve a rejection of parents' opinions and values.

The typical progression from family to peer to young adult can be upset when parental relationships fail to maintain a balance between supportive involvement and the encouragement of self-sufficiency. Adolescents who report less emotional support from their parents and less involvement in their families have been shown to be more susceptible to the influence of delinquent peers than adolescents who report more support from an involvement with their families. Similarly, excessive or premature autonomy from parental influence has been found to be related to adolescent girls' early initiation of sexual activity. Thus, it appears that the quality of both family and peer relations are related to adolescent development and adjustments.

As already noted, friendships during early adolescence are unstable. However, they become more stable as adolescents move through adolescence. This increased stability is due to social cognitive development, decreased egocentrism, and improved relationship management skills (Erwin, 1993). After age 18, friendships again typically fluctuate because students leave home for college, jobs, the armed services, or marriage.

Broadening Early Friendships

When young adolescents leave the confines of their neighborhood elementary schools and transfer to district or consolidated middle schools, they are immediately exposed to much broader and more heterogeneous friendships. They now have an opportunity to meet youths from other neighborhoods, social classes, and different ethnic and national origins. These youths may act, dress, speak, and think differently from those they have known before.

One social task at this stage of development is to broaden their acquaintances, to learn how to relate to and get along with many different types of people. During this early period, adolescents want many friends. Usually, there is an increase in the number of friends during early adolescence. After that, adolescents become more discriminating, and the number of reported friendships decreases.

Friendship Activities

What do adolescents do with their friends? How do they spend their time together? A large study of over 2,000 middle-class Canadian high school students conducted in the mid-1990s provided good answers to these questions (van Roosmalen and Krahn, 1996). One popular activity of these students was hanging around. When hanging around, some of the girls spent their time at their homes or at a friend's house. Also, when spending time just hanging around, they engaged in other activities at the same time. For example, on Saturday mornings, they hung around the house doing chores. Boys appeared to spend less time hanging around than girls.

Watching television was a common source of leisure for these young people. And while they spent many hours in front of the television, it was not their first choice in leisure pursuits. There were some gender differences in types of television viewing. Most female and male high school students spent much of their Saturday television viewing time watching cartoons. A greater proportion of males spent some time on Saturday watching sports. Few young women stated they watched sports on television.

Many of the young people in the Canadian study spent moderate amounts of time (anywhere between one and five hours a week) cruising around in a car. More males than females spent greater amounts of out-of-school hours "cruising around downtown," "just driving around," or cruising to pick up friends.

A larger proportion of females than males spent time at the mall with their friends. They would hang out, windowshop, try on clothes, watch other groups of teens, and snack. The adolescent girls also spent more time talking to friends and family members than did the boys. The girls were more likely to spend time "talking on the phone with my boyfriend," "going downstairs to talk to mom and dad," "talking with my grandmother," "talking to my sister," or "just hanging around and talking with my friends." When boys spent time talking, they "talked with friends," they "drank beer and talked with friends," they "sat around and talked," or they had friends sleep over and in the morning "sat around and talked." They seemed to spend less time talking on the phone than did girls and less time talking with family.

A sizable majority of the students consumed alcohol quite regularly, usually with friends. Of all the youths studied, 44 percent consumed alcohol at least once a week; 6 percent had never drunk alcohol. More males than females consumed alcohol and took drugs, although drinking is becoming more acceptable for girls. Young people perceived alcohol as helping them have more fun, especially when with their friends.

Because that study was conducted in the mid-1990s, we might expect some changes if it were repeated today. First, even more time would be spent talking to friends because many if not most of the teens would have cell phones. Second, communication among friends would be further augmented because they would be instant messaging each other when they were working or playing on their computers. Finally, at least for the boys, video game playing would likely displace some of the television watching time.

GROUP ACCEPTANCE AND POPULARITY

As their number of acquaintances broadens, adolescents become increasingly aware of their need to belong to a group. One study emphasized that boys were more concerned with status or attributes that led to acceptance by a group than were girls. Girls were more interested in affiliation, in being close to a relatively small group of girls (Benenson, 1990). However, both boys and girls want to be liked by peers. By midadolescence, the goal toward which they strive is acceptance by members of a clique or crowd they strongly admire. At this stage, they are sensitive to criticism or to others' negative reactions to them. They are concerned about what people think because their concepts of who they are and their degree of self-worth are partly a reflection of the opinions of others.

What Does It Take to Be Popular?

When the junior author's daughter was just starting high school, she was often upset because she didn't perceive herself as being popular. This surprised me no end, since she had literally dozens of friends, more invitations to go places and do things than she could possibly take advantage of, and her cell phone never stopped buzzing with calls for her. To me she appeared quite the social butterfly! When I tried to speak with her about the disconnect between her perceptions and mine, she would say, "But Mom, the *popular* kids don't like me; not that I really like them, either. So I'm not

RESEARCH HIGHLIGHT FRIENDSHIP EXPECTATIONS

Clark and Ayers (1993) studied friendship expectations during adolescence and came to the following conclusions:

1. Sharing mutual activities is important in friendships during early school years and remains an essential characteristic of friendships during adolescence. Mutual activities are perceived as rewarding and facilitate bonding between friends. Proximity and the sharing of activities facilitate interpersonal attraction.
2. Early adolescents felt that friends should be "morally good" and should be open and straightforward, especially about their feelings regarding the friendship. Early adolescents had high standards for conventional morality; however, they realized that many of their peers could not meet these idealized views, and, therefore, settled for those who had lower levels of conventional morality than they expected. They emphasized genuineness, which facilitated the growth of friendships, whereas the lack of genuineness, or phoniness, was one of the major reasons given by adolescents for the dissolution of adolescent friendships.
3. Early adolescents emphasized the importance of loyalty and commitment in the relationship.
4. Adolescents desired relationships in which there was empathetic understanding between them. However, there were some differences in expectations between boys and girls. The boys reported less empathetic understanding in their close friendships than did girls and indicated they required less understanding so that their expectations were still being met by their current relationships. In addition, boys did not require as much loyalty and commitment from their friends as girls did, so male friendships often surpassed their requirements for loyalty and commitment. In general, early adolescent friendships possess many of the qualities that adolescents believe are important for close friendships. Nevertheless, girls expected more from their friendships than they were getting. This emphasis on morality reinforces the view often expressed that early adolescents are more attached to friends who do not get into trouble (Gillmore, Hawkins, Day, and Catalano, 1992).

popular." Three years later, it's déjà vu all over again, as I am listening to my equally well-liked son say the exact same things. My children are apparently not alone: Many adolescents yearn to be popular (Jarvinen and Nichols, 1996), and middle and high school students spend a good deal of time talking about the popular kids (Eder, Evans, and Parker, 1995).

The discrepancy comes from the fact that adults (and, until recently, psychologists) did not mean the same thing as teenagers when they used the word *popular.* Popular people, to adults and (formerly) psychologists, are those that everyone else likes. Popular kids are those that have a lot of friends. They are *nice:* friendly, sociable, helpful, cooperative, generous, and trustworthy (Rubin, Bukowski, and Parker, 1998). When adolescents refer to "the popular kids," they mean something else entirely: They mean the socially dominant leaders. These students may or may not be liked at all, but they are the social center of the school. They are the trendsetters, the ones that others wish to be seen with (de Bruyn and van den Boom, 2005).

So what are the popular teens like? Popular teenagers are usually physically attractive (Lease, Musgrove, and Axelrod, 2002). Also, they spend a good deal of money on clothing and so are very fashionable and look good (LaFontana and Cillessen, 2002). Everyone knows who they are, they mingle with the other popular teens, and they are considered hot by members of the opposite sex (Lease, Muskgrove, and Axdral, 2002). They are also very socially savvy. They have good leadership skills and can be quite manipulative (Farmer, Estell, Bishop, O'Neal, and Cairns, 2003). They know how to turn on the charm, but they are not above using coercion to get what they want (Hawley, 2003). In other words, while they are always socially successful, they are not always nice. Many of their peers, while longing to be part of their crowd, at the same time consider them stuck up and mean.

Two tools that popular adolescents often employ to hold onto their high status are **relational** and **reputational aggression** (Xie, Swift, Cairns, and Cairns, 2002). Relational aggression involves using your friends to keep another in line; for example, you may get your friends to promise that they will snub that other person until you tell them to stop. Reputational aggression involves spreading lies and rumors about another to damage her or his social standing; for example, you might say that you know that Sarah had sex with the entire basketball team after last weekend's big game. Reputational aggression appears to be used first; if it proves insufficient, then relational aggression is used to ensure that the other is firmly put in her or his place. Girls are somewhat more likely to use relational aggression than boys, who more often resort to more direct verbal insults and physical aggression (Crick, 1997). Also, adolescents are more likely to use relational and reputational aggression than younger children (Rose, Swenson, and Waller, 2004): The social scene really does get more vicious when you enter middle school.

Routes to Social Acceptance

Conformity

Adolescents choose their friends so as to maximize the similarity within the friendship pair (Urberg, Degirmencioglu, and Tolson, 1998). If there is a state of imbalance such that the friend's attitude or behavior is incongruent, the adolescent will either break off the friendship and seek another friend or keep the friend and modify her or his own behavior.

Cliques and groups operate in the same way. Each group takes on a personality of its own: Members are characterized according to dress and appearance, scholastic standing, extracurricular participation, social skills, socioeconomic status, reputation, and personality qualifications (see Chapter 13). One way the individual can try to be liked by a particular group is to be like other members of the group. This may include using special slang, wearing a certain type of pin, bracelet or tattoo. When a fad is in fashion, every person in the group adopts it. Those who are different are excluded.

Of course, conformity can be a helpful, positive social influence or a negative one, depending on the group and its values. The adolescent boy who wants to belong to a juvenile gang and has to pull off a robbery to do so is obviously conforming, but to a peer code that may get him into trouble.

Conformity needs also depend on adolescents' family adjustments. Youths with a good family adjustment and who are fond of their parents have less need to conform to peer demands, at least in some areas, so that when confronted with decisions, parental rather than peer opinions are accepted. Total adjustment to parents influences the degree to which adolescents conform to parents versus peers.

Adolescent girls show a greater degree of conformity than do adolescent boys. Members of girls' groups are more concerned with harmonious relations, social approval and acceptance, and living up to peer expectations than are members of boys' groups. In one study of peer influence among high school students, this desire was a more dominant and influential feature of life for girls than for boys. The conformity needs reported by girls were much more intense than for boys (Brown, 1982). However, for girls, the pressure was to be active in organizations and to maintain a "nice girl" image. For boys, the pressure was to be a "macho" athlete, to use drugs or alcohol, and to become sexually involved.

How do peers encourage each other to conform? Surprisingly, most teens report little direct *pressure* to conform (Bradford-Brown and Klute, 2003). In other words, they don't order each other to conform and threaten retaliation or rejection if they do not. However,

ANSWERS WOULDN'T YOU LIKE TO KNOW...

Do adolescents pressure each other to conform?

Yes but not usually in overt ways. Instead, adolescents use nonverbal signals, approval, attention, and teasing to encourage one another to conform.

peers do exert **normative regulation** (Brown and Theobald, 1999). That is, there is an unspoken understanding that friends will stick together and behave in similar ways. They sometimes indicate their approval or disapproval of each other's actions through subtle nonverbal signals.

Two other techniques are also used to encourage conformity. *Modeling,* a concept first proposed by Bandura (1971), appears to be a significant avenue of influence. Teenagers copy each other's behavior—especially that of the most popular individuals. Friends also provide opportunities for each other to engage in particular activities. If a teenage boy calls all of his friends to ask them to come over and play football, those who accept the invitation will spend the afternoon engaged in the same activity.

Achievement

Another way of finding group acceptance and approval is through achievement—in sports, club membership, recreational activities, or academic subjects. The recognition and acceptance the individual achieves depends on the status accorded the activity by the peer group.

Research indicates consistently that high school athletes are awarded higher social status than are scholars. For example, Landsheer, Maasen, Bisschop, and Adema (1998) uncovered a negative relationship between academic competence in math and science and popularity with peers. These researchers speculated that the hours academically successful students spend studying take time away from peer interaction and decrease their ability to be spontaneous, which is valued by youths. Other researchers have concluded that gifted and talented teens spend more time alone than other adolescents but that they enjoy the activities they do when alone and hence are not lonely or unhappy (Csikszentmihalyi, Rathunde, and Whalen, 1993). Athlete-scholars are the most popular students of all, suggesting that some positive status is given to both academic and athletic achievements.

Participation

Joining in-school clubs and participating in a variety of out-of-school social activities are other ways the adolescent has of finding social acceptance (Dubois and Hirsch, 1993). One study found that the desire to belong was the most important motive for participating in out-of-school activities (Bergin, 1989). The most popular students are often joiners, usually in multiple activities in schools, but also as members of out-of-school, community-sponsored youth groups and as participants in every conceivable type of social and recreational activity among friends.

The group life of adolescents has been characterized as *herd life.* The herd assembles at the local hangout for refreshments and small talk. The herd goes joyriding in the car or to a movie, a dance, or a rock concert. The herd goes on a hayride, skiing, or to the beach. The herd hangs out at the local shopping mall (Anthony, 1985). To be part of the social scene, one has to join and be with the herd.

Physical Attractiveness

Physical attractiveness also influences popularity. In one study, 270 ninth-graders were asked to rate the acceptability of hypothetical same-sex peers with whom they might be paired to complete a school assignment. Participants consistently ranked the physically attractive partners as more acceptable than the less attractive ones, regardless of whether the attractive partner was presented as having high or low grades. Boys and girls were equally likely to value having a good-looking partner (Boyatzis, Baloff, and Durieux, 1998).

Even teachers have been found to rate physically attractive students more academically competent than less attractive students (Lerner, Delaney, Hess, Jovanovic, and von Eye, 1990). After getting to know less attractive students better, however, both adolescents and adults begin to place less emphasis on physical attractiveness and more emphasis on other qualities. The older they become, the more adolescents emphasize interpersonal factors and deemphasize achievement and physical characteristics in friendship bonds.

Deviance

Thus far, little has been said about achieving group acceptance through deviant behavior—that is, behavior different from that of the majority of youths but considered acceptable in a particular group that itself deviates from the norms. Whereas overtly aggressive, hostile behavior may be unacceptable in society as a whole, it may be required in a gang as a condition of membership. Likewise, what might be considered a bad reputation in the local high school (fighter, troublemaker, uncooperative, antisocial, sexually promiscuous) might be a good reputation among a group of delinquents.

relational aggression using your friends to help socially hurt another.

reputational aggression spreading rumors or doing other actions to hurt another's reputation.

normative regulation the process by which teens signal their approval and disapproval of each other, generally through unspoken means.

ANSWERS WOULDN'T YOU LIKE TO KNOW . . .

What makes some adolescents so popular?

Popular adolescents tend to be athletic (especially boys), to participate in a lot of activities, to get decent grades, and to be outgoing. Being physically attractive increases one's popularity, too.

One study of 12- to 16-year-old boys who were overaggressive and bullied younger, weaker youths showed that the bullies enjoyed average popularity among other boys (Olweus, 1994); those who were the targets of aggression were far less popular than the bullies. These findings illustrate that standards of group behavior vary with different groups so that popularity depends not so much on a fixed standard as on group conformity.

Although it might seem that antisocial adolescents would be incapable of being good friends, this is not true. In fact, the friendships among deviant youths are frequently quite close (Hussong, 2000). Unfortunately, due to the mechanisms described earlier—modeling, opportunity, and normative expectations—adolescents who are involved in friendships with delinquents often end up behaving badly themselves.

The Darker Side of Peer Interactions: Bullying

Bullying is unprovoked aggressive behavior that is intended to hurt another. It is usually repeated over and over again, and it stems from a perceived power difference between the bully and his or her victim (Olweus, 2001; Rigby, 2002). It is the most common form of aggression in schools (Smith, Walker, Fields, Brookins, and Seay, 1999) and it is distressingly common: More than half of adolescents report having both bullied another student and having been a victim of bullying themselves (Bond, Carlin, Thomas, Rubin, and Patton, 2001). Bullying can take many forms, including physical aggression, ridicule, or shunning (Tanaka, 2001). It can be done by a lone individual, but it is usually done in the presence of peers who either actively support it or passively condone it (Karatzias, Power, and Swanson, 2002; Salmivalli, Kaukiainen, and Lageropetz, 1999).

Victims of bullies are insecure, quiet, and shy (Olweus, 1994). They have few friends and are physically weak (Card, 2003). They may be physically unattractive (Sweeting and West, 2001) or come from a different ethnic or racial group than those who bully them (Siann, Callaghan, Glisson Lockhart, and Rawson, 1999). They are often poor students or very strong students (Horowitz et al., 2004).

Bullying has a major effect on the victims. In the short run, they lose friends because others are afraid that they will become targets if they associate with those who are being victimized (Batsche and Knoff, 1994). They may begin to avoid school (Kochenderfer and Ladd, 1997) and attempt or complete suicide (Tanaka, 2001). Even when older, they are more likely to become depressed (Bond, Carlin, Thomas, Rubin, and Patton, 2001).

Bullies, especially male bullies, are often poor students who have cold, rejecting, authoritarian parents

RESEARCH HIGHLIGHT CYBERBULLYING

While computers and the Internet have the potential to enhance student learning and foster positive communication among people, they also bring the potential for a new form of harassment: cyberbullying (Beran and Li, 2005). According to Willard (2004), cyberbullying involves sending or posting harmful or cruel text or images using the Internet or other digital communication devices. Specific examples include (1) sending derogatory or threatening messages; (2) posting stories or pictures that ridicule named others; (3) sending embarrassing or pornographic material to the one you wish to harass; (4) spreading rumors on a Web page about another; and (5) copying personal information that has been sent to you via e-mail or instant messaging from the person you wish to harass to others.

Cyberbullying has not yet been well studied, but it appears to be prevalent. Beran and Li (2005) found that one-fourth of the Canadian adolescents they studied had been cyberbullied, and 50 percent claimed to know at least one teenager who had been harassed online. A study done in Great Britain had very comparable findings (National Children's Home, 2002).

Males are more likely to bully, in the conventional sense, than females. Is this true in cyberspace? It appears that it is. Li (2006) found that adolescent boys were about twice as likely to admit to cyberbullying than girls.

In addition, Li (2006) found that about one-third of the victims were repeatedly cyberharassed. Most victims did not tell an adult, even when the harassment occurred at school. It is likely that the students did not believe that the cyberbullying could be stopped. Unfortunately, they are likely correct: It is very difficult to stop cyberharassment due to laws protecting freedom of speech.

PERSONAL ISSUES HELPING PAINFULLY SHY ADOLESCENTS

Several techniques can be used to effectively help shy adolescents develop more confidence in social situations. For instance, **cognitive-behavioral modification** can be used to help reduce the anxiety-provoking thoughts common among shy individuals. These people can be made aware of their self-defeating cognitions ("No one likes me"; "I always make a fool of myself when I try to talk to anyone"), and these feelings can then be gently disputed. Increased confidence results when individuals realize that things are not as bleak as they have been telling themselves. Individuals are also taught to substitute more positive messages when they catch themselves thinking destructive thoughts ("I have a good sense of humor; many people enjoy speaking with me").

Shy adolescents can also directly be taught social skills that will help them during social encounters. For instance, learning how to effectively enter a conversation, how to listen closely to others, and how to make eye contact when speaking can result in more pleasant interactions and increased self-confidence. With practice, these news skills will become habitual.

Shy adolescents can also learn how to remain calm when interacting with others. A variety of relaxation techniques, such as deep breathing and muscle relaxation, can be used before or during conversations to calm down. Conditioned fearful responses—the panic that some shy individuals fear because they have a history of negative social encounters—can be reduced or even eliminated using traditional extinction techniques.

Finally, in severe cases, drug therapy can be used to ameliorate feelings of social anxiety. Antidepressants such as Prozac and Paxil can be prescribed, as can beta-blockers such as Inderal, which are more useful for individuals who become socially anxious in only specific, limited circumstances.

No shy individual should suffer in silence. If people seek help, they can learn rather quickly ways to feel more comfortable as they go about their day. Most college counseling centers either conduct group sessions for persons with social anxiety or can refer individuals to someone who does. For a review of all treatment options, see Beidel and Turner (1998).

(Baldry and Farrington, 2000). There is disagreement in the literature about whether they have high or low self-esteem (Smith, 2004). Those who use physical aggression are likely to continue to do so as they get older (Olweus, 1993). A minority of bullies are also victims themselves. These adolescents look worse than either pure bullies or pure victims (Wolke, Woods, Bloomfield, and Korstadt, 2000); not only are they are hostile to others, but they are so disliked that they are picked on as well. A disproportionate number of these youth have attention deficit hyperactivity disorder (Griffin and Gross, 2003).

Fortunately, some very effective school-based antibullying programs have been devised. When fully implemented, these programs have reduced the rates of bullying by 50 to 75 percent (Olweus, 1994). Greene (2006) recently summarized the characteristics of the most effective interventions:

1. *All students must be actively involved, not just the bullies and victims.* They all need to be familiar with antibullying rules, they need to know who to go to if bullying does occur, and they need to develop antibullying attitudes. It helps if they can learn strategies that help diffuse potential bullying situations.
2. *Teachers must participate.* Not only must they control behavior within their classrooms, but they must teach social skills and monitor what is going on.
3. *Fair, school-wide policies must be enforced.* Administrators must be sure that teachers are trained to take bullying seriously and not view it as inevitable, normative behavior. They must be sure that teachers receive adequate training to handle bullying incidents. There must be consistent sanctions for those who bully.
4. *The best programs get parents and other members of the community involved.* Schools can only directly address what happens on their own turf; others must take over after hours.
5. *The specific motivations for bullying must be addressed in each individual school.* If the primary cause is racial, then that topic must be dealt with; if it is sexual harassment, then programs need to focus on that issue. Schools must also address the specific forms of bullying that occur (e.g., shunning).
6. *The efforts must be continued over time.* Short-term interventions rarely have lasting results.

cognitive-behavioral modification a therapeutic technique used to help control maladaptive, self-defeating thoughts.

HETEROSOCIALITY

Psychosocial Development

One of the most important social goals of midadolescence is to achieve heterosociality (Miller, 1990). In the process of psychosocial development, children pass through three stages:

1. **Autosociality:** The first stage, autosociality, is the early preschool period of development in which the child's chief pleasure and satisfaction is himself or herself. This is most typical of the 2-year-old who wants to be in the company of others but who plays alongside them, not with them. The adolescent who is still a loner, who does not have any friends, is still in this early stage of development.
2. **Homosociality:** The second stage, homosociality, is the primary school period of development in which the child's chief pleasure is in being with others of the same sex, not for sexual purposes but for friendship and companionship (Bukowski, Gauze, Hoza, and Newcomb, 1993). Every normal child passes through this important stage of forming same-sex friendships (Lempers and Clark-Lempers, 1993). Establishing same-sex friendships in preadolescence is crucial to identity formation. By establishing a "consensual exchange" with a same-sex friend, preadolescents are able to enrich their sense of self and validate their self-worth (Paul and White, 1990). During this stage, children actively avoid interacting with members of the opposite sex (Adler, Kleiss, and Adler, 1992) and sex segregation is pronounced, even when children are engaged in gender-neutral activities. When excursions into the "enemy camp" do occur in middle childhood, they often have romantic overtones. Thorne (1986) termed this "border work" and believes that it serves to further emphasize the boundaries between the sexes. This marked sex segregation is a near-universal phenomenon, occurring in cultures as disparate as those found in Sweden (Tietjen, 1982) and western Kenya (Harkness and Super, 1985).
3. **Heterosociality:** The final stage, heterosociality, is the adolescent and adult stage of development in which the individual's pleasure and friendships are found with those of both sexes (Goff, 1990). The development of intimacy is one of the important challenges of late adolescence (Paul and White, 1990). Failure to achieve close relationships with a member of the opposite sex may result in severe anxiety, fears about one's sexuality, and lower self-esteem. Older adolescents are particularly sensitive and vulnerable to feelings of heterosexual inadequacy.

ANSWERS WOULDN'T YOU LIKE TO KNOW ...

Is it good for adolescents to have cross-sex friendships?

Yes. Having cross-sex friendships is good for both adolescent girls and boys. Girls benefit by becoming comfortable around members of the opposite sex and by learning what boys think. Boys enjoy these benefits and also have the opportunity to disclose their feelings.

Getting acquainted and feeling at ease with the opposite sex is a painful process for some youths. The Personal Issues box that follows lists some of the questions that trouble midadolescents as they try to form cross-sex relationships.

With sexual maturity comes a biological-emotional awareness of the opposite sex, a decline in hostile attitudes, and the beginning of emotional responses. The girl who was looked upon before as a giggly, pain-in-the-neck kid now takes on a new allure. On the one hand, the now-maturing male is fascinated and mystified by this young woman; on the other hand, he is awed, terrified, and bewildered. No wonder he ends up asking "How do you go about talking to a girl?"

The boy's first effort is to tease by engaging in some sort of physical contact: swipe her books, pull her hair, hit her with a snowball. Her response is often a culturally conditioned, predictable one: scream, run (either away or after him), and pretend to be upset. The boy is not very good at talking to girls, but he knows how to roughhouse, so he uses this time-honored method of making his first emotionally charged heterosocial contacts.

Gradually, these initial contacts take on a more sophisticated form. Teasing is now kid stuff. To be "cool"—confident, poised, unemotional, a good conversationalist, and comfortable in social situations—is the order of the day. The group boy/girl relationships change into paired relationships, and these deepen into affectionate friendships and romance as the two sexes discover each other. Table 12.1 lists the usual stages of psychosocial development.

Overall, the average age for choosing opposite-sex companionship has been declining, probably because of earlier sexual maturity and changing social customs. A boyfriend/girlfriend relationship at early stages may not be reciprocal, and the object of affection may not be aware of the love affair. (One of the authors knew a preadolescent boy who sold his girlfriend to another boy for 100 baseball cards, but the girl was never aware of the

PERSONAL ISSUES QUESTIONS JUNIOR HIGH ADOLESCENTS ASK ABOUT SOCIAL DEVELOPMENT AND RELATIONSHIPS

The following questions were submitted by adolescents in family life education classes. They illustrate some of the concerns of junior high adolescents (grades seven, eight, and nine) about social development and relationships:

- How can I get over being shy in groups?
- Do you have to follow everybody else to be popular?
- Does a girl have to wait for a boy to actually say he likes her?
- Why am I so self-conscious when I meet new boys?
- Should you worry if you don't have dates right away?
- How can I get a boy to notice me and like me?
- Why do boys shy away from being introduced?
- How can I get others to like me?
- What do boys look for in a girl?
- At what age can you begin dating?
- What do you do if you're scared to ask a girl to go on a date?
- How should I go about talking to a girl?
- What can you do if you're a wuss and afraid to ask a girl on a date?
- How can I attract the opposite sex?

fact that she had been a girlfriend in the first place.) With advancing age, however, expected and actual reciprocity begin to converge.

Some gay and lesbian teens are aware of their sexual orientations from early adolescence. They, of course, may not feel the desire or need to develop romantic attachments to persons of the opposite sex. Still, homosexual adolescents need to develop friendships and other comfortable relationships with persons of the other gender. They also must learn to pursue same-sex romantic relationships. Due to prejudice and increased fear of rejection, gay and lesbian youths often find doing so even more difficult than negotiating cross-sex romantic attachments.

autosociality the period during which a child plays alongside other children, not with them.

homosociality the period during which children prefer the company of those of the same sex.

heterosociality the period during which adolescents and adults the company of both sexes.

TABLE 12.1 AGES AND STAGES IN PSYCHOSOCIAL DEVELOPMENT

AGE	STAGE
Infancy	Autosocial: Boys and girls are interested only in themselves.
About ages 2–7	They seek companionship of other children regardless of sex.
About ages 8–12	Homosocial: Children prefer to play with others of the same sex; some antagonism exists between the sexes.
Ages 13–14	Heterosocial: Girls and boys become interested in one another.
Ages 15–16	Some boys and girls pair off.
Ages 17–18	The majority of adolescents "go with" someone.

Adolescent Love and Crushes

Love and romance are common interests for adolescents. In one study, more than half of American 12- to 18-year-olds reported having been in a romantic relationship within the past 18 months (Furman and Shaffer, 2003). Most American teens fall in love for the first time when in early adolescence (Montgomery and Sorrell, 1998). Even when alone, high-schoolers report spending at least five hours per week thinking about a real or imagined romantic partner (Richards, Crowe, Larson, and Swarr, 1998). Boys begin falling in love at a younger age than girls, are more likely to have been in love at some time than girls, and as adolescents are more likely to currently be in love than girls (Montgomery and Sorrell, 1998), perhaps because boys base their love for girls more on physical attractiveness than girls do (Feiring, 1996).

Falling in love serves as a positive need in the lives of most people. If the love is reciprocated, it is associated with fulfillment and ecstasy. College dating couples who report they are in love are also the ones who report the greatest happiness. In addition, romantic involvement can foster the identity search and help adolescents break away emotionally from their parents (Gray and Steinberg, 1999).

Young adolescents may have an intense crush on someone they really do not know and will fantasize romantic encounters with this person. They often report being in love with a person that they do not know well and to whom they have rarely spoken. By late adolescence, teenagers are more cautious about labeling their feelings "love" (Montgomery and Sorrell, 1998).

ANSWERS WOULDN'T YOU LIKE TO KNOW ...

Do teenage boys fall in love as easily as teenage girls?

Teenage boys fall in love more easily than teenage girls. Namely, they report falling in love more quickly and more often.

Intense love can be risky business. Success sparks delight but failure invites despair. Unrequited love is associated with emptiness and anxiety. The loss of love can be a devastating experience for the adolescent.

Loss of Love

The loss of a romantic relationship constitutes a major life change, and adolescents are thus often devastated when a boyfriend or girlfriend leaves them. Parents and other adults commonly underestimate the grief that an adolescent feels over a breakup. From the adults' point of view, the relationship was brief and unimportant. Adults may seek to make various types of comforting statements: "You're too young to understand what love is; this wasn't the real thing," "You'll feel better tomorrow," "You're young; you have plenty of time to find a relationship," and "You'll look back and wonder what you ever saw in this person." But from the adololescent's perspective, this may have been the relationship of a lifetime. Experiencing a romantic breakup is among the most common causes of adolescent depression, suicide, and murder (Joyner and Udry, 2000).

RESEARCH HIGHLIGHT GAY AND LESBIAN ADOLESCENTS' ROMANTIC RELATIONSHIPS

Because gay and lesbian youths are in the minority and because of the prejudice they face, negotiating intimate relationships is even more difficult for them than for straight youths. Certainly, the majority of gay and lesbian adolescents would like to have same-sex romances (Savin-Williams, 1990), but it is difficult for them to do so. Fearing rejection, most are willing to approach only openly gay or lesbian peers, and there are not likely to be many in their school or even in their community. Even if they know two or three other same-sex homosexual teens, they face a range of issues: (1) They might not be attracted to those other teens; (2) the other teens might not be attracted to them; (3) they might not be interested in the same type of relationship (e.g., exclusive or open, intensive or casual); and (4) they may be afraid to risk losing the few friends to whom they can really relate (Diamond and Savin-Williams, 2003).

Given these difficulties, many homosexual adolescents date persons of the opposite sex, even though that is not their preference. In addition, adolescent lesbians may form extremely intense, passionate platonic friendships with other girls (Diamond, Savin-Williams, and Dubé, 1999). Gay adolescent boys may also form emotionally supportive platonic friendships with girls, who are generally less threatened by and more supportive of their sexual orientation than their straight male peers.

In actuality, adolescents are especially vulnerable to loss because their egos are still evolving and their range of coping skills may not be fully developed. Adolescents are also more vulnerable to loss because when they enter a romantic relationship, they tend to idealize their partner.

Emotionally disengaging from a relationship takes considerable time and effort. Youths often experience grief, which may result in reduced academic performance and health problems, as well as carelessness about home duties, employment responsibilities, schoolwork, and attire. Adolescents may withdraw and spend more time alone, even taking meals to their rooms. They may be thinking and fantasizing about the former partner while listening to sentimental music. They may express hopelessness of ever loving anyone else. They may also attempt to self-medicate with drugs or alcohol. Of equal concern are adolescents who exhibit no reaction to the loss, but who start living at a hectic pace and initiate new, intense relationships too quickly. The loss of a loved one has also been identified as a significant factor in adolescent suicide.

The following techniques, summarized from Kaczmarek and Backlund (1991), are things adults can do to help adolescents survive such a loss:

- Help them to view the intense feelings as normal, to be expected. Adolescents need to be given permission to feel and to grieve.
- Encourage them to express feelings and thoughts.
- Teach them about the process of grief.
- Encourage them to rely on a network of family and friends—those who will accept their pain and not offer comforting clichés. Friends who have also lost a love may prove empathetic and insightful.
- Give them permission to slow down and allow the healing process to begin.
- Encourage a balance between the need for connectiveness and the need for withdrawal.
- Encourage them to take care of themselves physically through rest, diet, and exercise.
- Suggest that they put away mementos. Doing this indicates that they relinquish some of the fantasy of being reunited.
- Help them view themselves as survivors who understand that the hurt will become less intense with the passage of time.
- Help them to understand that there will be up-days and down-days and to anticipate sadness occasionally.
- Suggest that they postpone major decisions and avoid other significant changes in their lives, that the period of grief is not the time to make major changes.
- Encourage them to find new ways to enjoy the extra time and new freedom. Propose ways to do this, such as taking up a hobby, making new friends, or engaging in additional work or activities. These can help rebuild confidence and self-esteem.

DATING

Dating is not a universal phenomenon. Many societies actually prohibit dating or even close premarital contact with members of the opposite sex (Hatfield and Rapson, 1996). In fact, dating as American adolescents practice it—by freely and independently choosing romantic partners and having no sense that the experience will culminate in marriage—is a recent cultural custom. What purpose, then, does dating serve? Why do adolescents (and adults) date? A number of reasons can be cited:

The purpose of dating among adolescents ranges from platonic recreation, to companionship, to mate selection, to intense sexual and/or romantic involvement.

1. *Recreation:* One major purpose of dating is to have fun. Dating provides amusement; it is a form of recreation and source of enjoyment. It can be an end in itself.
2. *Companionship without the responsibility of marriage:* Wanting the companionship of others is a strong motive for dating. Desiring the friendship, acceptance, affection, and love of others is a normal part of growing up.
3. *Status grading, sorting, and achievement:* Higher-status youths date more frequently than lower-status youths, and some use dating partly to achieve, prove, or maintain status. Membership in certain cliques is associated with the status-seeking aspects of dating. Although there has been a significant decline in dating as a means of gaining or proving status, there are still significant prestige dimensions to cross-sex socializing, especially with the "right" person.
4. *Socialization:* Dating is a means of personal and social growth. It is a way of learning to know, understand, and get along with many different types of people. Through dating, youths learn cooperation, consideration, responsibility, numerous social skills and matters of etiquette, and techniques for interacting with other people. This may not often be a reason for dating, but it is certainly a benefit often gained from that activity.
5. *Sexual experimentation or satisfaction:* Studies have shown that dating has become more sex oriented as more adolescents have sexual intercourse. Whether dating is used to have sex or sex develops out of dating depends on the attitudes, feelings, motives, and values of the youths involved. Most research, however, indicates that men want sexual intimacy in a relationship sooner than do women, and this discrepancy is a potential source of conflict.
6. *Achieving intimacy:* The development of intimacy is the primary psychosocial task of the young adult, but adolescents crave intimacy, as well. *Intimacy* is the development of openness, sharing, mutual trust, respect, affection, and loyalty, so that a relationship can be characterized as close, enduring, and involving love and commitment. The capacity to develop intimacy varies from person to person. Research indicates that intimacy is more valued by females than by males, although gender differences decrease in later adolescence as males become closer to and more supportive of their partners (Eaton, Mitchell, and Jolley, 1991). Usually, women find it easier than men to talk intimately.
7. *Mate selection:* Whether this is a conscious motive or not, mate selection is eventually what happens, especially among older adolescents. The longer a couple dates, the less they tend to overidealize each other and the greater are their chances of knowing each other. Dating provides an opportunity for two people to become a pair. If they are similar in role preferences, leisure interests, and personality characteristics, they are more likely to develop a compatible relationship than if they are dissimilar in physical attractiveness and psychological and social characteristics.

Dating affects and is affected by the other in youths' lives. One study found that daters had more autonomy from their parents and experienced more conflicts with them than nondaters (Dowdy and Kliewer, 1998). A second study determined that adolescents who felt emotionally distant from their parents were less satisfied with their dating relationships than those who were close to their parents (Larson, Peterson, Health, and Birch, 2000). An additional study found that casual daters felt closer to their other friends than those who had a steady boyfriend or girlfriend (Davies and Windle, 2000).

The Development of Dating

By late adolescence, most American teenagers have had at least one romantic relationship (Carver, Joyner, and Udry, 2003). Most do not start regularly dating until fairly late in adolescence, however, since only about one-third of 15- and 16-year-olds report having a current boyfriend or girlfriend (Feiring, 1996).

The general flow of events is that adolescents move from having primarily or exclusively same-sex friends to belonging to mixed-sex groups. Next, some members of these mixed-sex groups begin to date and "be together" in these mixed-sex groups. Finally, adolescents truly pair off and the pairs go their separate ways and spend a good deal of time by themselves (Dunphy, 1963). Although this had originally been construed as a rigid, fixed sequence of events, most researchers now recognize that the events are more fluid; there is more back-and-forth movement in terms of a teen's behavior (Connolly, Craig, Goldberg, and Peplar, 2004).

The benefits of this gradual immersion into the world of dating are obvious. First, because the teen is in a group, many of whom are the teen's friends, the teen is surrounded by supportive individuals whom he or she likes. There is little change for rejection by the group. Second, the teen has the opportunity to observe others of the opposite sex, to "size them up" and see who is of interest. Third, the

PERSONAL ISSUES QUESTIONS SENIOR HIGH ADOLESCENTS ASK ABOUT DATING

The following questions were submitted by adolescents in family life education classes. They reflect some of the concerns of senior high school adolescents (grades ten, eleven, and twelve):

- Is it all right to date several boys at once?
- How can you tell if you're really in love?
- How should a girl refuse a date?
- Will boys take you out if you're not willing to go all the way?
- How can you break up without hurting the other person?
- What do you do if your parents don't want you to go with your boyfriend because he's three years older (I'm 15; he's 18)?

teen can very gently test the waters and see if the person he or she is interested in seems at all interested in him or her as well; if not, the teen can casually move off. Fourth, the burden of carrying on a conversation and being amusing are spread among many people; there are fewer awkward gaps to fill. Fifth, there is only limited opportunity for intimacy—physical or emotional—for which the younger teen is likely unready.

With increasing comfort and maturity, these crutches are less needed and adolescents gradually desire to spend more time alone with their romantic partner.

Violence

Upon conducting a literature search to find current articles about adolescent romantic experiences, the junior author was appalled to find that more than 40 percent of the articles written since 2001 that were retrieved using the search terms "adolescent love," "adolescent romance," "adolescent dating," and "going steady" were about dating violence. Therefore, even though this topic is briefly discussed in Chapter 9, it seems worthwhile to revisit the topic in this chapter, as well.

Aggression—physical, emotional, and sexual—is all too common when adolescents date. A study of more than 900 Los Angeles high school students indicated that about 45 percent, both male and female, had experienced some sort of physical violence at least once while on a date. And while the numbers among boys and girls may be similar, the nature of the violence they experienced was not. The males were most likely to report being shoved, kicked, or pushed, whereas the females were most likely to report being forced to engage in unwanted sexual activities

Dating violence occurs more commonly than many adolescents realize. Girls, in particular, are at significant risk of being physically or sexually assaulted in the context of a dating relationship.

ANSWERS WOULDN'T YOU LIKE TO KNOW . . .

How common is dating violence among adolescents?

Dating violence is distressingly common. An estimated 1 in 4 adolescents has experienced sexual or physical violence while on a date.

(although not necessarily intercourse). Boys were more likely to initiate violence than girls, usually because they were jealous or angry. Girls who engaged in violence most often did so because they were angry or wanted to "get back" at a boy who had hurt them. Girls reacted to the violence they experienced with either fear or by being hurt; boys' reactions were closely divided between anger and thinking that the girls' attempts to hurt them were "funny" (O'Keefe and Treister, 1998).

Other research has confirmed the high risk of sexual aggression for adolescent girls involved in romantic relationships. It has been estimated that at least 25 percent of adolescent girls are victims of dating violence (Wolfe and Feiring, 2000). Furthermore, dating partners are responsible for between one-half and two-thirds of the sexual assaults committed on late adolescent females (Flanagan and Furman, 2000).

Dating violence is not confined to teens in the United States. One study conducted in the United Kingdom found that almost half of the 13- to 19-year-olds sampled had experienced some form of aggression while on a date (Hird, 2000). Similarly, a study of New Zealand teens found that almost 80 percent of the girls and 67 percent of the boys had engaged in unwanted sexual activity and that most had been subjected to emotional violence at least once. As in the American study, boys were less likely than girls to be troubled by these incidents (Jackson, Cram, and Seymour, 2000).

"Going Together"

There are different patterns of adolescent dating. One step up from "dating"— though in some locations the terms are used synonymously—is "going together." While dating does not necessarily imply fidelity and exclusiveness, going together does. If you are going with someone, at least for the time being, the presumption is that you are not romantically involved with anyone else. The term *going together* has largely replaced the term *going steady.* Whatever it's called, is it a good thing? Does it foster healthy development?

Because many parents worry that their children will make premature commitments, they sometimes urge their offspring to date a large number of partners. Research indicates, however, that those who date the greatest number of partners also have the greatest number of different, more committed, relationships. Because marital success is positively correlated with the number of friends of both sexes one has before marriage, there is some advantage in going with large numbers of partners, although the chances of being committed to any one are greater. Steady dating for a long period can limit the number of dating partners, and a community that accepts "going with" as the norm can make it harder for youths to avoid the pattern. In some cases, they either have to go with someone or not date at all. Another worry that parents have is that their children will become sexually active in the context of a steady relationship. This concern seems justified; in one study of 1,200 parochial school students, most teens reported first having sexual intercourse with their steady boyfriend or girlfriend (de Gaston, Jensen, and Weed, 1995).

ANSWERS WOULDN'T YOU LIKE TO KNOW . . .

Is going together good or bad for teenagers?

Going steady is good for teens in that it allows them to have security and experience a deeper, more meaningful relationship. Going steady is bad in that it limits teens' exposure to others, may require a level of emotional maturity that teens are not ready for, and increases the probability of sexual activity.

Youths also see advantages and disadvantages to going with someone. The primary motive seems to be to enjoy the company of someone else. Steady dating also provides security for some adolescents. Apparently, they go with someone because they need to, emotionally and socially. They try to find someone to love and be loved by—someone who understands and sympathizes with them. Steady dating often meets those emotional needs (McDonald and McKinney, 1994).

The disadvantages of going together are many. Some youths feel that it's confining and even boring and that they have more fun dating different people. One girl said, "Instead of going steady, I wound up staying home steady. Ted didn't take me out." Another issue is that some youths are not emotionally mature enough to handle such an intimate relationship and the problems that arise. Also, breaking up leads to hurt feelings. One boy asked, "How can I ditch Kathy without hurting her feelings?" This is a frequent remark from youths who are involved but who do not know how to get uninvolved. The problem of jealousy often arises, as well. Boys tend to be jealous over sexual issues; girls complain of lack of time and attention.

The basic problem may be that neither person is ready for an intense, intimate relationship with one person over a long period of time. Most youths admit that going together becomes a license for increasing sexual intimacy. "You get to feeling married, and that's dangerous" is the way one adolescent expressed it. Others feel that steady dating adds respectability to petting or even to intercourse and that this is an advantage rather than a disadvantage. Research indicates that those within a particular socioeconomic class who date the most frequently and who begin at the earliest ages are more likely to get married early, as well. Therefore, whenever steady dating pushes youths prematurely into early marriage, it is a serious disadvantage.

NONMARITAL COHABITATION

To many older adolescents, nonmarital cohabitation is just an extension of steady dating (Thornton, 1990).

Incidence

The rise in nonmarital sex has been accompanied by an increase in cohabitation. In 2004, there were 5.1 million unmarried cohabiting couples in the United States. About 20 percent of these included individuals who were under 25 years of age (Fields, 2004). Most college students say that they would be willing to cohabitate if they met the right person (Knox, Zusman, Snell, and Cooper, 1999).

In fact, more than half of young adults will live with someone prior to marriage (Bumpus and Lu, 2000). Living together is more common among African Americans, among people who are poor, and among people who are not religious. Cohabiting is also more prevalent among young adults whose parents were divorced, who are from single-parent homes, or whose parents displayed much marital discord. As Figure 12.1 illustrates, the number of cohabiting couples has increased astronomically during the past 40 years. Although many people view cohabitors as never-married, childless young adults, this image is not entirely accurate. Almost half of all cohabiting couples have one or more children (Fields, 2004), and many have been previously married.

Meanings Attached to Cohabitation

When couples decide to cohabit, the important questions are: What meaning do they attach to the relationship? Do they consider themselves in love? Are they committed to one another in an exclusive relationship? Are they testing their relationship? Are they preparing for marriage? Do they consider themselves married? There is a wide variety of patterns and meanings associated with cohabitation, which may be grouped as follows:

- Arrangements without commitment
- Intimate involvements with emotional commitment
- Living together as a prelude to marriage
- Living together as a trial marriage
- Living together as an alternative to marriage

Arrangements without Commitment

Sometimes, cohabitation arrangements are hastily or informally decided. After a weekend of fun and a short acquaintance, for example, the young man decides to

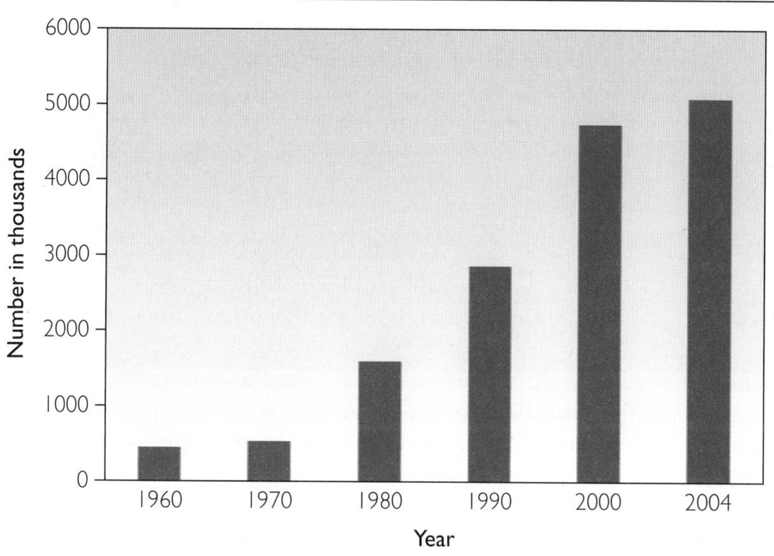

FIGURE 12.1 NUMBER OF COHABITATING U.S. COUPLES

Source: Data from Popenoe and Whitehead (2005).

move into his girlfriend's apartment. He ends up staying the rest of the semester. Sometimes, the arrangement is carefully worked out over a period of time as desirable for the couple. They simply want to live, sleep, and have fun together. They are very good friends and lovers but want no permanent, intimate commitment. Their living together includes sharing expenses, housekeeping chores, and the other economic and material necessities that a married couple do, as well as sleeping together. This type of arrangement usually is of short duration. Either it develops into a greater commitment or the couple breaks up.

Intimate Involvements with Emotional Commitment

The majority of cohabiting college couples place themselves in this category. Couples describe themselves as having a strong, affectionate relationship. Although some permit dating and sexual relationships outside the relationship, monogamy is the rule. And while there is a strong emotional commitment, there are no long-range plans for the future or for marriage. Such couples intend to continue the relationship indefinitely, but most involvements are of fairly short duration. Although dated, the only study of cohabitation in college found no statistically significant association between cohabitation and whether the couple married (Risman, Hill, Rubin, and Peplau, 1981). Cohabiting couples were not less likely to have married or more likely to have broken up by the end of the two-year study in contrast to those couples that had not cohabited.

Living Together as a Prelude to Marriage

In this type of relationship, the couple has already committed to legal marriage. The partners are engaged, formally or informally, but find no reason to live apart while they are waiting to be married or while they are making arrangements for their marriage. Many times, their living arrangements just develop over time, without conscious intent. Here is one student's story:

> My boyfriend and I never really *decided* we were going to live together before marriage. It just happened. He would come over to my apartment weekends. It would be late, so I'd put him up for the night. Then several weekends he stayed the whole time, it was easier than driving all that distance back home. After a while, we got thinking: "Isn't this silly, why should we be separated, why can't he just move in with me?" So he did. Finally, he gave up his own place, because it was cheaper for us to maintain only one apartment. Six months later we got married. If someone would ask: "What made you decide to live together before

Couples who cohabit may attach any of several meanings to their relationship. It might be a temporary arrangement without commitment, an emotionally committed relationship without long-range plans, a prelude to marriage, a test trial for marriage, or an alternative to marriage.

marriage?" my answer would be: "I don't know. It just happened."

Under these circumstances, there is never an intention that cohabitation will replace marriage or even be a trial period before marriage. It is just something the couple decides to do before they get married.

Living Together as a Trial Marriage

In this type of arrangement, the couple decides to live together to test their relationship—to discover if they are compatible and want to enter into legal marriage. This arrangement is "the little marriage before the big marriage that will last."

Living Together as an Alternative to Marriage

This arrangement has been called *companionate marriage, a covenant of intimacy,* or *a nonlegal voluntary association.* It is intended not as a prelude to marriage but as a substitute for it. This situation is more common among older adults than adolescents. It is not uncommon, for example, for someone who has been through a messy divorce to want to avoid any possibility of repeating that experience; such an individual may live with a partner indefinitely and never marry. In addition, elderly persons, especially widows and widowers, may find it economically more feasible to cohabitate without marriage than to get married. If they marry, their pension or Social Security benefits may decrease, and there may also be complications with maintaining individual assets and setting up wills.

Cohabitation versus Dating

There has been very little research comparing the satisfaction of those who are cohabitating with those who are dating while living separately. The benefits of cohabitation that have been identified include the convenience, the cost sharing, the increased amount of time spent together, the opportunity for more meaningful interaction, and enhanced sex lives. The downsides to cohabitation are mismatched expectations (e.g., one partner is more committed to the relationship than the other), arguments about dividing chores and sharing resources, the potential for feeling used, and lack of privacy.

Still, the majority of college students who have cohabited indicate positive feelings about the experience. Students report the experience as "pleasant," "successful," "highly productive." Many students indicate that it fostered personal growth and maturity, resulting in a deeper understanding of themselves or of what marriage requires (Rice, 1993). In comparison with noncohabiting couples in the Boston area, cohabiting men and women were more likely to report satisfaction with their relationships (Risman, Hill, Rubin, and Peplau, 1981). Cohabiting men were more likely to say that having sexual intercourse with their partner was satisfying. Cohabiting couples reported seeing each other more often, having sexual intercourse more often, feeling greater love for each other, and disclosing more to their partners.

Adjustments to Cohabitation

One major category of problems in cohabitation relates to the emotional involvement and feelings of the individuals concerned. A minority complain about overinvolvement, feeling trapped, losing identity, overpermissiveness of their partner, or the lack of opportunity to participate in activities with others. Without realizing it, these people became enmeshed in relationships for which they were not emotionally prepared. Once in, they did not know how to escape without hurting their partners. Others report being exploited or used by another person who did not care about them. Jealousy of others' involvements is common. One major worry is concern and uncertainty about the future. This uncertainty pressures some into marriage, others into breaking off the relationship.

The other problems youths face while living together unmarried are similar to those of any other people sharing the same quarters. Arranging to do the housekeeping chores is a challenge to unmarried as well as married couples. Traditional sex-role concepts and role specialization in the division of labor are quite evident among couples. Far greater percentages of women than men report cooking, dusting, dishwashing, vacuuming, doing laundry, feeding pets, and planning menus, which are traditionally considered feminine chores. Men report major responsibility for cutting the lawn, washing the car, doing repairs, cleaning the garage, shoveling snow, which are traditionally considered masculine chores. More men than women report an equal sharing of traditionally feminine chores, indicating that men reported they helped with these tasks more often than women felt they did.

It is obvious that nonmarital cohabitation is not a cure-all for sex-role inequality. Some tasks are shared, but generally the female partners do women's work and the male partners do men's work (as defined by traditional standards). This division leaves the women with most of the household duties regardless of whether they are going to school and are employed as well.

Cohabitation versus Marriage

Cohabitation is similar to marriage in many ways, but there are also significant differences. People who cohabit are more prone to split up than are married couples, for several reasons. Normally, people who are cohabiting have lower levels of commitment than do those who are married. Those who cohabit eschew tradition and are less committed to a traditional lifestyle. Greater commitment is required in marriage, and there are stronger social sanctions associated with deviation from tradition and marriage. Also, there is stronger social disapproval of deviant marital behaviors.

Taken together, this means that the relationship between a married couple is harder to dissolve. In marriage, there are more barriers that hold the relationship together (e.g., property interests). Therefore, lower levels of commitment are generally expected between cohabiting rather than married partners. The lack of social norms governing cohabitation also contributes to higher dissolution rates in such relationships.

Although most cohabiting individuals are happy with their living arrangement, they are significantly *less* happy than married people, even equating for demographic factors and the duration of the relationship (Brown and Booth, 1996; Nock, 1995). This is probably related to the lower levels of commitment associated with cohabitation.

One similarity between married couples and cohabiting couples is their likelihood of having children. More than 40 percent of cohabiting couples today have children, which is a large increase from the past (Fields and Casper, 2001). This is, of course, much less true of cohabiting adolescents than adults.

Effects on Subsequent Marriage

What effects does premarital cohabitation have on subsequent marital adjustment? One of the arguments used for cohabitation is that it weeds out incompatible couples and prepares people for more successful marriage. Is this true? No, according to several studies.

Compared to couples who do not cohabit prior to marriage, those who do score significantly lower on measures of marital quality (Booth and Johnson, 1988), have more extramarital affairs (Forste and Tanfer, 1996), and have a significantly higher risk of marital dissolution at any given marital duration (Teachman and Polonko, 1990; Wu, 1995a). The newest data suggest that the higher divorce rate occurs only when the spouses have cohabited multiple times with several different individuals prior to marriage (Teachman, 2003). Those who have cohabitated only with the person they eventually marry are no more likely to divorce than those who do not cohabit. This is most likely true because premarital cohabitation has become a normative behavior in modern American society. Therefore, those who are thoughtful and cautious in deciding to live with the person whom they eventually wed are no more likely to have a poor attitude toward marriage or a low ability to commit than those who do not live together.

> **ANSWERS WOULDN'T YOU LIKE TO KNOW ...**
>
> **Is living together a good test of marital compatibility?**
>
> No. Couples who live together before they are married are no more likely to have happy, stable marriages than couples who do not live together.

It is important to remember that comparisons between people who have and have not cohabited prior to marriage are correlational in nature. People *choose* whether to cohabitate with one another without getting married. This self-selection quite likely accounts for the differences in relationship satisfaction and divorce statistics that have been observed. For example, persons who live together without marriage are likely to be less religious and have lower educational levels than people who do marry. These factors might contribute their own negative outcomes, independent of or in addition to the experience of cohabiting per se.

Cohabitation and Premarital Childbearing

The question arises as to whether cohabitation is commonly a setting for procreation and care of the young. Research demonstrates that a substantial proportion of premarital pregnancies and births to U.S. women take place within cohabitation. Moreover, entry into motherhood is more likely among never-married women who are cohabiting than among those who are living alone. Premarital births to cohabiting women are less likely to be unplanned than premarital births to single (noncohabiting) women.

The rise of cohabitation has taken place in very different family contexts for various racial and ethnic groups. Cohabitation seems to operate differently for disadvantaged minorities than for Whites. One study documents sharp differences in the role of cohabitation across racial and ethnic groups. Cohabitation operates largely as a transitional stage before marriage for non-Hispanic Whites, but this is not the case for African Americans or Puerto Rican Americans. Nonmarital unions are a common family context for childbearing among Puerto Ricans; about half of the babies born premaritally have parents who live together. In contrast, African American women are much less likely to be in any union (cohabitation or marriage) when they become mothers. African Americans have markedly higher rates of premarital childbearing than Puerto Rican Americans. The historical prevalence of consensual unions among Puerto Ricans and their higher level of acceptance of cohabitation may partially explain why cohabitation plays a greater role in premarital childbearing for Puerto Rican Americans than for African Americans (Manning and Landale, 1996).

As the incidence of cohabitation continues to rise, the number of children born into these relationships will likely continue to increase, as well. Yet a study in the United States (Manning, 1995) found that the majority of women bear their first child within marriages and that many cohabiting women wait until their first marriage to have their first child (Wu, 1996). Cohabiting couples with children in the relationship are less likely to experience union disruption than are childless couples. Having children can encourage both married and unmarried couples to stay together.

Children born to cohabiting couples fare more poorly, on average, than those born to married couples. This is due, in part (but only in part), to their dire economic circumstances (Manning and Lichter, 1996). Children of cohabiting parents do not do as well in school as children being raised by married parents even when demographic and economic differences are accounted for (McLanahan and Sandefur, 1994). Children of cohabiting parents also exhibit more behavioral problems than those with married parents (Johnson, Stein, and Dadds, 1996).

ADOLESCENT MARRIAGE

To evaluate whether adolescent marriage is wise or unwise, desirable or undesirable, we must ask how successful these marriages are. If they are strong, happy, satisfying marriages, there is no cause for complaint or alarm. But if they are weak, unhappy, frustrating marriages, causing much personal suffering and numerous social problems, there is ample cause for concern.

Trends and Incidence

Figure 12.2 illustrates the median age at first marriage by sex. As can be seen, there have been steady increases in the ages at first marriage for both men and women since 1953. This increase has been most pronounced since 1960. Currently, men first marry when they are 26.8 years old and women first marry when they are 25.1 years old. The gap in marriage age between men and women has remained fairly constant, with men waiting an average of 2 to 2.5 years longer than women to marry.

Even so, some youths—especially girls—still marry young. Census figures for 2000 showed that 4.5 percent of girls and 1.5 percent of boys aged 18 and 19 are or had been married (Fields and Casper, 2001). Data also revealed that 25 percent of women and 14 percent of men aged 20 to 24 were or had been married. Hispanic youths were much more likely to be or have been married than non-Hispanic White or Black youths.

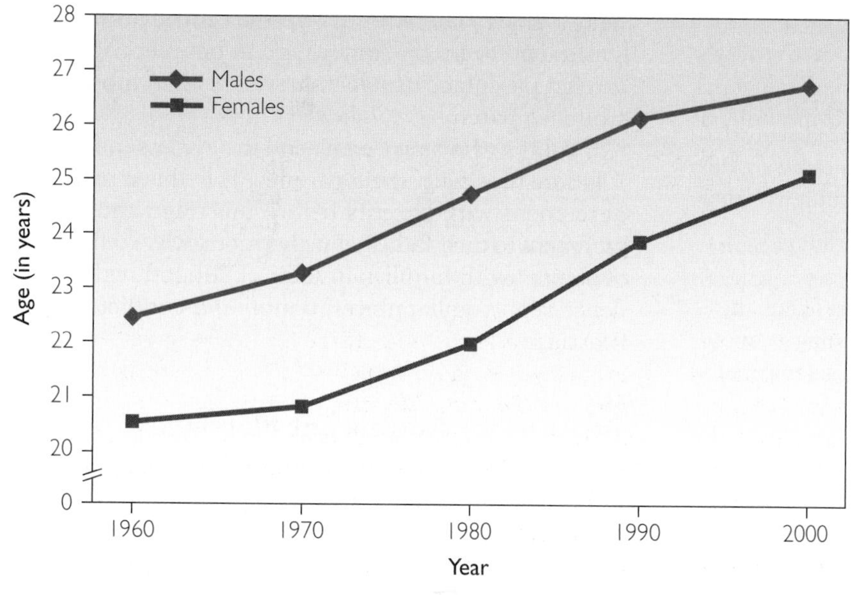

FIGURE 12.2 MEDIAN AGE AT FIRST MARRIAGE BY SEX

Source: U.S. Bureau of the Census, Current Population Survey, Annual Social and Economic Supplements, 2005 and earlier.

ANSWERS WOULDN'T YOU LIKE TO KNOW . . .

How many adolescents get married?

Fewer and fewer adolescents are getting married, probably due to the greater acceptability of nonmarital pregnancy. Regardless, this is a positive trend, since adolescent marriages are rarely happy or long lasting.

Prospects and Prognosis

Divorce statistics are a means of measuring marriage success or failure. Using this measure, adolescent marriages do not work out well. Numerous research studies indicate that the younger people are when married, the greater the chance of unhappy marriage and thus of divorce (Raley and Bumpus, 2003).

The older the couple at first marriage, the greater is the likelihood the marriage will succeed. But this direct correlation between age at first marriage and marital success diminishes for men at about age 27, when the decline in divorce rates slows considerably. For women, the divorce rate declines with each year they wait to marry until a gradual leveling off occurs at about age 25. Therefore, strictly from the standpoint of marital stability, men who wait to marry until at least age 27 and women who wait until about age 25 have waited as long as practical to maximize their chances of marital success.

Many couples marrying young may never get divorced, but some express deep dissatisfaction with their marriages. Here are some of their comments:

> "I don't think people should marry young. It's hard to get along when he is going to school. Our income is rather short. We probably should have waited."

> "We thought we were in love, we would get married and have good times. We had a very poor idea of what marriage was. We thought we could come and go, do as we pleased, do or not do the dishes, but it isn't that way."

> "I have missed several years of important living, the dating period, living with another girl, being away from home, working, maybe. I wouldn't get married so young again."

> "I would have waited to finish high school first. It has tied me down so. I've had no fun since I was married. I can't go to dances. I don't feel right there. . . . I guess I thought he was the only one in the world. I was badly mixed up."

A Profile of the Young Married

Early marriages primarily involve younger wives and older husbands. Typically, a high school girl will marry a boy who is past high school age, usually from 3.5 to 5.5 years older. Usually, the younger the bride, the larger the age difference between her and her husband. Early marriages disproportionately involve adolescents from lower socioeconomic backgrounds. Typically, their parents have less education and are of a lower occupational status.

There are several reasons that low socioeconomic status (SES) correlates with early marriage. As a group, low-SES youths are less interested in high school and post–high school education, so they see no need to delay marriage to finish their schooling, especially when marriage seems much more attractive than school. In some communities, marriage by age 18, especially for girls, is generally approved because the youths have reached a dead end in school and marriage seems to be an attractive course. Lower-SES parents are less likely to object to early marriage. Furthermore, premarital pregnancy, one of the principal causes of early marriage, is more common among youths from low-SES families.

Similarly, adolescents who get poor grades in school more often marry early. Furthermore, those who marry during school are more likely to drop out of school. It becomes a vicious cycle: The academically challenged marry earlier, and once married, they are less likely to continue their education. This is especially true of those who have children soon after marriage.

Place of residence seems to have some influence on age at marriage. Rural residents tend to marry a year earlier than urban residents. Those from the South tend to marry earlier than others, those from the Northeast tend to marry later, those from the central and western states tend to marry somewhere in between. Youths of foreign parentage usually marry later than those of native-born parents.

Youths who marry early tend to have less satisfactory relationships with their parents. They have more disagreement with parents before marriage and less attachment to their fathers. Furthermore, wives who report problems with families in their childhood and adolescence report unhappiness, doubt, and conflict in early marriage.

Reasons for Adolescent Marriage

The number-one reason for early marriage, particularly while still in school, is pregnancy. Pregnancy rates vary from study to study according to the age of the youths. The younger the adolescent is at the time of marriage, the more likely pregnancy is to be involved.

The number-one reason for early marriage, especially while still in school, is pregnancy. Many problems can be associated with these early marriages, including financial worries, lack of maturity, and resentment at being tied down.

Pregnancy rates may be as high as 50 percent when at least one of the partners is still in high school.

Social pressure from parents, friends, and society pushes adolescents toward early marriage. Educators report a chain reaction of early marriages in their schools. When one couple marries, there is increased pressure on others to do the same. No one wants to be left out. Pressure may also come from parents who do not want their daughters to bear children out of wedlock or who married young themselves.

Adolescents often hold very magical views of marriage. Marriage is seen as a fairytale in which a man and woman fall in love, marry, and live in bliss for eternity. Even adolescents whose parents are divorced and/or remarried have idealized concepts of marriage. Being in love in our culture is held to be so romantic and wonderful that many youths do not want to wait to enter this blissful state. The concept of marriage for love leads youths to feel that the goal of life is to find love, and that once found, they must hurry up and marry, at all costs, before it escapes. Girls who marry early often feel that marriage is their goal in life.

Marriage is also sometimes used as a means of escape from an unhappy home situation, lack of school achievement, personal insecurities or inadequacies, or unsatisfactory social adjustment with one's peers. The less attractive one's present situation is and the more attractive marriage seems, the more the emotionally insecure or socially maladjusted individual feels pushed toward marriage.

Adjustments and Problems

Many of the adjustments young couples must make or the problems they must solve are no different from those of other couples, but they are aggravated by immaturity. It is essentially the problem of immaturity, then, that is the great obstacle to successful teenage marriage.

The less mature are less likely to make a wise choice of mate. When the time span between first date and marriage is shortened, youths have less chance to gain experience in knowing and understanding the kind of person with whom they are compatible. The young adolescent girl or boy in the throes of a first love affair is at a distinct disadvantage in making an intelligent choice of spouse. Youths who marry young have spent insufficient time in the marital search process and tend to marry spouses who are relatively poor matches on a variety of unmeasured traits. Marriage at a young age often signifies a failure to search adequately for a well-matched spouse; thus, early marriages are disproportionately composed of poorly matched spouses (South, 1995).

Immature individuals are less likely to display the ultimate direction of their personality growth. Youths change as they mature and may find they have nothing in common with their partners as they grow older. Two young people who might genuinely find common interests and a good reciprocal interaction at a particular point in time could easily grow away from each other in the ensuing two or three years as their personalities unfold.

The most common example is the young woman who drops out of school to work to put her husband through college only to discover afterward that he has grown away from her intellectually and they can no longer enjoy talking together. The same holds true of a boy who marries young. He may marry a girl who has not yet found herself in life and runs the risk of living with a girl different from the woman she will be several years later. Many girls marry only to discover later that they resent having to give up a promising career.

The difficult and complex adjustments needed to solve the problems of marriage are not handled well by immature couples. There is ample evidence to show that emotional maturity and good marital adjustment go together. Many teenagers are still insecure, oversensitive, and somewhat tempestuous and unstable. Many are still rebelling against adult authority and seeking emotional emancipation from parents. If these youths marry, they carry their immaturities into marriage, making it difficult to adjust to living with their mates and making it harder to make decisions and solve conflicts as they arise.

Most youths have not yet become responsible enough for marriage. The average teenage boy is not ready to settle down. He wants to go out, have fun, be with the gang, and be free to do as he pleases. He may resent being tied down and possibly having to support a wife and child. He may not yet have developed a "monogamous attitude." Nor are many teenage girls ready to be wives and probably mothers, to manage a family budget, or to handle their share of the responsibility for the homemaking tasks.

One of the real problems and disadvantages of early marriage is that it is often associated with early parenthood. A majority of teenage couples have a baby within one year after marriage, if they have not already had a baby before marriage (Miller and Heaton, 1991; Moore and Stief, 1991). The younger the bride and groom, the sooner they start having children. Also, the earlier the age at marriage, the greater is the percentage of brides who are premaritally pregnant. Those who get married because of pregnancy have the poorest prognosis of marital success. Because premarital pregnancy and early postmarital pregnancy are followed by a higher-than-average divorce rate, large numbers of children of early marriages grow up without a secure, stable family life or without both a mother and a father. Apparently, many young marrieds are not mature enough to assume the responsibilities of marriage and early parenthood, so the marriages often fail and the children suffer.

Adolescent married couples not only begin having children at an earlier age, but they also have more children. The young women who are the least happily married are also the ones who experience unplanned pregnancies. Early motherhood creates many stresses in the lives of adolescents. Adolescent mothers are more likely to be out of school, unemployed, poor, and on public assistance. They experience loneliness and isolation from friends, with little time for themselves. Many are able to cope only by asking family members and community agencies for assistance, and many live with their parents after the birth of the baby (Ross and Aday, 2006).

In addition, the children born to adolescent mothers are more likely to be born premature, with low birth weight and with physical and neurological defects, than are infants born to mothers in their twenties. Perinatal, neonatal, and infant mortality have been found to be higher for children of young mothers ("Substantially Higher," 1984). The higher incidence of physical defects in children born to adolescent mothers is not due solely to the age of the mother. It is related also to the fact that these mothers usually receive inadequate nutrition and poor or inadequate prenatal care (Rogers, Peoples-Sheps, and Suchindran, 1996). Early pregnancy is also a medical risk for the young teenage girl. If she becomes pregnant while her own body is still growing and maturing, the growing fetus imposes an additional strain on her system, and she is more prone to complications during pregnancy.

One of the major problems of early marriage is financial worry. The primary difficulties are having an inadequate income and the fact that the income has not reached the level expected. Little education, inexperience, and youth do not bring high wages. Some couples marry without any income. With little or no income, couples receive part or all of their financial assistance from parents and from the government. Families usually give some assistance to their children in the first year of marriage, such as wedding gifts, clothing, home furnishings and equipment, food, loans of household equipment and car, babysitting services, money, and other gifts. Not only low income but also inexperience in financial management and naively optimistic expectations get young marrieds into financial trouble. Teenagers often unrealistically expect to be able to purchase immediately many of the items that probably took their parents years to acquire.

One of the most frequent complaints of immature wives is the husband who goes out with his friends and leaves her home alone. Also, in-law problems are more likely if young couples live with parents or accept financial help from them. When parents give assistance to married children, they often expect continual affectional response, inclusion in some of their children's activities, personal service and attention, and compliance with parental wishes. The more immature the young marrieds, the more likely parents are to try to "help"— to direct and interfere in their children's lives—and the more likely the young couple is to enact the residues of late adolescent conflicts over autonomy and dependence.

Early Marriage and Education

Early marriage diminishes educational attainment among those attending high school. Not only do young marrieds make less educational progress during the four-year period of high school, but they also tend to have lower educational aspirations for the future. The converse is also true: Those with lower educational aspirations tend to marry earlier than those with higher aspirations.

The dropout rate among married high school couples is high, reflecting the fact that the great majority of the girls are pregnant before marriage. Remember, however, that these are correlational data and do not necessarily mean that marrying causes girls to drop out of school. In many instances, the causality is reversed: Girls who had already dropped out of school or who were planning to drop out of school marry.

What are high schools legally permitted to do when a student marries? What are they permitted to do when they discover a student is pregnant? What are the student's constitutional rights? What are the rights of the school board? What does the law say?

With the implementation of the regulations issued under Title IX of the Education Amendments of 1972, all married students and unmarried girls and young mothers are entitled to complete their education with full access to the resources and facilities provided by the public school system (New York Civil Liberties Union, 2006). Specifically, these regulations require that any school system receiving federal funds cannot (1) apply any rule concerning a student's actual or potential parental, family, or marital status that treats students differently on the basis of sex or (2) discriminate against or exclude any student from its education program or activity on the basis of such student's pregnancy or pregnancy-related condition. Assignment of a student to a separate portion of the program or activity of the school can be made only if the student voluntarily requests such assignment or if a physician certifies inability to continue in the normal program. Any separate instructional program for pregnant students must be comparable to that offered to nonpregnant students.

SUMMARY

1. The need for close friends intensifies during adolescence. Having friends helps bridge the gap between being emotionally dependent on one's parents and achieving true emotional independence.
2. It is extremely common for adolescents to experience loneliness.
3. The ability to form close friendships is partly learned in the family. Adolescents who have close relationships with their parents tend to be the most socially adjusted.
4. Young adolescent friends are usually very similar to each other, for several reasons: They choose friends who are like them to begin with, and once they become friends, they encourage each other to be even more similar.
5. Young adolescents are sensitive to slights and hints of disloyalty, and so early adolescent friendships are volatile.
6. When adolescents leave the confines of their elementary schools, they broaden their friendships. Young adolescents want a lot of friends; as they get older, they become more discriminating and seek fewer but better friends.
7. Youths engage in a variety of leisure activities with their friends: They hang out, watch television, talk, go to the mall, and sometimes drink alcohol.
8. Adolescents find group acceptance and popularity by conforming, achieving, participating in school activities, developing and exhibiting personal qualities that others admire, and learning social skills that ensure acceptance. Being athletic enhances boys' popularity, in particular.
9. Having lots of friends does not necessarily make you "popular." Popular adolescents are the social leaders. They are not always well liked, and they often use relational and reputational aggression to maintain their social standing.
10. Bullying is an all too common experience for many teens. Adolescents who are different, quiet, and have few friends are most likely to be targeted. Fortunately,

there are programs that can greatly reduce the incidence of bullying.

11. Psychosocial development takes place in three stages: autosocial, homosocial, and heterosocial. One of the chief tasks is to develop heterosociality, wherein friendships are chosen from both sexes.
12. Most adolescents develop crushes on or fall in love with real or imagined partners.
13. Loss of love can be a major source of stress in the life of the adolescent.
14. Dating has several important purposes: to have fun; to provide companionship; to gain status; for sexual satisfaction; as a means of mate selection; and as a means of developing intimacy.
15. Dating begins gradually, shifting from mixed-sex group activities to one-on-one, private outings.
16. Dating violence is an unfortunately common occurrence. While boys and girls both engage in violence, boys more often initiate it. Boys are less intimidated than girls when their dates become violent. Dating violence appears to be a worldwide problem.
17. Adolescents who exclusively date someone are more likely to be sexually intimate than those who date a variety of others.
18. Most college students say that they would be willing to cohabitate under the right circumstances, and about half will cohabitate with a romantic partner before they marry.
19. Adolescents cohabitate for a variety of reasons: because it is satisfying; because they feel emotionally committed; as a prelude to marriage; as a trial marriage; and because they do not believe in marriage.
20. Cohabitation before marriage does not improve the quality of the subsequent marriage or decrease the probability of divorce.
21. More and more cohabiting couples are having children.
22. The younger people are when they get married, the greater the chance of having an unhappy marriage and getting divorced.
23. High school girls who marry are typically younger than their husbands. Early marriages disproportionately involve adolescents who are from low-socioeconomic-status groups, are less interested in education, are premaritally pregnant, get poor grades, are rural residents, and have less satisfactory relationships with parents.
24. Adolescents marry due to becoming pregnant, having an overly romantic view of marriage, trying to escape from their families, and feeling social pressure.
25. Young couples face many problems, including unwanted children, immaturity, financial hardships, and arguments with in-laws.
26. Early marriage diminishes educational attainment. The dropout rate among married high school couples is high, but all married students and unmarried girls and young mothers are entitled to an education.

KEY TERMS

attachment 270
cognitive-behavioral modification 277
autosociality 278
heterosociality 278
homosociality 278
normative regulation 275
relational aggression 274
reputational aggression 274

THOUGHT QUESTIONS

Personal Reflection

1. Were you often lonely when you were in middle school or high school? If you were, can you say why?
2. Compare the relationships you had/have with your closest friend in middle school, high school, and now. How have your friendships changed?
3. What sorts of things did you do to make yourself more popular when you were younger?
4. How did you feel about the "popular" students in your middle and high school? Did you like them? Admire them? Were they nice?
5. Reflect back on your first love. Why did you fall for him/her?
6. Would you cohabitate with someone prior to marriage? If so, under what conditions? If not, why not?

Group Discussion

7. How would you answer each of the following questions if you were asked it by a youth in middle school or high school?
   a. How can you get others to like you?
   b. What do you do if your best friend talks about you behind your back?
   c. What do boys look for in a girl?
   d. What do girls look for in a boy?
   e. How can I get over being shy?
   f. How do you know if you're really in love?
   g. How can you break up without hurting the other person?
8. What are the pros and cons of exclusively dating someone while in high school?
9. Would you advise other young people to cohabit? Why or why not?
10. How old do you think people should be before getting married? Explain.
11. Did your school take bullying seriously enough? How did they handle it?

Debate Questions

12. Little can be done to change the social structure of middle and high schools: There will also be popular and unpopular students.

13. Parents should discourage young teens from dating.
14. Premarital cohabitation should be discouraged.
15. States should raise the legal age of marriage to 21.

SUGGESTED READING

Furman, W., Brown, B. B., and Feiring, C. (Eds.). (1999). *The Development of Romantic Relationships in Adolescence.* Cambridge, England: Cambridge University Press.

Garbarino, J., and deLara, E. (2003). *And Words Can Hurt: How to Protect Adolescents from Bullying, Harassment, and Emotional Violence.* New York: Free Press.

Way, N., and Hamm, J. V. (Eds.). (2005). *The Experience of Close Friendship in Adolescence: New Directions for Child & Adolescent Development.* San Francisco: Jossey-Bass.

Wu, S. (2000). *Cohabitation: An Alternative Form of Family Living.* Oxford, England: Oxford University Press.

CHAPTER 13 ADOLESCENT SOCIETY, CULTURE, AND SUBCULTURE

CULTURE AND SOCIETY

THE ADOLESCENT SUBCULTURE

A False Dichotomy
Distinctive Social Relationships and Culture

ADOLESCENT SOCIETIES

Formal Societies
Informal Societies
Division by Grade
Social Class and Status

FORMAL AND SEMIFORMAL SUBSYSTEMS

The Formal Academic Subsystem
The Semiformal Activities Subsystem
The Friendship Subsystem

NOTABLE YOUTH SUBCULTURES

Flappers
RESEARCH HIGHLIGHT *The Straightedge Subculture*
Hippies
Skateboarders
Hip-Hop
Goths

MATERIAL CONCERNS OF ADOLESCENT CULTURE

Adolescents as Consumer Forces
PERSONAL ISSUES *Adolescent Credit Card Debt*
Clothing
Automobiles
PERSONAL ISSUES *Automobile Casualties*
Cell Phones
Computers and the Internet
PERSONAL ISSUES *Internet Addiction*

NONMATERIAL CONCERNS OF ADOLESCENT CULTURE

Slang
Music
RESEARCH HIGHLIGHT *Changing Tastes in Fashion, Music, and Movies*

WOULDN'T YOU LIKE TO KNOW . . .

- In what sense do adolescents have their own subculture?
- What is the most important identifier during adolescence?
- Does participating in sports benefit adolescents?
- Is it important for adolescents to belong to a clique?
- How tolerant are adolescents of people who are different from themselves?
- Why are fads important to teens?
- Does listening to antisocial music cause antisocial behavior?

Some researchers would assert that adolescents have both their own *society* and their own *culture*. **Adolescent society** refers to the structural arrangements of subgroups within an adolescent social system; in other words, it is the organized network of relationships and association among adolescents. **Adolescent culture** is the sum of the ways of living of adolescents; it refers to the body of norms, values, attitudes, and practices recognized and shared by members of the adolescent society as appropriate guides to action. Adolescent society consists of the interrelationships of adolescents within their social systems; their culture describes the way they think, behave, and live.

This chapter is concerned with both adolescent society and adolescent culture. We will focus on formal and informal adolescent societies both in and out of school. Factors that influence the adolescent's social position in a formal group are outlined and discussed, along with the subcultures that exist at the high school and college levels. The chapter concludes with a discussion of four important material aspects of adolescent culture—clothing, automobiles, cell-phones, the Internet—and two nonmaterial aspects of adolescent culture—slang and music.

CULTURE AND SOCIETY

Adolescent society is not one single, comprehensive, monolithic structure that includes all young people. There are usually numerous adolescent societies with wide variations among various age groups, socioeconomic levels, and ethnic or national backgrounds. Furthermore, adolescent societies are only vaguely structured. They exist without any formal, written codification and without traditions of organizational patterns. Individuals move into and out of each system within a few short years, contributing to structural instability. Each local group of adolescents is provincial, with few ties beyond school membership and its own crowd of peers. Although there are nationwide youth organizations, fan clubs, or competitive athletic events, most adolescent societies are primarily local, variably replicated in community after community.

The same cautions should be applied to adolescent culture. We cannot speak of U.S. adolescent culture as though it were a body of beliefs, values, and practices uniformly espoused by all youths throughout the country. Just as there are regional, ethnic, and socioeconomic versions of the national adult culture, so are there variations in expression of adolescent culture among differing segments of the population. Adolescent culture is not homogeneous; the popular image of adolescent culture usually refers to that of urban, middle-class youths. Actually, there may be substantial deviations from this pattern. A more accurate description would convey that there are numerous versions of teenage culture expressed by various segments of youths who share some common elements of a general middle-class youth culture but who participate selectively and in varying degrees in the activities of the organized adolescent society.

Before we can analyze adolescent society or culture, an important question should be addressed: Are adolescent society and culture unique and different from those of the adult world?

THE ADOLESCENT SUBCULTURE

According to one point of view, **adolescent subculture** describes a uniform peer group whose values are contrary to adult values. This subculture exists primarily in the high school, where it constitutes a small society—one that has most of its important interactions within itself, maintaining only a few threads of connection with the outside adult society. This happens because teenagers are set apart in schools, where they take on more and more peer-focused extracurricular activities. Segregated from the adult world, they develop subcultures with their own language, styles, and, most important, value systems that may differ from those of adults. As a result, the adolescent lives in a segregated society and establishes a subculture that meets with peer, but not adult, approval.

An opposite point of view is that the theory of an adolescent subculture, segregated and different from adult culture, is a myth. This view—that adolescents reflect adult values, beliefs, and practices—is substantiated by many studies. For example, when they are deciding what to do with their lives, adolescents turn to their parents for advice more than they turn to their friends or the media (Malmberg, 2001). When conflict *does* arise between the generations, it is usually centered in mundane, day-to-day issues such as noisiness, tidiness, punctuality, and living under the same roof, rather than on fundamental values such as honesty, perseverance, and concern for others (Smetana, 2002).

There continues to be disagreement, then, as to whether adolescent culture is different enough from adult culture to be distinct from it.

A False Dichotomy

The more studies that are conducted and the more closely these studies are analyzed, the more evident it becomes that adolescents choose to follow neither parents nor friends exclusively. One explanation is that, in many instances, parents and friends are quite alike, so the peer group serves to reinforce rather than violate parental values. Adolescents tend to choose friends whose values are like their own (Aloise-Young, Graham, and Hansen, 1994); thus, there may be considerable overlap between the values of parents and peers because of commonalities in their backgrounds—social, economic, religious, educational, even geographic.

And, as has been discussed previously, some teenagers are relatively more influenced by peers and others by parents—age, gender, socioeconomic status, and the quality of relationship between parent and child all come into play—but most of the basic values that adolescents hold are similar to those of their parents. There are some differences: Adolescents tend to value popularity, nonconformity with tradition, and hedonism (Boehnke, 2001) more than their parents do.

Distinctive Social Relationships and Culture

The system of social relationships in which adolescents are involved is a highly distinctive one, not in the sense that it is the only world to which they are responsive but in the sense that it is a society over which adults exercise only partial control. Most modern teenagers are *both* typically confused adolescents in the adult world and relatively self-assured and status-conscious members of their peer groups—depending on the set of interactions being analyzed.

These same conclusions might be reached with respect to other aspects of adolescent culture, as well. Adolescents reflect many adult values and norms. One study of high school students revealed that they were primarily parent oriented in matters of finance, education, career plans, and prejudices (Ritchey and Fishbein, 2001). In contrast, activities that were intrinsic to peer life were heavily influenced by peer guidance. Certain aspects of their lives were distinguishable from U.S. adult culture because in these areas, adolescents can exercise some control and make their own decisions. Such matters as styles of dress, tastes in music, language, preference of popular movie and recording stars, dating customs and practices, and behavior at youth hangouts are particular to the adolescent subculture, and they may sometimes run counter to adult preferences. It is therefore proper and possible to point to certain aspects of adolescent culture that are identifiable as separate, for they are developed and practiced predominantly by adolescents, sometimes in contradiction to adult norms. The further along adolescents are in school, the more likely they are to listen to peers rather than to parents in matters pertaining to social judgments.

Two especially notable areas of adolescent-adult disagreement are drugs and sexual behavior. The primary reason adolescents and adults disagree in these matters is that cultural change has been so rapid and so great that youthful behavior *is* different from adult values. For example, several attitude surveys have revealed that the sexual attitudes of adolescents are more liberal than

ANSWERS WOULDN'T YOU LIKE TO KNOW . . .

In what sense do adolescents have their own subculture?

In the sense that adolescents have different values and behaviors than the adults around them, then they have their own subculture. It is a matter of opinion, however, whether the differences that exist (such as so highly valuing popularity) are large enough to warrant this distinction.

those of adults (Le Gall, Mullet, and Shafighi, 2002). For example, today's teens are less likely to view oral sex as "having sex" than are adults (Remez, 2000). These youthful attitudes, therefore, may be regarded as subcultural. Parents do, however, continue to exert some influence on their adolescent children's sexual behavior. For instance, adolescents whose mothers are fundamentalist Protestants and those whose parents attend church regularly are significantly less likely than others to approve of premarital sexual intercourse (Regnerus, 2005).

Thus, whether a youthful subculture exists depends on what areas of concern are being examined. Overall, youth culture reflects adult culture. In specific areas, however, youth culture is a distinct subculture. Certainly teens have their own tastes in fashion, music, slang, and entertainers. The more rapid the social change, the more likely that youths' views become different from those of their parents. In this sense, certain aspects of adolescent life become subcultural—at least for a while. Eventually, as adolescents age and become adults, many aspects of youth culture are absorbed into mainstream adult society. (Nowadays, most adults enjoy rock and roll music and wear blue jeans.) What is novel and rebellious at first becomes staid and commonplace with the passage of time.

ADOLESCENT SOCIETIES

Like adult social structures, adolescent societies may be divided into two groups: formal and informal.

Formal Societies

Formal adolescent societies primarily include groups of in-school youths. Linkages with peers are determined by whether adolescents are enrolled in school,

adolescent society structural arrangements of subgroups within an adolescent social system.

adolescent culture sum of the ways of living of adolescents.

adolescent subculture values and way of life that are contrary to those found in adult society.

ANSWERS WOULDN'T YOU LIKE TO KNOW . . .

What is the most important identifier during adolescence?

The most important identifier during adolescence is not gender or race/ethnicity but grade level in school. Being a twelfth-grader is better than being a tenth-grader on any day, in any school.

which school they are enrolled in, and which student organizations they join. The youth is identified with his or her particular school, team, and teachers. There are also out-of-school religious or youth groups, but for the most part, only in-school youths participate in these activities. Therefore, any formal, well-defined social system to which adolescents belong is invariably related to their in-school associations.

Informal Societies

Informal adolescent societies generally describe those loosely structured groups of out-of-school youths who get together socially but who have little opportunity to participate in a formally structured network of social relationships. These youths are too scattered and too involved in trying to find their places in adult society to be characterized as a separate adolescent society. One exception might be the adolescent street gang, which exists as a subsociety all its own.

This does not mean that all adolescents who remain in school are actively participating members of the organized adolescent society. Some adolescents remain in school but are really excluded from school life. Those who finally drop out of school have poor attendance records and rarely hold school office or have been active in school affairs. There are some who are socially outside "the society," though they may still be physically in it.

Division by Grade

Most Western schools are strongly age graded; that is, adolescents are primarily identified by their grade or class in school. This identification allows adolescents to take certain courses and participate in certain school-sponsored activities (for which being a freshman or a senior, for instance, is a prerequisite for eligibility). Freshmen may compete with sophomores in sports or other events, but class membership is important in influencing friendship associations. Among pairs of friends, the one item that two members have in common far more often than any other—including religion, father's occupation, mother's education, common leisure interests, grades in school, and others—is class in school.

Social Class and Status

Evidence continues to mount that an individual's acceptance by and active involvement in adolescent society are influenced by socioeconomic background. Students from a higher social class far more often attend athletic events, dances, plays, and musical activities than those from the lower classes, especially in schools where children come from a variety of social classes. Furthermore, youths who identify themselves with organized youth groups (e.g., Boy Scouts, Girl Scouts) and church or synagogue youth fellowship groups are predominantly from middle-class rather than lower-class homes.

This does not mean that every individual from a low-socioeconomic-status family is rejected by people of middle socioeconomic status. Nevertheless, students whose fathers are college graduates (one clue to middle-class status) are far more likely than students whose fathers have only grade school education to be identified as members of the leading crowd, to be chosen as friends, and to be viewed as people whom one would wish to be like.

FORMAL AND SEMIFORMAL SUBSYSTEMS

In-school adolescent societies also may be divided into distinct **subsystems** in which adolescents participate and in which they are assigned status positions. Furthermore, students are often simultaneously involved in more than one of these distinct subsystems.

The Formal Academic Subsystem

Adolescents are involved in a formal academic subsystem shaped by the school administration, faculty, curriculum, classrooms, grades, and rules. As students, adolescents are concerned with intellectual pursuits, knowledge, achievement, and making the honor roll. In this system, seniors outrank freshmen, and the honor roll student outranks the D student. However, the degree to which students subscribe to this academic ranking varies according to gender, neighborhood, and ethnicity.

Many but not all studies have suggested that female adolescents value academic success more than male students, and so rate peers more highly if they do well in school than if they do not. Socioeconomic status also plays a role: Middle-class students are more likely to value academics than do poverty-class students. Finally, race comes into play as well—and, of course, each of these variables interacts with the others. For example, several authors (e.g., Fordham, 1996) have reported that there is tremendous pressure on lower-income Black males to do poorly in school, since academic success is seen as a "White" activity. Other research (e.g., Kennedy, 1995) indicates that both Black males and females very much respect their peers for being good students; however, there are only weak associations between these adolescents' evaluations of who is a good student and the grades their peers receive. Yet other research has shown that academic success by itself is not a good predictor of popularity, but that it interacts with an adolescent's other personal characteristics (athleticism, physical attractiveness, personality). In other words, you can be smart and popular if you don't seem to work hard and are on the soccer team; on the other hand, if you flatter the teachers too much and are clumsy, you won't be considered smart and popular.

The Semiformal Activities Subsystem

Most youths are involved in a semiformal activities subsystem, which includes all sponsored organizations and activities, such as athletics, drama, and departmental clubs. There are dozens of independent formal school organizations, ranging from varsity basketball to the community services club. Each group has a prestige ranking in the eyes of the students, which conveys a certain status rating to its members. Each group has specific offices, with the result that the individual's status is determined partly by which of these offices he or she holds; for example, the captain of the football team is accorded higher status than a benchwarmer. The amount of prestige that any position bestows depends on its rank within each respective group and the prestige standing of the group in relation to all other groups. There are also groups that meet outside of school, such as church-based groups.

As many as 75 percent of middle-school students participate in structured extracurricular activities (Mahoney, Schweder, and Stattin, 2002). The most common activities for high school students involve athletics; this is followed by arts, which is in turn followed by journalism (yearbook, the school newspaper or television program), and then vocational clubs (National Center for Education Statistics, 2002). Girls are more likely to participate in athletic activities than boys, although boys are more likely to participate in sports (Eccles and Barber, 1999).

Is it good for youth to be involved in these structured after-school activities? The answer is, in the main, yes (Feldman and Matjasko, 2005). Although there is some conflicting data, students who participate in structured extracurricular activities tend to do better in school than those who do not (Mahoney, Cairns, and Farmer, 2003; Marsh and Kleitman, 2003) and are less likely to drop out (Mahoney, 2000). Participants are also less likely to use drugs (Eccles and Barber, 1999) or engage in sexual intercourse (Miller, Sabo, Farrell, Barnes, and Melnick, 1998). Participants tend to carry enhanced self-esteem with them into young adulthood (Barber, Eccles, and Stone, 2001).

Involvement in extracurricular activities, such as athletics, can enhance the adolescent's development of sociability, popularity, competency, self-esteem, and commitment to goal achievement.

Why should participation in structured extracurricular activities be so beneficial? One can imagine several contributors. First, the self-confidence that comes from higher self-esteem could spill over into other areas of endeavor. Another possibility is that participants must develop time management skills that help them juggle all of their responsibilities. Most research (e.g., Eccles and Barber, 1999), however, has concentrated on the fact that involvement in extracurricular activities puts adolescents in the company of high-quality peers (i.e., those who are academically focused, avoid using drugs, don't break the law, etc.). Adolescents tend to spend a lot of time with the teens who are on their team or in their club, both during meetings and after hours; therefore, joining an extracurricular group helps ensure that peer influence will be positive rather than negative.

subsystems smaller segments of adolescent society within the larger social system.

ANSWERS WOULDN'T YOU LIKE TO KNOW . . .

Does participating in sports benefit adolescents?

For the most part, yes. Being on sports teams enhances adolescents' status and helps them feel good about themselves. Such participation instantly makes them part of a group. It is less clear, however, whether sports participation improves academic performance.

As mentioned before, more students participate in athletics than in any other activity. Given the obesity crisis facing our country, it is surely good for adolescents to have an outlet in which to be physically active. However, the positive benefits associated with athletic involvement are not quite as clear as the positive benefits of other types of extracurricular activities, as the data are more mixed. For example, some studies show that academic achievement *is not* increased by being on a sports team. Crosnoe (2001) found that there were two types of athletes, those whose friends were academically successful and those whose friends were interested more in partying. Not surprisingly, those who ran with an academically disinterested crowd did not do well in school themselves. Other research has found that athletes are more likely, not less likely, to drink and use drugs (e.g., Borden, Donnermeyer, and Scheer, 2001; Crosnoe, 2002). In addition, some studies show that male athletes are more likely to engage in sexual activity and have more sexual partners than nonathletes (Miller, Sabo, Farrell, Barnes, and Melnick, 1999). In general, girls seem to benefit more clearly from sports participation than boys do.

Again, much of the research concludes that being on a sports team is highly beneficial for the students involved; it is likely that the outcomes depend upon which sport is being considered, the characteristics of the students who select each sport, and the status that each sport has in a given school. We know more about this at the college level than we do at high school level. It is well established that college athletes as a whole drink considerably more than nonathletes (Nelson and Wechsler, 2001). They also drink more heavily, are more likely to report doing something they regret while drunk, drive after heavy drinking, and get into trouble for drinking than nonathletes. College athletes at large universities also have high rates of pathological gambling (Kerber, 2005). Athletes at Division I schools have high status and may develop a sense of entitlement, which increases the chance that they engage in problematic behaviors. In addition, they are under a good deal of stress and pressure to win.

The Friendship Subsystem

Adolescent students may be involved in an informal network of friendship subsystems that operate primarily within the boundaries of the school world. Friendship choices are directed overwhelmingly to other students in the same school, and the majority of these choices are directed to members of the same grade and sex group.

Of the three subsystems, membership in the informal friendship system is most important in the eyes of other students. This is the only subsystem unencumbered by adult sponsorship. This is the adolescent's world, and the status an individual enjoys in this world is of major importance. Status in the academic and activities subsystems is coveted but primarily for the prestige, acceptance, and standing it gives one within the network of informal peer groupings.

Cliques are relatively small, tightly knit groups of three to ten friends who spend considerable and often exclusive time with each other. Virtually all observational studies of adolescents have shown that the clique is the most prevalent and important friendship structure for adolescents. Studies also have indicated that cliques are characterized by members being similar to one another in age, gender, race/ethnicity, and social status, as well as in the types of interest and activities of the members (Ennett and Bauman, 1996). In particular, members tend to be equally disposed toward or against antisocial behavior (Cairns and Cairns, 1994).

Cliques, especially female cliques, have a very definite status hierarchy (Adler and Adler, 1995). The high-status members ridicule outsiders and low-status members to keep them in line. The high-status members also determine who is permitted to join the clique. Membership changes are frequent. In one study, only about 10 percent of the cliques showed no change of membership over a one-year period (Engles, Knibble, Drop, and de Haan, 1997).

Not everyone belongs to a clique; in fact, fewer than half of adolescents do. About 30 percent of students are **liaisons**—individuals who have friends from several different cliques but belong to none (Ennett and Bauman, 1996). These youths are generally well thought of, and many prefer their peripheral position. As one tenth-grader explained:

> If you're in a clique, you have to hang with everyone in the group. I always find that I like some of them but not others. Since I'm not in the clique, I can just be with the girls I like. It does make having parties difficult, because my friends don't like each other!

Liaisons serve as bridges between cliques. Liaisons become increasingly common as adolescents get older (Shrum and Cheek, 1987). The remaining students are *social isolates*—individuals with few friends.

Schools also contain **crowds.** A crowd is larger than a clique, often having about 20 members. Crowds are loose associations of cliques; it is unusual to be in a crowd if you are not in a clique. Whereas cliques get together all the time, crowds usually get together on weekends. They may all attend the same party, for instance,

ANSWERS WOULDN'T YOU LIKE TO KNOW . . .

Is it important for adolescents to belong to a clique?

Belonging to a clique is very important to adolescents. In fact, the clique is the most prevalent and significant friendship structure for this age group. Even so, only about half of all adolescents belong to a clique. Some have friends from several different cliques but don't belong to any of them.

or meet at a mall. During the week, the cliques process and discuss what transpired at the crowd event (Urberg, Degirmencioglu, Tolson, and Halliday-Scher, 1995).

In large part because of the shootings at Columbine and other high schools, there has been a resurgence of interest in the clique and crowd structures of schools. Past and current data (and almost everyone's personal experiences) leave little doubt that cliques vary dramatically in status. Aronson (2000) compared the social informal social structures at three high schools—one in Missouri, one in Arizona, and one in California—and found them to be nearly identical. In today's schools, "jocks" and "preppies" (obedient students who are active in school government and other sanctioned activities) rule the schools. Lower down in the pecking order are "techno nerds," and below them are the "Goths" (short for "gothics") and the "dirts" (drug users). The lowest of the low are those students who are loners, belonging to no crowd.

The observation that there are status differences among middle and high school students is old news. The surprising findings from these new studies are (1) how great these differences are, (2) the magnitude of the unhappiness and anxiety experienced by subordinate students, and (3) the number of students who feel put down and hassled by popular crowds.

Some friendship groups may be in active, open rebellion against the school's educational and social activities. Those in these groups reject the rules of the school system and flaunt authority.

ANSWERS WOULDN'T YOU LIKE TO KNOW . . .

How tolerant are adolescents of people who are different from themselves?

Adolescents are generally not tolerant of those who are different from themselves. This explains why a tremendous amount of teasing and bullying occurs in schools. Individuals from high-status cliques and crowds pick on, taunt, and ridicule those in lower-status cliques and crowds.

NOTABLE YOUTH SUBCULTURES

Because adolescents need to distinguish themselves from their elders, youth subcultures come and go. There have been a number of interesting, distinctive youth subcultures in the past 100 years. Five of the more interesting ones, two historical and three contemporary, are described below.

Flappers

> We are the Younger Generation. The war tore away our spiritual foundations and challenged our faith. We are struggling to regain our equilibrium. The times have made us older and more experienced than you were at our age. It must be so with each succeeding generation if it is to keep pace with the rapidly advancing and mighty tide of civilization.
>
> Ellen Welles Page, *Outlook* magazine, December 6, 1922

cliques relatively small, tightly knit groups of friends that spend a lot or even all of their time together.

liaisons individuals who have friends from several cliques but belong to none.

crowds loose associations of cliques that usually meet on weekends.

RESEARCH HIGHLIGHT THE STRAIGHTEDGE SUBCULTURE

The *Straightedge subculture* is an interesting offshoot of the hard-core and punk rock subcultures of the 1980s. The name derives from the title of a song sung by Minor Threat that argues against drug use and promiscuity. The Straightedge credo was originally "Don't drink; don't smoke; don't ****." In the 1990s, the movement broadened its philosophy to include promotion of topics such as animal rights and environmental issues (Irwin, 1999; Wood, 1999).

Although Straightedgers promote causes that are generally favored by mainstream society, they retain the trappings of hard-core rockers. Their appearance is often unconventional, their music is loud and harsh, and their concerts feature mosh pits. They may expound walking a straight and narrow line, but they appear deviant to many adults.

This modern-sounding plaint was written by a young flapper who was trying to explain her generation to her parents. **Flapper** was a term used to describe a certain type of rebellious teenage girl in the late 1910s–1920s. The war Welles Page refers to is World War I, an event that truly shocked the world's citizens and caused a rise of cynicism and pessimism about the future. Flappers were scandalous, especially compared to their Gibson Girl mothers and Victorian grandmothers. (These women wore tight corsets, were never seen without long sleeves, and wore floor-length dresses.) They went to jazz clubs (with men!) where they danced in highly inappropriate ways. They smoked cigarettes and wore make-up (something associated only with loose women). They cut their hair into short bobs and (gasp) dyed it. They wore skirts so short that their knees showed when they walked, they threw away their corsets, and they went sleeveless. They openly drank alcohol (even though it was against the law at the time). They threw "petting parties" where much societally frowned upon sexual activity took place.

Although the flapper era didn't last very long—the great Depression put an end to it—it had a lasting impact. Women would never be viewed in quite the same way again, nor would they ever go back to their bustles.

Hippies

As almost everyone knows, the word **hippie** refers to a particular kind of 1960s teenager. Hippie values were very distinct from those of mainstream America: Hippies were against the war in Vietnam, were interested in Eastern religions more than Christianity, were antimaterialistic, and were suspicious of government and what they termed the military-industrial complex. Because of these values, hippies held sit-ins to protest the war and burned their draft cards. They became vegetarians, meditated, and burned incense. They preferred to earn money by making crafts or by panhandling rather than by getting traditional jobs.

Hippies also believed in sexual freedom, interracial dating, communal living, and recreational drug use. They freely cohabitated. It was common to allow strangers to "crash" at your place if they needed a place to stay. Marijuana and LSD use were common. Hippie values were summed up well by the title of Timothy Leary's book *Turn On, Tune In, Drop Out. Turn on* referred to using drugs, *tune in* referred to getting in touch with one's inner self, and *drop out* meant to refuse to participate in the negative aspects of our culture.

Hippies had a distinct appearance. Both sexes tended to have long hair (often kept out of their faces with headbands), and men usually sported beards or mustaches. Women wore floor-length peasant skirts. Individuals of both sexes often wore flowers in their hair and bell-bottom or very wide blue jeans. Tie-dyed fabric was popular, as were other items that were hand made, such as beaded necklaces or crocheted vests. Clothing tended to look old and well worn rather than newly purchased.

San Francisco, especially the Haight-Ashbury district, was the spiritual home of the hippie movement. Tens of thousands of hippies gathered there during the summer of 1967 ("the summer of love"). The movement itself was really over by the early 1970s, but its legacy can be seen in such things as the sexual revolution, health food stores, large outdoor rock concerts, and the punk movement that followed the hippie movement.

The hippie movement was heavily influenced by a previous youth subculture, the *beatniks.* The beatniks were around in the 1950s and into the 1960s. Hippies were similar to beatniks in their use of marijuana (the beatniks were the first to call it "tea"), political liberalism, and antimaterialism. They differed from the beatniks in that beatniks preferred jazz to rock and roll, they wore different fashions (primarily black clothing and berets), and they were generally less intellectual.

Skateboarders

In 2002, there were 12.5 million skateboarders in the United States, a large majority of them males under the age of 18 (Fetto, 2002). About 15 percent of teens say they skateboard once in a while, while 8 percent are true devotees who skateboard whenever they can. Skateboards were actually invented in the 1950s, but skateboarding really didn't hit it big as a sport (or a subculture) until the 1980s and 1990s. The number of skateboarders continues to grow.

Skateboarders labor under a rather negative image. Many nonskaters assume that skateboarders are all slackers and thugs. In some ways, die-hard skateboarders match this unsavory image. For example, they are more likely to perceive themselves as being very different from their parents than other teens and are less likely to get along with their parents. However, in most ways skateboarders do not match this image. For example, they are just as serious about academics as other adolescents and are as likely to intend to go to college. As a group they are more technologically savvy than their peers (Fetto, 2002).

Early on, many skaters affected a punk look and listened to punk rock, although that has changed to a certain degree. Many skaters wear baseball caps, baggy jeans, over-sized shirts, and hooded sweatshirts. Often the clothing has holes. A newer style ("hesh") features tighter clothing.

Devoted skaterboarders work hard to perfect their performance. The backbone of skateboarding is the "ollie," a move in which the board is kicked off the ground and flies through the air; the rider manages to stay on even though he or she is not holding on and is not attached to the board in any way. Boarders also work on doing flips (when the board turns over) and grinds (sliding on surfaces such as stair railings). More and more communities are building skateparks, where skateboarders can practice these moves without loitering on private property, causing property damage, or endangering pedestrians. If enough of these facilities are developed, tensions between skateboarders and other community members might be reduced and skateboarders' image can improve.

Hip-Hop

The hip-hop subculture began about 30 years ago in New York City. It was originally confined to the Black and Latino communities but has now become a global phenomenon. The most important elements are listening and dancing to rap music (described later in this chapter) and wearing hip-hop fashion. Since hip-hop has been around for a long time, its fashions and slang have evolved. Early hip-hop artists characteristically wore African-inspired clothing, sneakers with exaggerated shoelaces, and much heavy gold jewelry. More recently, a tougher, gang-inspired look has become common. In particular, pants are worn baggy and pulled low, tee-shirts are oversized, sweatshirts with hoods are abundant, heads are covered with bandanas, and many males sport black tattoos.

Hip-hop dance is equally distinctive. It began with *breakdancing*. The name comes from the "breaks" in songs when there are drum solos. Breakdancing is unique in that it involves putting your hands or shoulders on the floors while kicking and spinning. Fewer dancers get down on the floor these days than in the past. Instead, they pop (contract and relax their muscles to make parts of their bodies twitch), boogaloo (roll their heads, knees, and hips), slide (glide without apparent stepping), strobe (move in quick starts and stops to make it appear as if they are being viewed under a strobe light), and do the wave (move in a continuous fashion to make it appear that a wave is moving through the dancer's body).

Adult concern with hip-hop culture has centered on the antisocial nature of the lyrics in many rap songs and the emulation of violent individuals. This will be discussed later in the chapter.

Goths

Another visible group of extreme youths are the *Goths*. *Goth* is short for *gothic*, and the movement originated in England in the early 1980s. Goths like to wear black velvet and black leather clothing. Girls favor pale complexions, black nail polish, and black lipstick. Goths tend to be interested in questions about good and evil, and some are fascinated by the macabre and funereal. Goth bands include Nine Inch Nails, Sisters of Mercy, and Marilyn Manson. Although some newspaper accounts described the shooters at Columbine High School as Goths (because of their black trench coats), most Goths are not violent.

flappers teenage girls in the late 1910s–1920s who dated, wore short skirts, and drank alcohol.

hippies youth in the late 1960s who held pro-drug, pacifistic, antimaterialistic values.

Clown dancing, and its offshoot, Krumping, were invented in South Central Los Angeles in the 1990s. They are a reaction to the commercialization of hip-hop and a form of non-violent competition.

MATERIAL CONCERNS OF ADOLESCENT CULTURE

Another way we can understand adolescent culture is by examining the material artifacts that youths buy, make, and use in their daily lives. Four items—clothes, cars, computers, and cell phones—have been selected for discussion because they are so important in the adolescent's life. First, though, we will give an overview of the total spending power that adolescents have.

Adolescents as Consumer Forces

Teenagers have more disposable income than ever before. Due to both higher earnings from their own jobs and the fact that families are spending more money on their adolescent children, the buying power of American teens reached $190 billion dollars in 2006. To put that in perspective, it is more than a 25 percent increase since 2001, and it is more than the gross domestic product of Russia (MarketResearch.com, 2005). This translates to about $74 dollars/weeks for each and every adolescent in America (Newspaper Association of America, 2005).

Where do teens get all this money? There are a number of sources. The majority of adolescents report getting money from their parents, whether it is in the form of irregular payments or a steady allowance or both. The majority of younger teens (ages 12–14) who receive an allowance get $20–$50 per month. The amount for older teens (ages 15–17) is more variable: about one-third get $20–$30 per month while about 20 percent get $50–$100 per month. Many adolescents also get cash as gifts for birthdays and other occasions. In addition, a large minority of teens work at any given time. Note that males are more likely to have money due to employment and females because it was given to them. Interestingly, a significant number of teenagers reported getting money by collecting spare change from around the house. This foraging typically yields about $14 dollars/month (Coinstar, 2003; Newspaper Association of America, 2005) (see Figure 13.1).

What do teenagers spend their money on? One poll found that the ten most common (major) purchases that adolescents said they planned to make within the next year were, in order, an MP3 player, a cell phone, a digital camera, a used car, contact lenses, a DVD burner, a car stereo, a video camera, sunglasses, and a digital video recorder (Newspaper Association of America, 2005). In fact, teenagers spend the most money in an average week on clothing and accessories (about one-third of their spending) and food (about one-fifth of their spending). A substantial number also buy prepaid minutes for their cell phones (Coinstar, 2003). It is clear from this list that little adolescent income goes either to savings or to help with basic household expenses.

So far we've been discussing middle and high school students. Does the situation change once teenagers head off to college? College students generally have more disposable income than secondary students. Most hold part-time jobs during the academic year and work during the summer. College students make, on average, about $169 per week. In addition, their parents continue to give them money. College students average about $210 dollars per week discretionary spending money. Like younger teens, they spend a large portion on their money on technology (cell phones, the latest computers, digital cameras, etc.) and another large portion on entertainment. College students spend almost $3 billion each year on movies, music, video games, and they spend more than twice as

FIGURE 13.1 TEENAGERS' SOURCES OF INCOME

Source: Newspaper Association of America (2005).

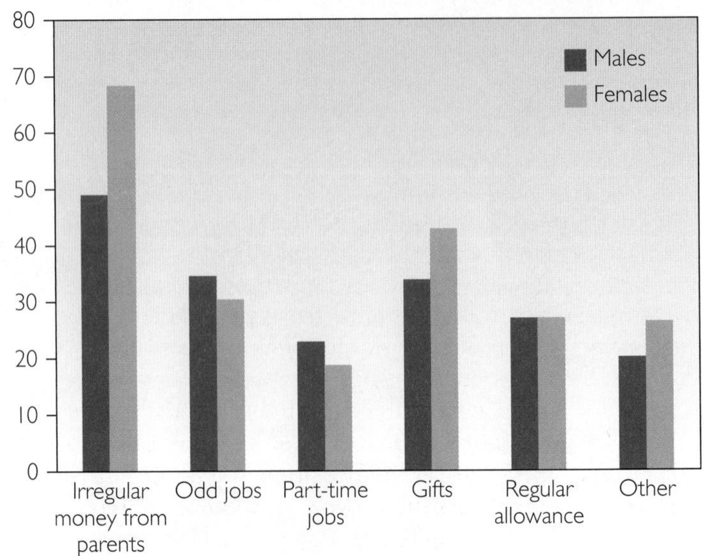

PERSONAL ISSUES ADOLESCENT CREDIT CARD DEBT

Going to college brings many new challenges, not the least of which, for many older teenagers, is the responsibility of owning their own credit card. Eighty-three percent of college students have at least one credit card, and most acquired them during their freshman year. Almost half of undergraduates leave college saddled with credit card debt—on average more than $3000 in credit card debt (Akaka, 2004). This, of course, is on top of whatever student loans they have taken out.

Credit card companies aggressively target college students. They offer sign-up gifts, and they flood student mailboxes with easy credit offers. Invitations are plastered in dorm hallways and in classroom buildings. These companies are not being altruistic; for them it makes good business sense to do so. For one, people often develop "brand loyalty" to their credit card; in other words, they tend to stick with whichever card they get first. Second, many if not most of the cards students acquire have annual fees. Third, because college students use their cards but then don't pay off the full balance at the end of the month, they rack up late payment penalties and interest debt. Because credit card interest rates are high, this is high profit for the credit card companies. Credit card companies encourage you to accrue interest charges by having a minimum monthly payment that is insufficient to reduce the principal quickly.

Credit cards are very useful to own if used wisely. They let you avoid carrying large sums of cash, are good sources of emergency funds, help you build up a good credit rating, and allow online purchases. On the other hand, they can become traps if used poorly. Carrying a large balance, delaying your payments, or defaulting on your credit card bill will adversely affect your credit rating, making it harder for you to take out loans in the future if you need them.

In order to try to avoid getting in over your head, it is often a good idea to own only one major credit card. Shop around to get the best terms (such as the interest rate you are being charged). It is also important to read your monthly statements carefully to make sure that the terms have not been changed. Never make purchases that you can't afford. Unless you have good reason, don't assume that you will be able to afford something next month that is out of your price range today (NellieMae Corporation, 2006). You'll sleep better!

much on movie theater tickets as the average American (Harris Interactive, 2004).

As the preceding discussion should make clear, there *are* material elements to youth culture. In order to fit in better with peers, teenagers are prepared to spend considerable sums of money to look right, own trendy gadgets, and be able to join their friends eating food in the right places. Some of these items—clothing, cars—have been around for some time; others, such as cell phones, MP3 players, and computers, are relatively new.

Clothing

One of the most noticeable aspects of adolescent culture is the preoccupation with clothing, hairstyles, and grooming (see also Chapter 5). Adults often accuse adolescents of being rebellious nonconformists or, at the other extreme, of being superficial in their values. Sociologists and social psychologists point out that neither accusation is true. Adolescents are conformists, especially when it comes to clothing and appearance within their own peer groups. Rather than showing superficiality because of their concern about appearance, youths are actually evidencing both their need to find and express their own individual identities and their need to belong to a social group.

Clothing is an important means by which individual adolescents discover and express their identities. As adolescent boys and girls search for self-images with which they can be comfortable, they are preoccupied with experimentation with their appearance (Littrell, Damhorst, and Littrell, 1990). Clothing and appearance are expressions of themselves as they strive to control the impressions that they make on others. Clothing is a visual means of communicating to others the kind of role a person wishes to play in life. By choosing which of the current popular brands to wear—for instance, PacSun, The Gap, Abercrombie and Fitch, Old Navy—or by avoiding all of them, teens make a statement about who they are and how they would like to be seen.

Appearance also plays an important role in social interaction, for it provides a means of identification. If a boy dresses like a tough delinquent, he is likely to be treated as one. Clothing enables one adolescent to discover the social identity of another person and to pattern his or her behavior and responses according to what is expected. As human beings within a society develop social selves, dress and adornment are intimately linked to their interacting with one another.

Clothing is one means by which adolescents express their dependence/independence conflicts or their conformity/individuality conflicts. Clothing can be a medium

Clothing helps adolescents discover and express their identities as well as ensure their sense of belonging in their peer group. A number of studies have shown a positive correlation between adolescents' appearance and their social acceptance.

of rebellion against the adult world. Adolescents who are hostile or rebellious toward their parents may express their contempt by wearing clothes or hairstyles they know their parents dislike. The more fuss the parents make, the more determined adolescents are to stick to their own styles. However, the dominant motives in selecting the styles are the desire to be recognized by others as cool or the desire to depend on and be like others (Piacentini and Mailer, 2004). Adolescents who buy clothes to show independence (from parents especially) wear clothes that will give them recognition or acceptance in their own peer groups.

Clothing and hairstyles have been used by some youths as an expression of rebellion against particular mores and values in adult society. Adult puritanical culture emphasized that cleanliness is next to godliness; therefore, some teenagers express their rejection of what they perceive as a hypocritical, materialistic, godless culture by choosing to remain unclean and unkempt. Youths of the 1960s chose various symbols of a youth culture that was predominantly antiwar and antiestablishment. Ban-the-bomb symbols; beads, flowers, and headbands; fringed leather, Native American–style jackets; granny dresses; moccasins or sandals; and beards and long, unkempt hair were an expression of independence, dissatisfaction with the status quo, and the determination of these youths to show solidarity against adult criticism. Such clothing symbolized youths' rejection of middle-class philosophy and values. Students of the 1980s who adopted punk-rock styles were expressing the same rebellion against middle-class society and conformity to their own peer groups. Currently, youths who wear baggy, oversized, hip-hop clothing; bare their navels; and sport tattoos and piercings also seek to express their independence. Clothing remains a basic expression of personality, lifestyle, and political philosophy.

For adolescents, the most important function of clothing is to assure their identity and sense of belonging with peer groups. Clothing is used to enhance self-concept, to make adolescents feel good about themselves, and to make a favorable impression on others (Jensen and Ostergaard, 1998). A number of studies have shown the relationship between adolescents' appearance and their social acceptance. Those who are defined by their peers as fashionable dressers have high status; well-dressed but not fashionable students occupy the middle ground; poorly dressed students have low status (Hinton and Margerum, 1984). Consciously or not, other students look down on those not dressed correctly.

Adolescents who are satisfied with the way they look also have more acceptable self-concepts and make more adequate personal adjustments. Preoccupations with clothing and appearance are not superficial or unimportant to youths who are concerned about peer-group acceptance. They must either conform or be rejected. Research has shown that females are more concerned about clothes and more involved in shopping than males (Chen-yu and Seock, 2002). This reflects differences in their socialization. Females are taught to place more emphasis on dress than are males.

ANSWERS WOULDN'T YOU LIKE TO KNOW . . .

Why are fads important to teens?

Following fads—whether in clothing, slang, or music—makes individuals feel secure. (You won't get teased about your taste in clothing if you wear the same thing everyone else does.) Following fads also lets others know something about you, such as which group you are in. Finally, having unique styles of dress and the like separates teens from adults and makes them feel independent.

One function of adolescent clothing is to indicate the clique to which an adolescent belongs. "Jocks" often wear jerseys and other casual items of dress. "Nerds" may wear clothing that is too adultlike or out of style; their pants may be too short or made of dated material. "Punks" often favor leather and chains; their hair may be dyed several vivid, unusual colors and they likely have multiple body piercings. In addition to wearing black, "Goths" like dangling-cross earrings and lace. "Preppies" wear expensive clothing, often favoring one or two particular brands; clothes from Abercrombie and Fitch have dominated the "preppie" scene for the past several years.

The importance of clothing wanes over the course of adolescence. One study found that 12- to 14-year-olds were more concerned than 15- to 18-year-olds about wearing the latest fashions, being in style, and having famous-label clothing (Simpson, Douglas, and Schimmel, 1998). By college, late adolescents generally dress in whatever style is most comfortable for them and are less concerned overall with their image.

Automobiles

Another material aspect of adolescent culture is the automobile. It has become important in the lives of adolescents for a number of different reasons:

1. *The automobile is a status symbol.* When boys are asked what impresses girls the most, they rank being an athlete first, followed by being in the leading crowd, followed by having a nice car. Owning or having access to a car adds to one's prestige in the eyes of one's peers. The type of car one owns or drives is important, and the status attached to various types changes over the years. Not long ago, to drive the family car—especially if it was a new, large, and expensive one—added greatly to prestige. Later, the big car was out, and the small, fast, expensive sports car was in. Now, sport utility vehicles (SUVs) are filtering down into the adolescent market. For the majority of youths—male and female—owning a car is still one of the most coveted symbols of status.

   Owning a car is becoming ever more common among high school students. Among 15- to 20-year-olds, ownership nearly doubled between 1985 and 2002, jumping from 22 percent to 42 percent. More than one-half million new cars were sold to teenagers in 2002. This increase can be attributed to the fact that parents are more willing to purchase cars for their teens and to pay their insurance premiums, as well (Higgins, 2003).

2. *The automobile is a means of freedom and mobility.* A car allows adolescents the opportunity to get away from home and drive to the neighboring town, to the big city, or to Florida during the spring break from school. It provides adolescents with a home away from home. If particularly devoted to a car, an adolescent may spend hours in it each day, eating, talking with friends, or even having sex in it. In addition, owning a car means adolescents don't have to rely on the school bus. They can stay after school for extracurricular activities and can get themselves to and from their job.

3. *For a number of youths, an automobile has become a hobby.* Fixing up an old clunker can be a satisfying way to spend a Saturday afternoon. Many adolescent boys share a love for power and speed. Drag-strip or stock-car races are opportunities to compete in socially sanctioned ways to see who can build the fastest engine or soup up an old car. Such races provide opportunities for boys to prove themselves as men and as expert mechanics. Fixing up an old clunker can be a satisfying way to spend a Saturday afternoon.

4. *The automobile has become a symbol of glamour and sexuality, of romantic conquest and acceptability.* Madison Avenue has been quick to use not only snob appeal but also sex appeal in promoting automobiles. Advertisements imply that any man who drives a certain car will automatically fill it with beautiful women or that any girl who drives up in a car with leather upholstery will be considered as glamorous and beautiful as the model in the ad. The automobile has also become a favorite lovers' retreat. It allows for mobility, a fair degree of privacy, and even some degree of comfort and warmth.

5. *For some, the automobile has become a means of expressing hostility and anger.* Psychiatrists have hypothesized that driving a powerful automobile provides an outlet for expression of frustration and hostility. Immature people who jump into their cars when frustrated and angry and go careening down the highway are unintentionally using the automobile as a convenient weapon. It has been widely publicized that hostile and explosive mental attitudes are major causes of injuries and deaths from automobiles and that the accident-prone driver rebels against authority. One study found that adolescents who were least likely to use seat belts were those who were most depressed, had decreased home support, had problems with school and the law, had been on probation, or, in general, felt that their lives were not going well (Schichor, Beck, Bernstein, and Crabtree, 1990). The way adolescents use cars and the attitudes with which they drive are indications and tests of their emotional maturity.

PERSONAL ISSUES AUTOMOBILE CASUALTIES

Adolescents are not very safe drivers. In fact, they are more likely to be in accidents than drivers of any other age, including the elderly. Youths are especially accident prone in these situations: right after they get their license, at night, after they have been drinking, and when they are horsing around with their passengers (McCartt, Shabanova, and Leaf, 2003).

Accident fatality rates for teens followed several clear trends in the 1990s. The good news was that the overall fatality rate fell during this period. The bad news was that the fatality rates for African American teens, Asian American teens, and Hispanic American girls rose slightly during the same period (Ozer, Park, Paul, Brindis, and Irwin, 2003).

Adolescents can take several steps to reduce their risk of becoming a motor vehicle fatality. First, they should wear a seat belt, whether driving or riding. The death rate is about twice as high for those who don't wear a seat belt compared to those who do. Most teens (about 85 percent) now report that they "usually" or "always" wear a seat belt, especially females (NHTSA, 2001), so "buckling up" should carry no sense of social stigma.

Second, teens should avoid driving after having drunk alcohol. Males are more likely to perform this risky behavior than females. Similarly, teens should avoid being a passenger in a car being driven by someone who has been drinking. Males and females report this behavior with equal frequency. Studies have shown that it is even more risky to ride with someone who is drunk than to drive while drunk yourself; the passenger seat is a more dangerous place to sit than the driver's seat, in part because cars are less likely to have passenger-side airbags. Almost 30 percent of adolescent traffic fatalities involve a collision due to drunk driving (NHTSA, 2001).

Finally, the 25 percent of adolescents who sometimes ride on motorcycles should wear a helmet, as doing so greatly increases the likelihood of surviving a motorcycle crash. Only about two-thirds of adolescents who ride on motorcycles do wear a helmet (Ozer, Park, Paul, Brindis, and Irwin, 2003).

Cell Phones

Adolescents love to use phones, as any parent will attest. They can be out all day with a good friend, only to come home and immediately call that same friend on the phone. They can spend literally hours and hours on the phone talking about every conceivable subject. Adolescents who receive a number of phone calls take this as an approval of their social standing. Those who don't get many phone calls experience feelings of rejection and sometimes loneliness.

In times gone by, it was socially acceptable for girls to call other girls or for boys to call girls, but it seemed to be inappropriate for girls to call boys. That pattern has changed as adolescent female gender roles in the United States have changed. Males' reports of receiving calls from girls parallels girls' reports of calling boys (Anderson, Arceneaux, Carter, Miller, and King, 1995).

It used to be a common joke that parents had to constantly yell at their adolescent children to get off the phone because they were tying up the family's only telephone line. With the expansion of cell phone use, adolescents spend even more time chatting with friends, but at least they are not annoying their parents.

In 2004 nearly half of all American teenagers owned their own cell phone; girls are slightly more likely than boys to do so. Older teens are more likely to have cell phones than younger teens. Adolescents who live in urban and suburban areas are more likely to own phones than adolescents who live in rural areas. Even though cell phones have become so popular, teens who own them are still more likely to use a land line when they make a call than to use a cell phone (Lenhart, Madden, and Hitlin, 2005).

One benefit of cell phones is the sense of security they provide both adolescents and their parents (Williams and Williams, 2005). With a cell phone, help is only a few button pushes away, regardless of one's location. Several years ago, pagers and beepers were standard in some high schools. The cell phone has replaced these devices because it guarantees access, allowing a parent to check up on a teen at any time. Because of this, parents are often willing to give their adolescents more freedom than they would if the teens did not have cell phones. For example, they let them stay out later or go places without clearing it first as long as they call in. Paradoxically, adolescents have given up a certain amount of true autonomy for this "increased freedom": They are never truly on their own, independent of their parents' supervision. There is always a safety line, a tether, home.

In any case, most adolescents are more concerned about social interaction than they are about safety. Thus, the majority of the calls they make and receive are to and from friends. Since cell phones are always at hand, teens can now spend even more time talking with their peers than previously.

In addition to allowing actual voice-to-voice communication, cell phones allow another means of communication as well: text messaging (TMing). About two-thirds of all American teens who own a cell phone have used text messaging. No one anticipated how popular TMing would become with adolescents: It is a cumbersome, slow process, and you can leave only short messages (Faulkner and Culwin, 2005). Older teens and girls are more likely to text message than younger teens and boys. In effect, it is the modern equivalent of "note passing" in that it is private and cannot be overheard (Davie, Panting, and Charlton, 2004).

Because many cell phones represent cutting-edge technology and not everyone has one, they are a new status symbol among youths. Adolescents can choose models in various colors and designs and with an array of features. For example, they can program the phone to play different melodies instead of the standard ring.

Talking on the phone is an important pastime for most adolescents and can occupy a large part of their day. The prevalence of the cell phone has only reinforced this behavior.

One downside of cell phones is that they can disturb others when they go off. Some schools have banned cell phones because they are too disruptive during class. A second downside is that it is more dangerous to drive when using a cell phone. Even with these caveats, however, it is clear that cell phones are a part of the adolescent scene and that they will likely be used more and more in the years to come.

Adolescent cell phone use is by no means limited to the United States. In fact, the teenagers in many European and Asian countries are even more likely to use cell phones than their American counterparts, for several reasons: They do not need parental consent for service, and calling rates are relatively less expensive (compared to fixed-line service) than in the United States (Anderson, 2002).

Computers and the Internet

Virtually all adolescents have access to computers and the Internet: If they do not have them at home (and most do), nearly every school in America not only has multiple computers for student use but is wired to the Web. Eighty-seven percent of American teenagers between the age of 12 and 17 go online, and half of the ones who say they don't used to use the Web but have quit. Internet use has become truly ubiquitous. Black youth are somewhat less likely to go online than other adolescents (about 77 percent do so), but even they use the Internet at higher rates than adults. This pattern is likely partially a product of socioeconomic differences, since adolescents whose parents earn more money, are married, and went to college are more likely to use the Web than those whose parents do not have those attributes (Lenhart, Madden, and Hitlin, 2005).

Not only do adolescents use the Web, but they use it frequently. About half of all teens say that they connect to the Internet about once per day; another quarter say they get on several times per day. The most common place to use the Web is one's own home, and about half of the teens' homes have high-speed, broadband connections. Most adolescents share their wired computer with other family members, and so these computers tend to be located in shared family spaces such as family rooms.

What do teens do while on the Web? How do they spend their Internet time? As Figure 13.2 illustrates, teenagers do a variety of activities while online. More adolescents send e-mails and visit entertainment sites than do any other Web-related activities. There are some gender differences in Internet usage: in particular, girls are more likely to seek health-related information, send e-mail, and go to entertainment sites whereas boys are more likely to play online games (Lenhart, Madden, and Hitlin, 2005). Also, teenagers as a whole in some ways

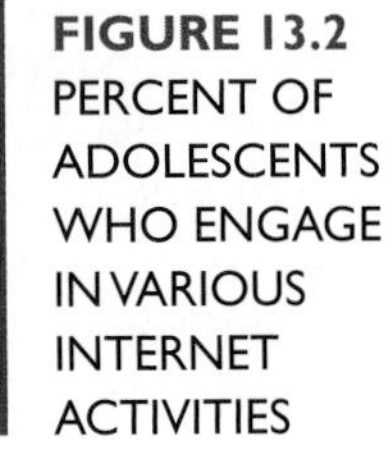

FIGURE 13.2
PERCENT OF ADOLESCENTS WHO ENGAGE IN VARIOUS INTERNET ACTIVITIES

Source: Lenhart, Madden, and Hitlin (2005).

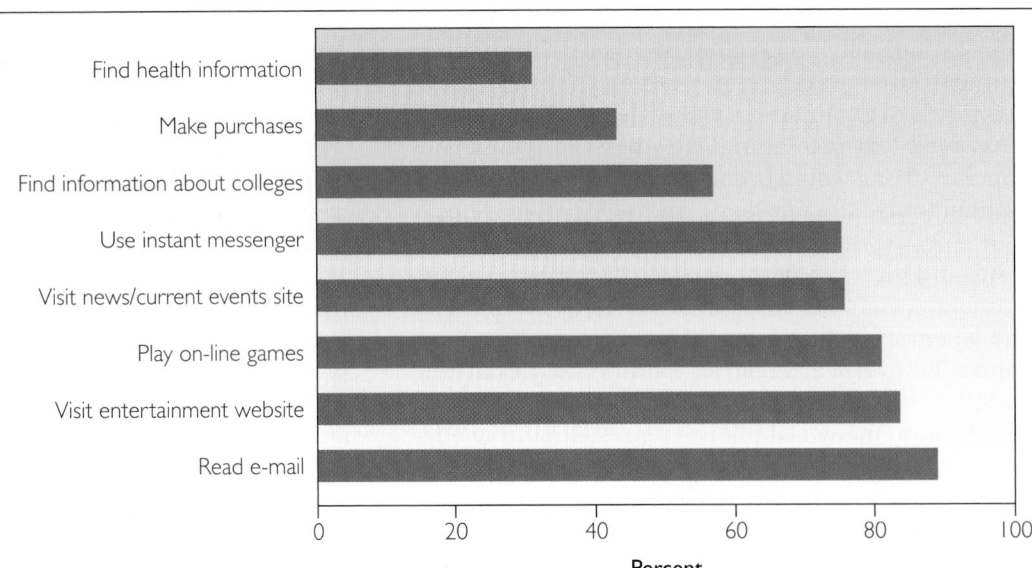

use the Internet differently than their parents. They are more likely than adults to download music or videos, read or create a blog, instant message (IM) another person, and play games (Fox and Madden, 2006).

Note, though, that all these statistics reflect the numbers of adolescents who do these activities, not the amount of time that they do them. It is hard to assess the relative amounts of time that teenagers spend doing different activities while online, partly because they are often multitasking. For example, I can be scanning a sports site to see how well my favorite team is doing while I am instant messaging and listening to a live-stream radio program. Therefore, it is not contradictory to say that even though more adolescents send e-mail, most prefer instant messaging and spend between half an hour to one hour a day using it. More than one-third of all teens have created and posted an IM profile. Teenagers report enjoying instant messaging because they can carry on several conversations at once and because it is more like a conversation. They also like to use instant messages for conveying awkward information that they'd rather not do face-to-face (Lenhart, Madden, and Hitlin, 2005). There is some research suggesting that IMing enhances relationships among friends and strengthens the bonds between them (Hu, Wood, Smith, and Westbrook, 2004).

Besides being able to keep in touch with friends from school, the Internet also allows adolescents to interact with strangers, some of whom may become friends or part of one's support network. This may be particularly useful for adolescents who find themselves in a minority in their community or who have some special interest or problem that is not widely shared by those around them. Adolescents can go on chat rooms and "speak" with others who share a hobby, root for the same sports team, share their lifestyle (e.g., bisexual, goth), have the same medical condition as themselves, have the same ethnicity, or share their religious or political beliefs. At present, there is little cause to worry that reasonable levels of computer use adversely affect adolescents' social skills or activities (Subrahmanyam, Greenfield, Kraut, and Grass, 2001).

Of course, it cannot be forgotten that interacting with strangers is not all good. There are chat rooms in which teenagers encourage each other to engage in harmful activities, such as eating-disordered behavior or self-mutilation. Also, several studies have revealed that about 15 percent of adolescents have actually met face-to-face with persons that they have initially had contact with online (e.g., Staksrud, 2003). This clearly carries significant risk, since there is no guarantee that a person is actually who he or she claims to be online.

This brings up the issue of how adolescents present themselves on the Web, and how these presentations might affect their identity development. Due to its anonymity, the Internet offers unprecedented opportunity to experiment with one's identity (Katz and Rice, 2002). You can present yourself in different ways, with minimal "real-life" consequences, to see how others react to you. You can pretend to be things you are not, and no one can know that you are not being truthful. Adolescents do seem to take advantage of the Web for identity experimentation (Calvert, 2002). Early adolescents experiment more than older ones, who spend more of their

PERSONAL ISSUES INTERNET ADDICTION

It is so common for college students to spend long hours using the Internet that it is possible to lapse into problematic behavior without being aware of it. Internet use becomes problematic if it becomes compulsive and begins to interfere with the rest of your life. It's not really the number of hours that you log on that matter; it's the attitude you have about those hours and the priority they have in your life.

If you are at all concerned that you are lapsing into Internet addiction, you should ask yourself the following questions:

1. Are you in control of the time you spend on the Internet, or do you find yourself logging on more than you'd like?
2. Do you frequently stay online longer than you intended, even if it means missing an appointment or losing needed sleep?
3. Do you neglect schoolwork or employment responsibilities so that you can stay online?
4. Do you cancel social activities so that you can spend more time on the Web?
5. Do you daydream about being online when you are not?
6. Do you find yourself lying about your Internet use, or minimizing it when you talk to others?
7. Have your friends complained to you about your computer usage, or suggested to you that you spend too much time online?
8. Do you get irritated when you can't be online as much as you'd like?

These questions are analogous to the questions you would ask yourself to evaluate any form of addiction, be it drug use or gambling or exercising.

There is more than one form of Internet addiction, since there are so many different things one can do on the Web. Some people participate in online gambling, others interact with others in chat rooms, others shop, others surf for information, yet others view pornography, and others play online games. Again, it is the desperation and need to be on the Web, rather than the activity itself, that makes the behavior hurtful.

Internet addiction can be treated, just as any other compulsive behavior can be treated. If you are worried about your Internet usage, you should speak to a counselor in your college or university's counseling center.

time communicating with their friends. Girls and boys both alter their personas to be more sexually stereotyped (i.e., girls describe themselves as more beautiful than they are, boys as more hypermasculine). The most common motivation for this deception appears to be to see how others react to you when aspects of yourself are changed; facilitating relationship formation is a secondary concern (Valkenberg, Schouten, and Peter, 2005).

NONMATERIAL CONCERNS OF ADOLESCENT CULTURE

Not all aspects of the adolescent subculture involve possessions. Using the latest slang terms and listening to peer-approved music also helps teens feel part of a subculture. Both also encourage others to perceive a teen as "cool/groovy/with it/crazy/a bull brahma/all that/bad/phat," depending on the era.

Slang

People in subgroups often use their own variety of slang terms. *Slang* is a shorthand way of expressing a concept that would take longer to express using conventional language. For instance, it takes less time to say *hot* than to say *sexually attractive.* The correct use of slang identifies one as a member of a subculture, just as clothing does. Using slang also provides teens a certain degree of privacy, since the adults around them may have difficulty understanding what they are saying to each other. Slang terms express the values of the subgroup; for example, in the 1960s, hippies used the word *psychedelic,* which refers to hallucinogenic drugs, to express approval for nondrug items. Using slang fosters a sense of cohesion among subgroup members.

Music

Music is an important part of adolescent culture. During the twentieth century, popular music took many forms: pop, rhythm and blues, rap, folk, country and western, jazz, and rock. Adolescents are drawn to a variety of types of popular music, perhaps due to the wide range of emotions expressed in today's songs.

Most adolescents spend a lot of time listening to music. Most studies reveal that adolescents spend somewhat more than 3 hours/day listening to music (e.g., Gentile, Lynch, Linder, and Walsh, 2004; Schwartz and Fouts, 2003). Much of that time, the music provided a background for doing other activities. Strasburger (1995) has identified four different reasons for youths' listening to music:

1. Music can help one relax and improve one's mood.
2. Music can enhance a social event, such as a party or gathering of friends.
3. Music can help pass the time and relieve boredom.
4. Music can allow one to express one's feelings about various issues and can provide something or someone (the singer) to identify with.

Given that it fills so many needs, it is really not surprising that music fills so much of many adolescents' time.

Although different genres of music emphasize different themes, in mainstream rock, pop, and country and western music, songs about love predominate. (This theme dominates the lyrics of songs directed at adults, as well.) Many songs depict love in a very romantic fashion, suggesting that true love can conquer all or that love is the greatest pleasure in life. Other songs deal with the downsides of love: breaking up, unrequited love, and betrayal. Moreover, songs have become more and more sexually explicit; it is not unusual for songs to be blatantly suggestive and to extol the joys of sexual contact. Both male and female singers frequently describe how good making love feels.

In addition to love and sexual themes, popular music sometimes discusses the problems that teenagers confront. Some artists sing about loneliness or being unable to find a job. Some urge listeners to reject the authority of their parents, their teachers, or the police. Song lyrics may encourage violence against perceived oppressors or rail against societal or world problems, such as war and hatred. Drinking and drugs are also frequently mentioned, either celebrating the fun in getting drunk or high or emphasizing the problems these behaviors can cause. So-called party songs encourage adolescents to let loose and have a good time.

Rock Music

When rock music was invented in the 1950s, it was the music of youth. Prior to this time, adults and adolescents listened to the same types of music, such as the crooners of earlier eras. Although jazz was once viewed as scandalous, it never had an exclusively adolescent audience. But beginning with Little Richard, Elvis, and Chuck Berry, teenagers had their own music and it often met with their parents' disapproval.

RESEARCH HIGHLIGHT CHANGING TASTES IN FASHION, MUSIC, AND MOVIES

Since the 1950s, American adolescents have worn clothing, listened to music, and favored movies that may or may not have been enjoyed by their parents. Here is a brief view of adolescent trends over the years.

Clothing

1950s: Rolled jeans, white T-shirts, saddle shoes, sweater sets
1960s: Torn jeans, headbands, Afros, granny glasses, tie-dyed T-shirts
1970s: Bell bottoms, Earth shoes, crocheted vests, disco styles
1980s: Acid-washed jeans, leg warmers, leggings, big hair
1990s: Baggy pants, tattoos, piercings, fleece, grunge
2000s: Lowcut jeans, fitted T-shirts, button-front shirts, straight hair, flat shoes

Movies

1950s: *From Here to Eternity;* 3-D horror films
1960s: *Lawrence of Arabia; To Kill a Mockingbird*
1970s: *American Graffiti; Star Wars; Jaws*
1980s: *Raiders of the Lost Ark; Top Gun*
1990s: *Jurassic Park; The Matrix*
2000s: *Lord of the Rings; American Pie; Pirates of the Caribbean*

Music

1950s: Elvis Presley, Buddy Holly, Little Richard, Chuck Berry, Bill Haley and the Comets
1960s: The Beach Boys, The Beatles, Bob Dylan, The Grateful Dead, Jimi Hendrix, Janice Joplin
1970s: Pink Floyd; Fleetwood Mac; America; Crosby, Stills, Nash, and Young; Talking Heads; Led Zeppelin
1980s: Michael Jackson, U2, Genesis, Journey, The Pretenders, Talking Heads, Metallica
1990s: Nirvana, Pearl Jam, Sonic Youth, Nine-Inch Nails, Phish, Radiohead, Fugazi, M. C. Hammer
2000s: Dave Matthews Band, Britney Spears, Usher, Jay-Z, 50 Cent

Attending rock concerts has been a tradition among youths for more than 50 years.

Although much rock consisted (and continues to consist) of rather gentle love songs, some of it extolled the virtues of sex, drug use, and rebellion. Early on, Elvis's gyrating hip movements were cause for alarm. In the 1960s, the Beatles' John Lennon scandalized the adult world by claiming that the group was more popular than Jesus (inspiring public record burnings), and the Rolling Stones were prevented from singing "Let's spend the night together" on television. (They had to change the lyrics to "Let's spend some time together.") Later on, the Jefferson Airplane and the Grateful Dead recommended drug use to their listeners, and Country Joe sang out against the war in Vietnam. Heavy metal performers such as Motley Crue and Metallica presented themselves as dangerous sexual predators, while glam rockers gloried in sexual ambiguity. The Seattle-based grunge bands of the early 1990s, such as Alice in Chains and Nirvana, were angry and full of despair. At the turn of the new century, new metal bands such as Linkin Park and Limp Bizkit continued the tradition of provocative lyrics.

Rock has lost much of its ability to shock the adult world, since the parents of today's teens grew up listening to some version of it. Many, if not most, adults still tune their radios to rock stations (even if they play hits from the 1970s or 1980s) and attend rock concerts. Because rock became so mainstream, a new type of youth sound was needed.

Rap Music

Rap has now been in existence for about 30 years. Its hallmark is its spoken lyrics, which are accompanied by a rhythmic beat.

Rap music is now by far the most popular music with Black, White, and Latino adolescents (Roberts, Foehr, and Rideout, 2005). Rap is the backbone of hip-hop culture. With its roots in African and Caribbean music, rap was invented in New York City by two disc jockeys, Afrika Bambaata and Kool Herc, who had immigrated from the islands. The first large commercial rap recording was the Sugar Hill Gang's "Rapper's Delight," released in 1979. As rap became more established, it diversified. Artists began to experiment with fusing rap with rock (especially metal), Latin, and techno sounds. One branch in particular, gangsta rap—exemplified by rappers such as Ice T, Tupac Shakur, and Public Enemy—became violent, sexist, and homophobic.

Inevitably, the same kinds of concerns about antisocial messages that had been reserved for rock music spilled over onto rap. Are these concerns justified? Does listening to music with violent or overtly sexual lyrics negatively affect teens?

The Effects of Antisocial Music

The principles of social learning theory suggest that being exposed to music with antisocial themes, especially when performed by one's heroes or idols, will be harmful. What is known about the effects of television exposure—a different form of media—also argues for caution. What does the research that directly examines the effects of music on adolescents indicate?

There is clearly a correlation between preference for antisocial music and alienation. Scheel and Westefeld (1999), for example, found that heavy metal fans had more positive views of suicide and saw less reason for living than nonfans. Atkin et al. (2002) found that adolescents who were aggressive or most prone to engaging in antisocial acts were also most likely to say that heavy metal was their favorite type of music. Other studies have linked alienation with school and preference for heavy metal music (Roe, 1995).

However, no study to date has demonstrated a direct causal link between the preference for songs with antisocial lyrics and harmful behavior (Kirsh, 2006). Stack (1998), for instance, found that while heavy metal fans were more accepting of suicide, this was no longer the case when differences in the religiosity of heavy metal fans and nonfans was taken into account. In other words, it was one's religious ideation, not his or her preference for heavy metal, that influenced attitudes toward suicide. Other research has found that when heavy metal fans listen to their preferred music, their mood improves, not darkens (Gowensmith and Bloom, 1997; Scheel and Westefeld, 1999). Nonfans who were new to heavy metal lyrics were likely to react with anger, however. Ballard and Coates (1995) failed to demonstrate that listening to heavy metal or rap had even a short-term effect on youths' suicide ideation.

In one study, adolescent boys 14 to 20 years of age were interviewed individually to find out why they liked heavy metal music and what effects they felt it had on them (Arnett, 1991). Heavy metal listeners reported liking the music for a variety of reasons but most of all for what they perceived as the talent and skill of the performers. They also favored heavy metal music because of the lyrical themes expressed in the songs—in particular, the dismal condition of the world as they see it. The songs they liked best were those concerned with social issues, such as the nuclear arms race and environmental destruction. Heavy metal songs often lament the state of the world but do not provide even a hint for hope of the future. Hopelessness and cynicism pervade the songs. Most heavy metal songs are never played in a major key; the songs are nearly all in minor keys—the keys of melancholy.

It is not difficult to see why many adults object to the heavy metal songs listened to by their adolescents. In fact, the adolescents in this study most often mentioned "Fade to Black," which describes suicidal despair, as their favorite song. It's remarkable that not even one subject reported that the music tended to make him feel sad or hopeless. Rather, heavy metal music served a purgative function, dissipating accumulative frustration and anger. Adolescents listened to it especially when they were angry, and it consistently had the effect of making them less angry and of calming them down.

The adolescent boys' enthusiasm for heavy metal music did not appear to be motivated by defiance or rebellion toward parents. Although most parents said they did not like the music, only in one case did a boy say his parents made any effort to stop or restrict him from listening to it.

In sum, the role of antisocial music in the lives of adolescents who like and listen to it is complex, reflecting their concern with the condition of the world and a certain pessimism with regard to the future, but it is also used by them to assuage unpleasant and unruly emotions. Songs about suicide, murder, radical despair, and the destruction of the world are the result. But rather than being the cause of recklessness and despair among adolescents, heavy metal music is a reflection of these and of the socialization environment.

> **ANSWERS WOULDN'T YOU LIKE TO KNOW ...**
>
> **Does listening to antisocial music cause antisocial behavior?**
>
> There are no causal data linking teen depression, suicide, and antisocial behavior to antisocial music. However, adolescents who are depressed or aggressive tend to listen to music that reflects those themes. In addition, exposure to music and music videos that depict stereotypes of women and minorities tends to increase belief in those stereotypes.

The popularity of antisocial music among adolescents is, among other things, a symptom of their alienation. Even though the lyrics are despairing and the music is angry, listening to it does not cause them to despair but, in fact, dissolves their anger. Ultimately, there is something consoling in the bond they feel to others through the music, even if that bond is based on a shared alienation (Arnett, 1991).

Similarly, there is correlational data showing that adolescents who listen to music that contains sexually degrading lyrics (but not sexual, nondegrading lyrics) are more likely to engage in early sexual intercourse than adolescents who do not listen to music with sexually degrading lyrics (Martino, Collins, Elliott, Strachman, Kanouse, and Berry, 2006). This appears to be true even though numerous other factors that could be responsible for the findings were statistically controlled. While this kind of analysis is more persuasive than a more typical purely correlational research design, it is still premature to conclude that listening to sexually degrading lyrics directly leads to increased early sexual activity (i.e., that there is a causal relationship between the two).

It is important to remember that preferences for violent rock and rap music are associated with participation in reckless behavior but do not necessarily *cause* adolescents to behave recklessly. Rather, both reckless behavior and heavy metal or rap music may appeal to adolescents who have an especially high propensity for sensation seeking. It is equally important to remember that only a few studies have tried to find causal links between music listening and antisocial outcomes. It is quite possible that these links will be demonstrated in the future, especially for those individuals who are subjected to antisocial music against their will.

Music Videos

With the advent of MTV (Music Television) in August 1981, an immensely popular new form of entertainment was spawned. No one can dispute the huge commercial success of MTV and its residual impact on the music industry. Still, today's adolescents do not spend nearly as much time watching music videos as those in the 1980s: most watch only 15–30 minutes per day (Roberts, Christianson, and Gentile, 2003). MTV itself devotes very little time to music videos. Adolescents now watch videos on other television stations and on their computers. However, 15–30 minutes each day adds up to 90–180 hours each year, so it is worthwhile to consider what we know about music videos' effects.

Targeted at teenagers and containing more violence and sex than conventional television, the music video industry attracted a notable group of critics. For example, the American Academy of Pediatrics, Women against Pornography, National Coalition on Television Violence, Parents Music Resource Center, National Parent Teachers Association, and others all expressed concern about the possible harmful effects of music videos on youths. Content analyses have revealed that more than half of concept videos have violent or sexual imagery or both (Strasburger, 1995).

Johnson and colleagues demonstrated several different negative effects of videos with these themes. In one study, African American male adolescents were exposed to violent rap videos, nonviolent rap videos, or no videos (the control condition). Afterward, the adolescents were presented with a scenario in which violence occurred. Those subjects who had watched the violent rap videos found the violence in the scenario more acceptable than did the other subjects. Moreover, they said that they were more likely to use violence themselves (Johnson, Jackson, and Gatto, 1995). A second study demonstrated that girls who watched videos in which females were sexually subordinate were less likely to disapprove of a scenario involving sexual violence than girls who had not been shown such videos (Johnson, Adams, Ashburn, and Reed, 1995). Finally, a third study showed that adolescents who watched violent rap videos developed more negative stereotypes about African American males than subjects who did not watch such videos (Johnson, Trawalter, and Dovidio, 2000).

The U.S. Senate held hearings in 1985 to examine the rock music industry and its effect on youthful consumers, but at the time, there was insufficient research to support the allegation of the critics or to allay the anxieties of concerned parents. There are good reasons, however, why music videos have the potential to affect youths more than any other popular medium. Consider the following (Strouse, Buerkel-Rothfuss, and Long, 1995):

1. Music can evoke very strong feelings; the mood-altering effects of music make people more susceptible to behavioral and attitudinal changes.
2. It is well known that a combined audio and visual presentation enhances learning and has a greater impact on attitudes and behavior than music alone.
3. Rock music has always contained rebellious, antisocial, and sexually provocative messages.
4. Concept music videos are frequently interspersed with unconnected segments of violence.
5. Some research reveals that a relatively short exposure to music videos can result in desensitization to violence and an increased acceptance of socially violent behavior.

Research on the effects of music videos on adolescents reveals some interesting gender differences. Females tend to listen to more music and prefer soft, romantic, danceable music, whereas males prefer hard rock, macho music (Toney and Weaver, 1994). Females describe greater personal importance of music and pay more attention to lyrics. Therefore, they report more personal involvement and participation in music imagery and are more likely to recall the images of the videos than listening to a song on the radio. Survey research finds a stronger association between the amount of exposure to music videos and premarital sexual permissiveness for females than for males (Strouse, Buerkel-Rothfuss & Lang, 1995).

Another important consideration is the environment of the family in which the youth dwells. Parental absence is associated with an increased use of television and radio by adolescents. Furthermore, adolescents who are heavy consumers of rock music tend to be more involved with their peers and less with their families than are adolescents who are light users of rock music. Thus, the family environment is an important moderator of the impact of music videos on youth. Thus, adolescents' perceptions and feelings about their level of satisfaction with their family may be a better moderator of the potential effects of music video exposure than other more objective entices of actual family functions. Unsatisfactory conditions in a family promote an affective need for youthful members to select and attend to music programming that enables them to escape into the fantasies of a seductive video. In summary, the potential effect of music videos as a dynamic, interactional process has a greater impact on youths who are at risk. Adolescents from family environments with a high level of satisfaction may be relatively unaffected by the sexual messages of music videos (Strouse, Buerkel-Rothfuss, and Long, 1995).

SUMMARY

1. Adolescent society is the organized networks of social interaction among adolescents. Adolescent culture is the sum of adolescents' ways of living.
2. There are wide variations in adolescent society and culture among various adolescent groups.
3. Some adults believe that adolescents have their own subculture; others believe that adolescent culture is a reflection of adult culture. Actually, both views are partially true. Certain aspects of adolescent culture (such as sexual behavior and use of marijuana) are subcultural because they run counter to adult culture. In many ways, however, adolescent culture reflects adult values, depending on parent versus peer orientation.
4. Adolescent societies may be divided into formal (primarily in-school) and informal (out-of-school) groups. Most in-school groups are age-grade specific—that is, they are identified with a particular age and grade in school.
5. In-school subsystems may be divided into three groups: the formal academic subsystem; the semiformal activities subsystem; and the friendship subsystem. Of the three, membership in the friendship subsystem is the most important in the eyes of students.
6. Athletes tend to be popular. Much research has found that being on a sports team benefits the athletes involved; however, the benefits may not be as great as for some other activities.
7. In addition to friendship pairs, adolescents arrange themselves into cliques and crowds. Not everyone belongs to a clique or a crowd—some by their own choice and others by rejection.
8. In many generations there are youth who form distinctive, visible groups. In the 1920s, flappers scandalized their parents with their short dresses, cigarette smoking, and drinking. In the 1960s, the hippies wore torn clothing, grew their hair long, used mind-altering drugs, and staged protests against the Vietnam War. Currently, goths, skateboarders, and members of the hip-hop culture are viewed with suspicion by many adults.
9. Adolescents are a powerful consumer force. They have a great deal of discretionary disposable income, which they largely spend on themselves for luxury items.
10. Clothing is one of the most noticeable aspects of adolescent culture. It is an important means by which adolescents discover and express their identities. It expresses their dependence/independence conflict with adults. It may even express a lifestyle and political philosophy and assure their sense of belonging with peer groups.
11. The automobile is another important material part of adolescent culture. It is a status symbol, a means of freedom and mobility, a symbol of power and independence, a hobby, a symbol of glamour and sexuality, and, for some, a means of expressing hostility and anger. Ready access to an automobile has a great influence on the adolescent's daily life, social activity, and freedom.
12. Talking on the telephone is a favorite pastime of adolescents. Cell phone use ensures even more constant contact with friends than was possible in the past. Cell phones are also used for text messaging.
13. Almost all teenagers make frequent use of the Internet; on it they communicate with friends, interact with strangers who sometimes become friends, look up information, and play games. They do not always present themselves honestly in online interactions.
14. Adolescents use slang to identify themselves as part of a group, for shorthand, for privacy, to foster cohesion, and to have privacy from adults.
15. Music is an important part of adolescent culture. Adolescents listen primarily to rock and rap.
16. Rock has been criticized by adults since it first began, since it sometimes promotes values considered antithetical to adult culture. It is not uncommon (although certainly not widespread) for lyrics to endorse casual sex, drug use, and opposition to authority.
17. Rap music is now more popular with youth than any other type of music. Many adults are equally concerned about the sexist and violent messages found in rap music.
18. Youths listen to antisocial music because it serves as a purgative function in dissipating their anger and because it is a reflection of alienation. Listening to heavy metal music or rap music and engaging in reckless behavior are correlated, although the former does not *cause* the latter. Rather, those who do both have a propensity for sensation seeking.
19. Music videos are watched by millions of youths. Many professional organizations are critical of some of these videos because they portray much sex and violence. The data suggest that watching such music videos can foster negative attitudes.

KEY TERMS

adolescent culture 298	crowds 302
adolescent society 298	flappers 304
adolescent subculture 298	hippies 304
	liaisons 302
cliques 302	subsystems 300

THOUGHT QUESTIONS

Personal Reflection

1. Do you feel that you were ever part of a distinct subculture? Did you feel alienated or just different?
2. Do you and your parents agree or disagree on most of your fundamental values? Do you agree more or less now compared with when you were younger?

3. What extracurricular activities did you participate in as an adolescent? Looking back, are you happy with the choices you made? Why or why not?
4. Did you belong to a clique, were you a liaison, or were you a loner? How did you treat others who were not part of your "inner circle"? How were you treated by others?
5. Are you satisfied that your own Internet use is not excessive? Do you show any signs of Internet addiction or use the Internet excessively?
6. Did you have a car in high school? How would your life have been different with or without it?
7. Do you feel that you personally were affected by the music you listened to as a younger adolescent? If not, why not?

Group Discussion

8. In what ways are adolescent society and culture unique and distinctive from adult society and culture? In what ways does adolescent culture reflect adult culture?
9. Do parents or peers exert the greatest influence on the lives of youths?
10. Was there much snobbishness and socioeconomic class discrimination in your high school? Explain.
11. Some of the studies discussed in this chapter presents the life and values of high school youths as quite superficial. Are adolescents more serious minded than these studies indicate? In your experience, are they less superficial and more concerned with world problems and academics?
12. Do extracurricular activities contribute to adolescent development? Explain.
13. Is clothing as important to the adolescent as this chapter claims? Why or why not?

Debate Questions

14. High school students should not be allowed to own cars.
15. Songs with antisocial lyrics do have harmful effects on adolescents.
16. Middle and high school students should be required to participate in some structured extracurricular activity.
17. Hip-hop culture is harmless.
18. Adolescent cell phone use is excessive and should be limited.

SUGGESTED READING

Bennett, A., and Kahn-Harris, K. (Eds.). (2004). *After Subculture: Critical Studies in Contemporary Youth Culture.* Hampshire, England: Palgrave.

Calvert, S., Jordan, A. B., and Cocking. R. R. (Eds.). (2002). *Children in the Digital Age: Influences of Electronic Media on Development.* Westport, CT: Praeger.

Chang, J. (2005). *Can't Stop Won't Stop: A History of the Hip Hop Generation.* New York: St. Martin's Press.

Crampton, L., and Rees, D. (2003). *Rock and Roll Year by Year.* London, England: D.K. Publishing.

Gentile, D. A. (Ed.). (2003). *Media Violence and Children: A Complete Guide for Parents and Professionals.* Westport, CT: Praeger.

Katz, J. E., and Rice, R. E. (2002). *Social Consequences of Internet Use: Access, Involvement, and Interaction.* Cambridge, MA: MIT Press.

Simmons, R. (2004). *Odd Girl Speaks Out: Girls Write about Bullies, Cliques, Popularity, and Jealousy.* Westminster CO: Harvest Books.

Skelton, T., and Valentine, G. (Eds.). (1997). *Cool Places: Geographies of Youth Cultures.* New York: Routledge.

CHAPTER 14 THE DEVELOPMENT OF MORAL VALUES

WOULDN'T YOU LIKE TO KNOW . . .

- How is children's moral thinking different from that of adults?
- What can be said about the moral development of someone who bases his or her behavior on what other people think?
- Are truly moral people ever willing to break the law?
- Do men and women think differently about moral issues?
- Do teens and their parents often disagree about basic moral issues?
- What should parents do to help their children grow into moral adults?
- How religious are most American teenagers?
- Does watching violence on television really affect people?
- How common is students' cheating on exams and papers?

This chapter discusses the development of moral judgments, behaviors, and values. Why is it placed here, after chapters about family and peer relationships? Morality is a topic that cannot be separated from personal relationships. Most of our moral beliefs are strongly influenced by those around us. We learn what is and is not ethical from our parents, our friends, and the people we see on television and on the Internet. We either come to believe what they believe, or if we are repelled by certain individuals, we actively reject their beliefs and form opposing views. In addition, morality regulates the way in which we behave toward others and how we expect them to behave toward us. Our moral code delineates both our rights and our responsibilities toward those around us. Morality cannot be discussed apart from social standards.

The process by which adolescents develop moral judgment is extremely interesting. A number of major theories have been developed and will be discussed in this chapter. Jean Piaget, Lawrence Kohlberg, and Carol Gilligan all produced theories that emphasize the development of moral judgment as a cognitive process stimulated by the increasing, changing social relationships of children as they get older. These so-called stage theories have been gradually supplanted by the social-cognitive domain model of moral behavior, which emphasizes the multiple influences that direct moral decision making. Yet other researchers have concentrated on an examination of various family correlates that influence moral development. In this chapter, we will discuss such factors as parental warmth, parent-teen interaction, discipline, parental role models, and independence opportunities outside the home in relation to their influence on moral learning. The transmission of religious beliefs and practices from parents to children is also an important consideration and depends on a number of religious and family variables. Finally, we will examine other social influences, such as peer and reference groups, television, and schools. The effects of these influences on the development of values and behavior are important and need to be understood.

COGNITIVE-SOCIALIZATION THEORIES OF DEVELOPMENT

The most important early research on the development of moral judgment of children was that of Piaget (1948) and Piaget and Inhelder (1969). Although some details of Piaget's findings have not been substantiated by subsequent research, his ideas formed the theoretical basis for later research. Piaget's work was with children, but the theoretical framework that outlines his stages of development may be applied to adolescents and adults, as well. It is important, therefore, to understand his discoveries.

Piaget and Children's Moral Development

Piaget's (1948) research into morality involved two types of studies. In one, he observed and questioned children about the need for rules when playing games: Could these rules be changed? If so, under what circumstances? In the second type of research, Piaget told children stories and required them to make moral judgments based on them; for example, is a child more naughty if he or she intentionally breaks one cup or accidentally breaks several? On the basis of this work, Piaget uncovered quite a number of issues for which there was developmental change.

In studying children's attitudes to the rules of the game when playing marbles, Piaget concluded that there is first a **morality of constraint** and second a **morality of cooperation.** In the early stages of moral development, children are constrained by the rules of the game. These rules are coercive because children regard them as inviolable and because the rules reflect parental authority. Rules constitute a given order of existence and, like parents, must be obeyed without question. Later, as a result of social interaction, children learn that rules are not absolute; they learn that they can alter them by social consensus. Rules are no longer external laws to be considered sacred because they are laid down by adults but are social creations arrived at through a process of free decision and thus deserving of mutual respect and consent.

Piaget's story-based research gave him additional insights into the reasoning behind children's moral judgments. He said there are first judgments based solely on the consequences of wrongdoing (**objective judgments**) and later judgments that take into account intention or motive (**subjective judgments**). Therefore, while his younger subjects thought that the child who had accidentally broken several cups was more deserving of punishment than the one who had intentionally broken one cup, the older subjects did not.

Piaget (1948) spoke of children moving from a stage of **heteronomous morality** to one of **autonomous morality.** Heteronomous morality is *received* morality, according to which you do what authority figures tell you to do. You do not question—just obey. You think that rules are absolute and inviolable, and because you believe in the omniscience of those who make rules (parents, God, teachers), you believe that you will inevitably be caught and punished if you transgress. Piaget termed this **immanent justice.** Autonomous morality, conversely, is both *independent* and *cooperative.* It is independent in the sense that you feel that you own your own moral beliefs; they come from within you, rather than having been given to you by others. It is cooperative in that it is based on mutual decisions made with others. For example, if we all agree that the person who rolls the lowest number, not the highest number, on the dice should go first before

ANSWERS WOULDN'T YOU LIKE TO KNOW ...

How is children's moral thinking different from that of adults?

There are two major differences between the moral thinking of children and adults. One is that children believe that rules are set and unchangeable, whereas adults see rules as open to discussion and change. Children also believe that behaviors should be judged by their consequences, whereas adults are more likely to consider the intentions behind behaviors.

we start playing a board game, there is no reason that the rule cannot be changed.

As children move toward autonomous morality, their conception of fairness changes. They begin to develop a sense of *reciprocity.* Initially, they come to believe in cooperation but only because they understand that they will benefit if they behave cooperatively. Ultimately, they appreciate that they should treat others as they wish to be treated because that is what is moral and correct.

Piaget (1948) believed that morality progresses because children are developing on two fronts. On one front, they are becoming smarter and more cognitively sophisticated. This increased thinking ability lets them consider alternatives, recognize inconsistencies, and better understand others so that they can experience empathy. On another front, they are immersed in an ever more complicated social world. Whereas very young children interact mostly with adults, older children interact with peers, as well. These interactions with age-mates provide more opportunities for cooperation and negotiation. When alone, with no adults present, groups of children make their own rules and set their own standards. Piaget believed that these kinds of interactions were crucial to the development of autonomous morality.

One of the best summaries of Piaget's conclusions was given by Kay (1969, p. 157) in a series of simple propositions about the moral lives of children:

1. Human beings develop an intelligent and informed respect for law by experiencing genuine social relationships.
2. Social relationships are found in two basic forms. They are first characterized by child subordination and adult supremacy and then slowly change until the relationship is reciprocal. In this case, the relationship can be based on equality or equity.
3. Social relationships are functionally linked with a system of moral judgment. When the relationship is one of subordination and supremacy, then the moral judgment exercised is based on authoritarian considerations that are objective and heteronomous. Equally, when the relationship is reciprocal, moral judgments are autonomous and reflect the subjective system of morality that now activates the child from within.
4. Judgment and conduct at the final stage of moral development are based not on subscription to an external code of law or even on the regulation of rigid reciprocity in human relationships. They consist of the recognition of the rights and needs of all individuals with due regard to the situational circumstances and the moral principles expressed in them.

Although Piaget's conclusions were deduced from research with children up to age 12, they bear some relationship to the moral life of adolescents. It has been emphasized that Piaget said that children move from a morality of constraint (or obedience) to a morality of cooperation (or reciprocity); children pass from heteronomy to autonomy in making moral judgments; and they move from objective to subjective responsibility. Piaget has said that this second stage of moral development gradually supersedes the first as children grow older.

Of course, there are adolescents and even adults who obey certain laws and rules only because of coercion and the threat of external punishment. They are constrained by authority, not by an inner conscience. If they break the rules, their concern is not remorse at doing wrong but at having been caught. In other words, they never move from heteronomy to autonomy, from objective judgment to subjective judgment, from a morality of constraint to a morality of cooperation. They remain, like young children, at a preoperational,

morality of constraint conduct that is coerced by rules or authority.

morality of cooperation conduct that is regulated by mutual respect and consent.

objective judgments judgments based solely on the consequences of wrongdoing.

subjective judgments judgments that take into account intentions or motives.

heteronomous morality the earlier of Piaget's two stages of moral development, in which individuals slavishly follow the rules they are given.

autonomous morality the latter of Piaget's two stages of moral development, in which individuals make their own moral judgments rather than blindly follow rules.

immanent justice the child's belief that immoral behavior inevitably brings pain or punishment as a natural consequence of the transgression.

premoral stage of development, for the rules have never been internalized, and they never desire to do the right thing from mutual respect and concern for the feelings and welfare of others.

It is unreasonable, then, always to attach age categories to the stages of moral development. There are children, adolescents, and adults at early stages of moral growth. This is one reason that Piaget's findings may be applied to adolescents as well as children.

Kohlberg and Levels of Moral Development

One of the principal deficiencies of Piaget's work was his exclusive concern with children under the age of 12. Kohlberg compensated for this deficiency by using adolescents in a series of studies (Kohlberg, 1963, 1966, 1969, 1970; Kohlberg and Gilligan, 1971; Kohlberg and Kramer, 1969; Kohlberg and Turiel, 1972). Kohlberg greatly extended Piaget's work and over time developed his own theory of moral development.

Kohlberg's (1963) initial study included 72 boys aged 10, 13, and 16. All groups were similar in IQ; half of each group was upper middle class. Data were collected through taped interviews in which 10 moral dilemmas were presented to each boy. In each dilemma, acts of disobedience to legal-social rules or the commands of authority figures conflicted with the human needs or welfare of others. The most famous of Kohlberg's stories involves a man named Heinz:

> In Europe, a woman was near death from a very bad disease, a special kind of cancer. There was one drug the doctors thought might save her. It was a form of radium that a druggist in the same town had recently discovered. The drug was expensive to make, but the druggist was charging ten times what the drug cost him to make. He paid $200 for the radium and charged $2,000 for a small dose of the drug. The sick woman's husband, Heinz, went to everyone he knew to borrow the money, but he could only get together about $1,000, which was half of what the drug cost. He told the druggist that his wife was dying and asked him to sell it cheaper or let him pay later. But the druggist said, "No, I discovered the drug and I'm going to make money from it." Heinz got desperate and broke into the man's store to steal the drug for his wife.
>
> Should the husband have stolen the drug? Was doing so right or wrong? (Kohlberg and Gilligan, 1971)

Each boy was asked to select one of two acts as the more morally correct solution and was then questioned about the reasons for his choice. Kohlberg's material and technique were Piagetian in form. In this study, Kohlberg was concerned not with moral behavior but with moral judgment and the process of thought by which the individual made his judgment. There were no right or wrong answers expected; the individual was scored according to mode of reasoning, regardless of the direction of the given response.

From an analysis of the interviews, Kohlberg (1970), and then Kohlberg and Gilligan (1971), identified three major levels of moral development, each level having two stages of moral orientation or judgment. The levels and stages are outlined in Figure 14.1. Kohlberg found that *preconventional moral reasoning,* Level I, declined sharply from the younger to the older age groups. Level II, *conventional moral reasoning,* increased until age 13 and then stabilized. Level III, *postconventional moral reasoning,* was essentially absent during the teenage years. Figure 14.2 shows the mean percentage of moral reasoning at each stage for males through 36 years of age.

In outlining his stages, however, Kohlberg was careful not to equate each type with a particular age. Within any one age group, individuals are at different levels of development in their moral thinking: Some are delayed and others are advanced. No person fits neatly into any one of the six types. Kohlberg and Gilligan (1971) indicated that the development of moral thought is a gradual and continuous process as the individual passes through a sequence of increasingly sophisticated moral stages.

The three major levels of morality are quite different from each other whereas the two stages within each level are more similar. Let's consider each in turn.

FIGURE 14.1 KOHLBERG'S LEVELS AND STAGES OF MORAL DEVELOPMENT

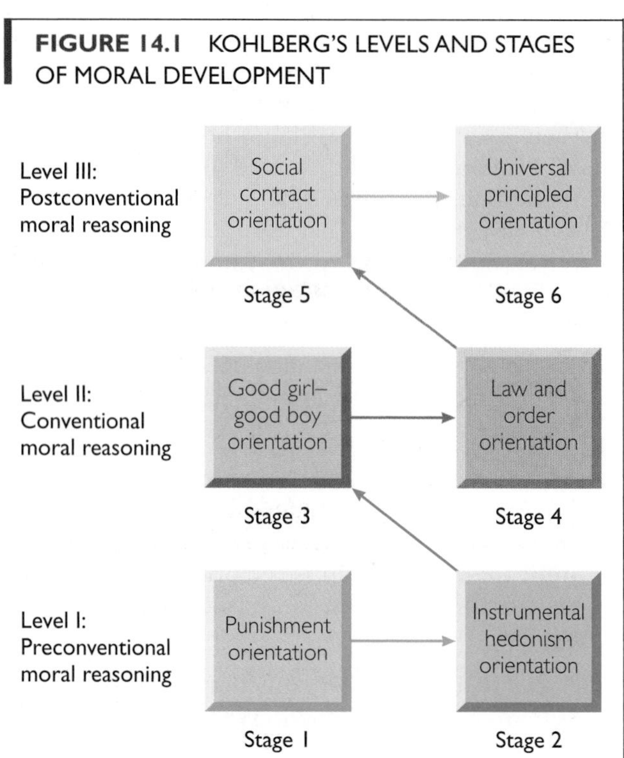

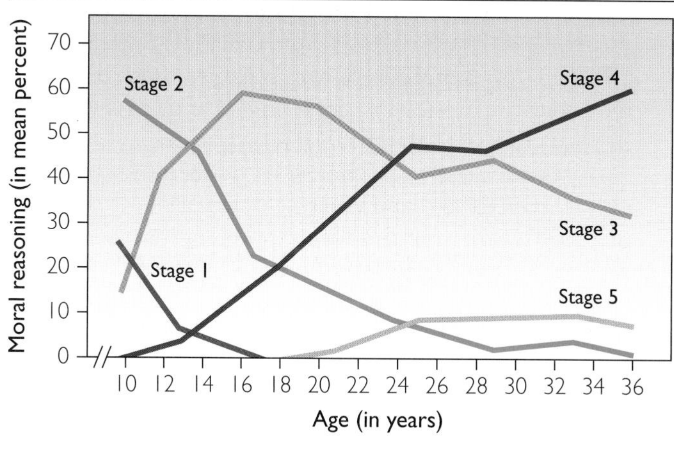

FIGURE 14.2 MORAL REASONING STAGE AND AGE LEVEL (FROM THE 20-YEAR LONGITUDINAL FOLLOW-UP OF KOHLBERG'S FIRST STUDY OF ADOLESCENT BOYS)

Source: From L. Kohlberg, *Moral Reasoning in Adolescence* (Boston: Allyn and Bacon, 1994), p. 200. Copyright © 1994 by Allyn & Bacon. Used with permission.

Level I

Preconventional moral reasoning is characterized by selfishness—it is, in fact, premoral rather than moral. People acting at this level of moral reasoning are motivated by self-interest. They "look out for number one": What's good for them is good and to be embraced, and what's bad for them is bad and to be avoided. In Stage 1, the **punishment orientation,** people act so as to avoid negative consequences. They obey not because of guilt or the desire to be nice but because they are afraid they will be punished if they don't. When presented with the Heinz dilemma, someone in Stage 1 might answer, "Heinz was foolish to steal the drug; if he had gotten caught, he would have surely gone to prison." He or she could also say, "Of course Heinz should have taken the drug. Think how miserable he would have been if his wife had died." These different responses illustrate that for most of the stages, it does not matter whether a person believes Heinz should or should not have taken the drug; rather, what matters is the explanation used to justify the decision.

When in the higher of the two preconventional stages—Stage 2, the **instrumental hedonism orientation**—people are motivated by the thought of payback and future gain. They do favors with the thought that favors will be returned. They obey because there is more gain than harm in doing so. An instrumental hedonist would think that Heinz should have taken the drug, reasoning that "If he saved his wife, think how grateful she would be. She'd treat him like a king forever." Almost all children are preconventional moral reasoners, as are many, if not most, young adolescents.

Level II

People at the **conventional moral reasoning** level of Kohlberg's sequence act so as to gain others' approval. They do what others think is right. In the lower of the two stages, Stage 3, or the **good girl–good boy orientation,** those others are family members, friends, teachers, co-workers, and other people important to the individual. Should Heinz have taken the drug? Of course not. "Think how embarrassed his family must have been when he got caught and his name was in the newspaper." On the other hand, maybe his action was justified. "His children must have been so proud that he was so brave and risked himself to save his wife."

Those in the **law and order orientation,** Stage 4, have a broader, more abstract conception of the term *others*. They are concerned with what society at large will say about their conduct, not just with how their circle of acquaintances will respond. They are motivated to follow rules and obey laws because that is what *others* have said is correct and moral. It is hard

preconventional moral reasoning according to Kohlberg, the first level of development of moral thought, based on reward and punishment.

punishment orientation the more primitive level of preconventional moral reasoning, in which one acts so as to avoid negative consequences.

instrumental hedonism orientation the more advanced of the two preconventional reasoning levels, in which one acts so as to gain a future reward.

conventional moral reasoning according to Kohlberg, the second level of development of moral thought, based on the desire to conform to social convention.

good girl–good boy orientation the first of the two levels of conventional moral reasoning, in which one acts so as to win others' approval.

law and order orientation the more advanced type of conventional moral reasoning, in which one unquestioningly obeys society's rules and laws.

ANSWERS WOULDN'T YOU LIKE TO KNOW . . .

What can be said about the moral development of someone who bases his or her behavior on what other people think?

Kohlberg would say that this reflects a middle, not a high, level of moral development. Most adolescents (and most adults) are at this conventional level of moral reasoning.

ANSWERS WOULDN'T YOU LIKE TO KNOW . . .

Are truly moral people ever willing to break the law?

Yes. Truly moral people *are* willing to break the law if they believe the law is unjust and violates their moral principles. Whereas immoral people break the law for their own benefit, moral people break the law to benefit others.

to imagine an individual in Stage 4 saying that Heinz should have stolen the medicine. A far more typical response would be: "Of course he shouldn't have taken the drug! It's against the law to steal! If everyone broke the law anytime it was convenient for them to do so, we'd have chaos and anarchy! None of us would be safe!" Most adolescents—and in fact, most adults—are conventional moral reasoners.

Level III

The highest level of moral reasoning, **postconventional moral reasoning,** occurs when people don't necessarily do what is best for themselves or what others think they should do but instead do what they believe is right and just. This is also termed *principled moral reasoning.* During the first of the two principled stages—Stage 5, **social contract orientation**—individuals understand that the purpose of rules and laws is to serve the greater societal good. At this stage, individuals define morality in terms of general principles such as individual rights, human dignity, equality, and mutual obligation. They believe that if a law doesn't further these aims, it should be changed. Stage 5 moral reasoners believe in *extenuating circumstances:* factors that allow one to violate a rule for valid moral grounds. They believe in following the spirit of the law. (In contrast, Stage 4 moral reasoners believe in following the letter of the law.) A Stage 5 moral reasoner might respond to the Heinz scenario by saying: "Stealing is wrong, but allowing someone to die is worse. The law shouldn't apply in this circumstance. Heinz did the right thing." The U.S. Declaration of Independence and Constitution both reflect a social contract morality.

Kohlberg originally included a sixth stage of moral reasoning in his scheme, that of **universal principled reasoning.** This type of person behaves so as to avoid self-condemnation. The approach to moral issues is based not on selfish needs or conformity to the existing social order but on autonomous, universal principles of justice that are valid beyond existing laws, social conditions, and peers' valves. Thus, individuals governed by universal ethical principles may break unjust civil laws because they recognize a morality higher than existing law.

The Reverend Martin Luther King, Jr. (1964) eloquently expressed Kohlberg's highest form of moral reasoning in his letter from a Birmingham jail:

> I do not advocate evading or defying the law. . . . That would lead to anarchy. One who breaks an unjust law must do so openly, lovingly, and with a willingness to accept the penalty. An individual who breaks the law that conscience tells him is unjust, and willingly accepts the penalty of imprisonment in order to arouse the conscience of the community over its injustice is, in reality, expressing the highest respect for the law. (p. 86)

Since very few persons employ Stage 6 moral reasoning, Kohlberg stopped discussing it in his later writings.

The Relation between Kohlberg's Stages and Thinking Ability

Since Kohlberg's theory is concerned with moral reasoning, it follows that advances in overall reasoning ability should open the door to higher levels of moral thought. Thus, there should be a relationship between cognitive level and moral reasoning. Kohlberg (Kuhn, Langer, Kohlberg, and Haan, 1977) believed that a high level of cognitive development was necessary for a high level of moral reasoning. He thought that advanced reasoning skills were necessary *but not sufficient* to ensure sophisticated moral reasoning. In other words, you must be able to think in a mature way to be a postconventional moral reasoner, but having mature thought processes does not guarantee this outcome.

Was Kohlberg correct in making this argument? It appears so. Cognitive level and moral reasoning level are certainly correlated (e.g., Krebs and Gillmore, 1982; Walker and Henning, 1997). In addition, researchers who have attempted to train children to morally reason above their cognitive level have failed in their efforts (Walker and Richards, 1979). Still, some who study moral development believe that the influence between cognitive development and moral development is more bidirectional: that each influences the other. These researchers (e.g., Gibbs, 2003) believe that children and adolescents can develop new cognitive capabilities if they continually grapple with difficult moral dilemmas.

One construct that has received little attention in the moral development literature is **metacognition.** Metacognition, or knowing about knowing, refers to insights children have about their own cognitive processes. By analogy to the discussions of metacognition, moral metacognition would refer to the knowledge that children have about their own morality. One investigation described the relationship between metamoral knowledge, moral reasoning, and moral behavior in three age groups: adolescents in grades seven, nine, and twelve (Swanson and Hill, 1993). These researchers found that older children had more accurate understanding of moral judgmental processes than young children and that the higher levels of moral metacognition are closely tied to more advanced moral reasoning and behavior. In regard to moral judgment, the researchers assumed and found that children who were better able to think about their moral reasoning processes were more likely to be aware of inconsistencies in this reasoning and were also more likely to attempt to resolve these inconsistencies. Likewise, moral metacognition affected behavior in that children who were better able to reason about their actions were more likely to recognize moral aspects of their behavior and thus implore moral reasoning in formulating plans for that behavior. Finally, moral metacognition served as a correlate between moral action and moral reasoning and as a prerequisite to using moral judgment to direct one's actions.

A recent research study has also succeeded in linking moral reasoning with epistemological development. (If you don't recall what that is, refer back to Chapter 7.) Krettenauer (2004) questioned 200 German seventh- through thirteenth-graders about their beliefs as to the certainty of moral judgments, whether they perceived moral judgments as relative or absolute, the reasons they felt justified changes in moral beliefs, and the kinds of information that should be taken into account when making moral assessments. Most of the subjects were quite consistent in their responses, falling neatly into one of the established epistemological categories. Krettenauer's youngest subjects were primarily *intuitionists,* or "realists" as they were termed in Chapter 7. They believed that moral judgments were either right or wrong, that you "just know" whether something is moral or not, and that you should listen to experts. High schoolers were primarily *subjectivists,* or "skeptics." They believed that moral judgments were completely subjective and that no moral position was more valid than any other. *Transsubjectivism,* or "postskeptical rationalism," emerged gradually after nineth grade. *Transsubjectivists* believed that moral judgments are more or less well founded, that all views are somewhat subjective, and that one should adjust one's views according to all of the available evidence.

Criticisms of Kohlberg's Theory

Criticisms of Kohlberg's theory raise three issues: (1) whether his stages are universal among humans or limited to people in Western cultures; (2) whether moral reasoning should be conceptualized as stage-like; and (3) whether his ideas are gender biased.

Are Kohlberg's Stages Universal? Kohlberg emphasized that a stage concept implies universality of sequence under varying cultural conditions (Jensen, 1995). That is, the development of moral judgment is not merely a matter of learning the rules of a particular culture; it reflects a universal process of development. In order to test this hypothesis, Kohlberg (1966) used his technique with boys 10, 13, and 16 years of age in a Taiwanese city, in a Malaysian (Atayal) aboriginal tribal village, and in a Turkish village, as well as in Great Britain, Canada, and the United States. The results for Taiwan and the United States indicate similar age trends in boys of both nationalities.

Although Kohlberg's findings showed a similar sequence of development in all cultures, the last two stages of moral thought do not develop clearly in preliterate village or tribal communities (Snarey, 1995). Principled moral reasoning develops only when individuals are exposed to differing, conflicting points of view. Therefore, cross-cultural study indicates that only those societies that have been urbanized or that provide formal education are likely to have citizens that develop principled moral reasoning (De Mey, Baartman, and Schulze, 1999).

In addition, some cultures have values that put them into conflict with Kohlberg's hierarchy. Persons raised in collectivist societies—those that emphasize each individual's responsibilities to the others around him or her—tend to find structural, macro-explanations for Kohlberg's dilemmas and do not blame the specific characters in the scenarios (Miller, 1997). For example, someone raised in such a culture might say that the problem lay not with Heinz but with the fact that he was placed in an awkward position due to such a limited supply of the drug.

postconventional moral reasoning according to Kohlberg, the third level of development of moral thought, based on adherence to universal principles.

social contract orientation the type of postconventional moral reasoning in which one believes that individual actions should serve the greater good.

universal principled reasoning the highest form of moral reasoning, in which one acts according to his or her abstract moral principles.

metacognition the ability to think about one's own thought processes.

Is Moral Development Stage-Like? In order to term any type of development *stage-like,* it must meet two criteria. First, the stages must be finite and consistent; for instance, someone must be either in Stage 1 or in Stage 2, not waffling back and forth between them. Second, the stages must emerge in an invariant, progressive sequence; Stage 1 must always come before Stage 2, Stage 2 must always come before Stage 3, and so on. Does moral reasoning meet these two criteria?

From early on, the data (even Kohlberg's own data) have indicated that people do *not* give consistent moral responses to Kohlberg's dilemmas (Boyes, Giordano, and Galperyn, 1993) nor do they always move upward through his sequence. Kohlberg and Kramer (1969), for example, found that many of their participants regressed from Stage 4 to Stage 2 over time. In fact, a number of studies have found that premoral reasoning re-emerges in mid and late adolescence, especially in circumstances in which personal cost is high (Eisenberg, 1998). In addition, when newer, alternative methods are used to test moral thought, individuals' answers tend to be inconsistent and dependent on the context of the situation (Gibbs, Basinger, and Fuller, 1992; Smetana and Turiel, 2003).

Critics have also argued that it is not true or fair to say that the higher the stage, the greater the level of morality (Callahan and Callahan, 1981). Stage 6 reflects liberal and radical political reasoning. Does this mean that liberals are more advanced morally than conservatives? There is little basis in empirical fact to conclude that this is so.

The most pervasive and serious challenge to Kohlberg's theory, however, is that it is biased against females.

IN THEIR OWN WORDS

"I was really blown away when I read Carol Gilligan's work. In my house, my mother is a doormat: She cooks and cleans and fixes everyone else's problems. She puts up with my brother being rude to her. She always asks everyone else what they want; it's never about what she wants. My family all praise her all the time and say what a great mother she is, and so I grew up thinking that this is what you were supposed to do for your husband and kids. So . . . this is how I used to act toward my boyfriends. We'd hang with their friends and do what they wanted to do. During the past few years, I've started to think that I never wanted to get married—I mean, why be someone else's slave? It was terrific to read that it's OK to put limits on what you give to other people."

Gilligan and Sex Differences in Moral Reasoning

Carol Gilligan (1977), an associate of Kohlberg's, pointed out that Kohlberg conducted his research about moral development on male subjects. The scoring method was developed from male responses, with the average adolescent female attaining a rating corresponding to Stage 3 (the good girl–good boy orientation). The average adolescent male was rated at Stage 4 (the law and order orientation). To Gilligan, the female level of moral judgment is not lower than that of the male but reflects the fact that females approach moral issues from a different perspective. Men emphasize justice—preserving rights, rules, and principles. Women emphasize concern and care for others and sensitivity to their feelings and rights. Women emphasize responsibility to human beings rather than to abstract principles. Thus, men and women speak with two different voices (Gilligan, 1982). In summarizing six studies, including four that were longitudinal, Gilligan (1984) revealed that men rely more heavily on a justice orientation, and women on an interpersonal network or care orientation.

This difference has been ascribed partially to differences in socialization experiences. Also, although the roles and opportunities for men and women are becoming increasingly equal, there are still more female models in the caregiving roles. For example, it is more common for a women than a man to be the primary caregiver of children as well as the elderly, and there are typically more women than men working in nurseries and elementary schools (Skoe and Gooden, 1993).

As a result of the difference in the way men and women think, Gilligan proposed a female alternative to Kohlberg's stages of moral reasoning. Table 14.1 compares Kohlberg's and Gilligan's levels.

At Level I, women are preoccupied with self-interest and survival, which requires obeying restrictions placed on them. Gradually, they become aware of the differences between what they want (selfishness) and what they ought to do (responsibility). This leads to Level II, in which the need to please others takes precedence over self-interest. The woman becomes responsible for caring for others, even sacrificing her own preferences. Gradually, she begins to wonder whether she can fulfill the needs of others and still remain true to herself. Still, she does not give her own needs full equality with those of others. At Level III, which many never attain, the woman develops a universal perspective, in which she no longer sees herself as submissive and powerless but active in decision making. She becomes concerned about the consequences for all, herself included, in making decisions.

Gilligan's work is not without its own critics. Many researchers have concluded that Kohlberg's tests are not, in fact, biased against women (Greeno and Maccoby,

TABLE 14.1 KOHLBERG'S VERSUS GILLIGAN'S UNDERSTANDING OF MORAL DEVELOPMENT

KOHLBERG'S LEVELS AND STAGES	KOHLBERG'S DEFINITIONS	GILLIGAN'S LEVELS
Level I: Preconventional morality		**Level I: Preconventional morality**
Stage 1: Punishment orientation	Obey rules to avoid punishment	Concern for the self and survival
Stage 2: Instrumental hedonism orientation	Obey rules to get rewards, share in order to get returns	
Level II: Conventional morality		**Level II: Conventional morality**
Stage 3: Good girl–good boy orientation	Conform to rules that are defined by others' approval/disapproval	Concern for being responsible, caring for others
Stage 4: Law and order orientation	Rigid conformity to society's rules, law-and-order mentality, avoid censure for rule-breaking	
Level III: Postconventional morality		**Level III: Postconventional morality**
Stage 5: Social contract orientation	More flexible understanding that we obey rules because they are necessary for social order, but the rules could be changed if there were better alternatives	Concern for self and others as interdependent
Stage 6: Universal principled orientation	Behavior conforms to internal principles (justice, equality) to avoid self-condemnation, and sometimes may violate society's rules	

Source: Adapted from J. S. Hyde, *Half the Human Experience* (Lexington, MA: D. C. Heath, 1985). Reprinted by permission.

ANSWERS WOULDN'T YOU LIKE TO KNOW . . .

Do men and women think differently about moral issues?

Men and women think far more similarly than differently when it comes to moral reasoning. However, women are somewhat more likely than men to exercise "damage control" and try to minimize harm, and men are somewhat more likely than women to base their decisions on contracts and established procedures.

1986). And although numerous studies have verified the existence of a caring moral orientation, it appears that males and females each use legalistic as well as caring reasoning (Perry and McIntire, 1995; Wark and Krebs, 1996), with women utilizing caring somewhat more than men (Jaffee and Hyde, 2000). Perhaps Gilligan's open-ended interview technique—which required much interpretation on the part of the researcher—allowed her own biases to accentuate gender differences rather than gender similarities (Colby and Damon, 1983). It also appears that the content of the dilemmas that the subjects chose to discuss affected the legalistic or caring nature of their answers; both men and women exhibited a caring orientation when speaking of personal concerns and a more legalistic orientation when speaking of impersonal issues (Walker, 1991).

Obviously, Kohlberg's and Gilligan's stages are parallel. Gilligan does not argue that her theory should replace Kohlberg's. She argues that her theory is more applicable to the moral reasoning of females and that the highest form of moral reasoning can utilize, combine, and interpret both the male emphasis on rights and justice and the female emphasis on responsibility and interpersonal care (Muuss, 1988a).

The Social-Cognitive Domain Approach to Moral Reasoning

Due to the problems with the stage theories described in the previous sections (especially the fact that individuals don't proceed through the stages in a consistent fashion), a new approach to moral thinking has emerged. This **social-cognitive domain model** goes beyond moral reasoning per se and analyzes social reasoning more broadly, but much of what its proponents

social-cognitive domain model an approach to moral development that stresses the contextual nature of moral decisions and distinguishes social conventions from moral rules.

ANSWERS WOULDN'T YOU LIKE TO KNOW . . .

Do teens and their parents often disagree about basic moral issues?

No. Teenagers usually agree with their parents about fundamental moral issues. What they disagree about are issues concerning social conventions and personal choice.

discuss is relevant to moral development (Killen, Lee-Kim, McGlothlin, and Stangor, 2002). Whereas Piaget believed that a rule was a rule was a rule and that all rules are moral in nature, we now know that not all rules are treated equivalently by children, adolescents, and adults.

The social-cognitive domain model holds that there are three types of rules, only one of which is similar to those studied by Piaget and Kohlberg (Turiel, 1998). That type of rule is a **moral rule.** A moral rule has to do with how people should behave toward each other; it is not okay, for example, for people to hurt one another. The second type of rule is a **social convention.** Such a rule has been agreed on by everyone and so helps ensure that society runs smoothly; people know what to expect from one another. Social conventions are less universal in nature than moral rules. For example, in some cultures, it is considered impolite to burp after eating; to do so signals disrespect for those around you. In other cultures, burping after a meal is seen as a sign that the food was ample and delicious; it indicates respect for the food that your host prepared. Moral rules and social conventions both serve to regulate social interactions, but they have very different essences. It is worse to transgress against a moral rule than a social convention. Finally, the third type of rule is a **personal preference.** This type of rule governs behaviors that are in the private sphere. No one else has the right to tell you how to behave in the personal domain. The color of clothing you like to wear, your taste in music, and the length of your hair are all personal preferences. From a very early age, children can distinguish among these three types of rules (Smetana and Turiel, 2003).

The social-cognitive approach emphasizes that social decisions are complex and that individuals must often weigh moral, social, and personal concerns when making decisions. The context in which a decision is made and the weight given to each factor is what determines social judgment, not the identification of a stage of reasoning. If adolescents seem to regress in moral development, it is because they weigh these competing factors differently as they age (Killen, Lee-Kim, McGlothlin, and Stangor, 2002).

Adolescents tend to believe that adults have the right to make rules about truly moral behavior and that those rules should be obeyed (Smetana, 1995). Adults are only allowed, however, to make and enforce moral rules in their own sphere of influence; teachers, for example, are not allowed to tell youths how to behave outside of school. Parents and adolescents rarely argue about topics they agree involve basic moral issues, but adolescents have much less respect than adults for social conventions. Early adolescents view social conventions as ways for authority figures to needlessly control adolescent behavior, and late adolescents see social conventions as superfluous, old-fashioned societal expectations (Smetana and Turiel, 2003). Parents and their adolescent children also frequently disagree as to whether an issue should be considered a personal choice or a social convention. A teenager, for example, may think that wearing revealing clothing is in the personal realm, whereas her parents may feel that doing so violates social norms. Adolescents universally agree—even those in traditional, non-Western cultures—that parents do not have the right to interfere in their personal choices (Fuligni, 1998; Smetana, 2002). Their parents, of course, often disagree with this premise.

Moral Reasoning and Prosocial Behavior

As the previous sections have indicated, most of the early research about morality focused on *moral reasoning*—the ability to make correct moral decisions. Although many studies are still being conducted about the development of moral-reasoning skills, the field has expanded to include the study of **prosocial behavior.** Prosocial behavior is the opposite of antisocial behavior; it consists of actions that benefit, help, and bolster others. Examples of prosocial behavior include complimenting a friend, doing a favor for a neighbor, helping a parent wash the dishes, and volunteering to clean up a local park.

There is a strong link between moral reasoning and prosocial behavior, but they don't always go together. On one hand, someone may make a good moral decision but then not carry through and act on it because of laziness, fear, or vested interest. Thus, good moral decision making is necessary but not sufficient to promote prosocial behavior. On the other hand, people can be selfishly motivated to act prosocially. For instance, someone might help his dad fix the car only so that he can borrow it or help a friend with her math homework today so that she will help him with chemistry next week. Still, there is no doubt that people are more likely to behave in a prosocial manner if they are good moral reasoners (Eisenberg, Carlo, Murphy, and Van Court, 1995).

Fabes and Carlo and their colleagues have delineated the major factors that influence adolescents' prosocial and moral behaviors (Carlo, Fabes, Laible, and Kupanoff, 1999; Fabes, Carlo, Kupanoff, and Laible, 1999):

Adolescents who have attained higher levels of moral maturity are less selfish than their more immature peers. Moral maturity may be expressed in a desire to help others.

1. *Pubertal status:* Postpuberty adolescents are larger and stronger, and so more actions are open to them. Also, with puberty comes feelings of sexual arousal and romantic love, both of which might prompt prosocial or antisocial actions.
2. *Perspective taking:* Cognitive maturation, combined with new kinds of experiences, allows adolescents to better understand others' points of view.
3. *Moral reasoning:* The more advanced an adolescent's moral-reasoning skills, the more likely he or she will make moral decisions.
4. *Empathy:* The more an adolescent can feel empathic toward others, the more likely he or she will engage in both moral and prosocial actions.
5. *Personality:* Anger-prone individuals are more likely to behave antisocially (Carlo, Roesch, and Melby, 1998).
6. *Family relationships:* Having a supportive family background promotes moral development.
7. *Peer relationships:* Peers can encourage either prosocial or antisocial actions.
8. *Schooling:* School size, class size, and school climate can influence prosocial tendencies. Schooling encourages the development of higher levels of moral reasoning.
9. *Culture and ethnicity:* Adolescents are influenced by the norms and values of their cultures. For example, in one study of British and Chinese adolescents, the Chinese were more likely to risk their lives to save someone else than were the British (Ma, 1989).

Several of these issues will be discussed more in the following sections; others will be discussed in later chapters.

How does prosocial functioning change from childhood into adolescent and then during adolescence itself? There are reasons to believe that it should increase (Eisenberg, Cumberland, Guthrie, Murphy, and Shepard, 2005). First, adolescents consider selfish behavior inappropriate and immature (Galambos, Barker, and Tilton-Weaver, 2003). Second, prosocial reasoning has long been linked with the ability to empathize and take another's point of view, and we know that perspective-taking abilities increase well into adolescence (Eisenberg, 1986). Third, cognitive development allows adolescents to increasingly empathize *abstractly,* with those they do not know and those who are different from themselves, thus broadening their motivation to perform altruistic actions (Hoffman, 2000). For, as just discussed, moral reasoning itself improves as individuals motive, making it more likely that adolescents will make prosocial rather than selfish decisions.

Previous research has shown that some but not all aspects of prosocial functioning improve from childhood into adolescence (Eisenberg and Fabes, 1998). In particular, the willingness to share and display empathy toward others increases, but the tendencies to offer comfort or to actually help others do not. The evidence that prosocial behavior improves from childhood through midadolescence is not strong: It appears only in lab studies (not naturalistic observations) and only when the target of the concern is a child, not an adult. Similarly, as adolescents move from mid to late adolescence, and from late adolescence into early adulthood, their prosocial tendencies improve in some ways but not in others. While prosocial moral reasoning and perspective taking do show development, helping behavior itself actually declines in the early

moral rules social rules that are concerned with how people behave toward one another.

social conventions social rules that dictate what is appropriate and expected.

personal preferences aspects of behavior that involve independent choices with which others have no right to interfere.

prosocial behavior actions that benefit, help, and bolster others.

twenties. Sympathetic responses do not exhibit systematic changes. Still, individuals show reasonable rank order consistency over time (Eisenberg et al., 2002); in other words, a person who is a highly prosocial child will be a high prosocial adolescent and adult, whereas a person who is selfish as a child will remain so.

FAMILY FACTORS AND MORAL LEARNING

The Family's Role

Studies of family socialization have demonstrated repeatedly that parents have a tremendous impact on the development of their children. Parents play a fundamental role in their children's transition from childhood to adulthood; in the development of their basic social, religious, and political values; and in encouraging them to adopt prosocial actions and empathetic responses to those in distress (Eisenberg and Murphy, 1995; McDevitt, Lennon, and Kopriva, 1991).

Much of the important research about the moral development of children and adolescents emphasizes the importance of parents and the family in the total process. A number of family factors correlate significantly with moral learning:

1. The degree of parental warmth, acceptance, mutual esteem, and trust shown the child
2. The frequency and intensity of parent-teen interaction and communication
3. The type and degree of discipline used
4. The role model parents offer the child
5. The independence opportunities the parents provide

Each of these factors needs elaboration, clarification, and substantiation. (For additional information on parent-adolescent relationships, see Chapters 10 and 11.)

Parental Acceptance and Trust

One important aid to moral learning is a warm, accepting relationship of mutual trust and esteem between parent and child. Young children who are emotionally dependent on their parents and have a strong emotional attachment to them develop strong consciences, whereas nondependent children grow up more lacking in consciences (Eisenberg and McNally, 1993).

There are a number of explanations for the correlation between parental warmth and moral learning. In a warm, emotional context, respected parents are likely to be admired and imitated by youths, resulting in similar positive traits in the adolescents. Youths learn consideration for others by being cared for, loved, and trusted by their parents. In an atmosphere of hostility and rejection, youths tend to identify with the aggressor, taking on the antisocial traits of the parent. In Sutherland and Cressey's (1966) theory of **differential association,** which outlines conditions that facilitate moral and criminal learning, the impact of a relationship varies according to its *priority, duration, intensity,* and *frequency.* The all-important parent-child relationship (high priority) over many years (long duration), characterized by close emotional attachment (high intensity) and a maximum amount of contact and communication (high frequency), has the maximum positive effect on the moral development of children. Similarly, a negative parent-child relationship existing for many years in an intense, repetitive way will have a disastrous and negative effect.

Frequency and Intensity of Parent-Teen Communication Role-modeling theory maintains that the degree of identification of the child with the parent varies with the amount of the child's interaction with the parent. Frequent interaction offers opportunities for the communication of meaningful values and norms, especially if the exchange is democratic and mutual. A one-sided form of autocratic interaction results in poor communication and less learning for the adolescent. It is important, therefore, for the channels of communication between parents and youths to be kept open. Certain types of communication appear to be especially good at fostering moral reasoning. Research has discovered, for example, that fathers who engage in Vygotskian/Socratic-style "transactive dialogues" with their adolescents—who push their thinking by challenging their reasoning—have adolescents who are more morally advanced than their peers (Pratt et al., 1999).

Type of Discipline

Research on the influence of parental discipline on the moral learning of youths indicates that discipline has the most positive effect when it is (1) consistent rather than erratic; (2) accomplished primarily through clear, verbal explanations to develop internal controls rather than through external, physical means of control; (3) just and fair and avoids harsh, punitive measures; and (4) democratic rather than permissive or autocratic (Zelkowitz, 1987).

One of the most important requirements is that discipline be consistent, both *intraparent* (within one parent) and *intraparent* (within one parent) and *interparent* (between two parents). Erratic parental expectations lead to an ambiguous environment and thus to poor moral learning, anxiety, confusion, instability, disobedience, and sometimes hostility and delinquency in the adolescent.

Although no one involved enjoys it, parents must sometimes discipline their adolescent children. The best kind of discipline involves a clear explanation as to why a certain behavior is unacceptable. When handled correctly, these interactions can enhance youths' moral development.

Parents who rely on clear, rational, verbal explanations to influence and control behavior—induction—have a more positive effect than those who use power assertion (Lopez, Bonenberger, and Schneider, 2001). This is primarily because cognitive methods result in the internalization of values and standards, especially if explanations are combined with affection so that the adolescent is inclined to listen and to accept them. Reasoning or praise used to correct or reinforce behavior enhances learning, whereas physical means of discipline, negative verbal techniques such as belittling and nagging, or infrequent explanations are more often associated with antisocial behavior and delinquency.

Parents who rely on harsh, punitive methods are defeating the true purpose of discipline: to develop a sensitive conscience, socialization, and cooperation (Hoffman, 1994). Cruel punishment, especially when accompanied by parental rejection, develops an insensitive, uncaring, hostile, rebellious, cruel person. Instead of teaching children to care about others, it deadens their sensitivities, so that they learn to fear and hate others and no longer care about them or want to please them. They may obey, but when the threat of external punishment is removed, they are antisocial.

Parents who are overly permissive also retard the socialization process and the moral development of their children (Boyes and Allen, 1993), for they give the children no help in developing inner controls. Without external authority, the child will remain amoral. Adolescents want and need some parental guidance. Without it, they may grow up as spoiled brats, disliked by their peers because of their lack of consideration for others, and lacking self-discipline, persistence, and direction.

ANSWERS WOULDN'T YOU LIKE TO KNOW . . .

What should parents do to help their children grow into moral adults?

Parents should be warm and supportive, avoid harsh discipline, explain the rationale of their rules, provide opportunities to make decisions, and model moral behavior.

Parental Role Models

It is important for parents to be moral people themselves if they are to offer positive role models for their children to follow. Children—even adolescent children—have a natural tendency to copy their mother's and father's behavior. And so no matter what parents may say about honesty, if they are observed cheating on their taxes, stealing a tip that was left on a table for a waiter, or walking out of a store knowing that they were given too much change, they will be teaching their children to be dishonest. Adolescents are much more likely to recognize and be affected by adult hypocrisy than children, and so it is even more important for parents to model moral behavior as their children get older. Parents can also encourage positive, prosocial actions in their children by behaving in caring, generous ways. Talk is not enough.

differential association Sutherland's theory that outlines conditions that facilitate moral or criminal learning.

Opportunities for Independence

The number and kinds of opportunities that parents give their children to make independent moral judgments also affects moral development. As we discussed in Chapter 7 (the second cognitive development chapter), making good decisions of any sort is a learned skill, for which practice is required. Adolescents need to be given chances to make decisions that affect their moral behavior and then to observe the results of their actions.

Of course, parents who provide too much independence—that is, who fail to monitor their children and provide guidance—cause their children to look to outsiders for moral guidance. A charismatic peer, for example, might encourage antisocial behavior. External forces of all sorts have greater impact if a moral vacuum is created by parental neglect and indifference.

Some adolescents engage in decidedly antisocial actions, often due to the influence of peers. Youths may turn to peers as a reaction against parental neglect and rejection.

EXTRAFAMILIAL INFLUENCES ON MORALITY

Peers

As has been previously discussed, sets of adolescent friends tend to behave in similar ways. This is true in regard to prosocial and antisocial behavior as well as to more morally neutral behaviors. Given this, there is great societal concern about the degree to which peers influence each other to engage in risky or deviant acts, such as drug use and delinquency. In fact, many youth intervention programs incorporate *peer-resistance training* as part of their curricula. Although this similarity among peers is caused, in part, by the fact that adolescents choose friends akin to themselves, it can also be explained by how peers directly and indirectly influence each other's actions.

Brown and Theobald (1999) have identified four ways that peers can influence each other's behavior: (1) peer pressure, (2) normative expectations, (3) structuring opportunities, and (4) modeling. Sometimes, all four of these forces act at once. For example, consider the case of a teenage girl, Lori, who had recently moved to a new high school and made a new group of friends. When they went to the movies together on a Friday night, Lori was in for a shock. She discovered that these girls never paid for the movies they watched. Instead, they would pool their money and buy one girl a ticket; she would legitimately enter the theater and then hold open an out-of-the-way door, through which the other girls would enter. Lori felt stuck, because although she disapproved of her friends' behavior, they clearly thought it was normal (normative expectations), they had worked out the means to avoid paying and did this weekly (opportunity), they all took turns entering illegally (modeling), and they gave her a hard time when she refused to join in (peer pressure).

Peers can encourage one another to engage in positive, prosocial actions, as well. In fact, there is a reciprocal relationship between peers and prosocial activities: Peers can encourage doing good deeds, and doing good deeds can make one more popular with peers (Wentzel and McNamara, 1999). The more close friends an adolescent has, the higher his or her level of moral reasoning is likely to be (Schonert-Reichl, 1999).

Religion

Religion certainly plays an important part in the lives of many Americans, including adolescents, and it is one avenue through which adolescents can learn a moral code. What determines how religious an adolescent is? What religion is he or she likely to follow? How religious is the average adolescent? Does religion influence adolescents to behave more morally? We will try to answer these questions in the sections that follow.

IN THEIR OWN WORDS

"I would like to point out that I most definitely feel a person can have strong morals without having a strong religious conviction. I am one of those people. My parents never forced religion on us, so as children we were fortunate. They offered to take us to any church we liked whenever we wanted, and so we often went along with our friends. I really appreciate the fact that my parents wanted me and my brothers to find our own religion in our own time, instead of just forcing us to follow theirs. I don't want to commit myself to a religion without taking some time to learn more about it and my other options. Clearly, there are so many religions in the world that I can explore until I find the one that I truly believe in."

"I entered church for the first time because my aunt had invited my family. As I heard the words of God spoken through the pastor at the time, I was very interested and intrigued by what he was saying. I kept going to church, and it was in college that I started to make my faith my own. I began to seriously study God's word and soak up every bit of pertinent information I came across. I have kept my focus on building my religious foundation and continue to do so at this point in my life."

What Determines How Religious an Adolescent Is?

The main determinant of an adolescent's religiosity is the strength and quality of the relationship with his or her family (Ream and Savin-Williams, 2003). Religious parents are most likely to raise religious offspring (King, Elder, and Whitbeck, 1997). Religious parents tend to expose their children to religion (whether the children want this or not) by making them attend religious services and Sunday school (Ozarak, 1989). Doing so provides the children with a sense of familiarity and comfort that facilitates their continued religiosity in later life.

Children are most likely to become religious if their parents practice the same faith than if they are of different faiths (Myers, 1996). Harmonious homes, in which the parents are nurturing and there is little parent-child or spousal conflict, tend to produce the most religious children. Girls are more likely to be religious than boys and to be more influenced by their mothers than their fathers (Ellis and Wagemann, 1993); boys are, as a group, less religious and more influenced by their fathers (Clark, Worthington, and Danser, 1988).

Race/ethnicity, place of residence, and denomination also influence religiosity. African American teens are more likely to be religious than teens of other races and ethnic groups. Adolescents from the southern states are, as a group, more religious than adolescents from other parts of the United States. Teens who belong to theologically conservative churches are more likely to claim religion is important to them than those who are either Catholic or who belong to more liberal Protestant denominations (Smith, Faris, and Denton, 2003).

What Religion Are Adolescents Likely to Follow?

Adolescents who have a close relationship with their parents usually remain in the faith in which they were raised, maintaining their parents' religion. Rejection of parents' religious values is often symptomatic of a strained parent-adolescent relationship (Dudley, 1999; Gameron, 1992). In fact, adolescents who convert to a different religion may do so because they crave forming a close attachment—something that seems to have been lacking in their lives (Kirkpatrick, 1998; Streib, 1999). Additionally, adolescents may change faiths because they feel that their current faith is not adequately helping them cope with their problems (Ream and Savin-Williams, 2003).

How Religious Is the Average Adolescent?

According to a major study, American teenagers are fairly religious (Smith, Faris, and Denten, 2003). About 60 percent say that religion is either "very" or "pretty" important to them. Eighty percent pray at least some of the time; 40 percent report daily prayer. Very few appear to be disaffected from religion. Only about 10 percent say that churches are doing a poor job serving the nation, and only about 20 percent would like to see religion exert less influence on society. All of these figures have remained nearly constant over the past 25 years, and so there is little basis on which to claim that today's teens are any more or less religious than those of one or two generations ago.

Nonetheless, as people move into their late teens and early twenties and leave home, their religious participation tends to decline (Gallup and Lindsey, 1999). For most individuals, this lapse is temporary. Once they marry, have children, and become a part of a permanent community, their religious affiliation will again increase (Stolzenberg, Blair-Loy, and Waite, 1995).

Does Religion Influence Adolescents' Moral Behavior?

The majority of research suggests that religion has a positive effect on adolescent behavior (e.g., Youniss, McClellan, and Yates, 1999). For example, religious youths have been found to be less likely to drink or use drugs than their less-religious counterparts (Wallace and Forman, 1998), and they also appear to engage less in other types of deviant behavior, such as vandalism, fighting, and using vulgar language (Litchfield, Thomas, and Li, 1997). Religious teens are also less likely to engage in premarital sex (Regnerus, Smith, and Fritsch, 2003). In addition to protecting

ANSWERS WOULDN'T YOU LIKE TO KNOW . . .

How religious are most American adolescents?

Most are reasonably religious. They believe in God, pray on a regular basis, and believe that religion benefits society.

against harmful behaviors, religiosity also promotes positive, prosocial concerns (Furrow, King, and White, 2004). It is associated with good academic achievement (Regnerus, 2000) and overall thriving (Dowling, Gestsdottir, Anderson, von Eye, Almerigi, and Lerner, 2004).

Why does being involved in religion provide such benefits? Many reasons have been proposed. First, being involved in an organized church provides a teenager with a good deal of **social capital,** or other persons willing to be there for him or her (King and Furrow, 2004). Second, it provides opportunities for helping others (Mattis, Jagers, Hatcher, Lawhan, Murphy, and Murray, 2000), and three, it surrounds teenagers with individuals who will praise them for their good works (Ellison, 1992). Finally, many (although not all) religions promote positive, prosocial values such as kindness (Hardy and Carlo, 2005).

Television

The increasingly large impact of the mass media on adolescents has already been discussed elsewhere in this book (see Chapters 1 and 13). But since so much attention has been devoted to worrying about the potentially harmful effects of television on adolescents' characters, it is worth examining those effects here. Adolescents spend an enormous amount of time watching television: more than 3½ hours daily during pre- and early adolescence, and almost 3 hours daily during mid and late adolescence (Roberts, 2000). By the time the typical teen graduates from high school, he or she will have spent considerably more time in front of the tube than he or she has in a classroom (Comstock and Paik, 1999)—20,000 versus 14,000 hours—and that doesn't take into account all of the time that minors played video games or watched movies. Almost 70 percent of American 8- to 18-year-olds have a television in their own bedroom (Roberts, Foehr, and Rideout, 2005).

Is it, then, any wonder that the public is worried about the effects of a such a steady television diet on adolescent values? Their unease centers on three issues: (1) the effects of viewing televised violence, (2) the effects of being exposed to sexually provocative stimulation, and (3) the effects of advertising on adolescents' material desires.

Violence

Public concern over the content of television shows has focused on the effect on children and youths of watching so much violence. Back in 1992, Althea Huston and her colleagues estimated that the average American child would have seen an average of 200,000 violent acts on television—rapes, assaults, murders—by

RESEARCH HIGHLIGHT THE POWER OF CULTS

In the course of searching for a religious identity, some adolescents turn to cults. What makes a group a cult? A *cult* frequently revolves around a single strong leader, and the group demands total obedience to this leader's dictates. Cults discourage questioning and individuality, and so they isolate members from outside influences (including family). Cults often demand that members turn over their money and property to the group. They often use deception to recruit members and intimidate those members who choose to leave. Some cults encourage their members to engage in antisocial behaviors.

Why are adolescents especially vulnerable to cults? While in the midst of their identity search, adolescents may feel lost and confused; a cult will provide definitive, ready answers to all their questions. Membership can make adolescents feel powerful and enhance their self-esteem. Also, it is normal for adolescents to feel more distant from their families than they did as children, sometimes leaving an emotional vacuum. A cult can both provide a sense of belonging and be a means of expressing rebellion (Clark, 1994). Finally, the idealism that is associated with entrance into the formal operations stage can leave individuals with a sense of dissatisfaction with established institutions that have failed to solve the world's problems. Furthermore, at this stage of cognitive development, individuals often believe in simple, overarching solutions to problems (Hunter, 1998).

Which adolescents are most likely to join cults? It is widely believed that being alienated from one's family (Wright and Piper, 1986) or having been abused (Belitz and Schacht, 1992) predisposes one to cult membership. Even so, most youths in cults do not come from dysfunctional families (Singer, 1992). Cult members come from a wide variety of socioeconomic backgrounds. A study by Walsh, Russell, and Wells (1995) suggested that cult members are more likely than others to have dependent personalities. At the present, however, there is no simple answer to the question of who will join a cult.

the time he or she was 18 years old. Given that it is well-established that American television has grown increasingly violent (in part because of cable networks), the number surely far surpasses that now. American television is the most violent in the world (Strasburger, 1995).

Almost all researchers and child advocacy groups who have examined the issue conclude that exposure to television violence *does* contribute to increased aggressiveness (Anderson and Bushman, 2002). Most of the classic studies on the relationship between television violence and aggression in children and adolescents support this association. In fact, more than 1,000 separate studies have linked television viewing with adolescent antisocial activity (Strasburger, 1995).

Violent television promotes violence in several ways. It makes aggression seem less shocking and more acceptable—even typical and normal. In many cases, it presents likable, attractive models who are acting aggressively (Center for Communication and Social Policy, 1998), and often, these characters are rewarded and admired for their aggressive behavior. In addition, action-oriented programming excites and arouses viewers, which makes them more prone to react aggressively if provoked (Cantor, 2000). Repeated exposure to violent actions desensitizes people, such that their arousal in the face of violence begins to decrease rather than to increase. This results in less distress at the thought of violence and less sympathy for the victims of violence. All in all, violence becomes more acceptable (e.g., Molitor and Hirsch, 1994).

Another effect of watching violent television is that viewers come to believe that the world is a place in which others are out to harm them (Gerbner, 1992). Children and adolescents may become frightened because of what they see on television, perhaps even resulting in nightmares and recurring thoughts that can last for years. Adolescents are especially troubled by scenes depicting supernatural forces and sexual assault (Harrison and Cantor, 1999). Many adults (including the junior author) can recall lingering fears after seeing such movies as *Psycho* and *The Exorcist.*

The sum of the data leaves little doubt that there is a *causal* link between watching violent television and behaving aggressively. Numerous laboratory and field experiments have been conducted that conclusively show, especially in aggregate, that violent television is a form of social pollutant that actively contributes to violent behavior. Many persons have trouble accepting this, because they feel that *they* watch violent TV and that *they* are not aggressive. However, remember that there are some people who smoke two packs of cigarettes each day and yet do not develop lung cancer. Does that mean

social capital the resources available to an individual through his or her interpersonal connections.

RESEARCH HIGHLIGHT WHY DO WE LIKE SCARY MEDIA?

Television executives wouldn't put violent television shows on the air, and movie executives wouldn't spend tens of millions of dollars producing horror movies, if people didn't watch them. At some level, then, people must enjoy frightening programs and movies. (And there is some data suggesting that adolescents like scary shows more than children or older adults; e.g. Cantor, 1998.) Why do teens and the rest of us like to be scared?

Several theories have been proposed. Zillman (1996) suggested that physiological arousal produced by the empathic distress we feel at seeing another in danger heightens the positive emotional response we feel when it all ends positively; the distress up front is worth the relief at the end. (This theory has trouble accounting for the fact that sometimes people enjoy frightening films even when there is no happy ending.) Conversely, Tamborini (1996) proposed that only those low in empathy could enjoy horror films, since those high in empathy would be too distressed at the protagonists' plight. Slater (2003) believes that frightening films satisfy a need for sensation-seeking, and Sparks (2001) views watching scary films as a means of escapism—a way to temporarily forget one's everyday problems. Cantor (1998) likens watching scary films to "forbidden fruit," stating that its appeal comes from the fact that it is not quite appropriate. Goldstein (1999) states that it is done for companionship, since the majority of the time these shows and movies are watched in groups. Many have suggested that watching death and mayhem is a means of vicarious aggression.

Hoffner and Levine (2005) conducted a meta-analysis of the research studies that have been conducted on this topic to date. They found that the bulk of the data suggests that males enjoy violent media more than females, and that adolescents enjoyed watching violence more than older adults did. (They did not include studies that examined children.) They also found that the more frightening a show was found to be, the more enjoyable it was rated, whether or not there was a positive resolution. Highly empathic individuals did enjoy these programs less than others, while aggressive individuals and sensation-seekers enjoyed them more.

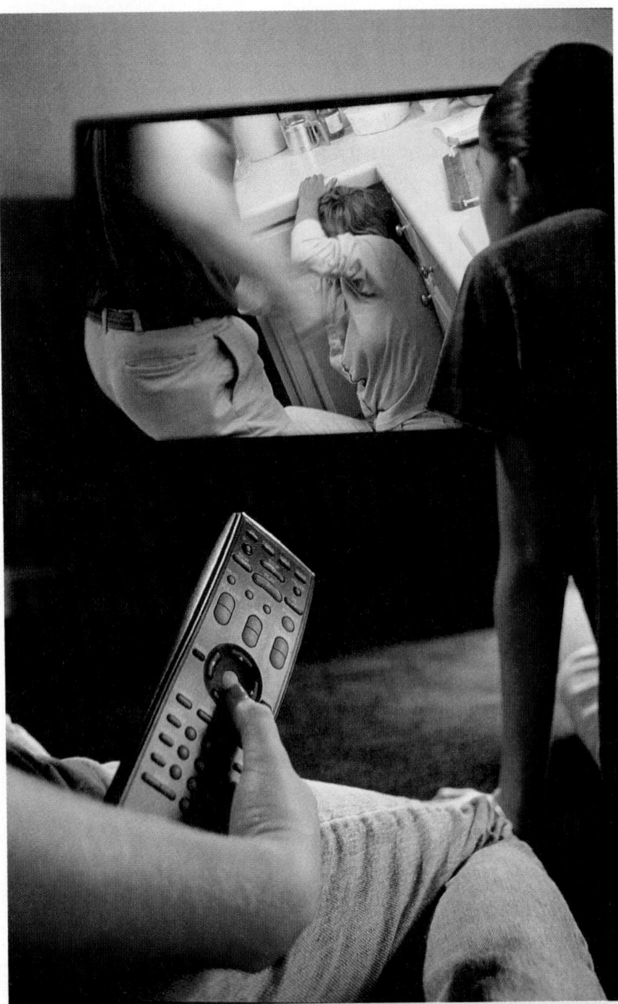

Watching violent television promotes violence in several ways. For instance violence seems commonplace and acceptable and even admirable when likable, attractive characters are rewarded for their violent actions.

ANSWERS WOULDN'T YOU LIKE TO KNOW ...

Does watching violence on television really affect people?

The data on the negative effects of watching violence on television are strong and compelling. Viewers who regularly see appealing characters save the day by using aggression eventually come to see aggression as commonplace and acceptable. Moreover, some become more likely to react aggressively themselves when provoked.

that smoking does not increase your cancer risk? No. Similarly, although not everyone who watches violent television is affected (although you may have been affected more than you realize), on a population level the amount of aggression has increased due to its prevalence.

Sexual Content

Just as television inundates youths with violent images, it also presents an abundance of sexual ones. The average American adolescent is exposed to almost 15,000 sexual references or behaviors each year while watching TV (Strasburger and Donnerstein, 1999). Sexual content on television has increased significantly, even during prime family-viewing time (Kunkel, Keven, Finnety, Biely, and Donnerstein, 2005.) Nearly one-third of the shows that air during the so-called family hour (from 8 to 9 P.M. Eastern Standard Time) contain sexual content, averaging eight or more such references per hour. Even worse, sex is usually presented either as exploitive or as trivial, harmless fun; the potential emotional and health consequences are rarely mentioned. In fact, only about 1 percent of the sexual incidents portrayed on television deal with issues such as the risk of pregnancy or sexually transmitted diseases, birth control, and abstinence (Zillman, 2000). The number of sex scenes shown on television has doubled since 1997–1998, and the shows that adolescents watch have even more sexual content than those that adults watch (Kunkel, Finnety, Biely, and Donnerstin, 2005). The number of portrayals of sexual risk has not, however, increased in that time.

This is troubling for the same reason that violence on television is troubling: Adolescents *are* affected by television's sexual content. Watching programs in which sex is merely discussed, not portrayed, has been shown to influence adolescents' beliefs as to what constitutes normative sexual behavior (Ward, 2002) and their attitudes about casual sex (Taylor, R.D. 2005). At least one well-designed, longitudinal study has demonstrated a link between heavy consumption of sexual television programming and early sexual activity, including intercourse (Collins et al., 2004).

Since studies parallel to those done on televised violence show that adolescents' concept of normal sexual activity can be skewed by what they view, the National Commission on Adolescent Sexual Health (SEICUS, 1996) recommends the following guidelines for the portrayal of sexuality in the media. The commission believes these changes will promote more beneficial adolescent sexual attitudes and behaviors. According to this group, society would benefit if the media would do the following:

1. Stop portraying only physically attractive people as desirable and capable of being involved in sexual relationships.
2. Depict sexually abstinent teens as well as sexually active ones.
3. Depict typical sexual relations as nonexploitive.
4. Represent the typical sexual encounter as planned, rather than impulsive.

5. Portray the use of contraceptives and display the negative consequences of failing to do so.
6. Depict scenes of parent-child communication about sexuality.

Materialism

American children and adolescents see about 40,000 commercials on television each year; this is a dramatic increase from the 1970s (Wilcox, Cantor, Dowrick, Kunkel, Linn, and Palmer, 2004). Some children and adolescents even view commercials while at school, since it is now quite common for schools to present packaged "current event" video programs that contain commercials. The fact that companies are willing to spend millions of dollars to buy air time to advertise their products suggests that these ads must be effective in changing people's consumer behavior. Unfortunately, much of the advertising directed at children and adolescents is for products that are not especially beneficial to them (e.g., sugary snack foods) or that are expensive (e.g., name-brand sports clothing). These ads help create a demand for these products and encourage teens to want to buy them.

Because they have been well studied, we know that advertisements for certain products (i.e., cigarettes, alcohol) do convince teenagers to go out and use these products. For example, one recent study found that, for each ad above the average that an adolescent saw, he or she was 1 percent more likely to drink (Snyder, Milici, Slater, Sun, and Strizhakova, 2006). Similarly, a study with early adolescents found that 12-year-olds who were more aware of televised beer advertisements had more favorable views of drinking and expressed more of an intention to drink as adults than other young adolescents (Grube, 1995).

On a more global level, television commercials promote the concept that living "the good life" entails having many material possessions. The message is that there is a product out there that will solve any and all of your problems. Unpopular? Try this acne cream or mouthwash or buy this car. Dissatisfied with your appearance? Try this shampoo and that brand of clothing. The role of possessions in bringing happiness is overemphasized in the media. In one study, Sirgy et al. (1998) found that the more television that American undergraduate students watched, the more materialistic they were and the more dissatisfied they were with their standard of living. It therefore appears that television advertising does have an effect upon viewers.

Other Concerns

Violence, promiscuity, and materialism are not the only complaints that have been raised about television. As discussed in Chapter 5 on body image, media portrayals of excessively slender individuals contribute to body dissatisfaction, especially in girls. In addition, the several hours a day spent watching television could be spent doing something else, such as exercising, being with friends, talking with family members, working on a hobby, or reading. Even watching good television is problematic if done to excess, since it siphons hours away from more beneficial activities.

Moral Education

Because we all are affected by the moral behavior of others, American schools have historically been concerned with instilling morality in their students. A number of the nation's founders—for example, Thomas Jefferson and John Adams—advocated public education as a means of transmitting democratic values to young citizens (Wynne, 1989). In the 1800s, as waves of immigrants who had not grown up in the democratic tradition came to the United States, the sense that the schools needed to teach democratic values increased (Titus, 1994). Over time, as societal concerns and values have evolved and changed, the approaches to moral education have changed, as well.

Superka, Ahrens, and Hedstrom (1976) have identified five different approaches to moral education. The earliest of these approaches (which became fashionable again within the past decade) involves **inculcation,** or teaching specific values and norms to students so that they will come to identify with these values and follow them. In a pluralistic society, an obvious question arises: Whose values will you teach? Proponents of inculcation insist that there are universally agreed on values that transcend culture, religion, and race/ethnicity. Numerous yet similar lists of universal values have been developed, including this one from the Josephson Institute of Ethics (2002), which proposes six pillars of morality:

1. *Trustworthiness,* which includes honesty, integrity, reliability, and loyalty
2. *Respect,* which includes treating others with dignity, civility, courtesy, and tolerance
3. *Responsibility,* which assumes that one is accountable for one's actions, perseveres, is diligent, and shows self-restraint
4. *Fairness,* which involves following due process, being impartial, and refusing to take unfair advantage of others
5. *Caring,* or the concern for others' welfare
6. *Citizenship,* or giving to the community and obeying its rules

inculcation an approach to moral education that teaches students to accept specific moral values, such as honesty and trustworthiness.

PERSONAL ISSUES ACADEMIC CHEATING IN COLLEGE

By all counts, cheating in college has reached epidemic proportions. Estimates range from a *low* of just more than 50 percent of students (Pino and Smith, 2003) to a high of in excess of 80 percent of students (Cochran, Wood, Sellers, Wilkerson and Chamlin, 1998). In addition, plagiarism appears to occur at least as frequently as cheating on exams (Wilson, 2001). Equally bad, more than 70 percent of students report making fraudulent excuses so as to have extra time to prepare for exams or to complete papers (Roig and Caso, 2005).

Given how many students cheat, at least occasionally, it might be better to ask who *doesn't* cheat rather than to ask who does. Women claim that they cheat less often then men (e.g., Jensen, Arnett, Feldman, and Cauffman, 2002), but there are few gender differences when cheating is measured more objectively (McCabe, Trevino, and Butterfield, 2001). Independent students—those not affiliated with fraternities or sororities—are less likely to cheat than those involved in the Greek system (Storch and Storch, 2002), perhaps because they have less opportunity to do so. Furthermore, the more heavily involved a student is with a fraternity or sorority, the more likely he or she is to cheat. In general, the brightest, most able students are less likely to cheat than those that are academically weaker—and by quite a margin (Nathanson, Paulhus, and Williams, 2006). Perhaps because so many students cheat, only weak associations have been found between personality variables and cheating (Whitley and Keith-Spiegel, 2002). Szabo and Underwood (2004) conjecture, however, that students who have a sincere desire to learn will be less likely to cheat.

Cheating can also be encouraged or discouraged by situational factors. Faculty can discourage cheating by making it difficult for students to cheat, so that it is simply not worth the effort (Szabo and Underwood, 2004). Teachers can give specific, rather than broad, general assignments (Davis, 1994). They can make the students believe that there is a real probability that they will be caught, and that the penalties will be severe if they are caught (Szabo and Underwood, 2004). They can make sure that students understand exactly what the rules governing cheating and plagiarism are (Roig, 1999), so that no one unintentionally misbehaves. They can be sure that students have adequate time to complete assignments (Szabo and Underwood, 2004), and they can make sure that they teach in such a way that they students feel that the course material is valuable to them and relevant to their lives (Kibler, 1993).

Fear of failure remained the most common reason for cheating. Math and science are the courses in which cheating most often occurs. The home is considered the best place and school the worst place to inculcate honesty. Over three decades, dishonesty has been viewed as increasingly necessary. More students admitted to cheating on tests and homework. Also, more parents are aiding and abetting students in avoidance of school rules (Schab, 1991).

Research has underscored the fact that students usually blame others—parents, teachers, school, and even society—for their cheating (Anderman, Griesinger, and Westerfield, 1998; McCabe, 1999). In addition, students are unlikely to believe that they will get caught for cheating and do not think they will be punished severely even if they are caught (McCabe and Trevino, 1997). The problem of cheating will not likely disappear soon, especially since the wealth of resources available on the Internet has created new opportunities for plagiarism (McCabe, 1999).

The second approach to moral education, known as **moral development,** grew directly out of Kohlberg's theories and research and first became popular in the early 1970s. The approach is based on the belief that adolescents must be exposed to higher-level reasoning in order to develop it themselves (Harding and Snyder, 1991). In this type of approach, the primary method used is to present case studies, or moral dilemmas, for the students to solve (Mills, 1987a, 1987b, 1988). Here is one dilemma used to promote thinking and discussion:

> Joe is a 14-year-old boy who wanted to go to camp very much. His father promised him he could go if he saved the money for it himself. So Joe worked hard at his paper route and saved the $40 it cost to go to camp and a little more besides. But just before camp was going to start, his father changed his mind. Some of his friends decided to go on a special fishing trip, and Joe's father was short of the money it would cost, so he told Joe to give him the money he had saved from the paper route. Joe didn't want to give up going to camp, so he thought of refusing to give his father the money. (Pagliuso, 1976, p. 126)

ANSWERS WOULDN'T YOU LIKE TO KNOW ...

How common is students' cheating on exams and papers?

All forms of student cheating are distressingly common. The most common reason given for cheating is the fear of failing or doing poorly.

The students are then presented with several questions (Pagliuso, 1976):

- Should Joe refuse to give his father the money? Why? Why not?
- What do you think of the father's asking Joe for the money?
- Does giving the money have anything to do with being a good son?
- Should promises always be kept?

Teachers need to invent other situations that relate to students' own lives and are meaningful to them.

The third approach to moral education, **values clarification,** was in its heyday in the 1970s and 1980s. It is not concerned with the *content* of values but with the *process* of valuing. It does not aim to instill any particular set of values; rather, the goal is to help students become aware of the beliefs and behaviors they prize and would be willing to stand up for, to learn to weigh the pros and cons and consequences of various alternatives, to choose freely after considerations of consequences, and to learn to match their actions with their beliefs in a consistent way.

A significant part of values clarification education, which can be viewed as either a strength or a weakness, is that students are allowed to choose their own values. Those who favor this approach assert that in a free, democratic society, individuals should be allowed to hold whatever values they wish; the state should not tell people what to think. Critics of this method argue that some moral choices are superior to others and that it is irresponsible to teach adolescents that all moral choices are equally valid.

Teachers who employ values clarification use a variety of methods. Students may be asked to think about their values and discuss them with each other; they may also be given real and hypothetical ethical dilemmas to consider. Another method is to ask students to make forced moral choices—for example, to decide whether people should be allowed to make as much noise as they want (individual freedom) or have their right to be noisy curtailed if they disturb others. Similarly, students are often asked to rank-order their priorities (Rice, 1980).

The fourth approach, **analysis,** has never become as popular as the others. In it, students are taught to employ critical thinking and reasoning when making moral decisions. Generally, lessons concentrate more on broad social values than on personal dilemmas. As is often the case with critical-thinking instruction, students are given practice in clarifying the issue, assembling and evaluating the truth of the facts used to support different positions on the issue, appraising the relevance of the facts, drawing appropriate conclusions, and thinking through the implications of their decision (Huitt, 2003).

The final approach to moral education, **action learning,** is the newest. It involves giving students the opportunity to participate in community service projects, thus bridging the gap between moral reasoning and moral action (Cottom, 1996). The idea behind action learning is that adolescents will come to value moral, caring behavior and develop an enhanced social consciousnesses if they observe social problems firsthand (e.g., poverty, pollution) and experience the self-satisfaction that comes from knowing that you have helped your community. More and more high schools are incorporating community service obligation into their set of graduation requirements. This issue is discussed more fully in Chapter 16.

moral development an approach to moral education that uses moral dilemmas and the like to give youths experience in higher-level reasoning.

values clarification a method of teaching values that helps students become aware of their own beliefs and values.

analysis an approach to moral education that emphasizes using logical reasoning to solve social dilemmas.

action learning an approach to moral education that emphasizes community service.

SUMMARY

1. This chapter has discussed four major aspects of moral development: (a) theories of development of moral judgment, represented by Piaget, Kohlberg, Gilligan, and those who take a social-cognitive approach; (b) family correlates to moral development; (c) transmission of religious beliefs and practices; and (d) the social influences of peers, television, and education on moral values and behavior.
2. Piaget outlined two stages of moral development: a morality of constraint (or obedience) and a morality of cooperation (or reciprocity). In between is a transitional stage during which rules become internalized as the individual moves from heteronomy to autonomy.
3. Kohlberg outlined three major levels of moral development: (a) preconventional, (b) conventional, and (c) postconventional.
4. Like Piaget, Kohlberg emphasized that the level of morality at which individuals operate depends on their *motives* for doing right. Piaget said that as children become more moral, they depend less on outside authority to constrain them and more on an inner,

subjective desire to cooperate and to consider the rights and feelings of others.

5. Essentially, Kohlberg said the same thing: Children's motives change gradually from a desire to avoid punishment, gain the reward of others, and avoid disapproval or censure, to a more positive motive of desire for individual and community respect and a desire to avoid self-condemnation.
6. Sufficient cognitive development is a prerequisite for advanced moral reasoning but does not guarantee it.
7. Kohlberg's theory better describes moral development in individuals from Western countries than those raised in other cultures. Also, people are not as consistent in their development moral reasoning as a stage theory would suggest.
8. Kohlberg based his theory on his research with male subjects. Later researchers raised the question of how applicable the theory was to females' moral development. One of Kohlberg's students, Carol Gilligan, made this issue the focus of her research.
9. Whereas Gilligan believes that women are more likely to resolve moral dilemmas using a caring perspective and men using a legalistic perspective, most researchers believe that the perspective both men and women take is a function of the particular dilemma being discussed and that both men and women use both caring and legalistic reasoning.
10. The moral progression is similar in all three theories: from amorality to outer control to inner control; from negative, selfish motivations to positive, altruistic motivations; from a desire to escape external punishment to a desire to escape self-condemnation.
11. The social-cognitive model identifies three types of rules: moral rules, social conventions, and personal preferences. Many of the disagreements between adolescents and adults stem from the fact that they view specific situations as fitting different of these domains.
12. Moral reasoning is needed for moral behavior but does not guarantee it. Many factors—such as pubertal status, degree of empathy, cultural background, and personality—act together to determine whether a person will behave morally.
13. Some aspects, but not all, of prosocial functioning improve during adolescence.
14. Moral growth and development cannot be isolated from other aspects of the adolescent's life. They have many correlates in the parent-child relationship especially and, to a lesser extent, in the adolescent peer relationship. What happens to children at home, with peers, and in the neighborhood will affect their moral development.
15. The majority of American teenagers believe in God and are fairly religious. They are most likely to be religious if their parents are religious and both follow the same faith. Although religiosity declines during very late adolescence/young adulthood, it re-emerges once a person marries and has children. Religious participation tends to positively influence adolescent behavior.
16. Teenagers spend more than 20 hours per week watching television. There is concern about this behavior, since many television shows promote violence, portray sex as impersonal and exploitive, and present commercials that encourage adolescents to spend their money unwisely.
17. An increasing number of people feel that schools should play a significant role in moral education. Some feel that the schools should teach selected moral values; others emphasize reasoning, values clarification, and learning through community service.
18. Cheating in school is widespread, and the practice seems to have gained more acceptance. Fear of failure is the most common reason given for cheating.

KEY TERMS

action learning 341
analysis 341
autonomous morality 322
conventional moral reasoning 325
differential association 332
good girl–good boy orientation 325
heteronomous morality 322
immanent justice 322
inculcation 339
instrumental hedonism orientation 325
law and order orientation 325
metacognition 327
moral development 340
moral rules 330
morality of constraint 322
morality of cooperation 322
objective judgments 322
personal preferences 330
postconventional moral reasoning 326
preconventional moral reasoning 325
prosocial behavior 330
punishment orientation 325
social capital 336
social-cognitive domain model 329
social contract orientation 326
social conventions 330
subjective judgments 322
universal principled reasoning 326
values clarification 341

THOUGHT QUESTIONS

Personal Reflection

1. Do you remember believing in immanent justice? Do you ever still feel that punishment is inevitable if you transgress?
2. Reflect on your own past and think of instances in which you and your parents disagreed as to whether a behavior was a personal preference or a social convention. Again, use examples to explain.
3. Think about an instance in which you behaved morally. Why did you behave that way? Think about an instance in which you behaved immorally. Why did you behave that way? Can you generalize about when and why you choose one path over the other?
4. Are you religious? By what criteria? Do your religious views influence the behavioral decisions that you make? If so, how?

5. Do you think that American teenagers watch too much television? Why or why not?
6. What are some of the specific concerns that psychologists have about the portrayal of sex on television? Do you agree with their characterizations?

Group Discussion

7. Compare and contrast the moral reasoning of a child who is a heteronomous moral reasoner with one who is an autonomous moral reasoner.
8. Do adults really make subjective moral judgments instead of objective moral judgments? If so, why does the crime of attempted murder carry a lighter sentence than that of a completed murder?
9. How would the thought processes of individuals at the preconventional, conventional, and postconventional moral levels differ if they were deciding whether to borrow their sibling's bicycle after having been told they could not?
10. Which criticisms of Kohlberg's theory do you agree with? Disagree with? Why?
11. How do you behave when you see someone violate a moral rule? A social convention? Use examples to make your point.
12. What family practices contribute positively to moral learning?
13. How does the type of discipline influence moral development?
14. How does modeling influence moral development?
15. What are the four ways in which peers can influence one another's moral behavior?
16. Imagine that your roommate mentions that he or she does not believe that televised violence really affects anyone. How would you respond?
17. What values are taught through television ads?
18. Which approach to moral education do you favor? Why?
19. What should schools do about academic cheating?

Debate Questions

20. Carol Gilligan was correct: A certain amount of self-protection is more moral than continual self-sacrifice.
21. A legalistic moral orientation is superior to a caring one.
22. Adolescents should be made to attend religious services whether they wish to or not.
23. Schools should teach moral values as part of their curricula.
24. It is impossible for schools to be morally neutral.

SUGGESTED READING

Brooks, B. D., and Goble, F. G. (1997). *The Case for Character Education: The Role of the School in Teaching Values and Virtue.* Northridge, CA: Studio 4 Productions.

Goodman, J. F., and Lesnick, H. (2000). *The Moral Stake in Education: Contested Premises and Practices.* Boston: Allyn & Bacon.

Hamilton, J. T. (2000). *Channeling Violence.* Princeton, NJ: Princeton University Press.

Killen, M., and Smetana, J. (Eds.). (2006). *Handbook of Moral Development.* Mahwah, NJ: Erlbaum.

Kirsh, S. J. (2006). *Children, Adolescents, and Media Violence: A Critical Look at the Research.* Thousand Oaks, CA: Sage.

Nucci, L. P. (2001). *Education in the Moral Domain.* Cambridge, England: Cambridge University Press.

Palmer, E. L., and Young, B. M. (Eds). (2003). *Faces of Televisual Media: Teaching, Violence, and Selling to Children.* Mahwah, NJ: Erlbaum.

Roehlkepartain, E. C., King, P. E., Wagener, L., and Benson, P. L. (Eds). (2006). *The Handbook of Spiritual Development in Childhood and Adolescence.* Thousand Oaks, CA: Sage.

Ryan, K., and Bohlin, K. E. (2003). *Building Character in Schools: Practical Ways to Bring Moral Instruction to Life.* San Francisco: Jossey-Bass.

USEFUL WEB SITES

Center for the Advancement of Ethics and Character
www.bu.edu/education/caec

The Center is located in the College of Education at Boston University. Its Web site contains information about character education, a suggested reading list (including books appropriate for children as well as adults), and links to other sites.

Character Counts!
www.charactercounts.org

Character Counts! is an offshoot of the Josephson Institute of Ethics, a consortium of prestigious organizations (e.g., the Red Cross, Big Brothers/Big Sisters, the Police Athletic League) that are concerned with fostering moral development. It was developed in the early 1990s to promote moral education in the schools. The group's Web site describes the group's beliefs and details the six moral virtues that the group believes are most important; it also includes free educational materials and links to other sites.

Character Education Partnership
www.character.org

This nonpartisan organization hosts an e-mail newsletter about character education and publishes a quarterly print newsletter. The site has a useful Question & Answer section and contains many links to other moral education sites.

National Study of Youth and Religion
http://www.youthandreligion.org

The National Study for Youth and Religion is conducted by researchers out of the University of North Carolina at Chapel Hill. The Web site includes many reports of the researchers' data and includes links to other Web pages about this topic. It contains information about a wide variety of topics related to adolescents and religion, and the quality of the reported research is very high.

CHAPTER 15 EDUCATION AND SCHOOL

WOULDN'T YOU LIKE TO KNOW . . .

- What is the purpose of public education?
- What is the difference between a *middle school* and a *junior high school?*
- Does fostering competition among students make them work harder and learn more?
- Do students fare better in large schools or small schools?
- What can teachers do to help students be successful in school?
- How many students drop out of high school?
- What can parents do to help their children be successful in school?
- Why do students drop out of school?
- What is the relationship between getting pregnant and dropping out of school?

Most American youths spend the bulk of their waking hours not at home but at school. And while there, they are exposed to the wide-ranging influence of peers and teachers. A successful school experience is the stepping stone to financial security. Most good jobs require having a high school diploma at the very least, and the best-paying jobs usually require even more education. Why do some students succeed while others do not? How are American schools structured? How satisfied are adolescents with the schooling they receive?

ANSWERS WOULDN'T YOU LIKE TO KNOW . . .

What is the purpose of public education?

Two perspectives must be considered in answering this question. Traditionalists believe that the purpose of public education is to teach reading, writing, and arithmetic. Progressives believe that the purpose of public education is to give students the skills they will need for adult life. Both traditionalists and progressives believe that public schools should turn out good citizens, although they disagree as to what that means. Traditionalists believe that good citizens embrace core American values, while progressives believe that good citizens actively participate in shaping society.

TRENDS IN U.S. EDUCATION

Let's take a look at the evolution of educational trends in the United States, particularly during the last half of the twentieth century through the present.

Traditionalists versus Progressives

Traditionalists argue that the purpose of education is to teach the basics—English, science, math, history, and foreign languages—to increase student knowledge and intellectual powers. **Progressives** urge that the purpose of education is to prepare students for life: citizenship, home and family living, a vocation, physical health, gratifying use of leisure time, effective personality growth. As envisioned by educational philosopher John Dewey and others (Westbrook, 1991), schools are to prepare students to be active, critical, engaged citizens. Progressive educators believe that students should be recognized as individuals, that they should be treated in a culturally sensitive manner, and that they should be trained in order to be capable of participating in the community.

The traditionalist-progressive debate has continued partly because of the insistence that education has an important role in reforming society and solving social problems. Each time a social problem has arisen, a new school program has been designed to deal with it. When traffic fatalities rose, driver education was introduced. A rise in premarital pregnancies and in divorce rates was followed by courses in family life education. Demands for racial integration led to African American studies and school busing. Feminists' demands for equality and liberation resulted in women's studies. A rise in crime rates resulted in new social problems classes. And so throughout history, as social needs have changed, the educational pendulum has been pushed first in one direction and then another.

Rise of Progressive Education

Until the 1930s, traditionalism was the dominant emphasis in U.S. schools. Then came the Depression, which destroyed the job market for adolescents, so that many who would have gone to work stayed in school instead (Ravitch, 1983). Most of these youths were non–college bound, uninterested in traditional academic subjects, and in need of different programs to deal with their own problems.

Progressive educators such as John Dewey felt the classroom should be a laboratory of living, preparing students for life. Under the progressive influence, many schools introduced vocational and personal service courses, restricting academic courses to the college-preparatory program. Life adjustment education centered around vocations, leisure activities, health, personal concerns, and community problems. Principals boasted that their programs adjusted students to the demands of real life, freeing them from dry academic studies. Developing an effective personality became as important as improving reading skills (Ravitch, 1983; Wood, Wood, and McDonald, 1988).

Sputnik and After

The United States was shocked when the Soviet Union launched *Sputnik*, the first space satellite, in the 1950s. Almost overnight, Americans became obsessed with the failure of the schools to keep pace with the technological advances of the Soviet Union. The schools were blamed for a watered-down curriculum that left U.S. youths unprepared to face the challenge of communism. As a result, Congress passed the National Defense Education Act and appropriated nearly $1 billion in federal aid to education, which supported the teaching of math, science, and foreign languages. Schools modernized their laboratories, and courses in physical sciences and math were rewritten by leading scholars to reflect advances in knowledge.

1960s and 1970s

By the mid-1960s, the so-called cold war with the Soviet Union had abated. The United States was swamped with the rising tide of social unrest, racial tension, and antiwar protests. Once again, society was in trouble, and the schools were called on to meet the challenge. Major school aid legislation was passed, primarily to benefit poor children, as part of the Johnson administration's War on Poverty. Once more, the educational clamor was for relevance. Educators claimed that schools were not preparing young people for adult roles and that adolescents needed to spend more time in community and work settings as well as in the classroom. Academic programs gave way to career and experimental education so that adolescents could receive hands-on experience. Elementary schools adopted open education, knocked down classroom walls, and gave students more choices as to what to do each day. High schools lowered graduation requirements. Enrollments in science, math, and foreign languages fell as traditional subjects gave way to independent study, student-designed courses, and a flock of electives. By the late 1970s, over 40 percent of all high school students were taking a general rather than college-preparatory or vocational course of study, and 25 percent of their educational credits came from work experience outside school, remedial course work, and classes aimed at personal growth and development (National Commission on Excellence in Education, 1983).

Soon, the nation became more alarmed at the steady, slow decline in academic indicators. **Scholastic Assessment Test (SAT)** scores showed a steady decline from 1963 to 1980. Verbal scores fell over 50 points and average math scores nearly 40 points. The College Entrance Examination Board administering the tests cited such in-school reasons as grade inflation, absenteeism, frivolous courses, absence of homework, and decline in reading and writing assignments as reasons for falling test scores. (Psychologists and educators cite other reasons also, such as family tensions, disorganization, and instability.) It became obvious that high school students were taking more nonacademic courses and fewer courses necessary for college preparation.

1980s

Parental and public outcry grew in the early 1980s, resulting in the appointment of the National Commission on Excellence in Education (1983). The commission drew these conclusions:

1. The number and proportion of students demonstrating superior achievement on the SATs (those with scores of 650 or higher) had declined.
2. Scores on achievement tests in such subjects as physics and English had declined.
3. There was a steady decline in science achievement scores of 17-year-olds by national assessments in 1969, 1973, and 1979.
4. The average achievement of high school students on most standardized tests was lower than when *Sputnik* was launched.
5. Nearly 40 percent of 17-year-olds could not draw inferences from written material; only one-fifth could write a persuasive essay; and only one-third could solve a mathematics problem requiring several steps.
6. About 13 percent of all 17-year-olds in the United States could be considered functionally illiterate. Functional illiteracy among minority youths ran as high as 40 percent.

This time, the reason given for demanding a back-to-basics education was not a threat from the Soviets but a fear that the nation was falling behind the economic competition from Japan and Western Europe and was losing its competitive edge in world markets. Educational reformers demanded more academic rigor in the schools; more required courses, particularly in math and science; longer school days; and tougher standards for graduation. Thus, the pendulum again swung back to a more traditionalist posture.

By the time the commission issued its report, however, the American Association of School Administrators (1983) pointed out the following:

1. The decline in SAT scores had stabilized and appeared to be reversing.
2. Students had been taking an increasing number of academic courses in each of the last six years.
3. Many states had already adopted stricter graduation requirements.
4. Many school districts had already raised expectations for students.
5. The percentage of adolescents enrolled in school continued to climb, and U.S. schools were educating a larger percentage of 17-year-olds than any other educational system in the world.
6. The average citizen was more literate and exposed to more math, literature, and science than the average citizen of a generation ago.
7. According to the United Nations, the United States had one of the highest literacy rates in the world.

traditionalists educators who emphasize that the purpose of education is to teach the basics.

progressives educators who emphasize that the purpose of education is to prepare pupils for life.

Scholastic Assessment Test (SAT) a test that measures aptitude to do academic work.

FIGURE 15.1 CHANGES IN SAT SCORES: 1971–2001

Source: Data from College Board (2003).

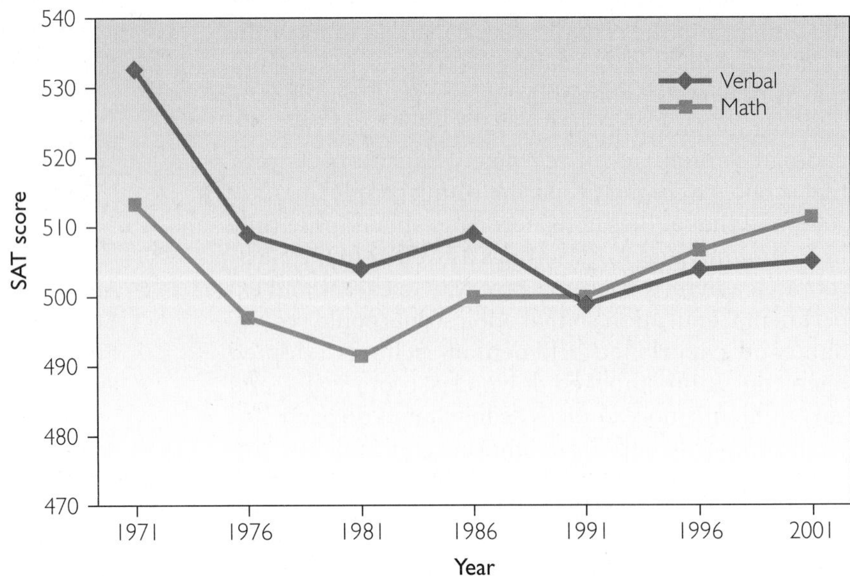

1990s

The optimism of the American Association of School Administrators in the middle 1980s was short lived. SAT scores did increase until 1986. However, after that, math scores leveled off for about five years. Verbal scores continued to fall until 1993, when they began to rise modestly. The SATs were renormed in 1993 to reflect changes in the characteristics of the students who are now taking them. Figure 15.1 illustrates how the SAT scores of college-bound high school seniors have changed since 1971. All pre-1993 scores have been adjusted to the revised scale.

Education in the 1990s was marked by a move toward *alternative forms* of instruction. Continuing dissatisfaction with public education and acknowledgment of the diversity of the U.S. student population encouraged parents and educators to experiment with a variety of novel approaches to teaching. In addition to the traditional public and private schools, a plethora of options were offered.**Magnet schools** have existed for decades, but enrollment in these schools jumped dramatically in the 1990s. Magnet schools are theme schools within public school systems; for instance, a magnet school might specialize in the arts or in African culture. Newer in concept are **charter schools.** Legal in 36 states, charter schools are a hybrid between public and private schools. They are public in the sense that they are supported by tax dollars and accountable to the government. They are private in the sense that they are free from most district-level rules and regulations, that they are founded and run by corporations or individuals who devise their own curricula, and that parents choose for their children to attend them. Charter schools are even more varied than magnet schools in terms of curricula and teaching format.

The distinction between public and private schools has become even more blurred by school districts' increasing use of **vouchers.** In a voucher system, the school district subsidizes the cost of a student attending a private school. Vouchers have existed for a long time, but their use is growing and expanding. Formerly, the only students who were given vouchers were those who lived in rural areas with no public schools or who needed special services because of disabilities. Now, voucher programs are much more widespread.

Another type of school, called a **tech-prep school,** is designed for students who are not interested in obtaining a four-year bachelor's degree after high school. High schools in more than 30 states have developed partnerships with community colleges so that their graduates can earn a career-focused, two-year associate's degree along with their high school diploma.

In addition, numerous states (for example, Minnesota, Delaware, and Iowa) have recently developed some form of **open enrollment** policy. In these states, students may attend any public school they wish, even if it is outside their own school district. In other words, if you live in Minneapolis but prefer to go to a St. Paul middle school because it offers a foreign language that is not available in your own middle school, you can. Proponents of open enrollment believe that the policy will improve public education because of increased competition for students. Since financial grants are often based on numbers of students, schools have more of an incentive to do well under open enrollment conditions.

Perhaps the most well-known educational innovation involves *home schooling.* The home-schooling movement began in the 1980s and was primarily endorsed by conservative Christians who wanted to shield their children from what they perceived to be immoral, secular influences. Today, it is a broad-based movement, and more than 1 million American children are currently home schooled. The experiences of home-schooled students vary widely. Some parents follow an established curriculum; some do not. Some parents keep their children home all day, while others strive to provide social opportunities for them. In certain states, home-schooled children are allowed to go to the public school for part of the day so that they can participate in activities such as drama, band, or team sports. Although some research has suggested that home-schooled children do well on standardized tests, those studies are inconclusive because of poor methodology. Given the variability of their experiences, it is likely that some home-schooled students will do well in college and the workplace but others will not.

Early Twenty-First Century

It is far too early to define the scope of the educational changes that will occur early in the twenty-first century, but a major new policy initiative was launched by President George W. Bush in 2001: the No Child Left Behind Act. It is based on four principles: (1) Schools should be made accountable for the success of their students and rewarded or punished commensurate with their success; (2) local control of the schools should be increased; (3) parents and students should have expanded options; and (4) specific teaching methods should be promoted. Another requirement of this new law is yearly testing of all students in grades three through eight to measure their abilities in core content areas. In addition, states will be given more leeway in choosing how they will spend federal education dollars, parents will be granted more choices as to which schools their children attend, and reading will become more of a priority in early education. In a sense, the No Child Left Behind legislation is a swing toward back-to-basics traditionalism: It emphasizes achievement in reading and other core subjects.

The No Child Left Behind Act is controversial. Opponents claim that testing is stressful and actually decreases the quality of education, since teachers "teach to the test." There is also the fear that schools that are below acceptable standards will lose funding and fall even further behind. The Act has not been adequately funded, and so many claim that the assessment requirements are actually draining money that could be spent on enhancing instruction. Others complain that the legislation shifts control of education from state authority, where it has traditionally resided, too far into federal hands. Finally, not everyone agrees with the specific reading methods that are being promoted. It will take several years to determine whether this new initiative is working to improve public education.

MIDDLE SCHOOLS

As we have discussed throughout this book, adolescents are considerably different from children, and early adolescents are considerably different from older adolescents. As the U.S. population increased, it was natural to progress from a one-room schoolhouse, which housed students of all ages, to a system in which the older students were separated from the younger ones. Perhaps the earliest model was to divide schools into *elementary schools* (grades one through six) and *secondary schools* (seven through twelve). Later, the most common model was to have *elementary schools, junior high schools,* and *high schools.* As the name implies, junior high schools were meant to be high schools for more junior adolescents. They were therefore structured much the same as high schools: Students changed teachers with every class period, the schools had larger enrollments, and students were more likely to be tracked according to ability level.

More recently, there has been a recognition that this junior high school model was not well suited to the special needs of early adolescents. Because of this, *middle schools* were developed. There is no single agreed-on structure for middle schools. Depending on the community, middle schools can include grades five through seven, five through eight, six and seven, six through eight, seven and eight, or seven through nine. Ideally, middle schools should not merely be renamed and reshuffled junior high schools; rather, they should be different in concept.

magnet schools theme schools that serve students within public school systems.

charter schools public schools that are funded and run by private corporations or individuals; accountable to government but relatively regulation free.

vouchers a method by which the public schools subsidize the cost of private school education.

tech-prep schools high schools that partner with community colleges to provide career preparation for non–college bound students.

open enrollment a policy that allows students to choose from among a large number of public schools, sometimes even those outside their own district.

ANSWERS WOULDN'T YOU LIKE TO KNOW ...

What is the difference between a *middle school* and a *junior high school?*

The term *junior high* really says it all. Junior high schools are high schools for younger students. The term *middle school* was created to indicate that younger adolescents need a different kind of education—one intended to help them in their transition to adolescence. In reality, the terms are used loosely, and many junior highs and middle schools are very similar in nature.

This has generally not been the case, however, and so many students still go into a slump when they enter middle school. They exhibit large declines in academic motivation, in perception of their own academic abilities, and in achievement after they leave elementary school (Roeser and Eccles, 1998; Roeser, Eccles, and Freedman-Doan, 1999).

Why does this happen? Middle schools are larger and more impersonal than elementary schools. Given this, students spend less time with friends and more time with relative strangers. In addition, when several elementary schools feed into the same middle school, which is usually the case, old peer networks break down. Friends often no longer see each other. This is exacerbated by individual scheduling. Rather than spend all day with the same 30 peers, as in elementary school, students in middle school often have little peer continuity during the seven or eight periods in their day. Students are less close to their teachers, too. A middle school math teacher might instruct 180 different students each day, as opposed to the 30 or so served by an elementary school teacher. Thus, middle school teachers do not have the time to get to know all of their students and to develop close rela-

RESEARCH HIGHLIGHT TRACKING

Tracking, or *ability grouping,* is an educational technique whereby students are separated into different classes based on their competency in a given subject area. (It differs from being placed in a curriculum, as discussed in the text, in that it refers to individual classes, not an entire program of course work.) Some classes, such as mathematics and science, are more commonly tracked than others.

Tracking, although practiced, is viewed with suspicion by many. One concern is that students are unfairly placed in lower tracks due to race, socioeconomic status, or other personal characteristics (Kubitschek and Hallinan, 1996). To compound that problem, once a student is placed in a lower-track class, it is hard to ever move into a higher track since the material is easier, the pace is slower, and he or she is viewed as less competent (Lucas and Good, 2001). Furthermore, it is widely feared that lower-tracked students will suffer from decreased self-esteem, since they (and others) have been given evidence that they are not talented in a subject.

On the other hand, tracking is believed by some to have benefits as well. The students in the higher tracks can learn more because the material is covered more quickly than it would be otherwise; students in the lower tracks can actually master material because they are given the time to do so. Students in the lower tracks are not subjected to daily feelings of discomfort as they struggle in front of their more-able peers.

Ultimately, however, one would want to know the long-term effects on achievement and self-esteem for students in both higher and lower tracks. Unfortunately, until recently truly excellent data were not available since most of the research that examined these issues used cross-sectional designs and lacked adequate control groups. However, in 2005 Mulkey and her colleagues (Mulkey, Catsambis, Steelman, and Crain, 2005) published an excellent longitudinal study that tracked 24,000 students over a 6-year period, from middle school through the end of high school. Some of these students were in schools where mathematics classes were tracked; others were not. Some of these students were in high tracks; others were in low.

Milkey and colleagues' counterintuitive findings were that tracking benefited lower-tracked students more than higher-tracked students. Although all students in the tracked schools demonstrated higher mathematics achievement than comparable students in the nontracked schools, the gains were greater for the initially weaker students. In addition, it was the higher-tracked students whose self-esteem suffered, not the lower-tracked students. Because the higher-tracked students shifted from being the best in their math class to being average, they had less and less trust in their math ability as time wore on; the lower-tracked students, in contrast, were now in with same-ability peers and so felt better about themselves. Tracking seemed to benefit males more than females.

One should always be cautious about jumping to conclusions based on any single study, but these results, if replicated, indicate that tracking may not be detrimental to lesser-ability students after all.

ANSWERS WOULDN'T YOU LIKE TO KNOW ...

Does fostering competition among students make them work harder and learn more?

Many researchers believe that fostering competition *among* students is less effective than fostering competition *within* students. That is, students do better if they are competing against themselves and trying to improve their own performance. According to this task mastery approach, students' grades should be based on their own improvement, not on how well they did in comparison with others.

tionships with them. In fact, large student enrollments usually mean that teachers don't even know all of their students by name. This lack of familiarity may also mean less effective supervision of student misbehavior (Carlo, Fabes, Laible, and Kupanoff, 1999). Given these changes, it is no wonder that many middle school students come to feel alienated and discouraged.

How might these problems be avoided? Eccles and Midgley (1989) believe that middle schools need to recognize early adolescents' special needs, including the fact that young teens are extremely self-conscious, that they desire autonomy, and that they need support from nonparental adults as they strive to break away from their parents. These researchers, as well as others, have suggested that the **performance goal structure** of most schools does not meet these needs and is actually detrimental to many adolescents. Schools with performance goal structures foster competition among students; the goal is to get the highest grade in the class. In contrast, schools with a **task mastery structure** are less competitive and highly value effort and improvement, rather than meeting preset standards (Middleton and Midgley, 1997). Data suggest that adolescents generally experience fewer problems in schools with task mastery structures (Roeser and Eccles, 1998; Roeser, Midgley, and Urdan, 1996). For example, students who are motivated by task mastery are more likely than goal-focused students to ask for help (and hence learn the subject matter) when they are confused; goal-focused students don't seek help because they are reluctant to seem dumb (Ryan and Pintrich, 1997).In addition, students whose teachers use task mastery standards come to value the academic subjects more and desire to learn them (Anderman, Eccles, Yoon, Roeser, Wigfield, and Blumenfeld, 2001). Moreover, due to the frustrations they feel, students in schools with a performance goal structure are more likely to feel angry and depressed and to be truant than students in schools that emphasize task mastery (Roeser and Eccles, 1998).

Drawing on the work of a large group of specialists, Jackson and Davis (2000) have summarized the attributes most characteristic of successful middle schools. Among their most important points are the following:

1. Teachers who work with early adolescents should have special training in interacting with this age group as well as opportunities for ongoing professional development.
2. The curriculum should be rigorous, and there should be high learning expectations.
3. The curriculum should be presented so that the students understand its relevance to their own lives.
4. The atmosphere of the school should be caring and supportive. Students should feel that they share a community with their peers and teachers.
5. Middle-schoolers need to feel that their opinions and thoughts are respected.
6. The school should strive to ensure the success of all of the students—academically weak and strong.
7. Parents should be involved in the school.
8. The school should be part of the larger civic community, and there should be interaction with businesses, community service centers, and the like.
9. Students should be encouraged to develop good health habits.

CHARACTERISTICS OF GOOD SCHOOLS

Jackson and Davis's list provides a good starting point for a discussion of what constitutes an ideal learning environment for middle and high school students. Other features have also been identified.

tracking an organizational technique that permits schools to create homogeneous groupings of students within a heterogeneous student population in order to facilitate instruction.

performance goal structure schooling in a competitive atmosphere in which the goal is to get the highest grade in the class.

task mastery structure schooling in a less competitive setting in which individual effort and improvement are rewarded.

ANSWERS WOULDN'T YOU LIKE TO KNOW ...

Do students fare better in large schools or small schools?

Small schools are generally better for students than large schools for several reasons: more students get to participate in activities such as band and sports, and students are less likely to feel lost and anonymous.

Size

As noted earlier, students do better and are more engaged in school if they feel part of a caring, supportive community. This is more likely to occur if the school is relatively small in size (less than 1,000 students) but not extremely small (Lee and Smith, 2001).

Students fare better in smaller schools for two reasons (Elder and Conger, 2000). First, in a small school, students will more likely be able to enjoy active, meaningful participation in activities. Clearly, there are only so many roles in the school play, running backs on the football team, and slots on the student council. This means that in larger schools, more students watch from the sidelines. Denied the opportunity to learn through doing, students may have feelings of disengagement.

The second reason students fare better in smaller schools is that the quality of monitoring by teachers is less adequate in larger schools. In small schools, most teachers know most students by name; students are not as anonymous as they often are in larger schools. It is obviously harder to slip through the cracks if teachers know you as an individual and frequently check on how you are doing. To address this issue, some large schools have started to divide themselves into self-contained subschools. Schools that are too small, however, may be problematic because of a lack of opportunities and because students cannot avoid peers and teachers they dislike.

Atmosphere

Although the teacher is in control of what happens in his or her individual classroom, the principal sets the tone for the entire school. A strong, competent principal who uses her or his leadership position to set high standards, to establish fair rules and discipline those students who break them, to make connections with the outside community, and to foster an upbeat spirit of cooperation and achievement is an enormous asset to the entire school. Students will be distracted if they do not feel safe in the hallways. They will be unhappy and uncooperative if they feel that they are constantly under scrutiny and suspicion. They will be angry if they believe that some students are treated preferentially. Thus, a school's overall climate can enhance or detract from achievement.

To enhance achievement, the school must create an atmosphere of learning. Too often, students do not perceive school as being primarily a place to go and learn. In many cases, even students who enjoy school do not like it because of the educating that takes place there; rather, they view it as a place to see friends and participate in activities (Anderson and Young, 1992). When parents ask their adolescents "How was school today?" they are more likely to hear about who was fighting with whom and how they had to go outside

In an atmosphere of learning, students feel they are responsible for their own learning, not held responsible for it. As such, they are interested in the course material and are willing to work.

during that day's fire drill than about what material was covered in their classes. An important aspect of school climate is how invested students are in learning. It is crucial that the school's curriculum be perceived by students as both relevant and challenging, for only then will learning become a priority.

A school is more likely to have an atmosphere of learning if students feel that *they are responsible* for their own learning rather than *being held responsible* for it. Students who feel responsible for their own learning and who are interested in the course material do not need to be constantly prodded to work; they choose to do so on their own. Students feel responsible when they are given sufficient autonomy and control (Bacon, 1993).

Teachers

Teachers can use many strategies to make students feel responsible for their own learning (Bransford, Brown, and Cocking, 1999; Eccles and Roeser, 2003). For instance, students generally do better and are more interested if they are allowed to discover answers for themselves rather than be expected to memorize large quantities of information. In addition, teachers can directly instruct their students about how best to learn. They can give students frequent feedback as to how they are doing, highlighting both accomplishments and areas that still need improvement. Teachers can also give students options for how to master course material and then demonstrate that mastery, allowing students to use their own individual strengths and learning styles.

ANSWERS WOULDN'T YOU LIKE TO KNOW ...

What can teachers do to help students be successful in school?

Teachers can help students succeed by being flexible and patient yet demanding high-quality work. To do well, students need to know that their teachers believe in their ability to master the course material and care about their success.

In addition, good teachers engage their students. They make information seem relevant and meaningful to their students and show students how to apply the course material and skills they are learning to their daily lives. They encourage students' questions, alternative points of view, and self-reflection. They allow students some time to explore areas of interest to them (National Middle School Association, 2005).

It is also important for teachers to demonstrate support and caring. Students do best when they believe that their teachers like them, care about them, and have faith in their ability to do well. Teachers can demonstrate such concern by being warm and friendly and by spending time with students. They can demonstrate

RESEARCH HIGHLIGHT SCHOOLS GET WIRED

Within the past decade, there has been a revolution in education: Computers have invaded our classrooms. In 2004, essentially 100 percent of American secondary schools had computers; middle schools had an average of 4 students/computer, high schools an average of 3.5 students/computer. Eighty-six percent of secondary schools had Internet access—in fact, more than half had wireless connections—and more than 90 percent of individual classrooms were linked to the Web. About 70 percent of secondary schools made computers available for their students outside of regular school hours, and, in addition, about two-thirds of students said they used computers at home to help them with school work (U.S. Bureau of the Census, 2006).

Computers and the Internet clearly have the potential to enhance learning. They make current information available to an extent never before possible. They allow students to see and hear images of things they would otherwise never experience. They allow students to collaborate with others who are at long distances and readily share information.

However, computer instruction is most likely not yet living up to its potential (e.g., Zhao, Pugh, Sheldon, and Byers, 2002). The reasons for this include lack of teacher training or commitment, inadequate technology or technical support, structural barriers in school schedules and policies, and lack of administrative support (Peck, Cuban, and Kirkpatrick, 2002). In addition, unless students are well monitored they can use computer time for nonacademic endeavors such as instant messaging or Web surfing. Other potential problems include the fact that many software packages are poor and do not stimulate thinking or creativity (e.g., the programs offer rote, repetitive drills) and that the Internet makes new forms of cheating and plagiarism possible.

With time, it is likely that most of the bugs will be worked out of the system and computers will truly enhance education. For now, all too often computers are misused or underused.

their belief in students' abilities by having high expectations, demanding high-quality work, having patience, and giving students the chance to redo work that is substandard. Teachers can undermine students' achievement if they indicate that they dislike them or lack faith in them. Negative teacher expectations fall disproportionately on girls, children from racial/ethnic minority groups, and children from lower-income families (Ferguson, 1998; Jussim, Eccles, and Madon, 1996).

Curriculum

The *curriculum* of a school consists of the aggregate of the courses of study offered. Most comprehensive high schools today offer three basic curricula: college preparatory/academic, vocational, and general (Hallinan and Kubitschek, 1999).

College Preparatory

Approximately half of high school students are enrolled in the college preparatory curriculum. Its goal is to prepare students for success in the type of college that leads to graduate school. Some high schools, particularly in middle- and upper-middle-class suburban communities, are particularly successful, boasting that 80 to 90 percent of their students go to college. Other schools, though enrolling large numbers of students in the college prep program, are unsuccessful because the majority of these students do not get into college. In such cases, the college prep program does not meet the needs of the majority of students; most do not go on to college, yet they are not employable without additional training.

Vocational

The vocational curriculum is designed to prepare students for gainful employment. Students spend about half of their time in general education, the rest in specialized courses, and, in some cases, in on-the-job training. Vocational teachers usually have work experience in the vocation they are teaching. The quality of the program varies from superb to mediocre. (More information on vocational education is presented in Chapter 16.)

General

Students in the general curriculum are often the castoffs from the other two curricula or are not committed either to college or to one of the vocations taught in the vocational curriculum. The curriculum has no goals other than to provide a general education for those who may be able to go onto some type of job

CROSS-CULTURAL CONCERNS JAPANESE EDUCATION

The Japanese educational system is known to be one of the finest in the world. Japan boasts high literacy rates, and its students excel in international math and science competitions. Why does the Japanese system work so well?

One reason is that the Japanese take education very seriously. Teachers have a higher professional status and enjoy higher salaries than in the United States. Another reason is that Japanese students spend more time in school; their school year is longer, and until very recently, they attended a half-day of school on Saturday. In addition, the Japanese people believe that academic success is more a function of hard work than innate ability, which fosters the belief that all children can learn successfully.

Three criticisms are regularly leveled against the Japanese educational model. First, it is extremely stressful on students. Japanese adolescents must take placement exams in order to get into the high school of their choice, and the competition for the best schools is fierce. Many students study long hours and attend *juku,* or "cram schools," to help them prepare for these tests. Students are well aware that the job they will eventually get and the university they will eventually attend (if any) is very much determined by which high school they go to. The second criticism against the Japanese system is that it is impersonal and rigid; little attention is paid to students' individuality. Finally, the Japanese schools have a tradition of emphasizing rote memorization rather than creative problem solving.

In order to address the latter two concerns, massive curricular changes were implemented in 2002. (Since the Japanese educational system is overseen by the national government, rather than at the local level, these changes were implemented nationwide.) A new subject, *integrated studies,* was introduced. Essentially, this provides a free time slot in which students are encouraged to learn about those topics that interest them. In addition, there has been discussion about making community service mandatory for high school students. These changes would move Japanese education from the traditional end of the continuum to the more progressive, but only time will tell whether they will prove successful.

Sources: Ellington (2001); Letendre (2000); Wray (1999).

In order to prepare students for gainful employment, most high schools offer a vocational curriculum that combines general education with specialized courses and possibly on-the-job training.

or some type of vocational school after graduation. Most dropouts and unemployed youths come from the general curriculum.Although students are assigned general education courses due to perceived low ability or motivation, all too often once placed there they are left to flounder. Numerous studies have shown that students in general education courses are taught by less experienced teachers who have low expectations of them (e.g., Pallas et al., 1994). They are surrounded by lackadaisical peers. If "no child is to be left behind," then extra attention must be paid to these students. We must find ways to motivate them to learn.

PRIVATE VERSUS PUBLIC SCHOOLS

The vast majority of pupils in the United States attend public schools. As Figure 15.2 indicates, about 88 percent of American high school students attend public schools. The majority of them attend their regular, neighborhood school; a much smaller percentage attend charter, magnet, or public schools in neighboring districts (U.S. Bureau of the Census, 2007). About 10 percent attend private schools, most of them church affiliated; about 2 percent are home schooled.

What determines which kind of education students receive? Ultimately, it is their and their parents' choice. Parents who choose private, religious schools tend to be devout, have higher incomes, be well educated, be older, be from the Northeast or Midwest, and be foreign born. Parents who select sectarian private schools tend to be wealthy and are more likely to be from the South than from the West (Yang and Kayaardi, 2004). Home-schoolers are at the present a diverse group, but they are more likely to be religious, conservative, White, better educated, and part of a two-parent family compared to the average American family. Home-schooling families tend to have more children and be middle class (Bielick, Chandler, and Broughman, 2001).

How good is each of these alternatives? Due to the fact that the backgrounds of the students who utilize the different choices are dissimilar—and we know that socioeconomic status, parent involvement, parents' educational level, and so on all help predict a student's academic success—it is actually not as simple to answer that question as you might imagine. We know that on average students who attend private schools, whether or not they are religiously affiliated, tend to do well on college entrance examinations and achievement tests (Hoffer, 1998; Persell, Catsambis, and Cookson, 1992). As of yet, there have been no large-scale studies of the

FIGURE 15.2 DISTRIBUTION OF HIGH SCHOOL STUDENTS, 2003

Source: U.S. Center for Education Statistics, 2005.

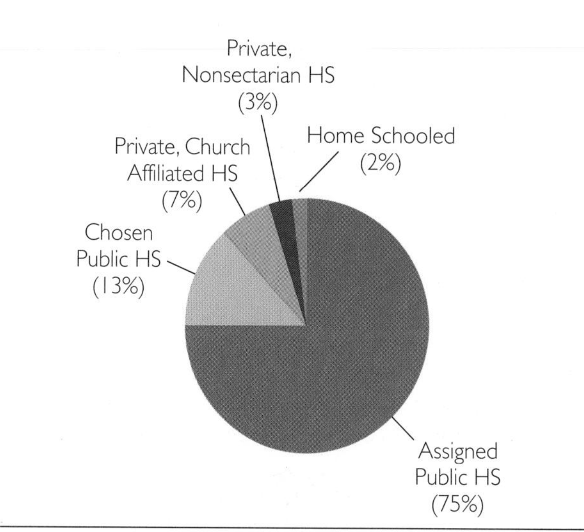

effectiveness of charter high schools—and by their nature, they vary tremendously from each other. The most comprehensive study that has been completed looked at elementary and middle school achievement. It concluded that students learned more if they were taught by certified teachers than by uncertified ones. (Charter schools are permitted to employ uncertified teachers.) In addition, the study determined that, on average, charter school students did not perform as well as students in traditional public schools (Nelson, Rosenberg, and van Meter, 2004). Although this might be partially due to self-selection in that parents whose children were already struggling opted to switch to charter schools, it is clearly not a strong endorsement. Those who are home schooled, however, appear to do well academically (Lines, 2001). There is some concern, however, that home schooling may hinder social development because home-schooled students spend less time than other adolescents interacting with peers. Many parents, though, ensure that their children have the opportunity to interact with peers by enrolling them in clubs, sports teams, and the like. Also, many states allow home-schooled students to attend classes part time.

ACHIEVEMENT AND DROPPING OUT

In this section, we'll discuss school achievement and those factors that are related to dropping out of school.

Enrollment Figures

Education for all youths has not always been the philosophy of the American people. A famous decision in Kalamazoo, Michigan, in 1874 established the now-accepted principle that public education need not be restricted to elementary schools. Prior to that, in 1870, the country's youths could choose from among only 800 public high schools. Most youths who were preparing for college attended private secondary schools, often called *preparatory (or prep) schools.* In 1970, 52 percent of Americans under the age of 25 had completed high school; in 2005, that figure stood at 85 percent (U.S. Bureau of the Census, 2006). There has been little overall change in dropout rates in the last 10 years. About 10 percent of those individuals with diplomas did not graduate from high school per se but instead received graduation equivalency degree (GED) certificates.

As Figure 15.3 illustrates, Hispanic American students are much more likely to drop out of high school than either Black or non-Hispanic White students. In addition, Hispanics are more likely to drop out at a younger age. Only about 20 percent of adolescent dropouts leave school by eighth grade (most leave by tenth grade); however, 40 percent of Hispanic dropouts do so by eighth grade (Schwartz, 1995). Hispanic students, of course, often face a language barrier, which makes academic success more difficult for them.

Who Drops Out and Why

A constellation of causes have been offered for adolescents dropping out of school or underachieving. The problem may begin before birth. Children who are born prematurely or with low birth weight may be at high risk for both biological and social factors. It is known that low-birth-weight children are at risk for subtle defects that may appear in school functioning. Neurological problems are found more frequently in preterm children than in full-term children. Specific cognitive processes such as attention and short-term memory may be affected, and these, in turn, have an impact on reading and arithmetic ability and social adaptation. A number of studies of elementary schoolchildren indicate that low-birth-weight children have more learning problems, visual-motor deficits, and grade retention (Cohen, Beckwith, Parmelee, Sigman,

FIGURE 15.3 DROPOUT RATES BY RACE AND ETHNICITY

Source: Data from U.S. Bureau of the Census 2000.

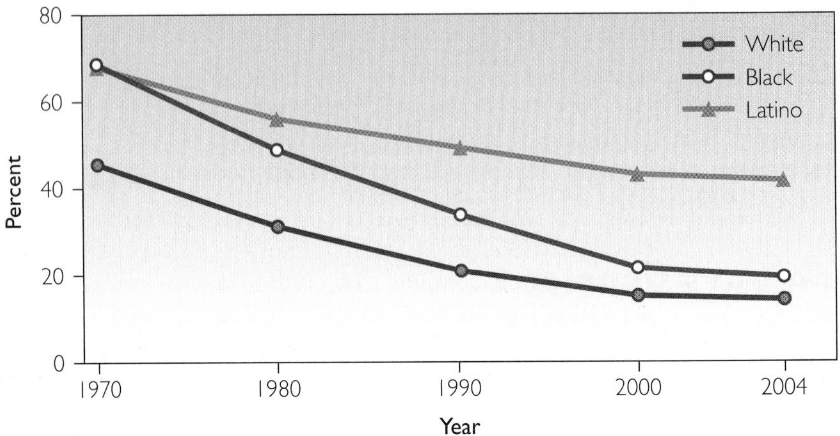

Asarnow, and Espinosa, 1996). Other research has found that children who were unhappy or poorly adjusted in elementary school have a more difficult time with the transition to middle school (Berndt and Mekos, 1995). In fact, Sroufe and his colleagues (Carlson, Sroufe et al., 1999) have shown that not only is middle childhood adjustment predictive of adolescent school functioning, but so are certain aspects of an adolescent's adjustment as a *toddler.*

So very many factors contribute to academic success or failure: socioeconomic status, racial and ethnic prejudice and discrimination, family background, parental influence and relationships, home responsibilities, personality problems, social adjustments, activities and associations, financial problems, health problems, pregnancy, marriage, intellectual difficulties, reading disability, school failure, misconduct, expulsion, low marks, and lack of interest in school (Connell, Halpern-Felsher, Clifford, Crichlow, and Usinger, 1995). Usually, problems accumulate over the years until withdrawal occurs, often after the legal requirement of age or number of years of schooling have been met.

The actual event or circumstance that precipitates withdrawal may be minor: a misunderstanding with a teacher, a disciplinary action, difficulty with peers, tension at home, or other reasons. For instance, one boy withdrew in the last semester of his senior year because his foster parents would not buy him a suit for graduation. Another boy was refused admittance to a class until a late excuse was obtained from his gym teacher in the prior period. The gym teacher would not give an excuse; the boy got angry, quit school, and never came back. In each incident like this, a whole series of prior events led to the final withdrawal: poor marks, grade retardation, conduct problems at school, strained family relationships, social maladjustment or isolation, and others.

ANSWERS WOULDN'T YOU LIKE TO KNOW . . .

How many students drop out of high school?

Only about 1 in 9 Americans does not complete high school or earn a GED, and this number has remained quite steady since the mid-1990s. Hispanic American students are much more likely to drop out than either Black or non-Hispanic White students, and they are more likely to drop out at an earlier age. The dropout rate for African Americans has decreased over the years, making it more similar to that of White students.

Here are some signs of possible early school withdrawal (Brooks-Gunn, Guo, and Furstenberg, 1993; Horowitz, 1992):

- Consistent failure to achieve in regular schoolwork
- Grade-level placement two or more years below average age for grade
- Irregular attendance
- Active antagonism to teachers and principals
- Marked disinterest in school with feeling of not belonging, meaninglessness
- Low scholastic aptitude
- Low reading ability
- Frequent changes of schools
- Nonacceptance by school staff; estrangement
- Nonacceptance by schoolmates
- Friends much younger or older

RESEARCH HIGHLIGHT PUSH AND PULL FACTORS

Using nationally representative high school student data, one study divided reasons why some adolescents drop out of school push factors and pull factors. *Push factors* are related to the school itself—when the school pushes students out. *Pull factors* are those reasons other than school that the student drops out.

There are several dimensions of school-related reasons for early withdrawal. School itself is defined as a push factor when the school becomes frustrating, punishing, or something a student wishes to avoid (and so is pushed toward quitting). There are three push dimensions in students' reasons for dropping out. First is a general student alienation from school, which includes failing in schoolwork, not getting along with teachers, and not liking or feeling welcome at school. The second push factor is school safety, meaning that the student is worried about attacks or hostile treatment from others at school or is having serious difficulties in getting along with schoolmates. The third push factor is having been expelled or suspended, which usually covers serious problems of discipline or confrontation with authorities by a student.

One important pull reason for dropping out is having to care for adult relatives, younger siblings, or one's own children. Clearly, this obligation mostly affects female dropouts. A second significant pull factor is employment—a reason given by female and male dropouts. Attraction of employment and the need to earn money definitely pulls many students away from school (Jordan, Lara, and McPartland, 1996).

- Unhappy family situation
- Marked differences from schoolmates with regard to size
- Inability to afford the normal expenditures of schoolmates
- Nonparticipation in extracurricular activities
- Inability to compete with or ashamed of brothers and sisters
- Performance consistently lower than potential
- Serious physical or emotional disability
- Discipline problems
- Record of delinquency

These signs must be interpreted cautiously; the presence of one or more of these symptoms of early school withdrawal may be a false alarm. At other times, only one symptom may be present but may be a real indication of possible withdrawal. When many of these symptoms appear together, a prognosis of school withdrawal is more reliable. Adolescents most at risk for dropping out need to be identified early in their school careers so that preventive measures can be taken. Large numbers of youths at risk need a lot more attention than they are getting in schools (Gregory, 1995).

Changing Schools

Changing schools is sometimes a factor in pupils' dropping out. When an adolescent changes schools, the ability of the parents and the adolescent to make wise decisions about schooling is reduced. They have less information about the new school and its teachers and classes. Also, they may be less able to take advantage of resources that the new school and teachers can provide. Additionally, teachers may be less committed to a youth who has only recently moved into the system and may be less willing to devote additional time and energy to that youth. Such an adolescent may feel separated from the educational process and may be more likely to seek marginalized social contacts (Teachman, Paasch, and Carver, 1996).

It may also be difficult for adolescents to merge into the social scene if they have moved from a distant geographic location, especially in the middle of an academic year. The junior author still shudders when she remembers how well her out-of-style clothes, Southern accent, and overly polite manners were received when she moved up North "to the big city." School was a nightmare, and academics wee the last thing on her mind.

Truancy

Those who drop out of school may have a high rate of truancy from school (Sheldon and Epstein, 2004). Truants, in general, score lower in academic ability and achievement, are less likely to live with both parents, and have more siblings than those who are not truant (Sommer and Nagel, 1991).

Bimler and Kirkland (2001) have identified several different types of truants. The first two types consist of adolescents who are truant because their parents either condone or encourage the behavior; for example, the truants' parents may wish them to stay home to care for younger siblings. The difference between the two groups is whether they are themselves intrinsically rebellious at school or not. Bimler and Kirkland term the third group "unmotivated loners": poorly adjusted loners who simply are uninterested in school. The fourth group is equally unmotivated and poorly adjusted but is part of a rebellious social circle. Finally, the fifth group is composed of "well-socialized delinquents." They are well adjusted and popular with other deviant youth, but their priorities do not include school.

Socioeconomic Factors

Research overwhelmingly indicates that low socioeconomic status (SES) correlates positively with early withdrawal from school. Why is the dropout rate higher among students from low-SES families? There are a number of considerations (Simons, Finley, and Yang 1991):

1. *Students from low-SES families often lack positive parental influences and examples.* Most parents want their children to have more education than they did. But if parents finished only fifth grade, they may consider graduating from junior high school sufficient. In general, sons of low socioeconomic status receive more encouragement to finish school than do daughters.
2. *Teachers are often prejudiced against youths from low-SES families, showing preferential treatment to students from higher-status families.* Students of higher-social-class backgrounds are chosen more often for little favors (e.g., running errands, monitoring, chairing committees), whereas students from lower-status groups receive more than their share of discipline. Teachers are usually from middle-class backgrounds and therefore often find it difficult to understand and accept the goals, values, and behavior of pupils from other social backgrounds.
3. *Low-SES students receive fewer rewards for doing well and for staying in school than do students from higher-status families* (Taylor, Casten, and Flickinger 1993). Rewards may take the form of academic grades, favors by teachers, social acceptance by peers, offices in school government, participation in extracurricular activities, or school prizes and awards. Lower-status students receive

these types of rewards less often than do higher-status students. Their grades are not as good, nor do they enjoy as much social acceptance and prestige by peers; they seldom are elected to positions of leadership; they are nonjoiners in extracurricular activities; and they are not often given special prizes or awards by the school.

4. *Low-socioeconomic-status students do not as often possess the verbal skills of their middle-class peers.* This in itself presents a handicap in learning to read or in almost all other academic work. Insofar as lack of verbal skills is associated with low socioeconomic status, lower-status youths do not do as well in school and are therefore more prone to drop out.

5. *Peer influences on low-SES youths are often anti-school.* Low-SES youths often have severed their ties with adult institutions and values, becoming involved instead with groups composed of jobless dropouts.

Racial and Ethnic Considerations

Hispanic American, African American, and Native American students have a much higher dropout rate than White students do (U.S. Bureau of the Census, 2006). The highest rates are among non-White students from inner-city high schools. In fact, the dropout rate in the inner-city high schools of the nation's largest cities is 50 percent (Orfield, Losen, Wald, and Swanson, 2004). The trying economic, social, and familial conditions of these youths are not conducive to continuing education. A variety of negative social, cultural, and psychological forces interfere with minority students' achievement and achievement orientation. Therefore, even though minority parents value and encourage education (Steinberg, Dornbusch, and Brown, 1992), their children are less apt to succeed.

Congruence between School and Home

Both economically disadvantaged and minority adolescents are likely to experience a lack of congruence between school and home (Arunkumar, Midgley, and Urdan, 1999). That is, the values and attitudes these students experience at home don't match those of their teachers; this is not a problem for middle-class, majority students.

Some areas of incongruence include attitudes toward competition, impulse control, and the appropriateness of emotional display (Trumbull, Rothstein-Fisch, Greenfield, and Quiroz, 2001). For example, expressions of anger are more tolerated among low-SES African American families than they are at school. Native American students may feel that it is boastful to raise your hand to indicate that you know the correct answer. When students feel this incongruence, they find themselves getting into trouble for behaviors they have been taught are acceptable. This leads to feelings of frustration, alienation, and anger. Students whose homes are dissonant from their schools are less hopeful about the future, have lower self-esteem, have less faith in their academic talents, and have lower grade point averages than students whose homes and schools are more congruent.

ANSWERS WOULDN'T YOU LIKE TO KNOW ...

What can parents do to help their children be successful in school?

Parents can best help their children do well in school by being enthusiastic, providing encouragement, and taking an active interest in their education. For instance, parents can make sure that their children get their homework done, and they can get to know their children's teachers. Parents should avoid putting too much pressure on their children, however, as this makes schoolwork unpleasant.

Family Relationships

The quality of interaction among members of the adolescent's family has a marked influence on his or her school success (Paulson, Marchant, and Rothlisberg, 1998). Studies of the family relationships of bright, high-achieving versus underachieving high school students show that the high achievers more often than the underachievers describe their parents as typically sharing recreation and ideas; as understanding, approving, trusting, affectionate, and encouraging (but not pressuring) with respect to achievement; and as not overly restrictive or severe in discipline. Parents of high achievers provide their children with learning opportunities at home, monitor their children's homework and achievement, and take time to volunteer at their children's schools (Paulson, 1994).

A large number of studies have examined the impact of parenting style on children's school success. *Authoritative parents* are most likely to have children who value school and get good grades (e.g., Spera, 2005). Authoritative parents are somewhat more likely than authoritarian parents and much more likely than permissive parents to be engaged in their children's education; they also have more contact with their children's teachers, spend more time helping their children do homework, and spend more time talking to their children about their school day (Melby and Conger, 1996).

Sense of Academic Competence

Adolescents who do well in school *believe* that they can succeed academically (Cadieux, 1996). Students who have faith in their academic ability are willing to expend the effort needed to do well, persist even when learning is difficult, are resilient and bounce back from failure, and get better grades than students who feel incapable (Patrick, Hicks, and Ryan, 1997). This sense of competence stems from many sources: feedback from parents (Bornholt and Goodnow, 1999), encouragement by teachers, a sense of fitting in, and a history of prior school success.

Adolescent boys and girls are equally likely to have faith in their academic strengths, even though girls tend to get better grades. Girls' academic confidence is more influenced by social factors than boys' (Patrick, Hicks, and Ryan, 1997).

Social Adjustment and Peer Associations

Peer associations often are a major factor in influencing a particular student to achieve in school. Most adolescents want to do what their friends are doing. If friends are dropping out of school to earn "big money" or to get married, the individual may be persuaded to do likewise (Schwartz, 1995). Similarly, the student who becomes acculturated into a subgroup that rejects education or into a delinquent group rebelling against the established system of education is strongly influenced by his or her peers to drop out of school. For example, in one study, boys' support from friends was negatively related to self-concept and educational plans (Cotterell, 1992a).

Developmental changes in relationships with peers are also likely to influence school motivation and engagement. The inclusion, acceptance, and approbation of the peer group have a marked influence on achievement motivation—especially during adolescence—and so those students with strong social skills do better in school than those who do not get along with their peers (Berndt and Keefe, 1995; Patrick, Hicks, and Ryan, 1997). Students need to feel that they belong. *Belonging* encompasses a student's sense of being accepted, valued, included, and encouraged by others (teacher and peers) in the academic classroom setting and of feeling like an important part of the life and activity of the class (Goodenow, 1993).

Employment and Money

Financial considerations are important in an individual's decisions about whether to stay in school. One study pointed to a relationship between family financial stress and academic achievement in sixth-, seventh-, and eighth-graders (Clark-Lempers, Lempers, and Netusil, 1990). Even high school is expensive. (For example, students feel they must have the "right" clothes to wear, and many schools charge for materials or charge participation fees for at least some of their courses.) This factor, plus financial pressures at home, force some adolescents to leave school to go to work. Sometimes, parents pressure youths to go to work to help support the family. At other times, there is the lure of being financially independent, having spending money for social activities, or saving to buy a car. The desire for clothes, a car, and other symbols of status in an affluent society lures many youths to opt for early employment. If at-risk students are able to get fairly good jobs without an education, they are more likely to do so (Stallmann and Johnson, 1996).

School Stress

A large body of research has demonstrated that continual high levels of stress debilitate psychological well-being, physical health, and task performance. A number of studies have focused on the sources of students' stress while in school, which are many.

One such source is safety. As has been discussed before, more and more students report that someone hit, kicked, or pushed them or threatened them with a knife or gun and that they feel unsafe in the school. Being made fun of in front of the class or by friends is also a source of stress, as is being criticized by teachers. Being made to feel inferior and ashamed, not being able to finish classroom work, and doing worse on a test than one should and experiencing a change of teachers in one or more classes are sources of stress. Other stressful situations are having something stolen from your locker and seeing other students throwing things and fighting in the lunchroom.

Anything that upsets the harmony and interferes with the classroom activities may be a source of stress and certainly affects academic functioning in the school situation (Ainslie, Shafer, and Reynolds, 1996).

School Failure, Apathy, and Dissatisfaction

Many school factors have been associated with dropping out of school (Evans, Cicchelli, Cohen, and Shapiro, 1995). Among these are poor reading ability, grade retardation, repetition, misplacement, low or failing marks (Goldschmidt and Wang, 1999), inability to get along with teachers, and misconduct. Students with learning disabilities and who have low IQs are also disproportionally likely to drop out (Dunn, Chambers, and Rabren, 2004). There is also a general, vague category that might be labeled apathy, lack of motivation, or a feeling that school is irrelevant. Some students are not necessarily emotionally or socially maladjusted—they simply lack interest in schoolwork, feel it is a waste of time, and would rather get married or go to work. Such youths may be capable of doing acceptable schoolwork but have no interest in doing so. Sometimes, such a student has been placed in the wrong type of program. A transfer to a vocational course that the student finds appealing and interesting is of help to the adolescent who has been wrongly placed in the college prep program. Many students do not drop out but are thrown out or given a temporary suspension, which they turn into a permanent absence.

Alienation

Student alienation—as manifested in a school context by poor academic performance, truancy, and rebellion—is a complex concept. One dimension of alienation is *powerlessness.* People feel powerless when they are controlled or manipulated by authority figures according to the rules of social institutions. In the school context, some students experience powerlessness when they can neither control nor change school policies, the classes into which they have been placed, and their marginal academic positions. They choose not to compete for rewards such as praise and academic grades and instead play truant from classes, rebel against rules, or merely attend but not participate in classes.

Meaninglessness is a second dimension of student alienation. In a school context, students may be unclear on the connection between subjects taught at school and their future roles in society.

The third dimension of alienation, *normlessness,* occurs when individuals have little sense of their cohesive goals and norms through social institutions. Official school norms reward students who achieve academically and who intend to pursue higher education. Many students from low-SES and minority groups perceive official school norms as unfair. Alienated students may readily reject official school norms in favor of peer and/or counterschool norms (Mau, 1992).

Pregnancy and Marriage

Leaving high school to get married is seldom a reason boys drop out of school, but pregnancy and marriage are among the most common reasons for girls. Thirty percent of teenage mothers drop out of school (Whitman, Bokowski, Keogh, and Weed, 2001). One study found that pregnant girls who didn't drop out were more likely to be better students, to be 16 years of age or older, and to be enrolled in vocational classes (DeBolt, Pasley, and Kreutzer, 1990). Schools can and do play an important role in meeting the many needs of teenage parents (Kiselica and Pfaller, 1993). Adolescent mothers who graduate from high school most resemble women who graduate and delay childbearing,

RESEARCH HIGHLIGHT SCHOOL VIOLENCE

School shootings such as the one that occurred in Littleton, Colorado, have caused many adolescents to wonder if they are safe in school. Are they?

They are not. Although students are considerably safer in school than they were in the mid-1990s, they are *relatively* less safe in school than they used to be. Because the juvenile crime rate has dropped faster outside of school than in it, adolescents today are about equally likely to be assaulted inside and outside of school (whereas in the past they were safer in school). About 9 percent of high school students report having been assaulted with a weapon while on school property; about 6 percent of students say that they have carried a weapon to school. Males and females, Whites, Blacks, and Latinos are all about equally likely to be assaulted while in school.

Students are more likely to be robbed than they are to be assaulted, and they are about half again as likely to be robbed inside of school as they are outside of it. About 30 percent of high school students will be robbed or have something stolen from them while on school grounds (Snyder and Sickmund, 2006).

Who is most likely to carry a gun to school? Older teens are more likely to carry guns than younger adolescents, and students from nontraditional families are more likely to do so than students from intact, two-parent homes. Adolescents who feel alienated and unpopular are more likely to carry guns, as are gang members. Students who attend a school whose climate is cold and hostile and where people are relatively uncivil to each other may respond by carrying guns. Many students who carry firearms to school say they do so for their own protection; they are afraid they will need to defend themselves (May, 1999).

Many students are afraid for their own safety at school. This fear is more common among urban, non-White, and female students (Harris and Associates, 1995). Fearful students often report that their anxiety affects their grades and sometimes causes them to skip school (Bowen and Bowen, 1999).

Schools are responding to their students' fears in several ways. Most middle and high school teachers and administrators are now more alert to potential problems. Almost 80 percent of schools now provide some sort of formal violence prevention program (Heaviside, Rowand, Williams, and Farris, 1998). Many have instituted new peer-mediation programs to resolve intrastudent conflicts. A growing number of schools employ security guards or have teachers monitor the school grounds. A small number of schools conduct periodic locker checks or have metal detectors installed inside the doors.

Fear of school violence is a problem that will not likely disappear soon. Fueled by alienation, the availability of weapons, and violence in the media, it is not a problem that can be solved by the schools alone.

ANSWERS WOULDN'T YOU LIKE TO KNOW . . .

Why do students drop out of school?

In short, students drop out of school because they are unhappy there. They may feel out of place socially or academically. Perhaps they are receiving too much negative and too little positive feedback from teachers and peers. Students may feel that school is not meeting their needs if the education they are receiving seems irrelevant to their lives. They may want to work full time and earn more money than they can at a part-time job.

ANSWERS WOULDN'T YOU LIKE TO KNOW . . .

What is the relationship between getting pregnant and dropping out of school?

For a girl, becoming pregnant increases the likelihood that she will drop out of school, and dropping out of school increases the likelihood that she will subsequently become pregnant. Adolescent boys who father children are also less likely to complete high school.

but are less likely to attend college than the latter (Aseltine and Gore, 1993). Not only does pregnancy encourage girls to drop out, but once they have dropped out, they are more likely to become pregnant (Manlove, 1998). Decreasing the high school dropout rate would therefore have the additional benefit of decreasing the teenage pregnancy rate.

What about teenage fathers? The data show that men who were teenage fathers completed fewer years of education and were less likely to finish high school compared to men who were not teen fathers. These educational deficits persist even after family and personal characteristics are taken into account. Teen fathers enter the labor market earlier and initially earn more money than do other men, but by the time teen fathers reach their mid-20s, they earn less. Teen fathers fare poorly in comparison to men who postpone having children until age 20 or later (Pirog-Good, 1996).

Dropouts and Employment

Contrary to the stereotype, many high school dropouts work (albeit at primarily unpleasant, low-wage jobs). Still, in 2004 the unemployment rate for dropouts was one and one-half time as high as it was for high school graduates (21 versus 13 percent). White dropouts are more likely to find work than Black dropouts, and male dropouts are more likely to be employed than female dropouts. (U.S. Bureau of the Census, 2006). This makes sense because many girls who drop out of school do because they have had a baby. Assuming they can find a job, at first dropouts earn almost as

Pregnancy and marriage are among the most common reasons for girls to drop out of school. Schools that provide special programs to meet the needs of teen mothers play an important role in keeping them in school.

PERSONAL ISSUES IS IT WORTHWHILE TO GET A COLLEGE DEGREE?

Since you are reading this text, it seems safe to assume that you are currently enrolled in college. You (and perhaps your parents) must be willing to invest what is likely a considerable amount of money in a college education, so you must believe that getting a degree will benefit you. Will it? The answer is an unequivocal yes.

The most obvious benefits concern knowledge and cognitive ability. Individuals who graduate from college certainly know more than they did before they entered college and likely more than they would if they had not continued their education. In addition, verbal and mathematical skills are enhanced, critical-thinking skills are improved, and the ability to engage in higher-order reasoning increases—although not by as much as you may imagine (Pascarella and Terenzini, 1991).

Many students go to college primarily because they believe that having a degree will help them get a good job. In fact, having a bachelor's degree does increase your chance of landing a desirable job along with your earning power. A college graduate can expect to earn $500,000 to $1,000,000 more over his or her lifetime than someone with only a high school diploma. This benefit applies to those who pursued liberal arts as well as more career-targeted programs. The earning power of women and minorities is particularly improved by having a bachelor's degree (Montgomery and Coté, 2003).

In addition, going to college changes people's attitudes. Students tend to leave college with a greater sense of civic responsibility (Ehrlich, 2000). They also tend to become more politically liberal (Pascarella and Terenzini, 1991), perhaps because they interact with politically liberal professors. (You may or may not view this change as positive.)

How many high school graduates continue on to earn a college degree? You may be surprised to learn that even in the United States, it is relatively rare for a young adult to obtain a college degree. According to the U.S. Bureau of the Census (2002), about 45 percent of American 18- to 21-year-olds are in college. Only about half of these (or 20 percent of all U.S. adolescents) will graduate in four years; another 25 percent or so will take longer but eventually earn their college degree. Putting these numbers together, at most about one-third of U.S. adults have an undergraduate degree. The trend is for more and more students to enter and complete college, and so this number will likely rise in the next decade. Right now, however, possessing a bachelor's degree places you in a privileged minority.

much as high school graduates ($20,000 versus $23,000 in 2004 for males). However, dropouts find themselves in dead-end jobs and their salaries do not rise, whereas those of graduates do; the wage gap, therefore, widens with age.

Whereas salaries for dropouts have roughly doubled in the past 20 years, they have tripled for those with a bachelor's degree. Low wages and high unemployment rates among low-SES and minority groups mean that dropouts are disproportionately likely to receive public assistance or to engage in criminal activity. About half of all heads of household on welfare and about half of all prison inmates are high school dropouts (Federal Interagency Forum on Child and Family Statistics, 2001).

SUMMARY

1. There are two opposing perspectives in American educational practice: traditionalism, which emphasizes teaching the basic academic subjects, and progressivism, which encourages the fostering of life skills and independent thought. These two perspectives wax and wane in popularity, depending on political and historical events.
2. Throughout the 1990s and continuing to the present time, dissatisfaction with the U.S. educational system has led to experimentation with new methods and tools that are intended to improve student learning and retention. Charter schools, open enrollment, and home schooling, for example, have all become more common. Most recently, in 2001, Congress passed the No Child Left Behind Act, which mandates stronger local control of schools, compulsory standardized testing, and an increased emphasis on reading and literacy. The measure is controversial.

3. Middle schools were developed to meet the special needs of early adolescents. Although the grades served by these schools vary, most are similar to high schools in structure. The larger size and more impersonal nature of middle schools, as compared with elementary schools, mean that students' achievement and engagement often decrease when they reach middle school.
4. The most successful middle schools share a number of features: a task mastery structure, specially trained teachers, a rigorous curriculum that is presented as relevant to students' lives, a caring and supportive atmosphere, and involved parents and community institutions.
5. All adolescents—high school students as well as those in middle school—benefit from attending smaller schools, where they feel safe, have opportunities to participate, and are treated fairly and with respect.
6. The average comprehensive high school offers three basic curricula: college preparatory, vocational, and general. Students in the general track tend to be more dissatisfied with their schools than students in the other two tracks.
7. As a whole, students who attend private schools or who are home schooled fare better academically than those who attend public schools. Charter schools have not yet proved to be more effective overall than more traditional public schools.
8. There are a number of reasons that pupils drop out of school: truancy, socioeconomic factors, racial and ethnic prejudices and discrimination, disturbed family situations and negative parental influences, incongruence between home and school, emotional problems, negative social adjustments and peer associations, financial reasons, school failure, school stress, apathy, student alienation and dissatisfactions, pregnancy and marriage, as well as other reasons.
9. Well-publicized incidents of school violence have focused attention on this issue. Students' fear is justified given the large numbers of individuals who carry weapons to school. Unhappy, alienated male youths from nontraditional families are the most likely to do so. Schools have become more security conscious in response to students' and parents' concerns.
10. Many dropouts find jobs, but they earn considerably less than high school graduates. Because of their poor economic prospects, a disproportionate number of dropouts go on welfare or engage in crime.
11. College attendance has a number of real benefits, such as becoming a better critical thinker and increasing one's social conscience. In addition, having a bachelor's degree is valuable in acquiring a good job and earning a good salary.

KEY TERMS

charter schools 348
magnet schools 348
open enrollment 348
performance goal structure 351
progressives 346
Scholastic Assessment Test (SAT) 347
task mastery structure 351
tech-prep schools 348
tracking 350
traditionalists 346
vouchers 348

THOUGHT QUESTIONS

Personal Reflection

1. Describe your middle school. Was it modeled after a high school? Do you feel that it was developmentally appropriate for you? Why or why not?
2. Describe your transition to middle school. Were you excited and pleased or anxious and distressed? What factors influenced your feelings?
3. Would you have benefited from an alternative type of middle or high school education? If you had had the options available today, what kind of school would you have selected and why?
4. In what ways did your high school program prepare you for college? In what ways was it deficient in preparing you for college?
5. What did you think of the teachers in your high school? What qualities did you most admire? What qualities did you like the least?
6. Did your high school have many dropouts? Why did these students leave school? What kept you in school when you sometimes felt you would rather leave and go to work?

Group Discussion

7. Do you believe that grades should be based on overall achievement or individual improvement? What are the pros and cons of each approach?
8. Describe the type of high school you attended. Evaluate the good things about it.
9. What curriculum options were available in your high school? Did these meet the needs of the students?
10. What are the most important attributes of a good teacher?
11. What sort of grade arrangements do you feel work best? That is, what classes should be placed in each building to achieve the maximum amount of learning and satisfactory adjustments of students?
12. What is your opinion of attending a private versus public school? Give examples from your own experience or the experience of others.
13. What, if any, aspects of the Japanese educational system would you like to see instituted in the United States? Why?
14. What can schools do to reduce the risk of violence on their grounds? What measures are counterproductive? Why?

Debate Questions

15. The progressive approach to education is superior to the traditional approach.

16. High schools cater too much to the students who are planning on going to college.
17. Middle schools and high schools are too lax in regard to discipline.
18. Students should help evaluate middle school and high school teachers.
19. Students should have a voice in the selection of their high school's curriculum.

SUGGESTED READING

Bonilla, D. M. (2000). *School Violence.* New York: H. W. Wilson.

Harris, S. (2006). *Best Practices of Award-Winning Secondary School Principals.* Thousand Oaks, CA: Corwin Press.

Krovetz, M. L., and Gilberto, A. (2006). *Collaborative Teacher Leadership: How Teachers Can Foster Equitable Schools.* Thousand Oaks, CA: Corwin Press.

Jackson, A. W., and Davis, G. A. (2000). *Turning Points 2000: Educating Adolescents in the Twenty-First Century.* New York: Teacher's College Press.

Lee, V. E., and Smith, J. (2001). *Restructuring High Schools for Equity and Excellence: What Works.* New York: Teacher's College Press.

McEwin, C. K., Dickinson, T. S., and Jenkins, D. M. (1998). *American Middle Schools in the New Century: Status and Progress.* Westerville, OH: National Middle School Association.

Orfield, G. (Ed.). (2004). *Dropouts in America: Confronting the Graduation Rate Crisis.* Boston: Harvard Education Press.

San Antonio, D. M. (2004). *Adolescent Lives in Transition: How Social Class Influences the Adjustment to Middle School.* Albany: State University of New York Press.

Sheets, R. H., and Hollins, E. R. (Eds.). (1999). *Racial and Ethnic Identity in School Practices: Aspects of Human Development.* Mahwah, NJ: Lawrence Erlbaum.

USEFUL WEB SITES

National Education Association (NEA)
www.nea.org

Probably best known for its "Read Across America" program, the NEA is an advocacy group dedicated to improving public education in the United States. Designed primarily for teachers and education students, the site contains position statements on educational issues and news releases. It also contains a section devoted to concerned parents. Quite useful is a "Legal Action Center," which makes it easy for interested individuals to contact their congressional representatives about educational issues.

National Middle School Association
www.nmsa.org

As its name implies, the National Middle School Association is concerned with the education of young adolescents. The site contains numerous online research articles and research summaries as well as current news about middle school education. It also provides position statements and has a useful online bookstore.

CHAPTER 16 WORK AND VOCATION

WOULDN'T YOU LIKE TO KNOW . . .

- How do you know whether a career will suit you?
- Do most teens think that their parents should have a say in their career plans?
- Who besides the parents can influence an adolescent's career choice?
- Do men and women today have equal career opportunities?
- Do most teenagers have jobs?
- Which teens are most likely to work?
- Is it good or bad for adolescents to have paying jobs?
- Do adolescents like doing unpaid volunteer work?
- What's the best thing you can do to avoid being unemployed later in life?

The choice of a vocation is one of the most important decisions that an adolescent has to make. In this chapter, we will examine the factors that influence that choice as well as other factors that should. We will also examine the major theories of vocational choice that have grown out of research discoveries and discuss the influence of parents, peers, school personnel, culture, sex-role concepts, intelligence, aptitudes, interest, job opportunities, job rewards and satisfactions, socioeconomic status, prestige factors, and race/ethnicity on career development. We will take a look at adolescents' work experiences, both salaried and volunteer, and discuss adolescent unemployment. The chapter concludes with a section on career education.

MOTIVES FOR CHOICE

There are some basic psychological reasons as to why the task of vocational choice is important. All people need to meet their emotional needs for recognition, praise, acceptance, approval, and independence. One way individuals do this is by taking on a vocation identity, by becoming "somebodies" whom others can recognize and by which others grant them emotional fulfillment. By identifying with a particular vocation, people find selfhood, self-realization, and self-fulfillment. High career aspirations are both a consequence of high self-esteem and a contributor to having a superior self-image (Chiu, 1990). To the extent that adolescents succeed in their own and others' eyes, they gain self-satisfaction and recognition. In their search for identity and self-satisfaction, they are strongly motivated to make a vocational choice that will contribute to their fulfillment (see Chapter 8).

For adolescents who are of a philosophical frame of mind, their vocation is one channel through which their life goals and purposes might be fulfilled. It is the reason for their existence, the niche they feel compelled to fill in the world (Homan, 1986). If adolescents believe life has meaning and purpose, they strive to find and to live out that meaning and purpose by the way they spend their time, talents, and energy. One way is through the work they perform. Vocational choice not only involves asking How can I make a living? It also involves asking What am I going to do with my life?

For adolescents whose concern is one of service—for meeting the needs of people or bettering the society in which they live—the choice of vocation will depend on the needs they recognize as most important and can best satisfy through their work. They thus seek a vocation in which they can help others. For adolescents who try to be practical, the choice involves discovering the types of work in which there are the most vacant positions, in which the best money and benefits package are offered, in which they are most interested, and for which they are best qualified. Such choices are based primarily on economic motives, practical considerations, and personal interests and qualifications. For other youths, seeking a vocation becomes a means by which they show they are grown up, financially independent, emancipated from parents, and able to make it on their own. For them, going to work becomes a means of gaining entrance into the adult world.

Sometimes, however, no rational choice of vocation is made at all. Adolescents just go out and get the first job they can find that pays well, or they accept a job because a friend has recommended them for it or because it happens to be the only one that opens up and that they hear about. Under such circumstances, vocational choice is happenstance rather than a thoughtful process. Adolescents may temporarily enjoy economic and other benefits such employment brings. Only later do they discover they are unhappy, ill suited to the tasks, and sacrificing their freedom and lives for doubtful benefits. They need to back up; reassess their goals, talents, and opportunities; and discover the ways these might be combined in meaningful, rewarding work.

Under the best of circumstances, choosing a vocation is an increasingly difficult task as society becomes more complex. The *Occupational Outlook Handbook* (2006) lists more than 1,000 different occupations, most of which are unfamiliar. If at all possible, adolescents need to make rational, considered choices of vocations. If they fail to identify themselves with the kind of work for which they are suited and in which they can find satisfaction and fulfillment, their vocational nonidentities will reflect their larger failure to discover their own identities. In a sense, they will have failed to discover what their own lives are all about.

THEORIES OF VOCATIONAL CHOICE

A number of theorists have sought to describe the process of vocational development. The particular theories that we will discuss are those of Ginzberg (1988), Holland (1985), and Gati (1998; Gati, Fassa, and Houminer, 1995).

Ginzberg's Compromise with Reality Theory

In his **compromise with reality theory,** Eli Ginzberg (1988) emphasized that making a vocational choice is a developmental process that occurs not at a single moment, but over a long period. It involves a series of *subdecisions* that together add up to a vocational choice. Each subdecision is important because each limits the individual's subsequent freedom of choice and the ability to achieve his or her original goal. For

During the fantasy stage, young children imagine the type of work they want to do without regard to training, ability, opportunity, or other realistic considerations.

example, a decision not to go to college and to take a commercial course in high school makes it difficult later to decide to go to college. Extra time, effort, and sometimes money must be expended to make up for deficiencies. As children mature, they gain knowledge and exposure to alternatives; they learn to understand themselves and their environment; and they are better able to make rational choices. Most of these choices involve making comparisons between an ideal and a reality. Ginzberg divided the process of occupational choice into three stages: fantasy, tentative, and realistic.

Fantasy Stage

The fantasy stage generally occurs up to age 11. During this time, children imagine workers they want to be without regard to needs, abilities, training, employment opportunities, or any realistic considerations. They want to be airline pilots, teachers, quarterbacks, ballerinas, and so forth. Most commonly, the careers they select are glamorous and easily identifiable because of particular costumes the workers wear.

Tentative Stage

The tentative stage spans ages 11 through 17 and is subdivided into four periods or substages. During the *interest period,* from ages 11 to 12, children make their choices primarily based on their likes and interests. This stage represents a transition between fantasy choice and tentative choice. The second period, the *capacities period,* occurs between about 13 and 14 years of age. During this period, adolescents become aware of role requirements, occupational rewards, and different means of preparation. However, they are primarily thinking of their own abilities in relation to requirements. During the third period, the *value period,* from ages 15 to 16, adolescents attempt to relate occupational roles to their own interests and values, to synthesize job requirements with their own values and capacities. They consider both the occupation and their own interests. The fourth and last stage, which occurs at around age 17, is a *transition period,* in which adolescents make transitions from tentative to realistic choices in response to pressures from school, peers, parents, colleges, and the circumstances of graduating from high school.

Realistic Stage

During the realistic stage, from age 17 on, adolescents seek further resolution of their problems of vocational choice. This stage is subdivided into a period of *exploration* (ages 17 to 18), during which they make an intensive search to gain greater knowledge and understanding; a period of *crystallization* (between ages 19 and 21), in which they narrowly define a single set of choices and commit themselves; and a period of *specification,* in which a general choice, such as physicist, is further limited to a particular type of physicist.

Ginzberg's interviews were conducted primarily with adolescents from upper-income families, who no doubt had a considerably great range of choices. The process would likely take longer for these youths than for others because they perceive themselves as having multiple and diverse opportunities. Lower-income youths often have an earlier crystallization of occupational choice, though

compromise with reality theory the theory of vocational choice proposed by Ginzberg.

their choices still seem to parallel those of the theoretical model. Also, Ginzberg's observations were primarily of boys, although he concluded that girls parallel the first two stages—fantasy and tentative. Other research indicates that the transition to realism applies to both boys and girls, but that girls tend to keep their vocational plans more tentative and flexible than do boys.

Ginzberg's theory suffers from rigidity with respect to the exact sequence, nature, and timing of the stages; thus, it may be too artificial and contrived. Much research, however, generally supports the broad outlines of the hypothesis, but not always the chronological ages, associated with Ginzberg's different stages.

Gottfredson (1996) proposed a theory of career development similar to that of Ginzburg. She suggested that early career development involves **circumscription** and then **compromise.** When quite young, children are intrigued by large, powerful individuals. They gradually realize that men and women tend to have different jobs and work roles. By late childhood, they are attuned to the values of society and the people around them and they recognize that different careers express different values. At this age they are also beginning to realize that some careers require abilities that they do not possess or require efforts that they are not willing to expend, and so they *circumscribe* their choices and begin rejecting careers on these bases. By early adolescence, personal interests and needs become the primary concern in career selection. However, adolescents compromise by modifying their choices to bring them in line with reality. Adolescents typically make *anticipatory* compromises, meaning that the modifications they make, are based on expectations, not actual experiences.

Armstrong and Crombie (2000) conducted a longitudinal study of eighth- through tenth-graders and found support for the movement to realism theorized by both Ginzberg and Gottfredson. Namely, adolescents who perceived a discrepancy between their ideals and their assessment of what was possible for them changed their career goals; the changes generally made their career selections more gender stereotyped and more realistic. Those who did not perceive a discrepancy did not modify their aspirations.

Similarly, Helwig's (2001) research also supported Ginsberg's and Gottfredson's theories. Helwig found that the tendency to select fantasy careers diminished over childhood and adolescence. Interestingly, boys lagged behind girls in this, in part because a number of them held onto the fantasy career of being a professional athlete into high school. In addition, careers that matched societal values peaked in eighth grade and then diminished. From this point onward, individual concerns began to take on more importance.

Ginzberg reformulated his theory to take new data and criticisms into account. He acknowledged that ca-

RESEARCH HIGHLIGHT DEVELOPMENTAL-CONTEXTUAL CONCEPTS

Research on career development emphasizes the dynamic interaction between individuals and their environments in their vocational quests. Specifically, there are three types of influences on development (Vondracek and Schulenberg, 1986, 1992):

1. *Normative, age-graded influences:* These influences, which vary with chronological time, might be biological or environmental. For example, certain types of careers, such as professional sports, demand requisite physical characteristics.
2. *Normative, history-graded influences:* These influences may be biological or environmental in nature, too. They could include such historical events as depression, war, famine, or even the launching of *Sputnik.*
3. *Nonnormative, life-event influences:* These influences might include an unexpected death of a family breadwinner, an illness, an injury, or a loss of scholarship, forcing alteration of career plans.

In other words, there may be significant influences on career choice over which the individual has minimal control. According to some researchers, *chance* plays a role in shaping career decisions (Cabral and Salomone, 1990). Such decisions are rarely purely rational; nor are they, in most instances, based purely on chance. Some combination of planning and happenstance seems to influence the decision. Individuals are most vulnerable to the effects of chance during life transitions, particularly those that occur early in one's career and that are not anticipated. However, the ability to cope with unforeseen events depends a great deal on the strength of the individual's self-concept and the sense of internal (or enabling) control. The accident theory of vocational choice emphasizes the effect of unexpected personal events on career development but would still emphasize that some individuals are better able to overcome negative contingencies and to take advantage of positive developments than are others (Scott and Hatalla, 1990).

TABLE 16.1 HOLLAND'S OCCUPATIONAL ENVIRONMENT THEORY

PERSONALITY TYPE	CHARACTERISTICS	SUGGESTED CAREERS
Artistic	Likes creative activities and the arts: music, drama, drawing. Views self as expressive and independent.	Composer, fashion designer, book editor, physician, art teacher, graphic designer
Conventional	Likes structure and order and working with numbers. Views self as systematic and organized.	Bookkeeper, bank teller, postal worker, court clerk, title examiner, secretary
Enterprising	Likes to lead, persuade, and be successful. Views self as ambitious and outgoing.	City manager, lawyer, real estate agent, salesperson, school principal
Investigative	Likes math and science. Views self as intellectual and exacting.	Architect, biologist, dentist, meteorologist, pharmacist, surveyor, veterinarian
Realistic	Likes to work with machines and animals, not people. Views self as practical.	Carpenter, police officer, electrician, firefighter, pilot, locksmith, mechanic

reer choices do not necessarily end with the first job and that some people remain occupationally mobile throughout their work histories. He emphasized that some people—those who are economically disadvantaged and who belong to minority groups especially—do not have as many choices as people in the upper classes do (Ginzberg, 1988). He also emphasized that there is variability in choice patterns and in the timing of crystallization that is really a deviation from normal sequences and timing. He acknowledged that some people may make a stable choice from the time they are young. Others are never able to make a choice because of psychopathology or because of so much pleasure orientation that necessary compromises cannot be made (Ginzberg, 1988).

Holland's Occupational Environment Theory

According to Holland's (1985) **occupational environment theory** of vocational choice, people select occupations that afford environments consistent with their personality types; they are more likely to choose and remain in a field when personal and environmental characteristics are similar (Vondracek, 1991).

Holland outlined six personality types—*realistic, intellectual, social, conventional, enterprising,* and *artistic*—and occupational environments compatible with these types (Lowman, 1991) (see Table 16.1). The personality types were measured with a *self-directed search system.* This system has six scales, each corresponding to one of Holland's personality types. Holland believed that responses to the lengthy inventory of items on each scale revealed individuals' vocational environmental preferences. Thus, individuals striving for a suitable career seek out those environments compatible with their patterns of personal orientations and exhibit these inclinations through their responses to the personality test items. According to Holland (1985), then, it is possible to ascertain occupational orientations by the scores on the personality scales.

Subsequent research has offered only partial support to Holland's theory (Brown, 1987). Even though personality often influences vocational choice, individuals sometimes elect and stay in occupations even when their personality does not match the vocational environment (Wallace-Broscious, Serafica, and Osipow, 1994). Thus, individuals may stay in a job because it offers more security, higher wages, or less travel; because it requires less education; because they are close to retirement; or because they don't want to move geographically. Many workers stay in

circumscription limiting one's career aspirations to a set of acceptable choices based on interests and values.

compromise modifying one's career choices to bring them in line with reality.

occupational environment theory the theory of vocational choice proposed by Holland.

ANSWERS WOULDN'T YOU LIKE TO KNOW ...

How do you know whether a career will suit you?

A career will most likely suit you if it matches your interests, abilities, and values (Ginsberg, Gottfredson, and Gati) and your personality (Holland).

jobs for which they are not perfectly fitted because of personal or family obligations (Salomone and Sheehan, 1985).

Gati's Sequential Elimination Model

Gati (1995; Gati et al., 1998) developed a model of career choice based on current theories of decision making. He divided the career search process into two broad phases—*prescreening* and *in-depth analysis*—which are not unlike Ginsberg's tentative and realistic stages. He diverged from Ginsberg, however, in combining interests, abilities, and values into what he terms *career aspects,* and he contrasts these with *within-aspect preferences,* or job-related characteristics. In Gati's view, career aspects should take precedence over within-aspect preferences.

Gati's theory, developed to help career counselors help clients make satisfying career decisions, contains a number of steps: defining the decision problem, identifying different career aspects, ranking those aspects by importance, identifying both optimal and acceptable levels of the aspects, eliminating those careers that are incompatible with the important aspects, collecting additional information on the remaining career options, ranking alternatives by overall desirability, and outlining the steps the client needs to take to move into that career. A key element of Gati's approach involves helping clients make the most acceptable compromises among the job characteristics that matter to them.

PEOPLE INFLUENCING VOCATIONAL CHOICE

Parents

Parents influence their adolescent's choice of vocation in a number of ways (Young and Friesen, 1992). One way is through direct inheritance: A son or daughter inherits the parents' business, and it seems easier and wiser to continue the family business than to go off on his or her own. Similarly, parents also exert influence by providing apprenticeship training. For example, a father who is a carpenter teaches his trade to his child by taking him or her along on the job or by arranging an apprenticeship with another carpenter. In the case of low-socioeconomic-status families, the adolescent may not have any other choices. Many mothers or fathers of such families have taught their skills to their children.

Parents influence children's interests and activities from the time they are young by the play materials provided, by the encouragement or discouragement of hobbies and interests, by the activities they encourage their children to participate in, and by the total experiences they provide in the family (Lent, Brown, and Hackett, 2000). Sibling influence also is important in stimulating masculine or feminine interests. A parent who is a musician exerts an influence on the child to take music lessons and to like music in a way that a nonmusician parent can never do. Similarly, a mother who is a lawyer usually wants her child to be exposed to that profession from the time the child is little.

Parents provide role models for their children to follow. Regardless of whether parents try to exert any conscious, direct influence, the influence by example is there. For example, Castellino, Lerner, Lerner, and von Eye (1998) found that a mother's feelings about her work—including its prestige and how satisfied she was in her role of an employed mother—predicted both male and female adolescents' career aspirations.

Parents sometimes direct, order, or limit the choices of their children by insisting they not go to school or go to a certain school, enroll in a particular major, or start out on a predetermined career. Parents who do so without regard for the talents, interests, and desires of their adolescent may be condemning the youth to a life of work to which she or he is unsuited. Often, an adolescent has no strong objections and accedes to parental wishes from a desire to please them and from not knowing what else to do. One of the motives of parents for taking such a course of action is to try to get the child to take up an occupation that the parents were always interested in but never got to do; the parents live vicariously through the child. Another motive is that the parents have a vocation in which they have found satisfaction, and so they urge the adolescent to share their goals because they are sure she or he would like it, too. Stories are legion of the father who insists his son attend his alma mater, join the same fraternity, play football as he did, and become a professional like himself. Some parents exert pressure by offering or withholding money or by getting their child into their alma maters. Other parents, of course, have very low educational and occupational expectations for their children, thus limiting the possible vocational choices (Galambos and Silbereisen, 1987).

It is also true, however, that of the one-third who do not choose an occupation in their parents' status cate-

PERSONAL ISSUES CAREER INDECISION AND FAMILY ENMESHMENT

Career development literature has largely ignored the role of family dynamics in making career decisions. Some adolescents are enmeshed and undifferentiated from their parents. In such situations, little individuation or differentiation has taken place, so adolescents have not extricated themselves from parental domination and have not developed autonomous self-identities. They suffer from low self-esteem, external locus of control, and anxiety and have trouble making career decisions. Decisions that are made are emotionally based and are reactions to the perceived wishes of parents (Kimmier, Brigman, and Noble, 1990).

gory, a number circumvent the entire status structure through extensive education in order to rise far above their parents. In this way, adolescents move from blue-collar positions into professions. Others become socially mobile downward, never aspiring or able to succeed as their parents have.

Teenagers believe that their parents have the right to try to influence their career decisions (Young, 1994), at least within limits. Although they believe that the decision should ultimately be theirs, adolescents think that it is appropriate for parents to intervene if their child is making an important vocational choice for a bad reason (e.g., because it is the easiest path or he or she wants to stay with a boyfriend or girlfriend). Teens do not think, however, that parents should use punishment or the threat of punishment when trying to change their children's minds (Bregman and Killen, 1999).

ANSWERS WOULDN'T YOU LIKE TO KNOW . . .

Do most teens think that their parents should have a say in their career plans?

Most teens believe that their parents should have *some* say in their career plans and are entitled to use gentle persuasion to guide them. Teens also believe, however, that unless they are being foolish, their parents should respect their choices.

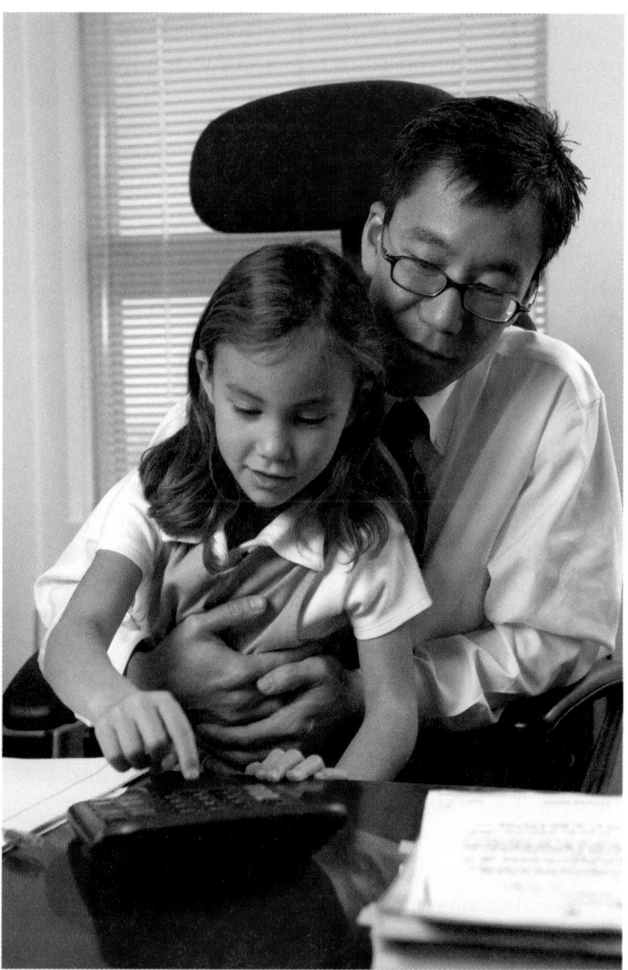

One way that parents can influence their adolescent's choice of vocation is by acting as a role model. "Take Your Children to Work" day gives a child the opportunity to see his or her parent on the job.

One study found that when two parents agree on educational expectations and goals for their adolescents, their children are more inclined to adopt the orientations held by both parents than are those who are supported by one parent and denied by the other (Smith, 1991). This same study indicated that agreement with the perceived educational goal of the mother is positively associated with the mother's formal education. In the case of the father, high occupational status—professional, managerial, or substantial business ownership—appears to increase adolescent agreement with perceived paternal educational goals. In summary, when the mother's education or the father's occupational status is high enough, it promotes adolescent agreement with the perceived educational goals of the parents (Smith, 1991).

An additional study found that family functioning dimensions, as evaluated by eleventh-grade students and their parents, were more frequent and stronger predictors of career development than gender, socioeconomic status, and educational achievement (Penick and Jepsen, 1992). In this study, *family functioning* was defined as the ability of the family to achieve objectives. It was measured by such factors as cohesion, expression, degree of conflict, organization, sociability, democratic government, enmeshment, and other factors that had to do with the family system. Families that show a democratic family style and are able to resolve conflict exert strong influences on career development of the adolescents in the family (Kracke and Schmitt-Rodermund, 2001). Other research has confirmed that adolescents who have strong attachments to their parents experience enhanced career development (Ketterson and Blustein, 1997).

ANSWERS WOULDN'T YOU LIKE TO KNOW ...

Who besides the parents can influence an adolescent's career choice?

Friends, teachers, coaches, and guidance counselors can all help influence an adolescent's career decision. Whether through encouragement or discouragement, such individuals can make a strong and lasting impression.

Peers

Studies of the relative influence of parents and peers on the educational plans of adolescents (relating to the level of vocation rather than to the particular job) reveal somewhat contradictory findings. Actually, the majority of adolescents hold plans in agreement with those of parents and their friends. Thus, friends reinforce parental aspirations because adolescents associate with peers whose goals are consistent with parental goals.

It has been found that the extent of upward mobility of working-class adolescents depends on the influences of both parents and peers. Working-class adolescents are most likely to aspire to high-ranking occupations if they are influenced in this direction by both parents and peers and are least likely to be high aspirers if they are subjected to neither of these influences.

In addition, Kracke (2002) found that friends could positively influence each other to think about career choices and to actively seek information about careers.

School Personnel

To what extent do school personnel influence adolescents' educational plans? In some instances, they have a great deal of influence. For example, a teacher or coach who acts as a student's mentor can provide information and advice about careers. Sometimes, a student's personal connection with a teacher makes him or her want to emulate that teacher, and a new career interest is born. Encouragement and praise from such individuals can give students a feeling of self-efficacy and competence with a particular subject, opening up the possibility of a related career.

Conversely, we probably all knew students who had the opposite experience: They were so bored or frightened by a teacher that they never pursued any more courses related to that teacher's topic again. Several girls in high school, for instance, stopped taking upper-level math courses because they were intimidated by a frankly sexist math teacher. He made them feel so stupid and self-conscious that they were convinced that they couldn't do math. The girls' ongoing refusal to take additional courses that even touched on mathematics (such as chemistry or physics) prevented them from being able to pursue science careers. Clearly, discouragement can be as powerful a tool as encouragement.

Teachers, coaches, and guidance counselors can help (or hinder!) students in conducting a realistic appraisal of their skills and abilities. These school personnel are likely to have knowledge about the types of skills needed for various occupations related to their disciplines. Given that, they can help students develop alternative, related goals if the students' initial goals do not seem plausible. In the field of psychology, for example, students should learn about the range of careers that exist in the helping profession. There are many alternative routes to working with people in need that most students don't know about. Giving these students advice as to how to build their résumés so that they will ultimately be employable is a large and enjoyable part of what college advisors do. Most colleges have a career services office that also can provide this sort of assistance.

GENDER ROLES AND VOCATIONAL CHOICE

Adolescents are strongly influenced by societal expectations as to the type of work that men and women should do (Jozefowicz, Barber, and Mollasis, 1994). Women have traditionally been channeled into a narrow range of careers: teacher, nurse, secretary, librarian, waitress, and so on. In 2002, only 29 percent of lawyers and 29 percent of physicians and surgeons were women (U.S. Bureau of Labor Statistics, 2005). See Figure 16.1 for a list of the jobs most and least likely to be held by American women.

Three types of barriers have been identified in efforts to explain why women are underrepresented in many high-paying professions (Fiorentine, 1988): *structural barriers, normative barriers,* and *cognitive differences.* **Structural barriers** are externally imposed limits on a woman's career success that result from gender discrimination. Some firms refuse to hire women for important jobs, deny them promotions even if they do well in the jobs they have, and deny them perks granted to male employees.

FIGURE 16.1 OCCUPATIONS WITH THE HIGHEST AND LOWEST PERCENTAGES OF FEMALE WORKERS

Source: Data from U.S. Bureau of the Census (2002).

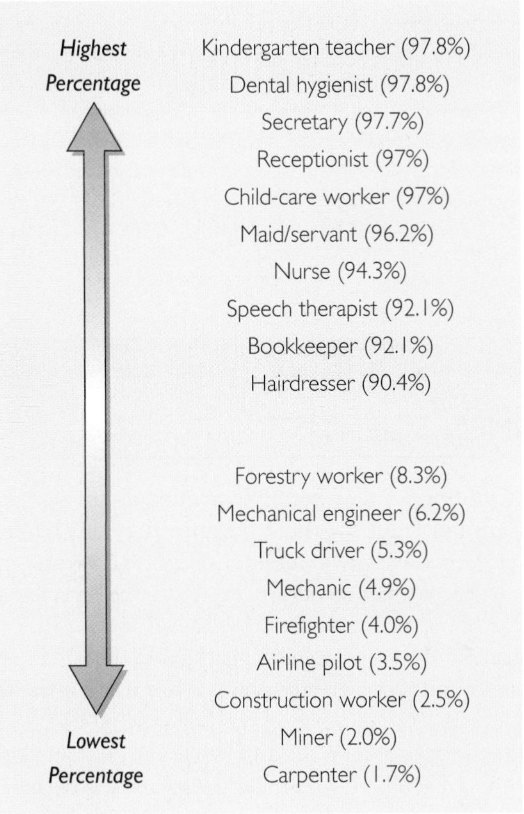

Adolescents are strongly influenced by societal expectations of what types of work women and men should do. That explains, in part, why there are many women kindergarten teachers but few women construction workers.

Normative barriers stem from how girls are socialized to want to be feminine, which for most includes valuing motherhood and placing great importance on the relationships in their lives. Having these goals can channel women away from high-powered careers, since caring for children while putting in 10-hour days at the office is a daunting prospect. Also, many women believe that their husbands' jobs come first, and so they make decisions that hurt their own career prospects.

The third barrier to women's professional success, cognitive differences, implies that women don't make it into executive and other high-level positions because they are different than men. Specifically, women are supposed to be less talented in certain domains or lack other traits, such as assertiveness, that are needed to climb to the top of the corporate ladder or make important scientific discoveries. If these views seem hopelessly old-fashioned, recall that the president of Harvard University, Larry Summers, was forced to resign in the summer of 2006 after he stated that he believed it's possible that women are cognitively incapable of being top-notch scientists.

Although diminishing, these structural and normative barriers also affect girls in high school and college. If girls are aware of these barriers or believe they exist (even if they do not), many will avoid career paths they perceive as difficult. While most female high school and college students say that their intention is to work until they reach retirement age, a large majority say they plan to get married and have children (Phillips and Imhoff, 1997). Since the burdens of child care continue to fall more heavily on women than men, in most cases, it is quite likely that adolescent girls weigh the demands of childrearing against their career plans differently than boys do, perhaps ruling out time-intensive careers or those with unpredictable hours.

structural barriers externally imposed limits on a woman's career success that result from sex discrimination.

normative barriers limitations on career choice that stem from how girls are socialized to be feminine.

As to cognitive differences, no significant gender differences in intelligence exist (see Chapter 7). Similarly, other potential differences—such as achievement, motivation, and self-confidence—are largely tied to how individuals perceive tasks. Both boys and girls are motivated to succeed when they believe that a given task is appropriate for their gender; both are more confident in their abilities when they perceive the task to be gender appropriate. Cognitive differences, such as they are, are not intrinsic to the sexes but result from gender stereotypes (Brannon, 1999).

Initially, girls have higher career aspirations than boys, perhaps because they are stronger students than

ANSWERS WOULDN'T YOU LIKE TO KNOW ...

Do men and women today have equal career opportunities?

Although the situation is gradually improving, many careers are still less available to women than men. Structural barriers include various types of gender discrimination, such as not promoting women to high-level positions. Normative barriers still exist, too. Women shoulder the bulk of family responsibilities and hence many shy away from having an intense, time-demanding career.

RESEARCH HIGHLIGHT WHY SO FEW WOMEN SCIENTISTS?

The path to becoming a scientist begins early—at the latest, while one is in high school. In order to pursue a science career, one must learn how to do science by taking the appropriate courses. Girls start off fine, succeeding as well or better than boys in math and science during elementary school. This begins to change in junior high school, although the differences at this point are small (American Association of University Women, 1992). Boys begin spending more time working on science activities during these years (Lee and Burkam, 1996), and by high school, boys have more positive attitudes than girls toward science (Weinburgh, 1995). When girls do elect to take science courses, they tend to limit themselves to biology, avoiding physics and chemistry.

This trend continues in college. Although 54 percent of the bachelor's degrees earned in the United States go to women, women earn only 47 percent of the math degrees, 41 percent of the chemistry degrees, and 17 percent of the physics degrees (National Science Foundation, 1996). Fewer than 10 percent of the graduate degrees in engineering and the natural sciences go to women (Betz and Schilano, 1999). The backgrounds of most women in high school and college who drop out of science suggest that they have the *ability* to succeed in science; what they seem to lack is the *desire* (Ware and Lee, 1988).

Why do girls avoid science? Many factors contribute, including sexism and discouragement from others. Girls who plan to pursue science are first and foremost interested in the topic but also have had a positive history with it: good grades, friends' support, extracurricular experiences, and encouraging mothers (Jacobs, Finken, Griffen, and Wright, 1998). Girls who shun science have not had this support. In addition, they perceive themselves as being different than "scientists" or "science students" (Lee, 1998); the career does not match their self-image, usually because the field is perceived as a masculine endeavor.

In addition, many young women feel that science careers are not right for them because they desire careers that let them have warm interactions with co-workers and help others. Women generally do not perceive science careers as being as conducive to these values as other types of careers and hence are less interested in them. Men place less value on these attributes and so are more attracted to the sciences (Morgan, Isaac, and Sansone, 2001).

Furthermore, girls tend to score lower than boys on measures of Holland's realistic personality type. Persons with realistic personalities like to tinker with objects, use their hands, and fix things. It follows that these individuals will likely gravitate toward careers in engineering and the natural sciences. Even when girls are interested in mechanical objects and manipulative kinds of activities, they often *feel less competent at them than boys.*

Betz and Schilano (1999) demonstrated that it is possible to raise young women's low levels of self-efficacy concerning mechanical objects. They devised a seven-hour intervention based on Bandura's (1977) four-part social learning model. During three sessions, college women were shown how to use various tools and to read blueprints. They were also given tasks with equipment and coached so that they succeeded in them, they were encouraged and rewarded for their efforts, and they practiced relaxation and anxiety reduction techniques. At the end of the intervention, the women felt more mechanically competent.

This study demonstrated that even a relatively short-term intervention can erase some of the negative feelings that limit women's occupational choices. If these sorts of activities were paired with encouragement, exploration opportunities, and female role modeling, more women would likely choose science careers.

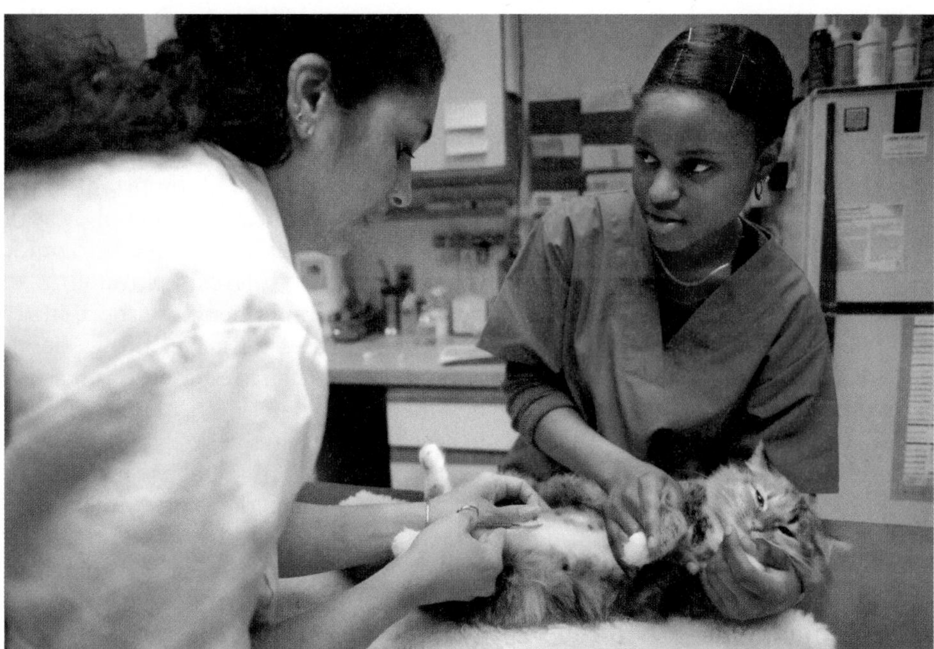

Adolescent girls are less likely than adolescent boys to be interested in science careers, in good part because working in the sciences is perceived as a masculine endeavor.

boys in their early years (Mau and Bikos, 2000). But after high school, girls' vocational aspirations drop, becoming more traditional and less prestigious. Many young women ultimately opt for careers that underutilize their talents and abilities (O'Brien, Friedman, Tipton, and Linn, 2000). The interplay of socialization, role expectations, discrimination (real or perceived), and different interests contributes to this drop.

OTHER CRUCIAL DETERMINANTS OF VOCATIONAL CHOICE

Mental ability has been shown to be important to vocational choice in several ways.

Intelligence

First, intelligence has been shown to be related to the decision-making ability of the individual. Bright adolescents are more likely to make vocational choices in keeping with their intellectual abilities, interests, capacities, and opportunities to receive training. The less bright are more likely to make unrealistic choices. They more often choose glamorous or high-prestige occupations for which they are not qualified or even interested except for the prestige. They more often choose what they think parents want them to do or what peers consider desirable rather than what they are capable of doing.

Second, intelligence has been shown to relate to the level of aspiration. Students who show superior academic ability and performance tend to aspire to higher occupational choices than those with lesser ability.

Third, intelligence is related to the ability of the individual to succeed or fail in a given occupation. For this reason, the vocational counselor usually measures level of intelligence as a beginning in assessing the vocational qualifications of a given student, because some occupations require a higher ability than others. However, a high intelligent quotient (IQ) is no guarantee of vocational success, nor is a low IQ a prediction of failure. Interest, motivation, other abilities, and various personality traits determine success as much as intelligence does. A high IQ shows only that the individual has the capacity to succeed as far as intelligence is concerned, but actual achievement must also be taken into account. Bright, high-achieving students are generally superior to bright, underachieving students in study habits, aspiration levels, and professionally oriented career expectations. A bright individual who is poorly motivated and indifferent may fail in an occupation, whereas an individual of average mental ability who is highly motivated, industrious, and conscientious may overachieve and far surpass the brighter person.

Furthermore, where do the IQ requirements for different occupations begin? There is actually a great deal of overlap in tested intelligence among workers in various jobs. How smart do you have to be to be a miner? an accountant? a physician? Some people who become successful physicians, teachers, engineers, or business executives show on tests that their intelligence is much below average for their professions.

Educational institutions are faced with a dilemma in deciding on the cutoff point below which they will not admit students. Although SAT scores are helpful in predicting possibilities of success or failure for groups of students, they are not sure indicators of the individual. Counselors must be extremely cautious in interpreting test results, particularly in predicting success or failure based on mental ability alone. Many individuals who are now successful in professional fields would not be admitted to the training programs if they had to pass the entrance exams today.

Aptitudes and Special Abilities

Different occupations require different aptitudes and special abilities. For instance, some occupations require strength, others speed, and still others good eye-hand coordination or good spatial visualization. Some require special talent such as artistic, musical, or verbal skills. Some fields require creativity, originality, and autonomy; others require conformity, cooperation, and ability to take direction. Possession or lack of certain aptitudes may be crucial in immediate job success or in the possibility of success with training and experience. Certainly, increasing technology requires more and more specialized training and abilities.

The measurement of some aptitudes, however, is not an exact science; therefore, it cannot always be determined which people are most likely to succeed in particular occupations. The fault lies generally with the tests used. Before relying too much on aptitude tests, counselors and students should be certain that the instruments used are valid measurements of the aptitudes tested.

Interests

Interest is another factor considered important to vocational success. The more interested people are in their work, the more likely they will succeed. To put it another way, the more their interests parallel those who are already successful in a field, the more likely they are to be successful, too, all other things being equal. Vocational interest tests are based on this last principle: They measure clusters of interests similar to those of successful people in the field to predict the possibilities of success. The individual is counseled to consider vocations in the fields of greatest interest.

Intelligence, ability, opportunities, and other factors must be related to interests for success in a field (Prediger and Brandt, 1991). Factor analysis of the **Strong Vocational Interest Blank** (Strong, 1943) indicates that interests may be subdivided and grouped to some degree by level. There are professional-scientific, professional-technical, and subprofessional-technical groups, as well as others. Interests are related to both the field and level of occupational choice. Interests that are based on abilities are stronger and more realistic than those influenced primarily by such things as prestige factors and group values. However, there is only a low correlation between interests and aptitudes.

CROSS-CULTURAL CONCERNS THE SCHOOL-TO-WORK TRANSITION FOR AMERICAN VERSUS EUROPEAN ADOLESCENTS

Kerckhoff (2002) has described a number of aspects of American adolescents' school-to-work transition that are unique to these youths or at least different from those faced by adolescents in most European countries. How do the American and European experiences differ?

1. Most American students pursue general courses of study that are not tied to specific careers, whereas European students tend to be more career focused.
2. American adolescents generally have less institutional support for their job searches.
3. In the United States, the two criteria that are most important in getting a job are having a high school diploma and having a college degree. These two accomplishments are usually attained years apart, and many adolescents drop out of college. Those who do graduate from college find that further study does not dramatically increase their employment prospects.
4. American adolescents are generally older than European adolescents when they begin working full time.
5. Having a college degree is more important for American than European adolescents. The gap in the kinds of jobs, pay scales, benefits, and promotional opportunities available to those with a bachelor's degree and those without is greater in the United States than in Europe.
6. American adolescents without a college degree are more likely to face periods of unemployment than their European counterparts.
7. American adolescents are more likely to return to school after they have been working full time than European adolescents.

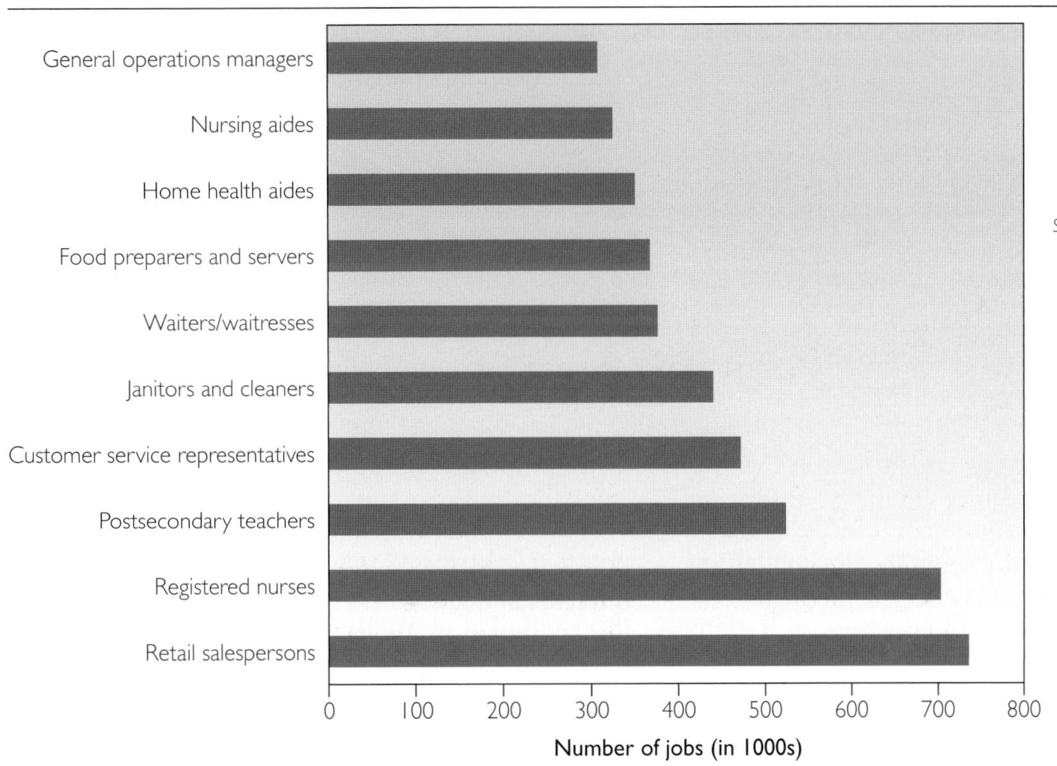

FIGURE 16.2 OCCUPATIONS PROJECTED TO GAIN THE MOST NEW JOBS, 2004–2014

Source: Data from Hecker (2005).

Job Opportunities

Being interested in a field does not mean that jobs are available in it. Some employment fields, such as agricultural workers, are becoming smaller; others, such as clerical workers, are becoming larger. There has been a continued shift toward white-collar and service occupations. This means youths need to control interests as well as be controlled by them, for interests and job availability are not synonymous (Mitchell, 1988).

What are the employment opportunities in various occupations? Figure 16.2 shows projected increases from 2004 to 2014 in selected occupations (Hecker, 2005). The jobs showing the greatest numbers of openings are (in declining order) retail salespersons, registered nurses, postsecondary teachers, customer service representatives, janitors, waiters/waitresses, food preparers and servers (e.g., fast food workers), home health aides, nursing aides, and general operations managers. Clearly, most of these jobs do not require having a bachelor's degree. Figure 16.3 lists the careers *that do require a college degree* and

Strong Vocational Interest Blank a test that measures suitability for different vocations according to interests.

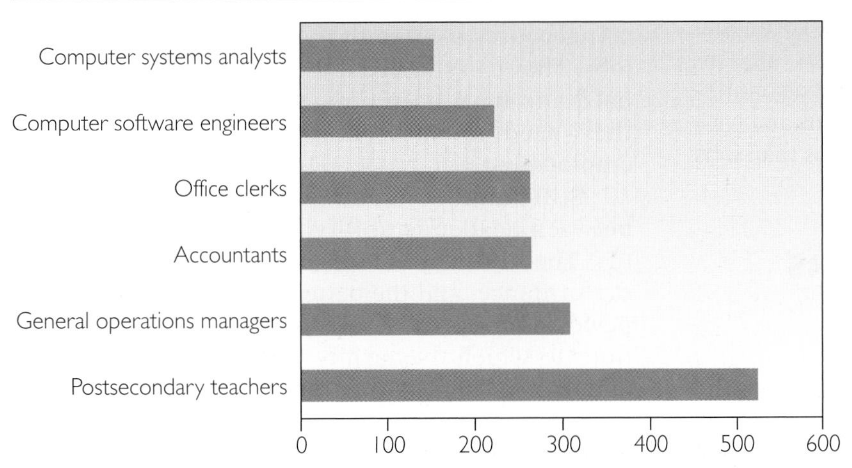

FIGURE 16.3 PROJECTED GAINS IN CAREERS REQUIRING COLLEGE DEGREES, 2004–2014

Source: Data from Hecker (2005).

TABLE 16.2 AVERAGE STARTING SALARIES OFFERED TO GRADUATES WITH BACHELOR'S DEGREES, 2005

FIELD	AVERAGE STARTING SALARY
Actuary	$52,741
Electrical engineer	$51,888
Computer scientist	$50,820
Chemist	$32,500
Advertising	$31,340
Teacher	$30,496
Forester	$27,950
Economist	$24,667

Source: Data from *Occupational Outlook Handbook,* U.S. Bureau of Labor Statistics (2006).

projected to have the most openings through 2014. Note that postsecondary teachers, general operations managers, and accountants head the list.

Salary

One factor that plays a role in vocational selection is the salary that can be expected. Salaries, of course, vary widely by profession; there are also regional variations in compensation. Table 16.2 shows the average starting salaries for 2005 graduates with bachelor's degrees in different fields.

Prestige

Some adolescents want to go into certain occupations because they sound glamorous or have high prestige. There are at least five commonly accepted assumptions about occupational values in U.S. culture: (1) White-collar work is superior, (2) self-employment is superior, (3) clean occupations are superior, (4) the importance of a business occupation depends on the size of the business, and (5) personal service is degrading (that is, it is better to be employed by an enterprise than to do the same work for an individual).

Another way to group values is to divide them into three major value clusters: people oriented, extrinsic reward oriented, and self-expression oriented. Vocational selection will depend partly on which values are considered more important. Community values also influence youths. Jobs considered most prestigious and with the highest status are more desired by youths than jobs with lower prestige and status.

SOCIOECONOMIC FACTORS

Familiarity

Socioeconomic status (SES) tends to influence the knowledge and understanding youths have of different occupations. Middle-SES parents are more able than lower-SES parents to develop broad vocational interests and awareness of opportunities beyond the local community. Adolescents from low-SES families have seen less, read less, heard less about, and experienced less variety in their environment in general and have fewer opportunities than youths from higher SES levels. As a result, low-SES adolescents are inclined to take the only jobs they know about at the time they enter the labor market. The socioeconomic and cultural backgrounds of youths influence their job knowledge and their job preferences (Weinger, 2000).

Social Status and Aspirations

Middle-SES youths tend to choose occupations with higher status than do lower-SES youths. There are a number of considerations in determining why this is so. To aspire to a position is one thing; to expect to actually achieve it is another. Poverty-level youths more often than middle-SES youths aspire to jobs they do not expect to achieve, but the fact that lower-SES youths realize the remoteness of reaching their goal makes them lower their level of aspirations. Of course, sometimes guidance counselors, teachers, parents, or others try to persuade lower-status youths to attempt to break into higher-paying jobs. They can succeed if they have the drive to work hard and have been provided with the basic skills they need to succeed in their chosen field of employment.

Still another factor enters in: a correlation between academic ability and socioeconomic status. The higher the status, the higher the academic performance; and the better the students' academic performances, the more prestigious the occupations to which they aspire (e.g., Watson, Quatman, and Edler, 2002). Apparently, students see their high academic ability as providing them access to high-prestige occupations. Occupational aspira-

IN THEIR OWN WORDS

"Am I glad I worked at a fast-food restaurant? Yeah, I definitely am (though I probably would have had a different answer if you had asked me that at six in the morning before work). I wasn't planning on working there—let me start with that. However, I learned very quickly that freedom of choice in the job market for precollege teens is basically nonexistent. So my good friend got me a job and that was that.

"What an eye-opener. It was a great thing to do before heading off to college. To be blunt, that is not a job I would want to wake up to every day of my life, so I had better not screw up the next four years because I need that degree. You know, I think one major fault in today's society is in what types of careers receive respect. World-famous doctors and lawyers and successful businesspeople all deserve a whole bunch of kudos for their talent, tenacity, and hard work. But at least when they drive off to work every morning in their BMWs from their nice homes, they are going to do something that not only pays well but that they genuinely enjoy doing. Fast-food workers, on the other hand, get a crappy job, no appreciation, and a whole lot less money for what they do. Now tell me, which would you prefer? I have enormous admiration for people who get up every day for a job they hate that doesn't even pay well but do it anyways so that they can support themselves and their families.

"I have no brilliant philosophy to sum it all up, but I seriously think the country would be a better place if everyone had to work fast food at least once in their lives. I learned a lot about the real world."

tion is related to both social class and academic aptitude.

Race/Ethnicity and Aspirations

When race and ethnicity are considered apart from socioeconomic status, there is little evidence that race or ethnicity alone is the determinative factor in occupational aspirations (Fouad and Byars-Winston, 2005). However, African American youths of lower socioeconomic status have lower aspirations, just as do White youths of lower status. Regardless of aspirations, there are fewer employment opportunities for youths than for adults and fewer opportunities for African Americans than for Whites—and they know it (Gloria and Hird, 1999).

Some studies have found differences between Asian Americans and White Americans in their occupational aspirations. Asian Americans place greater emphasis on extrinsic and security occupational value clusters (e.g., making more money and having a stable, prestigious, secure future) in comparison with White Americans (Leung, Ivey, and Susuki, 1994). This effect is much more pronounced for Asian American women than Asian American men (Song and Glick, 2004).

ANSWERS WOULDN'T YOU LIKE TO KNOW . . .

Do most teenagers have jobs?

Yes. If we count freelance jobs such as baby-sitting and lawn mowing, most teens begin working by age 14. More than 90 percent of teens work at some point before they graduate from high school.

YOUTH EMPLOYMENT

The vast majority of American teenagers today work before they graduate from high school. Is this a good trend? Do the short- and long-term benefits of working outweigh the costs? How much work is too much? How does uncompensated work (volunteering) benefit adolescent development? These are the questions we will address in this section.

Working for Wages

Scope of Youth Employment

The number of adolescents who work outside the home for wages has increased dramatically in the past few decades. In 1987, about one-third of high school sophomores and two-thirds of high school seniors held jobs during the school year. In the mid to late 1990s, however, more than three-fourths worked by age 16. And when irregular freelance work, such as baby-sitting and lawn mowing, are included, that figure rises to over 90 percent (Mihalic and Elliott, 1997).

Many teenagers begin working even before they enter high school, especially when those with irregular jobs are included in the count. In one study, more than half of 14-year-olds reported having had some kind of job, and among 15-year-olds, that figure rose to about 65 percent. In all, nearly 3 million 15- to 17-year-old adolescents work during the academic year, and 4 million work during the summer months (Herman, 2000).

What kinds of work do adolescents do? Many jobs are forbidden to adolescents, especially those younger than 16. Table 16.3 lists some of federal limits on adolescent employment.

Most adolescent girls work in restaurants and retail stores, especially grocery stores. They also work in entertainment venues (such as movie theaters), serve as maids and child-care workers, and are employed by

TABLE 16.3 FEDERAL LIMITS ON ADOLESCENT EMPLOYMENT

LIMITS ON 14- AND 15-YEAR-OLDS	LIMITS ON 16- AND 17-YEAR-OLDS
Cannot work in manufacturing, processing, and mining jobs	Cannot work with hazardous materials
Cannot work in transportation, construction, and warehouse jobs	Cannot operate motor vehicles
Cannot use power-driven machinery	Cannot operate most power-driven machinery
During academic year: Cannot work during school hours; Cannot work more than 18 hours/week; Cannot work more than 3 hours/day; Hours restricted to 7 A.M. through 7 P.M.	Cannot work in most excavating or demolition jobs
During summer months: Cannot work more than 40 hours/week; Cannot work more than 8 hours/day; Hours restricted to 7 A.M. through 9 P.M.	Cannot work in mines
	Cannot work in slaughterhouses

Source: Fair Labor Standards Act, as cited by National Consumer League (2000).

construction firms. Most boys also work in restaurants, retail stores, and construction, but they are more likely than girls to work as landscaping aids, with livestock, in factories, and in gas stations. Girls are more likely to work freelance than boys, and they are more likely to be employed by private individuals rather than by companies. Figure 16.4 illustrates the breakdown of school-year employment for male and female adolescents.

Other gender differences in employment include the fact that boys are more likely to work during the school year than girls, and boys work longer hours. However, these gender differences decrease as teenagers get older.

RESEARCH HIGHLIGHT WORK, MILITARY, OR COLLEGE?

One study took data from the Youth in Transition Study (YIT) directed by Jerald Bachman at the University of Michigan. The study attempted to identify those factors that led boys to enter the work force, the military, or college after graduation from high school.

Work was chosen by boys from large families who were in the lower socioeconomic strata, were enrolled in high school vocational tracks, and were working more hours in their senior year, as compared with those in the college group. Compared with members of any other context, workers tended to have the lowest intellectual ability and to have friends who were the least impressed by going to college. Boys who early on believed that their parents wanted them to enter the work force after high school were significantly more likely to enter work over the military context.

In relation to those who went into the *military,* this was chosen by boys who tended to express little desire to attend college, were generally from large families in the lower socioeconomic strata, were enrolled in a vocational track, and were poor students when contrasted to the boys headed for college. The military bound, as opposed to those headed for one of the other choices, were most likely to come from nonfarm backgrounds, to have failed a grade, and to believe their parents would be happy if they served in the military. The military group tended to express more hawkish attitudes, but were not significantly more hawkish than the college-bound group.

College choice was accepted by boys who came from the smallest families and the highest socioeconomic-status backgrounds, had the highest grade-point averages and were in a college track, had a strong intention of going to college, and worked the least number of hours in twelfth grade. Boys with higher intellectual ability and friends who were impressed by going to college were more likely to go to college instead of to work (Owens, 1992).

Other research indicates that African American teens are more likely to enlist than either Latino or non-Hispanic Caucasian youth, and that Latios are more likely to enlist than Caucasians. Those who join the military are more likely to come from one-parent homes and to be from the South (Bachman, Segal, Freedman-Doan, and O'Malley, 2000).

FIGURE 16.4 JOBS HELD BY 15- TO 17-YEAR-OLD MALES AND FEMALES DURING THE ACADEMIC YEAR

Source: Herman (2000), p. 36.

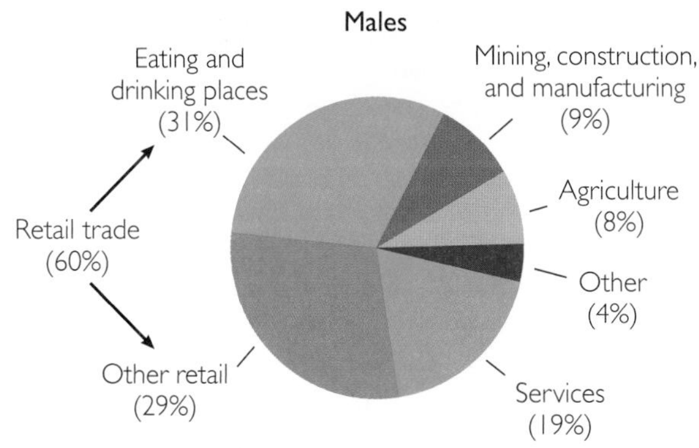

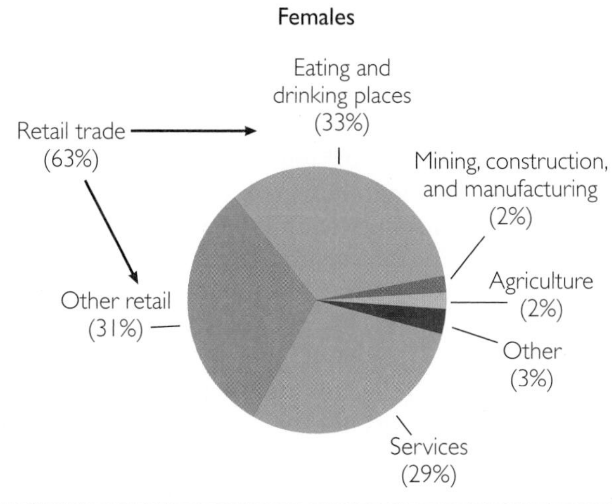

ANSWERS WOULDN'T YOU LIKE TO KNOW ...

Which teens are most likely to work?

White, middle-SES-level teenagers from intact families are more likely to work than adolescents from other SES and racial/ethnic groups. Why? They have more access to jobs, as it's easer for them to get hired and to have the transportation needed to get to work. These teens do not have a greater desire to work than others.

How long do adolescents work and how much do they get paid? Fifteen- to seventeen-year-olds who have jobs work an average of 17 hours a week during the school year (Herman, 2000), and 29 hours a week during the summer months (Stringer, 2003). In 1998, they earned an average of $5.57 an hour, which was more than the minimum wage of $5.15 an hour (Herman, 2000).

Usually the number of teenagers who work for wages increases dramatically during the summer months. (Adolescents obviously have more free time once school is no longer is session.) In recent years, this trend has become less evident. In July 2004, the proportion of 16- to 19-year-olds who were either employed or looking for work was 67.2 percent; this was the lowest percentage since 1966. Most economists attribute this to the fact that more and more students are attending summer school. Whereas summer school used to be something of a last resort for students who had fallen behind, summer courses are now taken by a much broader range of students (for example, those who wish to be able to fit in additional science courses before they graduate). Students who are enrolled in summer school are quite a bit less likely also to work than students who do not take summer classes (Bureau of Labor Statistics, 2004).

Correlates of Adolescent Employment

In addition to gender, other factors predict which adolescents will and will not work. White adolescents are more likely to be employed than minority adolescents. Adolescents from higher-SES homes are more likely to work than those from lower-SES homes, and those from intact families are more likely to work than those from single-parent families. Since teenagers living in low-SES neighborhoods likely cannot find work as readily as middle-SES teenagers, each of these differences is probably a matter of job availability rather than one of motivation.

Effects of Employment

Most people believe that working is good for teenagers (Mortimer, 2003). After all, it teaches them responsibility, exposes them to the world of work, and gives them the opportunity to manage their own money. Are these people correct? The cost/benefit ratio seems to depend on three factors: how many hours per week are spent at the job, the nature of the job itself, and how many weeks per year are spent working.

Most researchers agree that youths should not spend too many hours working. By any standard, however, American teens spend a lot of time working compared to teens in other industrialized nations. Whereas most American high school students work part time, only about 25 percent of Japanese and Taiwanese students do (Fuligni and Stevenson, 1995); almost no French or Russian teenagers work (Alsaker and Flammer, 1999). Moreover, U.S. adolescents work longer hours: 50 minutes per day for American students versus 15 minutes per day for Northern European students (Larson and Verma, 1999).

The first real job for many adolescents is at a fast-food restaurant. The boring nature of the work, the rapid pace, and the low pay may sour some adolescents' attitudes toward work but prompt others to continue with their education and prepare themselves for a better career.

The question is, How much is *too* much? There are two competing views. The first is that any employment is bad since it takes adolescents away from other, more important activities, such as schoolwork or family time. The second is that work is good in small doses, even though too much is harmful. Again, most adults believe this. If this were true, then teenagers who work only a few hours per week should look better than teenagers who do not work at all, but teens who work many hours should look worse.

Which view is correct? Although the data are somewhat contradictory, the best research converges on the same answer: The common wisdom is wrong. In most cases, *any* amount of working does more harm than good. For example, Marsh and Kleitman (2005) analyzed data collected on 12,000 students from the time they entered middle school until two years after high school graduation. Even after taking into account the effects causes by socioeconomic status, ethnicity, family constellation, and so on, the researchers found a strong, negative pattern of effects of working in grades eight, ten, and twelve on twelfth-grade and post-secondary outcomes. For example, those who worked were less likely to have assumed leadership roles, were more likely to have developed bad habits, had worse grades, participated in fewer extracurricular activities, took easier courses, and were less likely to go to college. Somewhat surprisingly, working as a senior was more harmful than working as a sophomore or as a middle school student. Fifteen of the twenty-three outcomes the researchers examined were adversely affected by working as a senior. The only positive effect was that those who worked were more likely to be employed after they left high school than those who had not. Furthermore, the hill-shaped function that one would expect with the commonsense model (a little is good, a lot is bad) was not seen for any of the variables the researchers examined; instead, the effects were largely linear and cumulative. In other words, two hours was worse than one, three hours was worse than two, and so on.

ANSWERS WOULDN'T YOU LIKE TO KNOW ...

Is it good or bad for adolescents to have paying jobs?

It's more good than bad for lower-income adolescents, as having had a job will help them get another job after high school. But working is more bad than good for middle-class adolescents, especially if they work long hours.

Other studies have had similar results in analyzing other outcome variables. Other negative outcomes that have been associated with working include increased absenteeism, less time spent with family, diminished parental control, and increased use of alcohol and marijuana (Manning, 1990; Steinberg and Dornbusch, 1991; Warren, 2002).

What explains the negative outcomes of employment? Since most of the studies were correlational rather than experimental—that is, they compared self-selected groups of working adolescents with self-selected nonworkers—it is legitimate to wonder the degree to which the differences in substance abuse, poor grades, and the like existed before the employed adolescents began working or if they resulted from working. The causality does appear to go in both directions: That is, students who are disengaged from school and family are more likely to work, and those who work are more likely to see their grades drop, spend less time at home, and so forth (Mihalic and Elliott, 1997). Working directly contributes to problem behavior by providing youths the income to spend on alcohol and drugs, the time away from home to privately engage in undesirable behaviors, and the opportunity to be with peers who are uninterested in school and prove to be delinquent.

Steinberg and his colleagues (Steinberg, Greenberger, Garduque, Ruggiero, and Vaux, 1982) were the first to suggest that adolescents who work are likely to develop cynical, negative attitudes about working, including tolerance for petty theft and for lying to the boss. Many adolescents develop negative attitudes when they work because they work at stressful, fast-paced, unpleasant jobs that they feel are irrelevant to their future career goals (Mortimer, Pimentel, Ryu, Nash, and Lee, 1996; Ritzer, 2000). When adolescents work in interesting, agreeable jobs, they don't become cynical. Unfortunately, even brief exposure to a noxious workplace can increase cynicism (Loughlin and Barling, 1998), and the longer one spends working in unsatisfying conditions, the more likely one will develop a pessimistic, unethical attitude (Mihalic and Elliott, 1997).

From the adolescent's point of view, of course, working has benefits. First and foremost, it provides them with money to buy things they would like. (Most of the money that teenagers earn goes to buying themselves luxury items rather than to helping support the family or to saving for college.) Besen (2006) claims that jobs also give adolescents a sense of control over their lives (due, in part, to having disposable income that is under their own control), a time when they can be in charge, outlets for creativity, and a time to be with and talk to friends. (This may explain why one often has to wait 10 minutes for a latte at a coffee bar.)

Several studies have suggested that working while in high school is not a risk factor for impoverished youth (National Research Council, 1998); in fact, it helps them find jobs once they leave school. (This ties back to Marsh and Kleitman's findings.) In addition, working during high school significantly increases students' earning power after high school (Ruhn, 1994). This is, in part, because students from low-income homes who work are more likely to complete high school than those who do not work (Carr, Wright, and Brody, 1996). Impoverished male adolescents who work are more likely to go on to college than their nonworking counterparts (Leventhal, Graber, and Brooks-Gunn, 2001), which might suggest that working during high school is indicative of high aspirations in poverty-class youth.

IN THEIR OWN WORDS

"I would strongly agree that a real problem with adolescent employment is the large number of stressful, boring, and irrelevant jobs. I worked one summer as a cashier at a pharmacy, and I spent a lot of my time there dealing with a hung-over manager, sweeping the floors, and getting yelled at by little old ladies because Revlon stopped making their favorite color lipstick. I never got any positive feedback, and I felt like a monkey could have done my job with enough training.

"The pharmacy job wasn't completely awful, but I had a much better experience doing occasional volunteer work during the school year. I worked with kids at Volunteers of America, and I actually felt useful there. I also got exposure to a lot of different kinds of people and situations, whereas the pharmacy only exposed me to other bored and frustrated teenagers. It would have been nice to do the volunteer-type work while also getting paid!"

ANSWERS WOULDN'T YOU LIKE TO KNOW . . .

Do adolescents like doing unpaid volunteer work?

Most adolescents who do volunteer work find it a good experience and say that they plan to continue volunteering in the future.

Volunteerism

Just as youths' participation in paid employment has increased over the past 30 years, so has their participation in *unpaid employment.* Between 50 percent and 65 percent of high school students do at least some volunteer work each year (Niemi, Hepburn, and Chapman, 2000). And given the benefits that volunteerism brings to self and society, support for volunteer programs is high. The federal government earmarked $30 million to fund community service programs for students in 1993, and youth volunteer work was a focus of the 1997 President's Summit for America's Future, chaired by General Colin Powell. Many high schools now require students to engage in some community service work.

Research has found that adolescents from two-parent homes, especially those in which the mother is a full-time homemaker, are most likely to donate their time (Raskoff and Sundeen, 1994). Adolescents are more likely to engage in public service work if their parents also do so, if they are from higher-level socioeconomic backgrounds, and if they have high grade point averages (Hart, Atkins, and Ford, 1998; Keith, Nelson, Schlabach, and Thompson, 1990). Some studies have found that girls are more likely to volunteer than boys, while other studies have found no gender differences in participation rates.

Community service appears to provide a number of benefits. Volunteers gain skills and knowledge.

Identity development is stimulated when individuals reflect on their place in society, their moral values, and their role in social change (Yates and Youniss, 1996). Community service is correlated with high self-esteem (Johnson, Beebe, Mortimer, and Snyder, 1998) and low levels of problematic behaviors (Eccles and Barber, 1999). Volunteering also increases the likelihood of attending college (Eccles and Barber, 1999). It encourages interest in knowledge of politics and prompts political discussions with parents and others (Niemi, Hepburn, and Chapman, 2000). Equally important, volunteering helps others in the community. One study found that 90 percent of the adolescent volunteers surveyed felt they had benefited from their service and would do it again (Hamilton and Fenzel, 1988).

Research into adolescent community service is only beginning. However, it is clear that some volunteer opportunities are more useful than others. While some teenagers stuff envelopes for a political candidate in a room with other students, others go out into the community and mingle with people different from themselves. Metz, McLellan, and Youniss (2003) compared adolescents who participated in social cause service (e.g., providing meals for elderly shut-ins) with those who participated in more standard youth service (e.g., tutoring fellow students; helping with office work). Although almost all of the volunteers found their experience enjoyable and planned to volunteer in the future, only those who had actively interacted with needy individuals showed enhanced social concern.

In any case, schools can enhance the benefits of community service by preparing the students beforehand and giving them opportunities for reflection afterward (Blyth, Saito, and Berkas, 1997).

ADOLESCENTS AND UNEMPLOYMENT

One of the major social problems in the United States is unemployment among youths.

Numbers of Unemployed Youths

In 2002, 12.7 percent of White 16- to 19-year-old adolescents were unemployed. Rates were even higher among minority youths: 29 percent of African American adolescents and 17.7 percent of Hispanic American adolescents were unable to find work (U.S. Bureau of the Census, 2003a). Figure 16.5 shows comparable figures for young adults 20 to 24 years of age. Altogether, this means that 2.6 million young people, aged 16 to 24, were out of work in 2002.

FIGURE 16.5 UNEMPLOYMENT RATE BY AGE AND RACE/ETHNICITY: 2002

Source: U.S. Bureau of the Census (2002).

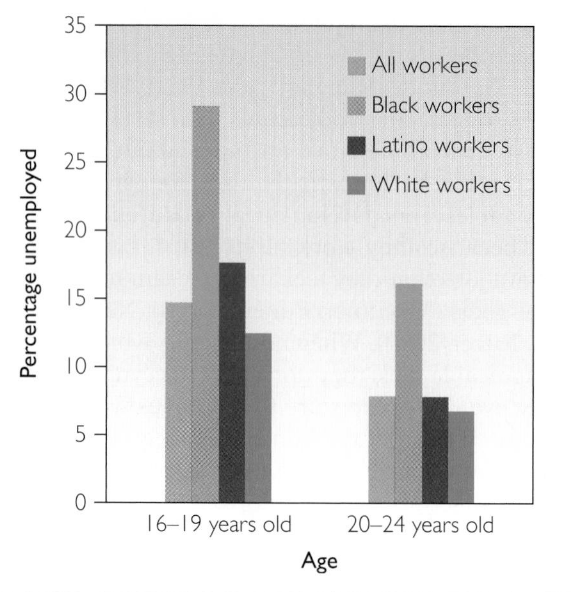

The highest unemployment is among African American teenagers, and this is true whether they are in school or not. Also, the jobless rate of Hispanic American youths is above the rate for their White counterparts but much lower than that for African Americans. These statistics probably underestimate the extent of the problem, for many adolescents who get discouraged and stop looking for work are not counted as unemployed. This high rate of joblessness means more crime, more drug addiction, more social unrest, and less income for many poor families.

Causes of Unemployment

Why is the rate of unemployment among youths so high? One reason is that they have little training and skill, little experience, and many are able to take only part-time jobs while in school. They are confined to a narrower range of the less-skilled occupations, at which many can work only part time. Youths with a high school diploma have better chances in the labor market than do dropouts, as is reflected by lower unemployment rates among graduates. Figure 16.6 shows the employment status of high school graduates and dropouts in the labor force. Many employers require educational degrees that have little relationship to job skills; dropouts are often denied work not because they cannot do the job but because they do not have the necessary credentials.

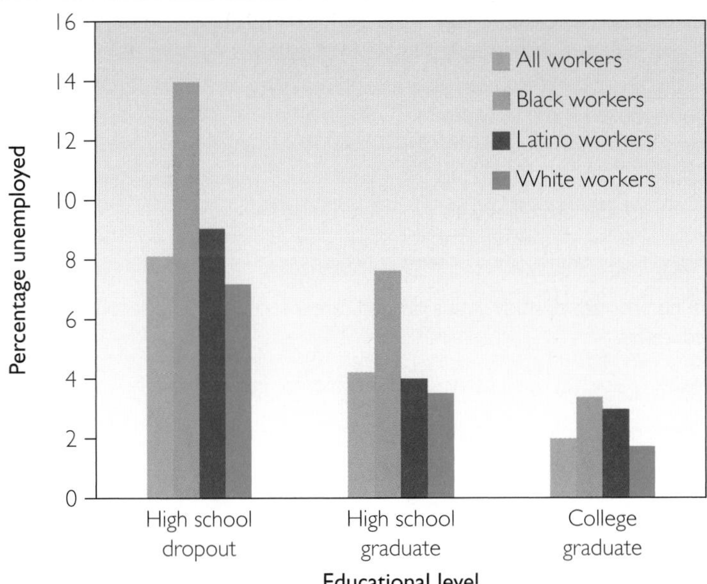

FIGURE 16.6 UNEMPLOYMENT RATE AS A FUNCTION OF EDUCATIONAL LEVEL AND RACE/ETHNICITY: 2001

Source: U.S. Bureau of the Census (2002).

ANSWERS WOULDN'T YOU LIKE TO KNOW . . .

What's the best thing you can do to avoid being unemployed later in life?

The best way to avoid unemployment is to graduate from college! The unemployment rate is much lower for college graduates than for people with less education.

Many unemployed youths are recent college graduates who are searching for first-time jobs. Some of these graduates have majored in subjects that do not directly prepare them for employment. For some, it is fairly normative to be out of work for a while before they can find something that is compatible with their education.

State licensing boards often operate to restrict entry into business. The Colorado Board of Cosmetology, for example, requires that a prospective hairdresser take 1,450 hours of instruction, including 100 hours of supervised practice at shampooing. Such requirements hit the young hardest, especially those who seek to combine work with schooling. Union requirements also limit participation of the young. It takes time and experience to acquire membership in a union; therefore, adolescents are not able to accept jobs in the construction industry, for example, which could be an important source of part-time and summer employment. Many unions also limit the number of apprentices that can be trained. In cases of layoffs, seniority rules work in favor of the older, more experienced workers; youths are the first to lose their jobs.

Minimum wage legislation may sometimes affect unemployment. When the minimum wage goes up relative to the low productivity of inexperienced youths, employers hesitate to hire them, often preferring older people if they are available. Furthermore, job turnover among youths is higher than among older, more stable workers. Some employers will not hire anybody under age 21 for steady jobs; they want those who have a greater degree of maturity.

On the other hand, the average period of unemployment among youths is shorter than among older workers. Females average somewhat shorter periods of unemployment than males, and Whites shorter periods than non-Whites. The fact that half of all unemployed youths have no more than four weeks without work reflects the seasonal and intermittent nature of their unemployment and the rapid turnover of jobs.

CAREER EDUCATION

Almost all Americans, men and women, work for wages for a significant portion of their adult lives. Individuals work to earn money, to achieve autonomy, and to enjoy self-fulfillment. Society needs workers to produce goods and perform services. It is crucial, therefore, that schools help prepare adolescents for careers. As discussed in Chapter 15, high schools offer different curricular tracks. Some students are college bound. Although the basic skills they will eventually need in the workplace are learned, in part, during primary and secondary school (reading, math, oral skills, etc.), it is expected that their college educations will

TABLE 16.4 TYPES OF SCHOOL-TO-WORK PROGRAMS

PROGRAM	DESCRIPTION
Job shadowing	Spending time with someone at his or her worksite
Mentoring	Being matched with an individual in a certain occupation
Cooperative education	Combining academic and vocational studies with a job in a related field
School-sponsored enterprise	Producing goods or services for sale or use by others
Technical preparation	Participating in a planned program of study with a defined career focus that links secondary and postsecondary education
Apprenticeship/Internship	Working for an employer to learn about a particular occupation or industry
Career major	Taking a defined sequence of courses to prepare for a specific occupation

Source: U.S. Bureau of Labor Statistics (2000).

prepare them for their careers. Many students, however, never go on to college. The job training and career skills they need must be acquired largely, if not exclusively, in high school.

In fact, many non–college bound youths are at a disadvantage when they try to enter the job market. Employers complain that teenagers lack basic academic skills and are unable to find information when they need it. Some are said to lack interpersonal skills, initiative, and effective work habits initiative (Taylor, 2005). To try to remedy this situation, Congress passed the School-to-Work Opportunities Act in 1994, which provides federal funds to schools that attempt to develop more effective job training.

Several types of programs have been developed to better link school with work and to improve the employment prospects of high school graduates (Lewis, Stone, Shipley, and Madzar, 1998) (see Table 16.4). **Tech-prep programs** involve partnerships between high schools and two-year, postsecondary vocational institutions. In this type of program, the student selects a career at the end of his or her sophomore year and then takes classes in the last two years of school that are directly applicable to that career. Upon high school graduation, he or she transfers to the technical school. One problem with these programs is that students must choose a career path before beginning their junior year. An alternative model, based on the system used in Germany,

Internships offer adolescents great opportunities to learn about different careers.

involves **apprenticeships or internships.** Students split their week among working at a company, taking career-related classes, and doing regular academic coursework. Again, students must make early, limiting career decisions. Finally, there are **school-based enterprises,** in which schools essentially set up shop and simulate small businesses. Although these enterprises do not get students into the real workplace, they allow students to participate in many aspects of a business and provide them with decision-making opportunities.

Stern and his colleagues (Stern, Rahn, and Chung, 1998) have differentiated between those programs that are "learn and stay" and those that are "learn and go." In learn-and-stay programs, students are channeled into a particular industry or company; in learn-and-go programs, students learn more general skills that can be transferred to any number of businesses. Stern and colleagues have recommended that schools convert students' existing part-time jobs to learn-and-go experiences. Since most students are employed in dead-end, low-paying work, the focus must shift to providing transferable job skills. Incentives would have to be provided to companies to secure their participation. Stern et al. also have suggested that schools work to create more firm-based learn-and-stay opportunities in industries that pay high wages. Finally, they have recommended an expansion of school-based enterprises, both learn and stay and learn and go.

tech-prep programs partnerships between high schools and two-year, postsecondary vocational institutions to provide career education.

apprenticeships or internships programs in which students split their time among working at a company, taking career-related classes, and doing regular academic coursework.

school-based enterprises programs in which schools set up small businesses to teach job skills.

SUMMARY

1. Choosing and preparing for a vocation is one of the most important development tasks of adolescence. Done wisely and realistically, it enables individuals to enter vocations for which they are well suited, in which they find satisfaction and fulfillment, and which are needed by society. Done haphazardly, it leads to frustration, discontent, unhappiness, and social disapproval.
2. The process of choosing a job or career is often a complicated one. Choices made early in high school affect the availability of later options. Adolescents from higher-socioeconomic-status groups are more fortunate because they have more options and more resources to use in taking advantage of options.
3. Ginzberg divides the process of occupational choice into three stages: fantasy stage (up to age 11), tentative stage (11 to 17 years), and realistic stage (from age 17 on). Research generally supports the broad outlines of this theory, though the sequence, nature, and timing of the stages may not always be the same. Also, one's career choices do not always end with one's first job.
4. Gottfredson proposed a theory of career development based on circumscription and then compromise.
5. Influences on development have been divided into three categories: normative, age-graded influences; normative, history-graded influences; and nonnormative, life-event influences.
6. Holland theorized that people select occupations that afford environments consistent with their personality types. He outlined six personality types: realistic, intellectual, social, conventional, enterprising, and artistic.
7. Parents exert a strong influence on their teenagers' career choices, especially those parents whose teens are strongly attached to them. Parents provide their children with opportunities, model certain behaviors, exhibit satisfaction or dissatisfaction with teens' careers, and encourage or discourage education.
8. Peers, teachers, and coaches also influence adolescents' career decisions.
9. Girls have traditionally been more narrowly channeled into careers than boys due to structural and normative barriers. The notion that cognitive differences restrict girls' and women's occupational success is rooted in stereotypes.
10. Women are underrepresented in careers involving the natural sciences.
11. Adolescent career decisions are influenced by intelligence, interests, aptitudes, job opportunities, job familiarity, salary, prestige, socioeconomic status, and, to some extent, race and ethnicity.
12. Almost all adolescents work at some point before they graduate from high school, primarily as cashiers and food servers. Working even only a few hours/week has harmful ramifications for adolescents.
13. Community service, or volunteer work, has increased greatly in the past 30 years. It appears to be quite beneficial for everyone involved.
14. One of the major social problems in the United States is unemployment among youths. Rates among African Americans and other minorities are higher than among Whites for numerous reasons. Lack of training, skills, and experience; restrictive licensing and union requirements; minimum wage legislation;

and lack of education all contribute to adolescent unemployment.

15. A variety of school-to-work programs have been developed to help adolescents develop job skills and become employable, including tech-prep programs, apprenticeships, and school-based enterprises.

KEY TERMS

- apprenticeships or internships 389
- circumscription 370
- compromise 370
- compromise with reality theory 368
- normative barriers 375
- occupational environment theory 371
- school-based enterprises 389
- Strong Vocational Interest Blank 378
- structural barriers 374
- tech-prep programs 388

THOUGHT QUESTIONS

Personal Reflection

1. What careers have you wanted at different points in your life, beginning in childhood? Why these careers?
2. Identify some of the normative age-graded, normative historical, and nonnormative, events that have affected your career plans.
3. Which of Holland's personality types best describes you? Are you planning to go into the kind of career he would suggest for you? If not, why not?
4. Have you ever attended a career education class? What was the result? In what ways was it helpful? In what ways was it not helpful?
5. How influential were or are your peers regarding your vocational choice?
6. Has any person at school been particularly influential in your choice of vocation? Discuss.
7. If you worked while in high school, how did the experience affect you? What, if any, valuable lessons did you learn from your job? How could the situation have been more instructive?

Group Discussion

8. Why is making a wise vocational choice one of the most important developmental tasks of adolescence?
9. Why do some adolescents make poor vocational choices?
10. Should parents have any voice about the vocation their adolescent chooses? What's the parental role in this regard?
11. Do you think that some vocations are unsuitable for women? For men? Explain.
12. Just because a person is interested in a particular vocation, does this mean he or she should go into it? What other factors ought to be taken into consideration?
13. How should you go about finding out if you have an aptitude or special ability suitable for a particular vocation?
14. Do you currently or did you perform any community service while in high school? How did the experience affect you?
15. What can be done about the high unemployment rate among adolescents, especially African American adolescents?
16. What kinds of school-to-work programs did your high school offer? How satisfied were the students who participated in these programs?
17. Is having a good education necessary to get a good job? Explain.

Debate Questions

18. Job prestige is a valid concern when selecting a career.
19. The military is a good option for adolescents who are uncertain what to do with their lives.
20. Getting a good education is necessary to getting a good job.
21. All high school students should be required to do community service.
22. All high schools should offer career exploration courses as part of their curriculum to teach students about available careers.

SUGGESTED READING

Barling, J., and Kelloway, E. K. (Eds.). (1999). *Young Workers: Varieties of Experience.* Washington, DC: American Psychological Association.

Csikszentmihalyi, M., and Schneider, B. (2000). *Becoming Adult: How Teenagers Prepare for the World of Work.* New York: Basic Books.

Eyler, J., and Giles, D. (1999). *Where's the Learning in Service Learning?* San Francisco: Jossey-Bass.

Howard, C. M., and Ill, P. J. (2003). *Career Pathways: Preparing Students for Life.* Thousand Oaks, CA: Sage.

Jacobsen, M. H. (1999). *Hand-Me-Down Dreams: How Families Influence Our Career Paths and How We Can Reclaim Them.* Bourbon, IN: Harmony Books.

Mortimer, J. (2003). *Working and Growing Up in America.* Cambridge, MA: Harvard University Press.

Siegel, S. (Ed.) (2003). *Career Ladders: Transitions from High School to Adult Life.* Austin, TX: Pro-Ed.

Watkins, M., and Braun, L. (2005). *Service Learning: From Classroom to Community to Career.* Indianapolis, IN: Jist.

Youniss, J., and Yates, M. (1997). *Community Service and Social Responsibility in Youth.* Chicago: University of Chicago Press.

USEFUL WEB SITE

United States Bureau of Labor Statistics
www.bls.gov

This site contains several different, helpful kinds of information. First, you can download The Occupational Outlook Handbook; *it details more than 1,000 careers, specifying the qualifications needed, employment prospects, salary ranges, and so on. You can browse or search specific careers. Second, you can download the bureau's report on youths in the labor force. Finally, in addition to reviewing myriad statistics about working and unemployment, you can explore links to other sites concerned with this topic.*

CHAPTER 17 ADOLESCENT ALIENATION

WOULDN'T YOU LIKE TO KNOW . . .

- Do most runaways leave home for good?
- Why do most runaways leave home?
- Who is more likely to commit suicide: adolescent boys or girls?
- What factors put a teen at risk for suicide?
- Is juvenile crime increasing or decreasing?
- How involved are girls in juvenile gangs?
- What usually happens to teens caught breaking the law?
- What can be done to reduce the rate of juvenile delinquency?

Sometimes, adolescents who are angry or unhappy turn outward, expressing pent-up emotions through various forms of acting-out behavior: truancy, aggression, promiscuity, theft, assault, even the destruction of one's own life or that of another. For the most part, such adolescents feel alienated from family and school. They do not function in the mainstream of adolescent or adult society. Their actions are an expression of their feelings of alienation, which they have found difficult to deal with in socially approved ways (Calabrese and Adams, 1990).

In this chapter, we will discuss three manifestations of disturbed, acting-out behavior: running away, suicide, and juvenile delinquency. Although these problems are quite different from each other, they stem from many of the same fundamental causes. There is a growing understanding that while the expressions of disturbance may vary, their roots are the same. Furthermore, adolescent problem behaviors—whether they involve substance abuse, pregnancy, delinquency, suicide, or dropping out—tend to *cluster.* In other words, teenagers who engage in one of these activities tend to engage in several of them (Lindberg, Boggess, Porter, and Williams, 2000; Ozer, Park, Paul, Brindis, and Irwin, 2003).

Clustering occurs for two separate reasons. The first is common causation. Family discord, association with deviant peers, poverty, and school failure all contribute to a host of behavioral problems (and, therefore, are mentioned multiple times throughout this and other chapters.) The second reason for clustering is that one problem can directly trigger another. For example, the stresses caused by running away can lead a youth to substance abuse, promiscuity, and criminal activity.

RUNNING AWAY

National estimates indicate that the number of adolescents who run away from home each year ranges from 1 to 2 million (Hammer, Finkelh; and Sedlak, 2002). It has been estimated that one in seven adolescents will run away at least once before his or her eighteenth birthday (Sedlak, Finkelhor, Hammer, and Schultz, 2002). Adolescents raised in single-parent homes are many times as likely to run as those from two-parent homes (Finkelhor, Hotaling, and Sedlak, 1990). A minority of adolescents who run away are running from foster care, group homes, and residential treatment facilities.

Most runaways are 15 or older, but 9 percent are less than 16 (Unger, Simon, Newman, Montgomery, Kipke, and Albornoz, 1998). These young teenagers find it particularly hard to cope with life on the street—even more so than their older counterparts. Young teens' small size leaves them especially vulnerable to victimization and makes it impossible for them to find legitimate work. They are unlikely to take advantage of social services (shelters, food banks, etc.) because they are afraid they will be turned over to their parents.

ANSWERS WOULDN'T YOU LIKE TO KNOW . . .

Do most runaways leave home for good?

No. About half stay away for only a day or two and go to a friend's or relative's house. Most of the more intent runaways, who are gone for long periods of time, eventually go home, as well.

Classes of Runaways

There are many different reasons for running away and many different typologies that classify runaways based on their motivation for leaving home. However, there are two primary classes of runaways: *intent runaways* and *transient runaways.* Intent runaways are those who, when they leave home, really mean to flee. They want to be gone—if not forever, then for a long time. Transient runaways are those who leave more at the spur of the moment and do not intend to stay away for more than a few hours or a day or two. These teens often leave homes because they are afraid; perhaps they think that their parents will beat them for getting failing grades, or maybe they have violated their curfew and are afraid to return home. Other teens are angry, perhaps over having been denied permission to do something or being disciplined.

The reason it is worthwhile at the outset of this discussion to distinguish these two groups is that about *half* of all runaways—the transient runaways—return home within two days (Finkelhor, Hotaling, and Sedlak, 1990). The vast majority run to friends' or relatives' houses, and often their parents know where they are (Snyder and Sickmund, 1995). The fact that an adolescent would take the rather extreme measure running away for even a short time does not speak particularly well of his or her family's dynamics, and it is quite possible that this behavior is an early warning of more serious problem to come. Still, transient running is a far less serious and less risky behavior than intent running with no plans of returning.

So, keeping in mind that a full 50 percent of runaways are gone only a night or two, let us examine the more serious intent runaways.

Reasons for Running Away

Rotheram-Borus, Parra, Cantwell, Gwadz, and Murphy (1996) have identified six reasons for youths' running away:

PERSONAL ISSUES PREVENTING TEENS FROM RUNNING AND FINDING THEM WHEN THEY DO

Most teens do not run away on the spur of the moment with the intent of staying away. Rather, their leaving is a dramatic move that they have usually considered for some time. This means that an alert parent or teacher who is aware of the warning signs might be able to speak with the adolescent and head off the behavior.

The most direct and obvious sign of planning to run is that the teen will have begun to accumulate the resources he or she will need to live on the street. He or she may be hoarding money or have packed a suitcase or backpack. In addition, he or she may gather personal mementos, such as photos of close friends.

Some runaways hint at or even directly state their intent to leave home. They sometimes confide their plans to friends. Hints, direct statements, and rumors reported by others should be taken seriously.

Other possible signs are less specific to running away but signal trouble. Changes in behavior, rebelliousness, a need for solitude, switching friends, and truancy often indicate that a problem is brewing and worth looking into.

If an adolescent has disappeared and is believed to have run away from home, the Office of Juvenile Justice and Delinquency Prevention (1998) recommends the following actions:

1. Check with persons who may know the child's whereabouts: friends, neighbors, and so on.
2. Check locations that the adolescent frequents to see if he or she is there.
3. Examine the youth's bedroom and school locker for clues (such as notes or maps) as to where he or she may have gone.
4. Check past telephone bills for unexplained long-distance calls the youth may have made.
5. Examine the child's e-mail account.
6. Call the police and make a report. Ask the police to put out a "Be on the lookout" alert.
7. Disseminate the news that the child is missing, including a photo of him or her.
8. Contact national runaway help hotlines and the National Center for Missing and Exploited Children to see if the child has been in contact with them.

---

1. Deserted by their parents due to parental death or divorce
2. Thrown out of their homes by their parents
3. Left home because their parents could not cope with their homosexuality
4. Left home after having been sexually abused by their parents
5. Left home or thrown out because they have substance abuse problems
6. Left home or thrown out because they have longstanding mental health problems

The most common thread running through the backgrounds of intent runaways is that they come from dysfunctional homes. They have a history of having been sexually or physically abused, neglected, and rejected by their parents. Their parents constantly fight and are frequently substance abusers (Baron, 1999; Terrell, 1997). Some estimates have suggested that 70 percent of runaways have been abused in some way (Jencks, 1994).

Most adolescents, then, have been *pushed out* of their homes. They flee from what they perceive to be an intolerable situation. The majority of intent runaway adolescents say that they tried to make their family situation work but failed in their attempt (Schaffner, 1998). Other teens are **throwaways;** that is, their parents have actively encouraged them to leave or have actually thrown them out of their homes (Gullotta, 2003). Only a relatively small number of youths are pulled toward a glamorous vision of life on the street.

Runaway girls generally view their parents as more controlling and punitive of their behavior in the home, whereas many runaway boys report minimal family control and supervision, which leads to outside forces, such as peers, becoming causal agents in running away. Thus, low levels of control of boys especially allows them opportunities to leave. Many parents of runaways are so absorbed with their own problems that they have little time to consider their children. Such youths report they are not wanted at home.

Given their poor family relationships, it is not surprising that most adolescents who run away exhibit a host of problem behaviors before they leave home (e.g., Robert, Pauzé, and Fournier, 2005). They often commit delinquent acts, do not get along well with peers, and are anxious or depressed. Many have experienced difficulties in school. Children who are slow learners, left back to repeat grades, or ostracized by school personnel seek to escape the school environment that rejects

throwaways adolescents who have been told to leave home.

them. An examination of the prevalence of arithmetic and reading difficulties in 16- to 21-year-old clients of a shelter for runaway and homeless street youths found that 52 percent had reading disabilities, 29 percent had trouble with arithmetic and written work, and only 20 percent were normal achievers (Barwick and Siegel, 1996).

ANSWERS WOULDN'T YOU LIKE TO KNOW ...

Why do most runaways leave home?

Most intent runaways leave home because of intolerable conditions there, such as being abused. Almost half of runaways, however, are told to leave or thrown out by their parents.

Throwaways

The largest study of runaways to date, the NISMART study (Hammer, Finkelhor, and Sedlak, 2002), found that not all runaways had, in fact, run away. Forty-four percent had been thrown out of their homes or asked to leave by their parents, and a large number of other teens had left voluntarily but then were not permitted to return when they wanted to. As noted earlier, these youths are more properly called *throwaways*.

What motivates a family to sever all ties with an adolescent child? Sometimes, the parents are distressed at their child's incorrigible behavior, whether it be substance abuse, promiscuity, delinquency, or the like. Sometimes, the child has a long-standing mental illness, such as conduct disorder, that makes him or her difficult to live with. Sometimes, the child has engaged in incest with a sibling or with one of the parents (Gullotta, 2003). Regardless, of the reason, the parents of a throwaway are not making a good, mature decision when they decide to abandon their child. If the family had been strong and healthy, the child's behaviors either would not have occurred or they would have been dealt with in a more proactive, healing manner. Shutting the door in a child's face may reduce the parents' problems, but it will only exacerbate the child's.

Another reason that parents ask their children to leave home is dire poverty. Some parents simply cannot afford to feed and clothe their children. In these cases, the parents will sometimes ask the older children to fend for themselves, so that the parents can concentrate on caring for the younger children (Shinn and Weitzman, 1996). Similarly, some youths are on the street because they have outgrown foster care and been discharged with no means of support (National Coalition of the Homeless, 1999).

Life on the Street

Adolescents who have run away quickly find that life on the street is extremely difficult. Homeless youths are likely to be victimized by others. One study found that 43 percent of the street-living adolescent boys and 39 percent of the adolescent girls they sampled had been assaulted with a weapon (Whitbeck and Simons, 1990). Boys were more often robbed and beaten whereas girls were more commonly sexually assaulted.

In order to get money for food, clothes, and shelter, adolescents who have been on the street for more than a few days are usually forced to turn to drug dealing, shoplifting, and theft (Terrell, 1997). Large numbers engage in prostitution, taking money for sex, or in so-called **survival sex,** swapping sexual favors for food or shelter. An estimated 75 percent of hard-core street youths engage in some form of crime and 50 percent engage in either prostitution or survival sex (Kipke, O'Connor, Palmer, and MacKenzie, 1995; Kipke, Palmer, LaFrance, and O'Connor, 1997). Street youths often go hungry (Antoniades and Tarasuk, 1998).

Engaging in these activities causes runaways to associate with deviant individuals, who further draw them into unhealthy lifestyles. The fact that many hard-core runaways use drugs and engage in sex with multiple partners, usually without condoms, puts them at high risk for contracting human immunodeficiency virus (HIV), which causes acquired immune deficiency syndrome (AIDS) (Booth, Zhang, and Kwiatkowski, 1999). Homeless youths are subject to high rates of psychological problems, as well. They experience low self-esteem and depression, engage in various forms of self-injurious behavior, and are at high risk for suicide (Molnar, Shade, Kral, Booth, and Watters, 1999; Yoder, 1999). One study of homeless youths in Los Angeles found that two-thirds were clinically depressed; in comparison, about 7 percent of the overall adolescent population is depressed (Unger, Kipke, Simon, Montgomery, and Johnson, 1997). Most studies report an attempted suicide rate of between 20 and 40 percent (Kidd, 2003). The mortality rate of street youths is estimated to be 40 times as high as that of at-home adolescents (Shaw and Dorling, 1998).

Help for Runaways

Runaway youths need a variety of services to help with their many problems. These services include but are not limited to short-term emergency shelters where they can find temporary food and shelter; medical, including psychological, care; access to social workers who can try to reunite them with their families if that is appropriate or help them make arrangements to live on their own; medical assistance; educational programs so that they can attend class and graduate from high school; long-term, stable residential placements; and job training and placement. Unfortunately, the services available to runaway and thrownaway youths are, at the current time, inadequate.

Worldwide Scope

Homeless youths are not just an American phenomenon. An estimated 100 million children and adolescents are homeless across the globe. Like their American counterparts, these children and adolescents suffer from malnutrition, self-destructive behaviors, and substance abuse. They eat out of garbage cans and steal or prostitute themselves to survive. Most of these children are from families living deep in poverty. Some have run away, some have been abandoned, and some have lost parents to death.

Le Roux and Smith (1998) blamed the increase in the numbers of street children on a combination of industrialization/urbanization and drought with its resulting famine. Urbanization breaks down the traditional extended family structure in rural communities, leaving mothers and fathers to care for children on their own. Famine destroys villages, kills parents, and forces families to make difficult choices when there is simply not enough food to feed them all.

SUICIDE

Suicide is an important adolescent topic because at the present, it is the third-leading cause of adolescent death (behind accidents and homicides) (Anderson and Smith, 2003). A well-cited survey of American adolescents found that in a 1-year period, 19 percent of adolescents had seriously considered suicide and 15 percent had made suicide plans (Kann et al., 2000).

Frequency of Suicide

The incidence of suicide among children, especially among those under age 13, is rare (Brent, Baugher, Bridge, Chen, and Chiappetta, 1999), for several reasons. First, *older* adolescents are more likely than children to have a psychological disorder, which is a significant risk factor for suicide. Second, older adolescents have more mature cognitive skills than children and can thus make more effective suicide plans (Shaffer et al., 1996).

Contrary to popular belief, the suicide mortality rate increases with age, reaching a peak in males over 85 years of age and in females at ages 45 to 54 (Centers for Disease Control, 2004c). Figure 17.1 shows these trends. As Figure 17.2 shows, the suicide rate in the 15- to 24-year-old age group tripled from 1950 to 1995—from about 4.5 deaths per 100,000 adolescents to nearly 14. Since then the adolescent suicide rate has declined to about 10 deaths per 100,000 (U.S. Bureau of the Census, 2003a).

Only a small percentage of attempted suicides succeed. Estimates of the ratio of adolescent suicide attempts to fatalities vary from 100 to 1 to 350 to 1

survival sex swapping sexual favors for food or shelter.

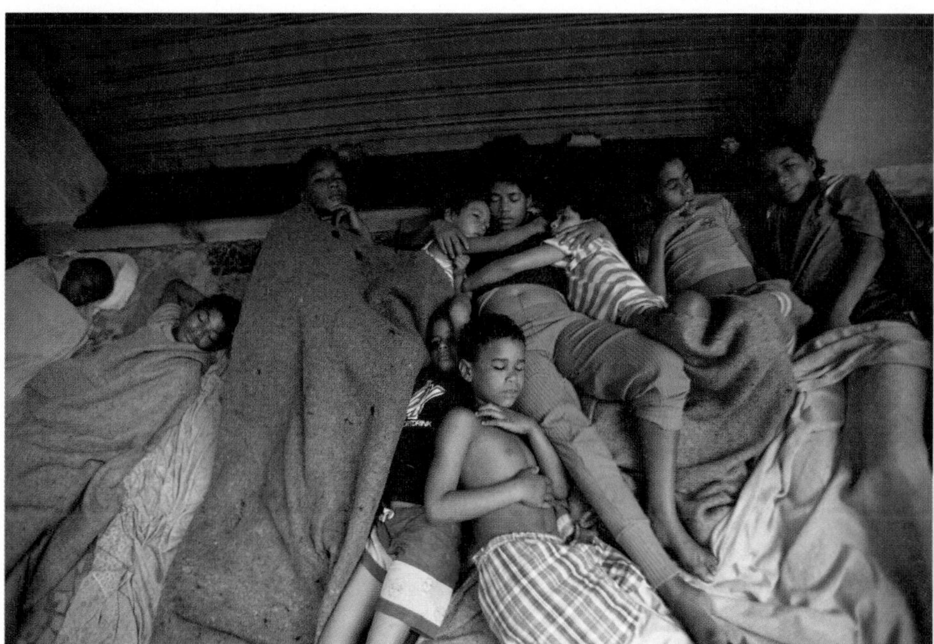

Homeless youths around the world sleep on the streets, eat out of garbage cans, and steal or prostitute themselves to survive.

FIGURE 17.1 SUICIDE MORTALITY BY SEX AND AGE GROUP: 2002

Source: Data from Centers for Disease Control (2004c).

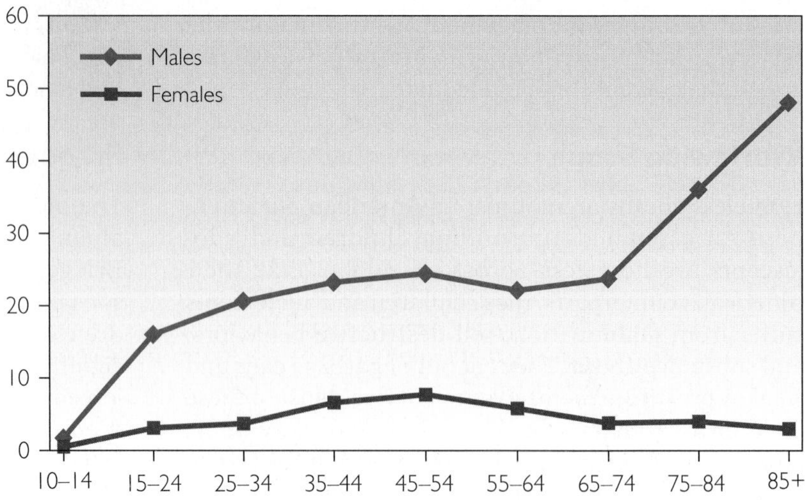

(Seroczynski, Jacquez, and Cole, 2003). About 5,000 young people between 15 and 24 years of age successfully commit suicide each year (U.S. Bureau of the Census, 2003). Girls are about twice as likely as boys to attempt suicide, but 85 percent of successful suicides are committed by boys (Anderson and Smith 2003). One of the reasons males succeed more often is that they frequently use more violent means—hanging, jumping from heights, single-vehicle automobile accidents, or shooting or stabbing themselves—whereas females more often use passive and less dangerous methods, such as taking pills. Females more often make multiple threats but less often really want to kill themselves or actually do it (Peck and Warner, 1995).

ANSWERS WOULDN'T YOU LIKE TO KNOW . . .

Who is more likely to commit suicide: adolescent boys or girls?

Girls are much more likely to attempt suicide, but boys are much more likely to succeed.

Suicide rates also vary by race and ethnicity. Native American adolescents have the highest suicide rate—four times that of White adolescents (Indian Health Service, 2000). White adolescents have a higher suicide rate than African American adolescents, and African Americans have a higher rate than Hispanic Americans (U.S. Bureau of the Census, 2003a). The suicide rate for African American males has doubled in the past 20 years (Centers for Disease Control, 1996).

FIGURE 17.2 ADOLESCENT SUICIDE RATES: 1950 TO 2001

Source: Data from U.S. Bureau of the Census (2003).

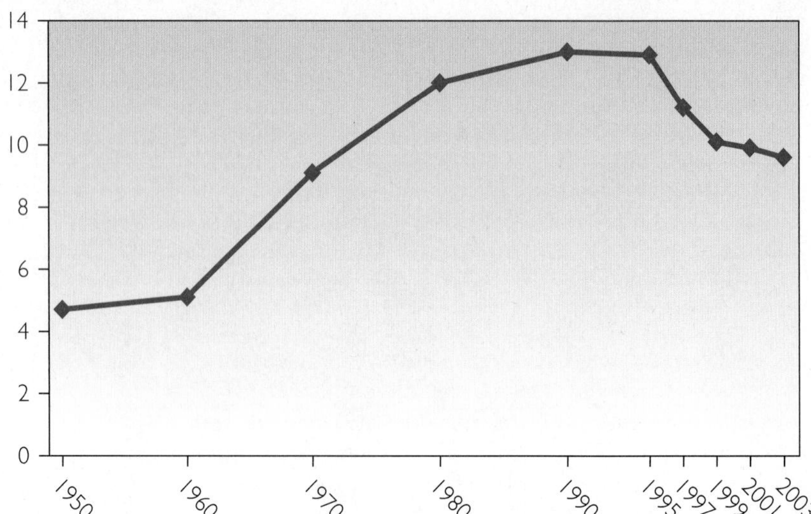

PERSONAL ISSUES WHY ARE ADOLESCENT GIRLS MORE LIKELY TO BE DEPRESSED THAN ADOLESCENT BOYS?

During childhood, boys and girls are equally likely to be depressed, but by adulthood, women are twice as likely to be depressed as men. It is thus during adolescence that this gender difference in the rates of depression first emerges. But why?

An obvious explanation would seem to be the hormonal fluctuations associated with women's menstrual cycle. Evidence for this hypothesis is weak, however (Seroczynski, Jacquez, and Cole, 2003). A second explanation for this gender difference has to do with body satisfaction. Both males and females become less satisfied with their bodies during adolescence, but females' dissatisfaction increases more than males'. Even so, since discontent with one's physique is associated with depression, this could account for the higher depression rate in adolescent females (Kostanski and Gullone, 1998).

Perhaps the most intriguing explanation has come from work linking biological and societal factors. Petersen and her colleagues (1993) noted that depression rates were highest when adolescents made the transition to middle school, or about the time they were experiencing puberty. Because girls hit puberty about two years earlier than boys, in most communities, girls are more likely than boys to begin middle school and to begin experiencing pubertal change at the same time. Experiencing these two significant stressors at once could be overwhelming. It is therefore likely that a confluence of factors—those described here and the social issues described in the body of the text—work together to contribute to girls' higher depression rates.

Causes and Motives of Suicide

Why do adolescents attempt to take their own lives? What are their motives? Many people are surprised to learn that 90 percent of persons who commit suicide have psychological disorders. Most commonly, they are depressed, but they also are likely to have a substance abuse problem or an anxiety disorder. In fact, the two best predictors of suicide are clinical depression and a previous suicide attempt (U.S. Department of Health and Human Services, 1999).

To put this in context, remember that although psychological disorders have a biological component, they are primarily caused by negative experiences and stressors in the environment. Thus, there are some commonalities in the backgrounds of most youths who commit suicide. In particular, a significant body of empirical literature suggests that suicidal behavior in the teenage years is largely associated with family processes (Koopmans, 1995).

Depression

Depression would be an important enough topic to cover in some depth even if it were not related to suicide. Clinical depression is a very serious condition that can make a person's life miserable—even unbearable—and trigger a host of other problems. When people are depressed, they feel both helpless—that there is nothing they can do to improve their terrible situation—and hopeless—that their situation will never change for the better. They feel sad and are self-critical; they also believe that others are critical of them. Depressed individuals feel overwhelmed at having to make even simple decisions. They often neglect their appearance and may act out their frustrations in an aggressive fashion (American Psychiatric Association, 2000).

Depression is quite common during adolescence: Between 15 and 20 percent of teenagers have been clinically depressed at least once by the time they enter young adulthood (Harrington, Rutter, and Fombonne, 1996). Furthermore, episodes of depression are frequently recurrent, with each bout usually lasting seven to nine months.

About two-thirds of adolescents who are clinically depressed have at least one other psychological disorder, as well—often substance abuse.

Depression runs in families. Depressed adolescents are three times more likely to have a close family member with depression as adolescents who are not depressed. The families of depressed youths are also more likely to be filled with discord, and divorce is more common. Their parents have a tendency to overprotect them (Nilzon and Palmérus, 1997).

Depression is equally common in boys and girls during childhood. However, girls' depression rates increase during adolescence whereas boys' rates do not (Wade, Cairney, and Pevalin, 2002). By adulthood, women are twice as likely as men to have depression (Angold and Rutter, 1992). Depression in boys and girls is typically triggered by different events. Girls are more likely than boys to become depressed due to problems

depression a serious psychological disorder marked by sadness, helplessness, and hopelessness.

PERSONAL ISSUES PREVENTING SUICIDE

Recognize the Precipitating Conditions

- The loss of a close friend or family member through death or relocation
- Other significant loss, such as a loss of job, home, status, and so on
- Substance abuse
- Depression
- A long-standing but recently exacerbated problem
- Feelings of worthlessness
- Social isolation

Recognize the Signs That Suicide May Be Imminent

- Depression that disappears for no reason
- Declining school or work performance
- Lack of interest in formerly enjoyed activities
- Deteriorating physical appearance
- Self-abusive, self-injurious behavior
- Explicit or veiled statements that the person is going to die or go away
- Preparation of a will or verbal statements giving away possessions
- Sentimental visits to favorite place
- Acquisition of lethal means, such as a gun, pills, poison, and so on

What You Can Do

- Do *not* ignore these signs. Speak to your friend. You will *not* encourage someone to commit suicide by asking about his or her problems or whether he or she has contemplated suicide.
- Listen to what your friend has to say. Be empathic and sympathetic. Do *not* belittle or trivialize his or her problems.
- Let your friend know that you care.
- Try to diminish feelings of hopelessness by helping your friend brainstorm solutions to his or her problem.
- Do *not* leave your friend alone if you believe that he or she is suicidal.
- Get rid of any means the person has to kill himself or herself. Ask to hold the means until you have had more time to try to help.
- Get help. Encourage your friend to speak to a counselor or call a crisis hotline. Let your friend know that you will not abandon him or her if he or she speaks to someone else.
- If you cannot get your friend to contact someone with training in this area, do it yourself.

with social relationships. For example, unpopular girls are more likely to be depressed than popular girls; this relationship is not true for boys (Oldenburg and Kerns, 1997). Girls are also more likely to feel others' pain and to become depressed due to the stresses that those they care about are experiencing (Eberhart, Shih, Hammen, and Brennan, 2006). Also, when boys have a problem, they tend to cope with it through denial and avoidance; that is, they try to distract themselves and not think about it. Girls, conversely, tend to ruminate on their problems. This latter coping strategy is more likely to lead to depression (U.S. Department of Health and Human Services, 1999). Girls who experience depression are more likely than boys to have that depression continue into adulthood (Gjerde and Westenberg, 1998).

Most kinds of stress increase the likelihood of depression. For example, students who do poorly in school are at heightened risk. It follows, then, that students with attention-deficit hyperactivity disorder, learning disabilities, and conduct disorder are at special risk. Loss of a loved one—whether a family member, close friend, boyfriend, or girlfriend—can also trigger depression, as can traumas such as assault (National Institute of Mental Health, 2000).

Some question remains as to whether depression in adolescents is the same condition as depression in adults. Although many commonalities have been identified, there are a few differences in how the disorder is manifested in the two age groups. For example, adolescents are more likely to have physical ailments as part of their depression than are adults but are less likely to be tired or to lose their appetites (Carlson and Kashini, 1988). In addition, some antidepressants that relieve symptoms in adults have little effect on adolescents (Birmaher et al., 1996). To some, these differences suggest a possible difference in the biological foundations of the disorders.

To tie depression back to suicide, there are two links. First, as mentioned before, depressed youths are at significantly increased risk for suicide (Birmaher, Arbelez, and Brent, 2002). Second, there is increasing concern that one of the most common treatments for depression—prescription SSRI (selective serotonin reuptake inhibitors) antidepressants such as Prozac—can trigger suicidal thoughts and behavior in adolescents. This is a real cause for alarm: in 2002, American physicians wrote nearly 11 million prescriptions for SSRIs for youths aged less than 17 years (Hampton, 2004). Concern grew to the point that, in October 2004, the U.S. Food and Drug

Administration issued a "black box" warning, stating that these medications put minors at increased risk for suicide and that they should be used with extreme caution in this population. (A number of European countries had previously restricted the use of SSRI antidepressants to adult patients.) The government's panelists determined that using these drugs doubled the risk of suicidal thoughts and behaviors in depressed adolescents receiving treatment who are using them.

Not all researchers are convinced that the dangers outweigh the benefits, however. For example, Vasa, Carlino, and Pine (2006) believe that the suicidal link has been exaggerated; they agree that the risk does double, but they note that the increase is from 2 percent to 4 percent and so is still small. In addition, they point out that the suicide risk of adolescents who are on psychotropic medications and are under treatment is still much less than that of untreated depressed adolescents. They also point to an inverse negative correlation between the number of prescriptions for these medications

ANSWERS WOULDN'T YOU LIKE TO KNOW ...

What factors put a teen at risk for suicide?

Most, but not all, teens who commit suicide are depressed. Many of them use drugs or alcohol, and many have a history of sexual abuse. Suicide is often triggered by the loss of someone or something important in the teen's life.

RESEARCH HIGHLIGHT A RAPID RISE IN SELF-MUTILATING BEHAVIOR

An unfortunate new behavior appears to be gaining ground with adolescents: self-injurious, or self-mutilating, behavior. Self-injurious behavior is defined as behavior that intentionally causes harm to the body for purposes not socially sanctioned (e.g., not for cosmetic purposes, such as body piercing) and without the apparent intent to commit suicide (Alderman, 1997). Self-injury most often takes the form of cutting with a knife or razorblade, but it also includes burning, picking at wounds, swallowing sharp objects, biting, inserting sharp objects into one's body cavities, scratching oneself, punching hard objects, and engaging in similar harmful actions (Burrows, 1992).

There is not a great deal of research on the prevalence of self-mutilation in the adolescent population. The relatively few studies that have been conducted have yielded results ranging from 14 to 39 percent for general, nonclinical populations and 40 to 61 percent in clinical, inpatient samples (cited in Nock and Prinstein, 2005). In several but not all of these studies girls have been found to self-injure more than boys (e.g., Ross and Heath, 2002). The behavior is so newly widespread in persons without other forms of psychopathology that it is not included in the American Psychological Association's *Diagnostic and Statistical Manual,* though some clinicians are calling for its inclusion in the next edition.

What motivates self-injurious behavior? It is closely linked to adolescent depression (Briere and Gil, 1998), borderline personality disorder (Sansone, Gaither, and Songer, 2002), and eating disorders (Thomas, Schroeter, Dahme, and Nutzinger, 2002), but clearly many adolescents who have not been diagnosed with full-blown psychological disorders are injuring themselves. Adolescents who have been sexually abused have high rates of self-harm (Zlotnick, Shea, Pearlstein, Simpson, Costello, and Begin, 1996). In general, self-harm seems to be a response to high levels of stress and unhappiness. Therefore, any adolescent who is coping with substantial problems—for example, homeless youth (Tyler, Whitbeck, Hoyt, and Johnson, 2003)—might be at risk.

Why has this behavior surfaced now? We can only speculate. It might be due to the fact that body piercing "opened the door" to the practice. We know that it, like suicide, is a copycat phenomenon, spreading once it has been identified in a community or given publicity (Yates, 2004).

Self-mutilation can help an adolescent deal with overwhelming stress in multiple ways (Suyemoto, 1998). First, it can be used to express one's pain in a visible form to oneself and to others. Second, it can be a means of achieving control over emotions that would otherwise be devastating. Nock and Prinstein (2005) found evidence for both of these motivations—cries for help and emotional control—but reported that the majority of the self-injurers they studied did so to "stop feeling bad" or "to become numb." Most self-mutilators feel little or no pain when they injure themselves (Zila and Kiselica, 2001).

Fortunately, a variety of therapies have been proven effective in helping self-mutilators stop their harmful behavior. Yaryura-Tobias, Neziroglu, and Kaplan (1995), for example, had success with an exposure then response prevention technique. This is an approach most commonly used to treat obsessive-compulsive disorder. Clients are monitored when they desire to injure themselves and are not permitted to do so; eventually the urge diminishes and the habit is eventually broken. Other forms of behavior modification and cognitive therapy can also be beneficial (reviewed by Zila and Kiselica, 2001). Most therapists use a multipronged approach (Suyemoto and MacDonald, 1995).

IN THEIR OWN WORDS

I feel out of control. I reach for my car keys, press one deep in the pale flesh of my forearm, and slowly drag it across my skin. As the metal carves through my arm, the tension increases to an almost unbearable level. When I finally pull the key away, I am rushed with a tremendous feeling of relief. My breathing slows and my muscles relax. All the tension I felt before is completely relieved and I sink into an almost catatonic calm.

I don't do it to mutilate myself; I did it to hurt myself. I think that is the most misunderstood aspect of self-injury. It's not a cry for help; it's not a suicide attempt. It is a way to deal with stress; a coping mechanism no different from drinking or cigarette smoking. It's a way to overwhelm emotional pain with physical pain. The relief is temporary but instant; it pours over you like warm rain and you feel nothing but quiet euphoria. It's a drugless high.

and the adolescent suicide rate in any given geographical region, a negative relationship that weakens the argument for a strong causal relationship between taking SSRIs and adolescent suicide. This linkage is under great scrutiny right now, and more will be known in a few years.

Family Relationships

Impaired family relationships are the second common factor observed in suicidal youth. Studies have indicated that many different aspects of family life can be implicated in suicide ideation, attempts, and completions (Bridge, Goldstein, and Brent, 2006). For example, parental psychopathology and substance abuse is correlated with attempted and completed adolescent suicide (Brent, 1995); in addition, suicidal behavior runs in families, and this appears to be at least in part due to genetic causes (Brent and Mann, 2005). Poor parent-child relationships clearly contributes to adolescent suicidal behavior (e.g., Yuen et al., 1996); the degree to which the child gets along and communicates with his or her father seems especially important (Gould, Fisher, Parides, Flore, and Shaffer, 1996). Parents who fail to monitor their children also put their children at increased risk (King et al., 2001). Adolescents from one-parent homes are more likely to attempt and commit suicide than adolescents from intact families (Weitoft, Hjern, Haglund, and Rosén, 2003), in part due to lessened monitoring and in part due to poorer parent-child relationships.

All of these factors sum to an absence of any warm, parental figure with whom to identify, and a sense of emotional and social isolation.

Suicide attempters often state that they do not feel close to any adult. Many times, they have trouble communicating with significant others around them (Stivers, 1988). There is no one to turn to when they need to talk to someone. Lack of closeness to parents leads to a lack of emotional support when needed (Dukes and Lorch, 1989). One study found three common characteristics of college students who had thoughts of suicide (Dukes and Lorch, 1989). They had poor relationships with parents, poor relationships with peers, and a conviction of personal helplessness and a sense of helplessness regarding the future. Where social integration is high, suicide rates for all age groups are lower (Lester, 1991).

The background of social isolation makes these adolescents particularly vulnerable to a loss of love object, which may trigger the suicide attempt. The loss of a parent in childhood makes any subsequent loss of a family member, mate, boyfriend, or girlfriend particularly hard to accept (Agerbo, Nordentoft, and Mortensen, 2002). Many studies have found that loss and low family support are good predictors of an adolescent's suicide attempt (Morano, Cisler, and Lemerond, 1993).

Other Psychological Correlates

The risk of suicide among adolescents especially males increases with alcohol and drug abuse (Brent, Baugher, Bridge, Chan, and Chiappettan, 1999). Under the influence of drugs or alcohol, adolescents are more likely to act on impulse (Sommer, 1984) or to overdose and kill themselves without intending to do so (Gispert, Wheeler, Marsh, and Davis, 1985). Other psychological problems—conduct disorder, posttraumatic stress syndrome, anxiety disorders, and eating disorders—also increase the likelihood of suicidal behavior (Bridge, Goldstein, and Brent, 2006).

A disproportionate number of adolescents who commit suicide have a history of sexual abuse (Pompili, Mancinelli, Girardi, Ruberto, and Taterelli, 2004).

Sexual Orientation

Gay and lesbian teens are more likely to attempt and actually complete suicide than heterosexual teens (Hershberger, Pilkington, and D'Augelli, 1997). As many as 30 percent of homosexual adolescents attempt suicide (Safren and Heimberg, 1999).

These youths have the same risk factors as their straight peers: substance abuse, depression, loss, family discord, and so on. The rates among homosexual teens are higher because as a group, they face the additional stressors of acknowledging their sexual orientation, of experiencing negative reactions by parents and friends, and of being victimized by hate-motivated individuals (Garland and Zigler, 1993; Savin-Williams, 1994).

IN THEIR OWN WORDS

"A year and a half ago, a friend of mine killed herself. We had known each other since seventh grade, and she and I became closer during college. Carrie was always a troubled girl, but no one knew the extent of her pain until it was too late. She had always been dramatic and a little eccentric, and people knew she loved attention. About a year before she killed herself, she became strangely morbid. She would talk about what her funeral would be like, who would come, who would be sorry, etc. She also became fairly promiscuous, sleeping with boyfriends of girls she knew casually. When we would be out, she would burn herself with cigarettes. Because her behavior was exhibitory, we all figured she was just doing it for attention.

"Apparently, Carrie had been diagnosed with depression. Little did we know she had stopped taking her medication a week before she killed herself. That week, she prepared herself. She apologized to our friend for not picking her for kickball in fourth grade. The next day, she got up, went for a run with her dog (her favorite thing to do), returned, and hung herself in her barn with her dog's leash.

"Not only was her suicide very sad, but I have realized how selfish it was, too. Not only did she leave behind two younger siblings (one of whom found her), but she left all her friends a mess. Her mother is now a chain smoker and drinks regularly."

Copycat Suicides

Copycat suicide is a real phenomenon (U.S. Department of Health and Human Services, 1999). Knowing someone who commits suicide not only increases one's feelings of loss but also disinhibits one's own restraints about suicide. One person's suicide, in effect, "gives permission" for others to commit suicide, too. This is especially true if the suicide was well publicized and resulted in extensive media coverage (Stack, 2003). In fact, fictional accounts of suicides presented on television or in movies can trigger copycat attempts (Gould, 2001).

Unsuccessful Attempts

Sometimes, attempted suicide is a cry for help to get attention or sympathy or an attempt to manipulate other people. Attempted suicide is not necessarily an effort to die but rather a communication to others in an effort to improve one's life. As a matter of fact, desired changes in the life situation as a result of attempted suicide may be accomplished. However, many suicidal gestures for help misfire and lead to death.

Contrary to common opinion, suicide attempts in a great majority of cases are considered in advance and weighed rationally against other alternatives. The attempter may have tried other means: rebellion, running away from home, lying, stealing, or other attention-getting devices. Having tried these methods and failed, the person turns to suicide attempts. Most adolescents who attempt suicide talk about it first. If others are alerted in time, if they pay attention to these developments and take them seriously enough to try to

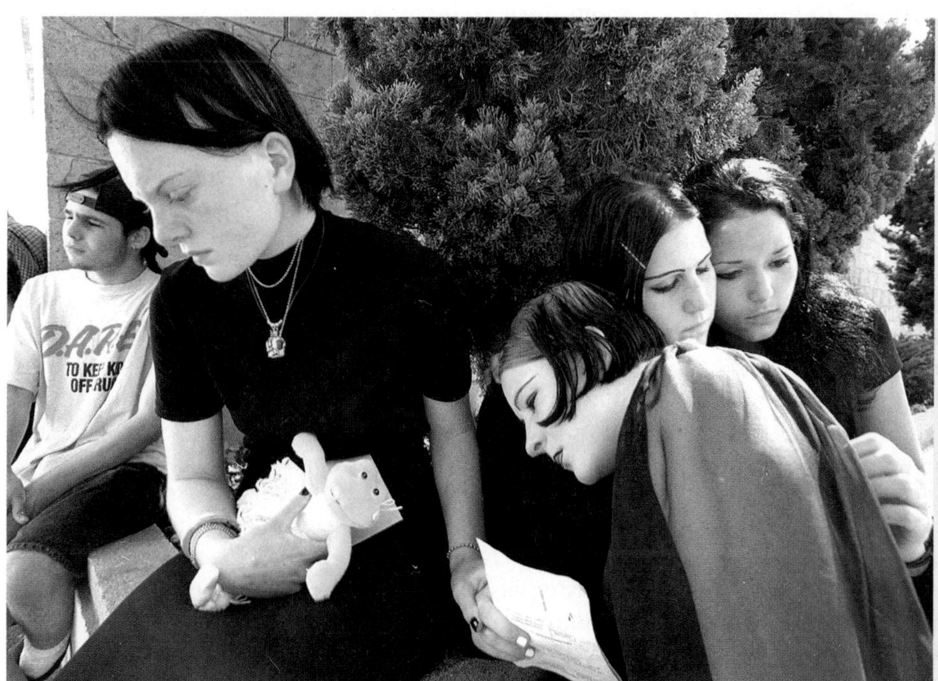

Adolescent suicide is particularly difficult for the family and friends who are left behind. They may suffer from loss and emptiness as well as from feelings of responsibility for not recognizing the problem.

remedy the situation, a death may be prevented; (Ghang and Jin, 1996).

Survivors

Adolescent suicide is particularly devastating for family and peers who are left behind. Survivors typically experience fear, rage, guilt, and depression. They feel responsible for not recognizing the signals that might have been given and preventing the suicide, and they feel angry at the victim for deserting them. Feelings of loss and emptiness and a sense of disbelief are often followed by bouts of self-doubt and recrimination. Survivors experience shock, disbelief, and numbness.

Recovering from the loss may take one to two years, depending on the survivor's personality and the events surrounding the suicide. Intense feelings have to be worked through as survivors come to terms with the loss (Baugher, 1999).

JUVENILE DELINQUENCY

The term *juvenile delinquency* refers to the violation of the law by a juvenile, which in most states means anyone under eighteen years of age. The legal term **juvenile delinquent** was established for young lawbreakers so that they could avoid the disgrace and stigma of being classified in legal records as criminals and to separate underage people and treat them differently from adult criminals. Most are tried in juvenile courts where the intent is to rehabilitate them.

A young person may be labeled a *delinquent* for breaking any of a number of laws, ranging from murder to truancy from school. Violations of laws that apply only to minors—for instance, underage drinking, curfew violations, and truancy—are called **status crimes.** Because laws are inconsistent, a particular action may be considered delinquent in one community but not in another. Furthermore, law enforcement officials differ in the method and extent of enforcement. In some communities, the police may simply talk to adolescents who are accused of minor crimes; in others, the police refer youths to their parents; and in still others, they may arrest them and refer them to juvenile courts. As with adults, many crimes adolescents commit are never discovered or, if discovered, are not reported or prosecuted. Most statistics therefore understate the extent of juvenile crime (Flannery, Hussey, Biebelhausen, and Wester, 2003).

Incidence of Delinquency

According to the Office of Juvenile Justice and Delinquency Prevention (2002), in 2002, juveniles were responsible for 15 percent of all violent crime arrests and 30 percent of all property crime arrests in the United States (Snyder, 2004). As Figure 17.3 indicates, juveniles contribute most to the total incidence rates of arson, vandalism, and motor vehicle theft; they are less involved in murder and aggravated assault. The rate at which juveniles commit violent crimes remained fairly constant between the mid-1970s and the mid-1980s but then rose sharply between 1985 and 1993. Since then, the juvenile violent crime rate has dropped and is, in fact, now lower than it has been since 1980 (see Figure 17.4, p. 405).

This trend also holds true for the juvenile homicide rate. Due to the increasing societal attention paid to killings by youths, there is the widespread misconception that the adolescent homicide rate has continued to rise. Instead, the juvenile homicide rate has dropped about 44 percent since it peaked in 1993. Most of this drop has resulted from a decrease in the use of firearms. Juvenile murders committed with other types of weapons have remained nearly constant, unfortunately.

African American youths are more likely to commit murder than their White counterparts. The vast majority of adolescents who murder kill someone of their own race or ethnic group, which means African American adolescents are also far more likely to be the victims of homicide than White youths. Adolescent males are considerably more likely than females to murder and to be murdered (Fox, and Zawitz, 2006).

Teenagers are two and a half times more likely to be the victims of violent crimes than adults. Teens are more likely to be the victims of property crimes, too. Crimes with juvenile victims are committed both by adults and by other teenagers. Only about one in four juvenile homicide victims is killed by another adolescent (Synder and Sickmund, 2006).

Currently, girls account for about 25 percent of all juvenile arrests. However, for many years, girls' arrest rate has been climbing faster than that for boys, and so the gap continues to narrow. In addition, boys are more likely to be referred for violations of the law, whereas girls are more likely to be referred for truancy, runaway behaviors, and social/personal problems. Boys tend to engage in serious delinquent behaviors, whereas the behaviors of girls tend to be more narrowly confined (Rhodes and Fisher, 1993). However, a greater proportion of females are involved in armed robbery, gang activity, and drug trafficking (Calhoun, Jurgens, and Chen, 1993). Girls are more likely to assault or murder a family member than an acquaintance or a stranger; the reverse is true for boys.

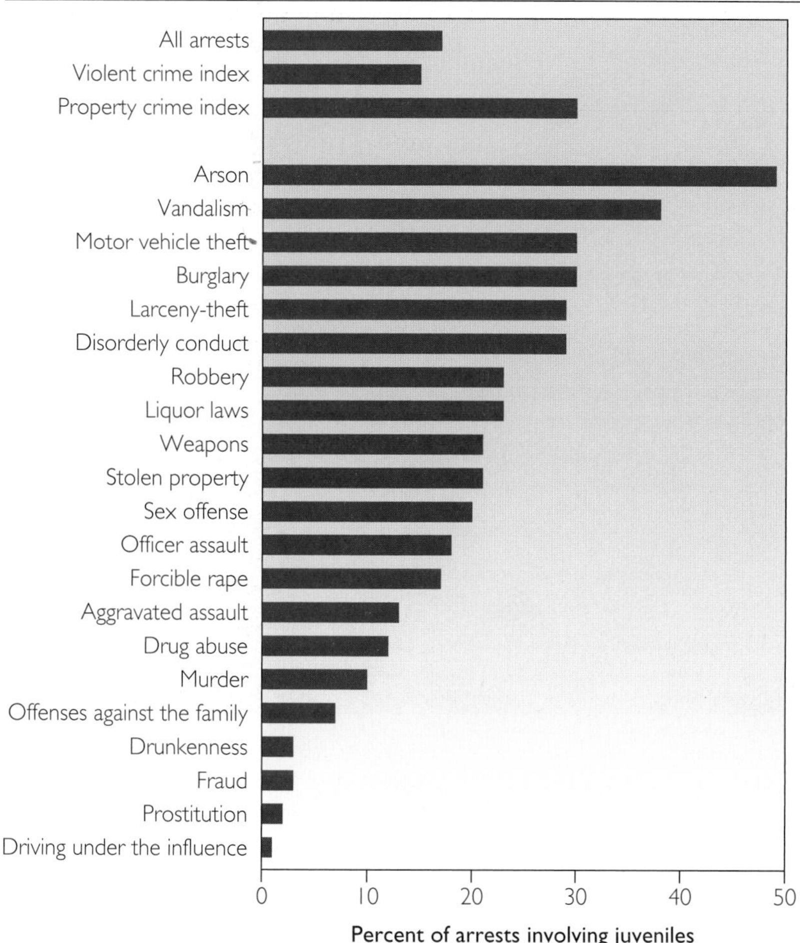

FIGURE 17.3 ARRESTS INVOLVING JUVENILES BY TYPE OF CRIME: 2002

Source: Data from Snyder (2004).

Adolescents are more likely to commit crimes and to be victimized when away from school than when at school. On school days, most crimes involving juveniles occur during the hours after school lets out, between 3 P.M. and 6 P.M. On weekends and

juvenile delinquent a juvenile who violates the law.

status crimes violations of laws that apply only to minors, such as underage drinking, violating curfews, and truancy.

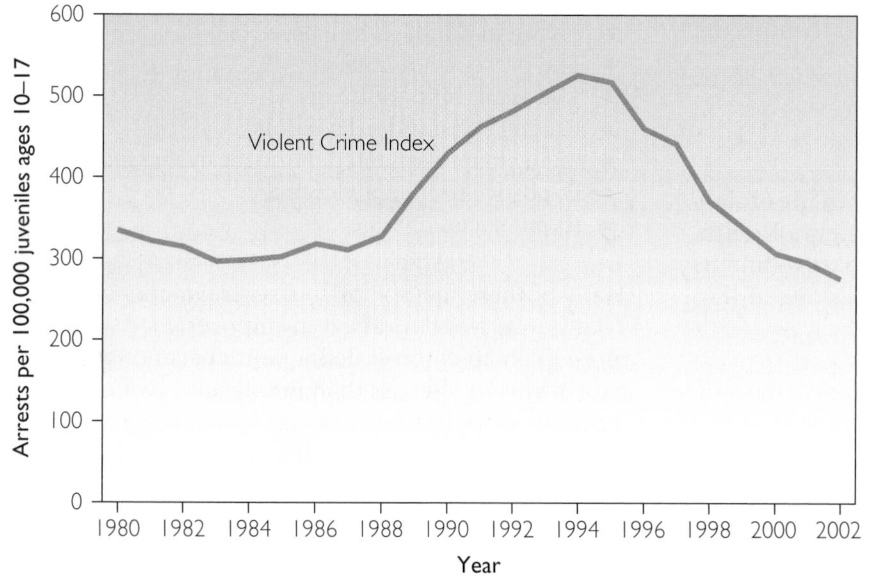

FIGURE 17.4 JUVENILE CRIME RATE: 1980–2002

Source: Data from Snyder (2004).

Many youths engage in status crimes, such as underage drinking.

ANSWERS WOULDN'T YOU LIKE TO KNOW . . .

Is juvenile crime increasing or decreasing?

Juvenile crime has been decreasing since the mid 1990s. This is true for both violent and nonviolent offenses.

holidays, most juvenile crime occurs between 8 P.M. and 10 P.M. This suggests that providing after-school programs would reduce crime more than enforcing curfews.

Causes of Delinquency

Antisocial behavior usually begins early in life (Tolan, Guerra, and Kendall, 1995). The problem of delinquency has motivated research efforts to try to find its causes. In general, the causes may be grouped into three major categories:

- *Environmental causes* include elements in the adolescent's neighborhood and community.
- *Interpersonal causes* refer to the influences of family, friends, siblings, and peers.
- *Personal causes* refer to personality traits and biological predispositions to antisocial behavior.

Also, as Bronfenbrenner (1979) explained in his ecological analysis of behavior, these three types of factors interact with each other in synergistic ways; they are not independent.

Environmental Causes

The most important environmental factors that have been investigated in relation to juvenile delinquency are the following:

- Poverty
- Living in a high-crime area
- The presence of gangs
- The availability of drugs
- Having substandard schools
- Living in a fragmented, noncohesive neighborhood
- Exposure to media violence
- Rapid social change

Many of these factors, of course, frequently co-occur. That is why youths raised in impoverished areas are more likely to commit delinquent acts and to participate in violent offenses than middle-class youths. Keep in mind, though, that some middle-class adolescents do get involved in crime, and that not all poor teenagers do.

What distinguishes those poverty-stricken teens who become delinquents from those who do not? This is where the interrelations between the different types of risk factors come into play. Chung and his colleagues (Chung, Hawkins, Gilchrist, Hill, and Nagin, 2002) have tried to answer this question by looking at the overall situations of poor children and seeing who became delinquent. They found, for example, that adolescents who avoided becoming delinquent had different temperaments, were closer to their parents, were more monitored by their parents, were less involved with antisocial peers, did better in school, and lived in neighborhoods in which drugs were not as ubiquitous as those who did begin to break the law. Furthermore, the circumstances of those youth who were only delinquent for a short time differed along many of the same dimensions, to a lesser degree, than those youth who were chronically delinquent.

Other research has shown that some school environments foster antisocial attitudes and behaviors. In particular, *disorganized schools*—in which rules are only sporadically enforced, there are problems with overcrowding, and after-school programs are unavailable—are the ones most prone to promote delinquency (Flannery, Hussey, Biebelhausen, and Wester, 2003).

Today's adolescents are also living in a period of rapid cultural change, disorganization, and unrest, which tends to increase delinquency rates (see Chapter 1). Values that once were commonly accepted are now questioned. Social institutions such as the family that once offered security and protection may exert an upsetting influence instead. The specter of social, economic, and political unrest stimulates anxieties and rebellion.

Interpersonal Causes

Family background has an important influence on adolescent development and adjustment and hence on social conduct. Disrupted homes and strained family relationships have been associated with delinquent behavior. Lack of family cohesion and troubled family relationships are particularly important correlates of delinquency (Bischof, Stiph, and Whitney, 1995; Lytton, 1995). Parents who model aggression or who reinforce the violent behavior that they observe in their children are most likely to have delinquent children (Patterson, DeBarysne, and Ramsey, 1989). Parents who physically abuse their children or their spouses model aggression most acutely, and so it is little wonder that their children are often aggressive (Flannery, Huff, and Manos, 1998).

Peer-group involvement is also a significant influence in delinquency (Mitchell, Dodder, and Norris, 1990). Adolescents become delinquent because they are socialized into it, particularly by peers (Kazdin, 1995). Youths who have a high degree of peer orientation are also more likely to have a high level of delinquency involvement (Elliott and Menard, 1996). Even so, close association with deviant peers usually occurs only after there are both established negative family interactions and a history of rejection by mainstream peers. In other words, peers can exacerbate and

Involvement in school and community organizations, such as the teen club shown here, is often a deterrent to delinquent activity.

encourage delinquency in youths who are already unhappy and poorly adjusted.

Personal Causes

There have been efforts also to determine whether certain personality factors predispose the adolescent to delinquency. No single personality type can be associated with delinquency, but it is known that those who become delinquent are more likely to be socially assertive, defiant, ambivalent to authority, resentful, hostile, and lacking in self-control (Caspi, Lynan, Moffitt, and Silva, 1993; Feldman and Weinberger, 1994). Individuals who have adequate self-control tend to have an entire constellation of personality and behavioral traits, each of which is negatively related to delinquency. Namely, they are (1) able to delay gratification, (2) persistent, (3) cautious, (4) able to set long-term goals for themselves, (5) aware of the importance of academic skills, and (6) sensitive to others' feelings (Gottfredson and Hirshi, 1990).

Some delinquents consistently exhibit low self-esteem and a negative self-image. Others maintain high self-esteem through denial of their problems and by failure to admit the incongruency between their behavior and their perceptions of self. Such adolescents become adept at denial. They refuse to accept responsibility for their actions and continually blame other people or circumstances for getting them into trouble. In many cases, delinquents have a psychological disorder such as ODD, conduct disorder, or ADHD (see the Highlight box).

Research has been conducted regarding to what extent delinquency is related to alcohol or drug usage among adolescents (Watts and Wright, 1990). Several studies have found that drinking is strongly associated with serious delinquency, especially when other factors were present, such as previous arrests, association with criminals or drug users, or heroin use by the adolescent. Furthermore, there is a strong relationship between adolescents who are raised by substance-abusive parents and juvenile delinquency. Adolescents from substance-abusive homes have been found to suffer from low self-esteem, depression, anger, and a variety of acting-out behaviors (McGaha and Leoni, 1995).

School performance is also an important factor in delinquency (Maguin and Loeber, 1996). In particular,

RESEARCH HIGHLIGHT CONDUCT DISORDER, ODD, AND ADHD

Conduct disorder is the psychological disorder most associated with juvenile delinquency. It can be described as a chronic behavior pattern in which the individual violates age-appropriate societal norms and tramples on others' rights. These long-standing disruptive behaviors impair the adolescent's ability to function in social, occupational, and academic settings.

In order to be diagnosed with conduct disorder, an individual must exhibit at least three different disruptive symptoms. The *Diagnostic and Statistical Manual of Mental Disorders* (4th ed.) clusters these symptoms in four broad groups:

1. Aggression toward people or animals (e.g., hitting or threatening classmates, throwing rocks at others' pets, etc.)
2. Destruction of property (e.g., vandalism, arson, graffiti, etc.)
3. Theft and/or deceitfulness (e.g., lying, conning, cheating, stealing, etc.)
4. Serious rule violations (e.g., repeated truancy, staying out all night, etc.) (American Psychiatric Association, 2000)

These symptoms may appear prior to adolescence or after it has begun.

Adolescents with conduct disorder often have poor social skills and don't know how to get along with others. They aren't good at handling frustration and can explode with anger. They are likely to begin using drugs at an early age and to be sexually precocious (Altepeter and Korger, 1999).

Conduct disorder is similar to both **oppositional defiant disorder (ODD)** and *attention-deficit hyperactivity disorder (ADHD)* in that persons with these disorders behave disruptively. But conduct disorder is different from both, as well. Persons with ODD are less likely to actually hurt others than are those with conduct disorder. Individuals with ODD argue and get angry. They blame others and may be defensive or disobedient, especially when interacting with authority figures. Youths with ODD go out of their way to annoy their teachers and parents but are less likely to pester peers. Individuals with ADHD often exhibit low frustration tolerance and poor impulse control, and so they may verbally or physically attack others when aroused. These antisocial behaviors are more by-products of their other symptoms, however, than symptoms in themselves. ADHD and ODD often co-occur, and many, if not most, children and adolescents with conduct disorder also have ADHD (Stewart, Cummings, Singer, and deBlois, 1981).

a lack of school success—poor grades, classroom misconduct, and an inability to adjust to the school program and to get along with administrators, teachers, and parents—is associated with delinquency (Huizinga and Jakob-Chien, 1998). Delinquent youths have also been found to score lower on social cognitive skills than nondelinquent youths (Edwards, 1996).

Delinquents experience greater conflict in all relationships, which reduces the quality and stability of friendships. Lochman and Dodge (1994), for example, found that aggressive adolescents are more likely to perceive others as being hostile than nonaggressive adolescents. If a person interprets others' behavior as threatening, then he or she will more likely behave aggressively himself or herself.

Although most delinquency is believed to have environmental causes, in some cases, organic or biological factors may be directly or indirectly influential. It has been found, for example, that some juvenile delinquents show evidence of a maturational lag in the development of the frontal lobe system of the brain (Chretien and Persinger, 2000). It is not that their cognition is impaired; rather, these juveniles cannot act on the basis of the knowledge they have.

Other researchers have emphasized the role of biological influences in delinquency, as well. There is some evidence to show that tendencies toward delinquency may be inherited, although shared family influences may include both environmental and genetic influences (Rowe, Rodgers, and Meseck-Bushey, 1992). It is true that certain personality characteristics, such as temperament, are genetically influenced, so that a child may have a predisposition to behave poorly. If the parents do not know how to cope, psychological disturbance in the adolescent may result.

High levels of testosterone and low levels of the neurotransmitter serotonin are also associated with aggressive behavior (Flannery, Hussey, Biebelhausen, and Wester, 2003). Furthermore, some research has linked these chemical imbalances with criminal activity. These chemicals likely work in conjunction with environmental and situational inputs; for example, having a low level of serotonin might make one less prone to feel happy and content, opening the door for destructive behavior.

Juvenile Gangs

During the 1980s and 1990s, youth gangs again surfaced as a major crime problem in the United States. News stories about violent crimes committed by youth gang members—crimes that often seem to involve

conduct disorder a psychological order typified by aggressive, hurtful, deceitful behavior.

oppositional defiant disorder (ODD) a psychological disorder that causes a person to get angry and argue, to blame and annoy others, and to disobey authority figures.

Males between the ages of 16 and 17 comprise the largest group of juvenile street gang members. They join gangs for a variety of emotional and social needs, including companionship, protection, and excitement.

random victims—appeared frequently in the mass media. What does research say about youth gang crime today?

According to the most recent National Youth Gang Survey (Egley and Ritz, 2006), there are about 24,000 youth gangs in the United States. Paralleling the decrease in juvenile crime overall, this is a significant drop since the peak in the mid-1990s. About 30 percent of the police districts sampled reported having gang activity within their jurisdictions. Gangs are more common in the West than in the East. A significant percentage of gangs are involved in the illegal drug trade.

A large body of research has characterized the typical gang member as a lower-income, minority male adolescent who does not get along with his family (Duke, Martinez, and Stein, 1997). In 2001, about half of all gang members were Latino and one-third were African American (Eagley, Howell, and Major, 2006). In the 1990s, gangs saw many changes: They moved into the suburbs, as well as staying in the inner city; female membership increased and more all-female gangs formed; and the age range of gang members widened.

Why do some individuals join gangs while others with similar backgrounds reject them? One theory says that a self-selection process is involved, such that youths who are already dysfunctional join gangs. A competing theory claims that normal adolescents join gangs and are then coerced into deviant behavior by their gang mates. These theories are not mutually exclusive, and both postulates appear correct: Adolescents who elect to join gangs are troubled to start with, but their level of delinquency increases once they join a gang. In particular, adolescents who join gangs have low self-esteem, poor relationships with their parents, and unresolved ethnic identities (Duke, Martinez, and Stein, 1997). They engage in antisocial activities to raise money, to gain status and approval, to bond with their gang peers, and to protect themselves.

ANSWERS WOULDN'T YOU LIKE TO KNOW . . .

How involved are girls in juvenile gangs?

As many as one-third of gang members are girls. Moreover, girls have cast aside their peripheral status and become increasingly similar to male gang members in their actions.

Until recently, it was taken for granted that there were few female gang members. It was also believed that when girls did join gangs, they were kept on the periphery; their main role was presumably as sex partners for the male gang members. A number of recent studies have produced findings that contradict these beliefs. Maxson and Whitlock (2002), for example, estimate that between one-quarter and one-third of all gang members are female. Although this is changing, female gang members are still less likely than male members to engage in violent activities, but they are likely to engage in criminal activity (Eagley, Howell, and Major, 2006). Girls tend both to join and leave gangs at younger ages than boys. Finally, girls, even more than boys, join gangs to fulfill a need for connections and relationships.

Youths who are members of gangs are more likely than nonmembers to steal, to commit assaults, to carry

Girls comprise an increasingly larger segment of the gang population and are less likely to be kept on the periphery than in the past.

ANSWERS WOULDN'T YOU LIKE TO KNOW ...

What usually happens to teens caught breaking the law?

When the police catch a teenager doing something illegal, they usually let him or her go after delivering a warning or contacting his or her parents or school officials. The teen is not usually sent through the criminal justice system. If a teen is arrested, tried, and found guilty by the courts, the most likely outcome is probation.

weapons, and to kill. Gang members are also more likely to be involved in an early pregnancy, to use drugs, to be assaulted, to be injured in a drive-by shooting, and to be killed at an early age (Flannery et al., 1998a; Morris, Harrison, Knox, Romanjhauser, Marques, and Watts, 1996). Thus, for some youths, joining a gang is a last-ditch effort to improve their life that backfires.

The Juvenile Justice System

Each state determines its own process for handling juvenile delinquents. Although this process varies among states, each system consists of three separate entities: the police, the juvenile court, and the correctional system.

The Police

The first contact any adolescent has with the juvenile justice system is the local police department. Charged with maintaining and enforcing the law, the police screen cases that may go before the courts. When offenses are discovered, the police may take any one of several actions: (1) Ignore the offenses; (2) let the juvenile go with a warning; (3) report the problem to parents; (4) refer the case to the school, a welfare agency, clinic, counseling or guidance center, or family society; (5) take the juvenile into custody for questioning, to be held or reprimanded by a juvenile officer; or (6) after investigation, arrest the juvenile and turn the matter over to a juvenile court. If arrested and awaiting trial, the juvenile may be released with or without bail or kept in a special detention center. If special juvenile facilities are not available, juvenile offenders are sometimes kept in jail with adult offenders.

One problem is that in the beginning of the process, the matter is left entirely to police discretion and so is inconsistent. Police must enforce the law, but they do so differentially. An individual officer may arrest adolescents who come from the so-called wrong section of town or have the wrong color skin but may release

parens patriae the philosophy that the juvenile court is to act in the best interests of the child.

RESEARCH HIGHLIGHT THE CASE THAT CHANGED JUVENILE COURT

Prior to the 1900s, the legal system treated juveniles as adults. If arrested, they appeared in adult courts; if sentenced, they went to adult prisons. Reformers working at the turn of the twentieth century were effective in changing this policy. They argued that minors could and should be rehabilitated rather than punished. The courts, they claimed, should assume the role of ***parens patriae*** and act in the best interests of the child. Although this was a noble intent, in practice it meant that juveniles were treated inconsistently and that their constitutional rights were often violated.

The case that changed the system involved a 15-year-old boy named Gerald Gault. In 1964, Gerald was arrested and detained by the police after a neighbor complained that he had made obscene phone calls to her. The police failed to notify Gerald's parents of his arrest. Neither Gerald's father nor the complainant was present at the hearing. Witnesses were neither sworn in nor cross-examined, and no official record was kept of the proceedings. The judge ordered that Gerald be sent to a juvenile detention center until his twenty-first birthday, a six-year sentence. In contrast, the maximum penalty that an adult could have received for the same offense would have been a $50 fine and two months in jail.

The case was appealed in the Arizona Supreme Court, but the appeal was denied. When presented to the U.S. Supreme Court in 1967, the Court found in Gerald's favor in a narrow 5 to 4 ruling. It decreed that minors are entitled to due process as outlined in the Bill of Rights and the Fourteenth Amendment. Since that time, even though juvenile court remains separate from adult court, minors are guaranteed the same judicial rights as adults; for example, they have the right to an attorney, they may cross-examine witnesses, and they cannot be made to incriminate themselves.

adolescents who come from well-to-do families or are neatly dressed. Some officers are far harder on juveniles than are other officers. One of the reasons adolescent offenders become bitter toward the police is because of unfair and differential treatment or harassment.

Many communities hire juvenile officers who are specialists in dealing with youths. Such officers go far beyond law enforcement functions and strive to assist adolescents and their families in solving problems. Some large cities have separate juvenile bureaus with five basic functions:

1. To discover delinquents, potential delinquents, and conditions contributing to delinquency
2. To investigate cases of juveniles who are delinquents or involved as accessories by association with adult criminals
3. To protect juveniles
4. To dispose of juvenile cases
5. To prevent juvenile delinquency

Police in many communities now go far beyond law enforcement, from sponsoring boys' and girls' clubs to offering drug education programs and safety education in local schools.

The Juvenile Court

As a last resort, the juvenile court is asked to make the disposition of a case, but procedures vary from state to state. How "parental" should the judge be? Cases are often dealt with informally in private hearings. The trial may consist of private talks in the judge's chambers. However, without any formal trial, what happens in such cases depends completely on the inclinations of the judge. Plea bargaining between lawyers is common, so that sometimes the attorneys decide the case.

The best juvenile court systems hire judges with special qualifications for juvenile court work, who understand not only the law but also child psychology and social problems. A variety of medical, psychological, and social services are available, along with adequate foster family and institutional care and recreational services and facilities (Stein and Smith, 1990). A qualified probation staff with limited caseloads and plans for constructive efforts works under state supervision. Detention of juveniles is kept at a minimum—if possible, outside of jails and police stations. An adequate record system is maintained and safeguarded against indiscriminate public inspection.

The Correctional System

The majority of juvenile offenders brought to court, especially those charged for the first time, are placed on probation, given suspended sentences, and/or ordered to get help from the proper medical, psychological, or social-service agency. The purpose of the court is not just to punish but also to ensure proper treatment and rehabilitation of the delinquent. Thus, the judge often must make quick decisions regarding the best treatment.

The backbone of the correctional procedure is the probation system, whereby the juvenile is placed under the care of a probation officer to whom she or he must report and who strives to regulate and guide his or her conduct. About two-thirds of convicted delinquents are placed on probation.

Probation based entirely on threat of punishment is poor rehabilitation. Programs that focus on positive behavior and positive reinforcement are more helpful. Studies show that juvenile offenders who are placed on probation have lower rearrest rates and generally better records than those detained in juvenile facilities. However, this is in part due to the fact that the most serious offenders—those least likely to be rehabilitated—are not placed on probation in the first place.

Most juvenile correction systems include detention centers. Many of these are reception and diagnostic centers where juveniles are placed under temporary restraint while awaiting a hearing. If hearings have already been held, the individuals are placed in the center for further diagnosis and evaluation before more permanent action is taken. About one-tenth of adolescents in detention centers are not even delinquents (Snyder and Sickmund, 2006). They are juveniles in need of supervision (JINS) who are wards of the court because their parents cannot, will not, or should not care for them. Some of the parents are ill or deceased; others have neglected, rejected, or abused the juveniles to the point where they have been taken out of the home. Some adolescents in detention facilities are those who have run away from home. Many are awaiting disposition by the court. Critics charge that overcrowded detention centers are no place for these juveniles. They have done nothing wrong—indeed, they have been victimized—and they are mixed in with juveniles who may have committed serious assault or even homicide. Similarly, one can question the wisdom of mixing the comparatively innocuous status offenders with more seriously criminal peers, as the potential for intimidation, harassment, and even inappropriate modeling seems substantial.

If a juvenile is sentenced to be held in a facility, there are a number of options. These include detention centers, long-term secure training schools, group homes, shelters, boots camps, and wilderness/ranch camps. About 30 percent of incarcerated juveniles are held in private, rather than public, facilities. The majority of incarcerated youths are in either detention centers or secure training schools (Snyder and Sickmund, 2006).

The system has been improved greatly by *the use of token economies,* which place the emphasis on a 24-hour positive learning environment (Miller, Cosgrove, and Doke, 1990). In this system, students earn points for good behavior, with points convertible to money that can be used to purchase goods or privileges. Money can be spent for room rental, for fines for misconduct, in the commissary or snack bar, or for recreation. Students earn points for academic accomplishments and schoolwork, for proper social behavior, for doing chores or other jobs, or for social development. Under this system, adolescents make great gains in academic achievement, on-the-job training, or eliminating assaultive, disruptive, and antisocial behavior.

One of the criticisms of these correctional institutions is that once the juveniles are released to the community, they often come under the same influences and face some of the same problems that led to detention in the first place. One suggestion has been to use more halfway houses and group homes where youths may live, going from there to school or to work. In this way, some control can be maintained over the adolescents until they have learned self-direction. One of the most important needs is to prepare youths for employment after discharge.

Only a small number of juvenile delinquents end up serving time in adult prisons. In 2003, 1 percent of persons admitted to adult prisons were less than 18 years of age (Snyder and Sickmund, 2006). This percentage climbed greatly in the 1990s, peaking in 1996, and has consistently dropped since then. The vast majority of adolescents incarcerated in adult facilities have committed serious person offenses, such as assault or homicide.

It is good that this number is so small, since sending adolescents to adult prisons is the worst way to rehabilitate them. A percentage of inmates of a prison population are violent individuals who prefer antisocial behavior, have no regard for the interests of others, and show little or no remorse. They are in contrast to adolescents, who are young and still developing. In spite of this, the average sentence for a juvenile is greater than for an adult who has committed the same crime (Cullen and Wright, 2002).

Once in prison, youths have no adequate adult male or female role models with whom they can have significant relationships. Furthermore, once they have a prison record, their chances of finding a useful life are jeopardized. They learn that fear, bribery, cheating, and sadism are ways of dealing with problems. In addition, many prisoners are harassed and bullied by fellow prisoners, who may use them in any number of ways, including for homosexual activities. If adolescents were not antagonistic toward authority and the system on arrival in prison, they soon become so.

Counseling and therapy, both individually and in groups, are important parts of any comprehensive program of treatment and correction of juvenile offenders. Individual therapy on a one-to-one basis is time consuming, with too few professionals and too many

Of all the options available in the juvenile correction system, sending a youth to an adult prison is the worst way to rehabilitate him or her.

delinquents, but it can be effective. Some therapists feel that group therapy reaches a juvenile sooner than individual therapy because the delinquent feels less anxious and defensive in the group situation. Group therapy is sometimes offered to both juvenile offenders and their parents, in which case it becomes similar to other types of family therapy. Work with parents is especially important in correcting family situations that contribute to the delinquency in the first place.

ANSWERS WOULDN'T YOU LIKE TO KNOW . . .

What can be done to reduce the rate of juvenile delinquency?

Programs that build life skills, create hope for the future, provide mentors, and instill prosocial values can and do reduce juvenile delinquency.

Critique of the Juvenile Justice System

The biggest criticism of the juvenile justice system is that it does not work. The present trend to try juveniles as adults has been proven ineffective (Lipsey and Wilson, 1998). Neither juvenile nor adult crime has been reduced as a result of the juvenile court system, nor has the system reduced the rates of recidivism (Ashford and LeCroy, 1990). Almost all critiques of the system point out the lack of coordination and definition in the system; the defective delivery of services; the confusion of roles and responsibilities of the judges, social workers, and police; and the system's failure to protect either the child or society. As long as the emphasis is on punishing the juvenile offender, treatment and rehabilitation will be neglected. In any case, it is far better to focus on primary prevention and stop delinquency before it starts.

The Restorative Justice Movement

In reaction to the long-standing failures of the juvenile justice system, a new approach to juvenile justice has gained momentum during the past 15 years the **restorative justice movement.** This approach tries to balance the needs of the victim (for reparation and confrontation), the community at large (for security and protection), and the juvenile perpetrator (to learn skills so he or she has alternatives to crime). To be sure, offenders are held accountable for their crimes: They are expected to understand the harm they have caused, to accept responsibility for that harm, and to repair the damage they have caused. In theory, by meeting with their victim and making restitution and by having opportunities for education, counseling, and community service, offenders become not only more morally mature but gain a feeling of integration into the community and the desire and skills to become productive members of that community (Office of Juvenile Justice and Delinquency Prevention, 1995).

The restorative justice approach is not without its critics (see Cullen and Wright, 2002). For example, it is unclear how such an approach could be implemented in the case of a serious crime, such as rape or murder, in which the victim might be understandably unwilling to confront the offender. Also, what happens if an offender promises to cooperate and then does not? What if he or she goes through the program and then commits additional offenses? To date, research on the effectiveness of the restorative justice approach has been mixed. More time will be needed to tell whether restorative justice is more effective than other rehabilitative approaches.

Prevention of Juvenile Delinquency

Prevention efforts are aimed at eliminating problem behaviors before they even occur. Many experts believe that greater efforts should be placed on prevention, for several reasons. First, a single program can effectively and concurrently reduce the risks of several undesirable behaviors, such as substance abuse and dropping out. In addition, prevention measures reduce the trauma experienced by adolescents as well as their families and their victims (if any). Finally, prevention programs can eliminate the spiral of defeat, whereby one problem leads to or at least exacerbates others.

Many different types of efforts have been aimed at reducing delinquency and other problems, but the greatest hope is held out for what are termed **youth development programs.** Although extremely varied, these programs are designed to provide skills, establish relationships, and increase self-esteem so that adolescents avoid delinquency and become well-functioning adults. In contrast, more narrowly focused prevention efforts, such as informational lectures on the dangers of unsafe sexual practices or substance abuse, do not give students the life skills they need for success (Roth, 2000).

A review of youth development programs found that successful programs share five features:

1. They enhance academic, social, and vocational competence.
2. They instill self-confidence and promote self-esteem.
3. They foster strong relationships between adolescents and adult mentors and between peers.
4. They build character and instill positive values.

5. They promote caring and compassion for others (Roth, Brooks-Gunn, Murray, and Foster, 1998).

Moreover, successful programs provide three different types of supports: emotional support and nurturance, motivational support from high expectations and standards, and strategic support in the form of help in planning and resources (Roth, 2000). The services must be sustained rather than short term. Research has suggested that adolescents are willing to participate in and benefit from participation in programs that challenge them and that they feel are relevant to their lives.

Unfortunately, it is hard to detail the characteristics of the most beneficial programs. How long must they last? What activities work best? Where should they be housed? At what age should they begin? The programs are very diverse, and the research on outcomes is scanty. Many of the studies that have been done are flawed in that they involve only small samples or lack control groups (Moote and Wodarski, 1997; Roth, Brooks-Gunn, Murray, and Foster, 1998). For the present, we can only conclude that what seems to work are activities that unite caring adults with adolescents in settings that stretch the youths and give them a sense of personal accomplishment.

restorative justice movement an approach to juvenile justice that addresses the needs of the victim, the community, and the perpetrator; it focuses on restitution for the victim and personal development for the offender.

youth development programs programs designed to provide skills, establish relationships, and increase self-esteem so that adolescents avoid delinquency and become well-functioning adults.

SUMMARY

1. Alienated adolescents feel estranged from family, friends, and school. They turn away from the mainstream of youth and adult society and express their feelings through various types of acting-out behavior, including running away, suicide, and juvenile delinquency.
2. Adolescents run away from home for a number of reasons. Most runaways come from dysfunctional families. Runaways may also have problems with delinquency, academics, and peer relationships.
3. About half of all runaways, called *transient runaways,* are gone only for a night or two. *Intent runaways* are generally more serious about leaving home and are gone for longer periods of time.
4. About half of intent runaways did not leave home voluntarily; rather, they were thrown out by their parents due to poverty, their own misbehavior, or family disintegration.
5. The consequences of running away may be disastrous. Runaways are likely to be victimized by others. They must often resort to drug dealing, theft, and prostitution to earn money for food and shelter. Because of unsafe sex practices and intravenous drug use, many are at risk for HIV and AIDS.
6. Assistance to runaway youths is inadequate. More emergency shelters, more comprehensive services, stable residential placements, and transitional programs for older adolescents are all needed.
7. Adolescent homelessness is a worldwide, rather than a national, problem.
8. Suicide is the third-leading cause of death among adolescents (after accidents and homicide). Girls are more likely to attempt suicide than boys, but boys are more likely to succeed because they use more violent means.
9. Most adolescents who commit suicide are clinically depressed or are substance abusers. Clinical depression is a serious psychological disorder. Girls are more likely to be depressed than boys, and girls' depression is more often triggered by social factors. Teenagers who have suffered a personal loss or who are having trouble at school are at heightened risk for depression.
10. Adolescents who commit suicide often have dysfunctional family backgrounds. In addition, these youths often lack impulse control. Because of the extra stresses they experience, gay and lesbian teens are especially likely to attempt or commit suicide.
11. Adolescent suicide is especially hard on survivors, who suffer fear, rage, guilt, and depression.
12. Juvenile delinquency is the violation of the law by anyone under legal age. From the mid-1980s to the mid-1990s, the juvenile crime rate rose sharply. It has since been declining. Males are more likely to commit offenses than girls, but girls' rates are rising faster than boys' rates.
13. The causes of delinquency may be grouped into three major categories: environmental, interpersonal, and personal.
14. Environmental factors leading to delinquency include poverty, living in a gang-infested neighborhood, and attending substandard schools. Not all delinquents are poor, however.
15. Interpersonal factors leading to delinquency include coming from an abusive, dysfunctional family and associating with deviant peers.

16. Personal factors leading to delinquency include poor self-control, psychological disorders, substance abuse, poor academic performance, and low social-cognitive skills.
17. Individuals may be predisposed to antisocial behavior due to maturation lags in the brain, genetic endowment, and biochemical imbalances.
18. Adolescents often organize themselves into juvenile gangs for protection, companionship, excitement, or status. Such gangs are a problem because they force members to engage in antisocial and illegal acts that they would not participate in if acting on their own. Dysfunctional youths are more prone to join gangs than psychologically healthy youths; after they join, youths are more likely to engage in deviant activities than they were before.
19. Female involvement in gangs is on the rise, and girls are beginning to engage in a wider variety of gang activities than they did in the past.
20. The juvenile justice system consists of the police, the juvenile court, and the correctional system (including the probation system, detention centers, training schools, ranches, forestry camps, farms, halfway houses, group homes, treatment centers, and prisons). The largest criticism of the juvenile justice system is that it does not work.
21. The newest approach to juvenile rehabilitation is the restorative justice approach. This model addresses the needs of the victim, the offender, and the community and incorporates both rehabilitation and punishment.
22. Rehabilitation should be reaffirmed as the foundation for treating juvenile delinquency.
23. The best prevention programs have several features in common. They provide youths with skills, instill self-confidence, foster strong relationships, and promote compassion.

KEY TERMS

conduct disorder 408	restorative justice 414
depression 399	status crimes 404
juvenile delinquent 404	survival sex 396
oppositional defiant disorder (ODD) 408	throwaways 395
parens patriae 411	youth development programs 414

THOUGHT QUESTIONS

Personal Reflection

1. Do you know an adolescent who ran away from home? What were the circumstances?
2. Have you or someone you've been close to battled with depression? Was there a specific cause? How were you/they helped?
3. Have you known an adolescent who committed suicide? What were the circumstances?
4. When you were growing up, were there any delinquent juvenile gangs in your area? If so, describe them.
5. Did you commit any status or criminal offenses when you were younger? Why? Were you ever caught? What happened, and how did the consequences effect you?
6. Have you known a juvenile offender who was sent to a training school or correctional institution who became a productive, law-abiding citizen? What factors made the difference?

Group Discussion

7. Should runaways be forced to return home? When should they? When should they not?
8. What can or should be done to help the parents or siblings of runaways?
9. What can or should be done to help runaways themselves?
10. How do you account for the fact that the percentages of those under age 18 who are arrested are decreasing?
11. Why do far greater number of males than females become delinquent? What factors may be exerting an influence?
12. Why do some adolescents who are brought up in crime-prone neighborhoods not become delinquent?
13. What should parents do if their adolescent is running around with a group whose members are known to be delinquent?
14. What is your opinion of the juvenile justice system? How could it be improved? What do you think is needed to reform known juvenile offenders?

Debate Questions

15. Parents whose child runs away from home for more than a day or two should be required to receive counseling.
16. Schools should take an active role in preventing delinquency.
17. Delinquents who have been diagnosed with conduct disorder should be treated differently by the system than delinquents who do not have this disorder.
18. Juvenile delinquency cannot be prevented.
19. It is impossible to rehabilitate juvenile delinquents with the present system.

SUGGESTED READING

Berman, A. L., Jobes, D. A., and Silverman, M. M. (2005). *Adolescent Suicide: Assessment And Intervention.* Washington, DC: American Psychological Association.

Empey, L. T., Stafford, M. C., and Hay, C. H. (1999). *American Delinquency: Its Meaning and Construction.* New York: Wadsworth.

Fassler, D. G., and Duman, L. S. (1998). *"Help Me, I'm Sad": Recognizing, Treating, and Preventing Childhood and Adolescent Depression.* New York: Penguin Books.

Flannery, D. J., and Huff, C. R. (1999). *Youth Violence: Prevention, Intervention, and Social Policy.* Washington, DC: American Psychiatric Press.

Heibrun, K., Goldstein, N. E. S., and Redding, R. E. (Eds.). (2005). *Juvenile Delinquency: Prevention, Assessment, and Intervention.* New York: Oxford University Press.

Howell, J. C. (2003). *Preventing and Reducing Juvenile Delinquency: A Comprehensive Framework.* Thousand Oaks, CA: Sage.

Hoyt, D., and Whitbeck, L. (1999). *Nowhere to Grow: Homeless and Runaway Adolescents and Their Families.* Somerset, NJ: Aldine.

Jackson, R. K., and McBride, W. D. (2000). *Understanding Street Gangs.* Belmont, CA: Wadsworth.

Jamison, K. R. (1999). *Night Falls Fast: Understanding Suicide.* New York: Knopf.

Koplewicz, H. (2003). *More Than Moody: Recognizing and Treating Adolescent Depression.* New York: Perigee.

Sikes, G. (1998). *Eight Ball Chicks: A Year in the Violent World of Girl Gangsters.* New York: Doubleday.

Wodarski, J. S., Wodarski, L. A., and Dulmus. C. N. (2002). *Adolescent Depression and Suicide: A Comprehensive Empirical Intervention for Prevention and Treatment.* Springfield, IL: Charles Thomas.

USEFUL WEB SITES

National Center for Missing and Exploited Children
http://missingkids.org

The site of this private, nonprofit organization has separate information sections for professionals and parents. It details the steps to take to report a missing adolescent and what to do if someone you love is missing. It also has a FAQs page and a newsroom.

National Strategy for Suicide Prevention
www.mentalhealth.org/suicideprevention/default.asp

This site, administered by the U.S. Department of Health and Human Services, contains facts, information about prevention programs, databases, and a newsroom.

Office of Juvenile Justice and Delinquency Prevention
www.ojjdp.ncjrs.org

This federal agency has an extensive Web site filed with the most current facts, statistics, and reports available on all aspects of juvenile delinquency.

CHAPTER 18 SUBSTANCE ABUSE, ADDICTION, AND DEPENDENCY

WOULDN'T YOU LIKE TO KNOW . . .

- What distinguishes *drug use* from *drug abuse?*
- What are the levels of risk for different types of drug users?
- Which drugs are most commonly used by adolescents?
- Does drug use increase or decrease in college?
- How many adolescents today use drugs?
- What demographic factors distinguish drug users from nonusers?
- What kinds of prevention and treatment programs are effective with adolescents?
- Why do teens smoke cigarettes when they know it's harmful?
- Why do so many adolescents begin to drink?
- Do most students who drink heavily in college keep drinking so heavily as adults?

This chapter focuses on a major health problem of adolescents: drug abuse. This particular problem has been selected because of its frequency and its importance in the lives of adolescents. Drug abuse is considered by many to be the greatest social health problem relating to youths. It is also significantly related to delinquency and crime among youths. We will take a look at the problem and answer a number of questions: Which drugs are most commonly abused? Has the abuse of drugs been overestimated? Who is using drugs and for what reasons?

In addition to illegal drugs, large numbers of youths also smoke tobacco and drink alcohol. What can be done to prevent them from starting? What are the harmful consequences of these behaviors? Because tobacco and alcohol use are so common, each is given its own section later in this chapter. But first, we need to distinguish between *drug use* and *drug abuse.*

DRUG USE AND ABUSE

The fact is, we use drugs all the time: We take a couple of aspirin when we have a headache, and we use a decongestant to dry up a stuffy nose. Virtually *all* drugs have the potential for abuse; even aspirin is lethal if taken in a sufficiently large quantity. How, then, can we distinguish between *use* and *abuse?*

There is no single, absolute heuristic for separating the two. But in commonsense terms, drug use qualifies as **drug abuse** when two criteria are met: (1) Using the drug puts someone at significantly increased risk for having bad things happen to him or her and (2) taking the drug interferes in some way with his or her normal, daily responsibilities and accomplishments. Unfortunately, depending on the drug in question, the first criterion is met quite readily. The second criterion is usually met with higher doses and more frequent use.

To be honest, most adolescents who experiment with drugs suffer no lasting negative consequences. The problem, however, is that we never know when we will be one of the people in the minority—the rare individual who has a heart attack the first time he or she tries crack or the more common individual who gets into the driver's seat drunk and causes a serious car accident. Likewise, no one knows before trying a drug if he or she is particularly susceptible to addiction and dependency. Added to this, of course, is the fact that most of the drugs used by adolescents are illegal for them to possess. Therefore, any adolescent who tries these drugs runs the risk of arrest, fine, probation, or even jail time.

In many ways, using drugs is like playing Russian roulette: If there is only one bullet in the eight chambers, the odds are that you will be fine. But if you get unlucky, the consequences can be fatal.

ANSWERS WOULDN'T YOU LIKE TO KNOW ...

What distinguishes *drug use* from *drug abuse?*

You have crossed the line between the two when your drug use hurts you—putting you at risk for danger or harm and making your behavior get out of control.

Physical Addiction and Psychological Dependency

As an individual continues to take a drug, he or she runs the risk of developing a physical addiction or a psychological dependency. A **physical addiction** to a drug results because the body builds up a physical need for the drug, so that its sudden denial results in withdrawal symptoms. In general, psychoactive drugs work by affecting the neurotransmitters that facilitate communication between nerve cells: They either enhance or diminish the effects of the neurotransmitters. Depending on which neurotransmitters are affected and whether their effects are increased or decreased, the neurons will fire more than they should or when they should not, or they will fail to fire or fire only weakly. **Psychological dependency** is the development of a persistent, sometimes overpowering psychological need for a drug, resulting in a compulsion to take it. A well-established habit of psychological dependency may be more difficult to overcome than one involving physical addiction, especially if someone becomes so deeply involved with a drug that he or she cannot function without it. A physical addiction to heroin, for example, may be broken, but individuals go back to it because of psychological dependence on it. It is a mistake, therefore, to assume that the only dangerous drugs are those that are physically addictive.

In either case, an addicted or dependent individual finds that his or her drug use interferes with his or her life. He or she may miss class, skip work, or do poorly on a test, for instance. Even someone who is not addicted or dependent can experience these consequences if he or she has a hangover or feels fuzzy headed the day after using the drug.

Patterns and Intensity of Drug Use

Most persons who use drugs can be fit into one of five categories, based on their motivation for taking the drug:

1. **Experimental use** is defined as the short-term, nonpatterned trial of one or more drugs, with a maximum frequency of 10 times per drug. It is motivated primarily by curiosity or by a desire to experience new feelings.

ANSWERS WOULDN'T YOU LIKE TO KNOW . . .

What are the levels of risk for different types of drug users?

Obviously, the risk increases as the user moves up the scale from experimental to compulsive use. As both the frequency and intensity of drug use increase, so do the nature and extent of the problems. Compulsive users, by definition, have serious problems.

2. **Social-recreational use** occurs in social settings among friends or acquaintances who wish to share an experience. This type of use tends to vary in frequency, intensity, and duration but not to escalate in either frequency or intensity to patterns of uncontrolled use. Users typically do not use addictive drugs such as heroin; they are therefore able to exercise control over their behavior.
3. **Circumstantial-situational use** is motivated by the desire to achieve a known and anticipated effect. This would include the student who takes stimulants to stay awake or the person who takes sedatives to relieve tension and go to sleep. Five common psychological conditions may lead to illicit drug use by adolescents: a depressed mood, normlessness (not having definite values, opinions, or rules to live by), social isolation, stress, and low self-esteem. The greatest danger from circumstantial use of marijuana is that the person will become accustomed to drug use to solve problems, and the habit will ultimately escalate to intensified use.
4. **Intensified drug use** is generally a long-term pattern of using drugs at least once daily to achieve relief from a persistent problem or stressful situation. Drug use becomes a customary activity of daily life, with people ordinarily remaining socially and economically integrated in the life of the community. Some change in functioning may occur, depending on the frequency, intensity, and amount of use.
5. **Compulsive drug use** is use at both high frequency and high intensity, of relatively long duration, producing physiological or psychological dependence, with disuse resulting in physiological discomfort or psychological stress. Motivation to continue comes from the physical or psychological comfort or relief obtained by using the drug. Users in this category include not only the street "junkie" or skid-row alcoholic but also the opiate-dependent physician, the barbiturate-dependent homemaker, and the alcohol-dependent business executive.

Types of Drugs

The drugs most commonly abused may be grouped into four categories: *narcotics, stimulants, depressants,* and *hallucinogens.* Some drugs bridge the categories.

Narcotics

Included in the **narcotics** are *opium* and its derivatives, such as *morphine, heroin,* and *codeine.* They work by mimicking **endogenous endorphins:** chemicals produced by the body to dull the sensation of pain. Opium is a dark, gummy substance extracted from the juice of unripe seed pods of the opium poppy. Opium is usually taken orally or sniffed—that is, it is heated and its vapor inhaled.

Morphine, the chief active ingredient in opium, is extracted as a bitter, white powder with no odor. Each grain of opium contains about one-tenth of a grain of morphine. Morphine is used medicinally to relieve extreme pain because of its depressant effect on the central nervous system. Addicts refer to it as "M" or "monkey." It may be sniffed, but the powder is usually mixed with water and injected under the skin with a hypodermic needle ("skin popping"). For maximum effect, it is injected directly into a vein ("mainlined").

Codeine is the mildest morphine derivative. Often used in cough syrups or to relieve mild body aches, it has the same but milder analgesic properties as other

drug abuse the use of drugs to the point of causing risk or harm, either due to legal risk or to the risk of harming oneself and others.

physical addiction a condition that develops from abusing a drug that forms a chemical dependency.

psychological dependency the development of a persistent, sometimes overpowering psychological need for a drug.

experimental use occasional drug use motivated by curiosity.

social-recreational use drug use primarily to relax and have fun at parties.

circumstantial-situational use drug use to produce a desired psychological mood.

intensified drug use daily drug use.

compulsive drug use drug use motivated by physical addiction or psychological dependency.

narcotics a class of opiate-based drugs that depress the central nervous system and thus relieve pain and induce sleep; in large doses, produce unconsciousness, stupor, coma, and possibly death; most are habit forming.

endogenous endorphins chemicals similar to narcotics that are produced by the body and cause euphoria and depress pain.

narcotics. Codeine is often used by young people who mistakenly think it is not addictive.

Heroin ("H," "horse," or "smack") was first refined from morphine in 1874. Like its relative, it is a white, odorless, bitter-tasting powder. It is rarely sold in pure form but is instead "cut," or mixed with, other white substances, such as powdered milk or corn starch. Unfortunately, it is sometimes mixed with quinine. Since quinine is bitter, like heroin, the user cannot tell by tasting how potent the mixture is. Heroin is not always white, however. Impurities can discolor it; in fact, black tar heroin, which ranges in color from dark brown to black, has become popular in the western United States. One reason heroin is so dangerous is that the amount of heroin in a "bag," or single dose, varies widely and an overdose can easily kill. The heroin being sold today is generally purer than that sold in previous decades. Because of this, usage patterns have changed. In the past, heroin was injected, either intravenously (into one's veins) or subcutaneously. Although many current users still inject heroin, more and more are snorting it or smoking it. Both of these options are perceived by many adolescents as safer ways to use the drug, since they eliminate the risk of contracting the human immunodeficiency virus (HIV) or hepatitis by sharing needles. Still, given that the amount of heroin needed to get high is close to the lethal dosage, use of this drug is dangerous in any form. It is particularly dangerous to mix heroin with alcohol and other depressants. Although it is the most widely used opiate, only a small minority of adolescents experiment with heroin. Heroin use rose over the course of the 1990s, but fewer than 1 percent of high school students report having taken the drug during the past year (Johnson, O'Malley, Bachman, and Schulenberg, 2006).

The synthetic opiates, *Demerol* (meperidine) and *Dolophine* (methadone), were created as chemical substitutes for the natural opiates and are used in medicine as pain relievers. They are addictive and restricted by law to medical use.

The consequences of morphine and heroin use are severe. They are the most physically addictive of all drugs. Users quickly develop tolerance and physical as well as psychological dependence and must therefore gradually increase the dosage. Because dependence becomes total and heroin is expensive (addicts spend several hundred dollars daily), many users turn to crime or prostitution to support their habits. Without the drug, withdrawal symptoms begin to appear within six to eight hours. The first symptoms are running eyes and nose, yawning, sweating, dilation of the pupils, and appearance of goose pimples on the skin (from which the expression "cold turkey" originated). Within 24 hours, addicts develop leg, back, and abdominal cramps, violent muscle spasms, vomiting, and diarrhea. The expression "kicking the habit" developed as a result of the muscle spasms during withdrawal. Bodily functions such as respiration, blood pressure, temperature, and metabolism, which have been depressed, now become hyperactive. These symptoms gradually diminish over a period of a week or more. Women who have babies while addicted deliver infants who are addicts or who are born dead from drug poisoning.

Addiction may have other effects, too. Addicts usually lose their appetite for food, which leads to extreme weight loss and severe malnutrition. They neglect their health, suffer chronic fatigue, and are in a general devitalized condition. Sexual interest and activity decline; most marriages end in separation or divorce. Addicts become accident prone—they may fall frequently, drown, or even set themselves on fire if they drop off to sleep while smoking. They lose the willpower to carry on daily functions and they pay little attention to their appearance. Their whole lives center on getting the next "fix."

Because the prognosis for curing heroin addiction is so discouraging, methadone is now given as a substitute drug through medically recognized methadone maintenance programs. The drug blocks the hunger for heroin and the effects of it, with the result that the majority of addicts no longer have a constant desire to obtain heroin. When they have no cravings, they do not get high or drowsy and can therefore function normally. Studies show outstanding success with methadone maintenance. The majority of patients who are regularly given medically prescribed doses of methadone become productive citizens, returning to work or school and avoiding any drug-related arrests (O'Brien and Cohen, 1984). Despite the success of these programs, only a minority of American heroin addicts receive methadone. Because it is currently the most effective treatment, in 1997 the National Institute of Health recommended that the law be changed to make access to methadone easier. In 1993, a newer drug, Levo-Alpha Acetyl Methadol (LAAM), was approved by the Food and Drug Administration (FDA) for use as a substitute for methadone. Its benefit is that it is longer acting, so that users need take it only three times a week rather than daily. If it lives up to its initial promise, its use will likely spread.

Stimulants

The term **stimulants** refers to a wide variety of drugs that "rev up" the central nervous system; they energize rather than tranquilize. Most work by increasing the amount of norepinephrine and/or **dopamine** available to the brain's neurons (McKim, 1997). Dopamine, in particular, is associated with feelings of pleasure.

One of the most well-known stimulants is *cocaine* ("coke," "snow," or "blow"). It is extracted from the leaves of the South American coca plant and is available as an odorless, fluffy, white powder. Even though it is expensive, it is widely used in the youth drug culture, as well as among more affluent groups. Cocaine depresses the appetite and increases alertness. It is not effective when taken orally, so users sniff or inject it intravenously into the bloodstream. Aside from financial depletion, the primary undesirable effects are nervousness, irritability, restlessness, mild paranoia, physical exhaustion, mental confusion, loss of weight, fatigue, depression when "coming down," and various afflictions of the nasal mucous membranes and cartilage. Taking large doses can lead to a severe psychosis while the person is still on the drug. Large doses can produce headaches, cold sweat, hyperventilation, nausea, tremors, convulsions, unconsciousness, and even death. Psychological dependence is severe; withdrawal is characterized by a profound depression for which cocaine itself appears to be the only remedy. One of the most famous cocaine addicts was Sigmund Freud, who escalated his use well into the twentieth century.

About 8 percent of high school seniors have used cocaine, about 5 percent of them within the past year (Johnson, O'Malley, Bachman, and Schulenberg, 2006). About 2 percent of young adults have used cocaine within the past year (Substance Abuse and Mental Health Services Administration, 2005). Hispanic students are significantly more likely to use cocaine than White students; African American students are less likely to use cocaine than students in the other two groups.

Cocaine can be further processed by heating it with ammonia or sodium bicarbonate to produce "crack," a form of the drug that can be smoked. (The name comes from the crackling sound it makes when heated.) Smoking crack produces a more intense but shorter-lasting high than ingesting powder cocaine. Crack is one of the most addictive of all drugs. It is so potent that users develop a craving for the drug very quickly. The craving can be so demanding that users will resort to theft, deceit, and violence to procure the drug. The health consequences of use may be severe, because the drug has destructive effects on brain neurotransmitters and acts as an excessive stimulant on the heart and other organs. Adolescent crack users are likely to make poor grades, be depressed, and be alienated from family and friends (Ringwalt and Palmer, 1989).

Amphetamines are stimulants that include such drugs as benzedrine, Dexedrine, Ritalin, and methedrine ("speed"). They are used medically for treating obesity, mild depression, fatigue, and other conditions. The drugs are usually taken orally in the form of tablets or capsules. Because they are stimulants, they increase alertness, elevate mood, and produce a feeling of well-being. Large doses may produce a temporary rise in blood pressure, palpitations, headache, dizziness, sweating, diarrhea, pallor and dilation of the pupils, vasomotor disturbances, agitation, confusion, apprehension, or delirium. Regular amphetamine users do not develop physical dependence, but users soon develop an intense psychological need to continue taking the drug and require larger doses as their tolerance develops. Mental depression and fatigue are experienced after the drug has been withdrawn, so psychic dependence develops quickly because the "high" is so enticing and the "low" so depressing. Patients usually need to be treated in mental hospitals, especially patients who inject the drugs into their veins. Some users end up swallowing whole handfuls of tablets instead of only one or two. The outcome of this or injecting the drugs intravenously can be amphetamine psychosis.

One of the amphetamines, called *methedrine* or *methamphetamine* ("speed," "meth," or "chalk"), is particularly dangerous because it is commonly injected under the skin or directly into a vein, often causing rupturing of the blood vessels and death. Other hazards are infections such as tetanus, HIV, syphilis, malaria, or hepatitis from dirty needles. The heavy user displays a potential for violence, paranoia, physical depiction, or bizarre behavior. Suicides are frequent during the periods of deep depression following withdrawal. Methedrine works by stimulating the release of dopamine; in the process, it damages the terminal branches of neurons that produce the neurotransmitters dopamine and **serotonin.** Methedrine is also available in a smokable, crystallized form ("ice," "crystal," or "glass"). About 2 percent of high school seniors have used methedrine within the past year (Johnson, O'Malley, Bachman, and Schulenberg, 2006).

Ritalin (methylphenidate) and Adderall (a mixture of amphetamine and dextroamphetamine) are stimulants that are readily available to teenagers, since both are widely prescribed to help children and adolescents who have **attention-deficit hyperactivity disorder (ADHD).** When prescibed and taken at low doses, these medications are very effective in helping youths with ADHD to concentrate and sit still. When taken in high doses, however, these two drugs have the same negative effects as other amphetamines and can be quite dangerous.

Depressants

In contrast to stimulants, **depressants** slow the functioning of the central nervous system. Barbiturates, tranquilizers, inhalants, and alcohol are all depressants.

stimulants agents that produce a temporary increase in the functioning of the body.

dopamine a neurotransmitter whose effects are enhanced by stimulants.

serotonin a neurotransmitter that is chemically similar to the hallucinogens.

attention-deficit hyperactivity disorder (ADHD) a behavioral disorder characterized by impulsivity, an inability to pay attention, and an inability to sit still.

depressants a class of drugs that work by slowing the functioning of the central nervous system (alcohol, inhalants).

PERSONAL ISSUES ECSTASY

One drug whose use has increased since the mid-1990s, when it first emerged as a so-called club drug, is *ecstasy* (also known as MDMA, XTC). Ecstasy is an amphetamine, but it also has mild hallucinogenic effects. It is derived from methamphetamine, and most of that found in the United States is imported from The Netherlands. Ecstasy comes in tablets that cost about $25 apiece; these tablets are often impure, containing methamphetamine, ephedrine, and cocaine (all other stimulants) in addition to the ecstasy. Each pill produces a four- to six-hour high, with peak effects about two hours after the pill is taken (Powell, 2003).

Ecstasy works by increasing the body's release of the neurotransmitters dopamine and norepinephrine (like other stimulants) as well as serotonin (like hallucinogens). It produces feelings of enhanced self-confidence and well-being, provides a burst of energy, and causes a loss of inhibitions. In the short run, ecstasy can also lead to confusion, depression, insomnia, anxiety, and paranoia. Blood pressure and heart rate often increase dramatically, and users may experience nausea, faintness, and blurred vision. A particularly dangerous effect of ecstacy is that it destroys the body's ability to regulate temperature, such that body temperature could rise to an unhealthy level. Since it can kill brain cells, it is not surprising that nonhuman primates exposed to ecstasy have been shown to exhibit learning and memory deficits, even after several years have passed (NIDA, 2001).

Unfortunately, the majority of high school seniors report that ecstasy is easy to obtain. Use of this drug increased from the mid-1990s until 2001, and then began declining in 2002. In 2005, approximately 5 percent of high school seniors and 2 percent of eighth-graders reported having used ecstasy during the previous year (Johnson et al., 2006).

Because they slow heartbeat and respiration rates, they can all be fatal if taken in large enough quantities.

Barbiturates are depressants that decrease the activity of the central nervous system, usually producing sedation, intoxication, and sleep. They include drugs commonly used in sleeping pills, such as *Quaalude, Nembutal, Seconal, Tuinal, Amytal,* and *phenobarbital.* Some of these drugs—Nembutal, Tuinal, and Seconal, for example—are short acting, meaning the effects set in soon and wear off quickly. Others, such as phenobarbital, are long acting. Barbiturates are widely prescribed medicinally for insomnia, nervousness, or epilepsy. When taken as directed, in small doses, there is no evidence that the long-acting barbiturates are addictive. There is a greater chance of addiction with the short-acting drugs. All barbiturates are dangerous when abused because they develop total addiction: both physical and psychological dependence. Dosages must be increased as tolerance develops. Barbiturates appear to work by making some of the brain's cells more susceptible to the effects of **GABA,** an inhibitory neurotransmitter.

Barbiturate users exhibit slurred speech, staggering gait, and sluggish reactions. They may be easily moved to tears or laughter, are emotionally erratic, and are frequently irritable and antagonistic. They are prone to stumble and drop objects and are often bruised or have cigarette burns on their bodies.

When the abuser has become physically dependent, withdrawal symptoms become severe in about 24 hours. Increasing nervousness, headache, muscle twitching, weakness, insomnia, nausea, and a sudden drop of blood pressure occur. Convulsions that can be fatal are an ever-present danger with barbiturate withdrawal. Delirium and hallucinations may develop. When barbiturates are taken in combination with alcohol or narcotics, the sedative effect is multiplied and can result in coma or death.

Tranquilizers such as *Miltown, Equanil, Placidyl, Librium,* and *Valium* are similar to barbiturates in their effects, for they, too, act to slow the central nervous system. The hazards of Valium are supplied to physicians by the manufacturer, Roche Laboratories. The product information supplied reads, in part:

> Warnings: . . . Patients receiving . . . Valium (diazepam) should be cautioned against engaging in hazardous occupations requiring complete mental alertness such as operating machinery or driving a motor vehicle. . . .
>
> Since Valium (diazepam) has a central nervous system depressant effect, patients should be advised against the simultaneous ingestion of alcohol and other central nervous system depressant drugs. . . .
>
> *Physical and Psychological Dependence:* Withdrawal symptoms (similar in character to those noted with barbiturates and alcohol) have occurred following abrupt discontinuance of diazepam (convulsions, tremor, abdominal and muscle cramps, vomiting and sweating). . . . Particularly addiction-prone individuals (such as drug addicts or alcoholics) should be under careful surveillance when receiving diazepam. (Valium package insert, 1988)

In short, these products, when abused, have the same dangers as barbiturates.

Inhalants are a subclass of depressants. There are three types of inhalants: (1) *solvents,* such as paint thinner, dry-cleaning fluid, gasoline, and some glues; (2) *gases,* such as the propellants used in spray paints and whipped cream dispensers ("whippets"); and (3) *nitrites,* such as amyl nitrate. Solvents and gases are primarily used by young adolescents to get high; nitrates are largely used by adults to enhance sexual experience. All three types of inhalants slow down the body's functions and, in large quantities, can cause coma and death. In addition, the use of inhalants can produce hearing loss, bone marrow damage, and liver and kidney damage (National Institute of Drug Abuse, 1999c). Some users increase the concentration of the drug they breathe by placing a plastic bag over their head when they inhale. This is especially dangerous, since if the user passes out, he or she can easily suffocate. Others stuff an inhalant-soaked rag into their mouth and inhale ("huffing"). Unlike nearly every other drug, young children and early adolescents are more likely to use inhalants than older adolescents, probably because they are inexpensive and easy to buy. About 8 percent of eighth-graders and 5 percent of high school seniors reported using inhalants in 2005 (Johnson, O'Malley, Bachman, and Schulenberg, 2006).

Finally, several depressants are now being used as so-called *date rape drugs. Rohypnol* ("roofies") and *GHB* ("scoop," "grievous bodily harm," "Vita-G") are sedatives that produce stupor, coma, or death when consumed with alcohol. Because these drugs are colorless, odorless, and tasteless, they can be slipped into a woman's drink without her knowledge, leaving her vulnerable to sexual assault. Spurred by reports of rape and death, in 1996 Congress passed the Drug-Induced Rape Prevention and Punishment Act, which increased federal criminal penalties for the use of any controlled substance as an aid to sexual assault (NIDA, 1999a). Rohypnol and GHB, together with Ecstasy (see Personal Issues box) and ketamine, are sometimes termed **club drugs.** Ketamine ("Vitamin K," "Special K") is an anesthetic that is primarily used by veterinarians. It can be injected or snorted.

Hallucinogens

Hallucinogens, or psychedelic drugs, include a broad range of substances that act on the central nervous system to alter perception and the state of consciousness. The most widely used and mildest hallucinogen is *marijuana.* Another well-known hallucinogen is *LSD (lysergic acid diethylamide),* a synthetic drug that must be prepared in a laboratory. Other hallucinogens include *peyote* and *mescaline* (derived from the peyote cactus plant) and *psilocybin* (derived from a species of mushrooms). Hallucinogens cause perceptual distortions because they are chemically similar to the neurotransmitter serotonin. When these substances are taken, parts of the brain that are involved in sensation and perception are activated.

Each compound has users who claim unique effects from ingesting it. In general, the drugs produce unpredictable results, including distortions of color, sound, time, and speed. A numbing of the senses in which colors are "heard" and sounds are "seen" is common. Some people experience "bad trips" that are intensely frightening and characterized by panic, terror, and psychosis. A majority of those who experience a bad trip report the feeling that no one anywhere can help, that they are no longer able to control their perceptions, or that they are afraid they have destroyed part of themselves with the drug. Users have been driven to suicide, violence, and murder, and have been permanently hospitalized as psychotic.

LSD, or "acid," is the most potent hallucinogen. Derived from a fungus, it was first produced in 1938. It is sold in many forms but most commonly in the form of "tabs," or squares of paper soaked with single doses of the drug. The purity and dosage varies, and thus so do the effects. Nonetheless, LSD is always a slow-acting, long-lasting drug. Its effects are generally not felt until 30 to 90 minutes after it's been ingested, and the "trip" lasts for 8 to 16 hours. Particularly problematic are "flashbacks"—hallucogenic episodes that occur at a later time even though no additional LSD has been used. Flashbacks are most common in but are not confined to heavy users. They occur when LSD that has been stored in fat cells is released into the bloodstream. LSD users may develop psychological but not physical dependency. In 2005, less than 2 percent of high school seniors reported having used LSD at least once during the previous year (Johnson, O'Malley, Bachman, and Schulenberg, 2006).

Marijuana (cannabis; also "grass," "pot," "dope," or "weed") is by far the most widely used illegal substance. More than 94 million Americans over the age of 12 have tried marijuana at least once (National Institute on Drug Abuse, 2005), and in 2002, about 34 percent of high school seniors reported having used marijuana during the past year (Johnson, O'Malley, Bachman, and Schulenberg, 2006). Marijuana is made from the dried leaves of the wild hemp plant. The plant is hardy and useful: It thrives in virtually every country of the world and produces a strong fiber for making cloth, canvas, and rope. The oil serves as a fast-drying paint base. For these reasons, U.S. farmers grew cannabis, and as late as World War II, the federal government licensed production of

GABA an inhibitory neurotransmitter; depressants increase its effectiveness.

Club drugs Collectively, ecstasy, rohypnol, GHB, and ketamine. They are part of the rave scene and are used in bars.

hallucinogens a class of drugs that act on the central nervous system to alter perception and state of consciousness, causing hallucinations; so-called psychedelic drugs.

Marijuana use remains popular with some adolescents. Although not as imminently destructive as other drugs, chronic heavy marijuana use may result in such negative outcomes as psychological dependency, damage to the lining of the lungs, and impairment of the immune system.

cannabis in the South and the West. Federal law now forbids growing marijuana, but illegal production in the United States continues at a high level.

The principal acting ingredient in cannabis is the chemical delta-9-THC, which will be referred to here as simply **THC.** The THC content of cannabis varies depending on the variety. In 1975, the THC content of "street" marijuana rarely exceeded 1 percent. More recently, new varieties have been produced, commonly containing THC content higher than 3 percent. These have more noticeable effects on users than did weaker strains. The THC content also varies with the part of the plant utilized. There is very little THC in the stem, roots, or seeds; the flowers and leaves contain more. *Ganja* or *sinsemilla,* which comes from the flower tops and small leaves, can range up to 24 percent in THC content. *Hashish,* derived from the resin extracted from unfertilized female flowers, may have a THC content as high as 28 percent. *Hashish oil,* a concentration of resin, has been found to have a THC content as high as 43 percent, with typical samples containing 16 percent (NIDA, 1998). The most common way to use marijuana is to roll it into a cigarette known as a "joint." It can also be smoked in a pipe or a water pipe, called a "bong," and in recent years, it has been made into "blunts," cigars whose contents have been replaced with marijuana.

This variability in the THC content of different varieties of plants, and in the different parts and preparations made from them, has made it difficult for scientists to determine physical effects and psychological effects of marijuana use. Studies often yield conflicting results because of a lack of standardized procedures. What do research studies show concerning marijuana?

Tolerance to cannabis, or diminished response to a given repeated drug dose, has now been well substantiated. Users are able to ingest ever larger quantities without disruptive effects. Physical dependency, as indicated by withdrawal symptoms, does not occur in ordinary users ingesting small or weak amounts. However, withdrawal symptoms can occur following discontinuance of high-dose chronic administration of THC. These symptoms include irritability, decreased appetite, sleep disturbance, sweating, vomiting, tremors, and diarrhea. It should be emphasized that these symptoms occur only after unusually high doses of orally administered THC under researchlike conditions. Psychological dependency may develop over a period of time and may make it difficult for chronic users to break the marijuana habit.

An increase in heart rate and reddening of the eyes are the most consistently reported physiological effects of marijuana. The heart rate increase is closely related to dosage. The risk of heart attack in the hour after smoking marijuana is approximately four times what it would normally be due to an increase in blood pressure (NIDA, 2005). However, the drug produces only minimal changes in heart function of young, healthy subjects.

Clinical studies have begun to point to various harmful effects of marijuana on the lungs and as a cause of lung cancer. The smoke contains much stronger tars and irritants than do regular cigarettes; one "joint" is the equivalent of smoking four cigarettes of tobacco, so heavy usage over a long period may harm the lungs. The tar from marijuana produces tumors when applied to the skin of test animals. Following exposure to marijuana smoke, the lung's defense systems against bacterial invasion have been shown to be impaired (NIDA, 2005).

Marijuana impairs the functioning of the **hippocampus,** a region in the brain responsible for learning, memory, and motivation. It is not surprising, therefore, that heavy users experience memory loss and that children exposed prenatally to marijuana suffer from poor memory and impaired learning abilities. In the short run, marijuana use interferes with a wide range of intellectual tasks in a manner that impairs classroom learning among student users. Marijuana also alters time and space sense, impairs vision, and retards reaction time and performance abilities.

Research has also suggested that heavy marijuana use may impair reproductive functioning in humans. Chronic use is associated with reduced levels of the male hormone testosterone in the bloodstream, which, in turn, may reduce potency and sexual drive and diminish sperm count and motility. It is also associated with possible interference with fertility in females. These preliminary findings may have greater significance for the marginally fertile. In addition, there is now substantial research evidence that marijuana use during pregnancy can harm fetal development. In one study, babies born to mothers who smoked marijuana while pregnant had unusual cries and atypical perceptual responses (Lester and Dreher, 1989). Even later, during preschool and grade school, the children born to these mothers were more likely to exhibit learning disabilities and symptoms of ADHD than other children (Fried, 1995).

How can a parent or teacher tell if an adolescent is using marijuana? When a person is high, he or she may appear uncoordinated and have trouble walking, be silly and giggly, have difficulty remembering things that were just said, and have red, bloodshot eyes. To disguise their red eyes, users may rely on eye drops, and in order to disguise pot's characteristic odor, they may use perfume or incense.

ANSWERS WOULDN'T YOU LIKE TO KNOW ...

What are the major types of drugs?

In sum, there are four major types of mind-altering drugs: (1) *narcotics*, which cause euphoria by mimicking naturally occurring endorphins; (2) *stimulants*, which energize the central nervous system; (3) *depressants*, which slow down the functioning of the central nervous system; and (4) *hallucinogens*, which cause perceptual distortions.

Frequency of Adolescent Drug Use

Research studies on adolescent drug use have consistently indicated that the drugs most frequently used by adolescents are *alcohol, tobacco,* and *marijuana,* in that order. Figures 18.1 and 18.2 show lifetime and 30-day drug use, respectively, among high school seniors from 1991 to 2005. Both graphs show the same basic pattern: that alcohol and tobacco use have declined *modestly* in the past decade, while illicit drug use (including use of marijuana) has risen somewhat. If you compare these graphs with the one in Figure 18.3, which illustrates 30-day use of other drugs by high school seniors, you will immediately notice a difference in the frequencies: Fewer than 5 percent of seniors use any other type of drugs on a monthly basis.

Are college students more likely to use drugs than high school students? College students are more likely

THC the active ingredient in marijuana.

hippocampus a part of the brain involved with learning, memory, and motivation.

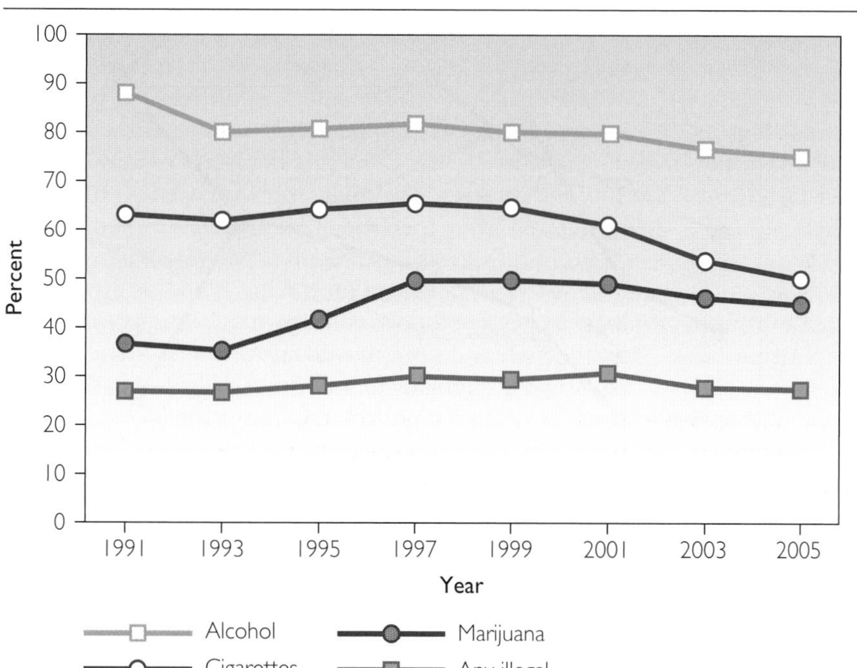

FIGURE 18.1 LIFETIME DRUG USE AMONG HIGH SCHOOL SENIORS: 1991 TO 2005

Source: Data from Johnson, O'Malley, Bachman, and Schulenberg (2006).

FIGURE 18.2 THIRTY-DAY DRUG USE AMONG HIGH SCHOOL SENIORS: 1991 TO 2005

Source: Data from Johnson, O'Malley, Bachman, and Schulenberg (2006).

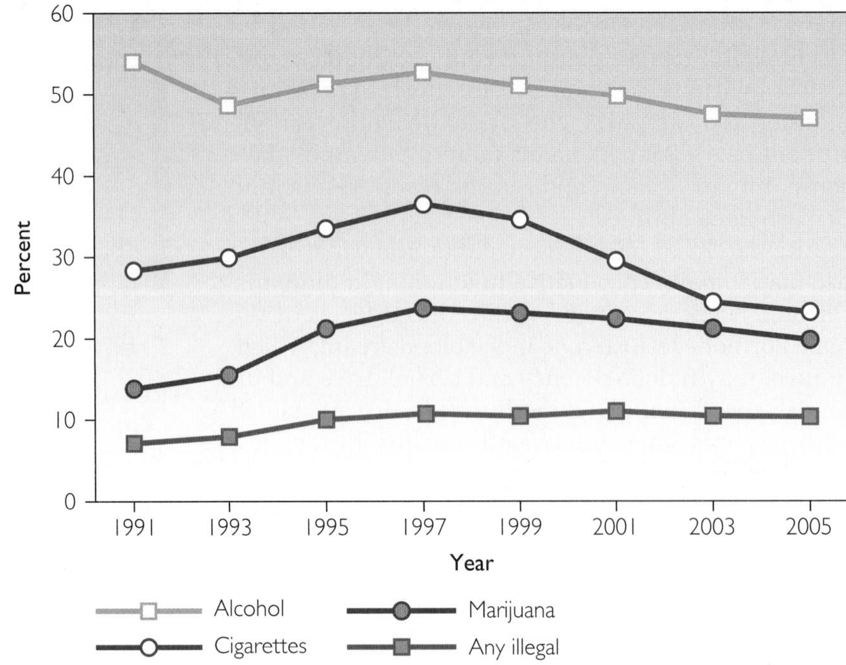

than high school students to drink alcohol, but they are about equally likely to smoke cigarettes and less likely to use illicit drugs (see Figure 18.4, p. 429). The decreased probability of using illegal drugs is most likely due to a selection factor: High school students who use speed, heroin, crack, and the like are less likely to have the grades to go on to college than their abstaining peers.

How do these rates of adolescent drug use compare with those from the past? In fact, drug use has been declining. Adolescents in the 1970s and 1980s were generally more likely to use drugs, especially marijuana and cocaine, than teenagers today (Johnson, O'Malley, Bachman, and Schulenberg, 2005). Nonetheless, drug use generally increased or held steady during the 1990s

FIGURE 18.3 THIRTY-DAY DRUG USE OF LESS COMMON DRUGS BY HIGH SCHOOL SENIORS: 1991 TO 2005

Source: Data from Johnson, O'Malley, Bachman, and Schulenberg (2006).

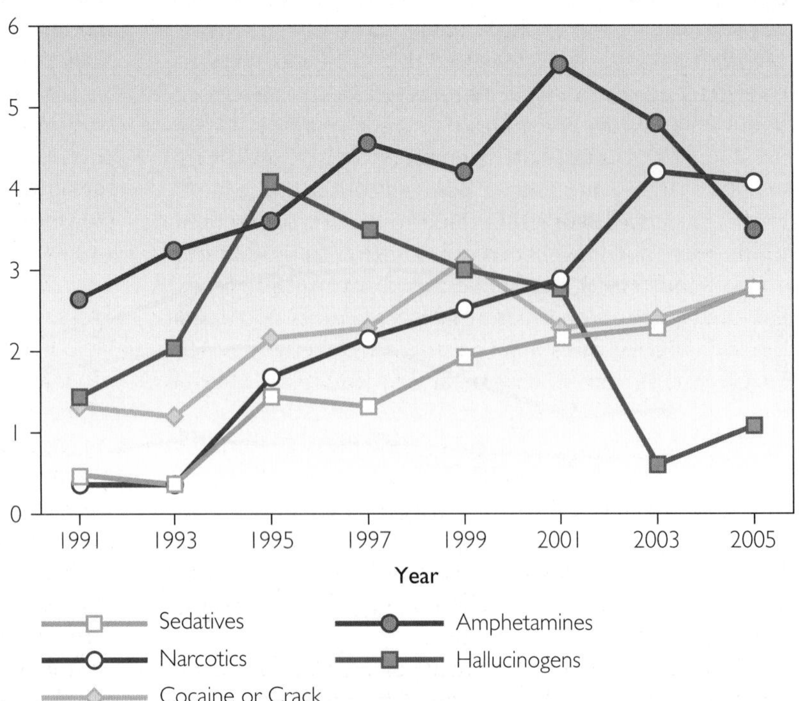

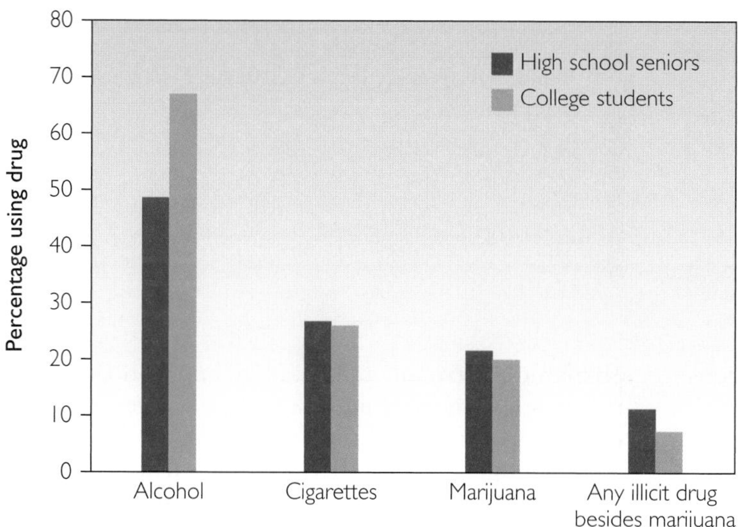

FIGURE 18.4 A COMPARISON OF DRUG USE BY HIGH SCHOOL SENIORS AND COLLEGE STUDENTS: 2002

Source: Data from Johnson, O'Malley, and Bachman, (2003).

ANSWERS WOULDN'T YOU LIKE TO KNOW . . .

Which drugs are most commonly used by adolescents?

About half of all American high school seniors report drinking within the past 30 days, about one-third report using tobacco during the same time period, and about one-fifth say they have smoked marijuana. All other types of drugs are used by only a small minority of adolescents on a regular basis.

(depending on the drug in question); for example, the use of marijuana, cocaine, stimulants, and hallucinogens all rose during the last decade.

One piece of bad news is that the reductions in drug use have been smaller for girls than for boys. Historically, males have not only been more likely to use most drugs than females, but they have been more likely to use drugs heavily. This is changing. Eighth-grade girls are now drinking as heavily as eighth-grade boys, and in 2004 they drank even more heavily than boys. Eighth-grade girls are now more likely to smoke than eighth-grade boys. However, young adolescent males are still using illicit drugs at higher rates than young adolescent females (Johnson, O'Malley, Bachman, and Schulenberg, 2006).

Reasons for First Drug Use

Why do adolescents first use drugs? The overwhelming majority try drugs out of curiosity—to see what they are like. If adolescents are more attracted by the promise of a drug than repelled by its potential harm, they may be led to experiment.

Other adolescents begin using drugs as a means of rebellion, protest, and expression of dissatisfaction with

ANSWERS WOULDN'T YOU LIKE TO KNOW . . .

Does drug use increase or decrease in college?

With the exception of alcohol, drug use does not go up in college.

traditional norms and values. This group includes activists and protestors whose lifestyles include involvement with drugs (Pedersen, 1990).

Another reason for trying drugs is for fun or sensual pleasure. Users may be seeking an exciting experience. Adolescents are growing up in a fun-oriented culture that emphasizes the need and value of having a good time. If smoking grass is thought to be fun, this becomes a strong motive for its use. Another aspect of having fun is to experience sensual pleasure. This pleasure may be sexual; many adolescents feel that pot makes the exploration of sex less inhibited and more enjoyable. The pleasure motive may involve seeking an increased sensitivity of touch or taste.

Another strong motive for trying drugs is the social pressure to be like friends or to be part of a social group. Whether friends use drugs or not is one of the most significant factors in determining adolescent drug usage (Hart, Robinson, and Kerr, 2001).

Research findings indicate that youths who use specific drugs almost invariably have friends who also use the same drugs (Dinges and Oetting, 1993). Adolescents say, "Many of my friends tried it and I didn't want to be different," or "Everybody is doing it." This motive is especially strong among immature adolescents who are seeking to belong to a crowd or gang (Johnson, Bachman, and O'Malley, 1994; McDonald and Towberman, 1993).

ANSWERS WOULDN'T YOU LIKE TO KNOW ...

How many adolescents today use drugs?

Drug use among adolescents peaked in the 1970s and 1980s and then declined. During the 1990s, drug use generally held steady, with some increases for drugs such as cocaine and marijuana. Unfortunately, youths are trying drugs at an increasingly younger age, and girls are catching up to the boys in patterns of use.

ANSWERS WOULDN'T YOU LIKE TO KNOW ...

What demographic factors distinguish drug users from nonusers?

Demographic factors such as gender, socioeconomic status, and residential area do not greatly distinguish drug users from nonusers, which is indicative of the fact that substance use is widespread among American teens.

Motives for trying drugs include to relieve tensions and anxieties, to escape from problems, or to be able to deal with or face them (Eisen, Youngman, Grob, and Dill, 1992). Students have cited the following reasons for using drugs:

"I needed to get away from the problems that were bugging me."
"I felt tired and depressed and needed a lift."
"I had to stay awake to study for exams."
"When I'm on grass, I have more self-confidence and can do anything."

One study found that adolescents who were shy but sociable were more likely to use drugs than those who were not shy. Drugs became a means of feeling more comfortable in social situations (Page, 1990).

Those who use drugs as an escape from tension, anxiety, problems, or reality, or to make up for personal inadequacies are likely to find themselves dealing with a drug habit (Simons, Whitbeck, Conger, and Melby, 1991).

There are those uses whose primary motive for trying a drug is to gain self-awareness, increased awareness of others, or more religious insight or to become more creative. The sense of increased awareness or greater creativity may be more imagined than real, but the person may truly believe that the drug provides this awareness. This is an especially strong motive for using the psychedelics.

There are some youths who begin selling drugs at an early age, prior to taking drugs. The bridge between drug dealing and drug using may eventually form. The motive for drug selling is obviously to make money, which may or may not, in the beginning, be spent on drugs for the seller (Feigelman, Stanton, and Ricardo, 1993).

Demographic Differences

If you ask many White, middle-income Americans to visualize a drug user, they will imagine a poor, inner-city adolescent of color. But quite to the contrary, African American youths are significantly less likely than White youths to use drugs, whether one considers overall illicit drug use or the use of alcohol, cigarettes, or specifically illicit drugs. By late adolescence, Hispanic Americans fall midway between the other two groups. In early adolescence, however, they are the group most likely to use drugs. (It is unclear whether this change reflects either earlier initiation rates or a tendency of users to drop out of school.) Urban youths are not more likely than suburban or rural youths to use drugs, including "crack" and heroin, and there are few socioeconomic differences in drug use (Johnson, O'Malley, Bachman, and Schulenberg, 2006). As mentioned before, males are somewhat more likely to use illicit drugs than females and are more likely to be frequent users of these substances.

In one sense, *all* American adolescents are at risk for substance use, since no demographic pockets are immune. As the following section will illustrate, however, certain factors do distinguish experimental and social-recreational users from those who become abusers.

Compulsive Drug Use

The reasons that adolescents first use drugs and then to continue to use them are varied. Those who continue to use nonaddictive drugs as a means of trying to solve emotional problems become psychologically dependent on them (Johnson and Kaplan, 1991). Drugs become a means of finding security, comfort, or relief (Andrews, Hops, Ary, Tildesley, and Harris, 1993). When individuals become psychologically dependent on drugs that are also physiologically addicting—such as alcohol, barbiturates, and heroin—dependence is secondarily reinforced by the desire to avoid the pain and distress of physical withdrawal.

Of all the risk factors that contribute to substance abuse, familial factors may be most important. The need to use drugs excessively originates within the families in which children grow up (Repetti, Taylor, and Seeman, 2002). Drug abusers are not as close to their parents and are more likely to have negative adolescent-parental relationships and a low degree of supportive interaction with them than are nonusers (Smart, Chibucos, and Didier, 1990). They are more likely to come from homes in which the parents have been divorced (Doherty and Needle, 1991), including those in which the parents have remarried (Jenkins and Zunguze, 1998). The parents of drug abusers are less likely to be authoritative than the parents of nonabusers (Adalbjarnardottir and Hafsteinsson, 2001; Fletcher and Jefferies, 1999). Drug abusers' parents are more likely either to use drugs themselves or to condone drug use (Andrews, Hops, Ary, Tildesley, and Harris, 1993). In addition, such parents less closely monitor their children (Martens, 1997; Svensson, 2003). Overall, research has found that the family relationships of adolescents who abuse drugs are similar to those of adolescents who are emotionally disturbed. The net effect of these family situations is to create personality problems that cause individuals to be more likely to run to drugs.

The other most commonly cited contributor to adolescent substance abuse (especially by parents) is peer influence. Many studies have found strong, positive correlations between peers' substance abuse patterns. In other words, users have friends and acquaintances who are users or at least *believe* that their friends are users (Thornberry and Krohn, 1997). It seems likely, however, that peer influence is only indirectly related to an adolescent's substance use (Bauman and Ennett, 1994, 1996). There is good reason to believe that teenagers choose friends who are like themselves. So if an adolescent plans to use drugs, he or she will find friends who approve of drug use. If he or she chooses to abstain, he or she will select friends from among the abstainers.

Why do youths plan to use drugs? The primary reason is family background and home life. Adolescents with strong, healthy family ties are less likely to select substance-abusing friends (Bahr, Marcos, and Maughan, 1995). Peer influence is apt to be more powerful for adolescents living in extreme poverty (McGee, 1992) for all of the reasons discussed in Chapter 3. Also, older adolescents are more likely than younger adolescents to listen to their peers (Bush, Weinfurt, and Iannotti, 1994). Finally, once adolescents have become drugs users, peer influence increases (Halebsky, 1987).

Some of these contributing factors, such as parenting style and poverty, appear to affect adolescents of both genders equally (Amaro, Blake, Schwartz, and Flinchbaugh, 2001), whereas others differ by gender. Boys, for example, are more influenced by deviant peers than girls (Svensson, 2003). Girls are more motivated by having poor self-esteem (Crump, Lillie-Blanton, and Anthony, 1997), by wanting to lose weight (French and Perry, 1996), and by having been physically or sexually abused (Sarigiani, Ryan, and Peterson, 1999).

Prevention and Treatment

Even before an adolescent begins to use drugs, preventive steps can be taken. Prevention programs target the risk factors that make drug use more likely. The National Institute on Drug Abuse has pulled together the results of numerous prevention efforts to develop a set of core principles that underlie the best programs (NIDA, 2003). Some of the most important are that prevention programs should:

CROSS-CULTURAL CONCERNS SUBSTANCE USE BY NATIVE AMERICAN ADOLESCENTS

Substance abuse is an especially large problem among Native American youths. Numerous studies have shown that drinking rates are higher among Native American adolescents than any other racial or ethnic group. Native American teenagers are also more likely than others to smoke marijuana and use inhalants. In fact, compared to youths from other racial and ethnic groups, Native American adolescents are more likely to use all of the major illegal drugs, with the exception of cocaine (see Novins, Spicer, Deals, and Spero, 2004).

Native Americans don't use drugs for different reasons than other people, and nothing inherent in their cultural traditions especially encourages drug use (Beauvais and LaBoueff, 1985). Instead, as discussed in Chapter 3, Native Americans are subjected to intense pressures due to their unique historical situation and generally low socioeconomic status. Native American youths are, as a whole, confronted with more risk factors than adolescents of other races and ethnicities. They are more likely to be economically disadvantaged, to feel alienated at school, to feel distant from both their own Native American and common American heritages, to feel hopeless and depressed, to associate with both parental and peer substance-using models, and to experience social and physical isolation. Moreover, prevention and intervention programs designed for other races and ethnicities may not work well among Native Americans.

The high alcoholism rate takes a high toll in health costs within the Native American community. Among adults, the death rate is high from liver damage associated with drinking. Frequent intoxication also puts people into poverty, which makes getting good health care less likely. Also, a disproportionately large number of Native American children are born with *fetal alcohol syndrome (FAS)*, which results in learning disabilities and behavioral problems that decrease their chance of success in school and life.

1. seek to enhance protective factors, such as good family functioning;
2. work to decrease risk factors, such as poverty school failure;
3. address all forms of substance abuse, including underage use of legal drugs;
4. focus on what is happening in the local community;
5. be targeted to the specific needs of the target population's age, ethnicity, and so on;
6. seek to have a positive effect on a wide variety of parenting issues;
7. begin early, perhaps as early as preschool;
8. target social skills;
9. seek to increase academic success;
10. be multipronged and long term;
11. include a teacher training component; and
12. use interactive techniques, such as peer discussions or role-playing.

(Note that this list is virtually identical to the characteristics of programs effective at preventing delinquency or adolescent pregnancy or school dropout that

RESEARCH HIGHLIGHT FAMILIES OF DRUG ABUSERS

Many studies have delineated the relationship between family factors and drug abuse. The following family factors have an impact on drug use:

Family Closeness

Isolation of adolescent from family
Lack of closeness with parents
Little parental support
Lack of love
Need for recognition, trust, love not filled
Parental rejection, hostility
Closeness bordering on enmeshment
Father not actively involved with family

Conflict

Marital conflict
Husband irresponsible
Unhappy home
Wife unhappy
Disharmony in family
Children as pawns in marital discord
High degree of stress, trauma

Scapegoating

Adolescent as scapegoat for inadequacy

Role Model

Parents as inadequate role models
Parents as drug users
Parents as models of drug abuse
No emulation of parents by adolescent

Divorce, Family Breakup

Broken home
One or both parents absent much of time
Father absence especially harmful
Single-parent home

Discipline

Parents showing lack of coping skills
Inconsistent discipline
Discipline too autocratic or laissez-faire
Lack of clear rules, limits, guidance
Excessive use of punishment

Hypocritical Morality

Double standard of behavior: one for selves, another for adolescents
Denial of problems with self and of parental faults

Psychological Crutches

Parents lacking confidence in coping with life; using drugs as psychological crutch
No effective coping skills learned from parents; adolescent follows parental model of coping by using drugs, alcohol

Communication Gap

Lack of ability to communicate
Lack of parental understanding
Lack of communication by parents for fear of hearing anything negative
Unheard cries for help

Research suggests that adolescents who are able to talk openly with their parents use illicit substances to a lesser extent than those who aren't able to talk with their parents (Kafka and London, 1991).

Religiosity

Research has revealed a negative relationship between religiosity and alcohol and marijuana use. Similarly, religious conservatism has a similar effect on alcohol and marijuana use.

Source: Based on Coombs and Landsverk (1988); Dunn (2005); Jurich, Polson, Jurich, and Bates (1985); Melby, Conger, Conger, and Lorenz (1993); Volk, Edwards, Lewis, and Sprinkle (1989).

IN THEIR OWN WORDS

"My first experiences with peers using substances happened in middle school. My best friend started smoking and experimenting with alcohol in about seventh grade, and over the next two years, she started using them more regularly and also started using marijuana. It was a very weird time. I still felt like a little kid, and she was telling me all these crazy things that she was doing with her other friends.

"I don't think there's any way I could've gotten away with drinking in seventh grade; my friend's mom never knew where she was or what she was doing, but mine did. It was obvious to me, even at that age, that the biggest factor in how much kids got involved with substance use was how much unsupervised time they had. If your parents knew where you were, drove you there, and picked you up, there was no way you were going to come stumbling in drunk at the age of 12."

you have seen before; effective programs all share the same features.)

Once an adolescent has become a drug abuser, different, more intrusive tactics are needed. Most teenagers (about 70 percent) who receive treatment do so as outpatients (Dennis, Muck, Dawud-No, and McDermeit, 2003); this means that they do not live full time in a hospital or treatment facility but instead go home between treatment sessions. Unfortunately, fewer than 10 percent of adolescents who report symptoms of substance use disorder receive any treatment (Muck, Zempolich, Titus, Fishman, Godley, and Schwebel, 2001).

Adolescents who have a drug abuse problem differ from adults in several ways. For instance, youths are more likely than adults to develop a psychological dependency and to have comorbid (i.e., co-occuring) psychological problems that existed before the drug abuse began (Winters, 1999) and do not disappear when it stops (Kandel et al., 1997). Adolescents are also less motivated than adults to stop using drugs and are usually referred by others for treatment, rather than choosing to work on their drug use (Muck, Zempolich, Titus, Fishman, Godley, and Schwebel, 2001). In order for a youth treatment program to be successful, it must take these differences into account.

There are various approaches to treating chemical dependency. These include the 12-step program of Alcoholics Anonymous (AA); behavioral therapy; professional counseling, medical treatment, and psychiatric care; family systems therapy; and therapeutic treatment. Let's look at these more in detail.

Alcoholics Anonymous

The most widely used approach in treating chemical dependency is the 12-step or **Alcoholics Anonymous (AA)** model. Sometimes called the *disease perspective,* it emphasizes the individual's inability to control drug consumption. The approach involves group therapy,

Alcoholics Anonymous (AA) an approach that uses a 12-step model and peer support to help people stop abusing alcohol.

RESEARCH HIGHLIGHT PROJECT DARE

Project DARE (Drug Abuse Resistance Education) is one of the most popular drug prevention programs in existence today. It employs trained police officers, who come in weekly over a four-month period to teach students the skills needed to resist peer pressure to use drugs. DARE also provides information about specific drugs and works on students' self-esteem and lifestyle choices.

Despite its popularity, there is little evidence that Project DARE is at all effective. For example, Donald Lynam and his colleagues conducted a 10-year follow-up study of 1,000 sixth-graders who had either gone through DARE training or had received other, much briefer forms of drug education (Lynam et al., 1999). At age 20, students who had experienced the DARE curriculum were no more likely to abstain from cigarettes, alcohol, or illicit drugs than other students. Moreover, they were not more immune to peer pressure nor did they have higher self-esteem than other students.

Given the results of this and other studies, why does DARE continue to be so popular? The authors offer two reasons. First, DARE is an innocuous, "feel good" program that is easy to support. In addition, Project DARE may *appear* to be working, since most adolescents who go through the program don't use drugs. The fact that most adolescents who do *not* go through the program also do not use drugs is less obvious.

Given the abundance of data that suggest that the roots of drug abuse lie within the family, it is not surprising that Project DARE—which does not address family relations—is so unsuccessful in preventing the problem.

individual counseling, education, family counseling, homework exercises, and attendance at meetings (Winters, Stinchfield, Opland, Weller, and Latimer, 2000).

Willful attempts at stopping on one's own are seen as futile and counterproductive. Recovery is thus largely a spiritual awakening process that is achieved through working the 12 Steps. The 12-step program begins by accepting one's powerlessness over drugs and then developing a sense of one's higher power, which enables one to control the drug habit.

ANSWERS WOULDN'T YOU LIKE TO KNOW ...

What kinds of prevention and treatment programs are effective with adolescents?

The best programs improve the overall quality of adolescents' lives, give them hope for the future, and help them get along with their parents. Unfortunately, only a small fraction of adolescents have the opportunity to participate in the most successful kinds of programs, whether in prevention or treatment.

Behavioral Therapy

Whether it is called **behavioral therapy** or *cognitive-behavioral therapy,* this approach is based on learning theory and focuses on building the skills needed to refuse drugs, resist peer pressure, and make good decisions. Two techniques are used in combination by behavioral therapists: *modeling* and *role-playing.* The therapist first models (or demonstrates) a desired behavior, and then the adolescent tries acting out that behavior himself or herself. The practicing continues until the client is comfortable and can respond effectively to challenging situations. A third technique, *behavioral contracting,* involves creating clear, specific agreements between the adolescent and his or her therapist or parents that detail what behaviors are acceptable, the rewards and privileges that will be earned by completing those behaviors, and the punishments that will accrue if the behaviors are not completed.

Professional Counseling, Medical Treatment, and Psychiatric Care

Rather than viewing chemical dependency as a disease in and of itself, traditional psychiatric and counseling approaches have tended to emphasize a host of emotional disorders as causal factors. Therefore, treatment is focused on understanding and resolving the emotional problems that underlie drug use, as well as medical treatment to restore health.

Family Systems Therapy

This approach focuses on family-of-origin conflicts and issues as central in developing and maintaining chemical dependency. **Family systems therapy** seeks to help families address separation issues and to help the family system adapt more effectively as the addict gives up drug-using behavior. A central goal is to help family members communicate more effectively and address conflicts that may have been ignored because of their focusing on the drug-using and antisocial behavior.

Therapeutic Community Treatment

The **therapeutic community treatment** model strongly emphasizes both abstaining from alcohol consumption and addressing emotional factors associated with drug use. This is a residential treatment model, and clients are typically expected to live in the facility for at least one year. At the center of the therapeutic community philosophy is the critical importance of involvement with one's peer group. Clients are involved in process groups, confrontation groups, support groups, and community meeting groups.

In sum, the drug treatment field seems to be moving in the direction of using multimodal approaches, which incorporate several different models simultaneously. This shift may reflect the increasing recognition that chemically dependent clients require a broad-based approach because of the various needs presented by them.

Effectiveness of Treatments

How effective are these treatments? All of them appear effective, at least in the short term (Muck, Zempolich, Titus, Fishman, Godley, and Schwebel, 2001). However, little research has examined how former drug users fare two or five years after treatment, and so it is difficult to say whether the positive outcomes are sustained.

Is any of the approaches superior to the others? Each has its adherents, but there has been little research directly comparing the effectiveness of these main approaches. Rather, in most research, patients completing these treatments are compared to controls who received no treatment, controls who received only minor interventions (such as education), or individuals who began but did not complete the program. There does seem to be some good, relatively long-term evidence in favor of both the family systems and cognitive-behavioral therapies, (Ozechowski and Liddle, 2000; Vaughn and Howard, 2004).

After reviewing the effectiveness of a large number of studies, Williams and colleagues (2000) concluded that the most successful programs were those that (1) minimized dropout rates, (2) provided follow-up and after-care, (3) were comprehensive in nature, and (4) included family therapy. These authors also emphasized the need to develop successful programs that could serve large numbers of adolescents, since the need is so great.

Treatment for chemical dependency is beginning to use multiple approaches simultaneously. A component of many of these multiple approaches is group counseling, such as shown here.

TOBACCO AND SMOKING

Incidence of Tobacco Use

Adolescent tobacco use rose sharply during the early and mid-1990s and has been decreasing since then. Even so, tobacco is the second most widely abused drug by youths age 12 to 17. About 9 percent of eighth-graders are current smokers (defined as having had at least one cigarette during the past 30 days), as are 15 percent of tenth-graders and 23 percent of twelfth-graders. About 4 percent, 8 percent, and 14 percent, respectively, of the youths in these groups smoke on a daily basis. Disapproval of cigarette smoking has increased: About half of all high school students say that they do not like to be around smokers, and three-fourths say that they have no interest in dating someone who smokes. Chewing tobacco has shown a similar decline in recent years (Johnson, O'Malley, Bachman, and Schulenberg, 2006).

White teenagers are more likely to smoke than Hispanic American teenagers, and members of both groups are more likely to smoke than African American teens. Rates for boys and girls are very similar (NIDA, 2000a).

About 80 percent of adult smokers began to smoke before they were age 18 (Smith and Stutts, 1999), and another 10 percent began between ages 18 and 21 (American Academy of Pediatrics, 1994). And so while many adolescents believe that they will eventually quit, they are deluding themselves: Most will not "grow out of it" and, in fact, will smoke more and more as they age (Perry and Staufacker, 1996; U.S. Department of Health and Human Services, 1994). Generally, the heaviest adult smokers are those who began at the youngest age (Escabedo, Marcus, Holtzman, and Giovino, 1986). Also, tobacco is an important so-called gateway drug; smokers are about three times more likely to use alcohol and at least ten times more likely to use illegal drugs than nonsmokers (De Civita and Pagani, 1994; Torabi, Bailey, and Majd-Jabbari, 1993).

Reasons Adolescents Start Smoking

Most youths are aware of the dangers of smoking. If so, why do they start and continue to smoke? Typical answers include the following:

"Because the rest of my crowd smokes."
"To feel sophisticated."
"I was curious."
"Because I was tense and nervous."
"Because I enjoy smoking."
"Because I wasn't supposed to."

These answers reflect the results of a recent study, in which teenagers were asked to describe their first smoking experiences (Delorme, Kreshel, and Reid, 2003). "Peer influence" was most often cited as the

behavioral therapy an approach that uses modeling, reinforcement, and situational inducement to alter behavior.

family systems therapy an approach to helping adolescents in which the emphasis is on enhancing family communication and improving family relationships.

therapeutic community treatment treatment in a residential situation with others who have similar problems; includes individual and group therapy and skills training.

One of the primary reasons so many adolescents start smoking is that they see adults smoking. Parents are especially influential.

reason to start smoking (see also Prince, 1995; Stanton and Silva, 1992). Almost as many explained that they wanted to "define their image." The two reasons are not unrelated, since image tending is often related to trying to enhance one's social status. Almost half of the respondents claimed that "being rebellious" was part of their motivation to smoke.

Girls and boys begin smoking for somewhat different reasons. In another study, girls were much more likely to report that the reason they had their first cigarette was to feel mature or to enhance their image; boys were more likely to indicate that they enjoyed being rebellious and that smoking made them feel relaxed. Girls are less likely than boys to stop smoking once they begin (Van Roosmalen and McDaniel, 1989, 1992).

In addition, many youths imitate their parents, older siblings, and other adults who smoke. There is little hope of changing teenage smoking habits unless the habits of parents and older siblings are changed. One of the primary reasons so many adolescents smoke is that they see adults smoking; they are striving to imitate adult behavior. Adolescents whose parents and older siblings smoke are far more likely to take up the habit than those whose parents do not (Bricker, Peterson, Leroux, Andersenn, Rajan, and Sarason, 2006; Rajan et al., 2003).

Effects of Cigarette Advertising

Adolescents are brainwashed from the early years of childhood by the huge advertising industry. Cigarette smoking has been identified with masculinity, independence, nature, beauty, youth, sex appeal, sociability, wealth, and the good life. Every conceivable gimmick has been used by the advertising industry to encourage smoking. The appeal is always to the emotions and to the desire for acceptability, popularity, and sexual allure. The sultry woman's voice, the society setting, the back-to-nature promises—all promise rewards the teenager seeks. As a result, adolescents are more strongly affected by tobacco advertising than adults and are far more likely to smoke the most heavily advertised brands than adults (Strasburger, 1995).

It has been recognized for decades that cigarette advertising influences adolescents. As far back as 1969, Congress passed a law that prohibited cigarette advertising on television. (That law, the Public Health Cigarette Smoking Act, took effect in 1971.) Since that time, tobacco companies have spread their message in other ways. In 1998, the tobacco industry spent nearly $7 billion—more than $18 million per day—to promote its products; only automobile manufacturers spent more money on product promotion (U.S. Department of Health and Human Services, 2000). Cigarettes are heavily advertised in magazines, and the manufacturers also hawk their brands using various

RESEARCH HIGHLIGHT THE HARMFUL EFFECTS OF LEGAL DRUGS

While the majority of Americans would say that it is bad to use "crack" or ecstasy or LSD, they would most likely also say that it is *less bad* to use tobacco and even *fine* to use alcohol (at least in moderation if you are over 21). After all, tobacco and alcohol are legal, while the other drugs are not. There must be some reason for this. Right?

A set of reasons—historical, cultural, and economic—can be offered as to why alcohol and tobacco are legal in the United States while cocaine, heroine, and marijuana are not. But *safety* does not enter into the discussion. Many people therefore incorrectly assume that legal drugs are less harmful and less risky to use than illicit drugs. The fact is, both nicotine and alcohol are addictive and can cause serious harm to the body. The message is not that illicit drugs are safe but rather that nicotine and alcohol are not entirely safe, either.

promotional activities: sponsoring sporting events and musical concerts and producing clothing and other items carrying logos and brand names.

In November 1998, the tobacco industry agreed, as part of a settlement with a number of states, to stop advertising to minors. (The industry also agreed to pay $206 billion over 25 years to help those states recoup the cost of Medicare payments due to tobacco-related illnesses, giving some indication of the magnitude of the health costs of tobacco use.) You might imagine, then, that there is less tobacco advertising than there was before. If so, you would be wrong. Between 1998 and 2003, the amount of money spent on tobacco advertising has risen 125 percent (Campaign for Tobacco Free Kids, 2005). In addition, after the settlement the companies increased the number of ads they place in magazines with large youth readership (Biener and Siegel, 2000). Instead of reducing advertisements, the industry shifted ads away from the prohibited billboards and into stores and magazines.

Do these advertisements matter? Yes, they do. Youths smoke the most heavily advertised brands (Arnett, 2001), and the advertisements for these brands—the ones young people smoke—feature models who look younger than advertisements targeted at older adults (Arnett, 2005). In one study, teenagers who could name a tobacco ad that had attracted their attention were twice as likely to begin smoking as those who could not (Biener and Siegel, 2000). Another study found that advertising had an even greater effect than peer pressure on smoking initiation (Evans, Farkas, et al., 1995).

Reasons Adolescents Continue Smoking

Once they begin to smoke, youths continue for the same reasons that adults do:

1. *Relief of tension:* Heavy smokers tend to be overly tense and restless people.
2. *Development of an unconscious habit:* A reflex action develops that is hard to break—the action of reaching for a cigarette.
3. *Association with sociability and pleasure:* Smokers associate the activity with after-dinner coffee, conversation, a social gathering, or pleasant surroundings.
4. *Social coping mechanism:* Smoking gives people something to do with their hands. In addition, inhaling and lighting up can provide several-second pauses in which to gather one's thoughts before speaking.
5. *Physical addiction to nicotine:* Numerous studies now support the conclusion that smokers not only become psychologically dependent on smoking but also physically addicted.

This final point bears elaboration. First, the body develops a physical craving for nicotine that can be alleviated by injecting nicotine or by increasing the nicotine content of cigarettes smoked. Second, only about 2 percent of smokers are able to use cigarettes intermittently or occasionally. The typical pattern of nicotine use is not only daily but hourly.

Third, withdrawal of nicotine produces nervousness, anxiety, lightheadedness, headaches, fatigue, constipation or diarrhea, dizziness, sweating, cramps, tremors, and palpitations. Fourth, smokers become tolerant of nicotine. Youthful smokers can tolerate only a few puffs. Gradually, they can tolerate one, then two, then three or more cigarettes. If they exceed their tolerance level, they show signs of acute anxiety. As tolerance levels rise, smokers may reach levels that would have been disastrous earlier in their smoking careers (Russell, 1971).

Also, when the supply of cigarettes is curtailed, smokers evidence unreasonable, antisocial behavior similar to that of heroin addicts. When the tobacco ration for men in Germany was cut to two packs per month after World War II, for example, it was noted that

> the majority of habitual smokers preferred to do without food even under extreme conditions of nutrition rather than to forgo tobacco. Thus, when food rations in prisoner-of-war camps were down to 900–1,000 calories, smokers were still willing to barter their food rations for tobacco. Of 300 German civilians questioned, 256 had obtained tobacco at the black market. . . . In disregard of considerations of personal dignity, conventional decorum, and esthetic-hygienic feelings, cigarette butts were picked up out of the street dirt by people who . . . would in other circumstances have felt disgust at such contact. Smokers also condescended to beg for tobacco, but not for other things. . . .
>
> Eighty percent of those questioned declared that it felt worse to do without nicotine than without alcohol. (Brill and Christie, 1974)

The conclusion is that cigarette smoking is a highly addictive habit that is difficult to break. Once started, it is not a habit that the majority of smokers can break by an effort of will.

Smokeless Tobacco

The use of chewing tobacco and snuff by American adolescents had been increasing since the 1970s, but fortunately its use has been declining since the mid-1990s (Boyle, Claxton, and Forster, 1997; Johnson, O'Malley, Bachman, and Schulenberg, 2006). Rural White males are the most common users (Tomar and Giovino, 1998). Use of smokeless tobacco usually begins at an earlier age than cigarette smoking (Boyle, Claxton, and Forster, 1997). Nicotine can be absorbed through the mucous membranes in the mouth, and so chewing tobacco is addictive and it is harmful to one's health. Although it is not associated with lung cancer, since no smoke is inhaled into the lungs, it does cause increases in mouth and throat cancer, coronary heart disease, ulcers, and neuromuscular diseases.

> **ANSWERS WOULDN'T YOU LIKE TO KNOW ...**
>
> **Why do teens smoke cigarettes when they know it's harmful?**
>
> Teens start smoking because it makes them look cool, because they want to be daring and rebellious, and because their friends encourage them to smoke. They keep smoking because they enjoy it, because it helps them feel at ease, and because they have become addicted to nicotine.

Keeping Adolescents from Starting

Clearly, the ideal is to keep adolescents from starting to use tobacco in the first place. A number of studies have been conducted to determine the most effective way to keep adolescents away from this habit and to help more of them to stop once they have started. Some of the most important suggestions and proposals are discussed here.

First, antismoking education should avoid extreme scare tactics that attempt to frighten adolescents into stopping. It is all right to point to the facts, such as the relationship between smoking and lung cancer, respiratory illnesses, and cardiovascular disease, and the dangers of smoking during pregnancy or while taking oral contraceptives. Moderate anxiety can be especially useful in preventing adolescents from starting. But extreme scare tactics lead adolescents to deny that smoking will cause physical harm and to reject the teachings of the person who is trying to scare them. Teachers who are against smoking are more effective in antismoking education than are teachers who are neutral. Teachers need to take a stand but not use extremely negative approaches, especially those that exaggerate.

Next, the primary appeal should be positive. The program should appeal to adolescents' vanity, their pride, their belief in themselves, and their sense of achievement. They should be encouraged to establish control over their own behaviors and not to blame others for their own habits (Sheppard, Wright, and Goodstadt, 1985). Appealing to their desire to maintain physical fitness has been proved to be an effective tactic.

Third, adolescents should be told all the facts as honestly as possible. A program should avoid half-truths and avoid creating a credibility gap. Even when adolescents have the facts about the hazards of smoking, some start or continue to smoke anyway because of the tendency to feel that lung cancer or other illnesses won't happen to them. Presenting factual information on the hazards does not often change behavior, but it usually has considerable influence on knowledge and attitudes.

Fourth, efforts should enlist the help of student leaders and of students themselves. Since peer pressure and the desire to appear cool are such strong motivators for smoking, having popular adolescents provide antismoking messages is often more effective than having adults deliver the same words.

Next, a program should begin early, when the child is young, and continue periodically over a span of years.

Since cigarette smoking is highly addictive and very difficult to stop, it is important to keep adolescents from starting to smoke.

A recurring program is more effective than a single mass exposure. Education laws in New York State require that antismoking education be started after grade eight. This is too late. Fourth or fifth grade is a better time to begin.

Sixth, students should be helped to discover and analyze their own inner, hidden, emotional, or social reasons for smoking and to deal with these problems so that the smoking crutch will not be needed.

Last, no one teaching method can be considered best. Antismoking education programs have been partly successful in changing smoking behavior among adolescents who already smoke.

Other measures are being taken to keep adolescents from starting smoking. Many states have passed laws making the smoking of cigarettes illegal before age 18. Also, cigarette taxes are being raised to make it harder for adolescents to afford cigarettes. Lawsuits against cigarette companies that use advertising to target youths or that distort the addictive power of nicotine seek to prevent companies from using false claims so they can sell tobacco products. More and more, smoking is being banned in public places. Together, these measures should reduce the use of cigarettes.

ALCOHOL AND EXCESSIVE DRINKING

Alcohol is the drug of choice among youths, yet it is often not recognized as the serious drug that it is.

Incidence of Alcohol Use

Studies of junior high, senior high, and college students reveal that a substantial proportion of adolescents drink. Findings from the 2005 Monitoring the Future Survey indicate that 41 percent of eighth-graders and 75 percent of high school seniors have had alcohol at some point in their lives, and that 17 percent and 47 percent of the same groups, respectively, have consumed alcohol within the past month (Johnson, O'Malley, Bachman, and Schulenberg, 2006).

Given that drinking is common in the United States, it is no surprise that a vast majority of adolescents have been introduced to alcohol.

The problem lies not so much in the drinking per se but in the frequent drinking of large quantities. In 2000, about 30 percent of high school seniors and 15 percent of eighth-graders reported at least one episode of **binge drinking** in the previous two weeks (Johnson, O'Malley, and Bachman, 2003). Binge drinking is defined as five drinks in a two-hour period for males and four drinks in the same time frame for females. The standard was set because research has shown that these are the quantities at which various risks greatly increase. In addition, a typical 160-pound man who has five drinks within two hours will attain a blood alcohol level of 0.08, a level high enough to qualify him as legally drunk in all 50 states (Substance Abuse and Mental Health Services Administration, 2003).

As noted, binge drinkers are at increased risk for many negative outcomes, and they place others at risk as well. For example, alcohol is a major contributor to traffic accidents and fatalities, and almost half of the persons who die each year in car crashes caused by drunk drivers were not the driver himself or herself (Hingston and Winter, 2003). Alcohol is also involved in more than 1,500 homicides involving minors each year, and nearly 40 percent of people under age 21 who are victims of fatal drownings, burns, and falls test positive for alcohol (Bonnie and O'Connell, 2004). The majority of sexual assaults involving youths take place when one or both participants are inebriated, and drunk individuals are less likely to follow safe sexual practices when engaging in consensual sexual behavior (Flanigan, McLean, Hall, and Propp, 1990). (One can only guess at the number of unwanted pregnancies that begin as a result of alcohol consumption.) Finally, drunk adolescents also damage other people's property, wake them up at night, and pick fights.

Beer is the preferred beverage among boys of all ages, regardless of the frequency with which they drink, and among girls of all ages who drink once a week or more. Older girls who drink infrequently prefer distilled spirits to beer (Bonnie and O'Connell, 2004). However, although many studies have specifically asked adolescents whether they drink wine coolers, few have asked about "alcopops" and other newer, sweet alcohol beverages. Usage of these flavored drinks appears to be high as well (Johnson, O'Malley, Bachman, and Schulenberg, 2006).

Although the social contexts in which adolescents drink are subject to legal restrictions, many drink before they can legally buy alcoholic beverages or patronize licensed premises. Most who begin to drink do so at home under parental supervision. Much of this drinking occurs on holidays and other special occasions. As youths grow older, they tend to drink more often outside the home, until the most likely drinking places are those where adults are not present. Common locations for teenage drinking are parties, the outdoors, and cars—all places where teens' activities will likely not be observed.

The prevalence of drinking among junior high and senior high youths motivated many states to reexamine their laws regulating legal drinking ages. After the Vietnam War, many states lowered the drinking age to 18. The argument was: If they're old enough to fight, they're old enough to vote and to drink. But authorities complained that giving 18-year-olds the right to purchase alcoholic beverages also made alcohol

binge drinking the consumption of five or more drinks at a sitting if you are male and four or more drinks at a sitting if you are female.

One of the biggest problems with alcohol is binge drinking, or the frequent drinking of large quantities. This is especially prevalent on college campuses.

available to their younger friends in junior and senior high school (the older seniors purchased it for the younger schoolmates). As a result, many states that lowered the drinking age raised it again to age 21 (Newman, 1987). Today, the drinking age in all 50 states is age 21.

Raising the minimum legal drinking age to 21 has had several positive effects. First, it has produced lower adolescent drinking rates and problems (see Wagenaar and Toomey, 2002, for a recent review of this literature). Second, it has prevented thousands of traffic fatalities (NHTSA, 1998). Finally, adolescents who do not begin to drink until they are 21 tend to drink less as adults than those who begin earlier (Grant and Dawson, 1997).

Reasons for Drinking during Adolescence

Why do so many adolescents begin to drink? And why does drinking so often begin at this point in life, rather than later or earlier? Schulenberg and Maggs (2002) suggest that a convergence of developmental changes sparks teenage alcohol consumption. Among the most important are the following:

1. The physical changes associated with puberty cause a person's tolerance to alcohol to increase, and so he or she can begin to drink in larger quantities without feeling ill.
2. Adolescents, who no longer view themselves as children, want to look more mature and adult like. They believe that having a drink in their hand will make them appear grown up.
3. The cognitive skills that emerge postpuberty allow teenagers to view issues—including whether or not to drink—in relative rather than absolute terms. They move beyond thinking about alcohol consumption in terms of yes or no and begin to think about when? and how much?
4. Cognitive conceit makes youths more likely to question the wishes of authority figures.
5. The personal fable (discussed in Chapter 6) makes adolescents feel invulnerable, and so they perceive that there is little threat of harm to themselves.
6. Increased inferential skills make teens more aware of adult hypocrisy. Teens may lose respect for adults who drink themselves but then tell their children or students that drinking is risky.
7. The process of finding an identity involves trying new experiences.
8. Adolescents have more freedom and independence than children; they are less closely supervised and monitored.
9. Adolescents spend more time with their peers and less with their families. This serves to increase peer influence and decrease family influence on behavior.
10. Teenagers mistakenly believe that the drinking rate is higher than it really is. The perception that "everyone drinks" encourages them to drink, too.
11. Adolescents are interested in romance and sex; this encourages them to frequent locations such as bars and parties, where alcohol is served.
12. Adolescents face many stresses, and drinking is perceived as a means of relaxing.

Dermen, Cooper, and Agocha (1998) would add that alcohol reduces inhibitions and can provide an excuse for behaving wildly. Drinking may allow a teenager to do something that he or she would not normally do—such as have sex with a stranger or vandalize school property.

PERSONAL ISSUES DRINKING ON COLLEGE CAMPUSES

In the past decade, much good research has been conducted on the magnitude of college drinking. About two-thirds of college students reported drinking at some point in the previous month (Johnson et al., 2005). Not all of these students drink heavily, however. In 2004, about 45 percent of college students reported binge drinking at least once during a two-week period; men were more likely to binge than women, with binge rates of 50 percent and 40 percent, respectively (Johnson, O'Malley, Bachman, and Schulenberg, 2005). Factors that are associated with the high consumption of alcohol by college students include membership in a sorority or fraternity; race/ethnicity (Blacks drink less than Whites); participation in athletics; going to a small college; going to a school located in the Northeast; and living in a dorm as opposed to off campus (Presley, Meilman, and Leichliter, 2002).

Nearly half (48 percent) of all the alcohol consumed by students attending four-year colleges is consumed by underage students (Wechsler, Lec, Kuo, Seibring, Nelson, and Lee, 2002). Young adults who are enrolled full time in college are more likely to drink heavily than their nonstudent agemates (Johnson, O'Malley, Bachman, and Schulenberg, 2005).

Binge drinkers are far more likely to experience negative consequences from their drinking than nonbingers. Binge drinkers' grades frequently suffer because cause they are too fuzzy headed to study and because they miss class. Their athletic performance declines, as well. Many experience blackouts and do not remember what they did or what others did to them. Students who binge drink are more likely to physically injure themselves by falling, fighting, or being in a car accident. Bingers more frequently develop colds and other short-term illnesses, and they are more likely to develop serious, long-term health problems. Heavy drinkers are more likely to engage in unintended and unprotected sexual activity, which causes increased risk for sexually transmitted diseases and pregnancy (Cooper, 2002; Perkins, 2002).

It is worth noting that bingers not only cause significant problems for themselves but for other students, as well. About 75 percent of students reported having at least one unwanted, unpleasant encounter with a drunken student (Wechsler, Lee, Kuo, and Lee, 2000). While most of these encounters were merely annoying (being interrupted while studying; being awakened; having to take care of a drunk friend), some were assaultive (being pushed or hit; experiencing unwanted sexual advances, or even date rape) (Abbey, 2002; Perkins, 2002).

Colleges, too, suffer because of student binging. Town-gown relationships can become strained, there may be increased legal fees and maintenance costs from alcohol-related problems, and student service personnel experience higher burnout rates due to the increased demands on their services. The negative impact truly can go beyond the drinking individual.

These findings may seem to document what many college students already feel: that most students they know are heavy drinkers. Yet these data indicate that *more than half of college students do not drink heavily,* at least on a regular basis. Students do not have to binge to be part of the crowd.

Adult and Peer Influences

Because drinking is a widespread adult custom, drinking by adolescents reflects their perceptions of the attitudes and behavior of adults in American society (Stevens, Mott, and Youells, 1996). Adolescents use alcohol as an integral part of adult role-playing, as a rite of passage into the adult community.

As discussed earlier regarding substance abuse, family factors play a significant role in alcohol misuse. Adolescents who drink to excess are more distant from their families than adolescents who do not (Crowe, Philbin, Richards, and Crawford, 1998). Youths who drink spend less time with their families and do not enjoy the time they do spend at home as much as nondrinking peers.

Parents who drink or who sanction drinking are more likely to have adolescents who drink (Barnes, Farrell, and Banerjee, 1995); parents who do not drink or who disapprove of drinking are more likely to have youths follow their example. Parents who are moderate to heavy drinkers are more likely to have adolescents who are moderate to heavy drinkers (Barnes, Reifman, Farrell, and Dintcheff, 2000). Furthermore, chronic alcoholism is more likely to run in families (Lieb, Merikangas, Hofler, Pfister, Isensee, and Wittchen, 2002). Children who are exposed to drinking

ANSWERS WOULDN'T YOU LIKE TO KNOW . . .

Why do so many adolescents begin to drink?

Adolescents' desire to drink alcohol seems to result from the convergence of a variety of physical, congnitive, and social changes. In simple terms, they are testing boundaries and trying to become adults, and they see drinking as helping them through that process. They do not, however, understand the risks of alcohol use.

by their parents, however, do not necessarily grow up to be problem drinkers. The highest rates of alcoholism among adolescents are found in groups that are under great pressure to refrain from drinking or who are in families, such as the Irish or Native Americans, who themselves have high rates of alcoholism (Gfellner and Hundelby, 1994; Huston, Hoberman, and Nugent, 1994). Recent research on family influences has focused on the role of parental monitoring: Not surprisingly, parents who monitor their children's behavior and set limits on their children's behavior are less likely to have children who drink (DiClemente et al., 2001).

Youths drink also because of peer-group pressure and the need for peer identification, sociability, and friendship (Sieving, Perry, and Williams, 2000). Drinking becomes a social custom of a particular group; therefore the adolescent who wants to be part of the group drinks, as well.

Many youths drink because they perceive it as normative and want to be part of the crowd (Olds and Thombs, 2001). One effective way to reduce underage drinking, then, is to spread the word that *not everyone drinks, and not all teens think that it is okay to get drunk.* A second peer-related tactic that has proven effective in reducing adolescent drinking is to teach refusal skills (the ability to say no in the face of peer pressure). Some research suggests that this may be even more effective than changing perceptions of norms (Connor, Young, Williams, and Ricciardelli, 2000).

Not all adolescents who get drunk become problem drinkers. Problem drinkers start to drink in excess for psychological rather than social reasons. Heavy, escapist drinking is symptomatic of serious adjustment problems. Such youths do not get along at home or at school; they receive more failing grades, are more prone to delinquency, participate less often in extracurricular activities, spend more nights out away from home, and are not as close to their parents as nonproblem drinkers. Only some youths who drink are problem drinkers, but they are already evidencing the psychological imbalance that prompts them to rebel or to seek escape through alcohol (Ralph and Morgan, 1991).

Physical Consequences of Alcohol Use

There is absolutely no doubt that the long-term, heavy consumption of alcohol harms the body. Most people know that alcohol abuse is associated with a type of liver damage known as **cirrhosis,** which is a potentially fatal illness. In addition, chronic heavy drinking impairs the functioning of the immune system; this means that abusers cannot fight off infections, including serious infections such as tuberculosis, as readily as people who do not drink. Long-term heavy alcohol use is also associated with high blood pressure, heart arrhythmia (irregular heartbeat), weakened heart muscle, and stroke. Women who drink large amounts of alcohol appear even more susceptible to its detrimental effects than men. Although heavy female drinkers typically consume less than heavy male drinkers, it takes less alcohol to harm a woman's body. In addition, heavy alcohol consumption is associated with an elevated rate of breast cancer. The National Institute on Alcohol Abuse and Alcoholism has recently prepared an excellent, detailed summary of what is known about the health consequences of consuming alcohol (NIAAA, 2000).

Alcohol also has well-documented behavioral and cognitive effects. Many behavioral effects—such as engaging in unprotected sex, missing classes, and so on—have already been discussed. Here, we will turn to alcohol's effects on more basic cognitive functioning.

Given that the brains of heavy drinkers actually shrink (i.e., become physically smaller), it is not surprising that most alcoholics exhibit a mild to moderate loss of intelligence. Most cell loss occurs in the cortex of the **frontal lobe,** the part of the brain most involved in higher-order thinking, such as planning and impulse control; in the *hippocampus,* a part of the brain involved in learning, memory, and motivation; and in the **cerebellum,** a part of the brain that helps control both balance, coordination, and learning. This cell damage leaves heavy drinkers with deficits in the ability to lay down new memories, to solve complex problems, and to perceive and remember the locations of objects. How about light and moderate drinkers? The data are mixed, but some studies have found that a long-term pattern of light to moderate consumption decreases cognitive abilities (NIAAA, 2001).

Since the adolescent brain is still growing, it is reasonable to ask if alcohol exposure alters brain development. Studies with both lab animals (see Spear, 2002) and humans suggest that alcohol may have that effect—at least if an adolescent drinks heavily. Adolescents who abuse alcohol have been found to have smaller hippocampi than those who do not use alcohol, and the heavier their drinking and the earlier they began, the smaller this area of the brain becomes (De Bellis et al., 2000). Since the hippocampus is a part of the brain that contributes to memory, it is not surprising that research has linked memory deficits and heavy drinking in adolescence (Brown, Tapert, Granhom, and Delis, 2000).

Drinking in Young Adulthood

Drinking tends to decrease as individuals move out of adolescence and into young adulthood. This is true of both youths who attend college and those who move directly from high school to the working world. Many, if not most, individuals who binge as college students cut down their consumption greatly once they graduate. Entering the work force is associated with decreased al-

ANSWERS WOULDN'T YOU LIKE TO KNOW . . .

Do most students who drink heavily in college keep drinking so heavily as adults?

No. The responsibilities of adult life and changes in socialization seem to reduce drinking among young adults.

cohol use (Wood, Sherman, and McGowen, 2000), although this is less true for post–high school students than for post–college students (Schulenberg, O'Malley, Bachman, and Johnson, 2000). Getting married further drops the drinking rate (Bachman, Wadsworth, O'Malley, Johnson, and Schulenberg, 1997).

At least two factors may be at play in these trends. First, the increased responsibilities of adult life may make it more difficult to sustain heavy drinking. One usually needs to get up earlier and work longer hours after graduation; there is also a house or apartment to keep clean, food to buy, and so on. Second, less time is spent socializing after graduation and after marriage, especially with exclusively same-age peers. Most people go out less and stay home more. If they do go out, it is more often with smaller groups of friends and couples, rather than to large parties. Some of that socializing might be with co-workers, who might be older and who might disapprove of heavy drinking.

In sum, although a portion of the adolescent drinkers who became addicted to or dependent on alcohol while in college will continue to drink heavily, most will greatly cut back their consumption.

cirrhosis an often fatal disease of the liver caused by heavy and chronic alcohol consumption.

frontal lobe the cerebral lobe that is the center for higher-order thinking, such as planning and impulse control.

cerebellum a part of the brain that controls balance, coordination, and learning.

alcohol abuse excessive use of alcohol so that functioning is impaired.

alcoholism chemical dependency on alcohol accompanied by compulsive and excessive drinking.

RESEARCH HIGHLIGHT ALCOHOL ABUSE AND ALCOHOLISM

Alcohol abuse is the use of alcohol to a degree that causes physical damage; impairs physical, social, intellectual, or occupational functioning; or results in behavior harmful to others. A person does not have to be an alcoholic to have problems with alcohol. The individual who drinks only once a month, but drives while intoxicated and has an accident, is an alcohol abuser—so is the man who gets drunk and beats up his children.

Alcoholism is dependence on alcohol—drinking compulsively and excessively, leading to functional impairment. Some alcoholics drink large amounts daily. Others drink heavily only on weekends. Still others may go through long periods of sobriety interspersed with binges of daily heavy drinking lasting for weeks or months. On some occasions, heavy drinking is limited to periods of stress, associated with periods of anxiety or strain.

The following are some warning signals that indicate a drinking problem is developing:

- You drink more than you used to and tend to gulp your drinks.
- You try to have a few extra drinks before or after drinking with others.
- You have begun to drink alone.
- You are noticeably drunk on important occasions.
- You drink the "morning after" to overcome the effects of previous drinking.
- You drink to relieve feelings of boredom, depression, anxiety, or inadequacy.
- You have begun to drink at certain times, to get through difficult situations, or when you have problems.
- You have weekend drinking bouts and Monday hangovers.
- You are beginning to lose control of your drinking; you drink more than you planned and get drunk when you did not want to.
- You promise to drink less but do not.
- You often regret what you have said or done while drinking.
- You are beginning to feel guilty about your drinking.
- You are sensitive when others mention your drinking.
- You have begun to deny your drinking or lie about it.
- You have memory blackouts or pass out while drinking.
- Your drinking is affecting your relationship with friends or family.
- You have lost time at work or school due to drinking.
- You begin to stay away from people who do not drink.

SUMMARY

1. A distinction needs to be made between *physical addiction* and *psychological dependency.* Some drugs are physically habit forming, meaning the body builds up a physical need for the drug. Psychological dependency is the development of an overpowering psychological need for a drug. Both physical addiction and psychological dependency are hard to break.
2. Teens who use drugs occasionally are less likely to develop a substance abuse problem than teens who use drugs to cope with the problems in their lives.
3. Abused drugs (in addition to alcohol and tobacco) may be grouped into a number of categories. The categories include the following drugs:
   - Narcotics—opium, morphine, heroin, codeine, and methadone
   - Stimulants—cocaine, amphetamines (benzedrine, Dexedrine, methedrine), and ecstasy
   - Depressants—barbiturates (Quaalude, Nembutal, Seconal, Amytal, or phenobarbital), tranquilizers (Miltown, Librium, and Valium); inhalants; and alcohol
   - Hallucinogens—LSD, peyote, mescaline, psilocybin; and marijuana in various forms (the plant cannabis, ganja, hashish, hashish oil)
4. The most frequently abused drugs among adolescents in the United States are alcohol, tobacco, and marijuana, in that order. Alcohol continues to be the drug of choice of all age groups.
5. Drug use is widespread throughout the adolescent population. However, White youths are more likely to use drugs than adolescents from other racial and ethnic groups, and males are more likely to use drugs than females. The gender gap is decreasing, however.
6. Adolescents begin to use drugs for a number of reasons: curiosity; fun and sensual pleasure; social pressure to be like friends; desire to relieve tensions, anxiety, and pressures; escape from problems; and desire to gain increased awareness, insight, and creativity. Those who continue to use drugs may build up a physical addiction and/or psychological dependency. Chronic abusers often have troubled family relationships and personal problems and turn to drugs to lessen pain and conflict and as a substitute for meaningful human relationships.
7. Treatment approaches to drug abuse include Alcoholics Anonymous, behavioral therapy, professional counseling and psychiatric care, family systems therapy, and therapeutic community treatment. Present approaches use several models simultaneously.
8. About 25 percent of high school seniors smoke cigarettes. Adolescents are influenced to start smoking by cigarette advertising, by modeling adults who smoke, by peer-group pressure, and by their own need for status. Some smoke as an expression of rebellion and autonomy and a desire to be grown up. Once they start, they continue to smoke to relieve tension; because smoking becomes an unconscious habit, as a means of social coping, and because of a physical addiction to nicotine. The best solution is to keep adolescents from starting in the first place by antismoking education.
9. Substantial portions of adolescents drink; 75 percent of high school seniors have had a drink. Frequent drinking of large quantities is a major factor in crime, homicides, traffic accidents, violence, pedestrian injuries, and unwed pregnancy. Binge drinking—having five or more drinks at one sitting if you are male and four or more drinks at one sitting if you are female—is especially frequent on college campuses.
10. Pubertal growth, cognitive development, the identity search, increased peer attachments, and the presence of more intense stressors all contribute to adolescents' desire and ability to drink.
11. Teens' drinking is highly influenced by cultural norms, their parents' behavior (both toward them and toward alcohol), their peers' behavior, and their own personality.
12. Heavy alcohol consumption carries with it great physical health risks as well as the likelihood of cognitive impairment.

KEY TERMS

alcohol abuse 443
Alcoholics Anonymous (AA) 433
alcoholism 443
attention-deficit hyperactivity disorder (ADHD) 423
behavioral therapy 434
binge drinking 439
cerebellum 442
circumstantial-situational use 421
cirrhosis 442
club drugs 425
compulsive drug use 421
depressants 423
dopamine 422
drug abuse 420
endogenous endorphins 421
experimental use 420
family systems therapy 434
frontal lobe 442
GABA 424
hallucinogens 425
hippocampus 426
intensified drug use 421
narcotics 421
physical addiction 420
psychological dependency 420
serotonin 423
social-recreational use 421
stimulants 422
THC 426
therapeutic community treatment 434

THOUGHT QUESTIONS

Personal Reflection

1. Was drug abuse a problem in the high school you attended? Explain. What drugs were most commonly used? Was drug abuse limited to any particular type of student? From what type of family background did abusers generally come?

2. What effect did drug abuse have on the lives of adolescents—both users and abstainers—in the school in which you were brought up?
3. Do you smoke regularly? How old were you when you started? Why do you smoke? Have you ever tried to stop? With what effect?
4. Do you drink to excess? On page 443 is a list of symptoms of problem drinking behavior. Do any of these characteristics fit you?
5. Have you ever tried any illegal drug? What was your motivation for doing so? Did the rewards outweigh the risks?

Group Discussion

6. What type of drugs are most commonly used among students you know?
7. What should parents do if they discover their adolescent is using marijuana? Narcotics? LSD? Speed? Cocaine? Inhalants?
8. Did your high school offer drug education? What type of program? With what effect?
9. What approaches do you think should be taken to combat drug abuse among adolescents?
10. How have cigarette advertisements influenced you or your friends? Which kinds of advertisements have been (or are) most persuasive? Why? Have ads affected the fact that you or your friends smoked (or smoke) or merely the brand chosen?
11. Discuss ways and means of how to quit smoking, such as attending smoking clinics or joining antismoking campaigns. Which way works the best?
12. What are some of the best ways of keeping adolescents from starting to smoke?
13. How common was drinking alcohol in your high school? Was the drinking level high enough to have noticeable consequences? Explain.
14. Discuss binge drinking on your college campus. What steps could college administrations take to reduce binge drinking? What steps would be ineffective? Why?
15. On pages 440, there is a list of reasons as to why drinking often begins during adolescence. How many of these do you think apply to smoking? To the use of illicit drugs? Which only apply to alcohol?

Debate Questions

16. Given all the problems that it causes, alcohol use should be outlawed.
17. Marijuana use should be legalized.
18. Tobacco companies should be prohibited from advertising.
19. All middle school students should be required to take a comprehensive drug education course.

SUGGESTED READING

Babbit, N. (2000). *Adolescent Drug and Alcohol Abuse: How to Spot It, Stop It, and Get Help for Your Family.* Cambridge, England: O'Reilly.

Bonnie, R. J., and O'Connell, M. E. (Eds.). (2004). *Reducing Underage Drinking: A Collective Responsibility.* Washington, DC: National Academies Press.

Faupel, C. E., Horowitz, A. M., and Weaver, G. (2003). *The Sociology of American Drug Use.* New York: McGraw-Hill.

Ross, G. R. (2002). *Treating Adolescent Substance Abuse: Understanding the Fundamental Elements.* Portland, OR: Resource Publications.

Wechsler, H., and Wuethrich, B. (2003). *Dying to Drink: Confronting Binge Drinking on College Campuses.* New York: Rodale.

Windle, M. (1999). *Alcohol Use among Adolescents.* Thousand Oaks, CA: Sage.

USEFUL WEB SITES

Core Institute
www.siu.edu/~coreinst/

This is the website of the Center for Alcohol and Drug Studies Program at Southern Illinois University at Carbondale. It contains information from the Core Alcohol and Drug Survey, which provides information about students' beliefs regarding alcohol consumption, the risks of alcohol use, and the secondary effects of drinking.

Higher Education Center for Alcohol and Other Drug Prevention
www.edc.org/hec

This site was developed by the U.S. Department of Education to assist colleges and universities in developing, implementing, and evaluating alcohol and other drug prevention programs.

Monitoring the Future Study
www.monitoringthefuture.org

This site, provided by the University of Michigan's Institute for Social Research, reports the findings of the Monitoring the Future Study, which has been annually tracking substance use by eighth- and tenth-graders since 1991 and by twelfth-graders since 1975.

National Clearinghouse on Alcohol and Drug Information (NCADI)
www.health.org

This site contains information from the Center for Substance Abuse Prevention of the U.S. Department of Health and Human Services and provides links to several alcohol and drug prevention databases.

National Institute on Drug Abuse (NIDA)
www.nida.nih.gov/

A branch of the National Institutes of Health, the NIDA's mission is to support the scientific investigation of substance abuse and to disseminate that information to the medical community as well as legislators and the public.

EPILOGUE

After reading this text, you have likely learned a lot about adolescents and the experiences they typically have. To close this book, we will briefly discuss the possible stages of life that come next.

Traditionally, we expected adolescents to move from adolescence into young adulthood—and, certainly, many still do. Ever greater numbers of adolescents, however, are moving into what has become a distinct, new stage of life: *emerging adulthood.* Since emerging adulthood precedes young adulthood, we will discuss it first.

Emerging adulthood was first conceptualized by J. J. Arnett (2000, 2004). It typically lasts from about 18 through the middle (or even late) twenties. Its existence came about because of the kinds of demographic changes we have already discussed: People are waiting longer to marry, they are more likely to continue their educations, and so on. They are postponing "settling down" and making permanent choices. Their lives are in constant flux; they move frequently, change jobs, and start and stop and restart their education. Emerging adults are a hard group to characterize, because whereas almost all middle-aged Americans are employed and almost all adolescents live with their families, "almost all" emerging adults don't have much in common. They are unique in their diversity.

Another reason to consider emerging adulthood a distinct time of life is that emerging adults themselves feel that they are neither really adolescents nor adults. When directly asked if they feel grown up, they are more likely to answer "both yes and no" than "yes." This is most likely due to the fact that they do not yet feel as if they are completely self-reliant, either financially or emotionally.

One appealing aspect of treating emerging adulthood as a separate stage of life is that it provides a time for the identity search to be completed. As you surely remember, Erikson believed that finding an identity was the singular achievement of adolescence. However, most individuals do not fully form their identities by the end of adolescence (unless you feel comfortable stretching adolescence into the twenties). If you are not planning to marry until you are nearly 30, you are not inclined to think seriously about what you are looking for in a life partner at 17. If college and even graduate school are on your horizon, you ruminate about career choices differently than if you plan to get a full-time job right after high school. Emerging adulthood is an extension of the psychological moratorium, the period of time in which one is actively thinking about one's goals and choices but has not yet come to any decisions.

Emerging adulthood is not a human universal. It exists only in societies in which development has been prolonged. This is likely to be true in Westernized rather than traditional cultures. Emerging adulthood may not endure as a phenomenon in industrialized societies. But, for now, it seems a fine way to conceptualize that betwixt-and-between period that many people go through in their twenties.

More customarily, individuals move from adolescence into young adulthood. Robert Havighurst (1972), who so elegantly described the life tasks of adolescents, also outlined the life tasks of young adulthood. Clearly, they are quite different from those of adolescents:

1. *Selecting a mate.* Dating takes on a different flavor for many people once they reach their twenties: It becomes more serious—more focused on finding a partner. It becomes common, when you are out with someone, to ask yourself, Would this person make a good spouse? A good mother/father someday? During adolescence, you date someone because he or she is fun, attractive, and available, but in young adulthood, that may not be enough.

2. *Learning to live with a marriage partner.** Living with someone takes many adjustments. In addition to the mundane disagreements about whether the toilet seat should be left up or down and whether it really is important to put the cap back on the toothpaste tube, it is important to learn how to juggle household tasks and integrate personal preferences: How much money should you be saving? How late should you stay up? How do you deal with the fact that your spouse is a complete grouch before having his or her morning coffee? Compromise is usually needed to balance the tastes and desires of both partners. It is extremely unusual for two persons to join their lives effortlessly.

3. *Starting a family.* As with all of Havighurst's tasks, not everyone has children; however, most people do. Having children causes profound changes in a couple's lifestyle: Money is tighter, sleep deprivation increases, time for romance decreases, spontaneity disappears, and stress skyrockets. Although there are few joys in life equal to that of holding a wanted, loved infant, it is unrealistic to

*Writing in the early 1970s, Havighurst did not consider the possibility of a long-term, committed, nonmarital relationship.

expect that life will otherwise go on as usual. Many adjustments must be made.

4. *Rearing children.* Life does not return to "prechildren normal" for quite some time. Most parents admit that parenting is the most difficult, most time-consuming, most rewarding job they have ever had. Trying to juggle a career or two, keeping up a household, and managing the chauffeuring, added shopping, tutoring, reading time, play time, coaching, and so on that make up a parent's job can be exhausting. Personal needs often seem to take a backseat to the demands of being a spouse and a parent. Most parents would say that the time and effort are well worth it and that they would become parents again in a second. Even so, rearing children is undoubtedly a major focus of life in early and mid adulthood.
5. *Managing a home.* Many college students take great satisfaction in the fact that they can fit everything they own into a car and drive off whenever they want. But when they go from living at home with their folks or in a dorm room to living on their own, they quickly discover that having a lot of material goods is, well, necessary. They come to covet items that they never even thought about before: dish towels, a lawn mower, and a dishwasher. They not only have to acquire some possessions that they did not previously own, but they also have to learn to perform all the little chores that keep a house running. They need to learn about circuit breakers and lint traps. Plus, they need to budget their money so that they can pay the electric bill. There is more to running a household than many youths probably imagine.
6. *Getting started in an occupation.* This life task is self-explanatory. Once schooling is over (however long that is), most people begin to work in earnest. They must learn to interact with their co-workers, master the job itself, and go to work every day. They need to impress the boss so as not to get fired, and, maybe, someday get promoted. Quite a large percentage of an adult's waking hours are spent at his or her place of employment.
7. *Taking on civic responsibilities.* Havighurst deemed this a life task of young adulthood, but it is becoming more common for adolescents to do this, as well. This task means to become a member of a neighborhood and community. You might join the PTA, become a Girl Scout troop leader, take meals to infirm shut-ins, or volunteer to keep a stretch of road clear of trash. The longer you participate in an activity, the more responsibility you are usually given. Doing community service not only helps others, but it provides personal satisfaction and strengthens ties to others.
8. *Finding a congenial social group.* When you are in school, you are surrounded mostly by people who are your own age and who are at the same point of life that you are. A sea of ready-made friends is available. Once you leave school, however, it becomes more difficult to find others like yourself. You may go to work in a business with only six other employees, all of whom are over 40 years of age. You may spend most of your day working alone. You may move to a new city and be the only unmarried, childless individual on your block. Therefore, it becomes necessary to learn how to seek out friends. Whether you do it by joining social organizations, by belonging to a religious institution, or simply by learning to introduce yourself to strangers, finding friends is often less automatic once you reach young adulthood.

Although not described by Havighurst, another change that is supposed to occur during young adulthood is becoming mature. Psychological maturity goes beyond being independent and having an identity (although both of those are necessary). In addition, it entails taking responsibility for your decisions and actions and accepting yourself for who you are. It means that you can look at both yourself and the world *realistically.* It involves being able to handle setbacks and bounce back from them. It involves caring for others, not only for yourself. Not everyone becomes psychologically mature during young adulthood, but it is a fine goal to strive for.

In addition to the issues just described, many people say that young adulthood *feels* different from adolescence. Adolescence very much has a flavor of "becoming" and "working toward." Many college students use phrases such as "When I join the real world . . ." and "When I'm grown up . . .". Late adolescence is rather future oriented; you feel like you are preparing for the life you will someday have. Young adulthood, in contrast, feels more like you have arrived; you are not becoming, you are. Enjoy it!

GLOSSARY

accommodation involves adjusting to new information by creating new structures to replace old.
achievement tests tests designed to assess mastery of specific subject matter or skills.
acne pimples on the skin caused by overactive sebaceous glands.
acquaintance rape forced, unwanted sexual intercourse with someone the victim knows.
action learning an approach to moral education that emphasizes community service.
adaptation including and adjusting to new information that increases understanding.
adolescence the period of growth from childhood to maturity.
adolescent culture sum of the ways of living of adolescents.
adolescent society structural arrangements of subgroups within an adolescent social system.
adolescent subculture values and way of life that are contrary to those found in adult society.
adrenal glands ductless glands, located just above the kidneys, that secrete androgens and estrogens in both men and women, in addition to the glands' secretion of adrenaline.
affect feelings that exist among family members.
affirmation a strategy used to confirm.
alcohol abuse excessive use of alcohol so that functioning is impaired.
Alcoholics Anonymous (AA) an approach that uses a 12-step model and peer support to help people stop abusing alcohol.
alcoholism chemical dependency on alcohol accompanied by compulsive and excessive drinking.
alternating biculturalism the state in which one vacillates between following one's ethnic beliefs and those of the societal mainstream.
amygdala the part of the brain that creates primitive emotional responses to the environment.
anabolic steroids the masculinizing hormone testosterone taken by athletes to build muscle mass.
anal stage the second psychosexual stage in Sigmund Freud's theory of development: the second year of life, during which the child seeks pleasure and satisfaction through anal activity and the elimination of waste.
analysis an approach to moral education that emphasizes using logical reasoning to solve social dilemmas.
analytic ability the aspect of creativity that involves evaluating ideas.
androgens a class of masculinizing sex hormones produced by the testes and, to a lesser extent, by the adrenals.
androgyny a blending of male and female characteristics and roles.
animism the preoperational belief that inanimate objects have humanlike properties and emotions.
anorexia nervosa an eating disorder characterized by an obsession with food and with being thin.
anovulatory without ovulation.
antiprostaglandins drugs that destroy prostaglandins and can reduce menstrual distress.
anxious attachments youths are nervous and insecure in relationships; fostered by inconsistent parenting.
apocrine glands sweat glands located primarily in the armpits and groin whose secretions cause body odor.
apprenticeships or internships programs in which students split their time among working at a company, taking career-related classes, and doing regular academic coursework.
assimilation incorporating a feature of the environment into an existing mode or structure of thought.
attachment style the kind of emotional bond an adolescent has with his or her parents; described as secure, anxious, or avoidant.
attachment the early emotional bond formed between child and parent.
attention-deficit hyperactivity disorder (ADHD) a behavioral disorder characterized by impulsivity, an inability to pay attention, and an inability to sit still.
authoritarian parents parents who set many rules and harshly enforce them.
authoritative parents parents who respect their children's wishes but who maintain control in the home.
autonomous morality the latter of Piaget's two stages of moral development, in which individuals make their own moral judgments rather than blindly follow.
autonomy independence or freedom.
autosociality the period during which a child plays alongside other children, not with them.
avoidant attachments youths are aloof and distant, afraid of being hurt; fostered by cold, rejecting parents.
Bartholin's glands glands on either side of the vaginal opening that secrete fluid during sexual arousal.
basal metabolic rate the speed at which the body burns calories when at rest.
behavioral autonomy becoming independent and free enough to act on one's own without excessive dependence on others.
behavioral therapy an approach that uses modeling, reinforcement, and situational inducement to alter behavior.
binge drinking the consumption of five or more drinks at a sitting if you are male and four or more drinks at a sitting if you are female.
blended biculturalism the state in which one finds the commonalities between one's ethnic and mainstream identities.
bulimia an eating disorder characterized by binge-eating episodes and purging.
centering the tendency of children to focus attention on one detail and their inability to shift attention to other aspects of the situation.
cerebellum a part of the brain that controls balance, coordination, and learning.
cerebrum the largest part of the human brain.
charter schools public schools that are funded and run by private corporations or individuals; accountable to government but relatively regulation free.
child abuse may include not only physical assault of a child but also malnourishment, abandonment, neglect, emotional abuse, and sexual abuse.
child neglect failure to provide even minimal care of a child, including adequate food, clothing, shelter, and medical care, as well as for the child's emotional, social, intellectual, and moral needs.
circumscription limiting one's career aspirations to a set of acceptable choices based on interests and values.
circumstantial-situational use drug use to produce a desired psychological mood.
cirrhosis an often fatal disease of the liver caused by heavy and chronic alcohol consumption.
class inclusion relationships understanding that objects can be fit into different levels of hierarchies.
cliques relatively small, tightly knit groups of friends that spend a lot or even all of their time together.
clitoris a small shaft containing erectile tissue, located above the vaginal and urethral openings, that is highly responsive to sexual stimulation.
club drugs Collectively, ecstasy, rohypnol, GHB, and ketamine. They are part of the rave scene and are used in bars.
cognition the act or process of knowing.
cognitive monitoring thinking about what you are doing, what you are going to do next, how the problem is going to be solved, and the approaches that you are going to take.
cognitive-behavioral modification a therapeutic technique used to help control maladaptive, self-defeating thoughts.
cohesion the degree to which family members are connected to one another.
cohort A group of individuals who are born at approximately the same time and who share traits because they experienced the same historical events.
coitus sexual intercourse.
colonias or barrios colonies or districts of Spanish-speaking people.
comparator the component of the identity control system that compares one's self-concept with one's identity standards.
compromise with reality theory the theory of vocational choice proposed by Ginzberg.
compromise modifying one's career choices to bring them in line with reality.
compulsive drug use drug use motivated by physical addiction or psychological dependency.
concrete operational stage the third stage of cognitive development, according to Piaget, lasting from 7 to 11 or 12 years of age.
conduct disorder a psychological order typified by aggressive, hurtful, deceitful behavior.
confirmation strategy looking for examples that match a hypothesis.

connection the presence of a warm, stable, loving, attentive bond between parents and child.

conservation problems tests used by Piaget to determine whether children had mastered concrete operations, such as understanding that changing an object's appearance does not alter its fundamental properties.

control the degree to which parents manage their child's behavior.

conventional moral reasoning according to Kohlberg, the second level of development of moral thought, based on the desire to conform to social convention.

corpus callosum a fibrous band of tissue that connects the two cerebral hemispheres of the brain.

corpus luteum a yellow body that grows from the ruptured follicle of the ovary and becomes an endocrine gland that secretes progesterone.

correlation a description of a relationship between two factors that does not imply a causal relationship between them.

Cowper's glands small twin glands that secrete a fluid to neutralize the acid environment of the urethra.

crowds loose associations of cliques that usually meet on weekends.

cultural determinism the influence of a particular culture in determining the personality and behavior of a developing individual.

cultural relativism variations in social institutions, economic patterns, habits, mores, rituals, religious beliefs, and ways of life from one culture to another.

cysts large, deep pimples that can cause scarring.

date rape forced, unwanted sexual intercourse with a date.

deductive reasoning beginning with an hypothesis or premise and breaking it down to see if it is true.

defense mechanisms according to Anna Freud, unrealistic strategies used by the ego to protect itself and to discharge tension.

defensive realism the belief that there are absolute truths but people are biased; differentiates between opinion and fact.

depressants a class of drugs that work by slowing the functioning of the central nervous system (alcohol, inhalants).

depression a serious psychological disorder marked by sadness, helplessness, and hopelessness.

developmental tasks the skills, knowledge, functions, and attitudes that individuals have to acquire at certain points in their lives in order to function effectively as mature persons.

dialectics an advanced form of reasoning that allows one to create new and better insights by integrating conflicting data.

differential association Sutherland's theory that outlines conditions that facilitate moral or criminal learning.

disengaged families those whose members are isolated from each other.

dogmatism clinging rigidly to one belief.

dopamine a neurotransmitter whose effects are enhanced by stimulants.

drug abuse the use of drugs to the point of causing risk or harm, either due to legal risk or to the risk of harming oneself and others.

ectomorph tall, slender body build.

ego according to Sigmund Freud, the rational mind that seeks to satisfy the id in keeping with reality.

egocentricism the inability to take the perspective of another or to imagine the other person's point of view.

elimination strategy looking for evidence that disproves a hypothesis.

emerging adulthood The stage of life, generally extending through one's twenties, in which one is between adolescence and full adulthood.

emotional abuse may include constant screaming at the child, calling him or her foul names, giving constant criticism and put-downs, making fun, constantly comparing the child with siblings, ignoring the child, and refusing to talk or listen to him or her.

emotional autonomy becoming free of childish emotional dependence on parents.

empathy the ability to identify with the thoughts, attitudes, and feelings of another person.

endocrine glands structures in the body that produce hormones.

endogenous endorphins chemicals similar to narcotics that are produced by the body and cause euphoria and depress pain.

endomorph short, heavy body build.

enmeshed families those whose members are too heavily connected with each other.

epididymis a system of ducts, running from the testes to the vas deferens, in which sperm mature and are stored.

epistemology one's beliefs about knowledge.

equilibrium according to Piaget, achieving a balance between schemas and accommodation.

estrogens feminizing hormones produced by the ovaries and, to some extent, by the adrenal glands.

exosystem that part of an ecological system that includes settings in which the adolescent does not have an active role as a participant but that influence him or her nevertheless.

expected selves the people we think we will likely be in the future.

experimental use occasional drug use motivated by curiosity.

fallopian tubes tubes that transport the ova from the ovaries to the uterus.

familialism devotion to one's family and respect for one's parents and grandparents.

family systems therapy an approach to helping adolescents in which the emphasis is on enhancing family communication and improving family relationships.

fatalism the belief that one cannot change one's destiny or fate.

feared selves the people we are afraid of becoming in the future.

femininity personality and behavior characteristics of a female according to culturally defined standards of femaleness.

flappers Teenage girls in the late 1910s–1920s who dated, wore short skirts, and drank alcohol.

follicle-stimulating hormone (FSH) a pituitary hormone that stimulates the maturation of the follicles and ova in the ovaries and of sperm in the testes.

foreclosure according to Marcia, establishing an identity without search or exploration, usually according to what has been handed down by parents.

formal operational stage the fourth stage of cognitive development, according to Piaget, during which people develop abstract thought independent of concrete objects.

frontal lobe the cerebral lobe that is the center for higher-order thought processes, such as planning and impulse control.

frontal lobe the cerebral lobe that is the center for higher-order thinking, such as planning and impulse control.

fusion the state in which one has merged one's ethnic traditions and those of the cultural mainstream into a new whole.

GABA an inhibitory neurotransmitter; depressants increase its effectiveness.

gender roles the behaviors that are supposedly characteristic of men and women.

gender schema theory a revised cognitive-developmental approach to gender that emphasizes the stages of labeling, attention, and interest.

gender the psychological/sociological construct of what it means to be a man or a woman.

genital stage the last psychosexual stage in Sigmund Freud's theory of development, during which sexual urges result in seeking other persons as sexual objects to relieve sexual tension

gonadotropic hormones hormones that are secreted by the pituitary and that influence the gonads, or sex glands.

gonadotropin-releasing hormone (GnRH) a hormone secreted by the hypothalamus that controls the production and release of FSH and LH from the pituitary.

gonads the sex glands: testes and ovaries.

good girl–good boy orientation the first of the two levels of conventional moral reasoning, in which one acts so as to win others' approval.

gynecomastia a phenomenon experienced by some young male adolescents in which their breasts temporarily swell as they enter puberty.

hallucinogens a class of drugs that act on the central nervous system to alter perception and state of consciousness, causing hallucinations; so-called psychedelic drugs.

heteronomous morality the earlier of Piaget's two stages of moral development, in which individuals slavishly follow the rules they are given.

heterosexuality sexual orientation to those of the opposite sex.

heterosociality the period during which adolescents and adults enjoy the company of both sexes.

hierarchical classification the ability to divide objects into nested series of categories.

hippies Youth in the late 1960s who held pro-drug, pacifistic, antimaterialistic values.

hippocampus a part of the brain involved with learning, memory, and motivation.

homosexuality sexual orientation to those of the same sex.

homosociality the period during which children prefer the company of those of the same sex.

hoped-for selves the people we hope to be in the future.

hormones biochemical substances secreted into the bloodstream by the endocrine glands that act as an internal communication system that tells the different cells what to do.

human growth hormone (HGH) a pituitary hormone that regulates body growth.
hymen the tissue partly covering the vaginal opening.
hypocrisy discrepancy between what people say and do.
hypothalamus a small area of the brain that controls motivation, emotion, pleasure, and pain in the body; that is, it controls eating, drinking, hormonal production, menstruation, pregnancy, lactation, and sexual response and behavior.
hypothetico-deductive reasoning a way to solve problems using the scientific method; only one factor at a time is varied while all else is held constant.
id according to Sigmund Freud, those instinctual urges that a person seeks to satisfy according to the pleasure principle.
ideal self the kind of person an individual would like to be.
identification the process by which an individual ascribes to himself or herself the characteristics of another person.
identification the taking on of parental values, beliefs, and behaviors.
identity achieved according to Marcia, those adolescents who have undergone a crisis in their search for an identity and who have made a commitment.
identity control system a construct that describes the process of developing an identity.
identity diffused according to Marcia, those adolescents who have not experienced a crisis and explored meaningful alternatives or made any commitments in finding an acceptable identity.
identity standards one's beliefs about how one should behave.
imaginary audience adolescents' belief that others are constantly paying attention to them.
immanent justice the child's belief that immoral behavior inevitably brings pain or punishment as a natural consequence of the transgression.
immigrants people who leave their native land to come to live in the United States for any reason.
inculcation an approach to moral education that teaches students to accept specific moral values, such as honesty and trustworthiness.
individuation the formation of personal identity by the development of the self as a unique person separate from parents and others.
induction parental control through offering alternative choices.
inductive reasoning gathering individual items of information and putting them together to form hypotheses or conclusions.
inference to develop new thoughts from old information.
information-processing approach an approach to studying cognition that focuses on the perception, attention, retrieval, and manipulation of information.
inhibin a hormone produced in the testes to regulate FSH secretion and sperm production.
instrumental hedonism orientation the more advanced of the two preconventional reasoning levels, in which one acts so as to gain a future reward.
intelligence quotient (IQ) calculated by dividing the mental age (MA) by the chronological age (CA) and multiplying by 100.
intensified drug use daily drug use.
introspection thinking about one's thoughts and feelings.
joint custody when two parents share decision-making privileges (joint legal custody) and/or living with a child (joint residential custody).
juvenile delinquent a juvenile who violates the law.
juvenile one who is not yet considered an adult in the eyes of the law.
labia majora major or large lips of tissue on either side of the vaginal opening.
labia minora smaller lips or tissue on either side of the vagina.
latency stage the fourth psychosexual stage in Sigmund Freud's theory of development: from about 6 to 12 years of age, during which sexual interests remain hidden while the child concentrates on school and other activities.
law and order orientation the more advanced type of conventional moral reasoning, in which one unquestioningly obeys society's rules and laws.
legal custody the parent has the right to make important decisions about the child's life, such as which school he or she will attend.
leptin a hormone that helps trigger puberty.
liaisons individuals who have friends from several cliques but belong to none.
long-term storage (long-term memory) the process by which information is perceived and processed deeply so it passes into the layers of memory below the conscious level (also called secondary memory).
luteinizing hormone (LH) a pituitary hormone that stimulates the development of the ovum and estrogen and progesterone in females and of sperm and testosterone in males.
machismo Spanish term for maleness or manhood.
macrosystem the ideologies, attitudes, mores, customs, and laws of a particular culture that influence the individual.
magnet schools theme schools that serve students within public school systems.
marianismo in Puerto Rican society, the implication that a woman finds her greatest satisfaction through motherhood.
masculinity personality and behavioral characteristics of a male according to culturally defined standards of maleness.
matrilineal descent through the mother's line.
melatonin the hormone that the brain produces to induce sleep.
menarche first menstruation.
mental operations abstract reasoning principles that allow children to think logically.
mental operations logical processes that allow for flexible thought.
merocrine glands sweat glands distributed over the entire body.
mesomorph medium, athletic body build.
mesosystem the reciprocal relationships among microsystem settings.
metabolic rate the rate at which the body utilizes food and oxygen.
metacognition the ability to think about one's own thought processes.
microsystem includes those persons with whom the adolescent has immediate contact and who influence him or her.
modeling learning by observing and imitating the behavior of another.
mons veneris mound of flesh (literally "mound of Venus") in the female located above the vagina, over which pubic hair grows.
moral development an approach to moral education that uses moral dilemmas and the like to give youths experience in higher-level reasoning.
moral rules social rules that are concerned with how people behave toward one another.
morality of constraint conduct that is coerced by rules or authority.
morality of cooperation conduct that is regulated by mutual respect and consent.
moratorium according to Marcia, a period of time in the life of adolescents who are involved in a continual crisis, who continue to search for an identity, and who have not made any commitments.
mortality rate the probability of dying.
naive realism the belief that there are absolute, universal truths; creates difficulty in distinguishing fact from opinion.
narcotics a class of opiate-based drugs that depress the central nervous system and thus relieve pain and induce sleep; in large doses, produce unconsciousness, stupor, coma, and possibly death; most are habit forming.
naturalistic intelligence the ability to identify plants and animals.
negation a strategy used to disprove.
negative affect a relationship characterized by negative feelings of emotional coldness, rejection, hostility, anger, and insensitivity among family member.
negative correlation a description of a relationship in which when one factor increases, the other decreases.
negative identity an identity based on rejecting parenting and societal values.
nocturnal emissions male ejaculation during sleep.
normative barriers limitations on career choice that stem from how girls are socialized to be feminine.
normative regulation the process by which teens signal their approval and disapproval of each other, generally through unspoken means.
obesity overweight; excessively fat.
objective judgments judgments based solely on the consequences of wrongdoing.
occupational environment theory the theory of vocational choice proposed by Holland.
open enrollment a policy that allows students to choose from among a large number of public schools, sometimes even those outside their own district.
oppositional defiant disorder (ODD) a psychological disorder that causes a person to get angry and argue, to blame and annoy others, and to disobey authority figures.
oral stage the first psychosexual stage in Sigmund Freud's theory of development: from birth to one year, during which the child's chief source of pleasure and satisfaction comes from oral activity
organismic psychologist someone like Piaget, who believes that both brain maturation and environmental experience are needed for cognitive development.
osteoporosis a condition in which the bones become brittle due to calcium loss
ovaries female gonads, or sex glands, that secrete estrogen and progesterone and produce mature egg cells.
papules tender, raised red bumps that are precursors to pimples.

parens patriae the philosophy that the juvenile court is to act in the best interests of the child.

parietal lobe the cerebral lobe that is the center for solving problems involving spatial relationships.

penis the male organ for coitus and urination.

performance goal structure schooling in a competitive atmosphere in which the goal is to get the highest grade in the class.

permissive parents parents who exercise little control over their children's behavior.

personal fable adolescents' belief that they are invulnerable and that their feelings are special and unique.

personal preferences aspects of behavior that involve independent choices with which others have no right to interfere.

phallic stage the third psychosexual stage in Sigmund Freud's theory of development: from about the fourth to the sixth year, during which the genital area is the chief source of pleasure and satisfaction.

physical addiction a condition that develops from abusing a drug that forms a chemical dependency.

pituitary gland master gland of the body located at the base of the brain.

pluralistic society a society in which there are many different competing standards of behavior.

positive affect a relationship characterized by emotional warmth, affection, love, empathy, care, sensitivity, and emotional support.

positive correlation a description of a relationship in which when one factor increases, so does the other.

possible selves the different selves we envision ourselves becoming.

postconventional moral reasoning according to Kohlberg, the third level of development of moral thought, based on adherence to universal principles.

postskeptical rationalism the belief that truth is constructed but that some beliefs are more valid than others.

practical ability the aspect of creativity that involves turning abstract ideas into practical applications.

preconventional moral reasoning according to Kohlberg, the first level of development of moral thought, based on reward and punishment.

preoperational stage the second stage of cognitive development, according to Piaget, lasting from 2 to 7 years of age.

principles abstract, theoretical guidelines.

problem-finding stage the fifth stage of cognitive development characterized by the ability to be creative, to discover, and to formulate problems.

processing speed the pace at which the brain perceives and manipulates information.

progesterone a female sex hormone produced by the corpus luteum of the ovary.

progressives educators who emphasize that the purpose of education is to prepare pupils for life.

proprium the self-identity that is developing in time.

prosocial behavior actions that benefit, help, and bolster others.

prostaglandins hormones that cause smooth muscle contractions and contribute to dysmenorrhea and menhorrhagia.

prostate glands two glands that secrete a portion of the seminal fluid.

pseudostupidity the tendency to approach problems at much too complex a level and to fail, not because the tasks are difficult, but because they're too simple. Adolescents appear stupid when they are, in fact, bright but not yet experienced.

psychoanalytical theory Freud's theory that the structure of personality is composed of the id, ego, and superego and that mental health depends on keeping the balance among them.

psychological autonomy the freedom to form one's own opinions, have privacy, and make decisions for oneself.

psychological dependency the development of a persistent, sometimes overpowering psychological need for a drug.

psychometric approach an approach to cognitive development that focuses on the measurement of knowledge and thinking ability.

psychosocial moratorium a socially sanctioned period between childhood and adulthood during which an individual is free to experiment to find a socially acceptable identity and role.

puberty the developmental stage at which one becomes capable of reproduction.

punishment orientation the more primitive level of preconventional moral reasoning, in which one acts so as to avoid negative consequences.

pustules the medical term for pimples.

quasi-experiment a study in which the researcher compares pre-existing groups.

reasoning logical, constrained, useful thinking.

refugees people who leave their native land to come to live in the United States because they are fleeing political oppression or death.

regulation parental monitoring, supervision, and rule setting.

reinforcement positive reinforcements are influences that increase the probability that the preceding response will occur again. Negative reinforcements are influences that increase the probability that the preceding response will stop.

Relational aggression Using your friends to help socially hurt another.

Reputational aggression Spreading rumors or doing other actions to hurt another's reputation.

residential custody where and with which parent the child will live.

resiliency an individual's ability to succeed in spite of adversity and hardship.

restorative justice movement an approach to juvenile justice that addresses the needs of the victim, the community, and the perpetrator; it focuses on restitution for the victim and personal development for the offender.

scaffolding the assistance provided to help a child master a task; it is gradually withdrawn as the child gains competence.

schema the original patterns of thinking; the mental structures that people use for dealing with what happens in the environment.

Scholastic Assessment Test (SAT), a test that measures aptitude to do academic work.

school-based enterprises programs in which schools set up small businesses to teach job skills.

scrotum the pouch of skin containing the testes.

sebaceous glands oil-producing skin glands whose secretions can cause acne if the glands' pores become blocked.

secondary sexual characteristics features not directly related to reproduction that distinguish male from female bodies.

secular trend the trend to mature sexually at earlier ages.

secure attachments youths are trusting and open to others; fostered by parents who were consistently warm and nurturing.

self a person's personality or nature of which that person is aware.

self-concept a person's conscious, cognitive perception and evaluation of himself or herself; one's thoughts and opinions about oneself.

self-enhancement thesis an explanation for delinquency based on the need for troubled youths to enhance their self-esteem.

self-esteem a person's impression or opinion of himself or herself.

self-reinforcement the act of learners rewarding themselves for activities or responses that they consider of good quality.

self-serving bias looking at the world in a way that favors one's own opinion.

semenarche a recently coined term for a boy's first ejaculation; derived from the term menarche.

seminal vesicles twin glands that secrete fluid into the vas deferens to enhance sperm viability.

sensorimotor stage the first stage of cognitive development, according to Piaget, lasting from birth to about 2 years of age.

sensory storage (sensory memory) the process by which information is received and transduced by the senses, usually in a fraction of a second.

separation-individuation the process by which the adolescent becomes separated from parents and becomes a unique individual.

seriation the ability to line things up in order from large to small or small to large.

serotonin a neurotransmitter that is chemically similar to the hallucinogens.

Sertoli cells cells in the testes that produce the hormone inhibin.

sex one's biological endowment as a male or a female.

sexual abuse may include very suggestive language, use of pornography, fondling, petting, masturbation, exhibitionism, voyeurism, oral sex, or full vaginal or anal intercourse.

short-term storage (short-term memory) the process by which information is still in the conscious mind, being rehearsed and focused on (also called primary memory).

skepticism the rejection of rationality; complete disbelief.

social capital the resources available to an individual through his or her interpersonal connections.

social cognition how people think and reason about their social world as they watch and interact with others; their understanding and ability to get along with other people.

social contract orientation the type of postconventional moral reasoning in which one believes that individual actions should serve the greater good.

social conventions social rules that dictate what is appropriate and expected.

social role taking according to Selman, the social roles that individuals take on that reflect their understanding of themselves, their actions to others, and their abilities to understand others' points of view.

social-cognitive domain model an approach to moral development that stresses the contextual nature of moral decisions and distinguishes social conventions from moral rules.

social-recreational use drug use primarily to relax and have fun at parties.

spermatogenesis the process by which sperm are developed.

status crimes violations of laws that apply only to minors, such as underage drinking, violating curfews, and truancy.

stimulants agents that produce a temporary increase in the functioning of the body.

stranger rape forced, unwanted sexual intercourse with someone the victim doesn't know.

Strong Vocational Interest Blank a test that measures suitability for different vocations according to interests.

structural barriers externally imposed limits on a woman's career success that result from sex discrimination.

sturm und drang "storm and stress"; used to describe the volatile adolescent temperament.

subjective judgments judgments that take into account intentions or motives.

subsystems smaller segments of adolescent society within the larger social system.

superego according to Sigmund Freud, that part of the mind that opposes the desires of the id by enforcing moral restrictions that have been learned to try to attain a goal of perfection.

survival sex swapping sexual favors for food or shelter.

syncretism the act of trying to link ideas.

synthetic ability the aspect of creativity that involves generating new ideas.

task mastery structure schooling in a less competitive setting in which individual effort and improvement are rewarded.

tech-prep programs partnerships between high schools and two-year, postsecondary vocational institutions to provide career education.

tech-prep schools high schools that partner with community colleges to provide career preparation for non–college bound students.

teenager in a strict sense, includes only the teen years: ages 13 to 19.

temporal lobe the cerebral lobe that is the center for producing and understanding language.

testes the male gonads that produce sperm and male sex hormones.

testosterone a masculinizing sex hormone produced by the testes and, to a lesser extent, by the adrenals.

THC the active ingredient in marijuana.

therapeutic community treatment treatment in a residential situation with others who have similar problems; includes individual and group therapy and skills training.

thinking the conscious, deliberate manipulation of information.

throwaways adolescents who have been told to leave home.

tracking an organizational technique that permits schools to create homogeneous groupings of students within a heterogeneous student population in order to facilitate instruction.

traditionalists educators who emphasize that the purpose of education is to teach the basics.

transductive reasoning proceeding from particular to particular in thought, without making generalizations.

transitive inferences the ability to solve problems such as "Tom is taller than Fred, and Fred is taller than Marty. Is Tom taller than Marty?"

true experiment a study in which the researcher maintains control to ensure there are no significant differences among his or her groups of participants before the study begins and that the different groups of participants have identical experiences (except for the one issue of interest).

uninvolved parents parents who seem disinterested in their children and thus do not supervise them or give them much affection.

universal principled reasoning the highest form of moral reasoning, in which one acts according to his or her abstract moral principles.

urethra the tube carrying the urine from the bladder to the outside; in males, it also carries the semen to the outside.

uterus the womb in which the baby grows and develops.

vagina the canal from the cervix to the vulva that receives the penis during intercourse and acts as the birth canal through which the baby passes to the outside.

values clarification a method of teaching values that helps students become aware of their own beliefs and values.

vas deferens the tubes running from the epididymis to the urethra that carry semen and sperm to the ejaculatory duct.

vestibule the opening cleft region enclosed by the labia minora.

vicarious reinforcement learning from observing the positive or negative consequences of another person's behavior.

vouchers a method by which the public schools subsidize the cost of private school education.

vulva collective term referring to the external genitalia of the female.

warmth the love, approval, and emotional support that parents give their children.

youth development programs programs designed to provide skills, establish relationships, and increase self-esteem so that adolescents avoid delinquency and become well-functioning adults.

zone of proximal development the level of learning at which a task that is too difficult for a child to complete by himself or herself is manageable with help.

BIBLIOGRAPHY

Aalsma, M. C., Lapsley, D. K., and Flannery, D. J. (2006). "Personal Fables, Narcissism, and Adolescent Adjustment." *Psychology in the Schools,* 43, 481–491.

Aaron, D. J., Storti, K. L., Robertson, R. J., Kriska, A. M., and LaPorte, R. E. (2002). "Longitudinal Study of the Number and Choice of Leisure Time Physical Activities from Mid to Late Adolescence: Implications for School Curricula and Community Recreation Programs." *Archives of Pediatric and Adolescent Medicine,* 156, 1075–1080.

Abassi, V. (1998). "Growth and Normal Puberty." *Pediatrics,* 102, 507–511.

Abbey, A. (2002). "Alcohol-Related Sexual Assault: A Common Problem among College Students." *Journal of Studies on Alcohol,* Supplement 14, 118–128.

Abell, E., Clawson, M. C., Washington, W. N., Bost, K. K., and Vaughn, V. E. (1996). "Parenting Values, Attitudes, Behaviors, and Goals of African American Mothers from a Low-Income Population in Relation to Social and Societal Context." *Journal of Family Issues,* 17, 593–613.

Abernathy, T. J., Massad, L., and Romano-Dwyer, L. (1995). "The Relationship between Smoking and Self-Esteem." *Adolescence,* 30, 899–907.

Abma, J. C., and Sonenstein, F. L. (2001). "Sexual Activity and Contraceptive Practices among Teenagers in the United States, 1988 and 1995." *Vital and Health Statistics,* 23, 1–79.

Ackard, D. M., Neumark-Sztainer, D., Story, M., and Perry, C. (2006). "Parent-Child Connectedness and Behavioral and Emotional Health among Adolescents." *American Journal of Preventative Medicine,* 30, 59–66.

Acock, A. C., and Bengtson, V. L. (1980). "Socialization and Attribution Processes: Active versus Perceived Similarity among Parents and Youth." *Journal of Marriage and the Family,* 42, 501–515.

ACT, (2006). ACT News: Facts about ACT. Retrieved from http://www.act.org/news/aapfacts.html.

Adalbjarnardottir, S., and Hafsteinsson, L. G. (2001). "Adolescents' Perceived Parenting Styles and Their Substance Use: Concurrent and Longitudinal Analyses." *Journal of Adolescent Research,* 11, 401–423.

Adam, K. S., Bouckams, A., and Streiner, D. (1982). "Parental Loss and Family Stability in Attempted Suicide." *Archives of General Psychiatry,* 39, 1081–1085.

Adams, G. R., Gullotta, T. T., and Montenayor, R. (Eds.). (1992). *Adolescent Identity Formation.* Newbury Park, CA: Sage.

Adams, G. R., and Jones, R. M. (February 1982). "Adolescent Egocentrism: Exploration into Possible Contributions of Parent-Child Relations." *Journal of Youth and Adolescence,* 11, 25–31.

Adams, G. R., and Marshall, S. K. (1996). "A Developmental Social Psychology of Identity: Understanding the Person in Context." *Journal of Adolescence,* 19, 429–442.

Adams, K., Sargent, R. G., Thompson, S. H., Richter, D., Corwin, S. J., and Rogan, T. J. (2000). "A Study of Body Weight Concerns and Weight Control Practices of 4th and 7th Grade Adolescents." *Ethnicity and Health,* 5, 79–94.

Adams, R., and Laursen, B. (2001). "The Organization and Dynamics of Adolescent Conflict with Parents and Friends." *Journal of Marriage & the Family,* 63, 97–110.

Adcock, A. G., Nagy, S., and Simpson, J. A. (1991). "Selected Risk Factors in Adolescent Attempts." *Adolescence,* 26, 817–828.

Adeyanju, M. (1990). "Adolescent Health Status, Behaviors, and Cardiovascular Disease." *Adolescence,* 25, 155–169.

Adler, P. A., and Adler, P. (1995). "Dynamics of Inclusion and Exclusion in Preadolescent Cliques." *Social Psychology Quarterly,* 58, 145–162.

Adler, P. A., Kleiss, S. J., and Adler, P. (1992). "Socialization to Gender Roles: Popularity among Elementary School Boys and Girls." *Sociology of Education,* 65, 169–187.

Agbayani-Siewart, P. (2002). "Filipino American Culture and Family Values." In N. V. Benokraitis (Ed.), *Contemporary Ethnic Families in the United States: Characteristics, Variations, and Dynatics* (pp. 36–42). Englewood Cliffs, NJ: Prentice Hall.

Agerbo, E., Nordentoft, M., and Mortensen, P. B. (2002). "Familial, Psychiatric, and Socioeconomic Risk Factors for Suicide in Young People: Nested Case-Control Study." *British Medical Journal,* 325, 74.

Agrawal, P. (March 1978). "A Cross-Cultural Study of Self-Image: Indian, American, Australian, and Irish Adolescents." *Journal of Youth and Adolescence,* 7, 107–116.

Ahlstrom, P. A., Richmond, D., Townsend, C., and D'Angelo, L. (1992). *The Course of HIV Infection in Adolescents.* Paper presented at the meeting of the Society for Adolescent Medicine, Washington, DC.

Ahn, N. (1994). Teenage childbearing and high school completion: Accounting for individual heterogeneity. *Family Planning Perspectives,* 26, 17–21.

Ainslie, R. C., Shafer, A., and Reynolds, J. (1996). "Mediators of Adolescents' Stress in a College Preparatory Environment." *Adolescence,* 31, 913–924.

Ainsworth, M. D. S., Blehar, M. C., Waters, E., and Wall, S. (1978). *Patterns of Attachment: A Psychological Study of the Strange Situation.* Hillsdale, NJ: Erlbaum.

Akaka, D. (2004). *Credit Card Minimum Payment Warning Act.* Press release retrieved from http://akaka.senate.gov/~akaka/speeches/2004521A11.html.

Akinboye, J. O. (Summer 1984). "Secondary Sexual Characteristics and Normal Puberty in Nigerian and Zimbabwian Adolescents." *Adolescence,* 19, 483–492.

Alan Guttmacher Institute. (1993). *National Survey of the American Male Sexual Habits.* Unpublished data.

Alan Guttmacher Institute. (1999). *Facts in Brief: Teen Sex and Pregnancy* <www.agi-usaorg/pubs/fb_teen_sex.html>.

Alan Guttmacher Institute. (2003). *State Policies in Brief: Parental Involvement in Minors' Abortions.* New York: Author.

Alan Guttmacher Institute. (2006). Parental Involvement in Minors' Abortions. *State Policies in Brief.* Retrieved from http://www.guttmacher.org/statecenter/spibs/spib_PIMA.pdf.

Alderman, T. (1997). *The Scarred Soul: Understanding and Ending Self-Inflicted Violence.* Oakland, CA: Harbinger.

Allen, L. S., and Gorski, R. A. (1992). "Sexual Orientation and the Size of the Anterior Commissure in the Human Brain." *Proceedings of the National Academy of Sciences,* 89, 7199–7202.

Allen, R. J. (1992). "Social Factors Associated with the Amount of School Week Sleep Lag for Seniors in an Early Starting Urban High School." *Sleep Research,* 21, 114.

Allgood-Merten, B., Lewinsohn, P. M., and Hops, H. (1990). "Sex Differences and Adolescent Depression." *Journal of Abnormal Psychology,* 99, 55–63.

Allport, G. W. (1950). *Becoming: Basic Considerations for a Psychology of Personality.* New Haven, CT: Yale University Press.

Aloise-Young, P. A., Graham, J. W., and Hansen, W. B. (1994). "Peer Influence on Smoking Initiation during Early Adolescence: A Comparison of Group Members and Group Outsiders." *Journal of Applied Psychology,* 79, 281–287.

Aloise-Young, P. A., Hennigan, K. M., and Leong, C. W. (2001). "Possible Selves and Negative Health Behaviors during Early Adolescence." *Journal of Early Adolescence,* 21, 158–181.

Alsaker, F. D. (1992). "Pubertal Timing, Overweight, and Psychological Adjustment." *Journal of Early Adolescence,* 12, 396–419.

Alsaker, F. D., and Flammer, A. (1999). *Time Use by Adolescents in an International Perspective: II. The Case of Necessary Activities.* Mahwah. NJ: Erlbaum.

Altchek, A. (1988). "Abnormal Uterine Bleeding in Teenage Girls." *Medical Aspects of Human Sexuality,* 22, 82–88.

Alter-Reid, K., Gibbs, M. S., Lachenmeyer, J. R., Sigal, J., and Massoth, N. A. (1986). "Sexual Abuse of Children: A Review of the Empirical Findings." *Clinical Psychology Review,* 6, 249–266.

Altpeter, T. S., and Korger, J. N. (1999). "Disruptive Behavior: Oppositional Defiant Disorder, and Conduct Disorder." In S. D. Netherton, D. Holmes, and C. E. Walker (Eds.), *Child and Adolescent Psychological Disorders: A Comprehensive Textbook* (pp. 118–139). New York: Oxford University Press.

Amaro, H., Blake, S. M., Schwartz, P. M., and Flinchbaugh, L. J. (2001). "Developing Theory-Based Substance Abuse Prevention Programs for Young Adolescent Girls." *Journal of Early Adolescence,* 21, 256–293.

Amato, P. (2000). "The Consequences of Divorce for Adults and Children." *Journal of Marriage and Family,* 62, 1269–1287.

Amato, P., and Gilbreth, J. (1999). "Nonresident Fathers and Children's Well-Being: A Meta-Analysis." *Journal of Marriage and the Family,* 61, 557–573.

Amato, P. R. (1986). "Marital Conflict, the Parent-Child Relationship, and Child Self-Esteem." *Family Relations,* 35, 403–410.

Amato, P. R. (1987). "Family Processes in One-Parent, Stepparent, and Intact Families: The Child's Point of View." *Journal of Marriage & the Family,* 49, 327–337.

Amato, P. R. (1988). "Long-Term Implications of Parental Divorce for Adult Self-Concept." *Journal of Family Issues,* 9, 201–213.

Amato, P. R. (1990). "Dimension of the Family Environment as Perceived by Children: A Multidimensional Scaling Analysis." *Journal of Marriage and the Family,* 52, 613–620.

Amato, P. R. (2000). "Diversity within Single-Parent Families." In D. H. Demo, K. R. Allen, and M. A. Fine (Eds.), *Handbook of Family Diversity* (pp. 149–172). Oxford, England: Oxford University Press.

Amato, P. R. (2001). "Children of Divorce in the 1990s: An Update of the Amato and Keith (1991) Meta-Analysis." *Journal of Family Psychology,* 15, 355–370.

Amato, P. R., and Booth, A. (2001). "The Legacy of Parents' Marital Discord: Consequences for Children's Marital Quality." *Journal of Personality and Social Psychology,* 81, 627–638.

Amato, P. R., and DeBoer, D. D. (2001). "The Transmission of Marital Instability across Generations: Relationship Skills or Commitment to Marriage?" *Journal of Marriage and the Family,* 63, 1038–1051.

Amato, P. R., and Keith, B. (1991). "Parental Divorce and Well-Being of Children: A Meta-Analysis." *Psychological Bulletin,* 110, 26–46.

Ambert, A. (1986). Being a stepparent: Live-in and visiting stepchildren. *Journal of Marriage & the Family, 48,* 795–804.

American Academy of Pediatrics, Committee on Substance Abuse. (1994). "Tobacco-Free Environment: An Imperative for the Health of Children and Adolescents." *Pediatrics,* 93, 866–868.

American Association of School Administrators. (1983). *The Excellence Report: Using It to Improve Your Schools.* Arlington, VA: Author.

American Association of University Women. (2001). *Hostile Hallways: Bullying, Teasing, and Sexual Harassment in School.* Washington, DC: American Association of University Women.

American Association of University Women (AAUW) Educational Foundation. (1992). *The AAUW Report: How Schools Short-Change Girls.* Washington, DC: Author and National Education Association.

American Association of University Women (AAUW) Educational Foundation. (1993). *Hostile Hallways: The AAUW Survey on Sexual Harassment in America's Schools.* Research Report no. 923012. Washington, DC: Harris/Scholastic Research.

American College Testing Program. (1995). *The ACT Assessment Program.* Iowa City, IA: American College Testing Program.

American Library Association. (2006). The *Children's Internet Protection Act.* Retrieved from http://www.ala.org/ala/washoff/WOissues/civilliberties/cipaweb/cipa.htm.

American Psychiatric Association. (2000). *Diagnostic and Statistical Manual of Mental Disorders.* 4th ed. (text revision) Washington, DC: Author.

American Psychological Association. (1995). *Lesbian and Gay Parenting: A Resource for Psychologists* <www.apa.org/pi/parent.html>.

American Society of Plastic Surgeons. (2004). *Plastic Surgery for Teenagers.* Retrieved from http://www.plasticsurgery.org/news_room/Plastic-Surgery-for-Teenagers-Briefing-Paper.cfm 6/8/06.

Amos, R. J., Pingree, S., Ashbrook, S., Betts, N. M., Fox, H. M., Newell, K., Ries, C. P., Terry, R. D., Tinsley, A., Voichick, J., and Athens, S. (1989). "Developing a Strategy for Understanding Adolescent Nutrition Concerns." *Adolescence,* 24, 119–124.

Anderman, E. M., Eccles, J. S., Yoon, K. S., Roeser, R., Wigfield, A., and P. (2001). "Learning to Value Mathematics and Reading: Relations to Mastery and Performance-Oriented Instructional Practices." *Contemporary Educational Psychology,* 26, 76–95.

Anderman, E. M., Griesinger, T., and Westerfield, G. (1998). "Motivation and Cheating during Early Adolescence." *Journal of Educational Psychology,* 90, 84–93.

Andersen, B. L., and LeGrand, J. (1991). "Body Image for Women: Conceptualization Assessment, and a Test of Its Importance to Sexual Dysfunction and Medical Illness." *Journal of Sex Research,* 28, 457–477.

Anderson, C. A., and Bushman, B. J. (2002). "The Effects of Media Violence on Society." *Science,* 295, 2377–2378.

Anderson, C. A., and Dill, K. E. (2000). "Video Games and Aggressive Thoughts, Feelings, and Behavior in the Laboratory and in Life." *Journal of Personality and Social Psychology,* 78, 772–790.

Anderson, E. R. (1999). "Sibling, Half Sibling, and Stepsibling Relationships in Remarried Families." In E. M. Hetherington, S. H. Henderson, and D. Reiss (Eds.), *Adolescent Siblings in Stepfamilies: Family Functioning and Adolescent Adjustment* (pp. 101–126). Monographs of the Society for Research in Child Development, 64, no. 4.

Anderson, E. R., Greene, S. M., Hetherington, E. M., and Clingempeel, W. G. (1999). "The Dynamics of Parental Remarriage: Adolescent, Parent, and Sibling Influences." In E. M. Hetherington (Ed.), *Coping with Divorce, Single Parenting and Remarriage: A Risk and Resiliency Perspective.* Hillsdale, NJ: Lawrence Erlbaum.

Anderson, H. L., and Young, B. M. (1992). "Holistic Attitudes of High School Students towards Themselves and Their School Experiences." *Adolescence,* 27, 719–729.

Anderson, J. E., Kann, L., Holtzman, D., Arday, S., Truman, B., and Kolbe, L. (1990). "HIV/AIDS Knowledge and Sexual Behavior among High School Students." *Family Planning Perspectives,* 22, 252–255.

Anderson, P. B., Arceneaux, E. R., Carter, D., Miller, A. M., and King, B. M. (1995). "Changes in the Telephone Calling Patterns of Adolescent Girls." *Adolescence,* 30, 779–784.

Anderson, R. E. (2002). "Youth and Information Technology." In J. T. Mortimer and R. W. Larson (Eds.), *The Changing Adolescent Experience* (pp. 175–207). Cambridge, England: Cambridge University Press.

Anderson, R. E., and Ronnkvist, A. (1999). "Teaching, Learning, and Computing, 1998." University of California, Irvine. Retrieved from http://www.crito.uci.edu/tlc/html/findings.html

Anderson, R. N., and Smith, B. L. (2003). "Deaths: Leading Causes for 2001." *National Vital Statistics Report,* 52, 1–86.

Anderson, S., Dallal, G., and Must, A. (2003). "Relative Weight and Racial Influence Average Age at Menarche: Results from Two Nationally Representative Surveys of US Girls Studied 25 Years Apart." *Pediatrics,* 111, 844–850.

Andrews, J. A., Hops, H., and Duncan, S. C. (1997). "Adolescent Modeling of Parent Substance Use: The Moderating Effect of the Relationship with the Parent." *Journal of Family Psychology,* 11, 259–270.

Andrews, J. A., Hops, H., Ary, D., Tildesley, E., and Harris, J. (1993). "Parental Influence on Early Adolescent Substance Use: Specific and Nonspecific Effects." *Journal of Early Adolescence,* 13, 285–310.

Angold, A., and Rutter, N. (1992). "Effects of Age and Pubertal Status on Depression in a Large Clinical Sample." *Development and Psychopathology,* 4, 5–28.

Ansuini, C. G., Fiddler-Woite, J., and Woite, R. S. (1996). "The Source, Accuracy, and Impact of the National Sexual Information on Lifetime Wellness." *Adolescence,* 31, 283–289.

Antoniades, M., and Tarasuk, V. (1998). "A Survey of Food Problems Experienced by Toronto Street Youth." *Canadian Journal of Public Health,* 89, 371–375.

Apfel, N. H., and Seitz, V. (1991). "Four Models of Adolescent Mother-Grandmother Relationships in Black Inner-City Families." *Family Relations,* 40, 421–429.

"Aptitude-Test Scores: Grumbling Gets Louder." (May 14, 1979). *U.S. News & World Report,* pp. 76ff.

Aquilino, W. S., and Supple, A. J. (2001). "Long-Term Effects of Parenting Practices during Adolescence on Well-Being Outcomes in Young Adulthood." *Journal of Family Issues,* 22, 289–308.

Archer, S. L. (1989b). "The Status of Identity: Reflections on the Need for Intervention." *Journal of Adolescence,* 12, 345–359.

Archer, S. L., and Waterman, A. S. (1990). "Varieties of Identity Diffusions and Foreclosures: An Exploration of Subcategories of the Identity Statuses." *Journal of Adolescent Research,* 5, 96–111.

Archibald, A. B., Graber, J. A., and Brooks-Gunn, J. (1999). "Parental Relations and Pubertal Development as Predictors of Dieting and Body Image in Early-Adolescent Girls: A Short Term Longitudinal Study." *Journal of Research on Adolescence,* 9, 395–415.

Archibald, A. B., Linver, M. R., Graber, J. A., and Brooks-Gunn, J. (2002). "Parent-Adolescent Relationships and Girls' Unhealthy Eating: Testing Reciprocal Relationships." *Journal of Research on Adolescence,* 12, 451–461.

Ardelt, M., and Day, L. (2002). "Parents, Siblings, and Peers: Close Social Relationships and Adolescent Deviance." *Journal of Early Adolescence,* 22, 310–349.

Ardila, A., Rosselli, M., Matute, E., and Guajardo, S. (2005). "The Influence of the Parents' Educational Level on the Development of Executive Functions." *Developmental Neuropsychology,* 28, 539–560.

Arellano, A. R., and Pedilla, A. M. (1996). "Academic Invulnerability among a Select Group of

Latino University Students." *Hispanic Journal of Behavioral Sciences,* 18, 485–507.

Argyle, M., and Henderson, M. (1985). *The Anatomy of Relationships.* Harmondworth, Middlesex, England: Penguin.

Arlin, P. K. (1975). "Cognitive Development in Adulthood: A Fifth Stage?" *Developmental Psychology,* 11, 602–606.

Armstrong, P. I., and Crombie, G. (2000). "Compromises in Adolescents' Occupational Aspirations and Expectations from Grades 8 to 10." *Journal of Vocational Behavior,* 56, 82–98.

Arnett, J. J. (1990). "Contraceptive Use, Sensation Seeking, and Adolescent Egocentrism." *Journal of Youth and Adolescence,* 19, 171–180.

Arnett, J. J. (1991). "Adolescents and Heavy Metal Music: From the Mouths of Metalheads." *Youth and Society,* 23, 76–98.

Arnett, J. J. (1992). "The Soundtrack of Recklessness. Musical Preferences and Reckless Behavior among Adolescents." *Journal of Adolescent Research,* 7, 313–331.

Arnett, J. J. (1997). "Young People's Conceptions of the Transition to Adulthood." *Youth and Society,* 29, 3–23.

Arnett, J. J. (1999). "Adolescent Storm and Stress, Reconsidered." *American Psychologist,* 54, 317–326.

Arnett, J. J. (2000). "Emerging Adulthood: A Theory of Development from the Late Teens through the Twenties." *American Psychologist,* 55, 469–480.

Arnett, J. J. (2001). "Adolescents' Responses to Cigarette Advertisements for Five 'Youth Brands' and one 'adult brand.'" *Journal of Research on Adolescence,* 11, 425–443.

Arnett, J. J. (2004). *Emerging adulthood: The winding road from the late teens through the twenties.* New York: Oxford University Press.

Arnett, J. J. (2005). "Talk Is Cheap: The Tobacco Companies' Violations of Their Own Cigarette Advertising Code." *Journal of Health Communication,* 10, 419–431.

Arnstein, H. S. (1978). *Brothers and Sisters/Sisters and Brothers.* New York: Dutton.

Aronson, E. (2000). *Nobody Left to Hate: Teaching Compassion after Columbine.* New York: Worth.

Arunkumar, R., Midgley, C., and Urdan, T. (1999). "Perceiving High or Low Home-School Dissonance: Longitudinal Effects of Adolescent Emotional and Academic Well-Being." *Journal of Research on Adolescence,* 9, 441–466.

Aseltine, R. H., and Gore, S. (1993). "Mental Health and Social Adaptation Following the Transition from High School." *Journal of Research on Adolescence,* 3, 247–270.

Asendorph, J. B., and van Aken, M. A. G. (1999). "Resilient, Overcontrolled, and Undercontrolled Personality Prototypes in Childhood: Replicability, Predictive Power, and the Trait-Type Issue." *Journal of Personality and Social Psychology,* 77, 815–832.

Ashford, J. B., and LeCroy, C. W. (1990). "Juvenile Recidivism: A Comparison of Three Prediction Instruments." *Adolescence,* 98, 441–450.

Asmussen, L., and Larson, R. (1991). "The Quality of Family Time among Adolescents in Single-Parent and Married-Parent Families." *Journal of Marriage and the Family,* 53, 1021–1030.

Astin, H. S. (1984). "The Meaning of Work in Women's Lives: A Sociopsychological Model of Career Choice and Work Behavior." *Counseling Psychologist,* 12, 117–128.

Atkin, C. K., Smith, S. W., Roberto, A. J., Fediuk, T., and Wagner, T. (2002). "Correlates of Verbally Aggressive Communication in Adolescents." *Journal of Applied Communication Research,* 30, 251–266.

Atkinson, R. (2001). *Achievement versus Aptitude Test in College Admissions.* Retrieved 6/24/06 from http://www.ucop.edu/pres/speeches/achieve.htm.

Attie, I., and Brooks-Gunn, J. (1995). "The Development of Eating Regulation across the Lifespan." In D. Cicchetti and D. J. Cohen (Eds.), *Developmental Psychopathology* (Vol. 2, pp. 332–368). New York: Wiley.

Austin, D., Lopes, L., Wales, K., Casey, H., and Finch, R. (1992, 1993). *Hat 2 Da Back.* EMI April Music, Inc., Darp Music, Diva One Music, K. Wales Music, Inc., Tiz Biz Music, and Wind Swept Pacific Entertainment Company, d/b/a Longitude Business Company.

Avery, A. W. (December 1982). "Escaping Loneliness in Adolescence: The Case for Androgyny." *Journal of Youth and Adolescence,* 11, 451–459.

Azevedo, R., Cromley, J. G., Winters, F. I., Moos, D. C., and Greene, J. A. (2005). "Adaptive Human Scaffolding Facilitates Adolescents' Self-Regulated Learning with Hypermedia." *Instructional Science,* 33, 381–412.

Azmitia, M., and Hesser, J. (1993). "Why Siblings Are Important Agents of Cognitive Development: A Comparison of Siblings and Peers." *Child Development,* 64, 430–444.

Azmitia, M., Kamparth, N., and Linnet, J. (1998). "Intimacy and Conflict: The Dynamic of Boys' and Girls' Friendships during Middle Childhood and Early Adolescence." In L. Meyer, H. Park, M. Grnot-Scheyer, I. Schwartz, and B. Harry (Eds.), *Making Friends: The Influence of Culture and Development* (pp. 171–189). Baltimore: Brooks Publishing.

Bachman, J. G., and Schulenberg, J. (1993). "How Part-Time Work Intensity Relates to Drug Use, Problem Behavior, Time Use, and Satisfaction among High-School Seniors: Are These Consequences or Merely Correlates?" *Developmental Psychology,* 29, 220–235.

Bachman, J. G., Segal, D. R., Freedman-Doan, P., and O'Malley, P. M. (2000). "Who Chooses Military Service? Correlates of Propensity and Enlistment in the U.S. Armed Forces." *Military Psychology,* 12, 1–30.

Bachman, J. G., Wadsworth, K. N., O'Malley, P. M., Johnson, L. D. and Schulenberg, J. E. (1997). *Smoking, Drinking, and Drug Use in Young Adulthood: The Impacts of New Freedoms and New Responsibilities.* Mahweh, NJ: Lawrence Erlbaum.

Backover, A. (1991). "Native Americans: Alcoholism, FAS Puts a Race at Risk." *Guidepost,* 33, 1–9.

Bacon, C. S. (1993). "Student Responsibility for Learning." *Adolescence,* 28, 199–212.

Bahr, S. J., Marcos, A. C., and Maughan, S. L. (1995). "Family, Educational and Peer Influences on the Alcohol Use of Female and Male Adolescents." *Journal of Studies on Alcohol,* 56, 457–469.

Bailey, J. M., and Zucker, K. J. (1995). "Childhood Sex-Typed Behavior and Sexual Orientation: A Conceptual Analysis and Quantitative Review." *Developmental Psychology,* 31, 43–55.

Bailey, J. M., Bobrow, D., Wolfe, M., and Mikach, S. (1995). "Sexual Orientation of Adult Sons of Gay Fathers." *Developmental Psychology,* 31, 124–129.

Baines, E. T., and Slade, P. (1998). "Attributional Patterns, Moods, and the Menstrual Cycle." *Psychosomatic Medicine,* 50, 469–476.

Baird, A. A., Gruber, S. A., Fein, D. A., Maas, L. C., Steingard, R. J., Renshaw, P. F., Cohen, B. M., and Yurgelun-Todd, D. A. (1999). "Functional Magnetic Resonance Imaging of Facial Affect Recognition in Children and Adolescents." *Journal of the American Academy of Child and Adolescent Psychiatry,* 38, 195–199.

Baker, C. D. (June 1982). "The Adolescent as Theorist: An Interpretative View." *Journal of Youth and Adolescence,* 11, 167–181.

Baldry, A. C., and Farrington, D. P. (2000). "Bullies and Delinquents: Personal Characteristics and Parental Styles." *Journal of Community and Applied Social Psychology,* 10, 17–31.

Balk, D. (April 1983). "Adolescents' Grief Reactions and Self-Concept Perceptions following Sibling Death: A Study of 33 Teenagers." *Journal of Youth and Adolescence,* 12, 137–161.

Ballard, M. E., and Coates, S. (1995). "The Immediate Effects of Homicidal, Suicidal, and Nonviolent Heavy Metal and Rap Songs on the Moods of College Students." *Youth and Society,* 27, 148–168.

Bandura, A. (1971). *Social Learning Theory.* Morristown, NJ: General Learning Press.

Bandura, A. (1973). *Aggression: A Social Learning Analysis.* Englewood Cliffs, NJ: Prentice-Hall.

Bandura, A. (1977). "Self-Efficacy: Toward a Unifying Theory of Behavioral Change." *Psychological Review,* 84, 191–215.

Bandura, A. (1986). *Social Foundations of Thought and Action: A Social Cognitive Theory.* Englewood Cliffs, NJ: Prentice-Hall.

Bandura, A. (1989). "Human Agency in Social Cognitive Theory." *American Psychologist,* 44, 1175–1184.

Banks, I. W., and Wilson, P. I. (1989). "Appropriate Sex Education for Black Teens." *Adolescence,* 24, 233–245.

Bankston, C. L. III, and Zhou, M. (1997). "Valedictorians and Delinquents: The Bifurcation of Vietnamese American Youth." *Deviant Behavior,* 18, 343–364.

Banyard, B. L., and Williams, L. M. (1996). "Characteristics of Child Sexual Abuse as Correlates to Women's Adjustment: A Perspective Study." *Journal of Marriage and the Family,* 58, 853–865.

Baranowski, M. D. (Fall 1982). "Grandparent-Adolescent Relations: Beyond the Nuclear Family." *Adolescence,* 17, 575–584.

Barber, B. K. (1997). "Introduction: Adolescent Socialization in Context—The Role of Connection, Regulation, and Autonomy in the Family." *Journal of Adolescent Research,* 12, 5–11.

Barber, B. K., and Delfabbro, P. (2000). "Predictors of Adolescent Adjustment: Parent-Peer Relationships and Parent-Child Conflict." *Child and Adolescent Social Work Journal,* 17, 275–288.

Barber, B. K., and Thomas, D. L. (1986). "Dimensions of Fathers' and Mothers' Supportive Behavior: The Case for Physical Affection." *Journal of Marriage and the Family,* 48, 783–794.

Barber, B. K., Chadwick, B. A., and Oerter, R. (1992). "Parental Behaviors and Adolescent Self-Esteem in the United States and Germany." *Journal of Marriage and the Family,* 54, 128–141.

Barber, B. K., Eccles, J. S., and Stone, M. R. (2001). "Whatever Happened to the Jock, the Brain, and the Princess? Young Adult Pathways

Linked to Adolescent Activity Involvement and Social Identity." *Journal of Adolescent Research,* 16, 429–455.

Barber, B. K., Maughan, S. L., Olsen, J. A., and Thomas, D. L. (2002, April). *Parental Support, Psychological Control, and Behavioral Control: Assessing the Nature of Effects.* Paper presented at the Society for Research in Adolescence Biennial Meeting, New Orleans, LA.

Bardone, A. M., Vohs, K. D., Abramson, L. Y., Heatherton, T. F., and Joiner, T. E. (2000). "The Confluence of Perfectionism, Body Dissatisfaction, and Low Self-Esteem Predicts Bulimic Symptoms: Clinical Implications." *Behavior Therapy,* 31, 265–280.

Barker, E. T., and Galambos, N. L. (2003). "Body Dissatisfaction of Adolescent Girls and Boys: Risk and Resources Factors." *Journal of Early Adolescence,* 23, 141–165.

Barker, E. T., and Galambos, N. L. (2005). "Adolescents' Implicit Theories of Maturity: Ages of Adulthood, Freedom, and Fun." *Journal of Adolescent Research,* 20, 557–576.

Barnes, G. M., Farrell, M. P., and Banerjee, S. (1995). "Family Influences on Alcohol Abuse and Other Problem Behaviors among Black and White Americans." In G. M. Boyd, J. H. Oward, and R. A. Ducker (Eds.), *Alcohol Problems among Adolescents.* Hillsdale, NJ: Erlbaum.

Barnes, G. M., Reifman, A. S., Farrell, M. P., & Dintcheff, B. A. (2000). "The Effects of Parenting on the Development of Adolescent Alcohol Misuse: A Six-Wave Latent Growth Model." *Journal of Marriage and the Family,* 62, 175–186.

Barnes, H. L., and Olson, D. H. (1985). "Parent-Adolescent Communication and the Circumplex Model." *Child Development,* 56, 438–447.

Barnes, M. A., Dennis, M., and Haefele-Kalvaitis, J. (1996). "The Effects of Knowledge Availability and Knowledge Accessibility on Coherence and Elaborative Inferencing in Children From Six to Fifteen Years of Age." *Journal of Experimental Child Psychology,* 61, 216–241.

Barnes, M. E., and Farrier, S. C. (Spring 1985). "A Longitudinal Study of the Self-Concept of Low-Income Youth." *Adolescence,* 20, 199–205.

Barnett, J. K., Papini, D. R., and Gbur, E. (1991). "Familial Correlates of Sexually Active Pregnant and Non-Pregnant Adolescents." *Adolescence,* 26, 456–472.

Baron, J. (1989). *Teaching Decision-Making to Adolescents.* Hillsdale, NJ: Erlbaum.

Baron, S. (1999). "Street Youths and Substance Abuse: the Role of Background, Street Lifestyle, and Economic Factors." *Youth and Society,* 31, 3–26.

Barry, J. (1993). *In All the Right Places.* Ensign Music Corporation, and Affirmed Productions, Inc. (BMI)/Big Life Music, Ltd. (BMI).

Barth, R. P. (1986). *Social and Cognitive Treatment of Children and Adolescents.* San Francisco: Jossey-Bass.

Bartle-Haring, S., and Strimple, R. E. (1996). "Association of Identity and Intimacy: An Exploration of Gender and Sex-Role Orientation." *Psychological Reports,* 79, 1255–1264.

Barwick, N. A., and Siegel, L. S. (1996). "Learning Difficulties in Adolescent Clients of a Shelter for Runaway and Homeless Street Youths." *Journal of Research on Adolescence,* 6, 649–670.

Basow, S. A., and Rubin, L. R. (1999). "Gender Influences on Adolescent Development." In N. G. Johnson and M. C. Roberts (Eds.), *Beyond Appearance: A New Look at Adolescent Girls* (pp. 25–52). Washington, DC: American Psychological Association.

Basseches, M. (1980). "Dialectical Schemata: A Framework for the Empirical Study of the Development of Dialectical Thinking." *Human Development,* 23, 200–421.

Batsche, G. M., and Knoff, H. M. (1994). "Bullies and Their Victims: Understanding a Pervasive Problem in Schools." *School Psychology Review,* 23, 165–174.

Bauer, B. G., and Anderson, W. P. (1989). "Bulimic Beliefs: Food for Thought." *Journal of Counseling and Development,* 67, 416–419.

Baugher, R. (1999). *A Guide for the Bereaved Survivor.* Philadelphia: Caring People Press.

Bauman, K. E., and Ennett, S. T. (1994). "Peer Influence on Adolescent Drug Use." *American Psychologist,* 49, 820–822.

Bauman, K. E., and Ennett, S. T. (1996). "On the Importance of Peer Influence for Adolescent Drug Use: Commonly Neglected Considerations." *Addiction,* 91, 185–198.

Baumeister, L. M., Flores, E., and Marin, B. V. (1995). "Sex Information Given to Latina Adolescents by Parents." *Health Education Research,* 10, 233–239.

Baumeister, R. (2000). "Gender Differences in Erotic Plasticity: The Female Sex Drive as Socially Flexible and Responsive." *Psychological Bulletin,* 126, 347–374.

Baumeister, R. F. (1991). "Identity Crisis." In R. M. Lerner, A. C. Petersen, and J. Brooks-Gunn (Eds.), *Encyclopedia of Adolescence.* Vol. 1. New York: Garland.

Baumrind, D. (1971). "Current Patterns of Parental Authority." *Developmental Psychology,* 4, 1–103.

Bauserman, R. (2002). "Child Adjustment in Joint-Custody versus Sole-Custody Arrangements: A Meta-Analytic Review." *Journal of Family Psychology,* 16, 91–102.

Baydar, N. (1988). "Effects of Parental Separation and Reentry into Union on the Emotional Well-Being of Children." *Journal of Marriage and the Family,* 50, 967–981.

Baydar, N., Brooks-Gunn, J., and Furstenberg, F. F. (1993). "Early Warning Signs of Functional Illiteracy: Predictors in Childhood and Adolescence." *Child Development,* 64, 815–829.

Bayley, N. (1968). "Behavioral Correlates of Mental Growth: Birth to Thirty-Six Years." *American Psychologist,* 23, 1–17.

Bayrakal, S., and Kope, T. M. (1990). "Dysfunction in the Single-Parent and Only-Child Family." *Adolescence,* 25, 1–7.

Beal, C. R. (1994). *Boys and Girls: The Development of Gender Roles.* New York: McGraw-Hill.

Beaty, E. A. (1995). "Effects of Paternal Absence on Male Adolescents' Peer Relations and Self Image." *Adolescence,* 30, 873–880.

Beaumont, S. L. (1996). "Adolescent Girls' Perceptions of Conversations with Mothers and Friends." *Journal of Adolescent Research,* 11, 325–346.

Beauvais, F., and Laboueff, S. (1985). "Drug and Alcohol Abuse Intervention in American Indian Communities." *International Journal of Addictions,* 20, 139–171.

Becker, A. E., Grinspoon, S. K., Klibanski, A., and Herzog, D. B. (1999). "Eating Disorders." *New England Journal of Medicine,* 340, 1092–1098.

Beer, W. R. (1992). *American Stepfamilies.* New Brunswick, NJ: Transaction.

Beidel, D. C., and Turne, S. M. (1998). *Shy Children, Phobic Adults: Nature and Treatment of Social Phobia.* Washington, DC: American Psychological Association.

Beilin, H. (1992). "Piaget's Enduring Contribution to Developmental Psychology." *Developmental Psychology,* 28, 191–204.

Beiswinger, G. L. (1979). "The High Court, Privacy, and Teenage Sexuality." *Family Coordinator,* 28, 191–198.

Belitz, J., & Schacht, A. (1992). "Satanism as a Response to Abuse: The Dynamics and Treatment of Satanic Involvement in Male Youths." *Adolescence,* 27, 855–872.

Bell, A. P., Weinberg, M. S., and Hammersmith, K. S. (1981). *Sexual Preference—Its Development in Men and Women.* Bloomington, IN: Indiana University Press.

Bell, C. S., and Battjes, R. (1985). *Prevention Research: Deterring Drug Abuse among Children and Adolescents.* NIDA Research Monograph 63. Rockville, MD: National Institute on Drug Abuse.

Bell, L. G., Cornwell, C. S., and Bell, D. C. (1988). "Peer Relationships of Adolescent Daughters: A Reflection of Family Relationship Patterns." *Family Relation,* 37, 171–174.

Bell, N. J., and Avery, A. W. (May 1985). "Family Structure and Parent-Adolescent Relationships: Does Family Structure Really Make a Difference?" *Journal of Marriage and Family Therapy,* 47, 503–508.

Bell, N. J., Avery, A. W., Jenkins, D., Feld, J., and Schoenrock, C. J. (1985). "Family Relationships and School Competence among Late Adolescence." *Journal of Youth and Adolescence,* 14, 109–119.

Belsky, J., Steinberg, L., and Draper, P. (1991). "Childhood Experience, Interpersonal Development, and Reproductive Strategies: An Evolutionary Theory of Socialization." *Child Development,* 62, 647–670.

Bem, S. L. (1974). "The Measurement of Psychological Androgyny." *Journal of Consulting and Clinical Psychology,* 41, 155–162.

Benedict, R. (1938). "Continuities and Discontinuities in Cultural Conditioning." *Psychiatry,* 1, 161–167.

Benedict, R. (1950). *Patterns of Culture.* New York: New American Library.

Benedikt, M. (1991). *Cyberspace: First Steps.* Cambridge, MA: MIT Press.

Benedikt, R., Wertheim, E. H., and Love, A. (1998). "Eating Attitudes and Weight-Loss Attempts in Female Adolescents and Their Mothers." *Journal of Youth and Adolescence,* 27, 43–57.

Benenson, J. F. (1990). "Gender Differences in Social Networks." *Journal of Early Adolescence,* 10, 472–495.

Benson, P. L., Donahue, M. J., and Erikson, J. A. (1989). "Adolescence and Religion: A Review of the Literature from 1970 to 1986." *Research in the Social Scientific Study of Religion,* 1, 153–181.

Beren, T., and Li, Q. (2005). "Cyber-Harassment: A New Method for an Old Behavior." *Journal of Educational Computing Research,* 32, 265–277.

Berge, Z. L. (2000). "Designing Discussion Questions for Online, Adult Learning." *Educational Technology,* 37, 35–47.

Berghold, K. M., and Lock, J. (2002). "Assessing Guilt in Adolescents with Anorexia Nervosa." *American Journal of Psychotherapy,* 56, 378–390.

Bergin, D. A. (1989). Student goals for out-of-school learning activities. *Journal of Adolescent Research, 4,* 92–109.

Bergin, D. A. (1989). "Student Goals for Out-of-School Learning Activities." *Journal of Adolescent Research,* 4, 92–109.

Bergman, S. J. (1995). "Men's Psychological Development: A Relational Perspective." In R. F. Levant and W. S. Pollack (Eds.), *A New Psychology of Men.* New York: Basic.

Berk, L. (2006). *Child Development* (7th ed.). Boston: Allyn & Bacon.

Berkow, R., (Ed.), (1987). "Acne." *The Merck Manual.* 15th ed. Rahway, NJ: Merck and Co.

Berndt, T. (1992). "Friendship and Friends' Influence in Adolescence." *Current Directions in Psychological Science,* 1, 156–159.

Berndt, T. J. (1990). "Intimacy and Competition in the Friendships of Adolescent Boys and Girls." In M. Stevenson (Ed.), *Gender Roles across the Lifespan.* Madison: University of Wisconsin Press.

Berndt, T. J. (2004). "Children's Friendships: Shifts over a Half-Century in Perspectives on Their Development and Their Effects." *Merrill-Palmer Quarterly,* 50, 206–223.

Berndt, T. J., and Keefe, K. (1995). "Friends' Influence on Adolescents' Adjustment to School." *Child Development,* 66, 1312–1329.

Berndt, T. J., and Mekos, D. (1995). "Adolescents' Perceptions of the Stressful and Desirable Aspects of the Transition to Junior High School." *Journal of Research on Adolescence,* 5, 123–142.

Berndt, T. J., and Perry, T. B. (1990). "Distinctive Features and Effects of Early Adolescent Friendships." in R. Montemayor, R. Adams, and T. P. Gullotta (Eds.), *From Childhood to Adolescence: A Transitional Period.* Newbury Park, CA: Sage.

Berndt, T. J., Miller, K. E., and Park, K. (1989). "Adolescents' Perceptions of Friends and Parents' Influence on Aspects of Their School Adjustment." *Journal of Early Adolescence,* 9, 419–435.

Berry, J. W., and Bennett, J. A. (1992). "Cree Conceptions of Cognitive Competence." *International Journal of Psychology,* 27, 73–88.

Berry, J. W., Poortinga, Y. H., Segall, M. H., and Dasen, P. R. (1992). *Cross-Cultural Psychology: Theories, Methods, and Applications.* Cambridge, England: Cambridge University Press.

Bersamin, M. M.,Walker, S., Fisher, D. A., and Grube, J. (2006). "Correlates of Oral Sex and Vaginal Intercourse in Early and Middle Adolescence." *Journal of Research on Adolescence,* 16, 59–68.

Berzonsky, M. D. (1989). "Identity Style: Conceptualization and Measurement." *Journal of Adolescence,* 4, 268–282.

Berzonsky, M. D. (1997). "Identity Development, Control Theory, and Self-Regulation: An Individual Differences Perspective." *Journal of Adolescent Research,* 12, 347–353.

Berzonsky, M. D., and Kuk, L. (2000). "Identity Status, Identity Processing Style, and the Transition to University." *Journal of Adolescent Research,* 15, 81–98.

Berzonsky, M. D., Macek, P., and Nurmi, J.-E. (2003). "Interrelationships among Identity Process, Content, and Structure: A Cross-Cultural Investigation." *Journal of Adolescent Research,* 18, 112–130.

Berzonsky, M. D., Nurmi, J.-E., Kinney, A., and Tammi, K. (1999). "Identity Processing Style and Cognitive Attributional Strategies: Similarities and Differences across Different Contexts." *European Journal of Personality,* 13, 251–263.

Besen, Y. (2006). "Exploitation or Fun? The Lived Experience of Teenage Employment in Suburban America." *Journal of Contemporary Ethnography,* 35, 319–340.

Betz, N., and Schilano, R. (1999). "Evaluation of an Intervention to Increase Realistic Self-Efficacy and Interests in College Women." *Journal of Vocational Behavior,* 56, 35–52.

Bielick, S., Chandler, K., and Broughman, S. (2001). "Homeschooling in the United States: 1999." *NCES Technical Report, 2001–033.* Washington, DC: U.S. Department of Education, National Center for Education Statistics.

Biener, L., and Siegel, M. (2000). "Tobacco Marketing and Adolescent Smoking: More Support for a Causal Inference." *American Journal of Public Health,* 90, 407–411.

Billy, J. O. G., and Udry, J. R. (Spring 1985). "The Influence of Male and Female Best Friends on Adolescent Sexual Behavior." *Adolescence,* 20, 21–32.

Billy, J. O. G., Brewster, K. L., and Grady, W. R. (1994). "Contextual Effects of the Sexual Behavior of Adolescent Women." *Journal of Marriage & the Family,* 56, 387–404.

Bimler, D., and Kirkland, J. (2001). "School Truants and Truancy Motivation Sorted Out with Multidimensional Scaling." *Journal of Adolescent Research,* 16, 75–102.

Bingham, C. R., Miller, B. C., and Adams, G. R. (1990). "Correlates of Age at First Intercourse in a National Sample of Young Women." *Journal of Adolescent Research,* 5, 18–33.

Bird, G. W., and Harris, R. L. (1990). "A Comparison of Role Strain and Coping Strategies by Gender: Family Structure among Early Adolescents." *Journal of Early Adolescence,* 10, 141–158.

Birmaher, B., Arbelaez, C., and Brent, D. (2002). "Course and Outcome of Child and Adolescent Major Depressive Disorder." *Child Adolescent Psychiatric Clinics of North America,* 11, 619–637.

Birmaher, B., Ryan, N., Williamson, D. E., Brent, D., Kaufman, J., Dahl, R., Perel, J., and Nelson, B. (1996). "Childhood and Adolescent Depression: A Review of the Past Ten Years. Part 1." *Journal of the American Academy of Child and Adolescent Psychiatry,* 35, 1427–1439.

Biro, F. M., Khoury, P., and Morrison, J. A. (2006). "Influence of Obesity on Timing of Puberty." *International Journal of Andrology,* 29, 272–277.

Bischof, G. T., Stiph, S. N., and Whitney, M. L. (1995). "Family Environment in Adolescent Sex Offenders and Other Juvenile Delinquents." *Adolescence,* 30, 157–170.

Bishop, J. A., and Inderbitzen, H. M. (1995). "Peer Acceptance of Friendship: An Investigation of the Relation to Self-Esteem." *Journal of Early Adolescence,* 15, 476–489.

Bjorklund, D. F., and Harnishfeger, K. K. (1990). "The Resources Construct in Cognitive Development: Diverse Sources of Evidence and a Theory of Inefficient Inhibition." *Developmental Review,* 10, 48–71.

Black, C., and DeBlassie, R. R. (1985). "Adolescent Pregnancy: Contributing Factors, Consequences, Treatment, and Plausible Solutions." *Adolescence,* 20, 281–290.

Black, M. M., Ricardo, I. B., and Stanton, B. (1997). "Social and Psychological Factors Associated with AIDS Risk Behaviors among Low Income, Urban African American Adolescents." *Journal of Research on Adolescence,* 7, 173–196.

Blain, M. D., Tompson, J. M., and Whiffen, V. E. (1993). "Attachment and Perceived Social Support in Late Adolescence. The Interaction between Working Models of Self and Others." *Journal of Adolescent Research,* 8, 226–241.

Blakc, M. M., Bentley, M. E., Papas, M. A., Oberlander, S., Teti, L. O., McNary, S., Le, K., & O'Connell, M. (2006). "Delaying Second Births Among Adolescent Mothers: A Randomized, Controlled Trial of a Home-based Mentoring Program." *Pediatrics,* 118, e1087–e1099.

Blake, S. M., Amaro, H., Schwartz, P. M., and Flinchbaugh, L. J. (2001). "A Review of Substance Abuse Prevention Interventions for Young Adolescent Girls." *Journal of Early Adolescence,* 21, 294–324.

Blake, S. M., Ledsky, R., Goodenow, C., Sawyer, R., Lohrmann, D., and Windsor, R. (2003). "Condom Availability Programs in Massachusetts High Schools: Relationship with Condom Use and Sexual Behavior." *American Journal of Public Health,* 93, 955–962.

Blake, S. M., Ledsky, R., Lehman, T., Goodenow, C., Sawyer, R., and Hack, T. (2001). "Preventing Sexual Risk Behaviors among Gay, Lesbian, and Bisexual Adolescents: The Benefits of Gay-Sensitive HIV Instruction in Schools." *American Journal of Public Health,* 91, 940–946.

Blakemore, J. E. O., and Centers, R. E. (2005). "Characteristics of Boys' and Girls' Toys." *Sex Roles,* 53, 619–633.

Blash, R., and Unger, D. G. (1992). *Cultural Factors and the Self-Esteem and Aspirations of African-American Adolescent Males.* Paper presented at the meeting of the Society for Research on Adolescents, Washington, DC.

Blasi, A., and Glodis, K. (1995). "The Development of Identity: A Critical Analysis from the Perspective of the Self as Subject." *Developmental Review,* 15, 404–433.

Blau, G. M., and Gulotta, T. P. (1993). "Promoting Sexual Responsibility in Adolescence." In T. P. Gulotta, G. R. Adams, and R. Montemayor (Eds.), *Adolescent Sexuality.* Newbury Park, CA: Sage.

Block, J., and Robins, R. W. (1993). "A Longitudinal Study of Consistency and Change in Self-Esteem from Early Adolescence to Early Adulthood." *Child Development,* 64, 909–923.

Block, J., Block, J. H., and Gjerde, P. F. (1986). "The Personality of Children Prior to Divorce: A Prospective Study." *Child Development,* 57, 827–840.

Block, J., Block, J. H., and Gjerde, P. F. (1988). "Parental Functioning and Home Environment in Families of Divorce: Prospective and Concurrent Analyses." *Journal of the American Academy of Child and Adolescent Psychiatry,* 27, 207–213.

Blos, P. (1979). *The Adolescent Passage: Developmental Issues.* New York: International Universities Press, 1979.

Blumberg, M. L., and Lester, D. (1991). "High School and College Students' Attitudes towards Rape." *Adolescence,* 26, 727–729.

Blyth, D. A., and Foster-Clark, F. S. (1987). "Gender Differences in Perceived Intimacy with Different Members of Adolescents' Social Networks." *Sex Roles,* 17, 689–718.

Blyth, D. A., Hill, J. P., and Thiel, K. S. (December 1982). "Early Adolescents' Significant Others: Grade and Gender Differences in Perceived Relationships with Familial and Nonfamilial Adults and Young People." *Journal of Youth and Adolescence,* 11, 425–450.

Blyth, D. A., Saito, R., and Berkas, T. (1997). "A Quantitative Study of the Impact of Service-Learning Programs." In A. S. Waterman (Ed.), *Service Learning: Applications from the Research* (pp. 39–56). Mahweh, NJ: Erlbaum.

Bode, J. (1987). "Testimony Before the U.S. House of Representatives Select Committee on Children, Youth, and Families." In *The Crisis of Homelessness: Effects on Children and Families.* G. Miller (Chairman). Washington, DC: U.S. Government Printing Office.

Boehm, K. E., Schondel, C. K., Marlowe, A. L., and Rose, J. S. (1995). "Adolescents Calling. A Peer-Listening Phone Service: Variation in Calls by Gender, Age, and Season of the Year." *Adolescence,* 30, 863–871.

Boehnke, K. (2001). "Parent-Offspring Value Transmission in a Societal Context: Suggestions for a Utopian Research Design—with Empirical Underpinnings." *Journal of Cross-Cultural Psychology,* 32, 241–255.

Bogenschneider, K., Wu, M-Y., Raffielli, M., and Tsay, J. C. (1998). "Parent Influences on Adolescent Peer Orientation and Substance Use: The Interface of Parenting Practices and Values." *Child Development,* 69, 1672–1688.

Boice, M. M. (1998). "Chronic Illness in Adolescence." *Adolescence,* 33, 927–939.

Boivin, M., Hymel, S., and Bukowski, W. M. (1995). "The Role of Social Withdrawal, Peer Rejection, and Victimization by Peers Predicting Loneliness and Depressed Mood in Childhood." *Development and Psychopathology,* 7, 765–785.

Bolognini, M., Plancherel, B., Bellschart, W., and Halfon, O. (1996). "Self-Esteem and Mental Health in Early Adolescence: Development and Gender Differences." *Journal of Adolescence,* 19, 233–245.

Bomar, J. A., and Sabatelli, R. M. (1996). "Family System Dynamics, Gender, and Psychosocial Maturity in Late Adolescence." *Journal of Adolescent Research,* 11, 421–439.

Bond, L., Carlin, J. B., Thomas, L., Rubin, K., and Patton, G. (2001). "Does Bullying Cause Emotional Problems? A Prospective Study of Young Teenagers." *British Medical Journal,* 323, 480–484.

Bonnie, R. J., and O'Connell, M. E. (Eds). (2004). *Reducing Underage Drinking: A Collective Responsibility.* Washington, DC: National Academies Press.

Boone, C., Williamson, E., and Lyras, N. (1992, 1993). *Come In Out of the Rain.* W. B. Music Corporation, M. Squared Music, Square-Lake Music, Songs of Polygram International, Inc., Tiverton Music, and Deep N' Hard Music.

Booth, A., and Edwards, J. N. (1985). "Age at Marriage and Marital Instability." *Journal of Marriage and the Family,* 47, 67–75.

Booth, A., and Johnson, D. (1988). "Premarital Cohabitation and Marital Success." *Journal of Family Issues,* 9, 255–272.

Booth, R. E., Zhang, Y., and Kwiatkowski, C. F. (1999). "The Challenge of Changing Drug and Sex Risk Behaviors of Runaway and Homeless Adolescents." *Child Abuse and Neglect,* 23, 1295–1306.

Borden, L. M., Donnermeyer, J. F., and Scheer, S. D. (2001). "The Influence of Extracurricular Activities and Peer Influence on Substance Abuse." *Adolescent and Family Health,* 2, 12–19.

Bornholt, L. J., and Goodnow, J. J. (1999). "Cross-Gender Perceptions of Academic Competence: Parental Expectations and Adolescent Self-Disclosure." *Journal of Adolescent Research,* 14, 427–447.

Bosma, H. A., and Kunnen, E. S. (2001). "Determinants and Mechanisms in Ego-Identity Development: A Review and Synthesis." *Developmental Review,* 21, 39–66.

Bosma, H. A., Jackson, S. E., Zijsling, D. H., Zani, B., Cicognani, E., Lucia Xerri, M., Honess, T. M., and Charman, L. (1996). "Who Has the Final Say? Decisions on Adolescent Behavior within the Family." *Journal of Adolescence,* 19, 277–291.

Bourne, E. (September 1978a). "The State of Research on Ego Identity: A Review and Appraisal. Part I." *Journal of Youth and Adolescence,* 7, 223–251.

Bourne, E. (December 1978b). "The State of Research on Ego Identity: A Review and Appraisal. Part II." *Journal of Youth and Adolescence,* 7, 371–392.

Bowen, G. L., and Chapman, M. V. (1996). "Poverty, Neighborhood Danger, Social Support, and the Individual Adaptation among At-Risk Youth in Urban Areas." *Journal of Family Issues,* 17, 641–666.

Bowen, N. K., and Bowen, G. L. (1999). "Effects of Crime and Violence in Neighborhoods and Schools on the School Behavior and Performance of Adolescents." *Journal of Adolescent Research,* 14, 319–342.

Bowman, S. A., Gortmaker, S. L., Ebbeling, C. B., Pereira, M. A., and Ludwig, D. (2004). "Effects of Fast-Food Consumption on Energy Intake and Diet Quality among Children in a National Household Survey." *Pediatrics,* 113, 112–118.

Boyatzis, C. J., Baloff, P., and Durieux, C. (1998). "Effects of Perceived Attractiveness and Academic Success on Early Adolescent Peer Popularity." *Journal of Genetic Psychology, 159,* 337–344.

Boyes, M. C., and Allen, S. G. (1993). "Styles of Parent-Child Interaction and Moral Reasoning in Adolescence." *Merrill-Palmer Quarterly,* 39, 551–570.

Boyes, M. C., and Chandler, M. (1992). "Cognitive Development, Epistemic Doubt, and Identity Formation in Adolescence." *Journal of Youth and Adolescence,* 21, 277–304.

Boyes, M. C., Giordano, R., and Galperyn, K. (1993). *Moral Orientation and Interpretative Contexts of Moral Deliberation.* Paper presented at the biennial meeting of the Society for Research in Child Development, New Orleans.

Boykin, A. W., and Toms, F. (1985). "Black Child Socialization: A Conceptual Framework." In H. McAdoo and J. McAdoo (Eds.), *Black Children: Social, Educational, and Parental Environments* (pp. 33–51). Newbury Park, CA: Sage.

Boyle, R. G., Claxton, A. J., and Forster, J. L. (1997). "The Role of Social Influences and Tobacco Availability on Adolescent Chewing Tobacco Use." *Journal of Adolescent Health,* 20, 279–285.

Bracey, J. R., Bámaca, M. Y., and Umaña-Taylor, A. J. (2004). "Examing Ethnic Identity and Self-Esteem among Biracial and Monoracial Youth." *Journal of Youth and Adolescence,* 33, 123–132.

Brack, C. J., Brack, G., and Orr, D. P. (1996). "Adolescent Health Promotion: Testing a Model Using Multi-Dimensional Scaling." *Journal of Research on Adolescence,* 6, 139–149.

Bradford-Brown, B., and Klute, C. (2003). "Friendships, Cliques, and Crowds." In G. R. Adams and M. D. Berzonsky (Eds.), *Blackwell Handbook of Adolescence* (pp. 330–348). Oxford, England: Blackwell Publishing.

Brage, D., Meredith, W., and Woodward, J. (1993). "Correlates of Loneliness among Midwestern Adolescents." *Adolescence,* 111, 685–693.

Bramlett, M. D., and Mosher, W. D. (2002). Cohabitation, Divorce, and Remarriage in the United States. National Center for Health Statistics, *Vital Health Statistics* 23 (22). Retrieved from http://www.cdc.gov/nchs/data/series/sr_23/sr23_022.pdf.

Brannon, L. (1999). *Gender: Psychological Perspectives.* Boston: Allyn and Bacon.

Brannon, R. (1976). "The Male Sex Role: Our Culture's Blueprint for Manhood and What It's Done for Us Lately." In D. S. David and R. Brannon (Eds.), *The Forty-Nine Percent Majority* (pp. 1–45). Reading, MA: Addison-Wesley.

Bransford, J. D., Brown, A. L., and Cocking, R. R. (Eds.) (1999). *How People Learn: Brain, Mind, Experience, and School.* Washington, DC: National Academy Press.

Braver, S. L., Ellman, I. M., and Fabricius, W. V. (2003). "Relocation of Children after Divorce and Children's Best Interests: New Evidence and Legal Considerations." *Journal of Family Psychology,* 17, 206–219.

Breedlove, S. (1995). "Another Important Organ." *Nature,* 378, 15–16.

Bregman, G., and Killen, M. (1999). "Adolescents' and Young Adults' Reasoning about Career Choice and the Role of Parental Influence." *Journal of Research on Adolescence,* 9, 253–275.

Brent, D. A. (1995). "Risk Factors for Adolescent Suicide and Suicidal Behavior: Mental and Substance Abuse Disorders, Family Environmental Factors, and Life Stress." *Suicide and Life-Threatening Behavior,* 25 (Supplement), 52–63.

Brent, D. A., and Mann, J. J. (2005). "Family Genetic Studies, Suicide, and Suicidal Behavior." *American Journal of Medical Genetics,* Part C, 133C, 13–24.

Brent, D. A., Baugher, M., Bridge, J., Chen, T., and Chiappetta, L. (1999). "Age and Sex-Related Risk Factors for Adolescent Suicide." *Journal of the American Academy of Child and Adolescent Psychiatry,* 38, 1497–1505.

Brent, D. A., Perper, J. A., Moritz, G., and Baugher, M. (1993). "Suicide in Adolescents with No Apparent Psychopathology." *Journal of the American Academy of Child and Adolescent Psychiatry,* 32, 494–500.

Bricker, J. B., Peterson, A. V., Leroux, B. G., Andersen, M. R., Rajan, K. B., and Sarason, I. G. (2006). "Prospective Prediction of Children's Smoking Transitions: Role of Parents' and Older Siblings' Smoking." *Addiction,* 101, 128–136.

Bridge, J. A., Goldstein, T. R., and Brent, D. A. (2006). "Adolescent Suicide and Suicidal Behavior." *Journal of Child Psychology and Psychiatry,* 47, 372–394.

Briere, J., & Gil, E. (1998). "Self-Mutilation in Clinical and General Population Samples: Prevalence, Correlates, and Functions." *American Journal of Orthopsychiatry,* 68, 609–620.

Brill, H. Q., and Christie, R. L. (1974). "Marijuana Use and Psychological Adaptation: Follow-Up Study of a Collegiate Population." *Archives of General Psychiatry,* 31, 713–719.

Brindis, C. D., Ozer, E. M., Handley, M., Knopf, D. K., Millstein, S. G., and Irwin, C. E., Jr. (1997). *Improving Adolescent Health: An Analysis and Synthesis of Health Policy Recommendations, Full Report.* San Francisco: University of California Press, National Adolescent Health Information Center. Retrieved from http://youth.ucsf.edu/nahic/odf.html#1

Brody, G. H., Stoneman, V., and Flor, D. (1995). "Linking Family Processes and Academic Confidence among Rural African American Youths." *Journal of Marriage and the Family,* 57, 567–579.

Brody, N. (1997). "Intelligence, Schooling, and Society." *American Psychologist,* 52, 1046–1050.

Brodzinsky, D. M. (1987). "Adjustment to Adoption: A Psychosocial Perspective." *Clinical Psychology Review,* 7, 25–47.

Bromley, D. (1967). "Youth and Sex." In F. R. Donovan (Ed.), *Wild Kids.* Harrisburg, PA: Stackpole Co.

Bronfenbrenner, U. (1979). *The Ecology of Human Development.* Cambridge, MA: Harvard University Press.

Bronfenbrenner, U. (1987 August). *Recent Advances in Theory and Design.* Paper presented at the American Psychological Association, New York City.

Brooks-Gunn, J., and Markman, L. B. (2005). "The Contribution of Parenting to Ethnic and Racial Gaps in School Readiness." *The Future of Children,* 15, 139–168.

Brooks-Gunn, J., and Warren, M. P. (1988). "The Psychological Significance of Secondary Sexual Characteristics in Nine- to Eleven-Year-Old Girls." *Child Development,* 59, 1061–1069.

Brooks-Gunn, J., Guo, G., and Furstenberg, F. F., Jr. (1993). "Who Drops Out of and Who Continues beyond High School? A Twenty-Year Follow-Up of Black Urban Youth." *Journal of Research on Adolescence,* 3, 271–294.

Brooks-Gunn, J., Petersen, A. C., and Eichorn, D. (1985). "The Study of Maturational Timing Effects in Adolescence." *Journal of Youth and Adolescence,* 14, 149–161.

Brown, B. B. (1982). "The Extent and Effects of Peer Pressure Among High School Students: A Retrospective Analysis." *Journal of Youth and Adolescence,* 11, 122–133.

Brown, B. B., Eicher, S. A., and Petrie, S. (1986). "The Importance of Peer Group ("Crowd") Affiliation in Adolescence." *Journal of Adolescence,* 9, 73–96.

Brown, B. B., Larson, R. W., and Saraswathi, T. S. (2002). *The World's Youth: Adolescence in Eight Regions of the Globe.* Cambridge, England: Cambridge University Press.

Brown, B. B., Mounts, N., Lamborn, S. D., and Steinberg, L. (1993). "Parenting Practices and Peer Group Affiliation in Adolescence." *Child Development,* 64, 467–482.

Brown, B. R., Jr., Baranowski, M. D., Kulig, J. W., Stephenson, J. N., and Perry, B. (1996). "Searching for the Magic Johnson Effect: AIDS, Adolescents, and Celebrity Disclosure." *Adolescence,* 31, 253–264.

Brown, B. V., and Theobald, W. E. (1999). *How Peers Matter: A Research Synthesis on Peer Influences on Adolescent Pregnancy.* Washington, DC: National Campaign to Prevent Teen Pregnancy.

Brown, D. (1987). "The Status of Holland's Theory of Vocational Choice." *The Career Development Quarterly,* 36, 13–23.

Brown, J. E., and Mann, L. (1988). "Effects of Family Structure and Parental Involvement on Adolescent Participation in Family Decisions." *Australian Journal of Sex, Marriage, and Family,* 9, 74–85.

Brown, J. E., and Mann, L. (1990). "The Relationship between Family Structure and Process Variables and Adolescent Decision Making." *Journal of Adolescence,* 13, 25–37.

Brown, J. E., and Mann, L. (1991). "Decision-Making Confidence and Self-Esteem: A Comparison of Parents and Adolescents." *Journal of Adolescence,* 14, 363–371.

Brown, S. A., Tapert, S. F., Granholm, E., and Delis, D. C. (2000). "Neurocognitive Functioning of Adolescents: Effects of Protracted Alcohol Use." *Alcoholism: Clinical Experimental Research,* 24, 164–171.

Brown, S. L., and Booth, A. (1996). "Cohabitation versus Marriage: A Comparison of Relationship Quality." *Journal of Marriage and the Family,* 58, 668–678.

Brown, U. M. (2001). *The Interracial Experience: Growing Up Black/White Racially Mixed in the United States.* Westport, CT: Praeger.

Browne, B. A., and Francis, S. K. (1993). "Participants in School-Sponsored and Independent Sports: Perceptions of Self and Family." *Adolescence,* 28, 383–391.

Brownell, K. D. (1982). "Obesity: Understanding and Treating a Serious, Prevalent, and Refractory Disorder." *Journal of Consulting and Clinical Psychology,* 50, 820–840.

Brownfield, D., and Sorenson, A. M. (1991). "Religion and Drug Use among Adolescents: A Social Support Conceptualization and Interpretation." *Deviant Behavior,* 12, 259–276.

Bruch, M. A., and Cheek, J. M. (1995). "Developmental Factors in Childhood and Adolescent Shyness." In R. G. Heimberg, M. R. Liebowitz, D. Hope, and F. R. Scheier (Eds.), *Social Phobia: Diagnosis, Assessment, and Treatment* (pp. 163–182). New York: Guilford Press.

Buchanan, C. M. (1991). "Pubertal Status in Early-Adolescent Girls: Relations to Moods, Energy, and Restlessness." *Journal of Early Adolescence,* 11, 185–200.

Buchanan, C. M., Eccles, J. S., Flanagan, C., Midgley, C., Feldlaufer, J., and Harold, R. D. (1990). "Parents' and Teachers' Beliefs about Adolescents: Effects of Sex and Experience." *Journal of Youth and Adolescence,* 19, 363–394.

Buchanan, C. M., Maccoby, E. E., and Dornbusch, S. M. (1991). "Caught between Parents: Adolescents' Experience in Divorced Homes." *Child Development,* 62, 1008–1029.

Buchanan, C. M., Maccoby, E. E., and Dornbusch, S. M. (1992). "Adolescents and Their Families after Divorce: Three Residential Arrangements Compared." *Journal of Research on Adolescence,* 2, 261–291.

Buchholz, E. S., and Catton, R. (1999). "Adolescents' Perceptions of Aloneness and Loneliness." *Adolescence,* 34, 203–213.

Buchman, D., and Funk, J. (1996). "Children's Time Commitment and Game Preference." *Children Today,* 24.

Buhrmester, D. (1992). "The Developmental Course of Sibling and Peer Relationships." In F. Boer and J. Dunn (Eds.), *Children's Sibling Relationships: Developmental and Clinical Issues* (pp. 19–40). Hillsdale, NJ: Erlbaum.

Buhrmester, D., and Fuhrman, W. (1990). "Perceptions of Sibling Relationships during Middle Childhood and Adolescence." *Child Development,* 61, 1387–1398.

Buis, J. M., and Thompson, D. N. (1989). "Imaginary Audience and Personal Fable: A Brief Review." *Adolescence,* 24, 773–781.

Bukowski, W. M., Gauze, C., Hoza, B., and Newcomb, A. F. (1993). "Differences and Consistency between Same-Sex and Other-Sex Peer Relationships during Early Adolescence." *Developmental Psychology,* 29, 255–263.

Bulcroft, R. A., Carmody, D. C., and Bulcroft, K. A. (1996). "Patterns of Parental Independence Given to Adolescents: Variations by Race, Age, and Gender of Child." *Journal of Marriage and the Family,* 58, 866–883.

Bumpass, L. L. (1984). "Some Characteristics of Children's Second Families." *American Journal of Sociology,* 90, 608–623.

Bumpass, L. L. (1990). "What's Happening to the Family? Interactions between Demographic and Institutional Change." *Demography,* 27, 483–498.

Bumpass, L. L., and Raley, R. K. (1995). "Redefining Single-Parent Families: Cohabitation and Changing Family Reality." *Demography,* 32, 71–82.

Bumpass, L., Raley, R., and Sweet, J. (1995). "The Changing Character of Stepfamilies: Implications of Cohabitation and Non-Marital Childbearing." *Demography,* 32, 425–436.

Bumpus, L., and Lu, H.-H. (2000). "Trends in Cohabitation and Implications for Children's Family Contexts in the United States." *Population Studies,* 54, 29–41.

Burger, J. M. (1995). "Individual Differences in Preference for Solitude." *Journal of Research in Personality,* 29, 85–108.

Buri, J. R. (1989). "Self-Esteem and Appraisals of Parental Behavior." *Journal of Adolescent Research,* 4, 33–49.

Burke, P. J. (1991). "Identity Processes and Social Stress." *American Sociological Review,* 56, 836–849.

Burlew, A. K., and Johnson, J. L. (1992). "Role Conflict and Career Advancement among African-American Women in Non-Traditional Professions." *The Career Development Quarterly,* 40, 302–312.

Burnett, D. (1999). "Physical and Emotional Well-Being of Custodial Grandparents in Latino Families." *American Journal of Orthopsychiatry,* 69, 305–318.

Burns, A., and Dunlop, R. (1999). " 'How Did You Feel about It?' Children's Feelings about Their Parents' Divorce at the Time and Three and Ten Years Later." *Journal of Divorce and Remarriage,* 31, 19–35.

Burnside, M. A., Baer, P. E., McLaughlin, R. J., and Pickering, A. D. (1986). "Alcohol Use by Adolescents in Disrupted Families." *Alcoholism: Clinical and Experimental Research,* 10, 272–278.

Burr, W. R., and Christensen, C. (1992). "Undesirable Side Effects of Enhancing Self-Esteem." *Family Relations,* 41, 460–464.

Burrows, S. (1992). "Nursing Management of Self-Mutilation." *British Journal of Nursing,* 17, 138–148.

Burton, W. (1963). *Helps to Education* (pp. 38, 39). Boston: Crosby and Nichols.

Bush, P. J., Weinfurt, K. P., and Iannotti, R. J. (1994). "Families versus Peers: Developmental Influences on Drug Use from Grade 4–5 to Grade 7–8." *Journal of Applied Developmental Psychology,* 15, 437–456.

Bussiere, A. (1998). "The Development of Adoption Law." *Adoption Quarterly,* 1, 1–36.

Button, E. (1990). "Self-Esteem in Girls Aged 11–12: Baseline Findings from a Planned Prospective Study of Vulnerability to Eating Disorders." *Journal of Adolescence,* 13, 407–413.

Button, E. J., Loan, P., Davies, J., and Sonuga-Barke, E. J. S. (1997). "Self-Esteem, Eating Problems, and Psychological Well-Being in a Cohort of Schoolgirls Aged 15–16: A Questionnaire and Interview Study." *International Journal of Eating Disorders,* 10, 39–47.

Byrne, B. (2000). "Relationships between Anxiety, Fear, Self-Esteem, and Coping Strategies in Adolescence." *Adolescence,* 35, 201–215.

Byrnes, J. P. (2003). "Cognitive Development during Adolescence." In G. R. Adams and M. D. Berzonsky (Eds.), *The Blackwell Handbook of Adolescence* (pp. 227–246). Oxford, England: Blackwell Publishing.

Byrnes, J. P., and Overton, W. F. (1988). "Reasoning about Logical Connectives: A Developmental Analysis." *Journal of Experimental Child Psychology,* 46, 194–218.

Byrnes, J. P., Miller, D. C., and Reynolds, M. (1999). "Learning to Make Good Decisions: A Self-Regulation Perspective." *Child Development,* 70, 1121–1140.

Cabral, A. C., and Salomone, P. R. (1990). "Chance and Careers: Normative versus Contextual Development." *The Career Development Quarterly,* 39, 5–17.

Cacciopo, J. T., Ernst, J. M., Burleson, M. H., McClintock, M. K., Malarkey, W. B., Hawkley, L. C., Kowalewski, R. B., Paulsen, A., Hobson, J. A., Hugdahl, K., Spiegel, D., and Bernston, G. G. (2000). "Lonely Traits and Concomitant Physiological Processes." *International Journal of Psychophysiology,* 35, 143–154.

Cadieux, A. (1996). "Relationship between Self-Concept and Classroom Behavior among Learning and Non-Learning Disabled Students in Regular Classrooms." *Perceptual and Motor Skills,* 82, 1043–1050.

Cairns, R., and Cairns, B. (1994). *Lifelines and Risks: Pathways of Youth in Our Time.* New York: Cambridge University Press.

Calabrese, R. L., and Adams, J. (1990). "Alienation: A Cause of Juvenile Delinquency." *Adolescence,* 25, 435–440.

Caldwell, C., and Antonucci, A. (1996). "Childbearing during Adolescence: Mental Health Risks and Opportunities." In J. Schulenberg, J. Maggs, and K. Hurrelmann (Eds.), *Health Risks and Developmental Transitions during Adolescence* (pp. 220–245). London, England: Cambridge University Press.

Calhoun, G. (1987). "Enhancing Self-Perception through Bibliotherapy." *Adolescence,* 88, 929–943.

Calhoun, G., Jurgens, J., and Chen, F. (1993). "The Neophyte Female Delinquent: A Review of the Literature." *Adolescence,* 28, 461–471.

Call, K. T., Aylin, A. R., Hein, K., McLoyd, V., Petersen, A., and Kipke, M. (2002). "Adolescent Health and Well-Being in the Twenty-First Century: A Global Perspective." *Journal of Research on Adolescence,* 12, 69–98.

Callahan, D., and Callahan, S. (April 1981). "Seven Pillars of Moral Wisdom." *Psychology Today,* 84ff.

Calvert, S. (1999). *Children's Journeys through the Information Age.* New York: McGraw-Hill.

Calvert, S. L. (2002). Identity construction on the Internet. In S. L. Calvert, A. B. Jordan, and R. R. Cocking (Eds.) *Children in the digital age: Influences of electronic media on development* (pp. 57–70). Westport, CT: Greenwood Publishing Group.

Camara, K. A., and Resnick, G. (1988). "Interparental Conflict and Cooperation: Factors Moderating Children's Post-Divorce Adjustment." In E. M. Hetherington and J. Arasteh (Eds.), *Impact of Divorce, Single Parenting, and Step-Parenting on Children* (pp. 169–195). Hillsdale, NJ: Erlbaum.

Campaign for Tobacco Free Kids. (2005). *Tobacco Company Marketing to Kids.* Retrieved from http://www.tobaccofreekids.org/research/factsheets/pdf/0008.pdf.

Canals, J., Carbajo, G., Fernandez, J., Marti-Henneberg, C., and Domenech, E. (1996). "Biopsychopathologic Risk Profile of Adolescents with Eating Disorder Symptoms." *Adolescence,* 31, 443–450.

Canavan, M., Meyer, W., and Higgs, D. (1992). "The Female Experience of Sibling Incest." *Journal of Marital and Family Therapy,* 18, 129–142.

Cancian, M., and Meyer, D. (1998). "Who Gets Custody?" *Demography,* 35, 147–157.

Cantor, J. (1998). "Children's Attraction to Violent Television Programming." In J. H. Goldstein (Ed.), *Why We Watch: The Attractions of Violent Entertainment* (pp. 88–115). New York: Oxford University Press.

Cantor, J. (2000). "Media Violence." *Journal of Adolescent Health,* 27, Supplement 2, 30–34.

Card, N. A. (April, 2003). *Victims of Peer Aggression: A Meta-Analytic Review.* Presented at the Biennial Meeting of the Society for Research in Child Development, Tampa, FL.

Carey v. *Population Services International.* (1977). 75–443.

Carey, M., and Walden, N. (1990). *I Don't Want to Cry.* Vision of Love Songs, Inc.

Carey, S., and Markman, E. M. (1999). "Cognitive Development." In B. M. Bly and D. E. Rumelhart (Eds.), *Cognitive Science* (pp. 201–254). San Diego: Academic Press.

Carlo, G., Eisenberg, N., and Knight, G. P. (1992). "An Objective Measure of Adolescents' Prosocial Moral Reasoning." *Journal of Research on Adolescence,* 2, 331–349.

Carlo, G., Fabes, R. A., Laible, D., and Kupanoff, K. (1999). "Early Adolescence and Prosocial/Moral Behavior II: The Role of Social and Contextual Influences." *Journal of Early Adolescence,* 19, 133–147.

Carlo, G., Roesch, S. C., and Melby, J. (1998). "The Multiplicative Relations of Parenting and Temperament on Prosocial and Antisocial Behaviors in Adolescence." *Journal of Early Adolescence,* 18, 148–170.

Carlson, E. A., Sroufe, L. A., Collins, W. A., Jimerson, S., Weinfield, N., Hennighausen, K., Egeland, B., Hyson, D. M., Anderson, F., and Meyer, S. E. (1999). "Early Environmental Support and Elementary School Adjustment as Predictors of School Adjustment in Middle Adolescence." *Journal of Adolescent Research,* 14, 72–94.

Carlson, G. A., and Kashini, J. H. (1988). "Phenomenology of Major Depression from Childhood through Adulthood: Analysis of Three Studies." *American Journal of Psychiatry,* 145, 1222–1225.

Carlson, M. (1996). *Childproof Internet: A Parent's Guide to Safe and Secure Online Access.* New York: Mis Press.

Carlson Jones, D., and Crawford, J. K. (2005). "Adolescent Boys and Body Image: Weight and Muscularity Concerns as Dual Pathways to Body Dissatisfaction." *Journal of Youth and Adolescence,* 34, 629–636.

Carlyle, W. (1970). *You're My Friend So I Brought You This Book.* Edited by John Marvin. New York: Random House.

Carpenter, P. A., Just, M. A., & Shell, P. (1990). "What One Intelligence Test Measures: A Theoretical Account of the Processing in the Raven Progressive Matrices Test." *Psychological Review,* 97(3), 404–431.

Carr, M., and Schellenbach, C. (1993). "Reflective Monitoring in Lonely Adolescents." *Adolescence,* 111, 737–747.

Carr, R. V., Wright, J. D., and Brody, C. J. (1996). "Effects of High School Work Experience a Decade Later: Evidence from the National Longitudinal Survey." *Sociology of Education,* 69, 66–81.

Carrier, J. M. (1989). "Gay Liberation and Coming Out in Mexico." *Journal of Homosexuality,* 17, 225–252.

Carruth, B. R., and Goldberg, D. L. (1990). "Nutritional Issues of Adolescents: Athletics and the Body Image Mania." *Journal of Early Adolescence,* 10, 122–140.

Carruth, B. R., Goldberg, D. L., and Skinner, J. D. (1991). "Do Parents and Peers Mediate the Influence of Television Advertising and Food-Related Purchases?" *Journal of Adolescent Research,* 6, 253–271.

Carskadon, M. A. (2002a). "Factors Influencing Sleep Patterns of Adolescents." In M. A. Carskadon (Ed.), *Adolescent Sleep Patterns: Biological, Social, and Psychological Influences* (pp. 4–26). Cambridge: Cambridge University Press.

Carskadon, M. A. (2002b). "Risks of Driving while Sleepy in Adolescents and Young Adults." In M. A. Carskadon (Ed.), *Adolescent Sleep Patterns: Biological, Social, and Psychological Influences* (pp. 148–158). New York: Cambridge University Press.

Carskadon, M. A., Harvey, M. K., and Duke, P. (1980). "Pubertal Changes in Daytime Sleepiness." *Sleep,* 2, 453–460.

Carskadon, M. A., Vieira, C., and Acebo, C. (1993). "Association between Puberty and Delayed Phase Preference." *Sleep,* 16, 258–262.

Carskadon, M. A., Wolfson, A. R., Acebo, C., Tzischinsky, O., and Seifer, R. (1998). "Adolescent Sleep Patterns, Circadian Timing, and Sleepiness at a Transition to Early School Days." *Sleep,* 21, 871–881.

Carver, K., Joyner, K., and Udry, J. R. (2003). "National Estimates of Adolescent Romantic Relationships." In P. Florsheim (Ed.), *Adolescent Romantic Relationships and Sexual Behavior: Theory, Research, and Practical Implications* (pp. 23–56). Mahwah, NJ: Erlbaum.

Case, R. (1992). "The Role of the Frontal Lobes in the Regulation of Cognitive Development." *Brain and Cognition,* 20, 51–73.

Case, R. (Ed.). (1992). *The Mind's Staircase.* Hillsdale, NJ: Erlbaum.

Casey, B. J., Giedd, J. N., and Thomas, K. M. (2000). "Structural and Functional Brain Development and Its Relation to Cognitive Development." *Biological Psychology,* 54, 241–257.

Caspi, A., Lynan, D., Moffitt, T. E., and Silva, P. A. (1993). "Unraveling Girls' Delinquency: Biological, Dispositional, and Contextual Contributions to Adolescent Misbehavior." *Developmental Psychology,* 29, 19–30.

Caspo, B. (1997). "The Development of Inductive Reasoning: Cross-Sectional Assessments in an Educational Context." *International Journal of Behavioral Development,* 20, 609–626.

Cassidy, L., and Hurrell, R. M. (1995). "The Influence of Victim's Attire on Adolescents' Judgements of Date Rape." *Adolescence,* 30, 319–323.

Castellino, D. R., Lerner, J. V., Lerner, R. M., and Von Eye, A. (1998). "Maternal Employment and Education: Predictors of Young Adolescent Career Trajectories." *Applied Developmental Science,* 2, 114–126.

Caughlin, J. P., and Malis, R. S. (2004). Demand/Withdraw Communication between Parents and Adolescents: Connections with Self-Esteem and Substance Use. *Journal of Social and Personal Relations,* 21, 125–148.

Cella, D. F., DeWolfe, A. S., and Fitzgibbon, M. (1987). "Ego Identity Status, Identification, and Decision-Making Style in Late Adolescents." *Adolescence,* 22, 849–861.

Center for Communication and Social Policy. (1998). *National Television Violence Study,* Vol. 3. Thousand Oaks, CA: Sage.

Center for Human Resource Research. (1987). *The National Longitudinal Survey Handbook.* Columbus: Ohio State University.

Centers for Disease Control (CDC), Division of STD/HIV Prevention. (1991a). *Sexually Transmitted Disease Surveillance, 1989.* Atlanta: Author.

Centers for Disease Control (CDC). (1991b). "Body-Weight Perceptions and Selected Weight-Management Goals and Practices of High School Students—United States, 1990." *Mortality and Morbidity Weekly Report,* 40, 741–750. Washington, DC: Department of Health and Human Services, Public Health Service.

Centers for Disease Control (CDC), Division of STD/HIV Prevention. (1993). *Annual Report, 1992.* Atlanta: Author.

Centers for Disease Control (CDC). (1996). "Suicide among Black Youth, United States, 1980–1995." *Morbidity and Mortality Weekly Report,* 47, 193–196.

Centers for Disease Control and Prevention. (1999). *1997 Youth Risk Behavior Surveillance System.* Washington, DC: Department of Health and Human Services, Public Health Service.

Centers for Disease Control (CDC). (2000a). *Tracking the Hidden Epidemics: Tracking STDs in the United States 2000.* Washington DC: Author.

Centers for Disease Control (CDC). (2000b). "Youth Risk Behavior Surveillance—United States, 1999." *Morbidity and Mortality Weekly Report Surveillance Summary,* 49(5). Available online: www.cdc.gov/mmwr/preview/mmwrhtml/ss4905a1.htm.

Centers for Disease Control (CDC), National Vital Statistics System. (2002). *Deaths, Percent of Total Deaths, and Death Rates for the 15 Leading Causes of Death in 5-Year Age Groups, by Race and Sex, United States, 2000.* Retrieved June 10, 2003, from http://www.cdc.gov/nchsdatawh/statab/unpubd/mortabs/gmwk210_10.htm.

Centers for Diseases Control (CDC). (2003). "Injury Mortality among American Indian and Alaskan Native Children and Youth—United States, 1989–1998." *Morbidity and Mortality Weekly Reports,* 52, 697–701.

Centers for Disease Control (CDC). (2004a). *Improving the Health of Adolescents and Young Adults: A Guide for States and Communities.* Atlanta, GA: Author.

Centers for Disease Control (CDC). (2004b). *Trends in reportable sexually transmitted diseases in the United States, 2004.* Retrieved from http://www.cdc.gov/std/stats/trends2004.htm.

Centers for Disease Control (CDC). (2004c). *WISQARS Injury Mortality Reports, 1999–2003.* Retrieved from http://webappa.cdc.gov/sasweb/ncipc/mortrate10_sy.html.

Centers for Disease Control (CDC). (2005). Deaths: Leadings causes for 20023. *National Vital Statistics Reports, 53, no. 17.*

Centers for Disease Control (CDC). (2006a). Deaths: Final data for 2003. *National Vital Statistics Reports, 54, no. 13.*

Centers for Disease Control (CDC). (2006b). *Health, United States, 2006.* Retrieved from http://www.cdc.gov/nchs/data/hus/hus06.pdf#074.

Centers for Disease Control (CDC). (2006c). Youth Risk Behavior Surveillance—United States 2005. *Morbidity and Mortality Weekly Report, 55,* No. SS-5. Washington, DC: Author.

Cerel, J., Fristad, M. A., Weller, E. B., and Weller, R. A. (2000). "Suicide-Bereaved Children and Adolescents: A Controlled Longitudinal Examination." *Journal of the American Academy of Child and Adolescent Psychiatry,* 38, 672–679.

Chan, C. G., and Elder, Jr., G. H. (2000). "Matrilineal Advantage in Grandchild-Grandparent Relations." *The Gerontologist,* 40, 179–190.

Chan, C. S. (1992). "Cultural Considerations in Counseling Asian American Lesbians and Gay Men." In S. Dworkin and E. Gutierrez (Eds.), *Counseling Gay Men and Lesbians: Journey to the End of the Rainbow* (pp. 115–124). Alexandria, VA: American Association for Counseling and Development.

Chandler, C. R., Tsai, Y.-M., and Wharton, R. (1999). "Twenty Years After: Replicating a Study of Anglo- and Mexican-American Cultural Values." *Social Science Journal,* 36, 353–367.

Chandler, M., Boyes, M. C., and Ball, L. (1990). "Relativism and Stations of Epistemic Doubt." *Journal of Experimental Child Psychology,* 50, 370–395.

Chapin, J. (2001). "Self-Protective Pessimism: Optimistic Bias in Reverse." *North American Journal of Psychology,* 3, 253–262.

Chassin, L. C., and Young, R. D. (Fall 1981). "Salient Self-Conceptions in Normal and Deviant Adolescents." *Adolescence,* 16, 613–620.

Chaucer, G. (1963). *Canterbury Tales.* (Translated by Vincent Hopper). New York: Barrons.

Chavkin, M. F., and Williams, D. W. (1993). "Minority Parents and the Elementary School: Attitudes and Practices." In N. F. Chavkin (Ed.), *Families and Schools in a Pluralistic Society.* Albany: State University of New York Press.

Chen-Yu, J. H., and Seock, Y. (2002). "Adolescents' Clothing Purchase Motivations, Information Sources, and Store Selection Criteria: A Comparison of Male/Female and Impulse/Nonimpulse Shoppers." *Family & Consumer Sciences Research Journal,* 31, 50–77.

Cherlin, A. J., and Furstenberg, F. F. (March 19, 1989). "Divorce Doesn't Always Hurt the Kids." *The Washington Post,* p. C1.

Cherlin, A. J., Chase-Lansdale, P. L., and McRae, C. (1998). "Effects of Parental Divorce on Mental Health throughout the Life Course." *American Sociological Review,* 63, 239–249.

Chiam, H. (1987). "Changes in Self-Concept during Adolescence." *Adolescence,* 85, 69–76.

Chiu, L. (1990). "The Relationship of Career Goals and Self-Esteem among Adolescents." *Adolescence,* 25, 593–597.

Chiu, M. L., Feldman, S. S., and Rosenthal, D. A. (1992). "The Influence of Immigration on Parental Behavior and Adolescent Distress in Chinese Families Residing in Two Western Nations." *Journal of Research on Adolescence,* 2, 205–239.

Choi, I., Land, S. M., and Turgeon, A. J. (2005). "Scaffolding Peer-Questioning Strategies to Facilitate Metacognition during Online Small Group Discussion." *Instructional Science,* 33, 483–511.

Chretien, R. D., and Persinger, M. A. (2000). " 'Prefrontal Deficits' Discriminate Young Offenders from Age-Matched Cohorts: Juvenile Delinquency as an Expected Feature of the Normal Distribution of Prefrontal Cerebral Development." *Psychological Reports,* 87, 1196–1202.

Chrisler, J. C., and Zittel, C. B. (1998). "Menarche Stories: Reminiscences of College Students from Lithuania, Malaysia, Sudan, and the United States." *Health Care for Women International,* 19, 101–110.

Christ, G. H., Siegel, K., and Christ, A. E. (2002). "Adolescent Grief: 'It Never Really Hit Me . . . Until It Actually Happened.' " *Journal of the American Medical Association,* 288, 1269–1278.

Christ, M. J., Raszka, Jr., W. V., and Dillon, C. A. (1998). "Prioritizing Education about Condom Use among Sexually Active Adolescent Females." *Adolescence,* 33, 735–744.

Christian, H. (1994). *The Making of Anti-Sexist Men.* London, England: Routledge.

Christopher, F. S., and Cate, R. M. (1988). "Premarital Sexual Involvement: A Developmental Investigation of Relational Correlates." *Adolescence,* 23, 793–803.

Chubb, N. H., Fertman, C. I., and Ross, J. L. (1997). "Adolescent Self-Esteem and Locus of Control: A Longitudinal Study of Gender and Age Differences." *Adolescence,* 32, 113–129.

Chung, I.-J., Hawkins, J. D., Gilchrist, L. D., Hill, K. G., and Nagin, D. S. (2002). "Identifying and Predicting Offending Trajectories among Poor Children." *Social Service Review,* 76, 663–685.

Ciccone, M., and Pettibone, S. (1992). *Bad Girl.* W. B. Music Corporation, Webo Girl Publishing, Inc., MCA Music Publishing.

Claes, M. E. (1992). "Friendship and Personal Adjustment during Adolescence." *Journal of Adolescence,* 15, 39–55.

Clark, C. A., and Worthington, E. V., Jr. (1987). "Family Variables Affecting the Transmission of Religious Values from Parents to Adolescents: A Review." *Family Perspectives,* 21, 1–21.

Clark, C. A., Worthington, E. L., Jr., and Danser, D. B. (1988). "The Transmission of Religious Beliefs and Practices from Parents to First Born Early Adolescent Sons." *Journal of Marriage and the Family,* 50, 463–472.

Clark, C. M. (1994). "Clinical Assessment of Adolescents Involved in Satanism." *Adolescence,* 29, 461–468.

Clark, K. B. (1953). "Desegregation: An Appraisal of the Evidence." *Journal of Social Issues,* 9, 2–76.

Clark, M. L., and Ayers, M. (1993). "Friendship Expectations and Friendship Evaluations. Reciprocity and Gender Effects." *Youth and Society,* 24, 299–313.

Clark-Lempers, D. S., Lempers, J. D., and Netusil, A. J. (1990). "Family Financial Stress, Parental Support, and Young Adolescents' Academic Achievement and Depressive Symptoms." *Journal of Early Adolescence,* 10, 21–36.

Clarke, J. I., Dawson, C. M., and Bredehoft, D. J. (2004). *How Much Is Enough? Everything You Need to Know to Steer Clear of Overindulgence and Raise Likeable, Responsible, and Respectful Children.* New York: Marlow and Company.

Claxton-Oldfield, S., and Butler, B. (1998). "Portrayal of Stepparents in Movie Plot Summaries." *Psychological Reports,* 82, 879–882.

Cobliner, W. G. (1988). "The Exclusion of Intimacy in the Sexuality of the Contemporary College-Age Population." *Adolescence,* 23, 99–113.

Cochran, J. K., Wood, P. B., Sellers, C.S., Wilkerson, W., and Chamlin, M. B. (1998). "Academic Dishonesty and Low Self-Control: An Empirical Test of a General Theory of Crime." *Deviant Behavior,* 19, 227–255.

Codega, S. A., Pasley, B. K., and Kreutzer, J. (1990)."Coping Behaviors of Adolescent Mothers: An Exploratory Study and Comparison of Mexican-Americans and Anglos." *Journal of Adolescent Research,* 5, 34–53.

Cohen, K. M., and Savin-Williams, R. C. (1996). "Developmental Perspectives on Coming Out to Self and Others." In R. C. Savin-Williams and K. M. Cohen (Eds.), *The Lives of Lesbians, Gays, and Bisexuals: Children to Adults* (pp. 113–151). Fort Worth, TX: Harcourt Brace.

Cohen, S. (1981). "Adverse Effects of Marijuana: Selected Issues." *Annals of the New York Academy of Sciences,* 362, 119–124.

Cohen, S. E., Beckwith, L., Parmelee, A. H., Sigman, M., Asarnow, R., and Espinosa, M. P. (1996). "Prediction of Low and Normal School Achievement in Early Adolescence Born Pre-Term." *Journal of Early Adolescence,* 16, 46–70.

Cohen, Y. (1991). "Gender Identity Conflicts in Adolescents as Motivation for Suicide." *Adolescence,* 26, 19–29.

Coinstar, Inc. (2003). *First Coinstar TEENS Talk Poll Reveals That Teens Spend at Least $264 Each Month.* Press release. Retrieved from http://www.coinstar.com/US/PressReleases/453946?OpenDocument.

Colby, A., and Damon, W. (1983). "Listening to a Different Voice: A Review of Gilligan's *A Different Voice.*" *Merrill-Palmer Quarterly,* 29, 473–481.

Cole, D. A., Maxwell, S. E., Martin, J. M., Lachlin, G. P., Seroczynski, A. D. Tram, J. M., et al. (2001). "The Development of Multiple Domains of Child and Adolescent Self-Concept: A Cohort Sequential Longitudinal Design." *Child Development,* 72, 1723–1746.

Cole, M. (1990). "Cognitive Development and Formal Schooling: The Evidence from Cross-Cultural Research." In L. C. Moll (Ed.), *Vygotsky and Education* (pp. 89–110). New York: Cambridge University Press.

Coleman, J. S. (1995). *Adolescent Sexual Knowledge: Implications for Health and Health Risks.* Paper presented at the meeting of the Society for Research in Child Development, Indianapolis, IN.

Coleman, M., Ganong, L. H., Clark, J. M., and Madsen, R. (1989). "Parenting Perceptions in Rural and Urban Families." *Journal of Marriage and the Family,* 51, 329–335.

Coley, R. L., and Chase-Lansdale, P. L. (1998). "Adolescent Pregnancy and Parenthood: Recent Evidence and Future Directions." *American Psychologist,* 53, 152–166.

College Board. (2003). *College Bound Seniors, Yearly Report 2002.* Retrieved from http://www.collegeboard.com/prod_downloads/about/news_info/cbsenior/yr2002/pdf2002Report.pdf.

Collins, P. H. (1990). "Homophobia and Black Lesbians." In P. H. Collins (Ed.), *Black Feminist Thought: Knowledge, Consciousness, and the Politics of Empowerment* (pp. 192–196). New York: Routledge.

Collins, R. L., Elliott, M. N., Berry, S. H., Kanouse, D. E., Kunkel, D., Hunter, S. B., and Miu, A. (2004). "Watching Sex on Television Predicts Adolescent Initiation of Sexual Behavior." *Pediatrics,* 114, 280–289.

Collins, W. A., and Russell, G. (1991). "Mother-Child and Father-Child Relationships in Middle Childhood and Adolescence: A Developmental Analysis." *Developmental Review,* 11, 99–136.

Collins, W. A., Laursen, B., Mortensen, N., Luebker, C., and Ferreira, M. (1997). "Conflict Processes and Transitions in Parent and Peer Relationships: Implications for Autonomy and Regulation." *Journal of Adolescent Research,* 12, 178–198.

Comer, J. (1993). *African-American Parents and Child Development: An Agenda for School Success.* Paper presented at the biannual meeting of the Society for Research in Child Development, New Orleans.

Commons, M. L., Richards, F. A., and Kuhn, D. (1982). "Systematic and Metasystematic Reasoning: A Case for Levels of Reasoning Beyond Piaget's Stage of Formal Operations." *Child Development,* 53, 1058–1069.

Comstock, G., and Paik, H. (1999). *Television and the American Child.* San Diego: Academic Press.

Comstock, J. (1994). "Parent-Adolescent Conflict: A Developmental Approach." *Western Journal of Communication,* 58, 263–283.

Conger, J. J. (1973). *Adolescence and Youth.* New York: Harper and Row.

Connell, J. P., Halpern-Felsher, B. L., Clifford, E., Crichlow, W., and Usinger, P. (1995). "Hanging in There: Behavioral, Psychological, and Contextual Factors Affecting Whether African-American Adolescents Stay in High School." *Journal of Adolescent Research,* 10, 41–63.

Connolly, J., Craig, W., Goldberg, A., and Peplar, D. (2004). "Mixed-Gender Groups, Dating, and Romantic Relationships in Early Adolescence." *Journal of Research on Adolescence,* 14, 185–207.

Connolly, J., White, D., Stevens, R., and Burstein, S. (1987). "Adolescents' Self-Reports of Social Activity: Assessment of Stability and Relations to Social Adjustment." *Journal of Adolescence,* 10, 83–95.

Connor, J.P., Young, R.M., Williams, R.J., and Ricciardelli, L.A. (2000). "Drinking Restraint versus Alcohol Expectancies: Which Is the Better Indicator of Alcohol Problems?" *Journal of Studies on Alcohol,* 61, 352–359.

Connors, L. J., and Epstein, J. L. (1995). "Parent and School Partnerships." In M. H. Bornstein (Ed.), *Children and Parenting.* Vol. 4. Hillsdale, NJ: Erlbaum.

Cook, K. V., Reiley, K. L., Stallsmith, R., and Garretson, H. B. (1991). "Eating Concerns on Two Christian and Two Nonsectarian College Campuses: A Measure of Sex and Campus Differences in Attitudes towards Eating." *Adolescence,* 26, 273–293.

Coombs, R. H., and Landsverk, J. (1988). "Parenting Styles and Substance Use during Childhood and Adolescence." *Journal of Marriage and the Family,* 50, 473–482.

Coombs, R. H., Fawzy, F. I., and Gerber, B. E. (1986). "Patterns of Cigarette, Alcohol, and Other Drug Use among Children and Adolescents." *International Journal of the Addictions,* 21(8), 897–913.

Cooper, M. L. (2002). "Alcohol Use and Risky Sexual Behavior among College Students and Youth: Evaluating the Evidence." *Journal of Studies on Alcohol,* Supplement 14, 101–117.

Corbett, K., Gentry, C. S., and Pearson, W., Jr. (1993). "Sexual Harassment in High School." *Youth and Society,* 25, 93–103.

Costa, F. M., Jessor, R., Donovan, J. E., and Fortenberry, J. D. (1995). "Early Initiation of Sexual Intercourse: The Influence of Psychosocial Unconventionality." *Journal of Research on Adolescence,* 5, 93–121.

Costin, S. E., and Jones, D. C. (1994). *The Stress-Protective Role of Parent and Friends' Support for Sixth and Ninth Graders Following a School Transition.* Paper presented at the meeting of the Society for Research on Adolescence, San Diego.

Cote, J. E., and Levine, C. G. (1992). "The Genesis of the Humanistic Academic. A Second Test of Erikson's Theory of Ego Identity Formation." *Youth in Society,* 23, 387–410.

Cote, J. E., and Levine, C. G. (February 1983). "Marcia and Erikson: The Relationships among Ego Identity Status, Neuroticism, Dogmatism, and Purpose in Life." *Journal of Youth and Adolescence,* 12, 43–53.

Cotterell, J. L. (1992a). "The Relation of Attachments and Supports to Adolescent Well-Being and School Adjustment." *Journal of Adolescent Research,* 7, 28–42.

Cotterell, J. L. (1992b). "School Size as a Factor in Adolescents' Adjustment to the Transition to Secondary School." *Journal of Early Adolescence,* 12, 28–45.

Cottom, C. (1996). "A Bold Experiment in Teaching Values." *Educational Leadership,* 53(8), 54–58.

Cox, F. D. (1994). *The AIDS Booklet.* 3rd ed. Madison, WI: Brown and Benchmark.

Crago, M., Shisslak, C. M., and Estes, L. (1996). "Eating Disorders among American Minority Groups: A Review." *International Journal of Eating Disorders,* 19, 239–248.

Crawford, E., Wright, M. O., and Masten, A. (2004). "Resilience and Spirituality in Youth." In E. Roehlkepartain, P. King, L. Wagener, & P. Benson (Eds.), *The Handbook of Spiritual Development in Children and Adolescents* (pp. 355–370). Thousand Oaks, CA: Sage.

Crawford, M., and Popp, D. (2003). "Sexual Double Standards: A Review and Methodological Critique of Two Decades of Research." *Journal of Sex Research,* 40, 13–26.

Crick, N. R. (1997). "Engagement in Gender Alternative versus Nonnormative Forms of Aggression: Links to Social-Psychological Adjustment." *Developmental Psychology,* 33, 610–617.

Crick, N. R., and Dodge, A. (1996). "Social Information-Processing Mechanisms in Reactive and Proactive Aggression." *Child Development,* 67, 993–1002.

Crocker, J., Cornwell, B., and Major, B. (1993). "The Stigma of Overweight: Affective Consequences of Attributional Ambiguity." *Journal of Personality and Social Psychology,* 64, 60–70.

Crockett, L. J., and Bingham, C. R. (1994). *Family Influences on Girls' Sexual Experience and Pregnancy Risk.* Paper presented at the meeting of the Society for Research on Adolescents, San Diego.

Crosnoe, R. (2001). "The Social World of Male and Female Athletes in High School." *Sociological Studies of Children and Youth,* 8, 87–108.

Crosnoe, R. (2002). "Academic and Health-Related Trajectories in Adolescence: The Intersection of Gender and Athletics." *Journal of Health and Social Behavior,* 43, 317–336.

Crosnoe, R., and Elder, G. H., Jr. (2002). "Life Course Transitions, the Generational Stake, and Grandparent-Grandchild Relationships." *Journal of Marriage and Family,* 64, 1089–1096.

Crowe, P. A., Philbin, J., Richards, M. H., and Crawford, I. (1998). "Adolescent Alcohol Involvement and the Experience of Social Environments." *Journal of Research on Adolescence,* 8, 403–422.

Crump, R. L., Lillie-Blanton, M., and Anthony, J. C. (1997). "The Influence of Self-Esteem on Smoking among African-American School Children." *Journal of Drug Education,* 27, 277–291.

Crystal, D. S., and Stevenson, H. W. (1995). "What Is a Bad Kid? Answers of Adolescents and Their Mothers in Three Cultures." *Journal of Research on Adolescence,* 5, 71–91.

Csikszentmihalyi, M., Rathunde, K., and Whalen, S. (1993). *Talented Teenagers: The Roots of Success and Failure.* New York: Cambridge University Press.

Cullen, F. T., and Wright, J. P. (2002). "Criminal Justice in the Lives of American Adolescents." In J. T. Mortimer and R. W. Larson (Eds.), *The Changing Adolescent Experience: Societal Trends and the Transition to Adulthood* (pp. 88–128). Cambridge, England: Cambridge University Press.

Cummings, E. M., and Davies, P. (1994). *Children and Marital Conflicts: The Impact of Family Dispute and Resolution.* New York: Guilford Press.

Cyr, M., McDuff, P., Wright, J., Theriault, C., and Cinq-Mars, C. (2005). "Clinical Correlates and Repetition of Self-Harming Behaviors among Female Adolescent Victims of Sexual Abuse." *Journal of Child Sexual Abuse,* 14, 49–68.

Dalterio, S. L. (November 1984). "Marijuana and the Unborn." *Listen,* 37, 8–11.

Daniels, J. A. (1990). "Adolescent Separation-Individuation and Family Transitions." *Adolescence,* 25, 105–116.

Daniels, S. R., McMahon, R. P., Obarzanek, E., Waclawiw, M. A., Similo, S. L., Biro, F. M., Schreiber, G. B., Kimm, S. Y. S., Morrison, J. A., and Barton, B. A. (1998). "Longitudinal Correlates of Change of Blood Pressure in Adolescent Girls." *Hypertension,* 31, 97–103.

Danielson, C. K., de Arellano, M. A., Kilpatrick, D. G., Saunders, B. E., and Resnick, H. S. (2005). "Child Maltreatment in Depressed Adolescents: Differences in Symptomatology Based on History of Abuse." *Child Maltreatment,* 10, 37–48.

Dare, C., Eisler, I., Russell, G. F. M., and Szmukler, G. I. (1990). "The Clinical and Theoretical Impact of a Controlled Trial of Family Therapy in Anorexia Nervosa." *Journal of Marriage and Family Therapy,* 16, 39–57.

Darling, C. A., and Davidson, J. K. (1986). "Coitally Active University Students: Sexual Behaviors, Concerns, and Challenges." *Adolescence,* 22, 403–419.

Darmody, J. P. (1991). "The Adolescent Personality, Formal Reasoning, and Values." *Adolescence,* 26, 732–742.

Darroch, J. E., and Singh, S. (1999). *Why Is Teenage Pregnancy Declining? The Roles of Abstinence, Sexual Activity, and Contraceptive Use.* Occasional Report no. 1. New York: Alan Guttmacher Institute.

Darroch, J. E., Frost, J. J., and Singh, S. (2001). *Teenage Sexual and Reproductive Behavior in Developed Countries: Can More Progress Be Made?* Occasional Report no. 3. New York: Alan Guttmacher Institute.

Darroch, J. E., Landry, D. J., and Singh, S. (2000). "Changing Emphasis in Sexuality Education in U.S. Public Secondary Schools, 1988–1999." *Family Planning Perspectives,* 32, 204–211.

Davidson, J. K., Sr., and Darling, C. A. (1988). "Changing Autoerotic Attitudes and Practices among College Females: A Two-Year Follow-Up Study." *Adolescence,* 23, 773–792.

Davie, R., Panting, C., and Charlton, T. (2004). "Mobile Phone Ownership and Usage among Pre-Adolescents." *Telematics and Informatics,* 4, 359–373.

Davies, P. T., and Windle, M. (2000). "Middle Adolescents' Dating Pathways and Psychosocial Adjustment." *Merrill-Palmer Quarterly,* 46, 90–118.

Davis, C. (1999). "Excessive Exercise and Anorexia Nervosa: Addictive and Compulsive Behaviors." *Psychiatric Annals,* 29, 221–224.

Davis, K. (1944). "Adolescence and the Social Structures." *Annuals of the American Academy of Political and Social Science,* 263, 1–168.

Davis, R., and Jamieson, J. (2005). "Assessing the Functional Nature of Binge Eating in the Eating Disorders." *Eating Behaviors,* 6, 345–354.

Davis, S. J. (1994). "Teaching Practices That Encourage or Eliminate Student Plagiarism." *Middle School Journal,* 25, 55–58.

Davison, T. E., and McCabe, M. P. (2006). "Adolescent Body Image and Psychosocial Functioning." *The Journal of Social Psychology,* 146, 15–30.

Dawson, D. A. (1986). "The Effects of Sex Education on Adolescent Behavior." *Family Planning Perspectives,* 18, 162–170.

Dawson, D. A. (1991). "Family Structure and Childrens' Health and Well-Being: Data from the 1988 National Health Interview Survey on Child Health." *Journal of Marriage and the Family,* 53, 573–584.

Day, R. D. (1992). "Transition to First Intercourse among Racially and Culturally Diverse Youth." *Journal of Marriage and the Family,* 54, 749–762.

De Bellis, M. D., Clark, D. B., Beers, S. R., Soloff, P. H., Boring, A. M., Hall, J., Kersh, A., and Keshavan, M. S. (2000). "Hippocampal Volume in Adolescent-Onset Alcohol Use Disorders." *American Journal of Psychiatry,* 157, 737–744.

De Bruyn, E. H., and van den Boom, D. C. (2005). "Interpersonal Behavior, Peer Popularity, and Self-Esteem in Early Adolescence." *Social Development,* 14, 555–573.

De Civita, M., and Pagani, L. (1996). "Familial Constraints on the Initiation of Cigarette Smoking among Adolescents: An Elaboration of Social Bonding Theory and Differential Association Theory." *Canadian Journal of School Psychology,* 12, 177–190.

De Gaston, J. F., Jensen L., and Weed, L. (1995). "A Closer Look at Adolescent Sexual Activity." *Journal of Youth and Adolescence,* 24, 465–479.

De Mey, L., Baartman, H. E. M., and Schulze, H-J. (1999). "Ethnic Variation and the Development of Moral Judgment of Youth in Dutch Society." *Youth and Society,* 31, 54–75.

DeBlassie, A. M., and DeBlassie, R. R. (1996). "Education of Hispanic Youth: A Cultural Lag." *Adolescence,* 31, 205–216.

DeBolt, M. E., Pasley, B. K., and Kreutzer, J. (1990). "Factors Affecting the Probability of School Dropout: A Study of Pregnant and Parenting Adolescent Females." *Journal of Adolescent Research,* 5, 190–205.

Decety, J., and Jackson, P. L. (2004). "The Functional Architecture of Human Empathy." *Behavioral and Cognitive Neuroscience Reviews,* 3, 406–412.

Deci, E. L. (March 1985). "The Well-Tempered Classroom." *Psychology Today,* 19, 52–53.

Deeks, S., Smith, M., Holodniy, M., and Kahn, J. (1997). "HIV-1 Protease Inhibitors." *Journal of the American Medical Association,* 277, 145–153.

DeGaston, J. F., Weed, S., and Jensen, L. (1996). "Understanding Gender Differences in Adolescent Sexuality." *Adolescence,* 31, 217–231.

Dekovic, M., and Meeus, W. (1997). "Peers Relations in Adolescence: Effects of Parenting and Adolescents' Self Concept." *Journal of Adolescence,* 20, 163–176.

Delorme, D. E., Kreshel, P. J., and Reid, L. N. (2003). "Lighting Up: Young Adults' Autobiographical Accounts of Their First Smoking Experiences." *Youth and Society,* 34, 468–496.

Dembo, R., Dertke, M., LaVoie, L., Borders, S., Washburn, M., and Schmeidler, J. (1987). "Physical Abuse, Sexual Victimization and Illicit Drug Use: A Structural Analysis among High Risk Adolescents." *Journal of Adolescence,* 10, 13–33.

Demetriou, A., Christou, C., Spanoudis, G., and Platsidou, M. (2002). "The Development of Mental Processing: Efficiency, Working Memory, and Thinking." *Monographs of the Society for Research in Child Development,* 67, vii–154.

Demick, J. (2002). "Stages of Parental Development." In M. H. Bornstein (Ed.), *Handbook of Parenting: Vol. 3: Being and Becoming a Parent* (2nd ed.), pp. 389–413. Mahwah, NJ: Erlbaum.

Demo, D. H., and Acock, A. C. (1988). "The Impact of Divorce on Children." *Journal of Marriage and the Family,* 50, 619–648.

Demo, D. H., and Acock, A. C. (1996). "Family Structure, Family Process, and Adolescent Well-Being." *Journal of Research on Adolescence,* 6, 457–488.

Demo, D. H., Small, S. A., and Savin-Williams, R. C. (1987). "Family Relations and the Self-Esteem of Adolescents and Their Parents." *Journal of Marriage and the Family,* 49, 705–715.

"Denial of Indian Civil and Religious Rights, The." (1975). *Indian Historian,* 8, 43–46.

Dennis, M. L., Muck, R. D., Dawud-Noursi, S., and McDermeit, M. (2003). "The Need for Developing and Evaluating Adolescent Treatment Models." In S. J. Stevens and A. R. Morral (Eds.), *Adolescent Substance Abuse Treatment in the United States: Exemplary Models from a National Evaluation Study* (pp. 3–35). New York: Haworth Press.

Dennison, B. A., Straus, J. H., Mellits, D., and Charney, E. (1988). "Childhood Physical Fitness Tests: Predictor of Adult Physical Activity Levels?" *Pediatrics*, 82, 324–330.

Denno, D. (Winter 1982). "Sex Differences in Cognition: A Review and Critique of the Longitudinal Evidence." *Adolescence*, 17, 779–788.

Dermen, K. H., Cooper, M. L., and Agocha, V. B. (1998). "Sex-Related Alcohol Expectancies as Moderators of the Relationship between Alcohol Use and Risky Sex in Adolescence." *Journal of Studies on Alcohol*, 59, 71–77.

deRosenroll, D. A. (1987). "Creativity and Self-Trust: A Field of Study." *Adolescence*, 22, 419–432.

DeSouza, M. J., and Metzger, M. S. (1991). "Reproductive Dysfunction in Amenorrheic Athletes and Anorexic Patients: A Review." *Medicine and Science in Sports Exercise*, 22, 575–582.

deTurck, M. A., and Miller, G. R. (August 1983). "Adolescent Perceptions of Parental Persuasive Message Strategies." *Journal of Marriage and the Family*, 34, 533–542.

Diamond, L. M., and Savin-Williams, R. C. (2000). "Explaining Diversity in the Development of Same-Sex Sexuality in Young Women." *Journal of Social Issues*, 56, 297–313.

Diamond, L. M., and Savin-Williams, R. C. (2003). "Explaining Diversity in the Development of Same-Sex Sexuality among Young Women." In L. D. Garnets and D. C. Kimmel (Eds.), *Psychological Perspectives on Lesbian, Gay, and Bisexual Experiences*, 2nd ed. (pp. 130–148). New York: Columbia University Press.

Diamond, L. M., Savin-Williams, R. C., and Dubé, E. M. (1999). "Sex, Dating, Passionate Friendships, and Romance: Intimate Peer Relations among Lesbian, Gay, and Bisexual Adolescents." In W. Furman and C. Feiring (Eds.), *The Development of Relationships during Adolescence* (pp. 175–210). New York: Cambridge University Press.

DiCindio, L. A., Floyd, H. H., Wilcox, J., and McSeveney, D. R. (Summer 1983). "Race Effects in a Model of Parent-Peer Orientation." *Adolescence*, 18, 369–379.

Dickens, C. (1959). *Oliver Twist*. London: Collins Publishers.

DiClemente, R. J., Hansen, W. B., and Ponton, L. E. (1996). "Adolescents at Risk: A Generation in Jeopardy." In R. J. DiClemente, W. B. Hansen, and L. E. Ponton (Eds.), *Handbook of Adolescent Health Risk Behavior* (pp. 1–4). New York: McGraw-Hill.

DiClemente, R. J., Wingood, G. M., Crosby, R., Sionean, C., Cobb, B. K., Harrington, K., Davies, S., Hook III, E. W., & Oh, M. K. (2001). "Parental Monitoring: Association with Adolescents' Risk Behaviors." *Pediatrics*, 107, 1363–1368

Dietrich, D. R. (1984). "Psychological Health of Young Adults Who Experienced Early Parent Death: MMPI Trends." *Journal of Clinical Psychology*, 40, 901–908.

Dietz, T. (1998). "An Examination of Violence and Gender Role Portrayals in Video Games: Implications for Gender Socialization and Aggressive Behavior." *Sex Roles*, 38, 425–442.

Dilorio, C., Kelley, M., and Hockenberry-Eaton, M. (1999). "Communication about Sexual Issues: Mothers, Fathers, and Friends." *Journal of Adolescent Health*, 24, 181–189.

Dinges, M. M., and Oetting, E. R. (1993). "Similarity in Drug Use Patterns between Adolescents and Their Friends." *Adolescence*, 28, 253–266.

Dino, S., Stick, G., and Troutman, R. (1993). *Knockin' Da Boots*. Pac Jam Publishing, Saja Music, and Troutman Music.

Dixon, J. A., and Moore, C. F. (1996). "The Developmental Role of Intuitive Principles in Choosing Mathematical Strategies." *Developmental Psychology*, 32, 241–253.

Dobson, H., Ghuman, S., Prabhakar, S., and Smith, R. (2003). "A Conceptual Model of the Influence of Stress on Female Reproduction." *Reproduction*, 125, 151–163.

Doherty, W. J., and Needle, R. H. (1991). "Psychological Adjustment and Substance Use among Adolescents Before and After a Parental Divorce." *Child Development*, 62, 328–337.

Dolan, B. (1994). "Why Women? Gender Issues and Eating Disorders: An Introduction." In B. Dolan and I. Gitzinger (Eds.),*Why Women? Gender Issues and Eating Disorders* (pp. 1–11). London: Athlone Press.

Dolcini, M. M., Cohn, L. D., Adler, N. E., et al. (1989). *Journal of Early Adolescence*, 9, 409–418.

Dolgin, K. G. (2006). "Music Education: Why Now More Than Ever." In J. Aten (Ed.), *String Teaching in America: Strategies for a Diverse Society* (pp. 101–104). Washington, DC: American String Teachers Association.

Dolgin, K. G., and Kim, S. (1994). "Adolescents' Disclosure to Best and Good Friends: The Effects of Gender and Topic Intimacy." *Social Development*, 3, 146–157.

Dolliver, M. 1999. "Getting and Spending, Junior Division." *Adweek*, 40, 20.

Domenech, E. (1996). "Biopsychopathologic Risk Profile of Adolescents with Eating Disorder Symptoms." *Adolescence*, 31, 443–450.

Donnellan, M. B., Trzesniewski, K. H., Robins, R., Moffitt, T. E., and Caspi, A. (2005). "Low Self-Esteem Is Related to Aggression, Antisocial Behavior, and Delinquency." *Psychological Science*, 16, 328–335.

Donnerstein, E., and Lint, D. (January 1984). "Sexual Violence in the Media: A Warning." *Psychology Today*, 18, 14, 15.

Donovan, F. R. (1967). *Wild Kids*. Harrisburg, PA: Stackpole Co.

Donovan, P. (1997). "Confronting a Hidden Epidemic: The Institute of Medicine's Report on Sexually Transmitted Diseases." *Family Planning Perspectives*, 29, 87–89.

Dori, G., and Overholser, J. C. (1999). "Depression, Hopelessness, and Self-Esteem: Accounting for Suicidality in Adolescent Psychiatric Inpatients." *Suicide and Life Threatening Behavior*, 29, 309–318.

Dorius, G. L., Heaton, T. B., and Steffen, P. (1993). "Adolescent Life Events and Their Association with the Onset of Sexual Intercourse." *Youth and Society*, 25, 3–23.

Doty, R. L. (2001). "Olfaction." *Annual Review of Psychology*, 52, 423–452.

Doueck, H. J., Ishisaka, A. H., and Greenaway, K. D. (1988). "The Role of Normative Development in Adolescent Abuse and Neglect." *Family Relations*, 37, 135–139.

Douvan, E., and Adelson, J. (1966). *The Adolescent Experience*. New York: Wiley.

Dowdney, L. (2000). "Annotation: Childhood Bereavement Following Parental Death." *Journal of Child Psychology & Psychiatry*, 41, 819–830.

Dowdney, L., Wilson, R., Maughan, B., Allerton, M., Schofield, P., and Skuse, D. (1999). "Bereaved Children: Psychological Disturbance and Service Provision." *British Medical Journal*, 319, 354–357.

Dowdy, B. B., and Kliewer, W. (1998). "Dating, Parent-Adolescent Conflict, and Behavioral Autonomy." *Journal of Youth and Adolescence*, 27, 473–492.

Dowling, E. M., Gestsdottir, S., Anderson, P. M., von Eye, A., Almerigi, J., and Lerner, R. M. (2004). "Structural Relations among Spirituality, Religiosity, and Thriving in Adolescence." *Applied Developmental Science*, 8, 7–16.

Downs, A. C., and Fuller, M. J. (1991). "Recollections of Spermarche: An Exploratory Investigation." *Current Psychology: Research and Reviews*, 10, 93–102.

Doyle, J. A., and Paludi, M. A. (1995). *Sex and Gender: A Human Experience*. 3rd ed. Dubuque, IA: Brown and Benchmark.

Drevets, R. K., Benton, S. L., and Bradley, F. O. (1996). "Students' Perceptions of Parents' and Teachers' Qualities of Interpersonal Relationships." *Journal of Youth and Adolescence*, 25, 787–802.

Dreyer, T. H., Jennings, C., Johnson, F., and Evans, D. (1994). *Culture and Personality in Urban Schools: Identity Status, Self-Concepts, and Loss of Control among High School Students and Monolingual and Bilingual Homes*. Paper presented at the meeting of the Society for Research on Adolescents, San Diego.

Dreyfus, E. A. (1976). *Adolescence. Theory and Experience*. Columbus, OH: Charles E. Merrill.

Dryfoos, J. G. (July–August 1984). "A New Strategy for Preventing Teenage Childbearing." *Family Planning Perspectives*, 16, 193–195.

Dubas, J. S., Garber, J. A., and Pedersen, A. C. (1991). "A Longitudinal Investigation of Adolescents' Changing Perceptions of Pubertal Timing." *Developmental Psychology*, 27, 580–586.

DuBois, D. L., and Hirsch, B. J. (1993). "School/Non-School Friendship Patterns in Early Adolescence." *Journal of Early Adolescence*, 13, 102–122.

DuBois, D. L., Felner, R. D., Brand, S., Phillips, R. S., and Lease, A. N. (1996). "Early Adolescent Self-Esteem: A Developmental-Ecological Frame Work and Assessment Strategy." *Journal of Research on Adolescence*, 6, 543–579.

Dudley, R. L. (1999). "Youth Religious Commitments over Time: A Longitudinal Study of Retention." *Review of Religious Research*, 41, 110–121.

Dudley, R. L., and Laurent, C. R. (1988). "Alienation from Religion in Church-Related Adolescents." *Sociological Analysis*, 49, 408–420.

Duffy, J., and Coates, T. J. (1989). "Reducing Smoking among Pregnant Adolescents." *Adolescence*, 24, 29–37.

Duke, R. L., Martinez, R. O., and Stein, J. A. (1997). "Precursors and Consequences of Membership in Youth Gangs." *Youth and Society*, 29, 139–165.

Dukes, R. L., and Lorch, B. D. (1989). "The Effects of School, Family, Self-Concept, and Deviant Behavior on Adolescent Suicide Ideation." *Journal of Adolescence*, 12, 239–251.

Dunn, C., Chambers, D., and Rabren, K. (2004). "Variables Affecting Students' Decisions to Drop Out of School." *Remedial and Special Education*, 25, 314–323.

Dunn, J., Slomkowski, C., and Beardsall, L. (1994). "Sibling Relationships from the Preschool Period through Middle Childhood and Early Adolescence." *Developmental Psychology*, 30, 163–172.

Dunn, M. (2005). "The Relationship between Religiosity, Employment, and Political Beliefs on Substance Use among High School Seniors." *Journal of Alcohol and Drug Education*, 49, 73–88.

Dunphy, D. (1963). "The Social Structure of Urban Adolescent Peer Groups." *Sociometry*, 26, 230–246.

Durbin, D. L., Darling, N., Steinberg, L., and Brown, B. B. (1993). "Parenting Style and Peer Group Membership among European-American Adolescents." *Journal of Research on Adolescence*, 3, 87–100.

Durston, S., Hulshoff, P., Hilleke, E., Casey, B. J., Giedd, J. N., Buitelaar, J. K., and van Engeland, H. (2001). "Anatomical MRI of the Developing Human Brain: What Have We Learned?" *Journal of the American Academy of Child and Adolescent Psychiatry*, 40, 1012–1020.

Dusek, J. B., and McIntyre, J. G. (2003). "Self-Concept and Self-Esteem Development." In G. R. Adams and M. D. Berzonsky (Eds.), *Blackwell Handbook of Adolescence* (pp. 290–309). Oxford, England: Blackwell Publishing.

Dvorchak, R. (December 11, 1992). "Without Wampum or Buffalo, Indians Rely on Blackjack, Bingo." *Prescott Courier.*

Dye, J. L. (2005). "Fertility of American Women: June 2004." *Current Population Reports, P20-555.* Washington, DC: U.S. Bureau of the Census.

Eagly, A., Jr., Howell, J. C., and Major, A. K. (2006). *National Youth Gang Survey 1999–2001.* Washington, DC: Office of Juvenile Justice and Delinquency Prevention.

Earl, W. L. (1987). "Creativity and Self-Thrust: A Field of Study." *Adolescence*, 22, 419–432.

Earle, J. R., and Perricone, P. J. (1986). "Premarital Sexuality: A Ten Year Study of Attitudes and Behavior in a Small University Campus." *The Journal of Sex Research*, 22, 304–310.

East, P. L. (1989). "Early Adolescents' Perceived Interpersonal Risks and Benefits: Relations to Social Support and Psychological Functioning." *Journal of Early Adolescence*, 9, 374–395.

East, P. L. (1996). "The Younger Sisters of Childbearing Adolescents: Their Attitudes, Expectations, and Behaviors." *Child Development*, 67, 267–282.

East, P. L., and Khoo, S. T. (2005). "Longitudinal Pathways Linking Family Factors and Sibling Relationship Qualities to Adolescent Substance Use and Sexual Risk Behaviors." *Journal of Family Psychology*, 19, 571–580.

East, P. L., Felice, M. A., and Morgan, M. C. (1993). "Sisters' and Girlfriends' Sexual Childbearing Behavior: Effects on Early Adolescent Girls' Sexual Outcomes." *Journal of Marriage and the Family*, 55, 953–963.

Eaton, Y. M., Mitchell, M. L., and Jolley, J. M. (1991). "Gender Differences in the Development of Relationships during Late Adolescence." *Adolescence*, 26, 565–568.

Ebbeling, C. B., Sinclair, K. B., Periera, M. A., Garcia-Lago, E., Feldman, H. A., and Ludwig, D. S. (2004). "Compensation for Energy Intake from Fast Food among Overweight and Lean Adolescents." *Journal of the American Medical Association*, 291, 2828–2833.

Ebenkamp, B. (1998). "Fashion en Mass?" *Brandweek*, 39, 22–30.

Eberhart, N. K., Shih, J. H., Hammen, C. L., & Brennan, P. A. (2006). "Understanding the Sex Difference in Vulnerability to Adolescent Depression: An Examination of Child and Parent Characteristics." *Journal of Abnormal Child Psychology*, 34, 495–508.

Eccles, J. S., and Barber, B. (1999). "Student Council, Volunteering, Basketball, or Marching Band: What Kind of Extracurricular Involvement Matters?" *Journal of Adolescent Research*, 14, 10–34.

Eccles, J. S., and Midgley, C. (1989). "Stage-Environment Fit: Developmentally Appropriate Classrooms for Young Adolescents." In C. Ames and R. Ames (Eds.), *Research on Motivation in Education.* Vol. 3, *Goals and Cognitions* (pp. 13–44). New York: Academic Press.

Eccles, J. S., Midgley, C., Wigfield, A., Duchanan, C. M., Reuman, D., Flanagan, C., and MacIver, D. (1993). "Development during Adolescence: The Impact of Stage-Environment Fit on Young Adolescents' Experiences in Schools and Families." *American Psychologist*, 48, 90–101.

Eccles, J. S., and Roeser, R. W. (2003). "Schools as Developmental Contexts." In G. R. Adams and M. D. Berzonsky (Eds.), *Blackwell Handbook of Adolescence* (pp. 129–148). Oxford, England: Blackwell Publishing.

Eder, D., Evans, C. C., and Parker, S. (1995). *School Talk: Gender and Adolescent Culture.* New Brunswick, NJ: Rutgers University Press.

Eder, D., and Kinney, D. A. (1995). "The Effect of Middle School Extracurricular Activities on Adolescents' Popularity and Peer Status." *Youth and Society*, 26, 298–324.

Educational Resource Information Center. (2000). *Straight Talk about College Costs and Prices* <www.eriche.org/government/talk.html>.

Edwards, S. (1994). "As Adolescent Males Age, Risky Behavior Rises and Condom Use Decreases." *Family Planning Perspectives*, 26, 45–46.

Edwards, W. J. (1996). "A Measurement of Delinquency Differences between Delinquent and Nondelinquent Youths between a Delinquent and Nondelinquent Sample: What Are the Implications?" *Adolescence*, 31, 973–989.

Egley, A., & Ritz, C. E. (2006). Highlights of the 2004 National Youth Gang Survey: Office of Juvenile Justice and Delinquency Prevention Fact Sheet. Washington, D. C.: U. S. Department of Justice.

Ehrhardt, A., and Meyer-Bahlburg, H. (1981). "Effects of Prenatal Sex Hormones on Gender-Related Behavior." *Science*, 211, 312–318.

Ehrlich, T. (2000). *Civic Responsibility and College Education.* Phoenix: Oryx Press.

Eisen, S. V., Youngman, D. J., Grob, M. C., and Dill, D. L. (1992). "Alcohol, Drugs, and Psychiatric Disorders. A Current View of Hospitalized Adolescents." *Journal of Adolescent Research*, 7, 250–265.

Eisenberg, N. (1986). *Altruistic Emotion, Cognition, and Behavior.* Hillsdale, NJ: Erlbaum.

Eisenberg, N. (1998). "Prosocial Development." In N. Eisenberg (Ed.) and W. Damon (Series Ed.), *Handbook of Child Psychology. Vol. 3: Social, Emotional and Personality Development*, 5th ed. (pp. 701–778). New York: Wiley.

Eisenberg, N., and Fabes, R. A. (1998). "Prosocial Development." In W. Damon (Series Ed.) and N. Eisenberg (Vol. Ed.), *Handbook of Child Psychology: Volume 3, Social, Emotional, and Personality Development* (5th ed.), (pp. 701–778). New York: Wiley.

Eisenberg, N., and McNally, S. (1993). "Socialization and Mothers' and Adolescents' Empathy-Related Characteristics." *Journal of Research on Adolescence*, 3, 171–191.

Eisenberg, N., and Murphy, B. (1995). "Parenting and Children's Moral Development." In M. H. Bornstein (Ed.), *Children and Parenting.* Vol. 4. Hillsdale, NJ: Erlbaum.

Eisenberg, N., Carlo, G., Murphy, B., and Van Court, P. (1995). "Prosocial Development in Late Adolescence: A Longitudinal Study." *Child Development*, 66, 1179–1197.

Eisenberg, N., Cumberland, A., Guthrie, I. K., Murphy, B. C., and Shepard, S. A. (2005). "Age Changes in Prosocial Responding and Moral Reasoning in Adolescence and Early Adulthood." *Journal of Research on Adolescence*, 15, 235–260.

Eisenberg, N., Guthrie, I., Cumberland, A., Murphy, B. C., Shepard, S. A., Zhou, Q., and Carlo, G. (2002). "Prosocial Development in Early Adulthood: A Longitudinal Study." *Personality and Social Psychology*, 82, 993–1006.

Elder, G. H., Jr., and Conger, R. D. (2000). *Children of the Land.* Chicago: University of Chicago Press.

Elkind, D. (1967). "Egocentrism in Adolescence." *Child Development*, 38, 1025–1034.

Elkind, D. (1970). *Children and Adolescents: Interpretive Essays on Jean Piaget.* New York: Oxford University Press.

Elkind, D. (1975). "Recent Research on Cognitive Development in Adolescence." In S. E. Dragastin and G. H. Elder, Jr. (Eds.), *Adolescence in the Life Cycle.* New York: Wiley.

Elkind, D. (Spring 1978). "Understanding the Young Adolescent." *Adolescence*, 13, 127–134.

Ellickson, P. L., et al. (1996). "Teenagers and Alcohol Misuse in the United States: By Any Definition, It's a Big Problem." *Addiction*, 1, 1489–1503.

Ellington, L. (2001). "Japanese Education." *The Japan Digest.* Retrieved from http://www.indiana.edu/~japan

Elliott, D. S., and Menard, S. (1996). "Delinquent Friends and Delinquent Behavior: Temporal and Developmental Patterns." In J. D. Hawkinds (Ed.), *Delinquency and Crime: Current Theories* (pp. 28–67). New York: Cambridge University Press.

Elliott, G. C., Avery, R., Fishman, E., and Hoshiko, B. (2002). "The Encounter with Family Violence and Risky Sexual Activity among Young Adolescent Females." *Violence and Victims*, 17, 569–591.

Ellis, B. J. (2004). "Timing of Pubertal Maturation in Girls: An Integrated Life History Approach." *Psychological Bulletin*, 130, 920–958.

Ellis, B. J., and Garber, J. (2000). "Psychosocial Antecedents of Variation in Girls' Pubertal Timing: Maternal Depression, Stepfather Presence, and Marital and Family Stress." *Child Development*, 71, 485–501.

Ellis, B. J., McFaden-Ketchem, S., Dodge, K. A., Pettit, G. S., and Bates, J. E. (1999). "Quality of Early Family Relationships and Individual Differences in the Timing of Pubertal Maturation in Girls: A Longitudinal Test of an Evolutionary Model." *Journal of Personality and Social Psychology, 77*, 387–401.

Ellis, L., and Wagemann, B. M. (1993). "The Religiosity of Mothers and Their Offspring as Related to the Offspring's Sex and Sexual Orientation." *Adolescence,* 28, 227–234.

Ellis, N. B. (1991). "An Extension of the Steinberg Accelerating Hypothesis." *Journal of Early Adolescence,* 2, 221–235.

Ellison, C. G. (1992). "Are Religious People Nice People? Evidence from the National Survey of Black Americans." *Social Forces,* 71, 411–430.

Elmen, J. (1991). "Achievement Orientation in Early Adolescence: Developmental Patterns and Social Correlates." *Journal of Early Adolescence,* 11, 125–151.

Emery, P. E. (Summer 1983). "Adolescent Depression and Suicide." *Adolescence,* 18, 245–258.

Emery, R. E. (1988). *Marriage, Divorce, and Children's Adjustment.* Newbury Park, CA: Sage.

Emick, M., and Hayslip, B. (1999). "Custodial Grandparenting: Stress, Coping and Relationships with Grandchildren." *International Journal of Aging and Human Development,* 48, 35–61.

Employment Policies Institute. (2006). *June Report.* Retrieved from http://www.epionline.org/index_gi.cfm.

Engles, R. C. M. E., Knibble, R. A., Drop, M. J., and de Haan, Y. T. (1997). "Homogeneity of Cigarette Smoking within Peer Groups: Influence or Selection." *Health Education and Behavior,* 24, 801–811.

Engstrom, C. A., and Sedlacek, W. E. (1991). "A Study of Prejudice toward University Student-Athletes." *Journal of Counseling and Development,* 70, 189–193.

Ennett, S. T., and Bauman, K. E. (1996). "Adolescent Social Networks: School, Demographics, and Longitudinal Considerations." *Journal of Adolescent Research,* 11, 194–215.

Ennis, R. H. (1991). "Critical Thinking: Literature Review and Needed Research." In L. Idol and D. S. Jones (Eds.), *Educational Values and Cognitive Instruction.* Hillsdale, NJ: Erlbaum.

Ensminger, M. E. (1990). "Sexual Activity and Problem Behaviors among Black, Urban Adolescents." *Child Development,* 61, 2032–2046.

Entwisle, D. R., Alexander, K. L., Olson, L. S., and Ross, K. (1999). "Paid Work in Early Adolescence: Developmental and Ethical Patterns." *Journal of Early Adolescence,* 19, 363–388.

Erickson, L., and Newman, I. M. (January 1984). "Developing Support for Alcohol and Drug Education: A Case Study of a Counselor's Role." *Personnel and Guidance Journal,* 62, 289–291.

Erikson, E. H. (1950). *Childhood and Society.* New York: W. W. Norton.

Erikson, E. H. (1959). *Identity and the Life Cycle.* New York: International Universities Press.

Erikson, E. H. (1968). *Identity: Youth, and Crisis.* New York: W. W. Norton.

Erikson, E. H. (1982). *The Life Cycle Completed.* New York: W. W. Norton.

Erkut, S., Marx, F., Fields, J. P., and Sing, R. (1999). "Raising Confident and Competent Girls: One Size Does Not Fit All." In L. A. Peplau, S. C. DeBro, R. C. Veniegas, and P. L. Taylor (Eds.), *Gender, Culture and Ethnicity* (pp. 83–101). Mountain View, CA: Mayfield Publishing.

Erwin, P. (1993). *Friendship and Peer Relations in Children.* New York: Wiley.

Escabedo, L. G., Marcus, S. E., Holtzman, D., and Giovino, G. A. (1986). "Sports Participation, Age at Smoking Initiation, and the Risk of Smoking among U.S. High School Students." *Journal of the American Medical Association,* 256(20), 2859–2862.

Estrada, P. (1992). *Socio-Emotional and Educational Functioning in Poor Urban Youth during the Transition to Middle School: The Role of Peer and Teacher Social Support.* Paper presented at the meeting of the Society for Research on Adolescence, Washington, DC.

Estrada, P. (1995). "Adolescents' Self-Reports of Pro-Social Responses to Friends and Acquaintances: The Role of Sympathy-Related Cognitive, Affective, and Motivational Processes." *Journal of Research on Adolescence,* 5, 173–200.

Etringer, B. D., Altmaier, E. M., and Bowers, W. (1989). "An Investigation into the Cognitive Functioning of Bulimic Women." *Journal of Counseling and Development,* 68, 216–219.

Etter, G. W., Sr. (1999). "Skinheads: Manifestations of the Warrior Culture of the New Urban Tribes." *Journal of Gang Research,* 6, 9–21.

Evans, E. D., and Craig, D. (1990). "Adolescent Cognitions for Academic Cheating as a Function of Grade Level and Achievement Status." *Journal of Adolescent Research,* 5, 325–345.

Evans, I. M., Cicchelli, P., Cohen, M., and Shapiro, M. (1995). *Staying in School.* Baltimore, MD: Paul Brookes.

Evans, N., Farkas, A., Gilpin, E., Berry, C., and Pierce, J. P. (1995). "The Influence of Tobacco Marketing and Exposure to Smokers on Adolescent Susceptibility to Smoking." *Journal of the National Cancer Institute,* 87, 1538–1545.

Fabes, R. A., Carlo, G., Kupanoff, K., and Laible, D. (1999). "Early Adolescence and Prosocial/Moral Behavior. I: The Role of Individual Processes." *Journal of Early Adolescence,* 19, 5–16.

Fagan, A. A. (2005). "The Relationship Between Adolescent Physical Abuse and Criminal Offending: Support for an Enduring and Generalized Cycle of Violence." *Journal of Family Violence,* 20(5), 279–290.

Fagot, B., Pears, K., Capaldi, M., Crosby, L., and Leve, C. (1998). "Becoming an Adolescent Father: Precursors and Planning." *Developmental Psychology,* 34, 1209–1219.

Fallone, G., Acebo, C., Arnedt, T. J., Seifer, R., and Carskadon, M. A. (2001). "Effects of Acute Sleep Restriction on Behavior, Sustained Attention, and Response Inhibition in Children." *Perceptual and Motor Skills,* 93, 213–229.

Farmer, T. W., Estell, D. B., Bishop, J. L., O'Neal, K. K., and Cairns, B. D. (2003). "Rejected Bullies or Popular Leaders? The Social Relations of Aggressive Subtypes of Rural African American Early Adolescents." *Developmental Psychology,* 39, 992–1004.

Farrington, D. P. (1990). "Implications of Criminal Career Research for the Prevention of Offending." *Journal of Adolescence,* 13, 93–114.

Farrow, P. (Spring 1978). "The Presymposial State." *Andover Review,* 5, 14–37.

Farruggia, S. P., Chen, C., Greenberger, E., Dhitrieva, J., and Macek, P. (2004). "Adolescent Self-Esteem in Cross-Cultural Perspective." *Journal of Cross-Cultural Psychology,* 15, 719–733.

Faulkenberry, J. R., Vincent, M., James, A., and Johnson, W. (1987). "Coital Behaviors, Attitudes, and Knowledge of Students Who Experience Early Coitus." *Adolescence,* 22, 321–332.

Faulkner, X., and Culwin, F. (2005). "When Fingers Do the Talking: A Study of Text Messaging." *Interacting with Computers,* 17, 167–185.

Federal Interagency Forum on Child and Family Statistics. (1999). *America's Children: Key National Indicators of Well-Being, 1998* <www.childstats.gov>.

Federal Interagency Forum on Child and Family Statistics. (2001). *America's Children: Key National Indicators of Well-Being, 2000* <www.childstats.gov>.

Feigelman, S., Stanton, B. F., and Ricardo, I. (1993). "Perceptions of Drug Selling and Drug Use among Urban Youths." *Journal of Early Adolescence,* 13, 267–284.

Feiring, C. (1996). "Concepts of Romance in 15-Year-Old Adolescents." *Journal of Research on Adolescence,* 6, 181–200.

Feldman, A. F., and Matjasko, J. L. (2005). "The Role of School-Based Extracurricular Activities in Adolescent Development: A Comprehensive Review and Future Directions." *Review of Educational Research,* 75, 159–210.

Feldman, N. A., and Ruble, D. N. (1988). "The Effect of Personal Relevance on Psychological Inference: A Developmental Analysis." *Child Development,* 59, 1339–1352.

Feldman, S. A., and Rosenthal, D. A. (1994). "Culture Makes a Difference . . . or Does It? A Comparison of Adolescents in Hong Kong, Australia, and the United States." In R. K. Silbereisen and E. Todt (Eds.), *Adolescence in Context* (pp. 99–124). New York: Springer.

Feldman, S. S., and Cauffman, E. (1999a). "Sexual Betrayal among Late Adolescents: Perspectives of the Perpetrator and the Aggrieved." *Journal of Youth and Adolescence,* 28, 235–258.

Feldman, S. S., and Cauffman, E. (1999b). "Your Cheatin' Heart: Attitudes, Behaviors, and Correlates of Sexual Betrayal in Late Adolescents." *Journal of Research on Adolescence,* 9, 227–252.

Feldman, S. S., and Gehring, T. M. (1988). "Changing Perceptions of Family Cohesion and Power across Adolescence." *Child Development,* 59, 1034–1045.

Feldman, S. S., and Quatman, T. (1988). "Factors Influencing Age Expectations for Adolescent Autonomy: A Study of Early Adolescents and Parents." *Journal of Early Adolescence,* 8, 325–343.

Feldman, S. S., and Rosenthal, D. A. (2000). "The Effect of Communication Characteristics on Family Members' Perceptions of Parents as Sex Educators." *Journal of Research on Adolescence,* 10, 119–150.

Feldman, S. S., and Weinberger, D. A. (1994). "Self-Restraint as a Mediator of Family Influences on Boys' Delinquent Behavior: A Longitudinal Study." *Child Development,* 65, 195–211.

Feldman, S. S., and Wentzel, K. R. (1990). "The Relationship between Parenting Styles, Sons' Self Restraint, and Peer Relations in Early Adolescence." *Journal of Early Adolescence,* 10, 439–454.

Feldman, S. S., and Wood, D. N. (1994). "Parents' Expectations for Preadolescent Sons' Behavioral Autonomy: A Longitudinal Study of Correlates and Outcomes." *Journal of Research on Adolescence,* 4, 45–70.

Feldman, S. S., Mont-Reynaud, R., and Rosenthal, D. A. (1992). "When East Moves West: Acculturation of Values of Chinese Adolescents in the United States and Australia." *Journal of Research on Adolescence,* 2, 147–173.

Feldman, S. S., Turner, R., and Araujo, K. (1999). "Interpersonal Context as an Influence on Sexual Timetables of Youths: Gender and Ethnic

Effects." *Journal of Research on Adolescence,* 9, 25–52.

Feltey, K. M., Ainslie, J. J., and Geib, A. (1991). "Sexual Coercion Attitudes among High School Students. The Influence of Gender and Rape Education." *Youth and Society,* 23, 229–250.

Fenzel, F. M. (1994). *The Perspective Study of the Effects of Chronic Strain on Early Adolescents' Self-Worth and School Adjustment.* Paper presented at the meeting of the society for Research on Adolescents, San Diego.

Fenzel, F. M., Blyth, D. A., and Simmons, R. G. (1991). "School Transitions, Secondary." In R. M. Lerner, A. C. Petersen, and J. Brooks-Gunn (Eds.), *Encyclopedia of Adolescence.* Vol. 2. New York: Garland.

Fenzel, L. M. (1989). "Role Strain in Early Adolescence: A Model for Investigating School Transition Stress." *Journal of Early Adolescence,* 9, 13–33.

Fenzel, L. M. (2000). "Prospective Study of Changes in Global Self-Worth and Strain during the Transition to Middle School." *Journal of Early Adolescence,* 20, 93–116.

Ferguson, R. F. (1998). "Teachers' Perceptions and Expectations and the Black-White Test Score Gap." In C. Jencks and M. Phillips (Eds.), *The Black-White Test Score Gap* (pp. 273–317). Washington, DC: Brookings Institute Press.

Fergusson, D. M., Lynskey, M., and Horwood, L. J. (1995). "The Adolescent Outcomes of Adoption: A 16–Year Longitudinal Study." *Journal of Child Psychology and Psychiatry and Allied Disciplines,* 36, 597–615.

Fernandez-Guasti, A., Kruijver, F. P. M., Fodor, M., and Swaab, D. F. (2000). "Sex Differences in the Distribution of Androgen Receptors in the Human Hypothalamus." *Journal of Comparative Neurology,* 425, 422–435.

Ferreiro, B. W., Warren, N.J., and Konanc, J. T. (1986). "ADAP: A Divorce Assessment Proposal." *Family Relations,* 35, 439–449.

Ferron, C. (1997). "Body Image in Adolescence: Cross-Cultural Research—Results of the Preliminary Phase of a Quantitative Survey." *Adolescence,* 32, 735–745.

Ferron, C., Narring, G., Cauderay, M., and Michaud, P. A. (1999). "Sport Activity in Adolescence: Association with Health Perceptions and Experimental Behaviors." *Health Education Research,* 14, 225–233.

Fertman, C. I., and Chubb, N. H. (1992). "The Effects of a Psychoeducational Program on Adolescents' Activity Involvement, Self-Esteem, and Locus of Control." *Adolescence,* 27, 517–533.

Fetto, J. (2002). "Your Questions Answered: Statistics about Skateboarders." *American Demographics, October.* Retrieved from http://www.findarticles.com/p/articles/mi_m4021/is_2002_Oct_1/ai_92087410.

Field, A. E., Camargo, C. A., Taylor, C. B., Berkey, C. S., Frazier, L., Gillman, M. W. et al. (1999). "Overweight, Weight Concerns, and Bulimic Behaviors Among Girls and Boys." *Journal of the American Academy of Child & Adolescent Psychiatry,* 38(6), 754–760.

Field, T., Lang, C., Yando, R., and Vendell, D. (1995). "Adolescents' Intimacy with Parents and Friends." *Adolescence,* 30, 133–140.

Fields, J. (2004). America's families and living arrangements: 2003. *Current Population Report # P20-553.* Washington, DC: Census Bureau.

Fields, J. M. (2003). "Children's Living Arrangements and Characteristics: March 2002." *Current Population Reports,* no. P20-547. Washington, DC: U.S. Bureau of the Census.

Fields, J., and Casper, L. M. (2001). "American Families and Living Arrangements: March, 2000." *Current Population Reports,* no. P20-537. Washington, DC: U.S. Census Bureau.

Fiering, C. (1996). "Concepts of Romance in 15-Year-Old Adolescents." *Journal of Research in Adolescence,* 6, 181–200.

Fine, M. A. (1986). "Perceptions of Stepparents: Variations in Stereotypes as a Function of Current Family Structure." *Journal of Marriage and the Family,* 48, 537–543.

Fine, M. A., Donnelly, B. W., and Voydanoff, P. (1991). "The Relation between Adolescents' Perceptions of Their Family Lives and Their Adjustment in Stepfather Families." *Journal of Adolescent Research,* 6, 423–436.

Fineran, S., and Bennett, L. (1999). "Gender and Power Issues of Peer Sexual Harassment among Teenagers." *Journal of Interpersonal Violence,* 14, 626–641.

Finkelhor, D. (1984). *Child Sexual Abuse: Theory and Research.* New York: Free Press.

Finkelhor, D. (1994). "Current Information on the Scope and Nature of Child Sexual Abuse." In *The Sexual Abuse of Children.* Retrieved from http://www.futureofchildren.org/information2826/informationshow.htm?doc_id=74217.

Finkelhor, D., Hotaling, G., and Sedlak, A. (1990). *Missing, Abducted, Runaway, and Throwaway Children in America.* Washington, DC: U.S. Department of Justice.

Finkelhor, D., Mitchell, K. J., and Wolak, J. (2000). *Online Victimization: A Report on the Nation's Youth.* Alexandria, VA: National Center for Missing and Exploited Children. Retrieved from http://missingkids.com/download/nc62.pdf.

Finkelstein, M. J. & Gaier, E. L. (1983). "The Impact of Prolonged Student Status on Late Adolescent Development." *Adolescence,* 18, 115–129.

Fiorentine, R. (1988). "Sex Differences in Success Expectancies and Causal Attributions: Is This Why Fewer Women Become Physicians?" *Social Psychology Quarterly,* 51, 236–249.

Fischer, J. L., and Crawford, D. W. (1992). "Codependency and Parenting Styles." *Journal of Adolescent Research,* 3, 352–363.

Fischman, J. (1988). "Stepdaughter Wars." *Psychology Today,* 22, 38–45.

Fisher, M., Fornari, V., Waldbaum, R., and Gold, R. (2002). "Three Case Reports on the Relationship between Anorexia Nervosa and Obsessive Compulsive Disorder." *International Journal of Adolescent Medicine and Health,* 14, 329–334.

Fisher, T. D. (1986). "Parent-Child Communication about Sex and Young Adolescents' Sexual Knowledge and Attitudes." *Adolescence,* 21, 517–527.

Fitzgerald, B. (1999). "Children of Lesbian and Gay Parents: A Review of the Literature." *Marriage and Family Review,* 29, 57–75.

Fitzgerald, J. M. (1991). "Memory." In R. M. Lerner, A. C. Petersen, and J. Brooks-Gunn (Eds.), *Encyclopedia of Adolescence.* Vol. 2. New York: Garland.

Fixico, D. L. (2000). *The Urban Indian Experience in America.* Albuquerque: University of New Mexico Press.

Flanagan, A. S., and Furman, W. C. (2000). "Sexual Victimization and Perceptions of Close Relationships in Adolescence." *Child Maltreatment,* 5, 350–359.

Flanigan, B., McLean, A., Hall, C., and Propp, V. (1990). "Alcohol Use as a Situational Influence on Young Women's Pregnancy Risk-Taking Behavior." *Adolescence,* 25, 205–214.

Flannery, D. J., Huff, C. R., and Manos, M. (1998). "Youth Gangs: A Developmental Perspective." In T. P. Gullotta, G. R. Adams, and R. Montemayor (Eds.), *Youth Violence: Prevention, Intervention, and Social Policy* (pp. 175–204). Thousand Oaks, CA: Sage.

Flannery, D. J., Hussey, D. L., Biebelhausen, L., and Wester, K. L. (2003). "Crime, Delinquency, and Youth Gangs." In G. R. Adams and M. D. Berzonsky (Eds.), *Blackwell Handbook of Adolescence* (pp. 502–522). Oxford, England: Blackwell Publishing.

Flannery, D. J., Rowe, D. C., and Gulley, B. L. (1993). "Impact of Pubertal Status, Timing, and Age on Adolescent Sexual Experience and Delinquency." *Journal of Adolescent Research,* 8, 21–40.

Flannery, D. J., Singer, M., Williams, L., and Castro, P. (1998). "Adolescent Violence Exposure and Victimization at Home: Coping and Psychological Trauma Symptoms." *International Review of Victimology,* 6, 29–48.

Flavell, J. H. (1992). "Cognitive Development: Past, Present, and Future." *Developmental Psychology,* 28, 998–1005.

Flavell, J. H., Miller, P. A., and Miller, S. A. (1993). *Cognitive Development.* 3rd ed. Englewood Cliffs, NJ: Prentice-Hall.

Fleck, J. R., Fuller, C. C., Malin, S. Z., Miller, D. H., and Acheson, K. R. (Winter 1980). "Father Psychological Absence and Heterosexual Behavior, Personal Adjustment and Sex-Typing in Adolescent Girls." *Adolescence,* 15, 847–860.

Fleming, W. M., and Anderson, S. P. (1986). "Individuation from the Family of Origin and Personal Adjustment in Late Adolescence." *Journal of Marriage and the Family,* 3, 311–315.

Fletcher, A. C., and Jefferies, B. C. (1999). "Parental Mediators of Associations between Perceived Authoritative Parenting and Early Adolescent Substance Use." *Journal of Early Adolescence,* 19, 465–487.

Fletcher, A., Steinberg, L., and Sellers, E. (1999). "Adolescents' Well-Being as a Function of Perceived Interparental Consistency." *Journal of Marriage and the Family,* 61, 599–610.

Flewelling, R. L., and Bauman, K. E. (1990). "Family Structure as a Predictor of Initial Substance Use and Sexual Intercourse in Early Adolescence." *Journal of Marriage and the Family,* 52, 171–181.

Flint, L. (1992). "Adolescent Parental Affinity-Seeking: Age- and Gender-Mediated Strategy Use." *Adolescence,* 27, 417–434.

Florsheim, P., Moore, D., Zollinger, L., MacDonald, J., and Sumida, E. (1999). "The Transition to Parenthood among Adolescent Fathers and Their Partners: Does Antisocial Behavior Predict Problems in Parenting?" *Applied Developmental Science,* 3, 178–191.

Flug, G. (1991). "Dangerous Toys: Hot N' Nasty." *Hit Parader,* 326, 34.

Flynn, T. M., and Beasley, J. (Winter 1980). "An Experimental Study of the Effects of Competition on the Self-Concept." *Adolescence,* 15, 799–806.

Folkenberg, J. (March 1984). "Bulimia: Not for Women Only." *Psychology Today,* 18, 10.

Foltz, C., Overton, W. F., and Ricco, R. B. (1995). "Proof Construction: Adolescent Development from Inductive to Deductive Problem-Solving

Strategies." *Journal of Experimental Child Psychology,* 59, 179–195.

Ford, D. Y. (1992). "Self-Perceptions of Underachievement and Support for the Achievement Ideology among Early Adolescent African Americans." *Journal of Early Adolescence,* 12, 228–252.

Ford, M. E., Wentzel, K. R., Wood, D., Stevens, E., and Siesfeld, G. A. (1989). "Process Associated with Integrated Social Competence: Emotional and Contextual Influences on Adolescent Social Responsibility." *Journal of Adolescent Research,* 4, 405–425.

Fordham, S. (1996). *Blacked Out: Dilemmas of Race, Identity, and Success at Capital High.* Chicago: The University of Chicago Press.

Fornari, V., and Dancyger, I. F. (2003). "Psychosexual Development and Eating Disorders." *Adolescent Medicine,* 14, 61–75.

Forrest, J. D., and Singh, S. (1990). "The Sexual Reproductive Behavior of American Women, 1982–1988." *Family Planning Perspectives,* 22, 206–214.

Forrest, L., and Mikolaitis, N. (1986). "The Relationship Component of Identity: An Expansion of Career Development Theory." *The Career Development Quarterly,* 35, 76–88.

Forste, R., and Tanfer, K. (1996). "Sexual Exclusivity among Dating, Cohabiting, and Married Women." *Journal of Marriage and the Family,* 58, 33–47.

Fouad, N. A., and Byars-Winston, M. (2005). "Cultural Context of Career Choice: Meta-Analysis of Race/Ethnicity Differences." *Career Development Quarterly,* 53, 223–233.

Fowler, B. A. (1989). "The Relationship of Body Image Perception and Weight Status to Recent Change in Weight Status of the Adolescent Female." *Adolescence,* 95, 557–568.

Fox, G. L., and Kelly, R. F. (1995). "Determinants of Child Custody Arrangements at Divorce." *Journal of Marriage and the Family,* 57, 693–708.

Fox, J. A., and Zawitz, M. W. (2006). *Homicide Trends in the United States.* Bureau of Justice Statistics. Retrieved from http://www.ojp.usdoj.gov/bjs/homicide/homtrnd.htm#contents.

Fox, S., and Madden, M. (2006). *Generations Online.* Data Memo. Washington, DC: Pew Internet and American Life Project.

Frank, D., and Williams, T. (1999). Attitudes about Menstruation among Fifth-, Sixth-, and Seventh-Grade Pre- and Post-Menarcheal Girls." *Journal of School Nursing,* 15, 25–31.

Fraser, K. (1994). *Ethnic Differences in Adolescents' Possible Selves: The Role of Ethnic Identity in Shaping Self-Concepts.* Paper presented at the meeting of the Society for Research on Adolescents, San Diego.

Frazao, E. (1999). "The High Costs of Poor Eating Patterns in the United States." In E. Frazao (Ed.), *America's Eating Habits: Changes and Consequences* (pp. 5–32). Washington, DC: U.S. Department of Agriculture.

Freedle, R. O. (2003). "Correcting the SAT's Ethnic and Social-Class Bias: A Method for Reestimating SAT Scores." *Harvard Educational Review,* 73, 1–43.

Freeman, C. (1998). "Drug Treatment for Bulimia Nervosa." *Neuropsychobiology,* 37, 72–79.

Freeman, D. (1983). *Margaret Mead and Samoa: The Making and Unmaking of an Anthropological Myth.* Cambridge, MA: Harvard University Press.

Freeman, S. F. N., and Alkin, M. C. (2000). "Academic and Social Attainments of Children with Mental Retardation in General Education and Special Education Settings." *Remedial and Special Education,* 21, 3–18.

French, S. A., and Perry, C. L. (1996). "Smoking among Adolescent Girls: Prevalence and Etiology." *Journal of the American Medical Women's Association,* 51, 25–28.

Freud, A. (1946). *The Ego and the Mechanism of Defence.* New York: International Universities Press.

Freud, A. (1958). *Psychoanalytic Study of the Child.* New York: International Universities Press.

Freud, P. A. (1995). "Prenatal Exposure to Marijuana and Tobacco during Infancy, Early and Middle Childhood: Effects and an Attempt at Synthesis." *Archives of Toxicology,* Supplement 17, 233–260.

Freud, S. A. (1925). "Three Contributions to the Sexual Theory." *Nervous and Mental Disease Monograph Series,* No. 7.

Freud, S. A. (1953a). *A General Introduction to Psychoanalysis.* Translated by Joan Riviere. New York: Permabooks.

Freud, S. A. (1953b). *Three Essays on the Theory of Sexuality,* vol. 7. London: Hogarth Press.

Friedman, I. A., and Mann, L. (1993). "Coping Patterns in Adolescent Decision Making: An Israeli-Australian Comparison." *Journal of Adolescence,* 16, 187–199.

Friedman, J., and Rich, A. (1991, 1992). *Run to You.* PSO Ltd., Music by Candlelight, and Music Corporation of America.

Frijns, T., Finkenauer, C., Vermulst, A. A., and Engels, C. M. E. (2005). "Keeping Secrets from Parents: Longitudinal Associations of Secrecy in Adolescence." *Journal of Youth and Adolescence,* 34, 137–148.

Froman, R. D., and Owen, S. V. (1991). "High School Student's Perceived Self-Efficacy in Physical and Mental Health." *Journal of Adolescent Research,* 6, 181–196.

Frost, J. J., and Forrest, J. D. (1995). "Understanding the Impact of Effective Teenage Pregnancy Prevention Programs. *Family Planning Perspectives,* 27, 188–195.

Frost, J., and McKelvie, S. (2004). "Self-Esteem and Body Satisfaction in Male and Female Elementary School, High School, and University Students." *Sex Roles,* 51, 45–54.

Fry, A. F., and Hale, S. (1996). "Processing Speed, Working Memory, and Fluid Intelligence: Evidence for a Developmental Cascade." *Psychological Science,* 7, 237–241.

Fu, V. R., Hinkle, D. E., Shoffner, S., et al. (Winter 1984). "Maternal Dependency and Childbearing Attitudes among Mothers of Adolescent Females." *Adolescence,* 19, 795–804.

Fuhrman, W., and Buhrmester, D. (1992). "Age and Sex Differences in Perceptions of Networks of Personal Relationships." *Child Development,* 63, 103–115.

Fuligni, A. J. (1998). "Authority, Autonomy, and Parent-Adolescent Conflict and Cohesion: A Study of Adolescents from Mexican, Chinese, Filipino, and European Backgrounds." *Developmental Psychology,* 34, 782–792.

Fuligni, A. J., and Eccles, J. S. (1993). "Perceived Parent-Child Relationships in Early Adolescents' Orientation toward Peers." *Developmental Psychology,* 29, 622–632.

Fuligni, A. J., and Stevenson, H. W. (1995). "Time Use and Mathematics Achievement among American, Chinese, and Japanese High School Students." *Child Development,* 66, 830–842.

Fuligni, A. J., Eccles, J. S., and Barber, B. L. (1995). "The Long-Term Effects of Seventh-Grade Ability Grouping in Mathematics." *Journal of Early Adolescence,* 15, 58–89.

Fuller, J. R., and LaFountain, M. J. (1987). "Performance-Enhancing Drugs in Sport: A Different Form of Drug Abuse." *Adolescence,* 22, 969–976.

Funk, J. B. (2000). *The Impact of Interactive Violence on Children.* U.S. Senate Committee on Commerce, Science, and Transportation hearing of "The Impact of Interactive Violence on Children." Retrieved from http://www.utoledo.edu/psychology/funktestimony.html.

Furby, L., Ochs, L. M., and Thomas, C. W. (1997). "Sexually Transmitted Disease Prevention: Adolescents' Perceptions of Possible Side Effects." *Adolescence,* 32, 781–810.

Furman, W., and Shaffer, L. (2003). "The Role of Romantic Relationships in Adolescent Development." In P. Florsheim (Ed.), *Adolescent Romantic Relations and Sexual Behavior: Theory, Research, and Practical Implications* (pp. 3–22). Mahwah, NJ: Erlbaum.

Furman, W., Wehner, E. A., and Underwood, S. (1994). *Sexual Behavior, Sexual Communications, and Relationships.* Paper presented at the meeting of the Society for Research on Adolescence, San Diego.

Furrow, J. L., King, P. E., and White, K. (2004). "Religion and Positive Youth Development: Identity, Meaning, and Prosocial Concerns." *Applied Developmental Science,* 8, 17–26.

Furstenberg, Jr., F., Maziarz Geitz, L., Teitler, J. O., and Weiss, C. (1997). "Does Condom Availability Make a Difference? An Evaluation of Philadelphia's Health Resource Centers." *Family Planning Perspectives,* 29, 123–127.

Fussell, E. (2002). Youth in Aging Societies. In J. T. Mortimer and R. W. Larson (Eds.), *The Changing Adolescent Experience: Societal Trends and the Transition to Adulthood* (pp. 18–51). Cambridge, England: Cambridge University Press.

Gainor, K. A., and Forrest, L. (1991). "African American Women's Self-Concept: Implications for Career Decisions and Career Counseling." *The Career Development Quarterly,* 39, 261–272.

Galambos, N. C., and Silbereisen, R. K. (1987). "Income Change, Parental Life Outlook, and Adolescent Expectations for Job Success." *Journal of Marriage and the Family,* 49, 141–149.

Galambos, N. L., and Vitunski, E. T. (2000). *Fun, Freedom and Responsibility: Adolescents' Expectations for Their Futures.* Paper presented at the Eighth Biennial Meeting of the Society for Research on Adolescence, Chicago, IL.

Galambos, N. L., Barker, E. V., and Tilton-Weaver, L. C. (2003). "Canadian Adolescents' Implicit Theories of Immaturity: What Does 'Childish' Mean?" In J. Arnett and N. Galambos (Eds.), *New Directions for Child and Adolescent Development: Exploring Cultural Conceptions for the Transition to Adulthood* (pp. 77–89). San Francisco: Jossey-Bass.

Galambos, N. L., Kolaric, G. C., Sears, H. A., and Maggs, J. L. (1999). "Adolescents; Subjective Age: An Indicator of Perceived Maturity." *Journal of Research on Adolescence,* 9, 309–337.

Galambos, N. L., Sears, H. A., Almeida, D. M., and Kolaric, G. C. (1995). "Parents' Work Overload and Problem Behavior in Young Adolescents." *Journal of Research on Adolescence,* 5, 201–223.

Galbo, J. J. (Summer 1983). "Adolescent's Perceptions of Significant Adults." *Adolescence,* 18, 417–427.

Galbo, J. J. (Winter 1984). "Adolescent's Perceptions of Significant Adults: A Review of the Literature." *Adolescence,* 19, 951–970.

Galbo, J. J., and Demetrulias, D. M. (1996). "Recollections of Nonparental Significant Adults during Childhood and Adolescence." *Youth and Society,* 27, 403–420.

Gallagher, J. (1997). "Blacks and Gays: The Unexpected Divide." *The Advocate,* December 9, 37–41.

Gallant, S. J., and Derry, P. S. (1995). "Menarche, Menstruation, and Menopause: Psychosocial Research and Future Directions." In A. L. Stanton and S. J. Gallant (Eds.), *The Psychology of Women's Health: Progress and Challenges in Research and Application* (pp. 199–259). Washington, DC: American Psychological Association.

Gallup, G., Jr., and Lindsay, D. M. (1999). *Surveying the Religious Landscape: Trends in U.S. Beliefs.* Harrisburg, PA: Morehouse.

Galotti, K., M., Komatsu, L. K., and Voelz, S. (1997). "Children's Differential Performance on Deductive and Inductive Syllogisms." *Developmental Psychology,* 33, 70–78.

Gambrill, E. (1996). "Loneliness, Social Isolation, and Social Anxiety." In M. Mattaini and B. Thyer (Eds.), *Finding Solutions to Social Problems: Behavioral Strategies for Change* (pp. 345–371). Washington, DC: American Psychological Association.

Gameron, A. (1992). "Religious Participation and Family Values among American Jewish Youth." *Contemporary Jewry,* 13, 44–59.

Gamoran, A., and Nystrand, M. (1991). "Background and Instructional Effects on Achievement in Eighth-Grade English and Social Studies." *Journal of Research on Adolescence,* 1, 277–300.

Ganong, L. H., and Coleman, M. (1994). *Remarried Family Relationships.* Thousand Oaks, CA: Sage.

Ganong, L. H., Coleman, M., Thompson, A., and Goodwin-Watkins, C. (1996). "African American and European American College Students' Expectations for Self and for Future Partners." *Journal of Family Issues,* 17, 758–775.

Gantman, C. A. (December 1978). "Family Interaction Patterns among Families with Normal, Disturbed, and Drug-Abusing Adolescents." *Journal of Youth and Adolescence,* 7, 429–440.

Gard, M. C. E., and Freeman, C. P. (1996). "The Dismantling of a Myth: A Review of Eating Disorders and Socioeconomic Status." *International Journal of Eating Disorders,* 20, 1–12.

Gardner, H. (1993). *Frames of Mind: The Theory of Multiple Intelligences.* 10th ed. New York: Basic Books.

Gardner, H. (1999). *Intelligence Reframed: Multiple Intelligences for the Twenty-First Century.* New York: Basic Books.

Gardner, R. M., Friedman, B. N., and Jackson, N. A. (1999). "Hispanic and White Children's Judgments of Perceived and Ideal Body Size in Self and Others." *Psychological Record,* 49, 555–564.

Garland, A. F., and Zigler, E. (1993). "Adolescent Suicide Prevention: Current Research and Social Policy Implications." *American Psychologist,* 48, 169–182.

Garland, A. F., and Zigler, E. (1999). "Emotional and Behavioral Problems among Highly Intellectually Gifted Youth." *Roeper Review,* 22, 41–44.

Garnefski, N., and Diekstra, R. (1997). "Child Sexual Abuse and Emotional and Behavioral Problems in Adolescence: Gender Differences." *Journal of the Academy of Child and Adolescent Psychiatry,* 36, 323–329.

Garner, D. M., Rosen, L. W., and Barry, D. (1998). "Eating Disorders among Athletes: Research and Recommendations." *Child and Adolescent Psychiatric Clinics of North America,* 7, 839–857.

Garrett, S. C., and Tidwell, R. (1999). "Differences Between Adolescent Mothers and Nonmothers: An Interview Study." *Adolescence,* 34, 91–105.

Garzarelli, P., Everhart, B., and Lester, D. (1993). "Self-Concept and Academic Performance in Gifted and Academically Weak Students." *Adolescence,* 28, 235–237.

Gates, G. J., and Sonenstein, F. L. (2000). "Heterosexual Genital Sexual Activity among Adolescent Males: 1988–1995." *Family Planning Perspectives,* 32, 295–304.

Gati, I. (1998). "Using Career-Related Aspects to Elicit Preference and Characterize Occupations for a Better Person-Environment Fit." *Journal of Vocational Behavior,* 2, 341–356.

Gati, I., Fassa, N., and Houminer, D. (1995). "Applying Decision Theory to Career Counseling Practice: The Sequential Elimination Approach." *Career Development Quarterly,* 43, 211–220.

Gavazzi, S. M., and Sabatelli, R. M. (1990). "Family System Dynamics, the Individuation Process and Psychosocial Development." *Journal of Adolescent Research,* 5, 500–519.

Ge, X., Conger, D., and Elder, G. H. (1996). "Coming of Age Too Early: Pubertal Influences on Girls' Vulnerability to Psychological Distress." *Child Development,* 67, 386–340.

Ge, X., Conger, R. D., and Elder, G. H., Jr. (2001). "The Relation between Puberty and Psychological Distress in Adolescent Boys." *Journal of Research on Adolescence,* 11, 49–70.

Gecas, V., and Pasley, K. (December 1983). "Birth Order and Self-Concept in Adolescence." *Journal of Youth and Adolescence,* 12, 521–533.

Gecas, V., and Seff, M. A. (1990). "Families and Adolescents: A Review of the 1980s." *Journal of Marriage and the Family,* 52, 941–958.

Gentile, D. A., Lynch, P. J., Linder, J. R., and Walsh, J. A. (2004). "The Effects of Violent Video Game Habits on Adolescent Hostility, Aggressive Behaviors, and School Performance." *Journal of Adolescence,* 27, 5–22.

George, T. P., and Hartman, D. P. (1996). "Friendship Networks of Unpopular, Average, and Popular Children." *Child Development,* 67, 2301–2316.

Gerbner, G. (1992). "Society's Storyteller: How Television Creates the Myths by Which We Live." *Media and Values,* 59/60, 8–9.

Gerrard, M., Gibbons, F. X., Benthin, A. C., and Hessling, R. M. (1996). "A Longitudinal Study of the Reciprocal Nature of Risk Behaviors and Cognitions in Adolescents: What You Do Shapes What You Think, and Vice Versa." *Health Psychology,* 15, 344–354.

Gertner, J. M. (1986). "Short Stature in Children." *Medical Aspects of Human Sexuality,* 20, 36–42.

Gesell, Arnold, and Ames, L. B. (1956). *Youth: The Years from Ten to Sixteen.* New York: Harper and Row.

Gfellner, B. M., and Hundelby, J. D. (1994). *Patterns of Drug Use and Social Activities among Native Indians and White Adolescents.* Paper presented at the Society for Research on Adolescence, San Diego.

Ghang, J., and Jin, S. (1996). "Determinants of Suicide Ideation: A Comparison of Chinese and American College Students." *Adolescence,* 31, 451–467.

Gibbons, J. L., Brusi-Figueroa, R., and Fisher, S. L. (1997). "Gender-Related Ideals of Puerto Rican Adolescents: Gender and School Content." *Journal of Early Adolescence,* 17, 349–370.

Gibbs, J. C. (2003). *Moral Development and Reality: Beyond the Theories of Kohlberg and Hoffman.* Thousand Oaks, CA: Sage.

Gibbs, J. C., Basinger, K. S., and Fuller, D. (1992). *Moral Maturity: Measuring the Development of Sociomoral Reflection.* Hillsdale, NJ: Erlbaum.

Gibbs, J. R., and Hines, A. M. (1989). "Factors Related to Sex Differences in Suicidal Behavior among Black Youth: Implications for Intervention and Research." *Journal of Adolescent Research,* 4, 152–172.

Gibson, J. W., and Kempf, J. (1990). "Attitudinal Predictors of Sexual Activity in Hispanic Adolescent Females." *Journal of Adolescent Research,* 5, 414–430.

Giedd, J. M., Blumenthal, J., Jeffries, N. O., et al. (1999a). "Brain Development during Childhood and Adolescence: A Longitudinal MRI Study." *Nature Neuroscience,* 2, 861–863.

Giedd, J. N., Blumenthal, J., Jeffries, N. O., Rajapakse, J. C., Vaituzis, C., Hung, L., Berry, Y., Tobin, M., Nelson, J., and Castellanos, F. X. (1999b). "Development of the Human Corpus Callosum during Childhood and Adolescence: A Longitudinal MRI Study." *Progress in Neuro-Psychopharmacology and Biological Psychiatry,* 23, 571–588.

Giedd, J. N., Castellanos, F. X., Rajapakse, J. C., Vaituzis, A. C., and Rapaport, J. L. (1997). "Sexual Dimorphism of the Developing Human Brain." *Progress in Neuro-Psychopharmacology and Biological Psychiatry,* 21, 1185–1201.

Gifford, V. D., and Dean, M. M. (1990). "Differences in Extracurricular Activity Participation, Achievement, and Attitudes toward School Between Ninth-Grade Students Attending Junior High School and Those Attending Senior High School." *Adolescence,* 25, 799–802.

Gigy, L., and Kelly, J. (1992). "Reasons for Divorce: Perspectives of Divorcing Men and Women." *Journal of Divorce and Remarriage,* 18, 169–187.

Giles-Sims, J. (1985). "A Longitudinal Study of Battered Children of Battered Women." *Family Relations,* 34, 205–210.

Gilger, J. W., Geary, D. C., and Eisele, L. M. (1991). "Reliability and Validity of Retrospective Self-Reports of the Age of Pubertal Onset Using Twin, Sibling, and College Student Data." *Adolescence,* 26, 41–53.

Gill, R. T. (1992). "For the Sake of the Children." *The Public Interest,* 108, 81–96.

Gilligan, C. (1977). "In a Different Voice: Women's Conceptions of Self and of Morality." *Harvard Educational Review,* 47, 481–517.

Gilligan, C. (1982). *In a Different Voice: Psychological Theory and Women's Development.* Cambridge, MA: Harvard University Press.

Gilligan, C. (1984). "Remapping the Moral Domain in Personality Research and Assessment." Invited address presented to the American Psychological Association Convention, Toronto.

Gilligan, C. (1992). *Joining the Resistance: Girls' Development in Adolescence.* Paper presented at the Symposium on Development and Vulnerability in Close Relationships, Montreal, Quebec.

Gilliland, H. (1995). *Teaching the Native American* (3rd ed.). Dubuque, IA: Kendall/Hall.

Gillmore, M. R., Hawkins, J. D., Day, L. E., and Catalano, R. F. (1992). "Friendship and Deviance: New Evidence of an Old Controversy." *Journal of Early Adolescence,* 12, 80–95.

Gilmartin, B. G. (1985). "Some Family Antecedents on Severe Shyness." *Family Relations,* 34, 429–438.

Ginsburg, S. D., and Orlofsky, J. L. (August 1981). "Ego Identity Status, Ego Development, and Loss of Control in College Women." *Journal of Youth and Adolescence,* 10, 297–307.

Ginzberg, E. (1988). "Toward a Theory of Occupational Choice." *The Career Development Quarterly,* 36, 358–363.

Giordano, P. C., Cernkovich, S. A., and DeMaris, A. (1993). "The Family and Peer Relations of Black Adolescents." *Journal of Marriage and the Family,* 55, 277–287.

Gispert, M., Wheeler, K., Marsh, L., and Davis, M. S. (1985). "Suicidal Adolescents: Factors in Evaluation." *Adolescence,* 20, 753–762.

Gjerde, P. F., and Westenberg, P. M. (1998). "Dysphoric Adolescents as Young Adults: A Prospective Study of the Psychological Sequelae of Depressed Mood in Adolescence." *Journal of Research on Adolescence,* 8, 377–402.

Glass, C. R., and Shea, C. A. (1986). "Cognitive Therapy for Shyness and Social Anxiety." In W. Jones, J. Cheek, and S. Briggs (Eds.), *Shyness: Perspectives on Research and Treatment* (pp. 315–327). New York: Plenum Press.

Glei, D. A. (1999). "Measuring Contraceptive Use Patterns among Teenage and Adult Women." *Family Planning Perspectives,* 31, 73–80.

Glenn, N. D., and Kramer, K. B. (1987). "The Marriages and Divorces of the Children of Divorce." *Journal of Marriage and the Family,* 49, 811–825.

Glodis, K. A., & Blasi, A. (1993). "The Sense of Self and Identity Among Adolescents and Adults." *Journal of Adolescent Research,* 8, 356–380.

Gloria, A. M., and Hird, J. S. (1999). "Influences of Ethnic and Nonethnic Variables on the Career Decision-Making Self-Efficacy of College Students." *Career Development Quarterly,* 48, 157–174.

Gnepp, J., and Chilamkurti, C. (1988). "Childrens' Use of Personality Attributions to Predict Other Peoples' Emotional and Behavioral Reactions." *Child Development,* 59, 743–754.

Goff, J. L. (1990). "Sexual Confusion among Certain College Males." *Adolescence,* 25, 599–614.

Goff, L. (1999). "Don't Miss the Bus!" *American Demographics,* 21, 48–54.

Goff, M., and Ackerman, P. L. (1997). "Personality-Intelligence Relations: Assessment of Typical Intellectual Engagement." *Journal of Educational Psychology,* 84, 537–552.

Goldman, J. A., Rosenzweig, C. M., & Lutter, A. D. (1980). Effect of similarity of ego identity status on interpersonal attraction. *Journal of Youth and Adolescence,* 9, 153–162.

Goldman, S. R., Pellegrino, J. W., Parseghian, P., and Sallis, R. (1982). "Developmental and Individual Differences in Verbal Analogical Reasoning." *Child Development,* 53, 550–559.

Goldscheider, F., and Goldscheider, C. (1999). *The Changing Transition to Adulthood: Leaving and Returning Home.* New York: Berkeley Press.

Goldschmidt, P., and Wang, J. (1999). "When Can School Affect Dropout Behavior? A Longitudinal Multilevel Analysis." *American Educational Research Journal,* 36, 715–738.

Goldstein, J. (1999). *Why We Watch: The Attraction of Violent Entertainment.* New York: Oxford University Press.

Golombok, S., and Tasker, F. (1996). "Do Parents Influence the Sexual Orientation of Their Children? Findings from a Longitudinal Study of Lesbian Families." *Developmental Psychology,* 32, 3–11.

Golub, S. (1992). *Periods: From Menarche to Menopause.* Newbury Park, CA: Sage.

Gonsiorek, J. C. (1988). "Mental Health Issues of Gay and Lesbian Adolescents." *Journal of Adolescent Health Care,* 9, 114–122.

Gonzales, N. A., and Kim, L. S. (1997). "Stress and Coping in an Ethnic Minority Context." In I. N. Sandler and S. A. Wolchik (Eds.), *Handbook of Children's Coping: Linking Theory and Intervention* (pp. 481–511). New York: Wiley.

Goodenow, C. (1993). "Classroom Belonging among Early Adolescent Students: Relationships to Motivation and Achievement." *Journal of Early Adolescence,* 13, 21–43.

Goodenow, C., and Espin, O. M. (1993). "Identity Choices in Immigrant Adolescent Females." *Adolescence,* 28, 173–184.

Goodwin, M. P., and Roscoe, B. (1990). "Sibling Violence and Agonistic Interactions among Middle Adolescents." *Adolescence,* 25, 451–467.

Goossens, L., and Marcoen A. (1999). "Adolescent Loneliness, Self-Reflection, and Identity: From Individual Differences to Developmental Processes." In K. J. Rotenberg and S. Hymel (Eds.), *Loneliness in Childhood and Adolescence* (pp. 225–243). Cambridge, England: Cambridge University Press.

Goossens, L., Seiffge-Krenke, I., and Marcoen, A. (1992). "The Many Faces of Adolescent Egocentrism. Two European Replications." *Journal of Adolescent Research,* 7, 43–48.

Gordon, C. P. (1996). "Adolescent Decision-Making: A Broadly Based Theory and Its Application to the Prevention of Early Pregnancy." *Adolescence,* 31, 561–584.

Gordon, M. (February 1981). "Was Waller Ever Right? The Rating and Dating Complex Reconsidered." *Journal of Marriage and the Family,* 43, 67–76.

Gore, S., Farrell, F., and Gordon, J. (2001). "Sport Involvement as Protection against Depressed Mood." *Journal of Research on Adolescence,* 11, 119–130.

Gottfredson, L. S. (1996). "Gottfredson's Theory of Circumscription and Compromise." In D. Brown and L. Brooks (Eds.), *Career Choice and Development.* 3rd ed. (pp. 179–232). San Francisco: Jossey-Bass.

Gottfredson, M., and Hirshi, T. (1990). A *General Theory of Crime.* Stanford: Stanford University Press.

Gottman, J. M. (1986). "The World of Coordinated Play: Same- and Cross-Sex Friendship in Young Children". In J. M. Gottman and J. G. Parkes (Eds.), *Conversations of Friends: Speculation on Affectional Bonds. Studies in Emotion and Social Interaction* (pp. 139–191). Cambridge: Cambridge University Press.

Gould, M. S. (2001). "Suicide and the Media." *Annals of the New York Academy of Sciences,* 932, 200–221.

Gould, M. S., Fisher, P., Parides, M., Flore, M., and Shaffer, D. (1996). "Psychosocial Risk Factors of Child and Adolescent Completed Suicide." *Archives of General Psychiatry,* 53, 1155–1162.

Gould, M. S., King, R., Greenwald, S., Fisher, P., Schwab-Stone, M., Kramer, R., Flisher, A. J., Goodman, S., Canino, G., and Shaffer, D. (1998). "Psychopathology Associated with Suicidal Ideation and Attempts among Children and Adolescents." *Journal of the American Academy of Child and Adolescent Psychiatry,* 37, 915–923.

Gowensmith, W. N., and Bloom, L. J. (1997). "The Effects of Heavy Metal on Arousal and Anger." *Journal of Music Therapy,* 34, 33–45.

Graber, J. A., Brooks-Gunn, J., and Galen, B. R. (1998). "Betwixt and Between: Sexuality in the Context of Adolescent Transitions." In R. Jessor (Ed.), *New Perspectives of Adolescent Risk Behavior* (pp. 270–316). Cambridge, England: Cambridge University Press.

Graber, J. A., Lewinsohn, P. M., Seeley, J. R., and Brooks-Gunn, J. (1997). "Is Psychopathology Associated with the Timing of Pubertal Development?" *Journal of the American Academy of Child and Adolescent Psychiatry,* 36, 1768–1776.

Graber, J. A., Petersen, A., and Brooks-Gunn, J. (1996). "Pubertal Processes: Methods, Measures, and Models." In J. A. Graber, J. Brooks-Gunn, and A. Petersen (Eds.), *Transitions through Adolescence: Interpersonal Domains and Context* (pp. 23–53). Mahwah, NJ: Erlbaum.

Graff, H. J. (1995). *Conflicting Paths: Growing Up in America.* Cambridge, MA: Harvard University Press.

Grant, B. F., and Dawson, D. A. (1997). "Age at Onset of Alcohol Use and Its Association with DSM-IV Alcohol Abuse and Dependence: Results from the National Longitudinal Alcohol Epidemiological Survey." *Journal of Substance Abuse,* 9, 103–110.

Grant, C. L., and Fodor, I. G. (April 1984). "Body Image and Eating Disorders: A New Role for School Psychologists in Screening and Prevention." Mimeographed paper. New York University, School of Education, Health, Nursing, and Arts Profession.

Grant, C. L., and Fodor, I. G. (1986). "Adolescent Attitudes toward Body Image and Anorexic Behavior." *Adolescence,* 82, 269–281.

Gray, M. R., and Steinberg, L. (1999). "Adolescent Romance and the Parent-Child Relationship: A Contextual Perspective." In W. Furman, B. B. Brown, and C. Feiring (Eds.), *The Development of Romantic Relationships in Adolescence* (pp. 235–265). Cambridge, England: Cambridge University Press.

Green, J. J., Bush, D., and Sahn, J. (December 1980). "The Effects of College on Students' Partisanship: A Research Note." *Journal of Youth and Adolescence,* 9, 547–552.

Green, R., Mandel, J. B., Hotvedt, M. E., Gary, J., and Smith, L. (1986). "Lesbian Mothers and Their Children: A Comparison with Solo Parent Heterosexual Mothers and Their Children." *Archives of Sexual Behavior,* 15, 167–184.

Greenberg, E. F. (1983). "An Empirical Determination of the Competence of Children to Participate in Child Custody Decision-Making." Doctoral dissertation, University of Illinois. *Dissertation Abstracts International,* 45, (0–1) 350–B.

Greendlinger, V., and Byrne, D. (1987). "Coercive Sexual Fantasies of College Men as Predictors of Self-Reported Likelihood of Rape and Overt Sexual Aggression." *Journal of Sex Research,* 23, 1–11.

Greene, A. L. (1990). "Age and Gender Differences in Adolescents' Preference for Parental Advice: Mum's the Word." *Journal of Adolescent Research,* 5, 396–413.

Greene, A. L., and Reed, E. (1992). "Social Context Differences in the Relation Between Self-Esteem and Self-Concept during Late Adolescence." *Journal of Adolescent Research,* 2, 266–282.

Greene, B., and Land, S. M. (2000). "A Qualitative Analysis of Scaffolding Use in a Resource-Based Learning Environment Involving the World Wide Web." *Journal of Educational Computing Research,* 23, 151–179.

Greene, M. B. (2006). "Bullying in Schools: A Plea for a Measure of Human Rights." *Journal of Social Issues,* 62, 63–79.

Greene, N. B., and Esselstyn, T. C. (1972). "The Beyond Control Girl." *Juvenile Justice,* 23, 13–19.

Greeno, C. G., and Maccoby, E. E. (1986). "How Different Is the 'Different Voice'?" *Signs,* 11, 310–312.

Gregory, L. W. (1995). "The 'Turn Around' Process: Factors Influencing the School Success of Urban Youth." *Journal of Adolescent Research,* 10, 136–154.

Grief, G. (1985). "Single Fathers Rearing Children." *Journal of Marriage and the Family,* 47, 185–191.

Grieser, M., Vu, M. B., Bedimo-Rung, A. L., Neumark-Sztainer, D., Moody, J., Young, D. R., and Moe, S. G. (2006). "Physical Activity Attitudes, Preferences, and Practices in African American, Hispanic, and Caucasian Girls." *Health Education & Behavior,* 33, 40–51.

Griffin, N., Chassin, L., and Young, R. D. (Spring 1981). "Measurement of Global Self-Concept versus Multiple Role-Specific Self-Concept in Adolescents." *Adolescence,* 16, 49–56.

Griffin, R. S., and Gross, M. (2004). "Childhood Bullying: Current Empirical Findings and Future Directions for Research." *Aggression and Violent Behavior,* 9, 379–400.

Griffiths, M. (1997). "Computer Game Playing in Early Adolescence." *Youth and Society,* 29, 223–237.

Grilo, C. M., and Pogue-Geile, M. F. (1991). "The Nature of Environmental Influences on Weight and Obesity: A Behavior Genetic Analysis." *Psychological Bulletin,* 110, 520–537.

Grob, M. C., Klein, A. A., and Eisen, S. V. (April 1983). "The Role of the High School Professional in Identifying and Managing Adolescent Suicidal Behavior." *Journal of Youth and Adolescence,* 12, 163–173.

Grohølt, B., Ekeberg,Ø., Wichstrøm, L., and Haldorson, T. (2000). Young Suicide Attempters: A Comparison between a Clinical and an Epidemiological Sample." *Journal of the American Academy of Child and Adolescent Psychiatry,* 39, 868–875.

Grossman, M., Chaloupka, F. J., Saffer, H., and Laixuthai, A. (1994). "Effects of Alcohol Price Policy on Youth: A Summary of Economic Research." *Journal of Research on Adolescence,* 4, 347–364.

Grotevant, H. D. (1987). "Toward a Process Model of Identity Formation." *Journal of Adolescent Research,* 2, 203–222.

Grotevant, H. D. (1992). "Assigned and Chosen Identity Components: A Process Perspective on Their Integration." In G. R. Adams, T. P. Gullotta, and R. Montemayor (Eds.), *Adolescent Identity Formation: Advances in Adolescent Development* (pp. 73–90). Newbury Park, CA: Sage.

Grotevant, H. D. (1997). "Family Processes, Identity Development, and Behavioral Outcomes for Adopted Adolescents." *Journal of Adolescent Research,* 12, 139–161.

Grotevant, H. D., and Cooper, C. R. (1985). "Patterns of Interaction in Family Relationships and the Development of Identity Exploration in Adolescence." *Child Development,* 56, 415–428.

Grotevant, H. D., and Cooper, C. R. (1986). "Individuation in Family Relationships." *Human Development,* 29, 82–100.

Grotevant, H. D., Ross, N. M., Marchel, M. A., and McRoy, R. G. (1999). "Adaptive Behavior in Adopted Children: Predictors from Early Risk Collaboration in Relationships within the Adoptive Kinship Network, and Openness Arrangements." *Journal of Adolescent Research,* 14, 231–247.

Grotevant, H. D., Thorbecke, W., and Meyer, M. L. (February 1982). "An Extension of Marcia's Identity Status Interview into the Interpersonal Domain." *Journal of Youth and Adolescence,* 11, 33–47.

Grover, K. M., Russell, C. S., Schumm, W. R., and Paff-Bergen, L. A. (1985). "Mate Selection Processes and Marital Satisfaction." *Family Relations,* 34, 383–386.

Grube, J. W. (1995). "Television Alcohol Portrayals, Alcohol Advertising and Alcohol Expectancies among Children and Adolescents." In S. E. Martin and P. Mail (Eds.), *Effects of the Mass Media on the Use and Abuse of Alcohol* (pp. 105–121). Bethesda, MD: National Institute on Alcohol Abuse and Alcoholism.

Grunbaum, J. A., Kann, L., Kinchen, S. A., Williams, B., Ross, J. G., and Lowry, R. (2002). "Youth Risk Behavior Surveillance—United States, 2001." *Morbidity and Mortality Weekly Report,* 51, 1–62.

Grunseit, A., Kippax, S., Aggleton, P., Baldo, M., and Slutkin, G. (1997). "Sexuality Education and Young People's Sexual Behavior: A Review of Studies." *Journal of Adolescent Research,* 12, 421–453.

Gruskin, E. (1994). *A Review of Research on Self-Identified Gay, Lesbian, and Bi-Sexual Youths from 1970–1993.* Paper presented at the meeting of the Society for Research on Adolescents, San Diego.

Guagliardo, M. F., Huang, Z., and D'Angelo, L. J. (1999). "Fathering Pregnancies: Marking Health-Risk Behaviors in Urban Adolescents." *Journal of Adolescent Health,* 24, 10–15.

Guidubaldi, J., and Perry, J. D. (1985). "Divorce and Mental Health Sequelae for Children. A Two-Year Follow Up of a Nationwide Sample." *Journal of the American Academy of Child Psychiatry,* 24, 531–537.

Guiney, K. M., and Furlong, N. E. (1999). "Correlates of Body Satisfaction and Self-Concept in Third- and Sixth-Graders." *Current Psychology: Developmental, Learning, Personality, and Social,* 18, 353–367.

Gullotta, T. P. (2003). "Leaving Home: The Runaway and the Forgotten Throwaway." In G. R. Adams and M. D. Berzonsky (Eds.), *Blackwell Handbook of Adolescence* (pp. 494–501). Oxford, England: Blackwell Publishing.

Gutman, I. M., Sameroff, A. J., and Cole, R. (2003). "Academic Growth Curve Trajectories from 1st Grade to 12th Grade: Effects of Multiple Social Risk Factors and Preschool Child Factors." *Developmental Psychology,* 39, 777–790.

Guttman, J., and Lazar, A. (1998). "Mother's or Father's Custody: Does It Matter for Social Adjustment?" *Educational Psychology,* 18, 225–234.

Guzmán, B. (2001). The Hispanic population. *Census 2000 Brief. Publication No. C2KBR/01-3.* Washington D.C.: U.S. Bureau of the Census.

Hafen, B. Q., and Frandsen, K. J. (1986). *Youth Suicide: Depression and Loneliness.* Provo, UT: Behavioral Health Associates.

Hafez, E. S. E. (Ed.), (1980). *Human Reproduction: Conception and Contraception.* Hagerstown, MD: Harper and Row.

Hahn-Smith, A. M., and Smith, J. E. (2001). "The Positive Influence of Maternal Identification on Body Image, Eating Attitudes, and Self-Esteem of Hispanic and Anglo Girls." *International Journal of Eating Disorders,* 29, 429–440.

Hairston, K., Gale, T., and Davis, J. (1991). *Running Back to You.* Zomba Enterprises, Inc./Hiss 'N' Tell Music/ Gale Warnings Music/Mideb Music.

Hajat, A., Lucas, J. B., and Kington, R. (2000). "Health Outcomes among Hispanic Subgroups: Data from the National Health Interview Survey, 1992–1995." National Center for Health Statistics, *Advance Data,* 310.

Hajcak, F., and Garwood, P. (1988). "Quick-Fix Sex: Pseudosexuality in Adolescents." *Adolescence,* 23, 755–760.

Hale, S. (1990). "A Global, Developmental Trend in Cognitive Processing Speed." *Child Development,* 61, 653–663.

Halebsky, M. A. (1987). "Adolescent Alcohol and Substance Abuse: Parent and Peer Effects." *Adolescence,* 22, 961–967.

Halgin, R. P., and Leahy, P. M. (1989). "Understanding and Treating Perfectionistic College Students." *Journal of Counseling and Development,* 68, 222–225.

Hall, G. S. (1904). *Adolescence: Its Psychology and Its Relation to Physiology, Anthropology, Sociology, Sex, Crime, Religion and Education.* 2 vols. New York: D. Appleton.

Hall, G. S., and Lindzay, G. (1970). *Theories of Personality.* 2nd ed. New York: J. Wiley.

Hallinan, M. T. (1991). "School Differences in Tracking Structures and Track Assignments." *Journal of Research on Adolescence,* 1, 251–275.

Hallinan, M. T., and Kubitschek, N. (1999). "Curriculum Differentiation and High School Achievement." *Social Psychology of Education,* 3, 41–62.

Halpern, C. T., and Udry, J. R. (1992). "Variation in Adolescent Hormone Measures and Implications for Behavioral Research." *Journal of Research on Adolescence,* 2, 103–122.

Halpern, C. T., Udry, J. R., Campbell, B., Suchrindran, C., and Mason, G. A. (1994). "Testosterone and Religiosity as Predictors of Sexual Attitudes and Activity among Adolescent Males: A Biosocial Model." *Journal of Biosocial Science,* 26, 217–234.

Halpern-Felsher, B. L., and Cauffman, E. (2001). "Costs and Benefits of a Decision: Decision-Making Competence in Adolescents and Adults." *Journal of Applied Developmental Psychology,* 22, 257–274.

Hamachek, D. E. (1985). "The Self's Development and Ego Growth: Conceptual Analysis and Implications for Counselors." *Journal of Counseling and Development,* 64, 136–142.

Hamilton, B. E., Ventura, S. J., Martin, J. A., and Sutton, P. D. (2005). *Preliminary Births for 2004.* Hyattsville, MD: National Center for Health Statistics.

Hamilton, J. A. (1983). "Development of Interest and Enjoyment in Adolescence: I. Attentional Capacities." *Journal of Youth and Adolescence,* 12, 355–362.

Hamilton, S. F., and Fenzel, L. M. (1988). "The Impact of Volunteer Experience on Adolescent Social Development: Evidence of Program Effects." *Journal of Adolescent Research,* 3, 65–80.

Hammer, H., Finkelhor, D. & Sedlak, A. J. (2002). *Runaway/Thrownaway children: National estimates and characteristics.* Bulletin of the Office of Juvenile Justice and Delinquency Prevention. Washington, D.C.: U.S. Department of Justice.

Hampton, T. (2004). "Suicide Caution Stamped on Antidepressants." *Journal of the American Medical Association,* 291, 2060–2061.

Hanson, S. L. (1992). "Involving Families and Programs for Pregnant Teens: Consequences for Teens and Their Families." *Family Relations,* 41, 303–311.

Hanson, T. L., McLanahan, S. S., and Thomson, E. (1996). "Double Jeopardy: Parental Conflict and Stepfamily Outcomes for Children." *Journal of Marriage and the Family,* 58, 141–154.

Hardcastle, G. W. (1998). "Joint Custody: A Family Court Judge's Perspective." *Family Law Quarterly,* 32, 201–219.

Harding, C. G., and Snyder, K. (1991). "Tom, Huck, and Oliver Stone as Advocates in Kohlberg's Just Community: Theory-Based Strategies for Moral Education." *Adolescence,* 26, 319–329.

Hardy, S. A., and Carlo, G. (2005). "Religiosity and Prosocial Behaviors in Adolescence: The Mediating Influence of Prosocial Values." *Journal of Moral Education,* 34, 231–49.

Harkness, S., and Super, C. (1985). "The Cultural Context of Gender Segregation in Children's Peer Groups." *Child Development,* 56, 219–224.

Harnishfeger, K. (1995). "The Development of Cognitive Inhibition: Theories, Definition, and Research Evidence." In F. Dempster and C. Brainard (Eds.), *Interference and Inhibition in Cognition* (pp. 175–204). San Diego: Academic Press.

Harper, J. F., and Marshall, E. (1991). "Adolescents' Problems and the Relationship to Self-Esteem." *Adolescence,* 26, 799–808.

Harrington, R., Rutter, M., and Fombonne, E. (1996). "Developmental Pathways in Depression: Multiple Meanings, Antecedents, and End Points." *Developmental Psychopathology,* 8, 601–616.

Harris Interactive. (2004). *College Students Tote $122 Billion in Spending Power Back to Campus This Year.* Press release. Retrieved from http://www.harrisinteractive.com/news/allnewsbydate.asp?NewsID=835.

Harris, K. M., and Marmer, J. K. (1996). "Poverty, Paternal Involvement, and Adolescent Well-Being." *Journal of Family Issues,* 17, 614–640.

Harris, L., and Associates. (1988). *Sexual Material on American Network Television During the 1987–1988 Season.* New York: Planned Parenthood Federation of America.

Harris, L., and Associates. (1995). *Between Hope and Fear: Teens Speak Out on Crime and the Community.* New York: Author.

Harrison, K. S., and Cantor, J. (1999). "Tales from the Screen: Enduring Fright Reactions to Scary Media." *Media Psychology,* 1, 97–116.

Hart, D., Atkins, R., and Fegley, S. (2003). "Personality and Development in Childhood: A Person-Centered Approach." *Monographs for the Society for Research in Child Development,* 68, vii–109.

Hart, D., Atkins, R., and Ford, D. (1998). "Urban America as a Context for the Development of Moral Identity in Adolescence." *Journal of Social Issues,* 54, 513–530.

Hart, J. L., & Helms, L. (2003). "Factors of Parricide: Allowance of the Use of Battered Child Syndrome as a Defense." *Aggression and Violent Behavior,* 8(6), 671–683.

Hart, S., Robinson, S. E. K., and Kerr, B. (August, 2001). *Adolescent At-Risk Behaviors: Effects of Parents, Older Siblings, and Peers.* Paper presented at the Annual convention of the American Psychological Association, San Francisco.

Harter, S. (1990). "Self and Identity Development." In S. S. Feldman and G. R. Elliott (Eds.), *At the Thresholds: The Developing Adolescent.* Cambridge, MA: Harvard University Press.

Harter, S., Stocker, T., and Robinson, N. S. (1996). "The Perceived Directionality of the Link between Approval and Self-Worth: Reliabilities of a Looking Glass Self-Orientation among Young Adolescents." *Journal of Research on Adolescence,* 6, 285–308.

Hartman, A., and Laird, J. (1990). "Family Treatment after Adoption: Common Themes." In D. Brodzinsky and M. Schechter (Eds.), *The Psychology of Adoption* (pp. 221–239). New York: Oxford University Press.

Hartos, J. L., and Power, T. G. (1997). "Mothers' Awareness of Their Early Adolescents' Stressors: Relation between Awareness and Adolescent Adjustment." *Journal of Early Adolescence,* 17, 371–389.

Hartup, W. (1983). "Peer Relations." In E. M. Hetherington (Ed.), *Handbook of Child Psychology.* Vol. 4, *Socialization, Personality, and Social Development.* New York: Wiley.

Hartup, W. W., and Stevens, N. (1999). "Friendships and Adaptation across the Lifespan." *Current Directions in Psychological Science,* 8, 76–79.

Harvey, S. M., and Spigner, C. (1995). "Factors Associated with Sexual Behavior among Adolescents: A Multivariate Analysis." *Adolescence,* 30, 253–264.

Harwood, J., Hewstone, M., Paolini, S., and Voci, A. (2005). "Grandparent-Grandchild Contact and Attitudes towards Older Adults: Moderator and Mediator Effects." *Personality and Social Psychology Journal,* 31, 393–406.

Hassler, M. (1992). "The Critical Teens—Musical Capacities Change in Adolescence." *European Journal for High Ability,* 3, 89–98.

Hatfield, E., and Rapson, R. L. (1996). *Love and Sex: Cross-Cultural Perspectives.* Boston: Allyn and Bacon.

Hauck, W. E., and Loughead, M. (1985). "Adolescent Self-Monitoring." *Adolescence,* 20, 567–574.

Hauck, W. E., Martens, M., and Wetzel, M. (1986). "Shyness, Group Dependence and Self-Concept: Attributes of the Imaginary Audience." *Adolescence,* 21, 529–534.

Haurin, R. J. (1992). "Patterns of Childhood Residence and the Relationship to Young Adult Outcomes." *Journal of Marriage and the Family,* 54, 846–860.

Havens, B., and Swenson, I. (1988). "Imagery Associated with Menstruation in Advertising Targeted to Adolescent Women." *Adolescence,* 23, 89–97.

Havens, B., and Swenson, I. (1989). "A Content Analysis of Educational Media about Menstruation." *Adolescence,* 24, 901–907.

Havighurst, R. J. (1972). *Developmental Tasks and Education.* 3rd ed. New York: David McKay.

Hawkins, J. D., Catalano, R. F., and Miller, J. Y. (1992). "Risk and Protective Factors for Alcohol and Other Drug Problems in Adolescence and Early Adulthood: Implications for Substance Abuse Prevention." *Psychological Bulletin,* 112(1), 64–105.

Hawley, P. H. (2003). "Prosocial and Coercive Configurations of Resource Control in Early Adolescence: A Case for the Well-Adapted Machiavellian." *Merrill-Palmer Quarterly,* 49, 279–309.

Hayward, C., Killen, J. D., Wilson, D. M., and Hammer, L. D. (1997). "Psychiatric Risk Associated with Early Puberty in Adolescent Girls." *Journal of the American Academy of Child and Adolescent Psychiatry,* 36, 255–262.

"Health Service Issues. AIDS Guidelines." (November 15, 1985). *Portland Press Herald.*

Heatherton, T. F., Herman, C. P., and Polivy, J. (1992). "Effects of Distress on Eating: The Importance of Ego-Involvement." *Journal of Personality and Social Psychology,* 62, 601–803.

Heaven, P. C. L. (1996). "Personality and Self-Reported Delinquency: A Longitudinal Analysis." *Journal of Child Psychology and Psychiatry and Allied Disciplines,* 37, 747–751.

Heaviside, K., Rowand, L., Williams, F., and Farris, K. (1998). *Violence and Discipline Problems in U.S. Public Schools: 1996–1997.* Washington, DC: Department of Education, National Center for Education Statistics.

Hecker, D. E. (November, 2005). "Occupational Employment Projections to 2014." *Monthly Labor Review,* 70–101.

Heide, K. M. (1993). "Parents Who Get Killed and the Children Who Kill Them." *Journal of Interpersonal Violence,* 8, 531–544.

Heilbrun, A. B., Jr., and Loftus, M. P. (1986). "The Role of Sadism and Peer Pressure in the Sexual Aggression of Male College Students." *The Journal of Sex Research,* 22, 320–332.

Heilman, E. (1998). "The Struggle for Self: Power and Identity in Adolescent Girls." *Youth and Society,* 30, 182–208.

Heiman, T. (2000). "Friendship Quality among Children in Three Educational Settings." *Journal of Intellectual and Developmental Disability,* 25, 1–12.

Hellenga, K. (2002). "Social Space, the Final Frontier: Adolescents on the Internet." In J. T. Mortimer and R. W. Larson (Eds.), *The Changing Adolescent Experience* (pp. 208–249). Cambridge, England: Cambridge University Press.

Helms, J. E. (1990). *Black and White Racial Identity Theory and Professional Interracial Collaboration.* Paper presented at the meeting of the American Psychological Association, Boston.

Helsen, M., Vollebergh, W., and Meeus, W. (2000). "Social Support from Parents and Friends and Emotional Problems in Adolescence." *Journal of Youth and Adolescence,* 29, 319–335.

Helwig, A. (2001). "A Test of Gottfredson's Theory Using a Ten-Year Longitudinal Study." *Journal of Career Development,* 28, 77–95.

Hendershott, A. B. (1989). "Residential Mobility, Social Support and Adolescent Self-Concept." *Adolescence,* 24, 217–232.

Henderson, G. H. (April 1980). "Consequences of School-Age Pregnancy and Motherhood." *Family Relations,* 29, 185–190.

Hendry, L. B., Roberts, W., Glendinning, A., and Coleman, J. S. (1992). "Adolescents' Perceptions of Significant Individuals in their Lives." *Journal of Adolescence,* 15, 255–270.

Henninger, D., and Esposito, N. (1971). "Indian Schools." In D. Gottlieb and A. L. Heinsohn (Eds.), *America's Other Youth: Growing Up Poor.* Englewood Cliffs, NJ: Prentice-Hall.

Henningfield, J. E., Clayton, R., and Pollin, W. (1990). "Involvement of Tobacco in Alcoholism and Illicit Drug Use." *British Journal of Addiction,* 85, 279–292.

Henriques, G. R., Calhoun, L. G., and Cann, A. (1996). "Ethnic Differences in Women's Body Satisfaction: An Experimental Investigation." *Journal of Social Psychology,* 136, 689–697.

Henry, C. S., and Lovelace, S. G. (1995). "Family Resources and Adolescent Family Life Satisfaction in Remarried Family Households." *Journal of Family Issues,* 16, 765–786.

Henry, C. S., Wilson, S. M., & Peterson, G. W. (1989). Parental power bases and processes as predictors of adolescent conformity. *Journal of Adolescent Research,* 4, 15–32.

Henshaw, S. K. (1997). "Teenage Abortion and Pregnancy Statistics by State, 1992." *Family Planning Perspectives,* 29, 115–122.

Henshaw, S. K. (1998). "Unintended Pregnancy in the United States." *Family Planning Perspective,* 30, 24–49.

Henshaw, S. K. (1999). *U.S. Teenage Pregnancy Statistics with Comparative Statistics for Women Aged 20–24.* New York: Alan Guttmacher Institute.

Henshaw, S. K. (2003). *U.S. Teenage Pregnancy Statistics with Comparative Statistics for Women Aged 20–24.* New York: Alan Guttmacher Institute.

Henshaw, S. K., and Kost, K. (1992). "Parental Involvement in Minors' Abortion Decisions." *Family Planning Perspectives,* 24, 196–207.

Hepworth, J., Ryder, R. G., and Dreyer, A. S. (January 1984). "The Effects of Parental Loss on the Formation of Intimate Relationships." *Journal of Marital and Family Therapy,* 10, 73–82.

Herbert, W. (April 1984). "Freud under Fire." *Psychology Today,* 18, 10–12.

Herman, A. M. (2000). *Report on Youth Labor Force.* Washington, DC: Department of Labor.

Herman, M. R., Dornbusch, S. M., Herron, M. C., and Herting, J. R. (1997). "The Influence of Family Regulation, Connection, and Psychological Autonomy on Six Measures of Adolescent Functioning." *Journal of Adolescent Research,* 12, 34–67.

Herring, R. D. (1994). "Substance Abuse among Native American Youth: A Selected Review of Causality." *Journal of Counseling and Development,* 72, 578–592.

Hershberger, S. L., Pilkington, N. W., and D'Augelli, A. R. (1997). "Predictors of Suicide Attempts among Gay, Lesbian, and Bisexual Youth." *Journal of Adolescent Research,* 12, 477–497.

Hertzler, A. A., and Frary, R. B. (1989). "Food Behavior of College Students." *Adolescence,* 24, 349–356.

Herzberger, S. D., and Tennen, H. (1985). "The Effect of Self-Relevance on Judgments of Moderate and Severe Disciplinary Encounters." *Journal of Marriage and the Family,* 47, 311–318.

Herzog, D. B., Dorer, D. J., Keel, P., Selwyn, S. E., Ekeblad, E. R., Flores, A. T., Greenwood, D. N., Burwell, R. A, and Keller, M. (1999). "Recovery and Relapse in Anorexia and Bulimia Nervosa: A 7.5 Year Follow-Up Study." *Journal of the American Academy of Child and Adolescent Psychiatry,* 38, 829–837.

Hetherington, E. M. (1972). "Effects of Father-Absence on Personality Development in Adolescent Daughters." *Developmental Psychology,* 7, 313–326.

Hetherington, E. M. (1987). "Family Relations Six Years after Divorce." In K. Pasley and M. Ihinger-Tallman, (Eds.), *Remarriage and Stepparenting: Current Research and Theory* (pp. 185–205). New York: Guilford.

Hetherington, E. M. (1991). "The Role of Individual Differences and Family Relationships in Children's Coping with Divorce and Remarriage." In P. A. Cowan and E. M. Hetherington (Eds.), *Family Transitions* (pp. 165–194). Hillsdale, NJ: Erlbaum.

Hetherington, E. M. (1993). "An Overview of the Virginia Longitudinal Study of Divorce and Remarriage with a Focus on Early Adolescence." *Journal of Family Psychology,* 7, 39–56.

Hetherington, E. M. (1999a). "Family Functioning and the Adjustment of Adolescent Siblings in Diverse Types of Families." In E. M. Hetherington, S. H. Henderson, and D. Reiss (Eds.), *Adolescent Siblings in Stepfamilies: Family Functioning and Adolescent Adjustment* (pp. 1–25). Monographs of the Society for Research in Child Development, 64, no. 4.

Hetherington, E. M. (1999b). "Family Functioning in Nonstepfamilies and Different Kinds of Stepfamilies: An Integration." In E. M. Hetherington, S. H. Henderson, and D. Reiss (Eds.), *Adolescent Siblings in Stepfamilies: Family Functioning and Adolescent Adjustment* (pp. 184–191). Monographs of the Society for Research in Child Development, 64, no. 4.

Hetherington, E. M. (1999c). "Should We Stay Together for the Sake of the Children?" In E. M. Hetherington (Ed.), *Coping with Divorce, Single Parenting, and Remarriage: A Risk and Resiliency Perspective.* (pp. 93–116). Mahwah, NJ: Lawrence Erlbaum.

Hetherington, E. M., and Clingempeel, W. G. (1992). "Coping with Marital Transitions: A Family Systems Perspective." Monographs of the Society for Research in Child Development, 57, no. 2–3.

Hetherington, E. M., and Jodl, K. M. (1994). "Stepfamilies as Settings for Child Development." In A. Booth and J. Dunn (Eds.), *Stepfamilies: Who Benefits? Who Does Not?* (pp. 55–79). Hillsdale, NJ: Erlbaum.

Hetherington, E. M., and Kelly, J. (2002). *For Better or for Worse.* New York: Norton.

Hetherington, E. M., and Stanley-Hagan, M. (1995). "Parenting in Divorced and Remarried Families." In M. Bornstein (Ed.), *Handbook of Parenting, Vol. 3: Status and Social Conditions of Parenting* (pp. 253–254). Hillsdale, NJ: Erlbaum.

Hetherington, E. M., and Stanley-Hagan, M. (1999). "The Adjustment of Children with Divorced Parents: A Risk and Resiliency Perspective." *Journal of Child Psychology and Psychiatry,* 40, 129–140.

Higgins, J. (2003). "More High School Students Driving Nicer, Bigger Cars." *Detroit Free Press,* March 4, 2003.

Hilgard, E. R. (1949). "Human Motives and the Concept of Self." *American Psychologist,* 4, 374–382.

Hill, A. J., and Pallin, V. (1998). "Dieting Awareness and Low Self-Worth: Related Issues in 8-Year-Old Girls." *International Journal of Eating Disorders,* 24, 405–413.

Hill, R. B. (1998). "Understanding Black Family Functioning: A Holistic Perspective." *Journal of Comparative Family Studies,* 29, 15–25.

Hillier, L., Harrison, L., and Warr, D. (1997). "'When You Carry a Condom, All the Boys Think You Want It': Negotiating Competing Discourses about Safe Sex." *Journal of Adolescence,* 21, 15–29.

Hillman, S. B., and Sawilowsky, S. S. (1991). "Maternal Employment and Early Adolescent Substance Use." *Adolescence,* 26, 829–837.

Hines, A. M. (1997). "Divorce-Related Transitions, Adolescent Development, and the Role of the Parent-Child Relationship: A Review of the Literature." *Journal of Marriage and the Family,* 59, 375–388.

Hines, S., and Groves, D. L. (1989). "Sports Competition and Its Influence on Self-Esteem Development." *Adolescence,* 24, 861–869.

Hingston, R., and Winter, M. (2003). "Epidemiology and Consequences of Drinking and Driving." *Alcohol Research & Health,* 27, 63–78.

Hinton, K., and Margerum, B. J. (Summer 1984). "Adolescent Attitudes and Values Concerning Used Clothing." *Adolescence,* 19, 397–402.

Hiraga, Y., Cauce, A. M., Mason, C., and Ordonez, N. (1992). *Ethnic Identity and the Social Adjustment of Biracial Youths.* Paper presented at the biennial meeting of the Society for Research on Child Development, New Orleans.

Hirch, B. J., and Rapkin, B. D. (1987). "The Transition to Junior High School: A Longitudinal Study of Self-Esteem, Psychological Symptomatology, School Life, and Social Support." *Child Development,* 58, 1235–1243.

Hird, M. J. (2000). "An Empirical Study of Adolescent Dating Aggression in the U. K." *Journal of Adolescence,* 23, 69–78.

Hirokane, K., Tokomura, M., Nanri, S., Kimura, K., and Saito, I. (2005). "Influences of Mothers' Dieting Behaviors on Their Junior High School Daughters." *Eating and Weight Disorders,* 10, 162–167.

Ho, C. S., Lempers, J. D., and Clark-Lempers, D. S. (1995). "Effects of Economic Hardship on Adolescent Self-Esteem: A Family Mediation Model." *Adolescence,* 30, 117–131.

Hobbs, F., & Stoops, N. (2002). "Demographic Trends in the 20th Century." *Census 2000 Special Report. Publication No. CENSR-4.* Washington D.C.: U.S. Bureau of the Census.

Hockenberry-Eaton, M., Richman, M. J., Dilorio, C., Rivero, T., and Maibach, E. (1996). "Mothers and Adolescent Knowledge of Sexual Development: The Effects of Gender, Age, and Sexual Experience." *Adolescence,* 31, 35–46.

Hoelter, J., and Harper, L. (1987). "Structural and Interpersonal Family Influences on Adolescent Self-Conception." *Journal of Marriage and the Family,* 49, 129–139.

Hoff, E., Laursen, B., and Tardif, T. (2002). "Socioeconomic Status and Parenting." In M. H.

Bornstein (Ed.), *Handbook of Parenting: Vol. 2: Biology and Ecology of Parenting* (2nd ed.,) (pp. 231–252). Mahwah, NJ: Erlbaum.

Hoffer, T. B. (1998). "Social Background and Achievement in Public and Catholic High Schools." *Social Psychology of Education*, 2, 7–23.

Hofferth S. L., Reid, L., & Mott, F. L. (2001). "The Effects of Early Childbearing on Schooling Over Time." *Family Planning Perspectives*, 33, 259–267.

Hofferth, S., Kahn, J. R., and Baldwin, W. (1987). "Premarital Sexual Activity among U.S. Teenage Women over the Past Three Decades." *Family Planning Perspectives*, 19, 46–53.

Hoffman, M. L. (1994). "Discipline and Internalization." *Developmental Psychology*, 30, 26–28.

Hoffman, M. L. (2000). *Empathy and Moral Development: Implications for Caring and Justice.* Cambridge, England: Cambridge University Press.

Hoffman, V. J. (Spring 1984). "The Relationship of Psychology to Delinquency: A Comprehensive Approach." *Adolescence*, 19, 55–61.

Hoffner, C. A., and Levine, K. J. (2005). "Enjoyment of Mediated Fright and Violence: A Meta-Analysis." *Media Psychology*, 7, 207–237.

Hogan, D. P., and Astone, N. M. (1986). "The Transition to Adulthood." *American Sociological Review*, 12, 109–130.

Hogan, H. W., and McWilliams, J. M. (September 1978). "Factors Related to Self-Actualization." *Journal of Psychology*, 100, 117–122.

Hoge, D. R., Smit, E. K., and Crist, J. T. (1995). "Reciprocal Effects of Self-Concept and Academic Achievement in Sixth and Seventh Grade." *Journal of Youth and Adolescence*, 24, 295–314.

Holden, G., Geffner, R., and Jouriles, E. (Eds.). (1998). *Children Exposed to Marital Violence.* Washington, DC: American Psychological Association.

Hole, J. W. (1987). *Human Anatomy and Physiology.* 4th ed. Dubuque, IA: William C. Brown.

Hole, J. W. (1992). *Anatomy and Physiology* (6th Edition). New York: McGraw-Hill.

Holifield, J. E., Nelson, W. M., III, and Hart, K. J. (2002). "MMPI Profiles of Sexually Abused and Nonabused Outpatient Adolescents." *Journal of Adolescent Research*, 17, 188–195.

Holland, J. L. (1985). *Making Vocational Choices: A Theory of Vocational Personalities and Work Environments.* 2nd ed. Englewood Cliffs, NJ: Prentice Hall.

Hollander, D. (1996). "Contraceptive Use Is Most Regular if Teenagers Have Conventional Lifestyles." *Family Planning Perspectives*, 28, 289–290.

Holleran, P. R., Pascale, J., and Fraley, J. (1988). "Personality Correlates of College-Age Bulimics." *Journal of Counseling and Development*, 66, 378–381.

Holman, N., and Arcus, M. (1987). "Helping Adolescent Mothers and Their Children: An Integrated Multi-Agency Approach." *Family Relations*, 36, 119–123.

Holmbeck G. (1996). "A Model of Familial Relational Transformations during the Transition to Adolescence: Parent–Adolescent Conflict and Adaptation." In J. Graber, J. Brooks-Gunn, and A. Petersen, (Eds.), *Transitions through Adolescence: Interpersonal Domains and Context* (pp. 167–199). Mahwah, NJ: Erlbaum.

Holmbeck, G. N., and Hill, J. K. (1991). "Conflictive Engagement, Positive Affect, and Menarche in Families with Seventh-Grade Girls." *Child Development*, 62, 1030–1048.

Holmbeck, G. N., Paikoff, R. L., & Brooks-Gunn, J. (1995). "Parenting Adolescents." In M. Bornstein (Ed.), *Handbook of Parenting, Vol. 1: Children and Parenting* (pp. 91–118). Hillsdale, NJ: Lawrence Erlbaum Associates.

Homan, K. B. (1986). "Vocation as the Quest for Authentic Existence." *The Career Development Quarterly*, 35, 14–23.

Hope, R. M., and Hodge, D. M. (2006). "Factors Affecting Children's Adjustment to the Death of a Parent: The Social Work Professional's Perspective." *Child and Adolescent Social Work Journal*, 23, 107–126.

Hopson, I., and Rosenfeld, A. (August 1984). "PMS: Puzzling Monthly Symptoms." *Psychology Today*, 18, 30–35.

Horowitz, J. A., Vessey, J. A., Carlson, K. L., Bradley, J. F., Montoya, C., McCullough, B., and David, J. (2004). "Teasing and Bullying Experiences of Middle School Students." *Journal of the American Psychiatric Nurses Association*, 10, 165–172.

Horowitz, R. (1983). *Honor and the American Dream.* Brunswick, NJ: Rutgers University Press.

Horowitz, T. R. (1992). "Dropout—Mertonian or Reproduction Scheme?" *Adolescence*, 27, 451–459.

Hortacsu, N. (1989). "Target Communication during Adolescence." *Journal of Adolescence*, 12, 253–263.

Hoyt, K. B. (1987). "The Impact of Technology on Occupational Change: Implications for Career Guidance." *The Career Development Quarterly*, 35, 269–278.

Hoyt, K. B. (1988). "The Changing Workforce: A Review of Projections—1986 to 2000." *The Career Development Quarterly*, 37, 31–39.

Hoza, B., Bukowski, W. M., and Beery, S. (2000). "Assessing Peer Network and Dyadic Loneliness." *Journal of Clinical Child Psychology*, 29, 119–128.

Hu, Y., Wood, J., Smith, V., and Westbrook, N. (2004). "Friendships through IM: Examining the Relationship between Instant Messaging and Intimacy." *Journal of Computer Mediated Communication, 10.* Retrieved from http://jcmc.indiana.edu/vol10/issue1/hu.html.

Huang, C., and Grachow, F. (n.d.). "The Dilemma of Health Services in Chinatown." New York: Department of Health.

Hubble, L. M., and Groff, M. G. (December 1982). "WISC-R Verbal Performance IQ Discrepancies among Quay-Classified Adolescent Male Delinquents." *Journal of Youth and Adolescence*, 11, 503–508.

Hubbs-Tait, L., and Garmon, L. C. (1995). "The Relationship of Moral Reasoning and AIDS Knowledge to Risky Sexual Behavior." *Adolescence*, 30, 549–564.

Hudson, L. M., & Gray, W. M. (1986). "Formal Operations, the Imaginary Audience and the Personal Fable." *Adolescence*, 84, 751–765.

Huerta-Franco, R., deLeon, J. D., and Malacara, J. M. (1996). "Knowledge and Attitudes towards Sexuality in Adolescence and Their Association with the Family and Other Factors." *Adolescence*, 31, 179–191.

Huffman, J. W. (1986). "Teenagers' Gynecologic Problems." *Medical Aspects of Human Sexuality*, 20, 57–61.

Hughes, M., Morrison, K., and Asada, K. J. K. (2005). "What's Love Got to Do with It? Exploring the Maintenance Rules, Love Attitudes, and Network Support on Friends with Benefits Relationships." *Western Journal of Communication*, 69, 49–66.

Huitt, W. (2003). "Values." Retrieved July 11, 2003, from http://chiron.valdosta.edu/whuitt.

Huizinga, D., and Jakob-Chien, C. (1998). "The Contemporaneous Co-Occurrence of Serious and Violent Juvenile Offending and Other Behavior Problems." In R. Loeber and D. P. Farrington (Eds.), *Serious and Violent Juvenile Offenders: Risk Factors and Successful Intervention* (pp. 47–67). Thousand Oaks, CA: Sage.

Hulanicka, B. (1999). "Acceleration of Menarcheal Age of Girls from Dysfunctional Families." *Journal of Reproductive and Infant Psychology*, 17, 119–132.

Hultsman, W. C. (1992). "Constraints to Activity Participation in Early Adolescence." *Journal of Early Adolescence*, 12, 280–299.

Humphrey, L. L., and Stern, S. (1988). "Object Relations and the Family System in Bulimia: A Theoretical Integration." *Journal of Marital and Family Therapy*, 14, 337–350.

Hunt, G. P., and Laidler, K. J. (2001). "Alcohol and Violence in the Lives of Gang Members." *Alcohol Research & Health*, 25, 66–71.

Hunt, W. A., and Matazarro, J. D. (1970). "Habit Mechanisms in Smoking." In W. A. Hunt (Ed.), *Learning Mechanisms in Smoking.* Chicago: Aldine.

Hunter, A. (1997). "Counting on Grandmothers: Black Mothers' and Fathers' Reliance on Grandmothers for Parenting Support." *Journal of Family Issues*, 18, 251–269.

Hunter, E. (1998). "Adolescent Attraction to Cults." *Adolescence*, 33, 709–714.

Hurrelmann, K., Engel, U., Holler, B., and Nordlohne, E. (1988). "Failure in School, Family Conflicts, and Psychosomatic Disorders in Adolescence." *Journal of Adolescence*, 11, 237–249.

Hussong, A. M. (2000). "Distinguishing Mean and Structural Sex Differences in Adolescent Friendship Quality." *Journal of Social and Personal Relationships*, 17, 223–243.

Huston, A. C., and Alvarez, M. M. (1990). "The Socialization Context of Gender Role Development in Early Adolescence." In R. Montemayor, G. R. Adams, and T. P. Gullota, (Eds.), *From Childhood to Adolescence: A Transitional Period?* (pp. 156–179). Newbury Park, CA: Sage.

Huston, A. C., Donnerstein, E., Fairchild, H., Feshback, N. D., Katz, P. A., Murray, J. P., Rubenstein, E. A., Wilcox, B. L., and Zuckerman, D. (1992). *Big World, Small Screen: The Role of Television in American Society.* Lincoln: University of Nebraska Press.

Huston, L., Hoberman, H., and Nugent, S. (1994). *Alcohol Use and Abuse in Native American Adolescents.* Paper presented at the meeting of the Society for Research on Adolescence, San Diego.

Hutchinson, R. L., Valutis, W. E., Brown, D. T., and White, J. S. (1989). "The Effects of Family

Structure on Institutionalized Children's Self-Concepts." *Adolescence,* 94, 303–310.

Huurre, T., Junkkari, H., & Aro, H. (2006). "Long-Term Psychosocial Effects of Parental Divorce: A Follow-up Study from Adolescence to Adulthood." *European Archives of Psychiatry and Clinical Neuroscience,* 256, 256–263.

Hyde, J. S. (1985). *Half the Human Experience.* Lexington, MA: D. C. Heath.

Hyde, J. S., and Delamater, J. D. (2000). *Understanding Human Sexuality.* 2nd ed. New York: McGraw-Hill.

Iceland, J., Weinberg, D. H, and Steinmetz, E. (2002). "Racial and Ethnic Residential Segregation in the United States: 1980–2000." Series no. CENSR-3. Washington, DC: Government Printing Office.

Ieit, D. (1985). *Anxiety, Depression, and Self-Esteem in Bulimia: The Role of the School Psychologist.* Paper presented an the Annual Meeting of the Educational Research Association, February, 1985, Virginia Beach, VA.

Ihinger-Tallman, M., and Pasley, K. (1986). "Remarriage and Integration within the Community." *Journal of Marriage and the Family,* 48, 395–405.

Indian Health Service. (2000). "Trends in Indian Health, 1998–1999." Retrieved September 24, 2003, from http://www.ihs.gov/publicinfo/publications/trends98/front.pdf.

Information Please Almanac, Atlas and Yearbook: 1992. (1992). 45th edition. Boston: Houghton Mifflin.

Inhelder, B., and Piaget, J. (1958). *The Growth of Logical Thinking from Childhood to Adolescence.* New York: Basic Books.

Internet World Stats. (2006). *Internet Usage Stats: The Big Picture.* Retrieved from http://www.internetworldstats.com/stats.htm.

Irwin, D. D. (1999). "The Straight Edge Subculture: Examining the Youths' Drug-Free Way." *Journal of Drug Issues,* 29, 365–380.

Ivchenkova, N. P., Efimova, A. V., and Akkuzina, O. P. (2001). "Teenage Attitudes towards the Beginning of Sex Life." *Voprosy Psikologii,* 3, 49–57.

Jaccard, J., Dittus, P. J., and Gordon, B. B. (1996). "Maternal Correlates of Adolescent Sexual and Contraceptive Behavior." *Family Planning Perspectives,* 28, 159–165.

Jackson, A. W., and Davis, G. A. (2000). *Turning Points 2000: Educating Adolescents in the 21st Century.* New York: Teachers College Press.

Jackson, D. N., & Rushton, P. (2006). "Males Have Greater g: Sex Differences in General Mental Ability from 100,000 17- to 18-year-olds on the Scholastic Assessment Test." *Intelligence,* 34(5), 479–486.

Jackson, M. (1991, 1992). *Heal the World.* Mijac Music. Jacobs, J. B. (1988). "Families Facing the Nuclear Taboo." *Family Relations,* 37, 432–436.

Jackson, S. M., and Cram, F. (2003). "Disrupting the Sexual Double Standard: Young Women's Talk about Heterosexuality." *British Journal of Social Psychology,* 42, 113–127.

Jackson, S. M., Cram, F., and Seymour, F. W. (2000). "Violence and Sexual Coercion in High School Students' Dating Relationships." *Journal of Family Violence,* 15, 23–36.

Jacobs, J. B. (1988). "Families Facing the Nuclear Taboo." *Family Relations,* 37, 432–436.

Jacobs, J. E., and Klaczynski, P. A. (2002). "The Development of Judgment and Decision Making during Childhood and Adolescence." *Current Directions in Psychological Science,* 11, 145–149.

Jacobs, J. E., and Potenza, M. (1990). *The Use of Decision-Making Strategies in Late Adolescence.* Paper presented at the meeting of the Society for Research in Adolescence, Atlanta.

Jacobs, J. E., Finken, L. L. Griffen, N. L., Lindsley, J. A., and Wright, J. D. (1998). "The Career Plans of Science Talented Rural Adolescent Girls." *American Educational Research Journal,* 35, 681–704.

Jacobs, J. F., and Potenza, M. T. (1991). "The Use of Judgment Heuristics to Make Social and Object Decisions: A Developmental Perspective." *Child Development,* 62, 166–178.

Jacobs, S. B., & Wagner, K. (1984). "Obese and Nonobese Individuals: Behavioral and Personality Characteristics." *Addictive Behaviors,* 9(2), 223–226.

Jacobson, K. C., and Crockett, L. J. (2000). "Parental Monitoring and Adolescent Adjustment: An Ecological Perspective." *Journal of Research on Adolescence,* 10, 65–97.

Jaffee, S., and Hyde, J. S. (2000). "Gender Differences in Moral Orientation: A Meta-Analysis." *Psychological Bulletin,* 126, 703–726.

Jahnke, H. C., and Blanchard-Fields, F. (1993). "A Test of Two Models of Adolescent Egocentrism." *Journal of Youth and Adolescence,* 22, 313–326.

James, W. (1890). *The Principles of Psychology.* New York: Holt.

Jamison, W., and Signorella, M. L. (1980). "Sex-Typing and Spatial Ability: The Association between Masculinity and Success on Piaget's Water-Level Task." *Sex Roles,* 6, 345–353.

Jang, S. J., and Thornberry, T. P. (1998). "Self-Esteem, Delinquent Peers, and Delinquency: A Test of the Self-Enhancement Thesis." *American Sociological Review,* 63, 586–598.

Jansen, P., Richter, L. M., and Griesel, R. D. (1992). "Glue Sniffing: A Comparison Study of Sniffers and Non-Sniffers." *Journal of Adolescence,* 15, 29–37.

Jarrell, A. (2000). "The Face of Teenage Sex Grows Younger." *New York Times,* April 2, 2000.

Jarrett, R. L. (1995). "Growing Up Poor: The Family Experiences of Socially Mobile Youth in Low-Income African American Neighborhoods." *Journal of Adolescent Research,* 10, 111–135.

Jarvinen, D. W., and Nichols, J. G. (1996). "Adolescents' Social Goals, Beliefs about the Causes of Social Success, and Satisfaction in Peer Relations." *Developmental Psychology,* 32, 435–441.

Jemmott, L. S., and Jemmott, J. B., III. (1992). "Family Structure, Parental Strictness, and Sexual Behavior among Inner City Black Male Adolescents." *Journal of Adolescent Research,* 7, 192–207.

Jencks, C. (1994). *The Homeless.* Cambridge, MA: Harvard University Press.

Jenkins, J. E., and Zunguze, S. T. (1998). "The Relationship of Family Structure to Adolescent Drug Use, Peer Affiliation, and Perception of Peer Acceptance of Drug Use." *Adolescence,* 33, 811–822.

Jenny, C., Roesler, T. A., and Poyer, K. L. (1994). "Are Children at Risk for Sexual Abuse by Homosexuals?" *Pediatrics,* 94, 41–44.

Jensen, A. F., and Ostergaard, P. (1998). "Dressing for Security or Risk? An Exploratory Study of Two Different Ways of Consumer Fashion." *European Advances in Consumer Research,* 3, 98–103.

Jensen, L. (1995). *The Moral Reasoning of Orthodox and Progressivist Indians and Americans.* Paper presented at the meeting of the Society for Research in Child Development, Indianapolis, IN.

Jensen, L. A., Arnett, J. J., Feldman, S. S., & Cauffman, E. (2002). "It's Wrong, but Everybody Does It: Academic Dishonesty Among High School and College Students." *Contemporary Educational Psychology,* 27, 209–228.

Jensen, L. A., Arnett, J. J., Feldman, S. S., and Cauffman, E. (2004). "The Right to Do Wrong: Lying to Parents among Adolescents and Emerging Adults." *Journal of Youth and Adolescence,* 33, 101–112.

Jessop, D. J. (February 1981). "Family Relationships as Viewed by Parents and Adolescents: A Specification." *Journal of Marriage and the Family,* 43, 95–106.

Johnsen, K. P., and Medley, M. L. (September 1978). "Academic Self-Concept among Black High School Seniors: An Examination of Perceived Agreement with Selected Others." *Phylon,* 39, 264–274.

Johnson, C. L., and Flach, R. A. (1985). "Family Characteristics of 105 Parents with Bulimia." *American Journal of Psychiatry,* 142, 1321–1324.

Johnson, E., Stein, R. E. K., and Dadds, M. R. (1996). "Moderating Effects of Family Structure on the Relationship between Physical and Mental Health in Urban Children with Chronic Illness." *Journal of Pediatric Psychology,* 121, 43–56.

Johnson, J. D., Adams, M. S., Ashburn, L., and Reed, W. (1995). "Differential Gender Effects of Exposure to Rap Music on African American Adolescents' Acceptance of Teen Dating Violence." *Sex Roles,* 33, 597–605.

Johnson, J. D., Jackson, L. E., and Gatto, L. (1995). "Violent Attitudes and Deferred Academic Aspirations: Deleterious Effects of Exposure to Rap Music." *Basic and Applied Social Psychology,* 16, 27–41.

Johnson, J. D., Trawalter, S., and Dovidio, J. F. (2000). "Converging Interracial Consequences of Exposure to Violent Rap Music on Stereotypical Attributions of Blacks." *Journal of Experimental Social Psychology,* 36, 233–251.

Johnson, J. G., Cohen, P., Kotler, L., Kasen, S., and Brook, J. S. (2002). "Psychiatric Disorders Associated with Risk for the Development of Eating Disorders during Adolescence and Early Adulthood." *Journal of Consulting and Clinical Psychology,* 70, 1119–1128.

Johnson, J. H. (1986). *Life Events as Stressors in Childhood and Adolescence.* Beverly Hills, CA: Sage.

Johnson, K. A. (1986). "Informal Control Networks and Adolescent Orientation toward Alcohol Use." *Adolescence,* 21, 767–784.

Johnson, L., Bachman, J., and O'Malley, P. (1994). *Drug Use Rises among American Teenagers.* News Release, Institute of Social Research, University of Michigan, Ann Arbor.

Johnson, L. D., O'Malley, P. M., and Bachman, J. G. (1985). *Use of Licit and Illicit Drugs by America's*

High School Students, 1975–1984. Rockville, MD: National Institute on Drug Abuse.

Johnson, L. D., O'Malley, P. M., and Bachman, J. G. (1987). *National Trends in Drug Use and Related Factors among American High School Students and Young Adults, 1975–1986.* Washington, DC: U.S. Government Printing Office.

Johnson, L. D., O'Malley, P. M., and Bachman, J. G. (1996). *National Survey Results on Drug Use from the Monitoring the Future Study; 1975–1994.* Rockville, MD: National Institute on Drug Abuse.

Johnson, L. D., O'Malley, P. M., and Bachman, J. G. (2003). *Monitoring the Future: National Results on Adolescent Drug Use: Overview of Key Findings, 2002* (NIH Publication no. 03-5374). Bethesda, MD: National Institute on Drug Abuse.

Johnson, L. D., O'Malley, P. M., Bachman, J. G., and Schulenberg, J. E. (2005). *Monitoring the Future National Results on Adolescent Drug Use, 1975–2004: Volume, ii: College Students and Adults Ages 19–45* (NIH Publication No. 05-5728). Bethesda, MD: National Institute on Drug Abuse.

Johnson, L. D., O'Malley, P. M., Bachman, J. G., and Schulenberg, J. E. (2006). *Monitoring the Future National Results on Adolescent Drug Use: Overview of Key Findings, 2005* (NIH Publication No. 06-5882). Bethesda, MD: National Institute on Drug Abuse.

Johnson, M. K., Beebe, T., Mortimer, J. T., and Snyder, M. (1998). "Volunteerism in Adolescence: A Process Perspective." *Journal of Research on Adolescence,* 8, 309–332.

Johnson, P. L., & O'Leary, D. (1987). "Parental Behavior Patterns and Conduct Disorders in Girls." *Journal of Abnormal Child Psychology,* 15, 573–581.

Johnson, R. E. (1987). "Mother's versus Father's Roles in Causing Delinquency." *Adolescence,* 22, 305–315.

Johnson, R. J., and Kaplan, H. B. (1991). "Developmental Processes Leading to Marijuana Use: Comparing Civilians and the Military." *Youth and Society,* 23, 3–30.

Jolliffe, D. (2004). "Extent of Overweight among US Children and Adolescents from 1971 to 2000." *International Journal of Obesity and Related Metabolic Disorders,* 28, 4–9.

Jones, R. K., Darroch, J. E., and Henshaw, S. K. (2002). "Patterns in the Socioeconomic Characteristics of Women Obtaining Abortions in 2000–2001." *Perspectives on Sexual and Reproductive Health,* 34, 226–235.

Jordan, N. (1989). "Spare the Rod, Spare the Child." *Psychology Today,* 23, 16.

Jordan, W. J., Lara, J., and McPartland, G. M. (1996). "Exploring the Causes of Early Drop Out among Race-Ethnic and Gender Groups." *Youth and Society,* 28, 62–94.

Jorm, A. F., Christensen, H., Rogers, B., Jacomb, P. A., and Easteal, S. (2004). "Association of Adverse Childhood Experiences, Age of Menarche and Adult Reproductive Behavior: Does the Androgen Receptor Gene Play a Role?" *American Journal of Medical Genetics Part B: Neuropsychiatric Genetics,* 125, 105–111.

Josephs, R. A., Markus, H. R., and Tafarodi, R. W. (1992). "Gender and Self-Esteem." *Journal of Personality and Social Psychology,* 63, 391–402.

Josephson Institute of Ethics. (2002). *The Six Pillars of Character.* Retrieved from http://www.josephsoninstitute.org/MED/MED-2sixpillars.htm

Josselson, R. (August 1982). "Personality Structure and Identity Status in Women as Viewed through Early Memories." *Journal of Youth and Adolescence,* 11, 293–299.

Josselson, R. (1987). *Finding Herself: Pathways to Identity Development in Women.* San Francisco: Jossey-Bass.

Josselson, R. (1988). "The Embedded Self: I and Thou Revisited." In D. K. Lapsley and F. C. Power (Eds.), *Self, Ego, and Identity: Integrative Approaches* (pp. 91–106.) New York: Springer-Verlag.

Jovanovic, J., Lerner, R., and Lerner, J. V. (1989). "Objective and Subjective Attractiveness and Early Adolescent Adjustment." *Journal of Adolescence,* 12, 225–229.

Joyner, K., and Udry, J. R. (2000). "You Don't Bring Me Anything but Down: Adolescent Romance and Depression." *Journal of Health and Social Behavior,* 41, 369–391.

Jozefowicz, D. M., Barber, B. L., and Mollasis, C. (1994). *Relations between Maternal and Adolescent Values and Beliefs: Sex Differences and Implications for Vocational Choice.* Paper presented at the meeting of the Society for Research on Adolescence, San Diego.

Juhasz, A. M. (1989). "Significant Others and Self-Esteem: Methods for Determining Who and Why." *Adolescence,* 24, 581–594.

Jurich, A. P., Polson, C. J., Jurich, J. A., and Bates, R. A. (Spring 1985). "Family Factors in the Lives of Drug Users and Abusers." *Adolescence,* 20, 143–159.

Jurich, A. P., Schumm, W. R., and Bollman, S. R. (1987). "The Degree of Family Orientation Perceived by Mothers, Fathers, and Adolescents." *Adolescence,* 22, 119–128.

Jurich, J. A., Adams, R. A., and Schulenberg, J. E. (1992). "Factors Related to Behavior Change in Response to AIDS." *Family Relations,* 41, 97–103.

Jussim, L., Eccles J. S., and Madon, S. (1996). "Social Perception, Social Stereotypes, and Teacher Expectations: Accuracy and the Quest for the Powerful Self-Fulfilling Prophesy." In L. Berkowitz (Ed.), *Advances in Experimental Social Psychology* (pp. 281–388). New York: Academic Press.

Kacerguis, M. A., and Adams, G. R. (April 1980). "Erikson Stage Resolution: The Relationship between Identity and Intimacy." *Journal of Youth and Adolescence,* 9, 117–126.

Kaczmarek, M. G., and Backlund, V. A. (1991). "Disenfranchised Grief: The Loss of an Adolescent Romantic Relationship." *Adolescence,* 26, 253–259.

Kafka, R. R., and London, P. (1991). "Communication in Relationships and Adolescent Substance Use: The Influence of Parents and Friends." *Adolescence,* 26, 587–598.

Kahn, J. R., and London, K. A. (1991). "Premarital Sex and the Risk of Divorce." *Journal of Marriage and the Family,* 53, 845–855.

Kail, R. (1991). "Developmental Change in Speed of Processing during Childhood and Adolescence." *Psychological Bulletin,* 109, 490–501.

Kail, R. (1997). "The Neural Noise Hypothesis: Evidence from Processing Speed in Adults with Multiple Sclerosis." *Aging, Neuropsychology, and Cognition,* 4, 157–165.

Kail, R. (2000). "Speed of Information Processing: Developmental Change and Links to Intelligence." *Journal of School Psychology,* 38, 51–61.

Kaiser Family Foundation. (1998). *National Survey of Teens: Teens Talk about Dating, Intimacy, and Their Sexual Experiences.* Publication No. 1373. Retrieved from http://www.kff.org/youthhivstds/1373-datingrep.cfm.

Kaiser Family Foundation. (2000). *Safer Sex, Condoms, and "The Pill": A Series of National Surveys of Teens about Sex.* Menlo Park, CA: Author.

Kalakoski, V., and Nurmi, J-E. (1998). "Identity and Educational Transitions: Age Differences in Adolescent Exploration and Commitment Related to Education, Occupation, and Family." *Journal of Research on Adolescence,* 8, 29–47.

Kalil, A., and Kunz, J. (1999). "First Births among Unmarried Adolescent Girls: Risk and Protective Factors." *Social Work Research,* 23, 197–208.

Kalmuss, D., Namerow, P. B., and Cushman, L. F. (1991). "Teenage Pregnancy Resolution: Adoption versus Parenting." *Family Planning Perspectives,* 23, 17–23.

Kanazawa, S. (2001). "Why Father Absence Might Precipitate Early Menarche: The Role of Polygyny." *Evolution and Human Behavior,* 22, 329–334.

Kandel, D. B., et al. (March 1978). "Antecedents of Adolescent Initiation into Stages of Drug Use: A Developmental Analysis." *Journal of Youth and Adolescence,* 7, 13–40.

Kandel, D. B., Johnson, J. G., Bird, H. R., Canino, G., Goodman, S. H., Lahey, B. B., Regier, D. A., and Schwab-Stone, M. (1997). "Psychiatric Disorders Associated with Substance Use among Children and Adolescents: Findings from the Methods for the Epidemiology of Child and Adolescent Mental Disorders (MECA) Study." *Journal of Abnormal Child Psychology,* 25, 121–132.

Kandel, J., Schwartz, J., and Jessel, T. (1991). *Principles of Neural Science,* 3rd ed. New York: Elsevier.

Kane, M. J. (1988). "The Female Athletic Role as a Status Determinant within the Social System of High School Adolescents." *Adolescence,* 23, 253–264.

Kanin, E. J., and Parcell, S. R. (1977). "Sexual Aggression: A Second Look at the Offended Female." *Archives of Sexual Behavior,* 6, 67–76.

Kann, L., Kinchen, S. A., Williams, B. I., et al. (2000). "Youth Risk Behavior Surveillance: United States, 1999." *Centers for Disease Control Surveillance Summary,* 49, 1–32.

Kaplan, H. B. (1980). "Deviant Behavior and Self-Enhancement in Adolescence." *Journal of Youth and Adolescence,* 7, 253–277.

Kaplan, R. M., & Saccuzzo, D. P. (2005). *Psychological Testing: Principles, Applications, and Issues.* Belmont, CA: Thomson Wadsworth.

Kaplowitz, P. B., Slora, E. J., Wasserman, R. C., Pedlow, S. E., and Herman-Giddens, M. E. (2001). "Earlier Onset of Puberty in Girls: Relation to Increased Body Mass Index and Race." *Pediatrics,* 108, 347–353.

Karatzias, A. Power, K. G., and Swanson, V. (2002). "Bullying and Victimization in Scottish Secondary Schools: Same or Separate Entities?" *Aggressive Behavior,* 28, 45–61.

Katchadourian, H. (1977). *The Biology of Adolescence.* San Francisco: W. H. Freeman.

Katz, J. E., & Rice, R. E. (2002). *Social Consequences of Internet Use: Access, Involvement, and Interaction.* Cambridge, MA: MIT Press.

Katzenstein, D. (1997). "Antiretroviral Therapy for Human Immunodeficiency Virus Infection in 1997." *Western Journal of Medicine,* 166, 319–325.

Kaufman, A. S., and Lichtenberger, E. O. (2002). *Assessing Adolescent and Adult Intelligence* (2nd ed.). Boston: Allyn & Bacon.

Kaufmann, D., Gesten, E., and Santa Lucia, R. C. (2000). "The Relationship between Children's Adjustment and Parenting Style: The Parents' Perspective." *Journal of Child and Family Studies,* 9, 231–245.

Kay, A. W. (1969). *Moral Development.* New York: Schocken Books.

Kazdin, A. E. (1995). *Conduct Disorders in Childhood and Adolescence.* 2nd ed. Newbury Park, CA: Sage.

Keating, D. (2004). "Cognitive and Brain Development." In R. Lerner and L. Steinberg (Eds.), *Handbook of Adolescent Psychology* (pp. 45–84). Chichester, England: Wiley.

Keating, D. P. (1990). "Adolescent Thinking." In S. S. Feldman and G. R. Elliott (Eds.), *At the Threshhold: A Developing Adolescent.* Cambridge, MA: Harvard University Press.

Keefe, K., and Berndt, T. J. (1996). "Relations of Friendship Quality to Self-Esteem in Early Adolescence." *Journal of Early Adolescence,* 16, 110–129.

Keelan, J. P. R., Dion, K. K., and Dion, K. L. (1992). "Correlates of Appearance Anxiety in Late Adolescence and Early Adulthood among Young Women." *Journal of Adolescence,* 15, 193–205.

Keesey, R. E, and Pawley, T. L. (1986). "The Regulation of Body Weight." *Annual Review of Psychology,* 37, 109–133.

Keith, A., Nelson, B., Schlabach, C., and Thompson, D. (1990). "The Relationship between Parental Employment and Three Measures of Early Adolescent Responsibility: Family-Related, Personal, and Social." *Journal of Early Adolescence,* 10, 399–415.

Keith, V. M., and Finlay, B. (1988). "The Impact of Parental Divorce on Children's Educational Attainment, Marital Timing, and Likelihood of Divorce." *Journal of Marriage and the Family,* 50, 797–809.

Keithly, D., and Deseran, F. (1995). "Households, Local Labor Markets, and Youth Labor Force Participation." *Youth and Society,* 26, 463–492.

Keller, J., and Keller, K. T. (1992, 1993). *Love Is.* Warner-Tamerlane Publishing Company, Checkerman Music, Pressmancherryblossom, W. B. Music Corporation, N. Y. M., and Pressmancherry Music.

Kelley, S. S., Borawski, E. A., Flocke, S. A., and Keen, K. J. (2003). "The Role of Sequential and Concurrent Sexual Relationships in the Risk of Sexually Transmitted Diseases among Adolescents." *Journal of Adolescent Health,* 32, 296–305.

Kelly, C., and Goodwin, G. C. (Fall 1983). "Adolescents' Perceptions of Three Styles of Parental Control." *Adolescence,* 18, 567–571.

Kelly, J. (2003). "Changing Perspectives on Children's Adjustment Following Divorce: A View from the United States." *Childhood,* 10, 237–254.

Kelly, R. (1992). *Quality Time.* Willesden Music/R. Kelly Publishing Inc. (Administered by Willesden Music) (BMI).

Kendall-Tackett, K. A., Williams, L. M., and Finkelhor, D. (1993). "Impact of Sexual Abuse on Children: A Review and Synthesis of Recent Empirical Studies." *Psychological Bulletin,* 113, 164–180.

Kendler, K. S., Walters, E. E., Neale, M., C., Kessler, R. C., Heath, A. C., and Eaves, L. J. (1995). "The Structure of the Genetic and Environmental Risk Factors for Six Major Psychiatric Disorders in Women: Phobia, Generalized Anxiety Disorder, Panic Disorder, Bulimia, Major Depression, and Alcoholism." *Archives of General Psychiatry,* 52, 374–383.

Keniston, K. (1971). "Youth: A New Stage of Life." *American Scholar,* 39, 4.

Keniston, K. "The Tasks of Adolescence." *In Developmental Psychology Today.* Del Mar, CA: CRM Books.

Kennedy, E. (1995). "Correlates of Perceived Popularity among Peers: A Study of Race and Gender Differences among Middle School Students." *Journal of Negro Education,* 64, 186–195.

Kennedy, S. H., Kaplan, A. S., Garfinkel, P. E., Rockert, W., Toner, B., and Abbey, S. E. (1994). "Depression in Anorexia Nervosa and Bulimia Nervosa: Discriminating Depressive Symptoms and Episodes." *Journal of Psychosomatic Research,* 38, 773–782.

Kenney, A. M., Guardado, S., and Brown, L. (1989). "Sex Education and AIDS Education in the Schools: What States and Large School Districts are Doing." *Family Planning Perspectives,* 21, 56–64.

Kenny, M. E. (1994). "Quality and Correlates of Parental Attachment among Late Adolescents." *Journal of Counseling and Development,* 72, 399–403.

Kenny, M. E., Lomax, R., Brabeck, M., and Fife, J. (1998). "Longitudinal Pathways Linking Adolescent Reports of Maternal and Paternal Attachments to Psychological Well-Being." *Journal of Early Adolescence,* 18, 221–243.

Keough, J., and Sugden, D. (1985). *Movement Skill Development.* New York: Macmillan.

Kerber, C. S. (2005). "Problem and Pathological Gambling among College Athletes." *Annals of Clinical Psychiatry,* 17, 243–247.

Kerckhoff, A. C. (2002). "The Transition from School to Work." In J. T. Mortimer and R. W. Larson (Eds.), *The Changing Adolescent Experience: Societal Trends and the Transition to Adulthood* (pp. 52–87). Cambridge, England: Cambridge University Press.

Kerpelman, J. L., Pittman, J. F., and Lamke, L. K. (1997). "Toward a Microprocess Perspective on Adolescent Identity Development: An Identity Control Theory Approach." *Journal of Adolescent Research,* 12, 325–346.

Kerr, B. A., and Colangelo, N. (1988). "The College Plans of Academically Talented Students." *Journal of Counseling and Development,* 67, 42–48.

Kerr, M., Stattin, H., and Trost, K. (1999). "To Know You Is to Trust You: Parents' Trust Is Rooted in Child Disclosure of Information." *Journal of Adolescence,* 22, 737–752.

Kershner, R. (1996). "Adolescent Attitudes about Rape." *Adolescence,* 31, 29–33.

Keshna, R. (1980). "Relevancy of Tribal Interests and Tribal Diversity in Determining the Educational Needs of American Indians." In *Conference on the Education and Occupational Needs of American Indian Work.* Washington, DC: U.S. Department of Education, National Institute of Education.

Keski-Rahkonen, A., Viken, R. J., Kapiro, J., Rissanen, A., and Rose, R. J. (2004). "Genetic and Environmental Factors in Breakfast Eating Patterns." *Behavior Genetics,* 90, 503–514.

Ketterlinus, R. D., Henderson, S., and Lamb, M. E. (1991). "The Effects of Maternal Age-at-Birth on Children's Cognitive Development." *Journal of Research on Adolescence,* 1, 173–188.

Ketterson, T. U., and Blustein, D. L. (1997). "Attachment Relationships and the Career Exploration Process." *Career Development Quarterly,* 46, 167–177.

Keye, W. R. (Fall 1983). "Update: Premenstrual Syndrome." *Endocrine and Fertility Forum,* 6, 1–3.

Khalique, A., and Rohner, R. P. (2002). "Reliability of Measures Assessing the Pancultural Association between Perceived Parental Acceptance-Rejection and Psychological Adjustment: A Meta-Analysis of Cross-Cultural and Intra-Cultural Studies." *Cultural Research,* 33, 87–99.

Kibler, W. L. (1993). "Academic Dishonesty: A Student Development Perspective." *NASPA Journal,* 30, 252–267.

Kidd, S. A. (2003). "Street Youth: Coping and Interventions." *Child & Adolescent Social Work Journal,* 20, 235–261.

"Kids and Contraceptives." (February 16, 1987). *Newsweek,* pp. 54–65.

Kidwell, J. S., Dunham R. M., Bacho, R. A., Pastorino, E., and Portes, P. R. (1995). "Adolescent Identity Exploration: A Test of Erikson's Theory of Transitional Crisis." *Adolescence,* 30, 785–793.

Kifer, E. (1985). "Review of the ACT Assessment Program." In J. V. Mitchell (Ed.), *Ninth Mental Measurement Yearbook* (pp. 31–45). Lincoln: Buros Mental Measurement Institute, University of Nebraska Press.

Kilbourne, J. (1995). "Beauty and the Beast of Advertising." In G. Dines and J. M. Humez (Eds.), *Gender, Race, and Class in Media* (pp. 112–125). Thousand Oaks, CA: Sage.

Killen, M., Lee-Kim, J., McGlothlin, H., and Stangor, C. (2002). *How Children and Adolescents Evaluate Gender and Racial Exclusion.* (p. 118). Monograph of the Society for Research in Child Development, 67, no. 4.

Killen, M., and Turiel, E. (1998). "Adolescents' and Young Adults' Evaluations of Helping and Sacrificing for Others." *Journal of Research on Adolescence,* 8, 355–375.

Kim, K. G., Conger, R. D., and Lorenz, F. O. (2001). "Parent-Adolescent Reciprocity in Negative Affect and Its Relation to Early Adult Social Development." *Developmental Psychology,* 37, 775–790.

Kim-Cohen, J., Moffett, T. E., Caspi, A., and Taylor, A. (2004). "Genetic and Environmental Processes in Young Children's Resilience and Vulnerability to Socioeconomic Deprivation." *Child Development,* 75, 651–668.

Kimmier, R. T., Brigman, S. L., and Noble, F. C. (1990). "Career Indecision and Family Enmeshment." *Journal of Counseling and Development,* 68, 309–312.

King, A., Staffieri, A., and Adelgais, A. (1998). "Mutual Peer Tutoring: Effects of Structuring Tutorial Interaction to Scaffold Peer Learning." *Journal of Educational Psychology,* 90, 134–152.

King, M. L. (1964). *Why We Can't Wait.* New York: Harper and Row.

King, P. (1989 March). "Living Together: Bad for Kids." *Psychology Today,* 23, 77.

King, P. E., and Furrow, J. L. (2004). "Religion as a Resource for Positive Youth Development: Religion, Social Capital, and Moral Outcomes." *Developmental Psychology,* 40, 703–713.

King, P. M., Kitchener, K. S., Davidson, M. L., Parker, C. A., and Wood, P. K. (1983). "The Justification of Beliefs in Young Adults: A Longitudinal Study." *Human Development,* 26, 106–118.

King, R. A., Schwab-Stone, M., Flisher, A. J., Greenwald, S., Kramer, R. A., Goodman, S. H., Lahey, B. B., Shaffer, D., and Gould, M. S. (2001). "Psychosocial and Risk Behavior Correlates of Youth Suicide Attempts and Suicidal Ideation." *Journal of the American Academy of Child & Adolescent Psychiatry,* 40, 837–846.

King, V., Elder, G. H., Jr., and Whitbeck, L. B. (1997). "Religious Involvement among Rural Youth: An Ecological and Life-Course Perspective." *Journal of Research on Adolescence,* 7, 431–456.

Kinsey, A., Pomeroy, W., and Martin, C. (1948). *Sexual Behavior in the Human Male.* Philadelphia: Saunders.

Kinze, J. D., Frederickson, R. H., Ben, R., Fleck, J., and Karls, W. (1984). "Post-Traumatic Stress Disorder among Survivors of Cambodian Concentration Camps." *American Journal of Psychiatry,* 141, 645–650.

Kipke, M. D., O'Connor, S., Palmer, R. F., and MacKenzie, R. G. (1995). "Street Youth in Los Angeles: Profile of a Group at High Risk for HIV." *Archives of Pediatric and Adolescent Medicine,* 149, 513–519.

Kipke, M. D., Palmer, R. F., LaFrance, S., and O'Connor, S. (1997). "Homeless Youths' Descriptions of Their Parents' Child-Rearing Practices." *Youth and Society,* 28, 415–431.

Kirby, D. D., and Brown, N. L. (1996). "Condom Availability in Programs in U.S. Schools." *Family Planning Perspectives,* 28, 196–202.

Kirby, D., Short, L., Collins, J., Rugg, D., Kolbe, L., Howard, M., Miller, B., Sonenstein, F., and Zabin, L. (1994). "School-Based Programs to Reduce Sexual Risk Behaviors: A Review of Effectiveness." *Public Health Reports,* 109, 339–360.

Kirby, D., Waszak, C., and Ziegler, J. (1991). "Six School-Based Clinics: Their Reproductive Health Services and Impact on Sexual Behavior." *Family Planning Perspectives,* 23, 6–16.

Kirkcaldy, B. D., Shephard, R. J., and Siefen, R. G. (2002). "The Relationship between Physical Activity and Self-Image and Problem Behavior among Adolescents." *Social Psychiatry and Psychiatric Epidemiology,* 37, 544–550.

Kirkpatrick, L. A. (1998). "God as a Substitute Attachment Figure: A Longitudinal Study of Adult Attachment Style and Religious Change in College Students." *Personality and Social Psychology Bulletin,* 24.

Kirschner, D. (1996). "Adoption Psychopathology and the 'Adopted Child Syndrome.' " In *The Hatherleigh Guide to Child and Adolescent Therapy* (pp. 103–123). New York: Hatherleigh Press.

Kirsh, S. J. (2006). *Children, Adolescents, and Media Violence: A Critical Look at the Research.* Thousand Oaks, CA: Sage.

Kiselica, M. S., and Pfaller, J. (1993). "Helping Teenage Parents: The Independent and Collaborative Roles of Counselor Educators and School Counselors." *Journal of Counseling and Development,* 72, 42–48.

Kiselica, M. S., and Sturmer, P. (1993). "Is Society Giving Teenage Fathers a Mixed Message?" *Youth and Society,* 24, 487–501.

Kisker, E. E. (March–April 1985). "Teenagers Talk about Sex, Pregnancy, and Contraception." *Family Planning Perspectives,* 17, 83–90.

Klaczynski, P. (2005). "Metacognition and Cognitive Variability: A Dual-Process Model of Decision Making and Its Development." In J. Jacobs and P. Klaczynski (Eds.), *The Development of Decision Making in Children and Adolescents* (pp. 39–76). Mahwah, NJ: Erlbaum.

Klaczynski, P. A. (1990). "Cultural-Developmental Tasks and Adolescent Development: Theoretical and Methodological Considerations." *Adolescence,* 25, 811–823.

Klaczynski, P. A. (1993). "Reasoning Schema Effects on Adolescent Rule Acquisition and Transfer." *Journal of Educational Psychology,* 85, 679–692.

Klaczynski, P. A., and Gordon, D. H. (1996). "Self-Serving Influences on Adolescents' Evaluations of Belief-Relevant Evidence." *Journal of Experimental Child Psychology,* 62, 317–339.

Klaczynski, P. A., Byrnes, J. E., and Jacobs, J. E. (2001). "Introduction to the Special Issue on the Development of Decision-Making." *Journal of Applied Developmental Psychology,* 22, 225–236.

Klaczynski, P., and Cottrell, J. (2004). "A Dual-Process Approach to Cognitive Development: The Case of Children's Understanding of Sunk-Cost Decisions." *Thinking and Reasoning,* 10, 147–174.

Klarcznski, P. A., and Narasimhan, G. (1998). "Representations as Mediators of Adolescent Deductive Reasoning." *Developmental Psychology,* 34, 865–881.

Klaw, E., and Saunders, M. (1994). *An Ecological Model of Career Planning in Pregnant African-American Teens.* Paper presented at the biennial meeting of the Society for Research on Adolescents, San Diego.

Klayman, J. (1985). "Children's Decision Strategies and Their Adaptation to Talk Characteristics." *Oganizational Behavior and Human Decision Processes,* 35, 179–201.

Klebanob, P. K., and Brooks-Gunn, J. (1992). "Impact of Paternal Attitudes, Girls' Adjustment and Cognitive Skills upon Academic Performance in Middle and High School." *Journal of Research on Adolescence,* 2, 81–102.

Klein, H. A. (1992). "Temperament and Self-Esteem in Late Adolescence." *Adolescence,* 27, 689–694.

Klein, H. A. (1995). "Self-Perception in Late Adolescence: An Interactive Perspective." *Adolescence,* 30, 579–591.

Klein, M. 1998. "Teen Green." *American Demographics,* 20, 39.

Klepinger, D. H., Lundberg, S., and Plotnick, R. G. (1995). "Adolescent Fertility and the Educational Attainment of Young Women." *Family Planning Perspectives,* 27, 23–28.

Kling, K. C., Hyde, J. S., Showers, C. J., and Buswell, B. N. (1999). "Gender Differences in Self-Esteem: A Meta-Analysis." *Psychological Bulletin,* 125, 470–500.

Klingman, L., and Vicary, J. R. (1992). *Risk Factors Associated with Date Rape and Sexual Assault of Young Adolescent Girls.* Paper presented at the meeting of the Society for Research on Adolescents, Washington, DC.

Klos, D. S., and Loomis, D. F. (June 1978). "A Rating Scale of Intimate Disclosure between Late Adolescents and Their Friends." *Psychological Reports,* 42, 815–820.

Klyman, C. M. (1985). "Community Parental Surrogates and Their Role for the Adolescent." *Adolescence,* 20, 397–404.

Knapp, M., and Shields, P. (1990). "Recovering Academic Instruction for the Children of Poverty." *Phi Delta Kappan,* 71, 753–758.

Knox, D., Zusman, M. E., Snell, S., and Cooper, C. (1999). "Characteristics of College Students Who Cohabitate." *College Student Journal,* 33, 510–512.

Kochenderfer, B. J., and Ladd, G. W. (1997). "Victimized Children's Responses to Peers' Aggression: Behaviors Associated with Reduced versus Continued Victimization." *Developmental Psychopathology,* 9, 59–73.

Koenig, L. J. (1988). "Self-Image of Emotionally Disturbed Adolescents." *Journal of Abnormal Child Psychology,* 16, 111–126.

Koenig, L. J., and Abrams, R. F. (1999). "Adolescent Loneliness and Adjustment—A Focus on Gender Differences." In K. J. Rotenberg and S. Hymel (Eds.), *Loneliness in Childhood and Adolescence* (pp. 296–322). Cambridge, England: Cambridge University Press.

Koff, E., and Rierdan, J. (1990). "Gender, Body Image, and Self-Concept in Early Adolescence." *Journal of Early Adolescence,* 10, 56–68.

Koff, E., and Rierdan, J. (1995). "Preparing Girls for Menstruation: Recommendations from Adolescent Girls." *Adolescence,* 30, 795–811.

Koff, E., Rierdan, J., & Stubbs, M. L. (1990). "Gender, body image, and self-concept in early adolescence." *Journal of Early Adolescence,* 10, 56–68.

Kohlberg, L. (1963). "The Development of Children's Orientations toward a Moral Order." *Vita Humana,* 6, 11–33.

Kohlberg, L. (1966). "Moral Education in the Schools: A Developmental View." *School Review,* 74, 1–30.

Kohlberg, L. (1969). *Stages in the Development of Moral Thought and Action.* New York: Holt, Rinehart and Winston.

Kohlberg, L. (1970). "Moral Development and the Education of Adolescents." In R. F. Purnell (Ed.), *Adolescents and the American High School.* New York: Holt, Rinehart and Winston.

Kohlberg, L. (1994). *Moral Reasoning in Adolescence.* Boston: Allyn & Bacon.

Kohlberg, L., and Gilligan, C. (Fall 1971). "The Adolescent as a Philosopher: The Discovery of the Self in a Postconventional World." *Daedalus,* 1051–1086.

Kohlberg, L., and Kramer, R. (1969). "Continuities and Discontinuities in Childhood and Adult Development." *Human Development,* 12, 93–120.

Kohlberg, L., and Turiel, E., (Eds.). (1972). *Recent Research in Moral Development.* New York: Holt, Rinehart and Winston.

Kolata, G. (1988). "Child Splitting." *Psychology Today,* 22, 34–36.

Koopmans, M. (1995). "A Case of Family Dysfunction and Teenage Suicide Attempt: Applicability of a Family System's Paradigm." *Adolescence,* 30, 87–94.

Kopera-Frye, K., and Wiscott, R. (2000). "Intergenerational Continuity: Transmission of Beliefs and Culture." In B. Hayslip, Jr., and R. Goldberg-Glen (Eds.), *Grandparents Raising Grandchildren: Theoretical, Empirical, and Clinical Perspectives* (pp. 65–84). New York: Springer-Verlag.

Koss, M. P. (1993). "Rape: Scope, Impact, Interventions, and Public Policy Responses." *American Psychologist,* 48, 1062–1069.

Koss, M. P., Gidyca, C. A., and Wisniewski, N. (1987). "The Scope of Rape: Incidence and Prevalence of Sexual Aggression and Victimization in a National Sample of Higher Education Students." *Journal of Consulting and Clinical Psychology,* 55, 162–170.

Kostanski, M., and Gullone, E. (1998). "Adolescent Body Image Dissatisfaction: Relationships with Self-Esteem, Anxiety, and Depression Controlling for Body Mass." *Journal of Child Psychiatry,* 39, 255–262.

Kracke, B. (2002). "The Role of Personality, Parents and Peers in Adolescents' Career Exploration." *Journal of Adolescence,* 25, 19–30.

Kracke, B., and Schmitt-Rodermund, E. (2001). "Adolescents' Career Exploration in the Context of Educational and Occupational Transitions." In J. E. Nurmi (Ed.), *Navigating through Adolescence: European Perspectives* (pp. 137–161). New York: Garland.

Kramer, L. R. (1991). "The Social Construction of Ability Perceptions: An Ethnographic Study of Gifted Adolescent Girls." *Journal of Early Adolescence,* 11, 340–362.

Kratzert, W. F., and Kratzert, M. Y. (1991). "Characteristics of Continuation of High School Students." *Adolescence,* 26, 13–17.

Krebs, D., and Gillmore, J. (1982). "The Relationship among the First Stages of Cognitive Development, Role-Taking Abilities, and Moral Development." *Child Development,* 53, 877–886.

Kreider, R. M. (2003). "Adopted Children and Stepchildren: 2000." *U. S. Census Special Report CENSR-6RV.* Washington, DC: U.S. Bureau of the Census.

Kreider, R. M., and Fields, J. M. (2002). "Number, Timing, and Duration of Marriages and Divorces: 1996." *Current Population Reports,* no. P70–80. Washington, DC: U.S. Bureau of the Census.

Krettenauer, T. (2004). "Metaethical Cognition and Epistemic Reasoning Development in Adolescence." *International Journal of Behavioral Development,* 28, 461–470.

Kroger, J. (1988). "A Longitudinal Study of Ego Identity Status Interview Domains." *Journal of Adolescence,* 11, 49–64.

Kroger, J. (1990). "Ego Structuralization in Late Adolescence as Seen through Early Memories and Ego Identity Status." *Journal of Adolescence,* 13, 65–77.

Kroger, J. (1995). "The Differentiation of 'Firm' and 'Developmental' Foreclosure Identity Statuses: A Longitudinal Study." *Journal of Adolescent Research,* 10, 317–337.

Kroger, J. (1997). "Gender and Identity: The Intersection of Structure, Content, and Context." *Sex Roles,* 36, 747–770.

Kroger, J. (2003). "Identity Development during Adolescence." In G. R. Adams and M. D. Berzonsky (Eds.), *Blackwell Handbook of Adolescence* (pp. 205–226). Oxford, England: Blackwell Publishing.

Krohn, F. B., and Bogan, Z. (2001). "The Effects Absent Fathers Have on Female Development and College Attendance." *College Student Journal,* 35, 598–608.

Ku, L., Sonenstein, F. L., and Turner, C. F. (1997). "The Promise of Integrated Representative Surveys about Sexually Transmitted Diseases and Behavior." *Sexually Transmitted Diseases,* 12, 299–309.

Kubitschek, W. N., and Hallinan, M. T. (1996). "Race, Gender, and Track Inequity in Track Assignment." *Research in Sociology of Education,* 11, 121–146.

Kuhn, D. (1979). "The Significance of Piaget's Formal Operations Stage in Education." *Journal of Education,* 161, 34–50.

Kuhn, D. (1989). "Children and Adults as Intuitive Scientists." *Psychological Review,* 96, 674–689.

Kuhn, D. (2006). "Do Cognitive Changes Accompany Development in the Adolescent Brain?" *Perspectives on Psychological Science,* 1, 59–67.

Kuhn, D., and Dean, D., Jr. (2005). "Is Developing Scientific Thinking All about Learning to Control Variables?" *Psychological Science,* 16, 866–870.

Kuhn, D., Langer, J., Kohlberg, L., and Haan, N. S. (1977). "The Development of Formal Operations in Logical and Moral Judgment." *Genetic Psychology Monographs,* 95, 97–188.

Kunkel, D., Keren, E., Finnety, K., Biely, E., and Donnerstein, E. (2005). *Sex on TV: 2005.* Menlo Park, CA: Kaiser Family Foundation.

Kuperminc, G. P., Allen, J. P., and Arthur, M. W. (1996). "Autonomy, Relatedness, and Male Adolescent Delinquency." *Journal of Adolescent Research,* 11, 397–420.

Kurtz, P. D., Kurtz, G. L., and Jarvis, S. D. (1991). "Problems of Maltreated, Runaway Youths." *Adolescence,* 26, 543–555.

Kuttler, A. F., La Greca, A. M., and Prinstein, M. J. (1999). "Friendship Qualities and Social-Emotional Functioning of Adolescents with Close, Cross-Sex Friends." *Journal of Research on Adolescence,* 9, 339–366.

Kuziel-Perri, P., and Snarey, J. (1991). "Adolescent Repeat Pregnancies: An Evaluation Study of a Comprehensive Service Program for Pregnant and Parenting Black Adolescents." *Family Relations,* 40, 381–385.

Lachenmeyer, J. R., and Muni-Brander, P. (1988). "Eating Disorders in a Nonclinical Adolescent Population: Implications for Treatment." *Adolescence,* 23, 303–312.

Lachman, M. E., and Burack, O. R. (1993). "Planning and Control Processes across the Life Span: An Overview." *International Journal of Behavioral Development,* 16, 131–143.

Lackovic-Grgin, K., and Dekovic, M. (1990). "The Contribution of Significant Others to Adolescents' Self-Esteem." *Adolescence,* 25, 839–846.

LaFontana, K. M., and Cillessen, K. H. N. (2002). "Children's Perceptions of Popular and Unpopular Peers: A Multimethod Assessment." *Developmental Psychology,* 38, 635–647.

LaFromboise, T. D., and Bigfoot, D. S. (1988). "Cultural and Cognitive Considerations in the Prevention of American Indian Adolescent Suicide." *Journal of Adolescence,* 11, 139–153.

Lagoni, L. S., and Cook, A. S. (1985). "Stepfamilies: A Content Analysis of the Popular Literature, 1961–1982." *Family Relations,* 34, 521–525.

Laing, J., Valiga, M., and Eberly, C. (1986). "Predicting College Freshmen Major Choices from ACT Assessment Program Data." *College and University,* 61, 198–205.

Laird, R. (2005). What Is It We Think We Are Trying to Fix and How Should We Fix It? A View From the Admissions Office. In Camara, W. J. & Kimmel, E. W. (Eds.), *Choosing Students: Higher Education Admissions Tools for the 21st Century.* pp. 13–32. Mahwah, NJ: Lawrence Erlbaum.

Lam, C-m. (2003). "Covert Parental Control: Parent-Adolescent Interaction and Adolescent Development in a Chinese Context." *International Journal of Adolescent Medicine & Health,* 15, 63–77.

Lambert, T. A., Kahn, A. S., and Apple, K. J. (2003). "Pluralistic Ignorance and Hooking Up." *Journal of Sex Research,* 40, 129–133.

Lamborn, S., Mounts, N., Steinberg, L., and Dornbush, S. (1991). "Patterns of Competence and Adjustment among Adolescents from Authoritative, Authoritarian, Indulgent, and Neglectful Homes." *Child Development,* 62, 1049–1065.

Lamke, L. K., Lujan, B. M., and Showalter, J. M. (1988). "The Case for Modifying Adolescents' Cognitive Self-Statements." *Adolescence,* 23, 967–974.

Land, S. M. (2000). "Cognitive Requirements for Learning with Open-Ended Learning Environments." *Educational Technology: Research and Development,* 48, 61–78.

Landry, D. J., and Camelo, T. M. (1994). "Young Unmarried Men and Women Discuss Men's Role in Contraceptive Practice." *Family Planning Perspectives,* 26, 222–227.

Landry, D. J., Kaeser, L., and Richards, C. L. (1999). "Abstinence Promotion and the Provision of Information about Contraception in Public School District Sexual Education Policies." *Family Planning Perspectives,* 31, 280–286.

Landsheer, H., Maasen, G. H., Bisschop, P., and Adema, L. (1998). "Can Higher Grades Result in Fewer Friends? A Reexamination of the Relation between Academic and Social Competence." *Adolescence,* 33, 185–191.

Langlois, J. H., Kalakanis, L., Rubenstein, J., Larson, A., Hallam, M., and Smoot, M. (2000). "Maxims or Myths of Beauty? A Meta-Analytic and Theoretical Review." *Psychological Bulletin,* 126, 390–423.

Lapsley, D. K. (1990). "Continuity and Discontinuity in Adolescent Social Cognitive Development." In R. Montemayor, G. R. Adams, & T. P. Gullotta (Eds.), *From Childhood to Adolescence: A Transitional Period?* (pp. 183–204). Newbury Park, CA: Sage Publications.

Lapsley, D. K. (1993). "Toward an Integrated Theory of Adolescent Ego Development: The 'New Look' at Adolescent Egocentrism." *American Journal of Orthopsychiatry,* 63, 562–571.

Lapsley, D. K., and Murphy, M. N. (1985). "Another Look at the Theoretical Assumptions of Adolescent Egocentrism." *Developmental Review,* 5, 201–217.

Lapsley, D. K., FitzGerald, D. P., Rice, K. G., and Jackson, S. (1989). "Separation-Individuation and the 'New Look' at the Imaginary Audience and Personal Fable: A Test of an Integrative Model." *Journal of Adolescent Research,* 4, 483–505.

Larson, J. H., and Lowe, W. (1990). "Family Cohesion and Personal Space in Families with Adolescents." *Journal of Family Issues,* 11, 101–108.

Larson, J. H., Peterson, D. J., Heath, V. A., and Birch, P. (2000). "The Relationship Between Perceived Dysfunctional Family-of-Origin Rules and Intimacy in Young Adult Dating Relationships." *Journal of Sex and Marital Therapy,* 26, 161–175.

Larson, N. C., Hussey, J. M., Gilmore, J. R., and Gilchrist, L. D. (May, 1996). "What about Dad? Fathers of Children Born to School Mothers." *Families in Society,* 279–289.

Larson, R. W. (1987). "On the Independence of Positive and Negative Affect within Hour-to-Hour Experience." *Motivation and Emotion,* 11, 145–156.

Larson, R. W., and Verma, S. (1999). "How Children and Adolescents Spend Time across the World: Work, Play, and Developmental Opportunities." *Psychological Bulletin,* 125, 701–736.

Larson, R. W., Csikszentmihalyi, M., and Graef, R. (1980). "Mood Variability and Psychosocial Adjustment of Adolescents." *Journal of Youth and Adolescence,* 9, 469–489.

Larson, R., Csikszentmihalyi, M., and Graef, R. (1982). "Time Alone in Daily Experience: Loneliness or Renewal?" In L. A. Peplau and D. Perlman (Eds.), *Loneliness: A Sourcebook of Current Theory, Research and Therapy* (pp. 40–53). New York: Wiley.

Larson, R., Richards, M., Moneta, G., Holmbeck, G., and Duckett, E. (1996). "Changes in Adolescents' Daily Interactions with Their Families from Ages 10–18: Disengagement and Transformation." *Developmental Psychology,* 32, 744–754.

Lask, B., Waugh, R., and Gordo, I. (1997). "Childhood-Onset Anorexia Nervosa Is a Serious Illness." *Annals of the New York Academy of Sciences,* 817, 120–126.

Laumann, E., Gagnon, J., Michael, R., and Michaels, S. (1994). *The Social Organization of Sexuality: Sexual Practices in the United States.* Chicago: University of Chicago Press.

Laursen, B. (1993). "The Perceived Impact on Conflict on Adolescent Relationships." *Merrill Palmer Quarterly,* 39, 535–550.

Laursen, B. (1995). "Conflict and Social Interaction in Adolescent Relationships." *Journal of Research on Adolescence,* 5, 55–70.

Laursen, B., and Collins, W. A. (1994). "Interpersonal Conflict during Adolescence." *Psychological Bulletin,* 115, 197–209.

Laursen, B., Coy, K. C., and Collins, W. C. (1998). "Reconsidering Changes in Parent-Child Conflict across Adolescence: A Meta-Analysis." *Child Development,* 69, 817–832.

Lawrence, F. C., Tasker, G. E., Daily, C. T., Orhiel, A. L., and Wozniak, P. H. (1986). "Adolescents' Time Spent Viewing Television." *Adolescence,* 21, 431–436.

Lazala, C., and Saenger, P. (2002). "Pubertal Gynecomastia." *Journal of Pediatric & Endocrinology & Metabolism,* 15, 553–560.

Lazarus, R. F. (1991). *Emotion and Adaptation.* New York: Oxford University Press.

Le Gall, A., Mullet, C., and Shafeghi, R. (2002). "Age, Religious Beliefs, and Sexual Attitudes." *Journal of Sex Research,* 39, 207–216.

Le Grange, D., and Lock, J. (2005). "The Dearth of Psychological Treatment Studies for Anorexia Nervosa." *International Journal of Eating Disorders,* 37, 79–91.

Le Roux, J., and Smith C. S. (1998). "Causes and Characteristics of the Street Child Phenomenon: A Global Perspective." *Adolescence,* 33, 683–688.

Leadbetter, D. J. (1994). *Reconceptualizing Social Supports for Adolescent Mothers, Grandmothers, Babies, Fathers, and Beyond.* Paper presented at the meeting of the Society for Research on Adolescents, San Diego.

Leadbetter, D. J., Way, M., and Raben, A. (1994). *Barriers to Involvement of Fathers of the Children of Adolescent Mothers.* Paper presented at the meeting of the Society for Research on Adolescents, San Diego.

Lease, A. M., Musgrove, K. T., and Axelrod, J. L. (2002). "Dimensions of Social Status in Preadolescent Peer Groups: Likability, Perceived Popularity, and Social Dominance." *Social Development,* 11, 508–533.

Lederman, L. C. (1993). "Gender and the Self." In L. P. Arliss and D. J. Borisoff (Ed.), *Women and Men Communicating.* Fort Worth, TX: Harcourt Brace Jovanovich.

Lee, B. E., Brooks-Gunn, J., Schnur, E., and Liaw, F. (1990). "Are Head Start Effects Sustained: A Longitudinal Follow-Up Comparison of Disadvantaged Children Attending Head Start, No Preschool, and Other Preschool Programs." *Child Development,* 61, 495–507.

Lee, B. E., Cloninger, R. G., Linn, E., and Chen, X. (1995). *The Culture of Sexual Harassment in Secondary Schools.* Paper presented at the meeting of the Society for Research on Child Development, Indianapolis, IN.

Lee, C. C. (Spring 1985). "Successful Rural Black Adolescents: A Psychological Profile." *Adolescence,* 20, 130–142.

Lee, E. (1982). "A Social Systems Approach to Assessment and Treatment for Chinese American Families." In M. McGoldrick, J. Pearce, and J. Giordana (Eds.), *Ethnicity and Family Therapy.* New York: Guilford Press.

Lee, E. (1988). "Cultural Factors in Working with Southeast Asian Refugee Adolescents." *Journal of Adolescence,* 11, 167–179.

Lee, E., and Chan, F. (1985). "The Use of Diagnostic Interview Schedule with Vietnamese Refugees." *Asian American Psychological Association Journal,* 1, 36–39.

Lee, J. D. (1998). "Which Kids Can "Become" Scientists? Effects of Gender, Self-Concepts, and Perceptions of Scientists." *Social Psychology Quarterly,* 61, 199–219.

Lee, M.-Y. (2002). "A Model of Children's Postdivorce Behavioral Adjustment in Maternal- and Dual-Residence Arrangements." *Journal of Family Issues,* 23, 672–697.

Lee, S. M., Daniels, M. H., and Kissinger, D. B. (2006). "Parental Influences on Adolescent Adjustment: Parenting Styles versus Parenting Practices." *Family Therapy: Counseling and Therapy for Couples and Families,* 14, 253–259.

Lee, T., Sixx, N., Mars, M., and Neil, V. (1991). *Primal Scream.* Electra.

Lee, V. E., and Burkam, D. T. (1996). "Gender Differences in Middle Grade Science Achievement: Subject Domain, Ability Level, and Course Emphasis." *Science Education,* 80, 613–650.

Lee, V. E., and Smith, J. (2001). *Restructuring High Schools for Equity and Excellence: What Works.* New York: Teachers College Press.

Lehman, E. B., Morath, R., Franklin, K., and Elbaz, V. (1998). "Knowing What to Remember and Forget: A Developmental Study of Cue Memory in Intentional Forgetting." *Memory and Cognition,* 26, 860–868.

Leiber, O. (1988). *Opposites Attract.* Virgin Music, Inc., and Oliver Leiber Music.

Leigh, B. C. (1989). "Reasons for Having and Avoiding Sex: Gender, Sexual Orientation, and Relationship to Sexual Behavior." *Journal of Sex Research,* 26, 199–209.

Leitenberg, H., Detzer, M. J., and Srebnik, D. (1993). "Gender Differences in the Relation of Masturbation Experience in Preadolescence and/or Early Adolescence to Sexual Behavior and Adjustment in Young Adulthood." *Archives of Sexual Behavior,* 22, 87–98.

Lemann, N. (2000). *The Big Test: The Secret History of the Meritocracy.* New York: Farrar, Straus, and Giroux.

LeMare, L. J., and Rubin, K. H. (1987). "Perspective Taking and Peer Interaction: Stuctural and Developmental Analysis." *Child Development,* 58, 306–315.

Lempers, J. D., and Clark-Lempers, D. G. (1992). "Young, Middle, and Late Adolescents' Comparisons of the Functional Importance of Five Significant Relationships." *Journal of Youth and Adolescence,* 21, 53–96.

Lempers, J. D., and Clark-Lempers, D. G. (1993). "A Functional Comparison of Same-Sex and Opposite-Sex Friendships During Adolescence." *Journal of Adolescent Research,* 8, 89–108.

Lenhart, A., Madden, M., and Hitlin, P. (2005). *Teens and Technology.* Washington, DC: Pew Internet and American Life Project.

Lent, R. W., Brown, S. D., and Hackett, G. (2000). "Contextual Supports and Barriers to Career Choice: A Social Cognitive Analysis." *Journal of Counseling Psychology,* 47, 36–49.

Leong, F. T. L. (1991). "Career Development Attributes and Occupational Values of Asian-American and White-American College Students." *Career Development Quarterly,* 39, 221–230.

Leong, F. T. L., and Hayes, T. J. (1990). "Occupational Stereotyping of Asian Americans." *The Career Development Quarterly,* 39, 143–154.

Lerner, H. R. M., Lerner, J. V., Hess, L. E., et al. (1991). "Physical Attractiveness and Psychosocial Functioning among Early Adolescence." *Journal of Early Adolescence,* 11, 300–320.

Lerner, R. M., and Galambos, N. L. (1998). "Adolescent Development: Challenges and Opportunities for Research, Programs, and Policies." *Annual Review of Psychology,* 49, 413–446.

Lerner, R. M., and Karabeneck, S. A. (1974). "Physical Attractiveness, Body Attitudes, and Self-Concept in Late Adolescents." *Journal of Youth and Adolescence,* 3, 307–316.

Lerner, R. M., Delaney, M., Hess, L. E., Jovanovic, J., & von Eye, A. (1990). "Early Adolescent Physical Attractiveness and Academic Competence." *Journal of Early Adolescence,* 10, 4–20.

Lester, B. M., and Dreher, M. (1989). "Effects of Marijuana Use during Pregnancy on Newborn Cry." *Child Development,* 60, 764–771.

Lester, D. (1988). "Youth Suicide: A Cross-Cultural Perspective." *Adolescence,* 23, 955–958.

Lester, D. (1991). "Social Correlates of Youth Suicide Rates in the United States." *Adolescence,* 26, 55–58.

Letendre, G. K. (2000). *Learning to Be Adolescent: Growing Up in U.S. and Japanese Middle Schools.* New Haven, CT: Yale University Press.

Leung, S., A., Ivey, D., and Susuki, L. (1999). "Factors Affecting the Career Aspirations of Asian

Americans." *Journal of Counseling and Development,* 72, 401–410.

Levant, R. F., and Pollack, W. S. (Eds.). (1995). *The New Psychology of Men.* New York: Basic.

LeVay, S. (1991). "A Difference in Hypothalamic Structure between Heterosexual and Homosexual Men." *Science,* 253, 1034–1037.

Leventhal, T., Graber, J. A., and Brooks-Gunn, J. (2001). "Adolescent Transitions to Adulthood: Antecedents, Correlates, and Consequences of Adolescent Employment." *Journal of Research on Adolescence,* 11, 297–323.

Levine, M., and Harrison, K. (2004). "Media's Role in the Perpetuation and Prevention of Negative Body Image and Disordered Eating." In J. K. Thompson (Ed.), *Handbook of Eating Disorders and Obesity* (pp. 695–717). New York: Wiley.

Levinson, R. A. (1995). "Reproductive and Contraceptive Knowledge, Contraceptive Self-Efficacy, and Contraceptive Behavior among Teenage Women." *Adolescence,* 30, 65–85.

Levy-Schiff, R., Zoran, N., and Shulman, S. (1997). "International and Domestic Adoption: Child, Parents and Family Adjustment." *International Journal of Behavioural Development,* 20, 109–129.

Lewin, K. (1939). "Field Theory and Experiment in Social Psychology: Concepts and Methods." *American Journal of Sociology,* 44, 868–897.

Lewis, R. E. (2004). "Resilience: Individual, Family, School, and Community Perspectives." In D. Capuzzi and D. Gross (Eds.), *Youth at Risk: A Prevention Resource for Counselors, Teachers and Parents* (pp. 35–68). Upper Saddle River, NJ: Pearson.

Lewis, T., Stone, J., III, Shipley, W., and Madzar, S. (1998). "The Transition from School to Work: An Examination of the Literature." *Youth and Society,* 29, 259–292.

Leyendecker, B., Harwood, R. L., Comparini, L., and Yalcinkaya, A. (2005). Socioeconomic Status, Ethnicity, and Parenting. In T. Luster and L. Okagaki (Eds.) *Parenting: An ecological perspective (2nd ed.)* (pp. 319–341). Mahwah, NJ: Lawrence Erlbaum Associates.

Li, Q. (2006). "Cyberbullying: A Research of Gender Differences." *School Psychology International,* 27, 157–170.

Liben, L. S., and Goldbeck, S. L. (1980). "Sex Differences in Performance on Piagetian Spatial Tasks: Differences in Competence or Performance?" *Child Development,* 51, 594–597.

Lidz, C. S. (2001). "Multicultural Issues and Dynamic Assessment." In L. A. Suzuki and J. G. Ponterotto (Eds.), *Handbook of Multicultural Assessment: Clinical, Psychological, and Educational Applications* (2nd ed., pp. 523–539). San Francisco: Jossy-Bass.

Lieb, R., Merikangas, K. R., Hofler, M., Pfister, H., Isensee, B., and Wittchen, H.-U. (2002). "Parental Alcohol Use Disorders and Alcohol Use and Disorders in Offspring: A Community Study." *Psychological Medicine,* 32, 63–78.

Lindberg, L. D., Boggess, S., Porter, L., and Williams, S. (2000). *Teen Risk-Taking: A Statistical Portrait.* Washington, DC: Urban Institute.

Lines, P. M. (2001). "Homeschooling." *ERIC Digest,* 151, 1–7.

Linver, M. R., and Silverberg, S. B. (1995). "Parenting as a Multidimensional Construct: Differential Prediction of Adolescents' Sense of Self and Engagement in Problem Behavior." *International Journal of Adolescent Medicine and Health,* 8, 29–40.

Linz, D. (1985). *Sexual Violence in the Mass Media: Effects on Male Viewers and Implications for Society.* Unpublished doctoral dissertation, University of Wisconsin, Madison.

Lipsey, M. W., and Wilson, D. B. (1998). "Effective Interventions for Serious Juvenile Offenders: A Synthesis of Research." In R. Loeber and D. P. Farrington (Eds.), *Serious and Violent Juvenile Offenders: Risk Factors and Successful Interventions* (pp. 313–366). Thousand Oaks, CA: Sage.

Litchfield, A. W., Thomas, D. L., and Li, B. D. (1997). "Dimensions of Religiosity as Mediators of the Relations between Parenting and Adolescent Deviant Behavior." *Journal of Adolescent Research,* 12, 199–226.

Litt, I. F., and Vaughn, V. C., III. (1987). "Growth and Development during Adolescence." In R. E. Behrman, V. C. Vaughn, and W. E. Nelson, (Eds.), *Textbook of Pediatrics.* 13th ed. (pp. 20–23). Philadelphia: Saunders.

Littrell, M. A., Damhorst, M. L., and Littrell, J. M. (1990). "Clothing Interests, Body Satisfaction, and Eating Behavior of Adolescent Females: Belated or Independent Dimensions?" *Adolescence,* 25, 77–95.

Liu, X., Kaplan, H. B., and Risser, W. (1992). "Decomposing the Reciprocal Relationships between Academic Achievement and General Self-Esteem." *Youth and Society,* 24, 123–148.

Lobdell, J., and Perlman, D. (1986). "The Intergenerational Transmission of Loneliness: A Study of College Females and Their Parents." *Journal of Marriage and the Family,* 48, 589–595.

Lochman, J. E., and Dodge, K. A. (1994). "Social-Cognitive Processes of Severely Violent, Moderately Aggressive, and Nonaggressive Boys." *Journal of Counseling and Clinical Psychology,* 62, 366–374.

LoCicero, K. A., and Ashby, J. S. (2000). "Mulitdimensional Perfectionism in Middle School Age Gifted Students: A Comparison to Peers from the General Cohort." *Roeper Review,* 22, 182–185.

Loeb, P. (1988). "Willful Unconcern." *Psychology Today,* 22, 59–62.

Logan, D. D., Calder, J. A., and Cohen, B. L. (1980). "Toward a Contemporary Tradition for Menarche." *Journal of Youth and Adolescence,* 9, 263–269.

Lopez, N. L., Bonenberger, J. L., and Schneider, H. G. (2001). "Parental Disciplinary History, Current Levels of Empathy, and Moral Reasoning in Young Adults." *North American Journal of Psychology,* 3, 1527–7143.

LoPresto, C., Sherman, M., and Sherman, N. (1985). "The Effects of a Masturbation Seminar on High School Males' Attitudes, False Beliefs, Guilt, and Behavior." *Journal of Sex Research,* 21, 142–156.

Lord, S. E., Eccles, J. S., and McCarthy, K. A. (1994). "Surviving the Junior High School Transition: Family Processes and Self-Perceptions as Protective and Risk Factors." *Journal of Early Adolescence,* 14, 162–199.

Loring, I. (1718). Duty and Interests of Young Persons. Boston.

Loughlin, C. A., and Barling, J. (1998). "Teenagers' Part-Time Employment and Their Work-Related Attitudes and Aspirations." *Journal of Organizational Behavior,* 19, 197–207.

Lowe, C. S., and Radius, S. M. (1987). "Young Adults' Contraceptive Practices: An Investigation of Influences." *Adolescence,* 22, 291–304.

Lowman, R. L. (1991). *The Clinical Practice of Career Assessment.* Washington, DC: American Psychological Association.

Lowney, J. (Winter 1984). "Correspondence between Attitudes and Drinking and Drug Behavior: Youth Subculture over Time." *Adolescence,* 19, 875–892.

Lowney, K. S. (1995). "Teenage Satanism as Oppositional Youth Subculture." *Journal of Contemporary Ethnography,* 23, 453–484.

Lucas, S. R., and Good, A. D. (2001). "Race, Class, and Tournament Track Mobility." *Sociology of Education,* 74, 139–156.

Lundholm, J. K., and Littrell, J. M. (1986). "Desire for Thinness among High School Cheerleaders: Relationship to Disordered Eating and Weight Control Behavior." *Adolescence,* 21, 573–579.

Lussier, G., Deater-Deckard, K., Dunn, J., and Davies, L. (2002). "Support across Two Generations: Children's Closeness to Parents Following Parental Divorce and Remarriage." *Journal of Family Psychology,* 16, 363–376.

Luster, T., and McAdoo, H. M. (1995). "Factors Related to Self-Esteem among African American Youths: A Secondary Analysis with a High/Scope Perry Preschool Data." *Journal of Research on Adolescence,* 5, 451–467.

Luster, T., and Small, S. (1997). "Sexual Abuse History and Problems in Adolescence: Exploring the Effects of Moderating Variables." *Journal of Marriage and the Family,* 59, 131–142.

Lynam, D. R., Milich, R., Zimmerman, R., Novak, S. P., Logan, T. K., Martin C., Leukefeld, C., and Clayton, R. (1999). "Project DARE: No Effects at 10-Year Follow-Up." *Journal of Consulting and Clinical Psychology,* 67, 590–593.

Lytton, H. (1995). *Child and Family Predictors of Conduct Disorders and Criminality.* Paper presented at the meeting of the Society for Research in Child Development, Indianapolis, IN.

Ma, H. K. (1989). "Moral Orientation and Moral Judgment in Adolescents in Hong Kong, Mainland China, and England." *Journal of Cross-Cultural Psychology,* 20, 152–177.

Macallair, D. (1993). "Reaffirming Rehabilitation in Juvenile Justice." *Youth and Society,* 25, 104–125.

Maccoby, E. E. (1990). "Gender and Relationships." *American Psychologist,* 45, 513–520.

Maccoby, E. E., and Mnookin, R. H. (1992). *Dividing the Child: Social and Legal Dilemmas of Custody.* Cambridge, MA: Harvard University Press.

Maccoby, E. E., Buchanan, C. M., Mnookin, R. H., and Dornbusch, S. M. (1993). "Postdivorce Roles of Mothers and Fathers in the Lives of their Children." *Journal of Family Psychology,* 7, 24–38.

MacDonald, W. L., and DeMaris, A. (1996). "Parenting Step-Children and Biological Children." *Journal of Family Issues,* 17, 5–25.

MacGregor, J., and Newlon, B. J. (1987). "Description of a Teenage Pregnancy Program." *Journal of Counseling and Development,* 65, 447.

MacKay, A. P., Fingerhut, L. A., & Duran, C. R. (2000). *Adolescent Health Chartbook. Health, United States, 2000.* Hyattsville, MD: National Center for Health Statistics.

Maehr, M. L., and Midgley, C. (1991). "Enhancing Student Motivations: A School-Wide Approach." *Educational Psychologist,* 26, 399–427.

Maguin, E., and Loeber, R. (1996). "Academic Performance and Delinquency." In M. Tonry (Ed.),

Crime and Justice: A Review of Research (pp. 145–264). Chicago: University of Chicago Press.

Mahoney, J. L. (2000). "School Extracurricular Activity Participation as a Moderator in the Development of Antisocial Patterns." *Child Development,* 71, 502–516.

Mahoney, J. L., Cairns, B. D., and Farmer, T. W. (2003). "Promoting Interpersonal Competence and Educational Success through Extracurricular Activity Participation." *Journal of Educational Psychology,* 95, 409–418.

Mahoney, J. L., Schweder, A. E., and Stattin, H. (2002). "Structured After-School Activities as a Moderator of Depressed-Mood for Adolescents with Detached Relations to Their Parents." *Journal of Community Psychology,* 30, 69–86.

Malamuth, N. M., and Check, J. B. P. (1985). "The Effects of Aggressive Pornography on Beliefs and Rape Myths: Individual Differences." *Journal of Research of Personality,* 19, 299–320.

Malmberg, L. E. (2001). "Future-Orientation in Educational and Interpersonal Contexts." In J. E. Nurmi (Ed.), *Navigating through Adolescence: European Perspectives* (pp. 119–140). New York: Routledge.

Manaster, G. J. (1977). *Adolescent Development and the Life Tasks.* Boston: Allyn & Bacon.

Mandara, J., Murray, C. B., and Joyner, T. N. (2005). "The Impact of Fathers' Absence on African American Adolescents' Gender Role Development." *Sex Roles,* 53, 207–220.

Manlove, J. (1998). "The Influence of High School Dropout and School Disengagement on the Risk of School-Age Pregnancy." *Journal of Research on Adolescence,* 8, 187–220.

Mann, L., Harmoni, R. V., and Power, C. N. (1989). "Adolescent Decision-Making: The Development of Competence." *Journal of Adolescence,* 12, 265–278.

Mann, L., Harmoni, R. V., Power, C. N., and Beswick, G. (1986). *Understanding and Improving Decision-Making in Adolescents.* Unpublished manuscript, Flinders University of South Australia.

Manning, M. L. (Winter 1983). "Three Myths Concerning Adolescence." *Adolescence,* 18, 823–829.

Manning, W. D. (1990). "Parenting Employed Teenagers." *Youth and Society,* 22, 184–200.

Manning, W. D. (1995). "Cohabitation, Marriage, and Entry into Motherhood." *Journal of Marriage and the Family,* 57, 191–200.

Manning, W. D., and Landale, N. S. (1996). "Racial and Ethnic Differences in the Role of Cohabitation and Premarital Childbearing." *Journal of Marriage and the Family,* 58, 63–77.

Manning, W. D., and Lichter, D. T. (1996). "Parental Cohabitation and Children's Economic Well-Being." *Journal of Marriage and the Family,* 58, 998–1010.

Manning, W. D., Longmore, M. A., and Giordano, P. C. (2004). "Adolescents' Involvement in Non-Romantic Sexual Activity." *Social Science Research,* 34, 384–407.

Marcia, J. E. (1966). "Development and Validation of Ego Identity Status." *Journal of Personality and Social Psychology,* 3, 551–558.

Marcia, J. E. (1976). "Identity Six Years After: A Follow Up Study." *Journal of Youth and Adolescence,* 5, 145–160.

Marcia, J. E. (1980). "Identity in Adolescence." In J. Adelson (Ed.), *Handbook of Adolescent Psychology* (pp. 159–187). New York: Wiley.

Marcia, J. E. (1987). "The Identity Status Approach to the Study of Ego Identity Development." In T. Hones and K. Gardley (Eds.), *Self and Identity: Perspectives Across the Lifespan* (pp. 161–172). London: Routledge and Kegan Paul.

Marcia, J. E. (1991). "Identity and Self Development." In R. M. Lerner, A. D. Petersen, and J. Brooks-Gunn (Eds.), *Encyclopedia of Adolescence.* Vol. 1. New York: Garland.

Marcia, J. E. (1994). "The Empirical Study of Ego Identity." In H. A. Bosma, T. L. G. Graafsma, H. D. Grotebanc, and D. J. DeLivita (Eds.), *The Identity and Development.* Newbury Park, CA: Sage.

Marcia, J. E., and Friedman, M. L. (1970). "Ego Identity Status in College Women." *Journal of Personality,* 38, 249–263.

Marcus, M. D., and Kalarchian, M. A. (2003). "Binge Eating in Children and Adolescents." *International Journal of Eating Disorders,* 34, S47–S57.

Marcus, R. F. (1996). "The Friendships of Delinquents." *Adolescence,* 31, 145–158.

MarkarketResearch.com. (2005). *By 2006, U.S. Teens Can Buy and Sell Russia.* Press release. Retrieved from http://www.marketresearch.com/Corporate/aboutus/Press_view.asp?SID=54650555-228592314-249687041&Article=143.

Markiewicz, D., Doyle, A. B., and Bregden, M. (2001). "The Quality of Adolescents' Friendships: Associations with Mothers' Interpersonal Relationships, Attachment to Parents and Friends, and Prosocial Behaviors." *Journal of Adolescence,* 24, 429–445.

Markovitz, H., and Bouffard-Bouchard, T. (1992). "The Belief-Bias Effect in Reasoning: the Development and Activation of Competence." *British Journal of Developmental Psychology,* 10, 269–284.

Markstrom-Adams, C. (1990). "Coming-of-Age among Contemporary American Indians as Portrayed in Adolescent Fiction." *Adolescence,* 25, 225–237.

Markstrom-Adams, C., and Spencer, N. B. (1994). "A Model for Identity Intervention with Minority Adolescents." In S. A. Archer (Ed.), *Intervention for Adolescent Identity Development.* Newbury Park, CA: Sage.

Markus, H. R., and Kitayama, S. (1994). "A Collective Fear of the Collective: Implications for Selves and Theories of Selves." *Personality and Social Psychology Bulletin,* 20, 568–579.

Maroufi, C. (1989). "A Study of Student Attitudes towards Traditional and Generative Models of Instruction." *Adolescence,* 24, 65–72.

Marsh, H. (1989). "Age and Sex Effects in Multiple Dimensions of Self-Concept: Preadolescence to Early Adulthood." *Journal Of Educational Psychology,* 81, 417–430.

Marsh, H. W., and Kleitman, S. (2005). "Consequences of Employment during High School: Character Building, Subversion of Academic Goals, or a Threshold?" *American Educational Research Journal,* 42, 331–369.

Marsiglio, W., and Mott, F. L. (1986). "The Impact of Sex Education on Sexual Activity, Contraceptive Use and Premarital Pregnancy among American Teenagers." *Family Planning Perspectives,* 18, 151–162.

Martens, P. L. (1997). "Parental Monitoring and Deviant Behavior among Juveniles." *Studies on Crime and Crime Prevention,* 6, 224–244.

Martin, C. L., Ruble D. N., and Szkrybalo, J. (2002). "Cognitive Theories of Early Gender Development." *Psychological Bulletin,* 128, 903–933.

Martin, M. J., and Walters, J. (1982). "Family Correlates of Selected Types of Child Abuse and Neglect." *Journal of Marriage and the Family,* 44, 267–275.

Martin, Q., Peters, R. J., Amos, C. E., Yacoubian, G. S., Johnson, R. G., Meschack, and Essien, E. J. (2005). "The Relationship between Sexual Abuse and Drug Use: A View of African-American College Students in Texas." *Journal of Ethnicity in Substance Abuse,* 4, 23–33.

Martinez, A. C., Sedlacek, W. E., and Bachhuber, T. D. (1985). "Male and Female College Graduates—7 Months Later." *The Vocational Guidance Quarterly,* 34, 77–84.

Martinez, A. J. C., Mosher, W. D., and Dawson, B. S. (2004). "Teenagers in the United States: Sexual Activity, Contraceptive Use, and Child Bearing, 2002." *Vital Health Statistic,* 23. Washington, D.C.: National Center for Health Statistics.

Martinez, E. A. (1988). "Child Behavior in American/Chicano Families: Maternal Teaching and Child-Rearing Practices." *Family Relations,* 37, 275–280.

Martinez, M. E. (2000). *Education as the Cultivation of Intelligence.* Mahwah, NJ: Erlbaum.

Martinez, R., and Dukes, R. L. (1991). "Ethnic and Gender Differences and Self-Esteem." *Youth and Society,* 3, 318–338.

Martino, S. C., Collins, R. L., Elliott, M. N., Strachman, A., Kanouse, D. E., and Berry, S. H. (2006). "Exposure to Degrading versus Nondegrading Music Lyrics and Sexual Behavior among Youth." *Pediatrics,* 118, 430–441.

Martson, A. R., Jacobs, D. F., Singer, R. D., Widaman, K. F., and Little, T. D. (1988). "Adolescents Who Apparently Are Invulnerable to Drug, Alcohol, and Nicotine Use." *Adolescence,* 23, 593–598.

Mason, C. A., Walker-Barnes, C. J., Tu, S., Simons, J., and Martinez-Arrue, R. (2004). "Ethnic Differences in the Affective Meaning of Parental Control Behaviors." *Journal of Primary Prevention,* 25, 59–79.

Mason, M. G., and Gibbs, J. C. (1993). "Social Perspective Taking and Moral Judgment among College Students." *Journal of Adolescent Research,* 8, 109–123.

Masselam, V. S., Marcus, R. F., & Stunkard, C. L. (1990). "Parent–Adolescent Communication, Family Functioning, and School Performance." *Adolescence,* 25, 725–737.

Masters, W. H., and Johnson, V. (1966). *Human Sexual Response.* Boston: Little, Brown.

Masters, W. H., and Johnson, V. (1979). *Homosexuality in Perspective.* Boston: Little, Brown.

Mathias, R. (1997). "NIH Panel Calls for Expanded Methadone Treatment for Heroin Addiction." *National Institute for Drug Abuse Notes,* Vol. 12 <www.nida.nih.gov/nidanotes/nnvol12n6/nihpanel.html>.

Maton, K. (1990). "Meaningful Involvement in Instrumental Activity and Well-Being." *American Journal of Community Psychology,* 18, 297–320.

Matthews, L. J., and Ilon, L. (July 1980). "Becoming a Chronic Runaway: The Effects of Race and Family in Hawaii." *Family Relations,* 29, 404–409.

Mattis, J. S., Jagers, R. J., Hatcher, C. A., Lawhon, G. D., Murphy, E. J., and Murray, Y. F. (2000). "Religiosity, Volunteerism, and Community Involvement among African American Men: An Exploratory Analysis." *Journal of Community Psychology,* 28, 391–406.

Mau, R. Y. (1992). "The Validity and Devolution of a Concept: Student Alienation." *Adolescence,* 27, 731–741.

Mau, W-C., and Bikos, L. H. (2000). "Educational and Vocational Aspirations of Minority and Female Students: A Longitudinal Study." *Journal of Counseling and Development,* 78, 186–194.

Mau, W-C., and Lynn, R. (2001). "Gender Differences on the Scholastic Aptitude Test, the American College Test, and College Grades." *Educational Psychology,* 21, 133–136.

Maxson, C., & Whitlock, M. (2002). "Joining the Gang: Gender Differences in Risk Factors for Gang Membership." In C. Huff (Ed.), *Gangs in America III* (pp. 19–35). Thousand Oaks, CA: Sage Publications.

May, D. C. (1999). "Scared Kids, Unattached Kids, or Peer Pressure: Why Do Students Carry Firearms to School?" *Youth and Society,* 31, 100–127.

Mayer, J. E., and Ligman, J. D. (1989). "Personality Characteristics of Adolescent Marijuana Users." *Adolescence,* 24, 965–976.

Mazor, A., and Enright, R. D. (1988). "The Development of the Individuation Process from a Social-Cognitive Perspective." *Journal of Adolescence,* 11, 29–47.

McAdams, D. P. (2001). "The Psychology of Life Stories." *Review of General Psychology,* 5, 100–122.

McAuliffe, G. J. (1991). "Assessing and Treating Barriers to Decision Making in Career Classes." *The Career Development Quarterly,* 40, 82–92.

McCabe, D. L. (1999). "Academic Dishonesty among High School Students." *Adolescence,* 34, 681–687.

McCabe, D. L., and Trevino, L. K. (1997). "Individual and Contextual Influences on Academic Dishonesty: A Multi-Campus Investigation." *Research in Higher Education,* 38, 379–396.

McCabe D. L., Trevino L. K., and Butterfield K. D. (2001). "Cheating in Academic Institutions: A Decade of Research." *Ethics and Behavior,* 11, 219–232.

McCabe, M. P. (1987). "Desired and Experienced Levels of Premarital Affection and Sexual Intercourse during Dating." *The Journal of Sex Research,* 23, 23–33.

McCartt, A. T., Shabanova, V. I., and Leaf, W. A. (2003). "Driving Experience, Crashes and Traffic Citations of Teenage Beginning Drivers. *Accident Analysis and Prevention,* 35, 311–320.

McCary, J. L., and McCary, S. P. (1982). *McCary's Human Sexuality.* 4th ed. Belmont, CA: Wadsworth.

McCreary, M. L., Slavin, L. A., and Berry, E. J. (1996). "Predicting Problem Behavior and Self-Esteem among African American Adolescents." *Journal of Adolescent Research,* 11, 216–234.

McCurdy, S. J., and Scherman, E. (1996). "Effects of Family Structure on the Adolescent Separation-Individuation Process." *Adolescence,* 31, 307–319.

McDevitt, T. M., Lennon, R., and Kopriva, R. J. (1991). "Adolescents' Perceptions of Mothers' and Fathers' Pro-Social Actions and Empathic Responses." *Youth and Society,* 22, 387–409.

McDonald, D. L., and McKinney, J. P. (1994). "Steady Dating and Self-Esteem in High School Students." *Journal of Adolescence,* 17, 557–564.

McDonald, R. M., and Towberman, D. B. (1993). "Psychosocial Correlates of Adolescent Drug Involvement." *Adolescence,* 28, 925–936.

McElroy, T., and Foster, D. (1992). *Love Don't Love You.* 2 Tuff-E-Nuff Songs (BMI).

McEvoy, M., Chang, J., and Coupey, S. M. (2004). "Common Menstrual Disorders in Adolescence: Nursing Interventions." *MCN: The American Journal of Maternal/Child Nursing,* 29, 41–49.

McGaha, J. E., and Leoni, E. L. (1995). "Family Violence, Abuse, and Related Family Issues of Incarcerated Delinquents of Alcoholic Parents Compared with Those of Nonalcoholic Parents." *Adolescence,* 30, 473–482.

McGee, Z. T. (1992). "Social Class Differences in Parental and Peer Influence on Adolescent Drug Use." *Deviant Behavior,* 13, 349–372.

McGrory, A. (1990). "Menarche: Responses of Early Adolescent Females." *Adolescence,* 25, 265–270.

McGue, M. (1999). "The Behavioral Genetics of Alcoholism." *Current Directions in Psychological Science,* 8, 109–115.

McKay, A. (2004). "Oral Sex among Teenagers: Research, Discourse, and Education." *Canadian Journal of Human Sexuality,* 13, 201–204.

McKay, A., Pietrusiak, M.-A., and Holowaty, P. (1998). "Parents' Opinions and Attitudes towards Sexuality Education in the Schools." *Canadian Journal of Human Sexuality,* 7, 139–145.

McKenry, P. C., Kotch, J. B., and Browne, D. H. (1991). "Correlates of Dysfunctional Parenting Attitudes among Low-Income Adolescent Mothers." *Journal of Adolescent Research,* 6, 212–234.

McKim, W. A. (1997). *Drugs and Behavior: An Introduction to Behavioral Pharmacology,* 3rd ed. Upper Saddle River, NJ: Prentice-Hall.

McKinnon, J. D., & Bennett, C. E. (2005). "We the People: Blacks in the United States." *Census 2000 Special Reports.* Washington D.C.: U.S. Bureau of the Census.

McLanahan, S. S., and Sandefur, G. (1994). *Growing Up with a Single Parent: What Hurts, What Helps.* Cambridge, MA: Harvard University Press.

McLeod, B. (1986). "The Oriental Express." *Psychology Today,* 20, 48–52.

McLoyd, V. C. (1990). "Minority Children: Introduction to the Special Issue." *Child Development,* 61, 260–263.

McManus, M. J. (1986). "Introduction." In *Final Report of the Attorney General's Commission on Pornography.* Washington, DC: U.S. Government Printing Office. Reprint. Nashville, TN: Rutledge Hill Press.

McMurran, M. (1991). "Young Offenders and Alcohol-Related Crime: What Interventions Will Address the Issues?" *Journal of Adolescence,* 14, 245–253.

McShane, D. (1988). An analysis of mental health research with American Indian youth. *Journal of Adolescence,* 11(2), 87–116.

McShane, D. (1988). "An Analysis of Mental Health Research with American Indian Youth." *Journal of Adolescence,* 11(2), 87–116.

McVey, G. L., Pepler, D., Davis, R., Flett, G. L., and Abdolell, M. (2002). "Risk and Protective Factors Associated with Disordered Eating during Early Adolescence." *Journal of Early Adolescence,* 22, 75–95.

Mead, M. (1950). *Coming of Age in Samoa.* New York: New American Library.

Mead, M. (1953). *Growing Up in New Guinea.* New York: New American Library.

Mead, M. (1970). *Culture and Commitment: A Study of the Generation Gap.* Garden City, NY: Doubleday.

Mead, M. (1974). "Adolescence." In H. V. Kraemer (Ed.), *Youth and Culture: A Human Development Approach.* Monterey, CA: Brooks/Cole.

Medora, N., and Woodward, J. C. (1986). "Loneliness among Adolescent College Students at a Midwestern University." *Adolescence,* 21, 391–402.

Meer, J. (March 1984). "Psychotherapy for Obesity." *Psychology Today,* 18, 10, 11.

Meer, J. (1986). "Yours, Mine, and Divorce." *Psychology Today,* 20, 13.

Meer, J. (July 1985). "Loneliness." *Psychology Today,* 19, 28–33.

Meeus, W., Iedama, M., Helsen, M., and Vollebergh, W. (1999). "Patterns of Adolescent Identity Development: Review of Literature and Longitudinal Analysis." *Developmental Review,* 19, 419–461.

Mehlisch, D. R., Ardia, A., and Pallotta, T. (2003). "Analgesia with Ibuprofen Arginate versus Conventional Ibuprofen for Patients with Dysmenorrhea: A Crossover Trial." *Current Therapeutic Research,* 64, 327–337.

Mehrens, W. A., and Lehmann, I. J. (January 1985). "Testing the Test. Interpreting Test Scores to Clients: What Score Should You Use?" *Journal of Counseling and Development,* 5, 317–320.

Meij, H., van der (1990). "Question Asking: To Know That You Do Not Know Is Not Enough." *Journal of Educational Psychology,* 82, 505–512.

Meij, H., van der (1998). "The Great Divide between Teacher and Student Questioning." In S. A. Karabenick (Ed.), *Strategic Help Seeking: Implications for Learning and Teaching* (pp. 195–218). Mahwah, NJ: Erlbaum.

Melby, J. N., and Conger, R. D. (1996). "Parental Behaviors and Adolescent Academic Performance: A Longitudinal Analysis." *Journal of Research on Adolescence,* 6, 113–137.

Melby, J. N., Conger, R. D., Conger, K. J., and Lorenz, F. O. (1993). "Effects of Parental Behavior on Tobacco Use by Young Male Adolescents." *Journal of Marriage and the Family,* 55, 439–454.

Meneses, L. M., Orrell-Valente, J. K., Guendelman, S. R., Oman, D., and Irwin, C. E. (2006). "Racial/Ethnic Differences in Mother-Daughter Communication about Sex." *Journal of Adolescent Sex,* 39, 128–131.

Menning, C. L. (2002). "Absent Parents Are More Than Money: The Joint Effects of Activities and Financial Support on Youths' Educational Attainment." *Journal of Family Issues,* 23, 648–671.

Mercer, R. J. Merritt, S. L., and Cowell, J. M. (1998). "Differences in Reported Sleep Needs among Adolescents." *Journal of Adolescent Health,* 23, 259–263.

Merskin, D. (1999). "Adolescence, Advertising, and the Ideology of Menstruation." *Sex Roles,* 40, 941–957.

Merten, D. E. (1996). "Visibility and Vulnerability: Responses to Rejection by Nonaggressive Junior High School Boys." *Journal of Early Adolescence,* 16, 5–26.

Metcalf, K., and Gaier, E. L. (1987). "Patterns of Middle-Class Parenting and Adolescent Underachievement." *Adolescence,* 23, 919–928.

Metz, E., McLellan, J., and Youniss, J. (2003). "Types of Voluntary Service and Adolescents'

Civic Development." *Journal of Adolescent Research*, 18, 188–203.

Meyer-Bahlburg, H., Ehrhardt, A., Rosen, L., Gruen, R., Veridiano, N., Vann, F., and Neuwalder, H. (1995). "Prenatal Estrogens and the Development of Homosexual Orientation." *Developmental Psychology*, 31, 12–21.

Meyers, J. E., and Nelson, W. M., III. (1986). "Cognitive Strategies and Expectations as Components of Social Competence in Young Adolescents." *Adolescence*, 21, 291–303.

Michael, G. (1989). *Praying for Time*. Morrison Leahy Music, Ltd.

Michaels, B., Dall, B., Rockett, R., and Kotzen, R. (1993). *Stand*. Cyanide Publishing (Administered by Willesden Music/Richie Kotzen Music) (Administered by Zomba Enterprises, Inc.).

Michelman, J. D., Eicher, J. B., and Michelman, S. O. (1991). "Adolescent Dress, Part I: Dress and Body Markings of Psychiatric Outpatients and Inpatients." *Adolescence*, 26, 375–385.

Middleton, M., and Midgley, C. (1997). "Avoiding the Demonstration of Lack of Ability: An Underexplored Aspect of Goal Theory." *Journal of Educational Psychology*, 89, 710–718.

Midgley, C., and Urdan, T. (1995). "Predictors of Middle School Students' Views of Self-Handicapping Strategies." *Journal of Early Adolescence*, 15, 389–411.

Mihalic, S. W., and Elliott, D. (1997). "Short- and Long-Term Consequences of Adolescent Work." *Youth and Society*, 28, 464–498.

Milan, R. J., Jr., and Kilmann, P. R. (1987). "Interpersonal Factors in Premarital Contraception." *The Journal of Sex Research*, 23, 289–321.

Miller, A. T., Eggertson-Tacon, C., and Quigg, B. (1990). "Patterns of Runaway Behavior within a Large Systems Context: The Road to Empowerment." *Adolescence*, 25, 271–289.

Miller, B. C., & Heaton, T. B. (1991). "Age at First Sexual Intercourse and the Timing of Marriage and Childbirth." *Journal of Marriage and the Family*, 53, 719–732.

Miller, B. C., and Bingham, C. R. (1989). "Family Configuration in Relation to the Sexual Behavior of Female Adolescents." *Journal of Marriage and the Family*, 51, 499–506.

Miller, B. C., and Moore, K. A. (1990). "Adolescent Sexual Behavior, Pregnancy, and Parenting: Research through the 1980s." *Journal of Marriage and the Family*, 52, 1025–1044.

Miller, B. C., and Sneesby, K. R. (1988). "Educational Correlates of Adolescents' Attitudes and Behavior." *Journal of Youth and Adolescence*, 17, 521–530.

Miller, B. C., Benson, B., and Galbraith, K. A. (2001). "Family Relationships and Adolescent Pregnancy Risk: A Research Synthesis." *Developmental Review*, 21, 1–38.

Miller, B. C., Norton, M. C., Curtis, T., Hill, E. J., Schvaneveldt, P., and Young, M. H. (1997). "The Timing of Sexual Intercourse among Adolescents: Family, Peer, and Other Antecedents." *Youth and Society*, 29, 54–83.

Miller, D. (1974). *Adolescence: Psychology, Psychopathology, and Psychotherapy*. New York: Jason Aronson.

Miller, J. G. (1997). "Culture and Self: Uncovering the Cultural Grounding of Psychological Theory." In J. G. Snodgrass and R. Thompson (Eds.), *Annals of the New York Academy of Sciences, 18* (pp. 217–231). New York: New York Academy of Sciences.

Miller, K. E. (1990). "Adolescents' Same-Sex and Opposite-Sex Peer Relations: Sex Differences in Popularity, Perceived Social Competence, and Social Cognitive Skills." *Journal of Adolescent Research*, 5, 222–241.

Miller, K. E., Sabo, D. F., Farrell, M. Pi, Barnes, G. M., and Melnick, M. J. (1998). "Athletic Participation and Sexual Behavior in Adolescents: The Different Worlds of Boys and Girls." *Journal of Health and Social Behavior*, 39, 108–123.

Miller, K. E., Sabo, D. F., Farrell, M. P., Barnes, G. M., and Melnick, M. J. (1999). "Sports, Sexual Behavior, Contraceptive Use, and Pregnancy among Female and Male High School Students: Testing Cultural Resource Theory." *Sociology of Sport Journal*, 16, 366–387.

Miller, P. H., and Aloise, P. A. (1989). "Young Children's Understanding of the Psychological Causes of Behavior: A Review." *Child Development*, 60, 257–285.

Miller, R. L. (1989). "Desegregation Experiences of Minority Students: Adolescent Coping Strategies in Five Connecticut High Schools." *Journal of Adolescent Research*, 4, 173–189.

Miller, R. P., Cosgrove, J. M., and Doke, L. (1990). "Motivating Adolescents to Reduce Their Fines in a Token Economy." *Adolescence*, 25, 97–104.

Miller-Johnson, S., Winn, D. M., Coie, J., Maumary-Gremaud, A., Hyman, C., Terry, R., and Lochman, J. (1999). "Motherhood during the Teenage Years: A Developmental Perspective on Risk Factors for Childbearing." *Development and Psychopathology*, 11, 85–100.

Miller-Jones, D. (1989). "Culture and Testing." *American Psychologist*, 44, 360–366.

Mills, R. K. (1987a). "Traditional Morality, Moral Reasoning and the Moral Education of Adolescents." *Adolescence*, 22, 371–375.

Mills, R. K. (1987b). "The Novels of S. E. Hinton; Springboard to Personal Growth of Adolescents." *Adolescence*, 22, 641–646.

Mills, R. K. (1988). "Using Tom and Huck to Develop Moral Reasoning in Adolescents: A Strategy for the Classroom." *Adolescence*, 23, 325–329.

Millstein, S. G., and Halpern-Felsher, B. L. (2002a). "Judgments about Risk and Perceived Invulnerability in Adolescents and Young Adults." *Journal of Research in Adolescence*, 12, 399–422.

Millstein, S. G., and Halpern-Felsher B. L. (2002b). "Perceptions of Risk and Vulnerability." *Journal of Adolescent Health*, 31, 10–27.

Minkler, M., and Fuller-Thomson, E. (1999). "The Health of Grandparents Raising Grandchildren: Results of a National Study." *American Journal of Public Health*, 89, 1384–1389.

Mitchell, C. E. (1988). "Preparing for Vocational Choice." *Adolescence*, 23, 331–334.

Mitchell, C. E. (1990). "Development or Restoration of Trust in Interpersonal Relationships during Adolescence and Beyond." *Adolescence*, 25, 847–854.

Mitchell, C. M., O'Nell, T. D., Beals, J., Dick, R. W., Keane, E., and Manson, S. M. (1996). "Dimensionality of Alcohol Use among American Indian Adolescents: Latent Structure, Construct Validity, and Implications for Developmental Research." *Journal of Research on Adolescence*, 6, 151–180.

Mitchell, J. E., Pyle, R. L., and Eckert, E. D. (1981). "Frequency and Duration of Binge-Eating Episodes in Patients with Bulimia." *America Journal of Psychiatry*, 138, 835, 836.

Mitchell, J., and Dodder, R. A. (August 1983). "Types of Neutralization and Types of Delinquency." *Journal of Youth and Adolescence*, 12, 307–318.

Mitchell, J., Dodder, R. A., and Norris, T. D. (1990). "Neutralization and Delinquency: A Comparison by Sex and Ethnicity." *Adolescence*, 25, 487–497.

Moffitt, T. E., Caspi, A., Belsky, J., and Silva, T. A. (1992). "Childhood Experience and the Onset of Menarche: A Test of the Sociobiological Model." *Child Development*, 63, 47–58.

Molitor, F., and Hirsch, K. W. (1994). "Children's Toleration of Real-Life Aggression after Exposure to Media Violence: A Replication of the Drabman and Thomas Studies." *Child Studies Journal*, 24, 191–207.

Molnar, B. E., Shade, S. B., Kral, A. H., Booth, R. H., and Watters, J. K. (1999). "Suicidal Behavior and Sexual/Physical Abuse among Street Youth." *Child Abuse and Neglect*, 22, 213–222.

Montemayor, R. (1986). "Family Variation in Parent-Adolescent Storm and Stress." *Journal of Adolescent Research*, 1, 15–31.

Montemayor, R., and Browler, J. R. (1987). "Fathers, Mothers, and Adolescents' Gender Based Differences in Parental Roles During Adolescence." *Journal of Youth and Adolescence*, 16, 281–291.

Montemayor, R., and Flannery, D. J. (1991). "Parent-Adolescent Relations in Middle to Late Adolescence." In R. Lerner, A. Petersen, and J. Brooks-Gunn (Eds.), *Encyclopedia of Adolescence* (pp. 729–734). New York: Garland.

Montepare, J. M., and Lachman, M. E. (1989). "'You're Only as Old as You Feel': Self-Perceptions of Age, Fears of Aging, and Life Satisfaction from Adolescence to Old Age." *Psychology and Aging*, 4, 73–78.

Montgomery, M. J., and Coté, J. E. (2003). "College as a Transition to Adulthood." In G. R. Adams and M. D. Berzonsky (Eds.), *Blackwell Handbook of Adolescence* (pp. 149–172). Oxford, England: Blackwell Publishing.

Montgomery, M. J., and Sorell, G. T. (1998). "Love and Dating Experience in Early and Middle Adolescence: Grade and Gender Comparisons." *Journal of Adolescence*, 21, 677–689.

Moore, D., and Hotch, D. F. (April 1982). "Parent-Adolescent Separation: The Role of Parental Divorce." *Journal of Youth and Adolescence*, 11, 115–119.

Moore, J. W., Jensen, B., and Hauck, W. E. (1990). "Decision-Making Processes of Youth." *Adolescence*, 25, 583–592.

Moore, J., and Pachon, H. (1985). *Hispanics in the United States*. Englewood Cliffs, NJ: Prentice Hall.

Moore, K. A., & Stieft, T. M. (1991). "Changes in Marriage and Fertility Behavior: Behavior versus Attitudes of Young Adults." *Youth and Society*, 22, 362–386.

Moore, K. A., Miller, B. C., Glei, D., and Morrison D. R. (1995). *Adolescent Sex, Contraception, and Childbearing: A Review of Recent Research*. Washington, DC: Child Trends.

Moore, S. M. (1995). "Girls' Understanding and Social Constructions of Menarche." *Journal of Adolescence*, 18, 87–104.

Moore, S. M., and Rosenthal, D. A. (1992). "The Social Context of Adolescent Sexuality: Safe Sex Implications." *Journal of Adolescence*, 15, 415–435.

Moore, S., and Cartwright, C. (2005). "Adolescents' and Young Adults' Expectations of Parental Responsibilities in Stepfamilies." *Journal of Divorce & Remarriage,* 43, 109–127.

Moote, G. T., Jr., and Wodarski, J. S. (1997). "The Acquisition of Life Skills through Adventure-Based Activities and Programs: A Review of the Literature." *Adolescence,* 32, 143–168.

Moran, P. B., and Eckenrode, J. (1991). "Gender Differences in the Costs and Benefits of Peer Relationships during Adolescence." *Journal of Adolescent Research,* 6, 396–409.

Moran, P. B., Vuchinich, S., and Hall, N. K. (2004). "Associations between Types of Maltreatment and Substance Use during Adolescence." *Child Abuse & Neglect,* 28, 565–574.

Morano, C. D., Cisler, R. A., and Lemerond, J. (1993). "Risk Factors for Adolescent Suicidal Behavior: Loss, Insufficient Family Support, and Hopelessness." *Adolescence,* 28, 851–865.

Morgan, C., Isaac, J. D., and Sansone, C. (2001). "The Role of Interest in Understanding the Career Choices of Female and Male College Students." *Sex Roles,* 44, 295–320.

Morris, G. B. (1992). "Adolescent Leaders: Rational Thinking, Future Beliefs, Temporal Perspective, and Other Correlates." *Adolescence,* 105, 173–181.

Morris, R. E., Harrison, E. A., Knox, G. W., Romanjhauser, E., Marques, D. K., and Watts, L. L. (1996). "Health Risk Behavioral Survey from 39 Juvenile Correction Facilities in the United States." *Journal of Adolescent Health,* 117, 334–375.

Morrison, D. A., and Coiro, M. J. (1999). "Parental Conflict and Marital Disruption: Do Children Benefit When High Conflict Marriages Are Dissolved?" *Journal of Marriage and the Family,* 61, 626–637.

Morrow, K. B., and Sorell, G. T. (1989). "Factors Affecting Self-Esteem, Depression, and Negative Behaviors in Sexually Abused Female Adolescents." *Journal of Marriage and the Family,* 51, 677–686.

Mortimer, J. (2003). *Working and Growing Up in America.* Cambridge, MA: Harvard University Press.

Mortimer, J. T., Finch, M., Shanahan, M., and Ryu, S. (1992). "Work Experience, Mental Health, and Behavioral Adjustment in Adolescents." *Journal of Research of Adolescence,* 2, 25–57.

Mortimer, J. T., Pimentel, E. E., Ryu, S., Nash, K., and Lee, C. (1996). "Part-Time Work and Occupational Value Formation in Adolescence." *Social Forces,* 74, 1405–1418.

Moser, M. R., Paternite, C. E., and Dixon, W. E., Jr. (1996). "Late Adolescents' Feelings toward Parents and Siblings." *Merrill-Palmer Quarterly,* 42, 537–553.

Mosher, W. D. (1990). "Contraceptive Practice in the United States, 1982–1988." *Family Planning Perspectives,* 22, 198–205.

Mosher, W. D., Chandra, A., and Jones, J. (2005). "Sexual Behavior and Selected Health Measures: Men and Women 15–44 Years of Age, United States, 2002." *Advance Data from Health and Vital Statistics,* No. 362. Retrieved from http://www.cdc.gov/nchs/data/ad/ad362.pdf.

Moshman, D. (1993). "Adolescent Reasoning and Adolescent Rights." *Human Development,* 36, 27–40.

Moshman, D. (1994). "Reason, Reasons, and Reasoning: A Constructivist Account of Human Rationality." *Theory and Psychology,* 4, 245–260.

Moshman, D. (1997). "Cognitive Development beyond Childhood." In W. Damon, D. Kuhn, and R. Siegler (Eds.), *Handbook of Child Psychology.* Vol. 2 (pp. 947–978). New York: Wiley.

Moshman, D. (1999). *Adolescent Psychological Development: Rationality, Morality, and Identity.* Mahwah, NJ: Erlbaum.

Moshman, D., and Franks, B. F. (1986). "Development of the Concept of Inferential Validity." *Child Development,* 57, 153–165.

Mott, F. L., Fondell, M. M., Hu, P. N., Kowaleski-Jones, L., and Menaghan, E. G. (1996). "The Determinants of First Sex by Age 14 in a High-Risk Adolescent Population." *Family Planning Perspectives,* 28, 13–18.

Moulton, P., Moulton, M., Housewright, M., and Bailey, K. (1998). "Gifted and Talented: Exploring the Positive and Negative Aspects of Labeling." *Roeper Review,* 21, 153–154.

Muck, R., Zempolich, K. A., Titus, J. C., Fishman, M., Godley, M. D., and Schwebel, R. (2001). "An Overview of the Effectiveness of Adolescent Substance Abuse Treatment Models." *Youth and Society,* 33, 143–168.

Mueller, M. M., Wilhelm, B., and Elder, G. H., Jr., (2002). "Variations in Grandparenting." *Research on Aging,* 24, 360–388.

Mueller, U., Sokol, B., and Overton, W. F. (1999). "Developmental Sequences in Class Reasoning and Propositional Reasoning." *Journal of Experimental Child Psychology,* 74, 69–106.

Mulkey, L. M., Catsambis, S., Steelman, L. C., and Crain, R. L. (2005). "The Long-Term Effects of Ability Grouping in Mathematics: A National Investigation." *Social Psychology of Education,* 8, 137–177.

Mullis, A. K., Mullis, R. L., and Normandin, D. (1992). "Cross-Sectional and Longitudinal Comparisons of Adolescent Self-Esteem." *Adolescence,* 27, 51–61.

Mullis, R. L., and McKinley, K. (1989). "Gender-Role Orientation of Adolescent Females: Effects on Self-Esteem and Locus of Control." *Journal of Adolescent Research,* 4, 506–516.

Mulsow, M. H., and Murry, V. M. (1996). "Parenting on Edge." *Journal of Family Issues,* 17, 704–721.

Munk, N. (1997). "Girl Power." *Fortune,* 8 December, pp. 132–140.

Munson, W. W. (1992). "Self-Esteem, Vocational Identity, and Career Salience in High School Students." *The Career Development Quarterly,* 40, 361–368.

Murdock, B. B., Jr. (1974). *Human Memory: Theory and Data.* Mahwah, NJ: Erlbaum.

Murray, A., and Sandkvist, K. (1990). "Father Absence and Children's Achievement from Age 13 to 21." *Scandinavian Journal of Educational Research,* 34, 3–28.

Murry, B. M. (1992). "First Pregnancy among Black Adolescent Females over Three Decades." *Youth and Society,* 23, 478–506.

Murry, B. M. (1995). "An Ecological Analysis of Pregnancy Resolution Decisions among African American and Hispanic Adolescent Females." *Youth and Society,* 26, 325–350.

Murry, B. M. (1996). "An Ecological Analysis of Coital Timing among Middle-Class African-American Adolescent Females." *Journal of Adolescent Research,* 11, 261–279.

Must, A., Jacques, P. F., Dallal, G. E., Bajema, C. J., and Dietz, W. H. (1992). "Long-Term Morbidity and Mortality of Overweight Adolescents: A Follow-Up of the Harvard Growth Study of 1922–1935." *New England Journal of Medicine,* 327, 1350–1355.

Muuss, R. E. (Fall 1982). "Social Cognition: Robert Selman's Theory of Role Taking." *Adolescence,* 17, 499–525.

Muuss, R. E. (1985). "Adolescent Eating Disorder: Anorexia Nervosa." *Adolescence,* 20, 525–536.

Muuss, R. E. (1986). "Adolescent Eating Disorder: Bulimia." *Adolescence,* 22, 257–267.

Muuss, R. E. (1988a). "Carol Gilligan's Theory of Sex Differences in the Development of Moral Reasoning during Adolescence." *Adolescence,* 23, 229–243.

Muuss, R. E. (1988b). *Theories of Adolescence.* 5th ed. New York: McGraw-Hill.

Muuss, R. E. (1995). *Theories of Adolescenc* (6th Edition). New York: McGraw Hill.

Myers, S. M. (1996). "An Interactive Model of Religiosity Inheritance: The Importance of Family Context." *American Sociological Review,* 61, 858–866.

Nadeem, E., and Graham, S. (2005). "Early Puberty, Peer Victimization, and Internalizing Symptoms in Ethnic Minority Adolescents." *Journal of Early Adolescence,* 25, 197–222.

Nævdal, F., and Thuen, F. (2004). "Residence Arrangements and Well-Being: A Study of Norwegian Adolescents." *Scandinavian Journal of Psychology,* 45, 363–371.

Nail, J. M., and Evans, J. G. (1997). "The Emotional Adjustment of Gifted Adolescents: A View of Global Functioning." *Roeper Review,* 20, 18–21.

Najman, J. M., Aird, R., Bor, W., O'Callaghan, M., Williams, G. M., and Shuttlewood, G. J. (2004). "The Generational Transmission of Socioeconomic Inequalities in Child Cognitive Development and Emotional Health." *Social Science & Medicine,* 58, 1147–1158.

Nakajima, Y., and Hotta, M. (1989). "A Developmental Study of Cognitive Processes in Decision-Making: Information Searching as a Function of Task Complexity." *Psychological Reports,* 64, 67–79.

Namerow, P. B., Kalmuss, D. S., and Cushman, L. F. (1993). "The Determinants of Young Women's Pregnancy-Resolution Choices." *Journal of Research on Adolescence,* 3, 193–215.

Nathanson, C., Paulhus, D. L., and Williams, K. M. (2006). "Predictors of a Behavioral Measure of Scholastic Cheating: Personality and Competence But Not Demographics." *Contemporary Educational Psychology,* 31, 97–122.

Nathanson, M., Baird, A., and Jemail, J. (1986). "Family Functioning and the Adolescent Mother: A Systems Approach." *Adolescence,* 21, 827–841.

National Center for Education Statistics. (2001). *National Mathematics Achievement-Level Results by Race/Ethnicity for Grade 12: 1990–2000.* Retrieved from http://nces.ed.gov/nationsreportcard/mathematics/results/natachieve-g12RE.asp.

National Center for Education Statistics. (2002). *Table 146: Percent of High School Seniors Who Participate in Selected School-Sponsored Extracurricular Activities, by Student Characteristics: 1980 and 1992.* Retrieved June 1, 2005, from http://nces.ed.gov.proxy.lib.ohio-state.edu/programs/digest/d02/dt145.asp.

National Center for Health Statistics. (2001). *Healthy People 2000: Final Review.* Hyattsville, MD: Public Health Service.

National Center for Health Statistics. (2002). *Vital Statistics of the United States, 2001 Volume I,*

Natality. Washington, DC: National Center for Health Statistics.

National Center for Injury Prevention and Control. (2000, February 3). *Facts on Adolescent Injury* <www.cdc.gov/ ncipc/duip/adoles.htm>.

National Center for Tobacco Free Kids. (2000). *Tobacco Company Marketing to Kids* <www .tobaccofreekids.org/research/factsheets/pdf/ 0008.pdf>.

National Children's Home. (2002). *NCH 2002 Survey.* Retrieved from http://www.nch.org.uk/ itok/showquestion.asp?faq=9andfldAuto=145.

National Coalition of the Homeless. (1999). *Homeless Youth.* Fact Sheet no. 11. Washington, DC: Author.

National Coalition of the Homeless. (2006). Why are people homeless? *Fact Sheet no. 1.* Retrieved from http://www.nationalhomeless.org/publications/ facts/Why.pdf.

National Commission on Excellence in Education. (1983). *A Nation at Risk: The Imperative for Educational Reform.* Washington, DC: U.S. Government Printing Office.

National Consumer League. (2000). *An Overview of Federal Labor Laws.* Retrieved from http://www .neinet.org/ child%20labor/factI.htm.

National Gambling Impact Study Commission. (1998). *Final Report* <www.ngisc.gov/research/ nagamng.html>.

National Highway and Traffic Safety Administration (NHTSA). (1997). *1995 Youth Fatal Crash and Alcohol Facts.* Washington, DC: Author/Department of Transportation.

National Highway Traffic Safety Administration (NHTSA). (1998). *Traffic Safety Facts 1997: Alcohol.* Report no. DOT HS 808 806. Washington, DC: U.S. Department of Transportation.

National Highway Traffic Safety Administration (NHTSA). (2001). *Traffic Safety Facts 2000: A Compilation of Motor Vehicle Crash Data from the Fatality Analysis Reporting System and the General Estimates System.* Washington, DC: U.S. Department of Transportation.

National Incidence Studies of Missing, Abducted, Runaway and Thrownaway Children. (2002). "Runaway/Thrownaway Children: National Estimates and Characteristics." *NISMART Bulletin,* October.

National Institute of Allergy and Infectious Diseases. (2002). *HIV Infection in Adolescents: Fact Sheet.* Rockville, MD: National Institutes of Health.

National Institute of Arthritis and Musculoskeletal and Skin Diseases. (2006). *Questions and Answers about Acne.* Retrieved from www.nih .gov/niams/healthinfo/acne/ acne.htm.

National Institute of Mental Health. (2000). *Depression in Children and Adolescents.* NIH Publication no. 00-4744. Retrieved from www .nimh.gov/publicat/dechildresfact.cfm.

National Institute on Alcohol Abuse and Alcoholism (NIAAA). (2000). *Tenth Special Report to the U.S. Congress on Alcohol and Health.* Rockville, MD: Author.

National Institute on Alcohol Abuse and Alcoholism. (2001). *Cognitive Impairment and Recovery from Alcoholism.* Publication no. 53. Rockville, MD: Author.

National Institute on Drug Abuse (NIDA). (1997). *National Institute on Drug Abuse Prevention Brochure.* Retrieved from www.165.112.78.61/ prevention.html.

National Institute on Drug Abuse (NIDA). (1998). *Marijuana: Facts Parents Need to Know.* Retrieved from www.nida.nih.gov/marijbroch/ parentpg3–4n.html.

National Institute on Drug Abuse (NIDA). (1999a). *Infofax: Rohypnol and GHD.* Report no. 13556. Retrieved from www.nida.nih.gov/infofax/ rohypnolghb.htm.

National Institute on Drug Abuse (NIDA). (1999b). *Infofax: Ecstasy.* Report no. 13547. Retrieved from www.nida.nih.gov/infofax/ecstasy.html.

National Institute on Drug Abuse (NIDA). (1999c). *Infofax: Inhalants.* Report no. 13549. Retrieved from www.nida.nih.gov/infofax/inhalants.html.

National Institute on Drug Abuse (NIDA). (1999d). *Infofax: LSD.* Report no. 13550. Retrieved from www.nida.nih.gov/infofax/lsd.html.

National Institute on Drug Abuse (NIDA). (1999e). *Infofax: Marijuana.* Report no. 13551. Retrieved from www.nida.nih.gov/infofax/marijuana.html.

National Institute on Drug Abuse (NIDA). (1999f). "NIDA Notes: Tracking Trends in Teen Drug Abuse over the Years." *Special Report,* 14(1). Washington, DC: Government Printing Office. Retrieved from www.nida.nih.gov/nida_notes/ nnvol14n1/tentrends.html.

National Institute on Drug Abuse (NIDA). (2000a). *Monitoring the Future National Results on Adolescent Drug Use: Overview of Key Findings, 1999.* NIH Publication no. 00-4690. Washington, DC: Government Printing Office.

National Institute on Drug Abuse (NIDA). (2000b) *National Institute on Drug Abuse Research Report Series: Anabolic Steroid Abuse.* Retrieved from www.165.112.78.61/research_reports/ steroids/html.

National Institute on Drug Abuse (NIDA). (2001). *Ecstasy: What We Know and Don't Know about MDMA.* Retrieved from http://www.drugabuse .gov/Meetings/MDMA/MDMAExSummary.

National Institute on Drug Abuse. (2003). *Preventing Drug Use among Children and Adolescents* (2nd ed.). NIH Publication no. 04-4212(A). Bethesda, MD: National Institute on Drug Abuse.

National Institute on Drug Abuse. (2005). *Marijuana Abuse.* NIH Publication no. 05-3859. Bethesda, MD: National Institute on Drug Abuse.

National Marriage Project. (2005). *The State of Our Unions 2005: The Social Health of Marriage in America.* Piscataway, NJ: Rutgers University Press.

National Middle School Association. (2005) *Position Statement on Curriculum, Instruction, and Assessment.* Retrieved from http://www .nmsa.org/AboutNMSA/PositionStatements/Curriculum/tabid/767/Default.aspx.

National Public Radio (NPR). (2003). *Poverty in America.* Washington, DC: Author. Retrieved from http://www.npr.org/programs/specials/ poll/results.html.

National Public Radio. (2000). "NPR/Kaiser/ Kennedy School Kids and Technology Survey." Retrieved from http://npr.org/programs/specials/ poll/technology/technology.kids.html.

National Research Council. (1998). *Protecting Youth at Work: Health, Safety and Development of Working Children and Adolescents in the United States.* Washington, DC: National Academy Press.

National Science Foundation. (1996). *Women, Minorities, and Persons with Disabilities in Science and Engineering: 1996.* Arlington, VA: Author.

Neapolitan, J. (Winter 1981). "Parental Influences on Aggressive Behavior: A Social Learning Approach." *Adolescence,* 16, 831–840.

Necessary, J. R., and Parish, T. S. (1995). "Relationships of Parents' Perceived Actions toward Their Children." *Adolescence,* 30, 175–176.

Needle, R. H., Su, S. S., and Doherty, W. J. (1990). "Divorce, Remarriage, and Adolescent Substance Use: A Prospective Longitudinal Study." *Journal of Marriage and the Family,* 152, 157–159.

Neighbors, B., Forehand, R., and Armistead, L. (1992). "Is Parental Divorce a Critical Stressor for Young Adolescents? Grade Point Average as a Case in Point." *Adolescence,* 27, 639–646.

Neimark, E. D. (1975). "Longitudinal Development of Formal Operations Thought." *Genetic Psychology Monographs,* 91, 171–225.

Neisser, U., Boodoo, G., Bouchard, T. J., Jr., Boykin, A. W., Brody, N., Ceci, S. J., Halpern, D. F., Loehlin, J. C., Perloff, R., Sternberg, R. J., and Urbina, S. (1996). "Intelligence: Knowns and Unknowns." *American Psychologist,* 51, 77–101.

NellieMae Corporation. (2006). *Credit Card Tips.* Retrieved from http://www.nelliemae.org/ managingmoney/cc_tips.html.

Nelson, C., and Keith, J. (1990). "Comparisons of Female and Male Early Adolescent Sex-Role Attitudes and Behavior Development." *Adolescence,* 25, 183–204.

Nelson, F. H., Rosenberg, B., and van Meter, N. (2004). *Charter School Achievement on the 2003 National Assessment of Educational Progress.* Washington, DC: American Federation of Teachers.

Nelson, T. F., and Wechsler, H. (2001). "Alcohol and College Athletes." *Medicine and Science in Sports and Exercise,* 33, 43–47.

Nelson, W. L., Hughes, H. M., Handal, P., Katz, B., and Searight, H. R. (1993). "The Relationship of Family Structure and Family Conflict to Adjustment in Young Adult College Students." *Adolescence,* 28, 29–40.

Nevid, J. S., and Gotfried, F. (1995). *Choices: Sex in the Age of STD.* Boston: Allyn & Bacon.

Nevil, R., Golden, L., and Faragher, T. (1992, 1993). *The Right Kind of Love.* W. B. Music Corporation, Dresden China Music, MCA Music Publishing.

New York Civil Liberties Union. (2006). *The Rights of Pregnant and Parenting Teens.* Retrieved from http://www.nyclu.org/rrp_rppt2.html.

Newburger, E. C. (1999). *Computer Use in the United States: Current Population Reports, October 1997.* U.S. Bureau of the Census Publication no. 20-522. Washington, DC: Government Printing Office.

Newcomb, M. D. (1986). "Sexual Behavior of Cohabitators: A Comparison of Three Independent Samples." *The Journal of Sex Research,* 22, 492–513.

Newcomb, M. D., Maddahian, E., and Bentler, P. M. (1986). "Risk Factors for Drug Use among Adolescents: Concurrent and Longitudinal Analysis." *American Journal of Public Health,* 76, 525–531.

Newell, G. K., Hammig, C. L., Jurick, A. P., and Johnson, D. E. (1990). "Self-Concept as a Factor in the Quality of Diets of Adolescent Girls." *Adolescence,* 25, 117–130.

Newman, B. M. (1989). "The Changing Nature of the Parent-Adolescent Relationship from Early to Late Adolescence." *Adolescence,* 96, 915–924.

Newman, B. S., and Muzzonigro, P. G. (1993). "The Effects of Traditional Family Values on the Coming Out Process of Gay Male Adolescents." *Adolescence,* 28, 213–226.

Newman, J. (1987). "Psychological Effects on College Students on Raising the Drinking Age." *Adolescence,* 22, 503–510.

Newspaper Association of America. (2005). *Targeting Teens.* Retrieved from http://www.naa.org/marketscope/TargetingTeensBrief.pdf.

Nielsen S. J., and Popkin B. M. (2003). "Patterns and Trends in Food Portion Sizes, 1977–1998." *Journal of the American Medical Association,* 289, 450–453.

Niemann, Y. F., Romero, A. J., Arredondo, J., and Rodriguez, V. (1999). "What Does It Mean to Be "Mexican"? Social Construction of an Ethnic Identity." *Hispanic Journal of Behavioral Sciences,* 21, 47–60.

Niemi, R. G., Hepburn, M. A., and Chapman, C. (2000). "Community Service by High School Students: A Cure for Civic Ills?" *Political Behavior,* 22, 45–69.

Nilzon, K. R., and Palmérus, K. (1997). "The Influence of Familial Factors on Anxiety and Depression in Childhood and Early Adolescence." *Adolescence,* 32, 935–943.

Nippold, M. (1994). "Third-Order Verbal Analogical Reasoning: A Developmental Study of Children and Adolescents." *Contemporary Educational Psychology,* 19, 101–107.

Noack, P., and Buhl, H. M. (2004). "Relations with Parents and Friends during Adolescence and Early Adulthood." *Marriage & Family Review,* 36, 31–51.

Noble, P. S., Adams, G. R., & Openshaw, D. K. (1989). "Interpersonal Communication in Parent–Adolescent Dyads: A Brief Report on the Effects of a Social Skills Training Program." *Journal of Family Psychology,* 2, 483–494.

Nock, M. K., and Prinstein, M. J. (2005). "Contextual Features and Behavioral Functions of Self-Mutilation among Adolescents." *Journal of Abnormal Psychology,* 114, 140–146.

Nock, S. L. (1995). "A Comparison of Marriages and Cohabiting Relationships." *Journal of Family Issues,* 16, 53–76.

Nock, S. L. (1998). "The Consequences of Premarital Fatherhood." *American Sociological Review,* 63, 250–263.

Nolen-Hoeksema, S., and Girgus, J. S. (1994). "The Emergence of Gender Differences in Depression during Adolescence." *Psychological Bulletin,* 115, 424–443.

Noller, P., and Callan, V. J. (1986). "Adolescent and Parent Perception of Family Cohesion and Adaptability." *Journal of Adolescence,* 9, 97–106.

Noller, P., and Callan, V. J. (1990). "Adolescents' Perceptions of the Nature of Their Communication with Parents." *Journal of Youth and Adolescence,* 19, 349–362.

Noom, M. J., Dekovic, M., and Meeus, W. H. J. (1999). "Autonomy, Attachment and Psychosocial Adjustment during Adolescence: A Double-Edged Sword?" *Journal of Adolescence,* 22, 771–783.

Norcini, J. J., and Snyder, S. S. (April 1983). "The Effects of Modeling and Cognitive Induction on the Moral Reasoning of Adolescents." *Journal of Youth and Adolescence,* 12, 101–115.

Novins, D. K., Spicer, P., Beals, J., and Spero M. M. (2004). "Preventing Underage Drinking in American Indian and Alaska Native Communities: Contexts, Epidemiology, and Culture." In R. J. Bonnie and M. E. O'Connell (Eds.), *Reducing Underage Drinking: A Collective Responsibility* (pp. 678–696). Washington, DC: National Academies Press.

Nwadiora, E., and McAdoo, H. (1996). "Acculturative Stress among Amerasian Refugees: Gender and Racial Differences." *Adolescence,* 31, 477–487.

Nye, F. I., and Edelbrock, C. (1980). "Some Social Characteristics of Runaways." *Journal of Family Issues,* 1, 1–11.

Nye, S. S., and Johnson, C. L. (1999). "Eating Disorders." In S. D. Netherton, D. Holmes, and C. E. Walker (Eds.), *Child and Adolescent Psychological Disorders: A Comprehensive Textbook* (pp. 397–414). New York: Oxford University Press.

O'Brien, K. M., Friedman, S. M., Tipton, L. C., and Linn, S. G. (2000). "Attachment, Separation, and Women's Vocational Development: A Longitudinal Analysis." *Journal of Counseling Psychology,* 47, 301–315.

O'Brien, R. W., and Iannotti, R. J. (1993). "Differences in Mothers' and Children's Perceptions of Urban Black Children's Life Stress." *Journal of Youth and Adolescence,* 22, 543–557.

O'Brien, R., and Cohen, S. (1984). *The Encyclopedia of Drug Abuse.* New York: Facts on File.

O'Brien, S. (1989). *American Indian Tribal Governments.* Norman, OK: University of Oklahoma Press.

O'Callaghan, M. F., Borkowski, J. G., Whitman, T. L., Maxwell, S. E., and Keogh, D. (1999). "A Model of Adolescent Parenting: The Role of Cognitive Readiness to Parent." *Journal of Research on Adolescence,* 9, 203–225.

O'Connor, B. P. (1995). "Identity Development and Perceived Parental Behavior as Sources of Adolescent Egocentrism." *Journal of Youth and Adolescence,* 24, 205–227.

O'Connor, T. G., Pickering, K., Dunn, J., and Golding, J. (1999). "Frequency and Predictors of Relationship Dissolution in a Community Sample in England." *Journal of Family Psychology,* 13, 436–439.

O'Dea, J. A., and Abraham, S. (1999). "Association between Self-Concept and Body Weight, Gender, and Pubertal Development among Male and Female Adolescents." *Adolescence,* 34, 69–79.

O'Donnell, C. R. (1995). "Firearm Deaths among Children and Youth." *American Psychologist,* 50, 771–776.

O'Keefe, M., and Treister, L. (1998). "Victims of Dating Violence among High School Students: Are the Predictors Different for Males and Females?" *Violence against Women,* 4, 195–223.

O'Koon, J. (1997). "Attachment to Parents and Peers in Late Adolescence and Their Relationship with Self-Image." *Adolescence,* 32, 471–482.

O'Sullivan, R. G. (1990). "Validating a Method to Identify At-Risk Middle School Students for Participation in a Dropout Prevention Program." *Journal of Early Adolescence,* 10, 209–220.

Obeidallah, D. A., Brennan, R. T., Brooks-Gunn, J., Kindlon, D., and Earls, F. (2000). "Socioeconomic Status, Race, and Girls' Pubertal Maturation: Results from the Project on Human Development in Chicago Neighborhoods." *Journal of Research on Adolescence,* 10, 443–464.

Offer, D., & Schonert-Reichl, A. (1992). "Debunking the Myths of Adolescence: Findings from Recent Research." *Journal of the American Academy of Child & Adolescent Psychiatry,* 31(6), 1003–1014.

Offer, D., and Offer, J. (1974). "Normal Adolescent Males: The High School and College Years." *Journal of the American College Health Association,* 22, 209–215.

Offer, D., Ostrov, E., and Howard, K. I. (August 1982). "Family Perceptions of Adolescent Self-Image." *Journal of Youth and Adolescence,* 11, 281–291.

Office of Economic Cooperation and Development. (2004). *Employment Outlook 2004: How Does the U.S. Compare?* Retrieved from http://www.oecd.org/dataoecd/41/15/32504422.pdf.

Office of Juvenile Justice and Delinquency Prevention. (1995). *Balanced and Restorative Justice: Program Summary.* Washington, DC: Author.

Office of Juvenile Justice and Delinquency Prevention. (1998). *When Your Child Is Missing: A Family Survival Guide.* Washington, DC: Author.

Office of Juvenile Justice and Delinquency Prevention. (1999). *1997 National Youth Gang Survey.* Washington, DC: Department of Justice.

Office of Minority Health. (2006). *American Indian and Alaska Native Populations.* Retrieved from http://www.cdc.gov/omh/Populations/AIAN/AIAN.htm.

Office of National AIDS Policy. (2000). *Youth and HIV/AIDS 2000: A New American Agenda.* Washington, DC: Author.

Office of Refugee Resettlement. (1982, 1985). *Refugee Resettlement Program: Report to the Congress.* Washington, DC: U.S. Government Printing Office.

Ogbu, J. (1992). "Understanding Cultural Diversity and Learning." *Educational Researcher,* 21, 5–14.

Ogden, C. I., Carroll, M. D., Curtin, L. R., McDowell, M. A., Tabak, C. J., and Flegal, K. M. (2006). "Prevalence of Overweight and Obesity in the United States, 1999–2004." *Journal of the American Medical Association,* 295, 1549–1555.

Ognibene, F. P. (October 1984). "Complications of AIDS." *Medical Aspects of Human Sexuality,* 18, 9.

Ogundari, J. T. (Spring 1985). "Somatic Deviations in Adolescence: Reactions and Adjustments." *Adolescence,* 20, 179–183.

Ogunwole, S. U. (2006). *We the People: American Indians and Alaska Natives in the United States.* Census 2000 Special Reports. Washington, DC: U.S. Census Bureau.

Ohannessian, C. M., & Crockett, J. (1993). "A Longitudinal Investigation of the Relationship Between Educational Investment and Adolescent Sexual Activity." *Journal of Adolescent Research,* 8, 167–182.

Ohannesian, C. M., and Lerner, R. M. (1995). "Discrepancies in Adolescents' and Parents' Perceptions of Family Functioning and Adolescent Emotional Development." *Journal of Early Adolescence,* 15, 490–516.

Okazaki, S. (2002). "Influences of Culture on Asian Americans' Sexuality." *Journal of Sex Research,* 39, 34–41.

Okum, M. A., and Sasfy, J. H. (Fall 1977). "Adolescence: The Self-Concept, and Formal Operations." *Adolescence,* 12, 373–379.

Okwumabua, J. O., Okwumabua, T. M., Winston, B. L., and Walker, H., Jr. (1989). "Onset of Drug

Use among Rural Black Youth." *Journal of Adolescent Research,* 4, 238–246.

Oldenburg, C. M., and Kerns, K. A. (1997). "Associations between Peer Relationships and Depressive Symptoms: Testing Moderator Effects of Gender and Age." *Journal of Early Adolescence,* 17, 319–337.

Olds, R. S., and Thombs, D. L. (2001). "The Relationship of Adolescent Perceptions of Peer Norms and Parent Involvement to Cigarette and Alcohol Use." *Journal of School Health,* 71, 223–228.

Olson, D. (1988). "Family Assessment and Intervention: The Circumplex Model of Family Systems." *Child and Youth Services,* 11, 9–48.

Olson, D. H. (1986). Circumplex Model VII: Validation Studies and FACES III. *Family Process,* 25, 337–351.

Olson, D. H., Portner, J., and Lavee, Y. (1985). "FACES III." In D. H. Olson, H. McCubbin, H. Barnes, A. Larsen, M. Muxen, and M. Wilson (Eds.), *Family Inventories* (pp. 7–42). St. Paul: Family Social Science, University of Minnesota.

Olweus, D. (1991). "Bully-Victim Problems among School Children: Basic Facts and Effects of a School-Based Intervention Program." In D. Pepler and K. Rubin (Eds.), *The Development and Treatment of Childhood Aggression* (pp. 411–448). Hillsdale, NJ: Erlbaum.

Olweus, D. (1993). *Bully in Schools: What We Know and What We Can Do.* Oxford, England: Basil Blackwell.

Olweus, D. (1994). "Annotation: Bullying at School: Basic Facts and Effects of a School-Based Intervention Program." *Journal of Child Psychology and Psychiatry,* 35, 1171–1190.

Olweus, D. (2001). "Peer Harassment: A Critical Analysis and Some Important Issues." In J. Juvenon and S. Graham (Eds.), *Peer Harassment in School* (pp. 3–20). New York: Guilford.

Olweus, D. (December 1977). "Aggression and Peer Acceptance in Adolescent Boys: Two Short-Term Longitudinal Studies of Ratings." *Child Development,* 48, 1301–1313.

Openshaw, D. K., and Thomas, D. L. (1986). "The Adolescent Self and the Family." In G. K. Leigh and G. W. Peterson (Eds.), *Adolescents in Families* (pp. 104–129). Cincinatti: South-Western.

Ordway v. *Hargraves.* (1971). 323 F. Supp. 1115.

Orfield, G., Losen, D., Wald, J., and Swanson, C. B. (2004). *Losing Our Future: How Minority Youth Are Being Left Behind by the Graduation Rate Crisis.* Cambridge, MA: The Civil Rights Project at Harvard University.

Orlofsky, J. L., and Ginsburg, S. D. (Spring 1981). "Intimacy Status: Relationship to Affect Cognition." *Adolescence,* 16, 91–99.

Ormond, C., Luszez, M. A., Mann, L., and Beswick, G. (1991). "Metacognitive Analysis of Decision Making in Adolescence." *Journal of Adolescence,* 14, 275–291.

Oropesa, R. S. (1996). "Normative Beliefs about Marriage and Cohabitation: A Comparison of Non-Latino Whites, Mexican Americans, and Puerto Ricans." *Journal of Marriage and the Family,* 58, 49–62.

Orr, M. T. (November–December, 1982). "Sex Education and Contraceptive Education in U.S. Public High Schools." *Family Planning Perspectives,* 14, 304–313.

Osborne, J. W. (1995). "Academics, Self-Esteem, and Race: A Look at the Underlying Assumptions of the Disidentification Hypothesis." *Personality and Social Psychology Bulletin,* 21, 449–455.

Ostermann, J., Sloan, F. A., and Taylor, D. H. (2005). "Heavy Alcohol Use and Marital Dissolution in the USA." *Social Science & Medicine,* 61, 2304–2316.

Overton, W. F., and Byrnes, J. C. (1991). "Cognitive Development." In R. M. Lerney, A. C. Petersen, and J. Brooks-Gunn (Eds.), *Encyclopedia of Adolescence.* Vol. 1. New York: Garland.

Owens, J. A., Stahl, J., Patton, A., Reddy, U., and Crouch, M. (2006). "Sleep Practices, Attitudes, and Beliefs in Inner City Middle School Children: A Mixed-Methods Study." *Behavioral Sleep Medicine,* 4, 114–134.

Owens, T. J. (1992). "Where Do We Go from Here? Post-High School Choices of American Men." *Youth and Society,* 23, 452–477.

Oxford, M. L., Gilchrist, L. D., Gillmore, M. R., and Lohr, M. J. (2006). "Predicting Variation in the Life Course of Adolescent Mothers as They Enter Adulthood." *Journal of Adolescent Health,* 39, 20–26.

Oyserman, D., and Markus, H. R. (1990a). "Possible Selves and Delinquency." *Journal of Personality and Social Psychology,* 59, 112–125.

Oyserman, D., and Markus, H. R. (1990b). "Possible Selves in Balance: Implications for Delinquency." *Journal of Social Issues,* 46, 141–157.

Oyserman, D., and Saltz, E. (1993). "Competence, Delinquency, and Attempts to Attain Possible Selves." *Journal of Personality and Social Psychology,* 65, 360–374.

Ozarak, E. W. (1989). "Social and Cognitive Influences on the Development of Religious Beliefs and Commitment in Adolescence." *Journal for the Scientific Study of Religion,* 28, 448–463.

Ozechowski, T. J., and Liddle, H. A. (2000). "Family-Based Therapy for Adolescent Drug Abuse: Knowns and Unknowns." *Clinical and Family Psychology Review,* 3, 269–298.

Ozer, E. M., MacDonald, R., and Irwin, C. E., Jr. (2002). "Adolescent Health Care in the U.S.: Implications and Projection in the New Millennium." In J. Mortimer and R. Larson (Eds.), *The Changing Adolescent Experience: Societal Trends and the Transition to Young Adulthood* (pp. 129–174). New York: Cambridge University Press.

Ozer, E. M., Park, M. J., Paul, T., Brindis, C. D., and Irwin, C. E., Jr. (2003). *America's Adolescents: Are They Healthy?* San Francisco: University of California, San Francisco, National Adolescent Health Information Center.

Paddack, C. (1987). "Preparing a Boy for Nocturnal Emissions." *Medical Aspects of Human Sexuality,* 21, 15, 16.

Padilla, A. M., and Baird, T. L. (1991). "Mexican-American Adolescent Sexuality and Sexual Knowledge: An Exploratory Study." *Hispanic Journal of Behavioral Science,* 13, 95–104.

Padilla, A. M., and Lindholm, K. J. (1992). *What Do We Know about Culturally Diverse Children?* Paper presented at the meeting of the American Psychological Association, Washington, DC.

Padilla-Walker, L. M., and Carlo. G. (2004). "'It's Not Fair!' Adolescents' Constructions of Appropriateness of Parental Reactions." *Journal of Youth and Adolescence,* 33, 389–401.

Page, E. W. (1922). "A Flapper's Appeal to Parents." *Outlook,* December 6.

Page, R. M. (1990). "Shyness and Sociability: A Dangerous Combination for Illicit Substance Use in Adolescent Males?" *Adolescence,* 25, 803–806.

Pagliuso, S. (1976). *Understanding Stages of Moral Development: A Programmed Learning Workbook.* New York: Paulist Press.

Palenski, J. E., and Launer, H. M. (1987). "The 'Process' of Running Away: A Redefinition." *Adolescence,* 22, 347–362.

Pallas, A. M., Entwisle, D. R., Alexander, K. L., & Stluka, M. F. (1994). Ability-group effects: Instructional, social, or institutional? *Sociology of Education, 67,* 27–46.

Panchaud, C., Singh, S., Feivelson, D., and Darroch, J. E. (2000). "Sexually Transmitted Diseases among Adolescents in Developed Countries." *Family Planning Perspectives,* 32, 24–32.

Paolucci, E. O., and Violata, C. (2004). "A Meta-Analysis of the Published Research on the Affective, Cognitive, and Behavioral Effects of Corporal Punishment." *Journal of Psychology,* 138, 197–221.

Paolucci, E. O., Genius, M. L., and Violato, C. (2001). "A Meta-Analysis of the Published Research on the Effects of Child Sexual Abuse." *Journal of Psychology,* 135, 17–36.

Papini, D. R., and Roggman, L. A. (1992). "Adolescent Perceived Attachment to Parents in Relation to Competence, Depression and Anxiety: A Longitudinal Study." *Journal of Early Adolescence,* 12, 420–440.

Papini, D. R., Farmer, F. F., Clark, S. M., Micka, J. C., and Barnett, J. K. (1990). "Early Adolescent Age and Gender Differences in Patterns of Emotional Self-Disclosure to Parents and Friends." *Adolescence,* 25, 959–976.

Papini, D. R., Mucks, J. C., and Barnett, J. K. (1989). "Perceptions of Intrapsychic and Extrapsychic Functioning as Bases of Adolescent Ego Identity Statuses." *Journal of Adolescent Research,* 4, 462–482.

Parish, J. G., and Parish, T. S. (Fall 1983). "Children's Self-Concepts as Related to Family Structure and Family Concept." *Adolescence,* 18, 649–658.

Parish, T. S. (1991). "Ratings of Self and Parents by Youth: Are They Affected by Family Status, Gender, and Birth Order?" *Adolescence,* 26, 105–112.

Parish, T. S. (1993). "The Relationships between Support System Failures and College Students' Ratings of Self and Family: Do They Vary across Family Configuration?" *Adolescence,* 28, 422–424.

Parish, T. S. (Fall 1980). "The Relationship between Factors Associated with Father Loss and Individuals' Level of Moral Judgment." *Adolescence,* 15, 535–541.

Parish, T. S., and Dostal, J. W. (August 1980). "Evaluations of Self and Parent Figures by Children from Intact, Divorced, and Reconstituted Families." *Journal of Youth and Adolescence,* 9, 347–351.

Parish, T. S., and Parish, J. G. (1991). "The Effects of Family Configuration and Support System Failures during Childhood and Adolescence on College Students' Self-Concept and Social Skills." *Adolescence,* 26, 441–447.

Parker, J. S., and Benson, M. J. (2005). "Parent-Adolescent Relations and Adolescent Functioning: Self-Esteem, Substance Abuse, and Delinquency." *Family Therapy,* 32, 131–142.

Parks, P. S. M., and Read, M. H. (1997). "Adolescent Male Athletes: Body Image, Diet, and Exercise." *Adolescence,* 32, 593–602.

Parrott, C. A., and Strongman, K. T. (Summer 1984). "Locus of Control and Delinquency." *Adolescence,* 19, 459–471.

Pascarella, E. T., and Terenzini, P. T. (1991). *How College Affects Students: Findings and Insights from 20 Years of Research.* San Francisco: Jossey-Bass.

Patrick, H., Hicks, L., and Ryan, A. M. (1997). "Relations of Perceived Social Efficacy and Social Goal Pursuit to Self-Efficacy for Academic Work." *Journal of Early Adolescence,* 17, 109–128.

Patrick, H., Ryan, A. M., Alfeld-Liro, C., Fredricks, J. A., Hruda, L., and Eccles, J. (1999). "Adolescents' Commitment to Developing Talent: The Role of Peers in Continuing Motivation for Sports and the Arts." *Journal of Youth and Adolescence,* 28, 741–763.

Patterson, C. J. (1994). "Children of the Lesbian Baby Boom: Behavioral Adjustment, Self-Concepts, and Sex-Role Identity." In B. Greene and G. M. Herek (Eds.), *Contemporary Perspectives on Lesbian and Gay Psychology: Theory, Research and Applications* (pp. 156–175). Beverly Hills, CA: Sage.

Patterson, G. R., DeBarysne, B. D., and Ramsey, E. (1989). A Developmental Perspective on Antisocial Behavior. *American Psychologist,* 44, 329–335.

Paul, E. L., and White, K. M. (1990). "The Development of Intimate Relationships in Late Adolescence." *Adolescence,* 25, 375–400.

Paul, E. L., McManus, B., and Hayes, A. (2000). "Hookups: Characteristics and Correlates of College Students' Spontaneous and Anonymous Sexual Experiences." *The Journal of Sex Research,* 37, 76–88.

Paul, M. J., and Fischer, J. L. (April 1980). "Correlates of Self-Concept among Black Early Adolescents." *Journal of Youth and Adolescence,* 9, 163–173.

Paul, T., Schroeter, K., Dahme, B., and Nutzinger, D. O. (2002). "Self-Injurious Behavior in Women with Eating Disorders." *American Journal of Psychiatry,* 159, 408–411.

Paulson, S. E. (1994). "Relations of Parenting Style and Parental Involvement with Ninth-Grade Students' Achievement." *Journal of Early Adolescence,* 2, 250–267.

Paulson, S. E., and Sputa, C. L. (1996). "Patterns of Parenting during Adolescence: Perceptions of Adolescents and Parents." *Adolescence,* 31, 369–381.

Paulson, S. E., Marchant, G. J., and Rothlisberg, B. A. (1998). "Early Adolescents' Perceptions of Patterns of Parenting, Teaching, and School Atmosphere: Implications for Achievement." *Journal of Early Adolescence,* 18, 5–26.

Paus, T., Zijdenbos, A., Worsley, K., Collins, D. L., Blumenthal, J., Giedd, J. N., Rapoport, J. L., and Evans, A. C. (1999). "Structural Maturation of Neural Pathways in Children and Adolescents: In Vivo Study." *Science,* 283, 1908–1911.

Paxton, S. J., Norris, M., Wertheim, E. H., Durkin, S. J., and Anderson, J. (2005). "Body Dissatisfaction, Dating, and Importance of Thinness to Attractiveness in Adolescent Girls." *Sex Roles,* 53, 663–675.

Paxton, S. J., Schultz, H. K., Wertheim, E. H., and Muir, S. L. (1999). "Friendship Clique and Peer Influences on Body Image Concerns, Dietary Restraint, Extreme Weight-Loss Behaviors, and Binge Eating in Adolescent Girls." *Journal of Abnormal Psychology,* 108, 255–266.

P.C. Games. (January 1997). Volume 4, Number 1.

Pearlman, M. (1995). "The Role of Socioeconomic Status in Adolescent Literature." *Adolescence,* 30, 223–231.

Pearson, C. A., and Gleaves, D. H. (2006). "The Multiple Dimensions of Perfectionism and Their Relation with Eating Disorder Features." *Personality and Individual Differences,* 41, 225–235.

Pearson, J. L., and Ferguson, L. R. (1989). "Gender Differences in Patterns and Spatial Ability, Environmental Cognition, and Math and English Achievement in Late Adolescence." *Adolescence,* 24, 421–431.

Peck, C., Cuban, L., and Kirkpatrick, H. (February, 2002). "Techno-Promoter Dreams, Student Realities." *Phi Delta Kappan,* pp. 472–480.

Peck, D. L., and Warner, K. (1995). "Accident or Suicide? Single-Vehicle Car Accident and the Intent Hypothesis." *Adolescence,* 30, 463–472.

Pedersen, W. (1990). "Adolescents Initiating Cannabis Use: Cultural Opposition or Poor Mental Health?" *Journal of Adolescence,* 13, 327–339.

Penick, N. I., and Jepsen, D. A. (1992). "Family Functioning and Adolescent Career Development." *Career Development Quarterly,* 40, 208–222.

Peretti, P. O. (Fall 1980). "Perceived Primary Group Criteria in the Relational Network of Closest Friendships." *Adolescence,* 15, 555–565.

Perkins, D. F., and Lerner, R. M. (1995). "Single and Multiple Indicators of Physical Attractiveness and Psychosocial Behaviors among Young Adolescents." *Journal of Early Adolescence,* 15, 269–298.

Perkins, H. W. (2002). "Surveying the Damage: A Review of Research on Consequences of Alcohol Misuse in College Populations." *Journal of Studies on Alcohol,* Supplement 14, 91–100.

Perlman, S. B. (1980). "Pregnancy and Parenting among Runaway Girls." *Journal of Family Issues,* 1, 262–273.

Perper, T., and Weis, D. L. (1987). "Proceptive and Rejective Strategies of U.S. and Canadian College Women." *Journal of Sex Research,* 23, 455–480.

Perry, C. L., and Staufacker, M. J. (1996). "Tobacco Use." In R. J. DiClemente, W. B. Hansen, and L. E. Ponton, (Eds.) *Handbook of Adolescent Health Risk Behavior* (pp. 53–81). New York: Plenum Press.

Perry, C. L., Telch, M. J., Killen, J., Burke, A., and Maccoby, N. (Fall 1983). "High School Smoking Prevention: The Relative Efficacy of Varied Treatments and Instructions." *Adolescence,* 18, 561–566.

Perry, C. N., and McIntire, W. G. (1995). "Modes of Moral Judgement among Early Adolescents." *Adolescence,* 30, 707–715.

Perry v. Granada. (1969). 300 F. Supp. 748 (Miss.).

Persell, C. H., Catsambis, S., and Cookson, P. W., Jr. (1992). "Family Background, School Type, and College Attendance: A Conjoint System of Cultural Capital Transmission." *Journal of Research on Adolescence,* 2, 1–23.

Pesce, R. C., and Harding, C. G. (1986). "Imaginary Audience Behavior and Its Relationship to Operational Thought and Social Experience." *Journal of Early Adolescence,* 6, 83–94.

Pestrak, V. A., and Martin, D. (1985). "Cognitive Development and Aspects of Adolescent Sexuality." *Adolescence,* 22, 981–987.

Petersen, A. C., Compas, B. E., Brooks-Gunn, J., and Stemmler, M. (1993). "Depression in Adolescence." *American Psychologist,* 48, 155–168.

Petersen, J. R., Kretchner, A., Nellis, B., Lever, J., and Hertz, R. (March 1983). "The Playboy Reader's Sex Survey, Part 2." *Playboy,* p. 90.

Peterson, G. W., and Rollins, B. C. (1987). Parent-Child Socialization: A Review of Research and Applications of Symbolic Interaction Concepts. In M. B. Sussman and S. K. Steinmetz (Eds.), *Handbook of Marriage and the Family* (pp. 471–507). New York: Plenum.

Peterson, G. W., Stiver, M. E., and Peters, D. F. (1986). "Family versus Nonfamily Significant Others for the Career Decisions of Low-Income Youth." *Family Relations,* 35, 417–424.

Peterson, J. L., and Zill, N. (1986). "Marital Disruption, Parent-Child Relationships and Behavior Problems in Children." *Journal of Marriage and the Family,* 48, 295–307.

Peterson, K. L., and Roscoe, B. (1991). "Imaginary Audience Behavior in Older Adolescent Females." *Adolescence,* 26, 195–200.

Peterson, R. R. (1996). "A Re-Evaluation of the Economic Consequences of Divorce." *American Sociological Review,* 61, 528–536.

Petridou, E., Syrigou, E., Toupadaki, N., Zavitzanos, X., Willet, W., and Trichopoulos, D. (1996). "Determinants of Age at Menarche as Early Life Predictors of Breast Cancer Risk." *International Journal of Cancer,* 68, 193–198.

Pett, M. A., and Vaughan-Cole, B. (1986). "The Impact of Income Issues and Social Status in Post-Divorce Adjustment of Custodial Parents." *Family Relations,* 35, 103–111.

Pfeffer, C. R. (1989). "Life Stress and Family Risk Factors for Youth Fatal and Nonfatal Suicidal Behavior." In C. R. Pfeffer (Ed.), *Suicide among Youth: Perspectives on Risk and Prevention* (pp. 143–164). Washington, DC: American Psychiatric Press.

Phelps, L. A., Johnston, L. S., Jimenesez, D. P., Wilczenski, F. L., Andrea, R. K., and Healy, R. W. (1993). "Figure Preference, Body Dissatisfaction, and Body Distortion in Adolescence." *Journal of Adolescent Research,* 8, 297–310.

Philliber, S. G., and Tatum, M. L. (Summer 1982). "Sex Education and the Double Standard in High School." *Adolescence,* 17, 272–283.

Phillips, E. L., Greydanus, D. E., Pratt, H. D., and Patel, D. P. (2003). "Treatment of Bulimia Nervosa: Psychological and Psychopharmacologic Considerations." *Journal of Adolescent Research,* 18, 261–279.

Phillips, S. D., and Imhoff, A. R. (1997). "Women and Career Development: A Decade of Research." *Annual Review of Psychology,* 48, 31–59.

Phinney, J. S. (1989). "Stages of Ethnic Identity Development in Minority Group Adolescents." *Journal of Early Adolescence,* 9, 34–49.

Phinney, J. S. (1992). "The Multigroup Ethnic Identity Measure. A New Scale for Use with Diverse Groups." *Journal of Adolescent Research,* 7, 156–176.

Phinney, J. S., and Alipuria, L. L. (1990). "Ethnic Identity in College Students from Four Different Ethnic Groups." *Journal of Adolescence,* 13, 171–183.

Phinney, J. S., and Alipuria, L. L. (1996). "At the Interface of Cultures: Multiethnic/Multiracial High School and College Students." *Journal of Social Psychology,* 136, 139–158.

Phinney, J. S., and Chavira, V. (1995)."Parental Ethnic Socialization and Adolescent Coping with Problems Related to Ethnicity." *Journal of Research on Adolescence,* 5, 31–63.

Phinney, J. S., and Devich-Navarro, M. (1997). "Variations in Bicultural Identification among African American and Mexican American Adolescents." *Journal of Research on Adolescence*, 7, 3–32.

Phinney, J. S., Chavira, V., and Williamson, L. (1992). "Acculturation Attitudes and Self-Esteem among High-School and College Students." *Youth and Society*, 23, 299–312.

Phinney, J. S., Dupont, S., Landin, J., and Onwughalu, M. (1994). *Social Identity Orientation, Bicultural Conflicts, and Coping Strategies among Minority Adolescents.* Paper presented at the meeting of the Society for Research on Adolescents, San Diego.

Phinney, V. G., Jensen, L. C., Olsen, J. A., and Cundick, B. (1990). "The Relationship between Early Development and Psychosexual Behaviors in Adolescent Females." *Adolescence*, 25, 321–332.

Piacentini, M., and Mailer, G. (2004). "Symbolic Consumption in Teenagers' Clothing Choices." *Journal of Consumer Behaviour*, 3, 251–262.

Piaget, J. (1948). *The Moral Judgment of the Child.* Glencoe, IL: Free Press. (Originally 1932).

Piaget, J. (1951). *Psychology of Intelligence.* London: Routledge and Kegan Paul.

Piaget, J. (1963). *The Origins of Intelligence in the Child.* New York: Norton. (Originally 1936)

Piaget, J. (1967). *Six Psychological Studies.* Translated by A. Tenzer and D. Elkind. New York: Random House.

Piaget, J. (1971). "The Theory of Stages in Cognitive Development." In D. R. Green (Ed.), *Measurement and Piaget.* New York: McGraw-Hill.

Piaget, J. (1972). "Intellectual Evolution from Adolescence to Adulthood." *Human Development*, 15, 1012.

Piaget, J., and Inhelder, B. (1969). *The Psychology of the Child.* Translated by Helen Weaver. New York: Basic Books.

Piaget, J., and Inhelder, B. (Winter 1976). "The Development of Formal Thinking and Creativity in Adolescence." *Adolescence*, 11, 609–617.

Piccinino, L. J., and Mosher, W. D. (1998). "Trends in Contraceptive Use in the United States: 1982–1995." *Family Planning Perspectives*, 30, 4–10.

Pillemer, D. B., Koff, E., Rhinehart, E. D., and Rierdan, J. (1987). "Flashbulb Memories of Menarche and Adult Menstrual Distress." *Journal of Adolescence*, 10, 187–199.

Pink, J. E. T., and Wampler, K. S. (1985). "Problem Areas in Stepfamilies: Cohesion, Adaptability, and the Stepfather-Adolescent Relationship." *Family Relations*, 34, 327–335.

Pino, N. W., and Smith, W. L. (2003). "College Students and Academic Dishonesty." *College Student Journal*, 37, 490–500.

Pinquart, M. (2003). "Loneliness in Married, Widowed, Divorced, and Never-Married Older Adults." *Journal of Social and Personal Relationships*, 20, 31–53.

Pipher, M. (1996). *The Shelter of Each Other: Rebuilding Our Families.* New York: Grosset/Putnam Book.

Pirog-Good, M. A. (1996). "The Education and Labor Market Outcomes of Adolescent Fathers." *Youth and Society*, 28, 236–262.

Pittman, F. S. (1991). "The Secret Passions of Men." *Journal of Marital and Family Therapy*, 17, 17–23.

Plake, B. S., Kaplan, B. J., and Steinbrunn, J. (1986). "Sex Role Orientation, Level of Cognitive Development, and Mathematics Performance in Late Adolescence." *Adolescence*, 83, 607–613.

Plant, T. M., Winters, S. J., Attardi, B. J., and Majumdar, S. S. (1993). "The Follicle Stimulating Hormone—Inhibin Feedback Loop in Male Primates." *Human Reproduction*, 8, 41–44.

Plastic Surgery Information Service. (2000a). *National Clearinghouse of Plastic Surgery Statistics* <www.plasticsurgery.org/ediactr/98agedist.htm>.

Plastic Surgery Information Service. (2000b). *Most Popular Surgeries among Teenagers: Nose Reshaping and Breast Reduction* <www.plasticsurgery.org>.

Pleck, J. H. (1976). "The Male Sex Role: Definitions, Problems, and Sources of Change." *Journal of Social Issues*, 32, 155–164.

Pliner, P., Chaiken, S., and Flett, G. L. (1990). "Gender Differences in Concern with Body Weight and Physical Appearance Over the Lifespan." *Personality and Social Psychology Bulletin*, 16, 263–273.

Plotnick, R., and Butler, S. (1991). "Attitudes and Adolescent Nonmarital Childbearing." *Journal of Adolescent Research*, 6, 470–492.

Plummer, L. C., and Koch-Hattern, A. (1986). "Family Stress and Adjustment to Divorce." *Family Relations*, 523–529.

Plummer, W. (October 28, 1985). "A School's Rx for Sex." *People*, pp. 39–41.

Pogarsky, G., Thornberry, T. P., and Lizotte, A. J. (2006). "Developmental Outcomes for Children of Young Mothers." *Journal of Marriage and Family*, 68, 332–344.

Polaneczky, M., et al. (1994). "The Use of Levonorgestrel Implants (Norplant) for Contraception in Adolescent Mothers." *New England Journal of Medicine*, 331, 1201–1206.

Pombeni, M., Kirchler, E., and Palmonari, A. (1990). "Identification with Peers as a Strategy to Muddle through the Troubles of the Adolescent Years." *Journal of Adolescence*, 13, 351–369.

Pomeroy, W. (May, 1965). "Why We Tolerate Lesbians." *Sexology*, pp. 652–654.

Pompili, M., Mancinelli, I., Girardi, P., Ruberto, A., and Taterelli, R. (2004). "Suicide in Anorexia Nervosa: A Meta-Analysis." *International Journal of Eating Disorders*, 36, 99–103.

Popenoe, D. (1996). *Life Without Father.* New York: Martin Kessler Books.

Popenoe, D., and Whitehead, B. D. (2005). *The State of Our Unions 2005.* Piscataway, NJ: The National Marriage Project.

Popkin, B. M., and Udry, J. R. (1998). "Adolescent Obesity Increases Significantly in Second and Third Generation U.S. Immigrants: The National Longitudinal Study of Adolescent Health." *Journal of Nutrition*, 128, 701–706.

Portes, P. R., Dunham, R. M., and Williams, S. (1986). "Assessing Child-Rearing Style in Ecological Settings: Its Relation to Culture, Social Class, Early Age Intervention, and Scholastic Achievement." *Adolescence*, 21, 723–735.

Postrado, L. T., and Nicholson, H. J. (1992). "Effectiveness in Delaying the Initiation of Sexual Intercourse in Girls Aged 12–14." *Youth and Society*, 23, 356–379.

Powell, A. (2003). *Infofacts Resources: Campuses and the Club Drug Ecstasy.* Higher Education Center for Alcohol and Other Drug Prevention. Retrieved from http://www.campusblues.com/drgus3.shtml.

Powers, D. E., and Rock, D. A. (1999). "Effects of Coaching on SAT I: Reasoning Test Scores." *Journal of Educational Measurement*, 36, 93–118.

Powers, P. S. (1980). *Obesity: The Regulation of Weight.* Baltimore: Williams and Wilkins.

Pratt, M. W., Arnold, M. L., Pratt, A. T., and Diessner, R. (1999). "Predicting Adolescent Formal Reasoning from Family Climate: A Longitudinal Study." *Journal of Early Adolescence*, 19, 148–175.

Prediger, D. J., and Brandt, W. E. (1991). "Project CHOICE: Validity of Interest and Ability Measures for Student Choice of Vocational Program." *The Career Development Quarterly*, 40, 132–144.

President's Advisory Commission on Educational Excellence for Hispanic Americans. (1996). *Hispanic American Education.* Washington, DC: Government Printing Office.

Presley, C. A., Meilman, P. W., and Leichliter, J. S. (2002). "College Factors That Influence Drinking." *Journal of Studies on Alcohol*, Supplement no. 14, 82–90.

Prince, F. (1995). "The Relative Effectiveness of a Peer-Led and Sdult-Led Smoking Intervention Program." *Adolescence*, 30, 187–194.

Princeton Survey Research Associates for the Association of Reproductive Health Professionals and the National Campaign to Prevent Teen Pregnancy. (1997). *National Omnibus Survey Questions about Teen Pregnancy.* Washington, DC: Author.

Pritchard, M. E., King, S. L., & Czajka-Narins, D. M. (1997). "Adolescent Body Mass Indices and Self-Perception." *Adolescence*, 32, 863–880.

Pritchard, M. E., Myers, B. K., and Cassidy, D. J. (1989). "Factors Associated with Adolescent Saving and Spending Patterns." *Adolescence*, 24, 711–723.

Prokopcakova, A. (1998). "Drug Experimenting and Pubertal Maturation in Girls." *Studia Psychologica*, 40, 287–290.

Protinsky, H. (1988). "Identity Formation: A Comparison of Problem and Nonproblem Adolescents." *Adolescence*, 23, 67–72.

Protinsky, H., and Farrier, S. (Winter 1980). "Self-Image in Pre-Adolescents and Adolecents." *Adolescence*, 15, 887–893.

Pruchno, R. (1999). "Raising Grandchildren: The Experiences of Black and White Grandmothers." *The Gerontologist*, 39, 209–221.

Pryor, D. W., and McGarrell, E. F. (1993). "Public Perceptions of Youth Gang Crime: An Exploratory Analysis." *Youth and Society*, 24, 399–418.

Pryor, J., and Rogers, B. (2001). *Children in Changing Families: Life after Parental Separation.* Oxford, England: Blackwell Publishing.

Ptacek, C. (1988). "The Nuclear Age: Context for Family Interaction." *Family Relations*, 37, 437–443.

Public Agenda. (1999). *Kids These Days '99.* Retrieved from http://publicagenda.org/research/pdfs/kids_these_days_99.pdf.

Putukian, M. (1998). "The Female Athlete Triad." *Clinics in Sports Medicine*, 17, 675–696.

Quadrel, M. J., Fischoff, B., and Davis, W. W. (1993). "Adolescent (In)vulnerability." *American Psychologist*, 48, 102–116.

Queralt, M. (1993). "Risk Factors Associated with Completed Suicide in Latino Adolescents." *Adolescence,* 28, 831–850.

Quinlin, R. J. (2003). "Father Absence, Parental Care, and Female Reproductive Development." *Evolution and Human Behavior,* 24, 376–390.

Quintana, S. M., and Lapsley, D. K. (1990). "Rapprochement in Late Adolescent Separation-Individuation: A Structure Equations Approach." *Journal of Adolescence,* 13, 371–385.

Quintana, S. M., Casteñeda-English, P., and Ybarra, V. C. (1999). "Role of Perspective-Taking Abilities and Ethnic Socialization in Development of Adolescent Ethnic Identity." *Journal of Research on Adolescence,* 9, 161–184.

Rabasca, L. (1999) "Not Enough Evidence to Support 'Abstinence-Only.' " *APA Monitor Online,* 30(11) <www.apa.org/monitor/dec99/pil.html>.

Rabin, D. F., and Chrousos, G. P. (1991). "Androgens, Gonadal." In R. M. Lerner, A. C. Petersen, and J. Brooks-Gunn (Eds.), *Encyclopedia of Adolescence.* Vol. 1. New York: Garland.

Rabinowitz, F. E. (1991). "The Male-to-Male Embrace: Breaking the Touch Taboo in Men's Therapy Groups." *Journal of Counseling and Development,* 69, 574–576.

Raffaelli, M., Bogenschneider, K., and Flood, M. F. (1998). "Parent-Teen Communication abut Sexual Topics." *Journal of Family Issues,* 19, 316–334.

Rahman, Q. Q., Glenn, G. D., and Wilson, D. (2003). "Born Gay? The Psychobiology of Human Sexual Orientation." *Personality and Individuals Differences,* 34, 1337–1382.

Rajan, K. B., Leroux, B. G., Peterson, A. V., Jr., Bricker, J. B., Andersen, M. R., Kealey, K. A, et al. (2003). "Nine Year Prospective Association between Older Siblings' Smoking and Children's Daily Smoking." *Journal of Adolescent Health,* 33, 25–30.

Raley, K., and Bumpus, L. (2003). "The Topography of the Divorce Plateau: Levels and Trends in Unity Stability in the United States after 1980." *Demographic Research,* 8, 245–259.

Ralph, N., and Morgan, K. A. (1991). "Assessing Differences in Chemically Dependent Adolescent Males Using the Child Behavior Check List." *Adolescence,* 26, 183–194.

Ramirez, R. R. (2004). *We the People: Hispanics in the United States.* Census 2000 Special Report. Washington DC.: U.S. Bureau of the Census.

Ramsey, C. E. "A Study of Decision-Making of Adolescence." Unpublished data.

Raphael, B., Cubis, J., Dunne, M., Lewin, T., & Kelly, S. (1990). "The Impact of Parental Loss on Adolescents' Psychosocial Characteristics." *Adolescence,* 25, 689–700.

Raschke, H. J., and Raschke, V. J. (May 1979). "Family Conflict and Children's Self-Concepts: A Comparison of Intact and Single-Parent Families." *Journal of Marriage and the Family,* 41, 367–374.

Raskoff, S., and Sundeen, R. (1994, July). *The Ties That Bind: Teenage Volunteers in the United States.* Paper presented at the International Sociological Association Meetings, Bielefeld, Germany.

Rathus, S. A., Nevid, J. S., and Fichner-Rathus, L. (1997). *Human Sexuality in a World of Diversity.* Boston: Allyn & Bacon.

Rathus, S. A., Nevid, J. S., & Fichner-Rathus, L. (2000). *Human Sexuality in a World of Diversity* (4th Edition). Boston: Allyn & Bacon.

Ravitch, D. (October 1983). "The Educational Pendulum." *Psychology Today,* 17, 62–71.

Ray, W. J., Georgiou, S., and Ravizza, R. (1979). "Spatial Abilities, Sex Differences, and Lateral Eye Movements." *Developmental Psychology,* 15, 455–457.

Ream, G. L., and Savin-Williams, R. C. (2003). "Religious Development in Adolescence." In G. R. Adams and M. D. Berzonsky (Eds.), *Blackwell Handbook of Adolescence* (pp. 51–59). Oxford, England: Blackwell Publishing.

Reardon, B., and Griffing, P. (Spring 1983). "Factors Related to the Self-Concept of Institutionalized, White, Male, Adolescent Drug Abusers." *Adolescence,* 18, 29–41.

Reeves, T. J., and Bennett, C. E. (2004). *We the People: Asians in the United States.* Census Bureau Special Report. Washington, DC: U.S. Bureau of the Census.

Regnerus, M. D. (2000). "Shaping Schooling Success: Religious Socialization and Educational Outcomes in Metropolitan Public Schools." *Journal for the Scientific Study of Religion,* 39, 363–370.

Regnerus, M. D. (2005). "Talking About Sex: Religion and Patterns of Parent-Child Communication about Sex and Contraception." *Sociological Quarterly,* 46, 79–105.

Reijonen, J. H., Pratt, H. D., Patel, D. R., and Greydanus, D. E. (2003). "Eating Disorders in the General Population: An Overview." *Journal of Adolescent Research,* 18, 209–222.

Reiner, W. (1997). "To Be Male or Female—That Is the Question." *Archives of Pediatric and Adolescent Medicine,* 151, 224–225.

Reinking, M. F., and Alexander, L. E. (2005). "Prevalence of Disordered-Eating Behaviors in Undergraduate Female Collegiate Athletes and Nonathletes." *Journal of Athletic Training,* 40, 47–51.

Reis, I. L. (1971). *The Family System in America.* New York: Holt, Rinehart and Winston.

Reisch, S. K., Bush, L., Nelson, C. J., Ohm, B. J., Portz, P. A., Abell, B., et al. (2000). "Topics of Conflict between Parents and Young Adolescents." *Journal of the Society of Pediatric Nurses,* 5, 27–40.

Remafedi, G. (1987). "Adolescent Homosexuality: Psychosocial and Medical Implications." *Pediatrics,* 79, 331–337.

Remez, L. (1992). "Adolescent Drug Users More Likely to Become Pregnant, Elect Abortion." *Family Planning Perspectives,* 24, 281–282.

Remez, L. (2000). "Oral Sex among Adolescents: Is It Sex or Is It Abstinence?" *Family Planning Perspective,* 32, 298–304.

Renk, K., Liljequist, L., Simpson, J. E., and Phares, V. (2005). "Gender and Age Differences in the Topics of Parent-Adolescent Conflict." *The Family Journal: Counseling and Therapy for Couples and Families,* 13, 139–149.

Repetti, R., Taylor, S., and Seeman, T. (2002). "Risky Families: Family Social Environments and the Mental and Physical Health of Offspring." *Psychological Bulletin,* 128, 330–366.

Resnick, M. D., Wattenberg, E., and Brewer, R. (1992). *Paternity of Avowal/Disavowal among Partners of Low Income Mothers.* Paper presented at the Meeting of the Society for Research on Adolescence, Washington, DC.

Rest, J. (1986). *Moral Development: Advances in Research and Theory.* New York: Praeger.

Rest, J. R. (1983). "Morality." In P. H. Mussen (Ed.), *Handbook of Child Psychology,* III. 4th ed. New York: Wiley.

Reuterman, N., A., and Burcky, W. D. (1989). "Dating Violence in High School: A Profile of the Victims." *Psychology: A Journal of Human Behavior,* 26, 1–9.

Reyes, O., Kobus, K., and Gillock, K. (1999). "Career Aspirations of Urban, Mexican American Adolescent Females." *Hispanic Journal of Behavioral Sciences,* 21, 366–382.

Rhein, L. M., Ginsburg, K. R., Schwartz, D., Pinto-Martin, J. A., Zhao, H., Morgan, A. P., and Slap, G. B. (1997). "Teen Father Participation in Child Rearing: Family Perspectives." *Journal of Adolescent Health,* 21, 244–252.

Rhodes, J. E., and Fisher, K. (1993). "Spanning the Gender Gap: Gender Differences in Delinquency among Inner-City Adolescents." *Adolescence,* 28, 879–889.

Rhynard, J., Krebs, M., and Glover, J. (1997). "Sexual Assault in Dating Relationships." *Journal of School Health,* 67, 89–93.

Ricciardelli, L. A., and McCabe, M. P. (2001). "Children's Body Image Concerns and Eating Disturbance: A Review of the Literature." *Clinical Psychology Review,* 21, 325–344.

Ricciardelli, L. A., and McCabe, M. P. (2004). "A Biopsychosocial Model of Disordered Eating and the Pursuit of Muscularity in Adolescent Boys." *Psychological Bulletin,* 130, 179–205.

Ricciardelli, L. A., McCabe, M. P., Holt, K., E., and Finemore, J. (2003). "A Biopsychosocial Model for Understanding Body Image and Body Change Strategies among Children." *Applied Developmental Psychology,* 24, 475–495.

Rice, F. P. (1980). *Morality and Youth.* Philadelphia: Westminster Press.

Rice, F. P. (1989). *Human Sexuality.* Dubuque, IA: Wm. C. Brown.

Rice, F. P. (1993). *Intimate Relationships, Marriages, and Families.* Mountain View, CA: Mayfield.

Rice, F. P. (1996). *Intimate Relationships, Marriages, and Families.* Moutain View, CA: Mayfield.

Rice, K. G. (1993). "Separation-Individuation and Adjustment in College: A Longitudinal Study." *Journal of Counseling Psychology,* 39, 203–213.

Rice, K. G., and Whaley, T. J. (1994)."A Short-Term Longitudinal Study of Within-Semester Stability and Change in Attachment and College Student Adjustment." *Journal of College Student Development,* 35, 324–330.

Rich, C. L., Sherman, M., and Fowler, R. C. (1990). "San Diego Suicide Study: The Adolescents." *Adolescence,* 25, 855–865.

Rich, Y., and Golan, R. (1992). "Career Plans for Male-Dominated Occupations and Female Seniors in Religious and Secular High Schools." *Adolescence,* 27, 73–86.

Richards, L. N., and Schmiege, C. J. (1993). "Problems and Strengths of Single-Parent Families." *Family Relations,* 42, 277–285.

Richards, M. H., and Larson, R. (1993). "Pubertal Development in the Daily Subjective States of Young Adolescents." *Journal of Research on Adolescence,* 3, 145–169.

Richards, M. H., Boxer, A. M., Petersen, A. C., & Albrecht, R. (1990). "Relation of Weight to Body Image in Pubertal Girls and Boys from Two Communities." *Developmental Psychology,* 26, 313–321.

Richards, M. H., Crowe, P. A., Larson, R., and Swarr, A. (1998). "Developmental Patterns and Gender Differences in the Experience of Peer Companionship during Adolescence." *Child Development,* 69, 154–163.

Richardson, K. (2002). "What IQ Tests Test." *Theory & Psychology,* 12, 283–314.

Rideout, V., Roberts, D. F., and Foehr, U. G. (2005). *Generation M: Media in the Lives of 8–18 Year Olds.* Washington, DC: Kaiser Family Foundation.

Riegel, K. F. (1973). "Dialectical Operations: The Final Period of Cognitive Development." *Human Development,* 16, 346–370.

Rierdan, J. and Koff, E. (1997). "Weight, Weight-Related Aspects of Body Image, and Depression in Early Adolescent Girls." *Adolescence,* 32, 615–624.

Rierdan, J., Koff, E., and Stubbs, M. L. (1989). "A Longitudinal Analysis of Body Image as a Predictor of the Onset and Persistence of Adolescent Girls' Depression." *Journal of Early of Adolescence,* 9, 454–466.

Rigby, K. (2002). *New Perspective on Bullying.* Philadephia: Kingsley.

Rigby, K., and Cox, I. (1996). "The Contribution of Bullying at School and Boys' Self-Esteem to Acts of Delinquency among Australian Teenagers." *Personality and Individual Differences,* 21, 609–612.

Riggio, H. R. (2001). "Relations between Parental Divorce and the Quality of Adult Sibling Relationships." *Journal of Divorce and Remarriage,* 36, 67–82.

Rind, B., and Tromovitch, P. (1997). "A Meta-Analytic Review of Findings from National Samples of Psychological Correlates of Child Sexual Abuse." *Journal of Sex Research,* 34, 237–255.

Ringwalt, C. L., and Palmer, J. H. (1989). "Cocaine and Crack Users Compared." *Adolescence,* 24, 851–859.

Risman, B. J., Hill, C. T., Rubin, Z., & Peplau, L. A. (1981). "Living Together in College: Implications for Courtship." *Journal of Marriage & the Family,* 43, 77–83.

Ritchey, P. N., and Fishbein, H. D. (2001). "The Lack of an Association between Adolescents' Friends' Prejudices and Stereotypes." *Merrill-Palmer Quarterly,* 47, 188–206.

Ritzer, G. (2000). *The McDonaldization of Society.* Thousand Oaks, CA: Pine Forge Press.

Robbins, D. (1983). "A Cluster of Adolescent Suicide Attempts: Is Suicide Contagious?" *Journal of Adolescent Health Care,* 3, 253–255.

Robert, M. M., Pauzé R., and Fournier, L. (2005). "Factors Associated with Homelessness of Adolescents under Supervision of the Youth Protection System." *Journal of Adolescence,* 28, 215–230.

Roberto, L. G. (1986). "Bulimia: The Transgenerational View." *Journal of Marital and Family Therapy,* 12, 231–240.

Roberts, D. F. (2000). "Media and Youth: Access, Exposure, and Privatization." *Journal of Adolescent Health,* Supplement to vol. 27, 8–14.

Roberts, D. F., Christianson, P. G., and Gentile, D. A. (2003). "The Effects of Violent Music on Children and Adolescents." In D. A. Gentile (Ed.), *Media Violence and Children: A Complete Guide for Parents and Professionals* (pp. 153–170). Westport, CT: Praeger.

Roberts, D. F., Foehr, U. G., and Rideout, V. G. (2005). *Generation M: Media in the Lives of 8–18 Year Olds.* Menlo Park, CA: Kaiser Family Foundation.

Roberts, D. F., Foehr, U. G., Rideout, V. J., and Brodie, M. (1999). *Kids and Media at the New Millennium: A Comprehensive National Analysis of Children's Media Use.* Menlo Park, CA: Kaiser Family Foundation.

Roberts, E., and DeBlossie, R. R. (Winter 1983). "Test Bias and the Culturally Different Early Adolescent." *Adolescence,* 18, 837–843.

Roberts, L. R., and Petersen, A. C. (1992). "The Relationship between Academic Achievement and Social Self-Image during Early Adolescence." *Journal of Early Adolescence,* 12, 197–219.

Roberts, L. R., Sarigiani, P. A., Petersen, A. C., and Newman, J. L. (1990). "Gender Differences in Relationship between Achievement and Self-Image during Early Adolescence." *Journal of Early Adolescence,* 10, 159–175.

Roberts, R. E., Phinney, J. S., Masse, L. C., Chen, Y. R., Roberts, C. R., and Romero, A. (1999). "The Structure of Ethnic Identity of Young Adolescents from Diverse Ethnocultural Groups." *Journal of Early Adolescence,* 19, 301–322.

Robertson, J. F., and Simons, R. L. (1989). "Family Factors, Self-Esteem, and Adolescent Depression." *Journal of Marriage and the Family,* 51, 125–138.

Robins, L. N. (1966). *Deviant Children Grown Up.* Baltimore: Williams and Wilkins.

Robinson, B. E., Skeen, P., Flake-Hobson, C., and Herman, M. (1982). "Gay Men's and Women's Perceptions of Early Family Life and Their Relationships with Parents." *Family Relations,* 31, 79–83.

Robinson, I. E., and Jedlicka, D. (February 1982). "Change in Sexual Attitudes and Behavior of College Students from 1965 to 1980: A Research Note." *Journal of Marriage and the Family,* 44, 237–240.

Robinson, N. S. (1995). "Evaluating the Nature of Perceived Support in Its Relation to Perceived Self-Worth in Adolescents." *Journal of Research on Adolescence,* 5, 253–280.

Robinson, S. E. (January 1983). "Nader versus ETS: Who Should We Believe?" *Personnel and Guidance Journal,* 61, 260–262.

Robinson, T. N., Killen, J. D., Litt, I. F., and Hammer, L. D. (1996). "Ethnicity and Body Dissatisfaction: Are Hispanic and Asian Girls at Increased Risk for Eating Disorders?" *Journal of Adolescent Health,* 19, 384–393.

Roche, J. P., and Ramsbey, T. W. (1993). "Premarital Sexuality: A Five-Year Follow-Up Study of Attitudes and Behavior by Dating Stage." *Adolescence,* 28, 67–80.

Rodgers, J. L., and Rowe, D. C. (1990). "Adolescent Sexual Activity and Mildly Deviant Behavior." *Journal of Family Issues,* 11, 274–303.

Rodgers, J. L., Rowe, D. C., and Harris, D. F. (1992). "Sibling Differences in Adolescent Sexual Behavior: Inferring Process Models from Family Composition Patterns." *Journal of Marriage and the Family,* 54, 142–152.

Rodriquez, C., Jr., and Moore, M. B. (1995). Perceptions of Pregnant/Parenting Teens: Reframing Issues for an Integrated Approach to Pregnancy Problems." *Adolescence,* 30, 685–706.

Roe, K. (1995). "Adolescents' Use of Socially Devalued Media: Towards a Theory of Media Delinquency." *Journal of Youth and Adolescence,* 24, 617–631.

Roeser, R. W., and Eccles, J. S. (1998). "Adolescents' Perceptions of Middle School: Relation to Longitudinal Changes in Academic and Psychological Adjustment." *Journal of Research on Adolescence,* 8, 123–158.

Roeser, R. W., Eccles, J. S., and Freedman-Doan, C. (1999). "Academic Functioning and Mental Health in Adolescence: Patterns, Progressions, and Routes from Childhood." *Journal of Adolescent Research,* 14, 135–174.

Roeser, R. W., Midgley, C., and Urdan, T. C. (1996). "Perceptions of the School Psychological Environment and Early Adolescents' Psychological and Behavioral Functioning in School: the Mediating Role of Goals and Belonging." *Journal of Educational Psychology,* 88, 408–422.

Rogers, C. R. (1961). *On Becoming a Person: A Therapist's View of Psychotherapy.* Boston: Houghton Mifflin.

Rogers, M. M., Peoples-Sheps, M. D., and Suchindran, C. (1996). "Impact of Social Support Program on Teenage Prenatal Care Use and Pregnancy Outcomes." *Journal of Adolescent Health,* 19, 132–140.

Rohner, R. P., and Veneziano, R. A. (2001). "The Importance of Father Love: History and Contemporary Evidence." *Review of General Psychology,* 5, 382–405.

Rohner, R. P., and Britner, P. A. (2002). "Worldwide Mental Health Correlates of Parental Acceptance-Rejection: Review of Cross-Cultural and Intracultural Evidence." *Journal of Cross-Cultural Research,* 36, 15–47.

Rohner, R. P., Bourque, S. L., and Elordi, C. A. (1996). "Children's Perceptions of Corporal Punishment, Caretaker Acceptance, and Psychological Adjustment in a Poor, Biracial Southern Community." *Journal of Marriage and the Family,* 58, 842–852.

Roig, M. (1999). "When College Students' Attempts at Paraphrasing Become Instances of Potential Plagiarism." *Psychological Reports,* 84, 973–982.

Roig, M., and Caso, M. (2005). "Lying and Cheating: Fraudulent Excuse Making, Cheating, and Plagiarism." *Journal of Psychology: Interdisciplinary and Applied,* 139, 485–494.

Roll, E. J. (Fall 1980). "Psychologists' Conflicts about the Inevitability of Conflict during Adolescence: An Attempt at Reconciliation." *Adolescence,* 15, 661–670.

Rolls, B. J., Federoff, I. C., and Guthrie, J. F. (1991). "Gender Differences in Eating Behavior and Body Weight Regulation." *Health Psychology,* 10, 133–142.

Romans, S. E., Martin, M., Gendall, K., and Herbison, G. P. (2003). "Age of Menarche: The Role of Some Psychosocial Factors." *Psychological Medicine,* 33, 933–939.

Roosa, M. W. (1991). "Adolescent Pregnancy Programs Collection: An Introduction." *Family Relations,* 40, 370–372.

Rose, A. J., Swenson, L. P., and Waller, E. M. (2004). "Overt and Relational Aggression and Perceived Popularity: Developmental Differences in Concurrent and Prospective Relations." *Developmental Psychology,* 40, 378–387.

Rosen, D. (2003). "Eating Disorders in Childhood and Early Adolescence: Etiology, Classification, Clinical Features, and Treatment." *Adolescent Medicine,* 14, 49–59.

Rosen, J. C., and Gross, J. (1987). "Prevalence of Weight Reducing and Weight Gaining in Adolescent Girls and Boys." *Health Psychology,* 6, 131–147.

Rosenblum, G. D., and Lewis, M. (1999). "The Relations among Body Image, Physical Attractiveness, and Body Mass in Adolescence." *Child Development,* 70, 50–64.

Rosenthal, D. A., and Feldman, S. S. (1991). "The Influence of Perceived Family and Personal Factors on Self-Reported School Performance of Chinese and Western High School Students." *Journal of Research on Adolescence,* 1, 135–154.

Rosenthal, D. A., and Feldman, S. S. (1999). "The Importance of Importance: Parent-Adolescent Communication About Sexuality." *Journal of Adolescence,* 22, 835–852.

Rosenthal, D. A., Biro, F. M., Succop, P. A., Bernstein, D. I., and Stanberry, L. (1997). "Impact of Demographics, Sexual History, and Psychological Functioning on the Acquisition of STDs in Adolescents." *Adolescence,* 32, 757–770.

Rosenthal, D. A., Moore, S. M., and Brumer, I. (1990). "Ethnic Group Differences in Adolescent Responses to AIDS." *Australian Journal of Social Science,* 25, 77–88.

Rosenthal, D. A., Moore, S. M., and Taylor, M. J. (April 1983). "Ethnicity and Adjustment: A Study of the Self-Image of Anglo-, Greek-, and Italian-Australian Working Class Adolescents." *Journal of Youth and Adolescence,* 12, 117–135.

Rosenthal, R., and Jacobson, L. (1968). *Pygmalion in the Classroom: Teacher Expectation and Pupil's Intellectual Development.* New York: Holt, Rinehart and Winston.

Rosenthal, S. L., and Simeonsson, R. J. (1989). "Emotional Disturbances and the Development of Self-Consciousness in Adolescence." *Adolescence,* 24, 689–698.

Rosenthal, S. L., Biro, F. N., Cohen, S. S., Succop, P. A., and Stanberry, L. R. (1995). "Strategies for Coping with Sexually Transmitted Diseases by Adolescent Females." *Adolescence,* 30, 655–666.

Rosenthal, S. L., Lewis, L. M., and Cohen, S. S. (1996). "Issues Related to the Sexual Decision-Making of Inner-City Adolescent Girls. *Adolescence,* 31, 731–739.

Ross, J. A. (1981). "Improving Adolescent Decision-Making Skills." *Curriculum Inquiry,* 11, 279–295.

Ross, M. E. T., and Aday, M. L. (2006). "Stress and Coping in African American Grandparents Who Are Raising Their Grandchildren." *Journal of Family Issues,* 27, 912–932.

Ross, S., and Heath, N. (2002). "A Study of the Frequency of Self-Mutilation in a Community Sample of Adolescents." *Journal of Youth and Adolescence,* 31, 67–77.

Rosseel, E. (1985a). "Work Ethic and Orientation to Work of the Young Generation: The Impact of Educational Level." *Social Indicators Research,* 17, 171–187.

Rosseel, E. (1985b). *Riders and Knights in the Empty Dawn: Evolution in the Work Ethic of the Youth.* Brussels: Free University Press.

Rosseel, E. (1989). "The Impact of Attitudes toward the Personal Future in Study Motivation and Work Orientations of Nonworking Adolescents." *Adolescence,* 24, 73–93.

Rostosky, S. S., Wilcox, B. L., Wright, M. L. C., and Randall, B. A. (2004). "The Impact of Religiosity on Adolescent Sexual Behavior: A Review of the Evidence." *Journal of Adolescent Research,* 19, 677–697.

Roth, J. (2000). *What We Know and What We Need to Know about Youth Development Programs.* Paper presented at the Biennial Meeting for the Society for Research on Adolescence, Chicago, IL.

Roth, J., Brooks-Gunn, J., Murray, L., and Foster, W. (1998). "Promoting Healthy Adolescents: Synthesis of Youth Development Program Evaluations." *Journal of Research on Adolescence,* 8, 423–459.

Rotheram-Borus, M. J. (1989). "Ethnic Differences in Adolescents' Identity Status and Associated Behavior Problems." *Journal of Adolescence,* 12, 361–374.

Rotheram-Borus, M. J., Hunter, J., and Rosaria, M. (1994). "Suicidal Behavior and Gay-Related Stress among Gay and Bisexual Male Adolescents." *Journal of Adolescent Research,* 9, 498–508.

Rotheram-Borus, M. J., Lightfoot, M., Moraes, A., Dopkins, S., and LaCouer, J. (1998). "Developmental, Gender, and Ethnic Differences in Ethnic Identity among Adolescents." *Journal of Adolescent Research,* 13, 487–507.

Rotheram-Borus, M. J., Parra, M., Cantwell, C. Gwadz, M., and Murphy, D. A. (1996). "Runaway and Homeless Youths." In R. J. Diclemente, W. B. Hansen, and L. E. Ponton (Eds.), *Handbook of Adolescent Health Risk Behavior* (pp. 369–391). New York: Plenum Press.

Rotherarm, M. J., and Armstrong, M. (Summer 1980). "Assertiveness Training with High School Students." *Adolescence,* 15, 267–276.

Rowe, D. C. (2002). "On Genetic Variation at Menarche and Age at First Sexual Intercourse: A Critique of the Belsky-Draper Hypothesis." *Evolution and Human Behavior,* 23, 365–372.

Rowe, D. C., Rodgers, J. L., and Meseck-Bushey, S. (1992). "Sibling Delinquency and the Family Environment: Shared and Unshared Influences." *Child Development,* 63, 59–67.

Rubin, K. H., Bukowski, W., and Parker, J. G. (1998). "Peer Interactions, Relationships, and Groups." In W. Damon (Series Ed.) and N. Eisenberg (Vol. Ed.), *Handbook of Child Psychology: Volume 3. Social, Emotional, and Personality Development* (5th ed., pp. 619–700). New York: Wiley.

Rubin, Z., Hill, C. T., Peplau, L. A., and Dunkel-Schetter, C. (May 1980). "Self-Disclosure in Dating Couples: Sex Roles and the Ethic of Openness." *Journal of Marriage and the Family,* 42, 305–317.

Rueter, M. A., and Conger, R. D. (1995). "Antecedents of Parent-Adolescent Disagreements." *Journal of Marriage and the Family,* 57, 435–448.

Ruhn, C. J. (1994). *High School Employment.* Department of Labor Discussion Paper. Report no. NLS94-19. Washington, DC: Department of Labor.

Rumbaut, R. G., and Weeks, Jr. (1985). *Fertility and Adaptation among Indochinese Refugees in the United States.* Research Paper No. 3. San Diego: University of California, San Diego, Indochinese Health and Adaptation Research Project.

Russell, J., Halasz, G., and Beumont, P. J. V. (1990). "Death Related Themes in Anorexia Nervosa: A Practical Exploration." *Journal of Adolescence,* 13, 311–326.

Russell, M. A. H. (1971). "Cigarette Smoking: Natural History of a Dependence Disorder." *British Journal of Medical Psychology,* 44, 9.

Ruuska, J., Kaltiala-Heino, R., Rantanen,m P., and Koivisto, A.-M. (2005). "Are There Differences in the Attitudinal Body Image between Adolescent Anorexia Nervosa and Bulimia Nervosa?" *Eating and Weight Disorders,* 10, 98–106.

Ryan, A. M., and Pintrich, P. R. (1997). " 'Should I Ask for Help?' The Role of Motivation and Attitudes in Adolescents' Help-Seeking in Math Class." *Journal of Educational Psychology,* 89, 1–13.

Ryan, B. A., Adams, G. R., Gullotta, T. P., Weissberg, R. P., and Hampton, R. L. (Eds.). (1995). *The Family-School Connection.* Newbury Park, CA: Sage.

Ryan, S., Franzetta, K., & Manlove, J. (2005). "Hispanic Teen Pregnancy and Birth Rates: Looking Behind the Numbers." *Child Research Brief,* February, 2005. Washington, DC: Child Trends.

Sabatelli, R. M., and Anderson, S. A. (1991). "Family System Dynamics, Peer Relationships, and Adolescents' Psychological Adjustment." *Family Relations,* 40, 363–369.

Sacks, J. H. (1994). "A New Age of Understanding: Allowing Self-Defense Claims for Battered Children Who Kill Their Abusers." *Journal of Contemporary Health Law and Policy,* 10, 349–388.

Sadker, M., and Sadker, M. (1985). "Sexism in the School of the 80s." *Psychology Today,* 19, 54–57.

Safren, S. A., and Heimberg, R. G. (1999). "Depression, Hopelessness, Suicidality, and Related Factors in Sexual Minority and Heterosexual Adolescents." *Journal of Consulting and Clinical Psychology,* 67, 859–866.

Sallis, J. F., Prochaska, J. J., Taylor, W. C., Hill, J. O., and Geraci, J. C. (1999). "Correlates of Physical Activity in a National Sample of Girls and Boys in Grades 4 through 12." *Health Psychology,* 18, 410–415.

Salmivalli, C., Kaukiainen, A., Kaistaniemi, L., and Lagerspetz, K. (1999). "Self-Evaluated Self-Esteem, Peer-Evaluated Self-Esteem, and Defensive Egotism as Predictors of Adeolscents' Participation in Bullying Situations." *Personality and Social Psychology Bulletin,* 25, 1268–1278.

Salmon, C. A., and Daly, M. (1998). "Birth Order and Familial Sentiment: Middleborns Are Different." *Evolution and Human Behavior,* 19, 299–312.

Salomone, P. R., and Sheehan, M. C. (1985). "Vocational Stability and Congruence: An Examination of Holland's Proposition." *The Vocational Guidance Quarterly,* 34, 91–98.

Salt, R. E. (1991). "Affectionate Touch between Fathers and Preadolescent Sons." *Journal of Marriage and the Family,* 53, 545–554.

Sandberg, D. E. (1999). "Experiences of Being Short: Should We Expect Problems of Psychosocial Adjustment?" In U. Eiholzer, F. Haverkamp, and L. D. Voss (Eds.), *Growth, Stature, and Psychosocial Well-Being* (pp. 15–26). Seattle: Hogrefe and Huber.

Sandler, I. (2001). "Quality and Ecology of Adversity as Common Mechanisms of Risk and Resilience." *American Journal of Community Psychology,* 29, 19–42.

Sansone, R. A., Gaither, G. A., and Songer, D. A. (2002). "Self-Harm Behaviors across the Life Cycle: A Pilot Study of Inpatients with Borderline Personality Disorder." *Comprehensive Psychiatry,* 43, 215–218.

Santelli, J. S., Duberstein Lindberg, L., Abma, J., Sucoff McNeally, C., and Resnick, M. (2000). "Adolescent Sexual Behavior: Estimates and Trends from Four Nationally Representative Surveys." *Family Planning Perspectives,* 32, 156–165.

Santelli, J. S., Warren, C. W., Lowry, R., Sogolow, E., Collins, J., Kann, L., Kaufmann, R. B., and Celentano, D. D. (1997). "The Use of Condoms with Other Contraceptive Methods among Young Men and Women." *Family Planning Perspectives,* 29, 261–267.

Santilli, N. R., and Hudson, L. M. (1992). "Enhancing Moral Growth: Is Communication the Key?" *Adolescence,* 27, 145–160.

Santrock, J. W. (1987). *Adolescence.* Dubuque, IA: Wm. C. Brown.

Sarigiani, P. A., Ryan, R. M., and Peterson, J. (1999). "Prevention of High-Risk Behaviors in Adolescent Women." *Journal of Adolescent Health,* 25, 109–119.

Sarigiani, P. A., Wilson, J. L., Petersen, A. C., and Vicary, J. R. (1990). "Self-Image and Educational Plans of Adolescents from Two Contrasting Communities." *Journal of Early Adolescence,* 10, 37–55.

Sassaroli, S., and Ruggiero, G. M. (2005). "The Role of Stress in the Association between Low Self-Esteem, Perfectionism, and Worry, and Eating Disorders." *International Journal of Eating Disorders,* 37, 135–141.

Saucier, J. F., and Ambert, A. M. (1983). "Adolescents' Self-Reported Mental Health and Parents' Marital Status." *Psychiatry,* 46, 363–369.

Savin-Williams, R. C. (1990). *Gay and Lesbian Youth: Expressions of Identity.* New York: Hemisphere.

Savin-Williams, R. C. (1994). "Verbal and Physical Abuse as Stressors in the Lives of Lesbians, Gay Male and Bisexual Youth: Associations with School Problems, Running Away, Substance Abuse, Prostitution, and Suicide." *Journal of Consulting and Clinical Psychology,* 62, 261–269.

Savin-Williams, R. C. (1996). "Ethnic- and Sexual-Minority Youth." In R. C. Savin-Williams and K. M. Cohen (Eds.), *The Lives of Lesbians, Gays, and Bisexuals: Children to Adults* (pp. 152–165). Orlando: Harcourt, Brace College.

Savin-Williams, R. C. (1998). "The Disclosure to Families of Same-Sex Attractions by Lesbian, Gay, and Bisexual Youths." *Journal of Research on Adolescence,* 8, 49–68.

Savin-Williams, R. C., and Dubé, E. M. (1998). "Parental Reactions to Their Child's Disclosure of Same-Sex Attractions." *Family Relations,* 47, 1–7.

Scales, P. (1990). "Developing Capable Young People: An Alternative Strategy for Prevention Program." *Journal of Early Adolescence,* 10, 420–438.

Scamvougeras, A., Witelson, S. F., Branskill, M., Stanchev, P., Black, S., Cheung, G., Steiner, M., and Buck B. (1994). "Sexual Orientation and Anatomy of the Corpus Callosum." *Society for Neuroscience Abstracts,* 20, 1425.

Scarr, S. (1997). "Behavior-Genetic and Socialization Theories of Intelligence: Truce and Reconciliation." In R. J. Sternberg and E. L. Grigorenko (Eds.), *Intelligence, Heredity, and Environment* (pp. 3–41). Cambridge: Cambridge University Press.

Schab, F. (1991). "Schooling without Learning: Twenty Years of Cheating in High School." *Adolescence,* 26, 839–847.

Schaffner, L. (1998). "Searching for Connection: A New Look at Teenaged Runaways." *Adolescence,* 33, 619–628.

Schaller, M. (1992). "In-Group Favoritism and Statistical Reasoning in Social Inference: Implications for Formation and Maintenance of Group Stereotypes." *Journal of Personality and Social Psychology,* 63, 61–74.

Scheel, K. R., and Westefeld, J. S. (1999). "Heavy Metal Music and Adolescent Suicidality: An Empirical Investigation." *Adolescence,* 34, 253–273.

Scheer, S. D., Unger, D. G., and Brown, M. P. (1996). "Adolescents Becoming Adults: Attributes for Adulthood." *Adolescence,* 31, 127–131.

Schichor, A., Beck, A., Berstein, B., and Crabtree, B. (1990). "Seat Belt Use and Stress in Adolescents." *Adolescence,* 25, 773–779.

Schlecter, T. M., and Gump, P. V. (1983). "Car Availability and the Daily Life of the Teenage Male." *Adolescence,* 18, 101–113.

Schlegel, A., and Barry, H., III. (1991). *Adolescence: An Anthropological Inquiry.* New York: Free Press.

Schmidley, A. D. (2001). *Profile of the Foreign-Born Population in the United States: 2000. Current Population Report,* no. P23-206. Washington, DC: U.S. Bureau of the Census.

Schneider, B. H., and Younger, A. K. (1996). "Adolescent-Parent Attachment in Adolescents' Relations with Their Peers." *Youth and Society,* 28, 95–108.

Schneider, F. W., and Couts, L. M. (1985). "Person Orientation of Male and Female High School Students: to the Educational Disadvantage of Males?" *Sex Roles,* 13, 47–63.

Schneider, W., Perner, J., Bullock, M., Stefanick, J., and Zeigler, A. (1999). "Development of Intelligence and Thinking." In F. E. Weinert and W. Schneider (Eds.), *Individual Development from 3 to 12: Findings from the Munich Longitudinal Study* (pp. 9–28). Cambridge, England: Cambridge University Press.

Schoen, R., and Weinick, R. M. (1993). "Partner Choices in Marriage and Cohabitations." *Journal of Marriage and the Family,* 55, 408–414.

Schonert-Reichl, K. A. (1999). "Relations of Peer Acceptance, Friendship Adjustment, and Social Behavior to Moral Reasoning during Early Adolescence." *Journal of Early Adolescence,* 19, 249–279.

Schulenberg, J. E., and Maggs, J. L. (2002). "A Developmental Perspective on Alcohol Use and Heavy Drinking during Adolescence and the Transition to Young Adulthood." *Journal of Studies on Alcohol,* Supplement 14, 54–70.

Schulenberg, J., Asp, E., and Petersen, A. C. (1984). "School from the Young Adolescents' Perspective: A Descriptive Report." *Journal of Early Adolescence,* 4, 107–130.

Schulenberg, J., O'Malley, P. M., Bachman, J. G., and Johnson, L. D. (2000). " 'Spread Your Wings and Fly': The Course of Well-Being and Substance Use during the Transition to Young Adulthood." In L. J. Crockett and R. K. Silbereisen (Eds.), *Negotiating Adolescence in Times of Social Change* (pp. 224–255). New York: Cambridge University Press.

Schuster, M. A., Bell, R. M., and Kanouse, D. E. (1996). "The Sexual Practices of Adolescent Virgins: Genital Sexual Activities of High School Students Who Have Never Had Vaginal Intercourse." *American Journal of Public Health,* 86, 1570–1576.

Schuster, M. A., Bell, R. M., Berry, S. H. and Kanouse, D. E. (1998). "Impact of a High School Condom Availability Program on Sexual Attitudes and Behaviors." *Family Planning Perspectives,* 30, 67–72.

Schvaneveldt, J. D., and Adams, G. R. (1983). "Adolescents and the Decision-Making Process." *Theory into Practice,* 22, 98–104.

Schwartz, I. M. (1999). "Sexual Activity Prior to Coitus Initiation: A Comparison between Males and Females." *Archives of Sexual Behavior,* 28, 63–69.

Schwartz, K. D., & Fouts, T. (2003). "Music Preferences, Personality Style, and Developmental Issues of Adolescents." *Journal of Youth and Adolescence,* 32, 205–213.

Schwartz, R. C. (1987). "Working with 'Internal' and 'External' Families in the Treatment of Bulimia." *Family Relations,* 36, 242–245.

Schwartz, W. (1995). "School Dropouts: New Information about an Old Problem." *ERIC Clearinghouse on Urban Education Digest,* 109.

Schweinhart, L. J., and Weikert, D. P. (1985). "Evidence That Good Early Childhood Programs Work." *Phi Delta Kappan,* 66, 545–551.

Scott, C. S., Shifman, L., Orr, L., Owen, R. G., and Fawcett, N. (1988). "Hispanic and Black American Adolescents' Beliefs Relating to Sexuality and Contraception." *Adolescence,* 23, 667–688.

Scott, J., and Hatalla, J. (1990). "The Influence of Chance and Contingency Factors on Career Patterns of College-Educated Women." *The Career Development Quarterly,* 39, 19–30.

Scott-Jones, D., and White, A. B. (1990). "Correlates of Sexual Activity in Early Adolescence." *Journal of Early Adolescence,* 10, 221–238.

Sears, H. A., Sheppard, H. M., Scott, D., Lodge, S., and Scott, L. (2000). "Adolescents' Participation in Physical Activity and Sport and Their Emotional and Behavioral Adjustment." Paper presented at the Biennial Meeting of the Society for Research in Adolescence, Chicago, IL.

Sebald, H. (Spring 1981). "Adolescents' Concept of Popularity and Unpopularity, Comparing 1960 with 1976." *Adolescence,* 16, 187–193.

Sebald, H. (1989). "Adolescent's Peer Orientation: Changes in the Support System during the Past Three Decades." *Adolescence,* 24, 937–946.

Sedlak, A. J., Finkelhor, D., Hammer, H., and Schultz, D. (2002). *National Estimates of Missing Children: An Overview.* Office of Juvenile Justice and Delinquency Prevention Bulletin Series. Washington, DC: U.S. Department of Justice.

Segal, S. D., and Fairchild, H. H. (1996). "Polysubstance Abuse—A Case Study." *Adolescence,* 31, 797–805.

Seginer, R. (1998). "Adolescents' Perceptions of Relationships with Older Siblings in the Context of Other Relationships." *Journal of Research on Adolescence,* 8, 287–308.

Seide, F. W. (Spring 1982). "Big Sisters: An Experimental Evaluation." *Adolescence,* 17, 117–128.

Seidman, S. N., and Reider, R. (1994). "A Review of Sexual Behavior in the United States." *Journal of Psychiatry,* 151, 330–341.

Seitz, V., and Apfel, N. H. (1994). "Parent-Focused Intervention: Diffusing Effects on Siblings." *Child Development,* 65, 677–683.

Selman, R. L. (1977). "A Structural-Developmental Model of Social Cognition: Implications for Intervention Research." *Counseling Psychologist,* 6, 3–6.

Selman, R. L. (1980). *The Growth of Interpersonal Understanding: Development and Clinical Analysis.* New York: Academic Press.

Senate Hearings. (1993). *Children and Gun Violence.* Washington, DC: Government Printing Office.

Seroczynski, A. D., Jacquez, F. M., and Cole, D. A. (2003). "Depression and Suicide during Adolescence." In G. R. Adams and M. D. Berzonsky (Eds.), *Blackwell Handbook of Adolescence* (pp. 550–572). Oxford, England: Blackwell Publishing.

Serow, R. C., and Dreyden, J. I. (1990). "Community Service among College and University Students: Individual and Institutional Relationships." *Adolescence,* 25, 552–566.

Sessa, F. M., and Steinberg, L. (1991). "Family Structure and Development of Autonomy during Adolescence." *Journal of Early Adolescence,* 11, 38–55.

Settertobulte, W., and Kolip, P. (1997). "Gender-Specific Factors in the Utilization of Medical Services during Adolescence." *Journal of Adolescence,* 20, 121–132.

Sexuality Education and Information Council of the United States (SEICUS). (2005). "On our Side: Public Support for Comprehensive Sexuality Education." *SEICUS Public Policy Fact Sheet.* Retrieved from http://www.siecus.org/policy/public_support.pdf.

Sexuality Information and Education Council of the United States (SEICUS). (1996). "Media Recommendations for More Realistic, Accurate Images Concerning Sexuality. *SIECUS Report,* 24, 22–23.

Sexuality Information and Education Council of the United States (SEICUS). (1999). *Sexuality Education in the Schools: Issues and Answers.* Retrieved from http://www.siecus.org/pubs/fact/fact0007.html.

Sexuality Information and Education Council of the United States (SEICUS). (2001). "Fact Sheet: Public Support for Sexuality Education." *SEICUS Report,* 28.

Seydlitz, R. (1988). "Suicidal Children." *Medical Aspects of Human Sexuality,* 22, 63.

Seydlitz, R. (1991). "The Effects of Age and Gender on Parental Control and Delinquency." *Youth and Society,* 23, 175–201.

Seydlitz, R. (1993). "Perplexity in the Relationships among Direct and Indirect Parental Controls and Delinquency." *Youth and Society,* 24, 243–275.

Shaffer, D., Gould, M. S., Fisher, P., Trautmant, P., Moreau, D., Kleinman, M., and Flory, M. (1996). "Psychiatric Diagnosis in Child and Adolescent Suicide." *Archives of General Psychiatry,* 53, 339–348.

Shakespeare, W. (1974). *Plays: The Riverside Shakespeare.* Boston: Houghton Mifflin.

Shane, P. G. (1989). "Changing Patterns among Homeless and Runaway Youth." *American Journal of Orthopsychiatry,* 59, 208–214.

Shapiro, S. H. (1973). "Vicissitudes of Adolescence." In S. L. Cope (Ed.), *Behavior Pathology of Childhood and Adolescence.* New York: Basic Books.

Sharlin, S. A., and Mor-Barak, M. (1992). "Runaway Girls in Distress: Motivation, Background, and Personality." *Adolescence,* 27, 387–405.

Sharp, J. G., and Graeven, D. B. (December 1981). "The Social, Behavioral, and Health Effects of Phencyclidine (PCP) Use." *Journal of Youth and Adolescence,* 10, 487–499.

Shaw, M., and Dorling, D. (1998). "Mortality among Street Youth in the UK." *Lancet,* 352, 743.

Sheinberg, M., and Penn, P. (1991). "Gender Dilemmas, Gender Questions, and the Gender Mantra." *Journal of Marriage and the Family Therapy,* 17, 33–44.

Shek, D. (2001). "Chinese Adolescents and Their Parents' Views on a Happy Family: Implications for Family Therapy." *Family Therapy,* 28, 73–104.

Sheldon, S. B., and Epstein, L. (2004). "Getting Students to School: Using Family and Community Involvement to Reduce Chronic Absenteeism." *School Community Journal,* 14, 39–56.

Shelton, C. M., and McAdams, D. P. (1990). "In Search of an Everyday Morality: The Development of a Measure." *Adolescence,* 25, 923–943.

Sheppard, M. A., Wright, D., and Goodstadt, M. S. (1985). "Peer Pressure and Drug Use—Exploding the Myth." *Adolescence,* 20, 949–958.

Sherrod, L. R., Haggerty, R. J., and Featherman, D. L. (1993). "Introduction: Late Adolescence and the Transition to Adulthood." *Journal of Research on Adolescence,* 3, 217–226.

Shibley-Hyde, J., and Delamater, J. D. (2000). *Understanding Human Sexuality.* New York: McGraw-Hill.

Shilts, L. (1991). "The Relationship of Early Adolescent Substance Use to Extracurricular Activities, Peer Influence, and Personal Attitudes." *Adolescence,* 26, 613–617.

Shinn, M., and Weitzman, B. (1996). "Homeless Families Are Different." In J. Baumohl (Ed.), *Homelessness in America* (pp. 109–122). Westport, CT: Greenwood Press.

Shon, P. C., and Targonski, R. (2003). "Declining Trends in U.S. Parricides, 1976–1998: Testing the Freudian Assumptions." *International Journal of Law and Psychiatry,* 26, 387–402.

Shreve, B. W., and Kunkel, M. A. (1991). "Self-Psychology, Shame, and Adolescent Suicide: Theoretical and Practical Considerations." *Journal of Counseling and Development,* 69, 305–311.

Shrier, L., Pierce, J., Emans, S., and DuRant, R. (1998). "Gender Differences in Risk Behaviors Associated with Forced or Pressured Sex." *Archives of Pediatric and Adolescent Medicine,* 152, 57–63.

Shrum, W., and Cheek, N. H. (1987). "Social Structure during the School Years: Onset of the Degrouping Process." *American Sociological Review,* 52, 218–223.

Siann, G., Callaghan, M. Glissov, P., Lockhart, R., and Rawson, L. (1999). "Who Gets Bullied? The Effect of School, Gender, and Ethnic Group." *Educational Research,* 36, 123–134.

Siegall, B. (August 21, 1977). "Incest: An American Epidemic." *Los Angeles Times.*

Siegel, J. M. (2002). "Body Image Change and Adolescent Depressive Symptoms." *Journal of Adolescent Research,* 17(1), 27–41.

Siegel, J. M., Yancy, A. K., Aneshensel, C. S., and Schuler, R. (1999). "Body Image, Perceived Pubertal Timing, and Adolescent Mental Health." *Journal of Adolescent Health,* 25, 155–165.

Siegler, R. S. (1991). *Children's Thinking.* 2nd ed. Englewood Cliffs, NJ: Prentice Hall.

Siegler, R. S. (1995). "Children's Thinking: How Does Change Occur?" In F. E. Weinert & W. Schneider (Eds.), *Memory Performance and Competencies: Issues in Growth and Development* (pp. 405–430). Hillsdale, NJ: Lawrence Erlbaum.

Sieving, R., McNeely, C., and Blum, R. (2000). "Maternal Expectations, Mother-Child Connectedness, and Adolescent Sexual Debut." *Archives of Pediatrics and Adolescent Medicine,* 154, 809–816.

Sieving, R. E., Perry, C. L., and Williams, C. L. (2000). "Do Friendships Change Behaviors, or Do Behaviors Change Friendships? Examining Paths of Influence in Young Adolescents' Alcohol Use." *Journal of Adolescent Health,* 26, 27–35.

Sigelman, C. K., Gurstell, S. A., and Stewart, A. K. (1992). "The Development of Lay Theories of Problem Drinking: Causes and Cures." *Journal of Adolescent Research,* 7, 292–312.

Signorielli, N. (1993). "Television and Adolescents' Perceptions about Work." *Youth and Society,* 24, 314–341.

Silverberg, D., and Sternberg, L. (1987). "Adolescent Autonomy, Parent-Adolescent Conflict and Parental Well-Being." *Journal of Youth and Adolescence,* 16, 293–311.

Sim, T. N. (2000). "Adolescent Psychosocial Competence: The Importance and Role of Regard for Parents." *Journal of Research on Adolescence,* 10, 49–64.

Simes, M. R., and Berg, D. H. (2001). "Surreptitious Learning: Menarche and Menstrual Product Advertisements." *Health Care for Women International,* 22, 455–469.

Simmons, R., and Blyth, D. (1987). *Moving into Adolescence: The Impact of Pubertal Change and Social Context.* New York: Adine de Gruyter.

Simons, J. M., Finley, R., and Yang, A. (1991). *The Adolescent and Young Adult Fact Book.* Washington, DC: Children's Defense Fund.

Simons, R. L., and Robertson, J. F. (1989). "The Impact of Parenting Factors, Deviant Peers, and Coping Style among Adolescent Drug Users." *Family Relations,* 38, 273–281.

Simons, R. L., and Whitbeck, L. B. (1991). "Sexual Abuse as a Precursor to Prostitution and Victimization among Adolescent and Adult Homeless Women." *Journal of Family Issues,* 12, 361–379.

Simons, R. L., Lin, K.-H., Gordon, L. C., Conger, R. D., and Lorenz, F. O. (1999). "Explaining the Higher Incidence of Adjustment Problems among Children of Divorce Compared with Those in Two-Parent Families." *Journal of Marriage and the Family,* 61, 1020–1033.

Simons, R. L., Whitbeck, L. B., Conger, R. D., and Melby, J. N. (1991). "The Effect of Social Skills, Values, Peers, and Depression on Adolescent Substance Use." *Journal of Early Adolescence,* 11, 466–481.

Simpson, L., Douglas, S., and Schimmel, J. (1998). "Teen Consumers: Catalog Clothing Purchase Behavior." *Adolescence,* 33, 637–644.

Simsek, F., Ulukol, B., and Gulnar, S. B. (2005). "The Secular Trends in Height and Weight of Turkish School Children during 1993–2003." *Child: Care, Health, and Development,* 31, 441–447.

Singer, M. T. (1992). "Cults." In S. B. Friedman, M. Fisher, and S. K. Schonberg (Eds.), *Comprehensive Adolescent Health Care* (pp. 699–703). St. Louis: Quality Medical.

Singh, S. (1986). "Adolescent Pregnancy in the United States: An Interstate Analysis." *Family Planning Perspectives,* 18, 210–220.

Singh, S., and Darrock, J. E. (2000). "Adolescent Pregnancy and Childbearing: Levels and Trends in Developed Countries." *Family Planning Perspectives,* 32, 14–23.

Sirgy, M. J., Lee, D-J., Kosenko, R., Meadow, H. L., Rahtz, D., Cicic, M., Jin, G. X., Yarsuvat, D., Blenkhorm, D. L., and Wright, N. (1998). "Does Television Viewership Play a Role in the Perception of Quality of Life?" *Journal of Advertising,* 27, 125–142.

Sirin, S. R. (2005). "Socioeconomic Status and Academic Achievement: A Meta-Analytic Review of Research." *Review of Educational Research,* 75, 417–453.

Skinner, B. F. (1938). *The Behavior of Organisms.* New York: Appleton-Century-Crofts.

Skoe, E. (1995). "Self Role Orientation and Its Relationship to the Development of Identity and Moral Thought." *Scandinavian Journal of Psychology,* 36, 235–245.

Skoe, E., and Gooden, A. (1993). "Ethic of Care and Real-Life Moral Dilemma Content in Male and Female Early Adolescents." *Journal of Early Adolescence,* 13, 154–167.

Slater, E. J., Stewart, K. J., and Linn, M. W. (Winter 1983). "The Effects of Family Disruption on Adolescent Males and Females." *Adolescence,* 18, 931–942.

Slater, M. D. (2003). "Alienation, Aggression, and Sensation Seeking as Predictors of Adolescent Use of Violent Film, Computer, and Website Content." *Journal of Communication,* 53, 105–121.

Slaughter-Defoe, D. T., Kuehne, V. S., and Straker, J. K. (1992). "African-American, Anglo-American, and Anglo-Canadian Grade 4 Children's Concepts of Old People and of Extended Family." *International Journal of Aging & Human Development,* 35, 161–178.

Slonim-Nevo, V. (1992). "First Premarital Intercourse among Mexican-American and Anglo-American Adolescent Women." *Journal of Adolescent Research,* 7, 332–351.

Small, S., and Kerns, D. (1993). "Unwanted Sexual Activity among Peers during Early and Middle Adolescence: Incidence and Risk Factors." *Journal of Marriage and the Family,* 55, 941–952.

Smart, L. S., Chibucos, T. R., and Didier, L. A. (1990). "Adolescent Substance Use and Perceived Family Functioning." *Journal of Family Issues,* 11, 208–227.

Smetana, J. G. (1995). "Context, Conflict, and Constraint in Adolescent-Parent Authority Relationships." In M. Killen and D. Hart (Eds.), *Morality in Everyday Life: Developmental Perspectives* (pp. 225–255). Cambridge, England: Cambridge University Press.

Smetana, J. G. (1996). "Adolescent-Parent Conflict: Implications for Adaptive and Maladaptive Adjustment." In D. Cicchetti and S. L. Toth (Eds.), *Rochester Symposium on Developmental Psychology: Volume 7. Adolescence: Opportunity and Challenges* (pp. 1–46). Rochester, NY: Rochester University Press.

Smetana, J. G. (2002). "Culture, Autonomy, and Personal Jurisdiction in Adolescent-Parent Relationships." In H. W. Reese and R. Kail (Eds.), *Advances in Child Development and Behavior,* vol. 2 (pp. 51–87). New York: Academic Press.

Smetana, J. G., and Asquith, P. (1994). "Adolescents' and Parents' Conceptions of Parental Authority and Adolescent Autonomy." *Child Development,* 65, 1147–1162.

Smetana, J. G., and Turiel, E. (2003). "Moral Development during Adolescence." In G. R. Adams and M. D. Berzonsky (Eds.), *Blackwell Handbook of Adolescence* (pp. 247–268). Oxford, England: Blackwell Publishing.

Smetana, J. G., Metzger, A., Gettman, D. C., and Campione-Barr., N. (2006). "Disclosure and Secrecy in Parent-Adolescent Relationships." *Child Development,* 77, 201–217.

Smith, A. M. A., Rosenthal, D. A., and Reichler, H. (1996). "High Schoolers' Masturbatory Practices: Their Relationship to Sexual Intercourse and Personal Characteristics." *Psychological Reports,* 79, 499–509.

Smith, C., Faris, R., and Denten, M. L. (2003). "Mapping American Adolescent Subjective Religiosity and Alienation toward Religion: A Research Report." *Sociology of Religion,* 64, 111–133.

Smith, E. (May 1989). "The New Moral Classroom." *Psychology Today,* 23, 32–36.

Smith, E. A., and Caldwell, L. L. (1989). "The Perceived Quality of Leisure Experiences among Smoking and Nonsmoking Adolescents." *Journal of Early Adolescence,* 9, 153–162.

Smith, E. A., and Zabin, L. S. (1993). "Marital and Birth Expectations of Urban Adolescents." *Youth and Society,* 25, 62–74.

Smith, E. J. (1991). "Ethnic Identity Development: Toward the Development of a Theory within the Context of Majority/Minority Status." *Journal of Counseling and Development,* 770, 181–188.

Smith, E. P., Walker, K., Fields, L., Brookins, C. C., and Seay, R. C. (1999). "Ethnic Identity and Its Relationship to Self-Esteem, Perceived Efficacy and Prosocial Attitudes in Early Adolescence." *Journal of Adolescence,* 22, 867–880.

Smith, K. H., and Stutts, M. A. (1999). "Factors That Influence Adolescents to Smoke." *Journal of Consumer Affairs,* 33, 321–357.

Smith, P. (2004). "Bullying: Recent Developments." *Child and Adolescent Mental Health,* 9, 98–103.

Smith, P. K., Morita, Y., Junger-Tas, J., Olweus, D., Catalano, R., and Slee, P. (1999). *The Nature of School Bullying.* New York: Routledge.

Smith, S. P. (1996). "Dating-Partner Preferences among a Group of Inner-City African-American High School Students." *Adolescence,* 31, 79–90.

Smith, T. E. (1988). "Parental Control Techniques." *Journal of Family Issues,* 2, 155–176.

Smith, T. E. (1990). "Parental Separation and the Academic Self-Concepts of Adolescents: An Effort to Solve the Puzzle of Separation Effects." *Journal of Marriage and the Family,* 52, 107–118.

Smith, T. E. (1991). "Agreement of Adolescent Educational Expectations with Perceived Maternal and Paternal Educational Goals." *Youth and Society,* 23, 155–174.

Snarey, J. R. (1985). "Cross-Cultural Universality of Social-Moral Development: A Critical Review of Kohlbergian Research." *Psychological Bulletin,* 97, 202–232.

Snarey, J. R. (1995). "In a Commuitarian Voice: The Sociological Expansion of Kohlbergian Theory, Research, and Practice." In W. R. Kurtines and J. L. Gewirtz (Eds.), *Moral Development: An Introduction* (pp. 109–134). Boston: Allyn & Bacon.

Sneddon, H. (2003). "The Effects of Maltreatment on Children's Health and Well-Being." *Child Care in Practice,* 9, 236–250.

Snodgrass, D. M. (1991). "The Parent Connection." *Adolescence,* 26, 83–87.

Snyder, H. (1999). *Juvenile Arrests 1998.* Washington, DC: Office of Juvenile Justice and Delinquency Prevention.

Snyder, H. N. (2004). *Juvenile Arrests 2002.* Washington, DC: Office of Juvenile Justice and Prevention.

Snyder, H. N., & Sickmund, M. (1995). *Juvenile Offenders and Victims: A National Report.* Washington, D.C.: U.S. Department of Justice.

Snyder, H., and Sickmund, M. (2006). *Juvenile Offenders and Victims: 2006 National Report.* Washington, DC: Office of Juvenile Justice and Delinquency Prevention.

Snyder, J., Dishion, T. J., and Patterson, G. R. (1986). "Determinants and Consequences of Associating with Deviant Peers during Preadolescence and Adolescence." *Journal of Early Adolescence,* 6, 29–43.

Snyder, L. B., Milici, F. F., Slater, M., Sun, H., and Strizhakova, Y. (2006). "Effects of Alcohol Advertising Exposure on Drinking among Youth." *Archives of Pediatrics and Adolescent Medicine,* 160, 18–24.

Snyder, S. (1995). "Movie Portrayals of Juvenile Delinquency: Part I—Epidemiology and Criminology." *Adolescence,* 30, 53–64.

Sobal, J. (1984). "Group Dieting, the Stigma of Obesity, and Overweight Adolescents: Contributions of Natalie Allon to the Sociology of Obesity." *Marriage and Family Review,* 7, 9–20.

Sobal, J. (1987). "Health Concerns of Young Adolescents." *Adolescence,* 87, 739–750.

Sobal, J., Nicolopoulos, V., and Lee, J. (1995). "Attitudes about Overweight and Dating among Secondary School Students." *International Journal of Obesity,* 19, 376–381. "Social Factors, Not Age, Are Found to Affect Risk of Low Birth Weight." (May–June, 1984). *Family Planning Perspectives,* 16, 142, 143.

Sodowsky, G. R., Lai, E. W., & Plake, B. S. (1991). "Moderating Effects of Sociocultural Variables on Acculturation Attitudes of Hispanics and Asian Americans." *Journal of Counseling & Development,* 70, 194–204.

Sommer, B. (1984). "The Troubled Teen: Suicide, Drug Use, and Running Away." *Women's Health,* 9, 117–141.

Sommer, B., and Nagel, S. (1991). "Ecological and Typological Characteristics in Early Adolescent Truancy." *Journal of Early Adolescence,* 11, 379–392.

Sonenstein, F. L., and Pittman, K. J. (January–February, 1984). "The Availability of Sex Education in Large School Districts." *Family Planning Perspectives,* 16, 19–25.

Sonenstein, F. L., Pleck, J. H., and Ku, L. C. (1989). "Sexual Activity, Condom Use, and AIDS Awareness among Adolescent Males." *Family Planning Perspectives,* 21, 152–258.

Song, C., & Glick, E. (2004). "College Attendance and Choice of College Majors among Asian-American Students." *Social Science Quarterly,* 85, 1401–1421.

South, S. J. (1995). "Do You Need to Shop Around?" *Journal of Family Issues,* 16, 432–449.

Sparks, G. G. (2001). *Media Effects Research: A Basic Overview.* Belmont, CA: Wadsworth.

Spear, L. P. (2002). "The Adolescent Brain and the College Drinker: Biological Basis of Propensity to Use and Misuse Alcohol." *Journal of Studies on Alcohol,* Supplement no. 14, 71–81.

"Special Issue: Mental Health Research and Service Issues for Minority Youth." (June 1988). *Journal of Adolescence,* 11.

Spencer, M. B., Dupree, D., Swanson, D. P., and Cunningham, M. (1998). "The Influence of Physical Maturation and Hassles on African American Adolescents' Learning Behaviors." *Journal of Comparative Family Studies,* 29, 189–200.

Spera, C. (2005). "A Review of the Relationship among Parenting Practices, Parenting Styles, and Adolescent School Achievement." *Educational Psychology Review,* 17, 125–146.

Spillane-Grieco, E. (Spring 1984). "Characteristics of a Helpful Relationship: A Study of Empathetic Understanding and Positive Regard between Runaways and Their Parents." *Adolescence,* 19, 63–75.

Sprecher, S., Barbee, A., and Schwartz, P. (1995). "'Was It Good for You, Too?': Gender Differences in First Sexual Intercourse Experiences." *Journal of Sex Research,* 32, 3–15.

St. Louis, G. R., and Liem, J. H. (2005). "Ego Identity, Ethnic Identity, and the Psychosocial Well-Being of Ethnic Minority and Majority College Students." *Identity,* 5, 227–246.

Stacey, B. G., Singer, M. S., and Ritchie, G. (1989). "The Perception of Poverty and Wealth among Teenage University Students." *Adolescence,* 24, 193–207.

Stack, S. (1998). "Heavy Metal, Religiosity, and Suicide Acceptability." *Suicide and Life-Threatening Behavior,* 28, 388–394.

Stack, S. (2003). "Media Coverage as a Risk Factor in Suicide." *Journal of Epidemiology and Community Health,* 57, 238–240.

Stager, J. M. (1984). "Reversibility of Amenorrhea in Athletes: A Review." *Sports Medicine,* 1, 337.

Stager, J. M., Ritchie, B. A., and Robertshaw, D. (1984). "Reversal of Oligo/Amenorrhea in Collegiate Distance Runners." *New England Journal of Medicine,* 310, 51.

Staksrud, E. (2003). *Parents Believe, Kids Act.* Presented at the 2003 SAFT Conference: Future Kids Online: How to Promote Safety, Awareness, Facts, and Tools. Sweden. Retrieved from http://www.saftonline.org.

Stallmann, J. I., and Johnson, T. G. (1996). "Community Factors in Secondary Educational Achievement in Appalacia." *Youth and Society,* 27, 469–484.

Stanton, B. F., Black, M., Kaljee, L., and Ricardo, I. (1993). "Perceptions of Sexual Behavior among Urban Early Adolescents: Translating Theory through Focus Groups." *Journal of Early Adolescence,* 13, 44–66.

Stanton, W. R., and Silva, P. A. (1992). "A Longitudinal Study of the Influence of Parents and Friends on Childrens' Initiation of Smoking." *Journal of Applied Developmental Psychology,* 13, 423–434.

Stapley, J. C., and Haviland, J. M. (1989). "Beyond Depression: Gender Differences in Normal Adolescents' Emotional Experiences." *Sex Roles,* 20, 295–308.

Stein, D. B., and Smith, E. D. (1990). "The 'Rest' Program: A New Treatment System for the Oppositional Defiant Adolescent." *Adolescent,* 25, 891–904.

Stein, D. M., and Reichert, P. (1990). "Extreme Dieting Behaviors in Early Adolescence." *Journal of Early Adolescence,* 10, 108–121.

Stein, D., Witztum, E., Brom, D., DeNour, A. K., and Elizur, A. (1992). "The Association between Adolescents' Attitudes towards Suicide and Their Psychosocial Background and Suicidal Tendencies." *Adolescence,* 27, 949–959.

Stein, J. H., and Reiser, L. W. (1994). "A Study of White Middle-Class Adolescent Boys' Responses to 'Semenarche' (the First Ejaculation)." *Journal of Youth and Adolescence,* 23, 373–384.

Stein, R. F. (1987). "Comparison of Self-Concept of Nonobese and Obese University Junior Female Nursing Students." *Adolescence,* 22, 77–90.

Stein, S. L., and Weston, L. C. (Winter 1982). "College Women's Attitudes toward Women and Identity Achievement." *Adolescence,* 17, 895–899.

Steinberg, L. (1990). "Autonomy, Conflict, and Harmony in the Family Relationship." In S. S. Feldman and G. R. Elliot (Eds.), *At the Threshold: The Developing Adolescent* (pp. 255–276). Cambridge, MA: Harvard University Press.

Steinberg, L. (2001). "We Know Some Things: Parent-Adolescent Relationships in Retrospect and Prospect." *Journal of Research on Adolescence,* 11, 1–19.

Steinberg, L., and Dornbusch, S. M. (1991). "Negative Correlates of Part-Time Employment during Adolescence: Replication and Elaboration." *Developmental Psychology,* 27, 304–313.

Steinberg, L., and Steinberg, W. (1994). *Crossing Paths: How Your Child's Adolescence Triggers Your Own Crisis.* New York: Simon and Schuster.

Steinberg, L., Blatt-Eisengart, I., and Cauffman, E. (2006). "Patterns of Competence and Adjustment among Adolescents from Authoritative, Authoritarian, Indulgent, and Neglectful Homes: A Replication in a Sample of Serious Juvenile Offenders." *Journal of Research on Adolescence,* 16, 47–58.

Steinberg, L., Dornbusch, S. M., and Brown, B. B. (1992). "Ethnic Differences in Adolescent Achievement: An Ecological Perspective." *American Psychologist,* 47, 723–729.

Steinberg, L., Fegley, S., and Dornbusch, S. M. (1993). "Negative Impact of Part-Time Work on Adolescent Adjustment: Evidence from a Longitudinal Study." *Developmental Psychology,* 29, 171–180.

Steinberg, L., Greenberger, E., Garduque, L., Ruggiero, M., and Vaux, A. (1982). "Effects of Working on Adolescent Development." *Developmental Psychology,* 18, 385–395.

Steinberg, L., Lamborn, S. D., Dornbusch, S. M., and Darling, N. (1992). "Impact of Parenting Practices on Adolescent Achievement: Authoritative Parenting, School Involvement, and Encouragement to Succeed." *Child Development,* 63, 1266–1281.

Steitz, J. A., and Owen, T. P. (1992). "School Activities and Work: Effects on Adolescent Self-Esteem." *Adolescence,* 27, 37–50.

Stephen, J., Fraser, E., and Marcia, J. E. (1992). "Moratorium Achievement, (Mama) Cycles in Life Span Identity Development: Value Orientations and Reasoning Systems' Correlates." *Journal of Adolescence,* 15, 283–300.

Stepp, L. S. (1999). "Parents Are Alarmed by an Unsettling New Fad in Middle School: Oral Sex." *Washington Post,* July 8, 1999.

Sterling, C. M., and Van Horn, K. R. (1989). "Identity and Death Anxiety." *Adolescence,* 24, 321–326.

Stern, D., Rahn, M. L., and Chung, Y-P. (1998). "Design of Work-Based Learning for Students in the United States." *Youth and Adolescence,* 29, 471–502.

Stern, M., and Alvarez, A. (1992). "Pregnant and Parenting Adolescents. A Comparative Analysis of Coping Response and Psychosocial Adjustment." *Journal of Adolescent Research,* 7, 469–493.

Sternberg, R. J. (1997). *Successful intelligence.* New York: Plume.

Sternberg, R. J., and Girgorenko, E. L. (2002). *Dynamic Testing.* New York: Cambridge University Press.

Sternberg, R. J., and Wagner, R. K. (Eds.). (1986). *Practical Intelligence: Nature and Origins of Competence in the Everyday World.* Cambridge, England: Cambridge University Press.

Sternberg, R. J., and Williams, W. M. (1996). *How to Develop Student Creativity.* Alexandria, VA: Association for Supervision and Curriculum Development.

Sternberg, R. J., Torff, B., and Grigorenko, E. L. (1998). "Teaching Triarchically Improves School Achievement." *Journal of Educational Psychology,* 90, 374–384.

Sternberg, R., and Nigro, G. (1980). "Developmental Strategies in the Solution of Verbal Analogies." *Child Development,* 51, 27–38.

Stevens, N. M., Mott, L. A., and Youells, F. (1996). "Rural Adolescent Drinking Behavior: Three-Year Follow-Up on the New Hampshire Substance Abuse Prevention Study." *Adolescence,* 31, 159–166.

Stevens, R., and Pihl, R. O. (1987). "Seventh-Grade Students at Risk for School Failure." *Adolescence,* 22, 333–345.

Stewart, M. A., Cummings, C., Singer, S., and de-Blois, C. S. (1981). "The Overlap between Hyperactive and Unsocialized Aggressive Children." *Journal of Child Psychology and Psychiatry and Allied Disciplines,* 22, 35–45.

Stivers, C. (1988). "Parent-Adolescent Communication and Its Relationship to Adolescent Depression and Suicide Proneness." *Adolescence,* 23, 291–295.

Stolzenberg, R. M., Blair-Loy, M., and Waite, L. J. (1995). "Religious Participation in Early Adulthood: Age and Family Life Cycle Effects on Church Membership." *American Sociological Review,* 60, 84–103.

Stoppelbein, L., and Greening, L. (2000). "Post-Traumatic Stress Symptoms in Parentally-Bereaved Children and Adolescents." *Journal of the American Academy of Child and Adolescent Psychiatry,* 39, 1112–1119.

Storch, E. A., and Storch, J. B. (2002). "Fraternities, Sororities, and Academic Dishonesty." *College Student Journal,* 36, 247–252.

Story, M. D. (Winter 1982). "A Comparison of University Student Experience with Various Sexual Outlets in 1974 and 1980." *Adolescence,* 737–747.

Stouthamer-Loeber, M, and Wei, E. H. (1998). "The Precursors of Young Fatherhood and Its Effects on Delinquency of Teenage Males." *Journal of Adolescent Health,* 22, 56–65.

Strang, R. (1957). *The Adolescent Views Himself.* New York: McGraw-Hill.

Strang, S. P., and Orlofsky, J. L. (1990). "Factors Underlying Suicidal Ideation among College Students: A Test of Teicher and Jacob's Model." *Journal of Adolescence,* 13, 39–52.

Strasburger, V. C. (1989). "Children, Adolescents, and Television 1989. Vol. 2: The Role of Pediatricians." *Pediatrics,* 83, 446–448.

Strasburger, V. C. (1995). *Adolescents and the Media: Medical and Psychological Impact.* Thousand Oaks, CA: Sage.

Strasburger, V. C., and Donnerstein, E. (1999). "Children, Adolescents, and the Media: Issues and Solutions." *Pediatrics,* 103, 129–139.

Straugh, B. (2003). *The Primal Teen: What New Discoveries about the Teenage Brain Tell Us about Our Kids.* New York: Doubleday.

Straus, M. A., and Yodanis, C. L. (1996). "Corporal Punishment in Adolescence and Physical Assaults on Spouses in Later Life: What Accounts for the Link?" *Journal of Marriage and the Family,* 58, 825–841.

Streetman, L. G. (1987). "Contrasts in Self-Esteem of Unwed Teenage Mothers." *Adolescence,* 23, 459–464.

Streib, H. (1999). "Off-Road Religion? A Narrative Approach to Fundamentalist and Occult Orientations of Adolescents." *Journal of Adolescence,* 22, 255–267.

Stringer, D. M., and Duncan, E. (1985). "Nontraditional Occupations: A Study of Women Who Have Made the Choice." *The Vocational Guidance Quarterly,* 33, 241–248.

Stringer, T. (2003). "Summer Time, Summer Teens." *Occupational Outlook Quarterly,* Winter, Washington, DC: National Bureau of Labor Statistics.

Strong, E. K. (1943). *Vocational Interests of Men and Women.* Palo Alto, CA: Stanford University Press.

Strouse, J. S., Buerkel-Rothfuss, N., and Long, E. C. J. (1995). "Gender and Families as Moderators of the Relationship between Music Video Exposure and Adolescent Sexual Permissiveness." *Adolescence,* 30, 505–521.

Stubbs, M. L., Rierdan, J., and Koff, E. (1989). "Developmental Differences in Menstrual Attitudes." *Journal of Early Adolescence,* 9, 480–498.

Stunkard, A., Sorensen, T., Hanis, S. C., Teasdale, T., Chakraborty, R., Schull, W., and Schulsinger, F. (1986). "An Adoption Study of Human Obesity." *New England Journal of Medicine,* 314, 193–198.

Subrahmanyam, K., Greenfield, P., Kraut, R., and Gross, E. (2001). "The Impact of Computer Use on Children's and Adolescents' Development." *Journal of Applied Developmental Psychology,* 22, 7–30.

Substance Abuse and Mental Health Services Administration. (2003). *Results from the 2002 National Survey on Drug Use and Health: National Findings* (Office of Applied Studies, NHSDA Series H-22, DHHS Publication No. SMA 03-3836). Rockville, MD: Author.

"Substantially Higher Morbidity and Mortality Rates Found among Infants Born to Adolescent Mothers." (March–April, 1984). *Family Planning Perspectives,* 16, 91, 92.

Substance Abuse and Mental Health Services Administration. (2005). *Results from the 2004 National Survey on Drug Use and Health: National Findings* (Office of Applied Studies, NSDUH Series H-28, DHHS Publication No. SMA 05-4062). Rockville, MD: Author.

Suitor, J. J., and Reavis, R. (1995). "Football, Fast Cars, and Cheerleading: Adolescent Gender Norms, 1978 through 1989." *Adolescence,* 30, 265–272.

Sullivan, M. L. (1993). "Culture and Class as Determinants of Out-of-Wedlock Childbearing and Poverty during Late Adolescence." *Journal of Research on Adolescence,* 3, 295–316.

Sun, S. S., Schubert, C. M., Liang, R., Roche, A. F., Kulin, H. E., Le, P. A., Himes, J. H., and Chumlea, W. C. (2005). "Is Sexual Maturity Occurring Earlier among U.S. Children?" *Journal of Adolescent Health,* 37, 345–355.

Superka, D., Ahrens, C., and Hedstrom, J. (1976). *Values Education Sourcebook.* Boulder, CO: Social Science Education Consortium.

Sutherland, E. H., and Cressey, D. R. (1966). *Principles of Criminology.* 7th ed. New York: J. B. Lippincott.

Suyemoto, K. L. (1998). "The Functions of Self-Mutilation." *Clinical Psychology Review,* 18, 531–554.

Suyemoto, K. L., and MacDonald, M. L. (1995). "Self-Cutting in Female Adolescents." *Psychotherapy,* 32, 162–171.

Svensson, R. (2003). "Gender Differences in Adolescent Drug Use: The Impact of Parental Monitoring and Peer Deviance. *Youth and Society,* 34, 300–329.

Swaab, D. F., and Hofman, M. A. (1995). "Sexual Differentiation of the Human Hypothalamus in Relation to Gender and Sexual Orientation." *Trends in Neurosciences,* 18, 264–270.

Swain, C. R., Acherman, L. K., and Ackerman, M. A. (2006). "The Influence of Individual Characteristics and Contraceptive Beliefs on Parent-Teen Sexual Communications: A Structural Model." *Journal of Adolescent Health,* 38, 753e.9–753e.18.

Swanson, H. L. (1999). "What Develops in Working Memory? A Life Span Perspective." *Developmental Psychology,* 35, 986–1000.

Swanson, H. L., and Hill, G. (1993). "Metacognitive Aspects of Moral Reasoning and Behavior." *Adolescence,* 28, 711–735.

Sweat, K., and Murray, R. (1992, 1993). *Freak Me.* WB Music Corporation, E/A Music Inc., Keith Sweat Publishing, Inc., EMI Blackwood Music, Inc., and Saints Alive Music.

Sweeting, H., and West, P. (2001). "Being Different: Correlates of the Experience of Teasing at Age 11." *Research Paper in Education,* 16, 225–246.

Swenson, C. C., and Kennedy, W. A. (1995). "Perceived Control and Treatment Outcome with Chronic Adolescent Offenders." *Adolescence,* 30, 565–578.

Swenson, I. E., Foster, B., and Asay, M. (1995). "Menstruation, Menarche, and Sexuality in the Public School Curriculum: School Nurses' Perceptions." *Adolescence,* 30, 677–683.

Szabo, A., and Underwood, J. (2004). "Cybercheats: Is Information and Communication Technology Fueling Academic Dishonesty?" *Active Learning in Higher Education,* 5, 180–199.

Szinovacz, M. E. (1998). "Grandparent Research: Past, Present, and Future." In M. E. Szinovacz (Ed.), *Handbook on Grandparenthood* (pp. 1–20). Westport, CT: Greenwood Press.

Talero, K., and Talero, A. (1996). *Foundations in Microbiology.* 2nd ed. Dubuque, IA: Brown.

Tamborini, R. (1996). "A Model of Empathy and Emotional Reactions to Horror." In J. Weaver and R. Tamborini (Eds.), *Horror Films: Current Research on Audience Preference and Reactions* (pp. 103–123). Mahwah, NJ: Erlbaum.

Tanaka, T. (2001). "The Identity Formation of the Victim of Shunning." *School Psychology International,* 22, 464–476.

Tanner, J. M. (1962). *Growth of Adolescence.* Springfield, IL: Charles C. Thomas.

Tanner, J. M. (1968). "Earlier Maturation in Man." *Scientific American,* 218, 21–27.

Tanner, J. M. (1971). "Sequence, Tempo, and Individual Variation in the Growth and Development of Boys and Girls Aged Twelve to Sixteen." *Daedalus,* 100, 907–930.

Tanner, J. M. (1990). *Foetus into Man,* 2nd ed. Cambridge, MA: Harvard University Press.

Tanner, J. M. (1991). "Adolescent Growth Spurt." In R. M. Lerner, A. C. Peterson, and J. Brooks-Gunn (Eds.), *Encyclopedia of Adolescence.* Vol. 2 (pp. 418–424). New York: Garland.

Tanner, J. M. (September 1973). *Scientific American,* p. 8.

Tarnowski, K. J., Brown, R. T., and Simonian, S. J. (1999). "Social Class." In W. K. Silverman and T. H. Ollendick, (Eds.), *Developmental Issues in the Clinical Treatment of Children* (pp. 213–230). Boston: Allyn & Bacon.

Tasker, F., and Golombok, S. (1995). "Adults Raised as Children in Lesbian Families." *American Journal of Orthopsychiatry,* 65, 203–215.

Taylor, A. (2005). "What Employers Look For: The Skills Debate and the Fit with Youth Perceptions." *Journal of Education and Work,* 18, 201–218.

Taylor, L. D. (2005). "Effects of Visual and Verbal Sexual Content and Perceived Realism on Attitudes and Beliefs." *Journal of Sex Research,* 42, 130–137.

Taylor, L. T. (1994). *Winning Combinations: The Effects of Different Parenting Style Combinations on Adolescent Adjustment.* Paper presented at the biennial meeting of the Society for Research on Child Development, San Diego.

Taylor, R. (2000). "Diversity within African American Families." In D. H. Demo, K. R. Allen, and M. A. Fine, (Eds.), *Handbook of Family Diversity* (pp. 232–251). New York: Oxford University Press.

Taylor, R. D., Casten, R., and Flickinger, S. M. (1993). "Influence of Social Support on the Parenting Experiences and Psychosocial Adjustment of African-American Adolescents." *Developmental Psychology,* 29, 382–388.

Taylor, R. J. (1994). "Black American Families." In R. L. Taylor (Ed.), *Minority Families in the United States: A Multicultural Perspective* (pp. 19–46). Englewood Cliffs, NJ: Prentice Hall.

Taylor, R., and Roberts, D. (1995). "Kinship Support and Maternal and Adolescent Well-Being in Economically Disadvantaged African American Families." *Child Development,* 66, 1585–1597.

Teachman, J. (2003). "Premarital Sex, Premarital Cohabitation, and the Risk of Subsequent Marital Dissolution among Women." *Journal of Marriage and Family,* 65, 444–455.

Teachman, J. D., and Polonko, K. A. (1990). "Cohabitation and Marital Stability in the United States." *Social Forces,* 69, 207–220.

Teachman, J. D., Paasch, K., and Carver, K. (1996). "Social Capital and Dropping Out of School Early." *Journal of Marriage and the Family,* 58, 773–783.

Tedesco, L. A., and Gaier, E. L. (1988). "Friendship Bonds in Adolescence." *Adolescence,* 89, 127–136. "Teenage Pregnancy and Birth Rate—United States, 1990." (1993). *Morbidity and Mortality Weekly Report,* 42, 733–737.

Terrell, F., Terrell, S. L., and Miller, F. (1993). "Level of Cultural Mistrust as a Function of Educational and Occupational Expectations among Black Students." *Adolescence,* 28, 573–578.

Terrell, N.-E. (1997). "Aggravated and Sexual Assaults among Homeless and Runaway Adolescents." *Youth and Society,* 28, 267–290.

Tevendale, H. D., Dubois, D. L., Lopez, C., and Prindiville, S. L. (1997). "Self-Esteem Stability and Early Adolescent Adjustment: An Exploratory Study." *Journal of Early Adolescence,* 17, 216–237.

Thanasiu, P. L. (2004). "Childhood Sexuality: Discerning Healthy from Abnormal Sexual Behaviors." *Journal of Mental Health Counseling,* 26, 309–319.

Thelen, E., and Adolph, K. E. (1992). "Arnold L. Gesell: The Paradox of Nature and Nurture." *Developmental Psychology,* 28, 368–380.

Thomas, G., Farrell, M. P., and Barnes, G. M. (1996). "The Effects of Single-Mother Families and Nonresident Fathers on Delinquency and Substance Abuse in Black and White Adolescents." *Journal of Marriage and the Family,* 58, 884–894.

Thomas, T. (1992, 1993). *Mr. Wendal.* EMI Blackwood Music, Inc., and Arrested Development Music.

Thompson, D. N. (1985). "Parent-Peer Compliance in a Group of Preadolescent Youths." *Adolescence,* 20, 501–508.

Thompson, L., Acock, A. C., and Clark, K. (1985). "Do Parents Know Their Children? The Ability of Mothers and Fathers to Gauge the Attitudes of Their Young Adult Children." *Family Relations,* 34, 315–320.

Thomson, E., McLanahan, S. S., and Curtin, R. B. (1992). "Family Structure, Gender, and Parental Socialization." *Journal of Marriage and the Family,* 54, 368–378.

Thornberry, T. P., and Krohn, M. D. (1997). "Peers, Drug Use, and Delinquency." In D. M. Stoff, J. Breiling, and J. D. Maser (Eds.), *Handbook of Antisocial Behavior* (pp. 218–233). New York: Wiley.

Thorne, B. (1986). "Girls and Boys Together . . . but Mostly Apart: Gender Arrangements in Elementary Schools." In W. Hartup and Z. Rubin (Eds.), *Relationships and Development* (pp. 167–184). Hillsdale, NJ: Erlbaum.

Thorne, C. R., and DeBlassie, R. R. (1985). "Adolescent Substance Abuse." *Adolescence,* 20, 335–347.

Thornton, A. (1990). "The Courtship Process and Adolescent Sexuality." *Journal of Family Issues,* 11, 239–273.

Thornton, B., and Maurice, J. (1997). "Physique Contrast Effect: Adverse Impact of Idealized Body Images for Women." *Sex Roles,* 37, 433–439.

Thornton, C., and Russell, J. (1997). "Obsessive Comorbidity in the Dieting Disorders." *International Journal of Eating Disorders,* 21, 83–87.

Thornton, L. P., and DeBlassie, R. R. (1989). "Treating Bulimia." *Adolescence,* 24, 631–637.

Thurlow, C. (2001). "The Usual Suspects? A Comparative Investigation of Crowds and Social-Type Labeling among Young British Teenagers." *Journal of Youth Studies,* 4, 319–334.

Tice, D. M., Buder, J., and Baumeister, R. F. (1985). "Development of Self-Consciousness: At What Age Does Audience Pressure Disrupt Performance?" *Adolescence,* 20, 301–305.

Tierno, M. J. (Fall 1983). "Responding to Self-Concept Disturbance among Early Adolescents: A Psychosocial View for Educators." *Adolescence,* 18, 577–584.

Tietjen, A. (1982). "The Social Networks of Preadolescent Children in Sweden." *International Journal of Behavioral Development,* 5, 111–130.

Tietz, C. C., Hu, S. S., and Arendt, E. A. (1997). "The Female Athlete: Evaluation and Treatment of Sports-Related Problems." *Journal of the Academy of Orthopaedic Surgeons,* 5, 87–96.

Tiggemann, M. (2005). "Body Dissatisfaction and Adolescent Self-Esteem: Prospective Findings." *Body Image,* 2, 129–135.

Timnick, L. (August 1982). "How You Can Learn to Be Likeable, Confident, Socially Successful for Only the Cost of Your Present Education." *Psychology Today,* 42ff.

Tisak, M. S., and Tisak, J. (1996). "My Sibling's but Not My Friend's Keeper: Reasoning about Responses to Aggressive Acts." *Journal of Early Adolescence,* 16, 324–339.

Titus, D. N. (1994). *Values Education in American Secondary Schools.* Paper presented at the Kutztown University Education Conference, Kutztown, PA.

Toder, N. L., and Marcia, J. E. (1973). "Ego Identity Status and Response to Conformity Pressure in College Women." *Journal of Personality and Social Psychology,* 26, 287–294.

Tolan, P. H., Guerra, N. G., & Kendall, P. (1995). "A Developmental-Ecological Perspective on Antisocial Behavior in Children and Adolescents: Towards a Unified Risk and Intervention Framework." *Journal of Consulting and Clinical Psychology,* 63, 579–584.

Tolson, J. M., and Urberg, K. A. (1993). "Similarity between Adolescent Best Friends." *Journal of Adolescent Research,* 8, 274–288.

Tomar, S. L., and Giovino, G. A. (1998). "Incidence and Predictors of Chewing Tobacco Use among U.S. Youth." *American Journal of Public Health,* 88, 20–26.

Tomas, P., Zijdenbos, A., Worsley, K., Collins, D. L. Blumenthal, J., Giedd, J. N., Rapoport, J. L., and Evans, A. C. (1999). "Structural Maturation of Neural Pathways in Children and Adolescents: In Vivo Study." *Science,* 283, 1908–1911.

Tomlinson-Keasey, C. (1972). "Formal Operations in Females from Eleven to Fifty-Four Years of Age." *Developmental Psychology,* 6, 364.

Toney, G. T., & Weaver, B. (1994). "Effects of Gender and Gender Role Self-Perceptions on Affective Reactions to Rock Music Videos." *Sex Roles,* 30, 567–583.

Torabi, M. R., Bailey, W. J., and Majd-Jabbari, M. (1993). "Cigarette Smoking as a Predictor of Alcohol and Other Drug Use by Children and Adolescents: Evidence of the 'Gateway Drug Effect.'" *Journal of School Health,* 63, 302–306.

Toray, T., Coughlin, C., Buchinich, S., and Patricelli, P. (1991). "Gender Differences Associated with Adolescent Substance Abuse: Comparisons and Implications for Treatment." *Family Relations,* 40, 338–344.

Torres, R., Fernandez, F., and Maceira, D. (1995). "Self-Esteem and Value of Health as Correlates of Adolescent Health Behavior." *Adolescence,* 30, 403–412.

Toufexis, A. (1992). "When Kids Kill Abusive Parents." *Time,* 140, 60–61.

Toy, V. S. (1999). "Teen-Agers and Cell Phones: A Match Made in Gab Heaven." *New York Times,* August 2.

Traub, S. H., and Dodder, R. A. (1988). "Intergenerational Conflict of Values and Norms: A Theoretical Model." *Adolescence,* 23, 975–989.

Traver, N. (October 26, 1992). "Children without Pity." *Time,* 140, 46–51.

Trepanier-Street, M. L., Romatowski, J. A., and McNair, S. (1990). "Development of Story Characters in Gender-Therapeutic and Non-Therapeutic Occupational Roles." *Journal of Early Adolescence,* 10, 496–510.

Trevoux, D., and Busch-Rossnagel, N. A. (1995). "Age Differences in Parents and Peer Influences on Female Sexual Behavior." *Journal of Research on Adolescence,* 5, 469–487.

Troiden, R. R. (1988). *Gay and Lesbian Identity: A Sociological Study.* Dix Hills, NY: General Hall.

Trotter, R. T. (Summer 1982). "Ethical and Sexual Patterns of Alcohol Use: Anglo and Mexican-American College Students." *Adolescence,* 17, 305–325.

Trumbull, E., Rothstein-Fisch, C., Greenfield, P., and Quiroz, B. (2001). *Bridging Cultures between Home and School: A Guide for Teachers.* Mahwah, NJ: Erlbaum.

Trussell, J. (1988). "Teenage Pregnancy in the United States." *Family Planning Perspectives,* 20, 262–272.

Trusty, J., Robinson, C. R., Plata, M., and Ng, K. M. (2000). "Effects of Gender, Socioeconomic Status, and Early Academic Performance on Post Secondary Educational Choice." *Journal of Counseling and Development,* 78, 463–472.

Tschann, J. M., Adler, N. E., Irwin, C. E., Jr., Milstein, S. G., Turner, R. A., and Kegeles, S. M. (1994). "Initiation of Substance Use in Early Adolescence: The Roles of Pubertal Timing and Emotional Distress." *Health Psychology,* 13, 326–333.

Tschann, J. M., and Adler, N. E. (1997). "Sexual Self-Acceptance, Communication with Partner, and Contraceptive Use among Adolescent Females: A Longitudinal Study." *Journal of Research on Adolescence,* 7, 413–430.

Tschann, J. M., Johnston, J. R., and Wallerstein, J. S. (1989). "Resources, Stressors, and Attachment as Predictors of Adult Adjustment after Divorce: A Longitudinal Study." *Journal of Marriage and the Family,* 51, 1033–1046.

Tse, L. (1999). "Finding a Place to Be: Ethnic Identity Exploration of Asian Americans." *Adolescence,* 34, 121–138.

Tsunokai, G. T. (2005). "Beyond the Lenses of the 'Model' Minority Myth: A Descriptive Portrait of Asian Gang Members." *Journal of Gang Research,* 12, 37–58.

Tucker, C. J., Barber, B. L., and Eccles, J. S. (1997). "Advice about Life Plans and Personal Problems in Late Adolescent Sibling Relationships." *Journal of Youth and Adolescence,* 26, 63–76.

Tudge, J., and Winterhoff, P. (1993). *The Cognitive Consequences of Collaboration: Why Ask How?* Paper presented at the biennial meeting of the Society for Research in Child Development, New Orleans.

Turiel, E. (1998). "Moral Development." In N. Eisenberg (Ed.) and W. Damon (Series Ed.), *Handbook of Child Psychology. Vol. 3: Social, Emotional and Personality Development,* 5th ed. (pp. 863–932). New York: Wiley.

Turnage, B. F. (2004). "African American Mother-Daughter Relationships Mediating Daughter's Self-Esteem." *Child & Adolescent Social Work Journal,* 21, 155–173.

Turner, H. A., and Finkelhor, D. (1996). "Corporal Punishment as a Stressor among Youth." *Journal of Marriage and the Family,* 58, 155–166.

Twenge, J. M., & Crocker, J. (2002). "Race and Self-Esteem Revisited: Reply to Hafdahl and Gray-Little (2002)." *Psychological Bulletin,* 128, 417–420.

Tyler, K. A., Whitbeck, L. B., Hoyt, D. R., and Johnson, K. (2003). "Self-Mutilation and Homeless Youth: The Role of Family Abuse, Street Experiences, and Mental Disorders." *Journal of Research on Adolescence,* 13, 457–474.

Tyrka, A. R., Graber, J. A., and Brooks-Gunn, J. (2000). "The Development of Disordered Eating: Correlates and Predictors of Eating in the Context of Adolescence." In A. J. Sameriff, M.

Lewis, and S. Miller (Eds.), *Handbook of Developmental Psychopathology,* 2nd ed. (pp. 607–627). New York: Plenum.

Tzeng, J. M., and Mare, R. D. (1995). "Labor Market and Socioeconomic Effects on Marital Stability." *Social Science Research,* 24, 329–351.

U.S. Bureau of Justice Statistics. (2000). *Violent Crime Rate Trends.* Retrieved from http://www.ojp.usdoj.gov/bjs/glance/viort/htm.

U.S. Bureau of Labor Statistics. (2000). *Report on the Youth Labor Force.* Retrieved from http://www.stats.bls.gov/opub/rylf/pdf.chapter3.pdf.

U.S. Bureau of Labor Statistics. (2001). "Occupational Employment." *Occupational Outlook Quarterly,* Winter, 8–23.

U.S. Bureau of Labor Statistics. (2003). *Occupational Outlook Handbook, 2002–2003.* Washington, DC: Author. Retrieved from http://www.bls.gov.

U.S. Bureau of Labor Statistics. (2003a). *Computer and Internet Use at Work in 2003.* Retrieved from http://www.bls.gov/news.release/ciuaw.nr0.htm.

U.S. Bureau of Labor Statistics. (2004). *Employment of Unemployment among Youth—Summer 2004.* Retrieved from http://www.bls.gov/news.release/archives/youth_08182004.pdf.

U.S. Bureau of Labor Statistics. (2005). "Women in the Labor Force: A Databook." *Report 985.* Washington, D.C.: U.S. Department of Labor.

U.S. Bureau of Labor Statistics. *Occupational Outlook Handbook, 2006–07 Edition,* accessed 1/28/07 at http://www.bls.gov/oco.

U.S. Bureau of the Census. (1998). "Marital Status and Living Arrangements: March 1998 (Update). In *Current Population Reports.* Series P20-514. Washington, DC: Government Printing Office.

U.S. Bureau of the Census. (1999a). *Statistical Abstract of the United States, 1999.* Washington, DC: Government Printing Office.

U.S. Bureau of the Census. (1999b). *Poverty in the United States, 1999.* Washington, DC: Government Printing Office.

U.S. Bureau of the Census. (1999c). *Current Population Reports, March 1999.* Washington, DC: Government Printing Office.

U.S. Bureau of the Census. (1999d). *Marital Status and Living Arrangements: March 1998 (Update).* No. P20-514. Retrieved from http://www.census.gov/prod/99pubs/p20-514u.pdf.

U.S. Bureau of the Census. (2000a). "The Foreign-Born Population of the United States." In *Current Population Reports, March 1999.* Washington, DC: Government Printing Office.

U.S. Bureau of the Census. (2000b). *Poverty Rate Lowest in 20 Years, Household Income at Record High, Census Bureau Reports.* Press Release, Department of Commerce News, September 26, 2000. Retrieved from www.census.gov/pressrelease/www/2000/cb00–158.html.

U.S. Bureau of the Census. (2000c). *Statistical Abstract of the United States, 2000.* Washington, DC: Government Printing Office.

U.S. Bureau of the Census. (2000d). *Census 2000 Supplemental Survey.* Retrieved from http://www.census.gov/population/socdemo/hh-fam/tabCH-7.txt.

U.S. Bureau of the Census. (2002). *Statistical Abstract of the United States: 2002.* Washington, DC: Government Printing Office.

U.S. Bureau of the Census. (2003a). *Statistical Abstract of the United States, 2003.* Washington, DC: Government Printing Office.

U.S. Bureau of the Census. (2003b). *Computer Use in 2003.* Population Profile of the United States. Retrieved from http://www.census.gov/population/pop-profile/dynamic/Computers.pdf.

U.S. Bureau of the Census. (2004). *U.S. Interim Projections by Age, Sex, Race, and Hispanic* Origin. Retrieved from http://www.census.gov/ipc/www/usinterimproj/natprojtab02a.pdf.

U.S. Bureau of the Census. (June, 2005a). *Families and Living Arrangements.* Retrieved from http://www.census.gov/population/www/socdemo/hh-fam.html.

U.S. Bureau of the Census. (August, 2005b). *Poverty: 2004 Highlights.* Retrieved from http://www.census.gov/hhes/www/poverty/poverty04/pov04hi.html.

U.S. Bureau of the Census. (2005c). "Income, Poverty, and Health Insurance Coverage in the United States: 2004." *Current Population Reports, P60-229.*

U.S. Bureau of the Census. (2005d). *Statistical Abstract of the United States: 2004.* Washington D.C.: U.S. Bureau of the Census.

U.S. Bureau of the Census. (2006). *Current Population Survey,* March 2006.

U.S. Bureau of the Census. (2007). *Statistical Abstract of the United States: 2007* (126th Edition). Washington, D.C.: Bureau of the Census.

U.S. Department of Commernce. (1999). "Falling through the Net: Defining the Digital Divide." Retrieved from http://www.ntia.doc.gov/ntiahome/fttn99/contents.html.

U.S. Department of Education. (1993). *Adult Literacy in America.* Washington, DC: Government Printing Office.

U.S. Department of Health and Human Services. (1994). *Preventing Tobacco Use among Young People: A Report of the Surgeon General.* DHHS Publication no. (CDC) 94-8926. Washington, DC: Government Printing Office.

U.S. Department of Health and Human Services. (1995). *Report to Congress on Out-of-Wedlock Childbearing.* DHHS Publication no. 95-1257. Washington, DC: Government Printing Office.

U.S. Department of Health and Human Services. (1996). *Trends in the Well-Being of America's Children and Youth: 1996.* Washington, DC: Office of the Assistant Secretary for Planning and Evaluation.

U.S. Department of Health and Human Services. (1999). *Mental Health: A Report of the Surgeon General.* Washington, DC: Government Printing Office.

U.S. Department of Health and Human Services. (2000). *Reducing Tobacco Use: A Report of the Surgeon General.* Washington, DC: Government Printing Office.

U.S. Department of Health and Human Services. (2001). *The Surgeon General's Call to Action to Prevent and Decrease Overweight and Obesity.* Rockville, MD: Government Printing Office.

U.S. National Center for Education Statistics. (2005). "Characteristics of Schools in the United States: Results from the 2003–2004 Private School Survey." *NCES 2006-319.*

U.S. National Center for Health Statistics. (2000). *Vital Statistics of the United States, March 2000.* Washington, DC: Government Printing Office.

Udry, J. R., and Cliquet, R. L. (1982). "A Cross-Cultural Examination of the Relationship between Ages at Menarche, Marriage, and First Birth." *Demography,* 19, 53–63.

Uhlenberg, P., and Hammill. B. G. (1998). "Frequency of Grandparent Contact with Grandchild Sets: Six Factors That Make a Difference." *The Gerontologist,* 38, 276–285.

Umaña-Taylor, A. J., Diversi, M., and Fine, M. A. (2002). "Ethnic Identity and Self-Esteem among Latino Adolescents: Making Distinctions among the Latino Populations." *Journal of Adolescent Research,* 17, 303–327.

Umberson, D. (1989). "Relationship with Children: Explaining Parents' Psychological Well-Being." *Journal of Marriage and the Family,* 51, 999–1012.

Underwood, M. K., Kupersmidt, J. B., & Coie, J. D. (1996). "Childhood Peer Sociometric Status and Aggression as Predictors of Adolescent Childbearing." *Journal of Research on Adolescence,* 6, 201–223.

Underwood, R. C., and Patch, C. (1999). "Siblicide: A Descriptive Analysis of Sibling Homicide." *"Homicide Studies: An Interdisciplinary & International Journal,* 3, 333–348.

Ungar, M. T. (2000). "The Myth of Peer Pressure." *Adolescence,* 35, 167–180.

Unger, J. B., Kipke, M. D., Simon. T. R., Montgomery, S. B., and Johnson, C. J. (1997). "Homeless Youths and Young Adults in Los Angeles: Prevalence of Mental Health Problems and the Relationship between Mental Health and Substance Abuse Disorders." *American Journal of Community Psychology,* 25, 371–394.

Unger, J. B., Simon, T. R., Newman, T. L., Montgomery, S. B., Kipke, M D., and Albornoz, M. (1998). "Early Adolescent Street Youth: An Overlooked Population with Unique Problems and Service Needs." *Journal of Early Adolescence,* 18, 325–348.

United Nations High Commissioner for Refugees. (2000). From Sudan to North Dakota. *Refugees, 2,* 5–11.

United Nations High Commissioner for Refugees. (2005). *Refugees by the Numbers, 2005 edition.*

United Nations Population Find. (2003). *Making I Billion Count: Investing in Adolescents' Health and Rights.* The State of the World's Population: 2003. Retrieved from http://www.unfpa.org/swp/2003/english/ch1/page2.htm.

University of California at Los Angeles Medical Center. (2000). *Acne.* Patient Learning Series <www.mednet.ucla. edu/healthtopics/pls/acne.htm>.

Upchurch, D. M. (1993). "Early Schooling and Childbearing Experiences: Implications for Post Secondary School Attendance." *Journal of Research on Adolescence,* 3, 423–443.

Upchurch, D. M., Aneshensel, C. S., Sucoff, C. A., and Levy-Storms, L. (1999). "Neighborhood and Family Contexts of Adolescent Sexual Activity." *Journal of Marriage and Family,* 61, 920–933.

Urberg, K. A., Degirmencioglu, S., Toloson, J. M., and Halliday-Scher, K. (2000). "Adolescent Social Crowds: Measurement and Relationship to Friendships." *Journal of Adolescent Research,* 15, 427–445.

Urberg, K. A., Degirmencioglu, S. M., Tolson, J. M., and Halliday-Scher, K. (1995). "The Structure of Adolescent Peer Networks." *Developmental Psychology,* 31, 540–547.

Urberg, K. A., Degirmencioglu, S. M., and Tolson, J. M. (1998). "Adolescent Friendship Selection and Termination: The Role of Similarity." *Journal of Social and Personal Relationships,* 15, 703–710.

Vachon, J., Vtaro, F., Wanner, B., and Tremblay, R. E. (2004). "Adolescent Gambling: Relationships with Parent Gambling and Parenting Practices." *Psychology of Addictive Behaviors,* 18, 398–401.

Valentine, S., and Mosley, G. (1998). "Aversion to Women Who Work and Perceived Discrimination among Euro-Americans and Mexican-Americans." *Perceptual and Motor Skills,* 86, 1027–1033.

Valentine, S., and Mosley, G. (1999). "Acculturation and Sex-Role Attitudes among Mexican Americans: A Longitudinal Analysis." *Hispanic Journal of Behavioral Sciences,* 22, 104–113.

Valium Package Insert. (1988). Roche Laboratories.

Valkenburg, P. M., Schouten, A. P., and Peter, J. (2005). "Adolescents' Identity Experiments on the Internet." *New Media & Society,* 7, 383–402.

Van den Broucke, S., and Vandereycken, W. (1986). "Risk Factors for the Development of Eating Disorders in Adolescent Exchange Students: An Exploratory Study." *Journal of Adolescence,* 9, 145–150.

van Der Molen, H. T. (1990). "A Definition of Shyness and Its Implications for Clinical Practice." In W. Crozier (Ed.), *Shyness and Embarrassment* (pp. 286–314). Cambridge, England: Cambridge University Press.

Van Halen, E., Van Halen, A., Anthony, M., and Hager, S. (1991). *In 'N' Out.* Yessup Music.

van Hoof, A. (1999). "The Identity Status Approach: In Need of Fundamental Revision and Qualitative Change." *Developmental Review,* 19, 497–556.

Van Roosmalen, E. H., and Krahn, H. (1996). "Boundaries of Youth." *Youth and Society,* 28, 3–39.

Van Roosmalen, E. H., and McDaniel, S. A. (1989). "Peer Group Influence as a Factor in Smoking Behavior of Adolescents." *Adolesence,* 24, 801–816.

Van Roosmalen, E. H., and McDaniel, S. A. (1992). "Adolescent Smoking Intentions. Gender Differences in Peer Context." *Adolesence,* 27, 87–105.

Van Thorre, M. D., and Vogel, F. X. (Spring 1985). "The Presence of Bulimia in High School Females." *Adolescence,* 20, 45–51.

Vandereycken, W. (1994). "Emergence of Bulimia Nervosa as a Separate Diagnostic Entity: Review of the Literature from 1960 to 1979." *International Journal of Eating Disorders,* 16, 105–116.

Vanderlinden, J., and Vandereycken, W. (1991). "Guidelines for the Family Therapeutic Approach to Eating Disorders." *Psychotherapy and Psychosomatics,* 56, 36–42.

Vargas, L. A., and Willis, D. J. (1994). "Introduction to the Special Section: New Directions in the Treatment and Assessment of Ethnic Minority Children and Adolescents." *Journal of Clinical Child Psychology,* 23, 2–4.

Vartanian, L. R. (1997). "Separation-Individuation, Social Support, and Adolescent Egocentrism: An Exploratory Study." *Journal of Early Adolescence,* 17, 245–270.

Vartanian, L. R. (2000). "Revisiting the Imaginary Audience and Personal Fable Constructs of Adolescent Egocentrism: A Conceptual Review." *Adolescence,* 35, 639–661.

Vartanian, L. R., and Herman, C. P. (2006). "Beliefs about the Determinants of Body Weight Predict Dieting and Exercise Behavior." *Eating Behavior,* 7, 176–179.

Vartanian, L. R., and Powlishta, K. K. (1996). "A Longitudinal Examination of the Social-Cognitive Foundations of Adolescent Egocentrism." *Journal of Early Adolescence,* 16, 157–178.

Vasa, R. A., Carlino, A. R., and Pine, D. S. (2006). "Pharmacotherapy of Depressed Children and Adolescents: Current Issues and Potential Directions." *Biological Psychiatry,* 59, 1021–1028.

Vaughn, M. G., and Howard, M. O. (2004). "Adolescent Substance Abuse Treatment: A Synthesis of Controlled Evaluations." *Research on Social Work Practice,* 14, 325–335.

Vazsonyi, A. T., Hibbert, J. R., and Snider, J. B. (2003). "Exotic Enterprise No More? Adolescent Reports of Family and Parenting Processes from Youth in Four Countries." *Journal of Research on Adolescence,* 13, 129–160.

Vega, W. A. (1990). "Hispanic Families in the 1980s: A Decade of Research." *Journal of Marriage and the Family,* 52, 1015–1024.

Venkdeswaran, R. (2000). "Nutrition for Youth." *Clinical Family Practice,* 2, 791–822.

Ventura, S. J., Mosher, W. D., Curtin, M. A., Abma, J. C., and Henshaw, S. (2001). "Trends in Pregnancy Rates for the United States, 1976–1997: An Update." *National Vital Statistics Reports,* 49, 1–9.

Verma, S., and Saraswathi, T. S. (2002). "Adolescence in India: Street Urichins or Silicon Valley Millionaires?" In B. Brown, R. Larson, and T. S. Saraswathi (Eds.), *The World's Youth: Adolescence in Eight Regions of the Globe.* New York: Cambridge University Press.

Vicary, J. R., and Lerner, J. V. (1986). "Parental Attributes and Adolescent Drug Use." *Journal of Adolescence,* 9, 115–122.

Villarruel, A. M. (1998). "Cultural Influences on the Sexual Attitudes, Beliefs, and Norms of Young Latina Adolescents." *Journal of the Society of Pediatric Nursing,* 3, 69–79.

Violato, C., and Wiley, A. J. (1990). "Images of Adolescence in English Literature: The Middle Ages to the Modern Period." *Adolescence,* 25, 253–264.

Vischof, G. P., Stith, S. M., and Wilson, S. M. (1992). "A Comparison of the Family Systems of Adolescent Sexual Offenders and Nonsexual Offending Delinquents." *Family Relations,* 41, 318–323.

Visser, J., and Geuze, R. H. (2000). "Kinesthetic Acuity in Adolescent Boys: A Longitudinal Study." *Developmental Medicine and Child Neurology,* 42, 93–96.

Vitaro, F., Brendgen, M., and Tremblay, R. E. (2000). "Influence of Deviant Friends on Delinquency: Searching for Moderator Variables." *Journal of Abnormal Child Psychology,* 28, 313–325.

Vodanovich, S. J., and Kramer, T. J. (1989). "An Examination of the Work Values of Parents and Their Children." *Career Development Quarterly,* 37, 365–374.

Voight, J. 1999. "Moving Target." *Mediaweek,* 9, 38–39.

Volk, R. J., Edwards, D. W., Lewis, R. A., and Sprinkle, D. H. (1989). "Family Systems of Adolescent Substance Abusers." *Family Relations,* 38, 266–272.

Vondracek, F. W. (1991). "Vocational Development and Choice in Adolescence." In R. M. Lerner, A. C. Petersen, and J. Brooks-Gunn (Eds.), *Encyclopedia of Adolescence.* Vol. 2. New York: Garland.

Vondracek, F. W., and Schulenberg, J. E. (1986). "Career Development in Adolescence: Some Conceptual and Intervention Issues." *The Vocational Guidance Quarterly,* 34, 247–254.

Vondracek, F. W., and Schulenberg, J. E. (1992). "Counseling for Normative and Nonnormative Influences on Career Development." *The Career Development Quarterly,* 40, 291–301.

Vroegh, K. S. (1997). "Transracial Adoptees: Developmental Status after 17 Years." *American Journal of Orthopsychiatry,* 67, 568–575.

Vygotsky, L. S. (1978). *Mind in Society: The Development of Higher Mental Processes.* Cambridge, MA: Harvard University Press.

Wade, T. J., & Cooper, M. (1999). "Sex Differences in the Links Between Attractiveness, Self-Esteem, and the Body." *Personality and Individual Differences,* 27, 1047–1056.

Wade, T. J., Cairney, J., and Pevalin, D. J. (2002). "Emergence of Gender Differences in Depression during Adolescence: National Panel Results from Three Countries." *Journal of the American Academy of Child & Adolescent Psychiatry,* 41, 190–198.

Wagenaar, A. C., and Toomi, T. L. (2002). "Effects of Minimum Drinking Age Laws: Review and Analyses of the Literature from 1960 to 2000." *Journal of Studies on Alcohol,* Supplement 14, 206–225.

Wagner, R. K. (1997). "Intelligence, Training, and Employment." *American Psychologist,* 52, 1059–1069.

Waite, B., Foster, H., and Hillbrand, M. (1992). "Reduction of Aggressive Behavior after Removal of Music Television." *Hospital and Community Psychiatry,* 43, 173–175.

Waksman, S. A. (Spring 1984). "Assertion Training with Adolescents." *Adolescence,* 73, 123–130.

Walcott, D. D., Pratt, H. D., and Patel, D. R. (2003). "Adolescents and Eating Disorders: Gender, Racial, Ethnic, Sociocultural, and Socioeconomic Issues." *Journal of Adolescent Research,* 18, 223–243.

Waldner-Haugrud, L. K., & Magruder, B. (1996). "Homosexual Identity Expression Among Lesbian and Gay Adolescents: An Analysis of Perceived Structural Associations." *Youth & Society,* 27, 313–333.

Walker, D. K., Cross, A. W., Heyman, P. W., Ruck-Ross, H., Benson, P., and Tuthill, J. W. G. (1982). "Comparisons Between Inner City and Private School Adolescents' Perceptions of Health Problems." *Journal of Adolescent Health Care,* 3, 82–90.

Walker, L. J. (1980). "Cognitive and Perspective-Taking Prerequisites for Moral Development." *Child Development,* 51, 131–139.

Walker, L. J. (1991). "Sex Differences in Moral Reasoning." In J. L. Gewirtz and W. M. Kurtines (Eds.), *Handbook of Moral Behavior and Development,* Vol. 2 (pp. 333–364). Hillsdale, NJ: Erlbaum.

Walker, L. J., & Taylor, H. (1991). "Family Interactions and the Development of Moral Reasoning." *Child Development,* 62, 264–283.

Walker, L. J., and Henning, K. H. (1997). "Moral Development in the Broader Context of Personality." In S. Hala (Ed.), *The Development of Social Cognition* (pp. 297–327). Hove, England: Psychology Press.

Walker, L. J., and Richards, B. S. (1979). "Stimulating Transitions in Moral Reasoning as a

Function of Stage of Cognitive Development." *Developmental Psychology,* 15, 95–103.

Walker-Barnes, C. J., and Mason, C. A. (2004). "Delinquency and Substance Use among Gang-Involved Youth: The Moderating Role of Parenting Practices." *American Journal of Community Psychology,* 34, 235–250.

Wall, J. A., Power, T. G., and Arbona, C. (1993). "Susceptibility to Antisocial Peer Pressure and Its Relation to Acculturation in Mexican-American Adolescents." *Journal of Adolescent Research,* 8, 403–418.

Wallace, J. M., Jr., and Forman, T. A. (1998). "Religion's Role in Promoting Health and Reducing Risk among American Youth." *Health Education & Behavior,* 25, 721–741.

Wallace-Broscious, A., Serafica, F. C., and Osipow, S. H. (1994). "Adolescent Career Development: Relationships to Self-Concepts and Identity Status." *Journal of Research on Adolescence,* 4, 127–150.

Wallerstein, J. S. (1983). "Children of Divorce: Stress and Developmental Tasks." In N. Garnezy and M. Rutter (Eds.), *Stress, Coping and Development in Children* (pp. 265–302). New York: McGraw-Hill.

Wallerstein, J. S. (1991). "The Long-Term Effects of Divorce on Children: A Review." *Journal of the Academy of Child Adolescence Psychiatry,* 30, 349–360.

Wallerstein, J. S., and Blakeslee, S. (1989). *Second Chances: Men, Women, and Children a Decade after Divorce.* New York: Ticknor and Fields.

Wallerstein, J. S., and Lewis, J. (1998). "The Long-Term Impact of Divorce on Children: A First Report from a 25-Year Study." *Family and Conciliation Courts Review,* 36, 368–383.

Wallerstein, J. S., and Lewis, J. M. (2004). "The Unexpected Legacy of Divorce: Report of a 25-Year Study." *Psychoanalytic Psychology,* 21, 353–370.

Wallis, C. (February 16, 1987). "You Haven't Heard Anything Yet." *Time.*

Walsh, A., and Beyer, J. A. (1987). "Violent Crime, Sociopathy, and Love Deprivation among Adolescent Delinquents." *Adolescence,* 22, 705–717.

Walsh, B. T., Haidgan, C. M., Devlin, M. J., Gladis, M., and Roose, S. P. (1991). "Long-Term Outcome of Anti-Depressant Treatment for Bulimia Nervosa." *American Journal of Psychiatry,* 148, 1206–1212.

Walsh, R. N., et al. (1981). "The Menstrual Cycle, Sex, and Academic Performance." *Archives of General Psychiatry,* 38, 219–221.

Walsh, Y., Russell, R. J. H., and Wells, P. A. (1995). "The Personality of Ex-Cult Members." *Personality and Individual Differences,* 19, 339–344.

Waltz, J. A., Knowlton, B. J., Holyoak, K. J., Boone, K. B., Mishkin, F. S., de Menzes Santos, M., Thomas, C. R., and Miller, B. L. (1999). "A System for Relational Reasoning in Human Prefrontal Cortex." *Psychological Science,* 10, 119–125.

Wang, S., Baillargeon, R., and Paterson, S. (2005). "Detecting Continuity Violations in Infancy: A New Account and New Evidence from Covering and Tube Events." *Cognition,* 95, 129–137.

Ward, L. M. (2002). "Does Television Exposure Affect Emerging Adults' Attitudes and Assumptions about Sexual Relationships? Correlational and Experimental Confirmation." *Journal of Youth and Adolescence,* 24, 595–615.

Ward, S. L., and Overton, W. F. (1990). "Semantic Familiarity, Relevance, and the Development of Deductive Reasoning." *Developmental Psychology,* 26, 488–493.

Ware, N. C., and Lee, V. E. (1988). "Sex Differences in Choice of College Science Majors." *American Educational Research Journal,* 25, 593–614.

Wark, G. R., and Krebs, D. L. (1996). "Gender and Dilemma Differences in Real-Life Moral Judgment." *Developmental Psychology,* 32, 220–230.

Warner, P. E., Critchley, H., Lumsden, M. A., Campbell-Brown, M., Douglas, A., and Murray, G. D. (2004). "Menorrhagia I: Measured Blood Loss, Clinical Features, and Outcome in Women with Heavy Periods: A Survey with Follow-Up Data." *American Journal of Obstetrics and Gynecology,* 190, 1216–1223.

Warren, D. (1992, 1993). *I'll Never Get Over You Getting Over Me.* Real Songs.

Warren, D. (1992, 1993). *Love Can Move Mountains.* Real Songs.

Warren, D. (1993). *Don't Take Away My Heaven.* Real Songs.

Warren, J. R. (2002). "Reconsidering the Relationship between Student Employment and Academic Outcomes." *Youth and Society,* 33, 366–393.

Warren, J. R., LePore, P. C., and Mare, R. D. (2000). "Employment during High School: Consequences for Students' Grades in Academic Courses." *American Educational Research Journal,* 37, 943–969.

Warren, M. P., and Perlroth, N. E. (2001). "The Effects of Intense Exercise on the Female Reproductive System." *Journal of Endocrinology,* 170, 3–11.

Warren, R., Good, G., and Velten, E. (Fall 1984). "Measurement of Social-Evaluative Anxiety in Junior High School Students." *Adolescence,* 19, 643–648.

Warshak, R. A. (1986). "Father-Custody and Child Development: A Review of Analysis of Psychological Research." *Behavioral Science and the Law,* 4, 185–202.

Washington State Department of Health. (2000). *Adolescent Nutrition.* Publication no. 910-117. Tacoma: Author.

Waterman, A. S. (1992). "Identity as an Aspect of Optimal Psychological Functioning." In G. R. Adams, T. P. Gullotta, & R. Montemayor (Eds.), *Adolescent Identity Formation* (pp. 50–72). Newbury Park, CA: Sage Publications.

Waterman, A. S. (1999). "Identity, the Identity Statuses, and Identity Status Development: A Contemporary Statement." *Developmental Review,* 19, 591–621.

Waterman, J. (1986). "Overview of Treatment Issues." In K. MacFarlane and J. Waterman (Eds.), *Sexual Abuse of Young Children: Evaluation and Treatment* (pp. 197–203). New York: Guilford.

Waters, E., and Cummings, M. (2000). "A Secure Base from Which to Explore Close Relationships." *Child Development,* 71, 164–172.

Watkins, B. (1992). "Youth Beliefs about Health and Physical Activity." *Journal of Applied Developmental Psychology,* 13, 257–269.

Watson, C. M., Quatman, T., and Edler, E. (2002). "Career Aspirations of Adolescent Girls: Effects of Achievement Level, Grade, and Single-Sex School Environment." *Sex Roles,* 46, 323–335.

Watson, R. E. L., and DeMeo, P. W. (1987). "Premarital Cohabitation vs. Traditional Courtship and Subsequent Marital Adjustment: A Reflection and Follow-Up." *Family Relations,* 36, 193–196.

Watts, W. D., and Wright, L. S. (1990). "The Relationship of Alcohol, Tobacco, Marijuana, and Other Illegal Drug Use to Delinquency among Mexican-American, Black, and White Adolescent Males." *Adolescence,* 25, 171–181.

Way, N., and Chen, L. (2000). "Close and General Friendships among African American, Latino, and Asian American Adolescents from Low-Income Families." *Journal of Adolescent Research,* 15, 274–301.

Way, N., and Greene, M. (March, 2005). *Exploring Adolescents' Perceptions of Parental Attitudes and Rules about Friendships.* Paper presented at the Biennial Meeting of the Society for Research on Child Development, Seattle, WA.

Wayment, H., & Zetlin, G. (1989). "Theoretical and Methodological Considerations of Self-Concept Measurement." *Adolescence,* 24, 339–348.

Webb, R. A. (1974). "Concrete and Formal Operations in Very Bright 6- to 11-Year-Olds." *Human Development,* 17, 292–300.

Weber, T. E. (January 16, 1997). "Mainstream Sites Accept Ads Selling X-Rated Fare." *The Wall Street Journal.*

Wechsler, H., Lee, J. E., Kuo, M., and Lee, H. (2000). "College Binge Drinking in the 1990s: A Continuing Problem. Results of the Harvard School of Public Health 1999 College Alcohol Study." *Journal of American College Health,* 48, 199–210 <www.hsph.harvard.edu/organizations/cas/test/rpt2000/cas2000rpt.html>.

Wechsler H., Lee, J. E., Kuo, M., Seibring, M., Nelson, T. F., and Lee, H. P. (2002). "Trends in College Binge Drinking during a Period of Increased Prevention Efforts: Findings from Four Harvard School of Public Health Study Surveys, 1993–2001." *Journal of American College Health,* 50(5), 203–217.

Wegner, K. E., Smyth, J. M., Crosby, R. D., Wittrock, D., Wonderlich, S.A., and Mitchell, J. E. (2002). "An Evaluation of the Relationship between Mood and Binge Eating in the Natural Environment Using Ecological Momentary Assessment." *International Journal of Eating Disorders,* 32, 352–361.

Wehmeyer, M. L., and Palmer, S. B. (1997). "Perceptions of Control of Students with and without Cognitive Disabilities." *Psychological Reports,* 81, 195–206.

Wehr, S. H., and Kaufman, M. E. (1987). "The Effects of Assertive Training on Performance in Highly Anxious Adolescents." *Adolescence,* 85, 195–205.

Weinbender, M. L. M., and Rossignol, A. M. (1996). "Lifestyle and Risk of Premature Sexual Activity in a High School Population of Seven-Day Adventists: Valuegenesis, 1989." *Adolescence,* 31, 265–281.

Weinberg, D. H. (2000). *U.S. Census Bureau Press Briefing on 1999 Income and Poverty Estimates, September 26, 2000* <www.census.gov/hhes/income/income99/prs00ase.html>.

Weinburgh, M. (1995). "Gender Differences in Student Attitudes toward Science: A Meta-Analysis of the Literature from 1970 to 1991." *Journal of Research in Science Teaching,* 32, 387–398.

Weinger, S. (2000). "Opportunities for Career Success: Views of Poor and Middle-Class Children." *Children and Youth Services Review,* 22, 13–35.

Weinreich, H. E. (1974). "The Structure of Moral Reason." *Journal of Youth and Adolescence,* 3, 135–143.

Weinstock, H., Berman, S., and Cates, W., Jr. (2004). "Sexually Transmitted Diseases among American Youth: Incidence and Prevalence Estimates, 2000." *Perspectives on Sexual and Reproductive Health,* 36, 6–10.

Weisfeld, G. (1997). "Puberty Rites as Clues to the Nature of Human Adolescence." *Cross-Cultural Research: The Journal of Comparative Social Science,* 31, 27–54.

Weisfeld, G. E., Bloch, S. A., and Ivers, J. W. (1984). "Possible Determinants of Social Dominance among Adolescent Girls." *Journal of Genetic Psychology,* 144, 115–129.

Weisman, C. S., Plichta, S., Nathanson, C. A., Ensminger, M., and Robinson, J. C. (1991). "Consistency of Condom Use for Disease Prevention among Adolescent Users of Oral Contraceptives." *Family Planning Perspectives,* 23, 71–74.

Weithorn, L. A., and Campbell, S. B. (1982). "The Competency of Children and Adolescents to Make Informed Treatment Decisions." *Child Development,* 53, 1589–1598.

Weitoft, G. R., Hjern, A., Haglund, B., and Rosén, M. (2003). "Mortality, Severe Morbidity, and Injury in Children Living with Single Parents in Sweden: A Population-Based Study." *Lancet,* 361, 289–295.

Wellman, H. M., and Gellman, S. A. (1998). "Knowledge Acquisition in Fundamental Domains." In W. Damon (Ed.), *Handbook of Child Psychology. Vol. 2: Cognition, Language, and Perception* (pp. 524–573). New York: Wiley.

Wellsand v. *Valparaiso Community Schools Corporation et al.* (1971). U.S.C.C., N.D., 71 Hlss (2) (Ind.).

Welte, J. W., and Barnes, G. M. (1987). "Youthful Smoking: Patterns and Relationships of Alcohol and Other Drug Use." *Journal of Adolescence,* 10, 327–340.

Wentzel, K. R. (1996). "Social and Academic Motivation in Middle School: Concurrent and Long-Term Relations to Academic Effort." *Journal of Early Adolescence,* 16, 390–406.

Wentzel, K. R., and Erdley, C. A. (1993). "Strategies for Making Friends: Relations to Social Behavior and Peer Acceptance in Early Adolescence." *Developmental Psychology,* 29, 819–826.

Wentzel, K. R., and McNamara, C. C. (1999). "Interpersonal Relationships, Emotional Distress, and Prosocial Behavior in Middle School." *Journal of Early Adolescence,* 19, 114–125.

Wentzel, K. R., Feldman, S. S., and Weinberger, D. A. (1991). "Parental Child Rearing and Academic Achievement in Boys: The Mediational Role of Social-Emotional Adjustment." *Journal of Early Adolescence,* 11, 321–339.

Werner, E. E. (1998). "Resilience and the Lifespan Perspective: What We Have Learned—So Far." *Resiliency in Action,* 3, 1–9.

West, C. K., Jones P. A., and McConahay, G. (Fall 1981). "Who Does What to the Adolescent in the High School: Relationships among Resulting Affect and Self-Concept and Achievement." *Adolescence,* 16, 657–661.

Westbrook, R. B. (1991). *John Dewey and the American Democracy.* Ithaca, NY: Cornell University Press.

Westney, O. I., Jenkins, R. R., Butts, J. D., and Williams, I. (Fall 1984). *Adolescence,* 19, 557–568.

Whitbeck, L. B., and Simons, R. L. (1990). "Life on the Streets: The Victimization of Runaway and Homeless Adolescents." *Youth and Society,* 22, 108–125.

Whitbeck, L. B., Hoyt, D. R., Miller, M., and Kao, M. (1992). "Parental Support, Depressed Affect and Sexual Experience Among Adolescents." *Youth and Society,* 24, 166–177.

Whitbeck, L. B., Yoder, K. A., Hoyt, D. R., and Conger, R. D. (1999). "Early Adolescent Sexual Activity: A Developmental Study." *Journal of Marriage and Family,* 61, 934–946.

White, K. M. (1980). "Problems and Characteristics of College Students." *Adolescence,* 15(57), 23–41.

White, M. A., Kohlmaier, J. R., Varnado-Sullivan, P., and Williamson, D. A. (2003). "Racial/Ethnic Differences in Weight Concerns: Protective and Risk Factors for the Development of Eating Disorders and Obesity among Adolescent Females." *Eating and Weight Disorders,* 8, 20–25.

White, S. H. (1992). "G. Stanley Hall: From Philosophy to Developmental Psychology." *Developmental Psychology,* 28, 25–34.

Whitley, B. E., and Keith-Spiegel, P. (2002). *Academic Dishonesty: An Educator's Guide.* Mahwah, NJ: Erlbaum.

Whitman, F. L., Diamond, M., and Martin, J. (1993). "Homosexual Orientation in Twins: A Report on 61 Pairs and 3 Triplet Sets." *Archives of Sexual Behavior,* 22, 187–206.

Whitman, T., Bokowski, J., Keogh, D., and Weed, K. (2001). *Interwoven Lives: Adolescent Mothers and Their Children.* Mahwah, NJ: Erlbaum.

Wichstrøm, L. (2001). "The Impact of Pubertal Timing on Adolescents' Alcohol Use." *Journal of Research on Adolescence,* 11, 131–150.

Wickens, C. D. (1974). "Limits of Human Information Processing: A Developmental Study." *Psychological Bulletin,* 81, 739–755.

Widmer, E. D., and Weiss, C. C. (2000). "Do Older Siblings Make a Difference? The Effects of Older Sibling Support and Older Sibling Adjustment on the Adjustment of Socially Disadvantaged Adolescents." *Journal of Research on Adolescents,* 10, 1–27.

Wierzbicki, M. (1993). "Psychological Adjustment of Adoptees: A Meta-Analysis." *Journal of Clinical Child Psychology,* 22, 447–454.

Wigfield, A., and Eccles, J. S. (1994). "Children's Competence Beliefs Achievement Values, and General Self-Esteem: Change across Elementary and Middle School." *Journal of Early Adolescence,* 14, 107–138.

Wigfield, A., and Eccles, J. S. (1995). "Middle School Grades, Schooling, and Early Adolescent Development." *Journal of Early Adolescence,* 5–8.

Wigfield, A., Eccles, J. S., MacIver, D., Reuman, D. A., and Midgley, C. (1991). "Transitions during Early Adolescence: Changes in Children's Domain-Specific Self-Perceptions and General Self-Esteem across the Transition to Junior High School." *Developmental Psychology,* 27, 552–565.

Wigfield, A., Eccles, J. S., and Pintrich, P. R. (1996). "Development between the Ages of 11 and 25." In D. C. Berliner and R. C. Calfee (Eds.), *Handbook of Educational Psychology* (pp. 148–185). New York: Macmillan.

Wilcox, B., Cantor, J., Dowrick, P., Kunkel, D., Linn, S., and Palmer, E. (2004). *Report of the APA Task Force on Advertising and Children: Summary of Findings and Conclusions.* Washington, DC: American Psychological Association.

Wilkins, R., and Lewis, C. (1993). "Sex and Drugs and Nuclear War: Secular, Developmental, and Type A Influences upon Adolescents, Fears of the Nuclear Threat, AIDS, and Drug Addiction." *Journal of Adolescence,* 16, 23–41.

Willard, N. *Cyberbullying.* Retrieved from http://cyberbully.org/.

Williams, J. M., and Currie. C. (2000). "Self-Esteem and Physical Development in Early Adolescence: Pubertal Timing and Body Image." *Journal of Early Adolescence,* 20, 129–149.

Williams, J. M., and Dunlop, L. C. (1999). "Pubertal Timing and Self-Reported Delinquency among Male Adolescents." *Journal of Adolescence,* 22, 157–171.

Williams, J. W., and White, K. A. (1983). "Adolescent Status Systems for Males and Females at Three Age Levels." *Adolescence,* 18, 381–389.

Williams, K. (1988). "Parents Reinforce Feminine Role in Girls." *Medical Aspects of Human Sexuality,* 22, 106–107.

Williams, L. (1992, 1993). *Passionate Kisses.* Warner-Tamerlane Publishing Corporation, Lucy Jones Music, and Noman Music.

Williams, M., Himmel, K. F., Sjoberg, A. F., and Torrez, D. J., (1995). "The Assimilation Model, Family Life, and Race and Ethnicity in the United States." *Journal of Family Issues,* 16, 380–405.

Williams, R. J., Chang, S. Y., and the Addiction Centre Adolescent Research Group. (2000). "A Comprehensive and Comparative Review of Adolescent Substance Abuse Treatment Outcome." *Clinical Psychology: Science and Practice,* 7, 138–166.

Williams, S., and Williams, L. (2005). "Space Invaders: The Negotiation of Teenage Boundaries through the Mobile Phone." *The Sociological Review,* 53, 314–331.

Williams, T., Connolly, J., Peplar, D., and Craig, W. (2005). "Peer Victimization, Social Support, and Psychosocial Adjustment of Sexual Minority Adolescents." *Journal of Youth and Adolescence,* 34, 471–482.

Wilson, D. M., Killen, J. D., Hayward, C., Robinson, T. N., Hammer, L. D., Kraemer, H. C., Varady, A., and Taylor, C. B. (1994). "Timing and Rate of Sexual Maturation and the Onset of Cigarette and Alcohol Use."*Archives of Pediatric Adolescent Medicine,* 148, 789–795.

Wilson, J. (2001). "Hi-Tech Plagiarism: New Twist on a Perennial Problem." *Acumen,* 1, 1–4.

Wilson, P. M., and Wilson, J. R. (1992). "Environmental Influences on Adolescent Educational Aspirations. A Logistic Transform Model." *Youth and Society,* 24, 52–70.

Wilson, S. M., and Medora, N. P. (1990). "Gender Comparisons of College Students' Attitudes toward Sexual Behavior." *Adolescence,* 25, 615–627.

Wilson, W. J. (1987). *The Truly Disadvantaged.* Chicago: University of Chicago Press.

Windle, M., Shope, J. T., and Bukstein, O. (1996). "Alcohol Use." In R. J. DiClemente, W. B. Hansen, and L. E. Ponton (Eds.), *Handbook of Adolescent Health Risk Behavior* (pp. 115–159). Thousand Oaks, CA: Sage.

Winters, K. (1999). "Treating Adolescents with Substance Abuse Disorders: An Overview of Practice Issues and Treatment Outcomes." *Substance Abuse,* 20, 203–223.

Winters, K., Stinchfield, R. D., Opland, E., Weller, C., and Latimer, W. W. (2000). "The Effectiveness of the Minnesota Model Approach in the Treatment of Adolescent Drug Abusers." *Addiction*, 95, 601–612.

Wittchen, H.-U., Becker, E., Lieb, R., and Krause, P. (2002). "Prevalence, Incidence and Stability of Premenstrual Dysphoric Disorder in the Community." *Psychological Medicine*, 32, 119–132.

Wodarski, J. S. (1990). "Adolescent Substance Abuse: Practice Implications." *Adolescence*, 99, 667–688.

Wolfe, D. A., and Feiring, C. (2000). "Dating Violence through the Lens of Adolescent Romantic Relationships." *Child Maltreatment*, 5, 360–363.

Wolfson, A. R., and Carskadon, M. A. (1998). "Sleep Schedules and Daytime Functioning in Adolescents." *Child Development*, 69, 875–887.

Wolke, D., Woods, S., Bloomfield, L., and Karstadt, L. (2000). "The Association between Direct and Relational Bullying and Behavior Problems among Primary School Children." *Journal of Child Psychology and Psychiatry*, 41, 989–1002.

Wolock, I., and Horowitz, B. (1984). "Child Maltreatment as a Social Problem: The Neglect of Neglect." *American Journal of Orthopsychiatry*, 54, 530–543.

Wonderlich, S. A., Lilenfeld, L. R., Riso, L. P., Engel, S., and Mitchell, J. E. (2005). "Personality and Anorexia Nervosa." *International Journal of Eating Disorders*, 37 (Suppl.), s68–s71.

Wong, W. W., Nicholson, M., Stuff, J. E., Butte, N. F., Ellis, K., J., Hergenroeder, A. C., Hill, R. B., and Smith, E. O. (1998). "Serum Leptin Concentrations in Caucasian and African-American Girls." *Journal of Clinical Endocrinology and Metabolism*, 83, 3574–3577.

Wood, M. D., Sherman, K. J., and McGowen, A. K. (2000). "Collegiate Alcohol Involvement and Role Attainment in Early Adulthood: Findings from a Prospective High-Risk Study." *Journal of Studies of Alcohol*, 61, 278–289.

Wood, N. L., Wood, R. A., and McDonald, T. D. (1988). "Integration of Student Development Theory into the Academic Classroom." *Adolescence*, 23, 349–356.

Wood, R. T. (1999). "'Nailed to the X': A Lyrical History of the Straightedge Youth Subculture." *Journal of Youth Studies*, 2, 133–151.

Woodside, D. B. (2005). "Treatment of Anorexia Nervosa: More Questions than Answers." *International Journal of Eating Disorders*, 37 (Suppl.), s41–s42.

Woodward, J. C., and Kalyan-Masih, V. (1990). "Loneliness, Coping Strategies and Cognitive Styles of the Gifted Rural Adolescent." *Adolescence*, 25, 977–988.

Wray, H. (1999). *Japanese and American Education: Attitudes and Practices*. Westport, CT: Bergin and Garvey.

Wright, R. (1937). "The Ethics of Living Jim Crow." In *American Stuff*. New York: Harper and Row.

Wright, S. A., and Piper, E. S. (1986). "Families and Cults: Familial Factors Related to Youth Leaving or Remaining in Deviant Religious Groups." *Journal of Marriage and the Family*, 48, 15–25.

Wrobel, G. M., Grotevant, H. D., and McRoy, R. G. (2004). "Adolescent Search for Birth Parents: Who Moves Forward?" and *Journal of Adolescent Research*, 19, 132–151.

Wu, Z. (1995a). "Premarital Cohabitation and Postmarital Cohabiting Union Formation." *Journal of Family Issues*, 16, 212–232.

Wu, Z. (1995b). "The Stability of Cohabitation Relationships: The Role of Children." *Journal of Marriage and the Family*, 57, 231–236.

Wu, Z. (1996). "Childbearing and Cohabitational Relationships." *Journal of Marriage and the Family*, 58, 281–292.

Wyatt, G. E. (1989). "Reexamining Factors Predicting Afro-American and White American Women's Age at First Coitus." *Archives of Sexual Behavior*, 18, 271–298.

Wyatt, G. E., and Newcomb, M. (1990). "Internal and External Mediators of Women's Sexual Abuse in Childhood." *Journal of Consulting and Clinical Psychology*, 58, 758–767.

Wynne, E. (1989). "Transmitting Traditional Values in Contemporary Schools." In L. Nucci (Ed.), *Moral Development and Character Education: A Dialogue* (pp. 19–36). Berkeley, CA: McCutchan.

Xie, H., Swift, D. J., Carins, R. B., and Cairns, B. D. (2002). "Aggressive Behaviors in Social Interaction and Developmental Adaptation: A Narrative Analysis of Interpersonal Conflicts during Early Adolescence." *Social Development*, 11, 205–224.

Yacoubian, J. H., and Lourie, R. S. (1973). "Suicide and Attempted Suicide in Children and Adolescents." In S. L. Copel (Ed.), *Pathology of Childhood and Adolescence*. New York: Basic Books.

Yang, P. Q., and Kayaardi, N. (2004). "Who Chooses Non-Public Schools for Their Children?" *Educational Studies*, 30, 231–249.

Yaryura-Tobias, J. A., Neziroglu, F. A., and Kaplan, S. (1995). "Self-Mutilation, Anorexia, and Dysmenorrhea in Obsessive-Compulsive Disorder." *International Journal of Eating Disorders*, 17, 33–38.

Yates, M., and Youniss, J. (1996). "Community Service and Political-Moral Identity in Adolescents." *Journal of Research in Adolescence*, 6, 271–284.

Yates, T. M. (2004). "The Developmental Psychology of Self-Injurious Behavior: Compensatory Regulation in Posttraumatic Adaptation." *Clinical Psychological Review*, 24, 35–74.

Yau, J., and Smetna, J. G. (1993). "Chinese-American Adolescents' Reasoning about Cultural Conflicts." *Journal of Adolescent Research*, 8, 419–438.

Yeh, C. J., and Huang, K. (1996). "The Collectivistic Nature of Ethnic Identity Development among Asian-American College Students." *Adolescence*, 31, 645–661.

Yoder, K. A. (1999). "Comparing Suicide Attempters, Suicide Ideators, and Nonsuicidal Homeless and Runaway Adolescents." *Suicide and Life-Threatening Behavior*, 29, 23–36.

Young, E. A., Clopton, J. R., & Bleckley, M. K. (2004). "Perfectionism, Low Self-Esteem, and Family Factors as Predictors of Bulimic Behavior." *Eating Behaviors*, 5(4), 273–283.

Young, E. W., Jensen, L. C., Olsen, J. A., and Cundick, B. P. (1991). "The Effects of Family Structure on the Sexual Behavior of Adolescents." *Adolescence*, 26, 977–986.

Young, M. H., Miller, B. C., Norton, M. C., and Hill, E. J. (1995). "The Effect of Parental Supportive Behaviors on Life Satisfaction of Adolescent Offspring." *Journal of Marriage and the Family*, 57, 813–822.

Young, R. A. (1994). "Helping Adolescents with Career Development: The Active Role of Parents." *Career Development Quarterly*, 42, 195–203.

Young, R. A., and Friesen, J. D. (1992). "The Intentions of Parents in Influencing the Career Development of Their Children." *The Career Development Quarterly*, 40, 198–207.

Youngs, G. A., Jr., Rathge, R., Mullis, R., and Mullis, A. (1990). "Adolescent Stress and Self-Esteem." *Adolescence*, 25, 333–341.

Youniss, J., McLellan, J. A., and Yates, M. (1999). "Religion, Community Service, and Identity in American Youth." *Journal of Adolescence*, 22, 243–253.

Youniss, J., and Smollar, J. (1985). *Adolescent Relations with Mothers, Fathers, and Friends*. Chicago: University of Chicago Press.

Yuen, N., Andrade, N., Nahulu, L., Makini, G., McDermott, J. F., Danko, G., et al. (1996). "The Rate and Characteristics of Suicide Attempters in the Native Hawaiian Adolescent Population." *Suicide and Life-Threatening Behavior*, 26, 27–36.

Zachry, E. M. (2005). "Getting My Education: Teen Mothers' Experiences in School before and after Motherhood." *Teachers College Record*, 107, 2566–2598.

Zald, D. H., and Iacono, W. G. (1998). "The Development of Spatial Working Memory Abilities." *Developmental Neuropsychology*, 14, 563–578.

Zambrana, R. E., and Silva-Palacios, V. (1989). "Gender Differences in Stress among Mexican Immigrant Adolescents in Los Angeles, CA." *Journal of Adolescent Research*, 4, 426–442.

Zarb, J. M. (Summer 1984). "A Comparison of Remedial Failure, and Successful Secondary School Students across Self-Perception and Past and Present School Performance Variables." *Adolescence*, 19, 335–348.

Zarbatany, L., Ghesquiere, K., and Mohr, K. (1992). "A Context Perspective on Early Adolescents' Friendship Expectations." *Journal of Early Adolescence*, 12, 111–126.

Zebrowitz, L. A., Hall, J. A., Murphy, N. A., and Rhodes, G. (2002). "Looking Smart and Looking Good: Facial Cues to Intelligence and Their Origins." *Personality and Social Psychology Bulletin*, 28, 238–249.

Zeidner, M. (1995). "Personality Trait Correlates of Intelligence." In D. H. Saklofske and M. Zeidner (Eds.), *International Handbook of Personality and Intelligence* (pp. 299–319). New York: Plenum.

Zelkowitz, P. (1987). "Social Support and Aggressive Behavior in Young Children." *Family Relations*, 36, 129–134.

Zellman, G. L. (January–February, 1982). "Public School Programs for Adolescent Pregnancy and Parenthood: An Assessment." *Family Planning Perspectives*, 14, 15–21.

Zern, D. S. (1989). "Some Connections between Increasing Religiousness and Academic Accomplishment in a College Population." *Adolescence*, 24, 141–153.

Zhao, Y., Pugh, K., Sheldon, S., and Byers, J. L. (2002). "Conditions for Classroom Technology Innovations." *Teachers College Record*, 104, 482–515.

Zhou, J., Hofman, M., Gooren, L., and Swaab, D. (1995). "A Sex Difference in the Human Brain and Its Relation to Transsexuality." *Nature*, 378, 68–70.

Zila, L. M., and Kiselica, M. (2001). "Understanding and Counseling Self-Mutilation in Female Adolescents and Young Adults." *Journal of Counseling and Development,* 79, 46–52.

Zill, N., Morrison, D. R., and Coiro, M. J. (1993). "Long-Term Effects of Parental Divorce on Parent-Child Relationships, Adjustment, and Achievement in Young Adulthood." *Journal of Family Psychology,* 7, 91–103.

Zillman, D. (1996). "The Psychology of Suspense in Dramatic Exposition." In P. Vorderer, H. J. Wulff, and M. Friedrichsen, (Eds.), *Suspense: Conceptualizations, Theoretical Analyses, and Empirical Explorations* (pp. 199–231). Mahwah, NJ: Erlbaum.

Zillman, D. (2000). "Influence of Unrestrained Access to Erotica on Adolescents' and Young Adults' Dispositions toward Sexuality." *Journal of Adolescent Health,* 27, Supplement no. 2, 41–44.

Zimmerman, P. (1999). "Structure and Functioning of Internal Models of Attachment and Their Role in Emotional Regulation." *Attachment and Human Development,* 1, 55–71.

Zimmermann, P. (2004). "Attachment Representations and Characteristics of Friendship Relations during Adolescence." *Journal of Experimental Child Psychology,* 88, 83–101.

Zimmerman, R. S., Sprecher, S., Langer, L. M., and Holloway, C. D. (1995). "Adolescents' Perceived Ability to Say 'No' to Unwanted Sex." *Journal of Adolescent Research,* 10, 383–399.

Zlotnick, C., Shea, M. T., Pearlstein, T., Simpson, E., Costello, E., and Begin, A. (1996). "The Relationship between Dissociative Symptoms, Alexithymia, Impulsivity, Sexual Abuse, and Self-Multilation." *Comprehensive Psychiatry,* 37, 12–16.

Zuckerman, D. (2005). "Teenagers and Cosmetic Surgery." *Virtual Mentor,* 7. Retrieved from http://www.ama-assn.org/ama/pub/category/14695.html 6/8/06.

Zuckerman, D. (January 1985). "Too Many Sibs Put Our Nation at Risk?" *Psychology Today,* 19, 5, 10.

PHOTO CREDITS

Chapter 1

p. xviii: ©David M. Grossman/The Image Works
p. 9: Britt Erlanson/Stone/Getty Images
p. 10: ©Peter Hvizdak/The Image Works
p. 14: HBO/The Kobal Collection/Picture Desk
p. 19: Pool Photo by Nancee E. Lewis/ Newsmakers/NewsCom

Chapter 2

p. 24: ©Image Source/SuperStock Royalty Free
p. 26: Michael Newman/PhotoEdit
p. 31: ©Image Source/SuperStock Royalty Free
p. 39: Tony Freeman/PhotoEdit
p. 45: ©Sean Sprague/The Image Works

Chapter 3

p. 48: ©Roy Morsch/zefa/Corbis
p. 54: ©Sean Cayton/The Image Works
p. 57: ©John Eastcott/Yva Momatiuk/The Image Works
p. 62: Brand X Pictures/Jupiter Images Royalty Free
p. 66: David W. Hamilton/The Image Bank/ Getty Images
p. 69: DAJ/Getty Images Royalty Free
p. 71: AP Images/Mike Elicson

Chapter 4

p. 74 & 90: Michael Newman/PhotoEdit

Chapter 5

p. 94: ©Birgid Allig/zefa/Corbis
p. 99: ©Jeff Greenberg/PhotoEdit
p. 101: ©Mark Savage/Corbis
p. 110: ©Esbin-Anderson/The Image Works

Chapter 6

p. 116: ©Syracuse Newspapers/Gary Walts/ The Image Works
p. 118: Nancy Sheehan/PhotoEdit
p. 123: Billy E. Barnes/PhotoEdit
p. 126: ©Tony Savino/The Images Works
p. 132: ©John Birdsall/The Image Works

Chapter 7

p. 136: Frank Siteman Photography
p. 144: Spencer Grant/PhotoEdit
p. 150: ©Mike Booth/Alamy
p. 152: ©Andrew Fox/Corbis

Chapter 8

p. 158: ©John Henley/Corbis
p. 165: ©Ariel Skelley/Corbis
p. 170: ©Jeff Greenberg/PhotoEdit
p. 176: Spencer Grant/PhotoEdit
p. 179: Jill Greenberg/Photonica/Getty Images
p. 182: © Thinkstock/Corbis Royalty Free

Chapter 9

p. 186: ©Stockbyte/SuperStock Royalty Free
p. 191: ©Kate Mitchell/zefa/Corbis
p. 200: Peter D. Byron/PhotoEdit
p. 201: Spencer Grant/PhotoEdit
p. 205: David Young-Wolff/PhotoEdit
p. 210: © Photofusion Picture Library/Alamy
P. 214: ©Marilyn Humphries/The Image Works

Chapter 10

p. 222: Zia Soleil/Iconica/Getty Images Rights-Ready
p. 227: Walter Smith/Corbis
p. 235: Buccina Studios/Photodisc/Getty Images Royalty Free
p. 238: ©Dennis Nett/Syracuse Newspapers/ The Image Works
p. 239: David Young-Wolff/PhotoEdit
p. 240: Bill Aron/PhotoEdit

Chapter 11

p. 244: Kayte Deioma/PhotoEdit
p. 254: ©Eryrie/Alamy
p. 259: David Young-Wolff/Stone/Getty Images
p. 261: ©PhotoAlto/Alamy Royalty Free

Chapter 12

p. 266: ©Rob Melnychuk/Brand X/Corbis Royalty Free
p. 271: Will Faller
p. 281: David Stewart/Stone/Getty Images
p. 283: Tom Prettyman/PhotoEdit
p. 286: ©Reed Kaestner/Corbis Royalty Free
p. 291: Nick Vedros & Assoc/Stone/Getty Images

Chapter 13

p. 296: Catherine Ledner/Stone/Getty Images
p. 301; ©Randy Faris/Corbis
p. 305: AP Images/Lauren Greenfield/VII
p. 308: ©Blend Images/SuperStock Royalty Free
p. 311: ©Bob Daemmrich/The Image Works
p. 315: ©Chuck Savage/Corbis

Chapter 14

p. 320: Michael Newman/PhotoEdit
p. 331: Michael Newman/PhotoEdit
p. 333: Novastock/PhotoEdit
p. 334: Maggie Leonard/Rainbow
p. 338: Ron Chapple/Getty Images

Chapter 15
p. 344: Lisa Pines/Photonica/Getty Images
p. 352: Michael Newman/PhotoEdit
p. 355: Lon C. Diehl/PhotoEdit
p. 362: ©Shepard Sherbell/Corbis Saba

Chapter 16
p. 366: Jeff Greenberg/PhotoEdit
p. 369: David Young-Wolff/PhotoEdit
p. 373: David Young-Wolff/PhotoEdit
p. 375: Spencer Grant/PhotoEdit
p. 377: ©Kathy McLaughlin/The Image Works
p. 384: Seth Resnick/Stock Boston
p. 388: DreamPictures/Stone/Getty Images

Chapter 17
p. 392: ©Kirk Condyles/The Image Works
p. 397: ©Viviane Moos/Corbis
p. 403: AP Images/Susan Sterner
p. 406: ©Scott Houston/Sygma/Corbis
p. 407: ©Chris Ware/The Image Works
p. 409: STR/AFP/Getty Images
p. 410: Jerome Sessini/In Visu/Corbis
p. 413: Joel Gordon Photography

Chapter 18
p. 418: ©Michael Dwyer/Alamy
p. 426: ©Photofusion Picture Library/Alamy
p. 435: Mary Kate Denny/PhotoEdit
p. 436: Richard Hutchings/PhotoEdit
p. 438: ©Brooks Kraft/Sygma/Corbis
p. 440: Colin Young-Wolff/PhotoEdit

INDEX

N

O

T